MEN

OF THE

BATTLE OF BRITAIN

The 1939-1945 Star
with Battle of Britain clasp

MEN
OF THE
BATTLE OF BRITAIN

A Who was Who of the Pilots and Aircrew,
British, Commonwealth and Allied,
who flew with Royal Air Force Fighter Command
July 10 to October 31 1940

KENNETH G. WYNN

With a foreword by Her Majesty Queen Elizabeth the Queen Mother
Patron of the Battle of Britain Fighter Association

Gliddon Books
Norwich • Norfolk
1989

By the same author

HONOUR THE LIGHT BRIGADE
  (with Canon WM Lummis)

A CLASP FOR THE FEW

First published in 1989

ISBN 0 947893 15 6

Printed and bound in Great Britain by
Biddles Ltd, Guildford and King's Lynn
and published by Gliddon Books
Skeetshill Farmhouse, Shotesham St Mary
Norwich NR15 1UR, Norfolk

CONTENTS

For Anah

For her constant encouragement,
unfailing support and invaluable
common-sense

CLARENCE HOUSE
S.W. 1

In the hearts of the British people there will always be a special place for The Few, the young men from Britain, the Commonwealth and Allied Countries who fought and won the Battle of Britain in 1940.

Without their courage, skill and determination in the face of fearful odds, who can tell what the final outcome of the War might have been. Many of them gave their lives, young lives which held so much promise for the future.

This book is a record of those men. They will always be remembered.

ELIZABETH R
Queen Mother

Patron
The Battle of Britain
Fighter Association

ACKNOWLEDGEMENTS AND THANKS

During the preparation of this book I have received a great deal of help from many people and organisations. It is impossible to list them all but I would like to thank the undermentioned, without some of whom the book probably would never have been done.

Group Captain Tom Gleave, Historian of the Battle of Britain Fighter Association, for his constant help and encouragement, apparently limitless patience and unfailing courtesy.

Wing Commander Pat Hancock, Hon Secretary of the Battle of Britain Fighter Association, for invaluable help given over a period of years.

The late Flight Lieutenant John Holloway. Without his efforts in compiling the roll of Battle of Britain participants there would have been no foundation on which to build our knowledge of the 'The Few'.

Andy Saunders, for generously supplying information and photographs over the years. With his encyclopaedic knowledge of the Battle of Britain he has been a good friend to have.

Peter Elliott, Librarian, Royal Air Force Museum, Hendon, for always supplying the answers, cheerfully.

Captain Waclaw Milewski and Mr Andrzej Suchcitz of the Polish Institute and Sikorski Museum, London, for making my research into the Polish pilots such a pleasure.

Mrs Sarah Whitfield of the Commonwealth War Graves Commission, for being so efficient and helpful.

Peter Vincent, for his tenacity in tracking down survivors of the Battle and passing on information.

Ted Sergison and Trevor Williams, for providing photographs and information.

Finally, the Men of the Battle of Britain, their widows and relatives, who have been so wonderfully helpful in providing me with records of service, photographs, information and in many cases hospitality over the years.

In the production of this book I have been more than fortunate in having the expert assistance of a team of quite remarkable ladies.

My wife, Anah, who has always been a major driving force and always been there with good advice and help when it was most needed.

My daughter, Elizabeth, who so efficiently typed the whole text from my rough drafts, a long and arduous task.

Janis Ord and the team at Comset, Auckland, New Zealand, who were so helpful, brilliantly transforming it all into print.

Barbara Ross, of GM Studios, Auckland, who spent many hours in the dark room patiently producing usable photographs from negatives of very varying quality.

I thank them all and hope that the reader will find the book to be a worthwhile addition to the literature of the Battle of Britain.

INTRODUCTION

It is not the intention of this book to give an account of the Battle of Britain, of the events which led up to it or of its undoubted effect on the subsequent course of the war. Nor will it go into any technical details or description of the aircraft which took part. All of these aspects have been more than adequately covered in hundreds of books over almost fifty years.

This book is a Roll of Honour of 'The Few', immortalised by Winston Churchill in his speech to the House of Commons on August 20 1940. Contrary to popular belief 'The Few' are not as few as many people think. A widely-held misconception is that the Battle of Britain was won by a few hundred dashing Spitfire pilots, whereas the truth is that almost three thousand men qualify for the 'Battle of Britain' clasp to the 1939-1945 Star, the mark of a participant in the Battle.

They were in certain eligible fighter squadrons or flights, or serving in the Coastal Command or Fleet Air Arm squadrons which flew in support of Fighter Command during the period of the Battle of Britain, July 10 to October 31 1940. The minimum requirement for the clasp is that at least one authorised operational sortie was flown between those dates whilst serving with an eligible unit.

Numbered amongst 'The Few' are many airmen in aircrew categories other than pilot; the air gunners, observers and radar operators of the Blenheim and Defiant squadrons, which served as day or night fighters as the situation demanded.

The vast majority of 'The Few' were British, many of them serving in the pre-war Royal Air Force, officers with permanent or short service commissions and NCO pilots, many of whom had originally joined as aircraft apprentices. Flying alongside these career airmen were the 'weekend fliers' of the Auxiliary Air Force, the Royal Air Force Volunteer Reserve and men from the University Air Squadrons. These were men who had trained in their spare time and who were called to full-time service at the outbreak of war. In addition there were many men who had volunteered for aircrew duties in the early months of the war and had completed their training in time to be posted to operational units to take part in the Battle. Finally there were fifty-three pilots of the Fleet Air Arm, serving either as individual volunteers with Royal Air Force fighter squadrons or in the two Fleet Air Arm Squadrons on dockyard defence.

The countries of the Commonwealth were well represented by pilots from Canada, Australia, South Africa and Rhodesia and by pilots, air gunners and observers from New Zealand. Many of the pilots had been in the Royal Air Force before the war on short service commissions. Apart from the Canadians serving in No 1 (RCAF) Squadron the men from the Commonwealth were spread throughout the squadrons of Fighter Command.

Completing the cosmopolitan make-up of 'The Few' were pilots who had escaped from Europe following the occupation of their countries by the Germans. The Poles and Czechs flew in their own squadrons and individually in Royal Air Force squadrons. The French and Belgian pilots flew individually.

In this book I have presented as many facts on each man as I have been able to find. It is a matter of regret that for many men, particularly aircrew members, I have found very little. The refusal of the Ministry of Defence to give any ungazetted information, such as units served with, except to immediate next of kin makes research for a book like this extremely difficult. Fortunately this incomprehensible attitude is not taken by most countries outside Great Britain and I am very grateful for the official help I have been given.

The search for more knowledge of 'The Few' is ongoing and I hope that this book will provide a foundation on which others will build. Inevitably in a book like this, with so many facts and dates, there will be errors but, hopefully, not too many.

I have an unbounded admiration for the men who won the Battle of Britain and this book is my attempt to record for posterity who they were and some account of what became of them after the Battle.

Ken Wynn

Headquarters, Fighter Command,
Royal Air Force,
Bentley Priory, Stanmore,
MIDDLESEX.

2nd June, 1940.

My Dear Fighter Boys,

I don't send out many congratulatory letters and signals, but I feel that I must take this occasion, when the intensive fighting in Northern France is for the time being over, to tell you how proud I am of you and the way in which you have fought since the "Blitzkrieg" started.

I wish I could have spent my time visiting you and hearing your accounts of the fighting, but I have occupied myself in working for you in other ways.

I want you to know that my thoughts are always with you, and that it is you and your fighting spirit which will crack the morale of the German Air Force, and preserve our Country through the trials which yet lie ahead.

Good luck to you.

H.C.T. Dowding.
Air Chief Marshal

"What General Weygand called the Battle of France is over. I expect that the Battle of Britain is about to begin. The whole fury and might of the enemy must very soon be turned on us. Hitler knows that he will have to break us in this island or lose the War. If we can stand up to him, all Europe may be free and the life of the world may move forward to broad sunlit uplands. But if we fail, then the whole world, including the United States, including all that we have known and cared for, will sink into the abyss of a new Dark Age made more sinister, and perhaps more protracted, by the lights of perverted science. Let us therefore brace ourselves to our duties, and so bear ourselves that, if the British Empire and its Commonwealth last for a thousand years, men will still say 'This was their finest hour.' "

Winston Churchill June 18 1940

THE MEN

"The gratitude of every home in our Island, in our Empire, and indeed throughout the world, except in the abodes of the guilty, goes out to the British airmen, who, undaunted by odds, unwearied in their constant challenge and mortal danger, are turning the tide of world war by their prowess and devotion. Never in the field of human conflict was so much owed by so many to so few."

Winston Churchill August 20 1940

On the pages that follow are 2927 men, awarded the Battle of Britain clasp for having flown at least one authorised operational sortie with an eligible unit of RAF Fighter Command during the period from July 10 to October 31 1940.

They came from the following countries:

Great Britain	2353
Australia	29
Belgium	29
Canada	97
Czechoslovakia	87
France	13
Ireland	9
Jamaica	1
Newfoundland	1
New Zealand	126
Palestine	1
Poland	145
Rhodesia	3
South Africa	22
United States	11

During the Battle of Britain 544 lost their lives.

Between November 1 1940 and August 15 1945 another 791 died in the course of their duties in all theatres of war.

For the Battle of Britain the following squadrons and units were eligible:

Squadrons: 1, 1 (RCAF), 3, 17, 19, 23, 25, 29, 32, 41, 43, 46, 54, 56, 64, 65, 66, 72, 73, 74, 79, 85, 87, 92, 111, 141, 145, 151, 152, 213, 219, 222, 229, 232, 234, 235, 236, 238, 242, 245, 247, 248, 249, 253, 257, 263, 264, 266, 302, 303, 310, 312, 501, 504, 600, 601, 602, 603, 604, 605, 607, 609, 610, 611, 615 and 616

Flights: 421, 422 and Fighter Interception Unit

Fleet Air Arm: 804 and 808 Squadrons

HUBERT HASTINGS ADAIR

580088   Sgt   Pilot   British   151 and 213 Squadrons

Adair, from Norwich, was born in 1917. He joined 151 Squadron at Digby on September 4 1940, moving to Tangmere on the 21st. After being involved in a night landing accident at Tangmere on November 5 Adair was in action the following afternoon and did not return from combat over the Southampton area. He was posted as 'Missing' and is named on the Runnymede Memorial, Panel 11.

Recent research indicates that the Hurricane, V 7602, which crashed and burned out at Pigeon House Farm, Widley, Hampshire was Adair's. When it was excavated on October 6 1979 the pilot's remains were found and later sent to Porchester Crematorium for disposal. This aircraft was almost certainly shot down by Major Helmut Wick of JG 2.

DENNIS ARTHUR ADAMS

90537   FO   Pilot   British   611 and 41 Squadrons

Adams joined 611 Squadron, AuxAF in 1938. He went to summer camp at Duxford on August 4 1939 and was called to full-time service on the 26th.

Over Dunkirk on June 2 1940 Adams probably destroyed a Ju 87. Flying from Tern Hill on July 22 he made a forced-landing on the beach at Colwyn Bay, in Spitfire N 3062. The aircraft was pushed on to the promenade to escape the incoming tide.

On September 21 Adams was sent up to investigate an unidentified aircraft over Liverpool and intercepted a Do 215 of 2 (F)/121 on photo-reconnaissance. He chased it for fourteen minutes before shooting it down at Dolgellau, Merioneth. It crash-landed at Trawsfynydd. One crew member was killed and the other three captured, wounded.

Adams was posted to 41 Squadron at Hornchurch on September 29. In a morning engagement over Folkestone on October 7 he was shot down by return fire from a Do 17 and baled out of Spitfire N 3267, landing at Douglas Farm, Postling.

Posted away from 41 in April 1941, Adams was in the RAF until 1945, when he was released as a Squadron Leader. He later went to live in South Africa.

APO (AuxAF) 11.10.38   PO 26.8.39   FO 3.9.40   FL 3.9.41
SL 1.7.44

ERIC HENRY ADAMS

742165   Sgt   Pilot   British   236 Squadron

Adams joined the RAFVR in May 1938 and did his elementary flying training at 29 E&RFTS, Luton. He was called up at the outbreak of war and posted to 2 FTS, Brize Norton. After completing his training Adams joined 236 Squadron in June 1940.

In December 1940 he went to Aldergrove when personnel from 236 were transferred to form 252 Squadron. Early in 1941 Adams contracted a throat virus and was in hospital for four months. He was taken off operational flying and in September 1941 went to RAF Henlow as a test pilot for newly-assembled Hurricanes, testing Packard-Merlin engines.

In mid-1943 Adams did a flying control course and was afterwards posted to N'dola, Northern Rhodesia, a staging post on

EH Adams (continued)

the South Africa/Egypt route. He returned to the UK in October 1944 and became a controller at RAF Carnaby.

Adams was released in April 1946, as a Warrant Officer. He was a successful estate agent until his retirement in 1982.

HUGH CHARLES ADAMS

85645   PO   Pilot   British   501 Squadron

Adams, from Oxted, Surrey, joined the RAFVR in 1938. Called up at the outbreak of war, he completed his training and joined 501 Squadron at Gravesend on July 17 1940, as a Sergeant-Pilot.

On September 2 Adams destroyed a Bf 109 and was then himself shot down in combat south of Ashford, in Hurricane V 7234. On the 6th he was shot down and killed in action over Ashford. His Hurricane, V 6612, crashed at Clavertye, near Elham.

Adams was 22. He is buried in St Peter's churchyard, Tandridge, Surrey. His commission was gazetted on the day he was killed and in the casualty list he was down as 'Killed in Action', as Sergeant, 741254.

PO 6.9.40

JACK SYLVESTER ADAMS

37728   FL   Pilot   British   29 Squadron

Adams, who was born on May 17 1911, began his flying training with the RAF in January 1936 and was commissioned in March. He was posted to 2 FTS, Digby on May 2 and on completion of his training joined 29 Squadron at Debden on January 10 1937. He was still with 29 in September 1939 and served with the squadron in the Battle of Britain.

One night in August 1940 Adams sighted an enemy aircraft and chased it for fifty minutes before making contact off the South Coast. After attacking his quarry over the sea and apparently destroying it Adams returned to Digby and landed with both fuel gauges reading nil. This action was mentioned in the citation for his DFC (24.9.40).

In early November Adams was posted to 303 Squadron at Leconfield as a Flight Commander. He was given command of 151 Squadron at Wittering in January 1941, an appointment he held until October, when he was posted to staff duties at HQ 12 Group. Adams returned to operations in April 1942, taking command of 256 Squadron at Squires Gate, as an Acting Wing Commander. He remained with 256 until October.

On April 5 1943 he was posted to a staff job at the Air Ministry, in the Directorate of Operations (Air Defence). A further tour of operations followed in 1944, with 226 Squadron, for which Adams was awarded a Bar to the DFC (29.8.44). In 1945 he was CFI at the OTU at Mitchels.

He stayed in the RAF after the war and retired on July 27 1958 as a Wing Commander, retaining the rank of Group Captain. In 1958 he was appointed Commander in the Order of Orange Nassau.

APO 30.3.36   PO 27.1.37   FO 27.10.38   FL 3.9.40
SL 1.12 41   WC 1.7.44   WC 1.10.46

REGINALD THOMAS ADAMS

759300   Sgt   Air Gunner   British   264 Squadron

Adams, from Marten in Wiltshire, went to Kirton-in-Lindsey on September 13 1940 to join 264 Squadron, then engaged in night-fighting operations.

In 1942, as a Flight Sergeant, he was with 405(Vancouver) Squadron, RCAF, flying in Halifaxes from Pocklington. Adams failed to return from operations on June 30 1942. He is 21 and is buried in the churchyard at Noordwolde, Weststevingwerf, Netherlands.

WILLIAM NATHAN ADDISON

622688   Sgt   Radar Operator   British   23 Squadron

On August 18 1940 Addison joined 23 Squadron at Wittering and served with it during the Battle of Britain. Operating as a night-fighter unit 23 was equipped with Blenheim 1fs.

In early 1941 he was posted to 85 Squadron at Debden and entered what was to be a long and highly successful partnership with a Canadian pilot, Flight Lieutenant Gordon Raphael. Having taken part in the destruction of three enemy aircraft at night Addison was awarded the DFM (15.7.41). He was promoted to Warrant Officer on May 1 1942 and later awarded the DFC (19.2 43) for participating in three more night victories. About this time Addison was posted away for a rest.

He returned to operations in July 1944, when he joined 488 Squadron at Colerne. He was to have flown with the CO but he was killed just prior to Addison's arrival. So he was teamed up with Flying Officer Douglas Robinson and when Robinson went for a rest Addison flew with Flight Lieutenant Cook until he returned to the squadron. During his time with 488 Addison assisted in the destruction of a Ju 88.

When 488 disbanded on April 26 1945 Addison went with Robinson to 219 Squadron, where they stayed until the war ended.

Addison was released in 1945, still holding the rank of Warrant Officer.

RAYMOND CHARLES AEBERHARDT

42781   PO   Pilot   British   19 Squadron

Aeberhardt, from Walton-on-Thames, joined the RAF on a short service commission in August 1939. He completed his flying training and was posted to 19 Squadron at Duxford in June 1940.

On August 31 the squadron intercepted an enemy force attacking Debden. In the ensuing combat Aeberhardt's Spitfire, R 6912, was hit and the glycol system damaged. He returned to Fowlmere and attempted a landing without flaps, which were not working. The aircraft went over on its back and caught fire.

Aeberhardt was killed. He was 19 years old and is buried in the churchyard of St Mary and St Andrew, Whittlesford, Cambridgeshire.

APO 23.10.39   PO 18.5.40

NOEL le CHEVALIER AGAZARIAN

72550   PO   Pilot   British   609 Squadron

Son of an Armenian father and a French mother, Agazarian was at Wadham College, Oxford in the late thirties. He was a good athlete, a boxing blue and a member of the University Air Squadron. However, in spite of his sporting achievments, he was sent down in 1939. Agazarian was called up in late September. At ITW he met Richard Hillary, who described him as 'cosmopolitan by nature, intelligent and a brilliant linguist'. They had been in the University Air Squadron together and in late 1939 both were posted to 15 FTS, Lossiemouth, and then to No 1 School of Army Co-operation, Old Sarum.

In early June 1940 Agazarian was posted to 5 OTU, Aston Down and on July 8 he joined 609 Squadron at Warmwell. His first victory came on August 11, when he destroyed a Bf 110. On the 25th he shared a Bf 110, shared a He 111 on September 25, destroyed a Bf 109 the following day and a Bf 110, off the coast near Warmwell, on the 27th. Agazarian shared a Bf 110 and a Do 17 with Flying Officer Nowierski on December 2, near Thorney Island.

In early 1941 Agazarian was posted to the Middle East and joined 274 Squadron on April 6 at Amriya, in the Western Desert. He shot down a Bf 109 over Tobruk on May 1, but on the 16th he was shot down and killed when 274 was intercepted by Bf 109s over Gambut. Agazarian is buried in Knightsbridge War Cemetery, Acroma, Libya

PO (RAFVR) 14.2.39   PO 26.9.39   FO 14.8.40

CHARLES ROBERT AINDOW

162980   AC 2   Radar Operator   British   23 Squadron

Aindow volunteered for the RAF in September 1939. He was called up on June 4 1940 and after basic training volunteered for aircrew duties. He went to Yatesbury for a radar course, after which he was posted to 23 Squadron at Wittering on August 28. He flew 26 night operations during the Battle of Britain but without success.

In March 1941 Aindow was posted to 85 Squadron at Debden but after a short navigation course at Cranage was transferred in July to Tangmere on Turbinlite Bostons. The aircraft were fitted with a searchlight in the nose. On patrols the Bostons were each accompanied by two fighters. When an enemy was located, approached and illuminated by the searchlight, the fighters would then destroy it. The scheme was not successful and eventually scrapped.

In early 1943 Aindow, now a Warrant Officer, joined 157 Squadron at Castle Camps. He flew on Mosquito intruder patrols over the Continent, patrolling enemy airfields and attacking trains. In November 1943 the squadron moved to Predannack, attached to Coastal Command and flying daylight patrols down to the Bay of Biscay. Aindow's pilot, Flying Officer Dyke, destroyed two enemy aircraft and probably two more during the first ten days. Commissioned in October 1943, Aindow was rested in February 1944 and became a navigation instructor. He was later with a Radar Ground-Controlled Approach Unit as an Air Controller. The unit transferred to Germany and he was released from there in December 1945

PO 30.10.43   FO 30.4.44   FL 30.10.45

ERIC DOUGLAS AINGE

751890   Sgt   Aircrew   British   23 Squadron

Joined 23 Squadron at Ford on October 3 1940.

No other service details traced. Ainge died on November 30 1979.

SIDNEY AINSWORTH

1002750   Sgt   Aircrew   British   23 Squadron

Joined 23 Squadron at Ford on September 20 1940.

No other service details traced. Ainsworth died on October 21 1975.

ARTHUR AITKEN

936218   Sgt   Aircrew   British   219 Squadron

Joined 219 Squadron at Catterick in September 1940.
No other service details traced.

HENRY ALOYSIUS AITKEN

129498   Sgt   Pilot   British   54 Squadron

On completion of his flying training Aitken joined 54 Squadron at Catterick on October 6 1940 and remained with it into 1941.

He was commissioned in July 1943 and released from the RAF, as a Flight Lieutenant, in 1946.

PO 20.7.42   FO 20.1.43   FL 20.7.44

The Hon JOHN WILLIAM MAXWELL AITKEN

90128   SL   Pilot   British   601 Squadron

The Honourable Max Aitken was born in Montreal on February 15 1910, the elder son of William Aitken, who was created 1st Baron Beaverbrook in 1916.

Educated at Westminster School and Pembroke College, Cambridge, Aitken joined the Auxiliary Air Force in 1935 and was commissioned in September, serving with 601 Squadron. He was a noted member of the social set and sportsman in the thirties and his photograph often appeared in society magazines.

Aitken was embodied for full-time service with 601 on August 26 1939. He took part in the squadron's first operation on November 27 when six of its Blenheims joined with 25 Squadron to attack the German seaplane base at Borkum.

On May 16 1940 Aitken flew to Merville in France with 'A' Flight of 601 to reinforce 3 Squadron. During the short period of this attachment he destroyed one He 111 and probably another over Brussels on May 18. The next day he shot down a He 111 and a Ju 87 and probably destroyed a second Ju 87 and a Bf 110. Aitken was promoted and given command of 601 in early June. He destroyed a He 111 at night on June 26. For this and his victories in May he was awarded the DFC (9.7.40).

Aitken's next victory came on July 7, when he shared a Do 17 with four other pilots. He was posted away from 601 on July 20 and did not return to operations until February 1941, when he took command of 68 Squadron at Catterick, newly-formed with Blenheim 1fs for night-fighting. After being declared operational in April it had some victories later in the year but not until April 1942, flying from Coltishall with mostly Czech crews, did it achieve much success. In that month Aitken destroyed five German bombers at night. On May 29 he shot down a Do 217 and destroyed two more enemy bombers on July 23. He was awarded the Czech Military Cross (11.8.42), the DSO (14.8.42) and the Air Efficiency Award (1.1.43). His tour completed, he was posted away in January 1943 and in February went to HQ Eastern Mediterranean, in the Fighter Tactics Branch.

On March 5 1944, in a Beaufighter of 46 Squadron, Aitken destroyed two Ju 52s and probably another over the Aegean Sea at night. He returned to the UK later in the year to command the Banff Mosquito Strike Wing, operating in Norwegian waters against enemy shipping.

After being released, as a Group Captain, in early 1946 Aitken was given command of 601 Squadron in June and held the post until 1948. He had been returned as Conservative Member of Parliament in the 1945 General Election, holding the seat until 1950, when he returned to newspapers.

In 1968 he became Chairman of Beaverbrook Newspapers and President in 1977, an appointment he held until his death on May 1 1985.

Max Aitken succeeded his father as Lord Beaverbrook in 1964 but on June 11 of that year disclaimed the barony.

PO (AuxAF) 11.9.35   FO (AuxAF) 14.4.37   FO 26.8.39
FL 24.5.40   SL 3.5.41   WC 1.9.42   SL (RAuxAF) 1.8.46

HAROLD JOHN AKROYD

86360   **PO**   **Pilot**   **British**   **152 Squadron**

Born on September 6 1913, Akroyd was serving as a Sergeant-Pilot with 152 Squadron at Acklington at the start of the Battle of Britain. In mid-July the squadron moved south to Warmwell, in Dorset.

On August 15 1940 Akroyd claimed a Ju 87 destroyed. On the same day he returned to Warmwell in the late afternoon after a combat over Portland, damaged and with a jammed rudder, in Spitfire R 6910.

In combat with enemy fighters over Lyme Regis in the afternoon of October 7 Akroyd was shot down. His aircraft, Spitfire N 3039, crashed and burned out at Nutmead, Shillingstone. He was severely burned and died the next day. He is buried in the churchyard of Holy Trinity, Warmwell.

PO 25.9.40

ANTHONY VICTOR ALBERTINI

119844   **Sgt**   **Pilot**   **British**   **600 Squadron**

Served with 600 Squadron from 1938 to 1941. He was commissioned in May 1942 and released from the RAF in 1946, as a Flight Lieutenant.

PO 13.5.42   *FO 29.6.43*   *FL 13.5.44*

ERIC STANLEY ALDOUS

82708   **PO**   **Pilot**   **British**   **610 and 41 Squadrons**

Aldous, from Sanderstead, Surrey, was posted to 610 Squadron at Biggin Hill on July 27 1940.

His aircraft, Spitfire R 6641, was damaged in combat off Dover on August 24 but Aldous returned safely to base. He claimed a He 111 destroyed on the 30th. After combat over Charing in the morning of September 28 he crash-landed at Pluckley, in Spitfire X 4345, and was slightly injured.

In 1941 Aldous was with 615 Squadron. Flying from Manston on October 16 he was shot down and killed during an attack on storage tanks at Flushing. He was an Acting Flight Lieutenant and 23 years old. Eric Aldous is buried in Vlissingen Northern Cemetery, Flushing, Netherlands.

PO 27.7.40   *FO 27.7.41*

FREDERICK JOSEPH ALDRIDGE

42381   **PO**   **Pilot**   **British**   **610 and 41 Squadrons**

Aldridge began training as a pupil pilot in the RAF in June 1939 and was commissioned in early August. He joined 610 Squadron at Acklington on September 3 1940 and moved to 41 Squadron at Hornchurch on October 1.

The squadron was heavily engaged and Aldridge claimed a Bf 109 destroyed on October 17 and another on the 30th.

He was released from the RAF in 1947, as a Squadron Leader.

APO 5.8.39   *PO 4.3.40*   *FO 4.3.41*   *FL 4.3.42*

KEITH RUSSELL ALDRIDGE

91039   **PO**   **Pilot**   **British**   **501 Squadron**

Born in April 1918, Aldridge joined 501 Squadron in 1937 and underwent part-time flying training. He was embodied for full-time service on August 24 1939 and when 501 was sent to France he completed his elementary training at Hanworth Air Park and then went to 3 FTS, South Cerney for advanced flying.

On July 12 Aldridge rejoined 501 Squadron at Middle Wallop. In an engagement with Bf 109s on August 24 near Maidstone he was shot down and baled out, suffering burns and multiple fractures of an arm and a shoulder. His Hurricane, L 1865, crashed near Pells Farm, West Kingsdown. He claimed a Ju 88 destroyed on this day.

After a spell in hospital Aldridge was posted to the operations room at Rudloe Manor and later went to Exeter as controller. In early 1942 he did a refresher course at Hawarden, converted to Spitfires and then joined 33 Squadron in the Western Desert. He later went to 206 (Maintenance) Group as a test pilot and became Chief Test Pilot, Middle East, responsible for supplying pilots to units from Cyprus down to Khartoum.

Released in 1946, Aldridge took up gliding, an interest he followed for the next forty years

APO 24.8.39   *PO 13.7.40*   *FO 27.5.41*   *FL 27.5.42*

AYLMER JAMES MARTINUS ALDWINCLE

83288   **PO**   **Pilot**   **British**   **601 Squadron**

After completion of his flying training and conversion to Hurricanes at OTU Aldwincle joined 601 Squadron at Exeter on September 11 1940.

In 1942 he transferred to the Technical Branch (Engineering) and remained there until his release in 1946, as a Wing Commander.

PO 17.8.40   *FO 17.8.41*   *FL (T)(e)1.9.42*   *SL (T)(e) 11.3.45*

EDWARD ARISS ALEXANDER

88648   **Sgt**   **Pilot**   **British**   **236 Squadron**

Alexander, of Steyning, Sussex, was with 236 Squadron in July 1940. He was commissioned in November and killed on February 25 1941, aged 22, still with 236.

He is remembered on the Runnymede Memorial, Panel 31.

PO 27.11.40

JOHN WILLIAM EDWARD ALEXANDER

42178   **PO**   **Pilot**   **British**   **151 Squadron**

Joining the RAF as a candidate for a short service commission, Alexander began as a pupil pilot in April 1939 and completed his training in early 1940. On July 1 he was posted to 151 Squadron at Martlesham Heath.

Flying from North Weald on August 28 Alexander's aircraft was set alight in a combat over the Thames Estuary and he baled out, badly burned. The burning Hurricane, L 2005, crashed into a bungalow at Millthorpe, Godmersham at 4.30 pm.

Alexander was released from the RAF in 1945, as a Flight Lieutenant.

APO 24.6.39   *PO 27.12.39*   *FO 27.12.40*   *FL 27.12.41*
FL (RAFRO) 1.1.43

GEOFFREY ALLARD

44551   **PO**   **Pilot**   **British**   **85 Squadron**

Born in York on August 20 1912, Allard joined the RAF at Halton on September 3 1929, as an aircraft apprentice. He passed out as an LAC Metal Rigger on August 19 1932 and was posted to the maintenance staff at RAF College, Cranwell, remaining there until March 3 1936, when he went to 2 Armament Training Camp, North Coates.

Allard had applied for pilot training. He was selected in 1936 and on December 21 began his ab initio course at 2 E&RFTS, Filton. He went on to 9 FTS, Thornaby on March 20 1937, moved with the unit to Hullavington on July 9, passed out as a Sergeant-Pilot on October 23 and joined 87 Squadron at Debden.

On June 1 1938 Allard was posted to 85 Squadron, then reforming with Gladiators at Debden. On September 9 1939 the squadron flew to France but saw little action before the blitzkrieg began in May 1940. Between the 10th and 16th Allard is believed to have destroyed at least ten enemy aircraft. After heavy losses 85 was withdrawn to Debden on May 21. Allard was awarded the DFM (31.5.40).

On July 8 he claimed a He 111 destroyed, on the 9th another, on the 30th shared Bf 110, on August 6 a shared Do 17, on the 24th a Bf 109, on the 26th a Do 215, on the 28th two Bf 109s, on the 30th two He 111s, on the 31st a Bf 109 and on September 1 a Do 17 and a Bf 109.

Allard was commissioned in August and in a squadron severely depleted by losses he was promoted to Acting Flight Lieutenant and given command of 'A' Flight. He was awarded a Bar to the DFM (13.9.40) and the DFC (8.10.40).

On November 6 the squadron returned to Debden and prepared for a night-fighting role. Conversion from Hurricanes to Havocs began in February 1941. On March 13 Allard, with Pilot Officer WH Hodgson and Sergeant FR Walker-Smith as passengers, took off from Debden in a Havoc. Shortly afterwards the aircraft crashed at Mill Field Ley, just south of Wimbish. The three pilots were killed. It is believed that an insecurely-fastened nose panel flew off and jammed in the rudder, causing the aircraft to become uncontrollable.

Allard is buried in Saffron Walden Borough Cemetery, Essex. His portrait was done by Eric Kennington and Cuthbert Orde.

PO 15.8.40

PETER OWEN DENYS ALLCOCK

42179   PO   Pilot   British   229 Squadron

Allcock, from Herne Hill, London, joined the RAF on a short service commission and began training as a pupil pilot in April 1939.

He was serving with 229 Squadron when the Battle of Britain started. On September 23 1940 he was shot down when he was acting as weaver on a squadron patrol. He baled out, wounded, and after landing at Westcliff he was admitted to Southend Hospital. His aircraft, Hurricane P 2789, crashed on St Mary's Marshes, Hoo.

Allcock went with 229 when it departed for the Middle East in May 1941. On December 17 they formed part of the escort for Hurribombers of 80 Squadron, detailed to attack enemy vehicles near Mechili. The raid was frustrated when the British aircraft were attacked by Bf 109s and Mc 202s. In the ensuing combat Allcock was shot down and killed by Leutnant Hoffmann of 1/JG27. He was 22 years old and having no known grave he is remembered on the Alamein Memorial, Column 240.

APO 10.6.39   PO 6.4.40   FO 6.4.41

HUBERT RAYMOND ALLEN

42582   PO   Pilot   British   66 Squadron

Born on March 19 1919, Allen entered the RAF on a short service commission, beginning his flying training in early June 1939 at 11 E&RFTS, Perth. In late August he was posted to Hullavington for kitting-out and a disciplinary course, after which he went to 15 FTS, Lossiemouth for further training.

Allen joined 66 Squadron at Duxford on April 13 1940. He shared in the destruction of a Do 17 on August 30, shared a He 111 on September 9, destroyed a He 111 on the 15th and a Bf 109 on the 18th. In October he was appointed 'B' Flight Commander and on November 14 he destroyed a Ju 87 and probably a second. On the 28th, in Spitfire P7492, Allen collided with Sergeant Willcocks over Edenbridge and baled out, unhurt. Willcocks was killed.

Allen was wounded in the right arm on February 14 1941 after being jumped by Bf 109s. He crashed at Biggin Hill. On June 20 he

destroyed a Bf 109 and shared a second. Awarded the DFC (22.7.41), he was promoted to Acting Squadron Leader in October and commanded 66 Squadron until December 1941. He was then posted away and did not fly operationally again. Allen commanded No 1 Squadron from January to October 1946 and 43 Squadron from December 1949 to February 1952. He was a graduate of the RAF Staff College and retired as a Wing Commander on January 1 1965. Allen died on May 31 1987.

*APO 2.9.39   PO 24.3.40   FO 24.3.41   FL 1.1.42
SL 1.8.47   WC 1.7.54*

JAMES HENRY LESLIE ALLEN

39957   FO   Pilot   New Zealander   151 Squadron

Born in Remuera, Auckland on November 13 1914, Allen was orphaned at the age of four. Brought up by his paternal aunt, he was educated at Huntly School, Marton and Napier Boys' High School.

In 1931 Allen went to England for sea training and he joined HMS 'Conway' in May. He won His Majesty's Gold Medal in July 1933 as the most efficient cadet and in August went to the Blue Funnel Line as a midshipman. In June 1936 Allen applied for a commission in the RAF. He was successful and began elementary flying training at No 1 E&RFTS, Hatfield on May 24 1937.

After the short induction course at Uxbridge Allen was posted to 10 FTS at Dumfries. In March 1938, his training completed, he went to the School of Naval Co-operation on flying duties, remaining there until February 1939, when he was posted to 151 Squadron at North Weald.

Allen went to France with other pilots of 151 on May 16 1940 to reinforce 87 Squadron, which had suffered heavy losses. After a week of confused fighting 87 was withdrawn to England and Allen rejoined 151 at Martlesham Heath on June 4.

The squadron was ordered off on July 12 1940 to protect convoy 'Booty' from an approaching German formation. They attacked two staffeln of Do 17s about 20 miles east of Orfordness. Allen's Hurricane, P3275, was caught in a withering crossfire and he was last seen gliding down with a dead engine. He is believed to have drowned and is remembered on the Runnymede Memorial, Panel 5.

APO 9.8.37   PO 24.5.38   FO 24.12.39

JOHN LAURANCE ALLEN

70008   PO   Pilot   British   54 Squadron

Allen joined the RAF in June 1937. He went to 8 FTS, Montrose on August 21. He was on a training flight on January 18 1938 when he disappeared in fog over Forfarshire. Search parties failed to find him. Early the next morning an RAF search plane spotted wreckage on Glen Dye moor, Kincardineshire. Beside the wreck was a rescue party, laying down, spelling out the word ALIVE. An ambulance plane picked up Allen, badly injured. After a long stay in hospital he finished his training and joined 54 Squadron at Hornchurch on December 5 1938.

On May 21 1940 between Dunkirk and Calais Allen probably destroyed a Ju 88, 54 Squadron's first victory. Two days later he and Alan Deere escorted Squadron Leader J Leathart, in a Master, to Calais Marck airfield to pick up the CO of 74 Squadron, who was stranded there. Twelve Bf 109s attacked the Master but were engaged by Allen and Deere, who between them shot three down and badly damaged three more. Allen destroyed one and damaged two others. On May 25 his engine was hit by a cannon shell and he baled out over the Channel near a destroyer. He returned to the squadron after three days, in sailor's uniform, carrying a kitbag. Allen was awarded the DFC (11.6.40) and received it from the King in a ceremony at Hornchurch on June 27, in company with Deere and Leathart, who were awarded the DFC and DSO respectively.

Allen shared in destroying a He 59 on July 9. His engine was

JL Allen (continued)

damaged in a combat with Bf109s over Margate on July 24 1940. He stalled while trying to reach Manston. He was then seen making for Foreness in a controlled descent with a dead engine, which suddenly restarted, causing him to again make for Manston. The engine stopped again and trying to turn for Foreness a second time he stalled and spun in and was killed when his Spitfire, R6812, crashed and burned out near the Old Charles Inn at Cliftonville. Allen was 24. He is buried in Margate Cemetery, Kent.

APO 9.8.37   PO 5.12.38

JOHN WATSON ALLEN

135866   Sgt   Pilot   British   266 Squadron

Joined the RAF in early 1940 and was posted to 266 Squadron at Wittering on October 7.

Allen was later with 256 Squadron, was commissioned in November 1942 and released from the RAF in 1946, as a Flight Lieutenant.

PO 23.11.42   FO 23.5.43   FL 23.11.44

KENNETH MERVYN ALLEN

146710   F/Sgt   Pilot   British   257, 43 and 253 Sqdns

A pre-war airman pilot, Allen joined 257 Squadron at Debden on September 1 1940, moved to 43 at Usworth on the 11th and to 253 at Kenley on the 28th.

He was commissioned in April 1943 and was released from the RAF in 1946, as a Flight Lieutenant. He died in 1984.

PO 24.4.43   FO 24.10.43   FL 24.4.45

LESLIE HENRY ALLEN

129967   Sgt   Air Gunner   British   141 Squadron

Allen joined the RAF in 1940 and after completing his gunnery training was posted to 141 Squadron at Turnhouse on September 13 1940. At that time the squadron's Defiants were flying convoy patrols but soon afterwards were put on to night-fighting duties.

Commissioned in August 1942, Allen was released from the RAF in 1946, as a Flight Lieutenant.

PO 21.8.42   FO 21.2.43   FL 21.8.44

HAROLD HENRY ALLGOOD

565462   F/Sgt   Pilot   British   85 and 253 Squadrons

Born in Cambridge in 1915, Allgood was educated at the Central School there. He left in July 1931 and joined the RAF at Halton as an apprentice metal rigger in September.

Allgood later volunteered for pilot training and was accepted on September 13 1938 but did not begin training until 1939. He was at 11 FTS, Shawbury from September 25 until April 6 1940. After converting to Hurricanes he was posted to 85 Squadron in France on May 14. When 85 returned to Debden on the 21st Allgood was not with them. He was officially reported back on June 22 and rejoined 85 at Martlesham Heath in early July.

On August 11 1940 Allgood claimed a Bf 109 but the same day returned to base with his mainplane damaged by a Bf 110, engaged over a convoy off the east coast.

He escaped unhurt from Hurricane P 2827, when he crashed making a dusk landing at Church Fenton on September 9.

Allgood was posted to 253 Squadron at Kenley on September 28. He was killed on October 10 when his aircraft, Hurricane L 1928, crashed into houses at Albion Place, Maidstone. The cause of the crash was never established. He is buried in St Mark's Burial Ground, Grantchester, Cambridge.

JACK WHITWELL ALLISON

104382   Sgt   Pilot   British   41,611 and 92 Squadrons

Hailing from Eltham, London, Allison was with 41 Squadron at Catterick at the beginning of June 1940 and on the 8th shared in the destruction of a Ju 88. He moved south to Hornchurch with the squadron at the end of the month.

In September Allison was posted to 611 Squadron, staying only for a few weeks before moving to 92 Squadron at Digby on October 27.

Commissioned in August 1941, Allison was killed on October 15 1942 but the unit he was with at the time of his death is not known. He was 26 years old and was cremated at Pontypridd Crematorium, Glamorganshire.

PO 15.8.41   FO 15.2 42

HAROLD GORDON LEACH ALLSOP

32184   SL   Pilot   British   66 Squadron

Born on October 25 1909, Allsop joined the RAF in June 1932. He was posted to 4 FTS, Abu Sueir on August 26 and joined 84 Squadron at Shaibah, Iraq on August 25 1933.

Allsop returned to the United Kingdom in 1936 and on November 30 went to 608 Squadron at Thornaby as adjutant and flying instructor. He was still with the squadron at the outbreak of war.

During the period of the Battle of Britain Allsop flew at least one operational sortie with 66 Squadron, but not as a member of the squadron.

He retired from the RAF on October 25 1956, as a Wing Commander.

APO 12.8.32   PO 12.8.33   FO 12.3.35   FL 12.3.37
SL 1.4.39   WC 1.3.41   WC 1.10.46

LESLIE CHARLES ALLTON

745436   Sgt   Pilot   British   266 and 92 Squadrons

Born in Nuneaton in 1920, Allton was educated at King Edward VI Grammar School from 1931 to 1937, where he excelled, being School Captain and Captain of Football, Hockey and Cricket. He joined the RAFVR in 1938 and was called for full-time service at the outbreak of war.

Allton joined 266 Squadron at Wittering on September 16 1940, moving to 92 Squadron at Biggin Hill on the 30th. He was killed on October 19 when he crashed at Tuesnoad Farm, Smarden. Although the circumstances were unknown his name appeared in the casualty list as 'Killed in Action'. The site of the crash was excavated in the late seventies and the propellor, engine and other items from the aircraft, Spitfire R 6922, were recovered.

Leslie Allton is buried in the Oaston Road Cemetery, Nuneaton.

CHARLES FRANCIS AMBROSE

42583   PO   Pilot   British   46 Squadron

Ambrose was born on January 27 1917 and began his flying training as a candidate for a short service commission in June 1939.   On completion of his training he joined 46 Squadron at Digby in March 1940.

On September 2 he shot down a Bf 109 near Eastchurch. It crash-landed at Tile Lodge Farm, Hoath and the pilot was captured. Two days later Ambrose was shot down by Bf 109s in combat over Rochford. He was in Hurricane P 3066 and baled out unhurt.

He was flying with Pilot Officer Lefevre of 46 in the early afternoon of November 3 near Gravesend when they intercepted a Do 17 of 8/KG 3, which was being fired on by anti-aircraft guns. They shot the bomber down and it crashed at Bexley, with four of the crew killed and one captured, who died of his wounds the following day.

On November 30 Ambrose had to bale out again when he was shot down in an engagement over Dungeness. In December he was awarded the DFC (24.12.40).

Posted away from 46 in June 1941, Ambrose went to the Middle East later in the year and served with 112 Squadron, flying Tomahawks in the Western Desert. On December 5 he claimed a Fiat G 50 as 'probably destroyed'.

Ambrose remained in the RAF after the war. He commanded 43 Squadron in Austria and Italy from March 1946 to May 1947, was awarded the AFC (29.10 48) and held various staff appointments in Britain and overseas. He qualified on the Senior Officers War Course at the Royal Naval War College, was a graduate of the RAF College of Air Warfare and was qualified in Staff Studies. Ambrose was made a CBE (8.6.68) and retired on January 27 1972, as a Group Captain. He died in 1986.

APO 2.9.39   PO 24.2.40   FO 24.2.41   FL 24.2.42
SL 1.8.47   WC 1.1.57   GC 1.1.62

RICHARD AMBROSE

73040   PO   Pilot   British   25 and 151 Squadrons

Commissioned in the RAFVR in June 1939, Ambrose was called for full-time service after the outbreak of war and given a war-time commission.

He was posted to 25 Squadron at Martlesham Heath on August 18 1940 but moved to Stapleford on the 26th to join 151 Squadron.

Ambrose was detailed to ferry Hurricane V 7406 to Digby on September 4. He was killed, when he crashed into a crane on take-off and the aircraft burned out. He was 21 years old and is buried in Epping Cemetery, Essex.

PO (RAFVR) 20.6.39   PO 21.10.39

JAN AMBRUS

81883   SL   Pilot   Czechoslovakian   312 Squadron

Ambrus was posted to command 312 Squadron at Duxford on September 9 1940. It was RAF policy that for a period after formation of Czech squadrons the command would be shared by a British and Czech officer. Ambrus shared his with Squadron Leader FH Tyson.

On October 15 Ambrus crashed near Dalton-in-Furness in Hurricane V 6846. During a routine patrol he had lost his bearings and was low on fuel.

Posted to the Czech Ministry of Defence on December 18 1940, Ambrus did not return to operational flying. He was appointed Czech Air Attaché in Ottawa in 1943, with the rank of Wing Commander. After the war he made his home in Canada.

DONALD JOHN ANDERSON

79739   PO   Pilot   British   29 Squadron

On April 5 1939 Anderson joined the RAFVR and began his flying training at 34 E&RFTS, Rochford. Called up in September, he went to 4 ITW, Bexhill at the end of October and then to 11 FTS, Shawbury on November 19 1939.

Anderson was posted to No 2 School of Army Co-operation, Andover on June 15 1940 but a week later went to 5 OTU, Aston Down for conversion to Blenheims, after which he joined 29 Squadron at Digby on July 6. He remained with the squadron until July 20 1941 and after an attachment to Kirton-in-Lindsey he was posted to 89 Squadron, then forming at Colerne with Beaufighters. The squadron flew out to the Middle East in late November 1941 and began operating from Abu Sueir in night defence of the Delta.

In early March 1942 Anderson was medically regraded A2B and posted to No 1 Section Aircraft Delivery Unit, Wadi Natrun. Six months later he lost his flying category and was posted to a ground radar unit. Over the next eighteen months he served at a number of units in the Middle East. From April 2 1944 Anderson was Camp Commandant at Makadini, a Catalina base on the coast of East Africa. In early September he returned to radar units and for a spell in October 1944 was Fighter Direction Officer on HMS 'Ulster Queen', scanning the Greek Islands. After five months as a station adjutant Anderson embarked for home on December 12 1945. He was at RAF Wartling until his release on June 28 1946, as a Flight Lieutenant.

PO 9.6.40   FO 9.6.41   FL 9.6.42

JAMES ALEXANDER ANDERSON

187307   Sgt   Pilot   British   253 Squadron

Anderson joined 253 Squadron at Kenley in early September 1940. In the evening of the 14th he was shot down in combat with Bf 109s and crashed at Stone, near Faversham, in Hurricane P 3804. Admitted to Faversham Hospital with severe burns, he was later moved to the Queen Victoria Hospital, East Grinstead.

Commissioned from Warrant Officer in September 1944, Anderson was released from the RAF in 1946, as a Flying Officer. He was a member of the Guinea Pig Club and died on May 28 1978.

PO 22.9.44   FO 22.3.45

JOHN DENIS ANDERSON

1052185   AC 2   Radar Operator   British   604 Squadron

Born on April 22 1922, Anderson joined the RAF on June 6 1940. At the end of the month he was at RAF Yatesbury for what he expected to be the start of a Wop/AG course. Instead he found himself learning about airborne radar and in late July he was posted to 604 Squadron at Gravesend, never having flown.

Anderson flew operationally with 604, firstly in Blenheims and then Beaufighters, until December 1940, when he was posted back to Yatesbury for another radar course. In these five months Anderson flew without rank or brevet, receiving three shillings per day, which included one shilling flying pay.

In January 1941 Anderson was posted to a radar station at Saligo, Islay, Scotland. He went to No 1 Radio School at Cranwell in May, as an instructor, initially as a Corporal but became a Sergeant in March 1942. Anderson volunteered for pilot training and was accepted in September 1942. In 1943 he was deputy controller at a small radar station at Goldsborough on the Yorkshire coast.

In September 1943 Anderson began his pilot training but with inevitable delays awaiting courses he had still not qualified when training was terminated in April 1945. Anderson was then posted to RAF Atherstone for a GCA course, after which he went to 10 GCA, RAF Hemswell in November 1945, as a Flight Sergeant.

Commissioned from Warrant Officer in June 1955, Anderson retired from the RAF on January 31 1973, as a Squadron Leader. He then joined Customs and Excise and retired again on April 22 1984.

PO 8.6.55   FO 8.12.55   FL 18.11.58

MICHAEL FREDERIC ANDERSON

90209   SL   Pilot   British   604 Squadron

A member of the Stock Exchange before the war, Anderson joined 604 Squadron, AuxAF on October 4 1930 and was commissioned a month later. In the pre-war years he attended camps and courses and spent two spells with 23 Squadron, at Biggin Hill in March 1935 and at Northolt in July 1937. Called to full-time service on August 24 1939, Anderson was then senior flight commander of 604. He took command of the squadron in March 1940, led it throughout the Battle of Britain and on October 30 flew the first operational patrol in a Beaufighter.

Anderson was awarded the DFC (25.3.41), the citation stating that he had carried out many night operational flights, in the course of which he had destroyed a He 111 and probably a Ju 88. He was also credited with one enemy aircraft destroyed in daylight.

In early April 1941 Anderson was posted to RAF High Ercall, to command. After three months he went to HQ 9 Group, Preston, then to the Middle East, to serve at HQ 250 Wing, Ismailia. A series of staff appointments followed, the last being at Air HQ, Levant.

Anderson was released from the RAF on October 3 1945, as a Wing Commander.

PO (AuxAF) 4.11.30   FO (AuxAF) 4.5.32   FL (AuxAF) 6.6.35
FL 24.8.39   SL 1.3.40   WC 1.6.42

CHRISTOPHER JOHN DRAKE ANDREAE
70018   FO   Pilot   British   64 Squadron

A Londoner, Andreae was educated at Shrewsbury School from 1930 to 1935 and then at Caius College, Cambridge. He joined the RAFVR and was commissioned in March 1937.

Andreae was called for full-time service late in 1939 and given a war-time commission. He joined 64 Squadron at Kenley in late July 1940 and was soon in action. On August 11 he returned to base, in Spitfire N 3293, with damage caused by cannon fire from an enemy fighter engaged off Dover.

Four days later Andreae failed to return from a combat with Bf 109s over the Channel. He was 23 years old. He was never heard of again and is remembered on the Runnymede Memorial, Panel 5.

PO (RAFVR) 16.3.37   PO 15.12.39   FO 10.5.40

STANLEY ANDREW
740169   Sgt   Pilot   British   46 Squadron

Andrew, from Swanland, Yorkshire, joined the RAFVR in 1937. He went into regular service in March 1939 and after completing his training he joined 46 Squadron at Digby.

On May 18 1940 the squadron sailed for Norway in HMS 'Glorious'. The Hurricanes flew off and landed at Skaanland on the 26th. The campaign was short-lived. On June 7 the surviving Hurricanes of 46 flew back on to the 'Glorious', the first time such a landing had been attempted. The carrier was sunk the following day when it met the 'Scharnhorst' and 'Gneisenau'. Only two of the squadron's pilots were among the few survivors. Andrew was one of the luckier ones, who were evacuated from Norway by sea on June 8.

Back at Digby the squadron reformed and was operational again on June 26. In early September 46 moved south to Stapleford and on the 8th Andrew shot down a Do 17 of 5/KG 2, which exploded over Leeds Castle, near Maidstone, killing the crew. In the same sortie Andrew's aircraft, Hurricane P 3525, was damaged by a Bf 109 over Sheppey but he got back safely to base.

During an uneventful patrol on September 11 Andrew, flying the same aircraft, was killed when the Hurricane crashed and burned out. He is buried in the churchyard of All Saints, North Ferriby, Yorkshire. He was 21.

MAURICE RAYMOND ANDREWS
40615   Sgt   Air Gunner   New Zealander   264 Squadron

At the outbreak of war Andrews owned a motor engineering and garage business in Hamilton. At 29, he was old by normal aircrew standards when he volunteered for flying duties.

He reported to the Air Observers' School, Ohakea on March 11 1940 to train as an observer but soon afterwards remustered to trainee air gunner. Andrews sailed for Britain on April 26, arrived in early June and was posted to 5 OTU, Aston Down in mid-August. At the end of the month he joined 264 Squadron at Kirton-in-Lindsey.

Andrews was commissioned in early June 1942 and when the squadron converted to Mosquitos later in the month he was posted away, joning 277 (Air Sea Rescue) Squadron on July 15. When he left 264 Andrews had flown 122 operational sorties.

Early in 1942 Andrews had applied for pilot training and on August 22 he left 277 for 13 ITW. After completing his ground course he moved to 26 EFTS, thence to Manchester to await a posting overseas. He sailed for Canada in March 1943, completed his training at various flying schools and passed out as a twin-engine pilot in January 1944. Two months later Andrews was repatriated to New Zealand.

He was posted as a staff pilot to the School of Navigation and Reconnaissance at New Plymouth, where he was eventually appointed a Flight Commander. He was transferred to the Reserve on December 24 1945 and returned to his garage business. Andrews died in Hamilton on March 24 1971.

PO 3.6.42   FO 3.12.42   FL 3.6.44

SYDNEY ERNEST ANDREWS
44567   PO   Pilot   British   32 and 257 Squadrons

Commissioned in early May 1940, Andrews joined 32 Squadron at Acklington in early September. He was posted to 257 Squadron at Martlesham Heath on the 22nd of the month.

The squadron had great success when it met the Italian Air Force, making its one and only raid on London on November 11 1940. Andrews shared in the destruction of a Fiat BR 20.

He was later posted to the Middle East and on August 9 1942 Andrews was killed in a flying accident whilst serving with 3 Aircraft Maintenance Unit. He is buried in Ismailia War Memorial Cemetery, Egypt.

PO 2.5.40   FO 2.5.41

TADEUSZ ANDRUSZKOW
P5125   Sgt   Pilot   Polish   303 Squadron

Born in Lwow on November 18 1920, Andruszkow entered the PAF NCOs' Training School at Bydgoszcz in 1936. He qualified as a fighter pilot at Krosno in 1939, was posted to the 6th Air Force Regiment, Lwow and joined 162 Fighter Squadron. After the fighting in September 1939 the unit was evacuated to Roumania. Andruszkow eventually reached France, where he began to train on French aircraft. When France fell he escaped to England, arriving in July 1940.

After a Hurricane conversion course Andruszkow was posted to 303 Squadron at Northolt on August 21. He claimed a share in destroying a Do 17 on September 15. On the same day he was himself shot down in combat with Bf 109s over Dartford and baled out, unhurt. His Hurricane, P3939, is believed to be the one which crashed that day in Lower Stoke.

Andruszkow claimed a He 111 destroyed on September 26. On the following morning he was shot down over Horsham and killed when his aircraft, Hurricane V7246, crashed in flames at Holywych Farm, Cowden. Andruszkow was 19 years old and is buried in Northwood Cemetery, Middlesex. He was posthumously awarded the KW (1.2.41).

JAMES ANGUS

55202   **Sgt**   **Aircrew**   **British**   **23 Squadron**

Born on May 21 1915, Angus joined 23 Squadron at Collyweston in early August 1940. He was commissioned in June 1943 and remained in the RAF after the war, serving in the Aircraft Control Branch.

Angus retired on June 1 1965, as a Flight Lieutenant. He died on October 14 1984.

PO 11.6.43   FO 11.12.43   FL 11.6.45   FL 11.12.47

ROBERT ALEXANDER ANGUS

748062   **Sgt**   **Pilot**   **British**   **611 Squadron**

Angus, of Edinburgh, was in the RAFVR before the war. He was posted to 611 Squadron at Tern Hill on September 29 1940.

In early 1941 Angus was with 41 Squadron at Hornchurch. He was shot down by Werner Molders on February 20 over Dover, in Spitfire P 7322. Angus was seen to bale out over the sea but was never found. He was 21 years old and is remembered on the Runnymede Memorial, Panel 38.

MICHAEL JOHN APPLEBY

90962   **PO**   **Pilot**   **British**   **609 Squadron**

Appleby joined 609 Squadron, AuxAF in December 1938. He was called to full-time service on August 24 1939. He was posted to 6 FTS, Little Rissington in October and after completing his training he rejoined 609, then at Northolt, in May 1940.

On August 8 Appleby claimed a Bf 110 destroyed, a Do 17 on September 15 and a Bf 109 on the 30th. He was posted away to CFS, Upavon in November 1940, for an instructor's course.

Appleby subsequently instructed at 11, 17 and 21 EFTSs from December 1940 until he was released from the RAF in September 1945, as a Flight Lieutenant. His portrait was done by Cuthbert Orde in November 1940.

APO 24.8.39   PO 4.5.40   FO 9.12.40   FL 9.12.41

ALEXANDER NELSON ROBIN LANGLEY APPLEFORD

42736   **PO**   **Pilot**   **British**   **66 Squadron**

As a candidate for a short service commission, Appleford began his ab initio training at 12 E&RFTS, Prestwick on August 8 1939. After an induction course at Uxbridge he was posted to 11 FTS, Shawbury on September 26. With his training completed Appleford joined 66 Squadron at Duxford on May 13 1940. He was shot down in combat over the Thames Estuary on September 4 and baled out, slightly wounded. His Spitfire, P9316, crashed near Howe Green Farm, Purleigh.

Posted from 66 Squadron on December 18 1940, Appleford went to 8 FTS, Montrose for an instructor's course, after which he went to Southern Rhodesia to instruct at 22 SFTS, Gwelo. He was hospitalised on November 3 1941, firstly in Nairobi and then Durban until mid-April 1942. Appleford went north and joined the Aircraft Delivery Unit, Cairo on June 2, staying with it until January 10 1943, when he went to 274 Squadron, Benghazi, to fly Hurricanes on coastal defence.

His tour completed, Appleford was posted to 71 OTU, Ismailia as an instructor. After six weeks he returned to the Aircraft Delivery Unit and on November 15 1943 went south again to the Central Flying School, Bloemfontein. From early February 1944 until May 1945 Appleford instructed at various Air Schools in South Africa. He returned to Britain on July 1 1945 and joined 587 Squadron at Weston Zoyland on August 24. He was released from the RAF in August 1946, as a Flight Lieutenant.

APO 9.10.39   PO 18.5.40   FO 18.5.41   FL 18.5.42

IVOR KENNETH ARBER

156944   **Sgt**   **Pilot**   **British**   **603 Squadron**

Arber was already with 603 when the Battle of Britain began. On July 3 he had shared in the destruction of a Ju 88 off the East Scottish coast and on the 12th he shared a He 111 with Pilot Officers Gilroy and Caister in an engagement over Aberdeen. The enemy aircraft, from 9/KG 26, crashed and burned out, killing the crew of four.

Commissioned in August 1943, Arber was awarded the AFC (1.1.45). He left the RAF after the war and was commissioned in the RAFVR in 1947. He died on September 1 1952

PO 22.8.43   FO 29.2.44   FL 30.8.45
FO (RAFVR) 31.10.47   FL (RAFVR) 31.12.48

PAUL WADE ARBON

41893   **PO**   **Pilot**   **British**   **85 Squadron**

Born in Sydenham, London on February 8 1921, Arbon was educated at Brockley County School and joined the RAF after leaving there. He went to 13 E&RFTS, White Waltham as a pupil pilot on January 23 1939 and finished his elementary training at 11 E&RFTS, Scone. After kitting out at RAF Depot, Uxbridge Arbon was posted to 6 FTS, Little Rissington.

On November 20 1939 he went to No 1 School of Army Co-operation, Old Sarum for a short course, after which he went to the Pilots Pool, Andover in early January 1940. Arbon returned to Old Sarum on the 16th of the month when he joined 16 Squadron. Equipped with Lysanders, the squadron went to France on April 8 but was withdrawn on May 19.

Arbon volunteered for Fighter Command and was posted to 5 OTU, Aston Down on September 8. On the 26th he joined 85 Squadron at Church Fenton. He was with the squadron until June 15 1942 and was posted soon afterwards to 54 OTU, Charter Hall as an instructor. A return to operations came on January 31 1943, when Arbon went to 29 Squadron at West Malling as a Flight Commander. He was awarded the DFC (14.4.44) and given command of the squadron on April 29 1944, as Acting Wing Commander.

With his tour completed Arbon was posted to RAF Bradwell Bay as Station Commander on July 11 1944. He moved to RAF Hunsdon to command on March 22 1945 but a month later was appointed to a staff job at HQ Transport Command. Arbon was posted to 216 Group, Heliopolis on June 11 1945, taking command of 249 Wing, Bari two weeks later. He returned to England at the end of the year and was released in 1946, as a Wing Commander.

Arbon started an Auction and Estate Agency business in Hertfordshire. In 1967 he was elected the first President of the National Association of Estate Agents. The Association's headquarters in Warwick is called Arbon House.

Paul Arbon died on November 21 1968, following a car accident in France.

APO 15.4.39   PO 6.11.39   FO 6.11.40   FL 6.11.41
SL 17.7.44

JOHN ARBUTHNOT

564104   **Sgt**   **Pilot**   **British**   **1 and 229 Squadrons**

An ex-apprentice and pre-war airman pilot, Arbuthnot came from Kirknewton, Midlothian. When the war started he was with 43 Squadron at Tangmere. On December 15 1939 he baled out of Hurricane L 1725 after spinning in cloud. The aircraft crashed on peat moorland and buried itself deeply. It was excavated in 1978.

On the evening of April 8 1940 the Germans sent a force of bombers to attack the naval base at Scapa Flow. 43 was scrambled from its base at Wick to intercept. Arbuthnot was one of the first to make contact and

J Arbuthnot (continued)

he emptied his guns into a He 111, which dived away into a layer of cloud.

Posted to France to join 1 Squadron on May 16 Arbuthnot was again in action, returning to base at Boos on June 4 with his radiator shot away.

At some time during the Battle of Britain Arbuthnot was posted to 229 Squadron. He was killed with the squadron on February 4 1941. He is buried in Wilton Cemetery, Carluke, Lanarkshire and was 26 at the time of his death.

HAROLD THORPE ARCHER

747939   Sgt   Air Gunner   British   23 Squadron

Archer joined 23 Squadron at Ford on October 1 1940. In 1941 he was with 7 Squadron, flying in Stirlings from Oakington, Cambridgeshire. He failed to return from operations on June 30 1941 and is buried in Becklingen War Cemetery, Soltau, Germany.

SAMUEL ARCHER

803473   Sgt   Wop/AG   British   236 Squadron

Joined 236 Squadron on July 19 1940.

Archer was a member of the crew of Blenheim Z 5729, which was flying over Pembroke Dock on the afternoon of August 20 when it was damaged by anti-aircraft fire. The captain, Pilot Officer GL Campbell, returned the aircraft safely back to base at St Eval.

Archer was released from the RAF as a Master Signaller. He died in 1980.

ELLIS WALTER ARIES

79555   PO   Pilot   British   602 Squadron

Joined 602 Squadron at Drem on July 5 1940. Aries went south to Westhampnett with the squadron in August. On the 26th he claimed a Do 17 destroyed over Biggin Hill but his own aircraft, Spitfire K 9839, was hit by return fire and the glycol tank damaged. Aries crash-landed at Wrotham and escaped unhurt. He claimed another Do 17 destroyed on September 7.

Awarded the AFC (1.1.45), Aries was released from the RAF in 1945, as a Flight Lieutenant. He is said to have claimed the destruction of five and a half enemy aircraft during the war. He was commissioned in the RAuxAF in 1947. Ellis Aries died in 1976.

PO 2.6.40   FO 2.6.41   FL 2.6.42   FO (RAuxAF) 1.4.47

DENNIS LOCKHART ARMITAGE

76573   PO   Pilot   British   266 Squadron

Commissioned in December 1939, Armitage was posted to 266 Squadron at Wittering in late June 1940. On August 12 he claimed the destruction of a Ju 88.

Armitage was posted from 266 in May 1941 and was awarded the DFC (18.7.41) for his work with the squadron. Promoted to Acting Squadron Leader in June 1941, he took command of 129 Squadron, then forming with Spitfires at Leconfield, and held the appointment until September 1941.

Armitage was released from the RAF in 1945, as a Squadron Leader.

PO 10.12.39   FO 4.11.40   FL 19.9.41

JOSEPH FOX ARMITAGE

741932   Sgt   Pilot   British   242 Squadron

Armitage was posted to 242 Squadron at Coltishall in late June 1940 and remained with the squadron until posted away in August.

He was killed on June 17 1941, whilst serving as a Flight Sergeant with 234 Squadron at Portreath. With no known grave Armitage is remembered on the Runnymede Memorial, Panel 35.

WILLIAM ARMSTRONG

41812   PO   Pilot   British   54 and 74 Squadrons

From Darlington, Co Durham, Armstrong entered the RAF on a short service commission and began training as a pupil pilot in January 1939. After completing his training he joined 54 Squadron at Rochford towards the end of the year.

Amstrong was posted to 74 Squadron at Biggin Hill on October 28 1940 and on November 14 he was shot down off Dover after destroying two Ju 87s, whether by a Bf 109 or anti-aircraft fire is not known. He baled out and his aircraft, Spitfire P 7836, crashed on Dover Road, Sandwich.

On February 5 1941 Armstrong shared a Do 17 with three other pilots and on May 8 he destroyed a Bf 109. He died, aged 21, on February 18 1943, as a Flight Lieutenant. He is buried in Dely Ibrahim War Cemetery, Algeria. The unit he was serving with at the time of his death is not known.

APO 1.4.39   PO 23.10.39   FO 23.10.40   FL 23.10.41

STANLEY JOHN ARNFIELD

46253   Sgt   Pilot   British   610 Squadron

Arnfield was born on October 3 1913. He was serving with 610 early in 1940. He shared in the destruction of an enemy aircraft with Flight Lieutenant John Ellis on June 12, when they shot it down into the sea off Margate.

Two Bf 109s were claimed by Arnfield on August 18 and on the 24th he baled out of Spitfire R 6686 after an attack by a Bf 109 off Ramsgate. He broke an ankle on landing and was admitted to Victoria Hospital, Deal. His stricken aircraft crashed in flames at Hammill, near Eastry.

Arnfield, who was commissioned in July 1941, was awarded the DFC (30.6.44), as a Flight Lieutenant with 166 Squadron. He retired from the RAF on February 12 1951, as a Flight Lieutenant but retaining the rank of Squadron Leader. His post-war service was in the Secretarial Branch. He died on September 24 1954.

PO 26.7.41   FO 26.7.42   FL 26.7.43   FL 1.9.45

CHARLES IAN ROSE ARTHUR

41241   FO   Pilot   Canadian   141 Squadron

Born in Fort Garry, Manitoba, Arthur sailed for England in the 'Athenia' on August 13 1938 to take up a short service commission in the RAF. After completing his flying training in mid-1939 he was posted as a staff pilot to 3 Air Observers' School, Aldergrove.

Arthur joined 141 Squadron, then being reformed at Turnhouse, on October 6 1939. In April 1940 141 was re-equipped with Defiants as a day-fighter unit. In July the squadron flew south to West Malling and on the 19th, in a disastrous action off Dover, lost six of its aircraft with most of their crews. A decision was made to withdraw 141 as a day-fighter unit from the South and the shaken remnants of the squadron went north to Grangemouth two days later to begin training for night operations.

On December 7 1940 Arthur was posted to 242 Squadron at Duxford. Most of its pilots were Canadian and it was commanded by Douglas Bader. Arthur left 242 on May 23 1941 and joined 145 Squadron at Merston, as a Flight Commander. Whilst with the squadron Arthur destroyed a Bf 109 on June 25 and shared another on the 30th. With his tour completed he was sent to CFS, Upavon for an instructor's course, after which he was posted to 5 FTS, Tern Hill, moving later to 7(P) AFU.

A return to operations came on November 22 1942 with a posting to 411 Squadron at Hornchurch, as a supernumerary Flight Lieutenant. He moved soon afterwards to 81 Squadron in North Africa and on March 9 1943 he rejoined 242 at Souk-el-Khemis, this time as a Flight Commander. Arthur was promoted to Acting Squadron Leader on June 1 and took command of 232 Squadron at Sousse. A few days later the squadron moved to Ta Kali, Malta. On June 29 Arthur shared in the destruction of a Bf 109.

He commanded 232 until January 1944. After a short rest he was given command of 72 Squadron at Lago, Italy on April 12 1944. He destroyed a Bf 109 on May 7 and shared another on the 16th.

Arthur was awarded the DFC (9.6.44). He shared a Me 410 on October 14 and on November 21 was promoted to Acting Wing Commander and posted to command 5 Refresher Flying Unit at Ferugia. He received a Bar to the DFC (29.12.44) for his work with 72 Squadron.

In July 1945 Arthur was made Wing Leader 239 Mustang Wing at Lavariano. After the war he commanded 19 Squadron from April 1946 to August 1948. He retired as a Squadron Leader on November 3 1954, retaining the rank of Wing Commander.

Arthur returned to Canada, where he ran a water transport business in British Columbia until 1971.

APO 29.8.38   PO 29.8.39   FO 3.9.40   FL 3.9.42
SL 1.7.44

CHARLES JOHN ARTHUR

42090   PO   Pilot   British   248 Squadron

Arthur, of Radyr, Glamorgan, was first commissioned in the RAF in May 1939. He was posted to 248 Squadron in October 1939, when it was reformed at Hendon.

As a Coastal Command squadron it was seconded to Fighter Command during the Battle of Britain.

Arthur was lost on August 27 1940 when his Blenheim failed to return from a reconnaissance flight to the south Norwegian coast. The aircraft is known to have crashed into the sea. The body of the air gunner, Sergeant RCR Cox, was washed up in Sweden, but Arthur and his observer, Sergeant EA Ringwood, were never found. Their names are on the Runnymede Memorial, Panels 7 and 22 respectively. Arthur was 22 years old.

APO 13.5.39   PO 6.11.39

ROBERT CLIFFORD VACY ASH

31023   FL   Air Gunner   British   264 Squadron

Ash was commissioned in the Stores Branch of the RAF in January 1933 and in August was posted to Cranwell on Supply duties.

On September 1 1934 he went overseas to the Aircraft Depot, Hinaidi, Iraq, moving to the Central Supplies Depot there on May 23 1936. In December 1938 Ash was serving as an Acting Flight Lieutenant at the Supplies Depot, Habbaniya but was back in England in 1939. He was posted on May 1 to the Equipment Branch, 24 (Training) Group at No 1 RAF Depot, Uxbridge.

Ash transferred to the General Duties Branch on October 30 1939, having volunteered for aircrew duties as an Air Gunner. He completed his training and was posted to 264 Squadron.

On the morning of August 28 1940 Ash was airborne in Defiant L 7021 with his pilot, Squadron Leader GD Garvin. They got into combat with Bf 109s and both baled out when the aircraft was shot down, afterwards crashing in flames at Luddenham Marsh, Faversham. Garvin landed with minor injuries but Ash was dead on landing, from bullet wounds, probably machine-gunned as he floated down. He was 31 years old and is buried in the Western Cemetery, St Andrews, Fife.

PO 6.1.33   FO 6.1.34   FL 14.4.39

ALFRED EDWARD ASHCROFT

112736   Sgt   Air Gunner   British   141 Squadron

Ashcroft, who came from Cobham, Surrey, joined 141 Squadron at Grangemouth in July 1940. When the squadron re-equipped with Beaufighters he retrained as a Radio Observer.

He was commissioned in November 1941. Later in the war Ashcroft was with 29 Squadron and was awarded the DFC (22.2.44) for his services.

In the second half of 1944 Ashcroft was flying with 157 Squadron from Swannington, intruding over German night-fighter airfields. On October 6 he failed to return from a sortie. He is buried in Brussels Town Cemetery, Belgium. He was 24 at the time of his death.

PO 26.11.41   FO 1.10.42   FL 26.11.43

GLYNN ASHFIELD

36225   FO   Pilot   British   FIU

Ashfield, from Oxted, Surrey, entered the RAF in September 1939 with a direct-entry Permanent Commission. He joined the Fighter Interception Unit at Tangmere on its formation in April 1940.

In the early hours of July 23 Ashfield, flying a Blenheim fitted with AI radar equipment, shot down a Do 17 of 2/KG 3 off the Sussex coast. The crew of four were rescued, wounded, from the sea.

Ashfield escaped unhurt when he forced-landed Beaufighter R 2059 at Tangmere on September 9 after his cockpit roof flew off during a night patrol and he collided with an unlighted truck on landing. For his work at FIU Ashfield was awarded the AFC (17.3.41).

In early 1942 he was senior flight commander in 157 Squadron at Castle Camps. He probably destroyed a Do 217 south of Dover on May 30. Ashfield was awarded the DFC (4.12.42)

He was killed on December 12 1942, aged 30. He is buried in St Peter's churchyard, Limpsfield, Surrey.

PO 27.9.39   FO 27.9.40   FL 27.9.41

DENNIS GARTH ASHTON

76574   PO   Pilot   British   266 Squadron

Ashton was commissioned in the RAF in December 1939 and was serving with 266 Squadron at Wittering at the start of the Battle of Britain.

On July 18 Ashton, in Spitfire N 3170, collided with a stationary tractor at base but was unhurt.

In combat with enemy aircraft off Portsmouth on August 12 Ashton was reported 'Missing' when his aircraft, Spitfire P 9333, was shot down in flames. His body was recovered in September by the minesweeper HMS 'Cedar' and buried at sea.

Ashton, who came from Keyworth, Nottinghamshire, was 20 years old. He is remembered on the Runnymede Memorial, Panel 7.

PO 10.12.39

DENNIS KENNETH ASHTON

741212 Sgt Pilot British 32 Squadron

Ashton, of Carlton, Nottinghamshire, was in the RAFVR before the war. In September 1939 the FAA was short of pilots and after Ashton was called up he was posted to Donibristle and joined the Torpedo-Spotter-Reconnaissance Flight. He was later posted to 770 Squadron for deck-landing training on HMS 'Argus', in the Western Mediterranean. He was offered a transfer to the FAA but declined and was posted to 3 BGS, Aldergrove as a staff pilot.

On May 4 1940 Ashton was recalled to the FAA and joined 759 (T) Squadron at Eastleigh for a refresher deck-landing course. He was later posted to 804 Squadron at Hatston. By mid-June the RAF was short of pilots and Ashton was recalled and posted to 7 OTU, Hawarden. After converting to Hurricanes he was posted to 32 Squadron at Biggin Hill in early July.

Within two weeks Ashton was told to report to Uxbridge and became one of a group of nine sergeants and one officer. They were flown to Hullavington, picked up Hurricanes, flew them to Abbotsinch and were embarked on the carrier HMS 'Argus', where they were joined by four more officers. They were told their destination was Malta and they were now 418 Flight.

The 'Argus' sailed on July 23, arrived at Gibraltar and sailed for Malta on July 31. At dawn on August 2 they flew off to Luqa. 418 Flight and the Malta Fighter Flight were amalgamated into 261 Squadron on August 16 1940.

Ashton was flying one of two Hurricanes, which intercepted three Fiat CR 42s on November 26 1940. He shot one down and was then shot down himself into the sea by one of the others and killed.

He was 26 years old. He is buried in the Capuccini Naval Cemetery, Malta.

JACK ASHWORTH

49946 Sgt Aircrew British 29 Squadron

Ashworth joined 29 Squadron at Digby in August 1940. He was commissioned from Warrant Officer in September 1942 and released in 1946, as a Flight Lieutenant.

PO 13.9.42   FO 13.3.43   FL 13.9.44

ARTHUR THOMAS RAYNER ASLETT

170758 Sgt Wop/AG British 235 Squadron

Born in 1920, Aslett began work as an apprentice printer with a Kent newspaper in 1934. In early 1939 he joined the RAFVR at Rochester. Called up on September 5 1939, he completed his basic training and went to Air Service Training, Hamble for initial wireless theory and operation. This was followed by advanced wireless work and flying experience at Cranwell.

After a three week course at 9 Bombing and Gunnery School, Penrhos Aslett was posted on August 10 1940 to No 1 (Coastal) OTU, Silloth, from where he joined 235 Squadron at Bircham Newton on September 23. He was a member of a Blenheim crew returning from a bombing attack on two armed enemy merchant vessels on November 23. During the action the pilot, PO JT Davison, had been wounded and the aircraft sufficiently badly damaged to make necessary a crash-landing at base. Unbeknown to Davison a bomb remained on the rack and this exploded on impact severely wounding Aslett and setting fire to the aircraft. Davison and his observer, Sergeant Brazier, jumped clear but on realising that Aslett was still in the blazing aircraft they went back, regardless of their own safety, and dragged him out. They were both badly burned and their gallantry was recognised in March 1941, Davison being awarded the GM and Brazier the BEM.

Aslett spent some time in Ely Hospital, eventually returning to Bircham Newton, where he was put on instruction duties. He later joined 279 (Air Sea Rescue) Squadron, was commissioned in December 1943 and on finishing his tour in early February 1944 was posted to No 1 (Coastal) OTU at Turnberry as an instructor. Later in the year Aslett went to 111 OTU, Nassau, Bahamas for Liberator crewing. He joined 224 Squadron on his return to Britain on January 9 1945 and remained with the squadron until the end of the year. Aslett was released in February 1946, as a Flight Lieutenant.

PO 20.12.43   FO 20.6.44   FL 20.12.45

DONALD JAMES ASLIN

102097 Sgt Pilot British 32 and 257 Squadrons

On August 4 1940 Aslin joined 32 Squadron at Biggin Hill.

He moved to 257 Squadron at Martlesham Heath on September 22. The following morning he was shot down during a patrol over the Thames Estuary and baled out. Aslin was admitted to Minster Hospital with burns. His aircraft, Hurricane P 2960, crashed at Grove, near Eastchurch.

Aslin was later moved to the Queen Victoria Cottage Hospital at East Grinstead, where he underwent surgery by Archie McIndoe, becoming a Guinea Pig in the process.

Commissioned in July 1941, Aslin was released in 1946, as a Flight Lieutenant. In February 1948 he was commissioned in the RAFVR. He died on July 3 1988.

PO 18.7.41   FO 18.7.42   FL 18.7.43   FO (RAFVR) 27.2.48

WILLIAM RADCLYFFE ASSHETON

41979 PO Pilot British 222 Squadron

Born on December 12 1917, Assheton joined the RAF with a short service commission in early 1939. He was posted to 222 Squadron at Duxford in early November.

In August 1940 the squadron was at Hornchurch. On the 30th Assheton crash-landed at Bekesbourne Aerodrome, in Spitfire R 6720, after combat over Canterbury. Twelve days later he forced-landed on Parsonage Farm, Fletching, in Spitfire R 6638, after an action over Maidstone.

Assheton's third escape came on September 20 when he baled out, with slight burns, after being shot down in a surprise attack by Bf 109s over the Thames Estuary. He landed at Latchingdon and was admitted to St Peter's Hospital, Maldon. His aircraft, Spitfire K 9993, crashed and burned out at Linkhouse Farm, West Hanningfield.

In 1945 Assheton was awarded the DFC (10.4.45) for service with 540 Squadron, a Mosquito photographic-reconnaissance unit. He remained in the RAF after the war, graduated from the RAF Staff College and retired on November 22 1957, as a Squadron Leader.

APO 6.3.39   PO 6.11.39   FO 6.11.40   FL 6.11.41
SL 1.7.45   SL 1.8.47

FREDERICK PETER JOHN ATKINS

903401 Sgt Air Gunner British 141 Squadron

Atkins was with 141 Squadron at Turnhouse in July 1940. He went south with the squadron and was in one of the nine Defiants attacked by Bf 109s of III/JG 51 off Dover on July 19.

His aircraft, Defiant L 7015, was shot down into the Channel. The pilot, Pilot Officer R Kidson, was never found but Atkins' body was washed up on the French coast. He was 26 years old and is buried in Boulogne Eastern Cemetery, France.

ALLAN ARTHUR ATKINSON

78740 PO Observer British 23 Squadron

Atkinson joined the RAF in 1939, was commissioned in April 1940 and posted to 23 Squadron at Wittering.

On October 30 1940, operating from Ford, Atkinson was one of the crew of Blenheim L 6721 on a routine night patrol. The aircraft crashed at Orchard Way Road, South Berstead after R/T failure in deteriorating weather conditions. All three of the crew were killed.

Atkinson, who was 32 years old, is buried in St Mary's churchyard, Clymping, Sussex.

PO 12.4.40

GEORGE ATKINSON

47413 Sgt Pilot British 151 Squadron

A pre-war airman pilot from Harlow, Essex, Atkinson was serving with 151 Squadron when the Battle of Britain started.

On August 14 1940, flying in Hurricane P 3310, Atkinson was shot down off Christchurch following an attack on a formation of Do 17s. He baled out, was rescued from the sea and admitted to hospital suffering from shock.

Atkinson was awarded the DFM (7.3.41) and commissioned in November 1941. He was killed on March 1 1945, as a Flight Lieutenant, whilst serving as a flying instructor.

He was 29 and is buried in Blyth Cemetery, Northumberland.

PO 24.11.41   FO 1.10.42   FL 24.11.43

GORDON BARRY ATKINSON

42091 PO Pilot British 248 Squadron

Born on July 7 1921, Atkinson entered the RAF as a candidate for a short service commission and began training as a pupil pilot in late February 1939. He completed his training and joined 248 Squadron at Hendon in early November.

A Blenheim unit of Coastal Command, 248 served with Fighter Command during the Battle of Britain. On November 3 1940 Atkinson returned to Sumburgh, in the Shetlands, with a damaged oil cooler caused by return fire from a He 111 attacked over the North Sea. He and his crew were unhurt.

In 1943 Atkinson was with 603 Squadron in the Mediterranean. Normally a fighter squadron, 603 was then operating as a Coastal Strike unit, with Beaufighters.

Atkinson was awarded the DFC (14.12.43), the citation stating that he had flown a large number of sorties, including many attacks on shipping.

He remained in the RAF after the war, graduated from Staff College, was made an MBE (1.1.63) and retired on March 18 1976 as a Wing Commander.

APO 13.5.39   PO 6.11.39   FO 6.11.40   FL 6.11.41
SL 1.7.54   WC 1.1.64

HAROLD DERRICK ATKINSON

33418 PO Pilot British 213 Squadron

Born at Wintringham, Yorkshire on August 19 1918, Atkinson was educated at Shrewsbury School from 1932 to 1937, where he was a member of the First XI. He entered RAF College, Cranwell as a flight cadet in September 1937 and graduated in July 1939.

Atkinson joined 213 Squadron at Wittering. He went with the squadron to Merville on May 17 1940. The stay was a short one, with 213 returning on the 21st, 'A' Flight going to Manston and 'B' Flight to Wittering. During the pre-Dunkirk period Atkinson was credited with the destruction of two enemy aircraft and assisting in destroying two others. Flying from Biggin Hill in late May Atkinson got a probable Bf 109 on the 25th, destroyed another on the 28th and claimed a probable He 111 on the 29th. For his successes during May he was awarded the DFC (25.6.40).

213 Squadron was based at Exeter in August 1940 and over a period of seven days Atkinson claimed the destruction of six enemy aircraft, on the 12th two Bf 110s, on the 13th a Bf 109 and on the 14th a He 111. In this last action he returned to Exeter, in Hurricane R 4099, damaged by return fire from a He 111 engaged over Lyme Bay. He was slightly wounded by shell splinters in the arm. On the 16th Atkinson claimed a Bf 109 and another two days later.

He failed to return from a combat over Warmwell on August 25. The aircraft, Hurricane P 3200, is believed to have crashed into the sea but Atkinson's body was recovered and he is buried in Market Weighton Cemetery, Yorkshire.

PO 29.7.39

MATTHEW RICHARD ATKINSON

39364 FL Pilot British 43 Squadron

Atkinson, from Gosforth, Northumberland, began his elementary flying training as a pupil pilot in November 1936. He was posted to 11 FTS, Wittering on February 6 1937 and after completing his training joined 52 Squadron at Upwood, Huntingdon on September 4 1937. At that time 52 was using Audax and Hart light bombers and was re-equipped with Battles in 1939. The squadron was disbanded in early April 1940.

Atkinson volunteered for Fighter Command and on September 20 1940 he joined 43 Squadron at Usworth. He was killed, as a Squadron Leader, on June 26 1942, but his unit at the time of his death is not known. With no known grave Atkinson is remembered on the Runnymede Memorial, Panel 65. He was 26 years old.

APO 25.1.37   PO 16.11.37   FO 16.6.39   FL 3.9.40
SL 1.12.41

RONALD ATKINSON

79530 PO Pilot British 242, 600, 111 and 213 Sqdns

A member of the RAFVR before the war, Atkinson, from Gillingham in Kent, was called up for full-time service in September 1939. He was commissioned in May 1940 and joined 242 Squadron at Biggin Hill. Atkinson was with 242 when it went to Chateaudun on June 8 to cover rearguard actions being fought by the Army on its retreat to the Atlantic coast. The squadron was withdrawn to Coltishall on the 16th.

Atkinson was posted to 600 Squadron at Manston on August 10 but stayed only a few days before moving to 111 Squadron at Debden. He went to Tangmere on September 19 to join 213 Squadron. He claimed the destruction of a Bf 109 on the 30th.

He was killed, aged 19, on October 17 1940 when he was shot down in combat with Bf 109s, in Hurricane P 3174. Atkinson crashed at Weeks Farm, near Pluckley. He is buried in Woodlands Cemetery, Gillingham.

PO 19.5.40

———— AUSTIN

No unknown PO Pilot British 151 Squadron

No service details traced.

ALBERT LAWRENCE AUSTIN

917258 LAC Radar Operator British 604 Squadron

Austin was with 604 Squadron at Northolt at the start of the Battle of Britain. On August 25 he was flying as a member of the crew of Blenheim L 6782, when the aircraft crashed near Witheredge, Exeter whilst on an operational sortie. The cause of the crash is unknown. Sergeants JGB Fletcher and C Haigh were killed and Austin died the next day. He was 25 and is buried in Northwood Cemetery, Middlesex.

ANTHONY THOMAS AUSTIN

129122 Sgt Air Gunner British 29 Squadron

Joined 29 Squadron at Digby on July 1 1940.

Commissioned in May 1942, Austin was released from the RAF in 1946, as a Flight Lieutenant.

PO 20.5.42   FO 20.11.42   FL 20.5.44

FREDERICK AUSTIN

39627   FO   Pilot   British   46 Squadron

Austin began his elementary flying training in February 1937 and was commissioned in early May. On May 8 he was posted to 3 FTS, South Cerney and after completing his advanced training he joined 3 Squadron at Kenley on November 27 1937.

Austin went to CFS, Upavon on August 7 1938 for a course, after which he was posted to 2 FTS, Brize Norton as an instructor.

He joined 46 Squadron at Digby on August 16 1940 and served with the squadron to the end of the year.

On March 17 1941 Austin was killed, whilst serving as a Flight Lieutenant at 5 BGS. He is buried in St Andrew's churchyard, Clevedon, Somerset.

APO 3.5.37   PO 1.3.38   FO 1.11.39   FL 1.11.40

SYDNEY AUSTIN

101002   Sgt   Observer   British   219 Squadron

Austin was posted to 219 Squadron at Catterick on August 8 1940. He was crewed up with Sgt HF Grubb and they had two lucky escapes in landing mishaps. On August 26, in Blenheim L 1524, they undershot the runway at Catterick, landing in a sudden rainstorm in the early hours of the morning. Landing at Redhill on October 16, in Blenheim L 1236, they overshot the runway and struck the boundary fence.

Austin was awarded the DFM (30.5.41) for assisting in the destruction of three enemy aircraft at night. He was posted to 85 Squadron at Hunsdon in 1941 and was commissioned in July. He was killed on October 30, as a Flying Officer. Austin is remembered on the Runnymede Memorial, Panel 29.

PO 14.7.41

DAVID HART AYERS

740696   Sgt   Pilot   British   600 and 74 Squadrons

Ayers, from Herne Bay, Kent, was educated at Kent College, Canterbury from 1926 to 1931. He was a pre-war member of the RAFVR and was called up at the outbreak of war.

With training completed Ayers joined 600 Squadron at Northolt. In August 1940 he was posted to 74 Squadron at Wittering. On September 23, whilst on a routine patrol in Spitfire P 7362, Ayers baled out into the sea south-east of Southwold. His body was recovered on October 4 and he was buried in Ipswich Cemetery, Suffolk. He was 26.

CHARLES ALBERT HENRY AYLING

561455   Sgt   Pilot   British   43 and 66 Sqdns, 421 Flight

An ex-apprentice and pre-war airman pilot, Ayling was with 43 Squadron at Tangmere in September 1939.

On June 7 1940 he was forced to crash-land his damaged Hurricane at Rouen-Boos airfield in France. He got away from Garnay airfield on the 10th in a Hurricane with a punctured wing tank and managed to reach Tangmere.

Ayling was posted to 66 Squadron at Kenley on September 10 and he moved on to 421 Flight at Gravesend on October 8. Three days later, in Spitfire P 7303, he was killed when he crashed at Newchurch following combat with enemy aircraft over Hawkinge.

Ayling was 28 and is buried in St Nicholas' Cemetery, Moncton, Pembroke.

CYRIL FREDERICK BABBAGE

89298   Sgt   Pilot   British   602 Squadron

Babbage was born in Ludlow, Shropshire on June 25 1917 and was with 602 Squadron at Drem at the start of the Battle of Britain.

In August 1940 602 was based at Westhampnett. On the 18th Babbage claimed a Ju 87 destroyed and on the 25th a Do 17 and a Bf 110. After destroying a Bf 109 in combat over Selsey Bill on August 26 Babbage was himself shot down by Hauptmann Mayer of 1/JG 53. He baled out and was picked up by the Bognor lifeboat and admitted to Bognor Hospital. His aircraft, Spitfire X 4188, crashed into the sea.

Back with the squadron Babbage was engaged in combat with Bf 110s over Selsey Bill on September 11. He shot one down and returned to Westhampnett, in Spitfire X 4269, with starboard wing damaged. On September 26 he destroyed a He 111 and on the following day he returned to Westhampnett, in Spitfire X 4160, after being damaged by Bf 109s which attacked him following his destruction of a Ju 88 off Dungeness.

Babbage's final victory in the Battle of Britain came on October 12, when he claimed a probable Ju 88 in an engagement over the Channel. However his Spitfire, X 4541, was damaged by return fire and Babbage overturned when he forced-landed at Iford Farm, near Lewes. He was unhurt.

Babbage was awarded the DFM (25.10.40) and in November 1940 he was commissioned. In June 1941 he was posted to 41 Squadron at Merston and on September 18 he claimed an enemy aircraft destroyed.

Babbage remained in the RAF after the war. He was a Qualified A1 Instructor, having completed the course at CFS. He retired from the RAF on June 25 1964, as a Wing Commander. He died in 1977.

PO 29.11.40   FO 29.11.41   FL 29.11.42   SL 1.8.47
WC 1.7.55

JACK HENRY BACHMANN

76568   PO   Pilot   British   145 Squadron

Joined the RAF at the outbreak of war and commissioned in early November 1939. Bachmann completed his training and was posted to 145 Squadron at Drem on August 20 1940.

In June 1942 Bachmann was given command of 67 Squadron, then reforming at Alipore, India with Hurricane 11cs. In February 1943 the squadron went to the Akyab Front, moving in early April to Chittagong. On April 9 1943 Bachmann was killed in action, aged 25. He is buried in Chittagong War Cemetery.

PO 6.11.39   FO 6.11.40   FL 23.9.41

CHARLES HARVEY BACON

74324   PO   Pilot   British   610 Squadron

A Demi of Magdalene College, Oxford, Bacon was born on January 15 1919. He joined the RAFVR in 1938 and was called for full-time service at the outbreak of war.

Commissioned in October 1939, Bacon was posted to 610 Squadron at Acklington on September 16 1940. Just two weeks later, on the 30th, he was killed in a flying accident when his Spitfire crashed on Alnmouth beach.

Bacon is buried in St Mary's churchyard, Windermere, Westmorland.

PO 4.10.39

DOUGLAS HIRAM BADDELEY

814205   Sgt   Air Gunner   British   25 Squadron

Baddeley, from Dalton, Huddersfield, was posted to 25 Squadron at North Weald in early October 1940.

He was a Flight Sergeant when he was killed, at the age of 25, on June 26 1942. He is buried in Kiel War Cemetery, Germany.

DOUGLAS ROBERT STEUART BADER

26151   SL   Pilot   British   242 Squadron

Probably the most widely-known participant in the Battle of Britain, Bader was born in St Johns Wood, London on February 21 1910. His early years were spent in India, where his father was in the Civil Service. Bader returned to England to go to preparatory school at Temple Grove, Eastbourne. He later won a scholarship to St Edward's School, Oxford. In 1928 he won a prize cadetship to RAF College, Cranwell and began the course there in September.

After passing out in July 1930 Bader was commissioned and on August 25 he was posted to 23 Squadron at Kenley. In 1931 he represented 23 in the pairs aerobatic competition at the Hendon Air Display, when the squadron won for the third year running. On December 14 1931 Bader crashed in a Bulldog, after attempting a roll at very low level. Miraculously he was not killed but lost both his legs, the right one above the knee and the left below.

After being fitted with artificial limbs Bader remained in the RAF, but most unhappily because he was not allowed to fly. He was retired by the Air Ministry on April 30 1933. He got a job with the Asiatic Petroleum Company, which later became Shell.

After the outbreak of war Bader became increasingly insistent about rejoining the RAF in a flying capacity. Finally, on October 18 1939, he went to CFS, Upavon for a flying test, which was conducted by Squadron Leader RHA Leigh. Bader passed the test and was re-employed as a regular officer on November 26. After a refresher course at Upavon he joined 19 Squadron at Duxford on February 7 1940, with the rank of Flying Officer. In March he was promoted to Flight Lieutenant and posted to 222 Squadron, also at Duxford, as a Flight Commander.

On June 1 Bader scored his first victory, when he shot down a Bf 109 near Dunkirk. Promoted to Acting Squadron Leader, Bader was given command of 242 Squadron at Coltishall, a unit made up mainly of Canadian pilots. Morale in the squadron was low and discipline was lax and Bader set about the task of bringing 242 back to a good operational standard.

Bader's next victory came on July 11 1940 when he shot down a Do 17 into the sea off Cromer. A repeat performance on August 21 saw another Do 17 go down into the sea. He claimed another seven enemy aircraft destroyed and one shared during the Battle of Britain. The claims were, on August 30 two Bf 110s, on September 7 a Bf 110, on September 9 a Do 17, on September 15 a shared Do 17, on September 18 a Do 17 and a Ju 88 and on September 27 a Bf 109.

Bader was promoted Acting Wing Commander and posted to Tangmere as Wing Commander Flying on March 18 1941. In June he began to add to his victories, on June 21 a Bf 109, on June 26 a Bf 109 and another shared, on July 2 a Bf 109 and another probable and on July 5, 9, 10, 12, 14, 19 and 23 Bf 109s destroyed.

On August 9 Bader led the Wing to escort bombers to Bethune. From the start things went wrong and he found himself alone and involved with several Bf 109s, one of which collided with him, shearing off the rear end of his fuselage. Bader baled out and was captured on landing, minus his right artificial leg. For the Germans he was a difficult prisoner and he eventually finished up in Colditz. He was released from there on April 14 1945.

After rest and recuperation leave Bader was posted to Tangmere, as Group Captain, to command the Fighter Leaders School. Many things had changed since 1941 and it was not a successful appointment and after a short period Bader was given command of the North Weald Sector, from where he organised and led the Battle of Britain flypast in September 1945.

Bader retired on July 21 1946, retaining the rank of Group Captain. He had received the following awards, DSO (1.10.40), Bar to the DSO (15.7.41), DFC (7.1.41), Bar to the DFC (9.9.41), Legion d'Honneur, Croix de Guerre, and three Mentions in Dispatches.

After retirement Bader rejoined Shell. In 1952 he was made Managing Director of the Shell aircraft fleet, an appointment which necessitated a lot of overseas travel. Somehow he always found time to encourage disabled people, particularly children and young people. For his public service Bader was made a CBE in 1956.

Bader became Sir Douglas when he was created a KBE in 1976. He flew his own aeroplane for the last time on June 4 1979 when he made a local flight from White Waltham.

On September 5 1982, after attending a dinner in honour of Marshal of the RAF Sir Arthur Harris, Bader died in the car as his wife drove him back to their Berkshire home.

PO 26.7.30   FO 6.6.32   Retired 30.4.33   FO 26.11.39
FL 12.3.40   SL 18.6.41   WC 1.7.45

IVOR JAMES BADGER

45975   F/Sgt   Pilot   British   87 Squadron

Born on September 12 1912, Badger joined the RAF as a technical apprentice in 1928. In the mid-thirties he volunteered for pilot training and in 1938 was a Sergeant-Pilot in 151 Squadron and a member of the squadron's aerobatic team.

In May 1940 Badger was with 87 Squadron in France and served with it in the Battle of Britain. On August 11 he claimed the destruction of an Bf 109. In early 1941 Flight Lieutenant DH Ward of 87, who had flown with Badger in the 151 aerobatic team, thought it would be good for 87 Squadron morale if it too had such a team and Badger found himself a member with Ward and PO RP Beamont. On May 19 1941 Badger shot down a He 114 floatplane off the Scilly Isles. He remained with 87 until late in the year when he was posted to 94 Squadron in the Western Desert. Badger, who had been commissioned in May 1941, was with 73 Squadron in early 1942. On March 20 he took part in an attack on Derna airfield, during which several enemy aircraft and an illuminated flare path were destroyed. He took part in other successful attacks on enemy airfields, on July 11 1942 destroyed a Bf 109 and was awarded the DFC (18.9.42) when his tour ended.

Badger returned to Britain and he later transferred to the Technical Branch in July 1944. He remained in the RAF after the war and retired on August 12 1961, as a Flight Lieutenant, retaining the rank of Squadron Leader.

PO 8.5.41   FO 10.3.42   FL 10.3.43   FL 1.9.45

JOHN VINCENT CLARENCE BADGER

33046   SL   Pilot   British   43 Squadron

Born in Lambeth, London in 1912, Badger entered the RAF College, Cranwell in September 1931 as a Flight Cadet. He graduated in July 1933, winning the Sword of Honour, and was posted to 43 Squadron at Tangmere on the 15th of the month.

At this time the RAF was supplying pilots for the Fleet Air Arm and on October 3 1934 Badger went to the School of Naval Co-operation, Lee-on-Solent, moving to 821 (Fleet Spotter-Reconnaissance) Squadron on May 4 1935, shore base at Eastleigh and at sea on the aircraft carrier, HMS 'Courageous'. Badger was posted to the Marine Aircraft Establishment at Felixstowe on October 25 1937.

In June 1940 he was posted to 43 Squadron at Tangmere, as supernumerary Squadron Leader, to gain operational and administrative experience. On July 9 the CO, Squadron Leader G Lott, was shot down and badly wounded and Badger assumed command. On August 14 he shared in destroying a Ju 88, on the 15th he claimed another destroyed, on the 16th three Ju 87s and on the 26th he shared a He 111.

Badger, in Hurricane V6548, was shot down in combat with Bf 109s on August 30. He crashed south of Woodchurch, grievously wounded, and was taken to Ashford Hospital. He died of his wounds on June 30 1941 and is buried in the churchyard of St Michael and All Angels, Halton, Buckinghamshire. Badger was 29. He was awarded the DFC (6.9.40) and received a Mention in Despatches.

PO 15.7.33   FO 15.1.35   FL 5.1.37   SL 1.4.39

17

CHARLES GORDON BAILEY

No unknown   PO   Pilot   British   152 Squadron

No service details traced.

COLIN CYRIL BAILEY

102088   AC 2   Radar Operator   British   23 Squadron

Joined 23 Squadron at Wittering on July 23 1940. Bailey later retrained as a Radio Observer and was promoted to Sergeant.

Commissioned in July 1941, Bailey was awarded the DFC (30.11.43), as a Flight Lieutenant with 219 Squadron. He was released from the RAF in 1946, as a Flight Lieutenant.

PO 13.7.41   FO 14.7.42   FL 14.7.43

GEORGE JOHN BAILEY

106355   Sgt   Pilot   British   234 and 603 Squadrons

Bailey joined the RAFVR on July 26 1938 and did his elementary flying at 9 E&RFTS, Ansty and 13 E&RFTS, White Waltham. Called up in early October 1939, he was posted to 5 FTS, Sealand and after completing his training he joined 234 Squadron at Leconfield on May 4 1940.

Bailey shared a Ju 88 on July 8 and another on the 27th. He was posted to 603 Squadron at Hornchurch on September 10, claimed a Bf 109 destroyed on the 15th and another on October 2.

In late October Bailey went to 7 FTS, Peterborough as an instructor. He was posted to Canada on January 7 1941 and as an instructor at 31 SFTS, Kingston, Ontario he taught FAA pilots dive bombing, formation flying and general advanced flying. He was commissioned in May 1941.

After his return to Britain in October 1943, Bailey was posted to 15 (P) AFU as an instructor on December 7. He left Training Command on May 2 1944 and went to 105 (Transport) OTU, Bramcote, then to 107 OTU at Leicester East before joining 271 Squadron at Down Ampney. Bailey was shot down in a DC 3 on November 20 1944.

He was released from the RAF on November 25 1945, as a Flight Lieutenant.

PO 27.5.41   FO 27.5.42   FL 27.5.43

GRAHAM GEORGE BAILEY

83987   PO   Pilot   British   79 and 56 Squadrons

Bailey, of Henleaze, Gloucestershire, joined 79 Squadron at Pembrey on September 13 1940, moving to 56 Squadron at Boscombe Down on October 15.

Posted to Malta, Bailey flew off HMS 'Ark Royal' on April 27 1941. He joined the newly-formed 185 Squadron at Hal Far on May 12. He shared in shooting down a SM 79 on July 27.

On November 9 1941 two Hurricanes from 185 went out to patrol over a returning naval force. They intercepted a force of enemy torpedo bombers attempting to attack the ships. Bailey, in one of the Hurricanes, did not return and was thought to have been hit by return fire, although he may have destroyed one of the bombers before he was himself shot down. He was 25 years old and is remembered on the Malta Memorial, Panel 1, Column 1.

PO 11.8.40   FO 11.8.41

HENRY NOEL DAWSON BAILEY

84957   PO   Pilot   British   54 Squadron

Born on December 15 1917, Bailey joined the RAFVR in September 1938 and did his elementary flying training at Derby. He was called up at the outbreak of war and after completing ITW was posted in March 1940 to EFTS at Hanworth and then to 5 FTS, Sealand in May.

In August Bailey went to 7 OTU, Hawarden and joined 54 Squadron at Catterick on September 28. As an Acting Flight Lieutenant he was posted to 58 OTU, Grangemouth in September 1941 as a Flight Commander instructor.

Bailey joined an Air Ministry Unit attached to Rolls Royce, Derby and Hucknall for flying duties in January 1942 and remained there until November 1945, when he was released from the RAF, as a Squadron Leader. He continued flying for Rolls Royce, eventually becoming Chief Test Pilot. He flew the first jet lift machine, known as the 'Flying Bedstead', in August 1954.

PO 7.9.40   FO 7.9.41   FL 7.9.42

JAMES RICHARD ABE BAILEY

74325   FO   Pilot   British   264 and 85 Squadrons

Bailey was born on October 23 1919, the youngest son of Sir Abe Bailey. He was educated at Winchester College and Christ Church College, Oxford. As a member of the University Air Squadron he was called up at the outbreak of war. In November 1939 he went to ITW, Cambridge and on December 30 was posted to Cranwell for flying training, on the second war course. Bailey completed his training at 5 FTS, Sealand and then went to No 1 School of Army Co-operation, Old Sarum. A week later he was posted to Aston Down to convert to Defiants, after which he joined 264 Squadron at Duxford in mid-June 1940.

Bailey took part in 264's last day-fighting engagements in late August. On the 28th his Defiant, N 1569, was severely damaged in combat with Bf 109s of JG 26. He forced-landed at Court Lodge Farm, Petham. Both he and his gunner, Sergeant OA Hardy, were unhurt.

In September Bailey was posted to 85 Squadron at Castle Camps, as it went over to night-fighting. He was with the squadron until July 1941, when he went to 1452 Flight, then forming at West Malling with Turbinlite Havocs. Soon afterwards, at his own request, he returned to 264 Squadron.

On January 1 1942 Bailey moved to 125 Squadron at Fairwood Common, as a Flight Commander. Flying a Beaufighter on November 10 1942 he destroyed a Ju 88. Bailey was attached to 615 Squadron USAAC on April 1 1943, as a liaison officer. In July he went to 54 OTU, Charter Hall, as an instructor, moving later to Honiley to help form a new OTU for night-fighter pilots.

Bailey was posted overseas in November 1943 and joined 600 Squadron at Monte Corvino on December 3. In February 1944 he destroyed a Ju 88, on June 3 a Ju 87 and a Bf 110, on July 7 another Ju 88 and on July 11 another Ju 87. With his tour completed he was awarded the DFC (8.9.44), returned to Britain and was given a staff job at Air Ministry.

After release from the RAF Bailey returned to Oxford, obtaining a BA in 1947 and an MA in 1949. He went farming in South Africa and later moved into publishing.

PO 14.10.39   FO 26.9.40   FL 26.9.41   SL 1.7.45

JOHN CYRIL LINDSAY DYSON BAILEY

74660   PO   Pilot   British   46 Squadron

Bailey, from Stockland, Devon, was educated at Tonbridge School from 1933 to 1937. He joined the RAF in October 1939 and after completing his training was posted to 46 Squadron at Digby in August 1940. On September 2, flying Hurricane P3067 from Stapleford, he was shot down in an engagement over the Thames Estuary. He died at Detling Aerodrome and was buried in Maidstone Cemetery on September 11. Bailey was 22 years old.

PO 23.10.39

PAUL ABBOTT BAILLON

86331   PO   Pilot   British   609 Squadron

A solicitor before the war, from Church Brampton, Northants, Baillon joined 609 Squadron at Middle Wallop in October 1940. On the 27th his Spitfire, P 9503, was severely damaged by return fire from an enemy aircraft engaged over Andover. Baillon baled out, unhurt, near Upavon.

In combat with Bf 109s over the Channel in the late afternoon of November 28 1940 Baillon was shot down into the Channel, in Spitfire R 6631. His body was later washed ashore on the French coast and he is buried in Bayeux War Cemetery. He was 26 when he was killed.

PO 7.9.40

GEORGE STOBIE PRESTON BAIN

85647 PO Pilot British 111 Squadron

A pre-war trainee pilot with the RAFVR in Edinburgh, Bain was called to full-time service in September 1939 and was posted to 3 ITW, Hastings in November. He went to 12 EFTS, Prestwick for his elementary flying and moved on to 5 FTS, Sealand. On completion of the course Bain converted to Hurricanes at OTU and joined 111 Squadron at Drem in early October 1940.

The squadron moved soon afterwards to Dyce and it was flying from here on May 8 1941 that Bain crashed, suffering injuries that barred him from further operational flying. While he was in hospital 111 moved south to North Weald and Bain was able to arrange a posting there as a trainee Operations Room Controller. He took over as Controller in September 1941 and continued there until February 1944 when he was posted to Tangmere as Deputy Controller. Bain received a Mention in Despatches for his work during the Invasion. He became Senior Controller at Tangmere and later at the amalgamated Tangmere and Middle Wallop operations rooms at Middle Wallop.

In early 1945 Bain was posted to HQ 11 Group, Uxbridge and in April he became CO at RAF Lerwick, Shetland. He closed the station in August 1945 and served as Staff Officer at Group HQ, Inverness until released in November 1945, as Squadron Leader.

PO 7.9.40   FO 7.9.41   FL 7.9.42

CYRIL EDGAR JOSEPH BAINES

26152 SL Pilot British 238 Squadron

Baines, who was born on November 24 1909, entered RAF College, Cranwell as a cadet in September 1928. He graduated in July 1930 and was posted to 32 Squadron at Kenley on the 26th of the month.

He was sent to RAF Calshot on October 2 1932 for a Flying Boat course, after which he joined 209 (Flying Boat) Squadron at Plymouth. Posted to 24 (Communications) Squadron at Hendon on November 13 1934, Baines' stay was short and he went to Cranwell on March 11 1935 as a flying instructor.

In May 1940 he was given command of 238 Squadron, about to be reformed at Tangmere. He was posted away on July 15 1940.

Baines, a career officer, retired from RAF on March 1 1958, as a Group Captain. He was made a CBE (1.6.53), was a graduate of the Joint Services Staff College, the Army Staff College and was a Qualified A1 Instructor, Central Flying School.

PO 26.7.30   FO 26.1.32   FL 26.1.36   SL 1.10.38
WC 1.12.40   GC 1.1.44   GC 1.7.47

GEORGE MAURICE BAIRD

42094 PO Pilot New Zealander 248 Squadron

Born in Foxton on October 28 1913, Baird applied for a short service commission in April 1938 and after provisional acceptance he sailed for the UK on February 1 1939 in the RMS 'Tainui'.

He began his ab initio course at 10 E&RFTS, Yatesbury on March 13 and went to 5 FTS, Sealand on May 30. Baird joined the newly-reformed 248 Squadron at Hendon on November 6 1939. The squadron was transferred from Fighter to Coastal Command in February 1940 but was seconded back in mid-June, providing fighter patrols in the Montrose/Aberdeen area in support of 603 Squadron.

Baird, who was 'B' Flight Commander, was on a reconnaissance flight off the south-west coast of Norway on the morning of October 20 1940, in Blenheim P 6952. After engaging and shooting down a Do 215 the Blenheim was attacked by three Bf 109s. One engine was put out of action and the cockpit filled with smoke. Baird got down to low level, flying blind and skimming the sea, feeling for the surface at a speed of 150 mph.

The aircraft struck and the silence was complete as the fuselage filled with water. Baird freed himself and opened the hatch. He then managed to float out the unconscious Sergeant DL Burton but was unable to rescue Sergeant R Copcutt, also unconscious, before the aircraft sank. Further back the Wop/AG, Sergeant SV Wood, managed to get out and launch the dinghy. The three survivors were made PoWs.

Baird's long captivity was spent in various camps and he returned to Britain on VE Day 1945. He was repatriated to New Zealand but in late 1947 applied to rejoin the RAF and was granted an extended commission. After refresher courses on Oxfords and Wellingtons he converted to Lincolns and joined 35 Squadron at Mildenhall, as a Flight Commander.

In February 1950 Baird went on an Air Traffic Control course. He served as a controller at stations in the UK, the Far East and Germany and retired from the RAF on December 2 1963, as a Flight Lieutenant.

APO 12.5.39   PO 16.3.40   FO 6.11.41   FL 6.11.42
FL 1.9.45

AUBREY CYRIL BAKER

64892 Sgt Pilot British 610 and 41 Squadrons

Baker joined 610 Squadron at Biggin Hill on July 27 1940. He claimed a Bf 109 destroyed on August 24 and another on the 29th. A month later he was posted to 41 Squadron at Hornchurch.

Commissioned in April 1941, Baker later went to the Middle East and served in the Western Desert with 112 Squadron. On the completion of his operational tour he was awarded the DFC (4.12.42).

Baker was released from the RAF in 1946 and died in 1978.

PO 24.4.41   FO 24.4.42   FL 24.4.43

BARRIE BAKER

935961 Sgt Air Gunner British 264 Squadron

Coming from Kings Norton, Birmingham, Baker joined the RAF in early 1940 and after completing his training was posted to 264 Squadron at Kirton-in-Lindsey in July.

After a period of night-fighting following heavy losses over Dunkirk 264 moved south to Hornchurch on August 21 1940 for daylight patrols. Five days later Baker was flying with Flight Lieutenant AJ Banham in Defiant L 6985. They had destroyed a Do 17 over Thanet, when they were attacked and shot down by Bf 109s. The aircraft crashed two miles off Herne Bay. Banham had baled out and was rescued from the sea but Baker was never found. He is remembered on the Runnymede Memorial, Panel 11. He was 27 years old.

CLIVE CONRAD MAHONEY BAKER

40499 PO Pilot British 23 Squadron

Born on October 7 1919, Baker began his flying training with the RAF in late November 1937. On March 5 1938 he was posted to 9 FTS, Hullavington, after which he joined 23 Squadron at Wittering on September 17 1938.

Baker was still with the squadron at the outbreak of war and served with it throughout the Battle of Britain. He remained in the RAF after the war, was made an MBE (9.6.49) and retired, as an Air Commodore, on July 31 1971. He was a graduate of the Joint Services Staff College, RAF Staff College, RAF Flying College and was a Qualified Instructor, Central Flying School.

APO 19.2.38   PO 29.11.38   FO 3.9.40   FL 29.8.41
SL 1.7.43   WC 1.1.53   GC 1.1.62   AC 1.7.68

ERIC DEBNAM BAKER

740005 Sgt Pilot British 145 Squadron

Baker, of Wimborne, Dorset, was already with 145 Squadron at the start of the Battle of Britain. On August 8 1940 he was reported 'Missing' after a combat over the Channel, south of the Isle of Wight. His Hurricane, P 3381, is believed to be that shot down into the sea by FW Müller of I/JG 27. Baker was 28. He is remembered on the Runnymede Memorial, Panel 11.

HENRY COLLINGHAM BAKER

41146   FO   Pilot   British   41 Squadron and 421 Flight

As a candidate for a short service commission, Baker began his flying training at 9 E&RFTS, Ansty in July 1938. Following kitting-out and a disciplinary course at Uxbridge he was posted to 9 FTS, Hullavington in September.

In May 1939 Baker was posted to No 1 Electrical and Wireless School, Cranwell as a staff pilot. After a brief spell with 616 Squadron at Doncaster in late September Baker went to OTU, Aston Down, flying Gladiators. In November he joined 19 Squadron at Duxford. Over Dunkirk on June 1 1940 he destroyed a Bf 110 and damaged another.

Following a two month stay in hospital Baker was posted to 41 Squadron in late August. On September 15 he shared in the destruction of a He 111 and on the 30th he claimed a Bf 109 destroyed. In October he went to the newly-formed 421 Flight. He destroyed a Bf 109 and probably another on November 1 and on the 24th he shared in the destruction of another. After a short period on loan to 306 Squadron at Tern Hill, Baker joined 74 Squadron at Biggin Hill in January 1941. Flying a 'Rhubarb' operation on May 26 he shot down a Bf 109.

With his tour completed at the end of July 1941 Baker spent the next six months instructing at OTUs, at Debden and Aston Down. After a period in hospital, followed by convalescence at Torquay Baker was posted to a fighter squadron in the Western Desert in May 1942. Promoted to Acting Squadron Leader, Baker took command of 229 Squadron at Ta Kali, Malta in September. He returned to the UK in December and in January 1943 was posted to HQ Northern Ireland as OC Tactics and Training.

In April Baker became an instructor at 55 OTU, Annan, Scotland. but in May went to Gibraltar to take part in ferrying 300 Hurricanes to Cairo. New pilots took them on to Teheran, where they were picked up by Russian pilots. Back in Britain in July Baker was posted to 118 Squadron, Coltishall as supernumerary Flight Lieutenant. In January 1944 he was based at Croydon as a ferry pilot and in March went to CFS, Montrose for an instructor's course, following which he was posted to Wrexham as Chief Flying Instructor. Baker's next posting was as Chief Ground Instructor at 17 FTS, Cranwell in January 1945 and after holding another ground job at Kimbolton for the latter part of the year he was released from the RAF on January 1 1946, as a Squadron Leader.

APO 17.9.38   PO 25.7.39   FO 3.9.40   FL 3.9.41
SL 1.7.44

LOUIS VICTOR BAKER

157151   Sgt   Aircrew   British   236 Squadron

Joined 236 Squadron at St Eval in August 1940. Baker was commissioned from Warrant Officer in March 1943 and he was released from the RAF in 1945, as a Flight Lieutenant.

PO 15.3.43   FO 15.9.43   FL 15.3.45

P BAKER

No unknown   PO   Pilot   British   600 Squadron

This name appears in the Squadron Operations Record Book but nothing else has been traced.

RONALD DAVID BAKER

518293   Sgt   Pilot   British   56 Squadron

A pre-war airman pilot, Baker was with 56 Squadron in early 1940. Over Dunkirk he damaged a He 111 on May 27 and another two days later. On July 13 he claimed the destruction of a Ju 87 and he, himself, had to make a forced-landing at Rodmersham following damage to his Hurricane, P 2985, in a combat over the Channel.

Baker was killed on August 11 1940. His Hurricane, N 2667, was said to have been shot down into the sea by a lone Spitfire during a convoy patrol. Baker baled out but was dead when picked up. He is buried in Letchworth Cemetery, Hertfordshire. He was 23.

STANLEY BAKER

80811   PO   Pilot   British   54 and 66 Squadrons

Joined 54 Squadron at Hornchurch on August 18 1940 and moved to 66 Squadron at Gravesend on September 23. He claimed a Bf 110 destroyed on the 27th and a Bf 109 on October 25.

Baker was reported 'Missing' on a sweep on February 11 1941. He was 21 and is remembered on the Runnymede Memorial, Panel 31.

PO 9.6.40

GEORGE ERIC BALL

39842   FO   Pilot   British   242 Squadron

Ball, from Tankerton, Kent, began his elementary flying training in April 1937. On July 17 he was posted to 7 FTS, Peterborough and on completion of the course he joined 19 Squadron at Duxford on February 19 1938. Over Dunkirk on May 26 1940 Ball destroyed a Bf 109 and was wounded himself. On June 19 he shot down a He 111. Five days later he was posted to 242 Squadron at Coltishall, as 'A' Flight Commander.

During the Battle of Britain Ball shared a He 111 on August 30, destroyed a Bf 110 on September 7, a Bf 109 on the 9th and a Ju 88 on the 18th. He was awarded the DFC (1.10.40), as an Acting Flight Lieutenant. Posted from 242 on January 29 1941, Ball went to the Middle East, to 73 Squadron in the Western Desert, as Flight Commander.

On April 11 1941, very soon after his arrival, Ball flew into a sandstorm and was forced down and taken prisoner. After his release Ball was given command of 222 Squadron at Fairwood Common in October 1945. He was killed in a flying accident on February 1 1946, aged 27. He is buried in Exeter Higher Cemetery.

APO 5.7.37   PO 10.5.38   FO 10.2.40   FL 10.2.41

CYRIL STANLEY BAMBERGER

116515   Sgt   Pilot   British   610 and 41 Squadrons

Born in Port Sunlight on May 4 1919, Bamberger won an electrical engineering apprenticeship at Lever Brothers in 1934. He joined 610 Squadron, AuxAF in 1936, on the ground staff. Accepted for pilot training with the RAFVR in late 1938, he soloed in mid-1939.

Bamberger was called up at the outbreak of war and on October 23 1939 was posted to 8 EFTS, Woodley and later went to 9 FTS, Hullavington to complete his training. He rejoined 610 at Biggin Hill on July 27 but with no experience on Spitfires was sent to 7 OTU, Hawarden for three weeks. Back with 610 Bamberger claimed a probable Bf 109 on August 28. He was posted to 41 Squadron at Hornchurch on September 17 1940 and on October 5 he claimed a Bf 109 destroyed.

After volunteering for Malta, Bamberger left 41 in mid-October 1940. He sailed from Glasgow in the aircraft carrier HMS 'Argus'. Luckily for him he did not fly off for Malta with the twelve Hurricanes and two navigating Skuas which did. Only five of the fourteen aircraft reached their destination. Bamberger eventually reached Malta on

November 28 on the destroyer HMS 'Hotspur' and on arrival he joined 261 Squadron. On January 18 1941 he destroyed a Ju 87, and another the next day. 261 Squadron was disbanded on May 21 1941. Bamberger had moved on the 12th to the newly-formed 185 Squadron at Hal Far. He was posted back to England on June 12 and sent to Central Gunnery School at Sutton Bridge. Commissioned in February 1942, he was posted to Northern Ireland as a Gunnery Officer with Americans, who were converting to Spitfires. In March 1943 Bamberger volunteered for North Africa, where he joined 93 Squadron, moving later to 243 Squadron, as Flight Commander. On July 13 1943 he destroyed a Ju 87 and on May 25 1944 he shot down a Bf 109 during a sweep over Viterbo, Italy.

He returned to the UK in July 1944 and was sent on an instructor's course, after which he was posted in early 1945 to the Gunnery School at Catfoss.

Bamberger was awarded the DFC (28.9.43), as a Flying Officer, 93 Squadron and a Bar (14.11.44), as a Flight Lieutenant, 243 Squadron. The Bar was presented to him at Buckingham Palace on July 3 1945, the citation stating that he had destroyed six enemy aircraft and damaged others.

Released in 1946, Bamberger returned to Lever Brothers and rejoined 610 Squadron at Hooton Park, becoming its CO in 1950. When the Korean crisis came he was recalled to the RAF. In February 1951 he was granted a Permanent Commission and in May 1952 moved to an Intelligence unit assessing strike capabilities of the Chinese and Koreans.

Bamberger retired on January 29 1959, as a Squadron Leader, and became Managing Director of a small packaging materials company he had started in 1954. On retirement from that he had an antique shop in Hampshire.

PO 9.2.42   FO 1.10.42   FL 9.2.44   SL 1.1.47
SL (RAuxAF) 1.4.50

JAMES JULIUS FREDERIC HENRY BANDINEL

74326   FO   Pilot   British   3 Squadron

Whilst an undergraduate at Oriel College, Oxford Bandinel joined the University Air Squadron. He was called to full-time service in October 1939 and after completing his training he joined 3 Squadron at Wick in July 1940.

In late 1941 Bandinel was serving with 260 Squadron in the Middle East. On December 12 he failed to return from operations over the Gazala area. He is remembered on the Alamein Memorial, Column 240.

PO 16.10.39   FO 26.9.40   FL 26.9.41

ARTHUR JOHN BANHAM

37565   FL   Pilot   British   264 and 229 Squadrons

Educated at Perse School, Cambridge, Banham entered the RAF as a candidate for a short service commission and began his training at 7 E&RFTS, Desford on November 25 1935. He was posted to 11 FTS, Wittering on February 22 1936 and as a newly-qualified pilot he joined 19 Squadron at Duxford on August 24.

Promoted to Acting Flight Lieutenant, Banham moved to 611 Squadron, also at Duxford, on September 25 1939. Posted to 12 Group Fighter Pool, Aston Down on January 18 1940, Banham later went to 5 OTU, as an instructor. In June he joined 264 Squadron at Duxford, as Flight Commander. On August 26 Banham was flying with Sergeant B Baker in Defiant L 6985. They had destroyed a Do 17 over Thanet when they were attacked and shot down by Bf 109s. The aircraft crashed two miles off Herne Bay. Having ordered Baker to bale out Banham did so himself. He was rescued from the sea but Baker was never found.

Banham was promoted on September 6 and given command of 229 Squadron, then at Wittering but moved soon afterwards to Northolt. On October 15 Banham was shot down in flames, in Hurricane P 3124. He baled out, badly burned, and the aircraft crashed on to buildings at South Street Farm, Stockbury. Banham underwent plastic surgery by Archie McIndoe at Queen Victoria Cottage Hospital, East Grinstead, becoming forever a Guinea Pig.

Banham was posted to Air Ministry in January 1941 and apart from three months spent at Staff College in early 1942 he remained there until April 1943, when he was posted to Cranwell for a flying refresher course. Some short courses followed at Grantham and 51

OTU, Cranfield, after which Banham went to 604 Squadron, Scorton as a supernumerary Squadron Leader. He was posted to command 108 Squadron in Malta on December 22 1943. Banham took command of 286 Wing at Grottaglie on July 19 1944, served at No 1 Base Area, Naples for two months from October 13 and on December 13 1944 took command of 287 Wing, Ancona, an appointment he held until returning to the UK for release in July 1945. Banham died in 1987. His portrait was done by Captain Cuthbert Orde in 1940.

APO 3.2.36   PO 25.11.36   FO 25.6.38   FL 25.6.40
SL 1.9.41   WC 1.7.43

THOMAS HENRY BANISTER

48228   Sgt   Air Gunner   British   219 Squadron

Banister joined 219 Squadron at Catterick in early August 1940. On the 15th of the month he was flying in Blenheim L 8698 with Sergeant OA Dupee when their aircraft was hit by return fire from a He 111 engaged off Scarborough. Dupee was wounded in the arm. Banister went forward, assisted Dupee from his seat and took control of the damaged aircraft. Dupee, though weak from loss of blood, directed Banister, who was thus enabled to make a forced-landing, with undercarriage retracted. For this action both men were awarded the DFM (24.9.40).

Banister was commissioned in March 1942 and released from the RAF in 1945.

PO 20.3.42   FO 1.10.42   FL 20.3.44

WILLIAM HENRY BANKS

47102   Sgt   Pilot   British   245, 32 and 504 Squadrons

Born on October 4 1916, Banks was with 245 Squadron early in 1940. He flew with the squadron on patrols over Dunkirk and on June 14 his aircraft was damaged by anti-aircraft fire on a patrol over France.

Banks was posted to 32 Squadron at Acklington on September 18 1940 but six days later moved to 504 Squadron at Filton. On the 30th of the month he made a forced-landing in Hurricane P 3774, following a combat over the Yeovil area.

Commissioned in October 1941, Banks remained in the RAF after the war, retiring on May 30 1958 as a Squadron Leader. He died on January 16 1980.

PO 29.10.41   FO 1.10.42   FL 29.10.43   FL 1.9.45
SL 1.7.52

ERIC SAMUEL BANN

741589   Sgt   Pilot   British   238 Squadron

A native of Macclesfield, Bann was educated at Athey Street School and studied aeronautical engineering at Manchester College of Technology. He joined the RAFVR in 1937 and was called up at the outbreak of war.

Bann joined 238 Squadron at Tangmere in June 1940. On August 11 he claimed the destruction of a He 111. Bann's aircraft, Hurricane V 6776, was severely damaged in combat over Fareham on September 28 and he baled out over Brading Marshes but was killed when his parachute failed to open.

Bann was 26. He is buried in Macclesfield Cemetery, Cheshire.

FERDINAND HENRY RAPHAEL BARALDI

86332   PO   Pilot   British   609 Squadron

A member of the RAFVR before the war, Baraldi was called up in September 1939 and after ITW training he was at No 1 EFTS, Hatfield from December 4 until May 10 1940. He joined 609 Squadron at Middle Wallop in late October.

In August 1942 Baraldi went to 111 Squadron, as a Flight Commander, and in October went with it to North Africa. He damaged a Ju 88 east of Bone on November 18. He was posted away from 111 on January 11 1943, having had some trouble with his eyes. He was then 30 years old.

Baraldi was released from the RAF in 1946, as a Squadron Leader. He died in 1988.

PO 7.9.40   FO 7.9.41   FL 7.9.42

WIENCZYSLAW BARANSKI

P 0249　　FL　　Pilot　　Polish　　607 Squadron

Baranski was born on September 19 1908 at Solec, Wisla, Poland and joined the PAF in 1930. He commanded 113 Squadron, in IV / 1 Dyon in September 1939 and during the German invasion he shared in the destruction of an enemy aircraft. When Poland fell Baranski escaped to Roumania, then to France, where he joined l'Armée de l'Air. In early 1940 he commanded a flight of three Polish pilots in Groupe de Chasse 111 / 6, flying D 520 Dewoitine fighters from Coulommiers and shared in the destruction of an enemy aircraft. In the middle of the month the unit moved to Perpignan and a few days later flew to North Africa.

Baranski escaped to England, via Gibraltar, went to 5 OTU, Aston Down on August 25 and joined 607 Squadron at Tangmere on October 11 1940. A month later he was posted to 303 Squadron at Leconfield. He was awarded the KW (1.2.41) and on February 22 1941 went to the newly-formed 316 Squadron at Pembrey, as Flight Commander.

His first operational tour over, Baranski went to 316's Operations Room on July 19 1941. A year later he moved to 308 Squadron's Operations Room at Heston. Baranski returned to operations on May 16 1943, when he took command of 302 Squadron at Hutton Cranswick. He was awarded a Bar to the KW (7.7.43) and a second Bar (20.10.43), when he was posted away to be Polish Liaison Officer at HQ 12 Group.

Baranski moved to HQ PAF at Blackpool on April 3 1944, was awarded the VM (5th Class)(15.5.44) and went to a course at Polish Staff College on November 28 1944. He was released from the PAF on November 20 1946.

ROBERT HUGH BARBER

42385　　PO　　Pilot　　British　　46 Squadron

Barber was born on December 19 1915 at Hatfield, Hertfordshire. He moved to Lincolnshire as a child and was educated at Oakham School. He went into estate agency but in 1935 joined the Metropolitan Police. Barber entered the RAF on a short service commission in June 1939. After completing his ab initio course at 22 E&RFTS, Cambridge he was posted to 12 FTS, Grantham in late August.

In early 1940 Barber went to RAF Manby for an armament course, in July was posted to 7 OTU, Hawarden to convert to Spitfires and on August 15 joined 46 Squadron at Digby. On September 4, acting as weaver, Barber was jumped by a Bf 109 over Rochford. His glycol system was damaged and he was soaked in fluid. He dived from 15000 feet and made a belly-landing at Chigborough Farm, Heybridge. Admitted to St Margaret's Hospital, Epping, Barber learned that he had fractured three vertebrae in his neck and broken his jaw in three places. He was in hospital for six months.

Barber's medical category barred him from operational flying and he went to HQ 10 Group as an assistant to the Controller. When Wing Commander AG Malan formed CGS at Sutton Bridge Barber was one of his early pupils. He then commanded Armament Practice Camps at Warmwell, Martlesham Heath and Southend. He was awarded the AFC (1.1.43). Early in 1944 Barber went to the Gun Research Unit at Exeter, flying with the new gyro gunsight. He was then given command of a non-operational Spitfire squadron at

Southend, to train pilots on the new sight, including some American P 51 pilots.

Later in the year the squadron moved to North Weald. Barber had to return to Southend to clear up some matters. He was flown there in an Oxford. The aircraft swung on take-off and crashed. The pilot was killed and Barber went to hospital for several months. He returned to the APC at Warmwell but joined a Disarmament Group about to go to Germany.

After a motor accident on a mined bridge and another spell in hospital Barber was posted to Sylt to set up an APC for squadron training.

Barber was released from the RAF in 1947 and did not live in the UK again. He settled in New Zealand.

APO 5.8.39　　PO 2.3.40　　FO 2.3.41　　FL 2.3.42

RICHARD GEORGE ARTHUR BARCLAY

74661　　FO　　Pilot　　British　　249 Squadron

Born at Upper Norwood, Surrey on December 7 1919, Barclay was educated at Stowe School and then went to Trinity College, Cambridge to read Geography. In 1938 he joined the University Air Squadron and transferred into the RAFVR in June 1939.

Called up for full-time service in October, Barclay went to 3 ITW, Hastings on November 8 1939. He began his RAF flying training at Cranwell on January 1 1940 and with this completed he was posted to No 1 School of Army Co-operation on June 2. Eight days later he moved to 5 OTU, Aston Down to convert to Hurricanes and on June 23 he joined 249 Squadron at Leconfield.

Barclay destroyed a Bf 109 on September 7 and on the same day he crash-landed at Potter Street, Harlow in Hurricane V 6610 after his engine was damaged by return fire from a He 111 engaged over Maidstone. On September 15 he destroyed a Do 17, shared a Do 215 on the 19th and destroyed a Bf 109 and a Ju 88 on the 27th. During the attack on Ju 88s on that day Barclay, in Hurricane V 6622, was shot down south of London and made a forced-landing at West Malling. He got a probable Bf 109 on October 15, two probable Bf 109s on November 7 and destroyed another on the 14th. He was awarded the DFC (26.11.40).

On November 29 1940 Barclay was shot down by a Bf 109 and wounded in ankle, legs and elbow. He was taken first to Pembury Hospital but spent six more weeks in other hospitals and did not return to 249 until March 1941. Barclay was posted to 52 OTU, Debden, as an instructor, on May 7. Three months later he joined 611 Squadron at Hornchurch, as Flight Commander. During a sweep over St Omer on September 20 1941 Barclay was attacked by Bf 109s and his engine damaged. He forced-landed at Buyschoeure after breaking high tension cables. With the help of the French Resistance he was passed over the Spanish frontier, arriving in Barcelona on November 7. He reached the British Embassy four days later, left there for Gibraltar on December 7 and two days later flew by Catalina to Stranraer.

After a short attachment at HQ Fighter Command Barclay was posted to HQ 9 Group as Tactics Officer. On April 4 1942 he was given command of 601 Squadron, then about to go to the Middle East. The squadron embarked at Liverpool on April 10 in HMT K6 (SS 'Rangitata') and reached Port Tewfik on June 4, having gone via South Africa and Aden.

Barclay did not get a chance to lead 601. He was posted to command 238 Squadron at Amriya from July 2 1942. In the afternoon of July 17 he destroyed a Ju 87. In the early evening he led 238 on a patrol of the Alamein area, acting as top cover for 274 Squadron. As 238 moved to attack some Ju 87s it was jumped by Bf 109s and Barclay was shot down and killed, possibly by Leutnant Werner Schroer of 111 / JG 27. Barclay is buried in the El Alamein Cemetery and he is commemorated on a plaque in Cromer Parish Church, where his father was vicar from 1939 to 1946.

PO 3.10.39　　FO 3.10.40　　FL 3.10.41

FREDERICK JAMES BARKER

178549   **Sgt**   **Air Gunner**   **British**   **264 Squadron**

Born in Bow, London, Barker joined 264 Squadron on its reformation on October 30 1939. He teamed up with Sergeant ER Thorn and they later became the most successful Defiant partnership of the war.

Over Dunkirk on May 28 1940 they destroyed three Bf 109s, the following day two Ju 87s and a Bf 110 and on May 31 a He 111 and another shared. Barker was awarded the DFM (14.6.40).

When 264 moved south to Hornchurch on August 21 1940 Thorn and Barker were again in action. On the 26th they destroyed two Do 17s and as they went for a third they were attacked by a Bf 109. With their aircraft damaged Thorn spun down and prepared to make a crash-landing. At 500 feet the Bf 109 attacked again, this time setting the Defiant on fire. Before crashing Barker shot the enemy fighter down and it crashed a short distance away. Thorn and Barker escaped with slight injuries. For this action they were each awarded a Bar to the DFM (11.2.41).

They destroyed a He 111 at night on April 9 1941. The partnership broke up when Thorn was posted to 32 Squadron in October 1941. Barker remained with 264 until 1943. He was then posted to the Middle East as an air gunnery instructor. He was commissioned in April 1944 and released from the RAF in 1946.

PO 25.4.44   FO 25.10. 44

GEORGE LEONARD BARKER

44571   **PO**   **Observer**   **British**   **600 Squadron**

Barker, of Diss, Norfolk, served with 600 Squadron in the Battle of Britain. He was awarded the DFM (13.9.40), as a Sergeant.

Barker was killed on July 18 1944, aged 30. He is buried in Diss Cemetery, Norfolk.

PO 28.8.40   FO 28.8.41   FL 28.8.42

JOHN KEETH BARKER

566251   **Sgt**   **Pilot**   **British**   **152 Squadron**

Barker served as a ground wireless operator in the pre-war RAF before being trained as a pilot. He was with 152 Squadron at the start of the Battle of Britain. On August 18 1940 he claimed a Ju 87 destroyed and on the 25th a Bf 109.

Barker did not return from a sortie on September 4 1940. He is believed to have been shot down by return fire from a Do 17 engaged 25 miles off Bognor. He baled out but was killed. His body was washed up on the French coast and he is buried in Etaples Military Cemetery, France. Barker was 23.

ERIC CHARLES BARNARD

178934   **Sgt**   **Air Gunner**   **British**   **600 Squadron**

Joined 601 Squadron, AuxAF on March 6 1936 for ground crew duties. Barnard later trained as an air gunner but in February 1940 601 exchanged its Blenheims for Hurricanes. He was posted to 600 Squadron at Manston on May 11 1940 as an AC 2 Air Gunner but was later promoted to Sergeant.

Barnard was flying as a member of the crew of Blenheim L 1111 on September 8 when they became lost following an R/T failure during a night patrol. With fuel exhausted the crew, Barnard, Pilot Officer HBL Hough and Sergeant A Smith, baled out safely. The aircraft crashed near Odiham.

On July 1 1941 Barnard went to 125 Squadron at Colerne, as an air gunner. He was with the squadron until January 28 1942, when he was posted to Training Command for training as a navigator.

Barnard qualified at 2 Air Observers' School, Edmonton, Canada on April 16 1943. He returned to the UK and qualified as an Observer Radio at 62 OTU, Ouston on September 14 and finished as a Navigator Radar at 63 OTU, after which he was posted to 25 Squadron at Acklington on January 18 1944.

Commissioned from Warrant Officer in April 1944, Barnard was posted to 85 Squadron, Swannington on April 27 1945 and remained with the squadron until his release on July 24 1946.

PO 24.4.44   FO 24.10.44   FL 24.4.46

JOHN GUY CARDEW BARNES

90101   **FL**   **Pilot**   **British**   **600 Squadron**

Joined 600 Squadron, AuxAF in 1937 and served with the squadron through the Battle of Britain period.

Barnes was released from the RAF in 1946, as a Wing Commander.

PO (AuxAF) 17.8.37   FO (AuxAF) 17.2.39   FO 24.8.39
FL 3.9.40   SL 1.12.41

LESLIE DENIS BARNES

60325   **Sgt**   **Pilot**   **British**   **257, 615 and 607 Squadrons**

Barnes was with 257 at the start of the Battle of Britain. He was posted to 615 Squadron at Prestwick on September 4 1940 and moved on to 607 at Tangmere on the 21st. He returned to 257 and took part in the engagement with the Italians on November 11 1940, in which he claimed the probable destruction of a Fiat CR 42.

Commissioned in January 1941, Barnes was with 46 Squadron when it sailed for the Middle East in late May 1941 in the carrier HMS 'Argus'. At Gibraltar pilots and aircraft were transferred onto HMS 'Ark Royal' and 'Furious'. They flew off to Hal Far, Malta on June 6. On June 27 Barnes destroyed two Mc 200s in a combat over Ta Kali and on December 30 shared a Ju 88 over Luqa.

Barnes was released from the RAF in 1946, as a Flight Lieutenant.

PO 15.1.41   FO 15.1.42   FL 15.1.43

WILKINSON BARNES

90294   **FO**   **Pilot**   **British**   **504 Squadron**

Joined 504 Squadron, AuxAF in 1938 and was called for full-time service on August 24 1939. After completing his flying training Barnes rejoined 504 at Castletown in July 1940.

No further service details have been traced and Barnes' name does not appear on an Air Force List after March 1944. He is believed to have died on May 19 1980.

PO (AuxAF) 2.8.38   PO 24.8.39   FO 2.8.40   FL 2.8.41

RICHARD EDGAR BARNETT

26222   **SL**   **Pilot**   **British**   **234 Squadron**

Barnett entered RAF College, Cranwell as a cadet in January 1930. After graduating in December 1931 he joined 54 Squadron at Hornchurch on the 19th of the month.

Posted overseas in September 1932, Barnett joined 6 Squadron at Ismailia on November 1. He went to the RAF Depot at Aboukir in July 1935. In the Coronation Honours List Barnett was made an MBE (11.5.37) for operations in Palestine from April to October 1936. After returning to the UK he was posted to the Aeroplane and Armament Experimental Establishment at Martlesham Heath on August 16 1938.

When the CO of the newly-formed 234 Squadron was badly injured in a car accident on November 2 1939 Barnett took command at short notice. He did not fly very often and relinquished his command on August 13 1940. He resigned his commission on August 11 1941. After the war he worked in Kenya and died on January 2 1970.

PO 19.12.31   FO 9.6.33   FL 7.9.36   SL 1.6.39

RUPERT VICTOR BARON

78741   **PO**   **Air Gunner**   **British**   **219 Squadron**

Baron, of Highbury, London, joined 219 Squadron at Catterick in June 1940. On October 12 he was flying as crew in Blenheim L 1113 on a routine night patrol. Unexpected engine vibration was experienced and the pilot, Sergeant GM Mead, throttled back. This action caused a high speed stall. Both men baled out but Baron's parachute failed to open. The aircraft crashed at Court Lodge Farm, Ewhurst.

     Baron is buried in Sittingbourne and Milton Cemetery. He was 40 years old.

PO 1.6.40

RONALD GEORGE VICTOR BARRACLOUGH

66487   **Sgt**   **Pilot**   **British**   **266 Squadron**

A pre-war airman pilot, Barraclough joined 266 Squadron at Sutton Bridge on December 18 1939. Commissioned in May 1941, he was posted away from the squadron on July 19 1941.

     Barraclough commanded 137 Squadron on the Continent from December 1944 until March 1945. He did not remain in the RAF after the war.

PO 1.5.41   *FO 25.11.41*   *FL 25.11.42*

STANLEY MICHAEL BARRACLOUGH

46029   **Sgt**   **Pilot**   **British**   **92 Squadron**

Born on April 2 1917, Barraclough was with 92 Squadron at the start of the Battle of Britain. He was commissioned in June 1941 and stayed in the RAF after the war, retiring on May 28 1958 as a Squadron Leader. He was a graduate of RAF Staff College and a Qualified A1 Instructor, Central Flying School.

PO 28.6.41   *FO 28.6.42*   *FL 28.6.43*   *SL 1.8.47*

PHILIP HENRY BARRAN

90323   **FO**   **Pilot**   **British**   **609 Squadron**

Barran was born at Chapel Allerton, Leeds on April 20 1909 and when he joined 609 Squadron, AuxAF in early 1937 he was a trainee mining engineer and manager of a brickworks at a colliery owned by his mother's family.

     Appointed 'B' Flight Commander early in 1939, Barran was embodied for full-time service on August 24 1939. He was to become one of the earliest casualties in the Battle of Britain. On July 11 1940 his aircraft, Spitfire L 1069, was severely damaged in a morning combat with Bf 109s of III / JG 27 over a convoy off Portland. Barran tried to reach the coast but was forced to bale out five miles off Portland Bill. He was picked up, wounded and badly burned, but died before reaching land.

     Barran, who was 31, is buried in Leeds Cemetery.

PO (AuxAF) 20.4.37   *FO (AuxAF) 20.10.38*   *FO 24.8.39*

WILLIAM ERIC BARRETT

751810   **Sgt**   **Aircrew**   **British**   **25 Squadron**

No service details traced.

NORMAN PERCY GERALD BARRON

88649   **Sgt**   **Pilot**   **British**   **236 Squadron**

Born in 1918, Barron joined the RAFVR in January 1938 and trained at No 1 E&RFTS, Hatfield. He was called up at the outbreak of war and went to 2 FTS, Brize Norton to finish his training, after which he joined 236 Squadron at Martlesham Heath on December 9 1939. Commissioned in November 1940, Barron was involved in combat with a Blohm and Voss floatplane on the 30th of the month. His Blenheim was damaged and two of his crew wounded.

     Posted away on October 7 1941, Barron went to 19 Group, firstly to a drogue-towing unit at Roborough and later to an Armament Practice Camp at Carew Cheriton, where he flew Lysanders.

     On August 1 1942 Barron was posted to 172 Squadron at Chivenor, flying Leigh-Light Wellingtons on anti-submarine work. He went with a squadron detachment to Malta on June 9 1943. In early September he was sent to 22 PTC, Almaza, Cairo, from where he was posted to Southern Rhodesia. After an instructor's course at 33 FIS, Norton Barron went to 22 SFTS, Thornhill on January 9 1944. He instructed there on Harvards until returning to the UK in September 1945.

     Barron spent a further year instructing, firstly at 17 SFTS, Spitalgate and then at 19 FTS, Cranwell before he was released in April 1947. He joined KLM Airlines in January 1948 and flew with them until retiring in 1978.

PO 27.11.40   *FO 27.11.41*   *FL 27.11.42*

HECTOR JACK RAYMOND BARROW

745659   **Sgt**   **Pilot**   **British**   **607, 43 and 213 Squadrons**

Barrow, from Isleworth, Middlesex, joined 607 Squadron at Usworth in June 1940. In August he was posted to 43 Squadron at Tangmere and transferred on September 20 to 213 Squadron, then also at Tangmere.

     On September 27 Barrow claimed a share in destroying a Bf 110. He was reported 'Missing' following a Wing patrol with 602 Squadron over Tangmere on November 28. His aircraft, Hurricane V 6691, probably went into the sea and Barrow's body washed up on the French coast. He is buried in Colleville-sur-Mer churchyard, France. He was 21.

NATHANIEL JOHN MERRIMAN BARRY

72514   **FO**   **Pilot**   **South African**   **3 and 501 Squadrons**

In 1938, as an engineering undergraduate at Pembroke College, Cambridge Barry joined the University Gliding Club. He later transferred to the RAFVR and was called up at the outbreak of war. After completing his flying training Barry was posted as ADC to Air Vice Marshal de Crespigny. He repeatedly requested a posting to a fighter squadron and was finally successful and was serving with 3 Squadron at the start of the Battle of Britain.

     On September 26 1940 Barry was posted to 501 Squadron at Kenley. Four days later he forced-landed at Pembury, in Hurricane L 1657, after a morning combat with Bf 109s over Maidstone. A week later, on October 7 Barry was shot down by a Bf 109 over Wrotham. He baled out but fell dead at Wilmington. His aircraft crashed at Lane End, Darenth.

     Barry was 22 years old. He is buried in the churchyard of St Andrew's, Finghall, Yorkshire.

PO (RAFVR) 5.11.38   *PO 3.9.39*   *FO 15.5.40*

PATRICK PETER COLUM BARTHROPP

41542 FO Pilot British 602 Squadron

Barthropp was born in Dublin on November 9 1920. He was educated at St Augustine's Abbey School, Ramsgate, St Joseph's College, near Market Drayton and Ampleforth College, North Yorkshire, after which he went to Rover's on an engineering apprenticeship.

As a candidate for a short service commission he began his elementary flying training at 13 E&RFTS, White Waltham on November 1 1938. Following a short induction course at Uxbridge he was posted to 7 FTS, Peterborough on January 31 1939 for six months flying training.

After a month at No 1 Armament Training Camp, Catfoss Barthropp went to No 1 School of Army Co-operation, Old Sarum on the day the war started. On October 9 1939 he was posted to 613 (Army Co-operation) Squadron at Odiham. Barthropp volunteered for Fighter Command on August 21 1940 and was sent to 7 OTU, Hawarden to convert to Spitfires and on September 8 he joined 602 Squadron at Westhampnett. He shared in destroying a He 111 on the 27th and on October 2 shared a Ju 88 with Flight Lieutenant RF Boyd.

Barthropp was posted to 610 Squadron on December 20 1940 and on February 5 1941 he went to 91 Squadron at Hawkinge. He destroyed a Bf 109 on August 17 1941 and damaged another. On August 24 he returned to 610 Squadron, as 'B' Flight Commander, was awarded the DFC (26.9.41) and posted away to 61 OTU, Heston on October 23.

A return to operations came on May 15 1942 when Barthropp joined 122 Squadron at Hornchurch. Two days later, on a Boston escort operation, he was shot down over Audruicq, near St Omer, baled out and was captured on landing. From early June 1942 until his release on May 2 1945, near Lubeck, Barthropp was in several prisoner-of-war camps, including Stalag Luft III. In early September 1945 he was sent to Norway to locate graves of shot-down airmen and confirm their identities.

On January 2 1946 Barthropp began a course at the Empire Test Pilots' School, Cranfield, followed by a posting on May 23 to 'A' Fighter Test Squadron at the Aeroplane and Armament Experimental Establishment at Boscombe Down. In January 1948 he was sent to the Sudan to test the Meteor III under tropical conditions. Barthropp returned to Britain later in the year and was posted to HQ Fighter Command at Bentley Priory as Ops Day.

In March 1952 he went to RAF Waterbeach as Wing Commander Flying, in March 1954 to Air HQ Hong Kong as Staff Officer i/c Admin, in April 1955 to RAF Honiley to command, in March 1957 to RAF Coltishall as Wing Commander i/c Admin. He was awarded the AFC (10.6.54) for his work at Waterbeach.

Barthropp retired on December 28 1957, as a Squadron Leader. He then started, what later became a very successful chauffeur-driven car hire business in London.

APO 14.1.39   PO 3.9.39   FO 3.9.40   FL 3.9.41
SL 1.7.44   SL 1.8.47

LEONARD HAROLD BARTLETT

102959 Sgt Pilot British 17 Squadron

Born on June 20 1916, Bartlett joined the RAFVR in May 1939. Called to full-time service at the outbreak of war, he completed his training and was posted to 17 Squadron at Debden on July 15 1940.

On August 28 Bartlett shared in the destruction of a Ju 88, on September 19 he shared another and on November 8 he destroyed a Ju 87 and probably a second.

Commissioned in July 1941, Bartlett was posted to 137 Squadron at Matlask in February 1942. In September he was given command of 253 Squadron at Hibaldstow. The squadron went to North Africa in November 1942. Bartlett destroyed a Ju 88 on January 10 1943.

The squadron moved to Monte Corvino in October. Bartlett was posted away in January 1944 and was awarded the DSO (3.3.44). He retired on June 20 1966, as a Group Captain.

PO 31.7.41   FO 11.5.42   FL 31.7.43   SL 30.4.44
SL 1.9.45   WC 1.7.53   GC 1.1.60

ANTHONY CHARLES BARTLEY

41816 PO Pilot British 92 Squadron

The son of a District Judge, Bartley was born in Dacca, Bengal in 1919. He was educated at Stowe School and learned to fly at West Malling Flying Club in 1938. Bartley joined the RAF on a short service commission, did his elementary flying at 6 E&RFTS, Sywell and in May 1939 was posted to 13 FTS Drem. After a three week conversion course on to Blenheims at Hendon he joined 92 Squadron at Tangmere on November 20 1939.

Over Dunkirk on May 24 Bartley damaged two Bf 110s and on June 2 he damaged four He 111s. Flying from Biggin Hill in September he claimed a Do 17 destroyed on the 18th and a Ju 88 on the 27th. Bartley was awarded the DFC (25.10.40) and in March 1941 he was posted to 74 Squadron, as a Flight Commander. It was not a happy posting and he left the squadron in May to go to 56 OTU, Sutton Bridge, moving soon afterwards to 53 OTU, Heston. In July he was posted to Vickers-Supermarine as a production test pilot.

Bartley returned to operations in February 1942 as a Flight Commander with 65 Squadron at Debden. In early May he took command of 65 after the CO was killed. In July 1942 he went to CGS, Sutton Bridge for a course and in August was given command of 111 Squadron at Kenley. The squadron was destined for overseas and on October 20 sailed for Gibraltar. Bartley led the squadron off on November 11 and flew to Algiers, moving to Bone three days later. He destroyed two Ju 87s on November 25, a Bf 109 on the 29th, a probable Bf 109 on December 4 and a Bf 109 on the 28th. In mid-January 1943 Bartley was posted from the squadron and on the 29th took off from Gibraltar in a Liberator for the UK. Following the loss of two engines the aircraft made a crash-landing on a Welsh airfield.

Bartley was awarded a Bar to the DFC (16.2.43) and was posted in May to HQ 83 Group, Redhill to help train squadrons in ground attack and army support. In early October he sailed for America for a course at the Command and General Staff School at Fort Leavenworth, Kansas, moving in February 1944 to the School of Air Tactics at Orlando, Texas. After returning to Britain in the 'Queen Elizabeth' in mid-April Bartley was posted as Liaison Officer to the 70th Fighter Wing of the US Ninth Air Force. On October 24 1944 he went to Transport Command to set up staging posts in Europe.

Bartley volunteered for service in the Far East and sailed from Liverpool in the 'Mauretania' on July 3 1945. He reached Sydney on August 8 and was posted a week later to the Palau Islands to set up a Transport Command staging post. He requested repatriation, was granted leave and returned home in a DC 4, which was returning to England for a major overhaul.

On November 28 1945 Bartley married film actress Deborah Kerr. After release from the RAF in 1946 he joined Vickers Armstrong as a test pilot and sales executive.

APO 1.4.39   PO 21.10.39   FO 21.10.40   FL 21.10.41
SL 1.7.45

ANTHONY RICHARD HENRY BARTON

30104 PO Pilot British 32 and 253 Squadrons

Barton, of Oakleigh Park, was a Sub-Lieutenant in the Royal Navy in early 1936. He transferred to the RAF, with the rank of Flying Officer, and on May 17 1936 was posted to No 1 FTS, Leuchars. On August 24 1937 he went to RAF Gosport as a supernumerary and on October 1 joined 823 (Torpedo Spotter-Reconnaissance) Squadron, with the rank of Lieutenant RN.

ARH Barton (continued)

Barton re-appeared in July 1940 when he was commissioned in the RAF as a Pilot Officer. After converting to Hurricanes he joined 32 Squadron at Biggin Hill on August 5. On the 11th he claimed a Bf 109 and the next day was shot down, in Hurricane N 2596, in a combat over Dover, crashing near Hawkinge. Two days later he forced-landed at Hawkinge after being attacked by Bf 109s. On August 16 he destroyed two Bf 109s and on the 18th a Ju 88.

A posting to 253 Squadron at Kenley came on September 10 and on the 15th Barton destroyed a Do 215 over the Channel but the damage his aircraft, Hurricane V 6698, sustained in the engagement necessitated a forced-landing at Hawkinge. Five days later Barton was shot down and his Hurricane, R 2686, crashed and burned out. He was severely wounded and admitted to Ashford Hospital. He returned to operational flying in February 1941. He was later posted to 124 Squadron at Castletown, as a Flight Commander.

Barton went to 126 Squadron in Malta in March 1942, flying the squadron's first Spitfire off the carrier HMS 'Eagle'. Having received the DFC (10.4.42), being then credited with five enemy aircraft destroyed in the Battle of Britain, Barton was awarded a Bar to the DFC (7.7.42) for having destroyed at least another five enemy aircraft, two in one combat, whilst operating from Malta. He commanded 126 Squadron from May to August 1942, when he was posted back to the UK. Barton was killed in a flying accident on April 4 1943, whilst serving as a Squadron Leader instructor. He was 29 years old and is buried in St Andrew's churchyard, Totteridge, Hertfordshire.

FO 17.5.36   PO 6.7.40   FO 6.7.41   FL 30.7.42

ROBERT ALEXANDER BARTON

37664   FL   Pilot   Canadian   249 Squadron

Born in Kamloops, British Columbia on June 7 1916, Barton joined the RAF on a short service commission in January 1936. After completing his ab initio training he went to 9 FTS, Thornaby on April 4.

Barton joined 41 Squadron at Catterick on October 11 1936 and remained with it until posted as Flight Commander to 249 Squadron at Church Fenton on its formation on May 16 1940. The squadron moved south to Boscombe Down on August 1 and the next day Barton destroyed a Bf 110. On September 2 he shared a Do 215 and on the 3rd he was himself shot down over the Thames Estuary, in Hurricane V 6625. Barton baled out, unhurt. His next victory was a Bf 110 destroyed on September 27 and he shot down the Bf 109 of Oberleutnant Otto Hintze on October 29, had a probable Bf 109 on November 7 and shot down a bomber into the sea on November 11, probably a BR 20.

Barton was awarded the DFC (20.10.40) and was decorated by the King at Duxford in January 1941. He had been promoted and given command of 249 in December 1940. On a convoy patrol on February 4 1941 Barton destroyed a Bf 110, his final victory flying from an English base. In mid-April the squadron re-equipped with Hurricane 11s and in early May sailed from Liverpool in the carrier HMS 'Furious'. At Gibraltar 249's aircraft were transferred to HMS 'Ark Royal' and on May 21 1941 flew off the carrier and after some mishaps eventually all reached Malta safely.

The squadron was very successful over the next few months with Barton destroying a SM 79 on June 3, a BR 20 at night on June 8, a Mc 200 on July 17 and another on the 25th, a probable Mc 200 and another damaged on September 4, a shared SM 81 on October 19 and a Mc 202 on November 22. He was awarded a Bar to the DFC (31.10.41) and posted away for a rest on December 8 1941.

Thereafter Barton served in non-flying staff appointments, although he did fly a few Mustang sorties in 1945. He was made an OBE (14.6.45) and remained in the RAF. He retired on February 27 1959, as a Wing Commander, and returned to Canada to live in 1965.

APO 23.3.36   PO 27.1.37   FO 27.10.38   FL 3.9.40
SL 1.12.41   WC 1.7.44   WC 1.7.47

JINDRICH BARTOS

83220   PO   Pilot   Czechoslovakian   312 Squadron

Bartos was born on November 16 1911. In Czechoslavakia he served with the Second Air Regiment. After the Nazis occupied his country in 1938 Bartos escaped and eventually reached France and joined l'Armée de l'Air.

In May 1940 he was posted to Groupe de Chasse 1/3 at Esbley, flying Dewoitine D 520s. On June 3 he damaged a He 111 over Paris. Two weeks later the unit flew to Algeria. Bartos made his way to Casablanca, then on to England, via Gibraltar. After conversion to Hurricanes he joined 312 Squadron at Duxford on September 5 1940.

Flying Hurricane V 6885 from Penrhos on a dog-fight practice on February 13 1941 Bartos spun into the ground near Prestatyn and was killed. He was 29 years old and is buried in West Derby Cemetery, Liverpool in a joint grave with another Czech pilot, Sergeant O Hanzlicek.

ERIC GORDON BARWELL

77454   PO   Pilot   British   264 Squadron

A member of the RAFVR from early July 1938, Barwell did his part-time elementary flying training at 22 E&RFTS, Cambridge. He was called up at the outbreak of war and posted to 2 FTS, Brize Norton on October 8 1939. Commissioned in December he went to the 12 Group Fighter Pool on New Year's Day 1940.

On February 5 Barwell joined 264 Squadron at Martlesham Heath. He took part in the successful actions of the squadron over Dunkirk, destroying a Bf 109, a Bf 110 and two Ju 87s on May 29 and a Bf 109 and a He 111 on the 31st. In the latter engagement Barwell was hit by return fire and turned for home but was unable to maintain height and landed on the sea between two destroyers, about five miles from Dover. The aircraft broke up and Barwell and his gunner, knocked unconscious in the crash, were thrown into the water. Barwell supported Pilot Officer Williams until they were picked up.

Credited with one enemy aircraft destroyed during the Battle of Britain, Barwell was awarded the DFC (11.2.41). Promoted to Acting Flight Lieutenant on July 1 1941, he was posted to the newly-formed 125 Squadron at Colerne, as a Flight Commander. He took command of the squadron in December 1941 and held it until February 1942, when it became a Wing Commander post. Barwell remained as Flight Commander until September 6 1942, when he went to HQ 10 Group as Ops Night. He returned to 125 Squadron at Fairwood Common on March 31 1943, again serving as a Flight Commander until he was posted to the Fighter Interception Unit on August 18 1944. He was awarded a Bar to the DFC (15.8.44).

A month later Barwell went to Main HQ 2nd TAF, as an Acting Wing Commander, moved to HQ 148 Wing on April 4 1945 and returned to his old squadron, 264, at Twente, Germany in late June. The squadron was disbanded there on August 25 and Barwell was released from the RAF on September 2 1945, as an Acting Wing Commander.

PO 10.12.39   FO 10.12.40   FL 10.12.41   SL 20.12.44

PHILIP REGINALD BARWELL

22062 WC Pilot British 242 Squadron

Barwell, of Peterborough, Northamptonshire, was born in 1907, commissioned into the RAF in September 1925 and posted to 19 Squadron at Duxford, under instruction. On September 9 1929 he went to a staff appointment at CFS, Upavon and on August 5 1930 was posted to the Home Aircraft Depot, Henlow for an engineering course. With this completed he went to the Aircraft Depot, Hinaidi, Iraq.

On June 1 1933 Barwell moved to the engineer section at Hinaidi, on the staff of Iraq Command. He returned to Britain in late 1934 and on January 7 1935 was posted to CFS, Upavon as an instructor.

Barwell took command of 46 Squadron at Digby on January 4 1937 and led it until late October 1939. He was awarded the DFC (28.11.39) for leading a flight of six aircraft on October 21 over the North Sea to intercept enemy bombers approaching a British convoy about thirty miles out. He shot down one enemy aircraft and shared in the destruction of another.

Whilst commanding RAF Coltishall in October 1940 Barwell flew three operational sorties with 242 Squadron on the 5th of the month, in Hurricane R 4115, thus qualifying for the Battle of Britain clasp. He took command of RAF Biggin Hill in June 1941 and sometimes flew as No 2 to Sailor Malan on fighter sweeps. On July 4 1941 he shared a probable Bf 109 with Malan and a week later he destroyed a Bf 109.

One day in early 1942 Barwell's engine cut out on take-off and he crash-landed just beyond the runway and broke his back. He still took part in operations and flew for several months encased in plaster, which made it difficult for him to turn his head.

On July 1 1942 Barwell, accompanied by Squadron Leader RW Oxspring, took off from Biggin Hill an hour before sunset on a standing patrol between Dungeness and Beachy Head. Control at Biggin Hill warned of unidentified aircraft in the area, which proved later to be two Spitfires from Tangmere flown by inexperienced pilots. Barwell, apparently oblivious to the warning, was attacked by one and shot down in flames into the sea. Although Oxspring saw him trying to open his hood Barwell did not bale out, perhaps being too hampered by his plaster cast. Despite intensive searches no trace of him was found. His body was washed up on the French coast and he is buried in Calais Canadian War Cemetery.

PO 28.9.25   FO 28.3.27   FL 14.5.30   SL 1.12.36
WC 1.1.40

RONALD EDWARD BARY

41818 PO Pilot New Zealander 229 Squadron

Born in New Plymouth on June 9 1915, Bary was employed as a law clerk at the Department of Justice in Palmerston North. He was accepted for an RAF short service commission and left New Zealand on December 16 1938.

Bary's training began at No 1 E&RFTS, Hatfield, was completed at 11 FTS, Shawbury and he joined the recently-reformed 229 Squadron at Digby on October 26 1939. Over Dunkirk on June 1 1940 Bary got a probable Ju 87 and during September and October he shared in destroying two enemy aircraft, probably another and damaged three more.

229 Squadron was posted to the Middle East in May 1941 and sailed in HMS 'Furious'. The pilots flew six aircraft off to Malta on May 21 and after refuelling flew on to Mersa Matruh. On arrival Bary was attached to 274 Squadron in the Western Desert, after which he was attached to the Ferry Pool at Takoradi. On September 1 229 was brought together as a unit and it began night defence duties in the Mersa Matruh area.

In early October Bary was posted to 250 Squadron at Sidi Heneish, as a Flight Commander. He was awarded the DFC (7.4.42) and soon afterwards went to No 1 Middle East Training School at Ballah as an instructor. In his time with 250 he had destroyed two enemy aircraft and probably another.

Bary took command of 80 Squadron at Bu Amoud, Libya on January 23 1943. In mid-June he took command of 239 Kittyhawk fighter-bomber Wing, which he took to Malta on July 9 to take part in the invasion of Sicily on the following day. The Allies invaded Italy on November 3 1943 and 239 Wing flew in support of the Army, based initially in Sicily and later in Italy.

In late January 1944, tour-expired, Bary returned to the UK. He was posted to the Fighter Leaders' School at Milfield for a course and on July 27 he was appointed as an instructor. He later joined the staff of the Central Fighter Establishment at Milfield.

Bary returned to operations when he flew to Naples in December 1944 to take command of 244 Wing, Desert Air Force, flying in support of the Eighth Army. On April 12 1945 he took off with two Spitfires of 92 Squadron to make a close-support bombing attack on a target north-east of Imola. On reaching the area Bary dived to drop his two 500 lb bombs. Between 4000 and 5000 feet his aircraft exploded and disintegrated. There was no flak, no enemy aircraft were seen and it is assumed that the explosion was caused by a faulty fuse, detonated when the bombs were released. Bary's body was recovered and he is buried in the British Empire Cemetery at Faenza. He was awarded the DSO (12.2.46), with effect from the day prior to his death. The citation described him as 'an outstanding Wing Leader'.

APO 1.4.39   PO 23.10.39   FO 23.10.40   FL 23.10.41
SL 16.10.43

HENRY BASHFORD

141156 Sgt Observer British 248 Squadron

Bashford joined 248 Squadron in March 1940 and served with it throughout the Battle of Britain. He was posted away in July 1941 to 404 (RCAF) Squadron at Skitten, a maritime reconnaissance and coastal strike unit. He served with it until April 1942.

Commissioned in January 1943, Bashford was released from the RAF in 1946, as a Flight Lieutenant. He joined the RAFVR in September 1948.

PO 14.1.43   FO 14.7.43   FL 14.1.44   FO (RAFVR) 27.9.48

FRANCIS BERNARD BASSETT

41982 PO Pilot British 222 Squadron

Bassett, of Wembley Park, Middlesex, joined the RAF on a short service commission in February 1939. He served with 222 Squadron throughout the Battle of Britain.

On November 14 1942 152 Squadron flew from Gibraltar to Algiers to take part in the invasion of North Africa. En route Bassett's engine failed and he baled out over the sea. His body was never found and he is remembered on the Malta Memorial, Panel 2, Column 1. He was 22 years old.

APO 29.4.39   PO 6.11.39   FO 6.11.40   FL 6.11.41

GORDON HERBERT BATCHELOR

86343 PO Pilot British 54 Squadron

Batchelor, of Higham, Kent, was posted to 54 Squadron at Catterick on October 14 1940. He was still with the squadron when he was killed, aged 23, on April 15 1942. He is buried in Hamburg Cemetery, Ohlsdorf, Germany.

PO 14.9.40   FO 14.9.41

LESLIE GORDON BATT

145514   **Sgt**   **Pilot**   **British**   **238 Squadron**

Batt, an engineering apprentice at Daimler's, joined the RAFVR in April 1938 and did his elementary flying training in Avro Cadets at 9 E&RFTS, Ansty. He was called up in September 1939 and after the intermediate and advanced course at 6 FTS, Little Rissington he joined 253 Squadron at Kenley on May 17 1940 but four days later moved to 238 Squadron at Tangmere.

On July 21 he shared in the destruction of a Do 17, on August 8 he claimed a Bf 109 and five days later he forced-landed at Eartham, in Hurricane P 2989, with a damaged oil tank after an attack by a Bf 109 south of the Isle of Wight.

Batt went to Egypt with 238 in May 1941 and remained with the squadron until December. In January 1942 he had his first long leave since May 1940, in Cairo, and in February he joined the Aircraft Delivery Unit there. In August Batt was posted away and returned to the UK in November. He went to 55 OTU, Annan as an instructor in early December 1942 and was commissioned from Warrant Officer in March 1943.

A return to operations came on August 11 1943 when Batt was posted to 198 Squadron, flying Typhoons from Martlesham Heath. He went for a course to 7 FIS, Upavon on November 24, after which he was posted to 15 (P) AFU, Babdown, remaining there until his release in 1945, as a Flight Lieutenant. His portrait was done by Cuthbert Orde.

PO 24.3.43   *FO 24.9.43*   *FL 24.3.45*

SIDNEY BAXTER

566388   **Sgt**   **Pilot**   **British**   **222 Squadron**

A pre-war airman pilot, Baxter was with 222 in early 1940 and over Dunkirk on June 1 he destroyed a Bf 110.

In the afternoon of September 14 1940 Baxter's aircraft, Spitfire X 4275, was severely damaged in combat with Bf 109s. He was killed attempting to land near Rochford.

Baxter was 23. He was cremated at West Road Crematorium, Newcastle-upon-Tyne and is remembered on Panel 1 there.

IAN NORMAN BAYLES

74327   **FO**   **Pilot**   **British**   **152 Squadron**

Born on August 13 1918, Bayles was educated at Winchester College and Trinity College, Oxford. He was a member of the University Air Squadron and was called to full-time service in October 1939.

Bayles was with 152 Squadron at Acklington in early July 1940. On September 25 he claimed a Ju 88 destroyed and shared a He 111.

He commanded 135 Squadron in India from February to November 1943 and 273 Squadron in Burma from December 1944 to April 1945.

Bayles was awarded the DFC (2.10.45). He was released from the RAF in 1946, as a Wing Commander.

PO 16.10.39   *FO 26.9.40*   *FL 26.9.41*   *SL 30.6.45*

EDWARD ALAN BAYLEY

741004   **Sgt**   **Pilot**   **British**   **32 and 249 Squadrons**

Born in Eastbourne, Bailey learned to fly at Wilmington in 1933 and later joined the RAFVR. He was called up at the outbreak of war and was with 32 Squadron in late 1939.

On July 3 Bayley shared in the destruction of a Do 17 and on August 18 he claimed a Do 215 destroyed. He was posted to 249 Squadron at North Weald in September 1940.

Bayley was killed on October 10 1940 when his Hurricane, V 7537, crashed at Shades House, Cooling Marsh during a routine patrol. The cause is not known but may have been caused by Bayley losing consciousness due to oxygen failure. He is buried in St Luke's Cemetery, Bromley, Kent. He was 29.

DEREK BAYLISS

42183   **PO**   **Pilot**   **British**   **604 Squadron**

Bayliss joined 604 Squadron at North Weald in late 1939. On October 8 1940 he crashed and wrecked Blenheim L 1281 when he overshot the flare path at Middle Wallop coming in from a night patrol. He and his crew were unhurt.

Bayliss came off flying in 1941 and was released from the RAF in 1946, as a Flight Lieutenant.

APO 10.6.39   *PO 18.11.39*   *FO 18.11.40*   *FL 18.11.41*

ERNEST JOHN BAYLISS

581431   **Sgt**   **Observer**   **British**   **248 Squadron**

A pre-war airman, Bayliss, of Christchurch, Hampshire, was with 248 squadron, while it was seconded to Fighter Command during the Battle of Britain.

On November 3 1940 he was a member of the crew of a Blenheim, which was last seen attacking a He 111 over the North Sea. It was presumed to have been shot down by return fire and its crew were reported 'Missing'. Bayliss is remembered on the Runnymede Memorial, Panel 11. He was 21 years old.

JAMES BAYLY

39899   **Sgt**   **Pilot**   **New Zealander**   **111 Squadron**

Bayly was born at Waitara on March 18 1917. He was educated at New Plymouth Boys' High School and after leaving in 1934 he became an apprentice electrician. On September 1 1938 he joined the Civil Reserve of Pilots and gained his 'A' license at the Western Federated Aero Club.

Called for full-time service at the outbreak of war, Bayly completed his ground training and then went to 2 EFTS, New Plymouth. In late January 1940 he was posted to 2 FTS, Woodbourne, gained his wings on May 2 and sailed for the UK on July 12. In late August Bayly went to 6 OTU, Sutton Bridge, afterwards joining 111 Squadron at Drem on September 28.

Bayly became ill in January 1941, spending a month in hospital. In his absence he was posted to RAF Kemble for a twin-engine conversion course and then to an aircraft ferry and maintenance unit at St Athan. In February 1942 he converted to Hudsons at RAF Oulton and in March was posted to India. He flew from Cornwall in a Hudson, via Gibralter, Mersa Matruh, Iraq, Persia and Karachi to Delhi. Bayly's first posting was as a staff pilot at a paratroop training school, flying Vickers Valentias at 70 mph. He returned to operations on January 4 1943, going to 62 (Bomber) Squadron at Cuttack.

On the night of March 16 he was detailed to attack Japanese positions at Magwe. The Hudson's radio was knocked out and the port engine badly damaged by heavy anti-aircraft fire over the target. Bayly decided to switch off the engine and head for Chittagong. The starboard fuel tank ran low and it was impossible to switch to the port one because of damage to the fuel lines. He could not reach Chittagong on the little fuel left and after some discussion with the crew it was decided to turn inland and bale out before the now-faltering starboard motor stopped, a forced-landing in the jungle being out of the question. After they had landed it took the four men two days to find each other. Friendly Bengalis helped them evade Japanese patrols and they eventually reached Chittagong. On return to Cuttack the subsequent Court of Enquiry found that Bayly had made an error of judgement in switching off the port engine too soon. The finding resulted in Bayly having a heated verbal exchange with his CO and it was recommended that he be reduced in rank and disciplined. At an interview the AOC told Bayly that he considered that the right action had been taken in the Hudson but that Bayly's insubordination could not be overlooked and he forfeited a year's seniority.

To his relief Bayly did not return to 62 Squadron but he and his crew were posted to 31 (Transport) Squadron. After a short leave in Calcutta Bayly remained behind to see the adjutant and his crew went ahead in a Dakota. The aircraft crashed soon after take-off and they were killed. Bayly flew Dakotas with 31 until April 9 1944, carrying out supply drops to the Army, often in hazardous conditions. He returned to New Zealand and in September 1944 became a staff pilot at the School of Navigation, New Plymouth. In late November Bayly again became a Dakota captain with 40 (Transport) Squadron at Whenuapai. He was released from the RNZAF in June 1945.

PO 19.10.43   FO 19.4.44

ALFRED WILLIAM ALEXANDER BAYNE

39014   FL   Pilot   British   17 Squadron

Bayne began his elementary flying training in June 1936. On September 5 he was posted to 10 FTS, Tern Hill and joined 54 Squadron at Hornchurch on April 24 1937. He was with 17 Squadron in the Battle of Britain.

On July 29 Bayne shared in the destruction of a He 111, on August 27 he claimed a probable Bf 110, a Bf 109 on August 31, another on September 5, a Bf 110 on the 11th and he shared a Do 17 on October 2. Bayne was himself shot down on August 25 in combat with Bf 109s and 110s. He baled out and was rescued from the sea, unhurt. His Hurricane, V 7407, crashed into the sea off Portland.

On November 8 1940 Bayne led 17 Squadron against a force of heavily-escorted Ju 87s which were attacking two destroyers. In the action he shot down one Ju 87 and probably another. He destroyed a Bf 110 on November 17 and damaged another. He was awarded the DFC (26.11.40).

Bayne commanded 132 Squadron from its formation on July 7 1941 at Peterhead until February 1942. He took command of 30 Squadron at Ratmalana, Ceylon in May 1942 and led it until February 1943. He then commanded 136 Squadron at Chittagong until May 1943. He was released from the RAF in 1946, as a Wing Commander, and died on May 28 1963.

APO 24.8.36   PO 29.6.37   FO 29.3.39   FL 3.9.40
SL 1.12.41

DAVID WALTER BAYNE

26077   SL   Pilot   British   257 Squadron

Born on April 17 1908, Bayne entered RAF College, Cranwell as a cadet in January 1927. On graduation in December 1928 he was posted to 12 Squadron at Andover. On January 21 1930 he went overseas to 5 (Army Co-operation) Squadron at Quetta, India, flying Bristol Fighters. A move to 20 (Army Co-operation) Squadron at Peshawar was made on September 1 1933. In 1935 Bayne had a flying accident and lost a leg. He returned to the UK and was non-effective sick at RAF Depot, Uxbridge for a long period.

On July 1 1937 he was appointed to the staff at Uxbridge and

moved on to the HQ staff at Kenley on August 8 1938. Although he had an artificial leg he was given the task of forming 257 Squadron at Hendon from May 17 1940. Bayne was posted away on July 22 1940.

In 1948 he was appointed Military and Air Attaché in Rio de Janeiro. Bayne retired from the RAF on August 29 1955, as a Group Captain. He was a graduate of the RAF Staff College.

PO 15.12.28   FO 15.6.30   FL 15.2.35   SL 1.8.38
WC 1.12.40   GC 1.7.43   GC 1.7.47

GEOFFREY THEODORE BAYNHAM

41518   FO   Pilot   British   234 and 152 Squadrons

Born in 1915, Baynham joined 234 Squadron at Middle Wallop in mid-September 1940. He was posted to 152 Squadron at Warmwell on October 5. In March 1941 he returned to 234, also then stationed at Warmwell.

Baynham destroyed a Bf 109 on May 19 1941 and on July 17 he shot down three more. He was posted back to 152 Squadron on April 17 1943, as a Flight Commander. The squadron was then at Souk el Khemis in North Africa. Baynham damaged a Bf 109 on April 25, shared another on May 8 and destroyed a Ju 52 on July 25. He was awarded the DFC (10.9.43).

Released from the RAF in 1945, Baynham later went to live in Rhodesia.

APO 14.12.38   PO 3.9.39   FO 3.9.40   FL 3.3.42

JAMES MICHAEL BAZIN

90281   FL   Pilot   British   607 Squadron

Bazin was born in Kashmir, India. He joined 607 Squadron, AuxAF at Usworth in May 1935, flew his first solo on November 11 and was commissioned in December 1935. He was called for full-time service on August 28 1939.

607 Squadron was ordered to France in November 1939. On the 13th they flew their Gladiators from Acklington down to Croydon and two days later flew to Merville. After suffering heavy losses in the Blitzkreig 607 was withdrawn to England and re-assembled at Croydon on May 22 1940. Bazin had at least one victory in France and claimed a Do 215 on September 15 and a Ju 88 on the 30th. However, when he was awarded the DFC (25.10.40) the citation stated that he had destroyed some ten enemy aircraft. He was himself shot down once in France and on October 5 1940 he crash-landed at Hurn when his engine failed.

In early 1941 Bazin was posted from 607 and at some time he served as a Controller in 14 Group Operations Room at Inverness. He did a flying refresher course in November 1943, a Beam Approach Training course in December and in January 1944 he was posted to 16 (Bomber) OTU. Bazin converted to Lancasters at 1660 Conversion Unit and after 5 Lancaster Finishing School he joined 49 Squadron at Fiskerton in May 1944. In late June he was posted to command 9 Squadron at Bardney. By the end of the war Bazin had carried out twenty-five operational sorties, including a raid on the German battleship 'Tirpitz'. He was released from the RAF in May 1945, as a Wing Commander, and was awarded the DSO (21.9.45). He resumed his career as an engineer and rejoined 607 in November 1946, commanding the squadron from late 1949 until 1951. Bazin died in 1985.

PO (AuxAF) 9.12.35   FO (AuxAF) 9.6.37   FO 24.8.39
FL 3.9.40   SL 1.12.41   SL (RAuxAF) 1.10.49

SYDNEY HOWARTH BAZLEY

90359   FL   Pilot   British   266 Squadron

A native of Southport, Lancashire, Bazley joined 611 Squadron, AuxAF in early 1937 and was commissioned in April of that year. He was called to full-time service on August 26 1939 and in May 1940 was with 266 Squadron at Martlesham Heath.

On August 12 Bazley claimed a Bf 110. Four days later his aircraft was set alight in combat and he baled out over Canterbury. The Spitfire, P 9312, is believed to be that which crashed near Wickhambreux. Bazley suffered burns and minor injuries.

Still with 266 Bazley was killed in a flying accident on March 2 1941, aged 27. He was cremated at Leicester City Crematorium.

PO (AuxAF) 4.4.37   FO 26.8.39   FL 3.9.40

PERCIVAL HAROLD BEAKE

84923   PO   Pilot   British   64 Squadron

Beake, who came from Bristol and was educated at Victoria Park School and Bristol Grammar School, joined the RAFVR in April 1939 and by the time he was mobilised in September he had completed almost fifty hours on Tiger Moths at 33 E&RFTS at Whitchurch, Bristol. He was posted to 3 ITW, Hastings but did not reach 15 EFTS, Redhill until March 26 1940. Two months later he went to 15 SFTS, Middle Wallop, finishing the course at its Advanced Training Squadron at Chipping Norton.

On August 31 Beake was posted to 7 OTU, Hawarden and joined 64 Squadron at Leconfield on September 22. He was with the squadron at various stations until posted to 92 Squadron at Biggin Hill on June 27 1941, moving from the squadron on December 29 to join 601 at Duxford.

Beake came off operations in late March 1942 and went to 58 OTU, Grangemouth as an instructor. He did an instructor's course at 7 FIS, Upavon in April/May 1942, following which he returned to Grangemouth, later moving to Balado Bridge.

Returning to operations Beake joined 193 Squadron, then forming at Harrowbeer, on December 22 1942, as a Flight Commander. He went to RAF Charmy Down on June 10 1943 for a short course at Fighter Command School of Tactics, afterwards returning to his squadron. Another short course at the Fighter Leaders' School, Milfield came in March 1944 and after a short spell at 84 Group Support Unit at Aston Down Beake took command of 164 Squadron at Thorney Island on May 30 1944. The squadron moved to France in mid-July. He was posted back to the Fighter Leaders' School on September 10 1944, this time as an instructor.

Beake was awarded the DFC (5.9.44), the citation stating that he was credited with two enemy aircraft destroyed. He was released from the RAF on January 21 1946, as a Squadron Leader.

PO 31.8.40   FO 31.8.41   FL 31.8.42

FRANCIS VICTOR BEAMISH

16089   WC   Pilot   Irish   151 and 249 Squadrons

Born at Dunmanway, Co Cork on September 27 1903, Beamish entered RAF College, Cranwell as a cadet on September 14 1921. He was posted to 4 (Army Co-operation) Squadron at Farnborough on September 18 1923 and in January 1925 moved to the School of Army Co-operation, Old Sarum.

Beamish went overseas later in the year, to 31 Squadron, Ambala on November 18 but only stayed four months before moving to 60 Squadron at Kohat. He was back in the UK in October 1926 for a course at Central Flying School, Wittering. This completed, he was posted to 5 FTS, Sealand as an instructor. On September 16 1927 Beamish went back to Cranwell, this time on the staff. He went to Canada on March 22 1929, on exchange with an RCAF officer and when he returned two years later he was posted to 25 Squadron at Hawkinge, as a Flight Commander. In January 1932 he was appointed Personal Assistant to the AOC-in-C ADGB at Uxbridge. A year later he went into hospital at Uxbridge suffering from tuberculosis and its effects caused him to retire on October 18 1933.

Desperately unhappy, Beamish got a job as civilian assistant at 2 FTS, Digby. He returned to Ireland in 1936 and became civilian adjutant at RAF Aldergrove on May 18. This was a non-flying appointment in Class C of the Air Force Reserve. Beamish was re-instated with full category as a Flight Lieutenant on January 27 1937 and was posted to command 2 Armament Training Camp and Met Flight at Aldergrove. His comeback was complete when he was given command of 64 Squadron at Church Fenton on December 8 1937. He was awarded the AFC (1.1.38) for establishing the Met Flight.

After a course at RAF Staff College, Andover Beamish took command of 504 Squadron at Digby on September 13 1939. He returned to Canada in mid-January 1940 on Air Staff duties but back in the UK he took over RAF North Weald on June 7. Beamish flew operations with his station squadrons whenever he could. On June 18 1940 he claimed a probable He 111, on the 30th two Bf 109s destroyed, on July 12 a Do 17, on August 18 a probable Ju 88 and on the 30th a probable Bf 110. On September 6 Beamish claimed a Ju 87 destroyed and another probable, on the 11th a probable He 111, on the 15th another probable He 111, on the 18th a probable Bf 109, with another on the 27th. In October he got a probable Bf 109 on the 25th and another on the 30th and his final victory claim for 1940 was a probable CR 42 on November 11. Beamish was awarded the DSO (23.7.40) and the DFC (8.11.40). On November 7 1940 he collided with Pilot Officer TF Neil of 249 whilst on patrol and made a forced-landing at Leeds Abbey. In all his sorties in 1940 Beamish was damaged by enemy action three times, on each occasion getting his aircraft down safely.

Beamish was posted to HQ 11 Group on March 17 1941. He claimed a probable Bf 109 on January 10 1941 but did not claim again until August 9 1941, with a probable Bf 109 near Mardyck. He was awarded a Bar to the DSO (25.9.41). On January 25 1942 Beamish went to RAF Kenley to command and again flew with his squadrons. With Wing Commander RF Boyd he took off on the morning of February 12 'to see what was happening on the other side'. After chasing two Bf 109s they saw the German Fleet making its 'Channel Dash'. The ships had been reported ten minutes earlier by two pilots of 91 Squadron but the news was received with complete incredulity at 11 Group. Beamish's confirmation was enough to set in motion a series of uncoordinated attacks on the Germans.

On February 13 Beamish had a share in the destruction of a He 114 over the Channel. On March 9 he claimed a FW 190 destroyed and another on the 26th. Leading the Kenley Wing and flying with 485 Squadron on March 28 Beamish saw a force of Bf 109s and FW 190s a few miles south of Calais. He turned the Wing toward them. In the ensuing engagement Beamish was seen to be attacked and damaged by a Bf 109. He requested a vector over the R/T and was last seen entering a cloud near Calais. It is presumed that he went into the Channel, possibly wounded and perhaps unconscious.

Victor Beamish was one of that small band of near-legendary figures in the RAF and was photographed by Cecil Beaton and had his portrait done by both Orde and Kennington. He is remembered on the Runnymede Memorial, Panel 64.

PO 15.8.23   FO 15.2.25   FL 12.12.28   FL (RAFO) 18.5.36
FL 27.1.37   SL 1.4.37   WC 1.3.40

RONALD BEAMISH

127044   Sgt   Pilot   British   601 Squadron

Joined 601 Squadron at Exeter on September 11 1940. He was commissioned from Warrant Officer in June 1942 and released from the RAF in 1945, as a Flight Lieutenant.

PO 26.6.42   FO 12.12.42   FL 26.6.44

ROLAND PROSPER BEAMONT

41819   FO   Pilot   British   87 Squadron

Beamont was born at Chichester on August 10 1920. He was educated at Eastbourne College and entered the RAF on a short service commission in January 1939. After elementary flying training at 13 E&RFTS, White Waltham and a short spell at RAF Depot, Uxbridge Beamont went to 13 FTS, Drem.

In September 1939 he was in the 11 Group Fighter Pool at St Athan and in November joined 87 Squadron in France. On May 13 1940 Beamont destroyed a Do 17. The squadron was withdrawn to England on May 20 and after a few days at Debden went to Church Fenton to refit. On July 5 it went south again, to Exeter, and on the 24th Beamont claimed a Ju 88 destroyed, on August 15 two Bf 110s and a Bf 109 and a Do 17 on the 25th.

Beamont was awarded the DFC (6.6.41) and posted to 79 Squadron at Fairwood Common, as a Flight Commander, staying until December 1941 when he went to the Special Duties List, reporting to Hawker Aircraft as a test pilot. In May 1942 he went as supernumerary Flight Lieutenant to 56 Squadron at Manston. On June 29 he joined 609 Squadron at Duxford and took command in mid-October 1942. He was awarded a Bar to the DFC (29.1.43) and the DSO (6.5.43).

A return to test flying came in May 1943 and Beamont returned to Hawker's but in February 1944 he was asked to form the first Typhoon Wing, No 150, at Castle Camps. He was leading the Wing when he was shot down over France on October 12 1944 and taken prisoner. Whilst with the Wing he destroyed two Bf 109s over Dieppe on June 8 1944 and a FW 190 on October 2. In the same summer period he destroyed 32 V1 Flying Bombs. He was awarded a Bar to the DSO (25.7.44).

After being released from the Germans Beamont was finally released by the Russians on May 21 1945. He formed the first Tempest Wing for service in the Far East but was then appointed to command the Air Fighting Development Squadron at the Central Fighter Establishment. Beamont left the RAF in January 1946 and went to Gloster Aircraft as No 3 Test Pilot, left there for de Havilland's to be a demonstration pilot and in May 1947 moved to English Electric as Chief Test Pilot. In this capacity Beamont established several records in Canberra and P 1 aircraft.

In 1955 he was made Manager of Flight Operations and Special Director of English Electric Aviation in 1960. Beamont became Director of Flight Operations, BAC Preston in November 1965, was made a CBE (1969) and later appointed Director of Flight Operations, Panavia Aircraft. In 1978 he resigned his BAC directorship to concentrate on development of the Tornado. Following the first flight of the first production aircraft he retired on July 31 1979. In addition to his British awards Beamont received the DFC (US)(14.6.46). He became Deputy Lieutenant for Lancaster in 1977.

APO 1.4.39   PO 21.10.39   FO 21.10.40   FL 21.2.42
SL 17.5.44

JOHN MAURICE BENTLEY BEARD

89588   Sgt   Pilot   British   249 Squadron

Born in 1919 in Shoreham, Sussex, Beard was educated at Leamington College. A bank clerk, he was a member of the RAFVR and was called to full-time service on September 1 1939.

Beard joined 249 Squadron, when it was reformed at Church Fenton on May 16 1940. He claimed a Do 215 destroyed on September 2, a Bf 109 on the 6th, a Bf 110 on the 18th, two Bf 109s and a Bf 110 on the 27th and another Bf 109 on the 28th. He was awarded the DFM (22.10.40).

On September 7 Beard baled out, unhurt, when his Hurricane, N 2440, was damaged during an attack on some Do 17s, possibly by anti-aircraft fire. He was shot down on October 25 by Bf 109s over north Kent. Beard baled out, wounded, and was admitted to Pembury Hospital. His Hurricane, P 3615, is believed to have crashed on Rankin's Farm, Linton.

Commissioned in December 1940, Beard did not fly operationally again. He was awarded the AFC (1.1.45) and released from the RAF in 1946, as a Squadron Leader.

PO 18.12.40   FO 18.12.41   FL 18.12.42

ERIC WALTER BEARDMORE

C 820   FO   Pilot   Canadian   1(RCAF) Squadron

Born in Berlin on August 29 1911, Beardmore joined the RCAF on September 1 1937. He was with No 1 (RCAF) Squadron when it arrived in the UK on June 20 1940.

Beardmore was shot down in combat over the Thames Estuary on September 18. He baled out, slightly wounded.

Repatriated to Canada in March 1941, Beardmore formed 118 (RCAF) Squadron at Rockcliffe, Ottawa. He was released from the RCAF on October 18 1945, as a Wing Commander. He died on August 23 1966.

ROBERT ARTHUR BEARDSLEY

100607   Sgt   Pilot   British   610 and 41 Squadrons

Born at Old Charlton, London on January 19 1920, Beardsley joined the RAFVR on April 2 1938 and carried out his elementary training at 20 E&RFTS, Gravesend. He was mobilised at the outbreak of war and after two months at 3 ITW, Hastings was posted to 15 FTS, Lossiemouth, later at Middle Wallop and Chipping Norton.

Beardsley went to 7 OTU, Hawarden on July 30 1940 and joined 610 Squadron at Biggin Hill on August 12. He claimed a Bf 109 destroyed on the 25th and a He 111 on the 30th. The next day the squadron flew north to Acklington but Beardsley went south again on September

RA Beardsley (continued)

18 to 41 Squadron at Hornchurch. He was attacked by Bf 109s off Dungeness on the 30th of the month and after his engine caught fire he made a forced-landing at Hawkinge, unhurt.

Again off Dungeness on October 25 1940 Beardsley was in hectic combat with Bf 109s. After shooting one down his Spitfire, P 7371, was hit and a cannon shell went through his starboard camshaft. He managed to make a forced-landing at Hawkinge, once again unhurt.

Commissioned in June 1941, Beardsley remained with 41 Squadron until November 22, the last four months at Merston as part of the Tangmere Wing. He was awarded the DFC (17.10.41). A period was spent instructing at a Spitfire OTU before going to Andreas, where 93 Squadron was being reformed in June 1942. Beardsley went with the squadron to the invasion of North Africa in November. After returning to England in 1943 he again went instructing at an OTU.

After the invasion of Europe Beardsley joined 222 Squadron at Tangmere and went with it to France. He later had a staff job in Cairo and was released from the RAF on December 20 1945.

Beardsley rejoined the RAF on April 19 1949, as a Flight Lieutenant, and after a flying refresher course and conversion to jets he served with 74 Squadron at Horsham St Faith, as a Flight Commander, during 1950 and 1951. Afterwards he transferred into Fighter Control, on trial and mobile convoys in Germany, Singapore and Borneo. He did two tours at the School of Fighter Control, the second as CO. When he retired on July 31 1970 Beardsley was stationed at HQ 11 Group, Bentley Priory.

*PO 28.6.41   FO 28.6.42   FL 28.6.43   FL 13.2.48
SL 1.7.65*

MARCUS ALFRED BEATTY

69455   Sgt   Pilot   British   266 Squadron

Beatty joined 266 Squadron at Wittering on September 30 1940. He was commissioned in June 1941 and released from the RAF in 1946, as a Flight Lieutenant. One research source indicated that he died in Cairo in 1959.

PO 19.5.41   FO 3.6.42   FL 3.6.43

STEPHEN GERALD BEAUMONT

90319   FL   Pilot   British   609 Squadron

Born in 1910, Beaumont learned to fly at West Riding Aero Club, Yeadon in 1935. He was junior partner in a firm of solicitors and was the first privately-trained pilot to join 609 Squadron, AuxAF, when it was formed at Yeadon on February 10 1936. Beaumont was commissioned in April and was one of the first three pilots trained with 609, gaining his wings in August 1937.

Beaumont was one of 609's original Flight Commanders but in January 1939 he handed over to Flying Officer PH Barran because of business and family commitments. He took over again after Barran was killed on July 11 1940. Mobilised on August 24 1939, Beaumont served with 609 until he was posted to 7 OTU, Hawarden as an instructor on August 2 1940. He was made an OBE (1.1.45) and was a Group Captain at 84 Group when he was released in 1945.

*PO (AuxAF) 24.3.36   FO (AuxAF) 24.10.37   FO 24.8.39
FL 12.3.40   SL 1.6.41   WC 1.6.42*

WALTER BEAUMONT

76308   PO   Pilot   British   152 Squadron

Beaumont was born in Dewsbury, Yorkshire. He had a BSc from the University of London, was a pre-war member of the RAFVR and was then living at Coulsdon, Surrey. He was called for full-time service at the outbreak of war and joined 152 Squadron at Acklington in the early months of 1940.

After the squadron moved to Warmwell in July Beaumont took part in many combats. He claimed two BF 109s destroyed on August 16, two Ju 87s and a shared Bf 109 on the 18th, a shared Ju 88 on the 23rd, another Bf 109 on the 25th and a shared He 111 on the 27th. On this day Beaumont was hit by return fire from a Ju 88 and baled out. His Spitfire, R 6831, crashed into the sea eight miles off Portland.

Beaumont failed to return from an operational sortie on September 23 1940. From an unknown cause his Spitfire, R 7016, is believed to have crashed into the Channel. He is remembered on the Runnymede Memorial, Panel 7. He was 26 years old and was awarded the DFC (22.10.40).

PO 10.12.39

HUGH JOHN SHERARD BEAZLEY

73023   FO   Pilot   British   249 Squadron

The son of a judge, Beazley was born on July 18 1916. He was educated at Cheltenham College and Pembroke College, Oxford. As a member of the RAFVR he was called up in September 1939 and posted to 249 Squadron, when it reformed at Church Fenton on May 16 1940.

On July 8 Beazley shared a Ju 88 and claimed a Bf 110 destroyed on August 8. He was shot down in flames in combat over Rochester on September 2 by a Bf 110 of 5/ZG 26. He baled out, unhurt, over Gillingham and landed in Boxleywood. His Hurricane, P 2988, crashed on Eccles Recreation Ground, near Rainham. On September 7 Beazley shared a Do 215 and destroyed another on the 15th.

In May 1941 249 Squadron sailed for Malta, arriving there on the 21st, having flown off HMS 'Ark Royal'. On June 8 Beazley shared a probable Fiat BR 20, on December 21 damaged a Bf 109 and on December 26 he assumed command of 249, when the CO was wounded.

Beazley was posted away on February 21 1942. He later served with 89 Squadron, as a Flight Commander, and was awarded the DFC (7.3.44). He was released from the RAF in 1946, as a Wing Commander.

PO 25.9.39   FO 25.9.40   FL 25.9.41   SL 13.6.44

ANTONI BEDA

P 1900   Sgt   Pilot   Polish   302 Squadron

Joined 302 Squadron at Leconfield on August 20 1940. Awarded the KW and one Bar (1.2.41), Beda was posted to 87 Squadron at Colerne on September 27 1941. He was with 307 Squadron at Exeter from April 22 1942, was awarded the C de G (7.7.43) and on July 7 1943 was posted for a course to 3 FIS but returned to 307 Squadron on September 15.

Rested from operations, Beda moved to HQ 216 Group. He went on to transport when he joined 301 Squadron on April 28 1945 and on January 24 1946 he was posted to 304 Squadron.

Beda left the PAF in December 1946 and went to the USA. He later moved to Canada, where he died in 1960.

PO 1.6.42   FO 1.6.43   FL 1.6.44

ERNEST HORACE BEE

751768   Sgt   Air Gunner   British   29 Squadron

Bee was posted to 29 Squadron at Debden on May 17 1940. He was one of the crew of Blenheim K 7135 flying off the east coast on October 13 when they were attacked at dusk by Hurricanes of 312 Squadron. Although the aircraft was damaged the pilot returned to base at Tern

Hill. Another Blenheim of 29 was not so lucky. It was shot down and the crew killed.

Bee was posted away on March 22 1941 and nothing further is known. He left the RAF as a Warrant Officer at the end of the war and died in 1987.

ALFRED FRANCIS BEECHEY

113913   Sgt   Air Gunner   British   141 Squadron

Beechey was with 141 Squadron at the start of the Battle of Britain. He was commissioned in December 1941 and posted to Bomber Command in 1942. He was awarded the DFC (12.1.43) and at that time was acting as Gunnery Leader with 101 Squadron, operating in Lancasters from Holme-on-Spalding Moor, Yorkshire.

Beechey was released from the RAF in 1946 but rejoined later as a Flying Officer in the Aircraft Control Branch.

PO 1.12.41   FO 1.10.42   FL 1.12.43   FO 18.7.47

CYRIL SYDNEY FRANK BEER

751495   Sgt   Wop/AG   British   235 Squadron

Beer, from Southend-on-Sea, joined 235 Squadron at Bircham Newton on August 23 1940. He was killed on September 10 1940 flying with 22 Squadron, Coastal Command.

He was 22 years old and is buried in Den Burg General Cemetery, Texel, Netherlands.

HENRY WILLIAM BEGGS

Sub-Lieutenant (FAA)   Pilot   British   151 Squadron

Beggs trained with the Fleet Air Arm before the war. He was seconded to the RAF in June 1940, converted to Hurricanes and joined 151 Squadron at Martlesham Heath on July 1.

He destroyed a Bf 109 of 4/JG 52 over Kent on August 14. The next day Beggs was shot down, in Hurricane P 3605, in combat with Bf 109s over Dover and crashed at Shorncliffe, wounded.

In January 1942 Beggs was posted to 883 Squadron, FAA and was reported 'Missing' when HMS 'Avenger' was sunk on November 15 1942. He was 25 and is remembered on the Lee-on-Solent Memorial, Bay 3, Panel 1.

Acting Sub-Lt 1.5.39   Sub-Lt 14.3.40   Lt 1.11.41

MARIAN BELC

P 1901   Sgt   Pilot   Polish   303 Squadron

Born in Poland on January 27 1914, Belc was in the PAF before the war and was credited with destroying one German aircraft in the fighting in September 1939.

He joined 303 Squadron at Northolt at its formation on August 2 1940. After a routine training flight on the 8th he crashed on landing in Hurricane R 4100. Belc's first victory was a Bf 109, claimed on September 26. Four days later he was himself shot down during combat with Bf 109s and baled out, unhurt. On October 5 he claimed a Bf 110 and on the 7th he claimed a Bf 109.

Belc was awarded the KW (1.2.41). He shared in damaging a Ju 52 taxying on an aerodrome near St Inglevert on May 15 1941, claimed a Bf 109 on June 24 and another on the 28th. He was awarded a Bar to the KW (15.7.41) and the VM (5th Class)(10.9.41). Belc's final victory, a Bf 109, was claimed on October 24 1941.

He was posted away to 58 OTU, Grangemouth in late April 1942. Belc was still with 58 OTU, but on August 27 1942 he was at Baladown, Gloucestershire on No 3 Instructors' Course there. He was flying dual with another trainee, in Master W 8664, when they made too low an approach. The plane lost height, crashed and both pilots were killed.

Belc is buried in Northwood Cemetery. He was awarded the DFC (15.11.42) and a further two Bars to the KW (31.10.47).

PO 21.5.42

LAWRENCE GEORGE BELCHEM

26172   SL   Pilot   British   264 Squadron

Belchem entered RAF College, Cranwell in September 1928, as a flight cadet. He graduated in December 1930 and was posted to 19 Squadron at Duxford.

On June 4 1933 Belchem went to 204 (Flying Boat) Squadron at Plymouth, moved to 3 FTS, Grantham on July 3 1934, as an instructor, went for a course to RAF Gosport on September 1 1935 and on October 23 1936 joined 824 (Fleet Spotter-Reconnaissance) Squadron, based on HMS 'Hermes' in the Far East.

Belchem possibly flew only one operational sortie with 264 Squadron during the Battle of Britain period, on July 18 1940, and was certainly not on the strength of the squadron. He was killed on July 14 1942, as a Squadron Leader with 119 Squadron, operating in Catalinas from Lough Erne. Belchem is remembered on the Runnymede Memorial, Panel 65.

PO 20.12.30   FO 20.6.32   FL 1.4.36   SL 1.12.38

ROBERT WILFRED GARTH BELEY

43022   PO   Pilot   Canadian   151 Squadron

Beley, from Rossland, British Columbia, was commissioned in the RAF in March 1940 and joined 151 Squadron at Martlesham Heath on July 14.

In an action with Bf 109s off Ramsgate on August 12 Beley was shot down, in Hurricane P 3304, and crashed into the sea. He was rescued but died of his wounds at RAF Manston. He was 20 and is buried in Margate Cemetery, Kent.

APO 23.3.40

CHARLES ALGERNON BELL

76595   PO   Air Gunner   British   29 Squadron

Bell was commissioned in February 1940 and posted to 29 Squadron at Digby in May. Nothing further has been traced.

PO 26.2.40

CHARLES HENRY BELL

754849   Sgt   Pilot   British   234 Squadron

Bell joined 234 Squadron in September 1940. On October 9 he crashed on landing at St Eval in Spitfire R 6621, following the destruction of a Do 17 off Newquay.

On March 2 1941 Bell was reported 'Missing', still with 234. He is remembered on the Runnymede Memorial, Panel 39.

DEREK BELL

621608   Sgt   Air Gunner   British   23 Squadron

Bell, of South Shields, Co Durham, served with 23 Squadron in the Battle of Britain. He was killed on December 27 1941, serving with 50 Squadron, which was operating in Hampden bombers from Skellingthorpe, Lincolnshire.

Bell was 23. He is remembered on the Runnymede Memorial, Panel 39.

JOHN SWIFT BELL

90051   FO   Pilot   British   616 Squadron

A pre-war member of the AuxAF, Bell joined 503 (Special Reserve) Squadron at Waddington early in 1935 and was commissioned in April. It was decided in late 1938 to disband 503 and absorb anyone interested into 616 Squadron, being formed as from November 1 at Doncaster as a bomber unit. The new squadron was transferred to

JS Bell (continued)

Fighter Command on December 15 1938.

Bell moved to 616 and he was called for full-time service on August 24 1939. Over Dunkirk on June 1 1940 he destroyed a Bf 109 and was then himself shot down into the sea and picked up by the Royal Navy. In mid-June Bell intercepted and damaged a He 115, which jettisoned its bombs and fled. On July 1 he shared in damaging a He 111 over Yorkshire.

On August 30 Bell was shot down in a head-on attack on Bf 109s over West Malling. His Spitfire, X 4248, crashed and burned out and Bell was killed. He was 23 and is buried in St Peter's Cemetery, Eastgate, Lincoln.

PO (AuxAF) 22.4.35   FO (AuxAF) 20.7.37   FO 24.8.39

RALPH BELL

565216   Sgt   Air Gunner   British   219 Squadron

A pre-war airman, Bell was with 219 at the start of the Battle of Britain. On August 2 1940 he was crew in Blenheim L 8962, which overshot the runway at RAF Leeming during a practice landing not using flaps. The pilot deliberately raised the undercarriage to avoid running on to the Great North Road. Both men were unhurt.

Nothing further is known of Bell's service.

DAVID BASIL BELL-SALTER

41895   PO   Pilot   British   253 Squadron

Bell-Salter began his elementary flying at 11 E&RFTS, Perth in February 1939. He completed his training at 2 FTS, Brize Norton and joined 253 Squadron at Manston in late 1939.

On September 2 1940 Bell-Salter was shot down in a combat over the Sussex coast. He attempted to get out of his cockpit but flying without gloves and with his hood open his hands were too cold to pull out the harness pin. Down to 1500 feet he finally managed it and shot out by kicking his feet on the floor. The aircraft, being in a full-throttle dive, made the airflow such as to render him unconscious as he went through it. Bell-Salter came to at only 100 feet from the ground, hanging upside down by one leg with a single rigging line caught behind his knee. The parachute was torn across and flapping and his harness was completely off and hanging beside him. On hitting the ground Bell-Salter passed out again. He sustained several badly-crushed vertebrae, both shoulders dislocated, one knee broken and a smashed right heel. He was in hospital for several months.

In June 1941 Bell-Salter was instructing at 53 OTU, Heston. He was released from the RAF in 1946 and died in New York in late 1985 or early 1986.

APO 15.4.39   PO 6.11.39   FO 6.11.40   FL 6.11.41

HOWARD JOHN BELL-WALKER

103515   Sgt   Pilot   British   72 Squadron

Born on August 7 1920, Bell-Walker was with 72 Squadron during the Battle of Britain. On September 14 1940 he baled out, unhurt, following a combat over Ashford. His Spitfire, K 9960, crashed and burned out at Orlestone.

Four days later Bell-Walker was shot down in a surprise attack by Bf 109s during a squadron patrol over Gravesend. He was seriously wounded and in hospital for some time. In 1941 he was posted to 602 Squadron and was commissioned in August. Bell-Walker took part in a Blenheim escort to Lille on August 12 1941. He was flying as No 2 to the CO, Alan Deere. The squadron was surprised by Bf 109s and Bell-Walker was shot down before he could break away. He was

wounded and taken prisoner.

Bell-Walker stayed in the RAF after his release. He transferred into the Engineering Branch, was made an MBE (30.4.54) and retired on December 1 1967, as a Squadron Leader.

PO 7.8.41   FO 7.8.42   FL 7.8.43   FL 30.5.48
SL 1.1.56

GORDON WILLIAM BENN

513418   Sgt   Air Gunner   219 Squadron

Joined the RAF October 16 1930 at the age of 18. After three months training at Uxbridge Benn was posted to a Vimy bomber squadron at Hawkinge. In July 1931 he went to 423 Flight, HMS 'Furious', with Fairey Flycatchers. The unit was transferred in 1932 to HMS 'Courageous', Mediterranean Fleet.

Benn left the FAA in 1933 and was posted to RAF Gosport, then on to HMS 'Hornet', a Repair Unit for Air Sea Rescue vessels. In 1935 he went to 28 Squadron, Ambala, India as a trainee air gunner in Wapitis. He served on the North-West Frontier during the tribal uprisings and got the India General Service Medal in 1937.

After returning to Britain in 1939 Benn joined 217 Squadron as a Corporal Air Gunner, flying in Ansons. At the outbreak of war he was posted to 219 Squadron, then being reformed at Catterick.

After flying operationally for three years Benn came off in 1942 and was posted to 53 MU, Charlwood, a depot supplying bombs to the squadrons on a 24 hour basis. In August 1945 Benn went to Singapore with 5353 Airfield Construction Wing to build metal runways at Changi. After this he joined 314 MU at Seletar, where fourteen RAF men, with the aid of two hundred Japanese PoWs, were dismantling or disposing of Japanese bombs.

Home again in 1948, Benn was posted to a Radar and Signals Unit at Chicksands, went to RAF Luqa, Malta in 1949, returned to the UK in 1952 and was discharged to pension on October 16 1954, as a Warrant Officer.

CLARENCE CHARLES BENNETT

42097   PO   Pilot   Australian   248 Squadron

Bennett, from Adelaide, began flying training with the RAF in February 1939. With this completed he was posted to 248 Squadron, which had been reformed at Hendon in 1939 as a Blenheim fighter squadron. It was later transferred to Coastal Command and then seconded to Fighter Command for a period during the Battle of Britain.

On October 1 1940 Bennett failed to return from a reconnaissance operation to the Norwegian coast, in Blenheim R 3626. He and his crew were posted 'Missing'. He is remembered on the Runnymede Memorial, Panel 12.

APO 13.5.39   PO 6.11.39

HECTOR ERNEST BENNETT

758075   Sgt   Pilot   British   43 Squadron

Bennett is believed to have flown with 43 Squadron in the Battle of Britain. His unit at the time of his death on February 4 1941 is not known. He was 22 and was cremated at Arnos Vale Crematorium, Bristol.

GEOFFREY RYDING BENNETTE

42387   PO   Pilot   British   17 Squadron

Bennette, of Carshalton, Surrey, joined 17 Squadron early in 1940. On July 9 he claimed a share in the destruction of a He 111. He was reported 'Missing' on August 19 1942, whilst serving as a Flight Lieutenant with 245 Squadron at Middle Wallop. With no known grave he is remembered on the Runnymede Memorial, Panel 65.

APO 5.8.39   PO 6.4.40   FO 6.4.41   FL 6.4.42

GEORGE HERMAN BENNIONS

43354   PO   Pilot   British   41 Squadron

Born at Burslem, Stoke-on-Trent in 1913, Bennions joined the RAF as an aircraft apprentice at Halton in 1929. Later recommended for a cadetship at Cranwell he was given ab initio flying training but the cadetship did not eventuate.

In 1935 Bennions completed his pilot training at 3 FTS, Grantham and in January 1936 he was posted to 41 Squadron at Khormaksar, Aden. He was promoted to Flight Sergeant in November 1938 and commissioned in April 1940.

Bennions destroyed a Bf 109 on July 28 1940 and with his own flaps damaged in combat he crashed on landing at Manston. On August 15 he claimed a Bf 110 and on September 6 two Bf 109s. He made a belly-landing at Rochford on this day when his undercarriage collapsed. Bennions was wounded by a shell splinter in his left heel on September 11. Four days later he shot down another Bf 109, two more on the 17th and the 18th and another on the 23rd.

In combat with Bf 109s over Henfield on October 1 1940 Bennions was shot down. His Spitfire, X 4559, crashed on Heatenthorn Farm, Alborne. He baled out, grievously wounded, landed at Dunstalls Farm and was admitted to Horsham Hospital with his left eye destroyed and a wound which left his brain exposed. Bennions was later transferred to Queen Victoria Hospital, East Grinstead, where he underwent plastic surgery by Archie McIndoe, becoming a Guinea Pig in the process. His DFC (1.10.40) was gazetted on the day he was shot down.

When fully recovered, Bennions was anxious to fly again and after being tested at CFS he was given an A2B non-operational category. This allowed him to fly only by day and then only with a passenger who could look out.

In 1943 he was posted to North Africa, where he was appointed Liaison Officer to an American Fighter Group, which had recently received Spitfires. In Sicily he was flying Spitfires on convoy patrols but took no further part in combat. In October 1943 Bennions suffered shrapnel wounds when the landing craft he was in at Ajaccio, Corsica was sunk by enemy action.

After release from the RAF in 1946, as a Squadron Leader, Bennions became a school teacher.

PO 1.4.40   FO 1.4.41   FL 1.6.42

ALAN BENNISON

130806   Sgt   Air Gunner   New Zealander   25 Squadron

Bennison was born in Ashburton on March 5 1918 and educated at the Hampstead School and the Technical School. He volunteered for aircrew duties in early 1939 but was not called until February 13 1940.

After completing his initial training Bennison sailed for the UK, arriving on June 8. He was posted to 5 OTU, Aston Down for further training in mid-July and after being awarded his air gunner's badge he joined 25 Squadron at North Weald on September 21 1940.

From October 1940 the squadron began to receive Beaufighters, equipped with Radar. Bennison remustered as a Radar Operator (Air) in late December and after a navigation course at Cranage he became a Navigator Radar in July 1941.

Bennison was posted to 89 Squadron, then forming at Colerne, in October 1941. The squadron flew to the Middle East as two flights in November. As well as night defence of the Delta 89 also flew long day patrols over the Mediterranean searching for FW Condors, which were preying on Allied shipping .

In August 1942 Bennison was posted to India but he fell sick and remained at Air HQ Middle East on Operations Room duties. He rejoined 89 in February 1943 but went to 46 Squadron at Edku on April 13. With his tour completed Bennison returned to the UK in October 1943, where he was posted to an instructor's course at 62 OTU, Ouston. In January 1944 he went to 51 OTU, Cranfield as an instructor and was commissioned in February.

Repatriated to New Zealand in early June, he went on to the Reserve on September 22 1944. He joined the Active Reserve at its inception in 1949 and continued until transferred to the General Reserve on December 31 1969. During this period he was awarded the Air Efficiency Medal and two clasps.

PO 26.2.44   FO 27.2.56

JAMES GILLIES BENSON

81365   PO   Pilot   British   141 Squadron

Benson completed his flying training at 8 FTS, Montrose in early July 1940 and after conversion to Defiants at 5 OTU, Aston Down he joined 141 Squadron at Grangemouth on July 25. The squadron was still stunned after its heavy daylight losses of six days earlier off Folkestone.

In the night-fighting role and operating from Gravesend 141 was more successful and on December 22 1940 Benson destroyed a He 111, which crashed at Underwoods House, Etchingham. For many months he had no further victories but in October 1941 he teamed up with Lewis Brandon, a highly successful partnership, which, except for a five month break in 1943, was to go on until they came off operations in 1945.

The team's first victory was a Do 217 on February 15 1942, on June 4 they got a probable Do 217 and another damaged. On July 23 1942 they were both posted to 62 OTU, Usworth as instructors. Benson was awarded the DFC (2.10.42). In October both men went to 54 OTU, Charter Hall to instruct. They returned to operations on February 16 1943 with a posting to 157 Squadron at Castle Camps. On April 15 they destroyed a Do 217 at night and on an intruder patrol on July 3 they shot down a Do 217 over St Trond airfield. In early August 1943 Brandon was posted away to another squadron but the team came together in January 1944, again with 157 at Predannack.

On June 12 they destroyed a Ju 188 and during the month they shot down several V1s at night. In July Benson was appointed Flight Commander and promoted to Acting Squadron Leader and several more V1s were destroyed. The final months of 1944 were very successful, with two Ju 188s shot down on September 11, a Ju 88 on November 11, another probably destroyed on December 23 and a Bf 110 on the 24th. Benson was awarded a Bar to the DFC (20.10.44).

The New Year brought the final victory, a He 219 on January 5. In February Benson was posted to RAF Great Massingham, as a Wing Commander, to form and command 1692 Bomber Support Training Unit, with Brandon as CGI.

Benson was awarded the DSO (13.3.45) and released from the RAF later in the year. He died in 1987.

PO 6.7.40   FO 6.7.41   FL 6.7.42   SL 20.4.45

NOEL JOHN VICTOR BENSON

33485 **PO** **Pilot** **British** **603 Squadron**

Benson entered RAF College, Cranwell in April 1938 as a flight cadet. After graduating in October 1939 he spent a week at St Athan in the 11 Group Pool and was then posted to 145 Squadron at Croydon.

In 1940 Benson moved to 603 Squadron. On August 28 he was shot down in combat with Bf 109s and killed when he crashed in flames on Great Hay Farm, Leigh Green, Tenterden.

Benson was 21. He is buried in St Mary's churchyard, Great Ouseburn, Yorkshire.

PO 23.10.39

BENJAMIN BENT

52078 **Sgt** **Radar Operator** **British** **25 Squadron**

Bent was born on August 22 1919 at Coatbridge, Scotland. He joined the RAF on November 8 1937 and began a Wireless operator course at No 1 Electrical and Wireless School at Cranwell on February 11 1938. After completing the course in November Bent was posted to Biggin Hill on January 9 1939.

In June 1940 he volunteered for aircrew duties and after a short radar course he joined 25 Squadron at Martlesham Heath on August 6. Bent began operational night flying a few days later, as an LAC without a flying badge. He was promoted to Sergeant on September 27 in the category of Wireless Operator (Air).

On his first operational tour Bent assisted in five successful interceptions, an unidentified enemy aircraft damaged on May 5 1941, a He 111 destroyed on the 8th, a Do 17 on the 9th, a He 111 damaged on the 12th and a Ju 88 destroyed on June 14. Bent remustered as a Radio Observer on July 10 1941. Tour-expired, he was posted to 54 OTU on April 29 1942, as an instructor.

On July 23 Bent was reclassified as a Navigator Radio and rejoined 25 Squadron, then at Church Fenton, on September 8 1942 for his second tour. He was commissioned from Warrant Officer in April 1943. On March 21 1944 Bent assisted in the destruction of two Ju 88s and at 00.43 hrs on June 6 a Bf 110 over the Dutch Islands, believed to be the first enemy aircraft shot down on D Day. Awarded the DFC (26.5.44), Bent finished his tour in July and then served as Night Fighter Liaison Officer in France with P 61 Squadron, USAF.

Bent was released from the RAF on February 2 1947, as a Flight Lieutenant. He rejoined on October 4 1950, on a short service commission in the Fighter Control Branch. Granted a Permanent Commission on April 1 1952, Bent retired from the RAF at his own request on December 5 1970, as a Flight Lieutenant.

PO 24.4.43   FO 24.10.43   FL 24.4.45   FO 23.12.47
FL 27.5.54

JOHN BENZIE

42185 **PO** **Pilot** **Canadian** **242 Squadron**

Benzie, from Winnipeg, served in Princess Patricia's Canadian Light Infantry for three years prior to joining the RAF on a short service commission. He began his training in April 1939 and was posted from 5 OTU, Aston Down to 242 Squadron at Church Fenton on February 3 1940.

On May 23 he was shot down by Bf 109s near Ypres. Benzie baled out south of Dunkirk, wounded, and was evacuated to England, via Dunkirk. He rejoined his squadron on July 11.

Benzie failed to return from a combat over the Thames Estuary on September 7 1940. He was 25 and is remembered on the Runnymede Memorial, Panel 7. Lake Benzie, in Canada, is named in his honour. Research led to an aircraft being excavated, which was thought to be his. Evidence was inconclusive and the pilot-remains found were buried in Brookwood Military Cemetery as 'an unknown pilot'.

APO 24.6.39   PO 9.12.39

HUGH RICHARD ADEN BERESFORD

37150 **FL** **Pilot** **British** **257 Squadron**

Born at Ampthill, Bedfordshire in 1915, Beresford was the son of the Rector of Hoby, Leicestershire. He joined the RAF on a short service commission in 1935 and after training was posted to 3 Squadron at Port Sudan on March 6 1936.

Beresford returned to the UK with the squadron in August and on April 1 1937 he was posted to the staff of No 1 Anti-Aircraft Co-operation Unit at Biggin Hill. On October 4 he was appointed Personal Assistant to the AOC 11 Group.

On May 17 1940 257 Squadron was reformed at Hendon and Beresford joined it as a Flight Commander. He shared in destroying a He 111 on August 18 and claimed a Bf 110 on the 31st.

In Hurricane P 3049 Beresford was shot down in combat over the Thames Estuary on September 7 1940. The aircraft crashed at Elmley, Spitend Point, Sheppey and Beresford was reported 'Missing'. Excavations in 1979 revealed that his remains were still in the cockpit. He was buried at Brookwood Military Cemetery on November 16 1979 with full military honours. He was 24 when he was killed.

APO 16.4.35   PO 16.4.36   FO 16.1.38   FL 16.1.40

VACLAV BERGMAN

81884 **PO** **Pilot** **Czechoslovakian** **310 Squadron**

Bergman was born on August 27 1915 and joined 310 Squadron at Duxford at its formation on July 12 1940. He was shot down on August 26 whilst attacking Do 17s over Clacton and baled out, slightly wounded. His Hurricane, P 3960, crashed and burned out at Rumbolds Farm, Goldsands, Southminster. In September Bergman claimed a Bf 110 destroyed on the 9th and a Do 215 on the 18th.

Bergman, who was awarded the DFC, commanded 313 Squadron at Mendlesham from February to May 1944.

Bergman was in the RAF after the war and received a Mention in Despatches (21.3.52) for distinguished service in Malaya. He was in the Aircraft Control Branch and retired on April 30 1969, as a Squadron Leader.

SL 1.1.63

THOMAS COLQHOUN EDMONDS BERKLEY

754377   **Sgt**   **Pilot**   **British**   **85 Squadron**

A pre-war member of the RAFVR, Berkley came from Tullahoge, Co Tyrone, Northern Ireland. He joined 85 Squadron at Croydon on September 2 1940 and was killed with the squadron on June 14 1941.

Berkley was 23. He is remembered on the Runnymede Memorial, Panel 35.

FRANTISEK ANTONIN BERNARD

120209   **Sgt**   **Pilot**   **Czechoslovakian**   **238 and 601 Squadrons**

Bernard, who was born on July 23 1914, joined 238 Squadron in August 1940. He was posted to 601 Squadron at Debden on September 6 but returned to 238 on October 8.

Commissioned in April 1942, Bernard was released after the war but rejoined the RAF in the fifties. He received a Mention in Despatches (6.3.56) for distinguished service in Kenya and was awarded the AFC (1.1.57). Bernard retired on July 23 1964, as a Flight Lieutenant.

FL 18.5.55

BRONISLAW BERNAS

76820   **PO**   **Pilot**   **Polish**   **302 Squadron**

Born in Poland in 1906, Bernas was in the PAF before the war. He joined 302 Squadron at Leconfield on September 23 1940. Over Selsey Bill on March 13 1941 he shared in damaging a Ju 88.

Bernas went to 58 OTU, Grangemouth on April 14 1941 as an instructor. He was posted to Digby on November 24 1941 to join the newly-formed 288 (Anti-Aircraft Co-operation) Squadron. Bernas came off flying in August 1943 and joined 5010 Airfield Construction Squadron. He spent the rest of his service with the Directorate of Works and Airfield Construction. He returned to Poland in late 1946 and died there on September 3 1980.

HORACE WALTER WILLIAM BERRIDGE

115634   **Sgt**   **Radar Operator**   **British**   **219 Squadron**

Berridge was posted to 219 Squadron at Catterick at some time during the Battle of Britain. In late 1940 he teamed up with Flying Officer JG Topham for what was to be a long and highly successful night-fighting partnership.

On March 13 1941 they destroyed a He 111, an unidentified enemy aircraft on June 14, a He 111 on May 8 1942, a Ju 88 on June 9, a Do 217 on July 6, two unidentified enemy aircraft on July 26 and a Do 217 on September 9. Berridge was commissioned in January 1942 and awarded the DFC (23.6.42) and a Bar (20.10.42).

In 1944 Berridge was with 125 Squadron and when he was awarded the DSO (17.8.45) the citation stated that he had taken part in the destruction of at least twelve enemy aircraft. He was released from the RAF in 1945, as a Flight Lieutenant.

PO 5.1.42   FO 1.10.42   FL 5.1.44

ALAN BERRY

968305   **Sgt**   **Air Gunner**   **British**   **264 Squadron**

Berry, from Longsight, Manchester, was with 264 at the start of the Battle of Britain. After a spell of night-fighting, following heavy losses over Dunkirk, 264 went south to Hornchurch on August 21 1940 for another try at daylight operations.

On August 24 the squadron was refuelling at Manston when a force of enemy bombers was reported. The Defiants took off as the first bombs fell. Before they could form up three were shot down by the fighter escort from JG 3. Berry's Defiant, L 7027, was one of the victims and he and his pilot, Flying Officer IG Shaw, were reported 'Missing'. Berry was 23 and is remembered on the Runnymede Memorial, Panel 12.

FREDERICK GEORGE BERRY

563426   **F/Sgt**   **Pilot**   **British**   **1 Squadron**

Berry was born in 1914 and joined the RAF as an aircraft apprentice in late 1929. He volunteered for pilot training, was accepted and after qualifying he joined 43 Squadron at Tangmere in 1936.

Early in 1938 Berry was posted to No 1 Squadron, also at Tangmere. He was with the squadron when it went to France at the outbreak of war. On No 1's final operational patrol in France on June 17 1940 Berry was leading a section over the docks at St Nazaire, when He 111s came in at low level to attack troopships loading there. Berry led his section to attack but could not stop the leading bomber from scoring direct hits on the 'Lancastrian' setting it on fire and causing it to sink later with heavy casualties to the 4000 troops aboard. Berry shot the He 111 down in flames into the river. For this action he was awarded the DFM (20.8.40).

On September 1 1940 Berry was shot down in combat with Bf 109s and killed when his Hurricane, P 3276, crashed at Brisley Farm, Ruckinge. Berry is buried in Pinner New Cemetery, Harrow, Middlesex.

RONALD BERRY

78538   **PO**   **Pilot**   **British**   **603 Squadron**

Born in Hull on May 3 1917, Berry was educated at Hull Technical School and afterwards worked in the City Treasurer's Deparment. He joined the RAFVR in 1937 and did his weekend flying training at 4 E&RFTS, Brough. Called up at the outbreak of war, Berry was posted to 603 Squadron at Turnhouse. In November he was one of a detachment sent to Montrose to protect the airfield there. On December 7 the 603 pilots drove off a formation of He 111s, damaging at least two of them.

Berry was commissioned in December 1939. In the Battle of Britain he shared a Ju 88 on July 3 1940, shared a He 111 on July 30, destroyed three Bf 109s on August 31, another Bf 109 on September 2, a Do 17 on the 15th, a Bf 109 and another shared on the 27th and two Bf 109s on September 30. He was awarded the DFC (25.10.40). Patrolling south-west of Dover on November 23 Berry was part of a 603 formation which intercepted Italian CR 42s, flying as escort for bombers attacking coastal shipping. Berry destroyed one and probably another.

After a rest Berry took command of 81 Squadron at Turnhouse in January 1942. The pilots had just returned from Russia, leaving their aircraft there. In October 1942 the squadron sailed for Gibraltar, picked up tropical Spitfire Vcs and on November 8 became one of the first two Allied squadrons to land in North Africa. On the 9th Berry destroyed a Ju 88 and shared a He 111, on the 28th he shared a Bf 109, on December 3 he shared a FW 190 and on the 6th he destroyed another.

R Berry (continued)

Berry was promoted and became Wing Leader 322 Wing on January 22 1943. He destroyed Bf 109s on January 31 and February 25 and shared another probable on March 2. Berry was awarded a Bar to the DFC (2.3.43) and on March 13 he took command of 322 Wing. On April 13 he claimed his final victory, a Bf 109 probably destroyed. He was awarded the DSO (1.6.43).

After returning to the UK Berry went to the Army Staff College, Camberley. He commanded RAF Acklington 1945 - 46, graduated from the Joint Services Staff College in 1955 and held a series of staff appointments in Fighter and Bomber Command before his retirement on January 29 1969. He was made an OBE (1.1.46) and a CBE (1965).

PO 1.12.39   FO 1.12.40   FL 1.12.41   `SL 23.2.43
SL 1.9.45   WC 1.7.52   GC 1.7.59   AC 1.1.66

ROBERT CHARLES BERWICK

745915   Sgt   Wop/AG   British   25 Squadron

Berwick, from Manor Park, Essex, served with 25 Squadron in the Battle of Britain. In early 1941 he was posted to 78 Squadron at Dishforth, as a Flight Sergeant, flying in Whitleys. He failed to return from operations on June 19 1941.

Berwick was 22. He is buried in Reichswald Forest War Cemetery, Germany.

CHARLES BEVERIDGE

54030   Sgt   Air Gunner   British   219 Squadron

Beveridge, who was born on June 7 1915, was posted to 219 Squadron at Catterick on August 1 1940. Five days later the Blenheim he was in collided with high tension cables and crashed into a river during a searchlight co-operation flight. Both he and the pilot escaped with superficial injuries.

Awarded the AFM (1.1.43), Beveridge was commissioned in August 1943 as a Flight Engineer. He was given an extended commission and retired on September 1.1952, as a Flight Lieutenant. He died on December 18 1984.

PO 22.8.43   FO 22.2.44   FL 22.8.45   FL 22.2.47

MICHAEL LEO ffRENCH BEYTAGH

39057   FL   Pilot   British   73 Squadron

Beytagh was born in Shanghai in 1916, the son of a prosperous Irish business man. When his parents separated Beytagh, his brother and sister were put in the care of Miss Esylt Newbery, who eventually became their guardian.

After very unsettled school days Beytagh was adopted at 13 by Mr Morton, a wealthy American and taken to the US. They did not get on and after a few years he returned to Miss Newbery. Beytagh took a job in Maidstone to learn insurance law and run a small office. After a few months he disappeared and Miss Newbery never saw him again.

Beytagh joined the RAF on a short service commission in June 1936 and after completing his training at 8 FTS, Montrose he joined 23 Squadron at Wittering on April 24 1937. He was posted to 73 Squadron at Church Fenton on July 24 1940. He claimed a Bf 110 destroyed on September 7.

In November 1940 73 Squadron sailed for the Middle East in the carrier HMS 'Furious'. It flew off to Takoradi and then in stages flew overland to Heliopolis. In December the pilots of 73 were attached to 274 Squadron in the Western Desert. In early January 1941 the squadron began to operate on its own account from Sidi Heneish.

On the 5th Beytagh destroyed a CR 42 near Tobruk and on April 5 he destroyed a Ju 87.

In Takoradi for a rest, Beytagh and four other pilots were ordered to fly a Blenheim and two Hurricanes to Freetown on June 21 1941. Compelled by bad weather to make a forced-landing in the jungle they were unable to take off again and they walked 72 miles in two days and three nights, eventually arriving at the Firestone Rubber Plantation, 35 miles from Monrovia, Liberia.

Beytagh returned to the UK in November 1941 and was posted to 55 OTU, Annan, as CFI. On October 2 1942 he took command of 602 Squadron at Skeabrae, stationed there for the defence of Scapa Flow. In January 1943 602 flew south to Perranporth for a more active role. Awarded the DFC (1.10.43), the citation stating that he had destroyed five enemy aircraft, Beytagh was posted in October 1943 to the Air Ministry in the Directorate of Air Transport Policy. Early in 1945 he went to Staff College and then returned to the Air Ministry as Deputy Director Plans, as a Wing Commander.

Beytagh left the RAF on January 10 1946 and in April went to Uganda as an Administrative Officer in the Colonial Service. He returned to Britain in 1948 for a Colonial Officers' Course at Jesus College, Cambridge. In March 1949 he was posted to Pemba, Zanzibar as District Commissioner. In 1950 he was recalled to Zanzibar proper. Stationed again at Pemba, Beytagh died there on August 12 1952 and at his own request was buried at sea off Pemba.

APO 24.8.36   PO 29.6.37   FO 29.1.39   FL 3.9.40
SL 1.3.42

JOHN LAURANCE BICKERDIKE

36266   PO   Pilot   New Zealander   85 Squadron

The son of a policeman, Bickerdike was born in Christchurch on February 11 1919. He was educated in Auckland at King's Preparatory School and then King's College. He was an outstanding athlete.

Bickerdike got a job in Christchurch as a radio announcer. He was accepted for an RNZAF short service commission in June 1939 and did his flying training at Wigram. He sailed for England in early March 1940 and at the end of April was posted to No 1 Fighter Pilot Unit at Meir, after which he converted to Hurricanes at 6 OTU, Sutton Bridge and joined 85 Squadron at Debden on May 25.

A section of the squadron was ordered off on July 12 to help protect convoy 'Booty' against an approaching raid by a large force of Do 17s and He 111s. The section intercepted the bombers before they could disperse. In his first encounter with the Luftwaffe Bickerdike attacked one and sent it down in flames into the sea.

On July 22 1940 he was killed when he crashed near Debden during an aerobatic exercise. He is buried in Wimbish Parish Church Cemetery, near Saffron Walden, Essex.

PO 12.2.40

———— BICKNELL

No unknown   Sgt   Aircrew   British   23 Squadron

Name appears in the ORB but no service details traced.

LESLIE CHARLES BICKNELL

33131   SL   Pilot   British   23 Squadron

Bicknell was born on April 9 1913 and entered RAF College, Cranwell as a flight cadet in January 1933. On graduation in December 1934 he joined 29 Squadron at North Weald on the 15th of the month.

He was posted to 65 Squadron at Hornchurch on December 30 1936 as a Flight Commander. In April 1938 Bicknell collided with Pilot

Officer RRS Tuck while they were practicing aerobatics and although his tail unit was sheared off he managed to bale out safely.

Bicknell went as a supernumerary to the School of Photography at Farnborough on January 1 1939. He took command of 23 Squadron at Wittering in January 1940 and held the appointment until August 9 1940. He later graduated from RAF Staff College and retired on June 20 1949.

PO 15.12.34   FO 15.6.36   FL 15.6.38   SL 1.8.39
WC 1.3.42   WC 1.10.46

ERIC GEORGE BIDGOOD

42098   PO   Pilot   British   253 Squadron

A Devonshire man, Bidgood entered the RAF in March 1939 on a short service commission. He joined 253 Squadron at Manston in November 1939 and remained with the squadron until posted away towards the end of the Battle of Britain.

In mid-November the carrier HMS 'Argus' sailed from Gibraltar with Hurricanes for Malta. Bidgood was one of the six pilots who flew off on November 16 in the second flight of Hurricanes, led by a FAA Skua. A series of mishaps saw the Hurricanes run out of fuel and fall one by one into the sea, with the loss of all six pilots.

Bidgood was 22. He is remembered on the Runnymede Memorial, Panel 5.

APO 13.5.39   PO 6.11.39

IVOR KENNETH JACK BIDGOOD

748111   Sgt   Pilot   British   213 Squadron

Bidgood, from Bristol, served with 213 Squadron in the Battle of Britain.

He was killed on June 2 1941, as a Flight Sergeant, aged 23. The unit he was serving with is not known. Bidgood is buried in Canford Cemetery, Bristol.

ARTHUR JAMES BIGGAR

32168   SL   Pilot   British   111 Squadron

Born on April 20 1914, Biggar joined the RAF in early 1932. On April 16 he was posted to 3 FTS, Grantham. He went on a further course at 2 FTS, Digby on March 21 1933, after which he joined 16 (Army Co-operation) Squadron at Old Sarum.

Biggar was posted to 20 (Army Co-operation) Squadron at Peshawar on October 18 1933. Back in Britain in 1936 he was appointed to the staff of No 1 Armament Training Camp at Catfoss on September 27. A move to the permanent staff of 604 Squadron, AuxAF came on July 31 1937.

Biggar took command of 111 Squadron in October 1940 and stayed with it until February 1941. He remained in the RAF after the war, graduating from the Joint Services Staff College and the Army Staff College. He was made a CBE (2.1.56) and retired from the RAF on June 1 1958, as a Group Captain. Biggar died in 1975.

APO 1.4.32   PO 1.4.33   FO 1.10.34   FL 1.10.36
SL 1.4.39   WC 1.3.41   GC 1.7.44   GC 1.7.50

JOHN EDWARD BIGNELL

616568   Sgt   Wop/AG   British   25 Squadron

Bignell, of Romford, Essex, joined 25 Squadron at Martlesham Heath on August 20 1940.

He was killed on September 4 1941, as a Flight Sergeant. Bignell was 23. He is buried in Romford Cemetery, Essex.

ARTHUR EDWARD BINHAM

161311   Sgt   Pilot   British   64 Squadron

Binham trained as a pilot with the RAFVR at 8 E&RFTS, Woodley from January 2 1938 until October 7 1939. The next day he was posted for final training to 2 FTS, Brize Norton and then joined 64 Squadron at Church Fenton on December 18 1939. He was in action with the squadron over Dunkirk.

On July 13 Binham's Spitfire, K 9795, was hit by anti-aircraft fire during combat with Bf 109s over Dover. He made a belly-landing at Hawkinge, unhurt. On the 29th his Spitfire, R 6643, was damaged by return fire from a Ju 87 over the Channel. Binham was escorted back to the coast by Gibson of 501. He made a forced-landing near St Margaret's Bay, again unhurt.

Binham was posted to 15 FTS, Chipping Norton on September 24 1940, as an instructor. He was sent to CFS, Upavon for an instructor's course in January 1941, returning to 15 FTS in March. Posted to 15 (P) AFU, Leconfield on February 10 1942, Binham was then sent as an instructor to 24 Air School, Nigel, South Africa, where he remained until August 1945. Commissioned from Warrant Officer in October 1943, Binham was awarded the AFC (14.6.45). He was released in 1946, as a Flight Lieutenant.

PO 24.10.43   FO 24.4.44   FL 24.10.45

COLIN NORMAN BIRCH

41519   FO   Pilot   British   1 Squadron

Birch was born on November 27 1918 and joined the RAFVR in 1937. He entered the RAF in September 1938 on a short service commission and completed his flying training at 2 FTS, Brize Norton.

In June 1939 Birch was posted to No 1 Squadron at Tangmere and he went with it to France at the outbreak of war. He returned to England on May 24 1940.

On August 19 Birch blundered into the London balloon barrage during a night patrol. He baled out and landed on the roof of a house. It took him a long time to convince the local people that he was British. His Hurricane, P 3684, crashed and burned out in Chatterton Road, Finsbury Park. Birch claimed a He 111 destroyed on August 30 and a Bf 109 on September 1.

He was posted to 56 OTU, Sutton Bridge on October 18 1940, moving eventually to RAF Tealing. In 1941 Birch did an instructor's course at CFS, Upavon. He was at HQ Fighter Command in 1942 and the Fighter Leaders' School at Aston Down in 1943. Awarded the AFC (8.6.44), Birch was posted to ADGB, Bentley Priory, moving in 1945 to the Central Fighter Establishment, West Raynham. In 1946 Birch served at Air HQ Northern Italy, was Commandant No 2 RAFVR Centre in 1947 and in 1948 he was granted a Permanent Commission.

From 1949 until he retired on March 28 1958 Birch held a number of appointments, the final one being at Air Ministry on Intelligence duties.

APO 14.11.38   PO 3.9.39   FO 3.9.40   FL 3.9.41
SL 1.7.44   SL 1.8.47

RONALD ARTHUR BIRD

Lieutenant (FAA)   Pilot   British   804 Squadron

Bird, from Largs, Ayrshire, joined the FAA in 1937. He was posted to 804 Squadron at Hatston on July 1 1940. The squadron was seconded to Fighter Command and its Sea Gladiators were employed on dockyard defence.

804 was later reformed as a Catapult Fighter unit. On October 4 1941 Bird was launched in a Fulmar from the 'Ariguani' against a FW Condor, which he intercepted and damaged.

Bird was awarded the DSC (26.6.45) for 'courage, daring and tenacity in air strikes whilst serving with HMS 'Searcher' off Norway'. He was awarded a Bar (7.8.45) for 'outstanding courage in air attacks against U-boat bases at Kilbotn, Norway'.

On April 10 1946 Bird was killed in a flying accident whilst serving in HMS 'Garnet', aged 29. He is remembered on the Fleet Air Arm Memorial at Lee-on-Solent.

Actg/Sub-Lt 1.9.37   Sub-Lt 1.1.38   Lt 1.4.39
Actg Lt-Cdr 1943

HAROLD ARTHUR COOPER BIRD-WILSON

40335   FO   Pilot   British   17 Squadron

Bird-Wilson was born at Prestatyn on November 20 1919. He was educated at Liverpool College and joined the RAF in September 1937. His elementary flying was done at 7 E&RFTS, Desford and he completed his training at 3 FTS, South Cerney.

In August 1938 Bird-Wilson joined 17 Squadron at Kenley. He was immediately sent to Brough on a navigation course. On September 19, flying back to Brough in a BA Swallow, he ran into a storm and made for Cranwell. In bad weather he crashed and his pilot passenger was killed. Bird-Wilson had severe facial injuries and was operated on four times by Archie McIndoe, the last in October 1939, making him one of the earliest Guinea Pigs.

17 Squadron spent two short periods in France, the first from May 18 to 24 1940 and from June 8 to 18. In between these excursions Bird-Wilson shared in destroying a Ju 88 on May 26. He shared a He 111 on July 29, shared a Ju 88 on August 21, destroyed a Bf 109 on the 25th, a Bf 109 and another probable on the 31st, shared a Do 17 on September 3 and got a probable Do 215 on the 15th. He was awarded the DFC (24.9.40).

Bird-Wilson was shot down by Adolf Galland on September 24. He baled out, burned, and was rescued from the sea by an MTB and admitted to the Royal Naval Hospital, Chatham. His Hurricane, P 3878, crashed into the sea off Chatham. He did not return to 17 Squadron but when recovered he was posted to 56 OTU, Sutton Bridge in November, as an instructor.

Bird-Wilson joined 234 Squadron at Warmwell in March 1941, as a Flight Commander. He went to 52 OTU, Aston Down on August 8 1941 and on December 16 took command of 'A' Squadron there. In April 1942 he was given command of 152 Squadron at Eglinton. On November 17 1942 he took command of 66 Squadron at Zeals.

In May 1943 Bird-Wilson was appointed Wing Leader 122 Wing. Awarded a Bar to the DFC (29.10.43), he was rested in January 1944 and went to a Command and General Staff Course at Fort Leavenworth, Kansas. He returned to the UK in April and was posted to 85 Group, Uxbridge as Wing Commander Training but on June 9 he was appointed to lead the Harrowbeer Spitfire Wing, moving later to lead the Bentwaters Mustang Wing. On August 11 1944 he shot down a Bf 109.

For his Wing activities Bird-Wilson was awarded the DSO (9.1.45). In February he was posted to 11 Group, Uxbridge and in May 1945 took command of 1335 Jet Conversion Unit, Colerne. In 1945 he was awarded the Czechoslovak Medal of Merit 1st Class and the Dutch DFC.

In a long post-war career Bird-Wilson reached Air Rank and held many responsible appointments. He was awarded the AFC (1.1.46) and a Bar (1.1.55) and was made a CBE in 1962. He retired on June 1 1974, as an Air Vice-Marshal.

APO 30.11.37   PO 27.9.38   FO 27.6.40   FL 27.6.41
SL 1.7.43   SL 1.8.47   WC 1.1.53   GC 1.1.58
AC 1.1.63   AVM 1.1.70

THOMAS BIRKETT

87634   PO   Pilot   British   219 Squadron

Birkett was serving as a Sergeant-Pilot with 219 Squadron at Catterick at the start of the Battle of Britain and was commissioned in October. On November 13 1940 his Beaufighter crashed in daylight near Edenbridge and he and Sergeant CEP Castle were killed.

Birkett was 26 and is buried in St Andrew's churchyard, near his home in Chew Magna, Somerset.

PO 9.10.40

MAURICE ANDREW BIRRELL

Midshipman (FAA)   Pilot   British   79 Squadron

In response to Churchill's request to the Admiralty for pilots Birrell was one of those loaned to the RAF in mid-June 1940. After conversion to Hurricanes he joined 79 Squadron at Biggin Hill. When the squadron was rested he was posted to 804 (FAA) Squadron at Hatston. After a short spell with 802 Squadron he returned to 804 when it became a Catapult Fighter Unit.

Birrell was the first pilot to be catapulted from a CAM ship. He sailed in the 'Michael E' on May 28 1941, bound for New York. Five days out from Belfast they were torpedoed by a U-boat and Birrell was among the survivors picked up after twenty hours in the boats. His next ship was the 'Ariguani'. On August 26 he was shot off in a Fulmar to deal with a FW Condor. He fired one burst before it vanished into cloud. Birrell headed for Northern Ireland, landed on a beach but on enquiry found that it was neutral Donegal. He took off again and reached Eglinton, almost out of fuel. In late October 1941 he survived when the 'Ariguani' was torpedoed 300 miles off Lisbon.

Birrell was awarded the DSC (3.10.52) for service in HMS 'Glory' in Korea. He retired in 1972 as a Commander.

Midshipman 1.7.39   Sub-Lt 23.4.42   Lt 25.5.43
Acting Lt-Cdr 1944   Lt-Cdr 25.5.51   Cdr 31.12.56

JOHN DEREK BISDEE

76575   PO   Pilot   British   609 Squadron

Born at Weston-super-Mare on November 20 1915, Bisdee was educated at Marlborough College and was an Exhibitioner at Corpus Christi College, Cambridge. He was a member of the RAFVR and was called to full-time service at the outbreak of war. He joined 609 Squadron at Kinloss on December 26 1939.

Bisdee claimed a Bf 110 destroyed on August 11 1940 and three more on September 7, 27 and October 7.

In sweeps over France he shared a Bf 109 on May 21 1941, destroyed two Bf 109s and probably a third in June and claimed a final Bf 109 on July 9. He was awarded the DFC (11.7.41) and was posted to 61 OTU on July 31 1941, as a Flight Commander.

Bisdee was given command of 601 Squadron on March 10 1942. On April 20 he led twelve 601 Spitfires off the US carrier 'Wasp', off Algiers, to Malta. The next day he destroyed a Ju 88, was then jumped by Bf 109s and shot down. He baled out and was picked up from his dinghy late the same night.

601 left Malta on June 23 1942 for the Western Desert and Bisdee was posted away on August 21. In 1943 he was appointed Military Governor of Lampedusa and in 1944 he was on the staff of 323 Wing, in charge of night-fighter personnel in Italy.

Bisdee was made an OBE (14.6.45) and released from the RAF in 1945, as a Group Captain.

PO 10.12.39   FO 10.12.40   FL 10.12.41   SL 18.6.43
WC 10.6.45

DOUGLAS LEONARD BISGOOD

41896   PO   Pilot   British   3 Squadron

Bisgood began training with the RAF in January 1939 and he was with 3 Squadron in late July 1939. At Wick on July 23 1940 he collided on take-off with a Hudson and crashed on the aerodrome. He was seriously injured and his Hurricane, P 2862, was written off.

Early in 1942 Bisgood was awarded the DFC (2.1.42) for carrying out a large number of met. flights, often in unfavourable weather conditions. On one occasion he saw three enemy bombers, made a surprise attack on one and sent it, burning, into the sea. At the time of the award he was credited with three enemy aircraft destroyed.

Bisgood was killed on April 18 1947, as a Squadron Leader with 202 Squadron. With no known grave he is remembered on the Runnymede Memorial, Panel 286. He was 27.

APO 15.4.39   PO 6.11.39   FO 6.11.40   FL 6.11.41

ERNEST RALPH BITMEAD

34139   SL   Pilot   British   29 and 611 Squadrons

Bitmead joined the RAF early in 1934. On April 3 he was posted to 5 FTS, Sealand, after which he joined 54 Squadron at Hornchurch on March 4 1935. He was sent as an instructor to 6 FTS, Netheravon on November 5 1936 and on July 16 1938 he was posted to 501 Squadron at Whitchurch, Bristol, on the permanent staff.

On July 8 1940 Bitmead took command of 29 Squadron at Digby but after a few days he was attached to 266 at Wittering, then attached to 310 Squadron at Duxford in August. Short attachments to 253 and 229 Squadrons occurred in September and finally Bitmead assumed command of 611 Squadron at Tern Hill on October 19. In January 1941 he destroyed a Bf 109 and a Do 215. In May 1941, after an engagement over the Channel, his aircraft was damaged and he forced-landed in a field near East Grinstead. An insecure hood fractured the base of his skull. Bitmead was posted from 611 and on August 14 he was given command of 71 Squadron at North Weald, but after a week felt that he was not fit enough and relinquished his command. He did not regain his full flying category.

Bitmead was awarded the DFC (21.11.44). He stayed in the RAF after the war and died whilst still serving, in 1955.

APO 16.3.34   PO 16.3.35   FO 16.9.36   FL 16.9.38
SL 1.6.40   WC 1.12.41   WC 1.10.46

ALLAN BLACK

107476   Sgt   Pilot   British   54 Squadron

Joined 54 Squadron at Catterick on September 28 1940. He was commissioned in September 1941 and killed on February 1 1944, as a Squadron Leader with 239 Squadron.

Black was 30. He is buried near his home, in Knadgerhill Cemetery, Irvine, Ayrshire.

PO 24.9.41   FO 6.7.42   FL 6.7.43

HERBERT ERNEST BLACK

740749   Sgt   Pilot   British   32, 257 and 46 Squadrons

Born in Measham, Leicestershire, Black joined the RAFVR in 1937 and gained his wings in late 1939. He was posted to France early in 1940 to join 226 Squadron, equipped with Fairey Battles. After the squadron was withdrawn to England in mid-June Black volunteered for Fighter Command. He was posted to OTU and joined 32 Squadron at Acklington in early September. Later in the month he went to 257 Squadron at Martlesham Heath and finally was posted to 46 Squadron at Stapleford in October.

On October 29 Black was shot down in combat with Bf 109s and is believed to have crashed in Hothfield Park, near Ashford. He was badly burned and wounded. His wife was by his bedside when he died in Ashford Hospital on November 9 1940. He was 26 and is buried in St Denys' churchyard, Ibstock.

WILLIAM FRANCIS BLACKADDER

90282   FL   Pilot   British   607 Squadron

Blackadder joined 607 Squadron, AuxAF in early 1936. He was called for full-time service at the outbreak of war and flew to France with the squadron on November 15 1939. He was awarded the DSO (4.6.40), the citation stating that he had shot down three enemy aircraft and carried out several very important reconnaissances of bridges and roads at a time when information was hard to come by.

On September 9 1940 Blackadder shared in the destruction of a Ju 88 and on the 26th he destroyed a He 111. On November 9 Blackadder was posted to Turnhouse as Sector Controller in the Operations Room, later doing the same job at Usworth, Ouston, Prestwick and Ayr. He commanded 245 Squadron at Aldergrove from June 1941 to July 13 1942, when he was posted to 10 Group, as Controller at Rudloe Manor.

Blackadder went for a course to the Army Staff College, Camberley on January 1 1943, after which he was posted to HQ Fighter Command, as Wing Commander Tactics, on May 7 1943. He moved to HQ Allied Expeditionary Air Forces on September 28.

Blackadder's final wartime posting was as CO of the Air Fighting Development Unit at Wittering. He was made an OBE (1.1.45) and was released from the RAF on November 19 1945. He rejoined 607 Squadron at Ouston in September 1946 and served with it until December 1948, after which he became CO of the Northumberland Wing, ATC until February 1 1951.

PO (AuxAF) 1.6.36   FO (AuxAF) 1.12.37   FO 24.8.39
FL 3.9.40   SL 1.12.41   FL (RAuxAF) 26.9.46

GEORGE DOUGLAS MORANT BLACKWOOD

32181   FL   Pilot   British   310 Squadron

Educated at Eton, Blackwood joined the RAF on a short service commission in early 1933. He did his flying training at 2 FTS, Digby. On August 26 1933 he was posted to 25 Squadron at Hawkinge and took part in the 1934 Hendon Air Display, flying one of the tied-together Furies.

In September 1934 he was seconded from the squadron to be Personal Assistant to the AOC Coastal Area, Lee-on-Solent. He returned to Hawkinge on July 1 1935. Six months later Blackwood was posted to 600 Squadron, AuxAF at Hendon as assistant adjutant and flying instructor in the Advanced Training Squadron.

In April 1938 his term of service ended and he joined a family business. Recalled at the end of August 1939, Blackwood was posted to 5 FTS, Sealand. A request for operational flying eventually led to a conversion course on to Hurricanes and he joined 213 as a supernumerary Squadron Leader in early June 1940. At the end of the month he was posted to Duxford to form 310, the first Czech fighter squadron. It became operational on August 17 1940 and on the 26th Blackwood claimed the destruction of a Do 17. He was himself shot down by return fire and baled out, unhurt. His Hurricane, P 3887, crashed at Maldon.

He was awarded the Czech Military Cross (24.12.40) and posted to HQ 12 Group in January 1941. Blackwood went to Northern Ireland for a year, commanded a station in 10 Group and then formed 134 Wing in preparation for the invasion of Normandy. He was

GDM Blackwood (continued)

released from the RAF early in 1945, as a Wing Commander.

PO 25.4.33   FO 25.10.34   FL 25.10.36   FL 1.9.39
SL 1.12.40   WC 1.3.42

CHARLES EDWARD BLAIR

78743   PO   Air Gunner   British   600 Squadron

Blair, from Wallington Surrey, joined 600 Squadron at Manston in May 1940. Posted away in late 1940 he was killed on April 25 1941, serving with 218 Squadron at Marham, Norfolk. He was 33 and with no known grave is remembered on the Runnymede Memorial, Panel 31.

APO 12.4.40   PO 1.6.40

KENNETH HUGHES BLAIR

39704   FL   Pilot   British   151 Squadron

Blair, born on February 15 1918 at Heaton Moor, Stockport, joined the RAF on a short service commission and began his flying training in March 1937. On June 5 he went to 11 FTS, Wittering and on June 1 1938 he joined 85 Squadron at Debden on its reformation. He went to France with the squadron at the outbreak of war. On May 10 1940 Blair destroyed two He 111s and he was awarded the DFC (31.5.40).

After return to Debden on May 22 Blair was posted to 151 Squadron at Martlesham Heath. He claimed a Bf 109 destroyed on August 5, a Bf 110 on the 18th, a He 111 on the 30th, a Do 215 on the 31st and on September 30 a shared Ju 88. On November 9 Blair and Sergeant Copeland intercepted a Do 17 on a pre-dawn sortie over the east coast, off Skegness. Although they claimed it as destroyed it managed to reach Gilze-Rijen, with two of the crew wounded.

On July 10 1941 Blair took command of 1453 Flight at Wittering, operating Turbinlite Havocs and working with 151 Squadron Hurricanes. He was posted away on September 4 1942. In June 1943 Blair returned to operations as a Flight Commander with 25 Squadron at Church Fenton. Promoted to Acting Wing Commander in October 1943, he was given command of 613 Squadron, at that time just transferred to 2 Group as a light bomber squadron with Mosquito VIs, specialising in low-level daylight attacks on particular buildings. The first operational sortie was made by Blair on December 19 1943. He was awarded a Bar to the DFC (23.5.44) at the end of his tour.

Blair stayed in the post-war RAF and died on October 31 1952, whilst still serving.

APO 18.5.37   PO 15.3.38   FO 15.10.39   FL 15.10.40
SL 1.12.41   SL 1.9.45   WC 1.1.52

PIERRE MICHEL BLAIZE

30490   Sous-Lt   Pilot   French   111 Squadron

Born on November 1 1915 at Saint Leocadie, Blaize was in the pre-war l'Armée de l'Air. After the fall of France he escaped to Britain and after conversion to Hurricanes joined 111 Squadron at Croydon in September 1940.

In March 1941 he was posted to 615 Squadron at Kenley. On April 15 on a squadron patrol at 30000 feet over Dungeness Blaize fell behind for some reason and was attacked and shot down by two Bf 109s. He baled out ten miles from the coast and his descent was covered down to the sea by one of his squadron. When rescue arrived only the parachute was found. Blaize was never seen again.

ARTHUR GILES BLAKE

Sub-Lieutenant (FAA)   Pilot   British   19 Squadron

Blake, who was born in 1917, was in the Navy in early 1939. In mid-June 1940 he was loaned to the RAF and after converting to Spitfires at 7 OTU, Hawarden he joined 19 Squadron at Duxford.

He destroyed a He 111 on September 9, a Bf 109 and a shared He 111 on the 15th and two Bf 109s two days later. Blake was acting as weaver during a squadron patrol over South London on October 29 1940, when he was shot down and killed, probably picked off by a Bf 109. His Spitfire, P 7423, crashed in London Road, Chelmsford. Blake is buried in St Mary's churchyard, Langley, Slough.

Midshipman (FAA)   Acting Sub-Lt 16.9.39   Sub-Lt 14.3.40

MINDEN VAUGHAN BLAKE

36095   SL   Pilot   New Zealander   238 and 234 Sqdns

Blake was born on February 13 1913 at Eketehuna and was educated at Southland Boys' High School and Canterbury University. He graduated in 1934 with an MSc, with Honours in mathematics. In 1935 he was appointed as a lecturer in Physics at Canterbury.

After narrowly missing a Rhodes Scholarship two years running Blake applied to join the RAF as a University Entrant. In face of stiff competition he was accepted, possibly because of his outstanding athletic record.

Blake sailed for England in November 1936 and after proving his aptitude for flying he was granted a Permanent Commission. In late March 1937 he was posted to 5 FTS, Sealand and after completing the course on October 20 he joined 17 Squadron at Kenley. He was appointed 'B' Flight Commander in June 1938. On September 8 1939 approaching Croydon to land Blake realised that he was going to overshoot, opened his throttle and the engine stopped. At 300 feet he slowed to stalling speed, hit the chimney of a nurses' home and flipped on to his back into the foundations of the new Purley Hospital. The cause of the engine failure was found to be hay in the air intake, the result of parking the aircraft in the open at Croydon for the first time. A modification by Rolls Royce prevented any further such occurrence. Blake escaped with a cut head.

On April 10 1940 he was posted to 10 FTS, Tern Hill as an instructor but in early August he converted to Hurricanes at 6 OTU, Sutton Bridge and took command of 238 Squadron at St Eval on August 16, as a Flight Lieutenant. On the 21st Blake destroyed a Ju 88, shared a Do 17 on the 27th, a Ju 88 on September 14 and a He 111 the next day.

Promoted to Acting Squadron Leader on September 22 Blake was given command of 234 Squadron. He shared in shooting down a Do 215 on November 24 and a Do 17 on the 29th, when 234 escorted the damaged destroyer HMS 'Javelin' into Plymouth. He was awarded the DFC (20.12.40).

Flying from Warmwell Blake shared a Bf 109 on March 11, destroyed a Ju 88 on May 8 and a Bf 109 three days later. On July 10 234 escorted Blenheims to attack shipping at Cherbourg. After shooting down two Bf 109s Blake was hit and ditched in the sea seven miles from the French coast. In twelve hours, with a favourable wind, he had paddled his dinghy to within two miles of the Isle of Wight and was picked up.

In late July 1941 he became Wing Leader of the Polish Wing at Exeter and two months later went as Wing Leader to Portreath. He was awarded the DSO (27.7.42). Over Dieppe on August 19 1942 Blake destroyed a FW 190 but was then himself shot down into the sea. He extricated himself and inflated his dinghy. After paddling all day and the following night he was picked up by a German launch when only five miles from Dover. Blake spent his captivity developing a new kind of rotary engine, which in post-war years proved to be too expensive to develop.

Released in May 1945, Blake remained in the RAF, holding staff appointments at home and overseas. He retired on January 28 1958, as a Wing Commander. He died in England on November 30 1981.

PO 24.3.37   FO 24.9.38   FL 24.3.39   SL 1.3.41
WC 1.10.46

JOHN WELLBURN BLAND

90895   PO   Pilot   British   601 and 501 Squadrons

Bland was the son of a parson and came from Bristol. He was a member of the AuxAF before the war and was called to full-time service on August 24 1939.

At the completion of his training Bland joined 601 Squadron and on July 11 1940 he shared in the destruction of a Do 215. The next day he was posted to 501 Squadron at Middle Wallop. On July 29 he claimed a Ju 87 shot down over Dover. His own port mainplane was hit by return fire but Bland returned to base at Gravesend.

On August 18 1940 Bland was shot down and killed by Oberleutnant Schoepfel of JG 26. He is buried in Gravesend Cemetery, Kent.

APO 24.8.39   PO 4.5.40

WILLIAM HIGGINS BLANE

1052333   AC 2   Radar Operator   British   604 Squadron

Joined the RAF in early June 1940 and after a short radar course at Yatesbury joined 604 Squadron at Gravesend on July 20, as aircrew but with no flying training, rank or brevet.

No further service details traced.

HOWARD PETER BLATCHFORD

37715   FL   Pilot   Canadian   17 and 257 Squadrons

Blatchford, from Edmonton, Alberta, was born in 1912. He joined the RAF on a short service commission in January 1936. On April 18 he was posted to 6 FTS, Netheravon and on January 10 1937 joined 41 Squadron at Catterick.

On October 17 1939 Blatchford gained the first Canadian victory of the war, when he shared in the destruction of a He 111 twenty-five miles east of Whitby. In April 1940 Blatchford went to 212 Squadron at Heston. A reconnaissance unit, 212 was preparing to work with the Photographic Development Unit, also at Heston. In early May the squadron was disbanded and the personnel went to PRU. Blatchford was sent to France to photograph bridges, troop concentrations and movements. He flew back to Heston in early June.

On September 30 1940 Blatchford joined 17 Squadron at Debden. He shared in destroying a Do 17 on October 2 and then had to make a forced-landing near Bacton, out of fuel. Six days later he was posted to 257 Squadron at North Weald. The squadron met the Italian Air Force on November 11 1940 and Blatchford destroyed a Fiat BR 20 and damaged a Fiat CR 42 by ramming it with his propeller because he was out of ammunition. On November 17 he shot a Bf 109 down into the sea. He was awarded the DFC (6.12.40). On March 19 1941 he got a probable Ju 88 and on the night of May 11/12 he sent a He 111 into the sea.

Blatchford took command of 257, when Tuck was promoted to lead the Duxford Wing. In September 1941 he too was promoted to lead the Canadian Wing at Digby, which he did until rested in April 1942.

A return to operations as Wing Leader of the Coltishall Wing came on February 5 1943. On March 18 he destroyed two FW 190s, with another probable on May 2. The Wing escorted bombers to attack the power station at Amsterdam on May 3 1943. Blatchford was shot down and ditched in the sea forty miles off the English coast. Searches failed to find him. He is remembered on the Runnymede Memorial, Panel 118.

APO 30.3.36   PO 3.2.37   FO 3.11.38   FL 3.9.40
SL 1.12.41

ADOLF JARVIS BLAYNEY

90538   FO   Pilot   British   609 Squadron

Blayney, who was educated at Stowe School, joined 609 Squadron, AuxAF in 1938. He was called for full-time service on August 24 1939 and continued to serve with the squadron.

On July 28 1940 he blacked out at 12000 feet, regained consciousness at 1000 feet and made a forced-landing at Boscombe Down. He was taken off operations and in August was posted away to Training Command, remaining with it until his release in 1945, as a Flight Lieutenant. For his services as an instructor Blayney was awarded the AFC (2.4.43).

APO (AuxAF) 20.11.38   PO 24.8.39   FO 3.9.40   FL 3.9.41

FRANK BLENKHARN

1002007   Sgt   Radar Operator   British   25 Squadron

Born on April 28 1920, Blenkharn joined the RAF in May 1940 and was posted to 25 Squadron at Martlesham Heath in September.

On December 7 1940 Blenkharn was one of the crew of a Blenheim, which was on a flight to test the black-out over Peterborough. They collided with an aircraft, which had been training pilots in night landings at the FTS at Peterborough. Blenkharn was seriously injured and his pilot, air gunner and the six trainee pilots in the other aircraft were all killed. He spent three weeks in

F Blenkharn (continued)

Peterborough Hospital and then four months in RAF Rauceby Hospital. He did not fly again and went on to Flying Control.

Blenkharn spent his last six months at Dum Dum, Calcutta, India and was released in early 1947.

DAVID HENRY BLOMELEY

40665   FO   Pilot   British   151 Squadron

Blomeley, born on May 12 1916, joined the RAF on a short service commission in December 1937. He was posted to 11 FTS, Shawbury on May 7 1938 and joined No 1 Squadron at Tangmere on December 17.

In April 1939 Blomeley moved to 151 Squadron at North Weald. He claimed a Bf 110 destroyed over Dunkirk on May 29 1940.

In 1943 he was with 605 Squadron at Castle Camps, flying Mosquitos on night intruder operations. He was awarded the DFC (26.10.43), having by that time destroyed four enemy aircraft.

Blomeley stayed in the RAF, was awarded the AFC (10.6.54) and retired on February 20 1958, as a Flight Lieutenant, retaining the rank of Squadron Leader.

APO 7.3.38   PO 7.3.39   FO 3.9.40   FL 3.9.41
SL 1.1.44   FL 21.5.46

ERNEST BLOOR

564830   Sgt   Pilot   British   46 Squadron

Joined the RAF as an apprentice in late 1929 and later volunteered for pilot training. Bloor was with 46 Squadron at the start of the Battle of Britain. On September 3 he was shot down in combat over Canewdon and baled out, with slight burns on his face. His Hurricane, P 3024, crashed into the sea wall at Beckney Farm, South Fambridge.

Bloor was killed on August 27 1941 when his Hurricane, Z 3843, crashed near Horsham while on a searchlight co-operation flight. At the time of his death he was 27 and serving with No 1 Squadron. He was buried near his home, in Stamford Cemetery, Lincolnshire.

KENNETH LESLIE OWEN BLOW

751684   Sgt   Observer   British   235 Squadron

With 235 Squadron in early July 1940 and served with it throughout the Battle of Britain.

In 1943 Blow was with 487 Squadron, as a Warrant Officer, flying in Venturas. Awarded the DFC (15.6.43), he was killed on December 10 1943.

Blow was 22. He is buried in Den Ham General Cemetery, Netherlands.

MICHAEL CHRISTOPHER BINDLOSS BODDINGTON

88017   PO   Pilot   British   234 Squadron

Joined the RAFVR on December 6 1936 and called up at the outbreak of war. Boddington, who was born at Hawkshead, Lancashire, joined 234 Squadron at Leconfield at its formation on October 30 1939.

He claimed a Ju 88 destroyed on August 14 1940, two Bf 110s on September 4, a Bf 109 on each of the following two days and he shared a Ju 88 on October 28. Boddington was commissioned at the end of October and awarded the DFM (26.11.40). He got a probable Ju 88 on February 15 1941 and soon afterwards was posted to 118 Squadron at Filton, as a Flight Commander.

In 1942 Boddington commanded 19 Squadron at Perranporth from September until December. In May 1943 he took command of 242 Squadron in North Africa, moving in June to Malta and in July to Lentini East in Sicily. He claimed a Bf 109 and a He 111 on July 10, shared a Ju 88 the next day and destroyed a Bf 110 on the 13th. He was awarded the DFC (10.9.43).

Boddington commanded 242 until its disbandment at Gragnano on November 4 1944. He was released from the RAF on February 13 1946, as a Squadron Leader. He died in 1977.

PO 30.10.40   FO 21.5.41   FL 21.5.42

CRELIN ARTHUR WALFORD BODIE

42790   PO   Pilot   British   66 Squadron

Born at Kirton, near Ipswich, Bodie joined 66 Squadron at Duxford in May 1940.

On August 20 he claimed a Bf 110, shared a Do 215 the next day, shared a He 111 on September 2, claimed another on the 11th, four Do 17s on the 15th, a He 111 on the 18th and a Bf 109 on October 11. Bodie was awarded the DFC (8.11.40) and on November 14 claimed a Bf 109 destroyed.

In March 1941 Bodie was posted to 310 Squadron at Duxford, as a Flight Commander. He moved to 152 Squadron at Portreath in June. Bodie was killed in a flying accident on February 24 1942, possibly while performing aerobatics. He is buried in the churchyard of St Canice, Eglinton, Co. Antrim, Northern Ireland. He was 21.

APO 23.10.39   PO 18.5.40   FO 18.5.41

DEREK PIERRE AUMALE BOITEL-GILL

28142   FL   Pilot   British   152 Squadron

Boitel-Gill was born in 1909 and joined the RAF in 1929, going to 5 FTS, Sealand on September 28 and joining 3 Squadron at Upavon on September 9 1930. He went on to the Reserve of Air Force Officers in September 1934 when his period of service ended.

Sometime personal pilot to the Nizam of Hyderabad, Boitel-Gill was a pilot with Imperial Airways before the war. He was recalled to the RAF in April 1940 and joined 152 Squadron at Acklington, as a Flight Commander.

Boitel-Gill claimed a Ju 88 destroyed on August 12, two Bf 110s and a Ju 87 on the 15th, another Ju 87 on the 18th, a Ju 88 on September 25 and a Bf 109 on September 25 and a Ju 88 on the 26th. He was awarded the DFC (22.10.40) and commanded 152 Squadron from November 1940 to June 1941.

On September 18 1941 Boitel-Gill was killed in a flying accident at Carlisle, as a Wing Commander. He was cremated at West Norwood Crematorium, Lambeth, London.

PO 13.9.29   FO 13.3.31   FO (RAFO) 13.9.34   FL 22.4.40
SL 1.12.40

HENRY ALBERT BOLTON

754530   Sgt   Pilot   British   79 Squadron

Bolton, from West Hartlepool, joined 79 Squadron in August 1940. On the 31st he was shot down in combat over Kenley, in Hurricane V 7200. He was killed whilst attempting a forced-landing at Haliloo Farm, Warlingham.

Bolton was 21. He is buried in Stranton Cemetery, Hartlepool.

———— BOMFORD

No unknown   Sgt   Pilot   British   601 Squadron

No service details traced.

CAMILLE ROBESPIERRE BONSEIGNEUR

42791   PO   Pilot   Canadian   257 Squadron

Bonseigneur was posted to 257 Squadron at its reformation at Hendon on May 17 1940.

He shared in the destruction of a Do 17 shot down into the sea off Brighton on July 19. Shot down in combat with Bf 109s over Essex on September 3 1940, Bonseigneur baled out but fell dead at The Grove, Ingatestone. His Hurricane, P 3518, crashed at Lodge Farm, Galleywood, Essex.

Bonseigneur was 22. He is buried in Saffron Walden Cemetery, Essex.

APO 23.10.39   PO 11.5.40

PETER VICTOR BOOT

76455   PO   Pilot   British   1 Squadron

Boot joined No 1 Squadron in France in April 1940. He claimed a Bf 109 destroyed on May 12 and a Bf 110 on the 15th. On June 4 Boot forced a He 111 to land in a field near Rouen. Having expended all his ammunition in combat he made diving passes on the straggling bomber until it went down. He flew back with the squadron to England on June 17.

On August 31 Boot damaged a Bf 110 and on September 1 he claimed a Bf 109 destroyed. He was awarded the DFC (1.10.40) and posted away on October 18 1940.

Boot was released from the RAF in 1946, as a Flight Lieutenant. He died in 1984.

PO 6.11.39   FO 6.11.40   FL 6.11.41

GLENDON BULMAR BOOTH

748586   Sgt   Pilot   British   85 Squadron

Booth, of Sydenham, was educated at Brockley County School and worked for the County of London Electricity Company. He joined the RAFVR in 1938 and was called up at the outbreak of war.

With training completed, Booth joined 85 Squadron at Martlesham Heath on July 15 1940. He damaged a Bf 109 in combat over the Sussex coast on August 29. The pilot made a forced-landing near Pevensey and was captured.

On September 1 1940 Booth was shot down by Bf 109s over Tunbridge Wells. He baled out, with burns and parachute alight and was further injured in a heavy landing. His Hurricane, L 2071, crashed at Kingswood, Sanderstead.

Booth died from his injuries on February 7 1941. He is buried in Crystal Palace District Cemetery. He was 20 years old.

JOHN JAMES BOOTH

171689   Sgt   Air Gunner   British   600 and 23 Sqdns

Booth was with 600 Squadron at Northolt in July 1940, moving on to 23 Squadron at Wittering on August 22.

He was commissioned in January 1944 and released from the RAF in 1946.

PO 21.1.44   FO 22.7.44

ROBERT JOHN BORET

42554   PO   Pilot   British   41 Squadron

Boret joined the RAF in 1939, was commissioned in early March 1940 and was with 41 Squadron in July. His father, Air Commodore JA Boret, commanded the squadron from May 1933 to February 1937.

In October 1940 Boret was posted overseas and was in the carrier HMS 'Argus', when it sailed from Gibraltar in mid-November for

Malta. He was one of the six pilots who flew off on November 16 in the second flight of Hurricanes, led by a FAA Skua. A series of mishaps saw the Hurricanes run out of fuel and fall one by one into the sea, with the loss of all six pilots.

Boret was 20. He is remembered on the Runnymede Memorial, Panel 7.

PO 2.3.40

JAN BOROWSKI

P 0250   FO   Pilot   Polish   302 Squadron

Borowski joined 302 Squadron at Northolt on October 17 1940. The next day he crashed in deteriorating foggy conditions on Kempton Park racecourse, when returning from a patrol. Borowski was killed and his Hurricane, P 3930, burned out.

He was 28 and is buried in Northwood Cemetery, Middlesex.

REGINALD ARTHUR BOSWELL

742295   Sgt   Pilot   British   266 and 19 Squadrons

Joined 266 Squadron at Wittering on September 16 1940 and went to 19 Squadron at Fowlmere on September 25.

No other service details traced.

ROGER JOHN ERIC BOULDING

41249   FO   Pilot   British   74 Squadron

Born on November 19 1919, Boulding joined the RAF on a short service commission in June 1938 and went to 6 E&RFTS, Sywell on August 29. He was posted to 8 FTS, Montrose in November, finished at 11 FTS, Shawbury in June 1939 and after a month at the Armament Training Camp at Penrhos he joined 52 Squadron at Upwood in July.

Posted to 98 Squadron at Hucknall in October, Boulding went to France to join 142 Squadron in November 1939. He returned to England when the squadron was withdrawn in late May 1940 and in August volunteered for Fighter Command. He was posted to 74 Squadron at Kirton-in-Lindsey on August 22.

Boulding shared in the destruction of a Do 215 on October 5, he damaged a Bf 109 on May 7 1941, shot down a He 111 at night on the 10th, which crash-landed, wheels up, in a field near Ashford, Kent. On a sweep over the French coast on June 17 1941 Boulding was shot down by a Bf 109 and taken prisoner.

Released in May 1945, Boulding went to 6 (P) AFU on September 25, was posted to 10 OTU, Abingdon on February 12 1946, converted on to Lancasters at 1553 Heavy Conversion Unit at North Luffenham and took command of 35 Squadron at Stradishall on January 30 1947. He was posted away to HQ Bomber Command on October 22 1948.

Boulding went to 203 AFT, Driffield in May 1950, followed by two months at the Central Fighter Establishment at West Raynham, then took command of 249 Squadron on October 24 1950 at Deversoir, Egypt, with Vampires. He commanded the squadron until May 2 1953. He retired from the RAF on November 29 1966, as a Wing Commander.

APO 29.8.38   PO 29.8.39   FO 3.9.40   FL 3.9.41
SL 1.7.44   WC 1.1.54

JOHN CLIFFORD BOULTER

37757   FL   Pilot   British   603 Squadron

Boulter was born in Barnes, London and joined the RAF in early 1936. He went to 7 FTS, Peterborough on April 18 and was posted to No 1 Squadron at Tangmere on October 25. He moved to 72 Squadron at Church Fenton at its reformation on March 23 1937.

In September 1939 Boulter joined 603 Squadron at Turnhouse. On October 16 he fired on a He 111 east of Aberdour. In March 1940 he was in hospital after his aircraft was involved in a taxying accident with an Oxford.

JC Boulter (continued)

On August 29 Boulter claimed a Bf 109 destroyed over Deal and he returned to Hornchurch, slightly wounded. On September 14 he claimed a Bf 109, another on the 23rd and a probable Fiat CR 42 on November 23. The citation for his DFC (6.12.40) credited him with five enemy aircraft destroyed.

Boulter was killed on February 17 1941 when his Spitfire was struck by a Hurricane as he was about to take off. He is buried in Dirleton Cemetery, East Lothian. He was 28. His portrait was done by Cuthbert Orde in February 1941.

APO 6.4.36   PO 10.2.37   FO 10.11.38   FL 3.9.40

JOHN ERIC BOULTON

40362   FO   Pilot   British   310 Squadron

Boulton joined the RAF late in 1937. He was posted to 2 FTS, Brize Norton on January 1 1938 and on August 20 went to 29 Squadron at Debden. He joined 310 Squadron at Duxford at its formation on July 10 1940.

In an engagement over Croydon on September 9 Boulton was killed when he collided with Flight Lieutenant GL Sinclair of 310, lost control, hit a Do 215 amidships and crashed in Woodmanstern Lane, Woodmanstern. He was 20 and is buried in Bandon Hill Cemetery, Beddington, Surrey. Boulton was awarded the Czech Military Cross (10.1.41).

APO 9.1.38   PO 25.10.38   FO 25.4.40

HENRI JACQUES BOUQUILLARD

30495   Adjutant   Pilot   French   245, 615 and 249 Sqdns

Born in Nevers on June 14 1908, Bouquillard was in l'Armée de l'Air. He was posted to 6 OTU, Sutton Bridge on August 19 1940 and then joined 245 Squadron at Aldergrove on September 12, going six days later to 615 at Prestwick, finishing on October 1 with 249 Squadron at North Weald.

Bouquillard ran out of fuel on the landing circuit on October 18 and forced-landed on Padfields Farm, Church Road, Thornwood Common. A week later he made a forced-landing at Rochester after a combat with Bf 109s over North Kent. Wounded, he was admitted to the Royal Naval Hospital at Chatham.

In December 1940 Bouquillard returned to 615 Squadron. He was commissioned in February 1941 and was shot down and killed on an evening scramble on March 10. He was buried on the 15th. His remains were repatriated to France after the war.

CHARLES EARLE BOWEN

39488   FL   Pilot   British   607 Squadron

Bowen, of Chelsea, London, joined the RAF in December 1936. He went to 9 FTS, Thornaby on March 20 1937, joined 77 Squadron at Honington on October 23 and on May 2 1938 was posted to 10 FTS, Tern Hill, as an instructor.

In July 1940 Bowen was with 607 Squadron at Usworth. Later, flying from Tangmere, he claimed a Do 215 destroyed and a Do 17 shared on September 15. On the 26th he was shot down in combat over the Isle of Wight. He baled out over Calbourne and landed unhurt.

On October 1 1940 Bowen was reported 'Missing' after a combat with Bf 110s over the Isle of Wight. He is remembered on the Runnymede Memorial, Panel 4. He was 24 years old.

APO 8.3.37   PO 21.12.37   FO 21.7.39   FL 3.9.40

NIGEL GREENSTREET BOWEN

41984   PO   Pilot   British   266 Squadron

Joined the RAF on a short service commission in February 1939 and was posted to 266 Squadron at Sutton Bridge early in 1940.

Over Dunkirk on June 2 Bowen damaged a Bf 109. On August 12 he claimed a Ju 88 destroyed. He was shot down and killed during a combat with Bf 109s on August 16 1940, in Spitfire N 3095, crashing in flames at Adisham. He was 20 years old and is buried in Wallingford Cemetery, Berkshire.

APO 29.4.39   PO 6.11.39

PETER DUNCAN BOWEN

42481   PO   Pilot   British   264 Squadron

Bowen, from Ashford, Kent, joined the RAF in May 1939 and went to 264 Squadron at Martlesham Heath in February 1940.

On March 18 1941 Bowen was seriously injured, when, as he was taking off, he hit another Defiant, which had just landed and was taxying down the flare path instead of turning off it.

Bowen was reported 'Missing' after a night operation with 169 Squadron on February 13 1944. He was 23 and is remembered on the Runnymede Memorial, Panel 201.

APO 19.8.39   PO 1.2.40   FO 1.2.41   FL 1.2.42

HUGH BOWEN-MORRIS

758084   Sgt   Pilot   British   92 Squadron

Joined the RAFVR in June 1939 and began flying training at 9 E&RFTS, Ansty. Bowen-Morris was called up at the outbreak of war and after ITW at Hastings was posted in November to 3 EFTS, Hamble.

In April 1940 he went to 14 FTS, Kinloss and completed his training at FTS, Cranfield. In August Bowen-Morris was posted to 7 OTU, Hawarden and joined 92 Squadron at Biggin Hill on September 12. He shared in the destruction of a Ju 88 on the 27th and crashed on landing back at Biggin Hill, with damage to his Spitfire, R 6760.

Bowen-Morris was shot down during a fighter sweep over Northern France on June 23 1941. He was captured, seriously wounded, and had his right arm amputated. In an exchange of prisoners in October 1943 Bowen-Morris was repatriated. He was discharged in November, as a Warrant Officer.

OSWALD ROBERT BOWERMAN

741649   Sgt   Pilot   British   222 Squadron

Bowerman, of Ealing, was in the RAFVR before the war. In September 1939 the FAA was short of pilots and after Bowerman was called up he was posted to Donibristle and joined the Torpedo-Spotter-Reconnaissance Flight. He was later posted to 770 Squadron for deck-landing training on HMS 'Argus', in the Western Mediterranean. He was offered a transfer to the FAA but declined and was posted to 3 BGS, Aldergrove as a staff pilot.

On May 4 1940 Bowerman was recalled to the FAA and joined 759 (T) Squadron at Eastleigh for a refresher deck-landing course. He was later posted to 804 Squadron at Hatston. By mid-June the RAF was short of pilots and Bowerman was recalled and posted to 7 OTU, Hawarden. After converting to Spitfires he was posted to 222 Squadron at Hornchurch in early July.

Within two weeks Bowerman was told to report to Uxbridge and became one of a group of nine sergeants and one officer. They were flown to Hullavington, picked up Hurricanes, flew them to Abbotsinch and were embarked on the carrier HMS 'Argus', where they were joined by four more officers. They were told their destination was Malta and they were now 418 Flight.

The 'Argus' sailed on July 23, arrived at Gibraltar and sailed for Malta on July 31. At dawn on August 2 they flew off to Luqa. 418 Flight and the Malta Fighter Flight were amalgamated into 261 Squadron on August 16 1940.

Bowerman left Malta for Egypt on April 7 1941. He ferried a Hurricane to Greece and then went to the Aircraft Delivery Unit at Takoradi. In July 1942 he was posted to 260 Squadron in the Western Desert and moved to 601 Squadron in October. He was killed on October 24 1942, when he crashed after being seen to spin during a turn.

Bowerman, aged 26, was a Warrant Officer. He is remembered on the Alamein Memorial, Column 249.

LEONARD DOUGLAS BOWMAN

174743   Sgt   Air Gunner   British   141 Squadron

Joined 141 Squadron at Turnhouse in early September 1940. Bowman later served with 410 (RCAF) Squadron on Defiants and 159, 160, 178 and 31 (SAAF) Squadrons on Liberators.

Whilst serving with 178 he was awarded the DFM (27.4.43). He had then flown many operational sorties, including eight daylight attacks on targets in the Middle East.

Commissioned in April 1944, Bowman was released in 1945, as a Flying Officer.

PO 5.4.44   FO 5.10.44

BENJAMIN HARVEY BOWRING

90105   FO   Pilot   British   600 and 111 Squadrons

Born in April 1918, Bowring was educated at Uppingham School and learned to fly at the Brooklands Flying Club in 1937. He joined 600 Squadron, AuxAF in 1938. Called to full-time service on August 24 1939 he served with it until August 24 1940, when he was posted to 111 Squadron at Debden.

On September 4 and 5 Bowring claimed Bf 109s destroyed and on the 6th a Ju 88. He was shot down in early November and admitted to hospital, wounded. Recovered, he joined 260 Squadron on the 22nd, then forming at Castletown, as 'B' Flight Commander.

In May 1941 the squadron embarked on the carrier HMS 'Victorious'. At Gibraltar it transferred on to HMS 'Ark Royal' and on June 14 flew off to Malta. After refuelling it went on to Egypt and eventually arrived in Haifa, to take part in the Syrian campaign. Bowring served with the squadron detachment at Beirut. He returned to the UK in October 1941 and was posted to an Armament Officer's course.

He later took command of 278 (ASR) Squadron at Coltishall. Bowring led the squadron until its disbandment in September 1945. By that time it had rescued 998 men from the sea.

Bowring was released in 1945, as a Squadron Leader.

PO (AuxAF) 18.7.38   PO 24.8.39   FO 18.1.40   FL 15.1.41
SL 1.3.42

WALTER STAFFORD BOWYER

39607   FL   Pilot   British   257 Squadron

Joined the RAF in March 1937. Bowyer was posted to 3 FTS, South Cerney on May 8 and went to 3 Squadron at Kenley on November 27 1937. He joined 257 Squadron, when it was reformed at Hendon on May 17 1940.

Bowyer was killed on January 24 1942, as a Squadron Leader. His unit at that time is unknown. He is buried in Ocklynge Cemetery, Eastbourne, Sussex.

APO 3.5.37   PO 1.3.38   FO 1.9.39   FL 3.9.40

ADRIAN HOPE BOYD

39101   FL   Pilot   British   145 Squadron

Born in 1913, Boyd enlisted in the Royal Navy as a cadet in 1926. In 1933 he became an Acting Sub-Lieutenant and in 1934 he retired. He entered the RAF in June 1936, was posted to 2 FTS, Digby on September 19 and joined 65 Squadron at Hornchurch on May 22 1937.

Boyd went to 145 Squadron at Croydon in October 1939, as 'B' Flight Commander. In operations over France he destroyed two Ju 87s and probably another on May 22 1940 and two Bf 110s and probably another on the 27th. The next day Boyd was shot down into the sea near Dunkirk and was picked up. On June 1 he destroyed a Bf 109 and a Bf 110. For these ten days of activity he was awarded the DFC (21.6.40)

On July 18 Boyd claimed a He 111 destroyed, on the 22nd shared a Do 17, on August 8 claimed two Bf 109s, two Bf 110s, a Ju 87 and damaged another and on the 23rd he shot down a He 111 at night over Edinburgh. On October 12 he shared an Arado Ar 196 and on the 15th claimed a Bf 109. He received a Bar to the DFC (20.8.40).

In December 1940 Boyd was posted away to an OTU, as an instructor, but returned to operations when he took command of 501 Squadron at Ibsley in mid-June 1941. On July 7 he destroyed a Ju 88 at night and on the 24th he claimed two Bf 109s.

Boyd was appointed Wing Leader at Middle Wallop on August 2 1941 and when he was awarded the DSO (2.12.41) he was credited with sixteen enemy aircraft destroyed. In 1944 Boyd commanded 281 Wing in Italy, as an Acting Group Captain. He left the RAF in 1947, as a Wing Commander, and died on January 21 1975. His portrait was done by Cuthbert Orde in October 1940.

APO 7.9.36   PO 13.7.37   FO 13.1.39   FL 3.9.40
SL 2.11.41   WC 1.1.44

ARCHIBALD DOUGLAS McNEILL BOYD

72461   FO   Pilot   British   600 Squadron

Born in Sheffield in 1918, Boyd was at Trinity College, Oxford and learned to fly with the University Air Squadron in 1938. He joined the RAFVR in October 1938 and continued his flying at 18 E&RFTS, Fairoaks.

Called up in September 1939, Boyd was posted in October to 2 FTS, Brize Norton and in April 1940 went to 12 Group Pool at Aston Down, from where he joined 600 Squadron at Manston in May. On September 30 he flew 600's first Beaufighter patrol with Pilot Officer RC Haine.

In November 1940 Boyd teamed up with Pilot Officer AJ Glegg, forming another of those long and successful night-fighting partnerships. On May 16 1941 they destroyed a Ju 88, on October 10 a He 111, on December 2 another He 111 and on January 25 1942 a He 111. They were both awarded the DFC (9.1.42). On March 7 they shot down a He 115 within sight of the airfield at Predannack.

Boyd was posted to HQ Fighter Command, as Squadron Leader Night Training, in September 1942. He took command of 219 Squadron in March 1943 at Scorton, again flying with Glegg. The squadron went to North Africa in early June 1943, became operational at Algiers on June 30 and on that day Boyd shot down two Ju 88s. On August 25 he destroyed another Ju 88, on September 6 a He 111 and on the 18th another. Boyd was awarded the DSO (3.3.44). The

ADM Boyd (continued)

squadron returned to the UK in February 1944 and Boyd continued to command until August, when he was posted to HQ Fighter Command, as Wing Commander Night Operations.

In May 1945 he was appointed Air Attaché in Dublin, demobilised in February 1946 and went to work for Vickers-Armstrong in March.

PO (VR) 18.10.38   FO 18.4.40   FL 18.4.41   SL 1.6.42

ROBERT FINDLAY BOYD

90165   FL   Pilot   British   602 Squadron

Born in East Kilbride, Scotland in 1915, Boyd joined 602 Squadron, AuxAF in 1935. He was called for full-time service in early September 1939.

Boyd shared in the destruction of a Ju 88 on July 7 1940, he claimed a Do 215 on August 15, a Ju 87 and a He 111 on the 16th, a Ju 87 and a Bf 109 on the 18th, two Bf 109s on the 25th, a Do 17 and a Bf 109 on September 4, a Bf 109 on the 11th and a Bf 109 on the 26th. Boyd shared a Ju 88 with Barthropp of 602 on October 2. Intercepted as it approached Shoreham, it was chased out to sea and shot down 35 miles out. Boyd's final victory in 1940 was a shared Ju 88 on November 13. He was awarded the DFC (24.9.40) and a Bar (25.10.40).

In December 1940 Boyd was given command of 54 Squadron at Catterick. On April 17 1941 he claimed a Bf 110. He was posted to 58 OTU, Grangemouth in July 1941, remaining there until December, when he went to Kenley as Wing Leader. Boyd was flying with Victor Beamish on February 12 1942, when they spotted the 'Scharnhorst' and 'Gneisenau'.

The citation for Boyd's DSO (10.4.42) stated that he had destroyed a total of twenty-two enemy aircraft. In June 1942 Boyd was posted to the Far East and at some time commanded 293 Wing in Burma. He was released from the RAF in 1945, as a Group Captain. His portrait was done by Cuthbert Orde in October 1940.

Boyd flew charter flights for Scottish Aviation, later tried pig farming and herring fishing and then moved to Skye, where he kept the Ferry Inn at Uig. He died in April 1975.

PO (AuxAF) 2.11.35   FO (AuxAF) 2.5.37   FL 3.9.39
SL 1.12.40   WC 1.3.42

CYRIL BOYLE

143495   Sgt   Aircrew   British   236 Squadron

Served with 236 Squadron in the Battle of Britain. Commissioned in January 1943, Boyle was released in 1945, as a Flight Lieutenant. He died on July 6 1971.

PO 24.1.43   FO 24.7.43   FL 24.1.45

JOHN GREER BOYLE

40204   FO   Pilot   Canadian   41 Squadron

The son of a doctor, Boyle, of Castlemain, Ontario, joined the RAF in August 1937. He was posted to 9 FTS, Hullavington on October 24 and after completing his training went as a staff pilot to No 1 Air Observers' School at North Coates on August 15 1938.

Boyle was with 611 Squadron in September 1939 but moved to 41 Squadron at Catterick in 1940. On August 11 he shared in the destruction of a Ju 88, on September 5 destroyed a Bf 109, on the 15th a Bf 109 and shared a Do 17 and on the 17th two Bf 109s.

On September 28 1940 Boyle was shot down and killed in a combat over Charing. His Spitfire, X 4426, crashed and burned out at Erriotts Farm, Dadmans, Lynstead.

Boyle was 26. He is buried in Lynstead New Churchyard, Kent.

APO 24.10.37   PO 23.8.38   FO 23.3.40

——— BRACTON

No unknown   Sgt   Pilot   British   602 Squadron

No service details traced.

JOHN RANDALL DANIEL BRAHAM

40667   FO   Pilot   British   29 Squadron

Braham was born in Bath on April 6 1920, the son of a vicar. He was educated at Taunton Grammar School, left in late 1936 and went to work as a boy clerk for the Lancashire County Police at Wigan. He applied for an RAF short service commission in December 1937 and was accepted. In late February 1938 Braham began his elementary flying at 7 E&RFTS, Desford, moving on to 11 FTS, Shawbury on May 7. At the end of the course he joined 29 Squadron at Debden on December 17 1938.

Braham's first victory came on August 24 1940, with a Do 17 shot down at night in the Humber area. He was awarded the DFC (17.1.41) and decorated by the King in a ceremony at Waddington.

On March 13 1941 Braham destroyed a Do 17 and on May 8 a He 111. In June 1941 he teamed up with Sergeant WJ Gregory. It was the start of a long and successful partnership. In July they shot a Ju 88 down into the Thames and in October a Do 217 into the sea. Awarded a Bar to the DFC (25.10.41), Braham was rested from operations but in June 1942, flying temporarily with 29 Squadron, he put a Do 217 into the sea off Sandwich. Later in the month he was posted to 29 as 'A' Flight Commander.

On August 9 Braham destroyed a Do 217, on October 19 a probable Do 217, on the 26th a Ju 88 and on the 31st a Do 217. He was awarded the DSO (9.10.42). In early January 1943 Braham was promoted to Acting Wing Commander and given command of 141 Squadron at Ford. He was awarded a second Bar to the DFC (15.6.43) and a Bar to the DSO (24.9.43). He led the squadron until October 1943, when he was sent for a course to the Army Staff College, Camberley. Braham was posted in February 1944 to a staff job at 2 (Light Bomber) Group to assist in the work of night interdiction. He was joined by Gregory and having obtained the AOC's permission to fly occasional sorties they shot down a He 177 on a daylight intruder operation to the airfield at Chateaudun on March 5.

On daylight intruder flights in March and April 1944 Braham's score rose to twenty-seven enemy aircraft destroyed. In early May he shot down a Ju 88 near Roskilde, Denmark and on May 12 he destroyed a FW 190 near Aalborg, then, damaged and out of fuel, he crash-landed on the sea and was picked up by a Royal Navy trawler. It was Braham's twenty-ninth and final victory.

He was awarded a second Bar to the DSO (13.6.44) and on June 25 1944 Braham was shot down by Leutnant Robert Spreckels in a FW 190. He crashed at Ringköbing Fiord and he and his Australian navigator were captured.

Braham was sent to Stalag Luft lll at Sagan, was later moved to Marlag Milag Nord, near Bremen and after a forced march to Lübeck he was released there on May 2 1945.

As well as his other awards Braham had the C de G (Belg). Granted a Permanent Commission after the war, he was awarded the AFC (1.1.51) and resigned in May 1952 to take up an appointment in the RCAF. In 1954 he commanded 432 Squadron, an all-weather jet fighter unit at North Bay, north of Toronto. In 1960 he was posted to SHAPE HQ, Paris. Braham retired from the RCAF in 1970, as a Group Captain. He settled in Nova Scotia and died there in 1973.

APO 7.5.38   PO 7.3.39   FO 3.9.40   FL 3.9.41
SL 22.3.43   SL 1.8.47

HENRY GEORGE KENELM BRAMAH

Sub-Lieutenant (FAA)   **Pilot**   **British**   **213 Squadron**

In the Fleet Air Arm in early 1939, Bramah was one of the pilots loaned to the RAF in mid-June 1940. After converting to Hurricanes he joined 213 Squadron at Exeter on July 1.

Bramah flew three times on July 15 1940. On the first, a scramble, he destroyed a Do 17. The second was a convoy patrol. On the third, another scramble, he was shot down by return fire from a Do 17 over Old Mill Creek, near Dartmouth. He baled out, badly wounded in the arm, and was rescued from the sea by the destroyer HMS 'Scimitar'. He refused to have his arm amputated. His recovery was slow and he did not return to 213 Squadron.

In 1945 Bramah was Flight Deck Officer on HMS 'Glasgow'. He remained in the Navy, retired in 1955 and died in 1973.

Midshipman 13.3.39   *Sub-Lt 14.3.40*   *Lt 13.7.42*
Lt-Cdr 13.7.49   *Cdr 31.12.52*

GUY RAUSTROM BRANCH

90137   **FO**   **Pilot**   **British**   **145 Squadron**

Educated at Eton, Branch joined 601 Squadron, AuxAF in late 1936. On February 11 1937 he was on an instructional cross-country flight in a Demon with Flying Officer Crawley. After refuelling at RAF Netheravon they took off in poor weather, just missed the hangars and crashed in flames on the road nearby. Branch extricated himself from the wreckage but, finding Crawley still trapped, went back into the flames and pulled him out. For this act he was awarded the Empire Gallantry Medal (25.3.38). This was later changed to the George Cross.

Branch was with 145 Squadron at the start of the Battle of Britain. On August 8 1940 he claimed the destruction of two Ju 87s. He failed to return from a combat south of Swanage on August 11. His Hurricane, P 2951, crashed into the sea and Branch's body was later washed up on the French coast. He was 26 and is buried in Quiberville churchyard, France.

PO (AuxAF) 7.5.37   *FO (AuxAF) 29.1.39*   *FO 24.8.39*

GEORGE BROWN BRASH

639109   **Sgt**   **Observer**   **British**   **248 Squadron**

Brash, from Edinburgh, joined 248 Squadron in July 1940. He was one of the crew of Blenheim R 3626, which failed to return from a reconnaissance sortie to the Norwegian coast on October 1 1940.

He was 18 and is remembered on the Runnymede Memorial, Panel 12.

REGINALD ARTHUR BREEZE

54089   **Sgt**   **Pilot**   **British**   **266 and 222 Squadrons**

Joined 266 Squadron at Wittering on September 16 1940. Breeze was posted to 222 Squadron at Hornchurch on October 1. In Spitfire N 3164 he was damaged in combat on November 8 and landed at Martlesham Heath. As he took off again the aircraft caught fire and crashed and burned out at Oakley Poultry Farm, Mundersley Heath. He escaped unhurt.

Breeze was commissioned in September 1943 and killed on January 28 1945, serving with 151 Repair Unit (Aircraft). He is buried in Calais Southern Cemetery, France.

PO 3.9.43   *FO 3.3.44*

VACLAV BREJCHA

787506   **Sgt**   **Pilot**   **Czechoslovakian**   **43 Squadron**

Nothing is known of his service with 43. He was killed on June 19 1941, serving with 257 Squadron. Brejcha was 26 and is buried in Scottow Cemetery, Norfolk.

JACK STEPHEN BRENNAN

391875   **Sgt**   **Air Gunner**   **New Zealander**   **23 Squadron**

Brennan was born in Auckland on July 18 1918. He volunteered for aircrew duties in September 1939 and reported for ground training at Weraroa on December 18, moving to Ohakea in mid-January 1940 for gunnery training.

On March 23 Brennan sailed for England in the SS 'Akaroa' and arrived at Tilbury on May 9. He was posted to 5 OTU, firstly at Chivenor and then Aston Down. Brennan joined 23 Squadron at Collyweston on July 6.

In the late evening of August 21 1940, whilst on flarepath duty, Brennan was struck by a Blenheim coming in to land and killed. He is buried in Wittering churchyard, Lincolnshire.

COLIN PETER NOEL BRETT

39850   **FO**   **Pilot**   **British**   **17 Squadron**

Joined the RAF in April 1937. Posted to 7 FTS, Peterborough on July 17 and after training joined 29 Squadron at Debden on February 19 1938.

Brett was posted from 29 to 17 Squadron at Debden on July 12 1940. He was posted away on August 16 1940 and released from the RAF in 1945, as a Flight Lieutenant.

APO 5.7.37   *PO 31.5.38*   *FO 31.1.40*   *FL 31.1.41*

JOHN BREWSTER

90995   **PO**   **Pilot**   **British**   **615 and 616 Squadrons**

Brewster, of Winsleyhurst, Yorkshire, joined the AuxAF before the war and was called to full-time service on August 24 1939. He was posted to 615 Squadron at Kenley in May 1940. On July 1 he shared in destroying a He 111.

Later in July Brewster went to 616 Squadron at Leconfield. He claimed a Bf 109 on September 1 and on November 5 crashed in a Spitfire at Kirton-in-Lindsey, landing in adverse weather conditions and poor visibility. He was unhurt.

Brewster was killed on April 6 1941, serving with 118 Squadron at Filton. He was 25 and is buried in St Giles' churchyard extension, Stanton St Quintin, Wiltshire.

APO 24.8.39   *PO 6.4.40*   *FO 3.12.40*

YVES BRIERE

30500   **Adjutant**   **Pilot**   **French**   **232 Squadron**

Joined 232 Squadron at Castletown on September 14 1940. In early 1941 Briere was posted to 615 Squadron at Kenley. He was killed on May 13 1941, when his plane crashed into the sea and he went down with it.

CARL E BRIESE

C 1591   **FO**   **Pilot**   **Canadian**   **1 (RCAF) Squadron**

Briese, of New Westminster, joined the RCAF on August 22 1935. He arrived in the United Kingdom with 1 (RCAF) Squadron on June 20 1940.

CE Briese (continued)

Repatriated to Canada in 1942, Briese was given command of 128 (RCAF) Squadron at Sydney, Nova Scotia on August 27, using Hurricanes on East Coast air defence. He was posted away on April 18 1943.

Briese retired from the RCAF on August 20 1962, as a Wing Commander. He died in Canada on November 20 1983.

DENNIS RUSHWORTH BRIGGS

580535 **Sgt** **Observer** **British** **236 Squadron**

A pre-war airman from Bradford, Yorkshire, Briggs joined 236 Squadron on July 24 1940. He failed to return from a reconnaissance sortie over Brest on December 21 1940. He was 24 and is buried with the other two members of his crew in Bayeux War Cemetery, France.

MICHAEL FEATHERSTONE BRIGGS

86346 **PO** **Pilot** **British** **234 Squadron**

Briggs, of Cookham, Berkshire, was educated at Oundle School, Liverpool. He joined the Test Section of the Fairey Aviation Company in 1939 and volunteered for the RAF at the outbreak of war.

On October 6 1940 Briggs joined 234 Squadron at St Eval and on November 4 was posted to 41 Squadron at Hornchurch. He was killed in a flying accident, in Spitfire P 8049, at Washington, near Richmond, Yorkshire on April 2 1941, aged 20. He is buried in Cookham Cemetery.

PO 21.9.40

VERNON MAXWELL BRIGHT

41240 **FO** **Pilot** **British** **229 Squadron**

Joined the RAF in August 1938 and went to 229 Squadron at Digby at its reformation on October 6 1939.

Over Dunkirk on May 29 1940 Bright destroyed a Bf 109 and two days later he claimed a probable Bf 110. On September 11 he claimed a Bf 109, on the 15th he shared a He 111 and on the 27th another He 111 and a shared Ju 88.

Bright was killed on September 24 1942, as a Squadron Leader. The unit he was with is not known. He was 26 and was cremated at Southampton Crematorium.

APO 29.10.38   PO 29.8.39   FO 3.9.40   FL 3.9.41

GEORGE WILLIAM BRIMBLE

745431 **Sgt** **Pilot** **British** **242 Squadron**

Brimble, from Ward End, Birmingham, joined 242 Squadron at Coltishall in late June 1940. On August 30 he claimed a Bf 110 destroyed and on September 18 a Do 17.

On November 6 Brimble was posted to 73 Squadron and immediately embarked on the carrier HMS 'Furious'. The squadron was destined for the Middle East and flew off on November 29 to Takoradi. It then flew in a series of hops to Heliopolis. On one of the later legs of the journey Brimble was killed in a flying accident on December 1 1940. He is buried in Khartoum War Cemetery, Sudan.

JOHN JOSEPH BRIMBLE

741563 **Sgt** **Pilot** **British** **73 Squadron**

Brimble, of Knowle, Bristol, served with 73 Squadron in France in May and June 1940.

He was shot down in combat over the Tonbridge area and killed on September 14 1940, aged 23. His Hurricane, P 2542, crashed at Parkhouse Farm, Chart Sutton.

Brimble's name appeared on the Runnymede Memorial, Panel 12 as having no known grave but when his aircraft was excavated on September 14 1980 Brimble's remains were still in the cockpit. He was buried with full military honours in Brookwood Cemetery on October 16 1980.

FRANCIS NOEL BRINSDEN

40338 **FO** **Pilot** **New Zealander** **19 Squadron**

Born in Auckland on March 27 1919, Brinsden was educated at Takapuna Grammar School and after leaving he worked as a bank clerk. He applied for a short service commission in 1937, was provisionally accepted and sailed for England in the RMS 'Arawa' in mid-August.

Brinsden did his elementary flying at 7 E&RFTS, Desford. In mid-December he was posted to 3 FTS, South Cerney and on July 9 1938 he joined 19 Squadron at Duxford. Over Dunkirk on May 26 1940 Brinsden destroyed a Ju 87 and shared another.

On August 31 Brinsden was late taking off. Trying to catch up with the squadron, he met a Bf 110 head-on at 22000 feet. The German pilot fired first and the Spitfire, R 6958, went into a dive. Brinsden baled out at 5000 feet and landed unhurt. On September 9 he shared a probable He 111.

In October 1940 Brinsden was posted to 303 Squadron at Leconfield, as RAF Liaison Officer. He returned to operations on March 26 1941, when he joined the newly-formed 485 Squadron at Driffield, as a Flight Commander. He went to the MSFU at Speke on July 22 as Port Loading Officer.

Brinsden took command of 3 ADU at High Ercall in mid-August 1942. He was posted to 54 OTU, Charter Hall in February 1943 for a night-fighting conversion course, after which he joined 25 Squadron at Church Fenton.

On August 17 1943 Brinsden was captain of a Mosquito supporting bombers raiding Peenemünde. He decided to bomb Sylt airfield and successfully attacked the hangars at rooftop height. He was then picked up and blinded by searchlights. With vision almost lost he headed out to sea but struck the surface of the water and broke both airscrews. Brinsden ditched the aircraft, he and the navigator got into their dinghy and attempted to sail out of the bay under an offshore breeze. Dawn brought a wind change and at mid-day on the 18th they were blown ashore into the arms of German troops, who had been watching them for six hours.

Eventually Brinsden found himself in Stalag Luft III. He was released on May 9 1945, went on a pilot refresher course and then took command of No 3 Missing Research and Enquiry Unit, tracing Allied aircrew. After a leave in New Zealand in March 1947 Brinsden was given a Permanent Commission in June.

He served in a number of ground and flying appointments before his retirement on December 31 1966. He later went to live in Western Australia.

APO 30.11.37   PO 27.9.38   FO 27.3.40   FL 27.3.41
SL 1.6.42   SL 1.8.47   WC 1.1.54

ALLAN WALTER NAYLOR BRITTON

72033 **FO** **Pilot** **British** **263 Squadron**

A Cambridge Honours graduate from Wallasey, Cheshire, Britton was commissioned in the RAFVR in November 1937.

He was called up in September 1939 and was with 263 Squadron at Grangemouth at the beginning of the Battle of Britain. Britton was killed on December 12 1940, when his Whirlwind crashed into the sea off Burnham. He was 23 and is remembered on the Runnymede Memorial, Panel 5.

PO (RAFVR) 23.11.37   PO 25.5.39   FO 3.12.39

HENRY WILFRED ARTHUR BRITTON

42458   PO   Pilot   British   17 Squadron

The son of a Major in the Royals Corps of Signals, Britton joined the RAF on a short service commission in May 1939 and after completing his training he was posted to 17 Squadron at Martlesham Heath in March 1940.

Britton was killed on August 6 1940, when his Hurricane, N 2456, crashed and burned out in Debden Park shortly after take-off on a routine air test, from an unknown cause. He was 19 years old and is buried in All Saints' churchyard, Wimbish, Essex.

APO 8.8.39   PO 24.2.40

HARRY BROADHURST

24035   WC   Pilot   British   1 Squadron

Born on October 28 1905 at Frimley, Surrey, Broadhurst joined the Army and was commissioned as a 2nd lieutenant in the Royal Artillery. In 1926 he transferred to the RAF and on October 1 was posted to 11 Squadron at Netheravon, under instruction. The squadron went out to India and Broadhurst received a Mention in Despatches for service on the North-West Frontier.

Back in Britain he was posted to 41 Squadron at Northolt on September 16 1931. Broadhurst went to RAF Calshot, under instruction, on September 18 1933, moved to 19 Squadron at Duxford on November 26 and was awarded the AFC (1.2.37). He was appointed to the Personnel Staff of 2 (Bomber) Group at Andover on September 2 1937, leaving there on January 24 1938 for a course at RAF Staff College, Andover.

In January 1939 Broadhurst took command of 111 Squadron at Northolt. He was awarded the DFC (2.1.40) for taking off alone in very bad weather conditions to intercept an approaching enemy aircraft. He found it and attacked, causing it to dive into cloud very close to sea level, so close that he almost went into the sea himself.

Broadhurst left 111 in January 1940. During the Battle of Britain he flew operational sorties with No 1 Squadron, thus qualifying for the clasp.

On December 23 1940 Broadhurst took command of RAF Hornchurch and apart from a few weeks in October/November 1941 he held it until May 1942. He was awarded the DSO (4.7.41) and a Bar (19.12.41), the citation for the latter crediting him with twelve enemy aircraft destroyed and probably another four. Broadhurst flew during the Dieppe Raid on August 19 1942, spending some eight hours in the area, during which time he destroyed an enemy fighter. For this day's work he was awarded a Bar to the DFC (29.9.42).

Posted to the Middle East as SASO to AOC Western Desert in late 1942 Broadhurst took over as AOC Allied Air Forces, Western Desert in 1943. He commanded 83 Group Allied Expeditionary Air Force in 1944-45.

Broadhurst retired from the RAF on March 1 1961, as an Air Chief Marshal, after a most distinguished career spanning thirty-five years. As well as his gallantry awards he was a GCB (1960)(KCB 1955, CB 1944), KBE (1945), Knight Grand Cross of Order of Orange Nassau, Legion of Merit (US). Broadhurst's portrait was painted by Captain Cuthbert Orde in 1941.

PO 1.10.26   FO 1.4.28   FL 1.6.32   SL 1.6.37
WC 1.6.40   GC 1.6.42   AC 31.1.44   AC 1.7.47
AVM 1.7.49   AM 1.1.54   ACM 14.2.57

JOHN WILLIAM BROADHURST

41898   PO   Pilot   British   222 Squadron

Broadhurst, from Crayford, joined the RAF in January 1939. He did his elementary flying at 11 E&RFTS, Scone and in April went to 2 FTS, Brize Norton. He was posted to 222 Squadron at its reformation at Duxford on October 5 1939.

Initially equipped with Blenheims, the squadron received Spitfires in March 1940. On May 29, after a patrol over Dunkirk, Broadhurst failed to find Hornchurch in bad visibility, ran out of fuel and crash-landed.

On August 31 Broadhurst claimed a Bf 109 destroyed, on September 4 a Bf 109 and two more on the 7th and 27th. He was shot down on October 7 1940 during an attack on enemy bombers. He baled out but fell dead at Longhurst. His Spitfire, P 9469, crashed and burned out at Baileys Reed Farm, Hurst Green, Salehurst. Broadhurst was 23 years old. He is buried in Hornchurch Cemetery, Essex.

APO 15.4.39   PO 6.11.39

RICHARD EDGAR PETER BROOKER

39931   FO   Pilot   British   56 Squadron

A school master from Willingdon, Sussex, Brooker joined the RAF in April 1937. On July 17 he was posted to 9 FTS, Hullavington and joined 56 Squadron at North Weald on February 19 1938.

On July 13 1940 Brooker claimed a Ju 87 destroyed and on August 21 a Do 17. In this engagement he was shot down by return fire but was only slightly injured when he forced-landed at Flowton Brook, Bramford. His Hurricane, P 3153, burned out.

In late 1940 Brooker was posted to CGS, Sutton Bridge, as an instructor. He took command of No 1 Squadron in late April 1941. On May 10 he shot down a He 111 over London at night and attacked three more bombers on the same sortie. He was awarded the DFC (30.5.41) and destroyed a Bf 109 on June 21.

Brooker was posted to the Far East on November 3 1941. He took command of 232 Squadron at Singapore on January 20 1942 after the CO was killed. On February 1 the squadron withdrew to Palembang, later in the month evacuating to Java, where it combined with 242. When the last Hurricane was destroyed Brooker and some pilots flew in a Lodestar to Australia. He was awarded a Bar to the DFC (27.3.42)

Brooker was on operations in Europe in 1944 and was awarded the DSO (1.12.44). In January 1945 he was appointed Wing Leader 122 Wing, Volkel. On April 16 1945 Brooker was leading 486 Squadron on a Wing operation, when he was shot down and killed. He was awarded a Bar to the DSO (12.2.46), which was given with effect from the day before his death.

Brooker is remembered on the Runnymede Memorial, Panel 264.

APO 12.7.37   PO 5.4.38   FO 5.1.40   FL 5.1.41
SL 1.3.42

RICHARD WALLER BROOKMAN

NZ 40186   Sgt   Observer   New Zealander   235 Sqdn

Born at Waitara on November 24 1912, Brookman was educated at New Plymouth Boys' High School and Wellington College. A commercial traveller, Brookman volunteered for aircrew duties at the end of September 1939 and was accepted as a trainee observer. He completed the ground course at Weraroa and flying training at the Air Observers' School, Ohakea.

Brookman sailed for the United Kingdom in the RMS 'Rangitata' on June 6 1940. Soon after arrival he was posted to 17 OTU, Upwood and on October 2 he joined 106 (Bomber) Squadron at Finningley but after ten days was sent to 235 Squadron at Bircham Newton.

On February 22 1941 Brookman was in a Blenheim on a patrol over the coast of Denmark. After attacking an enemy aircraft thirty miles west of Borkum the Blenheim was seen to crash into the sea and the crew were reported 'Missing'. Brookman is remembered on the Runnymede Memorial, Panel 63.

PHILIP WILLIAM BROOM

50924   Sgt   Aircrew   British   25 Squadron

Broom was with 25 Squadron at Martlesham Heath in early July 1940. He was promoted to Warrant Officer on March 1 1942, commissioned in December 1942 and released from the RAF in 1949, as a Flight Lieutenant.

PO 15.12.42   FO 15.6.43   FL 15.12.44   FL 16.6.46

PETER MALAM BROTHERS

37668   FL   Pilot   British   32 and 257 Squadrons

Brothers was born in Westerham, Kent, on September 30 1917. He learned to fly at 16 and joined the RAF in January 1936. He was posted to 9 FTS, Thornaby on April 4 and joined 32 Squadron at Biggin Hill on October 11 1936, becoming a Flight Commander in late 1938.

Still with the squadron in 1940 Brothers claimed a Bf 109 on May 19, a Bf 110 on the 23rd, a Bf 109 on July 19, another on the 20th, a Bf 110 on August 16, a Do 215 and a Bf 109 on the 18th and another Bf 109 on the 24th. He was posted to 257 Squadron at Debden on September 9, as a Flight Commander, and on the 15th destroyed two Do 17s. He was awarded the DFC (13.9.40) and posted to 52 OTU in January 1941.

Brothers was posted to Baginton in June 1941 to form 457 Squadron, with Australian pilots and RAF ground crews. On March 26 1942 he claimed a Bf 109 destroyed and on April 29 a probable FW 190. He took command of 602 Squadron at Redhill in June 1942 and on August 18 destroyed a FW 190.

In October 1942 Brothers was appointed Wing Leader at Tangmere. He was awarded a Bar to the DFC (15.6.43), posted to 61 OTU on July 29 and to a staff job at HQ 10 Group on November 22. He went back on operations in April 1944, when he was appointed Wing Leader at Exeter, later commanding the Wings at Milfield and Culmhead.

In October 1944 Brothers was posted away and awarded the DSO (3.11.44). He went to Fort Leavenworth, Kansas for a course at the Command and General Staff School. After returning to Britain he was posted to the Central Fighter Establishment, where he stayed until leaving the RAF in March 1947.

Brothers joined the Colonial Service and served in Kenya until 1949, when he rejoined the RAF. He held a number of appointments and commands before retiring on April 4 1973, as an Air Commodore. He was made a CBE in 1964.

APO 23.3.36   PO 27.1.37   FO 27.10.38   FL 3.9.40
SL 1.12.41   WC 1.7.45   SL 5.8.46   WC 1.1.53
GC 1.1.59   AC 1.7.66

ARCHIBALD WILKINSON BROWN

78744   PO   Air Gunner   British   25 Squadron

Brown was commissioned as an air gunner in April 1940 and posted to 25 Squadron at North Weald.

On September 14 1940 he was flying with Pilot Officer MJ Herrick in a night sortie over London. They intercepted and shot down a He 111. It crashed at Newmans End, near Sheering, Essex.

Brown was released from the RAF in 1945, as a Flight Lieutenant.

APO 12.4.40   PO 1.6.40   FO 1.6.41   FL 1.6.42

BERNARD WALTER BROWN

41548   PO   Pilot   New Zealander   610 and 72 Sqdns

Born at Stratford on December 6 1917, Brown was educated at Stratford Technical High School and after leaving he worked for the Post Office. He applied for a short service commission in February 1938, was provisionally accepted and sailed for England on September 22 in the RMS 'Rangitane'.

Brown began his training at 5 E&RFTS, Hanworth and in late January 1939 he was posted to 5 FTS, Sealand. At the end of August he went to No 1 School of Army Co-operation at Old Sarum for a course on Lysanders and then joined 613 Squadron at Odiham.

In May 1940 the squadron was made operational and moved to Hawkinge. On the 26th Brown was flying one of six Hectors detailed to dive-bomb gun emplacements near Calais. En route he test-fired his forward gun but the omission of a split pin caused the muzzle attachment to fly off, penetrate the fuselage and hole the main fuel tank. Brown jettisoned his two bombs and turned back, making a forced-landing on Herne Bay golf course.

He volunteered for Fighter Command in August 1940 and after converting to Spitfires joined 610 Squadron at Biggin Hill later in the month. On September 20 he went to 72 Squadron. Three days later he was shot down by a Bf 109 over Gravesend. Wounded, with no control over the aircraft, Brown baled out and landed on marshy ground near Eastchurch.

Returning to active duty in early 1941, Brown was sent to Montrose for an instructor's course, after which he was posted to Rhodesia, subsequently instructing at Cumalo, near Bulawayo.

Brown returned to England in early 1943 and did a Transport Command course at Bramcote. He became a ferry pilot flying between the United Kingdom and the Middle East. On January 1 1944 he transferred to the RNZAF and at the end of the year was flying Halifaxes. He was released in 1945 to be a first officer on Dakotas with BOAC.

Brown later joined BEA and flew with the airline until his retirement in 1972. He then returned to New Zealand to live.

APO 13.1.39   PO 15.11.39   FO 15.11.40   FL 15.11.41

CHARLES WALTER DRYBURGH BROWN

902211   Sgt   Air Gunner   British   236 Squadron

Brown, of Ightham Common, Kent, joined 236 Squadron in 1940. He was posted away in early 1941 and killed on June 30 1941, as a Flight Sergeant with 7 Squadron, aged 29.

Brown is buried in Becklingen War Cemetery, Soltau, Germany.

CYRIL BOB BROWN

109525   Sgt   Pilot   British   245 Squadron

Brown, who was born on January 17 1921, joined the RAFVR in May 1939 and did his elementary flying at 34 E&RFTS, Rochford. Called up at the outbreak of war, Brown completed his training at 11 FTS, Shawbury and 17 FTS, Cranwell and then joined 245 Squadron at Aldergrove in September 1940.

Brown was posted to 253 at Kenley in November 1940. He was commissioned in October 1941 and in early 1942 joined 616 Squadron at King's Cliff. On May 25 1942 Brown attacked a Do 17 over Leicester. Return fire shattered his hood and a splinter of perspex entered his right eye. He managed to land at North Luffenham. The eye was removed and Brown went back to 616 to continue his tour. He was checked in a dual trainer and then soloed in a Spitfire, staying on operations due to the intercession of Basil Embry.

Brown was later posted to 532 Turbinlite Havoc Squadron at Wittering. In 1943 he became a test pilot at the Aircraft and Armament Experimental Establishment at Boscombe Down. He was awarded the AFC (1.1.46). In late 1946 he went on a course at the Empire Test Pilots' School at Cranfield, after which he returned to Boscombe Down. In 1948 he was appointed as a tutor at the Empire Test Pilots' School.

Brown held a number of appointments and commands, including 220 (Maritime Reconnaissance) Squadron in 1954-56, before he retired on January 17 1972, as an Air Commodore. He was made a CBE in 1966.

PO 11.10.41   FO 11.10.42   FL 11.10.43   Sl 1.7.50
WC 1.7.56   GC 1.7.60   AC 1.1.67

De PEYSTER BROWN

C 1094   PO   Pilot   American   1 (RCAF) Squadron

Joined the RCAF on September 9 1939. Brown was posted to No 1 (RCAF) Squadron at Northolt on August 30 1940. On September 27 he claimed a Do 215 destroyed and shared a Ju 88.

Brown was transferred to the USAAF on May 25 1942.

FREDERICK SYDNEY BROWN

46784   F/Sgt   Pilot   British   79 Squadron

Brown, who was born on November 27 1912, joined the RAF as an aircraft apprentice and later volunteered for pilot training. He was with 79 Squadron at the outbreak of war.

On February 24 1940 he shared in shooting down a Do 17 over Hawkinge, which crashed into the Channel. On July 4 he damaged a Do 17.

Brown was commissioned in September 1941, from Warrant Officer, and retired on December 9 1946, as a Flight Lieutenant. He died on December 14 1956.

PO 30.9.41   FO 30.9.42   FL 30.9.43

GEORGE ALFRED BROWN

39851   FO   Pilot   British   253 Squadron

Born in India on July 6 1912, Brown joined the RAF on a short service commission in April 1937. After elementary flying at 13 E&RFTS, White Waltham he was posted to 5 FTS, Sealand on July 17 1937. On completion of his course Brown went to SHQ Duxford. He joined 66 Squadron there on January 30 1939.

Brown was posted to 253 Squadron at Kirton-in-Lindsey in May 1940. He forced-landed near Maidstone on August 30 in Hurricane P 3802, following combat with Bf 109s. Admitted to Preston Hall

Hospital, wounded in the shoulder and with shell splinters in the legs, he rejoined the squadron after two weeks.

In October 1940 Brown was posted to 71 (Eagle) Squadron, then being formed at Church Fenton, as 'A' Flight Commander. He was posted away on August 1 1941 to command 133 (Eagle) Squadron, then forming at Coltishall. In November 1941 he went to a staff job at HQ Fighter Command and was awarded the DFC (26.12.41).

Brown was posted later to 55 OTU, Annan as CFI. He was on the staff at HQ Eastern Mediterranean at Alexandria, commanded RAF Gaza and in 1945 commanded RAF Nicosia. He retired from the RAF on July 6 1962, as a Group Captain. From 1962 to 1967 he was Regional Liaison Officer, ATC, Wales and from 1967 to 1977 he was Commandant, ATC, Wales.

APO 5.7.37   PO 10.5.38   FO 10.12.39   FL 10.12.40
SL 1.3.42   WC 1.10.46   GC 1.7.53

JAMES WOOD BROWN

144933   Sgt   Pilot   British   600 Squadron

Brown, of Broadmayne, Dorset, joined 600 Squadron at Northolt on July 10 1940.

Commissioned in May 1943, Brown was killed on November 22 1943, as a Pilot Officer with 158 Squadron, operating in Halifaxes from Lissett, Yorkshire. He was 28 years old and is buried in Reichswald Forest War Cemetery, Cleves, Germany.

PO 26.5.43

MARK HENRY BROWN

37904   FL   Pilot   Canadian   1 Squadron

Brown was born on October 9 1911 at Portage la Prairie, Manitoba. He joined the RAF in May 1936 and went to 9 FTS, Thornaby on July 18, after which he joined No 1 Squadron at Tangmere on February 21 1937.

Brown went to France with the squadron following the outbreak of war. On November 23 1939 he shared in destroying a Do 17, on March 3 1940 he shared a He 111, on April 20 probably destroyed a Bf 109, on May 10 shared a Do 17, on the 11th two Bf 110s, on the 12th two Bf 109s, on the 14th a Bf 109 and a Ju 87, on the 15th a Bf 110, on the 17th a Bf 110 and a He 111, on the 18th a Hs 126, on the 19th a He 111, on the 21st a He 111, on June 4 a Do 17 and on June 14 a He 111 and a Bf 109. Brown was shot down on June 15 and baled out over France. He managed to get a lift to Brest and then got a boat to Southampton. The squadron pilots flew their Hurricanes to Tangmere on the 18th and Brown arrived there that evening. For his efforts in France he was awarded the DFC (30.7.40)

No 1 was fully operational again by the end of July. On August 11 Brown claimed a Bf 110 destroyed. Four days later he was shot down and baled out, slightly injured, into the sea and was rescued by a trawler. On October 24 he shared a Do 17.

Brown took command of the squadron on November 10 1940, when the CO was killed in a flying accident. At the end of April 1941 Brown was promoted and posted to 58 OTU, Grangemouth, as Squadron Leader Flying. Promoted again on July 1 he went to 57 OTU, Hawarden, as CO Training Wing. He was awarded a Bar to the DFC (23.5.41).

In late October 1941 Brown was posted to Malta, as Wing Commander Flying. On November 12 he was leading 249 Squadron over Sicily. Heavy flak was encountered and he was last seen gliding down. On the night of December 6 the Italians dropped a note saying that Brown had crashed and been killed and that he was buried with military honours.

APO 6.7.36   PO 11.5.37   FO 11.12.38   FL 3.9.40

MARVIN KITCHENER BROWN

42101   PO   Pilot   Canadian   242 Squadron

Brown, of Kincardine, Ontario, joined the RAF in March 1939. He was posted to 242 Squadron on November 6 at Church Fenton, shortly after its reformation. On May 16 1940 Brown was sent to France and attached to 85 Squadron. Two days later he was shot down and suffered bullet wounds in his right leg. He was evacuated to England and rejoined 242 on July 13.

Brown was on a local flight in Hurricane N 2476 on February 21 1941, when he crashed at Grange Farm, Alderton and was killed. He is buried in Ipswich Cemetery.

APO 13.5.39   PO 6.11.39

MAURICE PETER BROWN

40796   FO   Pilot   British   611 and 41 Squadrons

Joined the RAF in March 1938. Brown was with 611 Squadron in July 1940. He shared in destroying a Do 17 on August 21.

Brown was posted to 41 Squadron at Hornchurch on September 29 and he claimed a Bf 109 shot down on October 20.

Awarded the AFC (1.1.46), Brown was released from the RAF in 1946, as a Squadron Leader.

APO 4.6.38   PO 4.4.39   FO 3.9.40   FL 3.9.41
SL 1.1.44

PETER GEORGE FLEMING BROWN

120926   Sgt   Pilot   British   234 Squadron

Brown, of Pershore, Worcestershire, joined 234 Squadron at Middle Wallop on September 11 1940.

Commissioned in March 1942, he died on April 18 1944 of injuries sustained in a flying accident, whilst serving as a Flight Lieutenant with 54 Squadron at Night Cliff, Darwin.

Brown was 22. He is buried in the Adelaide River War Cemetery, Northern Territory, Australia.

PO 13.3.42   FO 1.10.42   FL 5.7.43

ROBERT SYDNEY BROWN

1003565   AC 2   Radar Operator   British   604 Squadron

Brown, who was born on October 2 1915, joined the RAF in early June 1940 and after initial training volunteered for flying duties. At the end of June he went to Yatesbury for a short course on airborne radar and on July 20 was posted to 604 Squadron at Gravesend, never having flown.

On the night of November 1 Brown was in a Blenheim on a fighter patrol. The aircraft went out of control and he and the air gunner were ordered to bale out, which they did and landed safely. The pilot regained control of the Blenheim and returned to Middle Wallop.

Brown flew operationally with 604, firstly in Blenheims and then Beaufighters, until December 1940, when he was posted back to Yatesbury for another radar course. In these five months he flew without rank or brevet, receiving three shillings a day, which included one shilling flying pay.

After completing the radar mechanic course and gaining practical experience Brown was attached to RAE, Farnborough, where he remained, until his release in February 1946.

RONALD CLIFFORD BROWN

41822   FO   Pilot   British   229 Squadron

Brown joined the RAF in January 1939. He was posted to 229 Squadron at Digby, when it reformed there on October 6 1939. Over Dunkirk on May 29 1940 Brown claimed a Bf 109 destroyed and another on October 15.

He was released from the RAF in 1945, as a Squadron Leader. He died on March 19 1988.

APO 1.4.39   PO 23.10.39
FO 23.10.40   FL 23.10.41

RONALD JOHN WALKER BROWN

44925   PO   Pilot   British   111 Squadron

Born on March 9 1914, Brown joined the RAF as an aircraft apprentice at Halton in September 1929. After an Engine Fitter course he was posted to the Flying Wing of RAF College, Cranwell, as an AC1, and received many 'unofficial' hours dual training on Tutor and Atlas aircraft there. He volunteered for pilot training and was selected in late 1935.

In December 1935 Brown was posted to 10 (Bomber) Squadron, Boscombe Down, solely on the strength of his soccer prowess as an RAF football representative. He was posted to 9 E&RFTS, Ansty in May 1936, then to 9 FTS, Thornaby in July and received his wings in November. He joined 111 Squadron at Northolt in February 1937. The squadron was the first to be equipped with Hurricanes, in December 1938, and was used a great deal in tactical trials.

In May 1940 it carried out daily patrols from French airfields, returning to Northolt in the evening. On May 31 over Dunkirk Brown got a probable Bf 109. On June 6 he was shot down by a Bf 109, when escorting Blenheims in the Abbeville area. He baled out and luckily was picked up by a Guards unit moving south, taken to a field hospital, put on a train and then sent in a hospital ship back to England. Brown rejoined the squadron on August 15 1940. Three days later he shared a Do 17, which crashed and burned out at Leaves Green, near Biggin Hill.

Brown was commissioned in September, but it was back-dated to April. He was posted to 260 Squadron at Castletown on December 7 1940 to train new pilots. On February 2 1941 he went to the AFDU at Duxford, where he flew many types of enemy and American aircraft. In October 1941 he was posted to the Ministry of Aircraft Production and transferred to the RAF Engineering Branch, closely involved with aircraft development and later the Martin Baker ejector seat.

Brown retired from the RAF on May 12 1947, as a Squadron Leader, retaining the rank of Wing Commander. He joined Percival Aircraft as Technical Sales Manager. In 1962 he moved to BAC and he retired from British Aerospace in April 1979 as Executive Director (Marketing and Sales). He was made an MBE for services to exports.

PO 25.4.40   FO 25.4.41   FL 25.4.42   SL 22.4.45
SL 1.7.45

CHARLES BROWNE

127561   Sgt   Air Gunner   British   219 Squadron

Joined the RAF on September 8 1939. Browne went to 3 BGS, Aldergrove on January 8 1940. On completion of a gunnery course he joined 235 Squadron on February 25.

Browne was posted to 219 Squadron at Catterick on May 23 1940. He crash-landed in a Blenheim on August 2, baled out of another on October 19 when ordered to do so by the pilot, who later successfully made a crash-landing, and on December 12 he crash-landed in a Beaufighter.

He was posted to 77 Squadron on June 3 1941, flying in Whitleys from Topcliffe, Yorkshire. Browne left the squadron on August 21 and was graded medically unfit for flying in January 1942. He was commissioned in the RAF Regiment in August 1942 and posted to the Middle East. He was released on October 26 1945, as a Flying Officer.

PO 28.8.42   FO 28.8.43

DENNIS OWEN MATTHEW BROWNE

41234   PO   Pilot   British   1 Squadron

Browne, of Portslade-by-Sea, Sussex, joined the RAF in August 1938 and was with No 1 Squadron in June 1940.

On July 19 his Hurricane, P 3471, was hit in the glycol tank by return fire from a He 111. Although out of ammunition he trailed the enemy aircraft to advise its position. Eventually he forced-landed in flames near Brighton and scrambled out before the fuel tanks blew up. The raider was later shot down by 43 Squadron.

Browne failed to return from an engagement with enemy fighters off Harwich on August 15 1940. His Hurricane, R 4075, is presumed to have crashed into the sea. He was 22 and is remembered on the Runnymede Memorial, Panel 7.

APO 17.10.38   PO 27.6.39

DAVID CAMPBELL BRUCE

39853   FO   Pilot   British   111 Squadron

Joined the RAF in May 1937. On July 17 Bruce was posted to 5 FTS, Sealand and on February 19 1938 he joined 111 Squadron at Northolt.

On April 8 1940 Bruce shared in probably destroying a He 111. Over Dunkirk on May 18 he got a Bf 109, on May 31 and June 2 he damaged Bf 109s and on June 11 he destroyed two Bf 109s and a Ju 88.

Promoted to Acting Flight Lieutenant on August 24, Bruce took command of 'A' Flight. The next day he claimed a Bf 110 and on September 2 he shared a He 111. Bruce was reported 'Missing' on September 4 after being shot down by Bf 109s. His Hurricane, R 4172, is believed to have crashed into the Channel five miles east of Folkestone. He was 22 years old and is remembered on the Runnymede Memorial, Panel 4.

APO 5.7.37   PO 10.5.38   FO 10.12.39

NORMAN BRUMBY

742228   Sgt   Pilot   British   615 and 607 Squadrons

Born in Kingston-upon-Hull, Brumby was educated at Boulevard Secondary School. He joined the RAFVR in 1938 and was called up at the outbreak of war.

Posted to 615 Squadron at Prestwick on September 4 1940, Brumby moved to 607 Squadron at Tangmere on the 21st. He was shot down in combat with Bf 110s over the Isle of Wight on October 1 and killed.

Brumby was 22. He is buried in Hull Northern Cemetery, Yorkshire.

GEOFFREY CLIFFORD BRUNNER

43941   PO   Pilot   British   43 Squadron

Born on April 7 1911, Brunner began his flying training at 2 FTS, Digby in July 1932 and joined 17 Squadron at Upavon in August 1933, as a Sergeant-Pilot.

In November 1936 Brunner went to 66 Squadron at Duxford. He took part in the Hendon Air Displays in 1935, 1936 and 1937 in converging dive-bombing, attack on a set-piece and formation aerobatics with smoke. In October 1937 Brunner was appointed a test pilot in the Performance Testing Section at the Aircraft and Armament Experimental Establishment, then at Martlesham Heath but from September 1939 at Boscombe Down.

Commissioned in May 1940, Brunner was posted to 6 OTU, Sutton Bridge on June 6. Four days later he joined 43 Squadron at Tangmere. On July 7 he damaged a Do 17 in a low-level chase across the Channel, until his ammunition was exhausted. Brunner was taken off operational flying on July 10 pending a posting back to the A&AEE but when it did not come he returned to operations on August 24.

Two days later 43 was deployed against a large raid on Portsmouth. After probably destroying a He 111 Brunner was hit and badly damaged by a Bf 109. Wounded in the ankle, he made a wheels-up landing at Tangmere and was admitted to the Royal West Sussex Hospital at Brighton.

Brunner returned to Boscombe Down on December 1 1940. He was awarded the AFC (1.1.42) and Bar (21.7.43), the latter for successfully landing the prototype Westland Welkin after engine and structural failure whilst on a test flight.

On January 8 1945 Brunner went to RAF Staff College. He transferred to the Aircraft Control Branch in September 1945. He retired on July 1 1966, as a Group Captain.

PO 2.5.40   FO 2.5.41   FL 2.5.42   FL 1.9.45
SL 1.7.49   WC 1.1.58   GC 1.7.63

LEOFRIC TREVOR BRYANT-FENN

40985   FO   Pilot   British   79 Squadron

Bryant-Fenn was born on April 9 1917 and began flying training with the RAF in June 1938. He was with 79 Squadron in July 1940 and on August 28 shared in the destruction of a He 59 floatplane.

On September 1 his aircraft was severely damaged in combat with Bf 109s over Biggin Hill. Bryant-Fenn baled out, wounded in the leg, landed at Dunton Green and was admitted to Sevenoaks Hospital.

In late 1942 Bryant-Fenn was a Flight Commander with 264 Squadron at Colerne. He was awarded the DFC (3.9.43) at the end of his tour. He stayed in the RAF and retired on October 19 1968, as a Group Captain.

APO 20.8.38   PO 27.6.39   FO 3.9.40   FL 3.9.41
SL 1.1.44   SL 1.8.47   WC 1.8.55   GC 1.1.61

JOHN BRYSON

41823   PO   Pilot   Canadian   92 Squadron

Bryson, from Westmount and formerly of the Royal Canadian Mounted Police, joined the RAF in January 1939. After completing his training at 13 FTS, Drem he joined 92 Squadron, when it was reformed at Tangmere on October 10 1939.

Over Dunkirk on June 2 1940 he damaged a He 111. On July 24 he shared in shooting down a Ju 88, which was bombing shipping in the Bristol Channel. It crashed on Martinhoe Common, near Lynton.

Bryson was shot down and killed by Bf 109s on September 24 1940. His Spitfire, X 4037, crashed and burned out near North Weald. He was 27 and is buried in St Andrew's churchyard, North Weald Bassett, Essex.

APO 1.4.39   PO 21.10.39

STANISLAW BRZEZINA

76782 FL Pilot Polish 74 Squadron

Born in Poland on March 5 1904, Brzezina was in the PAF before the war. He was posted to 5 OTU, Aston Down in July 1940 and joined 74 Squadron at Hornchurch on August 5. On the 13th he shot down a Do 17 and damaged another over the Thames Estuary but was hit by return fire, causing an explosion in the cockpit. Brzezina baled out, unhurt.

He was posted away on September 25 to take joint command of 308 Squadron, then being formed at Baginton. He was awarded the VM (5th Class)(1.2.41). Brzezina took command of 317 Squadron at Colerne in June 1941. On July 10 he destroyed a Bf 109. In August 1941 he was appointed Wing Leader of 2 Polish Wing at Exeter, made up of 302, 316 and 317 Squadrons. He was awarded the KW (10.9.41).

Brzezina went on to a series of staff jobs. On September 19 1945 he was posted to HQ BAFO for liaison duties, as a Group Captain. He was killed in a flying accident en route from Germany to England on February 13 1946. He is buried in St Mary Cray Cemetery, Orpington, Kent.

MICHAL BRZEZOWSKI

PO 5122 Sgt Pilot Polish 303 Squadron

Brzezowski, who was born at Dawidgrodek, Poland on February 26 1920, entered the PAF NCOs Training School at Bydgoszcz in 1936. He qualified as a fighter pilot at Krosno in 1939, was posted to the 5th Air Force Regiment at Lida and joined 151 Fighter Squadron. After the fighting in early September his unit was evacuated to Roumania on the 18th.

After escaping to France Brzezowski eventually reached England on July 7 1940. He went to 5 OTU, Aston Down and joined 303 Squadron at Northolt on August 21. He claimed the destruction of two He 111s on September 11. Four days later Brzezowski failed to return from a combat with Bf 109s over the Thames off Gravesend. His Hurricane, P 3577, is presumed to have crashed in the Estuary. He is remembered on the Polish Air Force Memorial at Northolt. He was awarded the KW (23.12.40).

JACK BUCHANAN

79735 PO Pilot British 29 Squadron

Joined the RAF in 1939 and was posted to 29 Squadron at Digby in June 1940. Buchanan was on an evening patrol on September 28, when his Blenheim's starboard wing was hit by British anti-aircraft fire. He returned safely to Digby.

He was killed on February 15 1941, still with 29 Squadron. Buchanan, who was 23 and came from Sandsend, is buried in Easington Cemetery, Yorkshire.

PO 2.6.40

JAMES RICHEBOURG BUCHANAN

77033 PO Pilot British 609 Squadron

Buchanan, from Iden, Sussex, was a fully-trained RAFVR pilot at the outbreak of war. He was commissioned in December 1939 and joined 609 Squadron at Kinloss on the 26th.

Flying from Drem on February 27 1940 Buchanan shared in destroying a He 111, which was attacking a convoy near St Abb's Head. Over Dunkirk on May 31 he destroyed a Bf 109 and damaged a He 111.

Buchanan was reported 'Missing' after being shot down by Oberleutnant Framm of 1/JG 27 on July 27 1940 in combat over a convoy off Weymouth. His Spitfire, N 3023, crashed into the sea. He was 25 years old and is remembered on the Runnymede Memorial, Panel 7.

PO 10.12.39

MAURICE SIMON HENRI CHARLES BUCHIN

81626 PO Pilot Belgian 213 Squadron

An instructor in the Belgian Air Force, Buchin escaped to France in May 1940 and was employed there in ferrying aircraft. In mid-June he flew to Bayonne and sailed in a Dutch cargo ship for Britain, arriving at Plymouth on June 23. After converting to Hurricanes he joined 213 Squadron at Exeter on July 23.

On August 11 Buchin shot down a Ju 88 off Portland. Four days later he was reported 'Missing' after a combat in the same area. He is remembered on the Runnymede Memorial, Panel 7 and has a memorial grave at the Pelouse d'Honneur Cemetery of Brussels at Evre. He was 34 years old.

JAMES ALAN BUCK

742235 Sgt Pilot British 43 Squadron

A member of the pre-war RAFVR, Buck, of Chorltonville, Manchester, was with 43 Squadron in early 1940. On a patrol over France on June 7 he landed at Rouen-Boos with a burst tyre, but managed to return to Tangmere the next day.

On July 19 Buck was shot down in combat with Bf 109s of III/JG 27 off Selsey. He baled out, wounded, but drowned. His Hurricane, P 3531, crashed into the sea. He was 24 and is buried in Stretford Cemetery, Lancashire.

JOHN STANLEY BUCKNOLE

745402 Sgt Pilot British 54 Squadron

Bucknole was in the RAFVR before the war. He joined 54 Squadron at Catterick on September 29 1940.

In 1941 he was serving with 103 Squadron, flying in Wellingtons from Newton. He failed to return from operations on July 24 1941 and is remembered on the Runnymede Memorial, Panel 40.

GEORGE OLIVER BUDD

90209   FL   Pilot   British   604 Squadron

Born at Reigate in 1911, Budd joined 604 Squadron, AuxAF at Hendon in June 1935. He was called for full-time service on August 24 1939 and continued with the squadron.

In July 1941, with his tour completed, Budd was posted to 54 OTU at Church Fenton, as an instructor. He was awarded the DFC (4.7.41), having then destroyed at least three enemy aircraft at night and damaged a further four.

Budd commanded 1455 Turbinlite Flight at Tangmere from January until August 1942. Thereafter until the end of the war he had a series of staff jobs, including Senior Air Liaison Officer with Anti-Aircraft Command from September 1943 until 1944. He was OC 141 Wing 1944, at HQ 46 Group 1944 to 1945 and at HQ 111 Wing 1945. Budd was released on September 8 1945, as a Wing Commander.

PO (AuxAF) 15.6.35   FO (AuxAF) 11.4.37   FO 24.8.39
FL 12.3.40   SL 1.6.41   WC 1.6.42

JAN BUDZINSKI

780665   Sgt   Pilot   Polish   145 and 605 Squadrons

Budzinski was born in Poland in 1916. He joined 145 Squadron at Westhampnett on August 12 1940. He went to 605 Squadron at Drem on August 31.

The squadron moved south to Croydon in early September and on the 11th Budzinski claimed a Bf 109 destroyed, on the 27th a Bf 110 and on October 7 he shared another Bf 109. He was awarded the KW (1.2.41) and on April 27 1941 he was posted to 302 Squadron at Kenley. He received a Bar to the KW (15.7.41) and on August 8 he went to 2 AOS, Millom as a staff pilot, moving a month later to 2 AGS, Dalcross.

Budzinski was posted to 2 FIS, Montrose on July 28 1942 and at the end of the course went as an instructor to 16 FTS, Newton. He remained there until November 20 1945, when he went to 3 PHU for release, as a Warrant Officer.

CECIL HALFORD BULL

37594   FO   Pilot   British   25 Squadron

Joined the RAF in January 1936 and posted to 3 FTS, Grantham on March 2 1936. After completing his training Bull was posted as a staff pilot to No 1 Anti-Aircraft Co-operation Unit at Biggin Hill on April 26 1937. He went on a course to the School of Air Navigation, Manston on November 14 1938.

Bull was with 25 Squadron in early 1940. On August 8 he was killed in a shooting accident whilst on leave.

APO 2.3 36   PO 6.1.37   FO 6.9.38

JOHN CECIL BULL

79227   PO   Air Gunner   British   600 Squadron

Born on April 5 1905, Bull joined 600 Squadron at Manston in June 1940. He stayed in the RAF after the war and transferred to the Secretarial Branch in 1946.

Bull retired on November 19 1962, as a Flight Lieutenant, retaining the rank of Squadron Leader. He went to live in Jamaica and died in 1965.

PO 15.6.40   FO 15.6.41   FL 15.9.42   FL 18.5.46

GEOFFREY GORDON ROBSON BULMER

Sub-Lieutenant (FAA)   Pilot   British   32 Squadron

Born on January 5 1920, Bulmer joined the FAA in July 1939, going to HMS 'President' at Greenwich and later to HMS 'Frobisher' and HMS 'St Vincent'. On October 9 he was posted to HMS 'Pembroke' and did his elementary flying training at 24 E&RFTS, Belfast.

Bulmer went to 7 FTS, Peterborough on December 11 1939, gained his wings there on March 14 1940 and on May 26 was posted

to Eastleigh for a fighter course and deck-landing training. He was one of the naval pilots loaned to the RAF in mid-June 1940. After converting to Hurricanes at 7 OTU, Hawarden Bulmer joined 32 Squadron at Biggin Hill on July 1.

He was shot down by Oberleutnant Priller in combat off Dover on July 20 1940. He baled out into the sea but was drowned. His Hurricane, N 2670, may have crashed at Lydden. Bulmer is remembered on the Fleet Air Arm Memorial at Lee-on-Solent, Bay 1, Panel 3.

Midshipman 1.7.39   Acting Sub-Lt 14.3.40

RONALD FREDERICK BUMSTEAD

53138   Sgt   Pilot   British   29 and 111 Squadrons

Born on August 7 1915 at Goudhurst, Kent, Bumstead entered the RAF in September 1935 as a trainee Rigger (Airframes). He joined 74 Squadron at Hornchurch in September 1936, as an AC 1 Rigger. In February 1937 he was posted to 64 Squadron at Martlesham Heath for flying and ground duties as a Rigger/Air Gunner.

Bumstead applied for pilot training and was selected in May 1938. On August 10 1939 he was posted to 12 E&RFTS, Prestwick and moved to 3 FTS, South Cerney on October 24.

He went to 5 OTU, Aston Down on May 3 1940 and converted to Blenheims, after which he joined 29 Squadron at Debden on June 8. Bumstead moved to 111 Squadron, also at Debden, on August 26 1940. He was posted away to 57 OTU, Hawarden on January 11 1941, as an instructor.

In preparation for a return to operations Bumstead went to 60 (Night Fighter) OTU on June 13 1941 and joined 409 Squadron at Coleby Grange on July 18. Two months later he was posted to 1451 Turbinlite Flight at Hunsdon but on December 9 Bumstead moved to 287 (Army Co-operation) Squadron at Croydon. He was commissioned from Warrant Officer in October 1943 and on December 15 joined 525 Squadron, newly-formed with Warwicks.

Bumstead's last posting was on September 5 1944, to 147 Squadron, being reformed at Croydon for transport duties with Dakotas. He was awarded the AFC (1.1.46), released in June 1946 and joined Sabena Airlines in December. In May 1953 he went as an Inspector of Air Accidents and in June 1955 joined the Goodyear Tyre Company, in the Aviation Division. He died on October 1 1977.

PO 24.10.43   FO 24.1.44   FL 24.7.45

DOUGLAS CAMPBELL BUNCH

115674   Sgt   Radar Operator   British   219 Squadron

Bunch was born on February 1 1920 and he joined 219 Squadron on August 2 1940. Still with 219, Bunch was commissioned in January 1942. Late in the year he teamed up with Flight Lieutenant JE Wilson and they had their first victory, a Do 217, on February 3 1943, destroyed two Do 217s and another probable on March 11 and a Do 217 on March 15.

The squadron went to North Africa in May 1943 and Bunch assisted in destroying a He 111 on June 30 and a Ju 88 on July 3. He then returned to the UK and was awarded the DFC (13.7.43).

In 1944 Bunch was posted to 157 Squadron at Swannington. On September 12 he made his first sortie with Flight Lieutenant RD Doleman, on a high-level bomber support patrol over the Frankfurt area and they destroyed a Bf 110. In the next six months they destroyed six more enemy aircraft and damaged another. Bunch was awarded a Bar to the DFC (9.3.45) and the DSO (21.9.45). He stayed in the RAF after the war and retired on May 1 1968, as a Squadron Leader, retaining the rank of Wing Commander. He died in 1972.

PO 5.1.42   FO 1.10.42   FL 5.1.44   FL 1.9.45
SL 1.1.51

SAMUEL HOSKIN BUNCH

Sub-Lieutenant (FAA)   **Pilot**   **British**   **804 Squadron**

Bunch, of Roehampton, was with 804 Squadron at Hatston in early July 1940, flying Sea Gladiators on dockyard defence.

He was killed in a night flying accident on May 11 1941, serving at RNAS Arbroath. Bunch was 22. He is buried in Arbroath Western Cemetery, Fife, Scotland.

Midshipman 1.5.39   Actg Sub-Lt 14.3.40

ROBERT WILTON BUNGEY

40042   **FL**   **Pilot**   **Australian**   **145 Squadron**

Bungey, born in Fullerton, South Australia on October 4 1914, trained with the RAAF and transferred to the RAF in August 1937. He was posted to 226 Squadron at Harwell on November 27 1937.

The squadron took its Battles to France on September 2 1939, was in action throughout the German blitzkrieg in May 1940 and withdrawn to England in mid-June.

In August Bungey responded to a call for volunteers for Fighter Command. After converting to Hurricanes he joined 145 Squadron at Drem on September 20 1940. He was shot down off St Lawrence, Isle of Wight by Bf 109s of JG 2 on November 7. He baled out, wounded. His Hurricane, V 6889, crashed into the sea.

Bungey was posted from 145 on March 30 1941 to go to hospital for an operation on an injured knee. He took command of 452 Squadron at Kirton-in-Lindsey on June 10. Awarded the DFC (7.10.41), Bungey destroyed a Bf 109 on December 6. He was posted away on January 25 1942 and repatriated to Australia later in the year. He died in Adelaide on June 10 1943, as a Wing Commander.

PO 26.8.37   FO 26.5.39   FL 3.9.40   SL 1.2.41

FRANTISEK BURDA

82540   **PO**   **Pilot**   **Czechoslovakian**   **310 Squadron**

Burda served with 310 Squadron in the Battle of Britain.

In April 1943 he was shot down by flak over Brest. He was captured and was in a number of different PoW camps, finally finishing up in Colditz.

After the war Burda returned to Britain and was later repatriated to Czechoslovakia. He died there in February 1988.

ALAN GEORGE BURDEKIN

143405   **Sgt**   **Air Gunner**   **British**   **600 Squadron**

Born on June 26 1917, Burdekin joined the RAFVR at Derby on March 29 1939 as a trainee Wop/AG. He was mobilised on September 1 and joined 266 Squadron at Sutton Bridge on October 31. The squadron was then equipped with Battles.

Burdekin was posted to 9 Air Observers' School, Penrhos on November 28 and after qualifying as an LAC air gunner he rejoined 266 on January 9 1940. He moved to 264 Squadron at Martlesham Heath on February 1, spent eight weeks in an Experimental Flight in April and May, was promoted to Sergeant on June 6 and then posted from 264 on the 13th to 5 OTU, Aston Down, to convert to Blenheims.

On July 7 1940 Burdekin joined 600 Squadron at Manston. He was posted to 10 Signals School at Blackpool on September 21, for a wireless course, which he finished at 2 Electrical and Wireless School at Yatesbury from January 4 to March 31 1941, qualifying as a wireless operator. Burdekin then rejoined 600 Squadron and remained with it until July 16, when he joined the newly-reformed 125 Squadron at Colerne, with Defiants.

On October 13 1941 Burdekin was posted to 278 (ASR) Squadron. He was commissioned in January 1943 and remained with the squadron until March 18 1944. He then went to 577 Squadron, on anti-aircraft co-operation duties.

Burdekin was released from the RAF on December 29 1945, as a Flying Officer. He emigrated with his family to New Zealand in October 1947, was in the RNZAF Active Reserve from 1953 to 1958 and then served in the 1st Battalion Nelson, Marlborough, West Coast Regiment, as a Captain, from April 1958 to October 1962.

PO 3.2.43   FO 3.8.43

JOHN HENRY BATEMAN BURGESS

67601   **Sgt**   **Pilot**   **British**   **222 Squadron**

Burgess, born in 1920, worked for an insurance company before the war. He joined the RAFVR on July 23 1938 and did his ab initio training at 21 E&RFTS, Stapleford. Called up at the outbreak of war, Burgess went to No 1 ITW, Cambridge on November 15 1939. He was posted to 11 FTS, Shawbury on February 1 1940. At the end of the course he went to 5 OTU, Aston Down on July 6 and joined 222 Squadron at Kirton-in-Lindsey on July 29.

Burgess claimed Bf 109s destroyed on September 7 and 15 and October 29. In the latter engagement his Spitfire, P 9318, was damaged in the glycol system and he made a forced-landing at a dummy aerodrome at Lenham. The Bf 109 crashed on Sheerlands Farm, Pluckley.

Commissioned in May 1941, Burgess was posted to 129 Squadron at Westhampnett on October 18, as a Flight Commander. On December 27 he went to 53 OTU, Llandow, as an instructor. In mid-February 1942 he was sent on a course at CFS, Upavon, returning in mid-March to Llandow.

Burgess was posted to 66 Squadron at Ibsley on August 6 but three weeks later sailed in the MV 'Leinster' to Gibraltar, where he was put in charge of a defence flight of six Spitfires and six Hurricanes on the North Front. He was posted to Luqa, Malta on October 26 1942, as a Flight Commander with 1435 Squadron. On a sweep across Sicily on November 25 to attack Comiso aerodrome Burgess was attacked by FW 190s at 25000 feet. He dived into cloud at 7000 feet but was followed by a FW 190. His Spitfire caught fire and he crashed in the sea just offshore from the beach at Gela and was captured.

After being entertained by the pilots of JG 2 at Santa Pietra Burgess was handed over to the Italians and imprisoned at Chieti. He was later in Stalag Luft 3. After repatriation to Britain in May 1945 Burgess was released from the RAF on November 23 1945. He returned to insurance but moved to banking, where he had a very successful career. He retired in 1980 but continued to work as a consultant with overseas banks. He died in 1988.

PO 27.5.41   FO 16.1.42   FL 16.1.43

ERIC BURGOYNE

42796   **PO**   **Pilot**   **British**   **19 Squadron**

Joined 19 Squadron at Duxford in June 1940.

Burgoyne was shot down and killed by Bf 109s in combat over Canterbury on September 27. His Spitfire, X 4352, crashed at Coldred.

He was 25 years old and is buried in St Mary's churchyard, Burghfield, Berkshire.

APO 23.10.39   *PO 18.5.40*

PETER SLATER BURLEY

551809   **Sgt**   **Aircrew**   **British**   **600 Squadron**

A pre-war airman, Burley was posted to 600 Squadron at Catterick in mid-September 1940.

No other service details traced. He died in 1978.

FRED PERCY BURNARD

45461   **F/Sgt**   **Pilot**   **British**   **616 and 74 Squadrons**

Burnard was born in 1915 and was an airman pilot in the pre-war RAF. He was with 616 Squadron at Leconfield in June 1940. On July 3 he shared in the destruction of a Do 17.

Posted to 74 Squadron at Biggin Hill on October 27 1940, he was taken by surprise by Bf 109s over Dover on November 1 and returned to base damaged, in Spitfire P 7501.

Burnard was commissioned in March 1941 and released from the RAF in 1947, as a Squadron Leader.

PO 5.3.41   *FO 5.3.42*   *FL 5.3.43*

PETER ANTHONY BURNELL-PHILLIPS

37848   **Sgt**   **Pilot**   **British**   **607 Squadron**

Born at Richmond, Surrey, Burnell-Phillips was educated at St George's School, Weybridge. He joined the RAF on a short service commission in February 1936. After completing his flying training at Cranwell he joined 54 Squadron at Hornchurch, later moving to 65 Squadron.

Burnell-Phillips was obliged to resign his commission on February 1 1939 for infringement of flying discipline, when, for a bet he flew at rooftop height along the main street at Crowborough. He joined the RAFVR on April 20 1939 and was called up on October 16.

Posted to 607 Squadron at Usworth in July 1940, Burnell-Phillips claimed his first enemy aircraft on August 15 and destroyed a Do 17 on September 9. In the latter engagement his engine seized and he made a forced-landing near Knockholt, in Hurricane P 2912. He was slightly wounded by a bullet in the ankle. On September 26 Burnell-Phillips forced a Do 215 to crash into the sea by making mock attacks, his ammunition being exhausted. He also claimed a Bf 110 destroyed on September 30.

Awarded the DFM (1.11.40), credited with at least five victories, Burnell-Phillips was commissioned in November 1940. He was killed on February 9 1941 in a flying accident at Haddington, East Lothian, aged 24. He is buried in Dirleton Cemetery, Peebleshire.

His portrait was done by Cuthbert Orde in February 1941.

APO 18.5.36   *PO 9.3.37*   *PO 14.11.40*

NORMAN WHITMORE BURNETT

70101   **FO**   **Pilot**   **British**   **266 and 46 Squadrons**

Burnett was commissioned in the RAFO, on Reserve Category AA 2, in August 1934. When the RAFVR came into being he transferred to it in January 1938. Called up at the outbreak of war, he was with 266 Squadron at Wittering in June 1940.

Burnett was posted to 46 Squadron at Digby on July 25. He crashed at Hollingbourne on September 8 1940 following a combat over Sheppey. He was wounded and admitted to hospital. His Hurricane, V 6631, was a write-off.

In late May 1941 46 Squadron sailed for the Middle East in the carrier HMS 'Argus'. At Gibraltar pilots and aircraft were transferred to the carriers HMS 'Ark Royal' and 'Furious'. On June 6 they flew off to Hal Far, Malta. Five days later Burnett was flying one of seven Hurricanes scrambled to meet a heavily-escorted Italian reconnaissance aircraft. In the ensuing combat Burnett was shot down. A search to within sight of the coast of Sicily failed to find any trace of him. He is remembered on the Malta Memorial, Panel 1, Column 1.

PO (RAFO) 13.8.34   *FO (RAFO) 13.2.36*   *FO (VR) 1.1.38*
FO 7.9.39   *FL 16.12.40*

OWEN VALENTINE BURNS

146278   **Sgt**   **Wop/AG**   **British**   **235 Squadron**

Born in 1915, Burns joined 235 Squadron in May 1940. Returning from a dusk patrol over the North Sea on February 14 1941, Burns was one of the crew of a Blenheim, which prepared to land at Bircham Newton. Suddenly the lights were put out because of enemy aircraft in the vicinity. The pilot, Pilot Officer JTR Chamberlain, flew on to the satellite at Langham, 15 miles away. As he was about to touch down the lights again went out. He hit a tree. The observer was killed, the pilot seriously injured and Burns escaped with only slight injuries.

He was later with 279 Squadron, an ASR unit flying Hudsons carrying the 24 feet long airborne lifeboat. Commissioned in February 1943, Burns remained in the RAF until 1949. His final posting was as PA to AVM CBS Spackman, AOC 19 Group.

PO 19.2.43   *FO 19.8.43*   *FL 19.2.45*   *FL 19.8.46*

WILLIAM RICHARD BURNS

NZ 40202   **Sgt**   **Air Gunner**   **New Zealander**   **236 Sqdn**

Born in Devonport, England on June 10 1912, Burns went to New Zealand in 1929 and worked on sheep and dairy farms. He joined the RNZAF in January 1940 and after training at Weraroa and Ohakea he sailed in the SS 'Akaroa' on March 23 and arrived at Tilbury on May 9.

After further gunnery instruction at 5 OTU, Aston Down he was posted on July 6 to 236 Squadron at Thorney Island. He joined 282 Squadron on November 14 1940 and moved to 221 Squadron in mid-December.

Burns came off operations on March 26 1941 to operate and maintain the searchlight on the first Wellington to be equipped with the Leigh Light, for anti-submarine work. He went to the Coastal Command Development Unit on July 10 to instruct on the Light. In late January 1942 he joined a searchlight development unit, 1417 Flight, which became 172 Squadron on March 8 and by June was fully operational. Burns was posted to 210 Squadron on January 15 1943, moving to 59 Squadron in early April and three weeks later to 279 Squadron at Bircham Newton.

Commissioned in December 1943, Burns was with 279 until November 1944, when he went to 5 (Coastal) OTU, at Turnberry. He was repatriated to New Zealand in September 1946 and released on December 21, as a Flight Lieutenant. He died on May 23 1949.

PO 5.12.43   *FO 5.6.44*   *FL 5.12.45*

ALFRED DENMARK BURT

49994 **Sgt** **Pilot** **British** **611 and 603 Squadrons**

Born on July 27 1916, Burt was educated at Brockenhurst Grammar School. He joined the RAF as an aircraft apprentice at Halton on September 7 1932, to train as a Fitter ll (Airframes and Aero Engines). He was posted to 4 Squadron on July 26 1935, as an LAC.

Burt volunteered for pilot training and on January 18 1938 he began flying at 2 E&RFTS, Filton, moving on to 10 FTS, Tern Hill on March 27 and on October 30 he was posted as a staff pilot to No 1 Electrical and Wireless School, Cranwell.

Immediately after the outbreak of war he joined 46 Squadron at Digby but two weeks later moved to 611 Squadron.

On August 21 1940 Burt shared in shooting down a Do 17 off the Lincolnshire coast. He was posted to 603 Squadron at Hornchurch on October 4 and on December 17 was sent to CFS, Upavon for an instructor's course, after which he was posted to 15 FTS, Kidlington. Burt was posted overseas on October 22 1941, going to 24 Air School, Nigel, South Africa, as an instructor. He was commissioned from Warrant Officer in August 1942. In September 1944 Burt returned to the UK and joined No 1 ADU, Redhill, as a ferry pilot.

On February 28 1945 Burt was posted to 512 Squadron. He was awarded the AFC (14.6.45). A year later he went to 271 Squadron as a pilot and squadron training officer.   271 was disbanded at the end of 1946 and re-numbered 77. Burt went to 241 OCU, North Luffenham on January 27 1948 and later took part in the Berlin Air Lift. He was appointed as an examiner in the Transport Command Examining Unit on October 1 1948. He held a number of staff appointments prior to his retirement on July 27 1958, as a Squadron Leader. He was awarded a Bar to the AFC (1.1.55) for work with the Far East Communications Squadron, Singapore.

Burt joined HM Customs in 1958 and retired from the service in 1976. He died on March 17 1980.

PO 24.8.42   FO 24.2.43   FL 24.8.44   SL 1.1.51

ALLAN ANTHONY BURTENSHAW

745616 **Sgt** **Pilot** **British** **54 Squadron**

Joined 54 Squadron at Catterick on September 29 1940.

Burtenshaw was killed on March 12 1941, aged 21. He is buried in Snodland Cemetery, Kent.

CYRIL GEORGE BURTON

45730 **F/Sgt** **Pilot** **British** **23 Squadron**

A pre-war airman pilot, Burton was with 23 Squadron at Collyweston in early July 1940.

Commissioned in May 1941, he was released from the RAF in 1945, as a Flight Lieutenant.

PO 8.5.41   FO 8.5.42   FL 8.5.43

DOUGLAS LAWRENCE BURTON

NZ 40187 **Sgt** **Observer** **New Zealander** **248 Sqdn**

Born in Opunake on December 14 1916, Burton was working as a salesman in Sydney at the outbreak of war. He returned to New Zealand and enlisted in the RNZAF as a trainee observer. With ground training at Weraroa and flying at the Air Observers' School at Ohakea completed Burton sailed for the UK in the RMS 'Rangitata' on June 7 1940.

At the end of July he was posted to 17 OTU, Upwood and he joined 106 Squadron at Finningley on October 2. Ten days later he went to Sumburgh, in the Shetlands, to join 248 Squadron.

On October 20 Burton was a member of a Blenheim crew, captained by Pilot Officer GM Baird, on a flight off the south-west coast of Norway. After engaging and shooting down a Do 215 they were themselves shot down by Bf 109s. Burton was wounded and sent to hospital at Stavanger. He was a prisoner in Stalag Luft 1 and Stalag Luft III, where he worked in the Red Cross store. He was promoted to Warrant Officer in May 1943.

Burton arrived back in New Zealand in January 1946, spent some time in hospital and went on to the Reserve in December. He became a partner in a sports-outfitting business in Wanganui. He died there on November 20 1974.

HOWARD FRIZELLE BURTON

33227 **FL** **Pilot** **British** **66 and 616 Squadrons**

Burton was born in Letchworth in 1916 and entered RAF College, Cranwell as a flight cadet in January 1935. He was awarded the Sword of Honour in December 1936 and on the 19th of the month he joined 46 Squadron at Digby.

In October 1939 Burton was posted to 66 Squadron at Duxford, as a Flight Commander. On May 12 1940 he shared a He 111 and on June 2 a probable He 111 over Dunkirk. Promoted to Acting Squadron Leader on September 3 he took command of 616 Squadron at Kenley. On June 2 1941 Burton shared a Bf 109, was awarded the DFC (19.9.41) and in September posted away for a rest.

In early 1942 Burton was posted to the Middle East and later became Wing Leader of 239 (Kittyhawk) Wing. On January 18 1943 he destroyed a Bf 109 and got another on February 26. He was awarded a Bar to the DFC (23.2.43) and at the end of his tour he got the DSO (6.4.43).

Burton was posted back to the UK in May 1943. He was returning as a passenger in a Hudson on June 3, when it was lost over the Bay of Biscay. He is remembered on the Runnymede Memorial, Panel 118.

PO 19.12.36   FO 19.6.38   FL 19.6.40   SL 1.9.41

LESLIE GILBERT BURTON

78081 **PO** **Observer** **British** **236 Squadron**

Burton, of Stanwell, Middlesex, joined 236 Squadron on July 19 1940.

He was killed on December 24 1940, aged 26. He is buried in St Peter's churchyard, Harborne, Birmingham.

PO 24.3.40

PERCIVAL ROSS-FRAMES BURTON

74348   PO   Pilot   South African   249 Squadron

Born in 1917 in Cape Province, Burton joined the South African Coast Garrison and Citizen Forces in 1935. He later went to Britain to study at Christ Church College, Oxford. He learned to fly with the University Air Squadron and was called up in October 1939.

Burton joined 249 Squadron at Church Fenton on July 21 1940. The squadron engaged a formation of Bf 110s of V/LG 1 on the morning of September 27. The Hurricanes broke the Germans' two defensive circles and the enemy aircraft went south at low level, heading for the Channel. Burton pursued one of the Bf 110s for about forty miles, often at little more than treetop height, but the German pilot, the Gruppe Kommandeur of V/LG 1, Hauptmann Horst Liensberger, was unable to shake him off.

Just north of Hailsham Burton's guns stopped and the two aircraft skimmed over the rooftops. The Hurricane, above and behind the Bf 110, banked and made what appeared to be an attack. Both machines lurched and an object spun away and the tail unit of the enemy aircraft dropped, followed by the rest of it, into a field. The object seen was the wingtip of Burton's Hurricane. His aircraft crashed into a huge oak tree on New Barn Farm, throwing its dead pilot clear and burning itself out in a field.

The Germans were buried in Hailsham Cemetery, but were exhumed and buried elsewhere after the war. Burton, who was 23, is buried in St Andrew's churchyard, Tangmere. The eye-witness reports indicate strongly that Burton deliberately rammed the German aircraft. In 1980 a road on a housing estate near to the site was named 'Burton Walk' in his memory.

PO 12.10.39

BASIL MARTIN BUSH

101038   Sgt   Pilot   British   504 Squadron

Bush was a member of the RAFVR in Cambridge and had carried out some training at 22 E&RFTS there before being called to full-time service at the outbreak of war. He completed his training at 8 FTS, Montrose and after converting to Hurricanes at 7 OTU, Hawarden he joined 504 Squadron at Castletown in early June 1940.

On September 7 Bush made a forced-landing at Eastchurch after a cannon shell went through his cockpit hood and petrol tank during a combat over the Thames Estuary. He was shot down on September 30 in an action over the south-west coast and crash-landed near Yeovil, in Hurricane P 3021.

Commissioned in July 1941, Bush spent a period instructing Army glider pilots. He then converted to Mosquitos and joined 139 Squadron at Upwood. He was later with a Spitfire Flight training Lancaster crews to cope with attacking fighters. Bush was awarded the DFC (23.3.45), serving with 128 Squadron in 8 (Pathfinder) Group, Bomber Command, in Mosquitos. He was released from the RAF in late 1945, as a Flight Lieutenant.

PO 12.7.41   FO 12.7.42   FL 12.7.43

CHARLES ROY BUSH

42691   PO   Pilot   New Zealander   242 Squadron

Born in Wellington on February 7 1918, Bush was educated at Wellington College and went to work for an insurance company. Early in 1939 he applied for an RAF short service commission and was provisionally accepted. He left New Zealand on June 15 and in late July began flying at 8 E&RFTS, Woodley, after which he went to 3 ITW at Hastings and finished his flying training at 10 FTS, Dumfries.

Bush was posted to 5 OTU, Aston Down, where he converted to Gladiators and then Spitfires. In mid-May 1940 he joined 615 Squadron at Abbeville and flew Gladiators on aerodrome defence until the 21st when 615's remaining aircraft were withdrawn to Kenley. On June 5 he was posted to 242 Squadron at Biggin Hill. Three days later he flew back to France with the squadron to provide cover for the Army falling back to St Nazaire. After several days patrolling the port 242 was withdrawn to Coltishall on the 18th.

Operational again, led by Douglas Bader, the squadron moved to Duxford at the end of August. On September 7 Bush damaged a He 111 and a Bf 110, on the 9th he destroyed a Bf 110, on the 18th a probable Ju 88 and on the 27th a Bf 109.

Bush joined 258 Squadron at Drem on December 5. On June 16 1941 he claimed a probable Bf 109. He was posted to 610 Squadron at Tangmere on July 19 but moved on a month later to 41 Squadron at Merston, as a Flight Commander. He destroyed a Bf 109 on August 22, shared a Hs 126 on September 18 and was awarded the DFC (30.9.41).

Posted to 58 OTU, Grangemouth on October 22, Bush was there until March 1942, when he was detached for special duties with the RNZAF. He arrived home on July 13 and was posted to the newly-formed 11 (Fighter) OTU at Ohakea. He joined 15 (Kittyhawk) Squadron at the end of October 1943 and went with it to New Georgia on December 16, as a Flight Commander. Bush returned to New Zealand on February 16 1944 and on May 1 he was given command on 21 Squadron, about to be formed at Ardmore with Corsairs. The squadron pilots flew in a transport to Santos on June 19 and got their Corsairs next day. Tour-expired, Bush returned to Whenuapai on September 20 and after a rest went to Guadalcanal for a second tour with 21, which he finished in February 1945.

He returned to the UK by air in July and was attached to No 1 AFDU at Andrews Field, Essex. He took part in the first Battle of Britain flypast on September 15 1945. At the end of March 1946 Bush transferred to the RNZAF and he arrived back in New Zealand in early November. He was given command of the General Purpose Communications Flight at Ohakea.

On November 30 1948 Bush was carrying out a photographic reconnaissance of the Gisborne area in an Oxford. He landed at Napier, took off again for Ohakea but never arrived. The crashed aircraft was finally located in the Ruahine Range. It is believed to have broken up in the air. Bush and his two crew were all killed.

PO 20.4.40   FO 24.4.41   FL 24.4.42

GEORGE DOWNS BUSHELL

745584   Sgt   Pilot   British   213 Squadron

Bushell, of Fenny Stratford, was with 213 Squadron in early July 1940. On August 12 he claimed two Bf 110s destroyed and another two days later. He was killed on December 31 1940, aged 24, when he crashed in a snowstorm at Risby Park, Suffolk in Hurricane P 3267. He is buried in Bletchley Cemetery, Buckinghamshire.

SAMUEL LESLIE BUTTERFIELD

563441   Sgt   Pilot   British   213 Squadron

Born in Leeds, Butterfield was a pre-war regular airman and was with 213 Squadron in early 1940. On May 17 the squadron was sent to Merville and took part in defensive patrols, bomber escorts and army support operations until it was withdrawn on the 21st. It continued to operate over France from Biggin Hill and in a period of several days Butterfield shared in the destruction of two Hs 126s and a Do 17.

On May 28 over Dunkirk 213 engaged a large enemy force. Butterfield shot down two Bf 109s and a Ju 88. He was then attacked by a Bf 110, which he destroyed but his Hurricane suffered three more hits and was set on fire. He baled out and was picked up by a passing ship. Three days later Butterfield destroyed a Bf 109 and probably another. He was awarded the DFM (14.6.40).

He failed to return from a combat over Portland on August 11 1940. His body was washed up on the French coast and he is buried in Boulogne Eastern Cemetery. Butterfield was 27 years old.

ALEC FRANK BUTTERICK

202121   Sgt   Pilot   British   3 and 232 Squadrons

Butterick was with 3 Squadron at Biggin Hill at the outbreak of war. On September 10 1939 he crashed his Hurricane in bad visibility and was admitted to Faversham Cottage Hospital with a broken ankle and injuries to the spine.

On July 17 1940 Butterick moved to Sumburgh in the Shetlands, when 'B' Flight of 3 Squadron went there to become 232 Squadron. Six days later Butterick ditched in the sea off the Shetlands after his engine failed.

He was commissioned in September 1945 and stayed in the RAF for several years after the war, being released as a Flying Officer.

PO 5.9.45   FO 5.3.46   FO 5.9.46

KENNETH BUTTERWORTH

1050688   Sgt   Aircrew   British   23 Squadron

No service details traced

PERCY BYNG-HALL

79224   PO   Air Gunner   British   29 Squadron

Joined 29 Squadron at Digby on July 7 1940. Byng-Hall transferred to the Administrative Branch in July 1942 and was released from the RAF in early 1946. He is believed to have died in British Columbia, Canada on May 21 1948.

PO 15.6.40   FO 15.6.41   FL 15.6.42

EDWARD LAWRENCE BYRNE

621878   Sgt   Radar Operator   British   FIU

Byrne, of Portsmouth, was with the Fighter Interception Unit at Shoreham in early July 1940.

He was in a Blenheim which failed to return from an operational patrol on the night of September 13. Byrne and the other two men aboard baled out and were captured. The Blenheim, Z 5721, crashed into the Channel off Calais.

Byrne was released from the RAF in 1945, as a Warrant Officer.

ANTHONY RICHARD CAIN

755057   Sgt   Wop/AG   British   235 Squadron

Cain, from Harpenden, Hertfordshire, served with 235 in the Battle of Britain. He was still with the squadron when he was killed on June 15 1941, aged 21. He is buried in Kriberg Cemetery, Gothenburg, Sweden.

JAMES RUSSELL CAISTER

44827   PO   Pilot   British   603 Squadron

Born on October 19 1906, Caister joined the RAF in the twenties. He saw service in Palestine between the wars, as a Sergeant-Pilot.

In early 1940 Caister was with 603 Squadron at Dyce. He shared in the destruction of a Do 215 on April 16, one hundred miles east-north-east of Aberdeen.

Caister shared a Ju 88 on July 3, shared a Do 215 on the 6th and shared a He 111 on the 12th. Commissioned in August, Caister claimed a He 111 destroyed on the 30th and a Bf 109 on September 3.

Three days later he was shot down by Hauptmann von Bonin of l/JG 54 in an action over the Channel off Manston. Caister landed his Spitfire, X 4260, in France and was captured.

He was awarded the DFM (13.9.40). Caister was released from captivity in May 1945 and left the RAF on June 8 1946, as a Flight Lieutenant.

PO 21.8.40   FO 21.8.41   FL 21.8.42

GEORGE DOUGLAS CALDERHEAD

86333   PO   Pilot   British   54 Squadron

Calderhead, from Glasgow, joined 54 Squadron at Catterick on September 28 1940. He was killed in a flying accident on January 12 1942, while serving with 31 (General Reconnaissance) Squadron in Newfoundland. Calderhead was 23 and is buried in Sherwood Cemetery, Newfoundland, Canada.

PO 7.9.40   FO 7.9.41

THOMAS MORROW CALDERWOOD

106757   Sgt   Pilot   British   85 Squadron

Joined 85 Squadron on September 23 1940. Calderwood was commissioned in July 1941 and released from the RAF in 1946. He died on September 28 1957.

PO 26.7.41   FO 26.7.42   FL 26.7.43

FRANCIS WALTER CALE

42104   PO   Pilot   Australian   266 Squadron

Cale joined the RAF on a short service commission in February 1939. He was with 266 Squadron at Wittering in July 1940. On August 15 he was shot down in combat over Kent, baled out into the River Medway and was killed. His Spitfire, N 3168, crashed in flames on the bank of the Medway at Teston.

Cale was 25. He is buried in Westminster City Cemetery, Ealing.

APO 13.5.39   PO 6.11.39

WILLIAM PERCIVAL CAMBRIDGE

37791   FO   Pilot   British   253 Squadron

The son of a civil servant, Cambridge was born in India in 1912. He was educated at Bromsgrove Public School and then returned to India and went to work in the sugar industry. He joined the RAF in February 1936.

Cambridge was posted to 10 FTS, Tern Hill on May 16 and he joined 29 Squadron at Debden on December 25 1936. At the end of 1938 he was 'B' Flight Commander. When 253 Squadron was formed at Filton on October 20 1939 Cambridge joined it, as a Flight Commander.

On August 30 1940 he claimed a Bf 110 destroyed. The next day, after Squadron Leaders Starr and Gleave were lost, Cambridge, as Senior Flight Commander, assumed command of 253.

During a routine squadron patrol on September 6 Cambridge's aircraft gave trouble. He baled out but was killed. The Hurricane, P 3032, crashed at Kingsnorth.

Cambridge is buried in Henley Road Cemetery, Reading, Berkshire.

APO 4.5.36   PO 9.3.37   FO 9.9.38

JAMES DOUGLAS CAMERON

747925   Sgt   Wop/AG   British   604 Squadron

Cameron, of Edinburgh, served with 604 Squadron in the Battle of Britain. Later posted to Bomber Command, he was killed on May 9 1942, while serving as a Flight Sergeant with 9 Squadron at Honington, Suffolk. Cameron was 23. He is buried in the Berlin 1939-45 War Cemetery, Germany.

MATTHEW CAMERON ✱

45540   F/Sgt   Pilot   British   66 Squadron

A pre-war airman pilot, Cameron was with 66 Squadron at Duxford early in 1940. On August 20 he claimed the destruction of a Bf 110, on September 27 a Ju 88 and on November 14 a probable Ju 87.

Cameron was commissioned in March 1941 and he was released from the RAF in 1945, as a Flight Lieutenant. His portrait was done by Cuthbert Orde.

PO 26.3.41   FO 26.3.42   FL 26.3.43

NEIL CAMERON

102585   Sgt   Pilot   British   1 and 17 Squadrons

Cameron was born in Perth, Scotland on July 8 1920. He was educated at Perth Academy, went to work as a bank clerk and joined the RAFVR in May 1939. He learned to fly at 11 E&RFTS, Perth. Called up at the outbreak of war, Cameron went to ITW, Hastings and in March 1940 to 15 EFTS, Redhill. In early June he was posted to 8 FTS, Montrose and after completing the course went to 5 OTU, Aston Down and then joined No 1 Squadron at Wittering on September 26 1940.

Cameron was moved to 17 Squadron at Martlesham Heath on October 15. He destroyed a Ju 87 and probably another on November 8 and claimed a Bf 110 on the 15th. He was one of the 17 Squadron personnel who were transferred to 134 Squadron, formed at Leconfield on July 31 1941 for service in Russia. They sailed on August 19 in the carrier HMS 'Argus' from Abbotsinch and on September 6 flew to Vaenga airfield. Some operations were flown in Russia and Cameron got a probable Ju 88 on October 6 but the main work was to train Russian pilots on Hurricanes.

The squadron left Russia on November 28 and reached Rosyth on December 6. It was given Spitfires and sent to Eglinton, Northern Ireland. In April 1942 134 sailed for the Middle East, arriving at Tewfik on June 6. In early July the CO and most experienced pilots were attached to 213 Squadron in the Western Desert, while the remainder of the squadron went to Palestine.

Cameron was posted to 335 (Hellenic) Squadron at Mersa Matruh on April 3 1943 for advisory and training duties. In early September he went to 224 Group, Burma as a Staff Officer and on January 4 1944 he was given command of 258 Squadron. He was awarded the DFC (21.11.44), left the Squadron on August 8 1945 and returned to the UK and was awarded the DSO (2.10.45). He was granted a Permanent Commission on September 1 1945.

Cameron went on to a most distinguished career in the RAF, the most successful achieved by any participant in the Battle of Britain, culminating in his becoming Marshal of the RAF on July 31 1977 and being created a life peer, Baron Cameron of Balhousie on January 1 1983. He died on January 29 1985. In addition to his gallantry awards he was created KT (1983), GCB 1976 (KCB 1975), CB (1971) and CBE (1967).

APO 31.7.41   FO 4.3.42   FL 4.3.43   FL 1.9.45
SL 1.1.50   WC 1.1.56   GC 1.7.60   AC 1.7.64
AVM 1.7.68   AM 1.7.74   ACM 1.11.75   MRAF 31.7.77

ALAN CAMPBELL

391857   Sgt   Air Gunner   New Zealander   264 Sqdn

Campbell was born in Nelson, Lancashire on January 23 1920 and was taken to New Zealand as a baby. He volunteered for the RNZAF in November 1939 and reported to the Ground Training School at Weraroa on December 18. After completing a gunnery course at the Air Observers' School, Ohakea he sailed for the UK at the end of March 1940 in the SS 'Akaroa', arriving at Tilbury on May 9.

Campbell was posted to 264 squadron at Duxford and in the course of continuing his training he flew two operational sorties, as an LAC and without his Air Gunner's badge. He was posted to 5 OTU, Aston Down on July 27 where he qualified. After rejoining 264 he was promoted to Sergeant.

In early November Campbell was posted to 75 Squadron at Feltwell. He made thirty operational flights in Wellingtons and at the end of his tour he went to 23 OTU, Pershore, as an instructor. He returned to operations at the end of April 1942 and joined the recently-formed 156 Squadron at Alconbury. At his own request he went back to 75 Squadron on May 19 to do his second tour.

Campbell was front gunner in a Wellington which failed to return from a raid on Soltau on the night of July 28/29. German evidence revealed that it received a direct hit from ground guns at 2.10 a.m on the 29th. It was Campbell's fifty-second operation. He was buried in Stade Cemetery but was later re-interred in Soltau Military Cemetery.

ALAN ROBERTS McLEOD CAMPBELL

42393   PO   Pilot   Canadian   54 Squadron

Campbell, of Sorrento, British Columbia, began his flying training with the RAF in June 1939 and was with 54 Squadron at Hornchurch in June 1940. On July 7 he forced-landed at Deal, slightly wounded, after an attack by Bf 109s. He claimed a Bf 109 destroyed on August 18 1940.

In May 1941 Campbell was with the MSFU at Speke. He sailed for Halifax, Nova Scotia on June 10th in the 'Empire Moon', the second ship to sail equipped with a catapult Hurricane.

Campbell later served with 80, 123 and 234 Squadrons. He was released from the RAF on October 30 1945, joined the RCAF in August 1951, retired in 1964 and died in September 1974.

APO 5.8.39   PO 6.4.40   FO 6.4.41   FL 6.4.42

ALEXANDER MIDDLETON CAMPBELL

34932   FL   Pilot   British   29 Squadron

Born on October 16 1917, Campbell joined the RAF on a short service commission in October 1936. He was posted to 2 FTS, Digby on February 6 1937 and joined 29 Squadron at Debden on January 8 1938. In June 1940 he was 'B' Flight Commander.

Campbell was posted away in February 1941. He stayed in the RAF after the war and retired on October 17 1956, as a Wing Commander. He died in 1979.

APO 31.1.37   PO 8.1.38   FO 8.10.39   FL 9.10.40
SL 1.12.41   SL 1.9.45   WC 1.1.52

DAVID BAILLIE CAMPBELL

NZ 40604   **Sgt**   **Air Gunner**   **New Zealander**   **23 Sqdn**

Campbell was born at Te Kopuru on June 8 1920, educated at Dargaville High School and after leaving became a postman. He joined the Territorial Army in 1936 and in January 1940 was serving on Home Defence at Fort Takapuna, Auckland. He volunteered for the RNZAF and began training as an air gunner at Weraroa on February 13 1940. He gained air experience and had gunnery training at the Air Observers' School at Ohakea, after which he sailed for the UK in the RMS 'Rangitiki' on April 24.

Campbell was posted to 5 OTU, Aston Down on July 17 and he joined 23 Squadron at Ford on September 28. He remained with the squadron, carrying out night intruder operations, until early March 1942, when he was posted to 116 (Army Co-operation) Squadron at Hooton Park. In May 1942 Campbell moved to 1653 Conversion Unit at Polebrook to crew up and convert to Liberators. On June 24 1942 Campbell's crew flew a Liberator of 159 Squadron en route for India, via the Middle East. They were retained in the Middle East for operations and were initially based at St Jean, Palestine, from where they carried out long-distance day and night raids against targets in Crete and Tobruk.

The squadron moved to Aqir on August 12 and made attacks on enemy convoys and targets along the south Mediterranean coast, as far away as Benghazi. 159 was merged with 160 Squadron in September and went to Shandur, in Egypt. Campbell's tour finished in March 1943 and he returned to the UK, where he was awarded the DFM in April.

At the end of May 1943 Campbell left for New Zealand, via America and Australia. After arriving on August 1 he spent a short while at No 1 OTU, Ohakea and then went to ITW at Rotorua, as an instructor. In mid-January 1944 Campbell was posted back to flying in 3 (General Reconnaissance) Squadron at Ohakea but he was found to be medically unfit for aircrew duties and took his discharge on April 8 1944. He had a number of businesses in the post-war years and was working for the Ministry of Works in Whangarei when he retired in 1980. He died in June 1984.

DONALD CAIRNIE OGILVIE CAMPBELL

741676   **Sgt**   **Pilot**   **British**   **66 Squadron**

No service details traced.

GILLIAN LORNE CAMPBELL

81680   **PO**   **Pilot**   **British**   **236 Squadron**

Campbell, from Bromley, Kent, joined 236 Squadron on August 5 1940. On the 20th his Blenheim was damaged by anti-aircraft fire over Pembroke Dock but he returned safely to St Eval.

In 1941 Campbell was with 272 Squadron. On July 24 he claimed two Ju 87s destroyed over a convoy near Sicily, one in flames. He was awarded the DFC (30.1.42) and was killed on December 23 1942 but the unit he was serving with is not known. He was 23, the son of Sir Edward Campbell, and is buried in Durrington Cemetery, Wiltshire.

PO 11.7.40   *FO 4.7.41*

NORMAN NEIL CAMPBELL

41824   **PO**   **Pilot**   **Canadian**   **242 Squadron**

From St Thomas, Ontario, Campbell joined the RAF in January 1939. Initially with 32 Squadron, he was posted to 242 Squadron at Biggin Hill on June 3 1940. Five days later he flew to France with the squadron to help cover the rearguard actions being fought by the British Army as it retreated to the Atlantic coast. Campbell flew back on June 18. Having no maps, he ran out of fuel and made a forced-landing on a beach near Minehead.

By mid-July 242 was operational again and on September 18 Campbell claimed a Ju 88 destroyed and shared in shooting down two others. On October 17 1940 Campbell was in Hurricane V 6575, which crashed into the sea after, presumably, being hit by return fire from a Do 17 engaged off Yarmouth. His body was later recovered and he was buried on October 31 in Scottow Cemetery, Norfolk. He was 27.

APO 1.4.39   *PO 23.10.39*

ERNEST WILLIAM CAMPBELL-COLQUHOUN

39301   **FL**   **Pilot**   **British**   **66 and 264 Squadrons**

Joined the RAF on a short service commission in October 1936. Campbell-Colquhoun was posted to 10 FTS, Tern Hill on January 16 1937 and joined 66 Squadron at Duxford on August 7.

Over Dunkirk on June 2 1940 he damaged a Bf 109. Promoted to Flight Lieutenant on August 21, he was posted to 264 Squadron at Kirton-in-Lindsey, as a Flight Commander. He was released from the RAF in 1946, as a Squadron Leader. He died in 1989.

APO 21.12.36   *PO 12.10.37*   *FO 12.7.39*   *FL 3.9.40*
SL 1.7.44

ROBERT JOHN CANDY

79229   **PO**   **Air Gunner**   **British**   **25 Squadron**

Joined 25 Squadron at Martlesham Heath in June 1940. At the end of July posted to Iceland with 98 Squadron.

Candy later served with 264 and 12 Squadrons and was released from the RAF in 1945, as a Flight Lieutenant.

PO 15.6.40   *FO 15.6.41*   *FL 15.6.42*

ARTHUR WILLIAM CANHAM

939269   **Sgt**   **Air Gunner**   **British**   **600 Squadron**

Enlisted in the RAF on October 25 1939 and after gunnery training at Jurby joined 600 Squadron at Manston in May 1940. In January 1941, with the advent of the Beaufighter, the air gunners were posted away. Canham went to 11 OTU, Bassingbourn and afterwards joined 9 Squadron at Honington, flying as a rear gunner in Wellingtons. In August 1942 the squadron converted to Lancasters.

Canham was discharged from the RAF on February 9 1943 following an operation at RAF Hospital, Ely for the removal of splintered bone from his head and a badly perforated ear drum. After the war he emigrated to New Zealand.

BERNARD CANNON

1052310   AC 2   Radar Operator   British   604 Squadron

Born in Bolton in 1915, Cannon joined the RAF in June 1940. He volunteered for flying duties and at the end of the month was at RAF Yatesbury for an airborne radar course and on July 20 was posted to 604 Squadron at Gravesend, never having flown.

Cannon was one of those who flew operationally without rank or brevet, receiving three shillings per day, which included one shilling flying pay. When other radar operators were posted away as surplus in December 1940 Cannon was flying with the CO, Squadron Leader MF Anderson, and was kept on.

He was awarded the DFM (24.6.41) and had at that time assisted in the destruction of at least three enemy aircraft. Cannon was released from the RAF in 1945, as a Warrant Officer. He died on September 17 1983.

BERNARD CAPEL

902479   Sgt   Air Gunner   British   23 Squadron

With 23 Squadron in June 1940. With the advent of airborne radar many air gunners went to Bomber Command. Capel was serving with 7 Squadron at Oakington in 1941 when he was awarded the DFM (15.8.41). The citation stated that he was rear gunner of an aircraft attacking the 'Scharnhorst' at La Pallice. His aircraft was engaged by six enemy fighters. He destroyed two and the others flew away.

No further service details traced

CARDALE FREDERICK ALEXANDER CAPON

42741   PO   Pilot   British   257 Squadron

Capon was born at Surbiton, Surrey on August 1 1920. He was educated at Arundel House Preparatory School, Surbiton and Kingston Grammar School. In July 1937 he went to work at Bobby's, Eastbourne to learn the retail trade. His weekends were spent flying with the Civil Air Guard.

On August 8 1939 Capon began elementary flying training at 19 E&RFTS, Gatwick as a candidate for a short service commission. He went on to 11 FTS, Shawbury on October 21. He joined 257 Squadron, when it reformed at Hendon on May 17 1940. Capon claimed a He 111 destroyed on August 12 and a Ju 88 the next day. On October 12 he was shot down in combat with Bf 109s over Dungeness and baled out, slightly wounded. His Hurricane, V 7298, crashed at High House Farm, Stone.

After Tuck took command of 257 in September 1940 Capon always flew as his No 2. On January 1 1941, after flying a night patrol, Capon was killed landing in a snow blizzard at Coltishall. He was 20 years old and is buried in Marsh Lane Cemetery, Surbiton.

APO 9.10.39   PO 11.5.40

HERBERT CAPSTICK

79176   PO   Observer   Jamaican   236 Squadron

Joined 236 Squadron on July 15 1940. Later qualified at a Specialist Navigation course and was released from the RAF in 1946, as a Squadron Leader.

PO 5.5.40   FO 5.5.41   FL 5.5.42

BRIAN JOHN GEORGE CARBURY

40288   FO   Pilot   New Zealander   603 Squadron

The son of a veterinary surgeon, Carbury was born in Wellington on February 27 1918. He was educated at New Lynn and King's College, Auckland and was a fine athlete. Tiring of his job as a shoe salesman Carbury went to England in 1937 and successfully applied for a short service commission. He began his flying training on September 27 and in June 1938 he joined 41 Squadron at Catterick.

Just before the outbreak of war Carbury was attached to 603 Squadron to assist with Spitfire training. His temporary posting became permanent in late September 1939. On December 7 he got a probable He 111, on January 19 1940 he shared another and on July 3 he shared a Ju 88.

On August 27 603 went south to Hornchurch and was soon in action. Carbury shot down a Bf 109 on the 29th, another the next day, on the 31st two He 111s and three Bf 109s, on September 2, 5 and 14 he destroyed Bf 109s, on October 2, 7 and 9 he destroyed four Bf 109s and finally on the 14th he damaged a Ju 88. Carbury's claimed tally of 15 1/2 enemy aircraft destroyed placed him among the five top scoring pilots of Fighter Command and he is one of the few who were awarded the DFC (24.9.40) and Bar (25.10.40) during the period of the Battle of Britain.

On December 30 1940 Carbury was posted to 58 OTU, Grangemouth as an instructor. He did not fly operationally again but served as an instructor until he left the RAF in 1944, as a Flight Lieutenant. He remained in England after the war and died in July 1962.

APO 28.11.37   PO 27.9.38   FO 27.4.40   FL 27.4.41

PHILIP MELVILLE CARDELL

80818   PO   Pilot   British   603 Squadron

Cardell, whose home was in Huntingdonshire, was posted to 263 Squadron at Drem in late June 1940. After a few days he went to 603 Squadron at Dyce. On September 27 Cardell was in combat with Bf 109s over the Channel. He destroyed one but it is believed he was himself wounded. He attempted to get back to the English coast but had to bale out a quarter of a mile off Folkstone and his parachute failed to open. His friend, Pilot Officer PG Dexter, tried to attract peoples attention to Cardell's plight. When he failed he made a forced-landing on Folkstone beach, commandeered a boat but Cardell was dead when they reached him.

Cardell was 23. He is buried in Holy Trinity churchyard, Great Paxton, Huntingdonshire.

PO 10.6.40

CHARLES FREDERICK CARDNELL

80807   PO   Pilot   British   23 Squadron

Joined 23 Squadron at Collyweston in June 1940. Flying a night patrol on August 8, Cardnell's Blenheim crashed near Peterborough from causes unknown. He and his gunner, Sergeant C Stephens, were both killed. Cardnell was 22. He is buried in Highgate Cemetery, St Pancras.

PO 2.6.40

FRANK REGINALD CAREY

43132   PO   Pilot   British   43 Squadron

Born in London on May 7 1912, Carey was educated at Belvedere School, Haywards Heath. He joined the RAF in September 1927 as an aircraft apprentice at Halton. After completing his training he went to 43 Squadron at Tangmere in late 1930 as an AC 1 Metal Rigger. In 1933 he returned to Halton for a conversion course to become a Fitter II (Airframes). In 1934 he was posted to Worthy Down as an LAC and served with 7 and 58 Squadrons.

Carey had applied for pilot training and was selected in 1935. He passed out as a Sergeant-Pilot from 6 FTS, Netheravon and joined 43 Squadron at Tangmere in September 1936. He was still with the squadron at the outbreak of war and on January 30 1940 he shared in destroying a He 111, which was attempting to bomb fishing boats. On February 3 he shared a He 111 and on the 12th he shared another. He was awarded the DFM (1.3.40) and commissioned.

In early April Carey was posted to 3 Squadron at Kenley. On May 10 his section was sent to France and within a few days he had destroyed six enemy aircraft and been wounded in the leg, crash-landing south-east of Brussels. He returned to England in early June to learn that officially he was 'Missing, believed Killed'. He was awarded the DFC and Bar, both being gazetted the same day (31.5.40).

Carey rejoined 43 in late June, as a Flight Commander. On July 9 he destroyed a Bf 110, on August 12 a Ju 88, on the 13th another and on the 16th two Ju 87s and two more probables. Two days later he crash-landed at Holme Street Farm, Pulborough, wounded in the right knee and was sent to the Royal West Sussex Hospital, Chichester. He returned to the squadron in September.

In November 1940 Carey was posted to 52 OTU as an instructor but returned to operations in February 1941, as a Flight Commander with 245 Squadron at Aldergrove. He was back at 52 OTU not long afterwards and was posted away on July 25 1941. Carey went to Baginton on August 15 to form and command 135 Squadron. It sailed on December 6 for the Far East and arrived at Rangoon on January 19 1942. Ten days later he destroyed a Nakajima Ki 27 over the city and on February 26 he shot down three Nakajima Ki 43s. He was awarded a second Bar to the DFC (24.3.42). Later in the year he was appointed to command RAF Alipore, as a Wing Commander.

By the end of 1942, when he was posted to Air HQ Bengal, Carey is reputed to have destroyed at least ten Japanese aircraft. In February 1943 he was given command of the Air Fighting Training Unit, Amarda Road. Carey was posted to 73 OTU, Abu Sueir in November 1944 to command, as a Group Captain. For his work in India he was awarded the AFC (1.1.45). He returned to England in July 1945 and was granted a Permanent Commission. Carey held various staff appointments until finally, in 1958, he was made Air Adviser to the British High Commission in Australia.

He retired on June 2 1960 as a Group Captain and was made a CBE (11.6.60). He went to work at the Rolls Royce Aero Division in Australia and returned to live in the UK on retirement. Carey's portrait was done by Cuthbert Orde.

PO 1.4.40   FO 1.4.41   FL 23.11.41   SL 6.5.43
WC 6.5.45   WC 1.7.47   GC 1.7.56

SYDNEY CARLIN

81942   PO   Air Gunner   British   264 Squadron

Born in 1889, Carlin was farming near Hull before the Great War. He joined the Army and won the DCM and MC as an infantryman. He later lost a leg but acquired a wooden one, causing him to be known ever after as 'Timbertoes'. He learned to fly and somehow got into the RFC.

Carlin was a Captain when he joined 74 Squadron on May 26 1918. He was a Flight Commander with eleven enemy aircraft to his credit when he was shot down and taken prisoner in October 1918. He was awarded the DFC.

In the early thirties Carlin was in Kenya, managing a farm for a German baron. He was an expert rider and organised a polo team. He returned to England in 1939 to join the RAF as a pilot. When he was turned down he persisted until he was accepted for training as an air gunner. Commissioned in July 1940, Carlin joined 264 Squadron at Kirton-in-Lindsey in August. He was one of the few men in the RAF entitled to wear RFC wings and an Air Gunner's brevet.

Carlin was with 151 Squadron in 1941. On May 9, running to get to his Defiant turret to fire at German aircraft attacking the aerodrome, Carlin was himself killed. He was cremated at Hull Crematorium at Kingston-upon-Hull.

PO 27.7.40

WILLIAM FLEMING CARNABY

90157   FO   Pilot   British   264 and 85 Squadrons

Carnaby, of Newmarket, joined 601 Squadron, AuxAF in late 1935. He went on to the Reserve of Officers on March 1 1938 and was recalled to active service on August 31 1939.

He was with 264 Squadron in July 1940 and took part in the squadron's last spell of day-fighting from Hornchurch in late August. On the 28th he returned to base, severely damaged by return fire from a He 111 engaged over Dover. In September Carnaby was posted to 85 Squadron at Castle Camps, as it went over to night-fighting.

Carnaby was killed on February 5 1943, serving as a Flight Lieutenant in 25 Squadron. He was 29 and is buried in Newmarket Cemetery, Suffolk.

PO (AuxAF) 3.1.36   PO 31.8.39   FO 3.9.40   FL 3.9.41

RALPH CARNALL

48169   Sgt   Pilot   British   111 Squadron

Born on August 23 1913, Carnall entered the RAF as an aircraft apprentice. He volunteered for pilot training, was selected in 1935 and began training in 1936. In February 1937 he was posted to 111 Squadron at Northolt.

Carnall was still with the squadron in 1940 and was in action over Dunkirk. On July 10 he crashed on landing at Hawkinge after his port wing was damaged during a combat off Folkestone. He was shot down over Kent on August 16 and crashed in Hurricane P 3029 at Palmers Green Farm, Brenchley. He suffered burns and was operated on by Archie McIndoe, making him a Guinea Pig. He did not return to 111 Squadron.

Commissioned in March 1942, Carnall stayed on in the RAF, in the Fighter Control Branch. He retired on August 24 1963, as a Squadron Leader. He died in 1984.

PO 16.3.42   FO 1.10.42   FL 16.3.44   FL 16.9.46
SL 1.1.57

JACK CONWAY CARPENTER

Sub-Lieutenant (FAA)   **Pilot**   **British**   **229 and 46 Sqdns**

Joined the Fleet Air Arm in July 1939. Loaned to the RAF, Carpenter joined 229 Squadron at Wittering on July 9 1940. Two weeks later he moved to 46 Squadron at Digby.

Carpenter destroyed a Bf 110 near North Weald on September 3. Two days later he shot down a Bf 109 in the Southend area. On September 8 he was shot down during an attack on enemy aircraft over Sheppey. He baled out but fell dead. His Hurricane, P 3201, crashed at Bearsted, Maidstone.

Carpenter's body was taken to the Royal Naval Dockyard at Chatham, from whence it was returned to his family at Llanfaethlu, Anglesey. He was buried at sea on September 16 1940. He was 21 years old.

Midshipman 1.7.39   *Sub-Lt 1.9.39*

JOHN MICHAEL VOWLES CARPENTER

42191   **PO**   **Pilot**   **British**   **222 Squadron**

Born on April 9 1921, Carpenter began elementary flying instruction with the RAF in February 1939. On completion of his training he joined 263 Squadron at Filton in November. On April 21 1940 the squadron embarked on HMS 'Furious' for Norway, flying off three days later to land on a frozen lake. By the 26th all Gladiators were either destroyed or unserviceable so 263 re-embarked for the UK.

In May another attempt was made. From the 21st until it re-embarked on HMS 'Glorious' on June 6 the squadron gave a good account of itself, covering the evacuation of the Army and flying offensive patrols. The carrier was sunk by enemy action soon after sailing and nearly all 263's pilots were lost. Carpenter had not flown on to the carrier and returned to the UK by another ship. He joined 222 Squadron at Hornchurch in late June 1940.

On August 31 he claimed a probable Bf 109, on September 1 he destroyed a Bf 109, on the 3rd a Bf 110 and on the 4th another Bf 109. Soon afterwards he was shot down and wounded and returned to the squadron in October. Carpenter stayed with 222 until April 1941, when he was posted to 46 Squadron, just as it prepared to go to the Middle East. The squadron embarked on HMS 'Argus', transferred to the 'Ark Royal' and the 'Furious' at Gibraltar and flew off to Hal Far, Malta on June 6.

46 was kept in Malta and re-numbered 126 Squadron. On June 30 Carpenter shot down a Mc 200, on September 4 he claimed another, on November 8 a Mc 202, on the 12th another Mc 202 and on December 27 he shot a Ju 88 down into the sea. Carpenter, who had been a Flight Commander since early October, was awarded the DFC (2.1.42) and posted to 112 Squadron in the Western Desert. In May 1942 he went to 92 Squadron at Heliopolis.

After a rest Carpenter was given command of 72 Squadron at Lago, Italy in January 1944. On April 11 he was posted away, received a Bar to the DFC (7.7.44) and returned to the UK. He went to Hawker's as a production test pilot. Carpenter was granted a Permanent Commission in September 1945 and he retired on December 31 1959, as a Flight Lieutenant, retaining the rank of Squadron Leader.

APO 1.5.39   *PO 27.12.39*   *FO 27.12.40*   *FL 23.12.41*
FL 1.9.45

WILLIAM JOSEPH CARR

36127   **FL**   **Pilot**   **British**   **235 Squadron**

Carr was commissioned in the RAF in February 1938 but must have entered under special circumstances because four days later he was posted to the staff of the Aeroplane and Armament Experimental Establishment at Martlesham Heath. He was with 235 at the start of the Battle of Britain and was later awarded the AFC (1.7.41).

Carr was killed on August 26 1942, aged 29. His unit at the time of his death is not known. He is buried in St Paul's churchyard, Mill Hill, Middlesex.

PO 24.2.38   *FO 24.8.39*   *FL 3.9.40*   *SL 1.12.41*

ROBERT ALBERT CARR-LEWTY

46026   **Sgt**   **Pilot**   **British**   **41 Squadron**

Born at Bradford, Yorkshire on July 6 1911, Carr-Lewty was educated at Carlton Grammar School, Bradford and Edinburgh University. In January 1936 he joined the RAF on the direct-entry pilot scheme, did his elementary flying at 6 E&RFTS, Sywell and completed his training at 4 FTS, Abu Sueir.

Carr-Lewty qualified as a Sergeant-Pilot/Navigator in August 1936 and was posted to 107 Squadron at Andover in December. He moved to 41 Squadron at Catterick in October 1937. During Dunkirk and the Battle of Britain Carr-Lewty flew over 100 operational sorties, claiming a Bf 109 destroyed on July 29. In December 1940 he was posted to 15 EFTS, Kingstown as an instructor, commissioned in June 1941 and in December he went to the staff of 5 FIS, Scone, moving to 10 FIS, Woodley in August 1942.

Carr-Lewty was recategorised A1 on all types in November 1943. He was offered the post of CFI to the Royal Turkish Air Force in 1944 and CFI to the Free French Flying Instructors' School in 1946 but he declined both. He was awarded the AFC (1.1.45) and left the RAF at his own request in 1946.

In 1958 Carr-Lewty went to Edinburgh University Medical School. He qualified as MB Ch B in July 1964.

PO 26.6.41   *FO 26.6.42*   *FL 26.6.43*

JEAN CHARLES CARRIERE

41825   **FO**   **Pilot**   **Canadian**   **219 Squadron**

Born in Quebec in 1915, Carriere joined the RAF on a short service commission in January 1939. He was posted to 219 Squadron when it was reformed at Catterick on October 4 1939.

Carriere was on a searchlight co-operation flight in a Blenheim on August 6 1940, when he collided with high tension cables and crashed into a river. The aircraft was written off but Carriere and his gunner, Sergeant C Beveridge, escaped with superficial injuries.

In January 1944 Carriere transferred to the RCAF and he was released on November 28 1945, as a Flight Lieutenant.

APO 1.4.39   *PO 23.10.39*   *FO 23.10.40*

MALCOLM KEITH CARSWELL

39780   **FL**   **Pilot**   **New Zealander**   **43 Squadron**

Carswell was born in Invercargill on July 25 1915 and educated at Southland Boys' High School. He was apprenticed to a chemist and began a course in pharmacy. In 1936 he began having flying lessons at the Invercargill Flying Club and in June his instructor arranged for him to have an interview for a short service commission.

There were no immediate vacancies so Carswell made his own way to the UK in early 1937. He applied on arrival and was provisionally accepted. On March 30 he began his flying training at 12 E&RFTS, Prestwick and in June was posted to 6 FTS, Netheravon. After completing the course he joined 43 Squadron at Tangmere in January 1938.

On February 9 1940 Carswell was one of a section chasing a He 111, which was attacking a cargo boat off the coast between Acklington and Rosyth. His engine suddenly failed and being too low to bale out he decided to ditch the Hurricane close to the boat. The aircraft went straight down but Carswell managed to extricate himself. He could not inflate his life jacket and tried to swim through the freezing choppy sea to the boat, about a mile away. He passed out and came to in the boat, now docked at Rosyth. His life had been saved

MK Carswell (continued)

by the crew giving him artificial respiration.

Carswell was off flying for three months but arrived back just in time to fly south to Tangmere on May 31. The next day he was shot down in flames over Dunkirk and baled out. He landed very near the front line and after convincing French soldiers that he was an ally he was taken to an emergency hospital in Dunkirk. He boarded a destroyer, under Stuka attack, and finally reached England where he was taken to hospital, arriving there in the evening of the same day he had taken off from Tangmere.

Carswell returned to 43. On September 2, in a combat over Ashford, Carswell's Hurricane was hit and caught fire. He baled out, burned on legs, arms, hands and face and with cannon shell splinters in chest and thigh. After leaving hospital Carswell was grounded for medical reasons and took up control duties. In October 1940 he went to Exeter as a Fighter Controller, moving in November to the Orkneys on Defence of Scapa Flow.

In March 1941 he went to Peterhead as Chief Fighter Controller and in May 1942 moved to Biggin Hill. He had a number of postings as Controller over the next three years. Carswell transferred to the RNZAF in January 1944. He regained his flying category in April 1945 and went to 17 SFTS for a combined refresher and twin-engine conversion course for night fighters.

Towards the end of the year Carswell applied for discharge in the UK and was released on January 26 1946. After a long working life in Italy he retired to Australia.

APO 30.5.37   PO 5.4.38   FO 5.10.39   FL 5.10.40
SL 1.12.41

CHARLES ALBERT WILLIAM CARTER

74594   PO   Pilot   British   611 Squadron

Carter was first commissioned in the RAF in September 1939 and until he was released in 1946 he was always in the Engineering Branch. He may have qualified as a pilot before the war but nothing is known. His name appears in the 611 ORB but whether or not he served with the squadron is also not known. He was released from the RAF, as a Flight Lieutenant and died in 1960.

APO 18.9.39   PO 19.11.39   FO 19.11.40   FL 1.12.41

LESLIE RAYMOND CARTER

754236   Sgt   Pilot   British   66, 610 and 41 Squadrons

Carter, of Shenley, Hertfordshire, was a member of the pre-war RAFVR. Called up at the outbreak of war he completed his training and joined 66 Squadron at Coltishall on August 28 1940. He was posted to 610 Squadron at Acklington on September 10 and moved to 41 Squadron at Hornchurch on October 1.

On October 11 Carter, whilst climbing to engage Bf 109s, collided with Flying Officer DH O'Neill. Both pilots baled out but O'Neill's parachute failed to open and he was killed. Carter's Spitfire, X 4554, crashed and burned out at South Ash Manor, West Kingsdown.

In early 1941 Carter was posted to 74 Squadron at Manston. He was reported 'Missing' on July 6 1941. He was 21 and is remembered on the Runnymede Memorial, Panel 35.

PETER EDWARD GEORGE CARTER

41375   PO   Pilot   British   73 and 302 Squadrons

Joined the RAF on a short service commission and began his flying training in October 1938. Carter was with 73 Squadron at Church Fenton at the beginning of July 1940. On August 15 he claimed the destruction of two Ju 88s. On the 24th he was posted to 302 Squadron at Leconfield.

On October 18 a patrol of the squadron became lost over the Surrey hills because of fog. The leader caught a glimpse of Kempton Park racecourse and ordered his pilots to make forced-landings. Carter was one of the four who were killed in the attempt. He tried to bale out at 50 feet. His Hurricane, P 3931, crashed on the racecourse. He was 21 and is buried in Queen's Road Cemetery, Croydon.

APO 14.12.38   PO 3.9.39

VICTOR ARTHUR CARTER

84966   PO   Pilot   British   607 Squadron

Born in 1917, Carter was commissioned in the RAF in September 1940 and joined 607 Squadron at Turnhouse in October.

He transferred to the Administrative Branch in 1942 and was released in 1945, as a Flight Lieutenant.

PO 7.9.40   FO 7.9.41   FL 7.9.42

GERALD CHARLES TREWALLA CARTHEW

42484   PO   Pilot   Canadian   253, 85 and 145 Sqdns

Carthew, from Mountain Park, Alberta, joined the RAF in June 1939. He was posted to 253 Squadron in March 1940. He moved to 85 Squadron at Castle Camps on September 20 and on to 145 Squadron at Drem on October 14.

Transferred to the Administrative Branch in 1942, Carthew was released from the RAF in 1946.

APO 19.8.39   PO 28.2.40   FO 28.2.41   FL 28.2.42

JOHN CHAMPION CARVER

72396   FO   Pilot   British   87 Squadron

Born on January 30 1916, Carver was educated at Winchester College and Christ Church College, Oxford. He was a member of the University Air Squadron and was commissioned in the RAFVR in August 1938. He was with ICI Singapore before the war and did some flying with the VR in Malaya in 1939.

Carver was called to full-time service at the outbreak of war. He joined 87 Squadron at Church Fenton on October 1 1940. He was a Flight Commander in 247 Squadron at Portreath in June 1941 and on August 31 he shared in the destruction of a Do 17. In September Carver was promoted to Acting Squadron Leader and posted to HQ 10 Group.

He returned to operations in January 1942, when he was given command of 118 Squadron at Predannack. Carver took part in the attack on the 'Scharnhorst' and 'Gneisenau' on February 12. On March 13 he baled out after his Spitfire was hit by return fire from a Ju 88. As he left the aircraft he struck his face against the hood and was stunned. His parachute opened and he came to in the sea. After some difficulty in disentangling himself from the shrouds he inflated his dinghy and set out to paddle the seventy miles to the English coast. After 57 hours, in wintry conditions, Carver was within seven miles of his objective, when he was picked up by a Royal Navy vessel, whose attention he had attracted by blowing his whistle.

Carver was awarded the DFC (10.4.42). He was reported 'Missing' on June 6 1942, in action over Cherbourg. He is remembered on the Runnymede Memorial, Panel 65.

PO (RAFVR) 16.8.38   PO 7.9.39   FO 16.2.40   FL 16.2.41

KENNETH MALTBY CARVER

79730   PO   Pilot   British   29 and 229 Squadrons

Commissioned in May 1940 Carver joined 29 Squadron at Digby in June. He was posted to 229 Squadron at Wittering on July 17. In an engagement with He 111s over Maidstone on September 11 Carver's aircraft was set alight. He baled out and landed near Flimwell and was taken to the casualty clearing station at Benenden Girls' School. He spent four weeks at Rumwood Court Hospital, near Maidstone and then moved to RAF Hospital, Wendover. His Hurricane, N 2466, crashed at Spelmonden, Goudhurst Road, Horsmonden.

Carver rejoined 229 and was with the squadron in 1941. He was with 605 Squadron in 1944 and was awarded the DFC (21.11.44). He was released from the RAF in 1946, as a Squadron Leader.

PO 26.5.40   FO 26.5.41   FL 26.5.42

RODNEY HAROLD POWER CARVER

Lieutenant (FAA)   Pilot   British   804 Squadron

Born on June 8 1916, Carver joined the Navy in 1935. He had been in action over Scapa Flow and in Norway before the Battle of Britain. In July 1940 he was with 804 Squadron, flying Gladiators from Hatston on dockyard defence.

On August 29 1942 Carver was given command of 885 Squadron, operating in defence of Malta convoys with Hurricanes from HMS 'Victorious'. He was awarded the DSC (10.11.42) for his services, during which he shot down at least two Ju 88s. In 1945 he was Air Group Commander in the 21st Aircraft Carrier Squadron in the Indian Ocean and received a Mention in Despatches for an air strike on Sumatra from HMS 'Khedive' on June 30.

He was made a CBE (13.6.59) and was at that time on loan to the Government of India. Carver was ADC to the Queen in the late fifties. He retired on March 1 1966, as a Captain.

*Midshipman 1.5.35   Sub-Lt 1.9.36   Lt 1.9.38
Lt-Cdr 1.12.45   Cdr 31.12.49   Capt 30.6.56*

HERBERT ROBERT CASE

83272   PO   Pilot   British   64 and 72 Squadrons

Joined 64 Squadron at Leconfield in September 1940 but posted soon afterwards to 72 Squadron at Biggin Hill.

Case was killed on October 12 1940, when he dropped out of formation and crashed at Capel-le-Fern, near Folkestone, in Spitfire P 9338. He was buried in St Nicholas' churchyard, near his home in Withycombe, Somerset. He was 24 years old.

PO 10.8.40

ERNEST CASSIDY

40507   FO   Pilot   British   25 and 249 Squadrons

Born on October 25 1916, Cassidy joined the RAF on a short service commission in December 1937. He completed his elementary flying training and on March 5 1938 was posted to 7 FTS, Peterborough, after which he joined 25 Squadron at Hawkinge on September 17.

Cassidy was posted to 249 Squadron at North Weald on October 21 1940. In May 1941 the squadron was ordered to the Middle East. It sailed in the carrier HMS 'Furious' on the 12th. At Gibraltar the Hurricanes were transferred to HMS 'Ark Royal', which then sailed into the Mediterranean. On May 21 249 flew off to Malta and once there was told that it would be staying. On July 9 Cassidy shot a SM 79 down into the sea. At the end of the month he was posted as a Flight Commander to the Malta Night Fighter Unit, then about to be formed.

On the night of August 5/6 he destroyed a Fiat BR 20, on the 26th he shared in damaging two more and on November 9 he damaged an enemy bomber. Cassidy was awarded the DFC (2.1.42) and returned to the UK, becoming a Flight Commander at 61 OTU, Rednal. He commanded 64 Squadron from November 1943 to April 1944 and 72 Squadron from May to July 1945.

Cassidy was granted a Permanent Commission in September 1945. Awarded the AFC (5.6.52), he retired on June 1 1958, as a Squadron Leader, retaining the rank of Wing Commander.

*APO 19.2.38   PO 29.11.38   FO 29.8.40   FL 29.8.41
SL 1.7.43   SL 1.9.45*

LIONEL HARWOOD CASSON

91000   PO   Pilot   British   616 Squadron

Born in Sheffield in 1915, Casson joined 616 Squadron, AuxAF at Doncaster on April 6 1939. He was called for full-time service on August 24, posted to 2 FTS, Brize Norton on October 7 and rejoined 616 Squadron at Leconfield on April 6 1940.

Casson was sent to 6 OTU, Sutton Bridge on April 28, after which he was posted to 501 Squadron in France on May 15. On his way to Arras the train was bombed at Amiens and the next day he lost all his kit when the train was heavily bombed at St Roche junction. He walked to the outskirts of Rouen and met an RAF vehicle going to Cherbourg. From there he got a ship to Southampton.

On May 27 Casson joined 79 Squadron at Biggin Hill but managed to get back to 616 at Leconfield on July 7. In late August 1940 Casson and Pilot Officer T Murray were loaned for two days to 615 Squadron, they being the only 616 pilots with Hurricane experience.

On September 1 he claimed the destruction of a Do 17. Casson was scrambled on February 26 1941, with Flying Officer R Marples. They attacked a Ju 88, killing the rear gunner. Casson's engine began to overheat and the cockpit filled with glycol fumes. He headed for Tangmere but crossing the coast at 1200 feet he feared the aircraft was on fire so he baled out. The Spitfire, P 7753, crashed at Priors Leas, north of Littlehampton. On May 5 he attacked a Ju 88 at dusk, was hit by return fire and baled out over Littlehampton. He shared a Bf 109 on June 23.

Casson was shot down on August 9 and captured. Soon afterwards he was awarded the DFC (16.9.41). Released from captivity, Casson returned to the UK and was demobilised on November 12 1945. He rejoined the RAuxAF on May 3 1947, as a Flying Officer with 616 Squadron at Finningley. In October 1950 Casson took command of the squadron, was awarded the AFC (1.6.53) and was released again in November 1954.

*APO (AuxAF) 23.7.39   APO 24.8.39   PO 6.4.40
FO 3.12.40   FL 3.12.41   FO (RAuxAF) 31.1.47
SL (RAuxAF) 2.10.50*

COLIN EWART PATRICK CASTLE

966825   Sgt   Air Gunner   British   219 Squadron

Castle was with 219 Squadron at Catterick at the beginning of July 1940. He was killed on November 13 1940, when the Beaufighter he was in crashed near Edenbridge, cause unknown. He is buried in Cathcart Cemetery, Renfrewshire.

JOHN GEOFFREY CAVE

39271   FL   Pilot   British   600 and 242 Squadrons

Born in Britain, Cave was educated in Calgary from 1927 to 1932 and worked there in 1934/35. In October 1936 he joined the RAF. On January 16 1937 he was posted to 8 FTS, Montrose and after completing his training he joined 25 Squadron at Hawkinge on August 7 1937.

Cave was with 600 Squadron at Northolt in early July 1940. He was posted to 242 Squadron at Coltishall on August 11 but flew no operations with it before being posted away on October 3 1940.

Towards the end of the war Cave went into Aircraft Control and when he died in early 1962 he was the senior Squadron Leader in the Aircraft Control Branch.

*APO 21.12.36   PO 12.10.37   FO 12.5.39   FL 3.9.40
SL 1.9.42   FL 1.3.45   SL 1.8.47*

FREDERICK NORMAN CAWSE

80543   PO   Pilot   British   238 Squadron

Cawse joined 238 Squadron at Middle Wallop on July 7 1940. He was killed on August 11 when he was shot down by a Bf 109 in a combat off Weymouth. His Hurricane, P 3222, crashed into the sea. Cawse's body was later washed up on the French coast. He was 25 and is buried in the Cayeux-sur-Mer Communal Cemetery, France.

PO 8.6.40

ARSEN CEBRZYNSKI

P 1416   FO   Pilot   Polish   303 Squadron

Born on March 2 1912, Cebrzynski was in the PAF before the war. He escaped to France and in May 1940 was commanding a flight of three Polish pilots in Groupe de Chasse II /6 at Chateauroux, flying Bloch MB 152s. In the fighting in May the flight was credited with two victories.

Cebrzynski arrived in England on July 7 1940 and joined 303 Squadron at Northolt on August 21. He was shot down in combat south of London on September 11 and severely injured. He died on the 19th and was buried in Northwood Cemetery, Middlesex. Cebrzynski was awarded the KW and Bar (23.12.40) and a second Bar (31.10.47).

FRANTISEK CHABERA

115117   Sgt   Pilot   Czechoslovakian   312 Squadron

Joined 312 Squadron on September 5 1940. Chabera was commissioned in December 1941 and was released after the war as a Flight Lieutenant.

PO 19.12.41

DENNIS FREDERICK CHADWICK

101519   Sgt   Pilot   British   64 Squadron

Served with 64 in the Battle of Britain. On December 5 1940 Chadwick forced-landed near Faversham after being attacked by a Bf 109.

He was commissioned in July 1941, transferred to the Administrative Branch in 1943 and was released in 1945, as a Squadron Leader. He died in 1973.

PO 17.7.41   FO 17.7.42   FL 17.7.43

RONALD IVOR CHAFFE

79528   PO   Pilot   British   245 and 43 Squadrons

Chaffe, from Bristol, joined 245 Squadron at Drem in May 1940. He was posted to 43 Squadron on September 18 but returned to 245 at Aldergrove in December 1940.

In late 1941 Chaffe was in Malta, serving with 1435 Flight. He took command of 185 Squadron at Hal Far in February 1942 but was killed on the 22nd, aged 27. He is remembered on the Malta Memorial, Panel 2, Column 1.

PO 19.5.40   FO 19.5.41

HARRY HUTCHINSON CHALDER

43691   PO   Pilot   British   266 and 41 Squadrons

Joined 266 Squadron at Martlesham Heath in April 1940. On August 12 the squadron moved temporarily to Eastchurch for possible anti-shipping operations. Early the next morning the Germans made a bombing attack, using thirty Do 17s. Severe damage to buildings and hangars was inflicted and six aircraft were destroyed on the ground. Five Do 17s were destroyed. Chalder was injured in the foot by a bomb.

On September 15 he was posted to 41 Squadron at Hornchurch. Two days later his Spitfire, N 3266, was badly damaged by a Bf 109 in an action off Dover. Chalder was shot down in a combat over Charing on September 28 1940 and baled out, seriously wounded, landing near Garlinge Green. He was admitted to Chartham Hospital and died there on November 10, aged 25. He is buried in St Nicholas' Cemetery, Newcastle-upon-Tyne. His Spitfire, X 4409, was possibly the one which exploded over East Stour Farm, Chilham.

PO 1.4.40

PATRICK CHALLONER-LINDSEY

41036   PO   Pilot   British   601 Squadron

Challoner-Lindsey, of Cheltenham, began his flying training with the RAF in June 1938. He was with 601 Squadron at the beginning of July 1940. On the 11th he claimed the destruction of a Bf 110.

He was shot down two miles off St Catherine's Point on July 27 1940 by Oberleutnant Dobislav of III /JG 27. Challoner-Lindsey's Hurricane, P 2753, crashed into the Channel and he was reported 'Missing'. His body was later washed up on the French coast and he is buried in Wimereux Communal Cemetery, France. He was 20 years old.

APO 20.8.38   PO 27.6.39

STANISLAW JOZEF CHALUPA

P 1300   PO   Pilot   Polish   302 Squadron

Born in 1915, Chalupa was in the PAF before the war and in the fighting in September 1939 he was credited with three victories. He escaped to France and flew with l'Armée de l'Air in Groupe de Chasse I/2, destroying another two enemy aircraft and sharing two more.

Chalupa escaped to England in June 1940 and joined 302 Squadron at Leconfield on July 23. He claimed a probable Ju 88 on August 21 and a Do 17 and another probably destroyed on September 15. He was awarded the VM (5th Class) (1.2.41).

Rested from operations on July 30 1942 Chalupa was posted to the Operations Room of 302, remaining there until June 24 1944, when he went to 16 SFTS, Newton for an instructor's course on Masters, after which he became an instructor there. On January 30 1945 Chalupa was posted to 3 (O) AFU for No 1 Pilot Navigation Course and he returned to Newton as a Navigation Instructor.

On September 25 1946 he was posted away to a Holding Unit, went to 6 RU on November 9 and was released from the PAF on December 30 1946, as a Flight Lieutenant. He was awarded the KW (31.10.47). Chalupa settled in Canada.

FO 1.3.41   FL 1.9.42

GEORGE PHILIP CHAMBERLAIN

16168   **WC**   **Pilot**   **British**   **FIU**

Born on August 18 1905, Chamberlain was educated at Denstone College. He entered RAF College, Cranwell in September 1923 and on graduating was posted on July 30 1925 to 25 Squadron at Hawkinge. On April 14 1927 Chamberlain went to India, joining 5 (Army Co-operation) Squadron at Risalpur, flying Bristol Fighters. He returned to the UK in August 1930 and was sent to the Electrical and Wireless School at Cranwell for a course.

Chamberlain went to Upavon on July 21 1931 as Station Signals Officer, moving on September 26 1932 to the staff of HQ ADGB and a year later to the SHQ Staff at RAF Netheravon. It was back to flying in 1934, with a posting to 17 Squadron at Kenley on March 14, as a Flight Commander.

In January 1936 Chamberlain went to RAF Staff College, Andover and a year later was appointed to the Signals Staff at HQ 16 Group, Coastal Command at Lee-on-Solent. He moved to 18 Group, Donibristle i/c Signals on November 7th 1938. In April 1940 Chamberlain was serving on the Night Interception Committee at Air Ministry, which acceded to Dowding's request for a night unit. Chamberlain was given the job and formed the Fighter Interception Unit at Tangmere, with Blenheims.

He was posted to HQ Coastal Command on July 17 1941, made an OBE (24.9.41), posted on January 4th 1943 to No 1 Radio School, Cranwell and in August 1943 went on a year's attachment to the RAAF in Melbourne. After a short spell at the Air Ministry from October 1944 Chamberlain was posted to HQ Transport Command until October 1946. He was made a CB (13.6.46). He held a series of staff appointments from then until his retirement on September 25 1960, as an Air Vice-Marshal.

PO 30.7.25   FO 30.1.27   FL 5.11.30   SL 1.2.37
WC 1.3.40   GC 1.3.42   AC 1.7.50   AVM 1.7.55

JOSEPH THOMAS RONALD CHAMBERLAIN

81677   **PO**   **Pilot**   **British**   **235 Squadron**

Chamberlain joined the RAFVR in June 1939 and began his flying training at 6 E&RFTS, Sywell. He was called up at the outbreak of war and on October 23 went to No 1 EFTS, Hatfield, remaining there until March 18 1940, when he was posted to 6 FTS, Little Rissington.

On July 13 Chamberlain went to 5 OTU, Aston Down to convert to Blenheims and on August 3 1940 he joined 235 Squadron at Bircham Newton. Returning from a dusk patrol over the North Sea on February 14 1941, Chamberlain prepared to land at Bircham Newton. Suddenly the lights were put out because of enemy aircraft. He flew on to the satellite at Langham, 15 miles away, and as he was about to touch down the lights there went out. The aircraft hit a tree. The navigator was killed and the air gunner, slightly injured. Chamberlain was seriously injured and spent the next eight months in hospital, at Ely and Torquay. In October 1941 he went to a ground job at RAF Langham.

On May 11 1942 he was attached to 2 Armament Practice Camp at Thorney Island, on flying duties. He was posted on administrative duties to the Air Ministry on May 1 1943 and remained there until his release from the RAF in 1946.

PO 11.7.40   FO 11.7.41   FL 11.7.42

HORATIO HERBERT CHANDLER

106245   **Sgt**   **Pilot**   **British**   **610 Squadron**

Chandler, who was born in 1917, joined 610 Squadron, AuxAF on March 10 1936. In April 1939 an NCO pilot-training scheme was started and Chandler had already had some flying training when he was called up at the outbreak of war. He qualified as a Sergeant-Pilot in March 1940 and after converting to Spitfires he rejoined 610 Squadron at Wittering in April.

On July 25 1940 he claimed a Bf 109 destroyed and another on August 14. He claimed a Do 215 on the 18th and another Bf 109 on the 30th. Chandler was awarded the DFM (22.10.40), then being credited with six enemy aircraft destroyed.

Commissioned in June 1941, Chandler was awarded the AFC (2.4.43). He was released in 1946, as a Flight Lieutenant, and recommissioned as a Pilot Officer in the Training Branch, RAFVR in June 1946.

PO 26.6.41   FO 26.6.42   FL 26.6.43   PO (RAFVR) 1.6.46

VICTOR RONALD CHAPMAN

754146   **Sgt**   **Air Gunner**   **British**   **264 Squadron**

Joined 264 Squadron in July 1940. On August 28 Chapman was gunner in Defiant L 6957, which had its petrol tank holed during an attack on a He 111 over Folkestone. He and his pilot, Sergeant AJ Lauder, were unhurt and returned safely to Hornchurch.

No further service details traced.

ALAN KINGSLEY CHAPPELL

80808   **PO**   **Pilot**   **British**   **236 Squadron**

Chappell, of South Croydon, was born on May 21 1914 and was at Marlborough College from 1928 to 1931.

Commissioned in the RAF in June 1940, he joined 236 Squadron on August 15.

His name disappears from the Air Force List after July 1944 and he has not been traced as a casualty.

PO 2.6.40   FO 2.6.41   FL 2.6.42

CHARLES GORDON CHAPPELL

40672   **FO**   **Pilot**   **British**   **65 and 609 Squadrons**

Joined 65 Squadron at Turnhouse on August 19 1940 and moved to 609 Squadron at Middle Wallop on October 9.

Chappell was released in 1945, as a Squadron Leader.

APO 7.5.38   PO 7.3.39   FO 3.9.40   FL 3.9.41
SL 1.1.44

DOUGLAS WILLIAM ERNEST CHAPPLE

902225   **Sgt**   **Air Gunner**   **British**   **236 Squadron**

Chapple, of Plymouth, joined 236 Squadron on July 19 1940.

He was killed on June 28 1941, as a Flight Sergeant with 7 Squadron, operating in Stirlings from Oakington.

Chapple was 24. He is remembered on the Runnymede Memorial, Panel 35.

WILFRED THOMAS CHARD

746805   **Sgt**   **Air Gunner**   **British**   **141 Squadron**

Chard was with 141 Squadron in early July 1940. Flying with Sergeant G Laurence, he shot down a Ju 88 at night on September 17 1940. It crashed at St Andrews Close, Maidstone, killing the crew of four.

Chard was a Warrant Officer in 1943 but nothing further has been traced.

EDWARD FRANCIS JOHN CHARLES

36198   **FO**   **Pilot**   **Canadian**   **54 Squadron**

The son of an RFC pilot, Charles was born in Coventry, England on February 6 1919. He was taken to Canada as a child and lived in Lashburn, Saskatchewan. In June 1937 he joined a territorial unit, the 16th/22nd Saskatchewan Horse.

Charles joined the RCAF in January 1938 and transferred to the RAF in May 1939. In December he was posted to 81 (Communications) Squadron. When it disbanded on June 15 1940 Charles joined 2 (Army Co-operation) Squadron.

EFJ Charles (continued)

When a call was made for fighter pilots he volunteered and was posted to 7 OTU, Hawarden to convert to Spitfires, after which he went to 54 Squadron at Hornchurch on September 3.

He claimed no victories until April 17 1941, when he shot down a Bf 110. Between June 17 and the end of September Charles destroyed five Bf 109s, probably destroyed five others and shared in the probable destruction of two more. He was awarded the DFC (15.7.41) and posted away in late September to an OTU, as an instructor.

In January 1943 Charles went to 64 Squadron, on March 27 he moved to 611 Squadron, as a Flight Commander and on April 22 he was promoted to Acting Squadron Leader and given the command.

Charles began scoring again. On May 14 he destroyed a FW 190, the next day two FW 190s. Commandant Mouchotte had shot down a FW 190 simultaneously with Charles' second one. Thus the two pilots shared the honour of shooting down Biggin Hill's 1000th victim. On May 17 Charles claimed a FW 190, on the 23rd another and on the 25th, after destroying a FW 190, his own aircraft was damaged and after gliding down from 10,000 to 1000 feet he baled out into the sea and was picked up by an ASR launch.

On August 9 1943 Charles was promoted to lead the Middle Wallop Wing. He claimed a FW 190 on August 31, was posted to Portreath on September 16 to command the Wing there and on the 24th he claimed his final victory, a Bf 110. Charles was awarded a Bar to the DFC (16.7.43), the US Silver Star (20.7.43) and the DSO (29.10.43). He was posted to staff duties at HQ 10 Group and on April 14 1944 he transferred to the RCAF.

After making a lecture tour of Canada Charles was on the staff of HQ Allied Expeditionary Air Forces. After release from the RCAF he lived in Canada.

PO 15.5.39   FO 3.9.40   FL 3.9.41

GERARD CHARNOCK

1002641   Sgt   Aircrew   British   25 Squadron

Joined 25 Squadron in late September 1940. Nothing further known.

HARRY WALPOLE CHARNOCK

147902   Sgt   Pilot   British   64 and 19 Squadrons

Born in 1905, Charnock was educated at Harrow. He entered RAF College, Cranwell in January 1924 and was commissioned in December 1925, joining 32 Squadron at Kenley on the 16th. He was posted to No 1 Squadron at Tangmere on August 18 1930. Charnock was cashiered by order of General Court Martial on December 12 1930 for a low-flying offence.

Two days after the outbreak of war he rejoined the RAF and later went to 64 Squadron at Church Fenton, as a Sergeant-Pilot. On September 6 1940 he crashed in Spitfire K 9903 during a routine patrol. Although the aircraft was written off he was unhurt. In October 1940 Charnock was posted to 19 Squadron at Fowlmere. He scored his first victory on November 11, when he claimed a Bf 109. He claimed Bf 109s destroyed on July 21 and August 7 1941. At the end of his tour with 19 Squadron he was awarded the DFM (7.4.42).

Charnock was posted to 72 Squadron in early August 1942. In November 72 moved to Gibraltar and on the 16th it flew to Algiers and began patrols the next day. Between November 25 and December 18 he claimed a FW 190, four Bf 109s and a probable Bf 109 destroyed. On December 18 he was himself shot down and landed in enemy territory. Charnock bribed an arab to lead him to the British lines. Once there he went to a base hospital. Commissioned from Warrant Officer in January 1943, he was awarded the DFC (26.2.43) and rejoined the squadron on March 17.

Posted away, Charnock returned to the UK and after a rest joined 222 Squadron in July 1944. Two days later he was injured in a car accident and did not return to operations until early 1945, when he was posted to 41 Squadron at Volkel, as a Flight Commander. He was released from the RAF on November 24 1945, as a Flight Lieutenant. He died on May 24 1974.

PO 12.1.43   FO 12.7.43   FL 12.1 45

GEORGE FREDERICK CHATER

34230   SL   Pilot   South African   247 and 3 Squadrons

Chater was first commissioned in September 1934. He completed his flying training at 3 FTS, Grantham and joined 23 Squadron at Biggin Hill on September 16 1935. He was posted overseas on February 21 1936, to 100 (Torpedo-Bomber) Squadron at Seletar, Straits Settlements.

At the beginning of 1940 Chater was a flying instructor at Cranwell. On August 1 he reformed 247 Squadron at Roborough, from Gladiators of the Sumburgh Fighter Flight. He was awarded the DFC (13.9.40). On September 22 he was given command of 3 Squadron at Turnhouse. Posted away in November 1940, Chater commanded 30 Squadron in Ceylon from February to May 1942 and a Hurricane Wing in Burma in 1944.

He was released from the RAF in 1949, as a Group Captain.

APO 14.9.34   PO 8.3.35   FO 8.11.36   FL 8.11.38
SL 1.9.40   WC 1.12.41

JOHN COWPER CHEETHAM

46208   Sgt   Aircrew   British   23 Squadron

Cheetham, of Dunbar, East Lothian, was with 23 Squadron at Collyweston in June 1940. He was commissioned in July 1941 and killed on July 15 1944, as a Flight Lieutenant, aged 35. His unit at the time of his death is not known. He is remembered on the Runnymede Memorial, Panel 201.

PO 26.7.41   FO 26.7.42   FL 26.7.43

MARIAN CHELMECKI

76690   PO   Pilot   Polish   56 and 17 Squadrons

Born on August 2 1916, Chelmecki was in the PAF before the war. He graduated from the Air Force Flying School, Deblin and was posted to 122 Fighter Squadron of the 2nd Air Regiment. In 1939 he was transferred to Deblin as an instructor. After Poland collapsed he escaped to Roumania, then to France and arrived in England in early 1940.

In mid-July 1940 Chelmecki was posted to 15 EFTS, Carlisle, in early August he converted to Hurricanes at 6 OTU, Sutton Bridge and on August 31 he joined 56 Squadron at North Weald, moving to 17 Squadron at Debden ten days later. Chelmecki destroyed a Ju 87 on November 8, shared in damaging a Do 17 on the 9th and destroyed a Bf 109 on the 11th. He was awarded the KW (1.2.41) and a Bar (1.4.41).

He went to 55 OTU, Annan on March 20 1941 and for the next eight months instructed at 55, 56 and 61 OTUs. On November 5 1941 Chelmecki joined 308 Squadron at Northolt, moved to 302 at Heston on June 13 1942, was awarded a second Bar to the KW (7.7.43) and joined 317 Squadron on September 21 1943.

In January 1944 Chelmecki was posted to HQ 18 Sector, on July 12 he went to HQ 131 Airfield (Northolt) and on August 31 took command of 317 Squadron at Plumetot in France. At the end of his tour he went back to HQ 131 Airfield and was awarded the VM (5th Class)(25.6.45). Chelmecki was posted on November 9 1945 to the Ferry Pool of the Enemy Aircraft Salvage and Service Unit at Hamburg-Fühlsbuttel for flying duties. He was released on August 8 1946, returned to Poland in 1948 and died there on March 28 1988.

PO 6.8.40   FO 1.3.41   FL 1.9.42

PETER CHESTERS

84960   PO   Pilot   British   74 Squadron

Chesters, of Thorpe Bay, Essex, was born on April 29 1919 and was at Haileybury College from 1933 to 1935. He joined 74 Squadron at Coltishall on September 28 1940.

He claimed a Bf 109 destroyed on October 27. In combat over Chatham on November 27 Chesters baled out, wounded in the leg. He stayed at the controls until his aircraft was steered away from a village. He was admitted to Orpington Hospital. His Spitfire, P 7306, crashed at Blacketts Marshes.

On February 5 1941 Chesters shared in destroying a Do 215 near Dover. He shot down a Bf 109 of JG 51 over Kent on April 10. So delighted was he with his success that he attempted a victory roll over Hornchurch, misjudged his height and crashed on the parade ground. Chesters was killed instantly. He is buried in Sutton Road Cemetery, Southend-on-Sea.

PO 7.9.40

CHARLES ARTHUR COPELAND CHETHAM

82946   PO   Pilot   British   1 Squadron

Chetham, from Newton Abbot, Devon, was commissioned in May 1940 and joined No 1 Squadron at Tangmere in June. On August 11 he shared a Bf 110 with Pilot Officer GE Goodman. He was on a night flight on the 27th when he was held by searchlights and lost control. Chetham baled out and landed, unhurt, at Amersham. His Hurricane, P 3897, crashed and burned out at Lacey Green, Buckinghamshire. Back in action, he claimed a Bf 109 on September 1 and damaged another the next day.

In 1941 Chetham was with 33 Squadron in Greece. He was killed on April 15, aged 21. He is buried in Phaleron War Cemetery, Athens.

PO 26.5.40

JOSEPH ARMAND JACQUES CHEVRIER

C 856   PO   Pilot   Canadian   1 and 1 (RCAF) Sqdns

Born in St Lambert, Province of Quebec on October 7 1917, Chevrier joined the RCAF on July 4 1938. He went to England in 1940 and was posted to No 1 Squadron at Wittering on October 3, moving to No 1(RCAF) Squadron at Prestwick on the 21st.

Chevrier was repatriated to Canada on January 9 1941. He was appointed ADC to His Excellency the Governor-General, the Earl of Athlone on August 8 and served in that capacity until March 31 1942. Posted to 130(RCAF) Squadron, Chevrier was reported 'Missing, presumed Killed' in a flying accident on July 6 1942, as a Squadron Leader, aged 25. He is remembered on the Ottawa Memorial, Panel 1, Column 4.

CLIFFORD ARCHIBALD CHEW

116439   Sgt   Pilot   British   17 Squadron

From Eton Wick, Buckinghamshire, Chew joined 17 Squadron at Debden on July 15 1940. On August 21 he claimed a share in the destruction of a Ju 88.

Chew went to 616 Squadron at Kirton-in-Lindsey in November 1940. He was commissioned from Warrant Officer in January 1942. One day in June 1944 Chew was captain of an aircraft on an instructional flight, making night landings. On the fifth one the starboard engine began to give trouble. Chew took over the controls and managed to climb to 800 feet, a very difficult feat on one engine. Excessive vibration made it impossible to maintain height. As the aircraft came down the starboard engine caught fire and the propellor flew off. The undercarriage mechanism did not work. Chew decided to land on the runway to avoid crashing into other aircraft. He brought the crippled and burning aircraft down. The whole body was blazing by this time and only Chew's promptitude and presence of mind enabled the pupils to jump clear without injury. For this action he was awarded the AFC (25.8.44).

Chew was killed on March 24 1945, as a Flight Lieutenant with 512 Squadron, a Dakota transport unit. He is buried in Hotton War Cemetery, Belgium.

PO 2.1.42   FO 1.10.42   FL 2.1.44

ROBERT ALEXANDER CHIGNELL

24171   WC   Pilot   British   145 Squadron

Chignell joined the RAF in December 1927. He went to 2 FTS, Digby on January 14 1928 and after training joined 12 Squadron at Andover on December 15. He was posted to 444(Fleet Spotter-Reconnaissance) Squadron at Lee-on-Solent on January 29 1930, moving to the School of Naval Co-operation in March 1932. At the end of the year Chignell went to SHQ RAF Calshot. He was posted to RAF Seletar, in the Straits Settlements, on March 25 1937 and was put in charge of a detachment at Trincomalee.

Chignell went to SHQ Biggin Hill on July 10 1938. He commanded 32 Squadron there from October 1939 to May 1940. Although he did not belong to 145 Squadron Chignell must have flown at least one operational sortie with it during the period of the Battle of Britain, thus qualifying for the clasp.

Posted to the Far East, Chignell was killed at Kallang on February 14 1942, as a Wing Commander, aged 36. He is remembered on the Singapore Memorial in Kranji War Cemetery. In recognition of gallant conduct in operations against the Japanese in early 1942 Chignell received a Mention in Despatches on October 1 1946.

PO 9.12.27   FO 9.6.29   FL 1.2.34   SL 1.12.37
WC 1.9.40

PATRICK CHARLES STUART CHILTON

Sub-Lieutenant (FAA)   Pilot   British   804 Squadron

Born on February 15 1921 Chilton joined the Navy in January 1939. He was posted to 804 Squadron at Hatston on July 1 1940, to fly Gladiators on dockyard defence.

Later Chilton served with 805, 881, 1843 and 1849 Squadrons. After the war he was a test pilot in the UK and with the US Navy. He commanded 806 Squadron, became CFI at the Fighter School at Lossiemouth, commanded the Naval Test Squadron, the Flying Wing at Bedford and the Empire Test Pilots' School. He was awarded the AFC (1.1.59) and retired on April 5 1971, as a Captain.

Midshipman 13.1.39   Acting Sub-Lt 13.7.40   Sub-Lt 15.2.42
Lt 13.1.43   Lt-Cdr 13.1.51   Cdr 30.6.56   Capt 31.12.65

DOUGLAS JAMES CHIPPING

67603   Sgt   Pilot   British   222 Squadron

With 222 Squadron at Hornchurch in August 1940. Chipping was hit by anti-aircraft fire over Dover on September 5 and baled out, wounded. His Spitfire, X 4057, crashed and burned out near Pineham.

Commissioned in May 1941, Chipping was awarded the AFC (1.1.46) and released from the RAF in 1946, as a Flight Lieutenant. He later went to the USA to live and he died there in 1985.

PO 27.5.41   FO 27.5.42   FL 27.5.43

RODERICK AENEAS CHISHOLM

90233   FO   Pilot   British   604 Squadron

Chisholm was born on November 23 1911 and educated at Ampleforth College and the Imperial College of Science and Technology. He joined 604 Squadron, AuxAF in 1930 and was commissioned in March 1931. He went on to the Reserve in January 1935 and in 1936 went to Persia to work in the oilfields there. At the outbreak of war Chisholm was passed as fit for flying at HQ RAF Iraq, left Teheran in January 1940 and on February 23 was posted to South Cerney for a refresher course and conversion to twins.

Chisholm rejoined 604 at Northolt in late June. On March 13 1941 he destroyed two He 111s at night, on April 9 another two and was awarded the DFC (11.4.41). On the night of April 11 he shot down a He 111 and a probable Ju 88, on the 29th a He 111 and on July 8 he destroyed a He 111 and damaged another. At the end of his tour in January 1942 Chisholm was posted as a controller to Middle Wallop and was awarded a Bar to the DFC (10.2.42). He had been a Flight Commander since August 1941 and flew with Sergeant WG Ripley as his operator.

Chisholm went to HQ 81 Group in March 1942 to organise the training of night-fighter crews at OTUs but in June he was posted to RAF Ford, to command. In late 1943 Chisholm went to a staff job at 100 Group Bomber Command to develop radio counter-measures and fighter support for the bombers raiding Germany by night. He was awarded the DSO (14.1.44), credited with nine enemy aircraft destroyed.

Chisholm was stationed in Germany immediately after the war with an RAF interrogation team to find out as much as possible about German radio and radar measures taken against our bombers. He was made a CBE (1.1.46) and released from the RAF on January 1 1946, as an Air Commodore.

PO (AuxAF) 16.3.31   FO (AuxAF) 16.9.32
FO (AuxAFRO) 24.1.35   FO 23.2.40   FL 22.6.41
SL 16.12.42   WC 3.6.44   GC 14.12.44

TADEUSZ CHLOPIK

76691   FL   Pilot   Polish   302 Squadron

Chlopik was born on June 18 1908 and served in the pre-war PAF. He escaped to England and after converting to Hurricanes at 6 OTU, Sutton Bridge he joined 302 Squadron at Leconfield on August 3 1940. He claimed the destruction of a Do 215 on his first day with the squadron.

On September 15 1940, after sharing in destroying a D0 17, Chlopik was shot down in a surprise attack by enemy aircraft over North Weald. He baled out but is believed to have injured himself doing so and he fell dead at Rawreth. His Hurricane, P 2954, crashed at Marks Farm, Woodham Road, Battlesbridge. Chlopik is buried in Sutton Road Cemetery, Southend-on-Sea. He was awarded the KW and Bar (1.2.41).

JOHN ALLISON GEORGE CHOMLEY

84668   PO   Pilot   Rhodesian   257 Squadron

Chomley, from Southern Rhodesia, joined 257 Squadron at Northolt on July 7 1940. He crashed on landing at Hendon on the 23rd in Hurricane P3641 but was unhurt.

He was reported 'Missing' following a combat with enemy aircraft off Portsmouth on August 12 1940. His Hurricane, P 3662, is believed to have crashed in the sea. Chomley was 20 and is remembered on the Runnymede Memorial, Panel 7.

MAURICE PHILIPE CESAR CHORON

30501   Adjudant   Pilot   French   64 Squadron

Born on November 7 1911 at Bethisey St Pierre, Choron lived in Corsica before the war and in 1937 was a flying instructor at the Aero Club de Corse.

He was posted to 64 Squadron at Biggin Hill on October 11 1940. In July 1941 Choron joined 609 Squadron at Gravesend. On August 24, whilst flying as No 2 to Wing Commander ML Robinson, he shot down a Bf 109 off Dunkirk. Awarded the C de G in 1941, Choron was posted to 53 OTU, Heston in mid-November, as an instructor.

He returned to operations when he was posted to 340 Squadron on April 8 1942. Two days later the squadron went on its first offensive sweep, as part of the Tangmere Wing. Wing Commander ML Robinson was leading the Wing, at the head of 340 Squadron, with Choron flying as his No 2. Both men failed to return and were reported 'Missing'. A report on Paris radio said Choron had been picked up dead in his dinghy but this was never confirmed. His rank at the time of his death was Lieutenant de Reserve.

GEORGE PATTERSON CHRISTIE

40081   FO   Pilot   Canadian   242 and 66 Squadrons

Christie was born in 1917 at Westmount, Quebec and joined the RAF on a short service commission in June 1937. He was posted to 2 FTS, Brize Norton on September 18 and joined 43 Squadron at Tangmere on May 7 1938.

In May 1940 Christie went to the Photographic Development Unit at Heston, which was pioneering photo-reconnaissance techniques using unarmed, high-altitude Spitfires. For his work with the unit he was awarded the DFC (21.8.40).

Christie joined 242 Squadron at Coltishall on July 21 1940 and he claimed a He 111 destroyed on August 30. He was posted to 66 Squadron, also at Coltishall, on September 3, as a Flight Commander. The next day Christie claimed a Bf 109 but his Spitfire, X 4052, was damaged in the combat over Thanet and he made a forced-landing outside Canterbury, slightly wounded. Up again the next day he was shot down in combat with Bf 109s, wounded, and was admitted to the Royal Naval Hospital, Gillingham.

Christie claimed a Ju 87 destroyed and another probable on November 14, a Bf 109 on the 26th and on December 20 he flew one of two Spitfires in a low-level attack on the airfield at Le Touquet, one of the RAF's first offensive actions. Awarded a Bar to the DFC (14.1.41), he was then credited with at least seven enemy aircraft destroyed.

In early 1941 Christie returned to Canada and in March he joined Ferry Command. He was killed near Point Clare, Quebec on July 6 1942, in a flying accident in a Hudson, as a Squadron Leader.

APO 5.9.37   PO 12.7.38   FO 12.2.40   FL 12.2.41
SL 1.3.42

JOHN McBEAN CHRISTIE

741898   Sgt   Pilot   British   152 Squadron

Joined 152 Squadron at Warmwell in August 1940. On September 26 Christie was shot down by Bf 109s in combat over the Channel off Swanage. His Spitfire, K 9882, crashed into the sea and he was picked up dead.

Christie was 22 and is buried in Arkleston Cemetery, Renfrew.

BEVERLEY E CHRISTMAS

C 925   PO   Pilot   Canadian   1 (RCAF) Squadron

Christmas, of Rouville, Quebec, joined the RCAF on January 1 1939 and was with No 1 (RCAF) Squadron when it arrived in the UK on June 20 1940.

He claimed a Bf 109 destroyed on August 31, damaged a He 111 on September 11, shared a Ju 88 on the 27th and claimed a Bf 109 destroyed on October 5.

Christmas commanded 133 (RCAF) Squadron in March/April 1943, flying Kittyhawks at Boundary Bay on west coast defence. He commanded No 4 Wing (No 1 Air Division, Europe) from April 1955 to July 1957. He retired on January 5 1973, as a Colonel, and died on May 17 1988 at Victoria, British Columbia.

COLIN CHRYSTALL

46538   Sgt   Wop/AG   New Zealander   235 Squadron

Chrystall was born at Foxton on November 21 1916, educated at Foxton High School and after leaving went farming with his father. Unsuccessful in his attempts to get a short service commission, he sailed in the RMS 'Rangitata' for England on April 7 1938.

In July Chrystall joined the RAF as a trainee wireless operator and qualified in April 1939. He remustered as a Wireless Operator (Air) on May 1, was posted to 23 Squadron at Wittering and flew his first operation on September 20. Chrystall went to No 1 Air Armament School for a gunnery course on October 7 and passed out with the rank of LAC. He returned to 23 Squadron and began North Sea patrols. On November 29 his Blenheim had engine failure and the crew baled out. The aircraft crashed at Ravensfleet, near Gainsborough.

In March 1940 Chrystall applied for pilot training, had a selection board in May and was accepted for training at some future date. He joined 235 Squadron at Bircham Newton in late May and was promoted to Sergeant. The squadron flew patrols over Dunkirk and operated in support of Fighter Command during the Battle of Britain. When Chrystall was posted away for pilot training on May 10 1941 he had flown 133 operational sorties, involving 450 flying hours.

After completing ITW he went to 9 EFTS, Ansty, where he was commissioned in August and received a Mention in Despatches (24.9.41) for services with 235 Squadron. Chrystall was posted to 8 FTS, Montrose on November 1, he completed the course on April 15 1942 and then went to 59 OTU, Crosby-on-Eden, where he converted to Spitfires. He joined 485 Squadron in June, flying his first operational sortie as a pilot on July 3 1942. Chrystall destroyed a FW 190 over Dieppe on August 19.

In mid-September he was posted away for service in the Middle East, arriving at El Ballah for a course on Hurricanes on November 23, after which he joined 123 Squadron at Mehrabad, Persia. In April 1943 the squadron returned to Egypt. In July Chrystall went to 322 Wing Training Flight at Sorman and on August 10 he flew a Spitfire to Lentini, Sicily to join 243 Squadron at Pachino.

In February 1944 he was posted to 206 Group as a test pilot but rejoined 243, then in Egypt. In April it moved to Corsica and then to the Italian mainland. On June 6 1944 Chrystall was leading his section in a low-level attack on enemy transport east of Cencina. His propellor was damaged by flak and he made a forced-landing behind enemy lines. With the help of peasants he avoided capture for two weeks. On his way to a pick-up point on the coast Chrystall was skirting a German gun emplacement when he stepped on a mine and lost the lower half of his right leg. German soldiers treated him kindly and after hospital treatment he went to Stalag XIIID in Germany. He was repatriated to the UK in September 1944.

After a further operation Chrystall was fitted with an artificial limb. He was awarded the DFC (15.1.45), transferred to the RNZAF on July 1 1945, returned to New Zealand in June 1946 and was released on July 20.

Chrystall became a successful farmer. On July 28 1961 he and a contractor were at the bottom of a ten feet deep hole when the sides caved in. Both men were killed.

PO 3.8.41   FO 3.8.42   FL 3.8.43

EDWARD WALTER GILLES CHURCHES

39900   PO   Pilot   New Zealander   74 Squadron

One of the youngest participants in the Battle of Britain, Churches was born in Auckland on July 17 1921. Educated at Onehunga Primary and Auckland Grammar Schools he went to work as a telegraph messenger and postman.

At the age of 15 he made his first application for a short service commission. When he was finally successful the scheme lapsed before he was called. Churches went to the Ground Training School at Weraroa on October 26 1939, moved on to 2 EFTS, Taieri in November and on January 16 1940 was posted to 2 FTS, Woodbourne. He sailed for the UK in the RMS 'Rangitata' on June 7, went to Uxbridge on arrival, then to 7 OTU, Hawarden and joined 74 Squadron at Kirton-in-Lindsey on August 21 1940.

Churches collided with Sergeant WM Skinner on August 30. Skinner baled out and got down safely and Churches managed to land. On October 28 he claimed a probable He 111, two days later shot a Bf 109 down into the Channel, got another Bf 109 on November 14, shared a Bf 110 on February 22 1941 and destroyed a Bf 109 on March 18.

Churches failed to return from a patrol on April 19 1941 and was later presumed dead. He is remembered on the Runnymede Memorial, Panel 63.

PO 28.5.40

WALTER MYERS CHURCHILL

90241   SL   Pilot   British   605 Squadron

Churchill, of Leamington, joined 605 Squadron, AuxAF in 1931. He was commissioned in January 1932, went on to the Reserve of Officers in June 1937 and was recalled for full-time service with 605 on August 24 1939. He was appointed Flight Commander with 3 Squadron at Croydon in November.

On May 10 1940 the squadron was attached to 63 Wing in France and Churchill was given command at short notice. He shared in destroying two Hs 126s on May 12, shot down a He 111 on the 13th and three Ju 87s on the 14th. After ten days of fighting the squadron was withdrawn to England. Churchill received the double award of the DSO and the DFC (31.5.40). In early June he returned to 605 Squadron at Drem, to command. He was posted away on September 29 to form and command 71(Eagle) Squadron at Church Fenton.

In late 1940 Churchill was suffering from sinus trouble and on January 23 1941 he handed over command of 71 Squadron and came off flying. He later commanded RAF Valley.

In July 1942 Churchill was posted to RAF Ta Kali, Malta. He planned the first offensive sweeps over Sicily and led the first one on August 23. Four days later, leading the second one, his Spitfire crashed in flames after being hit by flak and Churchill was killed, aged 35, as a Group Captain. He is buried in Syracuse War Cemetery, Italy. His portrait was done by Eric Kennington and Cuthbert Orde.

PO (AuxAF) 11.1.32   FO (AuxAF) 11.7.33
FL (AuxAFRO) 21.6.37   FL 24.8.39   SL 1.6.40
WC 1.12.41

EVZEN CIZEK

85921   **PO**   **Pilot**   **Czechoslovakian**   **1 Squadron**

Cizek was in the Czech Air Force in the twenties and thirties. He escaped to France in 1938 and served with l'Armée de l'Air. In May 1940 he was a Lieutenant in Groupe de Chasse lll/3.

After the fall of France Cizek got to England and on October 14 1940 he joined No 1 Squadron at Wittering. He was appointed joint CO of 312 Squadron at Speke on December 18 1940 and when Squadron Leader FH Tyson was posted away in April 1941 Cizek took sole command. He was posted from the squadron in July 1941.

Cizek was killed on November 26 1942, as a Group Captain. He was 37 and is buried in Brookwood Military Cemetery.

SL 1.3.41

DAVID LAURENCE CLACKSON

90087   **FL**   **Pilot**   **British**   **600 Squadron**

Clackson joined 600 Squadron at Hendon in 1935 and was mobilised on August 24 1939. He served with the squadron throughout the Battle of Britain and was posted away in January 1941 to form and command 68 Squadron at Catterick.

Made an MBE (14.6.45), Clackson was released in 1946, as a Wing Commander.

PO (AuxAF) 10.7.35   FO (AuxAF) 10.1.37   FO 24.8.39
FL 3.9.40   SL 1.12.41

JAMES ALBERT CLANDILLON

117778   **Sgt**   **Pilot**   **British**   **219 Squadron**

Clandillon, of Ilford, Essex, joined 219 Squadron at Catterick on August 22 1940. He was commissioned in March 1942 and was killed on February 18 1943, as a Flying Officer. The unit he was with at the time of his death is not known.

Clandillon was 28. He is buried in Littlehampton Cemetery, Sussex.

PO 2.3.42   FO 1.10.42

COLIN ANTHONY GORDON CLARK

42192   **PO**   **Pilot**   **South African**   **FIU**

Clark, from Johannesburg, joined the RAF on a short service commission in April 1939. He was with the Fighter Interception Unit at Tangmere in July 1940. On October 13 Clark was flying Blenheim L 6805, operating as a target aircraft for an AI-equipped Boston. Due to an error in the use of the fuel cocks he experienced engine failure and crash-landed near Lancing College. The aircraft was written off but he was unhurt.

Clark was killed on October 30 1941, as a Flight Lieutenant with 137 Squadron. Newly-formed and equipped with Whirlwinds, the squadron flew its first operation on October 24. Clark was lost when he went into the sea whilst on an operational flight. He was 28 and is buried in St Michael's churchyard, Geldeston, Norfolk.

APO 24.6.39   PO 9.12.39   FO 9.12.40

DAVID de BRASSEY CLARK

90086   **SL**   **Pilot**   **British**   **600 Squadron**

Joined 600 Squadron, AuxAF in early 1935 and commissioned in May. Clark was called to full-time service on August 24 1939 and took command of the squadron in May 1940. He led 'A' Flight on a daylight attack on Middlekerck-Zeebrugge-Flushing on May 10, during which a He 111 was destroyed on the ground.

Clark was posted away from the squadron on September 14 1940. He was made a CBE (1.1.45) and released later in the year, as a Group Captain.

PO (AuxAF) 27.5.35   FO (AuxAF) 27.11.36
FL (AuxAF) 15.1.39   FL 24.8.39   SL 1.9.40   WC 1.3.42

GODFREY PERCIVAL CLARK

144706   **Sgt**   **Air Gunner**   **British**   **60**

Joined 604 Squadron at Middle Wallop on August 1 commissioned in March 1943 and awarded the serving with 102 Squadron and flying in Halifaxes f He was released from the RAF in 1947, as a Fligh

PO 29.3.43   FO 29.9.43   FL 29.3.45

HUGH DESMOND CLARK

33382   **FO**   **Pilot**   **British**   **213 Squad**

Born on March 30 1919, Clark was at Wellington C to 1936 and entered RAF College, Cranwell as a fligh 1937 and later became a King's Cadet. He was December 1938 and joined 213 Squadron at Exeter o

Clark retired from the RAF on October 1

PO 17.12.38   FO 17.6.40   FL 17.6.41
WC 1.7.52

WILLIAM TERENCE CLARK

126026   **Sgt**   **Air Gunner**   **British**   **21**

Clark joined AuxAF at Ke trained as an Hawker He mobilised ju outbreak of w Squadron at 1940.

With the Beaufighter a the air gunn trained with Radio Observ qualified in th He was awa (8.7.41), havi destruction aircraft at nig was posted to 1455 Flight, then forming at Tangmer Havocs. In May 1942 he went to 1451 Flight at Huns job.

Commissioned in May 1942 from Warrant Offi to 60 OTU in October 1942, as a Navigation/Radar i 1943 he was posted to 488 Squadron at Ayr, as navig arrived 'A' Flight Commander, Squadron Leader D had been a successful team in 219 Squadron. On D Clark was flying with Pilot Officer D Robinson an a Me 410 over Sussex.

At the end of his tour in March 1944 Clark wa Weald Sector Operations, where he trained as a rejoined 488 in August 1944 but two months lat Honiley Ground Approach School, after which he Unit to RAF Prestwick, as second-in-command. C from the RAF in November 1945, as a Flight Lieu

PO 18.5.42   FO 18.11.42   FL 18.5.44

ARTHUR WILLIAM CLARKE

42485   **PO**   **Pilot**   **British**   **504 Squad**

Born in Altrincham on December 26 1919, Cl Squadron at Debden in April 1940. He was shot dov 11 1940 in combat over the Kent coast and reporte remembered on the Runnymede Memorial, Panel

However, an investigation of an aircraft wh burned out south of Rookelands, near Newchu Marsh, proved beyond any doubt that it was Hurri that items found confirmed the pilot's identity as be AW Clarke and also showed that he had not left th

of-kin decided that his remains should be left undisturbed and that a memorial should be erected close to the crash site. This memorial was dedicated on September 11 1986.

PO 1.2.40

GORDON STUART CLARKE

747818   Sgt   Air Gunner   British   248 Squadron

A member of the RAFVR, Clarke, of Bedford, was with 248 Squadron in July 1940. On October 1 1940 he was a member of the crew of Blenheim R 3626, which failed to return from a reconnaissance sortie to the Norwegian coast. The crew of three was reported 'Missing'.

Clarke, who was 19, is remembered on the Runnymede Memorial, Panel 12.

GORDON THOMAS CLARKE

748034   Sgt   Pilot   British   151 Squadron

Clarke joined 151 Squadron at Martlesham Heath on July 15 1940. He was shot down by Bf 109s over Ramsgate on August 24. He crashed, in Hurricane P 3273, at Plumford Farm, Ospringe, wounded and was admitted to hospital.

Awarded the AFC (7.9.45), as a Warrant Officer, Clarke was a Master Pilot in October 1949, commissioned in March 1953 and killed on August 11 1953.

PO 5.3.53

HENRY REGINALD CLARKE ✱

102587   Sgt   Pilot   British   66 and 610 Squadrons

Joined the RAFVR in Belfast in Spring 1939 and soloed at 24 E&RFTS there in July. Clarke was called up in September and on October 1 he went to 3 ITW, Hastings, moving on to 4 EFTS, Brough on December 18.

Clarke was posted to 14 FTS, Kinloss on April 10 1940. With training completed he went to 7 OTU, Hawarden on August 10 and joined 74 Squadron at Kirton-in-Lindsey on the 26th but stayed only three days before going to 66 Squadron at Coltishall. It was again a short stay and on September 11 Clarke joined 610 Squadron at Acklington.

Whilst with 610 Clarke had an amazing escape from death. During a practice dog-fight he had a head-on collision with another Spitfire. Their wings hit and Clarke's propeller probably hit the other's wing because his engine became so rough that he had to throttle back immediately. He trimmed his nose down, opened the hood, undid his Sutton harness and let go. Clarke believed that he must have struck the tailplane. He passed out and when he came to he was hanging upside down, suspended by one strap, which was fastened very insecurely round one leg. He managed to pull himself up and got hold of the rest of the harness but just before he reached the ground he fainted again. His only injury was a deep cut on the chin, caused by his helmet being wrenched off as he left the cockpit, and some bruises. His parachute pack must have caught on some part of the cockpit and been pulled off, breaking the harness straps, one of which pulled itself tight round his leg when the buckle caught in the loop. Clarke's parachute must have been pulled open when the pack was wrenched off because he did not remember pulling the rip-cord. The other pilot and plane went straight into the ground from 14000 feet.

Clarke spent a week with 602 at Prestwick in December, followed by a week with 266 at Wittering over the New Year and finally joined 255 Squadron at Kirton-in-Lindsey on January 3 1941, initially flying Defiants and later Beaufighters. Commissioned in August 1941, Clarke stayed with 255 until December 1942, finishing up in North Africa from mid-November.

With his tour completed, Clarke returned to the UK, became a test pilot and was posted to 23 MU, Aldergrove on April 18 1943, where he remained until released from the RAF on May 2 1947, as a Flight Lieutenant.

PO 2.8.41   FO 2.8.42   FL 2.8.43

RAYMOND WALKER CLARKE

70849   FO   Pilot   British   79 and 238 Squadrons

Clarke joined the RAF on a short service commission in January 1938. On completion of his training he was posted to 226 Squadron at Harwell. The squadron, equipped with Battles, flew to France at the outbreak of war as part of the AASF. After being heavily involved in the fighting it withdrew to England in mid-June 1940.

Clarke volunteered for Fighter Command and joined 79 Squadron at Biggin Hill in September. On the 27th he shared in the destruction of a He 111. He was posted to 238 Squadron at Chilbolton on October 3 1940.

In mid-November the carrier HMS 'Argus' sailed from Gibraltar with Hurricanes for Malta. Clarke was one of the six pilots who flew off on November 16 1940 in the second flight of Hurricanes, led by a FAA Skua. A series of mishaps saw the Hurricanes run out fuel and fall one by one into the sea, with the loss of all six pilots.

Clarke is remembered on the Runnymede Memorial, Panel 5.

APO 26.3.38   PO 17.1.39   FO 3.9.40

RONALD NEVILLE CLARKE

29063   SL   Pilot   British   235 Squadron

Joined the RAF in April 1930. Clarke went to 3 FTS, Grantham on April 26. He was posted to the School of Naval Co-operation, Lee-on-Solent on February 24 1933 and to 217 (General Reconnaissance) Squadron at Tangmere on March 28 1937. In July 1940 Clarke was commanding 235 Squadron, with one flight at Thorney Island and the other at Bircham Newton.

Awarded the DFC (17.1.41), Clarke disappears from the records. He may have died or been killed on March 4 1941 but there is no trace of him in casualty lists.

PO 11.4.30   FO 13.10.31   FL 13.10.35   SL 1.10.38

GORDON NEIL SPENCER CLEAVER

90135   FO   Pilot   British   601 Squadron

Cleaver, who was born in Stanmore, Middlesex, joined 601 Squadron, AuxAF in 1937 and was commissioned in April. He skied for Britain in the years before the war.

Mobilised on November 24 1939, Cleaver went to Merville with 'A' Flight on May 16 1940. On the 27th he destroyed a Bf 109 and claimed two other victories before the flight was withdrawn at the end of May.

Cleaver claimed a Ju 87 and a probable He 111 destroyed on July 11, a probable Bf 109 on the 26th, two Bf 110s on August 11 and another on the 13th. Two days later he was shot down in combat over Winchester. When his hood was shattered by a cannon shell Cleaver's eyes were filled with perspex splinters. He managed to return to Tangmere and was rushed to hospital, where his sight was saved but his operational flying days were over. Cleaver was awarded the DFC (13.9.40).

In 1941 he transferred to the Administrative Branch and was released from the RAF in late 1943, as a Squadron Leader.

PO (AuxAF) 8.4.37   FO (AuxAF) 8.10.38   FO 24.11.39   FL 24.11.40   SL 1.3.42

IAN CHARLES COOPER CLENSHAW

745067   Sgt   Pilot   British   253 Squadron

Joined the RAFVR in early 1939 and made his first flight in a Tiger Moth on February 19 at 34 E&RFTS, Rochford.

In June 1940 Clenshaw was with 253 Squadron at Kirton-in-Lindsey. On July 10, flying in bad visibility on a dawn patrol, he lost control and was killed when he crashed near the Humber coast, in Hurricane P 3359.

Clenshaw was 22. He was the first RAF casualty in the Battle of Britain. He is buried in St Mary's churchyard extension, Kelvedon, Essex.

RUPERT FRANCIS HENRY CLERKE

36108   **FL**   **Pilot**   **British**   **32 and 79 Squadrons**

Clerke was born on April 13 1916 and educated at Eton. He went into the RAF on a direct-entry Permanent Commission in July 1937. He was posted to 5 FTS, Sealand on October 25 and with training completed joined 32 Squadron at Biggin Hill in June 1938.

On July 9 1940 Clerke shared a He 111. He was posted to 79 Squadron at Acklington on July 25. He shared a Do 17 and a Bf 110 on August 15, shared a He 59 and destroyed a probable Bf 109 on the 28th, probably destroyed a Ju 88 on September 6 and shared a He 111 on the 27th.

Clerke was with No 1 PRU at Benson on July 13 1941 when the first Mosquito, W 4051, arrived and on September 17 he flew the first operational sortie, to photograph Brest and the Spanish-French frontier. In October he demonstrated the Mosquito to the King and Queen at Watton, in mock combat with a Spitfire. On October 15 Clerke made a record-breaking flight from Wick to Benson in a Mosquito in 1 hr 32 minutes and on November 4 he made one of the first Mosquito flights overseas, going to Malta in 4 hrs 45 minutes, using a camera as he crossed Italy.

In early 1942 Clerke was posted to 157 Squadron at Castle Camps, as a Flight Commander. On September 30 he had the first Mosquito day combat when he shot down a Ju 88 thirty miles off the Dutch coast. Clerke was given command of 125 Squadron at Fairwood Common in December 1942, as an Acting Wing Commander. He destroyed a Do 217 on February 17 1943 and a Ju 88 on June 13. Awarded the DFC (23.7.43), he was then credited with four enemy aircraft destroyed, two of them at night, and three shared.

Clerke was posted from 125 in October 1943. He commanded RAF Manston from September 1945 to October 1946 and he retired on August 9 1965, as a Group Captain.

PO 25.7.36   *FO 25.1.38*   *FL 25.1.40*   *SL 1.3.41*
WC 1.9.42   *WC 1.1.49*   *GC 1.1.58*

DOUGLAS GERALD CLIFT

41828   **FO**   **Pilot**   **British**   **79 Squadron**

Clift was born on March 15 1919 and joined the RAF in January 1939. He did his ab initio training at 5 E&RFTS, Hanworth, then went to 11 FTS, Shawbury, converted to Hurricanes at St Athan and joined 79 Squadron at Biggin Hill in November 1939.

On August 15 1940 Clift claimed a Bf 109 destroyed and on August 30 he shared in the destruction of a He 111. He was posted to CFS, Upavon in July 1941 for an instructor's course. Clift later volunteered for the MSFU and served with it until October 1942. He remained on flying duties for the rest of the war, finishing up in South-East Asia with the RIAF.

After the war Clift served with 34 Squadron until its disbandment in August 1947. He went later to Germany and Singapore, spent some years at the Royal Radar Establishment at Malvern and after a year spent as Adviser to the Imperial Iranian Air Force his last posting was to West Drayton on the 'Linesman' project.

Clift retired on July 2 1974, as a Squadron Leader.

APO 1.4.39   *PO 23.10.39*   *FO 23.10.40*   *FL 10.1.42*
FL 10.7.45   *FL 10.1.48*

JOHN KENNETH GRAHAME CLIFTON

41902   **PO**   **Pilot**   **British**   **253 Squadron**

Joined the R[...] service commis[...] 1939. Clifton [...] course at 11 [...] and his inte[...] advanced at [...] Norton.

He was wi[...] at Kirton-in-L[...] July 1940. On [...] was shot dow[...] combat with D[...] over Dun[...] Hurricane, P [...] to be that w[...] Clapper Lane [...] site investigatio[...] up no evidence [...]

or deny this.

Clifton was 21. He is buried in St John's churchy[...] Somerset.

APO 15.4.39   *PO 6.11.39*

ARTHUR EDMUND CLOUSTON

29162   **SL**   **Pilot**   **New Zealander**   **21[...]**

Born on A[...] Motueka, C[...] early ambitio[...] found that h[...] apparently [...] sickness. He [...] and secondha[...] Westport, wh[...]

Inspired [...] Kingsford-S[...] learned to [...] Marlborough [...] sold his busi[...] sailed for E[...] applied for [...] commission h[...] the Fairey Av[...] After some [...]

problems Clouston was accepted by the RAF and [...] training in early September 1930 and in late Octobe[...] South Cerney. Clouston joined 25 Squadron at H[...] 7 1931. He was posted to 24 (Communications) Squ[...] in early 1934 and when his commission ended in [...] considered returning to New Zealand but accep[...] Ministry offered him an appointment as a civilia[...] Royal Aircraft Establishment, Farnborough.

Clouston made his mark in civil aviation in th[...] war in races and record-breaking long-distance [...] awarded the AFC (1.1.38) for his work at the RAE [...] of barrage balloon cables on aircraft. Recalled t[...] outbreak of war, Clouston was appointed to the Ex[...] at Farnborough to carry on with his testing work[...]

The aircraft at RAE were unarmed and pilot[...] the air raid sirens sounded. This irked Clouston, n[...] when his brother, Falcon, was killed over Dunkirk [...] death Clouston chased a He 111, intending to ch[...] propellor. The enemy aircraft escaped into cloud an[...] above and below the cloud as far as the coast Clou[...] CO was angry and Clouston was grounded, althoug[...] an order came through for RAE aircraft to be armed [...] to reach the aircraft after the warning sounded [...] airfield. Clouston was generally one of the fir[...] uneventful patrols, when the next siren went he to[...] airfield and then headed for Guildford, where he co[...] in the sky. Some He 111s, with a Bf 110 escort, we[...] a raid on London. A Bf 110 dived down, pulled o[...] headed for the coast. Clouston gave chase and had [...]

when a He 111 flew across his path. A long burst sent it crashing in flames into a field. He resumed his pursuit of the Bf 110, silenced the rear gunner and set the starboard engine on fire. More bursts exhausted Clouston's ammunition and he veered away to let a Hurricane finish the job but he too must have been out of ammunition and the Bf 110 limped away across the Channel. Clouston returned to Farnborough and did two victory rolls. Again he was grounded by an irate CO.

From October 18 1940 Clouston was attached, at his own request, to 219 Squadron at Redhill, flying Beaufighters at night but without success. He returned to Farnborough on November 17 and in early December he was posted to the Directorate of Armament Development to work on airborne searchlight equipment. On May 12 1941 he was given command of 1422 Flight at Heston to test the 40 KW Helmore Light. For this work he was awarded a Bar to the AFC (1.1.42).

In late 1942 Clouston began pressing for a transfer to an operational squadron. He was given command of 224 Squadron at Beaulieu on March 19 1943. Equipped with Liberators, the squadron was on anti-submarine duties and for his part in their operations Clouston was awarded the DFC (1.10.43). With his tour completed he was posted to RAF Langham to command in late February 1944 and was awarded the DSO (14.4.44) and received a Mention in Despatches (14.6.45).

Granted a Permanent Commission in September 1945, Clouston was seconded for two years to the RNZAF in July 1947. He returned in 1949 to the UK and went for a Senior War Course at the Royal Naval College, Greenwich. In July 1950 Clouston was appointed Commandant of the Empire Test Pilots' School. He retired on April 7 1960, as an Air Commodore CB.

APO 10.10.30   PO 10.10.31   FO 10.4.32   FL 3.9.39
SL 1.6.41   WC 1.9.44   GC 1.7.47   AC 1.7.54

WILFRID GREVILLE CLOUSTON

39223	FO	Pilot	New Zealander	19 Squadron

Clouston was born in Auckland on January 15 1916 and learned to fly privately at Rongotai in 1935. After being provisionally accepted for a short service commission he sailed for the UK in June 1936.

With his ab initio training completed Clouston was posted to 7 FTS, Peterborough in October and he joined 19 Squadron at Duxford in June 1937. He became squadron adjutant in late 1938 and in mid-1939 was made a Flight Commander.

On May 11 1940 Clouston shared in the destruction of a Ju 88, on the 23rd he destroyed a Bf 109, on the 26th two Ju 87s, on the 27th a Do 17 and shared another probable and on June 1 a Bf 109 and another shared. He was awarded the DFC (24.6.40).

As part of the Duxford Wing 19 Squadron took an increasingly active role in August. On the 31st Clouston shared a Do 17, on September 9 he claimed two probable Bf 109s, on the 15th a Bf 110 and a Do 17 and on the 18th a Ju 88.

In November 1940 Clouston was given command of 258 Squadron, then reforming at Leconfield. On August 22 1941 he was appointed to command 488 Squadron, then being formed at Rongotai, New Zealand. He went out to Singapore to prepare for the arrival of its pilots and ground staff. They arrived on October 10 and the inexperienced pilots were sent to an OTU at Kluang to convert to Buffalos. The ground staff, based at Kallang, tried to make serviceable the twenty-one Buffalos left behind by 67 Squadron, which had moved up to Burma.

Clouston's orders were to get the squadron operational as soon as possible but lack of tools and spares coupled with the aircraft's poor performance made 488 a weak opponent for the Japanese. Out-flown and out-manoeuvred, the squadron dwindled in numbers in spite of being strengthened by nine Hurricanes on January 24 1942. A week later its aircraft were evacuated to Sumatra and in mid-February those that remained were handed over to 605 Squadron and 488 ceased to exist.

Clouston was posted to HQ RAF Singapore on January 23 and he was captured when the Japanese occupied the city. Freed in September 1945, he returned to the UK and was granted a Permanent Commission. He held a number of commands and appointments before retiring on March 20 1957, as a Wing Commander.

After his return to New Zealand Clouston took up farming in Hawke's Bay. The privations he suffered as a prisoner of the Japanese almost certainly contributed to the deterioration in his health in the late seventies. In May 1980 he was admitted to hospital in Waipukurau following a fall. He appeared to be making a good recovery but died suddenly on May 24.

APO 31.8.36   PO 30.6.37   FO 30.1.39   FL 30.1.41
SL 1.6.44   WC 1.7.50

ARTHUR VICTOR CLOWES

44780	PO	Pilot	British	1 Squadron

Born in New Sawley, Derbyshire, Clowes was serving with No 1 Squadron in France from the outbreak of war. On November 23 1939, whilst sharing in the destruction of a He 111, Clowes' Hurricane was struck by a French Morane, losing one elevator and most of the rudder. He managed to make a successful forced-landing back at Vassincourt.

Clowes destroyed a Ju 87 and damaged two more on March 29 1940, destroyed a Bf 109 and a Ju 87 on May 14, a Bf 110 on the 15th and a Bf 109 on June 14. The squadron was withdrawn to Tangmere on June 18 and was fully operational again by the end of July. Clowes claimed a Ju 88 destroyed on August 11, a He 111 and a Ju 88 on the 16th, damaged a He 111 and a Bf 110 on the 30th, damaged two Do 17s and a Bf 110 on the 31st, destroyed a Bf 110 on September 7 and shared a Do 17 on October 24. Awarded the DFM (20.8.40) for his work in France, Clowes was commissioned in September, promoted to Acting Flight Lieutenant and given command of 'A' Flight on October 10.

He led No 1's first offensive operation on January 1 1941, strafing German installations between Calais and Boulogne with two other pilots. Clowes was posted to 53 OTU, Heston on April 29 1941 and was awarded the DFC (13.5.41). He commanded 79 Squadron at Baginton from December 1941 to February 1942, 601 Squadron in the Western Desert from August 21 to November 22 1942 and 94 Squadron in the Eastern Mediterranean from June to September 1943.

Granted a Permanent Commission in the Secretarial Branch in September 1945, Clowes later went to RAF Staff College. He died on December 7 1949, whilst still serving.

PO 11.9.40   FO 3.2.41   FL 10.12.41   SL 1.9.45

WILLIAM PANCOAST CLYDE

90154	FL	Pilot	British	601 Squadron

Clyde joined 601 Squadron, AuxAF in 1935. He skied for Britain in the years before the war. He went on to the Reserve of Officers in February 1938 and left for Mexico, from whence he returned when recalled at the outbreak of war.

'A' Flight of 601 was posted to France on May 16 1940. Clyde destroyed a Bf 110 on the 27th. The flight was withdrawn at the end of May and Clyde was awarded the DFC (31.5.40). On June 6 he destroyed a Do 17, shared a Ju 88 with Max Aitken on July 7, claimed two Bf 110s on August

WP Clyde (continued)

13, shared a Ju 88 on the 15th, claimed a Ju 87 the next day, a Do 17 on the 31st and a Bf 110 on October 7.

Clyde was released from the RAF in 1945, as a Group Captain, and returned to Mexico. His portrait was done in 1940 by Captain Cuthbert Orde.

PO (AuxAF) 30.7.35   FO (AuxAF) 14.4.37
FO (AuxAFRO) 11.2.38   FO 8.9.39   FL 3.9.40
SL 21.11.41   WC 1.1.44

JAMES PATRICK COATES

Lieutenant (RN)   Pilot   British   808 Squadron

Joined the Royal Navy in late 1931. Coates was commissioned in the Engineer Branch in 1934. He was with 808 Squadron at Castletown in early July 1940, flying Fulmars on dockyard defence.

Coates was killed on November 26 1940, serving with HMS 'Ark Royal' in the Mediterranean.

Midshipman 1.1.32   Sub-Lt 1.12.34   Lt 1.2.37

DONALD GORDON COBDEN

41552   PO   Pilot   New Zealander   74 Squadron

Born in Christchurch on August 11 1914, Cobden was educated at Christchurch Boys' High School from 1927 to 1931. He was a fine rugby player and played for the All Blacks against the Springboks in August 1937.

Cobden went to England in late 1937 and early in 1938 he was playing for the Catford Bridge Club. He joined the RAF on a short service commission at the end of August 1938. After two weeks at Uxbridge he was posted to 5 FTS, Sealand on January 28 1939.

Cobden joined 3 Squadron on September 2 1939, moved to 615 Squadron at Croydon on the 8th and on October 6 he was posted to 74 Squadron at Hornchurch. The squadron began patrols over France and Belgium on May 10 1940. On the 24th Cobden shared a Do 17, on the 26th shared a probable Hs 126 and on the 27th a probable Do 17.

Officially the first day of the Battle of Britain, July 10 saw 74 Squadron sent to protect a convoy in the Dover area. In the engagement which followed Cobden got a Bf 109 and damaged a Do 17. On August 11 74 took off to patrol convoy 'Booty', twelve miles east of Clacton. In the combat between the Spitfires and forty Bf 110s Cobden was shot down and killed, on his twenty-sixth birthday. His body was recovered by the Germans and he is buried in Ostende Communal Cemetery.

APO 13.1.39   PO 13.11.39

ARTHUR CHARLES COCHRANE

42915   PO   Pilot   Canadian   257 Squadron

Cochrane, of Vancouver, joined the RAF in April 1939. He was posted to 257 Squadron at Hendon on May 23 1940, a few days after it was reformed. He claimed a Bf 109 on August 8, a probable Do 17 on the 18th, a Bf 110 on the 31st, a Do 215 on September 7 and a Do 17 and a shared He 111 on the 15th.

Cochrane was badly injured in a car accident on September 15 and spent some months in hospital. He joined 87 Squadron at Charmy Down in August 1942 and went to North Africa with it in November. On January 22 1943 Cochrane was scrambled from Djidelli at 06.30 hrs. Although it was still dark he found and shot a SM 79 down into the sea. Awarded the DFC (30.3.43), Cochrane was killed in action on March 31 1943, aged 24. He is remembered on the Malta Memorial, Panel 6, Column 1.

APO 24.6.39   PO 10.4.40   FO 10.4.41   FL 10.4.42

JOHN REYNOLDS COCK

40674   FO   Pilot   Australian   87 Squadron

Born in Renmark, South Australia on March 3 1918, Cock joined the RAF on a short service commission in March 1938. He was with 87 Squadron in France and in early April 1940 destroyed a He 111.

On July 27 Cock probably destroyed a He 11[...]
11 he claimed a Ju 88 destroyed and a Bf 109 dama[...]
he was himself shot down by enemy fighters off [...]
baled out, slightly injured, was machine-gunned b[...]
way down but reached the sea and swam ashore. C[...]
88 destroyed on September 30. He was awarded the [...]

Cock collided with Pilot Officer DT Jay on O[...]
a routine patrol. Jay was killed and Cock made a fo[...]
severely damaged tail surfaces.

In September 1941 Cock was posted to 9 FTS,[...]
He was posted to 453 Squadron at Drem, when it w[...]
on June 18 1942, as a Flight Commander. After a [...]
to 222 Squadron at Ayr in November Cock return[...]
December 1942. He was attached to 54 Squadron [...]
1943, as a supernumerary.

Cock returned to the UK in 1944. He was rel[...]
a Squadron Leader. On August 30 1983 the wr[...]
Hurricane, V 7233, shot down on August 11 1940 [...]
the sea. He returned to the UK for the event. Co[...]
29 1988.

APO 7.5.38   PO 7.3.39   FO 3.9.40   FL[...]
SL 1.1.44   FL 1.12.42

JOHN CLAYTON COCKBURN

Lieutenant-Commander (FAA)   Pilot   Bri[...]

Joined the Navy in 1926 and attached to the RAF i[...]
commanded 804 Squadron from December 9 1939 t[...]
during part of which the squadron served on docky[...]
RAF Command in the Battle of Britain.

On June 1 1941 Cockburn took command of [...]
in 1942 was Commander (Flying) on HMS 'Argu[...]
the same appointment on HMS 'Stalker', which w[...]
in the assault on Salerno. He led 26 Seafires of the [...]
to the airfield at Paestum on September 9 1943, to [...]
until the RAF squadrons arrived in Sicily. The W[...]
Asa to operate alongside 324 Wing of the RAF, v[...]
days before returning to its own ships. Cockbur[...]
DSC (23.5.44) for his part in the action.

From December 1944 Cockburn commande[...]
Air Station at Puttalam, Ceylon. In 1955 he was M[...]
and he retired in 1960, as a Captain.

Midshipman 15.9.26   Sub-Lt 1.1.29   Lt 1[...]
Lt-Cdr 1.3.39   Cdr 31.12.46   Cdr 31.12.5[...]

RICHARD COCKBURN COCKBURN

Lieutenant (FAA)   Pilot   British   808 [...]

Cockburn was educated at Wellington College fro[...]
then went to the Royal Military College, Sa[...]
commissioned in the Highland Light Infantry in [...]
in 1936 and at some time learned to fly with the [...]

At the beginning of July 1940 Cockburn was [...]
at Castletown, flying Fulmars on dockyard defer[...]
1940 he embarked with the squadron on HMS 'A[...]
awarded the DSO (25.11.41) for service in the ca[...]
Malta convoys.

On May 1 1942 Cockburn was appointed to H[...]
later commanded 734 Squadron at Worthy Dow[...]
from the Royal Navy in January 1946, as a Lieute[...]

Sub-Lt 3.10.39   Lt 3.10.40

JOHN COGGINS

44458   PO   Pilot   British   235 Squ[...]

Coggins, of Nacton, Suffolk, was a Sergeant-Pi[...]
He was awarded the DFM (22.11.38) and Bar ([...]
and distinguished services in Palestine.

He was with 235 Squadron at the beginnir[...]
September an aircraft carrying a full load of bor[...]
other aircraft and burst into flames. Coggins, [...]
Laughlin and another officer immediately ran to th[...]
the engines and taxied them away. During this tin[...]

on the burning plane had exploded. Three aircraft were taken to safety without damage and a fourth with only minor damage. The courage of Coggins and Laughlin was recognised with an MBE (21.1.41).

On December 16 1940 Coggins was captain of Blenheim Z 5754, on a minesweeper escort operation. He and his crew were lost when the aircraft crashed into the sea, cause unknown. He was 27 years old and is remembered on the Runnymede Memorial, Panel 7.

PO 7.8.40

JOHN HUNTER COGHLAN

37719   FO   Pilot   British   56 Squadron

Coghlan, of Southsea, was born in Shanghai and joined the RAF in January 1936. He was posted to 7 FTS, Peterborough on April 18 and joined No 1 Squadron at Tangmere on October 25.

When 72 Squadron was reformed at Church Fenton in February 1937 Coghlan joined it but in March 1938 he went back to No 1. After the outbreak of war he was posted to 56 Squadron. On May 18 1940 he claimed a probable Bf 109 and He 111, on the 27th he shared a He 111, two days later he damaged two Ju 88s and on July 13 he claimed a Ju 87 and a Bf 109 destroyed.

Coghlan, who was appointed 'A' Flight Commander in June 1940, was awarded the DFC (30.7.40) and posted away from 56 on August 7. He was killed in a Lysander on August 17 1940, with a Parachute Training Unit. His body was recovered by the Germans and he is buried in Boulogne Eastern Cemetery. Coghlan was 25.

APO 30.3.36   PO 3.2.37   FO 3.9.38

The Hon DAVID ARTHUR COKE

73042   FO   Pilot   British   257 Squadron

Son of the Fourth Earl of Leicester, Coke, of Holkham Hall, Norfolk, was born on December 4 1915. He was educated at Eton and Trinity College, Cambridge. As a member of the RAFVR he was called up on September 1 1939.

Coke joined 257 Squadron at Hendon, when it was reformed on May 17 1940. On August 12 his Hurricane, P 3776, was severely damaged in combat over Portsmouth. Slightly wounded, Coke crash-landed and was admitted to the Royal Naval Hospital, Haslar. He was posted away from 257 on September 12 but returned on the 27th. Coke destroyed a Bf 109 over the Channel on October 22.

In late 1941 he was with 80 Squadron in the Western Desert and was killed on December 9. He is buried in Knightsbridge War Cemetery, Acroma, Libya. Coke was awarded the DFC (26.12.41) for an attack on enemy transport on the El Adem-Acroma road one day in November 1941. A large number of vehicles, tanks and mechanised transport were bombed and machine-gunned and the damage inflicted played a large part in blocking the road.

PO (RAFVR) 27.6.39   PO 1.9.39   FO 3.9.40   FL 3.9.41

CHARLES FREDERICK JOHN COLE

745971   Sgt   Aircrew   British   236 Squadron

Joined 236 on September 3 1940. Nothing further known.

CHRISTOPHER COLEBROOK

86344   PO   Pilot   British   54 Squadron

Joined 54 Squadron at Catterick on October 14 1940. Colebrook was killed on April 20 1941, still serving with the squadron. He is remembered on the Runnymede Memorial, Panel 31.

PO 14.9.40

EDWARD JACK COLEMAN

42800   PO   Pilot   British   54 Squadron

Joined 54 Squadron at Rochford in June 1940. On July 7 Coleman made a forced-landing near Deal after an attack by Bf 109s, slightly wounded. He was killed on February 17 1941, still with the squadron.

Coleman was cremated at South London Crematorium, Mitcham.

APO 23.10.39   PO 10.6.40

PETER COLLARD

90402   FO   Pilot   British   615 Squadron

Born in London, Collard joined 615 Squadron, AuxAF in late 1937. He was called for full-time service on August 24 1939. Two weeks later he was sent on a Hurricane conversion course, having been used to Gladiators. However, he flew with 615 to Merville on November 15 in a Gladiator from Croydon. The squadron did not receive Hurricanes until April 1940.

During the May fighting in France Collard destroyed two enemy aircraft. He claimed a Ju 87 on July 14 and shared a He 59 on the 27th. Collard failed to return from a combat off Dover on August 14 1940. His Hurricane, P 3109, crashed into the sea. He was 24 and is buried in Oye-Plage Communal Cemetery, France. Collard was awarded the DFC (23.8.40).

PO (AuxAF) 4.2.38   FO 24.8.39

GEORGE RICHARD COLLETT

745500   Sgt   Pilot   British   54 Squadron

Joined 54 Squadron on July 15 1940. Collett claimed a Bf 109 destroyed on July 24. On the same day he ran out of fuel pursuing an enemy aircraft and forced-landed his Spitfire, N 3192, on the beach at Dunwich, north of Sizewell. The aircraft was a write-off and Collett was slightly injured.

He was shot down and killed in combat with enemy fighters on August 22 1940. His Spitfire, R 6708, crashed into the Channel, off Deal. Collett was 24 years old and is buried in Bergen-op-Zoom War Cemetery, Netherlands.

LEON WILLIAM COLLINGRIDGE

42196   PO   Pilot   British   66 Squadron

Born on August 25 1920, Collingridge joined the RAF on May 1 1939. After his elementary training he was posted to 8 FTS, Montrose on July 8 and after converting to Spitfires he joined 66 Squadron at Duxford on February 3 1940.

On July 29 Collingridge crashed on the beach at Orfordness after being hit by return fire from a He 111 he was attacking. He was rescued, injured, and admitted to Ipswich Hospital. Following a period of convalescence at Torquay he rejoined the squadron.

Collingridge was posted to CFS, Upavon on November 16 1940 for an instuctor's course, after which he went to 9 FTS, Hullavington to instruct on Masters and Tutors, moving later to 5 FTS, Tern Hill, on Masters. In late August 1943 Collingridge sailed in the 'Queen Elizabeth' to Canada, where he instructed at 41 SFTS, Weyburn; 37 SFTS, Calgary and 34 SFTS, Medicine Hat.

In December 1944 Collingridge did a course at 2 FIS, Pearce and then instructed at 10 SFTS, Dauphin and 18 SFTS, Gimli. He returned to the UK on the 'Ile de France' in October 1945 and was posted to the staff of 16 Reserve Centre, Sudbury.

From June 1946 to April 1949 Collingridge was with 607 Squadron at Ouston. He served in a number of flying and instructing appointments before his retirement on August 25 1963, as a Flight Lieutenant, retaining the rank of Squadron Leader.

APO 24.6.39   PO 9.12.39   FO 9.12.40   FL 27.3.42
FL 1.9.45

ANTHONY ROLAND COLLINS

20988   SL   Pilot   British   72 and 46 Squadrons

Collins was born on June 22 1908 and entered the RAF in late June 1930. He did his flying training at 2 FTS, Digby and then joined 3 Squadron at Upavon on June 23 1931. He was posted to 30 Squadron at Mosul, Iraq on February 28 1933.

AR Collins (continued)

Back in the UK, Collins went to No 1 Armament Training Camp at Catfoss on February 28 1935 and on August 10 1936 he was appointed PA to the AOC 25 (Armament) Group, Eastchurch. On January 2 1938 Collins was sent to the School of Photography, Farnborough, under instruction, and on October 28 was appointed Officer i/c Photography at Coastal Command, Lee-on-Solent.

Collins was given command of 72 Squadron at Acklington in July 1940. On September 2 he was slightly wounded and his aircraft damaged in combat with Bf 110s over Herne Bay. Posted away from 72 on October 5, Collins took command of 46 Squadron at Stapleford Tawney the following day but only held the appointment for a very brief period.

Collins retired from the RAF on June 22 1955, as a Wing Commander. He died on February 21 1976.

PO 27.6.30   FO 27.2.32   FL 27.2.36   SL 1.12.38
WC 1.6.41   WC 1.10.46

BASIL GORDON COLLYNS

391368   PO   Pilot   New Zealander   238 Squadron

Collyns was born in Greymouth on February 24 1913 and educated at Nelson College from 1925 to 1930. He spent two years at Lincoln Agricultural College and then went to work as a sheep farmer at Kaikoura.

In June 1939 Collyns enrolled in the Civil Reserve of Pilots and began flying at the Marlborough Aero Club. Called for full-time service he reported to the Ground Training School, Weraroa on November 19 1939. Collyns did his elementary training at No 1 EFTS, Taieri and 2 EFTS, New Plymouth, before going to 2 FTS, Woodbourne.

Qualified as a pilot and commissioned at the end of June, Collyns sailed in RMS 'Rangitane' on July 12 for the UK. He was posted to 6 OTU, Sutton Bridge on September 14 and joined 238 Squadron at Middle Wallop on the 28th.

Collyns was posted to No 1 Squadron at Redhill on May 3 1941. On June 21 he shot a Bf 109 down into the sea. At the end of his tour he was posted to 60 OTU on November 17, as an instructor. Collyns joined the newly-formed 243 Squadron at Ouston in late June 1942, moved on to 222 Squadron at Drem on September 2, became a Flight Commander in October and was posted to 485 Squadron at Kings Cliffe on November 11 1942. Four weeks later Collyns went as supernumerary Flight Lieutenant to the AFDU at Duxford, remaining there until June 7 1943, when he was posted to 1493 Flight, Eastchurch as a gunnery instructor.

Collyns returned to operations on January 15 1944 with a posting to 65 Squadron at Gravesend, newly-equipped with Mustangs. He damaged a Ju 52 and a Bf 109 on the ground on April 19 and destroyed a Bf 109 in the air on June 10. Four days later Collyns was posted to 19 Squadron at Ford, as a Flight Commander. On June 20 he shot down a FW 190. On the 22nd he was attacking gun positions at low level when he was hit by flak. Collyns pulled up sharply to 3000 feet hoping to reach the American lines but his engine began to spurt flames so he baled out, was picked up by American troops and flew back to England to rejoin the squadron.

On August 9 Collyns destroyed a FW 190 and shared another, on the 14th he got a probable Bf 109 and damaged two FW 190s, on the 20th he destroyed a FW 190 but was then himself shot down. He crashed about one kilometre from Rouvres and was killed instantly, his body being thrown about twenty metres from his aircraft.

Collyns' body was taken to the Mayor's house and he was buried on the 22nd in the presence of the entire village. There were so many flowers that the Germans protested. After the war his remains were re-interred in the Villeneuve St George Communal Cemetery.

PO 28.6.40   FO 28.6.41   FL 28.6.42

PETER WOODRUFF COMELY

41831   PO   Pilot   British   87 Squadr[on]

Comely joine[d] short service [commission in] January 1939. [...] his training [...] Shawbury he [...] Squadron a[...] October 23 19[...] squadron wa[s...] February 10 [...] Blenheim K 7[...] K 7114, flown [...] RM Hogg, [...] Both aircraft [...] base.

On May [...] in company [...] pilots, deliver[...] 87 Squadron [...] They remained to fly with the squadron and the two [...] and Flying Officer DH Ward, went on to the [...] withdrawn to Debden on May 20.

Comely claimed a Ju 88 destroyed on Augus[t...] a Bf 110 in a combat off Portland on the 15th bu[t...] down and killed, crashing into the sea in Hurrican[e...] 19 and is remembered on the Runnymede Memo[rial].

APO 1.4.39   PO 23.10.39

HARRY ALFRED GEORGE COMERF[ORD]

24051   FL   Pilot   British   312 Squa[dron]

Joined the RAF in January 1927. Comerford train[ed...] and was afterwards posted to 28 (Army Co-opera[tion]) Ambala, India. He moved to 31 (Army Co-opera[tion]) Quetta on March 18 1932.

In October 1934 Comerford went on to the R[...] He was recalled at the outbreak of war and w[...] Squadron at Speke on October 1 1940, as a Fligh[t...] the 15th, flying in Hurricane V 6542, he became lo[st...] during a routine patrol and baled out near Carn[...]

Awarded the AFC (30.9.41), Comerford resig[ned...] on April 10 1943.

PO 15.1.27   FO 30.11.28   FL 1.6.33   [...]

JOHN WILLIAM COMPTON

1157050   Sgt   Aircrew   British   25 S[quadron]

Joined 25 Squadron at North Weald in October [...]
No further service details traced.

WILLIAM CHARLES CONNELL

C 1159   PO   Pilot   Canadian   32 S[quadron]

Born in 1918, Connell joined the RCAF on Octo[...] posted to 32 Squadron at Acklington on October [...] from the RCAF on June 16 1946, as a Flight Li[eutenant].

FRANCIS HEBBLETHWAITE POWE[...]

39857   FO   Pilot   British   234 Squ[adron]

Born in 1917, Connor joined the RAF on a short [...] in May 1937. On July 17 he was posted to 9 FTS [...] on June 12 1938 he joined 22 (Torpedo Bomber) S[...] Island.

Connor went to 5 OTU, Aston Down on Ju[ne...] converting to Spitfires he joined 234 Squadron a[...] He shared in the destruction of a Ju 88 on July 27 [...] on August 16 during a combat with Bf 109s off Po[...] out and was rescued by a Royal Navy launch a[...] Naval Hospital, remaining there for two months. [...] crashed into the sea.

On November 3 1940 Connor was sent to CFS, Upavon for an instructor's course. From May 14 1941 until the end of the war he was a flying instructor in the UK and Canada. Connor's final posting was to the Air Staff at HQ 50 Group, Reading. He was released in July 1946, as a Squadron Leader.

For sixteen years Connor was with Air Traffic Control at the States of Jersey Airport. He died on May 1 1982.

APO 5.7.37   PO 10.5.38   FO 10.12.39   FL 10.12.40
SL 1.9.42

STANLEY DUDLEY PIERCE CONNORS

40349   FO   Pilot   British   111 Squadron

Born in Calcutta on April 8 1912 and educated at St Paul's School, Darjeeling, Connors joined 500 Squadron, AuxAF in early 1936. He applied for an RAF short service commission in 1937, was accepted and began his elementary flying in October. Posted to 5 FTS, Sealand on December 20 1937, he completed his training and joined 111 Squadron at Northolt on June 27 1938.

On May 18 1940 the squadron began flying patrols over France and Connors destroyed a Ju 88 and a Bf 109, on the next day he shot down three He 111s and a Ju 88, on June 2 he damaged two Bf 110s over Dunkirk and on June 7 he destroyed a Bf 109. He was awarded the DFC (31.5.40).

Connors was made a Flight Commander and on July 19 he claimed a Bf 109 destroyed, on the 28th a Ju 88, on August 11 another Bf 109, on the 15th another Ju 88 and a shared Bf 110 and on the 18th a Do 17. In this last engagement Connors was shot down by anti-aircraft fire whilst attacking Do 17s bombing Kenley. He was killed and his Hurricane, R 4187, is believed to be that which crashed at The Oaks, Wallington. Connors is buried in North Berwick Cemetery. After his death the award of a Bar to the DFC was announced (6.9.40).

APO 20.12.37   PO 19.2.38   FO 19.8.39

BRIAN BERTRAM CONSIDINE

79728   PO   Pilot   Irish   238 Squadron

In the RAFVR before the war, Considine did his early flying at 20 E&RFTS, Gravesend. He was called up in September 1939 and posted to ITW at Selwyn College, Cambridge in October.

Considine was posted to 3 FTS, Grantham in November, completed his training there on May 10 1940 and went to 6 OTU, Sutton Bridge, after which he joined 238 Squadron at Tangmere in June. On July 21 Considine claimed the destruction of a Bf 110 and on the 27th he shared a Do 17. He was shot down himself by Bf 109s over Bournemouth on November 5. He baled out, wounded, over Sturminster and his Hurricane, V 6792, crashed at Crab Farm, Shapwick.

In May 1941 238 was posted to the Middle East. It flew off HMS 'Victorious' on June 14 to Malta, refuelled and then flew on to LG 07 in Egypt. Considine went by troopship from the UK to Takoradi and on arrival he ferried a Tomahawk up to Abu Sueir, was flown back to Takoradi and ferried a Hurricane up, for squadron use in the Western Desert.

In January 1942 Considine was posted to 73 OTU, Aden. He later returned to Egypt and then went to a Met Flight in Palestine, flying

twice daily in Gladiators to record weather information. Considine joined 74 Squadron at Mehrabad on January 30 1943, as 'B' Flight Commander. He went to 111 Squadron in Malta in June 1943 and moved to Sicily after the invasion. He later joined 173 (Communications) Squadron at Cairo, remaining with it until December 1944, when he returned to the UK.

Considine was posted to 48 Squadron and flew a Dakota towing a glider in the Rhine crossing. The squadron flew out to India on February 15 1945 and carried out supply drops in Burma. After his return to the UK in December 1945 Considine was released from the RAF. He flew with Aer Lingus for four years, then went into advertising.

PO 14.5.40   FO 12.5.41   FL 12.5.42

MICHAEL HUGH CONSTABLE MAXWELL

36219   FO   Pilot   British   56 Squadron

Born on June 3 1917, Constable Maxwell was educated at Ampleforth College, Yorkshire and Hertford College, Oxford. He was a member of the University Air Squadron, as well as being a commissioned officer in the 4th Queen's Own Cameron Highlanders, a territorial regiment. In the years preceding the war Constable Maxwell attended both Army and OUAS camps. In March 1939 he had applied for a Permanent Commission in the RAF and on August 28 he heard of his being accepted. Called up at the outbreak of war, he spent a month as an Army officer but then resigned his commission and reported to 9 FTS, Hullavington on October 10 1939.

Constable Maxwell completed his training and was posted to 7 BGS at Stormy Down in March 1940 for a gunnery course, following which he joined 56 Squadron at North Weald on April 20.

On May 27 Constable Maxwell shot down a He 111 over Dunkirk and was then hit by Belgian anti-aircraft fire. He baled out, was taken to Ostend and returned to England in a trawler. He was wounded in the leg and foot by cannon shell splinters on June 8, when he was jumped by Bf 109s, whilst on a bomber escort. A tyre burst on landing and the aircraft slewed round. Constable Maxwell was admitted to Epping Hospital.

On September 27 he claimed a Do 17 destroyed. Three days later he crash-landed on Chesil Bank after being in combat with Do 215s and Bf 110s over Portland. The Hurricane, L 1764, was a write-off but he was unhurt.

Constable Maxwell was posted to 52 OTU, Debden on February 21 1941. In late March he went to CFS for an instructor's course and then returned to Debden. At the end of July he moved to 60 OTU, East Fortune to do more instructing but on October 8 he was posted to 604 Squadron at Middle Wallop. He was teamed with Sergeant J Quinton. In March 1942 Constable Maxwell was promoted to Squadron Leader and posted to command the AI Flight at 60 OTU, taking Quinton with him. They were to remain together for over four years. At the end of August 1942 they went to 54 OTU, Charter Hall, where Constable Maxwell was to command 'B' Squadron.

A return to operations came on December 12 1942 with a posting to 264 Squadron at Colerne, as a Flight Commander. On January 22 1943 Constable Maxwell damaged a Do 217 and on March 30 he probably destroyed a He 111. On April 23 he was promoted to Acting Wing Commander and given command of 604 Squadron. He was awarded the DFC (18.5.43).

On July 25 Constable Maxwell and Quinton damaged a Do 217, on August 23 they destroyed a Ju 88, on May 15 1944 a Ju 88, on July 2 a Ju 88 and on July 8 a Ju 88 and a probable Do 217. It was their final victory. Constable Maxwell was posted to HQ 85 Group at Uxbridge on July 19 1944, was awarded the DSO (22.9.44) and went back to 54 OTU, to command the Training Wing.

With the war in Europe over Constable Maxwell asked to be sent to the Far East. He was given command of 84 Squadron at Charra, Bengal but the Japanese surrendered before he led the squadron on

MH Constable Maxwell (continued)

operations. With the disbandment of 84 in December 1946 Constable Maxwell took command of 60 Squadron at Singapore. He was posted to England on December 8 1947. On arrival he took four months leave and on April 27 1948 he entered Ampleforth Monastery as a novice, with a leave of absence from the RAF. He stayed there four year and having decided to leave he rejoined the RAF in November 1952.

Constable Maxwell retired on June 3 1964, as a Wing Commander.

PO 7.10.39   FO 7.1.40   FL 7.1.41   SL 1.3.42
SL 10.11.46   WC 1.1.52

ALEXANDER NOEL CONSTANTINE

40893   FO   Pilot   British   141 Squadron

Constantine joined the RAF in May 1938 and was with 141 Squadron in June 1940. He commanded 273 Squadron in Ceylon from April 1942 to June 1943 on defence of the ports there. From June 1943 to March 1944 Constantine commanded 136 Squadron. On January 15 1944 he destroyed a Mitsubishi A6M-3 and damaged another, on the 20th a Nakajima Ki 43, on February 15 another A6M-3 and in March a Nakajima Ki 44.

Constantine was killed in an accident on July 29 1947.

APO 9.7.38   PO 16.5.39   FO 3.9.40   FL 3.9.41
SL 1.1.44

ARTHUR WILLSON COOK

131140   Sgt   Air Gunner   British   604 Squadron

Cook enlisted in the RAFVR at Hartlepool in July 1939 and was called up in December. Posted to 3 ITW, Hastings, he was there until April 1940. In June he went on a gunnery course at 5 BGS, Jurby, Isle of Man, then to 5 OTU, Aston Down, after which he joined 604 Squadron at Middle Wallop on August 20 1940.

Cook remained with the squadron until February 20 1941, when he went to No 1 School of Army Co-operation, Old Sarum. He was posted to the Overseas Air Delivery Flight, Kemble on April 26 and from July 14 to September 12 served with 216 and 223 Squadrons at Heliopolis and Shandur. After a short spell with 69 (General Reconnaissance) Squadron in Malta Cook joined 1437 Stategical Reconnaissance Unit in Libya on November 30 1941, later serving with it in Sicily, Italy and Persia.

Cook was awarded the DFM (2.6.42) for a sortie over Benghazi. His Baltimore was attacked by six enemy fighters. Although his gun was rendered useless by icing condition and he was in grave danger from enemy fire Cook gave cool and skilful directions to his pilot and endeavoured to take photographs of the enemy aircraft. Commissioned in July 1942, Cook returned to the UK in November 1943 and after a Specialist Armament Course at Manby he became an armament officer at Morpeth in May 1944. He was appointed Station Armament Officer at RAF Dalcross in January 1945 and released from the RAF in December 1945.

PO 16.7.42   FO 16.1.43   FL 16.7.44

HARRY COOK

126096   Sgt   Pilot   British   266 and 66 Squadrons

In July 1939 Cook joined the RAFVR and began his flying training on August 6. Called up on September 1, he was posted in October to 3 ITW, Hastings, after which he trained at 3 EFTS, Hamble and 14 FTS, at Kinloss and Cranfield.

Cook was awarded his flying badge on June 21 1940, completed the course, converted to Spitfires at 7 OTU, Hawarden and joined 266 Squadron at Eastchurch on August 26. He moved to 66 Squadron at Kenley on September 12. He claimed a Bf 109 probably destroyed on the

24th, a Bf 110 destroyed on the 27th and another pr the 30th. Cook crash-landed at Hornchurch on Octo a combat with Bf 109s over Maidstone. His Spitf written off but Cook was unhurt. On October 27 he destroyed.

In early 1941 Cook was posted to 7 OTU, as an in the year he was with 234 Squadron at Ibsley, serv the MSFU and in 1943 was with 41 Squadron. On o patrol Cook surprised a German destroyer, which : cannon fire turned and ran on to rocks. Commissio Cook had three confirmed victories, three pro damaged. He also destroyed a V1, a train, two armo twenty other types of vehicle. He was released in Lieutenant.

PO 18.6.42   FO 18.12.42   FL 18.6.44

ROBERT VINCENT COOK

755328   Sgt   Aircrew   British   219 Sc

Joined 219 Squadron on August 12 1940. No oth

CHARLES ALFRED COOKE

43634   PO   Pilot   British   66 Squadr

Born on June 7 1912, Cooke was commissioned i joined 66 Squadron at Duxford later in the montl shared in destroying a Do 17 and on August 20 he

On September 4 Cooke was shot down in com over Ashford. He baled out, slightly wounded, an Street. His Spitfire, R 6689, crashed on the crossroa Farm, Aldington. Cooke was promoted to Acting F on October 10 and given command of 'B' Flight. In he was posted from the squadron.

In December 1941 Cooke took command of Colerne. He destroyed a Ju 88 at night in July 194 of his tour was awarded the DFC (13.10.42).

Cooke stayed in the RAF, in the Secretarial B graduate of RAF Staff College and retired on Ju Squadron Leader. He died on January 28 1985.

PO 1.4.40   FO 5.1.41   FL 5.1.42   SL 1.

HERBERT REGINALD COOKE

161352   Sgt   Air Gunner   British   23

Cooke was with 23 Squadron at Collyweston in Ju commissioned in March 1943 and was awarded the as a Warrant Officer with 619 Squadron. The cit Cooke had taken part in a very large number of s attack on Kassel Cooke saw an aircraft being attac He informed his captain and they were able to shoo aircraft.

Cooke was released in 1946, as a Flying Offi

PO 29.3.43   FO 23.3.44

ERIC COOMBES

808380   Sgt   Aircrew   British   219 Sc

Joined 219 Squadron at Catterick on August 1 19
No other service details traced.

ROBERT JOHNSON COOMBS

60324   Sgt   Pilot   British   219 Squad

With 600 Squadron at Northolt in June 1940.

Commissioned in January 1941, Coombs was a (29.6.45), serving with 487 Squadron. He was releas in 1947, as a Flight Lieutenant.

Coombs died in 1951.

PO 15.1.41   FO 15.1.42   FL 15.1.43

CECIL JOHN COONEY

564567   F/Sgt   Pilot   British   56 Squ

Cooney, of Rhos Robin, Denbighshire, entered the I

apprentice. He later trained as a pilot and was with 56 Squadron in early 1940. Over Dunkirk on May 27 he claimed the probable destruction of a Bf 110.

On July 29 1940 Cooney was shot down by a Bf 109. His Hurricane, P 3879, crashed and exploded in the Channel off Dover and he was reported 'Missing'. Cooney was 26 years old. He is remembered on the Runnymede Memorial, Panel 10.

WILLIAM EDWIN COOPE

05201   SL   Pilot   British   17 Squadron

Coope joined the RAF in March 1930 in the Reserve of Officers. He was posted to 3 FTS, Grantham on October 24 1931 and joined 33 Squadron at Bicester on March 27 1932. In April 1935 Coope went to a staff job at No 1 Air Defence Group, London. He was appointed Assistant Air Attaché in Berlin on November 12 1935 and in early 1939 he was supernumerary at No 1 RAF Depot, Uxbridge.

Although Coope is linked to 17 Squadron as far as eligibility for the Battle of Britain clasp is concerned it seems unlikely that he was ever a member of the squadron but probably flew an occasional sortie with it. He was killed on June 4 1941, as a Wing Commander with 266 Squadron but again he was almost certainly not a member of the squadron.

Coope is remembered on the Runnymede Memorial, Panel 28.

*PO (RAFO) 21.3.30   FO 24.10.31   FL 24.10.35   SL 1.10.38
WC 1.12.40*

CHARLES FREDERICK COOPER

1003497   AC2   Radio Operator   British   600 Squadron

Cooper, from Wolverhampton, joined 600 Squadron at Redhill on September 26 1940. He was a member of the crew of Blenheim L 4905, which had engine failure during a routine patrol in heavy rain on October 2 1940. It crashed into trees on high ground at Broadstone Warren, Forest Row. All three men on board were killed.

Cooper was 20. He is buried in Holy Trinity churchyard, Heath Town, Wolverhampton.

DOUGLAS CLIFFORD COOPER

155877   Sgt   Air Gunner   British   235 Squadron

Joined 235 Squadron on August 13 1940. Commissioned in June 1943, Cooper stayed on in the RAF and went on to the Reserve in 1954, as a Flight Lieutenant.

PO 9.6.43   FO 9.12.43   FL 9.6.45   FL 9.12.46

JAMES ENERTON COOPER

745777   Sgt   Pilot   British   610 Squadron

Cooper, of Luton, Bedfordshire joined 610 Squadron at Acklington on October 6 1940.

He was killed on September 9 1941, as a Sergeant with 91 Squadron. He is buried in Luton Church Burial Ground.

ROY NORMAN COOPER

188171   Sgt   Pilot   British   610 and 65 Squadrons

Cooper, of Portsmouth, joined 610 Squadron at Acklington on October 6 1940 and moved to 65 Squadron at Turnhouse on the 11th.

Commissioned from Warrant Officer in July 1944, Cooper was killed on October 28 1945, as a Flying Officer with the Anti-Locust Flight.

He was 29 and is buried in the European Cemetery, Jinja Road, Kampala, Uganda.

PO 18.7.44   FO 18.1.45

SYDNEY FREDERICK COOPER

174121   Sgt   Pilot   British   253 Squadron

Born on July 14 1916, Cooper was with 253 Squadron at Kirton-in-Lindsey in June 1940. He was shot down in combat on August 30. His Hurricane, P 2631, crashed near Biddenden and was completely wrecked but Cooper was unhurt.

Commissioned from Warrant Officer on June 28 1943, Cooper stayed on in the RAF, was awarded the AFC (10.6.48) and retired on June 29 1958, as a Flight Lieutenant.

PO 28.6.43   FO 28.12.43   FL 28.6.45   FL 28.12.46

THOMAS ARTHUR COOPER

196692   Sgt   Pilot   British   266 Squadron

Cooper was born in 1920. He joined 266 Squadron at Wittering on September 30 1940.

Commissioned from Warrant Officer in March 1945, Cooper was released from the RAF in 1946, as a Flying Officer.

PO 3.3.45   FO 3.9.45

ASTON MAURICE COOPER-KEY

40802   PO   Pilot   British   46 Squadron

Joined the RAF on a short service commission in April 1938. Cooper-Key was posted to 23 Squadron at Wittering on January 14 1939. At the start of the Battle of Britain he was with 46 Squadron at Digby.

Cooper-Key was killed on July 24 1940. He crashed on a railway embankment west of Peartree Station, Derby, whilst attempting a forced-landing, in Hurricane P 2685. He was 21 and is buried in Scopwick Church Burial Ground, Lincolnshire.

APO 4.6.38   PO 4.4.39

THOMAS PAUL MICHAEL COOPER-SLIPPER

41555   FO   Pilot   British   605 Squadron

Cooper-Slipper was born at Kinver, Staffordshire, the son of the Vicar. He joined the RAF on a short service commission in November 1938. In early 1940 he was with 605 Squadron at Wick.

In May the squadron moved south to Hawkinge. On the 22nd Cooper-Slipper shared in the destruction of a He 111, on the 25th he destroyed a Ju 87 and on the 26th a Ju 88. On September 8 he claimed a Bf 109 destroyed and on the 15th he destroyed a Do 17 by ramming. Hit by return fire during an attack on German bombers, Cooper-Slipper lost control and collided amidships with a Do 17 over Marden, losing his port wing. He baled out and was slightly injured landing at Church Farm, Marden. His Hurricane, L 2012, crashed at The Leas, Yalding. He was awarded the DFC (26.11.40).

In September 1941 Cooper-Slipper was posted to 96 Squadron at Cranage, as a Flight Commander. He moved to 74 Squadron at Acklington in October and in November joined 135 Squadron, then preparing to go to Burma.

When the squadron reached Singapore Cooper-Slipper and several other pilots were held back to fly with 232 Squadron against the Japanese. He was invalided back to the UK in January 1942 and did not return to operations.

Released in 1946, as a Squadron Leader, Cooper-Slipper went to work for the De Havilland Canada Co, as a test pilot.

*APO 14.1.39   PO 3.9.39   FO 3.9.40   FL 3.9.41
SL 1.7.44*

LEONARD EDWARD MORGAN COOTE

138415   Sgt   Aircrew   British   600 Squadron

Coote, of Chiswick, Middlesex, joined 600 Squadron at Manston on July 18 1940.

Commissioned in October 1942, he was killed on October 3 1943, as a Flying Officer with 46 Squadron. He is remembered on the Runnymede Memorial, Column 267.

At some time Coote had undergone surgery at the Queen Victoria Hospital, East Grinstead and was a Guinea Pig.

PO 13.10.42   FO 13.3.43

RICHARD COPCUTT

581146 Sgt Observer British 248 Squadron

Copcutt, of Whetstone, Middlesex, was a pre-war regular airman. He was with 248 Squadron at Dyce in early July 1940.

He was a member of the crew of Blenheim P 6952, detailed to carry out a reconaissance off the south-west coast of Norway on October 20 1940. After engaging and shooting down a Do 215 the Blenheim was attacked by three Bf 109s. One engine was put out of action and the cockpit filled with smoke. The captain, Pilot Officer GM Baird, got down to low level, flying blind and skimming the sea, feeling for the surface at a speed of 150 mph.

The aircraft struck and the silence was complete as the fuselage filled with water. Baird freed himself and opened the hatch. He then managed to float out the unconscious Sergeant DL Burton but was unable to rescue Copcutt, also unconscious, before the aircraft sank.

Copcutt was 20. He is remembered on the Runnymede Memorial, Panel 13.

NORMAN DOWNEY COPELAND

54595 Sgt Wop/AG British 235 Squadron

Joined the RAF on March 16 1938 and after initial training Copeland was posted to No 1 Electrical and Wireless School at Cranwell, for a wireless operator's course, after which he joined 23 Squadron at Wittering. Copeland was later sent to RAF Manby for an air gunnery course and after qualifying returned to the squadron.

On May 23 1940 Copeland was posted to 235 Squadron at Bircham Newton. He went to 272 Squadron at Aldergrove on November 20 and then to 404 (RCAF) Squadron at Thorney Island on May 25 1941.

Copeland was posted to Canada on April 7 1942 to be an instructor at 31 OTU, Wibert, Nova Scotia. He returned to the UK in late November 1943 and went to 12 AGS, Bishopscourt, Northern Ireland. Commissioned in December 1943, Copeland was posted to 13 AGS, Ballah, Egypt in late May 1944 but soon after arriving was sent to Quastina, Palestine.

After the end of the war he went to Pamanzi Island in the Comoro Islands group in the Indian Ocean. Copeland was repatriated from there in December 1945 and released in January 1946.

PO 29.12.43   FO 29.6.44   FL 29.12.45

PERCY COPELAND

108956 Sgt Pilot British 616, 66 and 73 Squadrons

Copeland was with 66 Squadron at Leconfield in May 1940. Over Dunkirk on June 1 he damaged a He 111. On August 26 he was shot down in a surprise attack by a Bf 109. He made a forced-landing in Spitfire K 9827 and burned out at Crundale House Farm, Wye. Copeland was wounded and admitted to Ashford Hospital.

On October 14 1940 he was posted to 66 Squadron at West Malling, moving ten days later to 73 Squadron at Castle Camps. Copeland joined 151 Squadron at Digby in early November 1940. On the 9th he and Flying Officer KH Blair intercepted a Do 17 on a pre-dawn sortie over the east coast, off Skegness. Although they claimed it as destroyed it reached Gilze-Rijen, with two of the crew wounded.

Commissioned in November 1941, Copeland was serving with 250 Squadron in the Western Desert in mid-1942. On June 26 he was flying one of three Kittyhawks of the squadron, as part of an escort for Bostons west of Matruh. The Kittyhawks were attacked by Mc 202s. Copeland failed to return from this operation.

He was 25 and is remembered on the Alamein Memorial, Column 247.

PO 10.11.41

JACK HARRY HAMILTON COPEMAN

41257 PO Pilot British 111 Squadron

Joined the RAF on a short service commission in August 1938.

Copeman was with 111 Squadron at Croydon in June 1940. He claimed a Bf 109 destroyed on July 19. He was shot down and killed in a combat off Margate on August 11. His Hurricane, P 3105, crashed into the Channel.

Copeman was 27. He is buried in Middlekerke Communal Cemetery, Belgium.

APO 29.10.38   PO 29.8.39

GEORGE HENRY CORBETT

81366 PO Pilot Canadian 66 Squ

Corbett, of Oak Bay, Victoria, British Columbia, jo at Coltishall on July 26 1940. He was shot down by Grinstead on September 9. His Spitfire, N 3049, crashed at Cowden after he baled out, slightly in

On September 27 Corbett claimed a Ju 88 action he was hit by anti-aircraft fire and crash-lande unhurt. He was killed on October 8, shot down Spitfire, R 6779, crashed and burned out on E Upchurch. Corbett was 21 years old. He is bur churchyard extension, Upchurch, Kent.

PO 6.7.40

VAUGHAN BOWERMAN CORBETT

C 299 FL Pilot Canadian 1(RCA

Born on March 24 1911 in Toronto, Corbett joir December 30 1935. He arrived in the UK with No 1(on June 20 1940.

Corbett was shot down in combat with Bf 109 on August 31. He baled out, with burns, and landed level crossing. His Hurricane, P 3869, crashed a Biddenden. On January 1 1941 Corbett was po Squadron at Digby, as a Flight Commander. He t the unit in April 1941. It had been re-numbered as March 1 1941.

On a Blenheim escort to raid the power static on September 27 1941 Corbett shared in destroyin his tour ended he was awarded the DFC (13.2.42) an he was repatriated to Canada.

Corbett was killed in a flying accident on Feb a Group Captain. He is buried in St James' Ceme

WILLIAM JAMES CORBIN

126536 Sgt Pilot British 66 and 6

Corbin, who was born in Kent, joined the RAFVR did his weekend flying at 23 E&RFTS, Roches September 1939 he did his elementary training November until April 1940 and then moved to 14 Kinloss but later at Cranfield.

On August 10 1940 Corbin was posted to 7 OT conversion to Spitfires, after which he joined 66 Squa on August 26. Apart from six weeks spent with September/October 1940 he remained with 66 un 1941, when he went to 53 OTU, Llandow, as an Gunnery Flight. Promoted to Warrant Officer in M was commissioned in June. He returned to operatio 1942, joining 72 Squadron at Ayr. The squadron w North Africa and on November 8 it was in Gibralta flew to Maison Blanche, Algiers.

Corbin shared a probable Bf 109 on Novem another on April 19 1943 and was awarded the D was posted away from 72 on June 8 and arrived b July. He went to the Gunnery Flight at 57 OTU, 1943 and in April 1944 was appointed Chief Armament Practice Camp, Fairwood Common.

Released from the RAF in December 1945, Co RAFVR in March 1948, serving until 1952.

PO 16.6.42   FO 16.12.42   FL 16.6.44
FO (RAFVR) 19.3.48

HENRY CORCORAN

519958 Sgt Air Gunner British 23

Corcoran, of Higher Openshaw, Manchester, join on July 19 1940. The next day he was flying with Serg on an escort operation in Blenheim L 1300. They w Hauptmann Neumann of JG 27. Both men were re after their aircraft crashed into the Channel off C

Corcoran was 27 years old. He is remembered o Memorial, Panel 13.

HORACE ARTHUR CORDELL

100598   **Sgt**   **Pilot**   **British**   **64 and 616 Squadrons**

Initially with 64 Squadron, Cordell was posted to 616 Squadron at Kirton-in-Lindsey on October 13 1940.

Commissioned in June 1941, he was released from the RAF in 1947, as a Flight Lieutenant.

PO 19.6.41   *FO 19.6.42*   *FL 19.6.43*

DOUGLAS FREDERICK CORFE

810075   **Sgt**   **Pilot**   **British**   **73, 610 and 66 Squadrons**

Corfe, of Hoylake, Cheshire, was on the ground staff of 610 Squadron, AuxAF before the war. He transferred to the RAFVR in late 1938 to begin pilot training. He was called up at the outbreak of war and in June 1940 was serving with 73 Squadron at Church Fenton.

On July 25 Corfe rejoined 610 Squadron, then at Biggin Hill. He claimed a Bf 109 destroyed on August 14 and on the 22nd he was shot down in flames during a combat with Bf 109s over Folkestone. His Spitfire, R 6995, crashed and burned out at Hawkinge. Corfe jumped clear before it exploded.

Corfe was posted to 66 Squadron at Kenley on September 10 1940. On the 18th he was shot down in an action over the Canterbury area. His Spitfire, R 6603, is believed to have crashed in Denge Wood, Petham. Corfe was injured and admitted to Chartham Hospital.

In 1941 Corfe went to the Middle East with 229 Squadron and arrived in Malta with the squadron in March 1942. He was killed on April 25 1942, as a Warrant Officer, aged 24.

Corfe is buried in the Naval Cemetery, Capuccini, Malta.

RICHARD JOHN CORK

Sub-Lieutenant (FAA)   **Pilot**   **British**   **242 Squadron**

Cork joined the Navy in early 1939. He was loaned to the RAF in mid-June 1940 and after converting to Hurricanes he joined 242 Squadron at Coltishall on July 1. He claimed a Bf 110 destroyed on August 30, a Do 215 and a Bf 110 on September 7 and two Do 17s on the 15th. Cork was awarded the DFC (18.10.40) but this was later converted to the DSC by the Admiralty.

On November 23 1940 Cork was posted to 252 Squadron, Coastal Command but soon afterwards he went back to the FAA and joined 880 Squadron in HMS 'Indomitable', operating in the Mediterranean. He was serving in the carrier during Operation 'Pedestal', re-supplying Malta. On August 11 1942 Cork destroyed a Ju 88. The following day he shot down two Ju 88s, a Bf 110 and two SM 79s in four sorties. He was awarded the DSO (10.11.42).

In 1944 Cork was appointed Wing Leader of 15 Fighter Wing, made up of two Corsair squadrons operating from HMS 'Illustrious'. On April 14 1944 he was killed in a flying accident at China Bay airfield, Trincomalee, when he crashed into another aircraft, which was on the runway about to take off.

Cork is buried in the cemetery at Trincomalee.

Midshipman 1.5.39   *Sub-Lt 14.3.40*   *Lt 1.11.41*

ALLAN HENRY CORKETT

41903   **PO**   **Pilot**   **British**   **253 Squadron**

Born on August 9 1917, Corkett joined the RAF on a short service commission in February 1939, when he began his flying training at 11 E&RFTS, Perth. In June Corkett was posted to 2 FTS, Brize Norton and on November 6 1939 he joined the newly-reformed 253 Squadron at Manston.

On September 4 1940 Corkett claimed a Bf 110 destroyed and on October 5 he shared in the destruction of a Ju 88. He remained with the squadron until August 1941, when he was posted to 17 Squadron at Elgin. With his tour completed Corkett went as an instructor to 53 OTU in October 1941, initially at Llandow but later at Roose, Glamorgan.

In January 1943 he was posted to 64 Squadron at Hornchurch and in May was given command of 197 Squadron at Tangmere. In early July 1943 Corkett was shot down, taken prisoner and sent to Stalag Luft III. Repatriated to the UK after the war he went on to the RAFO on September 1 1945.

Corkett rejoined the RAF in September 1952 and was posted to CFS, South Cerney for an instructor's course. In April 1953 he went to 2 FTS, then at Cluntoe, Northern Ireland but later at Hullavington and Syerston, as an instructor on Jet Provosts, until September 1958. Corkett had two non-flying staff jobs, firstly at RAF Pitreavie Castle and finally at RAF Scampton prior to his retirement on January 15 1962, as a Flight Lieutenant, retaining the rank of Squadron Leader.

APO 15.4.39   *PO 6.11.39*   *FO 6.11.40*   *FL 6.11.41*
FL 1.9.52

MALCOLM CHARLES CORNER

78746   **PO**   **Air Gunner**   **British**   **264 Squadron**

Born in 1907 at Westmount, Quebec, Corner was commissioned in April 1940 and joined 264 Squadron at Kirton-in-Lindsey in September.

Corner died on April 23 1945 at Ambala, India, as a Squadron Leader. He is buried in Delhi War Cemetery.

APO 12.4.40   *PO 29.5.40*   *FO 29.8.41*   *FL 1.9.42*

NOEL HENRY CORRY ✠

80544   **PO**   **Pilot**   **British**   **25 Squadron**

Corry joined the RAFVR on February 22 1939 and did his elementary flying at 24 E&RFTS, Belfast. Called up after the outbreak of war, he was posted to ITW at Bexhill-on-Sea. In late November 1939 Corry went to 11 FTS, Shawbury. With training completed he was commissioned and posted to 5 OTU, Aston Down on June 8 1940 to convert to Blenheims.

Corry joined 25 Squadron at Martlesham Heath on June 26 1940 and remained with the squadron until January 29 1941, when he was posted to the Special Duties Flight, 72 Group, initially at Northolt and later at Denham and Eastchurch.

On February 19 1943 Corry went to 18 (P) AFU, Church Lawford for training in precision night landings, then on to 2 FIS, Montrose for a flying instructor's course, after which he was posted to 14 (P) AFU, Banff as a Flight Commander flying instructor, on Oxfords.

On March 14 1944 Corry went to 30 OTU, Hixon on Wellingtons, to prepare for operational flying in heavy bombers. He moved to 1656 Halifax Conversion Unit, Lindholme, where he joined a crew, who had lost their skipper. Two weeks at the No 1 Lancaster Finishing School at Hemswell and Corry and his crew then joined 12 Squadron at Wickenby, he as a Squadron Leader and 'A' Flight Commander.

As he was on his second tour Corry was required to do only 20 operations, but his crew, on their first tour, had to complete 30. Keen to stay with them Corry continued after his quota was up and he was posted away when it was discovered that he had done 24. He went to HQ Bomber Command Air Staff, attached to HQ No 1 Group, Bawtry as Air Crew Safety and Rescue Officer. He was awarded the DFC (8.12.44).

Corry was released from the RAF on November 27 1945, as a Squadron Leader.

PO 8.6.40   *FO 8.6.41*   *FL 8.6.42*

GUY WEBSTER CORY

40677   **FO**   **Pilot**   **British**   **41 Squadron**

Cory was born on September 2 1916 and joined the RAF on a short service commission in March 1938. He did his flying training at 11 FTS, Shawbury and was with 41 Squadron at Catterick in June 1940.

In early 1941 Cory was posted to CFS, Upavon for an instructor's course, after which he went to 6 FTS, Little Rissington. He was awarded the AFC (1.1.43).

After the war he went to Oxford to read English. At some period he commanded the University Air Squadron there. In January 1952 Cory was Admin Officer at Kai Tak, Hong Kong. He retired from the RAF on July 24 1954, as a Wing Commander, and died on June 20 1981.

APO 7.5.38   *PO 7.3.39*   *FO 3.9.40*   *FL 3.9.41*
SL 1.1.44   *SL 1.9.45*   *WC 1.7.53*

ERIC THOMAS COSBY

157403   Sgt   Pilot   British   3 and 615 Squadrons

Born on November 1 1916, Cosby joined the RAFVR in May 1939 and began his weekend flying at 8 E&RFTS, Reading, continuing it later at 3 E&RFTS, Hamble.

Called to full-time service at the outbreak of war Cosby was posted to 3 ITW, Hastings on November 20 1939, moved on to 10 FTS, Tern Hill on March 6 1940 and finished his course there on June 14. Cosby then went to 5 OTU, Aston Down and after converting to Hurricanes he joined 3 Squadron at Wick on July 31. He moved to 615 Squadron at Northolt on October 14. Cosby claimed a Bf 109 destroyed and a Ju 88 damaged on the 29th.

He was posted away to CFS, Upavon on December 29 1940, for an instructor's course. Cosby went to RAF Hamilton, Ontario on July 2 1941, remaining there until November 21 1942, when he was posted back to the UK. From January 28 1943 Cosby instructed at 3 (P) AFU, Lulsgate Bottom, 62 OTU, Usworth and 12 (P) AFU, Grantham.

On August 3 1943 he was posted to 60 OTU, High Ercall, for conversion to night-intruder Mosquitos. Commissioned in September, Cosby joined 605 Squadron at Bradwell Bay on November 2. He flew with the squadron until July 14 1944, returning then to 60 OTU as an instructor, moving on September 4 to 54 OTU, Charter Hall.

Cosby was released from the RAF on October 28 1945. He rejoined in September 1949 and retired on March 3 1967, as a Flight Lieutenant. He died on April 26 1978. Elder brother of IH Cosby.

PO 5.9.43   FO 5.3.44   FO 13.5.48   FL 7.5.59

IVOR HENRY COSBY

42293   PO   Pilot   British   610, 72 and 222 Squadrons

Cosby was born in London on August 19 1919 and educated at Bournemouth School. He learned to fly in 1938 at Air Service Training Ltd at Hamble and joined the RAFVR. In May 1939 he went into the RAF on a short service commission and after completing his flying training he joined 13 (Army Co-operation) Squadron in France in April 1940. The remnants of the squadron were withdrawn by road to Cherbourg in late May, returned to England by sea and went to Hooton Park to reform.

In August Cosby volunteered for Fighter Command. He converted to Spitfires at 7 OTU, Hawarden and joined 610 Squadron at Biggin Hill later in the month. In early September Cosby was posted to 72 Squadron, also at Biggin Hill. On the 23rd he shared in destroying a Bf 109. In October, when 72 went to Leconfield to reform, Cosby moved to 222 Squadron at Hornchurch and when it went to Coltishall in November he joined 602 Squadron at Westhampnett.

In January 1941 Cosby was posted to 141 Squadron at Gravesend and stayed with it for two years. He did an Air Gunnery course at CGS, Sutton Bridge in January 1943 and went as Chief Gunnery Officer at the Night Intruder OCU at High Ercall. Cosby returned to operations in September 1943, when he was posted to 264 Squadron at Fairwood Common, as a Flight Commander. He was awarded the DFC (4.8.44), being then credited with four enemy aircraft destroyed.

In 1945 Cosby was made OC Admin 6502 Air Disarmament Wing in Germany and in 1946 he joined 98 Squadron, flying Mosquitos. Granted a Permanent Commission in August 1947, he had a long post-war career, holding various staff appointments and commands before retiring on August 19 1974, as a Wing Commander. Cosby's portrait was drawn by Cuthbert Orde in the mess at Biggin Hill in October 1940. Younger brother of ET Cosby.

APO 8.7.39   PO 1.2.40   FO 1.2.41   FL 1.2.42
SL 1.8.47   WC 1.7.55

DIGBY VAWDRE CARTMEL COTES-PREEDY

41987   PO   Pilot   British   236 Squadron

Cotes-Preedy joined the RAF on a short service commission in February 1939 and in June 1940 he was with 236 Squadron.

One day in January 1941 he was pilot of an aircraft, which crashed shortly after a pre-dawn take-off. The aircraft burst into flames on impact and the observer was thrown out. Cotes-Preedy forced his way out and found his observer laying in burning petrol. He dragged him clear, rolled him in the grass to extinguish his burning clothing and then returned to the aircraft to look for the air gunner. Finding the gunner's escape hatch jammed Cotes-Preedy ripped the side of the fuselage and dragged the gunner out by his head. Although injured and suffering from burns Cotes-Preedy had saved the life of the gunner and also probably the observer's. His courage was recognised by the award of the GM (5.5.41).

In March 1942 Cotes-Preedy was a Flight Commander in 609 Squadron. He took command of 56 Squadron at Grimbergen in September 1944 and held it until his release from the RAF in 1946, as a Squadron Leader. Cotes-Preedy died in 1972.

APO 29.4.39   PO 6.11.39   FO 6.11.40   FL 6.11.41
SL 1.7.45

GERALD COTTAM

1050685   Sgt   Aircrew   British   25 Squadron

Joined 25 Squadron at North Weald in early October 1940. No further service details traced.

HUBERT WEATHERBY COTTAM

77790   PO   Pilot   British   213 Squadron

Cottam, of Sunderland, was with 213 Squadron at Exeter in June 1940. On August 12 he claimed the destruction of a Bf 110 and another three days later.

He was killed on December 5 1941, whilst serving as a flying instructor at 23 SFTS in Southern Rhodesia. Cottam was 22 years old and is buried in Bulawayo Cemetery, Zimbabwe.

PO 7.3.40   FO 7.3.41

JACK BURALL COURTIS

391343   Sgt   Pilot   New Zealander   111 Squadron

Born at Bluff on October 1 1914, Courtis was educated at Waihopai School and Southland Boys' High School and worked as a clerk for the Vacuum Oil Company at Invercargill.

In June 1939 Courtis joined the Civil Reserve of Pilots and began elementary training with the Southland Aero Club. He volunteered for the RNZAF at the outbreak of war and reported to the Ground Training School at Weraroa on November 19. Courtis did his ab initio training at No 1 EFTS, Taieri and then went to No 1 FTS, Wigram on January 13 1940.

A forced-landing in April put him in hospital for four weeks. He completed his course and sailed for the UK, arriving at Liverpool on August 27. In September Courtis was posted to 6 OTU, Sutton Bridge and on the 28th he joined 111 Squadron at Drem.

He was killed on December 5 1940, when his Hurricane crashed into a hill in bad weather thirty miles north-west of Edzello. Courtis is buried in Sleepyhillock Cemetery, Montrose.

RONALD NOEL HAMILTON COURTNEY

70852   FO   Pilot   British   151 Squadron

Courtney was born on December 25 1919 and joined the RAF on a short service commission in January 1938. He went to 8 FTS, Montrose on April 9 and after completing his training joined 151 Squadron at North Weald.

On May 29 1940 Courtney was attacked by Bf 109s over Dunkirk and baled out, wounded in the back of the neck and the right leg. He was picked up by the corvette HMS 'Shearwater' and taken to Ramsgate Hospital. He returned to 151 on July 18.

In February 1942 Courtney was posted to 610 Squadron at Hutton Cranswick. He was given command of 261 Squadron at Chittagong in July 1943, moving to command 113 Squadron at Manipur Road in January 1944. Courtney was awarded the DFC (8.9.44), the citation stating that he had taken a prominent part in the squadron's operations in the Imphal Valley and had destroyed three enemy aircraft. He was posted away from 113 in September 1944.

Courtney was awarded a Bar to the DFC (29.1.46). He commanded 130 Squadron from July 1946 to January 1947, 72 Squadron from February 1947 to February 1949 and 32 Squadron from November 1951 to May 1952. Awarded the AFC (1.1.54), Courtney led the 1954 Battle of Britain flypast. A graduate of the Joint Services Staff College and the RAF College of Air Warfare, Courtney was made a CB (1.1.67) and retired from the RAF on January 6 1968, as a Group Captain.

APO 26.3.38   PO 17.1.39   FO 3.9.40   FL 3.9.41
SL 1.1.41   SL 1.8.47   WC 1.1.53   GC 1.7.59

HERBERT WILLIAM COUSSENS

120161   Sgt   Pilot   British   601 Squadron

Coussens was born on May 18 1920. He joined 601 Squadron at Exeter on September 11 1940.

Commissioned in March 1942, he was with 607 Squadron in Burma in June 1944.

Released from the RAF in 1946, Coussens joined the RAFVR in 1947 and then rejoined the RAF in 1949, in the Aircraft Control Branch. He retired on May 18 1963, as a Flight Lieutenant.

PO 19.3.42   FO 1.10.42   FL 19.3.44
FO (RAFVR) 11.12.47   FL 21.11.49

GEORGE WALTER COUZENS

44823   PO   Pilot   British   54 Squadron

Born on May 31 1909, Couzens was a pre-war airman pilot. Commissioned in April 1940, he was with 54 Squadron at Hornchurch in June.

Couzens was awarded the AFC (14.6.45) and retired from the RAF on September 8 1946, as a Flight Lieutenant, retaining the rank of Squadron Leader.

PO 1.4.40   FO 1.4.41   FL 1.4.42

WILLIAM HUGH COVERLEY

70142   FO   Pilot   British   602 Squadron

Coverley was commissioned in the RAFO in October 1937 and called to full-time service at the outbreak of war. It seems he was in the AuxAF at this time. In June 1940 he was with 602 Squadron at Drem.

On July 7 1940 Coverley shared in destroying a Ju 88. He was shot down by enemy fighters over Dorchester on August 25 and baled out, unhurt. His Hurricane, P 9381, crashed and burned out on Galton Heath.

Coverley was shot down over the Biggin Hill area on

September 7. He baled out, badly burned but his descent was not seen and his body was not found until September 16. His Spitfire, N 3198, crashed in flames at Fosters Farm, Hayesden Lane, near Tonbridge. He is buried in Dean Road Cemetery, Scarborough. Coverley was 23.

PO (RAFO) 12.10.37   FO 3.9.39

AUBREY RICHARD COVINGTON

42591   PO   Pilot   British   238 Squadron

Born on January 22 1921, Covington was first commissioned in September 1939. He joined 238 Squadron at St Eval on August 20 1940. He claimed a Bf 110 destroyed on September 15. Covington's Hurricane, P 3833, was damaged in this combat over Kenley and he forced-landed, out of fuel, at Gulledge Farm, Imberthorne, unhurt.

On October 1 Covington claimed two Bf 110s destroyed but on this day he was himself shot down by Bf 109s west of Poole and is believed to have baled out at Sherbourne. Six days later he was shot down by Bf 109s over Blandford. Covington baled out, slightly wounded, and was admitted to Blandford Hospital. His Hurricane, V 6777, crashed at Meriden Wood Down, Winterbourne Houghton.

Covington stayed in the RAF, latterly in the Fighter Control Branch. He retired on January 22 1964, as a Flight Lieutenant.

APO 2.9.39   PO 6.4.40   FO 6.4.41   FL 6.4.42
FL 1.9.45

JAMES BAIRD COWARD

39412   FL   Pilot   British   19 Squadron

Coward was born on May 18 1915. He joined the RAF on October 16 1936 and did his elementary flying training at 9 E&RFTS, Ansty and his intermediate and advanced at 2 FTS, Digby from February 6 to September 7 1937, when he was posted to 19 Squadron at Duxford.

On November 6 1939 Coward was appointed 'A' Flight Commander in 266 Squadron, then forming at Sutton Bridge. Over Dunkirk on June 2 1940 he probably destroyed a Bf 109. After a spell in hospital Coward joined 19 Squadron at Fowlmere.

On August 31 he was shot down during an attack on Do 17s ten miles east of Duxford, baled out, badly wounded, and landed on the Royston-Newmarket Road. Coward was taken to Addenbrookes Hospital, Cambridge, where his left leg was amputated below the knee.

Fit again, Coward was posted to Mr Churchill's personal staff, in charge of roof-spotting at Chequers and Chartwell. In early January 1942 he went on a three month's refresher course at Hullavington, after which he was posted to 52 OTU, Aston Down to command a squadron. In October 1942 Coward went as CFI to 55 OTU, Annan. On November 21 1943 he took command of No 1 ADU at Croydon.

Coward was sent on a course at RAF Staff College on June 17 1944, following which he was posted to the Air Ministry, in charge of Fighter Operational Training. After the war he held a series of staff appointments and commands. Awarded the AFC (1.1.54), Coward retired on September 8 1969, as an Air Commodore.

APO 28.1.37   PO 16.11.37   FO 16.6.39   FL 3.9.40
SL 1.12.41   SL 1.8.47   WC 1.7.52   GC 1.7.58
AC 1.7.62

WILLIAM COWEN

1050707   Sgt   Aircrew   British   25 Squadron

Joined 25 Squadron at Martlesham Heath in late August 1940. No other service details traced. Died on June 29 1979.

JAMES COWLEY

49664   **Sgt**   **Pilot**   **British**   **87 Squadron**

Cowley was with 87 Squadron in June 1940. On August 14 he made a forced-landing at Symondsbury, near Bridport, following a combat over Portland. His Hurricane, P 3465, was written-off and Cowley was admitted to Bridport Hospital, slightly injured.

Posted away from 87 on October 14 1940, Cowley was commissioned in July 1942 and released from the RAF in 1946, as a Flight Lieutenant.

PO 2.7.42   *FO 2.1.43*   *FL 2.7.44*

JAMES ROY COWSILL

741936   **Sgt**   **Pilot**   **British**   **56 Squadron**

Cowsill, from Muncaster, Northumberland, was with 56 Squadron at North Weald in June 1940. On July 13 he damaged a Ju 87, which crash-landed on the beach at Cap Griz Nez. Following this action Cowsill was shot down into the Channel off Calais by Feldwebel John of 4/JG 51. He was never heard of again and is remembered on the Runnymede Memorial, Panel 13.

Cowsill was 20 years old.

DAVID GEORGE SAMUEL RICHARDSON COX

101041   **Sgt**   **Pilot**   **British**   **19 Squadron**

Cox, from Cambridge, was born on April 18 1920, educated at Bournemouth and worked in a solicitor's office. After failing an RAF medical he spent some months working as a fish porter at Billingsgate Market to build himself up. Cox joined the RAFVR and began training at 19 E&RFTS, Gatwick in April 1939. He was called up on September 1, completed his flying training at 10 FTS, Tern Hill and joined 19 Squadron at Duxford on May 23 1940.

On August 19 he claimed a Bf 110 destroyed and on September 9 he claimed a Bf 109 and another on the 15th. He was himself shot down on the 27th in an engagement over the Canterbury area, in Spitfire X 4237. The aircraft was written off after crashing at Wye Court Farm, Wye and Cox was wounded.

He claimed Bf 109s destroyed on June 27 and August 12 1941. He was commissioned in July 1941 and posted away on September 12 to instruct at 57 OTU, Hawarden. In late May 1942 Cox joined 72 Squadron at Biggin Hill. The squadron was posted to North Africa in November. On the 8th it was in Gibraltar and on the 16th flew into Maison Blanche, Algiers. Cox destroyed a Bf 109 on the 26th, got a probable the next day, a Ju 88 on the 29th, destroyed a He 111 on the ground at Djedeida airfield on December 2 and another Bf 109 in the air on the 4th.

Cox was appointed a Flight Commander in January 1943 and was awarded the DFC (16.2.43). He claimed a FW 190 on April 3 and a probable Bf 109 on the 12th. His tour expired on April 26 and Cox was posted back to the UK on May 15, becoming a Tactics Liaison Officer, instructing American pilots. He was awarded a Bar to the DFC (9.7.43).

In January 1944 Cox was posted to 504 Squadron at Biggin Hill, as a Flight Commander. After a three month spell at 84 Group Support

Unit, Aston Down he was given command of 222 Squadron at Selsey. On June 8 he damaged a FW 190. Cox returned to 84 Group SU, then at Thruxton, in mid-July and did not return to operations until October 3 1944, when he went to No 1 Squadron at Detling. He took command of the squadron on January 1 1945. On April 21 Cox was posted to the Far East to lead 909 Spitfire Wing in Burma. He went to HQ RAF Siam, Bangkok on September 29 1945 and was released from the RAF on March 11 1946. He received the C de G in September 1944.

PO 17.7.41   *FO 17.7.42*   *FL 17.7.43*

GILBERT PARISH COX

580644   **Sgt**   **Aircrew**   **British**   **236 Squadron**

Joined 236 Squadron on September 20 1940. No other service details traced.

GRAHAM JAMES COX

41668   **FO**   **Pilot**   **British**   **152 Squadron**

Born in Sparkhill, Birmingham in 1919, Cox joined the RAF on a short service commission in January 1939. He was with 152 Squadron at Acklington in June 1940. On August 12 he shared a Ju 88, on the 18th he claimed a Bf 109, on the 21st he shared another Ju 88 and on September 27 he claimed a Bf 110 destroyed.

Cox destroyed a He 111 on May 27 1941 and with his tour completed he was posted away and awarded the DFC (17.10.41). Returning to operations in September 1942 Cox went to 501 Squadron at Middle Wallop, as a Flight Commander. In May 1943 he was posted to 43 Squadron at Mateur, Tunisia. The squadron moved to Malta on June 8. On a bomber escort to Gerbini, Sicily on July 4 Cox destroyed a Bf109. On the way back he decided to fly at low level and he and his No 2 attacked a train at Vizzini station and blew up the engine. The next day Cox was promoted and took command of 229 Squadron at Krendi. On July 10 he destroyed three Mc 200s.

In October 1943 Cox was posted away for a rest. He returned to operations in February 1944, when he took command of 92 Squadron at Marcianise in Italy. He destroyed a FW 190 on May 13 and a Ju 88 on July 21. Posted away in August 1944, Cox was awarded the DSO (10.10.44). He was released from the RAF in 1946, as a Squadron Leader.

APO 4.3.39   *PO 2.10.39*   *FO 2.10.40*   *FL 2.10.41*

KENNETH HENRY COX

81367   **PO**   **Pilot**   **British**   **610 Squadron**

Cox joined 610 Squadron at Biggin Hill on July 27 1940. On August 12 he claimed a Bf 109 destroyed and another six days later.

On August 28 Cox was shot down and killed in combat with Bf 109s over Dover. His Spitfire, P9511, crashed into a house at Stelling Minnis.

Cox was 24. He was cremated at Birmingham Municipal Crematorium and his ashes were later scattered at Old Castle Bromwich aerodrome.

PO 6.7.40

PHILIP ANTHONY NEVILLE COX

33184   **FO**   **Pilot**   **British**   **501 Squadron**

Cox, of Brighton, Sussex, entered RAF College, Cranwell as a flight cadet in September 1935. He was awarded the RM Groves Memorial Prize in 1937. After graduating in July 1937 he joined 43 Squadron at Tangmere at the end of the month.

Cox was posted to 501 Squadron at Croydon on June 21 1940, as a Flight Commander. He claimed a Bf 109 destroyed and another shared on July 20. In combat over Dover Harbour on July 27 Cox was shot down by

Feldwebel Fernsebner of III/JG 52 and reported 'Missing'. He was 25 years old and is remembered on the Runnymede Memorial, Panel 5.

PO 31.7.37   FO 31.1.39

RALPH CYRIL RUPERT COX

747819   Sgt   Air Gunner   British   248 Squadron

Cox was with 248 Squadron in June 1940. On August 27 he was one of the crew of a Blenheim, which failed to return from a reconnaissance sortie to the southern coast of Norway. The aircraft crashed into the sea. The pilot and air gunner were reported 'Missing' and Cox was killed, aged 30. He is buried in Kriberg Cemetery, Göthenberg, Sweden.

WALTER EDWARD COX

747745   Sgt   Air Gunner   British   264 Squadron

Cox was with 264 Squadron at Duxford in June 1940. No other service details have been traced. He is believed to have died on February 23 1953.

JOHN HARRY COXON

749430   Sgt   Air Gunner   British   141 Squadron

Joined 141 Squadron on August 20 1940. In 1942 Coxon was with 103 Squadron, flying in Wellingtons from Elsham Wolds, Lincolnshire, as a Flight Sergeant. He failed to return from operations on June 6 1942. He was 33 years old and is buried in Reichswald War Cemetery, Germany.

DOUGLAS BARKER CRABTREE

125730   Sgt   Pilot   British   501 Squadron

Crabtree was with 501 Squadron at Filton in September 1939 and served with it in France in May 1940 and throughout the Battle of Britain.

He was later with 616 Squadron and on July 3 1941 was shot down over Lille. Sheltered by a French family, Crabtree evaded capture by the Germans. He returned to England after several months, bringing back with him detailed drawings of an arms factory on cigarette papers.

Commissioned in June 1942 from Warrant Officer, Crabtree did not return to operations but became an instructor. He was released in 1946, as a Flight Lieutenant, and was killed in a civil flying accident on June 24 1950.

PO 4.6.42   FO 4.12.42   FL 4.6.44

GEORGE DUDLEY CRAIG

90285   FL   Pilot   British   607 Squadron

Born on September 13 1914, Craig was educated at Winchester College and Pembroke College, Cambridge, where he obtained a BA in Law in 1936 and an MA in 1940. Before the war he was practicing as a solicitor. Craig joined 607 Squadron, AuxAF in 1937 and was commissioned in May.

Called to full-time service on August 24 1939, Craig was one of a section of three Gladiators which sighted a Do 18 flying boat 25 miles out to sea. Their attacks inflicted such damage as to cause it to crash 50 miles out. The crew were picked up by a trawler as PoWs. On November 13 607 flew south from Acklington to Croydon, going on two days later to Merville in France.

Craig served with 607 throughout the Battle of Britain and took command of the squadron in March 1941. He was shot down whilst making a low-level attack on Le Touquet airfield on November 4 1941 and captured. In 1942 he attempted to walk out of Stalag Luft III, disguised as a German guard, but was unsuccessful. At Oflag XXIB Craig was one of thirty-six officers who tunnelled their way out. With a companion he walked south towards Gneisen but was recaptured by military police after three days.

After returning to England in May 1945 Craig was released from the RAF later in the year. He received a Mention in Despatches (28.12.45) and was made an OBE (26.7.46) for distinguished service whilst a PoW.

Craig returned to his practice, later becoming a partner. He rejoined the RAuxAF in 1947, firstly in the Secretarial but later in the Fighter Control Branch. He died in 1974.

PO (AuxAF) 28.5.37   FO (AuxAF) 28.11.38   FO 24.8.39
FL 3.9.40   FO (RAuxAF) 30.5.47   FL (RAuxAF) 6.2.50

JOHN TEASDALE CRAIG

564573   Sgt   Pilot   British   111 Squadron

Craig, of Witton-le-Wear, Isle of Man, was born in Newcastle-upon-Tyne. He was a pre-war airman pilot and was with 111 Squadron in September 1939.

Over Dunkirk on May 24 1940 Craig destroyed a Bf 109 and on the 31st he probably destroyed another.

On August 13 he shared a Do 17, on the 15th he claimed a Bf 110 destroyed and probably three Ju 88s and on the 16th a Do 17 destroyed.

Craig was shot down in combat with Bf 110s over Felixstowe on August 31. He baled out, injured, and was admitted to Epping Hospital. He was awarded the DFM (6.9.40), having then destroyed at least eight enemy aircraft.

He was killed on June 2 1941, aged 27. Craig is buried in Crook and Willington Cemetery, Isle of Man.

EDWARD WILLIAM CRANWELL

141532   Sgt   Pilot   British   610 Squadron

Joined the RAFVR in August 1938 and did his weekend flying at 21 E&RFTS, Stapleford Abbots. Cranwell was called up in late 1939, went to 3 ITW, Hastings and in May 1940 was posted to 11 EFTS, Perth. In June Cranwell went to 15 FTS, Brize Norton, moving in August to Chipping Norton.

On September 24 Cranwell was posted to 7 OTU, Hawarden and he joined 610 Squadron at Acklington on October 6. In early 1941 he was injured in a crash and spent several months in hospital, after which he was posted to No 1 Anti-Aircraft Co-operation Unit, initially at Weston Zoyland and later at Aberporth.

In June 1942 Cranwell volunteered for Bomber Command and did some training on Oxfords at Little Rissington. In July he converted to Wellingtons at 15 OTU, Harwell and in October joined 102 Squadron at Pocklington, on Halifaxes. Commissioned from Warrant Officer in February 1943, Cranwell finished his tour in July and was awarded the DFC (13.8.43). From July 1943 until February 1944 Cranwell was at 82 OTU, Ossington, as a Flight Commander on fighter affiliation. In March he moved to 26 OTU, Wing on similar duties.

In February 1945 Cranwell went to 17 OTU, Turweston to convert to Wellingtons, in May to 1652 Heavy Conversion Unit, Acaster Malbis to convert to Halifaxes, in June to the Glider Towing Training Unit at Matching and from July to October 1945 he served with 190 Squadron at Great Dunmow.

Cranwell was released in late 1945, as a Flight Lieutenant.

PO 6.2.43   FO 1.8.43   FL 1.2.45

HECTOR HUGH CRAWFORD

39904   PO   Pilot   New Zealander   235 Squadron

Born at Hawera on August 25 1916, Crawford was educated at New Plymouth Boys' High School and afterwards worked as a clerk, until joining the Customs Department in 1937.

Crawford learned to fly privately in early 1938 and in May 1939 he joined the Civil Reserve of Pilots. On October 26 he went to the Ground Training School at Weraroa, was posted to 2 EFTS, New Plymouth in late November and on December 18 1939 he moved to 2 FTS, Woodbourne. After gaining his flying badge and being promoted to Sergeant Crawford completed the course and was commissioned in early May 1940. He sailed in the SS 'Mataroa' for the UK on the 24th and was posted soon after arriving to No 1 (Coastal) OTU, Silloth.

Crawford joined 235 Squadron at Bircham Newton on August 18 1940. With ninety operational sorties carried out and one enemy aircraft destroyed he was posted to 143 Squadron at Thornaby on July 14 1941. He moved to 272 Squadron at Kemble on August 19 and on the 30th took off in his Beaufighter from Portreath bound for Gibraltar and then the Middle East, via Malta. After arriving at Edku in Egypt Crawford was immediately attached to 252 Squadron and flew back to Malta to carry out operational sorties from Luqa against targets in Sicily and Sardinia.

Crawford rejoined 272 in Egypt on October 8 1941 and began operations, during the early course of which he shot down a Ju 52. On December 19 he took off to strafe along the Barce-Tocra road. His Beaufighter was damaged by ground fire and after coaxing it along he finally crash–landed in the desert fifty miles north-west of El Mechili. Another pilot, whom Crawford had picked up in similar circumstances, saw his plight and landed beside a mile away. After setting fire to their aircraft Crawford and his navigator ran towards their would-be rescuer. As they came over a rise they heard machine gun fire. The Beaufighter took off and the two men were captured by a convoy of German armoured cars. They travelled for two days but at dawn on the third day Crawford escaped after a sentry left him alone for a few minutes. The Germans chased him for half an hour but he eluded them by hiding next to a dead camel. Having injured his ankle he was soon unable to walk but was found by some Bedouin tribesmen, who fed and cared for him. Crawford met some British troops on the 27th and rejoined his squadron four days later.

On February 6 1942 Crawford was shot down by ground fire whilst making a low-level attack on enemy vehicles near Martuba. He attempted to land but crashed on uneven ground and the aircraft caught fire. Some time later his navigator returned to the squadron. Although wounded, he had managed to get clear after the crash. He could see Crawford lying amongst the wreckage but because of his wound, the intense heat and danger from exploding ammunition he could not reach him. He was then unconscious or already dead.

Crawford was reported by the Red Cross to have been buried in a military cemetery near Barce. After the war his remains were re-interred in Benghazi Military Cemetery.

PO 4.5.40   FO 4.5.41

DENIS GEORGE CRESSWELL

751880   Sgt   Air Gunner   British   141 Squadron

Cresswell, of Wollaton, Nottinghamshire, joined 141 Squadron at Drem on September 10 1940. He was killed on August 30 1941, as a Flight Sergeant with 410 (RCAF) Squadron, operating in Defiants from Drem.

Cresswell was cremated at Nottingham Crematorium, West Bridgford. He was 23.

EDWARD DIXON CREW

74700   FO   Pilot   British   604 Squadron

Born on December 24 1917, Crew was educated at Felsted School and Downing College, Cambridge, where he obtained an MA. He was a member of the University Air Squadron and was called to full-time service in October 1939.

Crew went to ITW, Hastings in November and moved on to FTS, Cranwell in January 1940. He converted to Blenheims, firstly at Andover and later 5 OTU, Aston Down in June.

He joined 604 Squadron at Gravesend on July 8 1940. In December Crew teamed up with Sergeant NH Guthrie and they had some successes. On the night of April 4 1941 they destroyed a He 111, on the 24th another, on the 28th yet another and on July 7 they destroyed a Ju 88, which was one of a force attacking Middle Wallop by night. Crew was awarded the DFC (29.7.41). Guthrie was posted away from 604 but Crew continued to find enemy aircraft at night. On April 2 1942 he shot down a He 111 and another unidentified enemy aircraft, on the 28th a He 111, on May 3 a Do 217 and another the following night. He was made 'A' Flight Commander in May 1942.

In October 1942 Crew became OC Radio Development Flight, conducting radio and radar anti-jamming trials and training. In March 1943 he joined 85 Squadron at Hunsdon, as a Flight Commander and on May 21 destroyed a FW 190. Crew was given command of 96 Squadron at Church Fenton in June 1943. On January 4 1944 he shot down a Me 410 and damaged another, on February 13 he destroyed a Ju 88 and between June and September 1944 he destroyed twenty-one V1s at night. He was awarded the DSO (26.9.44), being then credited with thirteen enemy aircraft destroyed. The squadron was disbanded on December 12 1944 and Crew was posted to RAF Staff College in January 1945 and later granted a Permanent Commission.

Between July 1948 and February 1950 Crew led 45 Squadron in operations against the terrorists in Malaya. He was awarded a Bar to the DSO (10.3.50). He held a series of appointments and commands prior to his retirement on March 3 1973, as an Air Vice-Marshal. Crew was made a CB (1.1.73).

PO 3.10.39   FO 3.10.40   FL 3.10.41   SL 29.9.43
SL 1.9.45   WC 1.7.52   GC 1.1.59   AC 1.7.65
AVM 1.7.69

JOHN LAWRENCE CRISP

112450   Sgt   Pilot   British   43 Squadron

Crisp joined 43 Squadron at Tangmere in July 1940. On a routine patrol on August 16 his Hurricane, L 1736, developed a glycol leak and caught fire. He baled out over Bognor but in a heavy landing broke his right thigh.

Crisp did not return to duty until June 1941. Commissioned in November, he was killed on June 8 1942, with 122 Squadron. He was 25 and is remembered on the Runnymede Memorial, Panel 68.

PO 21.11.41

RONALD FREDERICK CROCKETT

79177   PO   Observer   British   236 Squadron

Crockett, of Acton, London, joined 236 Squadron at Thorney Island on July 15 1940. He was killed on September 17 1942, as a Flight Lieutenant with 230 Squadron, a flying boat unit.

Crockett was 25. He is buried in Hadra War Memorial Cemetery, Alexandria, Egypt.

PO 5.5.40   FO 5.5.41   FL 5.5.42

PETER GUERIN CROFTS

33381   FO   Pilot   British   615 and 605 Squadrons

Crofts entered RAF College, Cranwell in January 1937, as a flight cadet. He was commissioned in September 1938 and joined the SHQ staff at RAF Gosport.

On September 4 1940 Crofts was posted to 615 Squadron at Prestwick and on the 13th he moved to 605 Squadron at Croydon. He was shot down by Bf 109s over Ticehurst on September 28, baled out but fell dead at Red Pale, a mile and a half from Dallington, East Sussex after his parachute failed to open. His Hurricane, V 6699, crashed in a paddock at Earls Down, Red Pale and exploded.

Crofts was 22. He is buried in All Saints' churchyard, Tilford, Surrey. There is a small stone memorial to him on the spot where he fell, a few yards from Red Pale.

APO 11.5.38   PO 17.9.38   FO 17.3.40

ERIC EUGENE CROKER

391826   Sgt   Pilot   New Zealander   111 Squadron

Born in Auckland on January 1 1917, Croker was educated at Henderson Valley Primary School and Mt Albert Grammar School and afterwards was an electrical apprentice with the Auckland Harbour Board.

In August 1938 he joined the Civil Reserve of Pilots. He volunteered at the outbreak of war and began the ground training course at Weraroa on December 18 1939. Croker went to No 1 EFTS, Taieri in mid-January 1940 and moved to No 1 FTS, Wigram on March 11. With his training completed he sailed for the UK in the RMS 'Rangitane' on July 12.

Two weeks after arriving Croker was posted to 6 OTU, Sutton Bridge and he joined 111 Squadron at Drem on September 28. He had flown fourteen operational sorties before being posted to 260 Squadron at Skitten on December 12 1940.

Croker went to 41 Squadron at Catterick in May 1941. On a training flight on June 1 he crashed into the side of a hill, sustained severe head injuries and was taken to Catterick Hospital, where he died the next day. He is buried in Catterick Cemetery.

ROBERT CROMBIE

903506   Sgt   Air Gunner   British   141 Squadron

Crombie, of Lightwater, Surrey, was with 141 Squadron at Turnhouse in June 1940. The squadron went south on July 12 and Crombie was in one of the nine Defiants attacked by Bf 109s of III/JG 51 off Dover on July 19. His aircraft, L 6974, was shot down into the Channel. The pilot, Pilot Officer JR Kemp, and Crombie were both reported 'Missing'.

Crombie was 29 and is remembered on the Runnymede Memorial, Panel 13.

DAVID MOORE CROOK

90478   PO   Pilot   British   609 Squadron

Crook, from Shrewsbury, was born in Huddersfield in 1914. He went to Cambridge University. In August 1938 Crook joined 609 Squadron, AuxAF at Yeadon and had done some flying training before he was called for full-time service on August 25 1939.

He was posted to 6 FTS, Little Rissington on October 7 and after completing his training he rejoined 609 Squadron in May 1940. On July 9 Crook claimed a Ju 87 destroyed and another damaged, on August 11 a probable Bf 110, on the 12th another probable Bf 110, on the 13th a Bf 109 destroyed, on the 14th a shared He 111, on September 27 a shared Bf 110 and on the 30th two Bf 109s and a shared probable. He was awarded the DFC (1.11.40).

On November 10 Crook was posted to CFS, Upavon for an instructor's course, after which he went to 15 EFTS, Carlisle, remaining there until April 1944 when he moved to AFU, Wheaton Aston. In July Crook was posted to AFU, Tern Hill, in September to 41 OTU, Hawarden and on December 1 to 8(Coastal) OTU, Dyce.

On December 18 1944 Crook took off in a Spitfire lX, EN 662, to fly a mid-morning high-level photographic sortie. At 10.52 am HQ 13 Group reported to Dyce that a Spitfire had been seen to dive into the sea near Aberdeen from 20000 feet. A search of the area found some of Crook's flying clothing but he was never found. He is remembered on the Runnymede Memorial, Panel 202.

Crook's portrait was drawn by Cuthbert Orde in November 1940.

APO 25.8.39   PO 4.5.40   FO 9.12.40   FL 9.12.41

HAROLD KAY CROOK

63789   Sgt   Pilot   British   219 Squadron

Crook was with 219 Squadron at Catterick at the start of the Battle of Britain. He was commissioned in April 1941 and went on to the RAFO in August 1947. He died on March 20 1988.

PO 9.4.41   FO 9.4.42   FL 9.10.43   SL (RAFO) 1.8.47

VALTON WILLIAM JAMES CROOK

NZ 40203   Sgt   Air Gunner   Australian   264 Squadron

Born in Orange, New South Wales on May 11 1913, Crook went to New Zealand in 1937 under a Government Building Scheme. After the outbreak of war he volunteered for aircrew duties and began his ground training at Weraroa on January 15 1940. After a Lewis gunnery course at the Air Observers' School, Ohakea he sailed for the UK in the SS 'Akaroa' on March 23.

Crook was at Uxbridge for a month before being posted to 264 Squadron at Duxford for further training. On July 26 1940 he was sent to 5 OTU, Aston Down, where he was awarded his air gunner's badge and promoted to Sergeant. He then rejoined 264 Squadron.

Posted away on March 20 1941, Crook went to 3 Group Training Flight at Stradishall, leaving there for the Middle East in early April. He joined 37 Squadron at Shallufa, Egypt to fly in Wellington bombers. In June Crook's aircraft was shot down into the sea and he was not picked up for 38 hours.

With his tour completed in early September 1941 Crook returned to the UK and went to HQ 25 Group at Stormy Down, as an instructor. He received a Mention in Despatches (1.1.42). After a course at CGS, Sutton Bridge he was posted to 7 AGS, Manby, again as an instructor. In late June 1942 Crook went to 1653 Conversion Unit at Polebrook and after a month moved to the Aircrew Pool at Snaith. With his crew he flew from Lyneham in a Liberator to join 160 Squadron at Aqir, Palestine. The squadron later moved to Egypt and in January 1943 became part of 178 Squadron at Shandur.

Crook completed his third tour in June 1943, returned to the UK and was repatriated to New Zealand in September. He was with No

VWJ Crook (continued)

1 (RNZAF) Squadron at Whenuapai in early 1944 but transferred to the RAAF and left for Melbourne in June. He was discharged in mid-February 1945, as a Warrant Officer, probably for medical reasons. He died in 1950.

MICHAEL ERNEST CROSKELL

42805	Sgt	Pilot	British	213 Squadron

Joined the RAFVR in June 1938 and was awarded his wings in August 1939. Croskell was called up on September 1 and posted in October to 11 FTS, Shawbury for assessment of flying capabilities.

In December Croskell joined 213 Squadron at Wittering. Over Dunkirk on May 29 1940 he probably destroyed a Ju 87. On August 11 he claimed the destruction of a Ju 88, a Bf 109 and a Bf 110.

Croskell was posted to CFS, Upavon for an instructor's course in February 1941. Commissioned in May 1942, he spent six years as an instructor, from April 1941 until released from the RAF in March 1947. He was commissioned in the RAFVR in December 1947 and instructed as a civilian until 1951, when he joined BEA, from which he retired in 1976.

PO 27.5.42   FO 27.11.42   FL 27.5.44
FO (RAFVR) 10.12.47

JAMES TERENCE CROSSEY

42805	PO	Pilot	British	249 Squadron

Born in Johannesburg on January 24 1918, Crossey joined the RAF on a short service commission in August 1939 and did his elementary flying training at 5 E&RFTS, Hanworth.

Crossey was posted to 3 ITW, Hastings on October 24 1939 and went on to 9 FTS, Hullavington on November 6. After completing his flying training he was sent to 7 BGS, Porthcawl on April 29 1940. This was followed by four weeks at 5 OTU, Aston Down, converting to Hurricanes. He joined 249 Squadron at Leconfield on June 10 1940 and served with it throughout the Battle of Britain.

The squadron sailed in the carrier HMS 'Furious' on May 10 1941. At Gibraltar they transferred on to HMS 'Ark Royal' on the 18th and three days later flew off to Ta Kali, Malta. On November 22 1941 Crossey claimed a Mc 202 destroyed and on December 24 he shared in the destruction of a Ju 88.

In February 1942 Crossey left 249 and went to Cairo, from where he was posted to South Africa, as an instructor. He served at various Air Schools until August 21 1944, when he was posted back to the UK. He joined the Aircraft Delivery Flight at Redhill on October 15 but three weeks later went to 105 OTU, Bramcote to convert to Dakotas. Crossey was posted to 216 Squadron at Cairo West on February 17 1945, served with 26 Squadron at Akyab from March 28 until August 1 1945, when he returned to 216, then at Almaza, Egypt.

He was released in 1946 and later went to live in Malta, where he was Manager of Malta Airlines.

APO 23.10.39   PO 18.5.40   FO 18.5.41   FL 18.5.42

MICHAEL NICHOLSON CROSSLEY

37554	FL	Pilot	British	32 Squadron

Crossley was born on May 29 1912 at Halford, Warwickshire. He was educated at Eton and afterwards studied at the College of Aeronautical Engineering at Chelsea. After graduating in 1933 he was employed by the Aero Club, Brooklands. He later worked as an assistant director at Elstree Film Studios.

In November 1935 Crossley joined the RAF on a short service commission. On February 15 1936 he was posted to 11 FTS, Wittering and after completing his flying training he joined 32 Squadron at Biggin

Hill on August 24. In the years immediately preceding the war Crossley spent some time as ADC to the Governor of Aden. He afterwards returned to 32 and in 1940 was a Flight Commander.

From May 18 1940 the squadron used Abbeville as a forward base. On the 19th Crossley shot down two Bf 109s, on the 23rd another two, on the 26th a Ju 88 and on a patrol over France on June 8 he destroyed two He 111s. Awarded the DFC (21.6.40), Crossley received it from the King at a special investiture at Biggin Hill.

On July 20 1940 Crossley claimed a Bf 109 and a Bf 110 destroyed, on August 12 two Bf 109s, on the 15th two Ju 88s, a Do 17 and another shared, on the 16th a Bf 109 and a Ju 88, on the 18th a Bf 109 and a Ju 88 and on the 25th a Bf 109 and a Do 215. Crossley was shot down twice in the Battle of Britain. On August 18 he baled out after being shot down by Bf 109s and landed at Gillingham. His Hurricane, N 2461, crashed at Wigmore. On August 24 he crashed at Lyminge after a combat over Folkestone. The Hurricane, P 3481, was written off but Crossley was unhurt.

In early August 1940 Crossley had been promoted to Acting Squadron Leader and given command of 32. He was awarded the DSO (20.8.40) and remained with the squadron until April 1941, when he was sent to America, as a test pilot with the British Air Commission. Back in the UK, Crossley led the Detling Wing in 1943. He contracted tuberculosis and was restricted to non-operational flying.

Crossley was made an OBE (1.1.46) and released from the RAF in 1946, as a Wing Commander. His portrait was painted by Eric Kennington. He later went farming in South Africa and died there in September 1987.

APO 3.2.36   PO 25.11.36   FO 25.5.38   FL 25.5.40
SL 11.8.41   WC 1.9.42

JOHN DALLAS CROSSMAN

43282	PO	Pilot	Australian	46 Squadron

Crossman, of Newcastle, New South Wales, joined 46 Squadron at Digby in September 1940. He was killed on September 30, crashing in flames at Tablehurst Farm, Forest Row after being shot down by enemy fighters.

He was 22 years old. Crossman is buried in Chalfont St Giles churchyard, Buckinghamshire.

APO 10.4.40

RICHARD GEORGE CROSSMAN

746701	Sgt	Wop/AG	British	25 Squadron

Crossman, of Watford, Hertfordshire, joined 25 Squadron at Debden in early October 1940. He was killed on July 8 1941, as a Flight Sergeant and still serving with 25. He is buried in Watford Cemetery.

HAROLD REGINALD CROWLEY

42971	PO	Air Gunner	British	219 and 600 Sqdns

Born on June 19 1915, Crowley was in the RAF before the war, flying in Harts at Andover with 12 Squadron. In September 1939 he was with 64 Squadron, then equipped with Blenheims at Church Fenton. He moved to 219 Squadron at Catterick in April 1940.

Crowley retrained as an AI Operator with the advent of airborne radar and the Beaufighter. In September 1940 he went on a short detachment to 600 Squadron at Redhill with a 219 Beaufighter to test out the new equipment operationally.

He later transferred to the Technical Branch, as a signals specialist. He stayed in the RAF after the war, holding responsible staff appointments in signals and communications.

Crowley retired on July 1 1965, as a Wing Commander, retaining the rank of Group Captain. He died in 1984.

PO 17.1.40   FO 17.1.41   FL 1.12.41   SL 1.7.45
SL 1.9.45   WC 1.1.56

DENIS CROWLEY-MILLING

78274   PO   Pilot   British   242 Squadron

Born March 22 1919, Crowley-Milling was educated at Malvern College. He became an apprentice at Rolls Royce and joined the RAFVR in November 1937. He was called up at the outbreak of war, completed his advanced training, converted to Gladiators and Spitfires and in mid-May 1940 joined 615 Squadron in France.

After the squadron was withdrawn Crowley-Milling was posted to 242 Squadron at Coltishall. He went with it to France on June 8 1940 to help cover the retreat of the Army to the Atlantic ports. The last of the 242 pilots left France on the 18th and returned to Coltishall.

On August 30 Crowley-Milling claimed a He 111 destroyed, on September 7 a Bf 110, on the 14th a Do 17 and on the 15th a Bf 109. He shared a Do 17 on February 8 1941, was awarded the DFC (11.4.41) and posted to 610 Squadron at Westhampnett on June 13 1941, as a Flight Commander. He was soon in action, sharing a Bf 109 on June 21 and probably destroying another four days later. On August 21 Crowley-Milling was shot down over France. With the help of the French underground he evaded capture and eventually reached Spain, where he was interned for three months, during which time he contracted para-typhoid. After being released he recovered in a Madrid hospital and arrived back in the UK in December 1941.

Crowley-Milling returned to 610 and took over his old flight. Over Dieppe on August 19 1942 he destroyed a Bf 109. He was awarded a Bar to the DFC (22.9.42) and on September 1 was promoted and posted to Duxford to form and command 181 Squadron, which he did until August 1943. He then briefly led 16 Typhoon Bomber Wing but came off operations in October to go to HQ USAAF at High Wycombe to coordinate fighter operations with B 17 daylight attacks. He was awarded the DSO (24.12.43).

In June 1944 Crowley-Milling was posted to Air Ministry, Operational Requirements. He was granted a Permanent Commission in 1945 and took part in the first Battle of Britain flypast in that year. He commanded 6 Squadron from November 1947 to July 1950 and led the Odiham Meteor Wing in the 1953 Coronation flypast.

Crowley-Milling retired from the RAF on July 29 1975, as an Air Marshal. He was made a CBE (1.1.63), KCB (1973) and appointed Gentleman Usher of the Scarlet Rod to the Order of the Bath in 1979.

PO 11.4.40   FO 11.4.41   FL 11.4.42   SL 11.7.43
SL 1.8.47   WC 1.7.54   GC 1.7.59   AC 1.1.64
AVM 1.7.67   AM 1.1.73

IAN JAMES ALEXANDER CRUICKSHANKS

80819   PO   Pilot   British   66 Squadron

Cruickshanks was with 66 Squadron at Coltishall in June 1940. On August 20 he shared a Bf 110 and on September 9 he shared a He 111. Two days later he made a forced-landing north-east of Ashford after being damaged in a combat and was slightly injured.

He was killed on June 8 1945, as a Flight Lieutenant but his unit is not known. Cruickshanks is buried in Milverton Cemetery, Leamington, Warwickshire.

PO 10.6.40   FO 10.6.41   FL 10.6.42

JOHN CRUTTENDEN

40895   PO   Pilot   British   43 Squadron

Cruttenden joined the RAF in May 1938 on a short service commission. He was posted to 43 Squadron at Tangmere in late June 1940 from OTU.

On July 7 Cruttenden baled out after a glycol leak caused his engine to catch fire. He was shot down in combat with enemy aircraft ten miles south of the Isle of Wight on August 8 1940 and reported 'Missing'.

He was 20 years old and is remembered on the Runnymede Memorial, Panel 7.

APO 9.7.38   PO 16.5.39

LAWRENCE ELWOOD CRYDERMAN

41674   FO   Pilot   Canadian   242 Squadron

Cryderman, a school teacher of Islington, Ontario, joined the RAF on a short service commission in December 1938. He did his ab initio training at 9 E&RFTS, Ansty.

On August 31 1940 Cryderman was posted to 242 Squadron at Coltishall but with his complete lack of Hurricane experience he was posted to 5 OTU, Aston Down on September 5 to acquire some. He rejoined 242 three weeks later.

Cryderman was scrambled on February 8 1941, with Flight Lieutenant Turner and Flying Officer Crowley-Milling, to search for an enemy aircraft forty miles east of Clacton. They located it and Turner attacked, damaging one engine. Shortly afterwards Cryderman called up saying he was returning to base, then that he was landing on the sea. Despite searches he was never found. He is remembered on the Runnymede Memorial, Panel 30.

APO 4.3.39   PO 2.10.39   FO 2.10.40

WILLIAM ARTHUR CUDDIE

42806   PO   Pilot   British   141 Squadron

Cuddie, of Regina, Canada, joined 141 Squadron at Turnhouse on August 19 1940.

He was killed on October 3 1943, as a Squadron Leader with 46 Squadron. With no known grave he is remembered on the Alamein Memorial, Column 267.

APO 23.10.39   PO 3.8.40   FO 3.8.41   FL 3.8.42

VACLAV ERIC CUKR

107245   Sgt   Pilot   Czechoslovakian   43 and 253 Sqdns

Cukr served in France in 1940 as a Sergeant Pilot with ll/3 Groupe de Chasse in l'Armée de l'Air. He was credited with the destruction of eight German aircraft before he was shot down and wounded.

After the collapse of France Cukr went to England and joined the RAF. He converted to Hurricanes, joined 43 Squadron at Usworth on September 10 1940 and moved to 253 Squadron at Kenley at the end of the month.

Commissioned in early 1941, Cukr remained with the squadron until September 1941. He was awarded the DFC and posted away to 52 OTU, Debden, later moving with the unit to Aston Down. In 1942 Cukr was posted to the Test Unit at Kemble, where he went on a conversion course to become a test pilot on multi-engined aircraft.

Cukr was afterwards stationed at 20 MU, Aston Down, as a test pilot. He also commanded a small flight which converted multi-engined pilots to single-engined fighters.

In July 1943 Cukr was test-flying a special Mustang when a pupil-pilot collided with him. He baled out but his parachute did not open and he was very seriously injured. Cukr was admitted to RAF Hospital, Wraughton and when the war ended he was at the Rehabilitation Centre at Loughborough. He was invalided out of the RAF in April 1946, as a Flight Lieutenant.

Cukr later emigrated to New Zealand. He changed his name to Cooper.

REGINALD WALKER CULLEN

752429   Sgt   Aircrew   British   23 Squadron

With 23 Squadron at Collyweston in June 1940. No further details traced.

JAMES DOUGLAS CULMER

177211   Sgt   Air Gunner   British   25 Squadron

Born on March 15 1913, Culmer was with 25 Squadron at Martlesham Heath in June 1940. He was awarded the DFM (24.12.40) and remained with the squadron until 1942.

Culmer was commissioned in August 1944 and stayed in the RAF after the war, in the Aircraft Control Branch. He retired on March 15 1963, as a Flight Lieutenant.

PO 24.8.44   FO 24.2.45
FO 24.8.46   FL 18.5.56

JOHN HENRY CULVERWELL

529270   Sgt   Pilot   British   87 Squadron

Born in Cardiff on September 30 1914, Culverwell joined the RAF on February 18 1936, as an Aircrafthand/Mate. He was posted to 3 School of Technical Training on May 8 1936, went to 2 Wing, Henlow on July 3 and after passing out as a Flight Rigger he returned to 3 S of TT and qualified as a Metal Rigger.

Culverwell was then posted, as an ACI, to the School of Air Gunnery on the maintenance staff. He volunteered for pilot training and was remustered as a Metal Rigger u/t Airman Pilot on June 26 1939. His rank was then Corporal. He began his elementary flying training at 12 EFTS, Prestwick on September 2 1939, moved on to 10 FTS, Tern Hill, where he completed the course and was promoted to Sergeant on January 27 1940.

Culverwell went to the 11 Group Pool, St Athan on February 1 and joined 87 Squadron in France on March 29 1940. He was killed in a night-flying accident on July 25 1940. He took off and appeared to climb too steeply, stalled and crashed back into the ground, in Hurricane P 3596. Culverwell is buried in Cathays Cemetery, Cardiff.

ALFRED BERNARD CUMBERS

118713   Sgt   Air Gunner   British   141 Squadron

Born in Southend in 1908, Cumbers joined 141 Squadron at West Malling in mid-July 1940. On the night of September 16 Cumbers was flying in Defiant N 1552 with Flying Officer J Waddingham. They destroyed a He 111 and probably shot down another into the sea.

Awarded the DFM (18.3.41), Cumbers later retrained as a Navigator Radar. He was commissioned in March 1942 and released from the RAF in 1945, as a Flight Lieutenant. He died on December 28 1985.

PO 17.3.42   FO 1.10.42   FL 17.3.44

JAMES CUNNINGHAM

1052182   Sgt   Aircrew   British   29 Squadron

No service details traced.

JOHN CUNNINGHAM

90216   FL   Pilot   British   604 Squadron

Cunningham was born at Addington on July 27 1917 and educated at Whitgift School. In 1935 he became an apprentice at the de Havilland Aircraft Co. He joined 604 Squadron, AuxAF in November 1935 and having learned to fly he was asked by de Havilland's to test light aircraft. He was soon appointed full-time assistant test pilot under Geoffrey de Havilland.

On August 24 1939 Cunningham was mobilised and in September was made 'B' Flight Commander. His first three victories were achieved flying with Sergeant JR Phillipson, a Ju 88 on November 19 1940 and He 111s on December 23 and January 3 1941. Cunningham teamed up with Sergeant CF Rawnsley on January 12 1941 and they became the best-known British night-fighting partnership of the war. Their first success was a He 111, shot down on February 15 1941. Another He 111, destroyed on April 3, was the first of twelve He 111s which the team would destroy by May 23 1942. Cunningham was awarded the DFC (28.1.41), the DSO (8.8.41) and a Bar to the DFC (19.9.41). He had taken command of 604 in August 1941 and led it until July 1942. He was awarded a Bar to the DSO (24.7.42) and posted to 81 Group to direct the work of night-fighter OTUs. Rawnsley went with him to assist.

In January 1943 Cunningham was given command of 85 Squadron at Hunsdon and Rawnsley again went with him, as Navigation Leader. On June 13 they destroyed a FW 190, another two on August 23 and September 8 and a Me 410 on January 2 1944. Cunningham was posted in March 1944 to 11 Group, Uxbridge as Group Captain Night Ops. He was awarded a second Bar to the DSO (3.3.44) and released from the RAF in 1945. In addition to his British awards he received the Order of Patriotic War 1st Class (USSR)(11.4.44) and the Silver Star (US)(14.6.46).

Cunningham rejoined de Havilland's and had a most distinguished career involving the development and testing of new aircraft, particularly the Comet. He rejoined the RAuxAF and commanded 604 Squadron from July 1946 until 1948. His portrait was done by Eric Kennington in 1941.

PO (AuxAF) 7.5.36   FO (AuxAF) 5.12.37   FO 24.8.39
FL 12.3.40   SL 1.6.41   WC 1.6.42   SL (RAuxAF) 1.8.46

JOHN LAURENCE GILCHRIST CUNNINGHAM

90194   FL   Pilot   British   603 Squadron

Cunningham, of Burntisland, Fife, joined 603 Squadron, AuxAF in early 1935. He was called to full-time service on August 23 1939. On December 7 he damaged a He 111, when he was serving with a 603 detachment protecting Montrose airfield.

On July 20 1940 Cunningham shared in shooting down a Do 17 into the sea thirty miles east of Aberdeen. He failed to return from a combat over Dover on August 28 1940 and was reported 'Missing'.

Cunningham was 23 and is remembered on the Runnymede Memorial, Panel 4.

PO (AuxAF) 6.5.35   FO (AuxAF) 6.11.36   FO 23.8.39
FL 12.3.40

WALLACE CUNNINGHAM

80545   PO   Pilot   British   19 Squadron

Cunningham, who was born in Glasgow, did his flying training at 11 FTS, Shawbury, converted to Spitfires at 5 OTU, Aston Down and joined 19 Squadron at Duxford in June 1940.

On August 16 Cunningham destroyed a Bf 110, on September 7 a He 111, on the 9th a Bf 109, another on the 15th and he shared a Ju 88 on the 18th. Awarded the DFC (8.10.40), Cunningham shared a Bf 110 on November 15.

One day in August 1941, escorting Blenheims on a low-level attack on shipping in Rotterdam Harbour, Cunningham was shot down by ground fire and taken prisoner. He was in several different PoW camps until freed by the Russians near Berlin and then properly released by the Americans.

Cunningham was released from the RAF in 1946, as a Flight Lieutenant.

PO 8.6.40   FO 1.6.41   FL 1.6.42

WILLIAM GEORGE CUNNINGTON

740754   Sgt   Pilot   British   607 Squadron

Cunnington was with 607 Squadron at Usworth in early July 1940. On September 14 he shared in the destruction of a Ju 88.

He was posted away in October and in mid-November was one of thirteen pilots in the carrier HMS 'Argus', heading for Malta. At dawn on November 17 1940 the first six Hurricanes took off, Cunnington amongst them. Led by a FAA Skua, they reached their first landfall, Galite Island, safely but nearly half an hour late and running low on fuel. They were led on the final leg by a Sunderland.

One of the Hurricanes ran out of fuel, the pilot baled out and was picked up by the Sunderland, which then hurried on to catch up with the others. By this time Cunnington had run out of fuel. He baled out but the Sunderland failed to find him.

Cunnington is remembered on the Runnymede Memorial, Panel 13.

THOMAS CUPITT

1052312   Sgt   Aircrew   British   29 Squadron

No service details traced.

JOHN CURCHIN

42396   PO   Pilot   Australian   609 Squadron

Curchin was born in Hawthorn, Victoria on January 20 1918 but in 1940 his parents were living in Enfield, Middlesex. He joined the RAF on a short service commission in June 1939.

Initially with 600 Squadron, Curchin joined 609 Squadron at Northolt on June 11 1940. He claimed a Bf 110 destroyed on August 8, a Bf 109 on the 25th, another on September 7, shared two Do 17s on the 15th, claimed a Bf 110 on the 24th, two He 111s on the 25th and another He 111 on the 26th.

Curchin was awarded the DFC (1.11.40) and was decorated by the King in February 1941. He was appointed a Flight Commander in April, destroyed a Bf 109 and shared another on May 8 and was reported 'Missing' on June 4.

He is remembered on the Runnymede Memorial, Panel 29.

APO 5.8.39   PO 6.4.40   FO 6.4.41

ALBERT GEORGE CURLEY

747968   Sgt   Air Gunner   British   141 Squadron

Curley, of Bushey, Hertfordshire, was with 141 Squadron at Turnhouse in June 1940. The squadron went south in July and Curley was in one of the nine Defiants attacked by Bf 109s of lll/JG 51 off Dover on July 19. His aircraft, L 6995, was shot down into the Channel. The pilot, Pilot Officer RA Howley, and Curley were both reported 'Missing'.

Curley was 33 years old and is remembered on the Runnymede Memorial, Panel 13.

CHRISTOPHER FREDERICK CURRANT

43367   PO   Pilot   British   605 Squadron

Born in Luton on December 14 1911, Currant joined the RAF in 1936 as a direct-entry pilot. He was with 46 Squadron at Kenley in 1937 and with 151 Squadron at North Weald in 1939.

Commissioned in April 1940, Currant joined 605 Squadron at Wick. On May 22 he was shot down on a patrol south of Arras. He made a forced-landing, burned his Hurricane and returned to the squadron, with a broken nose. Currant claimed a He 111 and shared another on August 15, shared a Bf 109 and a Bf 110 on September 9, destroyed a He 111 on the 11th, shared another on the 12th, destroyed two Do 17s and a Bf 109 on the 15th, a Bf 110 on the 27th, a Bf 109 on the 28th, shared a Ju 88 on October 4, shared another on the 8th and destroyed a Bf 109 on the 15th. He was awarded the DFC (8.10.40) and a Bar (15.11.40).

CF Currant (continued)

When McKellar was killed on November 1 Currant took temporary command of 605 until the new CO arrived. He destroyed a Bf 109 on December 1 1940. In early 1941 Currant was posted to 52 OTU, Debden and in July he was CFI. A return to operations came on August 14 1941, when he was given command of 501 Squadron at Ibsley. He appeared briefly as himself in the film 'The First of the Few', filmed at Ibsley.

Currant destroyed a Bf 109 on April 17 1942. He was promoted to Acting Wing Commander in June and appointed to lead the Ibsley Wing. He was awarded the DSO (7.7.42) for his work with 501.

From February 15 1943 until July 24 1944 Currant commanded 122 Wing TAF. He was awarded the C de G (Belg) (9.4.43). He stayed in the RAF and was a graduate of the Joint Services Staff College and the RAF Staff College. He retired on January 11 1959, as a Wing Commander.

PO 1.4.40   FO 5.12.40   FL 23.6.41   SL 23.9.42
WC 1.7.47

FRANK WILLIAM CURTIS

74679   Sgt   Aircrew   British   25 Squadron

Curtis joined 25 Squadron at North Weald in September 1940.

As a Navigator Radar he was in the Middle East with 89 Squadron and teamed up with Warrant Officer HFW Shead in October 1942 and they flew together for almost a year.

On a scramble on December 21 they destroyed a He 111, a Ju 88 and probably a second, on January 8 1943 a He 111, on the 21st damaged a Ju 88 and on March 16 destroyed a Ju 88.

Curtis was awarded the DFM (16.2.43). In February 1943 he was promoted to Warrant Officer.

No further service details traced.

JOHN WINTRINGHAM CUTTS

40804   FO   Pilot   British   222 Squadron

Cutts, of Felpham, Sussex, joined the RAF in April 1938 on a short service commission. He was with 222 Squadron at Kirton-in-Lindsey in July 1940. On the 25th he made a forced-landing four miles north of base out of fuel after a combat with a He 111 off Mabelthorpe.

The squadron moved to Hornchurch on August 29 and on September 4 Cutts was shot down by Bf 109s over Maidstone. His Spitfire, X 4278, crashed and burned out on Amberfield Farm, Chart Sutton and Cutts was reported 'Missing'. He was 20 years old and is remembered on the Runnymede Memorial, Panel 5.

APO 4.6.38   PO 4.4.39   FO 3.9.40

FRANCISZEK CZAJKOWSKI

76692   PO   Pilot   Polish   151 Squadron

Born in Poland on September 20 1916, Czajkowski was in the PAF before the war. He escaped to England, was commissioned in April 1940 and joined 151 Squadron at Martlesham Heath in early August.

On the 24th Czajkowski probably destroyed a Bf 109 and on August 31 he claimed another probable Bf 109 but was himself shot down in combat over the Thames Estuary. He made a forced-landing at Foulness, wounded in the right shoulder and was admitted to Shoeburyness Hospital. His Hurricane, P 3301, was a write-off.

Czajkowski made a forced-landing at Longtown aerodrome, near Carlisle, on April 19 1941 after his engine blew up when he was climbing on high boost. He was badly injured on June 2 1941 in a crash.

He died on October 25 1942 from injuries received when the hospital he was in at Torquay was bombed. He is buried in the Higher Exeter Cemetery. Czajkowski was awarded the KW (10.9.41) and a Bar (20.2.43).

PO 2.4.40   FO 1.3.41

JERZY MICHAL CZERNIAK

P 1283   PO   Pilot   Polish   302 Squadron

Czerniak was born on March 21 1913 and was in the PAF before the war. He was posted to 302 Squadron at Leconfield on August 20 1940.

Awarded the KW (23.12.40), Czerniak moved to the newly-formed 315 Squadron at Leconfield on January 25 1941. He was killed over France on August 9 1941, shot down in combat three miles from the French coast, in Spitfire P 8506. With no known grave Czerniak is remembered on the Polish Air Force Memorial at Northolt. He was awarded two Bars to the KW (31.10.47).

FO 1.3.41

Count MANFRED BECKETT CZERNIN

37148   FO   Pilot   British   17 Squadron

Born in Berlin on January 18 1913, Czernin was the son of an Austrian diplomat and his English wife, daughter of the 2nd Baron Grimthorpe. The couple separated in 1914 and the mother took her son to live in Rome.

Czernin was at Oundle School from 1923 until 1930. After leaving he worked at an engineering firm for a year and then in September 1931 went to Southern Rhodesia to work on a tobacco plantation.

In April 1935 Czernin joined the RAF on a short service commission, using the name Beckett. He did his flying training at 6 FTS, Netheravon and on February 24 1936 joined 57 Squadron at Upper Heyford. He moved to 83 Squadron at Turnhouse on December 5 1936 and on August 16 1937 he went on to the Class A Reserve.

Czernin was recalled at the outbreak of war and was posted to No 1 Ferry Pilots' Pool, Hucknall on September 22 1939. In December he was sent to 12 Group Fighter Pool, Aston Down for assessment, after which he joined 504 Squadron at Debden on January 23 1940. He moved to 213 at Wittering on February 6 and on May 9 joined 85 Squadron in France. On the 19th Czernin destroyed a He 111 and two Do 17s and a Hs 126 the next day. He returned to England on the 21st, by boat from Boulogne to Dover, left 85 on the 27th and was posted to 17 Squadron at Martlesham Heath on June 8 1940. He flew a Hurricane out to France on the 9th to join the squadron at Le Mans.

Czernin destroyed a He 111 on June 12 and the squadron was withdrawn to England on the 19th. On July 12 he destroyed a Do 17, shared a Ju 88 on August 16, destroyed two Bf 110s and shared another on the 25th, two Bf 110s on September 3, a Bf 109 and two shared He 111s on the 5th, a Bf 110 on the 11th, shared a Ju 88 on the 19th, a Bf 110 on the 27th and shared a Do 17 on October 24.

Awarded the DFC (1.10.40), Czernin was shot down by Adolf Galland on November 17 1940 whilst engaged with Bf 110s attacking Wattisham. He baled out, slightly wounded and his Hurricane, V 7500, crashed and burned out just west of Bradfield Church.

Appointed as 'A' Flight Commander on March 23 1941, Czernin was posted away to 52 OTU, Debden on May 31, as OC 'A' Squadron. Promoted to Acting Squadron Leader in mid-December he commanded 65 Squadron for a few days, was then posted to command 222 Squadron on December 22, left to be attached to 41 Squadron on January 19 and then on February 28 1942 was posted to India. Initially at 301 MU, he took command of 146 Squadron at Dinjan on March 16. Czernin built the squadron up to a good operational standard before he was posted to HQ 224 Group as a Staff Officer in Operations. He returned to the UK in April 1943 and was posted to HQ 28 Group at Uxbridge.

On September 30 Czernin was officially transferred to an Air Ministry Unit but in fact had gone to the Special Operations Executive. For the next eight months he trained for warfare behind enemy lines and on June 13 1944 he was parachuted into enemy-occupied Northern Italy, near to the Austrian frontier. Czernin operated secretly until returning to the UK in late 1944. He was awarded the MC (1.12.44). On March 21 1945 he went on a second mission and was dropped just south of the Swiss border. His operations there culminated in the surrender of the German forces at Bergamo.

After a short time at Bentley Priory Czernin went for a flying refresher course to Tangmere. He was released from the RAF on October 2 1945, as a Squadron Leader and was awarded the DSO (2.11.45).

Czernin did a variety of jobs in the post-war years, his final one being Sales Manager for Fiat in England for four years. He died in his sleep on October 6 1962. His portrait was done by Cuthbert Orde in September 1940.

APO 16.4.35   PO 16.4.36   FO 28.3.40   FL 28.3.41
SL 1.6.42

JAN TADEUSZ CZERNY

76789   FL   Pilot   Polish   302 Squadron

Born in Poland in 1908, Czerny was in the PAF before the war. He joined 302 Squadron at Leconfield on August 20 1940. He remained with the squadron until posted to CFS, Upavon for an instructor's course in mid-1941.

On October 27 1941 Czerny was posted to 25 EFTS, Hucknall and stayed there instructing until November 15 1945, when he went to 16 FTS, Newton. Czerny came off flying in September 1946 and was repatriated to Poland in February 1947. He was awarded the KW (29.5.43) and the AFC (9.2.45).

FO 1.3.41   FL 1.3.42   SL 1.3.44

TADEUSZ CZERWINSKI

P 1290   PO   Pilot   Polish   302 Squadron

Czerwinski was born in Poland on February 17 1910 and was in the PAF before the war. He joined 302 Squadron at Leconfield on July 23 1940 and on September 15 claimed a Do 17 destroyed.

Awarded the KW and Bar (1.2.41), Czerwinski was posted to 55 OTU, Usworth on May 3 1941, as an instructor. He moved to 58 OTU, Grangemouth on November 19. Czerwinski took command of 306 Squadron at Church Stanton on April 14 1942. He shot down a FW 190 south-east of Calais on April 26.

The squadron attacked St Omer airfield and Longuenesse on August 22 1942 and encountered very heavy ground fire. Czerwinski was last seen in an uncontrolled climb, in Spitfire EN 836. He is buried in Souvenir-Longuenesse Cemetery, St Omer, France. He was awarded a second Bar to the KW (20.9.42) after his death.

FO 1.3.41   FL 1.3.42

STANISLAW CZTERNASTEK

76693   PO   Pilot   Polish   32 Squadron

Born on May 6 1916, Czternastek joined 32 Squadron at Acklington on October 12 1940.

He was later posted to 615 Squadron at Kenley. Czternastek was returning from operations on February 5 1941, when he collided with another aircraft. He was killed when he crashed at Appleton Farm, Marlen, near Dover, in Hurricane V 7598.

Czternastek is buried in Hawkinge Cemetery.

ROBERT CHIPPINDALL DAFFORN

81674   PO   Pilot   British   501 Squadron

Dafforn, of Burchetts Green, was born at Horton, Windsor on March 2 1916. He was at Harrow from 1929 to 1934 and after leaving worked in the Exchange Equalisation Department of the Bank of England.

In 1936 Dafforn applied to join the RAFVR but was turned down because at over 6 feet 6 inches tall the doctors considered him too thin. He underwent a course of training, applied again and was accepted, beginning his flying training at 8 E&RFTS, Woodley in October 1937.

In late June 1939 Dafforn was selected for four months training with the regular RAF and was posted to the Air Fighting School at St Athan. In mid-September he joined 501 Squadron at Filton. Commissioned in April 1940, Dafforn went with the squadron to Bethienville in France on May 10. He claimed a Do 17 destroyed on the 11th, a He 111 on the 14th, a probable Bf 110 on the 19th, a probable He 111 on the 20th and on the 27th a He 111 destroyed and another shared.

On June 18 501 Squadron flew from France to St Helier, Jersey and then re-assembled at Croydon on the 21st. Dafforn claimed a Ju 87 destroyed on August 12. He was shot down by Bf 110s on the 18th in an action over Biggin Hill and baled out, unhurt, landing in an orchard near Sevenoaks. His Hurricane, R 4219, crashed at Cronks Farm, East Seal.

On August 24 Dafforn claimed a Ju 88 destroyed, on September 11 a shared Do 17 and on October 30 a Bf 109 destroyed. He was wounded on December 2 in an attack by Bf 109s and made a forced-landing at Detling, wrecking his Hurricane, V 6919. Dafforn was awarded the DFC (17.1.41). He was appointed 'B' Flight Commander in late April 1941.

On October 26 Dafforn was posted to 56 OTU, Sutton Bridge, as an instructor. He was the last of the original 501 pilots. In early January 1942 he was posted to the Middle East. Dafforn went to Takoradi and on March 1 took off on the multi-stage ferry route to Cairo, in a Hurricane ll.

On April 1 1942 Dafforn was attached to the Air Fighting School and Conversion and Refresher School at El Ballah to accustom himself to desert conditions. Instead of being sent to the Western Desert Dafforn was posted to 229 Squadron at Hal Far, Malta. He flew from El Ballah on April 19, via Gambut. Two days after arriving Dafforn was promoted to Acting Squadron Leader and took command of a very badly-depleted squadron.

On his second patrol, on the 26th, he was shot down and crash-landed at Hal Far, with cannon shell fragments in right leg, lower back and arm. Although his wounds were slight Dafforn was in hospital for fourteen weeks, with undulant fever. He flew out in a Hudson to Gibraltar on August 2 1942 and then on to Hendon on the 9th.

After two months' convalescence at Torquay Dafforn was posted to 52 OTU, Aston Down, as OC Night Flying Squadron. He went to CGS, Sutton Bridge in December 1942, for a course. On June 23 1943 Dafforn was posted to CGS, as CFI.

On the morning of September 9 he was flying Spitfire P 7289 in

RC Dafforn (continued)

an air-firing exercise. He was returning to the airfield when the aircraft was seen to do a steep turn at very low level, the port wing touching the ground. The aircraft crashed and Dafforn was killed.

He is buried in St Mary's churchyard, White Waltham, Berkshire.

PO 25.4.40   FO 25.4.41   FL 25.4.42

ROBERT WILLIAM DALTON

115715   Sgt   Observer   British   604 Squadron

Dalton, who was born on August 24 1918, joined 604 Squadron at Middle Wallop in August 1940. He later trained as a Radio Observer was awarded the DFM (2.12.41) for displaying great skill in night operations and was commissioned in January 1942.

Posted away from 604 in July 1942, Dalton stayed in the RAF after the war. He retired on March 31 1958, as a Squadron Leader.

PO 27.1.42   FO 1.10.42   FL 27.1.44   FL 1.9.45
SL 1.4.56

JOHN J DALY

751318   Sgt   Pilot   British   141 Squadron

Served with 141 Squadron in the Battle of Britain. No service details traced

JAMES EDWIN DANN

50772   Sgt   Pilot   British   23 Squadron

Dann served with 23 Squadron from 1936 until 1941. He was commissioned in June 1942 and awarded the DFC (23.3.45), as a Flight Lieutenant with 192 Squadron. He left the RAF in 1949 and died in 1986.

PO 16.6.42   FO 16.12.42   FL 16.6.44   FL 16.12.45

ALEXANDER GEORGE DANNATT

1003513   Sgt   Aircrew   British   29 Squadron

No service details traced. Died on December 16 1982.

BRIAN WILLIAM JESSE D'ARCY-IRVINE

72500   FO   Pilot   British   257 Squadron

D'Arcy-Irvine was commissioned in the RAFVR in October 1938. His parents lived in Serdang, Kedah, Malaya. He joined 257 Squadron on May 17 1940, when it was reformed at Hendon.

On August 8 1940 D'Arcy-Irvine was reported 'Missing' after a combat with Bf 109s of lll/JG 27 off St Catherine's Point, in Hurricane P 3058. He was 22 and is remembered on the Runnymede Memorial, Panel 5.

PO (RAFVR) 25.10.38   FO 25.4.40

ALBERT McDONALD SMITH DARGIE

966123   Sgt   Air Gunner   British   23 Squadron

Dargie, of Dundee, was with 23 Squadron at Collyweston in July 1940. He was killed on July 13 1941, as a Flight Sergeant with 38 Squadron, operating in Wellington bombers from Shallufa, Egypt. He was 24 and is remembered on the Alamein Memorial, Column 242.

HORACE STANLEY DARLEY

32191   SL   Pilot   British   609 Squadron

Born on November 3 1913 at Wandsworth, Darley joined the RAF in August 1932. He carried out his training at 2 FTS, Digby and afterwards joined 207 Squadron at Bircham Newton on August 20 1933. He was posted overseas on February 9 1935, going to 8 Squadron at Khormaksar, Aden and later Somaliland.

Darley was granted a Permanent Commission in 1936. He returned to the UK and on January 2 1937 went to CFS, Upavon for an instructor's course, after which he was posted to 7 FTS, Peterborough, as a Flight Commander. On June 6 1938 Darley was appointed adjutant and flying instructor at 602 Squadron, AuxAF at Abbotsinch, moving on December 2 1938 to 611 Squadron, AuxAF at Speke.

Soon after the outbreak of war Darley was made Controller at Debden and on May 9 1940 was posted to Merville as Controller. After returning to England in late May he went as supernumerary Squadron Leader to 65 Squadron at Hornchurch and on June 22 he took command of 609 Squadron at Northolt.

On August 8 Darley claimed a Bf 110 destroyed, on the 15th a probable Ju 88, on the 25th a Bf 109 and a Bf 110 and on September 25 a Do 17. He was posted away on October 4 1940 to become Station Commander at Exeter. He was awarded the DSO (22.10.40).

Darley was posted to Air HQ Singapore on May 17 1941, on Fighter Defence. He went to RAF Kuala Lumpur on December 11 as Station Commander, returned to 224 Group, Singapore on January 8 1942 as Ops 1, moved to 226 Group, Sumatra on February 3 and after the inevitable collapse caused by the Japanese advance he arrived at RAF Depot, Karachi on March 16.

Appointed Station Commander at RAF Risalpur on October 7 1942, Darley remained there until February 7 1943, when he was posted to 221 Group, Calcutta. On June 11 he returned to Risalpur to command 151 OTU there, as a Group Captain. Darley returned to the UK in July 1944 and was given command of 62 OTU, Ouston. He was made Station Commander at RAF Cranfield on June 15 1945 and went to RAF Staff College, Bracknell in August for a course.

Darley held a series of appointments and commands before he retired from the RAF on June 15 1959, as a Group Captain.

APO 12.8.32   PO 12.8.33   FO 12.3.35   FL 12.3.37
SL 1.4.39   WC 1.6.41   WC 1.10.46   GC 1.7.51

ANDREW SMITTON DARLING

740544   Sgt   Pilot   British   611 and 603 Squadrons

Darling, of Auchterarder, Perthshire, was with 611 Squadron at Digby in June 1940. On August 21 he shared in destroying a Do 17 off the Lincolnshire coast and on the 28th he claimed a Bf 109 destroyed.

He was killed on April 26 1941, as a Flight Sergeant with 91 Squadron. Darling was 28. He is buried in Auchterarder Cemetery.

EDWARD VIVIAN DARLING

65979   Sgt   Pilot   British   41 Squadron

Darling joined 41 Squadron at Catterick in early 1940 and took part in the operations over Dunkirk. On August 11 he shared in the destruction of a Ju 88 and destroyed a Bf 109 on September 18. He was himself shot down over the Channel on September 24, in Spitfire R 6604, and crashed outside Dover, unhurt. Three days later Darling was shot down over West Malling. This time he baled out, wounded in the shoulder and was admitted to Preston Hall Hospital.

Back with the squadron, Darling destroyed a Bf 109 on November 27 1940. Commissioned in January 1941, he was posted to 602 Squadron in June but was promoted in August and went to 616 Squadron at Westhampnett, as a Flight Commander. In September Darling returned to 602 at Kenley, as a Flight Commander. He was awarded the DFC (17.10.41). Early in 1942, tour-expired, he was posted to an OTU in Wales, as an instructor.

On May 9 1942 Darling joined 403 (RCAF) Squadron at Rochford, as a Flight Commander. He failed to return from a sweep on June 2 and was reported 'Missing'. Darling is remembered on the Runnymede Memorial, Panel 65.

PO 15.1.41   FO 10.11.41

CHRISTOPHER WILLIAM WHARTON DARWIN

42050   PO   Pilot   British   87 Squadron

Darwin, of Elston, Nottinghamshire, was born on July 30 1918, the son of Major CJW Darwin, who formed 87 Squadron at Upavon on September 1 1917. He was educated at Winchester College and Ecole Lemania, Lausanne.

In March 1939 Darwin joined the RAF on a short service commission. He was with 87 Squadron in France and served with it in the Battle of Britain. In 1942 he was with 274 Squadron in the Western Desert. On August 7 1942 he was attacked over the sea by two Bf 109s and shot down. Darwin baled out but he was dead when picked up. He is buried in El Alamein War Cemetery.

APO 27.5.39   PO 18.11.39   FO 18.11.40   FL 18.11.41

JAN KAZIMIERZ MICHAL DASZEWSKI

P 1503   PO   Pilot   Polish   303 Squadron

Born on April 5 1916, Daszewski was in the PAF before the war. He joined 303 Squadron at Northolt at its formation on August 2 1940. He claimed a Do 215 destroyed and another probably destroyed on September 7 but was then shot down himself by Bf 109s over the Thames Estuary. Daszewski baled out, severely wounded in the thigh and was admitted to Waldershire Hospital. His Hurricane, P 3890, crashed near Canterbury Gate, Selsted. He was awarded the VM (5th Class) (23.12.40).

Out of action for several months, Daszewski rejoined 303 in early 1941. On April 20 he claimed a probable Bf 109 and a week later he destroyed another. He was awarded the KW (30.10.41).

On April 4 1942 303 joined up with 316 and 317 Squadrons to provide an escort for Bostons detailed to bomb St Omer railway station. They were intercepted by Bf 109s and FW 190s and a general combat ensued. Daszewski, 'B' Flight Commander, sent out a distress call but was not heard of again. He was in Spitfire AD 455.

Daszewski is remembered on the Polish Air Force Memorial, Northolt. He was awarded a Bar to the KW (20.8.42) and two more Bars (31.10.47).

FO 1.3.41

BRIAN DAVEY

79537   PO   Pilot   British   32 and 257 Squadrons

Joined 32 Squadron in mid-September 1940. On the 23rd Davey was posted to 257 Squadron at Martlesham Heath. He shared a Fiat BR 20 with a pilot from 46 Squadron on November 11 1940.

Davey was killed on June 12 1941. He was 22 and is buried in St Andrew's churchyard, Rochford, Essex.

PO 19.5.40   FO 19.5.41

JOHN ARTHUR JOSEPH DAVEY

44182   PO   Pilot   British   1 Squadron

Davey, of Leamington, Warwickshire, was an aircraft apprentice at RAF Halton. He won a cadetship to RAF College, Cranwell and began training there in September 1939. He was granted a Permanent Commission on July 14 1940 and joined No 1 Squadron at Tangmere on the 15th.

Shot down in combat with Bf 110s on August 11 Davey was killed when he crashed and burned out attempting a forced-landing on Sandown golf course, in Hurricane P 3172.

Davey was 20 years old. He is buried in Sandown Cemetery, Isle of Wight.

PO 14.7.40

WILLIAM DENNIS DAVID

40805   FO   Pilot   British   87 and 213 Squadrons

Born in Surbiton, Surrey on July 25 1918, David joined the RAFVR in 1937 and entered the RAF with a short service commission in February 1938. He carried out his elementary flying training at 5 E&RFTS, Hanworth and after a short spell at RAF Uxbridge went to 5 FTS, Sealand. In late 1938 David was in the Fighter Pool at RNAS, Ford, awaiting a squadron vacancy.

In early 1939 he was posted to 87 Squadron at Debden and flew to France with it on September 9 1939. During the fighting in May 1940 David was credited with eleven enemy aircraft destroyed and was awarded the DFC (31.5.40) and Bar (4.6.40).

On August 11 David claimed a Bf 109 and a Ju 88 destroyed, on the 15th a Ju 87, on the 25th a Ju 88 and a Bf 109 and on September 15 he shared a He 111. David was posted to 213 Squadron at Tangmere, as 'B' Flight Commander, on October 16 1940. He destroyed a Ju 88 on the 19th. He went to 152 Squadron at Warmwell on November 13, as a Flight Commander.

At the end of his tour David was posted to 59 OTU, Usworth on March 23 1941, as CFI. He moved to 55 OTU on November 25 1941, as Chief Instructor, firstly at Usworth and later at Annan. Awarded the AFC (1.1.43), David was posted to the Middle East in February 1943, as SASO 209 Group.

On July 19 1943 he took command of 89 Squadron, a Beaufighter night-fighter unit. He flew the unit to Ceylon on October 15. David was appointed Sector Commander at Trincomalee on March 4 1944, he became Base Commander at Minneriya on May 5 and Base Commander at Kankesanturai on August 30. Later in 1944 David was promoted to Acting Group Captain and appointed Air Adviser to the Commander of the 15th Indian Corps at Arakan, Burma.

He was SASO 224 Group from January 6 1945 to November 16, when he became SASO Air HQ Dutch East Indies at Batavia. David returned to the UK in April 1946.

He held a series of appointments and commands in the post-war RAF, including Honorary Aide to Viscount Trenchard until his death and Air Attaché in Budapest during the Hungarian uprising in 1956.

David was made a CBE (1.1.60) and retired on May 26 1967, as a Group Captain.

APO 4.4.38   PO 4.4.39   FO 3.9.40   FL 3.9.41
SL 25.2.42   SL 1.9.45   WC 1.7.53   GC 1.1.60

HENRY JOHN DAVIDSON

61945   **Sgt**   **Pilot**   **British**   **249 Squadron**

Davidson, of Stretford, was with 249 Squadron in July 1940. On August 7 he claimed a Do 17 destroyed, on September 2 a Bf 110 and on the 27th a Ju 88 and a shared Bf 110.

Commissioned in March 1941, Davidson went to the newly-formed MSFU at Speke on May 9. He made the first experimental launch from the SS 'Empire Rainbow' on May 31. After launching the Hurricane dropped below the ship's bow and the port wing touched the sea but Davidson regained control and landed at Abbotsinch. With modifications to equipment and changes in pilot technique Davidson sailed for Nova Scotia on June 8 in the 'Empire Rainbow' but he saw no action on the voyage.

Davidson was killed on October 6 1942, as a Flying Officer with 285 Squadron. He was 27 and was cremated at Manchester Crematorium.

PO 5.3.41   *FO 5.3.42*

ALFRED ERIC DAVIES

90963   **PO**   **Pilot**   **British**   **610 and 222 Squadrons**

A member of 610 Squadron, AuxAF before the war, Davies was called for full-time service on August 24 1939. With his flying training completed he rejoined 610 Squadron at Acklington on September 3 1940 and moved to 222 Squadron at Hornchurch on the 28th.

He was killed on October 30 1940, when his wing was shot off in combat with Bf 109s. His Spitfire, N 3119, crashed and burned out at Upper Wilting Farm, Crowhurst. Davies was 23 and he is buried in St Mary Magdalene churchyard extension, Tamworth, Warwickshire.

APO 24.8.39   *PO 17.3.40*

GRAHAM GORDON AYERST DAVIES

41989   **PO**   **Pilot**   **British**   **222 Squadron**

The son of a journalist, Davies was born on March 6 1919 and lived in Paris as a young child. He was sent to school in Folkestone, afterwards working as an engineer with Imperial Airways, flying between Croydon and Amsterdam.

In March 1939 Davies joined the RAF on a short service commission and did his elementary flying at 7 E&RFTS, Desford. In May he was posted to 14 FTS, Kinloss and after a short spell with 236 Squadron in early November he joined 222 Squadron at Duxford at the end of the month.

Davies was over Dunkirk on May 31 1940 when his engine gave trouble. He decided to land on a beach, hoping that the sand would be hard. He landed safely in spite of being fired at by French soldiers, who thought him a Stuka. He was driven into Dunkirk, then told to go back and burn his aircraft, which he did and was then taken back and returned to England in a paddle steamer.

On August 30 Davies damaged a Do 17. Two days later he was shot down in flames by a Bf 109 over Ashford. He baled out, burned on the hands and face. His Spitfire, P 9337, is believed to have crashed near Huntbourne St Michaels, Tenterden.

Davies damaged a He 111 on May 14 1941. In November he was posted to CFS, Upavon for an instructor's course, after which he went to 5 FTS, Tern Hill in January 1942 and moved to 5 (P) AFU, Peterborough in June.

Posted to India in April 1943, Davies was initially at No 1 SFTS, Ambala but in August 1943 he was posted to 225 Group, Bangalore, then to RAF Cholavarum, Madras. In December he moved to the AFTU, Amarda Road, went to 136 Squadron at Rumkhapalong in February 1944 and then took command of 607 Squadron at the same base in March. The squadron was involved in the heavy fighting at

Imphal and when the siege was lifted Davies flew back to the UK for a Fighter Leader's course at Milfield. He rejoined 607 in November and led it until May 1945, when he was posted to 73 OTU, Fayid, Egypt. In October he took command of 294 Squadron, an air sea rescue unit.

Davies stayed in the RAF. From 1946 to 1948 he was Air Attaché in Paris, he later served at HQ Middle East Air Force as a liaison officer, commanded 73 Squadron in Malta, was OC 7 Wing British Air Force in Belguim and was serving with NATO in London, when he retired on June 17 1959, as a Squadron Leader.

APO 29.4.39   *PO 6.11.39*   *FO 6.11.40*   *FL 6.11.41*
FL 1.9.45   *SL 1.7.53*

JOHN ALFRED DAVIES

90212   **SL**   **Pilot**   **British**   **604 Squadron**

Davies joined 604 Squadron, AuxAF at Hendon in early 1935. He was called for full-time service on August 24 1939 and was with 604 until posted away on September 9 1940, to form and command 308 Squadron at Squires Gate.

On October 16 1940 Davies was killed after striking a barrage balloon cable above Coventry, when it was obscured by cloud. His Hurricane, P 3999, dived into the ground at Whitley Stadium. He is buried in St Nectan's churchyard, Hartland or Stoke, Devon.

PO (AuxAF) 10.3.35   *FO (AuxAF) 11.4.37*
FL (AuxAF) 25.4.39   *FL 24.8.39*   *SL 1.9.40*

LEONARD DAVIES

143088   **Sgt**   **Pilot**   **British**   **151 Squadron**

Joined 151 Squadron at Martlesham Heath on July 15 1940. He crash-landed at Eastchurch on August 28, following a combat over the Thames Estuary. He was wounded.

Davies arrived in Malta on January 30 1941 in a Sunderland from the Middle East and joined 261 Squadron at Ta Kali. On February 4 he damaged a Ju 88 and on May 9 a Ju 87. He returned to the Middle East later in the month.

Commissioned in December 1942, Davies was released from the RAF in 1946, as a Flight Lieutenant.

PO 2.12.42   *FO 2.6.43*   *FL 2.12.44*

MAURICE PETER DAVIES

119872   **Sgt**   **Pilot**   **British**   **213 and 1 Squadrons**

Davies was with 213 at Exeter in July 1940. He moved to No 1 Squadron in September and was posted away on October 10.

Commissioned in January 1942, Davies was released from the RAF in 1946, as a Flight Lieutenant. He died on July 22 1953.

PO 13.1.42   *FO 1.10.42*   *FL 13.1.44*

PETER FREDERICK McDONALD DAVIES

40088   **FO**   **Pilot**   **British**   **56 Squadron**

Davies was born on August 11 1919 and joined the RAF on a short service commission in July 1937. He did his ab initio training and on September 18 was posted to 2 FTS, Brize Norton, after which he went to the RAF Ferry Flight at Cardington.

In July 1939 Davies joined 56 Squadron at North Weald. On August 13 1940 he was shot down in combat with Bf 109s. His Hurricane, N 2429, was set on fire and he baled out at 20000 feet over Kent, with burns on hands, arms and legs and minor burns on the face. This resulted in a non-operational medical category.

Davies went to ferry pilot duties in December 1940. In April 1941 he was posted to 29 MU, High Ercall as Senior Test Pilot and apart from a six month illness he served as a test pilot until August 1945. He was then sent on a Signal Officers' Long War Course at RAF Cranwell, after which he held various appointments in Signals and Radar. In 1948 Davies served as Group Movements Officer at 205 Group, Abyad, Egypt. Back in the UK in early 1951 he became CGI at the Advanced Jet Training School, Valley. In October 1953 Davies was appointed to command the Armament Practice Squadron.

His last appointment was in December 1955, with a posting to the Ministry of Supply to work on Research and Development of Flight Simulators. Davies resigned his commission on August 11 1958, as a Squadron Leader.

APO 5.9.37   PO 12.7.38   FO 12.4.40   FL 12.4.41
SL 1.7.44   SL 1.8.47

ROY BLACKBURNE DAVIES

40995   FO   Pilot   British   29 Squadron

Joined the RAF on a short service commission in June 1938 and was with 29 Squadron at Digby in July 1940.

Davies was released from the RAF in 1946, as a Squadron Leader. He died in 1972.

APO 20.8.38   PO 27.6.39   FO 3.9.40   FL 3.9.41

PAUL JOHN DAVIES-COOKE

36167   FO   Pilot   British   610 and 72 Squadrons

Davies-Cooke was at Shrewsbury School from 1930 to 1935 and then Trinity College, Cambridge. He joined 610 Squadron, AuxAF in 1937 and was commissioned in July.

In December 1937 Davies-Cooke joined the RAF on a direct-entry Permanent Commission. He was posted to 610 Squadron at Acklington on September 3 1940 and moved to 72 Squadron at Biggin Hill on the 20th. Davies-Cooke was shot down by a Bf 109 over Sevenoaks on September 27. He baled out but fell dead near Hayes Station. His Spitfire, N 3068, crashed into Nos 70 and 72 Queensway, West Wickham.

Davies-Cooke was 23. He is buried in St John's churchyard, Rhydymwyn, Cilcain, Flintshire.

PO (AuxAF) 1.7.37   PO 18.12.37   FO 18.6.39

ALFRED STEWART DAVIS

744961   Sgt   Aircrew   British   235 Squadron

Joined 235 Squadron on July 18 1940. No further service details traced.

CARL RAYMOND DAVIS

90131   FO   Pilot   American   601 Squadron

Davis was born in South Africa of American parents. He went to Britain when he was 13 to attend Sherbourne School, later going to Trinity College, Cambridge and McGill University. He became a mining engineer.

In 1936 Davis joined 601 Squadron, AuxAF and was commissioned in August. He was called for full-time service with the squadron on August 27 1939. Davis took part in the raid on Borkum on November 27, when six Blenheims of 601 joined six of 25 Squadron to attack the seaplane base there.

On July 11 1940 Davis claimed a Bf 110 destroyed, on August 11 two Bf 110s, on the 13th three Bf 110s, on the 16th a Ju 87, on the 18th a Bf 109, a Ju 87 and another shared and on September 4 another Bf 110 destroyed. He was awarded the DFC (30.8.40).

Davis was shot down and killed on September 6 1940. His Hurricane, P 3363, crashed, inverted, and burned out in the back garden of Canterbury Cottage at Matfield, Brenchley, near Tunbridge Wells. He was 29 and is buried in St Mary's churchyard, Storrington, Sussex.

PO (AuxAF) 7.8.36   FO (AuxAF) 6.10.38   FO 27.8.39

CHARLES TREVOR DAVIS

33563   PO   Pilot   British   238 Squadron

Born in Cardiff, Davis entered RAF College, Cranwell as a flight cadet in April 1939. The war caused the course to be shortened and on leaving there he was commissioned in May 1940.

Davis joined 238 Squadron at Tangmere in June. On July 13 he shared a Do 17, on the 20th he claimed a Bf 109, on the 21st another shared Do 17, on the 27th a Ju 87, on August 8 a Bf 110, on the 13th two Bf 110s, on September 15 a He 111 and on the 21st a Ju 88. He was awarded the DFC (25.10.40).

Davis was killed on March 26 1941, when he flew into a hill coming down through a cloud near Winchester. He was 20 years old and was cremated at St John's Crematorium, Woking, Surrey.

PO 12.5.40

JACK DAVIS

50555   Sgt   Pilot   British   54 Squadron

Born on May 9 1916, Davis joined 54 Squadron at Hornchurch on August 9 1940. On the 31st Davis, Deere and Edsall of 54 were caught in a bombing attack on Hornchurch as they were taking off. Davis got off, just cleared the boundary fence and then crashed in the River Ingrebourne. His wrecked plane was seen but he had gone, turning up some time later carrying his parachute. Having found no gap in the boundary fence he walked right around back to the main gate.

Commissioned in October 1942 from Warrant Officer, Davis was awarded the AFC (3.4.45) and retired from the RAF on June 6 1959, as a Squadron Leader.

PO 28.10.42   FO 28.4.43   FL 28.10.44   FL 28.4.46
SL 1.7.52

J N DAVIS

No unknown   Sgt   Aircrew   British   600 Squadron

No service details traced.

PETER EDGAR DAVIS

551875   Sgt   Aircrew   British   236 Squadron

Joined 236 Squadron on October 24 1940. No other service details traced.

PHILLIP OSCAR DAVIS

115138   Sgt   Pilot   British   222 Squadron

Davis, of Ramsey, Huntingdonshire, joined 222 Squadron at Hornchurch in mid-October 1940. On the 26th he crashed on Purleigh Barns Farm, Latchingden, when his engine caught fire during a patrol. The Spitfire, R 6773, was wrecked but Davis was unhurt.

Commissioned in January 1942, Davis was killed on August 10 1943, serving with 511 Squadron, an Albemarle transport unit. He was 22 and is remembered on the Malta Memorial, Panel 6, Column 2.

PO 15.1.42   FO 1.10.42

WILLIAM L DAVIS

61922   Sgt   Pilot   British   249 Squadron

Commissioned in early February 1941 and shot down on the 10th and captured. No further service details traced. He died in 1984.

JOHN TREGONWELL DAVISON

70020　　PO　　Pilot　　New Zealander　　235 Squadron

Born at Ashburton on January 7 1914, Davison applied for a short service commission in the RNZAF in March 1939 and was accepted in July. Before he could be called war broke out and he did not report to the Ground Training School at Weraroa until October 17.

In late November Davison moved to No 1 EFTS, Taieri and went on to No 1 FTS, Wigram on January 16 1940. He passed out as a Sergeant-Pilot but was commissioned soon afterwards. Davison sailed for the UK in the 'Mataroa' on May 24. He was posted to No 1 (Coastal) OTU at Silloth, Cumberland on July 27 and after converting to Blenheims he joined 235 Squadron at Bircham Newton.

On November 23 1940 Davison was captain of a Blenheim, which took part in a bombing attack on two heavily-armed enemy merchant vessels. During the action he was wounded in the foot and the thigh. He regained his base but damage to his aircraft's hydraulic system necessitated that he make a crash-landing. Unknown to Davison a bomb remained on the rack and this exploded on impact, severely wounding the Wop/AG, Sergeant ATR Aslett, and setting fire to the aircraft. Davison and his observer, Sergeant Brazier, jumped clear but on realising that Aslett was still in the blazing aircraft they went back, regardless of their own safety and dragged him out. They were both badly burned and their gallantry was recognised in March 1941, Brazier being awarded the BEM and Davison the GM (13.3.41).

On May 5 Davison was posted away to form the Nottingham University Air Squadron at Newton, as Flying Instructor and Adjutant. He was appointed Chief Instructor to the Cambridge University Air Squadron at Duxford on January 1 1942. Davison was posted to the Empire CFS, Hullavington in February 1943 for a Chief Ground Instructor's course. On completing it in June he went to Uxbridge to await an overseas posting. He was picked for a CGI post in Rhodesia but the RNZAF requested that he return to New Zealand.

On September 4 Davison became CGI at the ITW at Rotorua, moving to a similar appointment at RNZAF, Delta on July 17 1944. He was posted to Melbourne for an RAAF War Staff Course on October 1 1944 and on his return Davison was appointed Deputy Director of Personnel Services on February 10 1945, at the Air Department in Wellington.

He was recalled to the UK for special duties in November 1945 and on the 20th he became CGI at the Empire CFS. Davison was made an OBE (1.1.48), returned with his family to New Zealand in late 1948 and retired from the RNZAF on June 24 1951, as a Wing Commander. He died at Matamata on October 9 1981.

PO 4.5.40　　FO 6.5.41　　FL 6.5.42　　SL 1.1.44
WC 1.10.47

THOMAS DANIEL HUMPHREY DAVY

41383　　FO　　Pilot　　British　　266 and 72 Squadrons

Davy joined the RAF on a short service commission in October 1938 and was with 12 Squadron in France in 1940, operating in Fairey Battles. On May 12 the squadron was ordered to bomb bridges over the Albert Canal. The attack was carried out in the face of intense ground fire. After making a dive-bombing attack Davy's aircraft was attacked by a Bf 109, which was fought off by his gunner. The port petrol tank of the Battle was thought to be on fire and Davy ordered the crew to bale out. He stayed with the aircraft and was eventually compelled to make a forced-landing eight miles short of base, his plane bursting into flames on landing. It was the only survivor of the six aircraft which set out. Davy was awarded the DFC (31.5.40). Garland and Gray received posthumous VCs for this action.

After volunteering for Fighter Command, Davy joined 266 Squadron at Wittering on August 28 1940. He moved to 72 Squadron at Biggin Hill on September 28.

Davy was killed on September 13 1942, as a Flight Lieutenant. The unit he was serving with is not known. He was 22 and is buried in Anfield Cemetery, Liverpool.

APO 14.12.38　　PO 3.9.39　　FO 3.9.40　　FL 3.9.41

VICTOR GEORGE DAW

41561　　FO　　Pilot　　British　　32 Squadron

Daw, who was born in Portsmouth, joined the RAF on a short service commission in November 1938. He was with 32 Squadron at Biggin Hill in 1940. On May 18 it began using Abbeville as a forward base. On May 19 Daw destroyed a Bf 110, on the 20th a Bf 109, on the 21st another, on June 8 two He 111s and a Bf 109 and on the 12th a Hs 126. Daw was awarded the DFC (25.6.40) and was decorated by the King at a special ceremony at Biggin Hill on June 27.

In Hurricane P 3677, Daw made a forced-landing near Dover on July 25 after a combat with Bf 109s. Slightly injured, he was admitted to hospital. After the Battle of Britain he served with 145 Squadron and on July 17 1941 went to 242 Squadron at North Weald but was posted away on August 8.

Awarded the AFC (1.1.45), Daw stayed on in the RAF. He was killed in a flying accident on March 24 1953, as a Flight Lieutenant.

APO 14.1.39　　PO 3.9.39　　FO 3.9.40　　FL 3.9.41
SL 1.7.44　　SL 1.8.47

PETER LESLIE DAWBARN

41905　　PO　　Pilot　　British　　17 Squadron

Joined the RAF on a short service commission in February 1939, did his elementary flying training at 11 E&RFTS, Perth, his intermediate and advanced at 2 FTS, Brize Norton and joined 253 Squadron at Manston in November.

Dawbarn spent a short period in France with 'B' Flight in April 1940. In May he joined 17 Squadron in France and returned to England when it was withdrawn after the French surrender. He was involved in a flying accident on July 15, crashing during a routine patrol, and was seriously injured.

After six months in hospitals Dawbarn was posted to 59 OTU, Crosby-on-Eden, as an instructor. He went for an instructor's course at CFS, Upavon and was posted in June 1941 to an EFTS near Derby. In 1943 he returned to operations, flying with a Hurricane squadron at Warmwell. In late 1943 Dawbarn joined No 1 ADF and served at various stations in the London area until posted to India in February 1945 to command No 1 AACU. He was released in 1946, as a Squadron Leader.

APO 15.4.39　　PO 6.11.39　　FO 6.11.40　　FL 6.11.41

KENNETH DAWICK

391828　　Sgt　　Pilot　　New Zealander　　111 Squadron

Born in Palmerston North on August 21 1916, Dawick worked as a printer from 1933 until he joined the RNZAF.

In 1938 he learned to fly privately at the Middle Districts Aero Club and early in 1939 was accepted for the Civil Reserve of Pilots. He was called for full-time service in November 1939 and reported to the Ground Training School, Weraroa on December 18.

Dawick did his elementary flying at No 1 EFTS, Taieri, moved to No 1 FTS, Wigram in March and after completing the course he sailed for the UK in the RMS 'Rangitane' in July. After a short spell at Uxbridge Dawick was posted to 6 OTU, Sutton Bridge and he joined 111 Squadron at Drem on September 30 1940.

He went to 605 Squadron at Croydon on December 23, remaining with it until August 19 1941, when he was posted to 55 OTU, Usworth, as an instructor. In October Dawick was posted overseas to 73 OTU, Aden, where he arrived on January 4 1942. Commissioned in February, he instructed until the OTU was disbanded in October. Dawick then went to the Middle East and joined 238 Squadron at Burg-el-Arab, flying in support of the Eighth Army moving forward after El Alamein.

Dawick sailed for New Zealand on November 9 1943. He went on a CFS course on Harvards at Tauranga, after which he was posted to 2 SFTS, Woodbourne. He moved to 1 SFTS, Wigram in October 1944 and was released from the RNZAF on November 14 1945.

PO 7.2.42   FO 7.11.42   FL 7.2.44

THOMAS DAWSON

629727   Sgt   Air Gunner   British   235 Squadron

With 235 Squadron in early July 1940. No other service details traced.

FRANK SAMUEL DAY

123055   Sgt   Observer   British   248 Squadron

Day, of Chesham, Buckinghamshire, was with 248 in early July 1940. Commissioned in May 1942, he was killed on July 24, aged 28 and serving with 86 Squadron, a general reconnaissance unit.

Day is buried in St Illogan's churchyard, Illogan, Cornwall. At some time he underwent plastic surgery at East Grinstead and was a Guinea Pig.

PO 4.5.42

ROBERT LIONEL FRANK DAY

41263   FO   Pilot   British   141 Squadron

In August 1938 Day joined the RAF on a short service commission and was with 141 Squadron in July 1940.

One night in May 1941 Day, flying with Pilot Officer FCA Lanning as his gunner, destroyed an enemy aircraft. On a second patrol on the same night they destroyed another. Both men were awarded the DFC (6.6.41).

Day was killed on June 18 1944, as a Flight Lieutenant, serving with 132 Squadron at Ford. He is buried in Connelles Cemetery, France.

APO 29.10.38   PO 29.8.39   FO 3.9.40   FL 3.9.41

ALBERT HENRY DEACON

49756   Sgt   Pilot   British   85 and 111 Squadrons

Deacon was with 85 Squadron at Martlesham Heath in early July 1940. In mid-August he went to 111 Squadron at Croydon. On the 18th he was shot down in combat over Kenley and baled out, unhurt. His Hurricane, N 2340, crashed at Oxted.

On September 16 Deacon was posted away and on January 9 1941 he flew a Hurricane off an aircraft carrier to Takoradi. The next day he was flying one of six aircraft which took off for the Middle East, led by a Blenheim. Deacon's Hurricane had a fuel pump fault and he took off late from Khartoum and flew the stages to Abu Sueir alone. On the 29th he flew across to Ta Kali, Malta with five other Hurricanes, to reinforce 261 Squadron.

On April 11 Deacon probably destroyed a Bf 109. His Hurricane was damaged and he went back to Ta Kali but was driven off by ground fire. He then made a crash-landing at Hal Far and was slightly injured.

Deacon later returned to the Middle East and after a spell with the ADU, Takoradi he was posted to South Africa, as an instructor. He was commissioned in May 1942.

In 1945 Deacon was with 31 Squadron. He stayed on in the RAF on an extended commission and was released in 1948, as a Flight Lieutenant.

PO 1.5.42   FO 1.11.42   FL 1.5.44   FL 1.5.46

HENRY GEORGE DEADMAN

902541   Sgt   Aircrew   British   236 Squadron

With 236 in July 1940. Later changed name by deed poll to Stewart. Nothing further known.

EDWARD CHRISTOPHER DEANESLY

90251   FL   Pilot   British   152 Squadron

Deanesly joined 605 Squadron, AuxAF in early 1937. He was called to full-time service on August 24 1939 and posted to 152 Squadron at Acklington.

On July 25 1940 in an action five miles south of Portland Deanesly's Spitfire, K 9901, was damaged by return fire from a Ju 87 and he ditched in the Channel, wounded. He was rescued by SS 'Empire Henchman' and landed at Lyme Regis, where he was admitted to hospital. He was shot down again on September 26 during a combat with Bf 109s twelve miles south of the Needles and baled out, wounded. Deanesly was rescued by a Royal Navy launch and landed at Swanage. His Spitfire, K 9982, crashed into the Channel.

On November 23 1940 256 Squadron was reformed at Catterick as a night-fighter unit and Deanesly joined it as a Flight Commander. Over the Birmingham area on April 10 1941 Deanesly, with Sergeant WJ Scott as his gunner, destroyed a He 111, on May 3 on the same patrol they shot down a Ju 88 over Merseyside and a Do 215, which crashed in North Wales and on May 7 they destroyed a He 111 over Manchester. Deanesly was awarded the DFC (30.5.41) and Scott the DFM. They were decorated by the King in October.

Deanesly took command of 256 in September 1941 and led it until April 1942. He was released from the RAF in 1945, as a Wing Commander.

PO (AuxAF) 18.3.37   FO (AuxAF) 21.11.38   FO 24.8.39
FL 3.9.40   SL 1.12.41

KENNETH BARRY LEMPRIERE DEBENHAM

81656   PO   Pilot   British   151 Squadron

Debenham, of Cambridge, joined 151 Squadron at Martlesham Heath on July 15 1940. He claimed a Bf 109 destroyed on August 15 and shared a Bf 110 three days later.

On August 24 Debenham was shot down in combat with Bf 109s over Ramsgate and was seriously wounded, when his Hurricane, R 4183, crashed and burned out. He was admitted to Ramsgate Hospital and later underwent plastic surgery at the Queen Victoria Hospital, East Grinstead, making him a member of the Guinea Pig Club.

Debenham took command of 126 Squadron at Grottaglie, Italy in November 1943. He was killed on December 16, aged 24. He is remembered on the Malta Memorial, Panel 6, Column 1.

PO 29.6.40   FO 29.6.41   FL 29.6.42

ROGER EMILE de CANNAERT d'HAMALE

No unknown   Sgt   Pilot   Belgian   46 Squadron

De Cannaert d'Hamale arrived in England on June 20 1940. After conversion to Hurricanes he joined 46 Squadron at Digby on August 13. He was shot down in combat over Kent on September 11 and baled out, landing at Court Lodge, Bodiam, with an injured forehead. His Hurricane, V 6549, crashed at School Fields, Sandhurst.

On October 17 de Cannaert d'Hamale made a belly-landing at Parkers Farm, Woodend, Abbess Roding, because of bad visibility and lack of fuel. He was killed on November 1 1940, shot down by Bf 109s over Hawkinge. His Hurricane, V 7616, crashed at Smersole Farm, Swingfield, near Dover.

De Cannaert d'Hamale was 19. His body was repatriated to Belgium after the war.

XAVIER de CHERADE de MONTBRON

No unknown   Sgt   Pilot   French   64 and 92 Squadrons

Born at Forsac on August 18 1916, de Cherade de Montbron went to 6 OTU, Sutton Bridge on August 19 1940. He joined 64 Squadron at Leconfield in September and moved to 92 Squadron at Biggin Hill on October 2.

X de Cherade de Montbron (continued)

De Cherade de Montbron shared in destroying a Bf 109 on November 1 and he got a probable Bf 109 on December 1.

Commissioned in March 1941, he was later shot down and captured, passing himself off to the Germans as a French-Canadian. De Cherade de Montbron died on April 21 1955, following a flying accident in a Vampire.

PO 16.3.41

ORLANDO JOHN DEE

906581   Sgt   Wop/AG   British   235 Squadron

Joined 235 Squadron on September 13 1940. He was killed on May 28 1941, aged 20, still with 235.

Dee is buried in Hamburg Cemetery, Ohlsdorf, Germany.

ALAN CHRISTOPHER DEERE

40370   FO   Pilot   New Zealander   54 Squadron

Deere was born in Auckland on December 12 1917. After leaving school he spent a year sheep farming before becoming a law clerk in Wanganui. In April 1937 he applied for a short service commission in the RAF and after being provisionally accepted he sailed for the UK on September 23 in the RMS 'Rangitane'.

In November he began his elementary flying training at 13 E&RFTS, White Waltham, moved to 6 FTS, Netheravon in late January 1938 and joined 54 Squadron at Hornchurch in September. The squadron began to receive Spitfires in March 1939 and on a flight in May Deere was overcome by anoxia and lost consciousness. His aircraft dived towards the sea and he came to just in time to pull out but he suffered a broken ear drum, which kept him off flying for three months.

On May 23 1940 Deere and Pilot Officer JL Allen acted as escort to Flight Lieutenant JA Leathart, who was flying a Master to Calais/Marck airfield to pick up the CO of 74 Squadron, who had made a forced-landing there. Despite interference by enemy fighters the rescue was effected and Deere shot down two Bf 109s and damaged another. He destroyed a third in the afternoon of the same day. On May 24 he shot down a Bf 109 and on the 26th two more.

Deere was leading eight Spitfires of 54 on a dawn patrol on May 28. Unable to keep up with the other two Hornchurch squadrons they crossed the Belgian coast alone. Sighting a Do 17, slightly out to sea, Deere gave chase with three members of his flight. He damaged the bomber but was hit by return fire and with his glycol tank holed and producing smoke Deere decided to make a forced-landing on a beach. He was knocked unconscious when his forehead struck the windscreen, as the Spitfire ploughed through the sand. Coming to, he got out of the now burning aircraft and was taken by a soldier to Oost-Dunkerke, where he had his head injury dressed. After setting out for Ostende Deere decided to make for Dunkirk, commandeered a bicycle and eventually met three British soldiers, heading for Dunkirk in a truck, which they abandoned on the outskirts of the port because of congestion on the road. Deere managed to get a boat back to Dover, caught a train to London, went by underground to Elm Park and arrived back at Hornchurch nineteen hours after he had taken off. He was awarded the DFC (12.6.40), which was presented to him by the King in a ceremony at Hornchurch on June 27.

On July 9 Deere destroyed a Bf 109 and after colliding with another he crash-landed in a cornfield, escaping with minor injuries. On August 11 he destroyed a Bf 109, on the 12th two Bf 109s and a Bf 110, on the 15th he destroyed another Bf 109 but had to bale out at a very low level after being chased back across the Channel by two enemy fighters. He escaped with a slight fracture of the wrist and after an overnight stay in the Queen Victoria Hospital, East Grinstead he returned to Hornchurch.

Deere was shot down by a Spitfire on August 28 and baled out.

On the 30th he shot down a Do 215. The next day he was the pilot of one of three Spitfires caught in a bombing attack as they were taking off from Hornchurch. Deere's aircraft was thrown on to its back and he was left suspended in his harness. He was released by one of the other two pilots, Pilot Officer EF Edsall, who, despite leg injuries, crawled across and released Deere, who then took his rescuer to Station Sick Quarters. On September 3 Deere destroyed a Bf 110. He was awarded a Bar to the DFC (6.9.40).

In January 1941 he was made Operations Room Controller at Catterick. His portrait was done by Orde in February. Deere joined 602 Squadron at Ayr on May 7, as a Flight Commander. On June 5 he crash-landed on the clifftop at the Heads of Ayr after his engine seized.

On August 1 Deere took command of 602 and on the same day destroyed a Bf 109 over Gravelines. He was posted away in January 1942 and sent to America to lecture on fighter tactics. He returned to operations on May 1, when he took command of 403 (RCAF) Squadron at North Weald. In August Deere was posted to HQ 13 Group on staff duties. He went for a course at RAF Staff College and then returned to 13 Group.

In February 1943, desperate to return to operations, Deere went as supernumerary to 611 Squadron at Biggin Hill. Whilst there he destroyed a FW 190. He was given command of the Kenley Wing but the posting was changed and he went as Wing Leader to Biggin Hill. Deere was awarded the DSO (15.7.43). He led the Wing until September 15 1943, when he became ill and went to hospital. He then had 22 confirmed victories, 10 probables and a further 18 enemy aircraft damaged.

Deere was posted to CGS, Sutton Bridge to command the Fighter Wing, in March 1944 he went to a staff job at HQ 11 Group, in early May he took command of 145 (French) Airfield of 84 Group 2nd TAF at Merston. Deere led the Wing on patrol over the invasion bridgehead early on the morning of D Day. The Wing moved to the Continent later in June and Deere was posted soon afterwards to HQ 84 Group Control Centre as Wing Commander Plans.

In July 1945 he was appointed Station Commander at Biggin Hill. He was granted a Permanent Commission in August and posted to command the Polish Mustang Wing at Andrews Field. When the Wing was disbanded in October he became Station Commander at Duxford.

Deere held a series of appointments and commands in the post-war RAF prior to his retirement on December 12 1967, as an Air Commodore. He was then offered a civilian appointment as Director of Sport for the RAF, which he held until retiring in December 1977. In addition to his other awards Deere received the DFC (US) and the C de G (Fr) in 1943 and was made an OBE (1.6.45). He was ADC to the Queen in 1962.

APO 9.1.38   PO 28.10.38   FO 28.7.40   FL 28.7.41
SL 14.6.43   SL 1.9.45   WC 1.7.51   GC 1.1.58
AC 1.7.64

BAUDOUIN MARIE GHISLAIN de HEMPTINNE

82516   PO   Pilot   Belgian   145 Squadron

Commissioned in July 1940, de Hemptinne was posted to 6 OTU, Sutton Bridge on the 30th and joined 145 Squadron at Drem on August 17. He attacked a He 115 of 1/506 over a convoy on October 2. The enemy aircraft landed on the sea off Kinnaird's Head and the crew were rescued from their dinghy.

On October 25 de Hemptinne made a forced-landing at High Beeches, Haywards Heath golf course due to engine failure. He got out, unhurt, before his Hurricane exploded.

De Hemptinne was posted to 609 Squadron at Biggin Hill on June 17 1941 and awarded the C de G (Belg)(21.7.41). He was killed on May 5 1942, as a Flight Lieutenant with 122 Squadron. His body was repatriated to Belgium after the war.

PO 30.7.40

Comte RUDOLPHE GHISLAIN CHARLES de HEMRICOURT de GRUNNE

82158   PO   Pilot   Belgian   32 Squadron

De Hemricourt de Grunne went to Spain in 1936 and fought on the Nationalist side, flying CR 42s and Bf 109s in the 3rd Escadra, the 'Blue Group', against the Republicans. He was reputed to have had fourteen victories before the war ended in 1939.

After Belgium was overrun de Hemricourt de Grunne went to France. On June 21 the French signed an Armistice with the Germans and the Belgians were told to stay put. With other pilots de Hemricourt de Grunne reached Port Vendres, where with the help of a British destroyer and the support of the Belgian Embassy in London they caught a passing convoy and embarked on the SS 'Apapa' on the 24th. After arriving in Liverpool on July 7 they were commissioned in the RAF on the 19th.

De Hemricourt de Grunne joined 32 Squadron at Biggin Hill on August 15. The next day he claimed a Bf 109 destroyed, on the 17th a Bf 109 and on the 18th a Do 17. He was shot down by Bf 109s on this day and baled out, badly burned and was admitted to hospital. His Hurricane, V 6535, is believed to have crashed at Ruckinge.

After recovery de Hemricourt de Grunne did not return to 32 but was sent on a special mission to Lisbon to find out what German intentions were in North Africa. He joined the Belgian Flight of 609 Squadron at Biggin Hill in April 1941. He was killed on May 25, when 609 escorted Blenheims to raid Bethune. De Hemricourt de Grunne was jumped by a Bf 109 and baled out into the sea. A rescue boat went out from Ramsgate but no trace of him was found. He is remembered on the Runnymede Memorial, Panel 32.

PO 19.7.40

LEOPOLD JOSEPH DEJACE

81632   PO   Pilot   Belgian   236 Squadron

Dejace, of Liege, joined 236 Squadron on August 5 1940.

He failed to return from a meteorological flight over enemy-occupied territory on July 26 1942. He was a Flight Lieutenant and flying a Mosquito of 1401 Flight.

Dejace was 33 years old. He is buried in Arendal Hogedal Cemetery, Norway.

PO 12.7.40

FRANCOIS HENRI EDMOND JOSEPH ANDRE de LABOUCHERE

30593   Adjudant   Pilot   French   85 Squadron

Born on September 18 1917 at Chateau d'Hauterive, de Labouchere, whose father was killed in action in the Battle of France, was training for aircrew duties when capitulation came in June 1940. He asked for permission to fly to England and when this was refused he escaped to Morocco and made his way to Britain.

De Labouchere joined 85 Squadron at Castle Camps on September 13 1940. He was posted to 242 Squadron at Stapleford Tawney on April 26 1941. He claimed a Bf 109 destroyed on June 23, whilst flying on a Blenheim escort. On September 13 1941 de Labouchere was posted to 615 Squadron at Manston. He shot down a Bf 109 on the 18th.

In November 1941 the first Free French fighter unit was formed, 340 Squadron at Turnhouse. De Labouchere joined the squadron, as a Flight Commander. He destroyed a Do 17 on August 19 1942 over Dieppe and was killed over Rouen on September 5, when Yellow Section was jumped from above by fifty FW 190s and wiped out.

VICTOR BRETON de la PERELLE

36211   PO   Pilot   New Zealander   245 Squadron

Born on May 7 1919 at Winton, Southland, de la Perelle was educated at Southland Boys' High School. In October 1938 he learned to fly at the Otago Aero Club and in November joined the RNZAF on a short service commission. Awarded his wings on April 19 1939, de la Perelle completed his training and sailed for the UK in the SS 'Tamaroa' on July 14.

On the voyage he developed pneumonia and was grounded for some months. Fit again, de la Perelle was posted to 6 OTU, Sutton Bridge on August 17 1940 and joined 245 Squadron at Aldergrove on September 7.

He went to 258 Squadron on November 25 1940 and was made a Flight Commander in mid-August 1941. The squadron was posted overseas in October and on the 30th the pilots, minus their aircraft, went to Abbotsinch and sailed two days later in HMS 'Athene' for Gibraltar, where they spent a weary five weeks before sailing again. They finally reached Takoradi on January 1 1942.

The pilots were flown to Port Sudan and there embarked on the carrier HMS 'Indomitable'. After sailing south for nearly three weeks they flew Hurricanes off on January 28 to Kemajoran, Java, moving on to Palembang, Sumatra after refuelling. The same afternoon de la Perelle led his flight to Seletar airfield, Singapore to face the Japanese. After a few days the order came to withdraw and the serviceable remnants of 258 Squadron returned to Palembang. De la Perelle was temporarily commanding the airfield in mid-February until a Japanese airborne invasion drove 258 away to Java, leaving six of its pilots behind to help reform a very much-depleted 605 Squadron at Tjillitan.

On February 21 1942 de la Perelle was promoted to Acting Squadron Leader and appointed Liaison Officer with the Dutch Air Force in Java. The situation deteriorated rapidly as he went into the hills with RAF and Dutch personnel, moving from one tea plantation to the next. On March 20 they were forced to surrender and were sent to prison in Batavia, with de la Perelle in charge, he being the only senior officer left.

De la Perelle was moved to Amboina, where he remained until September 1944, when he went to Bandung in Java. He was released from a prison camp in Jakarta on September 17 1945. The first aircraft to arrive was a New Zealand one and the first person off was a nurse, who accepted the surrender of the Japanese. She was carrying 400 cigarettes for de la Perelle from his brother.

Flown back to New Zealand, via Singapore and Australia, de la Perelle spent three months recuperating before returning to the UK and rejoining the RAF in February 1946. After a refresher course he was given command of 165 Squadron at Duxford.

De la Perelle continued to serve in the RAF, retiring in 1958, as a Squadron Leader. In the Korean War he was seconded to the USAF and was awarded the Bronze Star (US) for secret work carried out in Korea.

After retirement de la Perelle lived in England and was a Director and Company Secretary for a company in Cambridge. He died there on June 11 1983.

*APO 28.11.38   PO 16.8.39   FO 17.8.40   FL 17.8.41
SL 1.8.47*

ALAN LAWRENCE MARTIN DELLER

156643   **Sgt**   **Pilot**   **British**   **43 Squadron**

Deller was posted from 6 OTU, Sutton Bridge to 43 Squadron at Northolt on August 3 1940. On the 12th he made a forced-landing at Tangmere after an action over the Channel.

On September 7 Deller baled out, unhurt, following a combat over Ashford. His Hurricane, V 7309, crashed and burned out at Babylon Farm, Sutton Valence.

Commissioned from Warrant Officer in February 1943, Deller was released from the RAF in 1946. He later went to live in America.

PO 27.2.43   FO 27.8.43   FL 27.2.45

RICARDO ADRIANI de MANCHA

80546   **PO**   **Pilot**   **British**   **43 Squadron**

The son of an Italian father and an English mother, de Mancha joined 43 Squadron at Tangmere on July 6 1940, from OTU.

In a combat ten miles south of the Needles on July 21 de Mancha collided with a Bf 109, flown by Leutnant Kroker of 7/JG 27. Both men were killed.

De Mancha was 23. He is remembered on the Runnymede Memorial, Panel 8.

PO 8.6.40

RICHARD STEPHEN DEMETRIADI

90145   **FO**   **Pilot**   **British**   **601 Squadron**

Demetriadi joined 601 Squadron, AuxAF in 1938, was commissioned in July and called to full-time service on August 25 1939. He was shot down into the Channel and killed on August 11 1940 during a combat off Portland, in Hurricane R 4092.

The son of Sir Stephen Demetriadi KBE and brother-in-law of Flying Officer WH Rhodes-Moorhouse, Demetriadi was 21 years old. He is buried in Cayeux-sur-Mer Communal Cemetery, France. His father gave land at Ditchling Beacon to the National Trust in memory of his son.

PO (AuxAF) 25.7.38   PO 25.8.39   FO 25.1.40

RENE JEAN GHISLAIN DEMOULIN

116107   **Sgt**   **Pilot**   **Belgian**   **235 Squadron**

Demoulin, of Comblain-au-Pont, Liege, joined 235 Squadron on August 5 1940 and served with it in the Battle of Britain.

On July 19 1941 he flew from Edku, Egypt to Malta with 272 Squadron. On the 28th he shared in damaging Z 501s in an attack on the seaplane base at Marsala.

Commissioned in August 1941, Demoulin shared in damaging two Ju 52s over the Gulf of Bomba on September 24. Some time in 1942 he destroyed a Ju 52 and in July 1943 he shared in destroying another.

Demoulin was killed on April 6 1944, as a Squadron Leader with 272 Squadron. He was 23 and is remembered on the Malta Memorial, Panel 12, Column 2. He held the Croix Chevalier de l'Ordre de Leopold avec Palme and the Croix de Guerre avec Palme et Lion.

PO 16.8.41

JEAN DEMOZAY

FR 297   **2nd Lt**   **Pilot**   **French**   **1 Squadron**

Demozay was born in Nantes on March 21 1916. He joined l'Armée de l'Air in 1936 but was invalided out on medical grounds and became a pilot with a civil airline. In September 1939 he was a liaison officer at HQ RAF Rheims. He transferred to the Operations Room at 67 Wing, Dussy-Lacoge in December.

In January 1940 Demozay was appointed official interpreter to No 1 Squadron and was with them until the squadron was withdrawn to England on June 18. He was left on the airfield at Nantes with sixteen groundcrew, who were to go to La Rochelle in a truck. A Bristol Bombay stood on the airfield, with full fuel tanks but left because it had a broken tail-wheel. This defect was swiftly put right and Demozay flew himself and the airmen out of France, heading for Tangmere but at the request of his passengers he put down at Sutton Bridge.

At Free French HQ he requested to join the RAF and went to 5 OTU, Aston Down for conversion to Hurricanes and then joined No 1 Squadron at Wittering on October 16 1940. He destroyed a Ju 88 on November 8 and a Bf 109 a few days later. Demozay claimed a Bf 109 on March 24 1941, a He 111 at night on May 10 and a Bf 110, shot down into the sea on May 25.

Demozay was posted to 242 Squadron at North Weald on June 21 1941. The next day he destroyed a Bf 109 and another two days later. He left 242 on the 29th and joined 91 Squadron at Hawkinge, as a Flight Commander. He sank a minelayer on July 17, damaged a Bf 109 on the 25th, destroyed two Bf 109s and damaged another on the 31st and between August 9 1941 and January 2 1942 Demozay destroyed eight Bf 109s and probably two more.

Posted then to HQ 11 Group for a rest, he returned to 91 Squadron on June 25 1942, to command. Demozay destroyed a FW 190 on September 23 and two more on October 31. In February 1943 he was posted to North Africa to form a flying school for Free French pilots. Recalled to London in April 1944, he was sent on a mission to the USSR and on August 9 1944 he took command of a Free French bomber group.

Demozay was made Deputy Commander of all flying training schools in France on October 24 1945. He was killed on December 19 1945, when the aircraft in which he was flying back from London crashed at Le Duc. He was credited with 21 confirmed victories in over 400 operational sorties and received many honours and awards; the DFC (Nov 1941) and Bar (July 1942), the DSO (Dec 1942), Ordre de Liberation (May 1941), C de G (Fr), C de G (Belg), Legion d'Honneur (Dec 1944), the DFC (US) and the Czech Military Cross. His portrait was done by Cuthbert Orde in February 1941, using Demozay's nom-de-guerre 'Moses Morlaix'.

GORDON ALFRED DENBY

80812 PO Pilot British 600 Squadron

Denby, of Herne Hill, Middlesex, joined 600 Squadron on July 9 1940. On September 27 he claimed an enemy aircraft probably destroyed at night, after it disappeared into clouds on fire.

Awarded the DFC (22.4.41), Denby was credited with a He 111 destroyed one night in February 1941 and two other probables. In May 1942 he was posted away to instruct. He joined 125 Squadron at Fairwood Common in July.

Denby was killed on December 12 1942, as a Squadron Leader Flight Commander with 125 Squadron. He crashed off the Shetlands, when his Beaufighter developed engine trouble. He was 27 and is remembered on the Runnymede Memorial, Panel 65.

PO 9.6.40   FO 9.6.41   FL 9.6.42

HERBERT DAVID DENCHFIELD

748168 Sgt Pilot British 610 Squadron

Joined 610 Squadron at Acklington on October 7 1940. Denchfield was still with the squadron on February 4 1941, when he was shot down on a Blenheim escort to St Omer. He was reported as a PoW on February 20. No further details have been traced.

GEORGE LOVELL DENHOLM

90190 SL Pilot British 603 Squadron

Born at Bo'ness, West Lothian, Denholm joined 603 Squadron, AuxAF in 1933. He was called to full-time service on August 23 1939. Over the Firth of Forth on October 16 Denholm shared in the destruction of a He 111. It was the first enemy aircraft shot down over British territory in the war.

On July 3 1940 Denholm shared a Ju 88, destroyed a Bf 109 on August 28 and was shot down himself on the 30th, in combat with Bf 110s over Deal. He baled out, unhurt, and his Spitfire, L 1067, crashed at Hope Farm, Snargate. On September 15 he destroyed a Bf 109 and on the same day was hit by return fire from a Do 17 and baled out, unhurt, landing near Guestling Lodge. His Spitfire, R 7019, crashed on Warren Farm, Fairlight, Hastings. Denholm shared a Bf 109 on September 27 and was awarded the DFC (22.10.40). He commanded 603 Squadron from late August 1940 until posted away to Turnhouse on April 1 1941.

On December 15 1941 he took command of 1460 Flight, then forming at Acklington with Turbinlite Havocs. Denholm left in March 1942 and was given command of 605 Squadron at Ford in August, holding the appointment until May 1943. He was released from the RAF in 1947, as a Group Captain.

PO (AuxAF) 27.6.33   FO (AuxAF) 27.12.34   FL 23.8.39
SL 1.9.40   WC 1.3.42

RICHARD WARREN DENISON

37596 FL Pilot British 236 Squadron

Born in London, Denison was brought up in Vernon, British Columbia. He joined the RAF on a short service commission in December 1935. On March 14 1936 he was posted to 3 FTS, Grantham and joined 213 Squadron at Church Fenton on March 8 1937.

Denison was with 236 Squadron in July 1940. He commanded 80 Squadron in the Western Desert from April to September 1942 and commanded 46 Squadron from June to August 1944 and again in November/December 1944. He was awarded the AFC (1.1.45). He returned to Canada after release from the RAF.

In 1946 Denison joined Trans-Canada Airlines, but moved shortly afterwards to Canadian Pacific Airlines. He later joined Yellowknife Airways and was killed in a flying accident at Yellowknife on February 6 1951.

APO 2.3.36   PO 6.1.37   FO 6.8.38   FL 6.8.40
SL 1.9.41   WC 1.1.44

DENIS AUSTIN DENTON

650890 Sgt Wop/AG British 236 Squadron

Denton, from Lancashire, joined 236 Squadron on July 24 1940. He was killed on August 30 1944, as a Warrant Officer with 502 Squadron. He is buried in Escoublac-la-Baule War Cemetery, France.

JOHN MONTAGUE DERBYSHIRE

42110 PO Pilot British 236 Squadron

Derbyshire joined the RAF on a short service commission in January 1939 and did his elementary flying at 7 E&RFTS, Desford. On March 27 he was posted to 9 FTS, Hullavington, after which he joined 236 Squadron at Stradishall on November 6 1939.

Derbyshire crashed at St Eval on November 5 1940, when he ran out of fuel and hit high tension cables. He spent eighteen months in hospital and then went to a desk job at the Ministry of Aircraft Production. He later went as an instructor to 18 E&RFTS, Fairoaks but whilst there he lost his flying category.

Posted to India, Derbyshire became Senior Admin Officer at HQ RAF Calcutta. He was released from the RAF in May 1946, as a Squadron Leader.

APO 13.3.39   PO 6.11.39   FO 6.11.40   FL 6.11.41

———— DERMOTT

No unknown PO Aircrew British 600 Squadron

Joined 600 Squadron at Manston on July 12 1940.
No further service details traced.

CHARLES JEAN MARIE PHILIPPE de SCITIVAUX de GREISCHE

30653 Captain Pilot French 245 Squadron

Born on August 2 1911 at Rosnay, de Scitivaux joined the Navy and went into the French Naval Air Service. In action, as a fighter pilot, on May 10 1940 he shot down an enemy aircraft and was then badly wounded in one arm. In hospital at Boulogne he heard that the arrival of the Germans was imminent so he made his way to the port area, gathered together some sailors and then convinced a tug master to take them all to England. They landed at Hastings, where de Scitivaux collapsed. When he was better he returned to France but when capitulation came he took a transport plane and flew it to Gibraltar. Flown back to England, he was made ADC to Admiral Muselier. When his arm was finally healed he went into the RAF, reporting to 6 OTU, Sutton Bridge on September 29 1940.

After conversion to Hurricanes de Scitivaux joined 245 Squadron at Aldergrove on October 14. He went to 253 Squadron at Kenley on November 27, to 249 at North Weald on March 29 1941, to 242 at Stapleford on April 27 and finally to 615 Squadron at Manston on September 19.

De Scitivaux was posted on November 10 1941 to 340 Squadron, then forming at Drem, as a Flight Commander. He took command in January 1942. On April 10 he was shot down near St Omer, baled out, landed in a tree and was captured, wounded in both legs and both arms. His fiancée, who had taken eighteen months to reach England, via Algeria, Portugal, South America and the Bermudas, arrived two days later.

De Scitivaux, who was described by Mouchotte as 'an excellent pilot, alive with grand aggressive spirit, supported by long experience', escaped five times whilst a PoW, the last and successful one just before the end of the war. He died in Toulon on August 10 1986. He was a Vice-Admiral d' Escadre, Compagnon de la Liberation, Grand Officier de la Légion d'Honneur and had the DFC, C de G with six Palms and the Grand Croix du Mérite National.

JEAN-PAUL JOSEPH DESLOGES

C 788   FO   Pilot   Canadian   1 (RCAF) Squadron

Born in Hull, Quebec on April 25 1913, Desloges joined the RCAF on October 1 1937. He arrived in the UK on June 2 1940, with No 1 (RCAF) Squadron. He was shot down on August 31 during an attack on Do 215s and baled out, severely burned. His Hurricane, N 2530, crashed and burned out at Gravesend.

Desloges was killed in a flying accident in North Africa on May 8 1944, as a Wing Commander. He is buried in Dely Ibrahim War Cemetery, Algeria.

FRANCOIS XAVIER EGENOFF de SPIRLET

82163   PO   Pilot   Belgian   87 Squadron

De Spirlet escaped from Belgium and reached Gibraltar. He joined other Belgian pilots bound for England in the SS 'Apapa', when it docked there. They reached Liverpool on July 7 1940 and after converting to Hurricanes de Spirlet joined 87 Squadron at Church Fenton on August 12.

He moved to 56 Squadron at Middle Wallop on November 29 1940. In April 1941 de Spirlet joined 609 Squadron at Biggin Hill. He shot a Bf 109 down into the sea on June 17. De Spirlet was made a Flight Commander in August 1941. He was killed on June 26 1942, when one of his Typhoon's tyres burst on take-off and he collided with another aircraft.

De Spirlet's remains were repatriated to Belgium after the war.

PO 20.7.40

DERRICK CANUT DEUNTZER

111486   Sgt   Pilot   British   79 and 247 Squadrons

Deuntzer was born in Greenford, Middlesex on September 21 1919. He joined 79 Squadron at Pembrey on September 30 1940, moving to 247 Squadron at Roborough on October 26.

He was flying as No 2 to Flight Lieutenant KW Mackenzie, when the latter was shot down and captured during a dusk attack on Lannion airfield, Brittany on September 29 1941.

Commissioned in October 1941, Deuntzer was with 43 Squadron in North Africa in 1943 and on April 18 he destroyed a Me 210. He was posted from 43 in December 1943. He was released from the RAF in 1946, as a Flight Lieutenant.

PO 29.10.41   FO 1.10.42   FL 29.10.43

PETER KENNETH DEVITT

90080   SL   Pilot   British   152 Squadron

Devitt learned to fly privately at West Malling in 1931. He was commissioned in the RAFRO at Filton, Bristol and learned to fly Bristol Fighters. In 1933 he joined 600 Squadron, AuxAF at Hendon.

Called for full-time service on August 24 1939, Devitt was posted to the Operations Room at Tangmere. In February 1940 he was given command of 152 Squadron at Acklington.

On September 25 he was hit in the petrol tank by return fire from a He 111 engaged west of Bristol and forced-landed at Skew Bridge, Newton St Loe, near Bath. At the end of October 1940 Devitt was posted to HQ 9 Group. In April 1941 he went to HQ 14 Group as Senior Controller. In December 1941 he was posted to HQ 221 Group, Rangoon, leading the final withdrawal of troops out of Burma to Assam on May 8 1942.

Devitt was Wing Commander Training at HQ 224 Group, Calcutta until June 1943, when he became Station Commander RAF Ranchi. In January 1944 he was given command of 189 Wing at Silchar and in September he was promoted to Group Captain as Ops, SEAC, Barrackmore, Calcutta.

Invalided home in November 1944 Devitt went to Air Ministry, London until released in 1945. He commanded 615 Squadron, RAuxAF from 1949 to 1950.

PO (AuxAF) 13.7.33   FO (AuxAF) 13.1.35
FL (AuxAF) 13.7.36   FL 24.8.39   SL 1.6.40   WC 1.7.44
SL (RAuxAF) 1.4.49

JOHN MICHAEL FIRTH DEWAR

72462   PO   Pilot   British   229 Squadron

Dewar, of Hitchin, Herts, was born on May 2 1917 and educated at Rugby School and Trinity College, Cambridge, where he obtained his BA. He was commissioned in the RAFVR in September 1938.

On August 10 1940 Dewar joined 229 Squadron at Wittering. He claimed a Bf 110 destroyed on September 25 and a Bf 109 the next day. He was killed on March 30 1941, with 229. Dewar was 24. He is remembered on the Runnymede Memorial, Panel 30.

PO (RAFVR) 27.9.38   PO 6.3.40

JOHN SCATLIFF DEWAR

26029   WC   Pilot   British   87 and 213 Squadrons

Dewar was born at Mussoorie, Lahore Province, India in 1907. He was educated at King's College, Canterbury and entered RAF College, Cranwell as a flight cadet in January 1926. He was a brilliant student with 'exceptional' ratings. Dewar graduated in December 1927 and on the 17th of the month he joined 13 (Army Co-operation) Squadron at Andover.

He was posted to the School of Naval Co-operation, Lee-on-Solent on July 18 1929. Dewar joined 822 Squadron on the carrier HMS 'Furious' on May 6 1933 and was posted to 801 (Fleet Fighter) Squadron, also on the 'Furious', on July 10 1934. Dewar went to the Aircraft and Armament Experimental Establishment at Martlesham Heath as a test pilot on June 23 1936. He was posted to SHQ Thorney Island on March 26 1938.

In December 1939 Dewar took command of 87 Squadron in France. He broke his shoulder in a flying accident but continued to fly regularly. The squadron destroyed more than sixty enemy aircraft during its stay in France, of which Dewar was credited with five. He was one of the first four officers to receive the double award of DSO and DFC (31.5.40).

On July 11 1940 Dewar destroyed two Bf 110s, on August 13 he shared a Ju 88 and on the 25th he destroyed a Ju 88.

Dewar failed to arrive at Tangmere on a routine flight from Exeter on September 12 1940. He was reported 'Missing'. His body was washed up at Kingston Gorse, Sussex on September 30. He is buried in St John the Baptist churchyard, North Baddesley, Hampshire.

PO 17.12.27   FO 17.6.29   FL 1.2.34   SL 1.2.38
WC 1.3.40

ROBERT BASIL DEWEY

42815   PO   Pilot   British   611 and 603 Squadrons

Joined 611 Squadron in June 1940. On October 20 Dewey claimed a Bf 109 destroyed. On the 27th he was shot down by Bf 109s in a surprise attack south of Maidstone. His Spitfire, P 7365, crashed into a tree at Apple Tree Corner, Chartham Hatch and Dewey was killed.

He was 19, came from Portsmouth and is buried in Hornchurch Cemetery, Essex.

APO 23.10.39   PO 18.5.40

KENNETH SHORTLAND DEWHURST

41907   PO   Pilot   British   234 Squadron

Born on March 24 1914, Dewhurst went into the RAF on a short service commission in January 1939. He joined the recently-reformed 234 Squadron at Leconfield in late 1939.

On July 28 Dewhurst shared in the destruction of a Ju 88, shot down into the sea off Plymouth and on August 16 he claimed a Bf 109. On this day, following an attack by a Bf 109 over Gosport, his engine was set alight and he baled out, landing near Widley. His Spitfire, R 6967, crashed at Widley Farm, between Southwick and Widley. Dewhurst shared another Ju 88 on October 28. In December 1940 he was 'B' Flight Commander.

Awarded the AFC (3.4.45), Dewhurst was released from the RAF in 1946, as a Squadron Leader.

APO 15.4.39   PO 6.11.39   FO 6.11.40   FL 6.11.41
SL 1.7.45   FL 18.11.45

PETER GRENFELL DEXTER

41680   FO   Pilot   British   603 and 54 Squadrons

Dexter flew with a Lysander army co-operation squadron in France in 1940 and shot down a Bf 109 whilst carrying out a reconnaissance for the Army. For his service in France he was awarded the DFC (23.7.40).

In late June 1940 Dexter joined 603 Squadron at Dyce. He was posted to 54 Squadron at Hornchurch on September 3 but rejoined 603 on the 16th. He claimed a Bf 109 destroyed on the 27th. On this day Dexter flew back with Pilot Officer Cardell of 603, when the latter, after being wounded in an engagement over the Channel, tried to reach the English coast. Cardell was forced to bale out just off-shore at Folkestone. Dexter tried to draw attention to Cardell's plight but having failed to do so he made a forced-landing on Folkestone beach, commandeered a boat and went to his friend's rescue but Cardell was dead when they reached him.

On October 2 Dexter shot down a Bf 109 over Croydon but was then himself shot down. He baled out, wounded in the leg. He was trapped by his leg as he abandoned the aircraft and fell 15000 feet before wrenching his foot free of his flying boot. Dexter was just high enough for his parachute to open. He spent the next six months in hospital.

In June 1941 he was posted to 611 Squadron at Hornchurch. He was killed on July 14 1941 after colliding with a Spitfire of 54 Squadron over Boulogne. He managed to bale out but the Red Cross later reported that he had been picked up dead in his parachute.

Dexter's remains were repatriated to Britain after the war.

APO 4.3.39   PO 30.9.39   FO 30.9.40

ROLAND HAROLD DIBNAH

42675   PO   Pilot   Canadian   1 and 242 Squadrons

Dibnah, of Winnipeg, joined the RAF on a short service commission in June 1939. After completing his training he was posted to 6 OTU, Sutton Bridge and from there joined No 1 Squadron in France in May 1940. On May 29 Dibnah was wounded in the thigh in a combat over Ochamps and made a forced-landing at Nancy.

On August 31 1940 he damaged a Bf 110 and on September 5 claimed a Bf 110 destroyed. He was posted to 242 Squadron at Coltishall on September 21 and remained with the squadron until December 30 1940.

In January 1944 Dibnah joined 91 Squadron at Tangmere. He transferred to the RCAF on January 18 1945 and was released on October 21 1947, as a Flight Lieutenant.

APO 2.9.39   PO 28.2.40   FO 28.2.41   FL 28.5.42

WILLIAM GORDON DICKIE

80541   PO   Pilot   British   601 Squadron

Dickie, of Dundee, joined 601 Squadron at Middle Wallop in June 1940. On July 7 he shared in the destruction of a Do 17.

On August 11 he was reported 'Missing' following an action over the Channel off Portland. He was 24 years old and is remembered on the Runnymede Memorial, Panel 8.

PO 27.5.40

JOHN HOLT DICKINSON

740861   Sgt   Pilot   British   253 Squadron

With 253 Squadron in early July 1940. Dickinson was shot down on August 30 by Feldwebel Kock of II/JG 26 in an engagement over Dungeness. He baled out but is believed to have been killed by a Bf 109 on the way down. His Hurricane, P 3213, may be the one which crashed at Cuckolds Corner, Plurenden Manor, near Woodchurch.

Dickinson was 21. He is buried in St Mary's churchyard, Egton-with-Newland, Lancashire.

GIOVANNI DIEU

81633   PO   Pilot   Belgian   236 Squadron

An instructor in the Belgian Air Force, Dieu left Belgium in May 1940 and was employed in ferrying French aircraft. When France collapsed he flew to Bayonne and sailed in a Dutch cargo ship to England, arriving at Plymouth on June 23 1940.

Dieu joined 236 Squadron on August 5 1940. He left the squadron on August 4 1941 and went to the Belgian Flight of 609 Squadron at Gravesend.

At some later time he was awarded the AFC and released from the RAF after the war, as a Squadron Leader.

IVOR BENISON DIFFORD

39865   FO   Pilot   South African   85 and 607 Squadrons

Difford, of Johannesburg, joined the RAF on a short service commission in April 1937. After completing his elementary flying training he was posted on July 17 to 4 FTS, Abu Sueir.

On March 6 1938 he went to a job at SHQ RAF Kai Tak, Hong Kong. Difford joined 85 Squadron at Church Fenton on September 23 1940, moving to 607 Squadron at Tangmere on October 2.

He was killed on October 7 1940, when he crashed at Eartham Farm, Slindon in Hurricane L 1728. Difford was 30 years old and is buried in St Andrew's churchyard, Tangmere.

APO 5.7.37   PO 10.5.38   FO 10.12.39

MAXWELL PAUL DIGBY-WORSLEY

649007   Sgt   Air Gunner   British   248 Squadron

A pre-war airman, Digby-Worsley was with 248 Squadron in early July 1940. He was reported 'Missing' on August 19, when the Blenheim he was in failed to return from a reconnaissance of the south Norwegian coast.

Digby-Worsley, who came from Hornsey, Middlesex, was 18 years old. He is remembered on the Runnymede Memorial, Panel 13.

JOHN WILLIAM DITZEL

122553   Sgt   Wop/AG   British   25 Squadron

Born in London on March 26 1920, Ditzel joined the RAFVR in April 1939. He was called to full-time service at the outbreak of war and joined 29 Squadron at Debden in October 1939.

Ditzel was posted to 25 Squadron at North Weald in April 1940 and flew with the squadron until February 1941, when he went to 1417 Flight for a few weeks before being put on ferry duties. In April 1941 Ditzel was posted to 46 MU, Lossiemouth, where he took part in testing overhauled aircraft before their return to squadrons.

In September 1941 Ditzel joined 125 Squadron at Fairwood Common. Initially equipped with Defiants, the squadron began to receive Beaufighters in February 1942. Commissioned in May 1942, Ditzel began the process of retraining as a Navigator Radar in June and was posted away from 125. He went to 6 AOS, Staverton in August for a course, moved on to 62 OTU, Cranfield in October, then to 51 OTU there in March 1943.

In June Ditzel flew to Gibraltar on his way to North Africa. He joined 600 Squadron at Monte Corvino, Sicily in September 1943. On the night of January 29 1944, Ditzel picked up a Do 217 over the Anzio beaches. After a running fight his Beaufighter was shot down by anti-aircraft fire over Civitavecchia and he was captured.

Ditzel was released from the RAF in 1946, as a Flight Lieutenant.

PO 4.5.42   FO 4.11.42   FL 4.5.44

CHRISTOPHER ALEXANDER WILFRED DIXON

124628   Sgt   Pilot   British   601 Squadron

Dixon joined 601 Squadron at Debden on September 4 1940. He was commissioned in April 1942, left the RAF early in 1944 and died in 1977.

PO 9.4.42   FO 9.10.42

FREDERICK JOHN POWELL DIXON

742124   Sgt   Pilot   British   501 Squadron

Joined the RAFVR in 1938. Dixon was with 501 Squadron at Middle Wallop in early July 1940. On the 11th he was shot down by Oberleutnant Franziket of III/JG 27 in an action over a convoy ten miles south-east of Portland Bill. Dixon baled out but was drowned. The Weymouth lifeboat searched for him but in vain. He was 21 years old and is buried in Abbeville Communal Cemetery Extension, France.

GEORGE DIXON

59384   Sgt   Pilot   British   FIU

Born on October 12 1912, Dixon, of Shrewsbury, was with the Fighter Interception Unit in early July 1940.

He was in a Blenheim which failed to return from an operational patrol on the night of September 13. Dixon and the other two men aboard baled out and were captured. The Blenheim, Z 5721, crashed into the Channel off Calais.

Dixon was commissioned from Warrant Officer in June 1946, he retired on June 5 1948 and died on February 28 1972.

PO 26.6.46   FO 26.6.47

JOHN ANTONY DIXON

41683   FO   Pilot   British   1 Squadron

Dixon was born on March 23 1919. He joined the RAF on a short service commission in December 1938.

He was with No 1 Squadron at Northolt in early July 1940 and was posted away on August 10. Dixon's name does not appear in Air Force Lists after September 1941.

Dixon became a Master Pilot on March 1 1948 and was awarded the AFC (6.6.49). He was commissioned in March 1960 and retired on May 3 1973, as a Flight Lieutenant.

APO 4.3.39   FO 2.10.39   FO 2.10.40   FO 31.3.60
FL 31.3.63

LAWRENCE DIXON

116698   Sgt   Aircrew   British   600 Squadron

Joined 600 Squadron at Manston on July 25 1940. Dixon was

commissioned in November 1941 and in 1942 was with 125 Squadron. In October he teamed up with Squadron Leader FD Hughes and they shared a Ju 88 on November 4.

They were posted to 600 Squadron on January 13 1943 at Maison Blanche. They destroyed two Ju 88s on January 23 1943, claimed a Cant Z 1007 on February 12 and a Ju 88 on April 26. Dixon was awarded the DFC (13.4.43). He and Hughes destroyed a He 111 on July 13, a Ju 88 on the 21st, three Ju 88s on August 11 and a Ju 87 on August 18. Dixon was awarded a Bar to the DFC (28.9.43).

On July 19 1944 Dixon joined 604 Squadron at Colerne, to fly again with Hughes, who had just taken command of the squadron. On August 6 they destroyed a Ju 88 and finally on January 14 1945 a Ju 188 over Rotterdam.

Dixon was released from the RAF in 1947, as a Squadron Leader.

PO 21.11.41   FO 1.10.42   FL 21.11.43

NICHOLAS ROBERT DOBREE

75018   FO   Air Gunner   British   264 Squadron

Dobree was posted to 264 Squadron on September 18 1940. He was released from the RAF in 1945, as a Group Captain.

PO 6.10.39   FO 6.2.40   FL 6.2.41   SL 14.2.42
WC 1.3.44

JOHN DODGSON DODD

84322   PO   Pilot   British   248 Squadron

A chartered accountant from East Horsley, Surrey, Dodd joined 248 Squadron on September 29 1940.

He was reported 'Missing' on December 13 1940. Detailed to fly to Wick for operations, Dodd collided with another Blenheim whilst they were formating. His aircraft crashed into the sea and sank and Dodd and his crew of two were lost. He was 27 years old and is remembered on the Runnymede Memorial, Panel 8.

PO 24.8.40

CHARLES WILLIAM DODGE

507141   Sgt   Aircrew   British   219 Squadron

A pre-war airman, Dodge was with 219 Squadron at Catterick in July 1940. He became a Warrant Officer on March 1 1942.

Dodge died in 1982.

ROBERT FRANCIS THOMAS DOE

41908   PO   Pilot   British   234 and 238 Squadrons

Born on March 10 1920 at Reigate, Surrey, Doe started work as an office boy at the News of the World. In March 1938 he joined the RAFVR and began training at 5 E&RFTS Hanworth, soloing on June 4.

Doe applied for a short service commission, was successful and joined the RAF in January 1939. He did his elementary flying training at 15 E&RFTS, Redhill and went on to 6 FTS, Little Rissington, after which he joined 234 Squadron, then reforming at Leconfield, on November 6 1939.

Doe claimed two Bf 110s destroyed on August 15, Bf 109s on the 16th and 18th, a Ju 88 on the 21st, a Bf 109 on the 26th, three Bf 110s on September 4, Bf 109s on the 5th and 6th and a He 111 on the 7th. He was posted to 238 Squadron at Middle Wallop on September 27, claimed a Bf 109 destroyed on October 1 and a Ju 88 on the 7th. Doe was awarded the DFC (22.10.40) and a Bar (26.11.40).

He was shot down on October 10 over Warmwell and baled out, wounded in the shoulder and the leg, and after landing at Brownsea Island was admitted to Poole Hospital. His Hurricane, P 3984, crashed near Corfe Castle Viaduct. Doe rejoined 234 at the end of December.

On January 3 1941 he was up at night when the oil in the cooler froze. Doe headed for Warmwell. At 6000 feet his engine stopped and he glided down to make a rapid landing on the snow-covered airfield. His harness broke and Doe was thrown forward, breaking his arm and smashing his face against the reflector sight. He went eventually to Park Prewitt Hospital and into the care of Harold Gillies, a distinguished plastic surgeon from New Zealand. After twenty-two operations Doe went to 66 Squadron at Perranporth on May 15 1941, as a Flight Commander, but moved to 130 Squadron at Portreath on August 18.

With his tour completed Doe was posted to 57 OTU, Hawarden on October 22 1941, as an instructor. On June 9 1943 he went to the Fighter Leaders' School, Milfield and in July to 118 Squadron at Coltishall, as a supernumerary. From August to October Doe was with 613 Squadron, was then posted to Burma and in December was given the job of forming 10 (IAF) Squadron. He commanded the squadron throughout the Burma campaign and was awarded the Indian DSO (2.10.45), one of the only two men to be so honoured.

After leaving 10 in April 1945 Doe went to the Army Staff College, Quetta and in August joined the planning staff at Delhi. He returned to the UK in September 1946. He held a number of staff appointments and commands before his retirement on April 1 1966, as a Wing Commander.

APO 20.3.39   PO 6.11.39   FO 6.11.40   FL 6.11.41
FL 1.9.45   SL 1.1.49   WC 1.1.56

FRANTISEK DOLEZAL

82593   PO   Pilot   Czechoslovakian   19 Squadron

Dolezal escaped from Czechoslovakia in 1938 and went to France, where he joined l'Armée de l'Air. In the fighting in 1940 he is believed to have destroyed two German aircraft and probably two others.

After the collapse Dolezal went to England. He was commissioned in the RAF in August and posted to 310 Squadron but was immediately attached to 19 Squadron at Fowlmere. On September 7 he claimed a Bf 110 destroyed, on the 10th a Bf 109 and on the 18th a He 111. He was wounded in the leg and his aircraft severely damaged in combat over London on September 11.

In January 1941 Dolezal returned to 310 Squadron at Duxford. He commanded the squadron from April 1942. He probably destroyed a Do 217 over Dieppe on August 19. Dolezal was awarded the DFC in 1942. In January 1943 he was promoted to lead the Czech Wing.

Dolezal left the RAF, as a Wing Commander, on March 3 1945 to join the Czech forces. He was killed in a flying accident in Czechoslovakia on October 4 1945.

PO 2.8.40   FO 27.12.40

MARIAN BOGUSLAW DOMAGALA

P 1904   Sgt   Pilot   Polish   238 Squadron

Domagala was born on March 23 1909. He joined 238 Squadron at Middle Wallop on August 5 1940. On the 8th he claimed a Bf 109 and a Bf 110 destroyed and on the 11th another Bf 109. He was awarded the KW (23.12.40) and a Bar (1.2.41).

On April 6 1941 Domagala was posted to 302 Squadron at Westhampnett, moving on September 15 to 317 Squadron at Exeter. With his operational tour completed Domagala went to 58 OTU, Grangemouth on February 4 1942, as an instructor. He was sent to 2 FIS,

Montrose for an instructor's course and did further courses at 10 FIS, Woodley and 25 EFTS, Hucknall. He was commissioned in June 1942.

On March 12 1943 Domagala was appointed as an instructor at 25 EFTS. He was posted to 16 SFTS, Newton on December 18 1944 for a twin-engine conversion course, after which he was made a staff pilot there.

Posted away in November 1945, Domagala was released in December 1946, as a Flight Lieutenant. He was awarded a further two Bars to the KW (31.10.47). Domagala settled in Scotland.

PO 1.6.42   FO 1.12.42   FL 1.6.44

RALPH STIDSTON DON

81348   PO   Pilot   British   501 Squadron

Don, of Ferndown, Dorset, was commissioned from Sergeant in May 1940. He joined 501 Squadron at Croydon in June. On July 31 he was shot down in combat with Ju 87s and Bf 109s over Dover. Don baled out, injured, and was admitted to Canterbury Hospital. His Hurricane, P 3646, crashed and burned out at Lydden Marsh.

In October 1944 Don was given command of 142 Squadron on its reformation with Mosquito PR 16s for photo-reconnaissance duties. He was reported 'Missing' on January 22 1945. He was 25 and is remembered on the Runnymede Memorial, Panel 264.

Don was awarded the DFC (11.12.45) for his work with the squadron.

PO 26.5.40   FO 26.5.41   FL 26.5.42

ARTHUR GERALD DONAHUE

81624   PO   Pilot   American   64 Squadron

Born in St Charles, Minnesota in 1913, Donahue was educated at the High School there. He learned to fly privately and had his private and commercial pilot's licenses before he was 19. For several years he instructed trainee pilots, barnstormed and gave pleasure flights. In between-times he worked on the family farm.

In 1938 Donahue flew to Laredo, Texas to join a friend in starting a business to train pilots and do aerial taxi work. He worked in Texas in the winter and did similar work in Wisconsin in the summer. In mid-June 1940 he heard that pilots were being enlisted in Canada for the RAF. Donahue went up, was accepted and ten days later sailed for the UK. He signed forms at the Air Ministry and was fitted for a uniform.

Six days after landing Donahue was at 7 OTU, Hawarden. He joined 64 Squadron at Kenley on August 3 1940. Two days later he landed at Hawkinge with serious damage following a combat with Bf 109s off the French coast. On the 12th Donahue was shot down during an engagement off the South Coast. He baled out, with injuries to the right leg and burns. His Spitfire, X 4018, crashed and burned out at Sellinge.

After some time in hospital he rejoined 64 in mid-September. On the 29th he was posted to 71 Squadron, newly-reformed at Church Fenton from American volunteers. With no operations being flown Donahue was posted away on October 23 at his own request and he rejoined 64.

In late February 1941 he was posted to 91 Squadron at Hawkinge. Donahue went home to America on leave in March and arrived back in London on April 17 and rejoined 91. He destroyed a Bf 109 on August 17. In October 1941 Donahue was posted to 258 Squadron, then about to go overseas.

The squadron sailed in HMS 'Athene' for Gibraltar, where they spent a weary five weeks before sailing again. They finally reached Takoradi on January 1 1942. The pilots were then flown to Port Sudan and there they embarked on the carrier HMS 'Indomitable'. After sailing south for nearly three weeks the pilots flew Hurricanes off on January 28 to Kemajoran, Java, moving on to Palembang, Sumatra

AG Donahue (continued)

after refuelling. In the afternoon of the same day they flew on to Seletar airfield, Singapore to face the Japanese.

After a few days heavy fighting and heavy losses the squadron withdrew to Palembang. Donahue remained in Singapore and flew with 232 Squadron. When the Japanese invaded Singapore Island he just managed to escape in a Buffalo and landed at a jungle airfield 55 miles south-west of Palembang and on the following morning he rejoined 258 Squadron.

On February 16 1942 Donahue was badly wounded in the left leg whilst strafing boats carrying Japanese troops. He got back to Palembang and was flown out in a Hudson to the Dutch military hospital at Bandoeng, Java. He was evacuated in a hospital ship to India and eventually rejoined 258 in Ceylon in April 1942. Donahue was awarded the DFC (27.3.42).

He returned to the UK and in August was back with 91 Squadron at Lympne. On an early morning weather reconnaissance over the French coast on September 11 1942 Donahue shot down a Ju 88 but his Spitfire was damaged by return fire. He radioed back that his engine was overheating and that he was ditching in the Channel. The weather conditions were severe and ASR launches could not find him.

Donahue is remembered on the Runnymede Memorial, Panel 65.

IAN DAVID GRAHAME DONALD

33306   FO   Pilot   British   141 Squadron

Donald, of Epsom, Surrey, entered RAF College, Cranwell as a flight cadet in January 1936. After graduation he joined 64 Squadron at Church Fenton on December 18 1937.

During the 1938 Air Exercises Donald was pilot of one of a formation of 64 Squadron Demons caught by a dense fog, which descended suddenly over a wide area of England on August 7. They were routed over Digby and then all pilots and gunners were ordered to bale out.

Donald joined 141 Squadron, when it was reformed at Turnhouse on October 4 1939. He was flying one of the nine Defiants attacked by Bf 109s of lll/JG 51 off Dover on July 19 1940. Both Donald and his gunner, Pilot Officer AC Hamilton, were killed. Their Defiant, L 7009, crashed at Elmsvale Road, Dover.

Donald was 22. He is buried in All Saints' churchyard, Tilford, Surrey.

PO 18.12.37   FO 18.6.39

EDWARD MORTLOCK DONALDSON

32043   WC   Pilot   British   151 Squadron

The son of a judge, Donaldson was born in Negri Sembilan, Federated Malay States on February 22 1912. He went to England at the age of six and was educated at King's School, Rochester, Christ's Hospital and McGill University, Canada. He joined the RAF in March 1931 and did his flying training at 2 FTS, Digby.

On June 20 1932 Donaldson joined 3 Squadron at Upavon. He won the Brooke-Popham Air Firing Trophy in 1933 and 1934 and led the aerobatic displays at Hendon in 1935 and 1937 and at the International Rally at Zurich in 1937. Donaldson went to No 1 Squadron at Tangmere on July 2 1936, as a Flight Commander. In August 1938 he joined the staff at 7 FTS, Peterborough and on November 14 took command of 151 Squadron at North Weald.

Using Vitry as an advanced landing ground 151 took part in the fighting in France in May 1940. On the 17th Donaldson destroyed two Ju 87s, the next day a Bf 110 and on the 22nd another two Ju 87s. Over Dunkirk he shared a probable Bf 109 on May 29, damaged a Ju 88 on June 1, destroyed a Bf 110 on June 2 and two Bf 109s on the 7th. He was awarded the DSO (31.5.40).

On July 14 Donaldson claimed a Bf 109 destroyed. He was posted from 151 on August 5 to be CFI at 5 FTS, Sealand. In 1941 he was

sent to the USA to help organise gunnery schools and to teach combat techniques. He was awarded the AFC (30.9.41).

In 1944, after a period at the Empire Central Flying School, Donaldson was given command of RAF Colerne, the first permanent base for jet fighters in the UK. He later commanded RAF Milfield. Donaldson took command of the RAF High Speed Flight in early 1946 and on September 7 he gained the World's Speed Record in a Meteor at 616 mph. He was awarded the Britannia Trophy and received a Bar to the AFC (12.6.47).

Donaldson retired from the RAF on March 21 1961, as an Air Commodore. He was made a CBE (1.6.53), a CB (1.1.60) and received the US Legion of Merit (1948). After his retirement he was Air Correspondent for the Daily Telegraph until 1979.

PO 26.6.31   FO 26.6.33   FL 1.4.36   SL 1.12.38
WC 1.3.40   GC 1.1.44   GC 1.7.49   AC 1.7.55

WILLIAM STANLEY DOSSETT

49697   Sgt   Air Gunner   British   29 Squadron

Dossett was born on November 1 1919 and joined 29 Squadron in early 1940. He was posted away on July 27 1940.

In 1942 Dossett was with 107 Squadron, operating in Bostons from Great Massingham, Norfolk. He was awarded the DFM (22.9.42), as a Flight Sergeant.

Commissioned in August 1942, Dossett retired from the RAF on May 22 1954, as a Flight Lieutenant.

PO 10.8.42   FO 10.2.43   FL 10.8.44   FL 10.2.46

NEVILLE ANTHONY RICHARD DOUGHTY

72477   FO   Pilot   British   247 Squadron

Doughty was born on April 5 1919 and joined the RAF on a short service commission in July 1938. He was with 247 Squadron at Roborough during the Battle of Britain.

On April 27 1941 Doughty flew off HMS 'Ark Royal' to Malta. He went on to the Middle East in May and joined 261 Squadron when it reformed at Habbaniya on July 12 1941, as a Flight Commander.

Doughty was posted to the Air Ministry on November 13 1944 to serve in the Mechanical Transport and Marine Craft section of the Directorate of Organisation. He was released from the RAF in 1946 but later rejoined and finally retired on January 6 1958, as a Squadron Leader.

APO 13.9.38   PO 30.9.39   FO 30.9.40   FL 30.9.41
SL 1.7.45   SL 1.8.47

WILLIAM ANDERSON DOUGLAS

90896   PO   Pilot   British   610 Squadron

Born in Edinburgh in 1921, Douglas joined 603 Squadron, AuxAF on April 23 1939. He had done some flying training before he was mobilised on August 24 1939.

Douglas was posted to 7 FTS, Peterborough on October 7 and after completing his training he rejoined 603 Squadron at Montrose on March 17 1940. He was posted away to 3 BGS, Aldergrove as a staff pilot on May 7, moved to 8 BGS, Evanton on July 3 and on September 5 went to 7 OTU, Hawarden, after which he joined 610 Squadron at Acklington on September 16.

Douglas was posted back to 603, then at Drem, on February 27 1941. He damaged a Bf 109 on June 14, destroyed another on the 21st and was wounded on the 23rd by cannon shell splinters, on a patrol near Calais. He was off operations until November 1941 and became a Guinea Pig after being in Queen Victoria Hospital, East Grinstead.

In April 1942 603 was posted overseas and the pilots and aircraft were embarked on the USS 'Wasp' on the 12th. They flew off to Ta Kali, Malta on the 20th. Douglas destroyed a Ju 88 on the 25th, a Bf 109 on May 9, a probable Ju 87 on the 10th and shared a Bf 109 on the 11th. On this day he collided with another Spitfire and baled out.

Douglas took command of the squadron on July 20 1942. It was disbanded on August 3 and he was given command of a new unit, reformed as 229 Squadron. With his tour completed he flew back to the UK on September 23 and on October 2 was posted to 58 OTU, Grangemouth, as an instructor. Douglas was awarded the DFC (4.12.42).

He was attached to 453 Squadron at Hornchurch on May 7 1943 and got a probable Ju 87 on the 10th, went as an instructor to the

Fighter Command School of Tactics at Charmy Down on July 7 and on August 18 was given command of 611 Squadron at Kenley. On June 10 1944 Douglas destroyed a Ju 88 and four days later a Bf 109. In August he was appointed Wing Commander Flying at Coltishall. He destroyed a Ju 88 in September and was awarded a Bar to the DFC (26.9.44).

Douglas was released from the RAF on December 17 1945, as a Wing Commander.

APO 24.8.39   PO 17.3.40   FO 1.12.40   FL 1.12.41
SL 3.7.45

MICHAEL DUKE DOULTON

90235   FO   Pilot   British   601 Squadron

Reputed to be the tallest pilot in the RAF in his day, Doulton, a mechanical engineer, joined 604 Squadron, AuxAF in 1931. He went on to the Reserve in September 1936 and was recalled on August 24 1939.

Doulton was with 601 Squadron in early July 1940. On the 11th he shared a Do 215, on the 20th a He 59, on August 15 he shared a Ju 88 and the next day destroyed a Ju 87. He was shot down on August 31 1940 in action over the Thames Estuary and reported 'Missing'. He was 31 and is remembered on the Runnymede Memorial, Panel 5.

However, an aircraft excavated south of Wennington Church, near Romford on April 27 1984 proved to be Hurricane R 4215 and Doulton's remains were still in the cockpit. He was cremated in a private ceremony at Hastings in June 1984 and his ashes interred in Salehurst churchyard, East Sussex.

PO (AuxAF) 29.9.31   FO (AuxAF) 29.3.33
FO (AuxAFRO) 29.9.36   FO 24.8.39

BASIL DOUTHWAITE

44928   PO   Pilot   British   72 Squadron

Douthwaite was with 72 Squadron as a Sergeant-Pilot in May 1940. Over Dunkirk on June 2 he probably destroyed a Ju 87.

Commissioned in August 1940, Douthwaite claimed a Bf 109 destroyed on September 1. He was wounded on the 11th and returned to Croydon damaged, following an action over Gravesend. His Spitfire, R 6710, was a write-off.

On November 9 1940 Douthwaite shared a He 111. He was released from the RAF in 1945, as a Flight Lieutenant.

PO 21.8.40   FO 21.8.41   FL 21.8.42

GEORGES LOUIS JOSEPH DOUTREPONT

82157   PO   Pilot   Belgian   229 Squadron

After leaving Belgium in May 1940 Doutrepont went to France.

On June 21 the French signed an Armistice with the Germans and the Belgians were told to stay put. With other pilots Doutrepont reached Port Vendres, where with the help of a British destroyer and the support of the Belgian Embassy in London they caught a passing convoy and embarked on the SS 'Apapa' on the 24th. After arriving in Liverpool on July 7 Doutrepont was commissioned in the RAF on the 19th.

He was posted to 7 OTU,

Hawarden on July 24 and after converting to Hurricanes he joined 229 Squadron at Wittering on August 4. Doutrepont destroyed a Do 17 and shared a He 111 on September 11. On the 15th he was shot down and killed by enemy fighters over the Sevenoaks area. His Hurricane, N 2537, crashed on Staplehurst Station.

Doutrepont was 27. His remains were exhumed on October 20 1949 and re-interred in the Pelouse d'Honneur Cemetery of Brussels at Evere.

PO 19.7.40

DEREK HUGH TREMENHEERE DOWDING

33422   FO   Pilot   British   74 Squadron

Dowding was born on January 9, 1919, the son of Group Captain HCT Dowding, later Air Chief Marshal Lord Dowding. He was educated at Winchester College and entered RAF College, Cranwell as a flight cadet in September 1937. On graduation at the end of July 1939 Dowding was commissioned and posted to 74 Squadron at Hornchurch.

The squadron flew patrols over France from May 20 1940. On the 24th Dowding destroyed a Do 17, shared another and probably destroyed a Ju 88, on the 23rd he shared a Do 17 and on the 27th damaged a Do 17 after chasing it for 20 miles before being forced to break off by intense anti-aircraft fire. He claimed a share in destroying a He 111 on July 8.

Dowding was posted from 74 on August 6 1940. He was instructing in 1941 and became a Flight Commander with 135 Squadron later in the year. He served as a test pilot in the Middle East from 1942 to 1945 and held a number of appointments and commands before retiring on November 17 1956, as a Wing Commander.

PO 29.7.39   FO 3.9.40   FL 3.9.41   SL 1.10.46
WC 1.7.51

JOHN KNIGHT DOWN

133043   Sgt   Pilot   British   64 and 616 Squadrons

Joined the RAFVR at Bristol in March 1939 and started flying at 39 E&RFTS, Weston-super-Mare in July. Called up at the outbreak of war, Down was posted to 5 ITW, Hastings in November.

He moved to 11 EFTS, Perth in April 1940, went on to 15 FTS, Brize Norton in June and after two weeks at 7 OTU, Hawarden in September Down joined 64 Squadron at Leconfield on October 7 1940. The stay was short and he moved to 616 Squadron at Kirton-in-Lindsey on the 13th.

Down was posted to 611 Squadron at Hornchurch in December 1940 and to 91 Squadron at Hawkinge in February 1941. Whilst with 91 he damaged two enemy aircraft. He was posted to 52 OTU, Aston Down in November 1941, was sent on an instructor's course to CFS, Upavon in January 1942, after which he continued to instruct at 52 OTU until rejoining 91 Squadron at Hawkinge in August 1942. He was commissioned from Warrant Officer in September.

Down joined 1696 Flight, AFDU at Bourn in August 1943. He went to HQ ADGB, Kenley in May 1944 and was later with the Communications Squadron at Northolt. He was posted to the Indian Air Force at Karachi in February 1945, later returning to the UK, where he was demobilised at RAF Rugeley on November 30 1945.

PO 18.9.42   FO 18.3.43   FL 18.9.44

PETER DERRICK McLEOD DOWN

39934   FO   Pilot   British   56 Squadron

Down joined the RAF on a short service commission in May 1937, was posted to 9 FTS, Hullavington on July 17 and joined 56 Squadron at North Weald on February 19 1938. He was in the squadron's aerobatic team before the war.

On May 16 1940 Down went with 'B' Flight to Vitry-en-Artois to support the squadrons in France. He destroyed a He 111 east of Cambrai on the 17th and damaged another. The Flight was withdrawn after four days. Down claimed a Bf 110 destroyed on August 18 and a Bf 109 on the 19th. He was posted away from 56 on September 26.

Down went to the Middle East in December 1941, he commanded 112 Squadron at Gambut in April/May 1942. He returned to the UK in mid-1943, was later at 2 FIS, Montrose and became CFI at 5 ATS, Tern Hill in November 1943. He was released from the RAF in 1945, as a Squadron Leader.

APO 12.7.37   PO 18.5.38   FO 18.8.40   FL 18.8.41

──────── DRABY

No unknown   Sgt   Aircrew   British   25 Squadron

No service details traced.

BILLY DRAKE

39095   FL   Pilot   British   421 Flight

Born in London on December 20 1917, Drake joined the RAF on a short service commission in July 1936. He was posted to 6 FTS, Netheravon on September 19 and with training completed joined No 1 Squadron at Tangmere on May 22 1937.

Drake went to France with the squadron in September 1939. On April 20 1940 he destroyed a Bf 109, on May 10 a He 111 and on May 13 he shot down a Do 17 and probably another but was jumped by Bf 110s and shot down. He baled out, wounded, was taken to a French hospital and later flown back to an RAF hospital in England.

In late October Drake returned to operations, joining 421 Flight at Hawkinge, as a Flight Commander. On December 7 he shared a Do 17 and in January 1941 was awarded the DFC (7.1.41). He was posted to 53 OTU, Heston in February, as an instructor. He went overseas in early October to form and command 128 Squadron at Hastings in West Africa.

Drake went to Air HQ Middle East in April 1942 and was given command of 112 Squadron at Gambut on May 24. He claimed a probable Bf 109 on June 6, another probable on July 2, destroyed Bf 109s on July 8 and 24, destroyed two Ju 87s on September 1, a Bf 109 on the 13th, shared a Ju 87 and probably destroyed another on October 1, got a probable Bf 109 on October 22, destroyed another on the 26th, a Mc 202 on the 27th, a Ju 87 on the 31st, a Bf 109 on November 5, a He 111 on the 15th, a Bf 110 and another damaged on the 19th, a Mc 202 and à Bf 109 on December 11 and finally a shared Bf 109 on the 13th. Drake was awarded a Bar to the DFC (28.7.42) and the DSO (4.12.42).

In January 1943 Drake was promoted to Wing Commander and posted to HQ RAF Cairo. He took command of the Spitfire Wing in Malta in June 1943 and before returning to the UK was credited with another six enemy aircraft destroyed. He received the DFC (US)(22.10.43).

He was appointed Wing Leader 20 Wing, Typhoons, in late November 1943 and in May 1944 Drake was sent to America on special duties. Back in the UK he was made deputy commander at Biggin Hill and later went to HQ SHAEF to serve in the Operations Room.

Drake took part in the 1945 Battle of Britain flypast. He retired from the RAF on July 1 1963, as a Wing Commander, retaining the rank of Group Captain.

APO 7.9.36   PO 13.7.37   FO 13.4.39   FL 3.9.40
SL 1.12.41   SL 1.9.45   WC 1.1.53

GEORGE JAMES DRAKE

42398   PO   Pilot   South African   607 Squadron

Drake was born in Hugenot, Cape Province on July 27 1920, the son of the stationmaster. He matriculated at Paarl Boys' High School in 1938 and tried to enlist in the SAAF but was unsuccessful. He made his way to England and joined the RAF on a short service commission in June 1939.

With his training completed Drake joined 607 Squadron at Usworth on August 10. He was shot down in combat over the Mayfield area on September 9 and reported 'Missing'. He is remembered on the Runnymede Memorial, Panel 8. His Hurricane, P 2728, crashed at Bockingfold Farm, Goudhurst. When this aircraft was excavated on May 21 1972 Drake's remains were still in the cockpit. He was buried with full military honours at Brookwood Military Cemetery on November 22 1972.

APO 5.8.39   PO 24.3.40

BRYAN VINCENT DRAPER

76309   PO   Pilot   British   74 Squadron

Draper, from Barry, South Wales, was commissioned in the RAF in December 1939 and joined 74 Squadron at Rochford on February 17 1940.

On May 25 he shared a Do 17 with four other pilots and on June 10 damaged a Do 17 and a Bf 109. Draper claimed a Ju 88 destroyed on September 14 and on October 17 he shot down a Bf 109, which made a belly-landing at Manston. The pilot, Oberleutnant Rupp, a Staffel Kapitan of JG 53 was captured unhurt. Three days later Draper crash-landed himself after his Spitfire, P 7355, was severely damaged in combat over South London, in which he claimed the probable destruction of a Bf 109.

He claimed three Ju 87s destroyed and a Bf 109 damaged on November 14 and a Bf 109 destroyed the next day. He was awarded the DFC (24.12.40) and posted away to CFS, Upavon on December 30 1940.

Draper was killed on February 28 1945, as a Squadron Leader with 45 Squadron. He was 28 and is buried in Taukkyan War Cemetery, Rangoon.

PO 10.12.39   FO 10.12.40   FL 10.3.42

GILBERT GRAHAM FAIRLEY DRAPER

42742   PO   Pilot   British   610 and 41 Squadrons

Born in December 1920, Draper was at Uppingham School from 1934 to 1937. He joined the RAF in August 1939 and began his elementary flying training at 19 E&RFTS, Gatwick and finished it at 18 E&RFTS, Fair Oaks. In October Draper was posted to 3 FTS, South Cerney.

In April 1940 he went to the School of Army Co-operation, Old Sarum and in May joined 2 Squadron at Sawbridgeworth. Draper volunteered for Fighter Command in August and was posted to 7 OTU, Hawarden. He joined 610 Squadron at Acklington on September 3 and moved to 41 Squadron at Hornchurch on the 29th. During a combat over Ashford on October 30 Draper was shot down in Spitfire P 7282. He crashed at New Barn Farm, Postling, slightly injured, and was admitted to Willesborough Hospital.

On August 7 1941 Draper was shot down over Fruge, near Lille and captured. He was released at the end of the war and went on to the Reserve of Officers on September 1 1945.

APO 9.10.39   PO 28.4.40   FO 28.4.41   FL 28.4.42
FL (RAFRO) 1.9.45

R A DRAPER

No unknown   Sgt   Pilot   British   232 Squadron

No service details traced.

ALLAN SYDNEY DREDGE

63785   Sgt   Pilot   British   253 Squadron

Dredge was serving with 253 Squadron in early July 1940. In a combat south of Biggin Hill on August 30 he fired at a Bf 109, which then collided with another and both went down. After capture the two pilots would not speak to each other.

On September 4 Dredge claimed a Bf 110 destroyed and on the 14th a Bf 109, which exploded over Beacon Hill, Stone.

Commissioned in March 1941, Dredge went to Malta in April, flying off HMS 'Ark Royal' on the 27th and joining 261 Squadron. He was shot down in flames on May 6 and baled out, badly burned. He was posted back to the UK in mid-July and was treated at Queen Victoria Hospital, East Grinstead, becoming a Guinea Pig.

In 1943 Dredge served with 183 Squadron and was awarded the DFC (27.7.43). He was given command of 3 Squadron at Manston in October 1943 and led it until August 1944, during which time he had destroyed six V1 flying bombs. He was awarded the DSO (5.12.44).

Dredge was killed in a flying accident in a Mosquito on May 18 1945, as a Wing Commander, aged 27. He is buried at St Paul's Cathedral, Coventry. His portrait was done by Cuthbert Orde.

PO 12.3.41   FO 12.3.42   FL 12.3.43

NIGEL GEORGE DREVER

42399   PO   Pilot   British   610 Squadron

Joined the RAF on a short service commission in June 1939. Drever was posted to 610 Squadron at Acklington on September 22 1940. He was later transferred to the Administrative Branch and was released from the RAF in 1946, as a Flight Lieutenant.

APO 5.8.39   PO 24.3.40   FO 24.3.41   FL 24.3.42

PETER EDWARD DREW

26199   SL   Pilot   British   236 Squadron

The son of Air Commodore BCH Drew, Drew was born on July 16 1910 and was at Marlborough College from 1924 to 1929. He entered RAF College, Cranwell as a flight cadet in September 1929 and on graduation joined No 1 Squadron at Tangmere on July 25 1931.

Drew was posted to the staff at SHQ Heliopolis on February 28 1933, returned to the UK in June 1935 and went to 6 FTS, Netheravon on March 30 1936, as an instructor. He was posted to the staff of CFS, Upavon on March 24 1937 and in July 1940 was commanding 236 Squadron.

On August 1 1940 Drew was shot down and killed during a bomber escort operation to attack Querqueville aerodrome, possibly a victim of the ground defences. He is buried in Biville churchyard, France.

PO 25.7.31   FO 25.1.33   FL 1.4.36   SL 1.12.38

BOLESLAW DROBINSKI

76731   PO   Pilot   Polish   65 Squadron

Drobinski was born at Ostrog on October 23 1918. He joined 65 Squadron at Turnhouse on September 11 1940.

He was posted to 303 Squadron at Northolt on March 2 1941. Drobinski shared in damaging a Ju 52 on the ground on May 15, he destroyed six Bf 109s between June 18 and July 3, shared another on July 7, probably destroyed one on October 24 and got his final Bf 109 on March 13 1942.

He was awarded the KW and Bar (15.7.41), the VM (5th Class)(10.9.41) and the DFC (30.10.41). He was posted to 58 OTU, Grangemouth on March 18 1942, as an instructor. He rejoined 303 Squadron on August 9, was awarded a second Bar to the KW (20.8.42) and returned to 58 OTU on April 9 1943.

Drobinski was posted to 317 Squadron at Northolt on October 18 1943, as a Flight Commander. He was appointed ADC to the Polish Minister of Defence on April 3 1944. He was awarded a third Bar to the KW (5.1.46) and posted away from the squadron on February 1 1946 to 61 OTU. Drobinski went to HQ 11 Group on March 20 1946 as Polish Liaison Officer. He was released in 1948 as a Squadron Leader and settled in England.

JOHN FRASER DRUMMOND

40810   FO   Pilot   British   46 and 92 Squadrons

Joined the RAF on a short service commission in April 1938. After completing his training Drummond was posted to 46 Squadron at Digby on January 14 1939.

He was with the squadron when it went to Norway in late May 1940. On the 29th he destroyed a He 111, on June 2 another and on June 7 he destroyed another He 111 and damaged two more. He did not fly off on to the 'Glorious' when the squadron was withdrawn and escaped the fate of most of 46's pilots, who were lost when the carrier was sunk. For his successes in Norway Drummond was awarded the DFC (26.7.40).

Drummond was posted to 92 Squadron at Pembrey on September 5 and claimed Bf 109s probably destroyed on the 11th and 22nd, a Bf 109 destroyed on the 23rd, a Ju 88 destroyed and a He 111 shared on the 27th and destroyed a Bf 109 and a Hs 126 on October 5.

During an attack on a Do 17 over Tangmere on October 10 Drummond collided with Pilot Officer DG Williams of 92. He baled out, wounded in an arm and a leg, but was too low and was killed. His Spitfire, R 6616, crashed and burned out in Jubilee Field, Portslade. His portrait was done by Cuthbert Orde.

Drummond was 21. He is buried in Thornton Garden of Rest, Lancashire.

APO 4.6.38   PO 4.4.39   FO 3.9.40

JOHN HOWARD DUART

77352   PO   Air Gunner   British   219 Squadron

Duart was an articled clerk with a chartered accountant before the war. He obtained his pilot's 'A' License in 1938 and joined the Civil Air Guard in 1939.

He volunteered for aircrew duties after the outbreak of war and was commissioned in February 1940 as a trainee air gunner. After completing a gunnery course at Manby Duart was posted to 219 Squadron at Catterick on March 16. He did a Gunnery Leaders' course in May and rejoined the squadron on June 18.

Duart served with 219 throughout the Battle of Britain and in April 1942 went on a Senior Armament Officer's course at Manby, after which he became Station Armament Officer at RAF Turnberry and later Long Kesh. In October 1943 he was posted to Canada and went to Penfield Ridge as Senior Armament Instructor.

JH Duart (continued)

In 1944 Duart returned to the UK and was with the Ministry of Defence, London until he was released on November 23 1945, as a Flight Lieutenant. He completed his articles and in May 1948 became a chartered accountant. For several years he was Hon Secretary and Treasurer of the Battle of Britain Fighter Association.

APO 3.2.40   PO 16.3.40   FO 16.3.41   FL 16.3.42

RONALD EDWIN DUBBER

Petty Officer (FAA)   Pilot   British   808 Squadron

Dubber was with 808 Squadron at Castletown in early July 1940, flying Fulmars on dockyard defence.

He embarked with the squadron in HMS 'Ark Royal' on October 22 1940 and took part in several actions in the Mediterranean in 1941. Dubber was commissioned in January 1943 and stayed in the FAA after the war. He died on September 10 1951.

Sub-Lt 1.1.43   Lt 1.7.44

BYRON LEONARD DUCKENFIELD

43368   PO   Pilot   British   74 and 501 Squadrons

Born on April 15 1917, Duckenfield joined 74 Squadron at Hornchurch on April 5 1940. He was posted to 501 Squadron at Middle Wallop on July 22.

On the 29th Duckenfield claimed a Ju 87 destroyed, on August 15 a Do 215, on the 28th a Bf 109 and another on September 8. He was later posted away on instructional duties and awarded the AFC (24.9.41).

In October 1941 Duckenfield was given command of 66 Squadron at Perranporth. In February 1942 he took command of 615 Squadron at Fairwood Common and in March took it to the Far East. In late December 1942 Duckenfield failed to return from an attack on Magwe airfield and was later reported as captured. He was released from captivity in Burma in May 1945.

Duckenfield retired from the RAF on June 28 1969, as a Group Captain.

PO 1.4.40   FO 1.4.41   FL 17.3.42   FL 1.9.45
SL 1.1.49   WC 1.7.59   GC 1.1.66

JOSEF DUDA

83224   PO   Pilot   Czechoslovakian   312 Squadron

In August 1939 Duda was Czech CO in Paris, as a Staff Captain. He joined 312 Squadron at Duxford on September 5 1940.

In 1944 he was in charge of the Czech Liaison Office at Fighter Command, as a Group Captain. Duda was made a CBE and held the Czech Military Cross. He returned to Czechoslovakia after the war and died there in the early seventies.

PO 17.8.40   FL 1.3.41

STANLEY SUTHERLAND DUFF

42340   PO   Pilot   British   23 Squadron

Duff joined the RAF on a short service commission in April 1939. He did his ab initio training at 12 E&RFTS, Prestwick and was posted to 11 FTS, Shawbury on July 22 1939. He was posted to 5 OTU, Aston Down on February 10 1940 and remained there until July 23, when he joined 23 Squadron at Wittering.

On June 19 1941 Duff went to 1451 Flight at Hunsdon, recently-formed with Turbinlite Havocs. He was posted to 141 Squadron at Acklington on February 10 1942, flying Beaufighters on night operations.

Duff flew from Lyneham on January 23 1943 to the Reinforcement Pool at Setif, North Africa, from where he joined 153 Squadron at Maison Blanche on February 13. For his work with the squadron in the night defence of Algiers and Bone Duff was awarded

the DFC (20.8.43). He returned to the UK in July 1943 and was posted to No 1 ADU at Croydon on August 8. When the unit moved to North Weald on July 4 1944 Duff was appointed CO.

He was attached to HQ Fighter Command for three months in early 1945, went on a course to 2 FIS, Montrose on April 4, moved to 5(P) AFU at Tern Hill on July 7, as an instructor and was released from the RAF at Uxbridge on December 1 1945, as a Squadron Leader.

APO 22.7.39   PO 10.2.40   FO 10.2.41   FL 10.2.42

RAYMOND MYLES BEECHAM DUKE DUKE-WOOLLEY

33241   FL   Pilot   British   23 and 253 Squadrons

Born on August 18 1916, Duke-Woolley was educated at Marlborough and entered RAF College, Cranwell in January 1935 as a flight cadet. He graduated in December 1936 and was posted to 23 Squadron at Northolt.

Appointed a Flight Commander in April 1940, Duke-Woolley destroyed a He 111 at night on June 18. When his night-flying tour was completed he asked to be posted to a day squadron. After his second request he went to 253 Squadron at Kenley on September 12. He claimed a probable Do 17 on the 15th. Duke-Woolley was promoted on the 27th and took temporary command of 253 after the CO was shot down and wounded.

He shared in the destruction of a Do 17 on October 6, destroyed a Ju 88 on November 9 and shared a Do 17 on the 22nd. In late November Duke-Woolley relinquished his temporary command and was awarded the DFC (24.12.40).

He was posted away in January 1941 and in May went to RAF Castletown to form and command 124 Squadron. He claimed the squadron's first victory, a Ju 88 shot down on December 17 1941. He was awarded a Bar to the DFC (29.5.42).

In June 1942 Duke-Woolley was made Wing Leader of the Debden Wing. He flew four sorties with 71 Squadron over Dieppe on August 19 1942, shared a FW 190 on October 2, was awarded the DSO (8.1.43) and posted away in January 1943 to HQ 8th USAAF Bomber Command as Fighter Liaison Officer. He was awarded the DFC (US)(5.3.43), the first time it was ever given to a non-American.

In July 1943 Duke-Woolley was given the job of forming and working up a Mobile Group Control Centre in 84 Group. He went to Normandy in June 1944, as second-in-command. He returned to England in January 1945 to go to RAF Staff College.

Duke-Woolley retired on January 30 1961, as a Group Captain.

PO 19.12.36   FO 19.6.38   FL 19.6.40   SL 1.9.41
WC 1.7.43   WC 1.7.47   GC 1.1.54

WILLIAM HOWARD DULWICH

751992   Sgt   Aircrew   British   235 Squadron

Dulwich, of Southend-on-Sea, was in the RAFVR before the war. He joined 235 Squadron on August 24 1940.

He was killed on August 2 1941, as a Flight Sergeant with 22 Squadron. Dulwich was 21 and is remembered on the Runnymede Memorial, Panel 36.

—————— DUNCAN

No unknown   Sgt   Aircrew   British   29 Squadron

No service details traced.

HUGH SPENCER LISLE DUNDAS

91001   **FO**   **Pilot**   **British**   **616 Squadron**

Dundas was born at Doncaster on July 22 1920 and was a trainee solicitor. He joined 616 Squadron, AuxAF in May 1939 and had completed part of his training before he was called to full-time service on August 24 1939. He was awarded his wings on October 2.

He flew with the squadron over Dunkirk in late May and early June 1940. On July 3 he shared a Do 17 over a convoy and on August 15 he destroyed a Ju 88 and shared another. On the 22nd Dundas was shot down by Bf 109s over Dover. He baled out and was admitted to Kent and Canterbury Hospital with arm and leg wounds.

On May 17 1941 Dundas destroyed a Bf 109, one of three attacking Worthing. He became a Flight Commander on July 5, destroyed a Bf 109 on the 10th, shared another on the 19th, got a probable Bf 109 on the 21st and shared another on the 23rd. He was awarded the DFC (5.8.41) and in September went to 610 Squadron at Leconfield.

Dundas was promoted to Acting Squadron Leader in December 1941 and given command of 56 Squadron. In November 1942 he was posted to Duxford to form the first Typhoon Fighter-Bomber Wing. He went to Tunisia in January 1943 to lead 324 Spitfire Wing and took it to Malta in June. On July 4 Dundas shared a Bf 109. He took the Wing to Sicily on July 7, moved to an airfield in the Salerno beach head in September and on September 24 shared a Ju 88.

In January 1944 Dundas went on to the personal staff of AVM H Broadhurst in the Advanced HQ Desert Air Force in Italy. He was awarded the DSO (3.3.44). In June he was made Wing Leader 244 Wing and in October was promoted to Group Captain and given command of the Wing. He was awarded a Bar to the DSO (20.3.45).

Dundas returned to the UK in September 1946 and retired from the RAF on January 25 1947, as a Wing Commander, retaining the rank of Group Captain. He became Air Correspondent for the Daily Express. Dundas joined 601 Squadron (RAuxAF) in 1946 and commanded the squadron from 1948 to 1950.

APO (AuxAF) 23.7.39   APO 24.8.39   PO 2.3.40
FO 2.10.40   FL 2.10.41   SL 11.2.43   WC 11.5.45
FO (RAuxAF) 23.4.47

JOHN CHARLES DUNDAS

90334   **FO**   **Pilot**   **British**   **609 Squadron**

The brother of HSL Dundas, Dundas went to Stowe School on a scholarship. He won a scholarship to Oxford when he was 17 and gained a First in Modern History at Christ College. He also won an award, which took him to the Sorbonne and Heidelberg.

Dundas joined 609 Squadron, AuxAF in 1938. He was then a journalist on the Yorkshire Post. He was called to full-time service on August 24 1939. In operations over Dunkirk Dundas destroyed a He 111 and a Do 17 on May 31 and damaged a He 111 on June 1.

He claimed a Bf 110 destroyed on July 13, another on the 19th, two more Bf 110s on August 11 and 12, a Ju 87 on the 13th, a Do 17 destroyed and a Ju 88 shared on the 14th, a probable Bf 110 on the 25th, a Do 17 shared on September 15, a Bf 110 on the 24th, a Do 17 on the 25th, a Bf 109 on the 26th, a Bf 110 on the 27th, a probable

Bf 110 on October 7 and a Bf 109 on the 15th. Dundas was awarded the DFC (22.10.40).

On November 27 he probably destroyed a Ju 88 and on the 28th he destroyed a Bf 109, flown by Major Helmut Wick. Almost immediately Dundas was himself attacked by Wick's No 2 and shot down after being chased out to sea. He was not seen again.

Dundas was 24. He is remembered on the Runnymede Memorial, Panel 4. He was awarded a Bar to the DFC (7.1.41).

PO (AuxAF) 18.7.38   PO 24.8.39   FO 18.1.40

JACK TOWNLEY DUNMORE

741448   **Sgt**   **Pilot**   **British**   **266 and 222 Squadrons**

Dunmore, of Egham, Surrey, joined 266 Squadron at Wittering on September 16 1940, moving to 222 Squadron at Hornchurch on October 1. On the 15th he shared in destroying a Bf 109 but had to make a forced-landing at Hawkinge, having suffered damage as well as running low on fuel.

Dunmore was killed on May 17 1941, as a Flight Sergeant. He is buried in the churchyard of The Annunciation, Chislehurst.

IAN LOVE DUNN

49222   **Sgt**   **Observer**   **British**   **235 Squadron**

Born on June 5 1920, Dunn joined the RAF as a direct-entry observer on February 6 1939. He was posted to No 1 AOS on June 20, moving to 9 AOS, Penrhos on August 1.

After training Dunn joined 29 Squadron at Debden on September 6 1939. Before he was posted to 235 Squadron at Bircham Newton on May 22 1940 Dunn had qualified as a Gunnery Leader at CGS, Warmwell. He served with 235 throughout the Battle of Britain and on November 20 1940 he joined 272 Squadron at Aldergrove, on anti-shipping operations.

Dunn went to 254 Squadron at Sumburgh on April 11 1941 and on July 14 he was posted to 2(Coastal) OTU, Catfoss. He was commissioned in June 1942 and remained at Catfoss until December 4 1942, when he joined 201(Flying Boat) Squadron, operating in Sunderlands from Lough Erne. On October 30 1943 Dunn went over to Catalinas, joining 190 Squadron at Sollum Voe, which became 210 Squadron on January 1 1944.

He was posted to RAF Chivenor on April 4 1944 and spent his time on short attachments to various squadrons until seconded to BOAC in July 1945 and becoming a Qualified 1st Class Civil Air Navigator.

Dunn was granted a Permanent Commission in 1945, the first navigator to be awarded one after the war. He was a graduate of RAF Staff College, RAF Flying College and held various staff appointments in Coastal Command before his retirement on December 23 1964, as a Wing Commander.

An LL B (Hons), Dunn settled in Australia and became a partner in a law firm, continuing as a consultant after he retired.

PO 11.6.42   FO 11.12.42   FL 11.6.44   FL 11.12.45
SL 1.7.53   WC 1.1.60

PETER WILLIAM DUNNING-WHITE

90543   **PO**   **Pilot**   **British**   **145 Squadron**

Dunning-White was born at Hadley Wood on April 16 1915 and educated at Harrow School, 1929 to 1933, and Jesus College, Cambridge. He was in the University Golf Team in 1935. In August 1938 he joined 601 Squadron, AuxAF at Hendon and made his first flight in an Avro Tutor on August 5.

He was called to full-time service on August 24 1939 and posted later to 6 FTS, Little Rissington and with conversion completed at 5 OTU, Aston Down he joined 29 Squadron at Drem in early May 1940.

PW Dunning-White (continued)

Dunning-White was posted to 145 Squadron at Westhampnett on July 2. On the 18th he shared a He 111, on the 22nd shared a Do 17, on August 8 destroyed a Ju 87 and a Bf 110, on the 11th destroyed a Bf 109 and got a probable Bf 109 on October 29. On January 10 1941 Dunning-White shared in the probable destruction of a Ju 88. He went to 615 Squadron at Kenley on March 13, as a Flight Commander. After shooting down a Bf 109 over Dungeness on April 15 Dunning-White's aircraft was severely damaged and he baled out over Dymchurch and was picked up from the sea by an ASR launch.

In early May 1941 he was posted to 59 OTU, Crosby-on-Eden, as an instructor. Dunning-White was awarded the DFC (6.6.41) and was decorated by the King at Buckingham Palace on July 17 1941. He was attached to 409 (RCAF) Squadron in early 1942 for night-flying experience and in March was posted to 255 Squadron at High Ercall. In November the squadron went to North Africa and in March 1943 Dunning-White was promoted to Acting Squadron Leader and made a Flight Commander. He returned to the UK later in the year and was posted to the staff at HQ Fighter Command.

Dunning-White moved to 100 Group Bomber Command in July 1944 and was released from the RAF on October 8 1945, as a Wing Commander. He was re-commissioned in the RAuxAF in 1946.

APO (AuxAF) 27.11.38   APO 24.8.39   PO 4.5.40
FO 9.12.40   FL 9.12.41   SL 4.11.44
FL (RAuxAF) 28.11.46

RAYMOND DOUGLAS DUNSCOMBE

87403   PO   Pilot   British   213 and 312 Squadrons

Born at Croydon on November 11 1918, Dunscombe worked on the London Stock Exchange before the war. As a Sergeant-Pilot he was with 213 Squadron in early July 1940 and on August 15 he claimed a Bf 110 destroyed. Later in the month he was posted to 312 Squadron at Duxford.

Dunscombe's aircraft was damaged in combat on September 17 and he baled out, sustaining injuries when he landed in a tree. His Hurricane, V 7228, crashed near Edenbridge, Kent.

Commissioned in October 1940, Dunscombe underwent plastic surgery at some time at Queen Victoria Hospital, East Grinstead and was a Guinea Pig.

He was killed on Crete on May 31 1941, as a Pilot Officer with 33 Squadron. Dunscombe is remembered on the Alamein Memorial, Column 241.

PO 16.10.40

FELIX PATRICK RAPHAEL DUNWORTH

28185   FL   Pilot   British   66 and 54 Squadrons

Dunworth joined the RAF in 1929 and was posted to 3 FTS, Grantham on October 26. He joined 25 Squadron at Hawkinge on October 8 1930, was appointed PA to the AOC Fighting Area, Uxbridge on April 24 1933 and went on to the RAFO on October 11 1934.

Recalled on September 1 1939, Dunworth was with 66 Squadron at Coltishall in early July 1940. He was slightly wounded on September 4 in a combat over the Thames Estuary and made a forced-landing at Great Cowbridge Farm, near Billericay, in Spitfire N 3044.

Dunworth was promoted and given command of 54 Squadron at Catterick on September 9. He was posted away in December 1940.

He was awarded the AFC (3.4.45) and released from the RAF in 1946, as a Wing Commander.

PO 11.10.29   FO 14.4.31   FL (RAFO) 1.4.36   FL 1.9.39
SL 1.12.41

OSWALD ARTHUR DUPEE

123298   Sgt   Pilot   British   219 Squadron

Dupee was with 219 Squadron at Catterick in June 1940. On August 15 Dupee was flying in Blenheim L 8698 with Sergeant TH Banister, when their aircraft was hit by return fire from a He 111 engaged off Scarborough. Dupee was wounded in the arm. Banister went forward, assisted Dupee from his seat and took control of the damaged aircraft. Dupee, although weak from loss of blood, directed Banister, who was thus enabled to make a forced-landing, with undercarriage retracted. For this action both men were awarded the DFM (24.9.40).

Commissioned in May 1942, Dupee was awarded the DFC (21.1.44), as a Flying Officer with 684 Squadron, a Mosquito photographic-reconnaissance unit in the Far East. He was released from the RAF after the war and rejoined in 1948 in the Technical Branch (Signals).

On April 30 1968 he joined the Engineering Staff, Strike Command. His name did not appear in the Air Force List after Spring 1969.

PO 9.5.42   FO 9.11.42   FL 9.5.44   FL 20.12.48
SL 1.1.56

CARROLL RONALD DURRANT

NZ 40605   Sgt   Air Gunner   New Zealander   23 Sqdn

Born in Wellington on April 5 1919, Durrant was educated at Rongotai College and worked as a monotype operator at the Government Printing Office. He was in the Territorial Army for 2 years prior to volunteering for aircrew duties in November 1939.

Durrant reported to the Ground Training School, Weraroa on February 13 1940, going a month later to the Air Observers' School, Ohakea for a gunnery course. He sailed for the UK in the RMS 'Rangitiki' on April 26. After a period at Uxbridge Durrant was posted to 5 OTU, Aston Down, where he was awarded his air gunner's badge after further training. He joined 23 Squadron at Ford on September 21 1940.

Durrant was with the squadron until early March 1942, when he was posted to 116 Squadron at Hooton Park, flying in Lysanders on radar calibration duties. In May 1942 he went to 1653 Conversion Unit, Polebrook for crewing-up and conversion to Liberators. Commissioned in June, Durrant joined 1445 Flight, Ferry Command at Lyneham and flew in a Liberator on a delivery flight to Egypt, returning as a passenger in various civil aircraft, including a Boeing Clipper. On arrival back Durrant was sent to hospital, suffering from malaria.

He returned to duty in early October and was posted to 160 Squadron at Aqir, Palestine. Durrant arrived there in a Liberator on October 19 1942. Eight days later he took off on a night operational flight to Crete. Radio contact was lost in the early hours of the 28th and the crew are officially presumed to have been lost on this date. Another member of the crew was New Zealander Pilot Officer CC Reilly. He and Durrant had been together from the day they joined up.

After the war Durrant's remains were re-interred in the Suda Bay Military Cemetery, Crete.

PO 10.6.42

MARIAN DURYASZ

76750   FO   Pilot   Polish   213 Squadron

Duryasz was born on December 14 1911 at Budy Pobytkowskie, Warsaw. He joined the PAF in 1932. After arrival in Britain he was commissioned in January 1940 and posted to 213 Squadron at Exeter on August 17 1940.

On September 11 he claimed a Bf 110 destroyed, on the 15th a Do 17 and on the 26th a probable He 111. Duryasz was posted away on October 20 to the 302 Squadron Operations Room at Northolt. He was awarded the KW (23.12.40) and a Bar (1.2.41). He moved to 317 Squadron's Operations Room at Exeter on January 31 1942.

Duryasz returned to operations on March 20, with a posting as a Flight Commander to 317 Squadron at Exeter. He destroyed a FW 190 on April 28. Duryasz went to Polish Staff College on June 14 1942 and joined 316 Squadron at Northolt on June 1 1943. He moved to 302 Squadron at Llandbedr on January 14 1944, was posted as supernumerary to 303 Squadron on May 22 and took command of 302 on July 5 1944.

Duryasz was awarded the DFC. On January 30 1945 he was appointed to the Polish Staff at HQ 2nd TAF. He was awarded the VM (5th Class)(1.6.45), released in December 1946 and returned to Poland.

PO 27.1.40   FO 1.3.41   FL 28.4.42   SL 1.9.44

STANISLAW DUSZYNSKI

780674   Sgt   Pilot   Polish   238 Squadron

Joined 238 Squadron at St Eval on September 2 1940. Duszynski failed to return from combat with Ju 88s pursued over Romney Marsh on September 11 and was reported 'Missing'.

A Hurricane excavated at Little Scotney Farm, Lydd in 1973 proved to be R 2682, flown by Duszynski on his last flight. Although a shoe, pieces of uniform and personal notes were found there was no trace of human remains.

Duszynski was 24. He is remembered on the Polish Air Force Memorial, Northolt.

G W DUTTON

No unknown   Sgt   Aircrew   British   604 Squadron

No service details traced.

ROY GILBERT DUTTON

39072   FL   Pilot   British   145 Squadron

Dutton was born at Hatton, Ceylon on March 2 1917. He joined the RAF on a short service commission in June 1936. On September 5 he was posted to 8 FTS, Montrose and joined 111 Squadron at Northolt on April 24 1937.

In early 1940 Dutton was still with the squadron. On January 13 he shared a He 111 and on March 8 destroyed another. He was posted to 145 Squadron at Croydon on April 3. Over Brussels on May 18 he destroyed a He 111 and shared another and on the 19th and 22nd destroyed two more. Over Dunkirk on May 31 Dutton shot down a Bf 109 and shared another

and on June 2 he destroyed a Bf 110 and two more Bf 109s. He was awarded the DFC (31.5.40).

In the Battle of Britain Dutton was 'A' Flight Commander. He shared Do 17s on July 1 and 10, claimed a He 111 destroyed on the 11th, shared another on the 19th, claimed three Ju 87s on August 8, two Bf 110s on the 11th and a Ju 88 on the 12th. He was awarded a Bar to the DFC (20.8.40).

Dutton was posted away on April 12 1941 to Kirton-in-Lindsey to form and then command 452, the first RAAF fighter squadron. He left to command 19 Squadron at Fowlmere on June 15 but went to a staff job at Air Ministry on July 16. In preparation for a return to operations Dutton was posted to 54 OTU, Church Fenton on March 3 1942. After converting to Beaufighters he joined 141 Squadron at Acklington on April 17 as a Flight Commander.

Tour-expired, Dutton was attached to No 1 ADF, Croydon on November 26 1942 and soon afterwards joined the Overseas Staff. In early May 1943 he was posted to HQ Middle East and on September 9 took command of 4 Ferry Control at Habanir, Iraq. Dutton was appointed SASO 249 Wing on April 1 1944. He returned to the UK later in the year and on December 12 he went to HQ 46 Group, as Wing Commander Ops.

On January 25 1945 Dutton took command of 512 Squadron at Bitterswell and in March was detailed to lead a glider train, comprising well over 400 tug and glider combinations, conveying an airborne division to a point between Weser and Emmerich. Dutton was first to reach the area and his tug and glider combination came under heavy fire but he pressed on to the landing zone, several miles behind enemy lines. He only gave the order for the glider to be released when he was sure it would reach its objective. For this action Dutton was awarded the DSO (8.6.45).

He commanded 525 Squadron at Lyneham and Membury from June 15 1945 to March 28 1946. He held various appointments and commands in the post-war years. He was ADC to the Queen, was made a CBE, went to Moscow as a Defence and Air Attaché in May 1968 and retired on December 3 1970, as a Group Captain, retaining the rank of Air Commodore. He died on September 14 1988.

APO 24.8.36   PO 29.6.37   FO 21.3.39   FL 3.9.40
SL 1.12.41   WC 1.7.44   WC 1.7.50   GC 1.7.57

REGINALD ALBERT LLOYD DUVIVER

79370   PO   Pilot   British   229 Squadron

A member of the pre-war RAFVR, Duviver joined 229 Squadron at Wittering in June 1940.

He was killed on March 30 1941, still with 229. Duviver was 26 and is remembered on the Runnymede Memorial, Panel 32.

PO 19.5.40

ALOIS DVORAK

78762   Sgt   Pilot   Czechoslovakian   310 Squadron

Joined 310 Squadron at Duxford on September 19 1940. Dvorak crashed in Hurricane P 2795 at Debden on November 5 after being attacked by Bf 109s over the Thames Estuary but was unhurt.

He was killed on September 24 1941, aged 25. He is buried in Dyce Old Churchyard, Aberdeen.

BERTRAM ERNEST DYE

47873   Sgt   Air Gunner   British   219 Squadron

Dye, of Stakeford, was with 219 Squadron at Catterick in June 1940. With the advent of AI equipment and the Beaufighter many of 219's air gunners, Dye included, retrained as Radio Observers. In early 1941 he teamed up with Pilot Officer AJ Hodgkinson and they had great success.

On March 13 they destroyed a Do 17, on April 7 a probable He 111, on the 10th a probable Ju 88, on the 30th an unidentified enemy aircraft, on May 1 a He 111, on the 9th and the 16th two more, on June 21 and 25 two unidentified enemy aircraft and on the 27th a Ju 88. Dye was awarded the DFM (2.5.41) and a Bar (6.6.41).

Commissioned in December 1941, he was killed on August 31 1943, as a Flight Lieutenant with 96 Squadron. Dye was 23. He is buried in St Peter's New Burial Ground, Cambois, Northumberland.

PO 17.12.41   FO 1.10.42

HENRY DAVID PATRICK DYER

NZ 40758   **Sgt**   **Air Gunner**   **New Zealander**   **600 Sqdn**

The son of a policeman, Dyer was born at Paeroa on May 4 1919. In March 1939 he applied for a short service commission but was unsuccessful. He volunteered for aircrew duties at the outbreak of war.

Dyer reported to the Ground Training School, Weraroa on March 12 1940 and moved to 2 EFTS, New Plymouth on April 8. He did not settle to pilot training and remustered as a trainee air gunner. After a gunnery course at the Air Observers' School, Ohakea, Dyer sailed for the UK in the RMS 'Rangitata' on June 7.

He was posted to 5 OTU, Aston Down on July 30 and after completing his training and being awarded his air gunner's badge he joined 600 Squadron at Redhill on September 21. With the advent of airborne radar and the gradual arrival of Beaufighters the air gunners were flying less and less. At the end of the year those who did not wish to retrain, Dyer among them, asked for a transfer to Bomber Command.

Dyer was posted to 11 OTU, Bassingbourn on February 6 1941. He was crewed-up, converted to Wellingtons and joined 218 Squadron at Marham, Norfolk on April 19. The aircraft, in which he was flying as a gunner, failed to return from operations on the night of July 15/16 1941 and the crew was posted as 'Missing'. It was later learned from a German source through the International Red Cross that Dyer had been killed and was buried in Venlo Cemetery, Holland. After the war he was re-interred in the Jonkerbosch British Cemetery, Holland.

JOSEF DYGRYN

787678   **Sgt**   **Pilot**   **Czechoslovakian**   **1 Squadron**

Dygryn was born at Humpolec in 1918. He was posted to No 1 Squadron at Wittering on October 22 1940. Following an air drill on the 30th he crashed on landing and wrote off Hurricane P 5187.

On May 11 1941 Dygryn shot down a He 111 in the early hours of the morning and it crashed east of London, on the 16th he destroyed a Bf 109, on the 21st he damaged a Bf 109 over the Channel and on June 17 he shot a Bf 109 down into the sea off Boulogne. Awarded the Czech Military Cross and Medal for Gallantry in late May 1941, Dygryn went to 310 Squadron at Dyce in September.

He was awarded the DFM in March 1942 and in mid-May returned to No 1 Squadron, then at Redhill, as a Warrant Officer. On June 4 Dygryn took off on his first night intruder operation to patrol airfields around Evreux, in Hurricane Z 3188. He failed to return and may have been hit by flak as he crossed back over the French coast.

Three months later his body was washed up on the beach at Worthing. Dygryn was buried in Westwell Burial Ground, Kent on September 14 1942.

LESLIE ARTHUR DYKE

754831   **Sgt**   **Pilot**   **British**   **64 Squadron**

Dyke, of Sutton, Surrey, was with 64 Squadron at Leconfield in September 1940. On the 27th he failed to return from a routine sector patrol, in Spitfire X 4032. No details are known.

Dyke was 22. He is remembered on the Runnymede Memorial, Panel 13.

WILLIAM LAWRENCE DYMOND

580059   **Sgt**   **Pilot**   **British**   **111 Squadron**

Born at Twickenham, Middlesex, Dymond was a pre-war airman pilot. He was with 111 Squadron in September 1939.

On April 10 1940 Dymond shared in destroying a He 111. On patrols over France he shot down Do 17s on May 13, 18 and 19. Over Dunkirk he damaged two He 111s on May 31 and destroyed a Bf 109 on June 11.

In August 1940 the squadron was heavily engaged, flying from Croydon and Debden. Dymond shared a Do 17 on August 13, destroyed a Bf 110 and a Do 17 on the 15th, damaged another Do 17 on the 16th, destroyed another on the 18th, a He 111 on the 24th and damaged a Bf 110 on the 30th.

Dymond was shot down in combat over the Thames Estuary on September 2 1940, in Hurricane P 3875. He was 23 and is remembered on the Runnymede Memorial, Panel 13.

ARTHUR WILLIAM EADE

563253   **Sgt**   **Pilot**   **British**   **266 and 602 Squadrons**

Eade joined the RAF as an aircraft apprentice in the late twenties. He volunteered for observer training and went to the Air Observers' School, North Coates on March 13 1937. As a Corporal-Observer he was posted to 90 Squadron at Bicester on July 13 1937. Eade volunteered for pilot training and on March 13 1939 he began elementary flying at 9 E&RFTS, Ansty.

Two months later Eade was posted to 12 FTS, Grantham, after which he joined 266 Squadron, then reforming at Sutton Bridge, on November 5 1939. He moved to 602 Squadron at Westhampnett on September 13 1940 and then to 610 Squadron on December 16 1940. During a sweep off Calais on March 19 1941 Eade was jumped by a Bf 109 and shot down, with shrapnel wounds to a shoulder and an arm. He made a forced-landing near Hailsham.

He was posted to 58 OTU, Grangemouth on April 14 1941, as an instructor. Eade was promoted to Warrant Officer on October 1 and was posted to 65 Squadron at Westhampnett on November 3 1941. He had been with the squadron for more than a year when he went to the Maintenance Wing at 58 OTU, where he stayed until July 1944, moving then to 61 OTU, Keevil. Eade was awarded the AFC (2.6.43).

He was released from the RAF in September 1947, as a Warrant Officer.

RICHARD LLEWELLYN EARP

562541   **Sgt**   **Pilot**   **British**   **46 Squadron**

Born on January 3 1912, Earp joined the RAF as an aircraft apprentice in the late twenties. At some point he volunteered for pilot training and was serving with 46 Squadron at Digby in July 1940.

Earp was promoted to Warrant Officer on October 1 1941, commissioned in August 1953 in the Engineer Branch and retired on January 4 1967, as a Flight Lieutenant.

FO 20.8.53   FL 20.8.56

DAVID ALBERT EASTON

129240   **Sgt**   **Pilot**   **British**   **248 Squadron**

Easton joined 248 Squadron on September 25 1940. Commissioned in July 1942, he later served with 201 Squadron, flying Sunderland flying boats.

In 1945 Easton joined BOAC and flew with the airline until 1972, then with Olympic Airways and PIA.

PO 19.7.42   FO 19.1.43   FL 19.7.44

ALAN FRANCIS ECKFORD

41563   **FO**   **Pilot**   **British**   **242, 32 and 253 Squadrons**

Eckford, from Thame, Oxfordshire, entered the RAF on a short service commission in November 1938. With his training completed he joined 32 Squadron at Biggin Hill just before the outbreak of war. He damaged a Bf 109 on May 19 1940.

On June 3 Eckford was posted to 242 Squadron at Biggin Hill. Five days later the squadron flew to Le Mans to reinforce No 1, 73 and 501 Squadrons, but moved immediately to Chateaudun. After ten hectic days it was withdrawn to Coltishall on June 18.

Eckford rejoined 32 Squadron, then at Biggin Hill, on July 29 1940. He claimed a Do 17 and a Bf 109 destroyed on August 18. He was posted to 253 Squadron at Kenley on September 12. He claimed Bf 109s destroyed on the 27th and October 30, got a probable Bf 109 on November 5, shared a Do 17 on the 22nd and destroyed a Bf 109 and probably another on the 23rd. He was awarded the DFC (24.12.40).

In early 1941 Eckford was made a Flight Commander and in November was posted to 55 OTU, as an instructor. He went to 64 Squadron at Hornchurch in April 1942 and in June he joined 154 Squadron there. Eckford probably destroyed a FW 190 on August 27. He went with the squadron to North Africa in November 1942. On the 12th he shared a Do 217, destroyed a Ju 88 the next day and shared another. He was slightly injured by flying debris during an attack by Bf 109 fighter-bombers on the airfield at Djidelli.

After a rest Eckford was given command of 242 Squadron at Souk-el-Khemis on March 9 1943. He was posted away in May and released from the RAF in 1946, as a Squadron Leader.

APO 14.1.39   PO 3.9.39   FO 3.9.40   FL 3.9.41
SL 1.7.44

ALEXANDER ROTHWELL EDGE

90325   **FL**   **Pilot**   **British**   **609 Squadron**

Born in 1908, Edge trained up to 'A' License standard at the Yorkshire Aero Club in a scheme sponsored by the Daily Mail, as part of Amy Johnson's 'Get Air-Minded' campaign after her record solo flight to Australia. He joined 609 Squadron, AuxAF in 1936 and was commissioned in June 1937.

Edge was called to full-time service on August 24 1939. On January 29 he and two other pilots were sent to intercept a He 111 bombing a merchant ship off the mouth of the Tay. They inflicted damage but it is known that the enemy aircraft regained its base.

Over Dunkirk on June 1 Edge claimed a Bf 110 destroyed. In an engagement off Swanage on July 18 his glycol system was damaged by return fire from a Ju 88. Edge made a forced-landing on Studland Beach, which was mined. He was taken off by the Navy.

On August 2 1940 Edge was posted away to Training Command and did not return to operations. He was awarded the AFC (1.1.43) and released from the RAF in 1945. Edge died in 1985.

PO (AuxAF) 22.6.37   FO (AuxAF) 22.12.38   FO 24.8.39
FL 3.9.40   SL 1.12.41

GERALD RICHMOND EDGE

90249   **FL**   **Pilot**   **British**   **605 and 253 Squadrons**

Edge was at Oundle School from 1927 to 1931. He joined 605 Squadron, AuxAF in 1936 and was called for full-time service on August 24 1939.

He shared in the destruction of a Do 17 off Dunnet Head on May 9 1940, destroyed a Ju 87 on the 25th and shared another Do 17 the next day. He was promoted to Acting Squadron Leader and posted to Kenley to command 253 Squadron on September 5. Edge claimed the probable destruction of a He 111 on the 7th, shot down a Bf 109 and probably a He 111 on the 11th and was himself shot down in an action over the Channel on the 26th. He baled out, was picked up by a motor boat and admitted to Ashford Hospital. He was awarded the DFC (13.9.40).

On November 29 1940 Edge returned to 605 Squadron at Croydon, to command. He led the squadron until September 2 1941, when he was posted overseas, to form and command 73 OTU at Aden. When that unit was disbanded in October Edge went to a staff job at Group HQ. He returned to England in mid-1943, served at HQ 11 Group and was made an OBE (1.1.45).

Edge was released in 1945, as a Group Captain. He went farming in Kenya and returned later to live in Britain.

PO (AuxAF) 11.7.36   FO (AuxAF) 16.1.38   FO 24.8.39
FL 1.6.40   SL 1.9.41   WC 1.1.44

ALWYN EDGLEY

135393   **Sgt**   **Pilot**   **British**   **601 and 253 Squadrons**

Edgley joined 601 Squadron at Debden on September 4 1940 and moved later in the month to 253 Squadron at Kenley. On the 29th he was shot down by a Bf 109, baled out, wounded in the shoulder, landing at South Heighton and was admitted to Horton Hospital. His Hurricane, P 2677, crashed in flames at New Road, Denton, near Newhaven.

Commissioned in April 1942, Edgley later transferred to the Administrative Branch. He was released in 1946, as a Flight Lieutenant.

PO 4.4.42   FO 4.10.42   FL 4.4.44

GUY ARTHUR FOWNES EDMISTON

84955   **PO**   **Pilot**   **British**   **151 Squadron**

Born on March 18 1918, Edmiston was at Uppingham School from 1931 to 1935 and before the war worked at Lloyds. He joined 151 Squadron at Digby on September 29 1940.

In August 1941 Edmiston went to Russia with 81 Squadron. The Hurricanes flew off the carrier HMS 'Argus' on September 1 and landed at Vaenga airfield, to help in the defence of Murmansk. On September 26 Edmiston destroyed two Bf 109s. The squadron left Russia on November 29 1941, leaving their aircraft for use by the Russians.

Edmiston later transferred to the Administrative Branch. He was released from the RAF in 1946. He died in 1989.

PO 7.9.40   FO 7.9.41   FL 7.9.42

NORMAN DOUGLAS EDMOND

41564   **FO**   **Pilot**   **Canadian**   **615 Squadron**

Born in Winnipeg and brought up in Calgary, Edmond joined the RAF on a short service commission in November 1938. He was posted from 6 OTU, Sutton Bridge to 615 Squadron at Prestwick on September 24 1940.

Edmond was shot down and wounded on October 29. He did

ND Edmond (continued)

not return to 615 but joined 242 Squadron at Duxford on November 22. The squadron took off for a patrol over the Channel on April 20 1941. Close to North Foreland the CO, Squadron Leader WPF Treacy, sighted some aircraft and began a steep turn towards them. In so doing he collided with his No 2, Edmond. Both Hurricanes went down into the sea. Edmond's body was recovered and he is buried in St Andrew's churchyard, North Weald Bassett, Treacy was never found.

APO 14.1.39   PO 3.9.39   FO 3.9.40

ERIC RALPH EDMUNDS

42744   PO   Pilot   New Zealander   245 and 615 Sqdns

Edmunds was born in Wellington on March 5 1920. After leaving Palmerston North Boys' High School he became an apprentice chemist at a hospital.

In April 1939 Edmunds sailed for the UK in the RMS 'Rimutaka', accepted provisionally for an RAF short service commission. He did his elementary flying at 19 E&RFTS, Gatwick and later at Fairoaks. After two weeks at 3 ITW, Hastings Edmunds was posted to 3 FTS, South Cerney for intermediate and advanced training. In February 1940 he went to Porthcawl for a high-dive bombing and gunnery course on Harts.

Edmunds joined 245 Squadron at Drem on May 20 and served with it until early October, when he was posted to 615 Squadron at Prestwick. The squadron went south to Northolt on October 9 and three days later Edmunds was flying as weaver, when he was attacked by a Bf 109. With his engine damaged by a cannon shell he made a forced-landing near Chiddingfold.

On October 29, having been separated from the squadron in an earlier action, Edmunds met three Bf 109s at 29000 feet over the Channel, mid-way between England and France. A cannon shell exploded inside his cockpit, severely wounding him and causing him to be drenched in hot coolant fluid. As the Hurricane, V 6785, went down towards the English coast he lost consciousness but came to in time to make a crash-landing in the Romney Marsh area. Edmunds was taken to Shorncliffe Field Dressing Station, with a fractured skull and other head injuries, shell fragments in the lungs, back, head and legs and also a bullet in the right leg, which he believed came from a Bf 109 continuing to fire at him whilst he was unconscious.

Edmunds did not rejoin 615 but in February 1941 went to 258 Squadron at Jurby, recently-reformed and with a large number of New Zealand pilots. He was posted away to CFS, Upavon in April for an instructor's course, after which he was sent to 8 FTS, Montrose to instruct on Masters. At the end of July 1941 Edmunds sailed for South Africa, where he instructed at 24 and 22 Air Schools until posted to the Middle East in March 1942. He joined 213 Squadron in the Western Desert in late April 1942.

On June 12 he set off on a ground-strafing flight. He was attacked by a Bf 109, which he managed to shake off. The German then climbed and attacked a nearby Kittyhawk from below. The pilot baled out and Edmunds circled him protectively but soon decided he was dead. He then went down to attack a column of German vehicles. On his second run he was hit by ground fire, crash-landed on the desert and was captured.

Edmunds was handed over to the Italians two days later. He was in Italian PoW camps for a year, moved to Germany in 1943 and ended up in Stalag Luft III. He was liberated in Lubeck on May 2 1945. After leave Edmunds went on a refresher course to Wittering and was then posted to 9 PDC, Regents Park as an Admin Officer. He declined a Permanent Commission and transferred to the RNZAF. He arrived back in New Zealand on October 22 1946 and was released soon afterwards.

APO 8.10.39   PO 20.5.40   FO 20.5.41   FL 20.5.42

HILARY PATRICK MICHAEL EDRIDGE

41836   PO   Pilot   British   222 Squadron

Edridge joined the RAF on a short service commission in January 1939. He was with 222 Squadron at Duxford in 1940. Over Dunkirk on June 1 he probably destroyed a Bf 109.

On August 30 Edridge was shot down by Bf 109s. He baled out, with burns to the face, landing at Broome Park. His Spitfire, K 9826, crashed and burned out at Marley, near Barham.

Edridge made a forced-landing at Tillingham Hall, near Horndon on October 15 due to engine failure. He shared in the destruction of a Bf 110 on the 20th. After being severely damaged in combat with Bf 109s on October 30 1940 Edridge crashed in flames, attempting to land at Longwood Farm, Ewhurst. He was rescued from the wreckage but died of his injuries, aged 21.

Edridge is buried in the Roman Catholic Cemetery, Perrymead, Widcombe, Bath.

APO 1.4.39   PO 21.10.39

ERIC FRANK EDSALL

81368   PO   Pilot   British   54 and 222 Squadrons

Edsall was posted to 54 Squadron at Catterick on August 1 1940. He was damaged by a Bf 109 whilst carrying out a front gun exercise on a ditched enemy pilot in mid-Channel and made a forced-landing near Dartford.

On August 18 he claimed a Bf 110 destroyed, on the 24th a Bf 109 and on the 30th he shared a Do 215. On the 31st Edsall was pilot of one of three Spitfires caught in a bombing attack as they were taking off from Hornchurch. Edsall's aircraft finished the right way up and he managed to extricate himself but his legs were so badly injured that he could not walk. He crawled over to Alan Deere's Spitfire, which was upside down with Deere suspended by his harness straps. Edsall wrenched off the cockpit door and freed Deere, who then helped his rescuer to Station Sick Quarters.

Fit again, Edsall was posted on September 19 to 222 Squadron, also at Hornchurch. The next day his aircraft was badly damaged in a surprise attack by Bf 109s over the Thames Estuary and he crashed through the perimeter fence on landing. He destroyed a Bf 109 on September 30. In combat with Bf 109s on October 27 Edsall ran out of fuel and crash-landed after flying through high tension cables at Pattenden's Farm, Battle Road, Hailsham. He was seriously injured and admitted to Hellingly Hospital.

Edsall returned to operations with 602 Squadron. He was awarded the DFC (16.1.42). He later went to 261 Squadron in Ceylon. He died on April 12 1942, possibly as a result of operations against the Japanese, who had made a carrier-borne attack on Trincomalee three days earlier.

Edsall was 24. He is buried in Trincomalee War Cemetery, Sri Lanka.

PO 6.7.40   FO 6.7.41

──────── EDWARDS

No unknown   Sgt   Pilot   British   247 Squadron

Joined 247 Squadron on September 2 1940. No further details traced.

A J EDWARDS

No unknown   Sgt   Aircrew   British   604 Squadron

No service details traced.

FREDERICK EDWARDS

910834   **Sgt**   **Aircrew**   **British**   **29 Squadron**

No service details traced.

HARRY DAVIES EDWARDS

41837   **PO**   **Pilot**   **Canadian**   **92 Squadron**

Edwards, of Winnipeg, joined the RAF on a short service commission in January 1939. He was posted in May to 13 FTS, Drem and with training completed went to 92 Squadron at Tangmere in October 1939.

On May 23 1940 Edwards probably destroyed a Bf 110, over Dunkirk on June 2 he claimed a He 111 and on July 4 he shared in shooting down another.

Edwards was shot down and killed in combat with Bf 109s on September 11 1940. His Spitfire, P 9464, crashed into a wood at Evegate Manor Farm, Smeeth. The wreck was not discovered until October 7. Edwards was 24. He is buried in Folkestone New Cemetery, Kent.

APO 1.4.39   *PO 21.10.39*

HAROLD HARDING EDWARDS

128104   **Sgt**   **Observer**   **British**   **248 Squadron**

Joined 248 Squadron in May 1940. Edwards flew as observer with Flight Lieutenant REG Morewood, 'B' Flight Commander. In April 1941 he was detached and sent to join 404(RCAF) Squadron, then being formed at Thorney Island.

Commissioned in May 1942, Edwards was posted to an ASR Squadron, after which he went to Blackpool to instruct on navigation for air-sea rescue. He requested pilot training, was accepted and at the end of the war was in the Bahamas on Flying Fortresses.

Edwards was released in 1945, as a Flight Lieutenant.

PO 12.5.42   *FO 12.11.42*   *FL 12.5.44*

IVOR HERBERT EDWARDS

78978   **PO**   **Pilot**   **British**   **234 Squadron**

Joined 234 Squadron at St Eval in mid-September 1940. Edwards claimed a Ju 88 destroyed on November 29 1940.

Later with 19 Squadron, he was awarded the DFC (22.9.42), having then destroyed at least two enemy aircraft, damaged several more and participated with distinction in the combined operations at Dieppe on August 19 1942.

Edwards was released in 1946, as a Flight Lieutenant.

PO 30.4.40   *FO 30.4.41*   *FL 30.4.42*

KENNETH CHARLES EDWARDS

84680   **PO**   **Air Gunner**   **British**   **600 Squadron**

Edwards joined 600 Squadron, AuxAF in early 1936 and began training as an air gunner in April. He was promoted to Sergeant in early 1939 and called for full-time service on August 24.

Commissioned in August 1940, Edwards served with 600 until January 1941, when he was posted to 150 Squadron at Newton. He was operating as a gunner in Wellingtons until shot down over Germany in July 1941 and captured.

Freed in May 1945, Edwards was released from the RAF in August, as a Flight Lieutenant.

PO 8.8.40   *FO 8.8.41*   *FL 8.8.42*

ROBERT LEONARD EDWARDS

C 903   **FO**   **Pilot**   **Canadian**   **1 (RCAF) Squadron**

Edwards arrived in the UK with the squadron on June 20 1940. He was shot down by return fire from a Do 17 attacking Debden on August 26 1940. In Hurricane P 3874 he crashed at The Hydes, Little Bardfield and was killed. He is buried in Brookwood Military Cemetery.

ROBERT SYDNEY JAMES EDWARDS

33242   **FL**   **Pilot**   **Irish**   **56 Squadron**

Born on February 12 1916, Edwards entered RAF College, Cranwell in January 1935 as a flight cadet. He graduated in December 1936 and joined 79 Squadron at Biggin Hill on March 22 1937.

Edwards was posted to 56 Squadron at Boscombe Down on September 10 1940, as a Flight Commander. He was shot down on the 30th in a combat with Do 215s and Bf 110s over Portland, in Hurricane P 3088. He is believed to have baled out, unhurt.

In 1941 Edwards moved to Bomber Command and was awarded the DFC (21.11.41), serving with 9 Squadron at Honington.

Edwards retired from the RAF on February 12 1963, as a Wing Commander. He died on May 2 1974.

PO 19.12.36   *FO 19.6.38*   *FL 19.6.40*   *SL 1.9.41*
WC 1.7.53

GERALD HENRY EDWORTHY

564606   **Sgt**   **Pilot**   **British**   **46 Squadron**

A pre-war airman pilot, Edworthy, of Teignmouth, Devon, joined 46 Squadron at Digby in June 1940. He failed to return from combat over the Essex coast on September 3 1940. His Hurricane, P 3064, is believed to be the one which crashed in Redwood Creek, River Crouch.

Edworthy was 25. He is remembered on the Runnymede Memorial, Panel 13.

ALLEN LAIRD EDY

41566   **FO**   **Pilot**   **Canadian**   **602 Squadron**

Edy, from Winnipeg, joined the RAF on a short service commission in November 1938. After completing his training at 5 FTS, Sealand he joined 613 Squadron at Odiham in September 1939. With the call for more pilots for Fighter Command Edy volunteered and joined 602 Squadron at Westhampnett on September 8 1940.

He claimed a Do 17 destroyed on the 15th. Edy was awarded the DFC (5.11.40) for his services with 613 Squadron. He was shot down by Bf 109s near Folkestone on December 12 1940 and crash-landed at Shorncliffe, unhurt, in Spitfire X 4658.

Edy was posted to 315 Squadron at Acklington in January 1941. He moved to 457 Squadron, when it was formed at Baginton on June 16. He was killed on December 12 1941, when his aircraft caught fire. He baled out but was too low and his parachute failed to open.

He is buried in St Andrew's churchyard, Andreas, Isle of Man. Edy was 25 years old.

APO 14.1.39   *PO 3.9.39*   *FO 3.9.40*

EDWARD JAMES EGAN

74287   **Sgt**   **Pilot**   **British**   **600, 615 and 501 Squadrons**

Egan, of East Dulwich, London, was in the RAFVR before the war. He was with 600 Squadron at Northolt in June 1940, was posted to 615 Squadron at Prestwick on August 27 and on September 13 went to 501 Squadron at Kenley.

On the 15th Egan claimed a Bf 109 destroyed. Two days later he was killed, shot down in flames in a surprise attack by a Bf 109 over Ashford. His Hurricane, P 3820, crashed in Daniels Wood, Tuesnoad Farm, Bethersden. Egan was reported 'Missing' and is remembered on the Runnymede Memorial, Panel 14. He was 19 years old.

The crash site was excavated on September 11 1976. The pilot's remains could not be identified and he was buried as 'an unknown airman' in Brookwood Military Cemetery, with full military honours. The site was excavated again in November 1978 and this time evidence was found to prove that it was Egan's aircraft. The grave marker in Brookwood was changed to include his name.

WILLIAM THORPE EIBY

391347   PO   Pilot   New Zealander   245 Squadron

Eiby was born in Christchurch on November 23 1914. He obtained his 'A' license at Masterton and joined the Civil Reserve of Pilots.

After the outbreak of war courses were made up of short service candidates and Civil Reserve Pilots. Eiby went to the Ground Training School at Weraroa on November 20 1939 and moved to No 2 EFTS, New Plymouth on December 18. He was posted to 2 FTS, Woodbourne on March 8 1940, was awarded his flying badge on May 14 and commissioned in late June.

He sailed for the UK in the RMS 'Rangitane' on July 12 and on September 10 went to 6 OTU, Sutton Bridge. After converting to Hurricanes Eiby joined 245 Squadron at Aldergrove on the 28th. He was posted to 73 Squadron on November 6 and soon afterwards embarked on HMS 'Furious' for the Middle East. The squadron flew off to Takoradi on the 29th and then flew in easy stages to Heliopolis, via Lagos, Accra, Kano, Maidugari, Khartoum, Wadi Halfa and Abu Sueir. During December the pilots were attached to 274 Squadron in the Western Desert.

On March 5 1941 Eiby destroyed an enemy aircraft. He was posted away to No 1 ADU, Cairo in early May and returned to 73 Squadron on December 1. Eiby was shot down near Tobruk on February 13 1942 by Oberfeldwebel Schulz of JG 27. He made a forced-landing in the desert, escaping with only a few shell splinter scratches.

On February 28 Eiby left 73 and returned to No 1 ADU. Before he was posted back to New Zealand on January 19 1943 he had made sixteen ferry flights across Africa, each averaging four days, starting at Takoradi and ending at Cairo. This was an easier way to get aircraft to the Western Desert than through the Mediterranean or round the Cape, also avoiding risk of sinkings at sea. The aircraft generally flew in groups of six or eight, this having been found to be the best number as far as refuelling and navigational arrangements were concerned.

Eiby reached New Zealand in early March 1943. He did a series of staff jobs until November 8, when he was posted to the Catalina Conversion Flight at Lauthia Bay, Fiji. He joined 6 (Flying Boat) Squadron at Halavo Bay, Florida Island on December 23 1943. Eiby returned to New Zealand in early July 1944 and in mid-December joined 40 (Transport) Squadron at Whenuapai, flying C 47s. By 1946 the squadron was doing some civil work as well as its service operations.

Eiby was released from the RNZAF on February 12 1947 and joined the National Airways Corporation when it was formed later in the year. He retired in 1970.

PO 28.6.40   FO 28.6.41   FL 28.6.42

VICTOR HOWARD EKINS

63073   Sgt   Pilot   British   111 and 501 Squadrons

Born at St Neots in 1914, Ekins qualified as a chartered surveyor before the war. He joined the RAFVR in March 1939 and began flying training at 16 E&RFTS, Shoreham.

Ekins was called up on September 1 1939, went to 3 ITW, Hastings, then to 4 EFTS, Brough to complete his elementary training. After 8 FTS, Montrose he was posted to 7 OTU, Hawarden in late June 1940 and joined the Training Flight of 111 Squadron at Kenley on July 18. Two weeks later he went to Croydon to join the squadron.

On September 5 Ekins claimed a Bf 109 destroyed. Three days later 111 went north to Drem but he was posted back to Kenley on the 21st to join 501 Squadron. Ekins was shot down in combat by a Bf 110 over Godstone on the 27th, in Hurricane V 6672. He baled out, wounded, at 19000 feet, landed in woods in the middle of a Canadian Ambulance Unit and was taken to Sevenoaks Hospital.

Ekins returned to the squadron, then at Filton, on November 26 1940. He was commissioned in April 1941 and remained with 501, as a Flight Commander, until April 26 1942, when he was posted to HQ 10 Group, Box as Squadron Leader Ops. On May 19 1942 Ekins went to 286 Squadron at Colerne on anti-aircraft co-operation duties. He was awarded the DFC (23.6.42), posted as supernumerary to 66 Squadron at Zeals on September 29 and given command of 19 Squadron at Perranporth on November 27 1942.

The squadron destroyed its 100th enemy aircraft on November 11 1943 and Ekins made his last operational flight on December 5, escorting Fortresses to Lille. He was posted to 53 OTU, Kirton-in-Lindsey on January 20 1944, as an instructor, and went to HQ 12 Group, Watnall on January 1 1945, as a staff officer. Ekins made his last flight in a Spitfire on August 25 1945, was made an MBE (1.1.46) and released from the RAF in January 1946, as a Squadron Leader. He returned to the family farm-surveying business.

PO 2.4.41   FO 17.11.41   FL 20.8.42

DOUGLAS WILLIAM ELCOME

740713   Sgt   Pilot   British   602 Squadron

Elcome, of Leigh-on-Sea, Essex, was a member of the RAFVR before the war. He completed his flying training at 14 FTS, Cranfield in early June 1940 and after converting to Spitfires joined 602 Squadron at Drem on the 21st.

On August 12 1940 602 moved south to Westhampnett. Elcome claimed a Bf 109 destroyed over Dungeness on the 31st. He landed at Ford following this action with a damaged glycol tank. On September 10 he crashed on Felpham golf course during night-flying practice, wrecking Spitfire L 1040.

Elcome failed to return from a routine patrol on October 26, in Spitfire R 6839. He was reported 'Missing', aged 21. He is remembered on the Runnymede Memorial, Panel 14.

FREDERICK WILLIAM ELEY

745667   Sgt   Pilot   British   74 Squadron

Joined 74 Squadron at Rochford on February 15 1940. Eley was killed on July 31 1940, when he was shot down in flames off Folkestone Pier. Troops, sailors and boatmen pulled the Spitfire, P 9398, ashore and his body was recovered.

Eley was 21. He is buried in St Margaret's churchyard, Wrenbury Cum Frith, Cheshire and his name is in a memorial stained glass window in the church.

FRANK RICHARD CHARLES ELGER

42114   PO   Pilot   Canadian   248 Squadron

Elger, from Toronto, joined the RAF on a short service commission in March 1939. He joined 248 Squadron on November 6 1939 and was posted away on December 12 1940.

Elger was released from the RAF in 1946.

APO 13.5.39   PO 6.11.39   FO 6.11.40   FL 6.11.41

HUGH WILLIAM ELIOT

42490   **PO**   **Pilot**   **British**   **73 Squadron**

Eliot, of Bromley, Kent, entered the RAF in June 1939. He joined 73 Squadron in France in early May 1940. On the 11th he damaged a Bf 110, on the 16th he claimed two enemy aircraft destroyed, on June 3 a Bf 110 and on June 13 he shared two He 111s.

On September 6 Eliot was shot down in combat over the Thames Estuary. He baled out, burned, and was admitted to Twickenhurst Hospital. In early November Eliot embarked on the carrier HMS 'Argus'. He was in the first group of six Hurricanes, which flew off on a 400 sea miles flight to Malta on November 17. Eliot joined 261 Squadron at Hal Far. On February 26 1941 he claimed a Ju 87 destroyed and probably another.

On May 12 261 was disbanded and Eliot went into a new unit, 185 Squadron, becoming a Flight Commander in July. He was awarded the DFC (26.9.41) and returned to the UK, where he joined 242 Squadron at Valley on September 24. He was rested from operations on October 10 1941.

In late 1942 Eliot was posted to 255 Squadron at Honiley, as a Flight Commander. He went to North Africa with the squadron and was given command in August 1943. On September 8 he shot down an Me 210 and on January 30 1944 a Do 217. Eliot was posted away in February 1944. He returned to operations in late September, to command 256 Squadron at Foggia, Italy. On October 4 he destroyed a Ju 52 and two days later a Do 24.

Whilst attacking a bridge at night on March 4 1945 Eliot was shot down by flak and killed. He was 23 and is buried in Argenta Gap War Cemetery, Italy. An award of the DSO (23.5.44) was announced after his death.

APO 19.8.39   *PO 28.2.40*   *FO 28.2.41*   *FL 28.2.42*
SL 5.11.43

JOHN FRANCIS DURHAM ELKINGTON

44184   **PO**   **Pilot**   **British**   **1 Squadron**

Born on December 23 1920, Elkington entered RAF College, Cranwell in September 1939, as a flight cadet. He was granted a Permanent Commission on July 14 1940 and joined No 1 Squadron at Tangmere on the 15th.

Elkington shot a Bf 109 down into the sea on August 15 and was himself shot down the next day over Thorney Island. He baled out, injured, and was admitted to hospital. His Hurricane, P 3173, crashed and burned out at Manor Farm, Chidham.

In April 1941 Elkington was posted away from the squadron. He stayed on in the RAF and retired on December 23 1975, as a Wing Commander.

PO 14.7.40   *FO 14.7.41*   *FL 14.10.42*   *SL 1.8.47*
WC 1.7.61

JOHN LAWRENCE WEMYSS ELLACOMBE

43031   **PO**   **Pilot**   **British**   **151 Squadron**

Ellacombe was born in Livingstone, Northern Rhodesia on February 28 1920. He was educated at Diocesan College, Rondebosch, South Africa and joined the RAF in late 1939. He completed his flying training at 2 FTS, Brize Norton and was posted directly to 151 Squadron at Martlesham Heath on July 13 1940. Never having flown Hurricanes he was converted via the Station Flight Master by Pilot Officer FB Sutton of 56, who was slightly wounded and non-operational.

On August 24 Ellacombe shot down a He 111 over Hornchurch. A week later his aircraft was hit by return fire from a Ju 88 and he baled out as the gravity fuel tank exploded. He was admitted to Southend General Hospital with burns. His Hurricane, P 3312,

crashed at Eastwood, Southend. Ellacombe rejoined the squadron in late December and in February 1941 was promoted to Acting Flight Lieutenant and posted to 253 Squadron at Leconfield, as a Flight Commander.

Ellacombe was awarded the DFC (7.4.42) and on July 28 1942 he probably destroyed a Do 217, whilst co-operating with a Turbinlite Havoc of 1459 Flight. He later served with 487 Squadron and was awarded a Bar to the DFC (29.12.44).

In the post-war RAF Ellacombe held various appointments and commands prior to his retirement on April 16 1973, as an Air Commodore. He was made a CB (1970) and became Director of Scientific Services at St Thomas' Hospital in 1973 and appointed Administrator to the Special Trustees there in 1980.

APO 23.3.40   *PO 13.7.40*   *FO 13.7.41*   *FL 13.7.42*
FL 1.9.45   *SL 1.7.49*   *WC 1.7.55*   *GC 1.1.61*
AC 1.7.68

CYRIL CHARLES ELLERY

78747   **PO**   **Air Gunner**   **British**   **264 Squadron**

Ellery was with 264 Squadron in the Battle of Britain and took part in the squadron's final day-fighting operations from Hornchurch in late August 1940. He was flying as gunner for Pilot Officer WF Carnaby on the 28th, when their Defiant, N1576, returned to base severely damaged by return fire from a He 111 attacked over Dover. Both men were unhurt.

Ellery was released from the RAF in 1945, as a Squadron Leader. He died on March 20 1977.

APO 12.4.40   *PO 29.5.40*   *FO 29.5.41*   *FL 1.6.42*

G J ELLIOTT

C 1349   **PO**   **Pilot**   **Canadian**   **607 Squadron**

Joined the RCAF in November 1939 and was posted to 607 Squadron at Tangmere in October 1940.

Elliott was released from the RCAF on June 4 1946, as a Squadron Leader.

ROBERT DEACON ELLIOTT

76311   **PO**   **Pilot**   **British**   **72 Squadron**

Born on November 20 1914, Elliott was educated at Northampton and joined the RAFVR in 1938. Called up in September 1939 he was posted to 6 FTS, Little Rissington on October 7 for advanced training. At the end of the course he was commissioned and joined 72 Squadron at Drem on December 16.

Elliott operated with the squadron over Dunkirk. On September 4 1940 he claimed a Bf 110 destroyed, on the 6th a Bf 109, on the 9th a Bf 110 and on the 11th a He 111. He was shot down on September 6 in a head-on attack on a Bf 109 over Maidstone and baled out, unhurt. His Spitfire, N 3070, crashed and burned out at Wanshurst Green.

Posted to HQ Fighter Command in October 1941, Elliott was awarded the DFC (17.10.41). In 1944 he was with 84 Group 2nd TAF and in 1946 was OC Flying Wing and OC APC in Cyprus. Elliott was a graduate of the Joint Services Staff College, RAF Staff College and the RAF College of Air Warfare. He held a number of appointments and commands prior to his retirement on September 27 1968, as an Air Commodore, retaining the rank of Air Vice-Marshal. His portrait was done by Cuthbert Orde.

PO 10.12.39   *FO 10.12.40*   *FL 10.12.41*   *SL 1.9.45*
WC 1.7.48   *GC 1.1.57*   *AC 1.7.62*

GORDON ERIC ELLIS

41993   **PO**   **Pilot**   **British**   **64 Squadron**

Born in 1915, Ellis joined the RAF on a short service commission in February 1939. He was posted to 64 Squadron at Kenley on July 12 1940.

Ellis disappears from the Air Force List after February 1941.

APO 29.4.39   *PO 6.11.39*   *FO 6.11.40*

JOHN ELLIS

37850   **FL**   **Pilot**   **British**   **610 Squadron**

Born in Deal on February 28 1917, Ellis joined the RAF in March 1936. He was posted to 11 FTS, Wittering on June 2 and after a short spell with 66 Squadron he joined 213 Squadron, when it was reformed at Northolt on March 8 1937.

At the outbreak of war Ellis was posted to 610 Squadron at Wittering, as a Flight Commander. Over Dunkirk he destroyed a Bf 109 on May 29, a Bf 110 on the 31st and on bomber escorts in June he destroyed another Bf 109 on the 7th and shared in the destruction of an enemy aircraft on the 12th.

Ellis claimed a Do 17 shared on July 3, a Bf 109 destroyed on the 24th, three Bf 109s on the 25th, another on August 12, a He 111 on the 18th, a Bf 109 on the 26th and another on the 27th. He had been promoted to Acting Squadron Leader and given command of 610 on July 26 1940 and awarded the DFC (13.8.40), receiving it from the King on September 3. Ellis was posted away to 55 OTU to instruct in early May 1941 and was awarded a Bar to the DFC (2.5.41).

He went to the Middle East at the end of 1941 and served with the Desert Air Force until appointed to lead a Wing in Malta in 1943. Ellis was reported 'Missing' on June 13 1943, after his engine failed over the sea during the invasion of Sicily. He was later reported to be a PoW. Back in the UK in 1945 he took part in the first Battle of Britain flypast in September.

Ellis was made an OBE (31.5.56) and a CBE (11.6.60) and retired from the RAF on February 28 1967, as a Group Captain.

APO 18.5.36   PO 23.3.37   FO 23.9.38   FL 3.9.40
SL 1.12.41   WC 1.7.44   WC 1.1.51   GC 1.1.59

JOHN HUGH MORTIMER ELLIS

742068   **Sgt**   **Pilot**   **British**   **85 Squadron**

Ellis joined the RAFVR on September 28 1938 and became a Sergeant u/t pilot the following day. He had finished his elementary flying training before he was called up on September 3 1939.

Posted to 4 ITW on October 10, Ellis moved to 2 FTS, Brize Norton on December 9. With training completed he went to 6 OTU, Sutton Bridge on May 18 1940 and joined 85 Squadron at Debden six days later.

Ellis shared a Do 17 on August 6 and claimed a Bf 109 destroyed on the 18th.

In combat over the Channel on the 29th he was set on fire and glided back over land before baling out, unhurt. His Hurricane, L 1915, crashed at Brigden Hill Farm, Ashburnham.

Ellis failed to return from a combat with Bf 109s over the Kenley area on September 1 1940. He was 21 and is remembered on the Runnymede Memorial, Panel 14.

RONALD VERNON ELLIS

47416   **F/Sgt**   **Pilot**   **British**   **73 Squadron**

Ellis joined 73 Squadron in France in June 1940. He piloted the plane which carried General de Gaulle to England after the collapse of France.

On September 11 and 15 1940 Ellis shared in destroying enemy aircraft and he shared in the destruction of a Bf 109 on the 27th. In

November 1940 73 Squadron was posted to the Middle East and sailed in the carrier HMS 'Furious'. They flew off at Takoradi and then in stages flew overland to Heliopolis. In December the 73 pilots were attached to 274 Squadron in the Western Desert. In early January 1941 the squadron began to operate on its own account from Sidi Heneish.

Ellis destroyed three Ju 87s over Tobruk on April 14 1941. He was commissioned in October 1941 and posted to 127 Squadron at Hurghoda, on ferrying duties. He was awarded the DFM (2.1.42) and later in the year rejoined 73 Squadron. In November 1942 Ellis was commanding a detachment at Bu Amoud and from February 1943 he commanded the squadron. In July he returned to the UK. Ellis was later senior test pilot at Vickers Armstrong and was awarded the AFC (1.1.46) for his services there. He was released from the RAF in 1946 but later rejoined. He was a Qualified Instructor, CFS and retired from the RAF on October 11 1966, as a Flight Lieutenant, retaining the rank of Squadron Leader.

PO 14.10.41   FO 1.10.42   FL 16.5.43   FL 2.3.50

WALTER THOMAS ELLIS

110331   **Sgt**   **Pilot**   **British**   **266 and 92 Squadrons**

Born on September 8 1919, Ellis joined 266 Squadron at Wittering on August 26 1940 and moved to 92 Squadron at Biggin Hill on September 21. Three days later he crash-landed on Higham Marshes, damaged in starboard wing and glycol system by a Bf 109 in an action over Maidstone.

Ellis claimed a share in a Ju 88 on the 27th and on October 10 he crash-landed near Poynings Station after being damaged by return fire from a Do 17 engaged over Tangmere. His Spitfire, X 4552, was a write-off. On November 5 Ellis made a forced-landing at Gravesend after a combat with Bf 109s. He was unhurt. On December 1 1940 he got a probable Bf 109.

Ellis was commissioned in October 1941 and stayed in the RAF. He was awarded the AFC (2.1.50) and retired on June 8 1963, as a Wing Commander.

PO 15.10.41   FO 1.10.42   FL 15.10.43   FL 1.9.45
SL 1.7.51   WC 1.1.57

HARRY DONALD BUCHANAN ELSDON

743044   **Sgt**   **Air Gunner**   **British**   **236 Squadron**

Elsdon, of Southend-on-Sea, was with 236 Squadron in June 1940. On July 18 he was reported 'Missing' when his Blenheim, L 6779, failed to return from a photo-reconnaissance sortie over Le Havre. The weather was bad and intense anti-aircraft fire was encountered over Cap de la Hague. It is believed that the Blenheim was shot down by Major Schellmann of JG 2.

Elsdon was 28. He is remembered on the Runnymede Memorial, Panel 14.

THOMAS ARTHUR FRANCIS ELSDON

33308   **FL**   **Pilot**   **British**   **72 Squadron**

Born at Broughty Ferry on January 22 1917, Elsdon entered RAF College, Cranwell in January 1936, as a flight cadet. After graduation he was posted to 72 Squadron at Church Fenton on December 18 1937.

Elsdon destroyed a He 115 on October 21 1939, shared two He 111s with five other pilots on December 7 and over Dunkirk got a probable Ju 87 on June 2 1940. He claimed a Bf 110 on August 15, two Bf 109s on September 1, a Ju 87 and a Bf 110 on the 4th and a Bf 109 on the 7th. In this last action his aircraft was badly damaged in the combat over the Thames Estuary. He crash-landed at Biggin Hill, severely injured in knee and shoulder.

Awarded the DFC (8.10.40), Elsdon was out of action until July 15 1941, when he joined 257 Squadron at Coltishall, as a Flight Commander. He claimed a Bf 109 destroyed on July 24 and was again wounded, not seriously. On August 25 1941 Elsdon was posted to RAF Kirton-in-Lindsey to form and command 136 Squadron. The squadron left for India in November 1941 and became operational there in April 1942.

Elsdon was appointed Wing Leader 165 Wing, Dum Dum on September 8. He moved to Alipore on October 10 to lead 293 Wing. He took command of 169 Wing, Agarthla on February 10 1943, was posted to 185 Wing, Feni on October 8 and returned to 165 Wing, then at Arakan, to command, on November 22 1943. Elsdon was posted to the staff at HQ Eastern Air Command, Calcutta on July 12 1944. He returned to the UK two months later.

His first posting was to Transport Command and on April 13 1945 he became OC RAF Boreham. Elsdon was made an OBE (14.6.45). He held various appointments and commands before his retirement on October 22 1959, as a Wing Commander, retaining the rank of Group Captain.

PO 18.12.37   FO 18.6.39   FL 3.9.40   SL 1.12.41
WC 1.1.49

PETER ELSE

741332   Sgt   Pilot   British   610 Squadron

Else was born on February 28 1917. He joined the RAFVR on February 23 1938 and became a Sergeant u/t pilot the next day. He began his flying training at 22 E&RFTS, Cambridge. At that time Else was working as an engineer at Marshall's Flying School, the operators.

Called up at the outbreak of war, Else went to 6 FTS, Little Rissington on October 7 1939 for advanced training. At the end of the course he was posted direct to 72 Squadron at Church Fenton.

On June 6 1940 Else was attached to 610 Squadron at Gravesend because of pilot shortage in the squadron. On July 25 he destroyed a Bf 109 off Folkestone. The next day, whilst attacking a Bf 109 over the Dover/Folkestone area, Else was hit from behind and set on fire. As he tried to bale out he was hit by another burst, which shattered his left forearm. Else left the burning aircraft at 20000 feet and landed on Hawkinge aerodrome, about 200 yards from the dispersal point he had taken off from only a short time before.

Else was taken to the Kent and County Hospital at Canterbury, where his left arm was amputated just above the elbow and he was treated for burns to face and right hand. He was discharged on medical grounds on April 2 1941 and returned to Marshall's as an aircraft inspector at 22 EFTS. On May 24 1944 Else began test flying of Tiger Moths and Auster llls after repairs or overhauls, using a special attachment in place of the hand on his artificial left arm.

He made his last flight as pilot-in-command on October 1 1946 and let his 'A' License lapse in order to concentrate on the engineering side. He took over as Chief Engineer in April 1974 and retired on April 11 1987.

CLIFFORD STANLEY EMENY

NZ 40204   Sgt   Air Gunner   New Zealander   264 Sqdn

Emeny was born in Wellington on January 11 1920. He volunteered for aircrew duties after the outbreak of war and reported to the Ground Training School, Weraroa on January 15 1940.

He was posted to the Air Observers' School, Ohakea on February 9, for a Lewis gunnery course and air experience. Emeny sailed for the UK in the SS 'Akaroa' on March 23. He was posted to 264 Squadron at Duxford on June 3 1940 for further training. He was awarded his air gunner's badge on July 26, promoted to Sergeant the next day and served with the squadron until February 14 1941, when he was posted to join the recently-reformed 255 Squadron at Kirton-in-Lindsey.

On May 9 Emeny was credited with destroying a German bomber at night over Hull. He also had a probable to his credit when he left the squadron on June 26 1941 to join 409 Squadron, then being formed at Digby. After the squadron converted to Beaufighters later in the year Emeny retrained and qualified as a Radio Observer. He was commissioned in late November.

In January 1942 he was accepted for pilot training and posted to 13 ITW, Torquay. Emeny did a grading course at 22 EFTS, Cambridge and left for Canada in late May. He carried out his flying training at 37 SFTS, Calgary and 39 SFTS, Swift Current. Qualified as a pilot, he embarked at Halifax for the UK on February 3 1943.

After further training at 12 (P) AFU, Grantham Emeny converted to Blenheims at 60 OTU there and then went to High Ercall for a night intruder course on Mosquitos. He was posted to India on November 29 1943 and on January 5 1944 joined 27 Squadron, Agartala. Emeny went to 45 Squadron at Yelahanka, India on March 20 1944.

On November 9 Emeny led six Mosquitos in a dawn raid on the Japanese airfield at Meiktila. After destroying a bomber as it was taking off his aircraft was hit by ground fire, which set it alight and stopped one engine. He was then attacked by fighters and crashed in flames in the jungle. Trapped by his feet, Emeny protected himself

from the fire by covering himself with his parachute and putting on his oxygen mask. He finally struggled free and was pulled out of the wreckage by his navigator.

The two men were betrayed to the Japanese by villagers and taken to Rangoon, where they were separated. Emeny was taken to the University and interrogated at great length and with extreme cruelty, receiving no medical treatment for his burns and injuries. He was eventually put into the main prison at Rangoon and at one point was put on trial and sentenced to death.

Emeny was freed in early May 1945 and flown out to Calcutta, weighing 6st 10lbs. He returned to New Zealand in July and was released from the RNZAF in 1946, as a Flight Lieutenant.

PO 29.11.41   FO 1.10.42   FL 29.11.43

GEOFFREY EMMETT

148765   Sgt   Observer   British   236 Squadron

Emmett joined the RAFVR as a trainee observer on May 5 1939. Called up at the outbreak of war, he went to 3 ITW, Hastings on November 10 1939 and moved to 4 AONS, Coventry on January 1 1940. He was posted to 8 BGS, Evanton on June 3, went to No 1 (Coastal) OTU on July 28 and joined 236 Squadron at St Eval on August 16.

Emmett was posted to ferry duties in Canada on February 2 1941. He returned to the UK and joined 140 Squadron at Hendon on August 27 1941. Promoted to Warrant Officer on October 1 1942, Emmett was commissioned in May 1943. He remained with 140 until September 1 1944, operating from bases on the Continent after the invasion.

After leaving 140 Emmett was posted to HQ 34 Wing and finally to 5352 Airfield Construction Wing at Lübeck. He was released on November 23 1945, as a Flight Lieutenant. Emmett was awarded the C de G (Fr)(5.6.46) for his services in taking photographs of German troop concentrations during the campaign in Normandy.

PO 18.5.43   FO 18.11.43   FL 18.5.45

WILLIAM ALEXANDER COOTE EMMETT

39723   FL   Pilot   British   25 Squadron

Born on March 17 1916, Emmett joined the RAF on a short service commission in March 1937. He was posted to 2 FTS, Brize Norton on June 5 and joined 25 Squadron at Hawkinge on January 1 1938. He served with the squadron throughout the Battle of Britain.

Emmett was released from the RAF in 1946 but rejoined later. He retired on April 30 1958, as a Squadron Leader.

APO 18.5.37   PO 15.3.38   FO 15.10.39   FL 15.10.40
SL 1.3.42   FL 15.12.43   SL 1.7.51

CHARLES EDWARD ENGLISH

77791   PO   Pilot   British   85 and 605 Squadrons

English was born in Newcastle-upon-Tyne in 1912. He was with 85 Squadron at Martlesham Heath in June 1940.

On August 30 he claimed a Bf 110 destroyed and on September 1 a Do 215. English was posted to 605 Squadron at Croydon on September 12. He was shot down over Westerham on October 7 1940 and killed, when his Hurricane, P 3677, crashed and burned out at Park Farm, Brasted.

English was 28. He is buried in St Andrew's and Jesmond Cemetery, Newcastle-upon-Tyne. His brother was killed in 1941, as a Sergeant-Pilot.

PO 7.3.40

PHILIP STEPHEN BADDESLEY ENSOR

41003   FO   Pilot   British   23 Squadron

Ensor, of Gidleigh, Devon, joined the RAF on a short service commission in June 1938. After completing his training he joined 23 Squadron at Wittering in June 1939.

Awarded the DFC (18.2.41), Ensor had then taken part in numerous engagements with the enemy, including three at night. He was killed on September 8 1941, aged 21. He is buried in Kerfautras Cemetery, Brest.

APO 28.8.38   PO 27.6.39   FO 3.9.40

WILFRED JOHN ETHERINGTON

48899   **Sgt**   **Pilot**   **British**   **17 Squadron**

Etherington was born in Bromley, Kent in 1911. After losing his job when his company failed in the depression he joined the RAF on December 15 1931 as an aircraft hand. He took part in the Royal Tournament in 1932, as a member of the display team. He was then posted to 111 Squadron at Hornchurch on general duties.

Determined to progress, Etherington went on to an equipment course at Cranwell, after which he was posted as an ACI Storekeeper to 32 Squadron at Biggin Hill. He later went to 47 Squadron, Khartoum. Whilst there he applied for pilot training, was accepted and went to 4 FTS, Abu Sueir for training.

Back in the UK, Etherington joined 17 Squadron at Kenley in April 1936. He served with the squadron through the Dunkirk and France periods and for most of the Battle of Britain. On September 27 1940 he was posted to 5 FTS, Tern Hill, as an instructor on Ansons. In December he went with the unit to Moose Jaw in Canada.

Commissioned from Warrant Officer in February 1942, Etherington was posted to Lethbridge, Alberta, where 133 (RCAF) Squadron was being formed. He later went to Bagotville to help form No 1 OTU. In March 1943 Etherington returned to the UK and was posted to 59 OTU, Milfield. In late January 1944 he was sent to RAF Woodvale as a trainee Ops officer, a non-flying job. In late 1944 Etherington moved to Tern Hill, where he spent a period as unit test pilot with 5 (P) AFU. He went to 2 FIS, Montrose in March 1945 for a course, after which he was posted to Cranwell as an instructor. Etherington was released from the RAF in August 1945, as a Squadron Leader.

PO 21.2.42   FO 1.10.42   FL 21.2.44

CECIL ROY EVANS

745506   **Sgt**   **Pilot**   **British**   **235 Squadron**

Evans, of Kingston-on-Thames, Surrey, joined 235 Squadron on September 26 1940. He was killed on March 23 1941, still with 235. He was 20 and is remembered on the Runnymede Memorial, Panel 43.

DAVID EVANS

42491   **PO**   **Pilot**   **British**   **615 and 607 Squadrons**

Joined the RAF on a short service commission in June 1939. Evans was with 615 Squadron at Kenley in early June 1940.

His aircraft was damaged in combat with Bf 109s off Folkestone on August 15 and he landed at Hawkinge, unhurt. Evans was posted to 607 Squadron at Tangmere on September 8. He was shot down in combat with Bf 109s over Swanage on October 5 and baled out, unhurt. His Hurricane, P 3554, crashed at Woodhorn Farm, Aldingbourne.

Evans was killed on May 28 1943, as a Squadron Leader with 25 Squadron. He is buried in St Andrew's churchyard, Bebington, Cheshire.

APO 19.8.39   PO 1.2.40   FO 1.2.41   FL 1.2.42

GEORGE JOHN EVANS

123995   **Sgt**   **Air Gunner**   **British**   **604 Squadron**

Evans was born in Holloway, London in 1918. He was with 604 Squadron at the outbreak of war. With the advent of AI equipment and the Beaufighter he retrained as a Radio Observer. He was awarded the DFM (4.7.41), having then assisted in the destruction of three enemy aircraft.

Commissioned in May 1942, Evans was released from the RAF in 1946, as a Flight Lieutenant.

APO 1.5.42   FO 1.11.42   FL 1.5.44

HAROLD ARTHUR CHARLES EVANS

79178   **PO**   **Observer**   **British**   **236 Squadron**

Evans joined 236 Squadron on July 15 1940. He was released from the RAF in 1947, as a Flight Lieutenant, and died in October 1984.

PO 5.5.40   FO 5.5.41   FL 5.5.42

WALTER REGINALD EVANS

67607   **Sgt**   **Pilot**   **British**   **85 and 249 Squadrons**

Evans joined the RAFVR in January 1939. He began his weekend flying at 3 E&RFTS, Hamble in May and continued it at 10 E&RFTS, Portsmouth in August. Called up on September 2, Evans was posted to ITW at Bexhill and in December he went to 2 FTS, Brize Norton.

With training completed Evans was posted to 6 OTU, Sutton Bridge on May 20 1940 and four days later he joined 85 Squadron at Debden. He shared in the destruction of a Do 17 on August 6 and claimed a Bf 109 and a Bf 110 destroyed on September 1. Evans was posted to 249 Squadron at North Weald on September 11 and was airborne on a scramble within one hour of arriving.

In January 1941 he went to 55 OTU, Aston Down, as an instructor. After courses at CFS, Upavon and 9 FTS, Hullavington Evans was commissioned in June and posted to 71 OTU, Gordon's Tree, Sudan in October 1941. He spent two months at Air HQ Levant from September 1942, went to 138 MU in Iran as Liaison Officer and Instructor to the Iranian Air Force and in February 1943 joined 74 Squadron at Mehrabad, as 'B' Flight Commander.

After service in the Western Desert Evans went to South Africa in September 1943, to instruct. He was at CFS, Bloemfontein and 4 EFTS, Benoni until September 1944, when he was posted back to the UK. He instructed at 61 OTU, Rednal until February 1945, was at HQ Fighter Command, Uxbridge until April, did a Staff Navigation Course at the Empire Air Navigation School, Shawbury and then went to HQ 12 Group, Watnall as a Staff Navigation Officer.

Evans' last posting was in the Research Office of Air Traffic Control from January until September 1946, when he was released as a Squadron Leader.

PO 5.6.41   FO 5.6.42   FL 5.6.43

ALFRED DOUGLAS EVERETT

751702   **Sgt**   **Aircrew**   **British**   **235 Squadron**

Everett was with 235 Squadron in early July 1940. He left the RAF as a Warrant Officer and died in 1953.

GEOFFREY CHARLES EVERITT

751919   **Sgt**   **Wop/AG**   **British**   **29 Squadron**

Everitt, of Westminster, London, was with 29 in early July 1940. He was killed on August 6 1942, as a Flight Sergeant with 207 Squadron, operating in Lancasters from Bottesford, Leicestershire.

He was 25 years old and is buried in Oden War Cemetery, Netherlands.

PETER RAOUL EYLES

560889   **Sgt**   **Pilot**   **British**   **92 Squadron**

A pre-war airman pilot, Eyles, of Basingstoke, was with 92 Squadron in early 1940. Over Dunkirk on June 2 he damaged a He 111.

Eyles claimed a He 111 destroyed on September 11. He was shot down on the 20th by Major Mölders of JG 51. His Spitfire, N 3248, went into the Channel off Dungeness and Eyles was reported 'Missing'. He was 24 and is remembered on the Runnymede Memorial, Panel 14.

ANTHONY EYRE

90408	FO	Pilot	British	615 Squadron

Born in Lowestoft, Eyre was educated at Whitgift School, Croydon and was studying law before the war. He joined 615 Squadron, AuxAF in 1938 and was called for full-time service on August 24 1939.

Eyre went to France with 615 in November 1939. After ten hectic days of fighting in May 1940 the squadron was withdrawn on the 21st and was operational again in June. On the 11th Eyre claimed a probable Bf 109, on July 20 he claimed a Bf 109 destroyed, on August 14 he destroyed a Ju 87 and shared another, on the 15th shared a Bf 109, on the 20th destroyed a Do 17, on the 26th a Bf 109 and on the 28th a Do 17. He was awarded the DFC (30.8.40), credited with seven enemy aircraft shot down and several more damaged.

In December 1940 Eyre was appointed a Flight Commander and on February 26 1941 he took command of the squadron after the CO was killed, when his parachute caught fire and failed to open. Eyre was posted away for a rest in April 1941. He returned to operations in March 1942 to lead the North Weald Wing. Eyre was shot down on his first sortie as Wing Leader and captured.

He was killed on February 16 1946 in a flying accident during a practice flight in a Meteor.

PO (AuxAF) 26.7.38   PO 24.8.39   FO 26.1.40   FL 26.1.41
SL 1.12.41

FRANTISEK FAJTL

82544	PO	Pilot	Czechoslovakian	310 and 17 Sqdns

Fajtl joined 310 Squadron at Duxford on August 6 1940. He was posted to 17 Squadron at Debden on September 25 and shared in the destruction of a Do 17 on October 2 and a Do 215 on the 24th.

In April 1942 Fajtl was given command of 122 Squadron at Hornchurch. He failed to return from a sortie over France on May 5 but evaded capture and got back to England. He was awarded the DFC.

Fajtl was given command of 313 Squadron at Ibsley in September 1943. He volunteered for service in Russia and in February 1944 took twenty-one Czech pilots with him. He formed and became CO of a Czech Squadron, which operated in the Carpathians and Slovakia with the Russian Air Force, flying Lavochkin aircraft.

Fajtl returned to Czechoslovakia after the war.

PO 2.8.40   FO 27.12.40

JAN PAWEL FALKOWSKI

P 0493	FO	Pilot	Polish	32 Squadron

Falkowski was born in Pochulanka, Latvia on June 26 1912. In May 1932 he went to Lwow for a university students' pilot course. In 1934 he was attached to the PAF Officers' School and finished his training as a fighter pilot. Commissioned in Autumn 1936, Falkowski served in the Torun Fighter Squadron for two years and was then posted to the Flying School at Deblin as an aerobatics instructor.

After the fighting in September 1939 Falkowski left Poland, drove to Bucharest, then went via Yugoslavia and Italy to Paris, arriving there on October 9. In late January 1940 he was posted to an instructors' school in preparation for future training of Polish pilots at Lyons. After the German attack in May Falkowski was transferred to Cognac airfield in charge of aerodrome defence. He left France for England on June 23 in the Polish liner 'Batory'.

Falkowski joined 32 Squadron at Acklington on September 12. On an evening patrol on January 16 1941 he intercepted and shot down a He 111 returning from a raid on Portsmouth. His aircraft was seriously damaged by return fire and Falkowski baled out and broke his leg in a heavy landing on Hayling Island. He rejoined the squadron at the end of March 1941.

On July 29 1941 Falkowski was posted to 315 Squadron at Northolt. He claimed Bf 109s destroyed on August 14, 19 and 21, September 16 and 21 and October 24. He was awarded the KW (10.9.41) and two Bars (30.10.41). Appointed a Flight Commander on September 22 1941, Falkowski stayed with the squadron into 1942. He was awarded the VM (5th Class) (19.2.42) and on June 20 was posted for a course to the Polish Army Staff College in Scotland. He was awarded the DFC (15.11.42).

In April 1943 Falkowski was at Polish HQ, London, went to 316 Squadron at Northolt on May 18 and on July 3 was given command of 303 Squadron, also at Northolt. He claimed FW 190s destroyed on August 22 and September 6 and he probably destroyed another on September 23.

Falkowski was posted to HQ 11 Group on November 22 1943 as Polish Liaison Officer. He was awarded a third Bar to the KW (20.12.43). He went to HQ 84 Group on February 15 1944 and moved with it to Normandy on June 20. In late November Falkowski was promoted to lead the Peterhead Wing, which moved to Coltishall on January 30 1945.

Escorting bombers attacking V2 sites in Holland on March 9 Falkowski was hit by flak and baled out. He was wounded in the leg by small arms fire as he came down and was captured on landing. He escaped and was hidden by the Dutch Resistance. He eventually met the American Army and was flown back to England, where he rejoined the Wing.

Falkowski went to Canada in February 1948. He began farming there but later started a flying school.

WALTER RONALD FARLEY

29089	FL	Pilot	British	151 and 46 Squadrons

Farley, of Knightsbridge, London, joined the RAF in late December 1930. He was posted to 2 FTS, Digby on January 10 1931 and joined 13 (Army Co-operation) Squadron at Netheravon on December 29 1931. He moved to 2 (Army Co-operation) Squadron at Manston on April 3 1933. Farley was posted to the staff of 2 FTS, Digby on March 11 1935 and in late 1936 went on to the RAFO.

Recalled on September 1 1939, Farley flew operational sorties with both 151 and 46 Squadrons during the Battle of Britain period but it seems unlikely that he actually served with either squadron. On November 8 1940 he was attacked by a Bf 109 and baled out, breaking a leg on landing. His Hurricane, V 6922, crashed and burned out.

Farley was awarded the DFC (7.3.41), serving with 419 Flight. This unit was engaged on special duties, such as dropping agents in

WR Farley (continued)

occupied Europe and picking them up. It became 138 Squadron on August 25 1941. Farley was killed on April 21 1942, as a Wing Commander with 138. He was 38 years old and is buried in Durnbach War Cemetery, Germany.

PO 29.12.30   FO 29.7.32   FL 1.4.36   FL 1.9.39
SL 1.12.40   WC 1.3.42

JAMES NIGEL WATTS FARMER

37316   FL   Pilot   British   302 Squadron

Born on March 11 1915, Farmer was at Shrewsbury School from 1928 to 1933. He joined the RAF on a short service commission in August 1935. On October 19 he went to 5 FTS, Sealand and with training completed joined 57 Squadron at Upper Heyford on June 28 1936.

Farmer was posted to RAF Upwood on October 1 1938 on the SHQ Staff. He joined 302 Squadron at Leconfield on July 15 1940, as a Flight Commander. Awarded the DFC (7.3.41), he was posted away in April 1941 to join 610 Squadron at Westhampnett, as a Flight Commander.

Farmer stayed in the RAF and retired on February 6 1960, as a Group Captain, retaining the rank of Air Commodore.

APO 30.9.35   PO 6.3.36   FO 6.3.38   FL 6.3.40
SL 1.6.41   WC 1.6.42   WC 1.7.47   GC 1.1.54

ERIC FARNES

77374   PO   Air Gunner   British   141 Squadron

Farnes joined the RAF in 1940. He was with 141 Squadron at Turnhouse in early July and went south with it to West Malling on the 12th.

On the morning of July 19 twelve Defiants were ordered forward to Hawkinge. At 12.23 hrs they were ordered off to patrol twenty miles south of Folkestone but three dropped out with engine trouble. At about 12.45 hrs they were surprised by Bf 109s of lll/JG 51, attacking from a higher altitude out of the sun. Farnes' Defiant, L 7001, was badly damaged and crashed near Hawkinge due to engine failure, with the pilot, Flight Lieutenant MJ Loudon wounded. Farnes baled out and was rescued from the sea, uninjured. Only two of the nine aircraft which set out got safely back to base.

Farnes was released from the RAF in 1947, as a Squadron Leader. He died on September 23 1985.

PO 16.3.40   FO 16.3.41   FL 16.3.42

PAUL CASWELL POWE FARNES

88437   Sgt   Pilot   British   501 Squadron

Farnes, who was born at Boscombe, Hampshire on July 16 1918, joined the RAFVR in April 1938 and did his flying training at 19 E&RFTS, Gatwick. In July 1939 he took the opportunity of spending six months with the regular RAF and went to the 11 Group Pool at St Athan, where he converted to Hurricanes.

On September 14 1939 Farnes joined 501 Squadron at Filton. The squadron flew to Bethienville in France on May 10 1940. Farnes destroyed a He 111 and shared a Do 17 on the 12th and shared a probable Bf 109 on the 27th. After being withdrawn on June 17 the squadron regrouped at Croydon and Middle Wallop and on July 26 moved to Gravesend. On August 12 Farnes claimed a Ju 87 destroyed, on the 15th two more, on the 18th a Bf 110, on the 28th a Bf 109, on September 30 a Ju 88 and on October 29 and November 8 two Bf 109s probably destroyed. He was awarded the DFM (22.10.40).

Commissioned in November 1940, Farnes was posted to 57 OTU, Hawarden on February 13 1941, as an instructor. He went out to 73

OTU, Aden on November 9 1941, from where he was posted on February 27 1942 to 229 Squadron at El Firdan, as a Flight Commander. The squadron spent two months in Malta and whilst there, on April 2, he damaged a Ju 88.

Farnes was posted to Air HQ Iraq, Habbaniya on July 3 1942 and apart from seven months spent in Baghdad in 1943 he remained there until January 19 1945, when he returned to the UK. After a short refresher course at 53 OTU, Kirton-in-Lindsey Farnes went to 124 Squadron at Hawkinge for a month. He spent two months at the CFE, Tangmere and then took command of 611 Squadron at Peterhead on July 7 1945. He was given command of 164 Squadron at Turnhouse on August 14 and led the squadron until August 31 1946.

In the post-war years Farnes held a series of appointments prior to his retirement on June 27 1958, as a Squadron Leader, retaining the rank of Wing Commander.

PO 27.11.40   FO 27.11.41   FL 26.7.42   SL 1.5.44
SL 1.9.45

ANDREW DOUGLAS FARQUHAR

90158   WC   Pilot   British   257 Squadron

Farquhar joined 602 Squadron, AuxAF in 1927. He took command of the squadron in January 1939. He was called for full-time service on August 24 1939.

On patrol on February 9 1940 Farquhar engaged a He 111 twenty miles out to sea and put both its engines out of action. The pilot turned landwards and crash-landed near North Berwick. On February 22 Farquhar shot down a He 111 at Coldingham, Berwickshire. He followed it down and seeing that the enemy crew were about to set their aircraft on fire he landed in the same field. Unfortunately his Spitfire cartwheeled and went on to its back and Farquhar was pulled out by the Germans he had just shot down.

He was awarded the DFC (1.3.40), promoted to Wing Commander and posted to RAF Martlesham Heath, to command. Whilst there he flew sorties with 257 Squadron on September 1 and 18, thus qualifying for the Battle of Britain clasp. He also shared in the destruction of two Ju 87s on November 8 1940, whilst flying with 17 Squadron.

On March 15 1941 Farquhar became Wing Commander Flying Hornchurch Wing. He was posted away on June 2 to command the Training Wing at 53 OTU, Heston.

Farquhar was released from the RAF in 1945, as a Group Captain. He later emigrated to South Africa and became a fruit farmer. He died in the mid-sixties.

PO (AuxAF) 17.8.27   FO (AuxAF) 17.2.29
FL (AuxAF) 6.5.31   SL (AuxAF) 26.10.37
SL 24.8.39   WC 1.3.40

JOHN ROBINSON FARROW

745091   Sgt   Pilot   British   229 Squadron

Farrow, of Eastleigh, joined 229 Squadron at Wittering in September 1940. On October 8 he lost formation in cloud and fell, out of control, over Bovingdon. The Hurricane, V 6820, disintegrated at 200 feet and Farrow was killed, aged 24.

He is buried in Northwood Cemetery, Middlesex.

JOHN FARTHING

562114   Sgt   Pilot   British   235 Squadron

A pre-war airman pilot, Farthing was with 235 Squadron in early July 1940. Made an MBE (1.1.46), as a Warrant Officer. No other service details traced.

DEREK P FAWCETT

755949 **Sgt** **Air Gunner** **British** **29 Squadron**

Joined 29 Squadron in October 1940. Fawcett was killed on September 15 1941, serving with 75 Squadron, operating in Wellingtons from Feltwell.

Fawcett is buried in Hamburg Cemetery, Germany.

EMILE FRANCOIS MARIE LEONCE FAYOLLE

30516 **PO** **Pilot** **French** **85 Squadron**

The son of an admiral and the grandson of a general, Fayolle was born at Chateau de Saint Priest, par Issoire on September 8 1916. He flew to Gibraltar on June 30 1940 in a Simoun and sailed for Britain on July 3.

Fayolle joined 85 Squadron at Church Fenton on September 13. He was posted to 242 Squadron at Stapleford Tawney on April 26 1941 and left on October 14 to go to Turnhouse, where the first Free French fighter squadron, 340, was about to be formed. On May 3 1942 Fayolle claimed a FW 190 destroyed and on May 11 a Ju 88.

He took command of 174 Squadron at Warmwell in August 1942 but was killed on the 19th over Dieppe. It was his first operation as CO.

ALAN NORMAN FEARY

742301 **Sgt** **Pilot** **British** **609 Squadron**

Feary was born in Derby in 1912. He was educated at Derby Municipal Secondary School and worked in the Borough Treasurer's Department. He joined the RAFVR in July 1936 and did his flying training at Burnaston aerodrome. Awarded his flying badge on November 18 1938, Feary was called up on September 1 1939. He was posted to 9 FTS, Hullavington for advanced training in December.

In April 1940 Feary went to 5 OTU, Aston Down, where he converted to Blenheims before joining 600 Squadron at Manston. He was posted to 609 Squadron at Northolt on June 11 1940.

Feary shared in the destruction of a Ju 88 on July 18, destroyed a Bf 109 on August 12 and a Ju 87 on the 13th. The next day Feary shot down a Ju 88, which had just bombed Middle Wallop, killing some airmen who were trying to close the doors of one hangar. The bomb went through the roof, blew the doors off, which fell on the airmen, crushing them. Feary, already airborne, shot the enemy aircraft down about thirty seconds later. It crashed five miles away.

On August 25 he destroyed a Bf 110 and on September 24 a Do 17. Feary was killed on October 17 1940, when he was shot down in a surprise attack by Bf 109s over Weymouth. He baled out but was too low. His Spitfire, N 3238, crashed at Watercombe Farm, south of Warmwell.

Feary is buried in Holy Trinity churchyard, Warmwell.

JOHN LESLIE FEATHER

641705 **Sgt** **Wop/AG** **British** **235 Squadron**

Feather, of Liverpool, joined 235 Squadron on August 2 1940. He was killed on September 18, whilst flying as a passenger in an aircraft of 22 Squadron. The Germans recovered his body and he is buried in Bayeux War Cemetery, France.

EMIL FECHTNER

81887 **PO** **Pilot** **Czechoslovakian** **310 Squadron**

Born on September 16 1916, Fechtner escaped from Czechoslovakia in 1938 and joined l'Armee de l'Air. He arrived in England in June 1940 and was posted to 310 Squadron at Duxford on July 12.

Fechtner claimed a Bf 110 destroyed on August 26, a Do 215 on the 31st, a Bf 110 on September 3 and a Do 215 on the 18th. He was awarded the DFC (10.40). He was killed when he crashed near Duxford on October 29 1940, in Hurricane P 3889, after colliding with Pilot Officer JM Maly during a Wing patrol.

Fechtner was 24. He is buried in Brookwood Military Cemetery.

STANISLAV FEJFAR

82545 **PO** **Pilot** **Czechoslovakian** **310 Squadron**

Fejfar joined 310 Squadron at Duxford on August 6 1940. He claimed a Bf 110 destroyed on September 9, a Do 17 on the 15th and shared a Do 215 on the 18th.

He was killed on May 17 1942, as a Flight Lieutenant with 313 Squadron. Fejfar is buried in Pihen-les-Guines Communal Cemetery, France.

PO 2.8.40 *FO 27.12.40*

STANLEY ALLEN FENEMORE

745110 **Sgt** **Pilot** **British** **245 and 501 Squadrons**

Fenemore, of Whitewell, Co Antrim, Northern Ireland, joined 245 Squadron at Aldergrove on July 17 1940. He moved to 501 Squadron at Kenley in September.

In an action with Bf 109s over Redhill on October 15 1940 Fenemore was shot down and killed. His Hurricane, V 6722, crashed at Postern Gate Farm, Godstone. He was 20 years old and is buried in Allerton Cemetery, Liverpool.

CECIL FRANCIS FENN

126029 **Sgt** **Observer** **British** **248 Squadron**

Fenn served with 248 Squadron from May 1940 to June 1941. He was commissioned from Warrant Officer in May 1942 and was released from the RAF in 1945, as a Flight Lieutenant. In May 1950 Fenn was commissioned in the RAuxAF Regiment. He died on December 27 1987.

PO 20.5.42 *FO 20.11.42* *FL 20.5.41*
FO (RAuxAF) 20.5.50

HAROLD ARTHUR FENTON

27127 **SL** **Pilot** **British** **238 Squadron**

Born in Gallegos, Patagonia, Argentina on February 9 1909, Fenton graduated from Trinity College, Dublin in 1927 and joined the RAF on a short service commission in September 1928. He was posted to 5 FTS, Sealand on October 1. He joined 4 (Army Co-operation) Squadron at Farnborough in June 1929 and in March 1930 went to India to join 5 (Army Co-operation) Squadron at Kohat, to take part in operations against the Afridis.

Fenton returned to the UK in 1933 and went target towing at Sutton Bridge. He went on to the Reserve in September 1933 and became a flying instructor at Air Service Training, Hamble. Before he was recalled at the outbreak of war Fenton was CFI at 3 E&RFTS, Hamble, instructing RAFVR trainees.

In February 1940 Fenton was posted to 8 FTS, Montrose as a Flight Commander in the Advanced Training Squadron. He was promoted in June and took command of 238 Squadron at Middle

HA Fenton (continued)

Wallop. On July 21 Fenton shared in the destruction of a Do 17 and on August 8 he ditched in the Channel, in Hurricane P 2947, after an attack on a He 59 during a search operation for earlier squadron losses. He was picked up by HMS 'Bassett' and admitted to Haslar Hospital, Gosport. Fenton rejoined the squadron on September 13 and on the 26th forced-landed at Lee-on-Solent after a combat with Bf 110s over Southampton. He claimed a Bf 110 destroyed on October 7.

In May 1941 238 was posted to the Middle East. It sailed in HMS 'Victorious', flew off near Majorca on June 14 for Malta, refuelled and then went on to Egypt. Fenton was appointed Wing Leader 243 Wing, Western Desert in September 1941. He was awarded the DFC (28.7.42) and in July 1942 was promoted to Acting Group Captain and given command of 212 Group, which had twelve squadrons of Hurricanes. Awarded the DSO (16.2.43), Fenton returned to the UK in February 1943 and was made CO of the Kenley Sector.

In August 1943 he became Group Captain Ops at 2nd TAF, Bracknell and in December took command of 84 Group Control Centre, moving in early 1944 to 83 Group Control Centre. Fenton was the first senior RAF officer to land in France on D Day. He remained on the Continent and was promoted to Acting Air Commodore as SASO 83 Group. At the end of the war he was at Luneberg. Offered a Permanent Commission, Fenton declined and did not stay on but was released from the RAF in late 1945. He was made a CBE (1.1.46).

Fenton was Managing Director of Deccan Airways from 1946 to 1947, General Manager of Airways Training Limited 1947 to 1948, Operations Manager BOAC 1949 to 1952 and Managing Director of Peter Jones 1952 to 1958.

PO 14.9.28   FO 14.3.30   FO (RAFO) 14.9.33   FL 1.1.40
SL 1.6.40   WC 1.12. 41   GC 26.10.45

JOHN OLLIS FENTON

81679   PO   Pilot   British   235 Squadron

Fenton, of Sevenoaks, Kent, joined 235 Squadron on August 5 1940. He shared a He 59 off Cherbourg with Pilot Officer HAC Gonay on October 8. He was killed on May 28 1941, still serving with 235.

Fenton was 21. He is remembered on the Runnymede Memorial, Panel 32.

PO 11.7.40

WALTER GORDON FENTON

391858   Sgt   Air Gunner   New Zealander   604 Sqdn

The son of a farmer, Fenton was born in Gisborne on May 3 1916. Too late for a short service commission, he volunteered for war service in 1939 and reported to the Ground Training School, Weraroa as a trainee air gunner on December 18.

In mid-January 1940 Fenton did a Lewis gun course at AOS, Ohakea and gained ten hours flying experience. He left for the UK on March 23 in the SS 'Akaroa'. On May 29 he was posted to 5 OTU, Aston Down, where he was awarded his air gunner's badge and promoted to Sergeant. Fenton joined 604 Squadron at Northolt on July 6.

Returning from Gravesend to Middle Wallop on August 15 Fenton was in a Blenheim, which suddenly encountered a force of German bombers. Before any action could be taken a lone Spitfire, flown by Pilot Officer DM Crook of 609, came from behind and riddled the Blenheim with bullets. The 604 pilot crash-landed at Middle Wallop and Fenton was taken to hospital with flesh wounds.

By June 1941 604 was completely equipped with Beaufighters. On August 1 Fenton was posted to 3 Group Training Flight for a gunnery conversion course, after which he joined 75 Squadron at Feltwell. Commissioned in January 1942, Fenton completed his tour

in June and went to CGS, Sutton Bridge, as an instructor. He moved to 28 OTU, Wymeswold in August 1942 and in June 1943 was repatriated to New Zealand.

Fenton was posted to Ohakea on instructional duties but in October a medical board found him to be unfit and he was invalided out on November 15 1943. He returned to farming.

PO 1.1.42   FO 1.10.42

SAMUEL GREEN FENWICK

91060   PO   Pilot   British   601 Squadron

Fenwick joined 601 Squadron, AuxAF in 1939. He was called to full-time service in September 1939 and posted to 601 Squadron at Exeter on October 1 1940.

On June 1 1942 Fenwick was posted to the Directorate of Accident Prevention at Air Ministry. He was released from the RAF in 1946.

APO 28.9.39   PO 17.3.40   FO 1.12.40   FL 1.12.41

CHARLES RAYMOND FENWICK

85648   PO   Pilot   British   610 Squadron

Joined 610 Squadron at Acklington on September 29 1940. Fenwick was one of the first MSFU pilots. He joined the 'Empire Franklyn' on July 3 1941 and was reserve pilot on the 'Empire Tide' in the ill-fated convoy PQ 17, which sailed for Russia in late June 1942. The 'Empire Tide' was one of eleven ships which survived German attacks to reach Archangel on July 24. Its Hurricane was still on the catapult.

Fenwick was released from the RAF in 1946, as a Squadron Leader.

PO 7.9.40   FO 7.12.41   FL 7.12.42

ROY FREDERICK FERDINAND

80817   PO   Pilot   British   263 Squadron

Ferdinand, of Chesham Bois, joined 263 Squadron at Drem in June 1940. He was killed on June 12 1941, as a Flying Officer, still with 263. He was 21 and is buried in Chesham Bois Burial Ground, Buckinghamshire.

PO 9.6.40

ERIC HANNAH FERGUSON

116529   Sgt   Air Gunner   British   141 Squadron

Joined 141 Squadron at Drem on September 17 1940. Commissioned in February 1942, Ferguson was killed on April 11 1943, as a Flying Officer with 515 Squadron, a unit which flew ahead of Bomber Command raids to jam German radar.

Ferguson is buried in Lemvig Cemetery, Denmark.

PO 9.2.42   FO 1.10.42

PETER JOHN FERGUSON

90167   FL   Pilot   British   602 Squadron

Ferguson joined 602 Squadron, AuxAF in 1936. He was called to full-time service on August 24 1939 and shared in the destruction of a Ju 88 on October 16.

Ferguson claimed a Ju 87 destroyed on August 18 1940 over Selsey. He was then attacked by one of the Bf 109 escort and hit in the port wing, elevator and fuel tank. Wounded and shocked, he decided not to bale out but crash-landed at Norway Farm, Rustington after breaking through power lines. He had a badly-strained back and was taken to Chichester Hospital. As a result of this crash Ferguson lost his flying category and was appointed ADC to the Duke of Kent.

With recurring pain and periodic blackouts Ferguson was not allowed to fly and the problem defied diagnosis. The Duke arranged for him to be seen by his personal physician. It proved to be a small shell splinter lodged between two bones and pressing against the spinal column. This was removed by a successful operation. Whilst Ferguson was being treated the Duke of Kent was killed in a plane crash in Scotland.

Ferguson was released from the RAF in 1945, as a Wing Commander.

PO (AuxAF) 16.7.36   FO (AuxAF) 16.1.38   FO 24.8.39
FL 3.9.40   SL 1.12.41

MIROSLAW FERIC

P 1387   PO   Pilot   Polish   303 Squadron

Feric was born on June 17 1915. He was in the PAF before the war and was credited with one enemy aircraft destroyed and another shared in September 1939. After the fall of Poland Feric escaped to France and joined l'Armée de l'Air.

He was posted to 303 Squadron, when it was formed at Northolt on August 2 1940. On August 31 he destroyed a Bf 109, on September 2 a probable Bf 109, on the 6th a Bf 109, on the 15th a Bf 109 and a Bf 110, on the 27th a Bf 109 and a Bf 110 and on October 5 a Bf 110. Feric was awarded the VM (5th Class)(23.12.40) and the KW (1.2.41).

He destroyed a Bf 109 on June 22 1941 and was awarded a Bar to the KW (10.9.41) and the DFC (30.10.41). Feric was killed on February 14 1942, still serving with 303. On a training flight his Spitfire, BL 432, broke up in the air and fell on Northolt aerodrome. The cause is unknown.

Feric is buried in Northwood Cemetery. He was awarded two more Bars to the KW (31.10.47).

FO 1.3.41

HENRY MICHAEL FERRISS

40099   FO   Pilot   British   111 Squadron

Born at Lee, London on August 1 1917, Ferriss was educated at St Joseph's, Blackheath and Stoneyhurst College. He began flying while he was at London University in 1935. He was later a medical student at St Thomas' Hospital.

Ferriss joined the RAF on a short service commission in July 1937. He was posted to 6 FTS, Netheravon on September 18 and joined 111 Squadron at Northolt on May 7 1938.

He shared in probably destroying a He 111 on April 8 1940 and shared another on the 10th. During patrols over France in May Ferriss destroyed a Bf 110 on the 13th, four more on the 18th, got a probable Bf 109 on the 31st, two Bf 109s on June 2 and another on the 10th. He was awarded the DFC (21.6.40).

Ferriss destroyed a Bf 109 and shared a Do 17 on July 10, shared a He 59 on the 28th, claimed a Do 215 on August 13 and a probable Do 17 on the 15th. In a head-on attack over Marden on August 16

1940 Ferriss collided with a Do 17 and was killed. He crashed on Sheephurst Farm, in Hurricane R 4193. The Do 17, of 7/KG 76, crashed at Moatlands, Brenchley, Paddock Wood.

Ferriss is buried in St Mary's churchyard, Chislehurst, Kent.

APO 5.9.37   PO 12.7.38   FO 12.1.40

FRANK FILDES

162675   Sgt   Aircrew   British   25 Squadron

Joined 25 Squadron at Debden in October 1940. Fildes was commissioned in the Administrative Branch in February 1944. He was released from the RAF in 1945.

PO 17.2.44   FO 17.8.44

T R H FINCH

No unknown   FO   Pilot   British   151 Squadron

No service details traced.

DONALD OSBORNE FINLAY

36031   SL   Pilot   British   54 and 41 Squadrons

Born on May 27 1909, Finlay was a well-known Olympic hurdler before the war. He joined the RAF on a direct-entry Permanent Commission in April 1935 and on May 13 was posted to 17 Squadron at Kenley. On March 16 1936 Finlay went to 54 Squadron at Hornchurch and on August 29 1937 he was posted to the RAF School of Aeronautical Engineering, Henlow for a course.

Finlay was posted to 54 Squadron, to command, on August 26 1940. Two days later he was shot down by Bf 109s over Ramsgate and baled out, wounded. His Spitfire, X 4053, is believed to be that which crashed at Westbere Lake, near Canterbury.

In September Finlay took command of 41 Squadron at Hornchurch. On the 23rd he claimed a Bf 109 destroyed, shared a Do 215 on October 7 and two more Bf 109s destroyed on November 23 and 27.

In August 1941 Finlay was promoted to Acting Wing Commander and posted away. He destroyed a Bf 109 on March 3 1942 and was awarded the DFC (10.4.42). He assumed temporary command of 608 Squadron at Montecorvino on April 1 1944 but was promoted to Group Captain soon afterwards and posted as SASO to 210 Group British North Africa Forces. He was awarded the AFC (1.9.44).

Finlay stayed on in the RAF, in the Engineer Branch. He retired on February 23 1959, as a Group Captain. He died in 1970.

PO 30.4.35   FO 30.10.36   FL 30.10.38   SL 1.6.40
WC 1.12.41   WC 1.10.46   GC 1.1.50

ARCHIBALD FINNIE

79158   PO   Pilot   British   54 Squadron

Finnie joined 54 Squadron at Rochford on July 8 1940. On the 24th he made a forced-landing at Great Bainden Farm, Mayfield after sustaining damage attacking Do 17s bombing a convoy in the Channel off Dover. He later returned to Rochford.

Finnie was shot down and killed the next day during combat with Bf 109s off Dover. He was 24 years old and is buried in Margate Cemetery, Kent.

PO 5.5.40

JOHN FREDERIC FORTESCUE FINNIS
SR 80035   FL   Pilot   British   1 and 229 Squadrons

Finnis was in the Southern Rhodesian Air Force. He transferred to the RAF and was given a commission for the duration. He was gazetted as a Pilot Officer/Temporary Flight Lieutenant on August 1 1940, with seniority from January 1 1940.

He joined No 1 Squadron at Northolt in early September 1940. On the 7th he damaged a Do 17. Finnis later served with 229 Squadron during the period of the Battle of Britain.

On June 9 1942 he was posted to 127 Squadron in the Western Desert, as a Flight Commander but was given command of 33 Squadron on July 20, an appointment he held until October 31 1942.

Finnis returned to the SRAF on September 8 1945.

FL (SRAF) 5.12.39   PO/FL 1.1.40   SL 1.3.41

BRENDAN EAMONN FERGUS FINUCANE
41276   FO   Pilot   Irish   65 Squadron

Finucane was born on October 16 1920 in Dublin. He joined the RAF on a short service commission in August 1938. He was posted to 65 Squadron at Hornchurch on July 13 1940.

Finucane claimed Bf 109s destroyed on August 12 and 13. He did not claim again until January 1941, on the 4th a Bf 110, on the 19th he shared a Ju 88, on February 4 destroyed a Bf 109 and another on April 15. He was awarded the DFC (13.5.41).

In late April 1941 Finucane was posted to 452 Squadron, then forming at Kirton-in-Lindsey, as a Flight Commander. On July 11 he claimed a Bf 109 destroyed, the squadron's first victory. Between August 3 and the end of October 1941 Finucane claimed eighteen Bf 109s destroyed. He was awarded a Bar to the DFC (9.9.41), a second Bar (26.9.41) and the DSO (21.10.41).

In January 1942 Finucane was given command of 602 Squadron at Redhill. He was wounded on February 20 in an engagement with FW 190s over the Channel. He destroyed a FW 190 and shared another on March 13 and destroyed three more on March 28, April 26 and May 17.

Finucane was appointed Wing Commander Flying at Hornchurch on June 27 1942. After attacking ships at Ostend and a German airfield on July 15 the Wing reformed to return to Hornchurch. As it passed at low level over the beach at Pointe du Touquet Finucane's Spitfire was hit by machine gun fire from the ground and his radiator was damaged. His engine began to overheat and Finucane apparently prepared to bale out but was too low. The engine stopped and he crashed into the sea, never to be seen again. He is remembered on the Runnymede Memorial, Panel 64. His portrait was done by Cuthbert Orde in October 1941.

APO 20.10.38   PO 29.8.39   FO 3.9.40   FL 3.9.41

ANTONY GEORGE ANSON FISHER
73708   FO   Pilot   British   111 Squadron

Fisher was born in 1915 and educated at Eton. He read Engineering at Cambridge and joined the RAFVR in 1939. He was called to full-time service at the outbreak of war and after completing his training he joined 111 Squadron at Wick in March 1940. He was posted away on August 24 1940.

Awarded the AFC (1.9.44), Fisher was released from the RAF in 1945, as a Squadron Leader. In 1955 he founded the Institute of Economic Affairs, which greatly influenced Britain's economic policy under Mrs Thatcher.

Fisher was knighted in June 1988 and died in San Francisco in early July. Brother of BM Fisher.

PO (RAFVR) 1.8.39   PO 25.9.39   FO 25.9.40   FL 25.9.41
SL 1.7.45

BASIL MARK FISHER
73282   FO   Pilot   British   111 Squadron

Fisher was educated at Eton and joined the RAFVR in 1938. He was with 111 Squadron at Croydon in early July 1940.

On August 15, in an action with Ju 88s and Bf 110s over Selsey, Fisher was shot down in flames. He baled out but was killed. His Hurricane, P 3944, crashed at Greenwood's Farm, Sidlesham.

He was 23 and is buried in St John's Church Cemetery, Eton. Brother of AGA Fisher.

PO (RAFVR) 26.7.38
PO 10.10.39   FO 26.1.40

GERALD FISHER
41570   FO   Pilot   British   602 Squadron

Fisher joined the RAF on a short service commission in November 1938. He did his ab initio training at 13 E&RFTS, White Waltham and moved on to 7 FTS, Peterborough on January 31 1939.

He was at 7 OTU, Hawarden in August 1940 and joined 602 Squadron at Westhampnett on September 8. Fisher claimed a Bf 109 destroyed on October 29.

He was released from the RAF in 1946, as a Squadron Leader. He died in 1973.

APO 14.1.39   PO 3.9.39   FO 3.9.40   FL 3.9.41
SL 1.7.45

WILLIAM MEAD LINDSLEY FISKE

78092   **PO**   **Pilot**   **American**   **601 Squadron**

The son of an international banker living in Paris, Fiske was at Cambridge University in the early thirties. He excelled in winter sports and driving fast cars. He set a record for the Cresta Run at St Moritz and captained the US Olympic team that won the bobsled event in 1932. He drove the first Stutz car to be entered in the Le Mans 24 hour race when he was 19.

Two weeks after the outbreak of war Fiske volunteered for the RAF and with his training completed he joined 601 Squadron at Tangmere on July 12 1940. He claimed a Ju 88 destroyed on August 13. Three days later he crash-landed in flames back at Tangmere following an engagement with a Ju 87 over Bognor. Fiske was grievously burned. He was taken to hospital but died of shock and injuries the next day, August 17 1940. He was 29 years old and is buried in Sts Mary and Blaise churchyard, Boxgrove, Sussex.

A bronze memorial plaque was unveiled in St Paul's Cathedral on July 4 1941. Beneath his name are the words 'An American citizen who died that England might live'.

APO 23.3.40

THOMAS BERNARD FITZGERALD

40783   **FO**   **Pilot**   **New Zealander**   **141 Squadron**

Fitzgerald was born at Temuka, South Canterbury on July 11 1919 and was educated at Timaru Boys' High School, after which he went farming with his father. He joined the RNZAF on a short service commission on June 8 1937 and carried out his flying training at Wigram.

On April 23 1938 Fitzgerald sailed for the UK in the SS 'Tamaroa' and on arrival transferred to the RAF and joined 103 Squadron at Usworth on June 15. At the end of the year the squadron converted to Battles. It flew to France on September 2 1939, as part of the AASF.

On May 12 1940 Fitzgerald was leading a section of three Battles, as part of a bomber force attacking bridges and roads near Sedan. Attacked by Bf 110s they went down to low level, flew along the Meuse and bombed from twenty feet while their gunners fired at German troops. In his next action, two days later, Fitzgerald shot down two Bf 109s, which attacked him at 4000 feet. Wounded in the shoulder and left hand he managed to make a forced-landing among French troops, without injury to his crew. He returned to England in a hospital ship. For these two actions Fitzgerald was awarded the DFC (13.6.40).

He volunteered for Fighter Command and on August 10 was posted to 141 Squadron at Turnhouse, as a Flight Commander. He joined 23 Squadron at Ford in late April 1941 and when his tour ended in mid-July Fitzgerald went to 54 OTU. Whilst there he converted to Hurricanes and in September was posted to 607 Squadron at Martlesham Heath, as a Flight Commander, moving in November to 41 Squadron at Merston.

In late February 1942, at the end of his third tour, Fitzgerald was placed on the Special Duties List and went to Hawker Aircraft at Langley, as a test pilot. On August 3 1942 Fitzgerald was flying the original prototype Hurricane, then camouflaged and with a three-bladed propellor, when he was fired on by a Do 17, which he then attacked and damaged. Other fighters shot it down into the sea.

Fitzgerald returned to New Zealand in late January 1943, was attached to the RNZAF and given command of 14 (RNZAF) Squadron, which went to Santo in the Solomon Islands in early April. He returned to New Zealand in June, to go to Staff College at Palmerston North. On October 2 1943 his attachment ceased. He returned to the UK and in mid-November went to de Havilland's as a test pilot.

In June 1944 Fitzgerald spent several weeks at the AFDU, Wittering flying Bf 109s and FW 190s. He returned to operations on June 11, when he was made Wing Leader at Coltishall. At the end of his fifth tour Fitzgerald was posted to HQ 2nd TAF in January 1945. He transferred back to the RNZAF in February 1946, returned to New Zealand in March 1947 and was released on December 15 1947.

PO (RNZAF) 8.6.37   *PO 1.6.38*   *FO 1.1.40*   *FL 1.1.41*
SL 1.3.42

JOSEPH FRANCIS FIZEL

1002702   **AC 1**   **Radar Operator**   **British**   **29 Squadron**

Fizel was posted to 29 Squadron in August 1940. On October 13 he was one of the crew in Blenheim K 7135, which was damaged in an attack by Hurricanes of 312 Squadron off the east coast. The aircraft returned to Tern Hill, with its crew of three unhurt.

Fizel is believed to have left the RAF during the war. He died on August 29 1976.

JOHN FLEMING

36195   **FO**   **Pilot**   **New Zealander**   **605 Squadron**

Born in Scotland on July 29 1915, Fleming was taken to New Zealand as a child. He graduated as a Bachelor of Commerce in 1935 from Victoria College, Wellington and got his Master's degree there two years later.

In 1938 Fleming was nominated for one of the small number of direct-entry Permanent Commissions, offered each year to graduates of British and Commonwealth universities. He was accepted and sailed for the UK on May 6 1939.

Fleming began his flying training at 5 E&RFTS, Hanworth on June 12, moving on August 19 to 2 FTS, Brize Norton. In January 1940, with flying training completed, he was posted to Manby for a Specialist Armament Course. He converted to Hurricanes at 6 OTU, Sutton Bridge in May and joined 605 Squadron at Drem on June 15 1940.

The squadron moved south to Croydon on September 7. The following morning they were ordered off and met a force of enemy bombers, escorted by Bf 109s, over Tunbridge Wells. In the ensuing combat Fleming was shot down in flames. He baled out, made a delayed drop of 20000 feet and landed, badly burned and shocked. Fleming was taken to Wrotham Cottage Hospital, at that time housing twelve expectant mothers. He was transferred to RAF Hospital, Halton, where he was put aside as a hopeless case after refusing to have both his legs amputated at the hip. With burned eyeballs, laying blindfolded in a small room having injections of morphine every four hours he was, in his own words, 'left to rot'. Fleming was found by Archie McIndoe. The surgeon suggested that as he was far too badly burned for plastic surgery he might like to go to Queen Victoria Hospital at East Grinstead to try the Saline Bath treatment. McIndoe pointed out that the treatment was still largely experimental but by then Fleming had nothing to lose. He transferred from Halton in October and within ten days of starting the bath treatment microscopic dots of skin began to grow, although initially they could only be seen with a magnifying lens.

Fleming was at East Grinstead until August 1941, when he was discharged to RAF Kenley. In September he was posted to 23 OTU, Pershore as Chief Armament Instructor and Station Armament Officer. Two years later Fleming was seconded to 12 Group RCAF to take up the post of Inspector of Bombing and Gunnery at OTUs formed in Canada. He was awarded the MBE in 1944. In March 1945 he was recalled to the UK to join one of the specialist teams tracking down V1 and V2 sites in France and Belgium, in the wake of the advancing allied armies. He went to Manby in September for the first Advanced Empire Air Armament Course, after which he was sent to RAF Staff College, Bracknell for a course. In June 1946 Fleming returned to New Zealand on leave, his first visit for over seven years.

He held a series of appointments in Britain and overseas prior to retiring at his own request on February 5 1959. Fleming settled in England.

PO 5.8.39   FO 1.4.40   FL 1.12.40   SL 1.12.41
WC 1.12.43   WC 1.7.48

ROBERT DAVID SPITTAL FLEMING

74672   PO   Pilot   British   249 Squadron

Fleming went to ITW, Cambridge in November 1939 and moved to FTS, Cranwell on January 1 1940. He was posted to No 1 School of Army Co-operation at Old Sarum on June 2 but eight days later went to 5 OTU, Aston Down to convert to Hurricanes, after which he joined 249 Squadron at Leconfield on June 23 1940.

Fleming was shot down and killed in combat with Bf 109s over Maidstone on September 7 1940. His Hurricane, R 4114, crashed at Hollingbourne. He was cremated at Golders Green Crematorium. Fleming was 20 years old.

PO 8.11.39

—————— FLETCHER

No unknown   Sgt   Pilot   British   3 Squadron

No service details traced.

ANDREW WILLIAM FLETCHER

37280   SL   Pilot   Canadian   235 Squadron

Fletcher, of Cardston, Alberta, joined the RAF on a short service commission in July 1935. He went to 5 FTS, Sealand on September 28 and after training was posted to SHQ RAF Calshot on July 20 1936.

In July 1940 Fletcher was with 235 Squadron as 'B' Flight Commander. He was awarded the DFC (22.10.40) and posted away in November 1940 to 272 Squadron, to command. In May 1941 the squadron went to the Middle East and Fletcher led a detachment to Malta in mid-July. On the 28th he destroyed four SM 79s and damaged two CR 42s on the ground at Borizzo airfield, on the 30th he destroyed three SM 79s on the ground at Elmas airfield and on September 28 he probably shot down two enemy aircraft at night.

At the end of his tour in October Fletcher was awarded a Bar to the DFC (31.10.41) and posted away. He was released from the RAF in 1946, returned to Canada and went farming in Warner, Alberta.

APO 16.9.35   PO 29.2.36   FO 29.8.37   FL 29.8.39
SL 1.9.40   WC 1.3.42

JOHN GORDON BOWLEY FLETCHER

800635   Sgt   Air Gunner   British   604 Squadron

Fletcher, of Wadhurst, was with 604 Squadron in June 1940. He was one of the crew of Blenheim L 6872, which crashed at Witheridge, Exeter on August 25 1940, whilst on an operational sortie. All three men on board were killed.

Fletcher was 20. He is buried in Forest Row Cemetery, Sussex.

WALTER THOMAS FLETCHER

NZ 40606   Sgt   Air Gunner   New Zealander   23 Sqdn

Born in Wairoa on October 14 1917, Fletcher was educated at Tauranga District High School and after leaving trained as an electrician.

In late September 1939 Fletcher volunteered for aircrew duties. He went to the Ground Training School at Weraroa on February 11 1940 as a trainee air gunner. In March he moved to the Air Observers' School, Ohakea for a Lewis gunnery course and air experience. He sailed for the UK in the RMS 'Rangitiki' on April 26.

Fletcher was posted to 5 OTU, Aston Down on July 17 and joined 23 Squadron at Ford on September 21. After the Battle of Britain the squadron began night intruder operations against airfields in France. On the night of April 9 1941 Fletcher's Blenheim bombed a column of enemy vehicles on the Goderville-Bolbec road. In late April he was in a Blenheim approaching the French coast on the way home when a four-engined bomber was sighted flying on the same course. It was identified as a FW Condor and was probably on its way to attack Allied shipping in the Atlantic. Closing in the Blenheim opened fire and the first bursts hit the Condor's bomb load and it exploded with a blinding flash, filling the air with debris and throwing the Blenheim about. After landing the crew found a piece of armour plate, nearly three feet square, sticking out of the leading edge of one wing.

On the night of May 3, in a Havoc, Fletcher damaged a Ju 88 and a He 111. In March 1942 he was posted to 116 Squadron, flying in Lysanders on radar calibration duties. In May Fletcher went to 1653 Conversion Unit at Polebrook for crewing-up and conversion to Liberators. After a spell in the Air Crew Pool at Snaith Fletcher's crew flew a Liberator to the Middle East to join 160 Squadron at Aqir, Palestine in September. The squadron was combined with 159 Squadron in mid-January 1943 to form 178 Squadron.

Fletcher left Egypt in mid-March, flew down to Freetown and sailed for the UK on the 27th. After leave he was posted to 11 OTU, Bassingbourn, as a Warrant Officer instructor. In mid-May 1944 he joined 282 Squadron on ASR duties, serving with it until November. He elected to take his discharge from the RNZAF in London on April 5 1945. Fletcher later returned to live in New Zealand.

JOHN FLINDERS

81333   PO   Pilot   British   32 Squadron

Joined 32 Squadron at Biggin Hill in April 1940. On May 19 Flinders claimed a Bf 109 destroyed on a patrol over France and another enemy aircraft shot down in early June.

He claimed a Do 17 on August 18 and is said to have had two more victories during the Battle of Britain period.

Flinders was released in 1946, as a Squadron Leader.

PO 1.4.40   FO 1.4.41
FL 1.4.42

FREDERICK WILLIAM FLOOD

37582   FL   Pilot   Australian   235 Squadron

Flood transferred from the RAAF to the RAF in February 1936. He was posted to 32 Squadron at Biggin Hill on March 6 and moved to

8 Squadron at Khormaksar, Aden on October 24 1936. Flood was appointed PA to the AOC British Forces in Aden on April 4 1938. He returned to his squadron on October 18.

In June 1940 Flood was a Flight Commander with 235 Squadron. On August 24 his Blenheim was damaged in an attack by Hurricanes of No 1 (RCAF) Squadron over Thorney Island. He landed safely, with his crew unhurt.

Flood failed to return from an escort operation for FAA Albacores attacking Calais on September 11 and he and his crew were reported 'Missing'. He was 25 years old and is remembered on the Runnymede Memorial, Panel 4.

PO 21.2.36   FO 21.9.37   FL 21.9.39

HUBERT LUIZ FLOWER

551866   Sgt   Aircrew   British   248 Squadron

Joined 248 Squadron in late July 1940. Reported to have died on August 23 1941 but no details traced.

VACLAV FOGLAR

138057   Sgt   Pilot   Czechoslovakian   245 Squadron

Joined 245 Squadron at Aldergrove on October 18 1940. Foglar was commissioned in May 1942 and at some time was awarded the Czech Military Cross. He returned to Czechoslovakia after the war and is believed to have been killed in an aircraft accident in December 1947.

PO 25.5.42

EMIL ANTONIN FOIT

83225   PO   Pilot   Czechoslovakian   310 Squadron

Foit joined 310 Squadron at Duxford on August 21 1940. He commanded the squadron from January 1943 to March 1944 and was awarded the DFC at the end of his tour. He also received the Czech Military Cross.

Foit was released after the war, as a Squadron Leader. He died in England in 1976.

PO 17.8.40   FO 27.12.40

RONALD HENRY FOKES

88439   Sgt   Pilot   British   92 Squadron

Fokes, of Hillingdon, Middlesex, was with 92 Squadron at Northolt in May 1940. Over Dunkirk on June 2 he claimed a He 111 destroyed. On July 4 he shared another He 111, on September 10 shared a Do 17, on October 15 destroyed two Bf 109s and a He 111 and destroyed three more Bf 109s on October 26, November 15 and 17. Fokes was awarded the DFM (15.11.40) and commissioned in late November.

On February 5 1941 he shared a He 111 and soon afterwards was posted to 53 OTU, Heston, as an instructor. In November Fokes joined 154 Squadron, then being formed at Fowlmere, as a Flight Commander. He was posted away in March 1942 to 56 Squadron at Duxford.

Fokes was given command of 257 Squadron at Warmwell in July 1943. He was awarded the DFC (10.3.44), then being credited with at least ten enemy aircraft destroyed. On June 12 1944 Fokes was killed over France, aged 33. He is buried in Banneville-la-Campagne War Cemetery, France.

PO 29.11.40   FO 29.11.41   FL 29.11.42

JAMES HENRY FOLLIARD

149657   Sgt   Aircrew   British   604 Squadron

Joined 604 Squadron at Middle Wallop on July 14 1940. Folliard was commissioned in July 1943, as a Flight Engineer. He was released from the RAF in 1945, as a Flight Lieutenant. He died in late 1981 or early 1982.

PO 7.7.43   FO 7.1.44

DESMOND FOPP

112448   Sgt   Pilot   British   17 Squadron

Born on March 13 1920, Fopp joined the RAFVR in November 1938. He was called up at the outbreak of war and posted to 2 FTS, Brize Norton. In May 1940 Fopp went to 6 OTU, Sutton Bridge and at the end of the month joined 17 Squadron at Debden, operating with it in France in June.

On July 12 Fopp shared in destroying a He 111. He was himself shot down in flames on September 3 and baled out, burned, landing at Pressey's Farm, Hutton. His Hurricane, P 3673, crashed and burned out near Handley's Dairy Farm, Ingrave, Essex. After three months in hospital Fopp went to 3 School of General Reconnaissance, Blackpool. He rejoined 17 Squadron, then at Elgin, in July 1941.

Commissioned in November, Fopp was posted to 132 Squadron at Peterhead. He was appointed 'A' Flight Commander in May 1942, received a Mention in Despatches (1.1.43) and remained with the squadron until the end of 1943, when he went as Fighter Tactics Liaison Officer to the 8th and 9th USAF. In May 1944 Fopp was posted to CFS, Upavon for an instructor's course on Oxfords, after which he went to an AFU at Wrexham. He was awarded the AFC (29.9.44) and in August 1945 moved to 12 FTS, Grantham, to instruct on Harvards.

Fopp stayed in the RAF after the war. He left in 1950 and spent a year as a civilian, instructing naval pilots on Mosquitos. He rejoined the RAF in March 1951 and held a series of appointments, latterly concerned with helicopters, prior to retiring on March 13 1975, as a Squadron Leader.

PO 3.11.41   FO 21.7.42   FL 21.7.43   FL 1.9.45
FL 10.6.46   SL 1.9.65

ATHOL STANHOPE FORBES

37499   FL   Pilot   British   303 and 66 Squadrons

Forbes was born in Hanover Square, London in 1912. He was educated at Throwthorne Towers, Berkshire and Dover College. In November 1935 he joined the RAF on a short service commission and was posted to 10 FTS, Tern Hill on February 1 1936. After completing his flying training Forbes went to the School of Army Co-operation, Old Sarum, under instruction and was posted to the School staff on August 28 1937.

Forbes joined 303 Squadron at Northolt at its formation on August 2 1940, as a Flight Commander. He claimed a Ju 88 destroyed on September 5, a Bf 109 on the 6th, a Do 215 on the 7th, two Do 17s on the 11th and He 111s on the 26th and 27th. He was awarded the DFC (22.10.40). Promoted to Acting Squadron Leader, Forbes was given command of 66 Squadron at West Malling on October 17. He was awarded the VM (5th Class)(24.12.40) for his services with 303 Squadron.

Forbes shared in destroying a Bf 109 on August 20 1941 and was posted away in October to a staff job at HQ 10 Group, Box. Forbes was awarded a Bar to the DFC (4.11.41).

AS Forbes (continued)

Awarded the OBE (1.1.44), Forbes was with 165 Wing in the Far East in 1944. He was posted to HQ 221 Group, Burma on August 16 1944 as SASO.

Forbes was released from the RAF in 1948, as a Group Captain. His portrait was done by Eric Kennington in 1940. He died in 1981.

APO 20.1.36   PO 25.11.36   FO 25.5.38   FL 25.5.40
SL 1.12.41   WC 1.7.43

ERNEST GEORGE FORD

81636   PO   Pilot   Canadian   3 and 232 Squadrons

Joined 3 Squadron at Kenley in May 1940. Ford was posted to 232 Squadron at its reformation at Sumburgh on July 17 but returned to 3 Squadron on September 10.

Ford was later repatriated to Canada and was killed there on December 12 1942, aged 28, as a Flight Lieutenant. He is buried in Burnsland Cemetery, Calgary.

PO 15.5.40   FO 22.2.41   FL 22.2.42

ROY CLEMENT FORD

88214   Sgt   Pilot   British   41 Squadron

Ford joined the RAFVR in June 1938 and did his flying training at 20 E&RFTS, Gravesend. Called up in September 1939 he was posted to 6 FTS, Little Rissington on October 6 for assessment of flying capabilities, after which he joined 41 Squadron at Catterick on December 15 1939.

On September 7 1940 Ford made a forced-landing between Confield Tye and Tinsley's Farm at West Hanningfield after a combat. He was unhurt. Commissioned in November 1940, Ford was posted on April 5 1941 to 4 Delivery Flight, Grangemouth but volunteered for the MSFU, then about to be formed at Speke. He joined the unit on May 23 1941 and served in the SS 'Empire Sun', 'Empire Shackleton', 'Empire Heath' and 'Dalton Hall' on North Atlantic crossings and Gibraltar convoy escort.

Ford went to Hawker's at Langley on June 23 1942, as a production test pilot. He completed 447 'first flights'. On June 17 1943 he was posted for a course to No 1 Empire Test Pilots' School, Boscombe Down, after which he joined 20 MU, Aston Down, as a test pilot.

Ford was released from the RAF on October 23 1945 and commissioned again in the RAFVR from September 1947 until May 11 1952, during which time he instructed at 18 Reserve Flying School at Fair Oaks and from April 1948 at 15 RFS, Redhill.

PO 6.11.40   FO 6.11.41   FL 6.11.42   FO (RAFVR) 13.9.47

DEREK NIGEL FORDE

41526   FO   Pilot   British   145 and 605 Squadrons

Born on October 17 1917, Forde joined the RAF on a short service commission in August 1938. He was with 145 Squadron in May 1940 and on the 27th was shot down over Dunkirk in combat with Bf 110s. He was unhurt and rejoined the squadron.

Forde was posted to 605 Squadron at Croydon on September 26. He was with 72 Squadron in 1942 and went with it to North Africa in November. He was awarded the DFC (26.2.43), being then credited with at least three enemy aircraft destroyed. On April 24 1943 Forde damaged a Bf 109.

He stayed on in the RAF and retired on February 8 1953, as a Squadron Leader. Forde died on January 16 1979.

APO 6.10.38   PO 3.9.39   FO 3.9.40   FL 3.9.41
SL 1.7.44   SL 1.8.47

DUDLEY HENRY FORREST

115218   Sgt   Pilot   British   66 Squadron and 421 Flight

Forrest was with 66 Squadron at Coltishall in early July 1940. On September 27 he claimed a share in destroying a Do 17.

On October 7 Forrest was posted to 421 Flight at Hawkinge and on December 18 he shared a Do 17, destroyed off Dover.

Commissioned in December 1941, he was released from the RAF in 1947, as a Flight Lieutenant.

PO 31.12.41   FO 1.10.42   FL 31.12.43

GEORGE MATHWIN FORRESTER

81369   PO   Pilot   British   605 Squadron

Born in Newcastle on February 17 1914, Forrester lived at Upper Bassett, near Southampton. He was at Haileybury College from 1927 to 1930.

Commissioned from Sergeant in July 1940, Forrester joined 605 Squadron at Drem. On September 9 he was shot down by crossfire in an engagement with He 111s over Farnborough and collided with one of Stab lll/KG 53. His Hurricane, L 2059, fell, minus its starboard wing, north of Alton, crashing at Southfield Farm. Forrester was killed. He is buried in Odiham Cemetery, Hampshire.

PO 6.7.40

TERENCE HENRY TRIMBLE FORSHAW

39165   FL   Pilot   British   609 Squadron

Forshaw was born on August 29 1916 and joined the RAF on a short service commission in August 1936. He was posted to 5 FTS, Sealand on October 31 and after completing his training joined 73 Squadron at Digby on June 30 1937. Forshaw was posted to the SHQ Staff there on February 2 1939.

He joined 609 Squadron at Middle Wallop on September 8 1940 and was made a Flight Commander on November 29. Forshaw was posted away for a rest in April 1941. He was given command of 603 Squadron at Hornchurch in October. Scrambled to search for a suspected raider on December 15, Forshaw crashed into the sea southeast of Newburgh. He was injured and did not return to the squadron.

Forshaw retired from the RAF on November 29 1957, as a Squadron Leader. He later went to live in South Africa.

APO 12.10.36   PO 17.8.37   FO 17.5.39   FL 3.9.40
SL 1.12.41   SL 1.8.47

ANTHONY DOUGLAS FORSTER

90290   FO   Pilot   British   151 and 607 Squadrons

Born at Bishop Middleham, Durham on April 17 1914, Forster joined 607 Squadron, AuxAF in early 1938. Called up on August 24 1939, he flew to France with the squadron in November and before 607 was withdrawn on May 20 1940 he was credited with four enemy aircraft destroyed.

In June Forster was posted to 151 Squadron at Martlesham Heath and on July 9 shared in the destruction of a Bf 110. Awarded the DFC (30.7.40), he was credited with a total of six enemy aircraft destroyed. Forster returned to 607 Squadron on August 12 1940.

He retired from the RAF on April 24 1962, as a Wing Commander.

PO (AuxAF) 31.5.38   PO 24.8.39   FO 30.11.39
FL 30.11.40   SL 1.12.41   WC 1.7.47

COLIN LEO MALCOLM FORSYTH

NZ 40607   Sgt   Air Gunner   New Zealander   23 Sqdn

Forsyth was born in Tauranga on February 11 1914. He was educated at Te Kuiti District High School and was employed at the Oropi saw mills.

He volunteered for aircrew duties in late 1939 and began his ground training at Weraroa on February 12 1940. He completed a Lewis gunnery course at Ohakea and sailed from Auckland for the UK in the RMS 'Rangitiki' in late April.

In mid-July Forsyth was posted to 5 OTU, Aston Down and he joined 23 Squadron at Ford on September 21 1940. The squadron began night intruder operations in December and on March 8 1941 Forsyth's crew damaged a He 111 and a Do 17.

On July 26 1941 Forsyth suffered injuries and burns in a crash during take-off and was admitted to Margate General Hospital and although he rejoined the squadron he was rested from operations. He was posted on December 1 to 418 (RCAF) Squadron, newly-formed at Debden for intruder work. From March 22 1942 it flew regular night sorties over the Continent, attacking strategic targets and intruding over enemy airfields.

Forsyth was awarded the DFM (15.11.42) and commissioned in December. He was posted to 180 Squadron at Foulsham on July 5 1943, operating in Mitchells on daylight raids. He moved to Dunsfold on March 11 1944, to join 98 Squadron, also flying Mitchells. On May 8 1944 Forsyth was one of the crew in an aircraft captained by the CO, Wing Commander RKF Bell-Irving. After attacking the target the Mitchell had turned for home, when it was hit by anti-aircraft fire. The nose was blown off, the Mitchell fell from 12000 down to 7000 feet and then banked and crashed in flames in a field at Cambron, near Abbeville. All aboard were killed.

Forsyth is buried in Notre Dame de la Chappelle Cemetery, Abbeville. He was awarded the DFC (12.4.45).

PO 3.12.42   FO 3.6.43

RONALD VICTOR FORWARD

172323   Sgt   Pilot   British   257 Squadron

Forward was with 257 Squadron at Hendon in June 1940. On a dawn patrol on July 9 he intercepted a Do 17. He fired all his ammunition but without any apparent result. The enemy aircraft finally crashed near Antwerp. On July 28 Forward's Hurricane, P 3622, was seriously damaged in combat with Bf 109s over the Channel off Dover and he crash-landed at Hawkinge, slightly injured, writing the aircraft off.

At the end of August Forward was rested from operations, severely shocked. In March 1944 he was commissioned in the Administrative Branch and released in 1946, as a Flying Officer.

APO 16.3.44   PO 11.5.44   FO 11.11.44

ROBERT WILLIAM FOSTER

80815   PO   Pilot   British   605 Squadron

Foster joined the RAFVR on May 1 1939 and did some part-time flying training at 9 E&RFTS, Ansty. He was called up at the outbreak of war and posted to No 1 ITW, Cambridge on November 10 1939, moving in late December to 12 FTS, Grantham.

Commissioned in June 1940, Foster went to 6 OTU, Sutton Bridge for conversion to Hurricanes and joined 605 Squadron at Drem on July 9. He claimed a Bf 109 destroyed on October 7 and another probably destroyed on the 15th.

Foster was posted to 55 OTU, Usworth on September 25 1941, as an instructor. He joined 54 Squadron at Castletown on April 14 1942 and sailed with it for Australia in HMT F6 on June 18, the first RAF fighter squadron sent to assist in the country's defence.

After a working-up period 54 moved to its operational base at Darwin on January 17 1943. Foster got the squadron's first victory on February 6, a Mitsubishi 'Dinah'. Between March 15 and July 6 1943 he destroyed 4 Mitsubishi Bettys and probably destroyed two more. He was awarded the DFC (13.8.43).

Foster left Australia on February 2 1944 for the UK. He joined the Air Information Unit on April 29 and went with it to the Continent on July 1 1944. He was posted to HQ Fighter Command on October 7 1944, staying there until June 11 1945, when he went to RAF Bentwaters.

Foster was released from the RAF on February 27 1947, as a Wing Commander. He served with 3613 FCU, RAuxAF from 1948 to 1958.

PO 9.6.40   FO 9.6.41   FL 9.6.42

ALAN COOK FOTHERINGHAM

754241   Sgt   Pilot   British   3 Squadron

Fotheringham served with 3 Squadron during the Battle of Britain.

In early 1941 he was with 615 Squadron at Kenley. On a Rhubarb operation on February 15 Fotheringham was shot down over Vlissingen, Holland in Hurricane V 7651 and captured.

Freed in May 1945, he was released from the RAF later in the year, as a Warrant Officer.

ALFRED LAWRENCE FOWLER

42116   PO   Pilot   New Zealander   248 Squadron

Fowler was born at Foxton on June 21 1918. He was educated at Foxton and Levin District High School and after leaving qualified as an electrician. From October 1937 he worked in Wellington as a Neon sign erector.

In June 1938 Fowler volunteered for an RAF short service commission, was provisionally accepted and sailed for the UK in the RMS 'Tainui' on February 1 1939. He carried out his elementary training at 10 E&RFTS, Yatesbury and went on to 5 FTS, Sealand on May 30. After high-dive and low-level bombing exercises at Aldergrove Fowler joined 248 Squadron at Hendon on November 6 1939. Originally in Fighter Command the squadron went over to Coastal Command in February 1940 but was seconded to Fighter Command during the Battle of Britain.

On October 3 1940 Fowler was on a North Sea patrol. He engaged a Do 215 and a combat started. Although wounded in the hand, face and eyes he pressed home his attacks until the enemy broke off the engagement. He then flew his badly damaged aircraft back to base. A radio message was picked up from the Dornier, reporting that it was returning to base, badly damaged and with members of its crew killed and injured. For this action Fowler was awarded the DFC (24.1.41).

In June 1941 he was posted to 119 Squadron at Bowmore for Catalina training. In July he joined 413 (RCAF) Squadron at Stranraer, then forming for general reconnaissance work. On August 23 Fowler took off from Loch Ryan on night-flying practice. A few seconds after take-off the aircraft crashed. Two of the crew were saved but Fowler was lost. He is buried in the Glebe Cemetery, Stranraer.

A subsequent Court of Enquiry found that the crash could have been caused by incorrect positioning of the elevator trimming tab control and recommended that illumination should be provided for night use. All Catalina units were so advised.

APO 12.5.39   PO 6.11.39   FO 6.11.40

REGINALD JOHN FOWLER

120330   Sgt   Pilot   British   247 Squadron

Joined 247 Squadron at Roborough on August 15 1940, a Gladiator unit for the day and night defence of Plymouth. Fowler was with the squadron until May 1941.

On September 13 1941 he flew a Hurricane off HMS 'Ark Royal' to Malta, to join 126 Squadron. Fowler was with 1435 Flight there in December 1941. Commissioned from Flight Sergeant in March 1942, he was released from the RAF in 1946, as a Flight Lieutenant.

PO 22.3.42   FO 22.9.42   FL 22.3.44

LAWRENCE FOX

1002697   Sgt   Aircrew   British   29 Squadron

Joined 29 Squadron at Digby on October 4 1940. Fox was promoted to Warrant Officer on October 1 1942. No further details traced.

PETER HUTTON FOX

754399   Sgt   Pilot   British   56 Squadron

Fox joined the RAFVR in Oxford in June 1939 and began training at 26 E&RFTS, Kidlington. On March 28 1940 he went to 13 EFTS, Fair Oaks and moved to 10 EFTS, Yatesbury on May 28 for a pre-fighter course.

Advanced training was carried out by Fox at 8 FTS, Montrose, after which he went to 5 OTU, Aston Down to convert to Hurricanes and then joined 56 Squadron at Boscombe Down on September 17 1940.

Fox was shot down in combat with Do 215s and Bf 110s over the Portland area on September 30. He is believed to have baled out, wounded in the leg. His Hurricane, N 2434, crashed at Okeford Fitzpaine. On November 16 Fox and Pilot Officer MR Ingle-Finch were flying to Kidlington in a Magister, when they crashed near Tidworth. Both were injured and admitted to Tidworth Hospital.

On June 28 1941 Fox joined 234 Squadron at Warmwell. He was shot down over France on October 20 1941 and captured. Freed on April 16 1945, Fox left the RAF in 1946, as a Warrant Officer.

CHRISTOPHER NEIL FOXLEY-NORRIS

70225   FO   Pilot   British   3 Squadron

Born on March 16 1917, Foxley-Norris was educated at Winchester College and Trinity College, Oxford. Whilst there he joined the University Air Squadron. In 1939 he won a Harmsworth Scholarship to the Middle Temple.

In early September 1939 Foxley-Norris was called up and posted to 9 FTS, Hullavington. With training completed, he went to the School of Army Co-operation at Old Sarum and then joined 13 Squadron at Douai in France. Back in England after the collapse of France Foxley-Norris volunteered for Fighter Command and was posted to 5 OTU, Aston Down in August, to convert to Hurricanes. He joined 3 Squadron at Turnhouse on September 27 1940 and moved to 615 Squadron at Northolt on November 19.

On February 26 1941 Foxley-Norris was jumped by Bf 109s and shot down in flames. He baled out, landing near Ashridge, Kent, where he met with a hostile reception from the locals. In June 1941 Foxley-Norris was posted to CFS, Upavon for an instructor's course, after which he went to 10 FTS, Tern Hill. He was later posted to Canada, to instruct in the Commonwealth Air Training Scheme.

In early 1943 Foxley-Norris went to Ferry Command to transport Hudsons across the Atlantic. He was with 143 Squadron at North Coates in mid-1943, flying Beaufighters on anti-shipping duties, as a Flight Commander. After being court-martialled for an alleged

breach of security and acquitted Foxley-Norris was posted to 252 Squadron in the Middle East, remaining with it until September 23 1944, when he went to 603 Squadron to command.

He returned to the UK in early 1945 and was given command of 143 Squadron, then part of the Banff Mosquito Strike Wing. Foxley-Norris was awarded the DSO (25.9.45).

In a long and distinguished post-war career Foxley-Norris held various appointments and commands before he retired on April 22 1974, as an Air Chief Marshal. He was made an OBE (2.1.56) and a GCB (1973)(KCB 1969; CB 1966). He became Chairman of the Battle of Britain Fighter Association in 1978.

PO (RAFO) 22.12.36   PO 9.9.39   FO 3.11.39   FL 17.3.41
SL 1.6.42   SL 1.9.45   WC 1.7.51   GC 1.7.57
AC 1.7.61   AVM 1.1.64   AM 1.7.68   ACM 1.12.70

DENNIS HUMBERT FOX-MALE

78660   PO   Pilot   British   152 Squadron

Educated at Wellington College and Trinity College, Oxford, Fox-Male was a solicitor before the war. He joined 152 Squadron at Warmwell on September 29 1940 and remained with it until 1941.

Fox-Male was released from the RAF in 1946, as a Flight Lieutenant. He died in 1986.

APO 15.3.40   PO 7.9.40   FO 7.9.41   FL 7.9.42

———— FRANCIS

No unknown   Sgt   Pilot   British   3 Squadron

No service details traced.

CLARENCE WILLIAM FRANCIS

115712   Sgt   Pilot   British   74 Squadron

Posted to 74 Squadron at Rochford on June 24 1940. Francis was commissioned in January 1942 and released from the RAF in 1946, as a Flight Lieutenant.

PO 6.1.42   FO 1.10.42   FL 6.1.44

COLIN DUNSTAN FRANCIS

42211   PO   Pilot   British   253 Squadron

Francis, of Stoke d'Abernon, Surrey, joined the RAF on a short service commission in April 1939. He was with 253 Squadron in early July 1940. The squadron moved south from Prestwick to Kenley on August 29.

On the morning of the 30th Francis took off in a section of three aircraft to join the rest of the squadron in attacking a force of bombers, which were escorted by some thirty fighters. It was his first encounter with the Luftwaffe and he was shot down and reported 'Missing'. His name appears on the Runnymede Memorial, Panel 8.

In August 1981 an aircraft was excavated at Wrotham, on land which had been Percival's Farm in 1940. It proved to be Hurricane L 1965 and Francis' remains were still in the cockpit. They were buried with military honours at Brookwood Military Cemetery. Francis was 19 when he was killed.

APO 24.6.39   PO 16.12.39

DOUGLAS NORMAN FRANCIS

745507   Sgt   Pilot   British   257 Squadron

Joined 257 Squadron on September 13 1940. No further service details traced. He died on January 7 1961.

JOHN FRANCIS

528890 Sgt Aircrew British 23 Squadron

Joined 23 Squadron in early July 1940. No further service details traced.

NOEL INGLIS CHALMERS FRANCIS

40817 FO Pilot British 247 Squadron

Francis, of Brighton, Sussex, joined the RAF on a short service commission in April 1938. He was with 247 Squadron at Roborough from its formation on August 1 1940.

At St Eval on November 22 Francis crashed on take-off. His Gladiator, N 5649, was written off.

Francis was killed on December 9 1941, aged 23. His unit at the time of his death is unknown. He is buried in St Peter's churchyard, Stoke-upon-Tern, Shropshire.

APO 4.6.38   PO 4.4.39   FO 3.9.40

WALTER DERRICK KERR FRANKLIN

40217 FO Pilot British 74 Squadron

Franklin, from Jamaica, joined the RAF on a short service commission in August 1937 and did his elementary flying at 12 E&RFTS, Prestwick. On October 24 he was posted to 9 FTS, Hullavington and on August 20 1938 he joined 142 Squadron at Andover.

On September 2 1939 the squadron flew its Battles out to France and after suffering heavy losses in May 1940 it was withdrawn to England in June. Franklin volunteered for Fighter Command and on August 21 joined 74 Squadron at Kirton-in-Lindsey. He claimed a Ju 87 destroyed on November 14 and on December 30 Franklin was posted to CFS, Upavon for an instructor's course.

He was instructing until 1945, when he went for a course at the Empire Test Pilots' School at Cranfield, after which he was posted to RAE, Farnborough.

Franklin resigned his commission in 1947 and returned to Jamaica to run the family hotel, which he eventually owned. He later sold out and returned to England in 1967.

APO 24.10.37   PO 23.8.38   FO 23.4 40   FL 23.4.41

WILLIAM HENRY FRANKLIN

44753 PO Pilot British 65 Squadron

Franklin was born in 1911 in Poplar, London. He joined the RAF in the late twenties as an aircraft apprentice. He was with 65 Squadron at the outbreak of war.

Over Dunkirk on May 22 1940 Franklin damaged a Ju 88, on the 24th he shared a Hs 126, on the 26th he destroyed a Bf 109 and a Bf 110, on the 27th a Do 17 and a Ju 88 and on the 28th he shared a probable Do 17. Franklin destroyed two Bf 109s on June 25 and was awarded the DFM (9.7.40).

Between July 7 and August 16 Franklin destroyed eight Bf 109s and was awarded a Bar to the DFM (13.8.40). He was commissioned from Flight Sergeant in September and was reported 'Missing' on December 12 1940, after chasing an enemy bomber in heavy cloud.

Franklin is remembered on the Runnymede Memorial, Panel 8.

PO 18.9.40

JOSEF FRANTISEK

793451 Sgt Pilot Czechoslovakian 303 Squadron

Born at Otaslavice on October 7 1912, Frantisek was in the Czech Air Force in the thirties. When the Germans moved in to Czechoslovakia in 1938 Frantisek is said to have machine-gunned columns of troops before flying off to Poland. He joined the PAF in March 1939 and may have destroyed some German aircraft in the September invasion.

Frantisek escaped to Roumania, where he was interned. He escaped and made his way to France, via the Balkans and Syria, and arrived there in early May 1940. He immediately joined a French fighter squadron and during the fighting is reported to have destroyed eleven enemy aircraft. He was awarded the C de G (Fr).

After the collapse of France Frantisek made his way to England. He converted to Hurricanes and joined 303 Squadron at Northolt at its formation on August 2 1940.

Frantisek was the highest scorer in the Battle of Britain, with seventeen victories. On September 2 he claimed a Bf 109 destroyed, on the 3rd another, on the 5th a Bf 109 and a Ju 88, on the 6th a Bf 109, on the 9th a Bf 109 and a He 111, on the 11th two Bf 109s and a He 111, on the 15th a Bf 110, on the 18th a Bf 109, on the 26th two He 111s, on the 27th a He 111 and a Bf 110 and on the 30th a Bf 109. He was awarded the DFM (1.10.40) and was decorated by the King at Northolt on September 20.

During a routine patrol on October 8 1940 Frantisek was killed, when his Hurricane, R 4175, crashed at Cuddington Way, Ewell, Surrey from an unknown cause. He is buried in Northwood Cemetery, Middlesex. Frantisek was awarded the VM (5th Class)(23.12.40), the KW and three Bars (1.2.41) and the Czech Military Cross (15.7.41). His portrait was done by Cuthbert Orde in September 1940.

ROBERT HENRY BRAUND FRASER

741810 Sgt Pilot British 257 Squadron

Fraser, of Glasgow, was with 257 Squadron at Hendon in early July 1940.

He was shot down and killed in combat with Bf 109s over Folkestone on October 22 1940. His Hurricane, V 6851, crashed and burned out at Moat Farm, Shadoxhurst.

Fraser was 20 years old. He is buried in Craigton Cemetery, Glasgow.

JOHN CONNELL FREEBORN

70854 FO Pilot British 74 Squadron

Freeborn was born in Middleton, Yorkshire. He joined the RAF on a short service commission in January 1938, was posted to 8 FTS, Montrose on April 9 and joined 74 Squadron at Hornchurch on October 29 1938.

Three days after the outbreak of war the squadron was scrambled. Freeborn and Flying Officer VG Byrne dived to attack what they thought were Bf 109s, but were in fact Hurricanes of 56 Squadron. They shot down two, killing one of the pilots. This incident became known as 'The Battle of Barking Creek'. Freeborn and Byrne came up before a General Court Martial on October 7 1939 and were acquitted.

On May 21 1940 Freeborn claimed a Ju 88, on the 22nd he shared a Ju 88, on the 24th a probable Bf 109 and on the 27th a Bf 109 destroyed and another probably destroyed. During the Battle of Britain Freeborn claimed a Bf 109 destroyed on July 10, another on the 28th, two Bf 109s and two Bf 110s on August 11, a Do 17 on the 13th and a Do 215 on September 11. He was awarded the DFC (13.8.40) and made a Flight Commander on August 29.

JC Freeborn (continued)

Freeborn shared a Bf 109 on November 17 and destroyed two more on December 5. He was awarded a Bar to the DFC (25.2.41) and posted from 74 to 57 OTU, Hawarden on June 6 1941, as an instructor.

In December 1942 Freeborn was posted to 602 Squadron at Skeabrae, as a Flight Commander. On June 1 1943 he took command of 118 Squadron at Coltishall and led it until January 1944.

Freeborn was released from the RAF in 1946, as a Wing Commander. His portrait was done by Cuthbert Orde.

APO 26.3.38   PO 17.1.39   FO 3.9.40   FL 3.9.41
SL 1.1.44

RICHARD POWELL FREEMAN

812312   Sgt   Aircrew   British   29 Squadron

Joined 29 Squadron at Digby on August 7 1940. No other service details traced.

PETER FOSTER FREER

65990   Sgt   Pilot   British   29 Squadron

Freer, of Cottingham, was with 29 Squadron at Digby in early July 1940. Commissioned in April 1941, he was killed on May 11, aged 22 and still serving with the squadron.

He is buried in Cottingham Cemetery, Haltemprice, Yorkshire.

PO 24.4.41

LAURENCE ERIC FREESE

742586   Sgt   Pilot   British   611 and 74 Squadrons

Freese, of Ilford, Essex, was posted to 611 Squadron at Tern Hill on September 29 1940. He moved to 74 Squadron at Biggin Hill on October 26 and on November 14 claimed a Ju 87 destroyed.

On January 10 1941 the squadron went on an anti-shipping strike but were sent too far and ran out of fuel on the return trip. Freese was fatally injured, attempting a forced-landing at Detling. He was 24 and is buried in Rippleside Cemetery, Barking, Essex.

THOMAS LENNOX FRENCH

65991   Sgt   Pilot   British   29 Squadron

Joined 29 Squadron at Digby on July 8 1940. French was commissioned in April 1941 and killed on December 14 1942, aged 24. The unit he was serving with is not known.

French is buried in Corstorphine Hill Cemetery, Edinburgh.

PO 24.4.41   FO 24.4.42

JULIUSZ FREY

P O322   FL   Pilot   Polish   607 Squadron

Born in Poland on July 14 1907, Frey was in the PAF before the war and in September 1939 was commanding 114 Squadron in lV/1 Dyon of the Dispositional Air Force.

Frey joined 607 Squadron at Turnhouse on October 11 1940. He was posted to 303 Squadron at Leconfield on November 12 and went to Pembrey on February 19 1941 to form and command 316 Squadron. Frey destroyed a Bf 109 on July 24, when the squadron escorted Hampdens in Operation 'Sunrise'. He was posted to 16 FTS, Newton as CO Training Squadron on August 10 1941.

In early January 1942 at the Polish Depot, Blackpool Frey was awarded the KW (19.2.42). He was sent to CFS, Upavon on March 1 1942 for an instructor's course, after which he returned to Newton. On November 17 1942 Frey went to 51 OTU, Cranfield to convert to Mosquitos and joined 418 (RCAF) Squadron at Ford on March 18 1943 for night intruder operations.

Frey returned to Blackpool on December 28, was posted to HQ ADGB on August 8 1944 and moved to HQ Fighter Command on December 18. He was released in 1946 and later settled in Canada. He was awarded two Bars to the KW (31.10.47).

JACK RICHARD FRIEND

904234   Sgt   Air Gunner   British   25 Squadron

Friend, of Norwich, joined 25 Squadron at North Weald in early October 1940. In the evening of December 7 he was one of the crew of a Blenheim, which had flown over Peterborough testing the black-out. It crashed near Wittering, from causes unknown, and Friend and the pilot were killed.

He was 26 and is buried in All Saints' churchyard, Wittering.

ALFRED HENRY BASIL FRIENDSHIP

81637   PO   Pilot   British   3 Squadron

Born in St Albans, Hertfordshire, Friendship was with 3 Squadron at Kenley in early 1940. He went with it to France on May 10, when it was attached to 63 Wing.

Friendship claimed two Hs 126s destroyed on the 12th, a Bf 109 and a Ju 87 on the 14th and a Bf 109 on the 15th. The squadron was withdrawn on the 20th and Friendship was commissioned in mid-May and awarded the DFM (31.5.40) and a Bar (4.6.40).

The squadron was in Scotland throughout the Battle of Britain. In March 1941 Friendship was posted to 605 Squadron at Tern Hill, as a Flight Commander. He went to an OTU in July 1941, as an instructor. In July 1942 he joined 126 Squadron at Luqa, Malta and moved to 1435 Squadron at Luqa on August 2, when it was expanded to squadron strength.

Friendship returned to the UK in September 1942 and joined 501 Squadron at Middle Wallop, as a Flight Commander. In December he was posted to 65 Squadron at Drem and finished his second tour there.

In April 1944 Friendship went to 604 Squadron at Church Fenton. He was posted away on August 1 to CGS, Catfoss, as an instructor. He commanded 80 Squadron in Germany from November 1945 to May 1946.

Friendship was released from the RAF in 1947, as a Squadron Leader.

PO 15.5.40   FO 15.5.41   FL 15.4.42

JOFFRE HARRY FRIPP

120212   Sgt   Pilot   British   248 Squadron

Fripp was with 248 Squadron in early July 1940.

Commissioned in April 1942, he was released from the RAF in 1945, as a Flight Lieutenant.

After the war he was commissioned in the RAFVR. He died in 1973.

PO 8.4.42   FO 8.10.42
FL 8.4.44
FO (RAFVR) 8.9.49

EDWARD MURRAY FRISBY

90507   FO   Pilot   British   504 Squadron

Frisby, of Cropston, Leicestershire, joined 504 Squadron, AuxAF in 1938. He was called to full-time service on August 28 1939.

He served with 504 throughout the Battle of Britain and was killed on December 5 1941, as a Flight Lieutenant. His unit at the time of his death is not known.

Frisby is buried in St Cuthbert's churchyard, Great Glen, Leicestershire.

APO (AuxAF) 31.10.38   PO (AuxAF) 14.5.39   PO 28.9.39
FO 3.9.40

ERIC THOMAS GEORGE FRITH

742091   Sgt   Pilot   British   611 and 92 Squadrons

Frith, of Cowley, was educated at Bedford House and Southfields, Oxford. He worked for Morris Motors Ltd.

On July 29 1940 Frith joined 611 Squadron at Tern Hill and on September 21 was posted to 92 Squadron at Biggin Hill. He was shot down on October 9 and baled out, badly burned. His Spitfire, X 4597, is believed to be that which crashed at The Ridgeway, Smeeth, Ashford.

Frith was admitted to Willesborough Hospital, where he died from his injuries on October 17 1940. He was 26 and is buried in Oxford Cemetery, Botley, Berkshire.

CHARLES GEORGE FRIZELL

42831   PO   Pilot   Canadian   257 Squadron

Frizell was born on October 3 1921 and joined the RAF on a short service commission in August 1939. With training completed, he was posted to 257 Squadron at its reformation at Hendon on May 17 1940. He then had four hours experience on Spitfires.

On August 15 his Hurricane, L 1703, caught fire during a routine patrol. Frizell baled out, unhurt, and the aircraft crashed at Watford Way, Edgware. On September 15 he was injured in an accident at Martlesham Heath, when Squadron Leader RRS Tuck drove into the back of his car. Frizell was in hospital for three months.

In 1941 he instructed at 10 FTS, Tern Hill; FTS, Cranwell and 8 FTS, Montrose. Frizell returned to operations in March 1942, when he joined 91 Squadron at Hawkinge. In June he was posted to 124 Squadron at Eastchurch, staying with it until November. In December 1942 Frizell went to 152 Squadron at Souk-el-Arba, Tunisia. He damaged a Bf 109 on April 11 1943.

In June 1943 Frizell was posted to command 1676 Fighter Defence Flight at Gibraltar, carrying out long-range Atlantic shipping patrols. He was instructing and carrying out liaison duties in America in 1944 and in 1945 was in South East Asia Command in Ceylon and India. He carried out liaison duties with the Chinese Air Force and was awarded the Order of the Cloud and Banner Mochi Medal by the Chinese (14.6.46).

Frizell was released on March 6 1946, as a Squadron Leader. He returned to Canada to live.

APO 23.10.39   PO 20.4.40   FO 20.4.41   FL 20.4.42

JACK LYNCH FROST

84681   PO   Air Gunner   British   600 Squadron

Frost was with 600 Squadron at Northolt in June 1940. He was commissioned in August. There is no trace of him in Air Force Lists after January 1942 and he was not a casualty, so presumably he left the RAF in early 1942.

PO 8.8.40   FO 8.8.41

DAVID FULFORD

63787   Sgt   Pilot   British   64 and 19 Squadrons

Fulford, from Dinnington, Yorkshire, did his intermediate and advanced flying training at FTS, Cranwell from April to July 1940 and then joined 64 Squadron at Kenley. He was posted to 19 Squadron at Fowlmere on September 25.

Commissioned in March 1941, Fulford was with 118 Squadron at Ibsley later in the year and was awarded the DFC (4.11.41). When the squadron did the flying for the film 'The First of the Few' he appeared as himself in a short sequence.

Fulford was killed on November 2 1942, as a Flying Officer with 611 Squadron. He is remembered on the Runnymede Memorial, Panel 67.

PO 10.3.41   FO 11.3.42

ROBERT CARL FUMERTON

C 1352   PO   Pilot   Canadian   32 Squadron

Fumerton was born on March 21 1913 at Fort Coulonge, Quebec. From the age of 18 he worked for prospecting and mining companies. He got his private pilot's license in 1939 and joined the RCAF at the outbreak of war. After completing his training at Camp Borden he was posted to the UK and joined 112 (RCAF) Squadron, an army co-operation unit with Lysanders.

Fumerton volunteered for Fighter Command, converted to Hurricanes at OTU and joined 32 Squadron at Acklington on October 5 1940.

In December he was posted to No 1 (RCAF) Squadron at Castletown. In June 1941 Fumerton went to 406 (RCAF) Squadron, newly-formed at Acklington. He teamed up with Sergeant LPS Bing and their first victory came on September 1, a Ju 88 at night. A week later they damaged a He 111.

In October 1941 Fumerton and Bing were posted to 89 Squadron at Colerne and went with it to Abu Sueir, Egypt in November. The team destroyed a He 111 on March 3 1942. Fumerton was awarded the DFC (27.3.42). On the night of April 7/8 he destroyed two He 111s. On June 22 the squadron established a detachment at Luqa, Malta. Flying from there on the 24th Fumerton destroyed a Ju 87 and a Ju 88, on the 29th two Ju 88s, on July 1 a Ju 88 and on July 2 another. He was awarded a Bar to the DFC (21.7.42). On July 22 he destroyed a Ju 88 and on August 14 a Cant Z 1007. The team's final victory was on August 28, a Ju 88 destroyed on the ground at Castelvetrano aerodrome, Sicily.

Posted back to Canada in December 1942, Fumerton went to No 1 OTU, Bagotville, Quebec. In June 1943 he moved to RAF Ferry Command on staff duties and when he returned to the UK in July he was promoted to Acting Wing Commander and on August 25 took command of 406 (RCAF) Squadron at Valley. On the night of May 14/15 1944 Fumerton destroyed a Ju 188, his final victory. He left 406 on July 26 1944, was repatriated to Canada and given command of 7 OTU, Debert, Nova Scotia. He was there until June 1945 and was awarded the AFC.

After leaving the RCAF in July 1945 Fumerton returned to mining. In 1948 he went to Hankow to train Chinese pilots on Mosquitos, then being sold by de Havilland's to the Nationalist Government. It was not a successful venture and he left China in early 1949.

Fumerton became a successful real estate broker in Canada.

REX HORTON FURNEAUX

103486   **Sgt**   **Pilot**   **British**   **3 and 73 Squadrons**

With 3 Squadron at Wick in June 1940. Furneaux was posted to 73 Squadron at Castle Camps on September 25. He was commissioned in July 1941 and released from the RAF in 1946, as a Flight Lieutenant.

PO 31.7.41   *FO 31.7.42*   *FL 31.7.43*

BOHUMIR FURST

68152   **Sgt**   **Pilot**   **Czechoslovakian**   **310 and 605 Sqdns**

Furst joined 310 Squadron at Duxford in August 1940. On September 3 he claimed a Bf 110 destroyed, on the 7th a Bf 109 and on the 15th a He 111. He was commissioned in June 1941 and awarded the Czech Military Cross.

Furst left the RAF in 1946, as a Flight Lieutenant. He returned to Czechoslovakia and died there in the seventies.

PO 12.6.41

ALEKSANDER KLEMENS GABSZEWICZ

P 0163   **FO**   **Pilot**   **Polish**   **607 Squadron**

Born in Szawle, Kowno, Poland on December 12 1911, Gabszewicz joined the PAF in 1934. When the Germans invaded Poland he was commanding a flight of 114 Squadron and he shot down the first enemy aircraft in the Battle of Warsaw, a He 111.

After the fall of Poland Gabszewicz escaped to France and joined l'Armée de l'Air. He led a flight in a Caudron C 714 Squadron at Lyons and later in Groupe de Chasse lll/10, flying Bloch 151s. He was credited with one victory and awarded the KW (11.6.40).

Gabszewicz was posted to 607 Squadron at Turnhouse on October 11 1940. He moved to 303 Squadron at Leconfield on November 13, was awarded a Bar to the KW (23.12.40) and went to 316 Squadron at Pembrey at its formation in February 1941, as a Flight Commander. On April 1 Gabszewicz shared a He 111 and on July 24 he shared a Bf 109 destroyed and probably destroyed another. He was awarded a second Bar to the KW (15.7.41) and given command of 316 squadron on November 14 1941. He claimed FW 190s destroyed on April 10, 25 and 27, a probable FW 190 on May 5 and shared a probable Bf 109 on the 6th.

Gabszewicz was posted to HQ 11 Group on June 4, was awarded the DFC (20.8.42), the VM (5th Class)(28.8.42) and on September 25 went to 58 OTU, Grangemouth, as an instructor. He was promoted on January 27 1943 to lead No 2 Polish Wing at Heston, moving later to lead No 1 Wing. On April 4 1943 he destroyed a FW 190, on July 4 another and on July 6 a Bf 109. He was awarded the C de G (Fr)(7.7.43).

He left the Wing on December 12 1943 and was attached to 56th Fighter Group, USAAF. Gabszewicz was promoted to Acting Group Captain on February 29 1944 and posted to command HQ 18 Fighter Sector. Awarded the VM (4th Class)(13.3.44) and the DSO (15.5.44), he moved to HQ 131 Wing to command on July 12 1944 and ten days later the advance party of the Wing landed in France.

Gabszewicz went to HQ 84 Group on June 19 1945, was given command of RAF Coltishall on February 2 1946 and was released from the PAF in January 1947. He was awarded a third Bar to the KW (31.10.47) and was invested with the Order of Orange-Nassau in 1947. Gabszewicz settled in Britain after his release.

FO 1.3.41   *FL 1.3.42*   *SL 1.9.42*   *WC 1.9.44*

JAMES EDWARD GADD

801453   **Sgt**   **Pilot**   **British**   **611 Squadron**

Gadd joined 601 Squadron, AuxAF at Hendon in 1937 as a wireless operator. Called up at the outbreak of war, he applied for pilot training and in March 1940 was posted to No 1 EFTS, Hatfield. In June he went to 5 FTS, Sealand and then to 7 OTU, Hawarden in September to convert to Spitfires.

On October 12 Gadd joined 611 Squadron at Tern Hill. He was posted away on June 16 1941 to No 1 ADF, Hendon, remaining with it until July 1942, when he went to 2 Signals School, as a staff pilot.

In August 1942 Gadd was posted to 5 FIS, Perth for a course, following which he instructed at 10 FIS, Reading from September to November 1942, then 24 EFTS, Sealand from November 1942 to February 1945 and finally at 11 EFTS, Perth from February to November 1945, when he was released from the RAF, as a Warrant Officer.

Gadd served with 601 Squadron, RAuxAF from June 13 1947 to September 18 1948, as a Warrant Officer.

DOUGLAS HUGH GAGE

83248   **PO**   **Pilot**   **British**   **602 Squadron**

Gage, of Staines, Middlesex, was at Shrewsbury School from 1931 to 1935 and was an architect before the war. He joined 602 Squadron at Westhampnett on September 21 1940.

On the 27th Gage was jumped by a Bf 109 and hit in the glycol tank. He made a forced-landing at Bivelham Forge Farm, Mayfield, unhurt. After being damaged by Bf 109s in a surprise attack over Dungeness on October 30 Gage forced-landed at Millbank Farm, Newchurch, again unhurt.

He was killed on June 6 1941, aged 23, serving with 91 Squadron at Hawkinge. He is remembered on the Runnymede Memorial, Panel 32.

PO 21.7.40

PAWEL PIOTR GALLUS

794124   **Sgt**   **Pilot**   **Polish**   **303 and 3 Squadrons**

Born at Szczawina, Poland on April 28 1920, Gallus went to the PAF NCOs Training School at Bydgoszcz in 1936. He qualified as a fighter pilot at Krosno in 1939. He was posted to No 1 Air Regiment, Warsaw and joined 112 Fighter Squadron. Gallus was evacuated to Roumania on September 19 and reached France on December 30 1939. He joined l'Armée de l'Air and was attached to a Polish flight of MB 152s defending Chateauroux airfield and the Bloch aircraft factory.

When France fell Gallus went to England, arriving there on June 23 1940. He was posted to 303 Squadron at Northolt at its formation on August 2. On the 12th he made a belly-landing after a training flight. Gallus went to 3 Squadron at Turnhouse on September 27 1940.

He was posted to 316 Squadron at Pembrey on March 27 1941, staying with it until October 22, when he went to 87 Squadron at Colerne for night-flying training. Gallus was attached to 317 Squadron at Exeter on March 15 1942, moving on April 5 to 316 Squadron at Heston. He was awarded the KW (3.9.42), claimed a FW 190 probably destroyed on January 21 1943, received a Bar to the KW (25.6.43) and claimed a Bf 109 destroyed on July 6. On August 26 Gallus was rested from operations and became an air traffic controller in the Operations Room at 306 Squadron.

Gallus joined 302 Squadron at Deanland on April 14 1944. He was posted away on February 8 1945, spent a short while with 639 and 595 Squadrons, was awarded the DFC (26.5.45), the VM (5th Class)(1.6.45) and went to 309 Squadron at Coltishall on August 23 1945.

Gallus was released from the PAF in 1948, as a Warrant Officer.

DOUGLAS ROBERT GAMBLEN

39657 FO Pilot British 41 Squadron

Gamblen joined the RAF on a short service commission in March 1937. He was posted to 10 FTS, Tern Hill on May 9 and joined the SHQ staff at Catterick on June 10 1938.

He was with 41 Squadron at Catterick in early July 1940. On the 29th he was reported 'Missing' following a combat with Ju 87s and Bf 109s over Dover.

Gamblen was 25. He is remembered on the Runnymede Memorial, Panel 5.

APO 9.5.37 PO 8.3.38 FO 8.10.39

SYDNEY RUSSELL GANE

42117 PO Pilot British 248 Squadron

Joined the RAF on a short service commission in March 1939. He did his elementary training at 10 E&RFTS, Yatesbury and the intermediate and advanced at 5 FTS, Sealand.

On November 6 1939 Gane was posted to 248 Squadron at Hendon. In February 1940 the squadron joined Coastal Command. Flying from Sumburgh in the Shetlands, Gane failed to return from a reconnaissance sortie over the Norwegian coast on October 20 1940. He had been searching for a Blenheim of 248, which had been lost earlier in the day.

Gane was 20. He is buried in Stavne Cemetery, Trondheim, Norway.

APO 13.5.39 PO 6.11.39

ERNEST GANT

52007 Sgt Air Gunner British 236 Squadron

Gant joined 236 Squadron on September 3 1940. He was commissioned in March 1943 and released in 1946, as a Flight Lieutenant.

PO 18.3.43 FO 18.9.43 FL 18.3.45

ERIC CECIL GARDINER

562691 Sgt Radar Operator British 219 Squadron

With 219 Squadron at Catterick in early July 1940. Gardiner was flying with Pilot Officer KW Worsdell in Beaufighter R 2065 on October 30 1940. In bad visibility the aircraft hit trees, crashed and exploded just south of Balcombe Place. Both men were killed.

Gardiner was 27. He is buried in Pontefract Cemetery, Yorkshire.

FREDERICK THOMAS GARDINER

72100 FO Pilot British 610 Squadron

Gardiner was a member of the RAFVR and was commissioned in February 1938. Called to full-time service in late September 1939, he was with 610 Squadron at Gravesend in early July 1940.

On August 12 Gardiner was slightly wounded in the leg and his aircraft damaged in an attack by a Bf 109 over New Romney. Further damage was caused by a heavy landing at Biggin Hill. He claimed a Bf 110 destroyed on the 18th. Gardiner was shot down in combat with Bf 109s over Dover on August 25. He baled out, slightly wounded, and was admitted to Waldershare Hospital. His Spitfire, K 9931, crashed and burned out on Stoneheap Farm, near Northbourne.

In early 1944 Gardiner was commanding 254 Squadron at North Coates. He was awarded the DFC (10.3.44). He was released from the RAF in 1946, as a Squadron Leader, and later settled in Canada.

PO (RAFVR) 15.2.38 PO 25.9.39 FO 16.2.40
FL 1.6.41 SL 1.6.42

WILLIAM NAIRN GARDINER

121234 Sgt Pilot British 3 Squadron

PO 22.3.42 FO 1.10.42 FL 22.3.44

BERNARD GEORGE DERRY GARDNER

740601 Sgt Pilot British 610 Squadron

Gardner, of Bassett, joined 610 Squadron at Biggin Hill on July 27 1940. He claimed three Bf 109s destroyed on August 12 and another on the 14th. After this latter combat off Folkestone he made a forced-landing at Wye and was admitted to Ashford Hospital, with bullet wounds in the arm.

On June 28 1941 Gardner was killed, as a Flight Sergeant. His unit at that time is unknown. He was 24 and is buried in Hollybrook Cemetery, Southampton.

JOHN RUSHTON GARD'NER

41841 PO Pilot New Zealander 141 Squadron

Gard'ner was born in Dunedin on June 14 1918. He was at Nelson College from 1931 to 1935 and was afterwards employed as an apprentice draughtsman in the Lands and Survey Department.

In 1938 Gard'ner applied for a short service commission and did some flying at Nelson Aero Club. He sailed for the UK on December 16 1938 in the RMS 'Rangitata' and began training at No 1 E&RFTS, Hatfield on January 23 1939, moving to 11 FTS, Shawbury on April 15.

Gard'ner joined 141 Squadron at Grangemouth on October 23. The squadron had no aircraft of its own but gradually two flights were formed, one of Gladiators, the other of Blenheims. In March 1940 141 began to receive Defiants, becoming operational on June 3 and moving south to West Malling on July 12.

On the morning of July 19 Gard'ner was flying one of the nine Defiants attacked by Bf 109s of lll/JG 51 off Dover. He was in one of the four rear aircraft and was shot down immediately but did not catch fire as did the other three rear aircraft. He landed on the sea four miles off Dover and the aircraft sank. Gard'ner managed to extricate himself and was picked up after fifteen minutes but his gunner, Pilot Officer DM Slatter, was not seen again. Gard'ner was admitted to Union Road Hospital, Dover with a badly cut head. He rejoined the squadron in late October.

On November 1 1941 Gard'ner joined 409 (RCAF) Squadron at Coleby Grange. Promoted to Acting Squadron Leader in July 1942, he joined 488 Squadron at Ayr on August 14, as a Flight Commander. With his second tour completed in November, Gard'ner was posted to HQ 13 Group, Newcastle as Ops Night. Whilst there he did a course at RAF Staff College.

Gard'ner transferred to the RNZAF on January 1 1944, went to 51 OTU, Bedford on April 25 for a refresher course on Beaufighters and then joined 219 Squadron at Bradwell Bay as a supernumerary. He returned to 488 in late October, as a Flight Commander. The squadron moved across to the Continent on November 15. Operating from Amiens-Glisy, Gard'ner destroyed a FW 190 in December. On the 31st he made a one-engine landing at Brussels-Melsbroek, after being damaged by anti-aircraft fire. The following day his aircraft was destroyed on the ground there by a German strafing attack.

Gard'ner was with 488 until its disbandment at Gilze-Rijen on April 26 1945. He returned to England and was posted to Air Ministry, Directorate of Organisational Establishments. He received a Mention in Despatches (1.1.46), returned to New Zealand in March 1947 and went on the Reserve on June 12.

Offered a Permanent Commission in September Gard'ner returned to the UK in February 1948. He held a series of appointments and commands prior to his retirement on June 14 1965, as a Wing Commander, retaining the rank of Group Captain.

APO 1.4.39 PO 23.10.39 FO 23.10.40 FL 23.10.41
SL 1.7.45 SL 1.8.47 WC 1.1.54

PETER MELVILL GARDNER

40527   FO   Pilot   British   32 Squadron

Born at Grimsby on July 1 1918, Gardner joined the RAF on a short service commission in November 1937. He was posted to 5 FTS, Sealand on March 5 1938 and joined 32 Squadron at Biggin Hill on September 17 1938.

In May 1940 Gardner was attached to 3 Squadron in France. On the 15th he claimed a Do 17 destroyed, on the 19th a He 111 and on the 20th another Do 17. Back with 32 Squadron he claimed a share in a Do 17 on July 3, two Bf 109s destroyed on August 12, a Ju 88 on the 15th and a Bf 109 on the 16th.

Gardner was awarded the DFC (30.8.40). In June 1941 he was posted to 54 Squadron at Hornchurch, as a Flight Commander. He destroyed a Bf 109 on June 17. During a sweep on July 11 1941 Gardner was shot down and captured. After being freed he stayed on in the RAF, retiring on July 31 1948, as a Squadron Leader. He died on May 23 1984.

APO 19.2.38   PO 29.11.38   FO 29.8.40   FL 29.8.41
SL 1.7.43   SL 1.8.47

RICHARD EXTON GARDNER

Sub-Lieutenant (FAA)   Pilot   British   242 Squadron

Joined the FAA in 1939. In mid-June 1940 Gardner was one of the pilots loaned to the RAF. He converted to Hurricanes at 7 OTU, Hawarden and joined 242 Squadron at Coltishall on July 1.

Gardner claimed a He 111 destroyed on July 10, shared a Do 17 on August 21, destroyed a Do 215 on September 7 and a Do 17 on the 18th. He was damaged in combat with Bf 109s off Sheerness on November 5 but returned, unhurt, to Coltishall, in Hurricane P 3054. On November 28 1940, Gardner was posted away from 242.

In March 1941 he joined 807 Squadron, then in HMS 'Furious' but later in 'Ark Royal'. In May the carrier took part in Operation 'Tiger', a convoy to reinforce Egypt. On May 8 Gardner destroyed two Ju 87s and shared a SM 79. He was awarded the DSC (29.7.41), shared a Ju 52 on August 23, shared a Cant Z 506 B on September 27 and shared a Fiat BR 20 on October 18.

In December 1942 Gardner was given command of 889 Squadron in the Western Desert. He later returned to the UK and was posted to the School of Naval Air Warfare at St Merryn. He commanded the school from November 1944.

Gardner was made an OBE (14.6.45) and retired on March 13 1946.

Sub-Lt 7.9.39   Lt 7.9.40   Lt-Cdr 1943   Cdr 1945

WALTER JAMES GARFIELD

740997   Sgt   Pilot   British   248 Squadron

Garfield, of Sutton-in-Ashfield, Nottinghamshire, was with 248 Squadron at Sumburgh in the Shetlands in early July 1940. He was captain of a Blenheim, which failed to return from a reconnaissance of the Feje-Stadlandet sector of the Norwegian coast on September 13 1940. Garfield was 25. He is buried in Mollendal Cemetery, Bergen, Norway.

ANTHONY HUGH HAMILTON GARRARD

42119   PO   Pilot   British   248 Squadron

Garrard joined the RAF on a short service commission in March 1939. After carrying out his elementary flying training at 10 E&RFTS, Yatesbury, he was posted to 5 FTS, Sealand, after which he joined 248 Squadron at Hendon on November 6 1939.

In February 1940 the squadron joined Coastal Command. Flying from Sumburgh in the Shetlands, Garrard failed to return from a sortie on November 3 1940, in Blenheim L 9392. He was last seen attacking a He 111 over the North Sea and is presumed to have been shot down by return fire.

Garrard was 19 years old. He is remembered on the Runnymede Memorial, Panel 8.

APO 13.5.39   PO 6.11.39

GEOFFREY GARSIDE

936021   Sgt   Observer   British   236 Squadron

Joined the RAF in September 1939. After a ground navigation course Garside was posted to Squires Gate in February 1940 for flying training. He then went on a bombing and gunnery course at Penrhos in May and joined 236 Squadron at Thorney Island on July 19 1940.

Flying with Sergeant EA Alexander, Garside carried out passenger flying boat escorts, reconnaissances of the French coast and fighter patrols. In December 1940 he was posted to 209 Squadron, operating in Lerwicks from Stranraer. Garside went to Andover in March 1941 for retraining and in April he joined 59 Squadron at Bircham Newton, from where he flew in Hudsons, mainly concerned in searching for and bombing E boats, particularly at Ymuiden, Holland.

When his tour finished Garside went to Catfoss, as an instructor. In July 1942 he was posted to RAF Cranwell to train for service in anti-submarine Whitleys and in late August he joined 58 Squadron at St Eval, moving soon afterwards to Stornaway.

In September 1942 Garside was in a Whitley which crashed soon after take-off and caught fire. All aboard escaped but Garside's face and hands were very badly burned. He was admitted to Bangour Hospital, West Lothian.

Garside was released from the RAF in 1946, as a Warrant Officer.

GEOFFREY WILLIAM GARTON

67034   **Sgt**   **Pilot**   **British**   **73 Squadron**

Garton was with 43 Squadron in early 1940. In May he was posted to 73 Squadron in France and on the 23rd he claimed a Bf 110 destroyed. The squadron was withdrawn to England in mid-June.

On September 7 Garton claimed a Bf 110 probably destroyed and on the 27th another, confirmed. Garton was posted to the Middle East with 73 in November 1940. The squadron embarked on the carrier HMS 'Furious' and flew off to Takoradi on the 29th. It then flew in easy stages to Heliopolis, via Lagos, Accra, Kano, Maidugari, Khartoum, Wadi Halfa and Abu Sueir.

On April 5 1941 Garton destroyed a Ju 87, on the 9th he shared a Hs 126 and on the 21st he destroyed another Ju 87. Commissioned in late April, he was posted to 112 Squadron at Sidi Aziez in early June, destroyed a probable Bf 109 on the 17th and was awarded the DFC (28.7.42).

Garton claimed a Mc 202 destroyed on September 16, he shared a Ju 87 and probably destroyed another on October 1, destroyed another Ju 87 on November 1, destroyed a Ju 52 on the ground on the 11th and on the 16th was posted to HQ 239 Wing as Squadron Leader Flying.

On January 15 1943 Garton was given command of 112 Squadron and in May was posted to 73 OTU at Abu Sueir, as an instructor. He commanded 232 Squadron in Tunisia from January to April 1944 and 87 Squadron in Italy from August 1944 until April 1945. Garton was awarded the DSO (21.8.45).

He stayed in the RAF and retired on February 13 1962, as a Squadron Leader, retaining the rank of Wing Commander. Garton died in November 1976.

PO 26.4.41   *FO 26.4.42*   *FL 1.6.44*   *SL 1.9.45*
SL 1.7.50

LEONARD ARTHUR GARVEY

740340   **Sgt**   **Pilot**   **British**   **41 Squadron**

Garvey, from Birmingham, was well known in athletic circles in the Midlands in the thirties. He was also a member of the RAFVR.

He was with 41 Squadron in the Battle of Britain. On October 30 1940 Garvey was shot down and killed in combat with Bf 109s over Ashford. His Spitfire, P 7375, is believed to have crashed on Church Farm, Stanford. Garvey was 26. He is buried in Wilton Cemetery, Birmingham.

GEORGE DESMOND GARVIN

34237   **SL**   **Pilot**   **British**   **264 Squadron**

Born on April 4 1916, Garvin joined the RAF in July 1934. He was posted to 3 FTS, Grantham on September 29 and joined 70 (Bomber Transport) Squadron at Hinaidi, Iraq on November 9 1935, under instruction. Back in the UK Garvin was posted to 215 Squadron at Driffield on June 4 1936.

Garvin joined 264 Squadron at Kirton-in-Lindsey on August 8 1940. He took command on the 24th when the CO was killed. On this day he claimed two Ju 88s destroyed. Four days later Garvin was shot down in flames and baled out, with minor injuries. His gunner baled out but was killed. Their Defiant, L 7021, crashed in flames on Luddenham Marsh, Faversham.

Garvin was posted away from 264 in November 1940. He formed and then commanded 154 Squadron at Fowlmere from November 17 1941 until the end of the year.

He stayed on after the war and retired from the RAF on June 28 1961, as a Group Captain, retaining the rank of Air Commodore. Garvin was made a CBE (13.6.57).

APO 14.9.34   *PO 14.9.35*   *FO 14.3.37*   *FL 14.3.39*
SL 1.9.40   *WC 1.12.41*   *WC 1.7.47*   *GC 1.1.53*

FRED GASH

146840   **Sgt**   **Air Gunner**   **British**   **264 Squadron**

Joined 264 Squadron at Kirton-in-Lindsey in August 1940. Gash teamed up with Pilot Officer FD Hughes and on August 26 they destroyed two Do 17s in daylight.

On October 16 they destroyed a He 111 but overshot the runway in mist on return to Luton and crashed. Both men were unhurt. During the night of November 23 they attacked a He 111 but Gash's turret jammed and it was claimed only as a probable. They destroyed a He 111 on March 12 1941, damaged another on April 8 and destroyed a Ju 88 on the 10th. Gash was awarded the DFM (18.4.41).

Commissioned in May 1943, Gash was released from the RAF in 1945, as a Flight Lieutenant.

PO 6.5.43   *FO 6.11.43*   *FL 6.5.45*

RICHARD STUART GASKELL

42832   **PO**   **Pilot**   **British**   **264 Squadron**

Born on July 25 1919, Gaskell joined the RAF in August 1939. He was posted to 264 Squadron at Duxford in June 1940.

On August 24 Gaskell was shot down by Bf 109s of JG 51 over Hornchurch. He was slightly injured but his gunner, Sergeant WH Machin, died of his wounds. The Defiant, L 6965, was written off.

Released from the RAF in 1946, Gaskell rejoined in 1952 and retired on January 4 1963, as a Flight Lieutenant.

APO 23.10.39   *PO 17.5.40*   *FO 17.5.41*   *FL 17.5.42*
FL 17.7.52

LIONEL MANLEY GAUNCE

37632   **FL**   **Pilot**   **Canadian**   **615 Squadron**

Gaunce, from Lethbridge, Alberta, served in the Loyal Edmonton Regiment from 1933 to 1935. He joined the RAF on a short service commission in January 1936 and was posted to 9 E&RFTS, Ansty. On March 21 he moved to 5 FTS, Sealand and at the end of the course joined 3 Squadron at Kenley.

Appointed a Flight Commander in April 1939, Gaunce was posted to 615 Squadron in France in February 1940.

He claimed Bf 109s destroyed on July 20 and 25 and August 12 and 26. Gaunce was awarded the DFC (23.8.40). He was shot down on August 18 by Bf 109s and baled out, with slight burns, and was admitted to Holmesdale Hospital. His Hurricane, P 2966, crashed into Hobsacks Wood, Sevenoaks Weald. On August 26 Gaunce was shot down in flames and baled out. He was rescued from the sea and taken to Herne Bay Hospital, suffering from shock. His Hurricane, R 4111, crashed west of Herne Bay pier.

On October 31 1940 Gaunce was promoted and given command of 46 Squadron at Stapleford Tawney. The squadron intercepted an Italian force on November 11 and Gaunce claimed a Fiat CR 42 destroyed, probably another and shared a Fiat BR 20. He left 46 in December and did not return to operations until July 1941, when he took command of 41 Squadron at Merston.

Gaunce shared a probable Bf 109 on August 21. He was killed on November 19 1941, when he was shot down into the sea near St Lo after a surprise attack by Bf 109s. He was 25 and is remembered on the Runnymede Memorial, Panel 28. Gaunce's portrait was done by Cuthbert Orde in July 1941.

APO 9.3.36   *PO 6.1.37*   *FO 6.8.38*   *FL 6.8.40*
SL 1.9.41

GEOFFREY NORMAN GAUNT

91230   PO   Pilot   British   609 Squadron

Gaunt completed his flying training at FTS, Cranwell, went to 7 OTU, Hawarden and after converting to Spitfires he joined 609 Squadron at Warmwell on August 16 1940.

He shared in the destruction of a Bf 110 on the 25th, with Pilot Officer N le C Agazarian. Gaunt was killed on September 15 1940, when he was shot down during an attack on German bombers over London. His Spitfire, R 6690, crashed and burned out near Kenley and he was identified four days later.

Gaunt was 24 years old. He is buried in Salendine Nook, Baptist Chapel Yard, Huddersfield, Yorkshire.

APO 10.4.40

WILLIAM EDWIN GAUNT

115719   Sgt   Air Gunner   British   23 Squadron

Born on August 7 1918, Gaunt joined 23 Squadron at Middle Wallop on September 16 1940. He was commissioned in January 1942 and released from the RAF in 1946.

Gaunt rejoined in 1955, in the Secretarial Branch, and retired on May 29 1965, as a Flight Lieutenant.

PO 27.1.42   FO 1.10.42   FL 27.1.44   FL 26.5.55

ARTHUR GAVAN

115126   Sgt   Pilot   British   54 Squadron

Gavan was posted to 54 Squadron on September 17 1940. He was commissioned in December 1941 and released from the RAF in 1946.

He rejoined in 1952 and was killed in a car accident on June 22 1967.

PO 26.12.41   FO 1.10.42   FL 26.12.43   FL 6.8.52

ALAN ANTILL GAWITH

41012   FO   Pilot   New Zealander   23 Squadron

Born in Masterton on May 9 1916, Gawith was educated in Wellington and Nelson and studied law at Victoria College from 1935 to 1937. He was working for a law firm in Wellington when he applied for an RAF short service commission in November 1937.

Gawith was provisionally accepted and sailed for the UK in the RMS 'Arawa' on May 20 1938. He went to 11 E&RFTS, Perth on June 27 for his ab initio training and in early September moved to 6 FTS, Little Rissington, after which he joined 23 Squadron at Wittering on April 15 1939.

Flying from Ford on October 11 1940, Gawith damaged a Ju 88. On March 8 1941, on an intruder flight over Beauvais aerodrome, he damaged a He 111 and a Do 17. In a bombing attack in early May Gawith destroyed the entire telephone communication system of the German bomber group at Deurne, near Eindhoven. Awarded the DFC (15.5.41), he was posted in June to command 1451 Flight at Hunsdon, operating with Turbinlite Havocs.

In December 1941 Gawith was rested and in January 1942 he was posted to HQ 9 Group, Preston as Ops Night. He went to RAF Staff College, Gerrards Cross for a course in August 1943 and afterwards joined the staff at HQ ADGB to work on plans for the invasion of Europe.

Gawith transferred to the RNZAF on January 1 1944. In mid-April he became Senior RAF Liaison Officer at the US 9th Air Defence Command, London, spent six weeks in the beach-head area after the invasion and then returned to liaison duties in London. On December 20 1944 Gawith was posted to RAF, Cleave, to command.

He returned to New Zealand in October 1945 and went on to the Reserve in January 1946. Gawith resumed his law studies and after qualifying in 1949 he joined the family firm of solicitors in Masterton. On August 2 1949 he received the Bronze Star (US) from the American ambassador in Wellington for meritorious service in 1944.

APO 20.8.38   PO 27.6.39   FO 3.9.40   FL 3.9.41
SL 1.1.44

JOHN RICHARD HENSMAN GAYNER

90399   FL   Pilot   British   615 Squadron

Gayner joined 615 Squadron, AuxAF at Kenley at its formation on June 1 1937 and was one of four candidates for pilot training.

He was called for full-time service on August 24 1939 and flew with the squadron to Merville on November 15, in a Gladiator. On July 14 1940 Gayner shared in the destruction of a Ju 87. He left 615 Squadron in November 1940.

Gayner commanded 153 Squadron in North Africa from December 1943 to July 1944. He was awarded the DFC (9.6.44) and released from the RAF in 1946, as a Wing Commander. He died in 1987.

PO (AuxAF) 14.9.37   FO (AuxAF) 14.3.39   FO 24.8.39
FL 3.9.40   SL 1.6.42

ALAN WALTER GEAR

144002   Sgt   Pilot   British   32 Squadron

Gear joined the RAFVR in April 1939 and carried out his elementary training on Magisters at 15 E&RFTS, Redhill. Called up on September 20 1939, he was posted to 8 EFTS, Woodley on October 23. Whilst there Gear had a motor cycle accident and was badly concussed.

On May 16 1940 he went to 9 EFTS, Ansty for a refresher course before being posted to 12 FTS, Grantham. Gear moved to 5 OTU, Aston Down on September 17 and joined 32 Squadron at Acklington on October 1 1940. He stayed with the squadron until October 18 1941, when he was posted to CFS, Upavon for an instructor's course.

Gear instructed at 9 FTS, Hullavington on Masters from December 15 1941 until July 15 1942, then at 58 OTU, Balado Bridge for a few weeks and finally at 9 (P) AFU, Errol, where he instructed FAA pupils on the Swordfish, Albacore and Walrus.

On October 18 1942 Gear was posted to 72 Squadron at Ouston and went with it to North Africa in November. On December 10 Gear damaged a Ju 88, but this was probably the one reported lost by KG 60 on that day. He claimed a Ju 87 destroyed on January 5 1943, damaged a Bf 109 on April 11 and claimed one destroyed on April 22.

Gear was commissioned from Warrant Officer on January 11 1943, awarded the DFC (27.7.43) and posted away from 72 on October 14 1943 to become a test pilot at 59 RSU, Foggia. In early January 1944 he crashed after his engine failed and suffered severe injuries, including a broken back. Gear was invalided out of the RAF in early 1945, as a Flying Officer.

PO 11.1.43   FO 12.7.43

KEITH IRVINE GEDDES

73045   FO   Pilot   British   604 Squadron

Born in Woking in 1918, Geddes began flying with the Cambridge University Air Squadron on October 22 1937. He soloed on March 3 1938, was commissioned in the RAFVR in June 1939 and after being called to full-time service at the outbreak of war he was posted to FTS, Cranwell on October 24 1939.

Geddes went to 5 OTU, Aston Down on June 24 1940 and converted to Blenheims. He joined 604 Squadron at Gravesend on July 8. He destroyed a Ju 88 on March 12 1941, a He 111 on the 14th, damaged another on the 16th, destroyed a He 111 on June 6, another on the 14th and a Ju 88 on July 8. He was awarded the DFC (4.7.41).

Geddes left 604 in October 1941 and from early December 1941 commanded GCI stations in the south-west. On March 18 1944 he was posted to the staff at HQ Fighter Command and was released from the RAF on November 25 1945, as a Squadron Leader.

PO (RAFVR) 20.6.39   PO 9.11.39   FO 5.9.40   FL 5.9.41

VICTOR DAVID GEE

742767   Sgt   Pilot   British   219 Squadron

Gee joined 219 Squadron at Catterick on July 7 1940. He was killed on March 21 1941 and is buried in St Bartholomew's churchyard in his home village, Hanworth, Norfolk.

TERENCE GENNEY

79204   PO   Air Gunner   British   604 Squadron

Genney, of Fulstow, Lincolnshire, served in the 1914-18 war and won the MC. He joined 604 Squadron at Northolt in June 1940. He teamed up with Flight Lieutenant A Hunter and after the arrival of Beaufighters retrained as a Radio Observer.

On February 6 1941 they took off in the dark for a belated air test. The Beaufighter spun in as it approached to land. Both men were killed. Genney was 44. He is buried in St Nicholas' churchyard, Grimsby.

PO 1.6.40

RAYMOND JOHN KITCHELL GENT

754361   Sgt   Pilot   British   32 and 501 Squadrons

Gent, of Midhurst, Sussex, was with 32 Squadron in early July 1940. He was posted to 501 at Kenley in late August and claimed a Bf 109 destroyed on October 25.

He was killed on January 2 1941 in a flying accident, when ferrying the squadron Magister from Kemble to Filton. Gent was 24. He is buried in St Martin's churchyard, Ashurst, Kent.

DUDLEY GUY GIBBINS

119136   Sgt   Pilot   British   54 and 222 Squadrons

Joined the RAFVR in June 1939 and began flying at 20 E&RFTS, Gravesend. Called up at the outbreak of war, Gibbins was posted to No 1 ITW, Cambridge, moved to 5 EFTS, Hanworth in November, to 3 FTS, South Cerney in April 1940 and to 7 OTU, Hawarden in July.

On August 10 Gibbins joined 54 Squadron at Catterick. After destroying a Bf 109 on the 31st Gibbins was himself shot down, possibly by a Hurricane. He baled out, unhurt, and landed at Tinley Lodge, Shipbourne. His Spitfire, X 4054, crashed and burned out near Great Hollanden Farm, Hildenborough. Gibbins was posted to 222 Squadron at Hornchurch on September 11 and shared in the destruction of a Bf 109 on October 15.

In January 1941 he was posted to 611 Squadron at Rochford and in April went to 14 FTS, Cranfield, as an instructor. Commissioned in November 1941, Gibbins instructed at 19 (P) AFU, Dalcross from June 1942 to June 1943 and from July 1943 until October 1944 he was at 7 FIS, Upavon.

Gibbins went to 83 Group Support Unit at Westhampnett in November 1944. He joined 130 Squadron at Fassberg in May 1945 and was with the squadron for four months in Norway prior to his release in December 1945, as a Flight Lieutenant.

PO 20.11.41   FO 1.10.42   FL 20.11.43

CHARLES MARTIN GIBBONS

61012   Sgt   Observer   British   236 Squadron

Born in 1914, Gibbons worked for ten years as a solicitor's clerk. He joined the RAFVR as a trainee observer in July 1939. Called up in September, he completed his training in May 1940 and was posted to 3 GRU, Coastal Command, flying in Wellingtons.

Gibbons joined 236 Squadron on July 19 1940. He was commissioned in February 1941 and posted in May to 2 (Coastal) OTU, as an instructor. In July 1942 Gibbons went to 280 Squadron, as Squadron Navigation Officer. He became Station Navigation Officer at RAF Thornaby in March 1944 and two months later was posted to Air Ministry for Air Crew Selection Board duties.

Gibbons left the RAF in 1954, as a Flight Lieutenant, retaining the rank of Squadron Leader.

PO 12.2.41   FO 12.2.42   FL 12.2.43   FL 19.2.47

JOHN ALBERT AXEL GIBSON

40969   FO   Pilot   New Zealander   501 Squadron

Gibson was born in Brighton, England on August 24 1916 and went to New Zealand in 1920. He was educated in Auckland and New Plymouth Boys' High School.

In late 1937 Gibson applied for an RAF short service commission and after provisional acceptance sailed for the UK on April 7 1938 in the RMS 'Rangitata'. He began his flying training at 4 E&RFTS, Brough on May 16 and moved on to 3 FTS, South Cerney on July 23. With training completed he was posted to Farnborough in early 1940 on army co-operation duties.

Gibson joined 501 Squadron at Tangmere in early May 1940 and flew with the squadron to France on the 10th. He destroyed a He 111 and shared a second on May 27, during which action he was himself shot down, crash-landing in a field. The squadron was withdrawn from France on June 18, operated from Jersey on the 19th and re-assembled at Croydon on the 21st.

Gibson claimed a Do 17 on July 13, a Ju 87 and another probable on the 29th, a Ju 87 and a Bf 109 on August 12 and another Ju 87 on the 15th. In this action Gibson's Hurricane, P 3582, was set alight by return fire from a Ju 87. He steered it away from Folkestone, bringing it down to 1000 feet before baling out. Gibson claimed a Ju 88 on August 24 and a Bf 109 on the 29th. In this combat he was again set on fire and baled out over the sea, two miles offshore, and was picked up by a motor boat. He was awarded the DFC (30.8.40). On September 7 he claimed a Bf 109 as probably destroyed.

Later in the month Gibson was wounded and went to hospital. He was posted to 53 OTU, Heston on May 28 1941, as an instructor. In early January 1942 he joined 457 Squadron at Jurby, as a Flight Commander. On the expiry of his short service commission he returned to New Zealand in late May 1942 and was attached to the RNZAF from June 13. Gibson joined the newly-formed 15 Squadron and went with it to Tonga, where it took over P 40s of the 68th Pursuit Squadron, USAAF, with which it eventually became operational.

Gibson returned to New Zealand in mid-December 1942, to a staff job at Air HQ Control Group. In May 1943 he went on a course at the Army Staff College at Palmerston North. On December 15 he returned to 15 Squadron, this time as CO. The squadron took part in the heavy fighting of the Bougainville landings. Gibson destroyed a Zeke fighter on January 23 1944. The squadron returned to New Zealand for a rest on February 11 and returned to Guadalcanal in May 1944, moving in June to Bougainville. Tour-expired, Gibson returned with the squadron to New Zealand in late July and was posted away in mid-August. He left for the UK on October 31.

Gibson flew with 80 Squadron at Volkel from March 3 to April 2 1945 and was involved in the Rhine crossing, covering the airborne operation. He was awarded the DSO (11.3.45). On December 1 1945 he ceased his attachment to the RAF and transferred to the RNAZF but on December 24 1946 he rejoined the RAF.

In 1947 Gibson was pilot of Montgomery's personal aircraft, in 1948/49 he was personal aide and pilot to Marshal of the RAF Lord Tedder. He retired from the RAF in 1954 and went to live in South Africa, where he began flying with the Chamber of Mines in Johannesburg. Gibson later moved to their forward base in Bechuanaland, where he operated nine DC 3s and four DC 4s, both

JAA Gibson (continued)

as CFI and until 1965 as a Line Captain. He then formed Bechuanaland National Airways and was its General Manager.

In 1969/70 Gibson took part in 'sanction-busting' after UDI in Rhodesia. He flew supplies in and brought refugee children out of Biafra during the war there. On these flights his son, Michael, flew as co-pilot. Gibson later formed an air charter company, Jagair, operating from Kariba, Zimbabwe.

APO 9.7.38   PO 16.5.39   FO 3.9.40   FL 3.9.41
SL 1.7.44   FL 1.12.42

HERBERT SELWYN GIDDINGS

37283   FL   Pilot   British   615 and 111 Squadrons

Giddings, of Knaresborough, Yorkshire, joined the RAF in July 1935. After his elementary flying training he was posted to 3 FTS, Grantham on September 28 1935 and joined 65 Squadron at Hornchurch on August 5 1936.

Following the outbreak of war Giddings joined 615 Squadron and flew with it to Merville on November 15 1939. He was posted from 615 on August 18 1940 to 111 Squadron at Debden, as a Flight Commander. On the 31st Giddings claimed a Do 17 destroyed. He made a forced-landing at Detling in the middle of a bombing attack on September 2, following an attack on He 111s over the Thames Estuary. Giddings claimed two Bf 109s destroyed in a combat over the Channel on September 4. His oil system was damaged and he made a forced-landing at Catts Green Farm, Ewhurst.

Giddings was given command of 135 Squadron at Dum Dum, India in July 1942. He was killed on January 23 1943, aged 28. He is remembered on the Singapore Memorial, Column 423.

APO 16.9.35   PO 16.9.36   FO 16.6.38   FL 16.6.40
SL 1.9.41

JOZEF GIL

76765   PO   Pilot   Polish   229 and 145 Squadrons

Gil was born on January 30 1914. He was with 229 Squadron and later 145 Squadron late in the Battle of Britain. On December 29 1940 Gil was injured when he crashed at East Dean, Sussex, whilst low flying after dark looking for Tangmere.

On March 12 1941 Gil was posted to 53 OTU at Heston. He joined 315 Squadron at Speke on April 13. Flying from Northolt he claimed a Bf 109 probably destroyed on August 9 and another destroyed on the 14th. He was awarded the KW (10.9.41). On October 24 1941 he probably destroyed a Bf 109.

Gil was awarded a Bar to the KW (15.2.42) and on June 13 1942 he was posted to 306 Squadron at Northolt. He destroyed a FW 190 and damaged a Bf 109 on October 9 and was awarded a second Bar to the KW (15.11.42).

On a high cover operation over the Abbeville area on December 31 1942 Gil was shot down by a FW 190, in Spitfire BS 455. He was last seen heading towards the Channel and almost certainly crashed into the sea. There in no record of any known grave. Gil is remembered on the Polish Air Force Memorial at Northolt. He was awarded the VM (5th Class) (20.2.43).

ERNEST GEORGE GILBERT

44548   PO   Pilot   British   64 Squadron

Gilbert was born on November 4 1912 and joined the RAF as an aircraft apprentice, beginning at 2 Wing, School of Technical Training, Halton on September 6 1928. He qualified in August 1931 and was posted to RAF Eastchurch.

Having volunteered for pilot training, Gilbert was selected and went to 5 FTS, Sealand on October 1 1934. As a Sergeant-Pilot he went to 6 Squadron, Ismailia, when its Fighter Flight was reformed in October 1935. At Heliopolis on March 1 1936 the Flight joined with a Flight from 29 Squadron and reformed as 64 Squadron.

The newly-formed unit returned to the UK in September 1936, to Martlesham Heath, and Gilbert was with it for the next four years. On August 15 1940 he made a forced-landing at Hawkinge, damaged in a combat with Bf 109s over Dungeness. On the 18th he shared in the destruction of a He 111 and was commissioned later in the month.

Gilbert was posted to CFS, Upavon on December 1, for an instructor's course. From January 1941 until September 29 1944, when he came off flying on medical grounds, he instructed at 14 EFTS, Elmdon; 17 EFTS, North Luffenham and Peterborough and 21 (P) AFU, Wheaton Aston.

Gilbert transferred to the Air Traffic Control Branch, serving at home and overseas prior to his retirement on November 4 1962, as a Squadron Leader.

PO 26.8.40   FO 26.8.41   FL 26.8.42   FL 27.10.47

HUMPHREY TRENCH GILBERT

40530   FO   Pilot   British   601 Squadron

Born on November 3 1919, Gilbert, of Revesby Abbey, Lincolnshire, was at Cheltenham College from January 1934 to July 1937. He joined the RAF on a short service commission in December 1937, was posted to 9 FTS, Hullavington on March 5 1938 and then went to 73 Squadron at Digby on September 17 1938.

Gilbert joined 601 Squadron at Debden on August 16 1940. On the 18th he shared a Ju 87, on the 30th shared a He 111 and on the 31st claimed a Bf 110 destroyed and was himself shot down over the Thames Estuary. He baled out, unhurt, and his Hurricane, V 7260, crashed and burned out. On September 4 Gilbert claimed a Bf 110 destroyed. Two days later he was shot down by a Bf 109 over Mayfield. He baled out, wounded, and his Hurricane, V 6647, crashed at Kippings Cross, near Pembury.

In September 1941 Gilbert was posted to 71 Squadron, as a Flight Commander. He was given command of 65 Squadron at Debden on December 22. He claimed a Bf 109 destroyed and damaged a second on February 12 1942 and damaged a FW 190 on April 12.

Gilbert crashed on May 2 1942, attempting to take off from Debden in a Spitfire, with the Controller on his lap. They were said to be going to a party. Both men were killed. Gilbert is buried in Saffron Walden Cemetery, Essex. He was awarded the DFC (29.5.42).

APO 19.2.38   PO 6.12.38   FO 3.9.40   FL 3.9.41

PETER ROBERT JOSEPH GILBERT

Midshipman (FAA)   Pilot   British   111 Squadron

Gilbert joined the FAA in September 1939. He was loaned to the RAF on June 29 1940 and posted to 111 Squadron at Croydon on September 22.

He was with 787 Squadron at Yeovilton in June 1942 and was released from the service on September 11 1946.

Midshipman 11.9.39   Sub-Lt 25.2.42   Lt 1.4.43

JOHN STANLEY GILDERS

741587   **Sgt**   **Pilot**   **British**   **72 Squadron**

Born at Deal, Kent on October 4 1919, Gilders was educated at Bancroft School, Woodford Green. He joined the RAFVR in May 1938 and began flying at 18 E&RFTS, Fair Oaks. Called up after the outbreak of war, Gilders was posted to No 1 ITW, Cambridge on November 6 1939. He went to 3 FTS, South Cerney on February 1 1940 and joined 72 Squadron at Acklington on June 19 1940. He was slightly injured in a night landing crash on August 22.

Gilders claimed a Do 17 damaged on September 2, a Bf 110 destroyed on the 4th, he shared a Do 215 on the 10th, claimed a Bf 109 on the 11th, damaged a Do 17 on the 24th, damaged a Do 215 on the 25th and claimed a Bf 109 and a Ju 88 destroyed on the 27th.

Posted to 41 Squadron at Hornchurch on November 26 1940, Gilders was killed on February 21 1941. His aircraft crashed at Chilham, Kent and Gilders was reported 'Missing'. He is remembered on the Runnymede Memorial, Panel 43. When the site was excavated no trace of remains was found.

JAMES VIVIAN GILL

759007   **Sgt**   **Air Gunner**   **British**   **23 Squadron**

Gill, of Bawtry, Yorkshire, joined 23 Squadron at Middle Wallop on September 29 1940. He was killed on July 2 1941, aged 19 and serving with 115 Squadron, flying in Wellingtons from Marham, Norfolk.

Gill is buried in Becklingen War Cemetery, Soltau, Germany.

DENYS EDGAR GILLAM

37167   **FL**   **Pilot**   **British**   **616 and 312 Squadrons**

Gillam was born at Tynemouth on November 18 1915. He was educated at Bramcote, Scarborough and Wrekin College, Shropshire. He got his 'A' license at Public School Aviation Camp at Norwich on September 12 1934. He joined the RAF in February 1935 and was posted to 6 FTS, Netheravon on May 7. With training completed, he went to 29 Squadron at North Weald on March 6 1936.

Gillam was posted to the Met Flight at RAF Aldergrove on January 25 1937. He was awarded the AFC (9.6.38) for flying food to Rathlin Island, isolated by a gale for three weeks. He made two perilous landings in a Westland Wallace. On September 18 1939 Gillam was posted to 616 Squadron at Finningley. Over Dunkirk on June 1 1940 he damaged a Ju 88.

On August 15 Gillam claimed a Ju 88 destroyed, on the 26th a Bf 109, on the 29th a Bf 110, on the 30th and 31st two Bf 109s, on September 1 a Do 17 and on the 2nd a Bf 110. In this last action his engine was set alight by a Bf 110 over the Maidstone area. Gillam baled out, unhurt. His Spitfire, X 4181, crashed on Brook Farm, Capel.

Gillam was posted to 312 Squadron at Speke on September 6 1940, as a Flight Commander. He destroyed a Ju 88 as he took off on October 8, the squadron's first victory and probably the fastest confirmed victory of the war. He was awarded the DFC (12.11.40). In December Gillam took command of 306 Squadron at Tern Hill. He was posted to HQ 9 Group on March 2 1941 and returned to operations in July. He destroyed two He 59s on the water on October 9, was awarded a Bar to the DFC (21.10.41) and the DSO (12.12.41). Gillam was shot down on November 23 by ground fire at Dunkirk

and baled out, wounded in legs and arms. He got into his dinghy and was protected by aircraft of 615 until an ASR launch arrived from the Goodwins.

In January 1942 Gillam went to the USA to lecture American aircrews. He returned to the UK in March and was posted to Duxford to form the first Typhoon Wing, which made its first operational appearance at Dieppe on August 19 1942. Gillam went to RAF Staff College in October and then was posted to HQ 12 Group in February 1943. He was sent to the Command and General Staff School, Fort Leavenworth, Kansas in August and after his return was appointed Wing Leader 146 Wing in December.

Gillam took command of 20 Sector 2nd TAF in April 1944 and on July 17 146 Wing. He was awarded a Bar to the DSO (11.8.44). On October 24 he led the Wing against a building in Dordrecht, where a conference of high-ranking German officers was taking place. Gillam dived from 6000 feet and dropped a marker bomb, followed by two 500lb bombs. He was followed by five Typhoons, which bombed from 15 to 20 feet. Among the dead were two Generals, seventeen senior officers and 55 other officers of HQ, German Fifteenth Army.

Awarded a second Bar to the DSO (23.1.45), Gillam was posted in February to HQ 84 Group as Group Captain Ops, in August he went to 84 Group Disbandment Centre and was released from the RAF in October 1945. Gillam rejoined 616 Squadron, RAuxAF in 1946, as a Flight Lieutenant.

APO 16.4.35   PO 16.4.36   FO 16.11.37   FL 16.11.39
SL 1.12.40   WC 1.3.42   FL (RAuxAF) 8.10.46

ERNEST GILLAM

746755   **Sgt**   **Aircrew**   **British**   **248 Squadron**

Gillam, of Bury, Lancashire, was with 248 Squadron in early July 1940. He was killed on October 19 1941, serving as a Flight Sergeant with 404 (RCAF) Squadron, a maritime reconnaissance and coastal-strike unit.

Gillam was 30. He is remembered on the Runnymede Memorial, Panel 36.

JAMES GILLAN

37675   **FO**   **Pilot**   **British**   **601 Squadron**

Joined the RAF in January 1936 on a short service commission. On April 9 Gillan was posted for intermediate and advanced training to 4 FTS, Abu Sueir and he joined 55 Squadron at Dhibban, Iraq on December 15 1936,

Back in the UK, Gillan was supernumerary at RAF Depot, Uxbridge in November 1938. He joined 601 Squadron at Tangmere on August 5 1940. He failed to return from a combat off Portland on the 11th, in Hurricane P 3783, and was reported 'Missing'.

Gillan was 26. He is remembered on the Runnymede Memorial, Panel 5.

APO 23.3.36   PO 27.1.37   FO 27.10.38

THOMAS WILLIAM GILLEN

70245   **FO**   **Pilot**   **British**   **247 Squadron**

Gillen joined the RAF in May 1937 and was posted to 8 FTS, Montrose on August 21. At the end of his training he went on to the RAFO on May 31 1938.

Called up on September 2 1939, Gillen was with 247 Squadron at its formation at Roborough on August 1 1940. No more service details have been traced. He was released in 1948, as a Wing Commander, and died in 1969.

APO 9.8.37   PO (RAFO) 31.5.38   PO 2.9.39   FO 30.11.39
FL 30.11.40   SL 1.12.41

JAMES LYON GILLESPIE

76902   **PO**   **Air Gunner**   **British**   **23 Squadron**

Gillespie joined 23 Squadron at Collyweston on August 12 1940. He died in St Richard's Hospital, Chichester on October 1 1940, aged 34, not as a result of active service. He is buried in Chichester Cemetery.

APO 30.12.39   PO 13.5.40

JAMES GILLIES

47317   F/Sgt   Pilot   British   602 Squadron, 421 Flight

Joined 602 Squadron at Westhampnett on September 18 1940. Gillies shared in the destruction of a Ju 88 on the 21st and claimed a Bf 110 on the 26th.

Gillies was posted in early October 1940 to 421 Flight, then forming at Hawkinge. On the 17th he crashed in a Hurricane on landing after a combat with Bf 109s, injured. On December 7 he chased a Dornier to the French coast, with another pilot. He ran out of fuel on the way back and crashed 421 Flight's special blue Spitfire just short of Hawkinge.

The Flight was re-numbered 91 Squadron on January 11 1941. On April 11 Gillies was on a reconnaissance patrol when he saw a He 115 floatplane being towed by an 800 ton tender, near the coast off Cap Griz Nez. He returned to Hawkinge, reported the incident and later escorted a section of fighters to the area. Despite bad visibility he located the tender and then participated in the attack, which resulted in the floatplane being destroyed and the tender severely damaged. Returning to base Gillies engaged and destroyed a Bf 109. For this action he was awarded the DFM (30.5.41). He destroyed another Bf 109 on September 18 1941.

Commissioned in November, Gillies was posted to 615 Squadron at Fairwood Common in February 1942 and went to India with the squadron in March. He is believed to have destroyed two Japanese aircraft on May 29 1943.

On the night of March 27 1944 Gillies, with a small patrol, penetrated into the enemy ammunition dump at Indaw, Burma. After he had rejoined the main force he explained to the RAF the layout of the dump area. Gillies also arranged to indicate the target for the bombers. On April 4 he flew as passenger in a light aircraft and placed smoke bombs around the target area from a height of 50 feet, enabling the bombers to attack the target with great precision.

Gillies was killed on April 21 1944, said to be a Flight Lieutenant with 136 Squadron but when he was gazetted for the MC (13.2.45) for the ammunition dump operation he was listed as serving with 79 Squadron. He was 29 years old and is remembered on the Singapore Memorial, Column 431.

PO 17.11.41   FO 1.10.42   FL 17.11.43

KENNETH McLEOD GILLIES

37799   FL   Pilot   British   66 Squadron

Gillies joined the RAF on a short service commission in March 1936. He was posted to 8 FTS, Montrose on May 16 and joined 66 Squadron at Duxford on December 25 1936.

He was still with the squadron in July 1940. On August 20 Gillies shared a Bf 110 and on the 31st shared a Do 215. He was appointed 'A' Flight Commander on September 7, claimed a Do 17 destroyed on the 15th, a He 111 on the 18th and he shared three Do 17s on the 27th.

Gillies was reported 'Missing' after the interception of a He 111 off the east coast on October 4 1940. His Spitfire, X 4320, crashed into the sea. His body was washed ashore at Covehithe on October 21. Gillies was 27 and is buried in Thornton Garden of Rest, Lancashire.

APO 4.5.36   PO 3.3.37   FO 9.9.38   FL 9.9.40

KEITH REGINALD GILLMAN

42053   PO   Pilot   British   32 Squadron

Born in Dover on December 16 1920, Gillman attended the County School there from 1933 to 1938. He joined the RAF in March 1939 and began his flying training at 22 E&RFTS, Cambridge. On June 10 Gillman was posted to 15 FTS, Lossiemouth, was awarded his wings on October 6 and went to 11 Group Pool at St Athan on November 20 1939.

Gillman was sent to RAF Manby for No 1 Air Armament Course on January 1 1940. After the course ended he joined 32 Squadron at Biggin Hill on May 10. He flew his first operational sortie on June 7, a Blenheim escort to Abbeville.

On July 19 Gillman claimed a Bf 109 destroyed. He failed to return from combat over the Channel off Dover on August 25 1940 and was reported 'Missing'. He is remembered on the Runnymede Memorial, Panel 8.

APO 27.5.39   PO 18.11.39

GEORGE KEMP GILROY

90481   FO   Pilot   British   603 Squadron

A sheep farmer before the war, Gilroy was born in Edinburgh in 1915. He joined 603 Squadron, AuxAF in 1938 and was called to full-time service on August 23 1939.

Gilroy shared in the destruction of a He 111 over the Firth of Forth on October 16 1939, the first enemy aircraft shot down on British soil in the war. On the 28th he shared another He 111 and on January 19 1940 another.

Flying from Dyce, Gilroy claimed a share in the destruction of a Ju 88 on July 3, a shared Do 215 on the 6th and a shared He 111 on the 12th. The squadron went south to Hornchurch on August 27. Gilroy claimed Bf 109s destroyed on the 28th and 31st. On this day he was shot down in combat over London and baled out, wounded. He was attacked by a crowd on landing and later admitted to King George Hospital, Ilford. His Spitfire, X 4271, crashed into 14 Hereford Road, Wanstead.

Gilroy was awarded the DFC (13.9.40). He claimed a Bf 109 destroyed on October 28 and shared a He 111 on November 21. On December 17 he was badly injured in an accident.

On July 29 1941 Gilroy took command of 609 Squadron at Gravesend. He claimed two Bf 109s on October 27, another on November 8 and a FW 190 on April 15 1942. He was posted away from the squadron on May 31 and awarded a Bar to the DFC (23.6.42) and the C de G (Belg)(3.3.42).

In November 1942 Gilroy was posted to 325 Wing in East Africa but on the 29th he went to North Africa instead, to take command of 324 Wing. On January 2 1943 he claimed a Bf 109 destroyed and shared others on the 11th and 18th. He was in collision with Flight Lieutenant EB Mortimer-Rose over Souk-el-Khemis on January 28 and baled out slightly injured. Gilroy got a probable Bf 109 on February 3, shared another probable on the 23rd and was awarded the DSO (2.3.43). He destroyed a Bf 109 on April 3, shared a Fiat G 12 on the 22nd, destroyed a Bf 109 on the 24th, shared a He 111 on May 1 and destroyed a Mc 202 on September 4.

In November 1943 Gilroy was promoted to Group Captain and returned to the UK, where he took command of RAF Wittering and later RAF Blakelow. He was awarded the DFC (US)(14.11.44). After release from the RAF Gilroy rejoined the RAuxAF and commanded 603 Squadron from June 1946 to September 1949.

APO (AuxAF) 10.11.38   PO 23.8.39   FO 3.9.40   FL 3.9.41
SL 23.12.42   WC 19.1.44   SL (RAuxAFRO) 1.8.46

HAROLD ROY GILYEAT

1063606   Sgt   Aircrew   British   29 Squadron

No service details traced.

ALEXANDER GEORGE GIRDWOOD

741908   Sgt   Pilot   British   257 Squadron

Girdwood was with 257 Squadron at Hendon in early July 1940. On August 13 he claimed a Ju 88 destroyed and shared a He 111 on the 18th. On this day he was shot down by a Bf 110 over the Thames Estuary and baled out, wounded in the foot, and was admitted to Foulness Hospital. His Hurricane, P 3708, crashed at Nazewick Farm, Foulness.

On October 29 Girdwood was killed, when he was caught in a low-level bombing attack as he was taking off from North Weald. His Hurricane, V 6852, crashed and burned out. He was 22 years old and is buried in Hawkhead Cemetery, Paisley, Renfrewshire.

ERNEST DEREK GLASER

82178   PO   Pilot   British   65 Squadron

Born on April 20 1921, Glaser joined 65 Squadron at Hornchurch on July 13 1940.

He was awarded the DFC (25.8.42), as an Acting Flight Lieutenant with 234 Squadron. He commanded 548 Squadron at Darwin Civil from February 1945 until its disbandment in September 1945.

Glaser retired from the RAF on June 26 1953, as a Squadron Leader.

PO 11.7.40   FO 11.7.41
FL 11.7.42   FL 1.9.45

THOMAS PERCY GLEAVE

29137   SL   Pilot   British   253 Squadron

Born on September 6 1908, Gleave was educated at Westminster High School and Liverpool Collegiate School and joined the Sefton Tanning Co in 1924. He first flew with the Liverpool and Merseyside Flying Club at Hooton in 1927, as a Founder-Member, and began instruction in early 1929, gaining his 'A' licence on July 6.

Later in the year Gleave went to Canada and worked for a tanning company in Acton, Ontario. He flew at the Toronto Flying Club. He returned to the UK in 1930 and joined the RAF in September.

Gleave was posted to 5 FTS, Sealand on September 27 and after training joined No 1 Squadron at Tangmere on September 8 1931. In an attempt to be the first man to fly to Ceylon, Gleave left Lympne

on October 11 1933 in a Spartan, G-AAMH. Four days later he was forced down in a down-draught in the mountains east of Kutahya, in Anatolia, Turkey. He forced-landed in a tree on the side of a ravine, not far from Sarbona Pinar and had to abandon his attempt.

From February 1934 Gleave was at CFS, Upavon on an instructor's course. He was posted to the staff of 5 FTS, Sealand on May 13 and went on loan to the Oxford University Air Squadron for a short period soon afterwards. On December 17 1936 Gleave was appointed as the Flying Instructor to 502 (Ulster) Special Reserve Squadron at Aldergrove. He converted the squadron to Auxiliary status and was re-posted as Adjutant and CFI. On January 1 1939 Gleave joined Air Staff, Bomber Command and carried out liaison duties in the Fighter Command Operations Room at Stanmore. On September 3 he was posted for full-time service there as Bomber Liaison Officer.

On June 2 1940 Gleave was given command of 253 Squadron at Kirton-in-Lindsey. He was posted away on August 9 but allowed to stay with the squadron until called upon by AOC 14 Group. On August 30 Gleave claimed five Bf 109s destroyed but was credited with one destroyed and four probables. The following morning Squadron Leader HM Starr, CO of 253, was shot down and killed. Command of 253 reverted to Gleave once more but he himself was shot down at about 1.00 pm, during a massive air attack on Biggin Hill by a German bomber force. He baled out, grievously burned, and was admitted to Orpington Hospital.

Gleave later went to Queen Victoria Hospital, East Grinstead, where he underwent plastic surgery by Archie (later Sir Archibald) McIndoe and his brilliant colleague Percy Jayes. On July 20 1941 the Guinea Pig Club was formed at the Queen Victoria Hospital, with McIndoe as President and Gleave as Vice-President and a Founder-Member.

In August 1941 he was given a temporary non-operational flying category and on the 19th began flying once more, with a grafted face and limbs, less than twelve months after being burned. He became operational again in October. Gleave took command of RAF Manston on October 5 and was there when the 'Scharnhorst' and 'Gneisenau' made their 'Channel Dash' on February 12 1942. Aircraft took off from Manston to attack the battleships. After the action Gleave recommended Esmonde for a posthumous VC and other awards for the five survivors of the Swordfish attack. All were granted.

Gleave went to RAF Staff College on April 13 1942 and returned to Manston on July 10, in time for the Dieppe operation, for which Manston was a main refuelling and re-arming base. On September 9 Gleave was promoted to Group Captain and posted to the Special Planning Staff at Norfolk House, St James Square, London. He was made Group Captain Air Plans for the Allied Expeditionary Air Force under Leigh-Mallory in November 1943. With Colonel Phillips Melville of the USAAF as co-operator he wrote the Overall Overlord Air Plan. For his outstanding work Gleave was made a CBE and awarded the US Legion of Merit, later changed to the Bronze Star because of protocol difficulties. In the wake of the invasion Gleave moved across to France.

On October 1 1944 Gleave was made Head of Air Plans under Eisenhower at Supreme HQ Allied Expeditionary Force. He returned to East Grinstead in mid-July 1945 for further plastic surgery and in September became SASO to the RAF Delegation to France.

Gleave returned to the UK in early November 1947 and went to Reserve Command, later Home Command, where he held various staff appointments. In February 1952 he joined the directing staff at RAF Staff College, Bracknell. After further plastic surgery he was invalided out of the RAF on November 14 1953. He joined the Historical Section in the Cabinet Office, as a member of the Mediterranean and Middle East team, engaged on official histories of the 1939-45 war.

On March 31 1974 Gleave ceased to be a full-time Official Historian and became a consultant to the Cabinet Office. He continued as Vice-President of the Guinea Pig Club, with the title of Chief Guinea Pig. In addition to his other awards Gleave received two Mentions in Despatches, the Légion d'Honneur (Fr), the C de G (Fr), was made an honorary pilot of l'Armée de l'Air and the Polish Air Force and was also honoured by the Government of Belgium.

Post-war research has shown that all five Bf 109s claimed by Gleave on August 30 1940 were doubtless destroyed and that on the 31st he destroyed a Ju 88, which crashed at Provins in France and another 'possible' crashed at Chateaudun.

PO 12.9.30   FO 12.4.32   FL 1.4.36   SL 1.12.38
WC 1.3.41   GC 1.1.44   GC 1.7.47

GEOFFREY GLEDHILL

742857   Sgt   Pilot   British   238 Squadron

Gledhill joined 238 Squadron at Middle Wallop on August 4 1940. He was killed on August 11, shot down in combat two miles east of Weymouth, in Hurricane P 2978.

He was 19. Gledhill is buried in Criquebeuf-en-Caux churchyard, France.

IAN RICHARD GLEED

37800   FL   Pilot   British   87 Squadron

The son of a doctor, Gleed was born in Finchley, London on July 3 1916. He was educated at Tenterden Preparatory School and Epsom College. He learned to fly privately and flew his first solo at the London Aeroplane Club, Hatfield on November 16 1935. Gleed joined the RAF on a short service commission in March 1936 and carried out his ab initio training at 2 E&RFTS, Filton. On May 16 he went to 8 FTS, Montrose and then joined 46 Squadron at Digby on December 25 1936.

Gleed was posted to 266 Squadron as 'B' Flight Commander on September 9 1939, when it was being reformed at Sutton Bridge. He was testing a Spitfire on February 18 1940, when it broke up in the air. He was thrown out and lost consciousness. He came to and pulled his ripcord and the parachute opened. Gleed did not return to 266 until late April and was only allowed to fly dual. He regained his full flying category on May 14 and was posted on the same day to 87 Squadron in France, as 'A' Flight Commander.

On May 18 Gleed claimed two Bf 110s destroyed, on the 19th a Bf 109, two Do 17s, a He 111 and a probable Bf 109 and on the 20th a Ju 88. The squadron was withdrawn to Debden on May 22.

Operational again on June 21, the squadron moved to Exeter in early July. On August 15 Gleed claimed two Bf 110s destroyed and on the 25th another two. He was awarded the DFC (13.9.40). On September 30 he probably destroyed a Ju 88.

Gleed took command of 87 on December 24 1940. He claimed a Do 17 destroyed on May 7 1941, a Do 18 on the 24th and a probable Ju 88 on the 28th. He was appointed Wing Leader at Middle Wallop on November 18. Gleed claimed a Ju 88 probably destroyed on March 13 1942, a Ju 88 on the 23rd, a Bf 109 and another probable on April 17 and a probable FW 190 on May 5. He was awarded the DSO (22.5.42) and posted to HQ Fighter Command on July 16, as Wing Commander Tactics, becoming Wing Commander Operations on December 7.

Posted to the Middle East on January 1 1943, Gleed was attached to 145 Squadron in North Africa from the 13th to gain experience of desert operations before taking command of 244 Wing, which he did on January 31. He claimed a Bf 109 destroyed on March 17.

On an afternoon patrol over the Cap Bon area on April 16 1943 Gleed was shot down, probably by Leutnant Reinert of JG 77. After being hit Gleed headed for the Tunisian coast. His Spitfire, AB 502, was found on sand dunes near the sea on the western coastline of Cap Bon. His body was not there but it is known that he was buried at Tazoghrane. He was re-buried in the Military Cemetery at Enfidaville on April 25 1944. Gleed was awarded the C de G (Belg)(9.4.43) and the C de G (Fr)(5.6.46).

*APO 4.5.36   PO 9.3.37   FO 9.10.38   FL 3.9.40
SL 1.12.41*

ALEXANDER JOSEPH GLEGG

84021   PO   Air Gunner   British   600 Squadron

Born in London in 1908, Glegg was in the AuxAF for four years in the thirties. He joined the RAF at the outbreak of war and was posted to 600 Squadron at Hornchurch on September 18 1940.

In November Glegg teamed up with Flying Officer ADM Boyd. They destroyed a Ju 88 on May 16 1941, a He 111 on October 10, another on December 2 and another on January 25 1942. Both were awarded the DFC (9.1.42).

When Boyd took command of 219 Squadron at Scorton in March 1943 Glegg was with him. They went to North Africa in early June and destroyed two Ju 88s on June 30, and He 111s on September 6 and 18.

Glegg was released from the RAF in 1945, as a Squadron Leader.

PO 9.5.40   FO 9.5.41   FL 9.5.42

JOHN NIXON GLENDINNING

740032   Sgt   Pilot   British   54 and 74 Squadrons

Glendinning was born at Benfieldside, Co Durham on July 7 1912. He joined the RAFVR on January 25 1937 and obtained his 'A' license on March 18 1938. He was called up on September 1 1939 and sent to 5 FTS, Sealand on October 7 for assessment of his flying capabilities.

On December 17 Glendinning was posted to 9 BGS, as a staff pilot. He went to 7 OTU, Hawarden on September 3 1940 and joined 54 Squadron at Catterick on September 16 and then joined 74 Squadron at Biggin Hill on October 21 and destroyed two Ju 87s on November 14, a Bf 109 on the 15th, another on December 2 and another on March 1 1941.

Whilst patrolling Dungeness on March 12 1941, Glendinning was shot down and killed by Bf 109s. His Spitfire, P 7506, crashed at Ivychurch, Kent. He was 28 and was cremated at West Road Crematorium, Newcastle-upon-Tyne.

NORMAN GLEW

107955   Sgt   Pilot   British   72 Squadron

Glew, from Derby, joined 72 Squadron at Gravesend on June 19 1940. On September 23 he claimed a share in a Bf 109 and on the 27th destroyed a Do 17.

Commissioned in August 1941, Glew was with 260 Squadron in the Western Desert in December. On January 2 1942 he damaged a Bf 109 and was himself badly damaged by Bf 109s on March 26 on his way back from Martuba to Tobruk.

Glew took command of 1435 Squadron in Italy in March 1944. He was killed on May 17, aged 27. He is buried in Bari War Cemetery.

PO 22.8.41   FO 22.8.42   FL 22.8.43

ANTONI GLOWACKI

P 1527   Sgt   Pilot   Polish   501 Squadron

Glowacki was born in Warsaw on February 10 1910. He joined the Warsaw Aero Club in 1926 and became a cadet in the PAF. Between 1931 and 1939 Glowacki flew about 5000 hours as a pilot. He was posted to 6 OTU, Sutton Bridge on July 5 1940 and joined 501 Squadron at Gravesend on August 4.

Glowacki claimed a Ju 87 destroyed and a Do 215 damaged on August 15, three Bf 109s and two Ju 88s on the 24th, a Bf 109 on the 28th, a Do 215 on the 31st and a probable Bf 109 on September 18. He was himself shot down on August 31, crashing and burning out on the aerodrome at Gravesend, in Hurricane V 6540.

In late 1940 Glowacki was posted to 55 OTU, Usworth, as an instructor. He was awarded the VM (5th Class)(23.12.40) and the DFM (30.10.41). He returned to operations on November 7 1941 when he was posted to 303 Squadron at Northolt. On April 27 1942 he claimed a probable FW 190 and on August 19, over Dieppe, Glowacki claimed a FW 190 destroyed and shared a He 111. He was awarded the KW and Bar (20.8.42) and the DFC (15.11.42).

Glowacki joined 308 Squadron at Northolt on February 7 1943 and remained with it until February 22 1944. After a trip to the USA he returned to 61 OTU, as a Flight Commander. He took command of 309 Squadron at Acklington on September 9 1944. He was awarded two more Bars to the KW (25.9.44). After a short spell at RAF Keevil from July 16 1945, Glowacki was with 307 Squadron at Horsham St Faith from October 5 until November 29 1945, when he was posted to 13 Group as a liaison officer.

Glowacki remained in the RAF after the war. He transferred to the RNZAF in 1954 and took his family to New Zealand. In 1960 he joined the Department of Civil Aviation in Wellington and was responsible for light aircraft in the region until his retirement in 1975. He died in May 1980.

FL 16.1.45

WITOLD JOZEF GLOWACKI

76739   PO   Pilot   Polish   145 and 605 Squadrons

Joined 145 Squadron at Westhampnett on August 12 1940 and moved to 605 Squadron at Drem on August 31.

Glowacki claimed a Bf 110 destroyed on September 11. With another pilot he chased a Do 17 to the French coast on September 24 1940. They were jumped by three Bf 109s and Glowacki was shot down and killed. He was 26 and is buried in the Guines Communal Cemetery, France. He was awarded the VM (5th Class)(1.2.41)

RICHARD LINDSAY GLYDE

39983   FO   Pilot   Australian   87 Squadron

Glyde was born on January 29 1914 in Perth, Australia. He joined the RAF on a short service commission in June 1937. He was posted to 3 FTS, South Cerney on August 21 and went to No 1 AACU at Farnborough on March 26 1938, as a staff pilot.

On October 24 1938 Glyde joined 87 Squadron at Debden. He went to France with the squadron at the outbreak of war. On May 19 1940 he destroyed a Bf 109 and a Hs 126. He was awarded the DFC (4.6.40), being then credited with four enemy aircraft destroyed.

Glyde claimed a Bf 110 on July 11 south of Portland and returned to Exeter damaged. On August 13 1940 Glyde was hit by return fire from a Ju 88 engaged south of Selsey Bill. His Hurricane, P 3387, crashed into the sea and he was reported 'Missing'. He was 26 years old and is remembered on the Runnymede Memorial, Panel 5.

APO 9.8.37   PO 24.5.38   FO 24.11.39

FELIKS GMUR

780678   Sgt   Pilot   Polish   151 Squadron

Joined 151 Squadron at Stapleford on August 21 1940. Gmur was shot down and killed in combat over the Thames Estuary on August 30. His Hurricane, R 4213, crashed at Jacks Hatch, Epping Green.

Gmur was 25. He is buried in Epping Cemetery, Essex.

WLADYSLAW GNYS

P 1298   PO   Pilot   Polish   302 Squadron

Born in Sary, Kielce, Poland on August 24 1910, Gnys joined the PAF in 1931. He began flying training in 1933 and then went on to a fighter pilot's course. After squadron service he was posted to Deblin in 1935, as an instructor. In 1938 Gnys went to Officers' School at Deblin and in early 1939 joined 121 Fighter Squadron, flying PZL PIIc aircraft.

Early in the morning of September 1 Gnys destroyed two Do 17s returning from a raid on Cracow. They were the first German aircraft shot down in the war. When Poland collapsed Gnys crossed into Roumania. He embarked on a ship sailing for Marseilles, via Malta. In France he trained on French aircraft and in February 1940 he was with Groupe de Chasse 3/1. Gnys shared in destroying a German bomber in May.

In June the Poles were ordered to England by General Sikorski. Gnys went in a British ship to Algiers, then by train to Casablanca, then took a ship for Liverpool, arriving there on July 14 1940. He joined 302 Squadron at Leconfield on July 28. He was awarded the KW (1.2.41).

Gnys was rested from operations on January 30 1942, going to 302's Operations Room, moving in August to 303's. On December 22 1942 he resumed flying with 302 and was posted to 316 Squadron at Hutton Cranswick on February 10 1943, as a Flight Commander. In August he moved to 309 Squadron and at the end of his tour was awarded a Bar to the KW (20.10.43) and posted to 18 Fighter Wing, HQ 84 Group.

In early August 1944 Gnys was given command of 317 Squadron at Plumetot, France. On the 27th he was shot down and wounded. He crash-landed and was captured. He was in a German hospital, when it was captured by the French Resistance. Gnys was flown back to hospital in Swindon. He did not return to operations and after a period at HQ PAF, Blackpool he was posted to HQ Fighter Command on September 17 1945, as a liaison officer.

Gnys was awarded the VM (5th Class)(1.6.45) and two more Bars to the KW (31.10.47). He left the PAF in 1947 and went to Canada to live on March 15 1948. He died there in 1983.

PO 1.3.41   FO 1.3.42   FL 1.3.43

HENRY GORDON GODDARD

70252   FO   Pilot   British   219 Squadron

Goddard was an architect before the war. Whilst at Wadham College, Oxford in the late twenties he learned to fly with the University Air Squadron. He was a member of the RAFO from 1932, later in the RAFVR and was called to full-time service on September 8 1939.

With 219 Squadron from December 1939, Goddard destroyed a Ju 88 at night in November 1940 after attacking it at point-blank range at 20000 feet. He was awarded the DFC (18.2.41).

Goddard was awarded the AFC (11.6.42) and commanded 153 Squadron at Portreath for a short time in December 1942. Posted overseas, he was given command of 176 Squadron at Baigachi, India in June 1943 and was posted away in March 1944 to lead 170 Wing in the Imphal Valley. On May 1

HG Goddard (continued)

Goddard was promoted to Acting Group Captain and took command of HQ 906 Wing. He was awarded the DSO (14.11.44).

He was released from the RAF in 1945, as a Wing Commander, and died in 1972.

PO (RAFO) 4.7.32   FO (RAFO) 4.1.34   FO 8.9.39
FL 16.12.40   SL 1.3.42   WC 1.3.45

WILLIAM BERNARD GODDARD

36126   FL   Pilot   British   235 Squadron

Goddard, of Ipswich, Suffolk, joined the RAF in February 1938 with a direct-entry Permanent Commission. He was posted immediately to the Aeroplane and Armament Experimental Establishment at Martlesham Heath.

In June 1940 Goddard was with 235 Squadron. On November 18, whilst on an escort operation, he engaged two He 115s. He was severely wounded in one foot by return fire, eventually losing three toes. He pressed home his attack and although suffering from loss of blood he got his aircraft and crew safely back to base. For this action Goddard was awarded the DFC (6.12.40).

He was killed on June 15 1941, aged 27. He is remembered on the Runnymede Memorial, Panel 29.

PO 24.2.38   FO 24.8.39   FL 3.9.40

STEPHEN FREDERICK GODDEN

05222   SL   Pilot   British   3 Squadron

Born on December 26 1910, Godden was commissioned in the RAFO in March 1931 and joined the RAF in October 1932. He was posted to 3 FTS, Grantham and after training joined 19 Squadron at Duxford on August 26 1933.

Godden went on to the staff at 2 FTS, Digby on December 16 1935 and in late 1938 was posted to the staff of the Inspector General RAF. He was given command of 3 Squadron at Wick in June 1940 and was posted away on September 6.

A graduate of the Military Staff College and a Qualified Instructor, CFS, Godden retired from the RAF on September 2 1957, as a Wing Commander. He died in August 1966.

PO (RAFO) 16.3.31   PO 10.10.32   FO 10.4.33   FL 10.4.36
SL 1.12.38   WC 1.3.41   WC 1.10.46

CLAUDE WALLER GOLDSMITH

72152   FO   Pilot   South African   603 and 54 Squadrons

Commissioned in the RAFVR in 1938, Goldsmith was called to full-time service on October 10 1939.

He was with 603 Squadron at Dyce in early July 1940 and was posted to 54 Squadron at Hornchurch on September 3. He rejoined 603 there on the 28th.

Goldsmith was shot down in a surprise attack by Bf 109s south of Maidstone on October 27 1940. His Spitfire, P 7439, crashed near Waltham. He died of his injuries the next day, aged 23. He is buried in Hornchurch Cemetery, Essex.

PO (RAFVR) 29.3.38   PO 10.10.39   FO 9.12.39

JOHN ERNEST GOLDSMITH

901859   Sgt   Air Gunner   British   236 Squadron

Born at Sudbourne, Suffolk on November 14 1921, Goldsmith volunteered for aircrew duties and joined the RAF in late 1939, as a trainee air gunner.

In early January 1940 Goldsmith was posted to AGS at Jurby. In seven weeks of gunnery training there he made fourteen flights and had logged 8 hrs 45 mins before he joined 236 Squadron in late March. At this time the squadron was in Coastal Command but in early July it was seconded to Fighter Command for the Battle of Britain.

Goldsmith flew his first operational patrol on July 6. On an offensive patrol on September 23 Goldsmith, flying with Pilot Officer GH Russell, shot down a He 111. Two days later on a sortie to Brest and again flying with Russell, Goldsmith shot down a Do 18 flying boat.

On October 30 1940 Goldsmith made his last flight with 236. In early March 1941 he was at 54 OTU, Church Fenton converting to Defiants. He teamed up with Sergeant Angell and they were posted to 96 Squadron at Cranage in early April.

On April 27 1941 they were on a night cross-country flight to Digby. The Defiant, T 3389, crashed four miles south of Wellingore and both men were killed. The cause was believed to be pilot disorientation.

Goldsmith was a Flight Sergeant at the time of his death. He is buried in All Saints' churchyard, Sudbourne.

HENRI ALPHONSE CLEMENT GONAY

81635   PO   Pilot   Belgian   235 Squadron

An instructor in the Belgian Air Force, Gonay left Belgium in May 1940 and went to France, where he was employed ferrying French aircraft. He later flew to Bayonne and sailed in a Dutch cargo ship for England, arriving at Plymouth on June 23.

Commissioned in July, Gonay was posted to 235 Squadron on August 5. On October 8 1940 he shared a He 59 destroyed off Cherbourg. He was awarded the C de G (Belg)(21.7.41).

Gonay commanded 129 Squadron from September 1942 to September 1943 and 263 Squadron from February 1944 until June 14 1944, when he was killed. Gonay's remains were repatriated to Belgium after the war.

HAROLD INGHAM GOODALL

79159   PO   Pilot   British   264 Squadron

Goodall was with 264 Squadron in early July 1940. Flying with Sergeant RBM Young as his gunner, Goodall shared in the destruction of a Ju 88 on August 24 and claimed a Do 17 on the 26th.

They were both killed on October 8 1940, when their Defiant, N 1627, crashed at Marlow, possibly as a result of enemy action.

Goodall was 25. He is buried in Parkstone Cemetery, Poole, Dorset.

PO 12.5.40

ALBERT THOMAS GOODERHAM

742957   Sgt   Pilot   British   151 and 46 Squadrons

Joined 151 Squadron at Stapleford on August 26 1940 and moved to 46 Squadron there on September 15.

Gooderham was shot down in combat with Bf 109s over the Thames Estuary on October 15 and baled out, slightly wounded. His Hurricane, V 6789, crashed at Gravesend.

He was killed on November 2 1941, as a Flight Sergeant with 615 Squadron. Gooderham is remembered on the Runnymede Memorial, Panel 36.

GEOFFREY GOODMAN

45491 Sgt Pilot British 85 Squadron

Goodman was born in Taunton on June 21 1916 and was a commercial pilot in the mid-thirties. He was a pre-war airman pilot and joined 85 Squadron at Debden, when it was reformed on June 1 1938. He went with the squadron to France in September 1939.

Injured in April 1940, Goodman did not fly operationally again until rejoining 85 at Martlesham Heath in July. On August 30 he claimed a Bf 110 destroyed and on September 1 a Bf 109. Commissioned in March 1941, he remained with 85 until April 19 1942, when he was posted to 51 OTU, Cranfield, as an instructor.

Goodman was posted to 29 Squadron at West Malling in November 1942, later becoming a Flight Commander. He damaged a Do 217 on December 16 and destroyed another on March 8 1943. Awarded the DFC (26.10.43), Goodman was posted to 151 Squadron at Middle Wallop in October 1943, to command. He destroyed eight enemy aircraft at night in a two month period, a Ju 88 and a He 177 on March 1 1944, a Ju 88 on April 1, a Ju W34 on the 20th and four He 111s on May 4. Goodman left the squadron in December 1944.

He stayed in the RAF after the war and moved later to the Engineer Branch. Goodman was made an MBE (1.1.46) and an OBE (13.6.59). He retired on June 1 1969, as a Wing Commander, and died in 1976.

PO 12.3.41   FO 12.3.42   FL 12.3.43   SL 1.8.47
WC 1.7.56

GEORGE ERNEST GOODMAN

42598 PO Pilot Palestinian 1 Squadron

Goodman, of Lagos, Nigeria, was born in Haifa, Palestine. He joined the RAF on a short service commission in June 1939.

He was posted to No 1 Squadron in France in March 1940. On May 13 Goodman destroyed a He 111 and shared a Bf 110, on the 14th he shared a He 111 and on the squadron's last day in France, June 17, he destroyed another He 111.

Goodman claimed a Bf 109 destroyed on July 25, shared a Bf 110 on August 11, claimed a He 111 on the 16th, a Bf 110 and a shared Do 17 on the 18th and a Bf 110 on September 6. In this engagement he was shot down by return fire and baled out, with a sprained shoulder. His Hurricane, P 2686, may be the one which crashed at Brownings Farm, Chiddingstone Causeway. Goodman shared a Ju 88 on October 8, destroyed a Do 17 on the 27th and was awarded the DFC (26.11.40).

In early November 1940 Goodman was posted to 73 Squadron and embarked for the Middle East in HMS 'Furious'. The squadron flew off to Takoradi on the 29th and then flew in easy stages to Heliopolis, via Lagos, Accra, Kano, Maidugari, Khartoum, Wadi Halfa and Abu Sueir. During December the pilots were attached to 274 Squadron in the Western Desert. The squadron became operational as a unit in early January 1941.

On February 4 Goodman destroyed a Fiat CR 42, on April 9 he claimed a Bf 110 and crash-landed behind British lines after being hit by ground fire, on the 14th he shared a Hs 126, on the 21st destroyed a Ju 87 and shared another and on the 22nd destroyed a Fiat G 50. Goodman was shot down and killed on June 14 1941, in a strafing attack on Gazala, where heavy flak was encountered. He was 20 and is buried in the Knightsbridge War Cemetery, Acroma, Libya.

APO 2.9.39   PO 28.2.40   FO 28.2.41

MAURICE VENNING GOODMAN

135476 Sgt Air Gunner British 604 Squadron

Goodman was with 604 Squadron at Northolt in early July 1940.

Commissioned in October 1942, he was awarded the DFC (12.11.43), as a Flying Officer with 192 Squadron. He was released from the RAF in 1946, as a Flight Lieutenant. Goodman died on January 8 1988.

PO 23.10.42   FO 23.4.43   FL 23.10.44

CHARLES GOODWIN

754024 Sgt Pilot British 219 Squadron

Goodwin, of Kingston-upon-Hull, joined 219 Squadron at Catterick on August 20 1940.

He was killed on September 30, when his Blenheim, L 1261, disintegrated and crashed during a routine night patrol. He and his crew of two were killed.

Goodwin was 21. He is buried in Hull Northern Cemetery.

HENRY MacDONALD GOODWIN

90269 FO Pilot British 609 Squadron

Goodwin was commissioned in the RAFO in May 1935. It was the forerunner of the RAFVR, which came into being in 1936. He joined 605 Squadron, AuxAF in May 1938 and was called to full-time service with the squadron on August 24 1939. Goodwin was posted to 609 Squadron at Northolt on May 20 1940.

He claimed a Bf 110 destroyed on August 12 and two Ju 87s over Lyme Bay on the 13th. He failed to return from combat on the 14th, in Spitfire N 3024. Ten days later Goodwin's body was washed up on the Isle of Wight.

He was 25 and is buried in St Cassian's churchyard, Chaddesley Corbett, Worcestershire.

PO (RAFO) 8.5.35   FO (RAFO) 6.7.36
FO (AuxAFRO) 8.5.38   FO 24.8.39

ROY DANIEL GOODWIN

120495 Sgt Pilot British 64 Squadron

Served with 64 Squadron in the Battle of Britain. Commissioned in April 1942, Goodwin was released from the RAF in 1946, as a Flight Lieutenant. He was commissioned in the RAFVR in September 1947 and died in 1983.

PO 13.4.42   FO 13.10.42   FL 13.4.44
FO (RAFVR) 20.9.47

STANLEY ALBERT GOODWIN

172607 Sgt Pilot British 266 and 66 Squadrons

Goodwin was born in 1921. He joined 266 Squadron at Wittering on September 30 1940 and moved to 66 Squadron at Gravesend on October 14.

Commissioned in December 1943, Goodwin was released from the RAF in 1946, as a Flight Lieutenant. He died on March 7 1982.

PO 22.12.43   FO 22.6.44   FL 22.12.45

JOHN ARTHUR GERALD GORDON

36075   **SL**   **Pilot**   **Canadian**   **151 Squadron**

Gordon, of Red Deer, Alberta, joined the RCAF in June 1934. He transferred to the RAF in July 1936 and went to 9 FTS, Thornaby, under instruction. He joined 19 Squadron at Duxford on October 25 1936.

Gordon took command of 151 Squadron at Martlesham Heath on August 5 1940. He claimed a Bf 109 destroyed on the 14th. He was shot down in combat with Bf 110s over Rochford on August 18, baled out, badly burned, and was admitted to Rochford Hospital. His Hurricane, P 3940, crashed and burned out at Tabriums Farm, Battlesbridge.

On June 1 1942 Gordon failed to return from a sweep, flying with 350 Squadron, as a Wing Commander. He is remembered on the Runnymede Memorial, Panel 64.

PO 22.7.36   FO 22.10.36   FL 22.10.38   SL 1.3.40
WC 1.12.41

STANLEY GORDON

939014   **Sgt**   **Aircrew**   **British**   **235 Squadron**

Joined 235 Squadron on October 25 1940. Gordon, of Heaton, Yorkshire, was killed on May 28 1941, aged 20. He is remembered on the Runnymede Memorial, Panel 44.

WILLIAM HUGH GIBSON GORDON

42120   **PO**   **Pilot**   **British**   **234 Squadron**

Born in Aberdeen in 1920, Gordon joined the RAF on a short service commission in March 1939.

He was with 234 Squadron at St Eval in early July 1940 and claimed a Bf 109 destroyed on August 24.

Gordon was shot down and killed in combat with Bf 109s on September 6. His Spitfire, X 4036, crashed on Howbourne Farm, Hadlow Down. He is buried in Mortlach Parish churchyard, Banff.

APO 13.5.39   PO 6.11.39

WILLIAM ERNEST GORE

90279   **FL**   **Pilot**   **British**   **607 and 54 Squadrons**

An electrical engineer from Stockton-on-Tees, Gore joined 607 Squadron, AuxAF in 1934. He was called to full-time service on August 24 1939 and flew to France with the squadron on November 15.

Leading a section on a dawn patrol in May 1940, Gore intercepted three He 111s, which were all shot down. Hit by return fire, his aircraft caught fire and he baled out, wounded. Gore was awarded the DFC (31.5.40).

He was posted to 54 Squadron at Catterick on August 6 but returned to 607 in early September. On the 28th Gore was shot down by Bf 109s, in an action east of Selsey. He was reported 'Missing', believed to have crashed into the sea, in Hurricane P 3108.

Gore was 25. He is remembered on the Runnymede Memorial, Panel 5.

PO (AuxAF) 18.6.34   FO (AuxAF) 18.12.35   FO 24.8.39
FL 3.9.40

DAVID GEORGE GORRIE

80542   **PO**   **Pilot**   **British**   **43 Squadron**

Gorrie, of Montrose, was posted to 43 Squadron at Tangmere in early July 1940, from OTU. On July 12 he shared in the destruction of a He 111 and on September 6 claimed a Bf 109 destroyed.

On April 4 1941 Gorrie was killed, aged 23. The unit he was serving with is not known. He is buried in the Smithbank extension of Barry Parish churchyard, Scotland.

PO 27.5.40

MIECZYSLAW GORZULA

76695   **PO**   **Pilot**   **Polish**   **607 Squadron**

Born in Cracow on August 1 1919, Gorzula joined the PAF in 1938. He was commissioned in January 1940 and posted to 607 Squadron at Turnhouse in October.

Gorzula was posted to 302 Squadron at Kenley on May 16 1941. He moved to 87 Squadron at Colerne on November 4 but rejoined 302, then at Harrowbeer, on March 16 1942. He was awarded the KW (20.8.42), posted to 58 OTU, Grangemouth on April 23 1943, as an instructor, and awarded a Bar to the KW (7.7.43).

On November 10 1943 Gorzula returned to operations, with a posting to 315 Squadron at Ballyhalbert, as a Flight Commander. He went to 84 Group Support Unit on May 8 1944, was with 306 Squadron for two months from July 31, after which he was attached to HQ PAF, Blackpool before joining 309 Squadron at Andrews Field on November 17 1944, as a Flight Commander.

Gorzula destroyed a Me 262 on April 9 1945. He went back to Blackpool on May 25, went to HQ 133 Wing on June 14 and was posted to RAF Coltishall on August 8 1945. Awarded a second Bar to the KW (5.1.46), Gorzula was released from the PAF in January 1947.

PO 24.1.40   PO 1.3.41   FO 1.3.42   FL 1.3.43

REGINALD CLIVE GOSLING

85245   **PO**   **Pilot**   **British**   **266 Squadron**

Gosling joined the RAFVR in November 1938 and was called to full-time service in October 1939. He was posted to 3 ITW, Hastings, went to 7 EFTS, Desford on April 16 1940, completed his flying training at RAF College, Cranwell from June 10 to August 29, converted to Spitfires at 7 OTU, Hawarden and joined 266 Squadron at Wittering on September 28.

Posted from the squadron on June 30 1941, Gosling joined 72 Squadron at Biggin Hill. He went to Vickers-Supermarine on January 10 1942, as a test pilot, remaining there until July 4 1944.

Gosling was posted to 616 Squadron at Manston on July 10 and was with the squadron, flying Meteors on the Continent and in Germany, until its disbandment at Lübeck on August 29 1945. He was released from the RAF on December 31 1945, as a Flight Lieutenant. He served in the RAFVR from January 1948 until the end of 1950.

PO 7.9.40   FO 7.9.41   FL 7.9.42   FO (RAFVR) 30.1.48

VILEM GOTH

81945   **PO**   **Pilot**   **Czechoslovakian**   **310 and 501 Sqdns**

Göth was born on April 22 1915. He joined 310 Squadron at Duxford at its formation on July 10 1940. He was posted to 501 Squadron at Kenley in August.

On September 7 Göth claimed two Bf 110s destroyed over Southend but his Hurricane was damaged by return fire and he made a forced-landing on Whitmans Farm, Purleigh. Göth was killed on October 25 1940. He collided with Pilot Officer KW Mackenzie during a combat over Tenterden and crashed in an orchard at Manor Farm, Staplehurst, in Hurricane P 2903.

Göth is buried in Sittingbourne and Milton Cemetery, Kent.

———— GOTHORPE

No unknown   **Sgt**   **Aircrew**   **British**   **25 Squadron**

No service details traced.

DERRICK LESLIE GOULD

41173   FO   Pilot   British   607 and 601 Squadrons

Joined the RAF on a short service commission in July 1938. Gould served in France as a bomber pilot in 1940 and after withdrawal to England volunteered for fighters.

He was with 607 Squadron at Usworth in early July 1940 and moved to 601 Squadron at Exeter on October 5. Gould was with 213 Squadron at Tangmere in November and claimed a Bf 109 destroyed on November 15.

In 1941 Gould was posted to the Middle East. He was attached to 274 Squadron at Gerawla in August and went to 33 Squadron there in October, as a Flight Commander. He took command of the squadron in December 1941 and led it until May 1942, when he went to HQ Middle East. Gould was awarded the DFC (18.9.42).

He commanded 274 Squadron from July until October 1943. Gould was released from the RAF in 1946, as a Squadron Leader.

APO 17.9.38   PO 25.7.39   FO 3.9.40   FL 3.9.41
SL 1.7.44

GORDON LESLIE GOULD

939718   Sgt   Aircrew   British   235 Squadron

Joined 235 Squadron on September 27 1940.
No other service details traced.

RONALD JOSEPH GOULDSTONE

812360   Sgt   Air Gunner   British   29 Squadron

Gouldstone, of Ryarsh, Kent, joined 29 Squadron at Digby on August 7 1940.

He was a member of the crew of Blenheim L 1330, which crashed into the sea on August 25, possibly shot down in combat over Wainfleet. All three men on board were lost.

Gouldstone's body was washed ashore at Gibraltar Point, Skegness on September 5. He was 19 years old and is buried in St Martin's churchyard, Ryarsh.

GEOFFREY KENNETH GOUT

41918   PO   Pilot   British   234 Squadron

Gout was educated at New Beacon School, Sevenoaks. He was a keen motorist and raced at Brooklands. He joined the RAF on a short service commission in February 1939 and after completing his training joined 234 Squadron at Leconfield at its reformation there on October 30 1939.

Gout was killed on July 25 1940, when his Spitfire, P 9493, crashed near Porthtowan during a routine flight, cause unknown. He was 24 and is buried in St Eval churchyard, Cornwall.

APO 15.4.39   PO 6.11.39

ARTHUR VINCENT GOWERS

40166   FO   Pilot   British   85 Squadron

Gowers, of Boscombe, Hampshire, joined the RAF on a short service commission in August 1937. He was posted to 5 FTS, Sealand on October 24 and joined 85 Squadron at Debden on August 10 1938. He served with the squadron in France from the outbreak of war until it was withdrawn on May 22 1940.

On August 30 Gowers claimed a Bf 110 destroyed and a Bf 109 the next day. He was shot down in combat with Bf 109s over Oxted on September 1, baled out, badly burned, and was admitted to Caterham Hospital. His Hurricane, V 7343, crashed near Merstham Tunnel.

Awarded the DFC (1.7.41), Gowers was posted to form and command 183 Squadron at Church Fenton on November 1 1942. He led the squadron until he was killed on October 24 1943, aged 30. He is remembered on the Runnymede Memorial, Panel 118.

APO 24.10.37   PO 19.2.39   FO 3.9.40   FL 3.9.41

EDWARD JOHN GRACIE

29090   FL   Pilot   British   56 Squadron

Born in Acton in 1911, Gracie learned to fly with the RAFO, in which he was commissioned in March 1937. He was called to full-time service on September 3 1939 and in early 1940 was with 79 Squadron at Manston.

Gracie joined 56 Squadron at North Weald in late June 1940, as 'B' Flight Commander. He claimed a Bf 110 destroyed on July 10, a probable Do 17 on the 15th, a Ju 88 on the 20th, a Ju 87 on the 25th, a Bf 110 on August 18, a Do 17 on the 27th and another Do 17 on the 28th. After destroying a He 111 in an action over Essex on August 30 Gracie was himself shot down, crashing and burning out near Halstead, in Hurricane P 3554. Gracie believed himself unhurt but discovered next day that he had a broken neck and was admitted to hospital. He rejoined the squadron on October 8 1940. He was awarded the DFC (1.10.40).

Posted from 56 for a rest on January 7 1941, Gracie was given command of 23 Squadron at Ford in March and then took over 601 Squadron at Northolt in late April and remained with the squadron until December 24 1941. He was posted to Malta and took command of 126 Squadron at Ta Kali in March 1942, when he led Spitfires off the carrier HMS 'Eagle' to replace 126's Hurricanes.

Gracie claimed a Ju 88 probably destroyed on April 2. He went to Gibraltar soon afterwards to join the carrier USS 'Wasp' and on April 20 he flew off, leading twelve Spitfires of 601 Squadron to Malta. The next day Gracie claimed two Ju 88s and another probable and on the 23rd he shared a Ju 87 and probably destroyed another. On the 29th Gracie was promoted to Acting Wing Commander and appointed Station Commander at Ta Kali.

He returned to the UK in June 1942 and commanded 32 Squadron at West Malling briefly in September. Gracie was posted to Ayr on October 1 1943 to form and command 169 Squadron, to operate in Mosquitos on bomber support. He flew the squadron's first operational sortie on January 20 1944, a night escort to Hamburg during a Berlin raid.

Gracie was killed over Germany on February 15 1944, as a Wing Commander. He is buried in Hanover War Cemetery. His portrait was drawn by Cuthbert Orde.

FO (RAFO) 23.3.37   FO 3.9.39   FL 20.3.40   SL 1.12.42

EDWARD GRAHAM

37449   FL   Pilot   British   72 Squadron

Graham was born on June 21 1911 and joined the RAF in September 1935. He was posted to 4 FTS, Abu Sueir on November 23 and went to 41 Squadron at Northolt on April 24 1936.

He joined 72 Squadron, when it was reformed at Tangmere on March 22 1937. Graham was appointed 'B' Flight Commander in June 1940 and he shared in the destruction of a He 59 on July 1. He took command of the squadron in late September 1940 and led it until April 1941.

Graham retired from the RAF on December 27 1958, as a Wing Commander, retaining the rank of Group Captain. He later went to live in Australia.

APO 6.11.35   PO 24.4.36   FO 24.11.37   FL 24.11.39
SL 1.12.40   WC 1.3.42   SL 1.7.45   WC 1.7.54

JAMES GRAHAM

47909   Sgt   Air Gunner   British   236 Squadron

Joined 236 Squadron on September 3 1940. Graham was with 7 Squadron at Oakington in 1941. In June he was rear gunner of a Stirling, which was attacked by two fighters twenty miles west of Texel. They came in simultaneously from the port and starboard quarters. During the action Graham's reflector sight stopped working and two

J Graham (continued)

of his guns jammed. Despite continuous attacks he repaired his sight, cleared his stoppages and then shot down one of the enemy fighters into the sea. For this action he was awarded the DFM (4.7.41).

Graham was commissioned in February 1942 and killed on June 26 1942, whilst with 1651 Conversion Unit. He is remembered on the Runnymede Memorial, Panel 69.

PO 19.2.42

KENNETH ALFRED GEORGE GRAHAM

78737   PO   Pilot   British   600 and 111 Squadrons

Graham, of East Ham, London, was with 600 Squadron at Northolt in early July 1940. He was posted to 111 Squadron at Debden on August 24 and killed on February 8 1941, as a Pilot Officer with 263 Squadron.

Graham was 20 and is remembered on the Runnymede Memorial, Panel 32.

PO 28.4.40

LESLIE WILLIAM GRAHAM

81912   PO   Pilot   South African   56 Squadron

Graham joined 56 Squadron at North Weald on July 29 1940. His Hurricane, V 7368, was set alight in a surprise attack by enemy aircraft during a section patrol on August 16. Graham baled out, slightly injured. He was posted away three days later.

He was released from the RAF in 1946, as a Squadron Leader.

PO 14.7.40   FO 14.4.42   FL 4.11.42

JOHN GRANDY

32078   SL   Pilot   British   249 Squadron

Born at Northwood, Middlesex on February 8 1913, Grandy was educated at University College School, London. He joined the RAF in September 1931 and was posted on the 26th to 5 FTS, Sealand.

Grandy joined 54 Squadron at Hornchurch on August 29 1932. He was posted to 604 Squadron, AuxAF at Hendon on April 15 1935, as Flying Instructor. He went to the Station Flight, Northolt on November 2 1936 but early in 1937 was posted to the London University Air Squadron as Adjutant and Flying Instructor.

In May 1939 Grandy became CFI at 13 FTS, Drem.

On May 16 1940 Grandy took command of 249 Squadron, when it was reformed at Church Fenton. He was shot down in combat over Maidstone on September 6, baled out, slightly wounded, and was admitted to Maidstone Hospital. He left the squadron in December 1940 and went to HQ Fighter Command on staff duties.

In July 1941 Grandy was OC Training Wing at 52 OTU, Debden. He was Wing Commander Flying at Coltishall later in the year and in 1942 was Station Commander at Duxford. Grandy was posted to HQ 210 Group in the Middle East in 1943 and commanded 73 OTU at Abu Sueir. He went to South East Asia Command in 1944 and commanded 341 Wing, Dakotas. With the Japanese out of Rangoon, he dropped a Union Jack and a Stars and Stripes over Government House there on May 2 1945 before landing at Mingaladon in a Dakota. He then supervised the repair of the airfield to receive the supply aircraft shortly to arrive. Grandy was awarded the DSO (19.10.45).

He went on to a most distinguished post-war career in the RAF, becoming a Marshal of the RAF in April 1971. Grandy was invested as GCB (1967)(KCB 1964; CB 1956) and KBE (1961). He was made Constable and Governor of Windsor Castle in 1978.

PO 11.9.31   FO 11.6.33   FL 11.6.36   SL 1.2.39
WC 1.3.41   GC 1.7.44   GC 1.1.50   AC 1.1.56
AVM 1.7.58   AM 1.1.62   ACM 1.4.65   MRAF 1.4.71

DONALD GRANT

Sub-Lieutenant (FAA)   Pilot   British   804 Squadron

With 804 Squadron at Hatston in July 1940, flying Gladiators on dockyard defence. No further service details traced. Grant was released from the Navy in 1946, as a Lieutenant.

Midshipman 21.2.39   Sub-Lt 27.7.40   Lt 27.1.43

EDWIN JOHN FORGAN GRANT

749872   Sgt   Aircrew   British   600 Squadron

Joined 600 Squadron at Manston on July 18 1940. Grant was killed on December 1 1941, aged 21, as a Sergeant with 600 Squadron. He is remembered on the Runnymede Memorial, Panel 44.

IAN ALLAN CHARLES GRANT

391351   Sgt   Pilot   New Zealander   151 Squadron

Born in Woodville on November 21 1915, Grant was educated in Auckland and then employed as a sheet-metal worker. He volunteered for aircrew duties at the outbreak of war and went to the Ground Training School at Weraroa on November 19 1939.

He was posted to 2 EFTS, New Plymouth on December 18 and then to 2 FTS, Woodbourne on March 11 1940. With training completed Grant sailed for the UK in the RMS 'Rangitane' on July 12. Posted to 6 OTU, Sutton Bridge on September 9, he converted to

Hurricanes and joined 151 Squadron at Digby on September 21.

Grant was posted to 7 BGS, Stormy Down on November 23, as a staff pilot. He was commissioned in October 1941 and on July 12 1942 was posted to 52 OTU, Debden for conversion to Spitfires. In October Grant joined 501 Squadron at Middle Wallop and on November 19 was posted to Kingscliffe, to 485 Squadron, then commanded by his older brother, Reg.

On February 13 1943 the squadron went on a sweep. After crossing the French coast they were directed to a force of FW 190s. A further twenty enemy fighters attacked out of the sun and three Spitfires were shot down, including Ian Grant's. An aircraft crashed in the vicinity of Cucq and buried itself deeply in marshy ground. Attempts were made after the war to recover the pilot's body but were unsuccessful so it is not known whether it was Grant. He is remembered on the Runnymede Memorial, Panel 197. Reg Grant was killed on operations on February 28 1944.

PO 27.10.41   FO 1.10.42

STANLEY BERNARD GRANT

33417   FO   Pilot   British   65 Squadron

Grant was born on May 31 1919 and educated at Charterhouse. He entered RAF College, Cranwell in January 1937, as a flight cadet, and graduated in December 1938.

In early 1940 Grant was posted to 65 Squadron at Northolt. Over Dunkirk he claimed a Bf 110 destroyed on May 26 and a Bf 110 probably destroyed and a Do 17 shared on the 27th. He claimed a Bf 109 probably destroyed on July 7.

In August 1941 Grant was made a Flight Commander. He moved to 601 Squadron at

Duxford in December and in March 1942 went to 249 Squadron at Ta Kali, Malta. On March 11 and 25 he claimed Bf 109s destroyed and on April 1 a Ju 87 and a Ju 88. Grant was given command of the squadron in mid-April. On the 21st he claimed a Ju 88, another on May 10 and a Reggiane 2001 on June 10. He was awarded the DFC (5.6.42) and promoted to be Wing Commander Flying Ta Kali.

Grant went back to the UK in August 1942 but returned to Malta later in the year and took command of the Spitfire Wing there. He destroyed two Bf 110s on December 11 1942 and was awarded a Bar to the DFC (29.1.43). Grant later went to 203 (Training) Group in the Middle East and in 1944 was at Advance HQ Mediterranean Allied Air Force in Italy, as Command Training Officer.

Created a CB (1969), Grant retired from the RAF on June 6 1970, as an Air Vice-Marshal. He died in July 1987.

PO 17.12.38   FO 17.6.40   FL 17.6.41   SL 1.7.43
WC 1.7.50   GC 1.1.57   AC 1.1.62   AVM 1.1.66

ROBERT DAVIDSON GRASSICK

41579   FO   Pilot   Canadian   242 Squadron

Grassick, of London, Ontario, joined the RAF on a short service commission in November 1938. He did his intermediate and advanced training at 5 FTS, Sealand and joined 242 Squadron, then reforming at Church Fenton, on November 5 1939.

Grassick went to France on May 14 1940, on attachment to 607 Squadron. He moved to 615 Squadron on the 16th and returned to England on the 19th. Whilst in France he is believed to have destroyed two Bf 109s and a Ju 88. Over Dunkirk on May 29 and 31 Grassick destroyed two Bf 109s.

242 was posted to France on June 8 to reinforce No 1, 73 and 501 Squadrons. Grassick did not go over until June 12 and he returned with the other pilots to England on the 16th. In late August he was injured in a motorcycle accident and was off flying for some time.

On April 1 1941 Grassick shared in destroying a Ju 88, on May 11 he destroyed a He 111, on June 17 a Bf 109 and probably another and on the 23rd probably another. Grassick was made a Flight Commander on June 17 1941, awarded the DFC (15.7.41) and posted away to 73 OTU, Aden on September 28. He was with 260 Squadron in the Western Desert in March 1942 and in June was posted to a Communications Flight.

In January 1943 Grassick was on test pilot duties. He transferred to the RCAF in early 1945.

APO 14.1.39   FO 3.9.39   FO 3.9.40   FL 3.9.41

EDWARD ARTHUR GRAVES

632826   Sgt   Air Gunner   British   235 Squadron

Joined 235 Squadron on August 23 1940. Graves was killed on a training flight on August 30. The Blenheim he was in went into a sustained spin and crashed at Barwick Farm, near Bircham Newton. He was 21 and is buried in Langney Cemetery, Eastbourne.

RICHARD COURTNEY GRAVES

83289   PO   Pilot   British   253 Squadron

Graves joined 253 Squadron at Kenley on September 9 1940. He was posted to 85 Squadron on the 14th but rejoined 253 on the 28th.

During a combat with Bf 109s over Weybridge on September 29 Graves' aircraft was set alight in an attack by another Hurricane. He baled out, burned, and was admitted to Brockley Park Hospital, Haywards Heath. His Hurricane, V 6621, crashed and burned out on Longridge Farm, Chailey.

Graves was flying one of twenty-four Hurricanes, which flew off HMS 'Ark Royal' to reinforce Malta on April 27 1941. He joined 261

Squadron and went to the Middle East when the squadron was disbanded in May. He joined 30 Squadron and served with it in Egypt, the Western Desert and later in Ceylon in 1942.

Released from the RAF in 1947, as a Squadron Leader, Graves was killed in a car accident in 1978.

PO 17.8.40   FO 17.8.41   FL 17.8.42

ANTHONY PHILIP GRAY

90155   FL   Pilot   British   615 Squadron

Gray joined 601 Squadron, AuxAF in 1932 and went on to the Reserve in November 1937. He was recalled to full-time service on September 4 1939.

In early July 1940 Gray was with 615 Squadron at Kenley. On August 26 he claimed a Bf 109 destroyed.

Gray was released from the RAF in 1946, as a Squadron Leader. He died in 1986.

PO (AuxAF) 5.11.32   FO (AuxAF) 5.5.34
FO 4.9.39   FL 16.2.40   SL 1.3.42

COLIN FALKLAND GRAY

41844   FO   Pilot   New Zealander   54 Squadron

Born in Christchurch on November 9 1914, Gray and his twin brother, Kenneth, applied for short service commissions in April 1937. His brother was accepted but Gray failed for medical reasons. In January 1938 he failed again but in September he passed. Declining the chance to immediately start training in New Zealand he sailed for the UK on December 16 in the RMS 'Rangitata'.

Gray began his ab initio training at No 1 E&RFTS, Hatfield on January 24 1939, moving to 11 FTS, Shawbury on April 18. After two weeks at AGS, Penrhos he was posted to 11 Group Pool at St Athan, where he converted to Hurricanes.

On November 20 1939 Gray joined 54 Squadron at Hornchurch. He shared in the destruction of a Bf 109 on May 24 1940 and returned to Kenley badly damaged, without brakes, flaps, airspeed indicator or guns.

Gray destroyed a Bf 109 on July 13, two Bf 109s on the 24th, a probable Bf 109 on the 25th, two Bf 109s on August 12 and two Bf 109s on the 15th. He was awarded the DFC (15.8.40). On August 18 Gray destroyed a Bf 110, shared another, damaged two more and damaged a Do 17. He shot down a Bf 110 on the 24th, and Bf 109s on the 25th and 31st, another Bf 109 and a probable He 111 on September 1, a Bf 109 and a Bf 110 on the 2nd and a Bf 109 and a shared Bf 110 on the 3rd.

In mid-December 1940 Gray was posted to 43 Squadron at Drem as 'B' Flight Commander but returned to 54 Squadron at Catterick on January 16 1941 to be 'A' Flight Commander. Gray went to No 1 Squadron at Redhill on June 12 as 'B' Flight Commander and shared in the destruction of a He 59 on the 16th. Flying with 41 Squadron on a sweep on August 2 1941 he shot down a Bf 109, which crashed on its own airfield at Le Havre. He was awarded a Bar to the DFC (20.9.41).

Posted to Debden on September 28 to command 403 Squadron, Gray was recalled to Tangmere three days later to take command of 616 Squadron at Westhampnett. At the end of this tour Gray was posted to HQ 9 Group, Preston as Squadron Leader Tactics on February 25 1942. He went to 64 Squadron at Fairlop as a supernumerary on September 28 and took command of the squadron on November 1.

Gray was posted overseas in late December and reported to HQ 333 Group at Algiers on January 19 1943. He joined 81 Squadron at Gibraltar as CO on the 24th and three days later flew across to Tingley

CF Gray (continued)

airfield, south-west of Bone. On February 22 Gray probably destroyed a Bf 109, on March 2 shared in the probable destruction of another, on the 23rd destroyed a Mc 202, on the 25th and 27th two Bf 109s, on April 3 a Bf 109, on the 18th a probable Bf 109, on the 20th a Bf 109 and another shared and two more Bf 109s on the 23rd and the 28th. Gray was awarded the DSO (15.5.43).

Promoted to Acting Wing Commander on June 1, Gray was made Wing Commander Flying 322 Wing at Ta Kali, Malta. He shot down a Bf 109 on June 14, a Mc 202 on the 17th and a Bf 109 on July 10, the day the invasion of Sicily took place. The wing moved to Lentini airfield on July 19. On the 25th Gray led the Wing to attack a large force of Ju 52s, which were landing supplies on the beaches near Milazzo. Twenty one were destroyed, two by Gray, and four of the fighter escort were shot down.

On September 7 1943 Gray was posted to HQ MEF, Cairo and returned to the UK in early October. He was given command of 2 CTW, Balado Bridge on October 30 1943, received his DSO from the King on November 9 and was awarded a second Bar to the DFC (15.11.43). Gray was posted to 61 OTU, Rednal on December 4, as OC Training Wing. He went to the Fighter Leaders' School at Milfield on June 8 1944, as OC Spitfire Wing and on July 27 was appointed Wing Leader at Detling, moving two weeks later to the Lympne Wing.

Gray led the Wing until January 1945, when he was posted to Cranwell for a Senior Commanders' Course, after which he became Station Commander at RAF Skeabrae. Granted a Permanent Commission in April 1945, Gray stayed on in the RAF and held a series of appointments and commands before retiring at his own request on March 31 1961, as a Group Captain. He returned to New Zealand and worked for the Unilever Company, retiring as Personnel Director on November 9 1979.

APO 1.4.39   PO 23.10.39   FO 23.10.40   FL 23.10.41
SL 1.1.43   WC 1.7.47   GC 1.1.55

CLIFFORD KEMPSON GRAY

81370   PO   Pilot   British   43 Squadron

Born on September 8 1916, Gray joined the RAFVR on January 9 1939 and began his flying training at 5 E&RFTS, Hanworth. Called to full-time service in November he was posted to No 1 ITW, Cambridge on the 10th, moving to 11 FTS, Shawbury on January 29 1940.

Gray went to 6 OTU, Sutton Bridge on July 6 to convert to Hurricanes and then joined 43 Squadron at Tangmere on August 2. He claimed Ju 87s destroyed on August 16 and 18. Gray was shot down over Portsmouth on the 26th and baled out, wounded in the right arm. His Hurricane, P 3202, crashed at Ratham Mill, Bosham.

On September 8 Gray crashed at Gedney Dye, Lincolnshire after his engine seized during a ferry flight to Usworth.

Gray was posted to 73 Squadron on November 2. Later in the month the squadron embarked on the carrier HMS 'Furious', bound for the Middle East and flew off to Takoradi on the 29th. It then flew by easy stages to Heliopolis, via Lagos, Accra, Kano, Maidugari, Khartoum, Wadi Halfa and Abu Sueir. On arrival on December 13 Gray went to the Middle East Pool, Ismailia. After a bout of malaria he flew a Hurricane to Malta on March 6 1941 and joined 261 Squadron at Ta Kali.

Gray was shot down on May 6 and baled out, wounded in the left thigh. He joined 185 Squadron, when it was reformed at Hal Far on May 12. He damaged two Mc 200s on July 11 and was posted back to the UK at the end of the month. He went to 61 OTU, Heston on September 1, moved to 56 OTU, Sutton Bridge on October 30 and on June 17 1942 joined 307th Pursuit Squadron, USAAF.

On August 30 Gray was posted to 222 Squadron at Drem and stayed with it until February 23 1943, when he went to 61 OTU, Rednal, as an instructor. He returned to operations on December 12 1943, joining 124 Squadron at West Malling. Awarded the DFC (17.8.45), Gray was with 124 until April 3 1946, when he was given command of 91 Squadron at Duxford.

In the post-war years he held a number of flying and staff appointments before his retirement on August 1 1963, as a Wing Commander.

PO 6.7.40   FO 6.7.41   FL 6.7.42   SL 1.8.47
WC 1.7 55

DONALD McINTOSH GRAY

83255   PO   Pilot   British   610 Squadron

Joined 610 Squadron at Biggin Hill on July 27 1940. Gray was shot down by a Bf 109 in combat over Dover on August 24. He crash-landed near Shepherdswell in Spitfire X 4102, wounded, and was admitted to Waldershare Hospital.

Gray was killed in a flying accident on November 5 1940, aged 21. He is buried in Chevington Cemetery, East Chevington, Northumberland.

PO 27.7.40

KENNETH WILLIAM GRAY

127525   Sgt   Pilot   British   85 Squadron

Gray, of Basford, Newcastle-under-Lyme, joined 85 Squadron at Castle Camps on September 16 1940.

Commissioned in June 1942, he was killed on June 9 1944, aged 23, serving as a Flying Officer with 25 Squadron. Gray is remembered on the Runnymede Memorial, Panel 206.

PO 26.6.42   FO 29.3.43

MALCOLM GRAY

741816   Sgt   Pilot   British   72 Squadron

With 72 Squadron at Acklington in early July 1940. Gray was shot down and killed on September 9, aged 20. His Spitfire, N 3093, crashed into Elham Park Wood. He is buried in Fulford Cemetery, North Yorkshire.

TREVOR GRAY

85236   PO   Pilot   British   64 Squadron

Posted to 64 Squadron at Leconfield on September 16 1940. Gray was released from the RAF in 1946, as a Flight Lieutenant.

PO 24.8.40   FO 24.8.41   FL 24.8.42

CHARLES GRAYSON

46769   F/Sgt   Pilot   British   213 Squadron

A pre-war airman pilot, Grayson, of Lewes, was with 213 Squadron at Exeter in early 1940. Over Dunkirk on May 29 he destroyed a Ju 87 and damaged a He 111. On August 18 he claimed a Bf 110 destroyed.

Promoted to Warrant Officer on April 1 1941, Grayson was commissioned in June. He was killed on July 8 1945, aged 32, as a Flight Lieutenant with 328 Squadron. Grayson is buried in Lewes Cemetery, Sussex.

PO 21.6.41   FO 1.4.42   FL 1.4.43

ALEXANDER WILLIAM VALENTINE GREEN

78082   PO   Observer   British   235 Squadron

Green, of Craigavad, Co Down, joined 235 Squadron on July 11 1940.

He was one of the crew of a Blenheim shot down by a Bf 109 on September 11 1940, whilst escorting FAA Albacores to attack Calais. The aircraft crashed into the sea and all three men on board were reported 'Missing'.

Green was 21. He is remembered on the Runnymede Memorial, Panel 8.

PO 10.3.40

CHARLES PATRICK GREEN

90134   FL   Pilot   British   421 Flight

Born on March 30 1914, Green was at Harrow School from 1927 to 1932 and then Trinity College, Cambridge. He was in the University ski team from 1932 to 1934 and the athletic team in 1934/35.

Green was made an FRGS in 1935 and joined 601 Squadron,

AuxAF in 1937. In the British ski team, Green broke his leg skiing in the President's Cup at St Moritz in 1937.

Called to full-time service at the outbreak of war, Green was posted from 601 in October to 92 Squadron at Tangmere. Over Dunkirk on May 23 1940 he destroyed a Bf 109 but was then himself shot down, with a leg wound which kept him off operations until posted to command 421 Flight at its formation at Hawkinge in early October 1940. During a spotting flight on the 12th, Green was jumped by Bf 109s. He baled out, wounded in the neck and arm, and was admitted to hospital. His Spitfire, P 7441, crashed at Coldbridge, Boughton Malherbe.

Green destroyed a Do 17 on November 25 and when the Flight was re-numbered as 91 Squadron in January 1941 he took command. Awarded the DFC (18.4.41), Green was posted away in June. He returned to operations in November 1941, joining 600 Squadron at Colerne, as 'A' Flight Commander. In June 1942 Green was given command of 125 Squadron, also at Colerne. On December 26 1942 he was posted to Maison Blanche, to take command of 600 Squadron.

On May 5 1943 he probably destroyed a Ju 88, on July 13 a Ju 88 and a He 111, on the 14th another He 111, on the 15th four more and on August 11 a Ju 88. Green was awarded the DSO (20.8.43). He got a probable He 111 on September 9 and destroyed a Ju 88 on January 25 1944.

In February 1944 he was promoted to Acting Group Captain and posted to Italy to command No 1 Mobile Operations Unit of the Desert Air Force. Green was awarded the Order of Patriotic War 1st Class (USSR)(11.4.44) and the DFC (US)(28.7.44). He was released in 1947, as a Group Captain.

PO (AuxAF) 26.3.37   FO (AuxAF) 6.10.38   FO 24.8.39
FL 3.9.40   SL 1.12.41   WC 6.9.44

FREDERICK WILLIAM WOODRIDGE GREEN

747797   Sgt   Aircrew   British   600 Squadron

Green served with 600 Squadron from November 1939 until February 1941. No further service details traced.

GEORGE GRAHAM GREEN

902540   Sgt   Aircrew   British   236 Squadron

With 236 Squadron in early July 1940. No further service details traced.

HERBERT EDWARD GREEN

50679   Sgt   Pilot   British   141 Squadron

Born on May 6 1914, Green was with 141 Squadron in early July 1940. He was promoted to Warrant Officer on April 1 1941 and commissioned in November 1942.

Green stayed on in the RAF, was made an MBE (31.5.56) and retired on May 1 1965, as a Squadron Leader.

PO 9.11.42   FO 9.5.43   FL 20.10.45   FL 14.2.48
SL 1.7.62

MAURICE DAVID GREEN

78263   PO   Observer   British   248 Squadron

Green joined 248 Squadron in April 1940. He was in Blenheim L 9453, which failed to return from a reconnaissance sortie over the Norwegian coast on October 20 1940, searching for a Blenheim of 248 which had been lost earlier in the day.

Green was reported 'Missing'. He was 20 years old and is remembered on the Runnymede Memorial, Panel 8.

PO 24.3.40

WILLIAM JAMES GREEN

135002   Sgt   Pilot   British   501 Squadron

Green joined 501 Squadron, AuxAF at Bristol in December 1936 as an AC 2 u/t Fitter (Aero Engines). With the introduction of a scheme for the AuxAF to have NCO pilots in October 1938 Green became

an LAC u/t Pilot. Partly trained before being called up at the outbreak of war, Green was posted to 5 EFTS, Hanworth in October 1939, where he got 50 hours on Magisters.

In March 1940 he went to 3 FTS, South Cerney and did 110 hours on Harts on intermediate and advanced flying training, was promoted to Corporal when awarded his wings and Sergeant on the completion of the course. On July 1 Green rejoined 501 Squadron at Middle Wallop. Having bypassed OTU he was entirely without Hurricane experience and taught himself to fly it before being taken officially on to the strength of 501 on August 20 1940.

Four days later Green crashed at Hawkinge after being hit by anti-aircraft guns during combat with Ju 88s and Bf 109s attacking Manston. On August 29 he was shot down by Bf 109s and baled out at 16000 feet, falling to some 300 feet above the ground before his parachute opened properly, the pilot chute cords having been severed by cannon shell splinters. He was rescued from the sea off Folkestone and his Hurricane, R 4223, crashed near Hawkinge.

Green was posted to 504 Squadron at Filton in November 1940. He went to 4 FIS, Cambridge in March 1941, after which he instructed at 10 EFTS, Locking and 3 EFTS, Shellingford. He was commissioned from Warrant Officer in October 1942. In June 1943 Green was posted to 5 FTS, Cranwell to instruct on Masters and in November to 39 OTU, Tealing on Spitfires.

From March 1944 he was at 1682 DTD, Enstone on Tomahawks. In preparation for a return to operations Green went to 3 TEU, Aston Down in October for conversion to Typhoons, went on to Tempests at Thorney Island and then joined 56 Squadron at Volkel in November.

Green was shot down in February 1945 and was a PoW until May. Posted back to instruct at 3 EFTS, Shellingford, he was released from the RAF in November 1945. He joined the RAFVR in June 1947 and instructed at 6 RFS, Sywell until July 1953.

PO 30.10.42   FO 30.4.43   FL 30.10.44
FO (RAFVR) 6.6.47

HENRY la FONE GREENSHIELDS

Sub-Lieutenant (FAA)   Pilot   British   266 Squadron

Born in 1918, Greenshields, of Axminster, Devon, was rejected by the RAF with defective eyesight. He joined the RNVR and was called to full-time service in September 1939.

In mid-June 1940 Greenshields was one of the FAA pilots loaned to the RAF. He converted to Spitfires and joined 266 Squadron at Wittering on July 1.

On August 15 Greenshields destroyed a Bf 109 south-east of Dover. The following day he failed to return from a combat with Bf 109s pursued out over the Channel. He was shot down and killed by Leutnant Müller-Duhe of JG 26. Greenshield's Spitfire, N 3240, crashed and burned out in the suburbs of Calais. He was 22 and is buried in the Calais Southern Cemetery. Müller-Duhe was killed two days later, when he was shot down by pilots of 32 Squadron.

Sub-Lt 20.9.39

JOHN PETER BOWTELL GREENWOOD

41920   PO   Pilot   British   253 Squadron

Greenwood joined the RAF on a short service commission in February 1939 and began his flying training at 11 E&RFTS, Perth. In April he moved to 2 FTS, Brize Norton and with training completed joined 253 Squadron at Manston, when it was reformed there on October 30 1939.

In February 1940 the squadron began to receive Hurricanes. On May 16 'A' Flight was sent to France, based at Lille. Greenwood destroyed a Bf 109 on the 19th. 253 returned to England on the 21st to build up again after heavy losses.

JPB Greenwood (continued)

On August 30 Greenwood destroyed a He 111, which had been attacking Farnborough. He was was posted to 5 FTS, Sealand, in December 1940, as an instructor. In February 1941 he went to Turnhouse, where 59 OTU was being formed, which moved in March to Crosby-on-Eden.

Greenwood volunteered for MSFU and joined the unit at Speke on May 20 and boarded the 'Empire Flame' on June 18. He was posted to 55 OTU, Usworth in November and went to 615 Squadron at Fairwood Common in February 1942.

The squadron left for India in March and after arriving in June and acclimatising to jungle conditions it flew its first operation on December 5 1942. In January 1943 Greenwood was posted to 17 Squadron at Alipore, as a Flight Commander. He went to 151 OTU, Risalpur in April and after malaria and dengue fever in October he was posted to 223 Group, Peshawar.

Greenwood joined 9 (IAF) Squadron in February 1944 and in July went to a job in the War Room at 221 Group. He volunteered for Visual Control Post duties, concerning the front line direction of strike aircraft on to specific targets in support of the Army. He did a parachute jumping course and was attached to an Airborne artillery brigade and took part in operations in Indonesia after the war against the Japanese ended.

In March 1946 Greenwood returned to the UK and was released from the RAF in June 1947, as a Flight Lieutenant.

APO 15.4.39   PO 6.11.39   FO 6.11.40   FL 6.5.42

ALBERT EDWARD GREGORY

133005   Sgt   Air Gunner   British   219 Squadron

Gregory was with 219 Squadron at Catterick in early July 1940. He was commissioned in August 1942 and awarded the DFC (13.7.43), as a Flying Officer with 275 Squadron , an ASR unit.

Gregory was released from the RAF in 1946 but rejoined in July 1947.

PO 31.8.42   FO 3.3.43   FL 3.9.44   FL 2.7.47

ALFRED HENRY GREGORY

758172   Sgt   Pilot   British   111 Squadron

Joined 111 Squadron at Drem on September 28 1940. Gregory, of Hulland, Derbyshire, was killed on July 23 1941, aged 24 and still serving with 111. He is buried in Christ Church churchyard, Hulland.

FELIX STAFFORD GREGORY

81044   PO   Pilot   British   65 Squadron

Gregory joined 65 Squadron at Hornchurch on July 6 1940. He claimed a Bf 109 destroyed on August 12. He was killed the following day, when he baled out too low during a night-flying practice for an unknown reason. His Spitfire, R 6766, crashed at Eastry.

Gregory was 21. He was cremated at Enfield Crematorium, Middlesex.

PO 15.6.40

WILLIAM JAMES GREGORY

115577   Sgt   Observer   British   29 Squadron

Born in West Hartlepool on November 23 1913, Gregory joined the RAFVR there in 1938. He did navigation and bombing and gunnery training at Prestwick and Penrhos.

Called to full-time service at the outbreak of war, Gregory was posted to 29 Squadron at Debden in May 1940. On August 18 he was a member of a Blenheim crew, which shot down a He 111 into the sea off Spurn Head in the early hours of the morning.

In June 1941 Gregory, now retrained as a Navigator Radar, teamed up with Flying Officer

JRD Braham. In July they shot a Ju 88 down into the Thames and in October a Do 217 into the sea. Gregory was awarded the DFM (17.10.41) and at the end of his tour in December he was posted to 51 OTU, Cranfield, as an instructor.

Commissioned in January 1942, Gregory revisited 29 Squadron in early June for a few days and he and Braham destroyed a Do 217, which went into the sea off Sandwich. Later in the month they were posted to 29, Braham as 'A' Flight Commander.

Gregory was awarded the DFC (4.8.42). On August 9 Braham and he destroyed another Do 217, on October 19 probably another, on the 26th a Ju 88 and on the 31st a Do 217. In early January 1943 Braham was given command of 141 Squadron at Ford and Gregory went with him. On January 20 they destroyed a Do 217, on June 14 a Bf 110 and on June 24 and August 19 two more. Gregory was awarded a Bar to the DFC (16.7.43).

In February 1944 he was posted to 2 Group to assist Braham in the work of night interdiction. Whilst there they flew the occasional sortie. On March 5 they destroyed a He 177 on a daylight intruder operation and in April two more enemy aircraft.

On May 12 they went on an intruder flight to Denmark and destroyed a FW 190 near Aalborg. On the way back, damaged and out of fuel, they crash-landed on the sea and were picked up by a Royal Navy trawler. The FW 190 was Braham's, and the team's, last victory.

Gregory was posted to RAF West Raynham as Navigation Officer later in 1944. He was awarded the DSO (17.7.45) and posted to HQ 12 Group in September 1945. Granted a Permanent Commission in 1947; Gregory held a number of appointments at home and overseas before his retirement on June 1 1964, as a Wing Commander.

PO 22.1.42   FO 1.10.42   FL 22.1.44   FL 1.9.45
SL 1.1.52   WC 1.1.59

HORACE EUSTACE GRELLIS

82501   PO   Air Gunner   British   23 Squadron

Grellis was with 23 Squadron at Collyweston in early July 1940. He was released from the RAF in 1946, as a Flight Lieutenant, and died on March 7 1950.

PO 17.1.40   FO 17.1.41   FL 17.1.42

KENNETH GASTON GRESTY

552727   Sgt   Air Gunner   British   219 Squadron

Gresty, of Handforth, Cheshire, was with 219 Squadron at Catterick in early July 1940. He was lost on April 17 1941, serving as a Sergeant with 105 Squadron, flying in Blenheims from Swanton Morley.

Gresty was 19. He is remembered on the Runnymede Memorial, Panel 19.

REGINALD HENRY GRETTON

754187   Sgt   Pilot   British   266 and 222 Squadrons

Gretton joined the RAFVR in 1939. In August he was called up for an ab initio course at 10 E&RFTS, Yatesbury, followed by intermediate and advanced training at 3 FTS, South Cerney. After converting to Hurricanes at 5 OTU, Aston Down he joined 266 Squadron at Wittering at the end of May 1940. He moved to 222 Squadron at Hornchurch on September 12.

During a patrol over Maidstone on September 27 Gretton was jumped by Bf 109s and shot down. He crashed near Winnington, Rainham, Essex in Spitfire R 6720, seriously wounded in the back. Gretton was admitted to Oldchurch Hospital and spent the next five months recovering from a fractured pelvis and spine.

In June 1941 he was posted to the ADF at Hendon and in September went to 58 OTU, Grangemouth, as an instructor. Gretton returned to operations in November 1941, joining 91 Squadron at Hawkinge. He was posted away in February 1942 for further treatment and rehabilitation and awarded the DFC.

In April 1942 Gretton rejoined ADF, then at Croydon, and stayed with the unit until June 1945. He spent his final six months at the air-to-ground firing ranges at Bulmer and Kirton Marsh and was released from the RAF in Birmingham in January 1946, as a Warrant Officer.

DORIAN GEORGE GRIBBLE

40695   FO   Pilot   British   54 Squadron

Gribble, from Ryde, Isle of Wight, joined the RAF on a short service commission in March 1938. He was posted to 11 FTS, Shawbury on May 19 1938 and at the outbreak of war was with 54 Squadron at Hornchurch.

Over France on May 23 and 24 he destroyed Bf 109s and on the 25th his aircraft was shot up and damaged. Gribble made a forced-landing on a beach near Dunkirk. He returned to England by ship, carrying his radio, which he considered was still too secret to fall into German hands.

On July 24 Gribble claimed a Bf 109 destroyed and probably another, on August 15 a Bf 109, on the 18th he claimed another Bf 109 and shared a Bf 110, on the 24th a Bf 109, on the 28th two more and on the 31st he shared another. He was awarded the DFC (13.8.40).

Gribble was killed on June 4 1941, aged 21. After attacking some Bf 109s over the Channel his engine failed. He crashed into the sea and was drowned. He is remembered on the Runnymede Memorial, Panel 29.

APO 7.5.38   PO 7.3.39   FO 3.9.40

DENNIS NEVE GRICE

70266   FO   Pilot   British   600 Squadron

Grice, of Ealing, joined the RAFO in 1931. It was the forerunner of the RAFVR, which came into being in 1936. He was called to full-time service on September 25 1939 and joined 600 Squadron at Northolt on July 9 1940.

On August 8 Grice was captain of Blenheim L 8665, which was shot down in flames by Oberleutnant Sprick of Ill/JG 26. He stayed at the controls of his burning aircraft, guiding it clear of Ramsgate before crashing into the sea. Grice and the two members of his crew were all killed. He was 28 and was cremated at Charing Crematorium, Kent.

PO (RAFO) 17.3.31   FO (RAFO) 17.9.32   FO 25.9.39

DOUGLAS HAMILTON GRICE

40534   FO   Pilot   British   32 Squadron

Born in Wallasey Village, Cheshire, Grice joined the RAF on a short service commission in December 1937. After carrying out his elementary flying training at 8 E&RFTS, Woodley he was posted to 5 FTS, Sealand on March 3 1938.

Grice joined 32 Squadron at Biggin Hill on September 17 1938. During the Battle of France the squadron used Abbeville as a forward base from May 18 1940. On that day Grice probably destroyed a Bf 110, on the 19th he claimed two Bf 109s destroyed and on the 20th and 22nd two more. He was shot down by return fire from He 111s on June 6. He glided 15 miles and landed near a small village 10 miles from Rouen. Having found no one in the village he returned to his aircraft and met some British soldiers, who drove him to Rouen. With another officer he drove from aerodrome to aerodrome until in a few days they had travelled 400 miles across France. At Dreux Grice found an aircraft and set off across the Channel but finding his way crossed by black smoke drifting from burning oil tanks he diverted to Jersey and flew away next day to rejoin his squadron. Grice was awarded the DFC (25.6.40) and was decorated by the King on June 27 in a special ceremony at Biggin Hill.

On July 4 Grice was shot down by Bf 109s and forced-landed at Manston. On the 8th he claimed a Bf 109 probably destroyed, on August 12 a Do 17 and on the 15th a Bf 109. On this day Grice was shot down in flames and baled out, burned about the face and wrists. He was rescued from the sea by an MTB and admitted to the Royal Naval Hospital, Shotley. His Hurricane, N 2459, crashed into the sea at Pye Sands, Pennyhole Bay, south of Harwich.

When he was fit again Grice became Controller at Biggin Hill. He was a Controller at Northolt from June 1941 until February 1942, Senior Controller at North Weald until December 1943, Senior Controller at Tangmere until August 1945, a Controller at 11 Group until February 1946 and a Staff Officer at HQ Fighter Command until he retired in April 1947, as a Wing Commander. He was made an MBE (1.1.46).

APO 19.2.38   PO 29.11.38   FO 26.9.40   FL 16.6.41
SL 1.7.43

ROBERT VICTOR GRIDLEY

46124   Sgt   Air Gunner   British   235 Squadron

Joined 235 Squadron on August 3 1940. Commissioned in June 1941, Gridley was killed on January 13 1942, as a Pilot Officer with 69 Squadron. He was 20 years old and is remembered on the Malta Memorial, Panel 3, Column 1.

PO 4.6.41

THOMAS GRIER

40907   FO   Pilot   British   601 Squadron

Grier, from Stow-on-the-Wold, Gloucestershire, was born in Glasgow in 1918. He joined the RAF on a short service commission in May 1938 and was with 601 Squadron at Tangmere in early July 1940.

On July 7 Grier claimed a share in the destruction of a Do 17, on the 16th he shared a Ju 88, on the 20th he shared a He 59, on August 13 he destroyed two Bf 110s, a Ju 88 and shared another, on the 18th two Ju 87s, on the 30th he shared a He 111, on the 31st claimed a Bf 110, on September 6 claimed two Bf 109s and on the 25th a Ju 88. He was awarded the DFC (1.10.40).

In October 1941 Grier was given command of 32 Squadron at Angle. He was killed on December 5 and is remembered on the Runnymede Memorial, Panel 28.

APO 9.7.38   PO 16.5.39   FO 3.9.40   FL 3.9.41

JOHN JAMES GRIFFIN

742304   Sgt   Pilot   British   73 Squadron

Griffin, of Twickenham, Middlesex, joined 73 Squadron at Church Fenton in early July 1940. He claimed a Ju 88 destroyed on August 15.

In an action over Maidstone on September 14 Griffin was shot down and baled out. He was admitted to West Kent Hospital, with a dislocated shoulder. His Hurricane crashed at Clapper Lane, Staplehurst.

Griffin was killed on April 7 1942, as a Warrant Officer with 273 Squadron at China Bay. He was 32 years old and is buried in Trincomalee War Cemetery, Sri Lanka.

———— GRIFFITHS

No unknown   Sgt   Pilot   British   32 Squadron

No service details traced.

GLYN GRIFFITHS

135394   Sgt   Pilot   British   17 Squadron

Born in 1918 in Llandudno, Griffiths was with 17 Squadron in June 1940. On July 9 he shared in the destruction of a He 111, on the 12th he claimed a He 111 destroyed and shared another, on August 11 he shared a Bf 110, on September 5 got a probable He 111, on the 19th shared a Ju 88 and on September 27 claimed a Bf 110 and Bf 109. He was awarded the DFM (26.11.40).

Griffiths was posted away from 17 in early 1941 and became an instructor. Commissioned from Warrant Officer in April 1942, he later went to Canada, to instruct. After his return to the UK he flew operationally in 1944 with 4 Squadron, an Army Co-operation unit. When returning from a sortie over France his No 2 collided with him over their base at Odiham. Griffiths was badly burned before he baled out and he had not recovered from his injuries before the war ended.

He was released from the RAF in 1946, as a Flight Lieutenant, and died in 1983.

PO 4.4.42   FO 4.10.42   FL 4.4.44

GEORGE JACQUES GROGAN

42972   PO   Air Gunner   British   23 Squadron

Born on October 24 1909, Grogan was commissioned in January 1940 and joined 23 Squadron at Wittering in February. He was with the squadron until March 1941.

Grogan stayed in the RAF and retired on November 1 1956, as a Squadron Leader. He died in 1983.

PO 17.1.40   FO 17.1.41   FL 17.1.42   SL 1.8.47

BERNARD GROSZEWSKI

P 0544   FO   Pilot   Polish   43 Squadron

Born on October 9 1909, Groszewski was in the PAF before the war. In September 1939 he was commanding 162 Squadron of III/6 Fighter Dyon at Lodz.

Groszewski was posted to 307 Squadron at Kirton-in-Lindsey on September 10 1940. After a spell at Old Sarum he joined 43 Squadron at Usworth on October 26 1940. He was posted to 315 Squadron at Acklington at its formation on January 21 1941. Groszewski went to 61 OTU, Heston on September 8 1941, as an instructor but moved to 58 OTU, Grangemouth on the 29th.

He returned to 315 Squadron, then at Northolt, on November 2 1941. The squadron was flying high cover near the French coast on December 12 1941. Groszewski, in Spitfire BL 323, was shot down near Le Touquet and Berck. He was seen in the water but drowned before help arrived. His body was washed up on the beach and buried in Boulogne-sur-Mer Cemetery.

Groszewski was awarded the KW (20.8.42).

FO 1.3.41

HARRY CYRIL GROVE

580202   Sgt   Pilot   British   3 and 501 Squadrons

Grove, of Herne Hill, London, joined 3 Squadron at Wick in August 1940. He was posted to 501 Squadron at Kenley on September 29.

Grove was shot down in flames by Bf 109s on November 8 1940. He baled out but was killed when his parachute failed to open. His Hurricane, V 6805, crashed and burned out at Pound Farm, Blackham. He was 29 and is buried in St Luke's churchyard, Whyteleafe, Surrey.

ERNEST GEORGE GRUBB

123639   Sgt   Pilot   British   219 Squadron

With 219 Squadron at Catterick in early July 1940. Promoted to Warrant Officer on October 1 1941, Grubb was commissioned in May 1942 and released from the RAF in 1945, as a Flight Lieutenant. He joined the RAFVR in September 1948.

PO 25.5.42   FO 25.11.42   FL 25.5.44
FO (RAFVR) 27.9.48

HENRY FRANK GRUBB

123640   Sgt   Pilot   British   219 Squadron

With 219 Squadron at Catterick in early July 1940. Promoted to Warrant Officer on October 1 1941, Grubb was commissioned in May 1942 and released from the RAF in 1945, as a Flight Lieutenant. He died in 1981. Brother to EG Grubb.

PO 25.5.42   FO 25.11.42   FL 25.5.44

FRANCISZEK GRUSZKA

76785   FO   Pilot   Polish   65 Squadron

Joined 65 Squadron at Hornchurch on August 7 1940. Gruszka was killed on August 18, aged 30. His Spitfire, R 6713, crashed at Westbere, near Canterbury during a flight patrol. The site was excavated in 1976 and the pilot's remains were found. Originally remembered on the Polish Air Force Memorial at Northolt, Gruszka is now buried in Northwood Cemetery, Middlesex.

BOHDAN GRZESZCZAK

P 1391   FO   Pilot   Polish   303 Squadron

Born on August 10 1908, Grzeszczak joined 303 Squadron at Northolt on August 21 1940. He claimed a He 111 probably destroyed on September 26 and a Bf 109 probably destroyed on the 27th. He was awarded the KW (1.2.41).

Grzeszczak was posted to 58 OTU, Grangemouth on April 21 1941, as an instructor. On August 28 1941 he was instructing a pupil in a simulated dog-fight, in Master T 8581. They made a sudden avoiding action at 1500 feet and went into a long dive. The aircraft did not pull out and exploded at Polmont, near Grangemouth. Both men were killed. Grzeszczak is buried in Northwood Cemetery.

CHARLES PAUL GUERIN

30526   Adjudant   Pilot   French   232 Squadron

Guerin was born in Paris on August 9 1916. He was in l'Armée de l'Air in 1940 and in early June was ordered to go to Algeria, as an instructor. He went to Oran and flew to Gibraltar on June 30, in a stolen plane piloted by Mouchotte.

They sailed for Britain on July 3. Guerin went to RAF St Athan on the 25th, moved to Old Sarum on the 30th, went to 6 OTU, Sutton Bridge on August 19 and joined 232 Squadron at Castletown on September 14.

Guerin was posted to 615 Squadron at Northolt on December 17 1940. He was killed on May 8 1941, whilst on a convoy patrol. He had a glycol leak and his engine seized. Instead of baling out Guerin decided to land on the sea near to the convoy. At 50 feet the aircraft suddenly lurched to the right, hit the sea, turned over and disappeared. Guerin received a posthumous Mention in Despatches.

THOMAS FRANCIS GUEST

42985   PO   Pilot   British   79 and 56 Squadrons

Guest was born in 1918 and was a 2nd Lieutenant in the Gloster Regiment (TA) before joining the RAF. He was posted to 79 Squadron on September 17 1940 and moved to 56 Squadron at Boscombe Down on October 8.

He claimed a Bf 109 destroyed on November 6 1940 and on the 23rd he collided with Sergeant W Szafraniec during a formation practice near Middle Wallop. Guest landed, unhurt but the other pilot was killed.

Guest was released from the RAF in 1945, as a Flight Lieutenant.

PO 7.3.40   FO 7.3.41   FL 7.3.42

KENNETH CRADOCK GUNDRY

81371   PO   Pilot   British   257 Squadron

Joined 257 Squadron at Northolt on August 3 1940. Gundry was slightly wounded by shell splinters on October 12 and made a forced-landing at Detling, with damage sustained in combat with Bf 109s over Deal.

Gundry was killed on May 22 1942, as a Flying Officer with 112 Squadron. He was 25 and is remembered on the Alamein Memorial, Column 248.

PO 6.7.40   FO 6.7.41

HAROLD RAYMOND GUNN

43067   PO   Pilot   British   74 Squadron

Gunn, of Oxley, Herts, joined 74 Squadron at Hornchurch on April 18 1940.

He claimed a Bf 109 destroyed on July 28 and was shot down into the Channel off Folkestone on the 31st, in Spitfire P 9379, possibly by Oberleutnant Fözö of 4/JG 51.

Gunn was 27. His body was recovered by the Germans and he is buried in Ostende New Communal Cemetery, Belgium.

PO 1.4.40

PETER STACKHOUSE GUNNING

43474   PO   Pilot   British   46 Squadron

With 46 Squadron at Digby in early July 1940. Gunning was shot down and killed in combat with Bf 109s over the Thames Estuary on October 15 1940. His Hurricane, N 2480, crashed and burned out in a chalk pit at Little Thurrock.

Gunning was 29. He is buried in St Andrew's churchyard, North Weald Bassett.

PO 1.4.40

EDWARD MAURICE GUNTER

83988   PO   Pilot   British   43 and 501 Squadrons

Gunter joined 43 Squadron at Usworth on September 10 1940 and moved to 501 Squadron at Kenley on the 22nd.

He was shot down attacking Do 17s, with a Bf 109 escort, on September 27. He baled out but was killed when his parachute failed to open. His Hurricane, V 6645, crashed near Teynham Court, Sittingbourne.

Gunter was 20. He is buried in St Mary's churchyard, Aldeby, Norfolk.

PO 17.8.40

JOHN VINTER GURTEEN

81918   PO   Pilot   British   504 Squadron

Born on February 10 1916, Gurteen, of Haverhill, Suffolk, was at Marlborough College from 1929 to 1933. He won a scholarship to the USA, sponsored by the English Speaking Union.

Gurteen joined 504 Squadron at Castletown in June 1940. He was shot down and killed in combat over the southern outskirts of London on September 15 1940. His Hurricane, N 2481, dived under full throttle on to a house at Hartley, near Longfield.

Gurteen was 24. He was cremated at Hendon Crematorium and his ashes were scattered over his house by Flight Lieutenant WB Royce of 504.

PO 18.6.40

GILES CONNOP McEACHARN GUTHRIE

Lieutenant (FAA)   Pilot   British   808 Squadron

Born on March 21 1916, Guthrie was the son of Sir Connop Guthrie, 1st Baronet. He was educated at Eton and Magdalene College, Cambridge. He was the winner, with CWA Scott, of the Portsmouth-Johannesburg Air Race in 1936.

Guthrie joined the Fleet Air Arm in 1939 and was with 808 Squadron at Wick in July 1940, flying Fulmars on dockyard defence. He embarked with the squadron in 'Ark Royal' on October 22 1940 and took part in the operations in the Mediterranean in 1941, including Operation 'Tiger' on May 8. He was awarded the DSC (25.11.41).

Guthrie, was made an OBE (1.1.46) and released from the Navy on January 30 1946, as a Lieutenant Commander (A). He succeeded to the baronetcy in 1945 and died on December 31 1979.

Sub-Lt 11.3.40   Lt 9.9.40

NORMAN HENRY GUTHRIE

133533   Sgt   Air Gunner   British   604 Squadron

Born in Plumstead in 1916, Guthrie was in the AuxAF before the war. He was with 604 Squadron in June 1940 and with the advent of AI he retrained as a radar operator.

In December 1940 Guthrie teamed up with Flying Officer ED Crew. On the night of April 4 1941 they destroyed a He 111, on the 24th another, on the 28th another and on July 7 they destroyed a Ju 88, which was one of a force attacking Middle Wallop by night. Guthrie was awarded the DFM (24.6.41).

Promoted to Warrant Officer on March 1 1942, Guthrie was commissioned in September 1942 and released from the RAF in 1946, as a Flight Lieutenant. He died on February 17 1981.

PO 8.9.42   FO 8.3.43   FL 8.9.44

LEONARD NORTHWOOD GUY

758823   Sgt   Pilot   British   601 Squadron

Guy, of Weston-Super-Mare, was with 601 Squadron at Tangmere in early July 1940.

On August 11 Guy claimed two Bf 110s destroyed, on the 13th a Bf 110 and another shared, on the 15th a shared Ju 88 and on the 16th two Ju 87s. Guy failed to return from a combat with Bf 109s off the Sussex coast on August 18 1940, in Hurricane R 4191. He was 25 and is remembered on the Runnymede Memorial, Panel 14.

PETER GUY

Midshipman (FAA)   Pilot   British   808 Squadron

Guy, of Kirbymoorside, was with 808 Squadron at Wick in early July 1940, flying Fulmars on dockyard defence. He embarked with the squadron in HMS 'Ark Royal' on October 22 and took part in all the carrier's actions in the Mediterranean in 1941. On September 27 he shared in destroying a Fiat BR 20 torpedo bomber and on October 17 shared a Cant Z 506B.

Guy was killed on January 28 1942 in a deck-landing accident on HMS 'Merlin'. He was 20 years old and is buried in Douglas Bank Cemetery, Dunfermline.

Midshipman 1.5.39

ERIC NORMAN LAURENCE GUYMER

119503   Sgt   Pilot   British   238 Squadron

Joined 238 Squadron at St Eval on September 7 1940 and served with it until March 1941.

Guymer was commissioned in January 1942 and released from the RAF in 1945, as a Flight Lieutenant.

PO 15.1.42   FO 1.10.42   FL 15.1.44

GERALD HENRY HACKWOOD

42217   PO   Pilot   British   264 Squadron

Hackwood, from Newbury, Berkshire, joined the RAF on a short service commission in April 1939. He was with 264 Squadron at

GH Hackwood (continued)

Martlesham Heath early in 1940.

Over Dunkirk on May 29 he destroyed a Bf 109 and shared a Bf 110 and on the 31st destroyed a He 111 and probably another. He was killed on November 20 1940, when his Defiant, N 1626, crashed on take-off just east of Blatches Farm, Rochford.

Hackwood was 20. He is buried in the churchyard of St Mary and St John, Newtown, Hampshire.

APO 24.6.39   PO 9.12.39

JOHN GALLOWAY EDWARD HAIG

90189   FL   Pilot   British   603 Squadron

Haig joined 603 Squadron, AuxAF in 1932. He went on to the Reserve of Officers in June 1938 and was recalled for full-time service on August 24 1939.

On September 2 1940 Haig claimed a Bf 109 destroyed but had to make a forced-landing himself at Hornchurch when his aircraft was damaged in combat. He was posted to 58 OTU, Grangemouth on December 30 1940, as an instructor.

Haig was released from the RAF in 1945, as a Squadron Leader.

PO (AuxAF) 11.6.32   FO (AuxAF) 11.12.33
FO 24.8.39   FL 3.9.40   SL 1.12.41

CYRIL HAIGH

566171   Sgt   Pilot   British   604 Squadron

Haigh was with 604 Squadron at Northolt in early July 1940. On August 25 he was captain of Blenheim L 6782, which crashed near Witheridge, Exeter whilst on an operational sortie. Haigh and Sergeant JB Fletcher were killed and LAC AL Austin died the next day.

Haigh was 23. He is buried in St Margaret's churchyard, Swinton, Yorkshire.

RICHARD CUMMINS HAINE

43147   PO   Pilot   British   600 Squadron

Born on October 1 1916, Haine learned to fly at the Cotswold Aero Club, Staverton, whilst still at school. He joined the RAF as an NCO pilot in 1935 and in September began his elementary flying training at the Bristol Flying School at Filton. In November Haine moved to 11 FTS, Shawbury and after completing the course he joined 25 Squadron at Hawkinge. He was in the squadron aerobatics team at the Hendon Air Display in 1937.

The squadron converted to Blenheims in December 1938 and moved to Northolt in August 1939. Haine flew what could be the first defensive patrol of the war, in the early hours of September 4 1939. On December 28 he flew one of the six Blenheims of 25 Squadron, which went with six from 601 to attack the German seaplane base at Borkum, the first fighter attack on Germany.

Haine was commissioned in April 1940 and posted to 600 Squadron at Manston. On May 10 he flew one of the six Blenheims, which attacked Rotterdam airfield in daylight. Only one returned to base. Haine claimed a Bf 109 destroyed and two Ju 52s damaged before he was shot down and made a forced-landing in Holland. He and his gunner evaded capture and got back to England in the destroyer evacuating the Dutch Royal Family. For this action Haine was awarded the DFC (9.7.40).

In January 1941 he was posted to 68 Squadron at Catterick, as a Flight Commander. He moved to HQ 9 Group in June and on December 30 1941 was given command of 96 Squadron at Wrexham. Haine went to HQ Fighter Command in March 1943, spent time in North Africa on attachment in June and was posted to 54 OTU, Charter Hall in July 1943, as Wing Commander Training.

In January 1944 Haine took command of 488 Squadron at Bradwell Bay. On August 4 he destroyed a Ju 88 and on September 1 a Ju 188. In November 1944 he was posted to 147 Wing at Odiham, as a test pilot. Haine returned to 54 OTU in March 1945, to command. In May he commanded the Spitfire OCU at Eshott, moved to 302 Wing at Ibsley in June and in September 1945 became Station Commander at Kai Tak, Hong Kong.

Over the next twenty-five years Haine held a series of appointments and commands. He retired on October 1 1970, as a Group Captain. He was made an OBE (1.1.62).

PO 1.4.40   FO 1.4.41   FL 25.11.41   SL 1.9.45
WC 1.1.52   GC 1.7.62

LEONARD ARCHIBALD HAINES

40297   FO   Pilot   British   19 Squadron

From Melcombe Regis, Weymouth, Haines joined the RAF on a short service commission in September 1937.

He was with 19 Squadron at Duxford in early 1940. Over Dunkirk on June 1 he destroyed a Bf 109 and on a later patrol damaged a He 111. On August 19 Haines shared a Bf 110, on September 3 he destroyed a Bf 110, on the 5th a Bf 109, on the 11th a Bf 110, on the 15th a Bf 109 and a Bf 110 and on the 18th he shared a Ju 88 and probably destroyed a Bf 109. He was awarded the DFC (8.10.40).

Haines shared a Bf 109 on November 5, shared a Bf 110 on the 15th and destroyed a Bf 109 on the 28th. He was posted away in late 1940 to be an instructor at OTU and was killed in a flying accident on April 30 1941.

He is buried in the Heston and Isleworth Cemetery, Twickenham, Middlesex.

APO 28.11.37   PO 27.9.38   FO 27.5.40

JOHN KEATINGE HAIRE

748611   Sgt   Pilot   British   145 Squadron

Born in Belfast on September 25 1920, Haire began his elementary flying training at No 1 EFTS, Hatfield on December 4 1939. He joined 145 Squadron at Drem on September 11 1940.

In October the squadron moved to Tangmere and on the 27th Haire's Hurricane, V 6888, was damaged in combat with Bf 109s east of the Isle of Wight. He ditched in the sea offshore at Bembridge and waded ashore, unhurt.

On November 6 1940 Haire was killed in a combat over the Isle of Wight. His Hurricane, V 6627, crashed at Heasley Farm, Arreton. He was probably shot down by Major Helmut Wick.

Haire is buried in Dundonald Cemetery, Belfast.

PETER RAYMOND HAIRS

76316   PO   Pilot   British   501 Squadron

Hairs joined the RAFVR in October 1937 and carried out his flying training at 19 E&RFTS, Gatwick. Called up at the outbreak of war, he went to 6 FTS, Little Rissington in October 1939 to complete his training, after which he was commissioned.

On December 27 Hairs was posted to the Fighter Pool, St Athan, where he converted to Hurricanes before joining 501 Squadron at Tangmere on January 25 1940. The squadron flew to France on May 10 and on the 15th Hairs shared in probably destroying a Do 17.

He claimed a Bf 109 destroyed on September 5.

Hairs was posted to 15 FTS, Kidlington on October 13 1940, as a flying instructor. He went to 2 CFS, Cranwell for an instructor's course on February 23 1941, after which he moved to 11 FTS, Shawbury to instruct on April 14. He spent a short while at 10 EFTS, Weston-super-Mare in May and was then posted to Canada on June 13, as a flying instructor and Assistant CFI (EFTS).

In mid-December 1943 Hairs returned to the UK and joined 276 (ASR) Squadron at Harrowbeer. He was posted away on May 5 1944 to 19 OTU, Kinloss as OC Bomber Defence Training Flight. His final posting was to India on July 18 1945 on admin duties.

Hairs was released from the RAF on October 30 1945, as a Flight Lieutenant. He received a Mention in Despatches (14.6.45) and was made an MBE (1.1.46).

PO 10.12.39   FO 10.12.40   FL 10.12.41

——— HALL

No unknown   Sgt   Aircrew   British   235 Squadron

No service details traced.

——— HALL

No unknown   Sgt   Aircrew   British   29 Squadron

No service details traced.

NOEL MUDIE HALL

33166   FL   Pilot   British   257 Squadron

Hall entered RAF College, Cranwell in September 1933 as a flight cadet. On graduation in July 1935 he was posted to 3 Squadron at Kenley. On November 2 1936 Hall went to the Station Flight at Mildenhall, where he joined the Meteorological Flight. For his work there he was awarded the AFC (2.1.39).

On January 14 1939 Hall was posted to the Wireless Flight at RAE, Farnborough. He went to 257 Squadron at Hendon at its reformation on May 17 1940, as a Flight Commander. In July he was recalled to RAE but managed to return to 257.

Hall was shot down and killed on August 8 1940, in combat with Bf 109s off St Catherine's Point, in Hurricane P 2981. His body was recovered by the Germans and he is buried in Criel Communal Cemetery, France. Hall was 24 years old.

PO 27.7.35   FO 27.1.37   FL 27.1.39

ROSSWELL CLIFFORD HALL

42964   PO   Air Gunner   British   219 Squadron

With 219 Squadron at Catterick in early July 1940. Hall last appears in the January 1943 Air Force List and no trace of him has been found as a casualty, so presumably he left the RAF in early 1943.

PO 17.1.40   FO 17.1.41   FL 17.1.42

ROGER MONTAGU DICKENSON HALL

43009   PO   Pilot   British   152 Squadron

Born on August 12 1917, Hall was at Haileybury College from 1931 to 1935. He entered the Royal Military Academy, Sandhurst in 1936 as an officer cadet. Hall was gazetted as a 2nd Lieutenant Royal Tank Regiment in early 1938. Soon afterwards he became ill and did not rejoin his regiment until the end of the year.

In March 1940 Hall applied to transfer to the RAF and after acceptance was posted to 7 EFTS, Desford for his ab initio course. He completed his training and in early August he went to the School of Army Co-operation at Old Sarum.

Hall volunteered for Fighter Command, was posted to 7 OTU, Hawarden and after converting to Spitfires joined 152 Squadron at Warmwell on September 1. In early December 1940 Hall went to 255 Squadron, then forming at Kirton-in-Lindsey with Defiants. He destroyed a He 111 over the Humber on February 10 1941, the squadron's first victory.

In September Hall joined 72 Squadron at Gravesend, as a Flight Commander. He was posted away in December. In April 1942 he went to 91 Squadron at Hawkinge. Hall made his last operational flight on September 17, left the squadron in October and was awarded the DFC (24.11.42). He lost his flying category for medical reasons and transferred to the Administrative Branch.

Hall was released from the RAF in 1944, as a Flight Lieutenant. He joined the RAFVR in 1960.

PO 8.3.40   FO 8.3.41   FL 8.3.42   FO (RAFVR) 11.7.60

WILLIAM CLIFFORD HALL

78264   PO   Pilot   British   248 Squadron

Hall, of Ovington, Northumberland, was with 248 Squadron in early July 1940. He was killed on April 14 1941, as a Flying Officer with No 1 PRU, aged 30.

Hall is buried in Vlissingen Northern Cemetery, Flushing, Netherlands.

PO 24.3.40   FO 24.3.41

IAN LEWIS McGREGOR HALLAM

39730   FL   Pilot   British   610 and 222 Squadrons

Joined the RAF on a short service commission in March 1937. Hallam was posted to 2 FTS, Brize Norton on June 5 and after training joined 2 (Army Co-operation) Squadron at Hawkinge.

On September 3 1940 Hallam was posted to 610 Squadron at Acklington. He moved to 222 Squadron at Hornchurch on September 30.

Hallam stayed on in the RAF after the war. He was killed on May 10 1952, when his aircraft crashed near Methlick, Aberdeenshire, whilst on a training flying from Dyce. At that time Hallam was a Squadron Leader and CO of the Aberdeen University Air Squadron.

APO 18.5.37   PO 15.3.38   FO 15.10.39   FL 15.10.40
SL 1.12.41   SL 1.8.47

ANTONY BURTON HALLIWELL

77354   PO   Air Gunner   British   141 Squadron

Born in 1905, Halliwell was with 141 Squadron at Turnhouse in early July 1940. He was in one of the nine Defiants, which were attacked by Bf 109s off Dover on July 19. His was one of the only two aircraft which returned safely to base and he claimed a Bf 109 destroyed in the action.

Halliwell was released from the RAF in 1946, as a Squadron Leader. He died in 1974.

APO 3.2.40   PO 16.3.40   FO 16.3.41   FL 16.3.42

HERBERT JAMES LEMPRIERE HALLOWES

45010   PO   Pilot   British   43 Squadron

Born in Lambeth, London on April 17 1912. As a boy he spent three years in the Falklands, where his father was a medical officer. Hallowes joined the RAF in January 1929 as an apprentice metal rigger at Halton. He passed out in 1932 and in 1934 volunteered for pilot training. He was accepted and after qualifying as a Sergeant-Pilot he joined 43 Squadron at Tangmere in August 1936.

On February 3 1940 Hallowes shared in destroying a He 111, the first enemy aircraft to crash on English soil in the war. On April 4 he damaged a He 111 and was surprised when it followed him down to the aerodrome at Wick. The pilot believed he was landing on water and after stopping let go his dinghy and emerged, minus his boots, into the snow, only to be confronted by a soldier with a fixed bayonet. Both rear gunners were dead.

Near Dunkirk on June 1 Hallowes destroyed a Bf 110, two Bf 109s and damaged another. On the 7th his aircraft was set alight in combat. As he was about to bale out a Bf 109 overtook him. Hallowes resumed his seat, shot down the enemy fighter and then baled out, dislocating his ankle on landing. Soldiers told him the Bf 109 had crashed and they were not sure which pilot he was. Hallowes was taken to No 4 Base Hospital at La Bause and rejoined 43 Squadron soon afterwards.

On August 8 Hallowes claimed two Bf 109s destroyed, on the 13th a Ju 88 destroyed and another Ju 88 and a Do 17 probably destroyed, on the 15th a Ju 88 probably destroyed, on the 16th three Ju 87s destroyed, on the 18th another three and he shared a He 111 on the 26th. Hallowes was awarded the DFM and Bar (6.9.40).

Commissioned in September 1940, he was posted to 65 Squadron at Biggin Hill in November, later becoming a Flight Commander. In early 1942 Hallowes was with 122 Squadron at Scorton. He was given command of 222 Squadron at North Weald in June 1942. In August he took command of 165 Squadron and led it in the Dieppe operation on the 19th, destroying a Do 217. Hallowes was awarded the DFC (19.1.43).

In October 1943 he took command of 504 Squadron at Peterhead. Hallowes was promoted to Acting Wing Commander in March 1944 and became Station Commander at Dunsfold.

He stayed on in the RAF, in the Secretarial Branch, and retired on July 8 1956, as a Squadron Leader, retaining the rank of Wing Commander. He went to work for the Ministry of Transport. Hallowes died on October 20 1987.

PO 18.9.40   FO 22.8.41   FL 22.8.42   SL 1.7.44
SL 1.9.45

DERRICK WILSON HALTON

748212   Sgt   Pilot   British   615 Squadron

With 615 Squadron at Kenley in early July 1940. Halton was shot down in combat on August 15 and reported 'Missing'. His Hurricane, P 2801, crashed and burned out at Seal.

Halton was 21. He is remembered on the Runnymede Memorial, Panel 14.

JACK ROYSTON HAMAR

70898   PO   Pilot   British   151 Squadron

Born at Knighton, Radnorshire, Hamar joined the RAF on a short service commission in May 1938. He was with 151 Squadron at North Weald in early 1940.

Over Dunkirk on May 18 Hamar destroyed a Ju 87 and on the 22nd shot down two more. He shared a Bf 110 on July 9 and claimed a Bf 109 destroyed on the 14th.

Hamar was killed on July 24 1940, when he stalled attempting an upward roll prior to landing. He crashed, inverted, on North Weald aerodrome from 500 feet. He was 25 and is buried in Knighton Cemetery. Hamar was awarded the DFC (30.7.40).

APO 9.7.38   PO 16.5.39

RICHARD KAYE HAMBLIN

16223   WC   Pilot   British   17 Squadron

Born on December 16 1906 Hamblin entered RAF College, Cranwell in September 1924. On graduation he was commissioned and joined 56 Squadron at Biggin Hill on July 30 1926. He was sent on a course to the Electrical and Wireless School, Cranwell on April 28 1930.

Hamblin was posted to 26 (Army Co-operation) Squadron at Catterick on July 21 1931 and on October 4 1932 he joined 31 (Army Co-operation) Squadron at Quetta. He moved to 5 (Army Co-operation) Squadron at Chakala, Rawalpindi on July 20 1935 and after returning to the UK Hamblin was given command of 142 Squadron at Andover. He was posted to a course at the Army Staff College, Camberley on January 23 1939.

During the Battle of Britain period Hamblin flew one patrol with 17 Squadron, in the afternoon of October 29 1940, thus qualifying for the clasp. He was made a CBE (1.1.46) and retired from the RAF on May 25 1956, as an Air Commodore.

PO 30.7.26   FO 30.1.28   FL 1.6.32   SL 1.8.37
WC 1.6.40   GC 1.6.42   GC 1.10.46   AC 1.7.52

RUSSEL CHAPMAN HAMER

566261   Sgt   Pilot   British   141 Squadron

Hamer was a pre-war airman pilot. He began his flying training at 8 E&RFTS, Woodley on July 25 1938 and moved to 7 FTS, Peterborough on October 1. With training completed he was posted to 3 AOS, Aldergrove as a staff pilot.

On October 7 1939 Hamer joined 141 Squadron, then reforming at Turnhouse. He was to remain with the squadron until his death. On September 8 1942 Hamer, then a Warrant Officer, was directed to a He 111 fifteen miles south-east of St Alban's Head at 01.40 hrs. He attacked the bomber and strikes were seen. Hamer expended his cannon ammunition and the Heinkel's starboard engine caught fire, but a burst of return fire ignited the Beaufighter's starboard engine. It is then likely that Hamer was wounded but he kept firing his machine guns until the return fire ceased.

The enemy aircraft crashed into the sea and Hamer asked for a homing. He was at 6000 feet and fifty miles south of Tangmere. The navigator suggested baling out but Hamer said he thought they could cope. He was under great strain and would not allow the navigator to transmit or open the front (pilot's) escape hatch. They were down to 2000 feet when the Isle of Wight was seen. Hamer told the navigator to bale out but said he was staying. Suddenly the port engine stopped and Hamer held the Beaufighter at 1000 feet, while the navigator baled out, landing on the beach near Newtown, Isle of Wight. The Beaufighter dropped and in his weakened condition Hamer was unable to get out. He crashed near Lymington and was killed. He knew that his navigator was a non-swimmer and it is thought that this influenced him to stay with the aircraft until they were over land even though it would mean his own death.

Hamer may have been recommended for the VC but if so, it was not granted. He received a Mention in Despatches (2.6.43). He is buried in Dolhasren Cemetery, Montgomeryshire.

JOHN WARREN HAMILL

40909   FO   Pilot   New Zealander   229 Squadron

Born in Hamilton on March 16 1916, Hamill was educated at Wanganui Collegiate School. He went to work for a newspaper and in July 1936 became manager of the Opera House cinema in Oamaru.

Hamill applied for an RAF short service commission in December 1937 and was provisionally accepted. He sailed for the UK on April 7 1938 in the RMS 'Rangitata'. In mid-May he began his elementary flying at 4 E&RFTS, Brough and was posted to 3 FTS, South Cerney on July 23 and then went to No 1 AACU at Henlow on March 4 1939, as a staff pilot.

On May 26 1940 Hamill was posted to 6 OTU, Sutton Bridge and after converting to Hurricanes he joined 229 Squadron at Digby. On December 11, with his tour completed, Hamill went to 4 Ferry Pilot's Pool at Kemble.

On Christmas Eve he was detailed to deliver a Hurricane from 20 MU to 247 Squadron at Roborough. The weather was bad, with rain and low cloud. After apparently losing his way Hamill crashed in the Mendip Hills, about three miles from Cheddar Gorge and was killed. He is buried in Wells Cemetery, Somerset.

APO 9.7.38   PO 16.5.39   FO 3.9.40

ALEXANDER LEWIS HAMILTON

42121   PO   Pilot   Australian   248 Squadron

Born on December 17 1914, Hamilton joined the RAF on a short service commission in March 1939. He was with 248 Squadron in early July 1940.

Hamilton stayed on in the RAF after the war, in the Fighter Control Branch. He retired on April 5 1961, as a Wing Commander.

APO 13.5.39   PO 6.11.39
FO 6.11.40   FL 6.11.41
FL 1.9.45   SL 1.7.51
WC 1.1.58

ARTHUR CHARLES HAMILTON

78543   PO   Air Gunner   British   141 Squadron

Hamilton, of North Harrow, Middlesex, was with 141 Squadron when it moved south from Turnhouse to West Malling on July 12 1940.

He was in one of the nine Defiants attacked off Dover by Bf 109s of lll/JG 51 on July 19. Hamilton's pilot, Flying Officer IDG Donald, was killed in the aircraft and Hamilton baled out but was drowned in the sea. Their Defiant, L 7009, crashed at Elmsvale Road, Dover.

Hamilton was 28 and is buried in Folkestone New Cemetery, Kent.

APO 15.3.40

CHARLES BLACKLEY HAMILTON

174685   Sgt   Aircrew   British   219 Squadron

Hamilton, of Girvan, Ayrshire, joined 219 Squadron at Catterick in early September 1940. Commissioned in February 1944, Hamilton was awarded the DFC (26.9.44), as a Pilot Officer with 85 Squadron. He had then assisted in the destruction of four enemy aircraft.

Hamilton was killed on April 13 1945, still with 85. He was 23 and is buried in Hamburg Cemetery, Ohlsdorf, Germany.

PO 22.2.44   FO 22.8.44

CLAUD ERIC HAMILTON

90964   PO   Pilot   British   234 Squadron

Hamilton, of Cairns, Midlothian, was in the AuxAF before the war. He was called to full-time service on August 23 1939.

He joined 234 Squadron at St Eval on September 12 1940. In mid-November Hamilton sailed from Gibraltar on the carrier HMS 'Argus'. He was in the first flight of six Hurricanes, which flew off on November 17 to Ta Kali, Malta, where he joined 261 Squadron. On the night of April 11/12 1941 Hamilton claimed a Ju 87 destroyed.

261 Squadron was disbanded on May 12 1941 and Hamilton was attached to 185 Squadron. He was shot down on the 14th by Oberleutnant Von Kageneck of lll/JG 27 and fatally wounded.

Hamilton was 20 years old. He is buried in the Naval Cemetery, Capuccini, Malta.

APO 23.8.39   PO 17.8.40

HARRY RAYMOND HAMILTON

39316   FL   Pilot   Canadian   85 Squadron

Hamilton, of Kings County, New Brunswick, joined the RAF on a short service commission in October 1936. He was posted to 3 FTS, Grantham on January 11 1937 and joined 46 Squadron at Digby on August 7.

In early 1940 Hamilton was with 611 Squadron and was posted to 85 Squadron at Debden on May 25, as a Flight Commander. On July 30 he shared in the destruction of a Bf 110, on August 18 he claimed a Bf 110 destroyed and shared a He 111 and on the 29th he destroyed a Bf 109 and was then himself shot down and killed, over Winchelsea. Hamilton's Hurricane, V 6623, crashed near the ruins of Camber Castle. He was 23 years old and is buried in Folkestone New Cemetery, Kent.

APO 21.12.36   PO 12.10.37   FO 12.5.39   FL 12.5.40

JAMES SUTHERLAND HAMILTON

754020   Sgt   Pilot   British   248 Squadron

Joined 248 Squadron on September 25 1940. Hamilton was captain of a Blenheim detailed to fly from Sumburgh to Wick for operations on December 13 1940. He collided with another Blenheim, whilst formating, and crashed into the sea and sank. The crew of three and two ground staff men were all lost.

Hamilton was 22. He is remembered on the Runnymede Memorial, Panel 15.

RONALD FAIRFAX HAMLYN

45277   Sgt   Pilot   British   610 Squadron

Born in Harrogate on February 26 1914, Hamlyn joined the RAF as a direct-entry for pilot training in 1936. He carried out his flying training at 11 E&RFTS, Perth and 8 FTS, Montrose.

At the outbreak of war Hamlyn joined 72 Squadron at Church Fenton. After Dunkirk he was attached to 610 Squadron at Gravesend on June 6 1940 and this attachment became a posting. On July 3 Hamlyn shared a Do 17, on August 14 he claimed a Bf 109 destroyed, on August 24 a Ju 88 and four Bf 109s and he claimed Bf 109s destroyed on August 26, 27, 28 and 30. He was awarded the DFM (13.9.40).

Commissioned in January 1941, Hamlyn was posted to 242 Squadron at North Weald on June 13. On a Blenheim escort to Bethune on July 4 he destroyed a Bf 109 and on the 27th he shot another down into the sea. He was made a Flight Commander in late July and remained with the squadron until October 15 1941, when he was posted to 275 (ASR) Squadron at Valley, to command.

Hamlyn later took command of 276 (ASR) Squadron at Harrowbeer. He was awarded the AFC (1.1.43) and went to the staff of Bomber Command as ASR Officer. In 1944 he was Tactics Liaison Officer with the 9th Air Force USAF in Normandy and later in the year was posted to Air Ministry on Air Staff Policy.

In February 1945 Hamlyn was appointed CGI at 41 and later 58 OTUs and in September became Station Commander RAF Maidugari, West Africa. He retired from the RAF on October 19 1957, as a Squadron Leader.

PO 29.1.41   FO 28.9.41   FL 28.9.42   SL 1.8.47

JACK HAMMERTON

745227   Sgt   Pilot   British   3 and 615 Squadrons

Hammerton joined 615 Squadron at Prestwick in early October 1940 from 3 Squadron. He was killed on November 6, when he crashed in bad visibility near the railway line at Noah's Ark, near Sevenoaks.

Hammerton is buried in Stoke Road Cemetery, Slough, Buckinghamshire.

DEREK JOHN HAMMOND

42601   PO   Pilot   British   54, 245 and 253 Squadrons

Hammond joined 54 Squadron at Catterick in September 1940, moved to 245 Squadron at Aldergrove on the 27th and then to 253 Squadron at Kenley on October 16.

Hammond went to the Middle East in late 1940 and on January 29 1941 flew a Hurricane to Malta and joined 261 Squadron there. He returned to the Middle East in early May because of ill health.

In 1942 Hammond was with 272 Squadron in the Western Desert and on May 11 he probably destroyed a Ju 88 and shared a He 111. He was released from the RAF in 1947, as a Squadron Leader.

PO 24.3.40   FO 24.3.41   FL 24.3.42

CYRIL EDWARD HAMPSHIRE

49529   Sgt   Pilot   British   85, 111, 249 Sqdns, 422 Flt

Hampshire joined the RAF on September 2 1930 as an aircraft apprentice and went to Halton to train as a metal rigger. He passed out in July 1933 and was posted to 3 FTS, Grantham as an ACI. In March 1936 Hampshire went to 810 (Torpedo Bomber) Squadron. He passed his Central Trade Test Board and was promoted to LAC.

Having been accepted for pilot training he was posted to 12 E&RFTS, Prestwick in October 1937 and moved to 11 FTS in January 1938, firstly at Wittering and later at Shawbury. In August 1938 Hampshire joined 85 Squadron, newly-formed at Debden. The squadron moved to Rouen-Boos on September 9 1939. In the fighting in France between May 10 and 22 Hampshire destroyed two enemy aircraft, probably destroyed two and damaged another.

On August 11 he claimed a Bf 110 destroyed. On the 17th he was posted to 111 Squadron at Croydon, moved to 249 Squadron at North Weald on September 10 and then to 422 Flight at Shoreham. From June to mid-November 1940 Hampshire flew 119 sorties by day and 11 by night and destroyed, probably destroyed or damaged four more enemy aircraft. 422 Flight became 96 Squadron on December 21. Hampshire remained with the squadron until February 7 1942, when he was posted to 60 OTU, East Fortune, as a Warrant Officer instructor on multi-engined aircraft.

Commissioned in July 1942, Hampshire joined 286 Squadron, an anti-aircraft co-operation unit at Zeals. Taking off from Locking in an Oxford on February 13 1943 he crashed. One man was killed, one died of his injuries and Hampshire was paralysed and spent a year in hospital. He lost his flying category and finished the war as an admin officer in the 2nd TAF Personnel Department. He was released from the RAF in January 1946, as a Flying Officer.

PO 2.7.42   FO 2.1.43

BRUCE ALEXANDER HANBURY

C 1329   PO   Pilot   Canadian   1 and 1 (RCAF) Sqdns

Born in Vancouver on April 22 1911, Hanbury joined the RCAF on August 16 1939. He was posted to No 1 Squadron at Wittering on October 3 1940 and moved to No 1 (RCAF) Squadron at Prestwick on the 21st.

Hanbury was killed in a flying accident on March 27 1942, as a Squadron Leader with 409 Squadron. He is buried in Scopwick Church Burial Ground, Lincolnshire.

OSGOOD VILLIERS HANBURY

81357   PO   Pilot   British   602 Squadron

Hanbury, of Herriard, Hampshire, was educated at Eton. He was commissioned in June 1940 and posted to a Lysander army co-operation squadron. He joined 602 Squadron at Westhampnett on September 3 1940.

Hanbury claimed a Do 17 destroyed on September 15, shared a Ju 88 on the 21st, claimed a Ju 88 on the 30th and a Bf 109 on October 30. In May 1941 he joined 260 Squadron at Drem, then about to go to the Middle East. The squadron spent some months in Palestine before going to the Western Desert in October.

On December 14 Hanbury destroyed a Ju 88. He was given command of the squadron in March 1942, shared a Bf 109 on April 3, destroyed a Ju 87 and a Mc 202 on the 25th and was then hit himself and made a forced-landing near Gazala. Hanbury was awarded the DFC (22.5.42) and destroyed a Bf 109 and probably another on June 27. He was rested on July 19 and awarded a Bar to the DFC (28.7.42). He took command of 260 Squadron again on November 5 1942.

Hanbury claimed a Bf 109 destroyed on January 2 1943 and a Bf 110 on April 17. He was awarded the DSO (30.4.43) and posted away. He was killed on June 3 1943, flying with 117 Squadron. He was 25 and is remembered on the Runnymede Memorial, Panel 118.

PO 30.6.40   FO 30.8.41   FL 23.6.42

ERNEST LINDSAY HANCOCK

70278   FO   Pilot   British   609 Squadron

Whilst at Lincoln College, Oxford Hancock was a member of the University Air Squadron and was commissioned in the RAFVR in December 1936.

Called to full-time service at the outbreak of war, Hancock joined 609 Squadron at Middle Wallop on September 23 1940 and was posted away on January 23 1941.

Hancock was released from the RAF in 1945, as a Wing Commander. He was awarded the DFC (16.11.45), as an Acting Wing Commander with 186 Squadron, a Lancaster bomber unit, which operated from Stradishall prior to its disbandment on July 17 1945.

PO (RAFVR) 1.12.36   PO 4.9.39   FO 5.12.39   FL 5.12.40
SL 1.9.42

NORMAN EDWARD HANCOCK

83266   PO   Pilot   British   65 and 152 Squadrons

Hancock joined the RAF at the outbreak of war. He was posted to ITW at Trinity Hall College, Cambridge on September 5 1939, moved to 12 EFTS, Prestwick on March 26 1940, then to 5 FTS, Sealand on May 26.

With training completed Hancock went to 7 OTU, Hawarden on August 11 to convert to Spitfires, after which he joined 65 Squadron at Hornchurch on September 3, moving on to 152 Squadron at Warmwell on October 10. Hancock probably destroyed a Bf 110 off the Isle of Wight on November 28.

He was posted to 56 OTU, Sutton Bridge on October 22 1941, as an instructor, and went to 55 OTU, Usworth on February 2 1942. Hancock went to Northern Ireland on July 11 to instruct at the 52nd Pursuit Group USAF. He returned to operations on October 18 1942, when he joined 128 Squadron at Hastings, Sierra Leone, as a Flight Commander.

Back in the UK, Hancock was posted to 198 Squadron at Matlask on April 27 1943 and was with it until July 15, when he went to 56 Squadron at Martlesham Heath, as a Flight Commander. At the end of his tour on May 31 1944 Hancock was posted to 85 Group and awarded the DFC (23.6.44).

In May 1945 he took command of 276 (ASR) Squadron at Knocke and his final appointment was as Squadron Leader Admin at RAF Cranfield. He was released from the RAF in March 1946.

PO 10.8.40   FO 10.8.41   FL 10.8.42

NORMAN PATRICK WATKINS HANCOCK

42122   PO   Pilot   British   1 Squadron

Born on August 4 1919, Hancock joined the RAF on a short service commission on February 6 1939. He did his ab initio course at 15 E&RFTS, Redhill and 11 E&RFTS, Perth. Hancock went to 9 FTS, Hullavington on May 28 1939 and after completing his training joined 266 Squadron at Sutton Bridge on November 7.

He was posted to No 1 Squadron at Berry-au-Bac in France on May 12 1940. After two days he was detached to 501 Squadron but did not fly, spending his days moving around in lorries. Hancock rejoined No 1 on May 18 and served with it until the squadron was withdrawn from Nantes to Tangmere on June 18.

Flying from Northolt on August 16 1940 he returned to base with two longerons of his Hurricane severed in an attack by a Bf 110 over the South Downs. On the 30th Hancock damaged a He 111. He was posted away to 85 Squadron at Gravesend on December 23 but returned to No 1, then at Kenley, on January 29 1941.

On April 7 Hancock went to the RAF Depot at Uxbridge. On the 14th he embarked on HMS 'Argus' at Greenock and sailed for Gibraltar, where, on the 24th pilots and aircraft were transferred on to HMS 'Ark Royal'. Hancock led seven Hurricanes off to Malta on the 27th to join 261 Squadron at Hal Far. When the squadron was disbanded in May Hancock joined the newly-reformed 185 Squadron on the 12th. He was appointed 'B' Flight Commander the next day, when Flight Lieutenant IB Westmacott was wounded.

Hancock crash-landed on May 20 after his engine failed due to a fuel-supply fault. He probably destroyed a He 111 in the early hours of June 6, shared a BR 20 on July 25 and shared a SM 79 on the 27th.

He was posted away to AHQ, Cairo on September 17 1941 and went to instruct at 71 OTU, Gordon's Tree, Sudan on October 1. The unit moved to RAF Carthago, Port Sudan on April 26 1942 and on June 8 Hancock was posted to Almaza. He did a short refresher course at El Ballah, was attached to 5 (SAAF) Squadron on July 1 and then joined 250 Squadron at LG 91 on July 9, as a Flight Commander. Hancock shot down a SM 79 at sea level on the 27th. He took command of the squadron on November 28 and on December 15 received an immediate award of the DFC (29.12.42). This award was for an operation flown on November 17. Hancock led twelve Kittyhawks of 250 and six from 405 (RAAF) Squadron from Gazala to Benina airfield. Intelligence had reported that converted bombers from Crete were delivering petrol for the Afrika Korps. After a flight through bad weather and low cloud the Kittyhawks arrived as seven enemy bombers, He 111s and SM 79s, were in the circuit and five had landed. 250 Squadron accounted for the bombers still in the air, Hancock destroying a He 111. The Kittyhawks then strafed the airfield, destroying three SM 79s on the ground. They all returned safely and the squadron's score passed the 100 mark, of enemy aircraft destroyed in the air.

On February 4 1943 Hancock was posted away and in March he was seconded to the Turkish Air Force, as liaison officer to the TAF Kittyhawk Squadron and also giving fighter tactics training. He returned to Egypt in January 1944, for a course at ABGS, El Ballah. Hancock was then seconded to 2 Squadron of the Royal Egyptian Air Force, as liaison officer and instructor.

He went to HQ 216 Group, Transport Command, Heliopolis in February 1945, as an Air Staff Officer. He attended a course at Netheravon in June, his first visit to the UK since April 1941.

Hancock returned to the UK in January 1946 and became Station Commander at RAF Aberporth and CO of 595 Squadron. He retired from the RAF on August 12 1958, as a Squadron Leader, retaining the rank of Wing Commander. In 1980 he became Hon Secretary and Treasurer of the Battle of Britain Fighter Association.

APO 6.2.39   PO 6.11.39   FO 6.11.40   FL 6.11.41
SL 1.7.45   SL 1.8.47

GEORGE HENRY HANNAN

79237   PO   Air Gunner   British   236 Squadron

Hannan, of Dumfriesshire, joined 236 Squadron in June 1940. He was one of the crew of a Blenheim, which failed to return from a reconnaissance sortie over Brest on December 21 1940. The pilot, Squadron Leader GW Montagu, the observer, Sergeant DR Briggs and Hannan were all reported 'Missing'. Their bodies were recovered by the Germans.

Hannan was 30 years old. He is buried in Bayeux War Cemetery, France.

PO 15.6.40

DAVID HARRY WELLSTED HANSON

33363   FO   Pilot   British   17 Squadron

Born on January 25 1918, Hanson was educated at Winchester College He entered RAF College, Cranwell in September 1936 as a flight cadet. He graduated in December 1938 and in early 1940 was with 17 Squadron at Debden.

Over Dunkirk on May 26 he damaged a Do 17, on the 29th he was slightly wounded in the right leg, on June 3 he damaged a Ju 87 and on the 14th probably destroyed a Bf 109.

Hanson claimed a share in destroying a Do 17 on July 12. After destroying a Do 17 on September 3 Hanson was himself shot down. He baled out at 100 feet and was killed. His Hurricane, P 3539, crashed at Blockhouse Farm, Foulness. Hanson is buried in All Saints' churchyard, Mappleton, Yorkshire.

PO 17.12.38   FO 17.6.40

JOSEF JAN HANUS

82546   PO   Pilot   Czechoslovakian   310 Squadron

Born on September 13 1911, Hanus joined the Czech Air Force in 1932. He trained as an observer/navigator but later retrained as a pilot. In 1939 he left his country and travelled to France, via Poland. The only unit open to the Czechs was the French Foreign Legion.

At the outbreak of war Hanus was seconded to l'Armée de l'Air as a Sergeant-Pilot. He trained all over again and was afterwards posted to a French fighter squadron, as a lieutenant, flying Ms 406s. After the German blitz in May 1940 Hanus retreated through France, eventually reaching the Spanish border. He took a French ship to Oran, a train to Casablanca, sailed in a collier to Gibraltar and then got on a troopship, which sailed in a convoy for sixteen days to Liverpool.

In early August Hanus was commissioned and posted to 6 OTU, Sutton Bridge, where he converted to Hurricanes, afterwards joining 310 Squadron at Duxford in early September. He remained with the squadron until May 21 1941, when he went to 32 Squadron at Angle. On September 15 1941 Hanus moved to 245 Squadron at Chilbolton.

He was posted to 54 OTU, Church Fenton on January 1 1942, to convert to Beaufighters. Hanus joined 600 Squadron at Predannack on February 17 and was attached for a while to 125 Squadron at Fairwood Common for further training. He went to 68 Squadron at Coltishall on September 13, was posted away later and on December 25 1942 was in transit to North Africa, in a Beaufighter.

Hanus arrived at Setif on January 10 1943 and rejoined 600 Squadron. On March 16 he damaged a Do 217, destroyed Ju 88s on April 4,21 and 24 and was given an immediate award of the DFC (26.5.43). He destroyed a Ju 88 on September 16, was posted back to the UK on December 8 1943, arrived on February 28 1944 and went to HQ Fighter Command as Technical Liaison Officer.

On August 22 1944 Hanus flew back to Prague in an Auster. He served in the Czech Air Force and left Czechoslovakia again on July 8 1948. His wife and two children had preceded him some months earlier. He rejoined the RAF and was posted on November 2 1948 to 23 Squadron at Coltishall. Hanus did a Control course at Middle Wallop, served with 141 Squadron from January 1949 and in June 1951 went on to Flying Control. He lost his flying category in late 1954 and trained as an Equipment Officer, serving in this capacity until retiring on September 19 1968, as a Flight Lieutenant, retaining the rank of Squadron Leader.

PO 2.8.40   FO 27.12.40   FL 27.12.41   FL 11.9.49

OTTO HANZLICEK

787697   Sgt   Pilot   Czechoslovakian   312 Squadron

Born on June 18 1911, Hanzlicek escaped to Poland in the summer of 1939. He later went to France and after some training at the Central Fighter School at Chartres he joined Groupe de Chasse ll/5 at Toul-Croix-de-Metz in December 1939, flying Curtis Hawk 75s.

On April 23 he probably destroyed a Do 17, on May 11 destroyed a He 111 and on the 18th shared a Bf 109 but was himself shot down and baled out. He was awarded the C de G (Fr) and the Czech Military Cross.

After the fall of France Hanzlicek escaped with other Czechs to North Africa and reached England, via Gibraltar. He joined 312 Squadron at Speke on September 19 1940. During a routine patrol on October 10 Hanzlicek's aircraft caught fire and he baled out into the river at Oglett and was killed. The Hurricane, L 1547, crashed into the mud of the River Mersey. Hanzlicek is buried in a joint grave with Pilot Officer J Bartos in West Derby Cemetery, Liverpool.

JOHN REGINALD HARDACRE

41405   FO   Pilot   British   504 Squadron

Born in Birmingham on June 26 1916, Hardacre joined the RAF on a short service commission in October 1938. He was with 504 Squadron in France in May 1940.

Hardacre was shot down twice on May 16, the first time crash-landing in a field and the second time baling out safely from a flaming aircraft.

On September 7 he claimed a Bf 110 destroyed and on the 15th a Do 215. Hardacre was shot down in combat over the south-west coast on September 30 1940 and killed. His Hurricane, P 3414, crashed into the sea. Hardacre's body was washed ashore on October 10. He is buried in All Saints' churchyard, Fawley, Hampshire. His logbook showed five confirmed victories and two enemy aircraft damaged.

APO 14.12.38   PO 3.9.39   FO 3.9.40

JACK HARDCASTLE

627887   Sgt   Wop/AG   British   219 Squadron

Joined 219 Squadron at Catterick on July 13 1940. Hardcastle was killed in an accident on October 28 1940, serving as a Sergeant with 105 Squadron at Swanton Morley.

He is buried in Whitkirk Cemetery, Leeds, Yorkshire.

HARDIE

No unknown   **Sgt**   **Pilot**   **British**   **232 Squadron**

No service details traced.

NELSON MAXWELL HARDING

39519   **FL**   **Pilot**   **British**   **23 Squadron**

Harding joined the RAF on a short service commission in January 1937. He was posted to 5 FTS, Sealand on March 20, joined 23 Squadron at Wittering on October 23 1937 and was still serving with the squadron in early July 1940.

Harding was killed on September 16 1944, serving as a Flight Lieutenant with 78 Squadron, operating in Halifaxes from Breighton, Yorkshire. He is remembered on the Runnymede Memorial, Panel 202.

APO 8.3.37   *PO 21.12.37*   *FO 21.9.39*   *FL 21.9.40*

NOEL DOUGLAS HARDING

116522   **Sgt**   **Aircrew**   **British**   **29 Squadron**

With 29 Squadron at Digby in early July 1940. Commissioned in February 1942, Harding transferred to the Administrative Branch later in the year. He was released in 1945.

PO 9.2.42   *FO 1.10.42*

HARRY GORDON HARDMAN

40535   **PO**   **Pilot**   **Australian**   **111 Squadron**

Joined the RAF on a short service commission in October 1937. Hardman was posted to 5 FTS, Sealand on March 5 1938 and joined 111 Squadron at Northolt on September 17 1938.

Hardman was posted away from the squadron in early September 1940.

He was released from the RAF in 1945, as a Squadron Leader.

APO 19.2.38   *PO 25.10.38*   *FO 25.7.40*   *FL 6.12.41*
SL 1.1.44

WILLIAM ROBERT HARROLD HARDWICK

801495   **Sgt**   **Aircrew**   **British**   **600 Squadron**

With 600 Squadron at Northolt in early July 1940. Hardwick was commissioned in the Training Branch of the RAFVR in late 1945. (Officer's Number 202458).

APO (RAFVR) 18.11.45   *PO (RAFVR) 1.7.46*
FO (RAFVR) 28.6.54

OSWALD ANTHONY HARDY

133487   **Sgt**   **Air Gunner**   **British**   **264 Squadron**

Hardy joined 264 Squadron at Kirton-in-Lindsey in early August 1940. Later in the month Hardy took part in 264's last day-fighting engagements. On the 28th he was in Defiant N 1569, flying with Pilot Officer JRA Bailey, when it was severely damaged in combat with Bf 109s of JG 26. Bailey made a forced-landing at Court Lodge Farm, Petham.

In 1941 Hardy broke both legs baling out over London after being shot down by anti-aircraft fire. Commissioned in August 1942, he was awarded the DFC (23.3.45), as a Flight Lieutenant with 550 Squadron, operating in Lancasters from North Killingholme, Lincolnshire.

Hardy was released from the RAF in 1947, as a Squadron Leader.

PO 31.8.42   *FO 3.3.43*   *FL 31.8.44*

RICHARD HARDY

41921   **PO**   **Pilot**   **British**   **234 Squadron**

Joined the RAF on a short service commission in February 1939. After completion of training Hardy joined the newly-reformed 234 Squadron at Leconfield on November 6 1939.

In combat with enemy fighters off Swanage on August 15 1940, Hardy's Spitfire, N 3277, was severely damaged. He was forced to land by Bf 109s near Cherbourg and was captured.

Freed in May 1945, Hardy was released from the RAF in 1946.

APO 15.4.39   *PO 6.11.39*   *FO 6.11.40*   *FL 6.11.41*

MAXWELL HARE

758138   **Sgt**   **Pilot**   **British**   **245 Squadron**

Hare, of Portsmouth, joined 245 Squadron at Aldergrove on October 4 1940. In June 1941 he was in the carrier HMS 'Furious', bound for Malta. On the 30th his was the second Hurricane to take off. Half way along the deck he swerved, hit the navigating position, his long range tanks burst and the petrol caught fire. Three naval men were killed and fourteen naval and nine RAF men were injured.

Hare died from his injuries. He was 19 and is buried in the North Front Cemetery, Gibraltar.

FREDERICK NORMAN HARGREAVES

42502   **PO**   **Pilot**   **British**   **92 Squadron**

Hargreaves joined the RAF on a short service commission in June 1939. He was posted to 92 Squadron at Croydon in March 1940.

Having lost his bearings during night flying from Bibury on August 27 Hargreaves baled out and landed at Red House Farm, Blaxhall. His Spitfire, P 9548, crashed near Marlesford, Suffolk.

Hargreaves failed to return from a combat over Dungeness on September 11 and was reported 'Missing'. His Spitfire, K 9793, is presumed to have crashed into the sea. He was 21 and is remembered on the Runnymede Memorial, Panel 8.

APO 19.8.39   *PO 10.2.40*

ALAN STUART HARKER

63791   **Sgt**   **Pilot**   **British**   **234 Squadron**

Born in Bolton, Lancashire, Harker joined the RAFVR in 1937 and carried out his training at 18 E&RFTS, Fair Oaks. Called up at the outbreak of war, he was posted to 10 FTS, Tern Hill on September 12 1939 for a twin-engine course on Ansons.

Harker volunteered for night-fighters and joined the newly-formed 234 Squadron at Leconfield on November 5. The squadron converted from Blenheims to Spitfires in May 1940.

On August 18 Harker claimed two Bf 109s destroyed, on September 4 a Bf 110, on the 6th two Bf 109s, on the 7th a Bf 109 and on the 22nd a Ju 88. He was awarded the DFM (22.10.40) and commissioned in March 1941.

During a low-level attack by He 111s on Warmwell on April 1 1941 Harker was wounded in the arm. He was shot down on a convoy patrol near Weymouth on May 19 and crash-landed in a field near Warmwell.

Harker was posted to 53 OTU, Llandow on August 4 1941, as a Flight Commander. He went to CGS, Sutton Bridge on June 27 1942, as an instructor, and moved to Llanbedr in December 1943 to form a Rocket Projectile School. On July 15 1944 Harker was posted to Italy, where he served as an MT Officer with a mobile radar unit and later as an Operations Officer with US Liberator and Polish supply-dropping squadrons. He was released from the RAF in November 1945, as a Flight Lieutenant.

PO 19.3.41   *FO 19.3.42*   *FL 19.3.43*

HILL HARKNESS

29208   SL   Pilot   Irish   257 Squadron

Harkness joined the RAF in December 1930. He was posted to 2 FTS, Digby on January 10 1931 and went to 54 Squadron at Hornchurch on December 29 1931. He joined the staff at the School of Naval Co-operation at Lee-on-Solent on January 6 1935 and went on to the RAFO on December 29 1936.

Recalled in October 1939, Harkness was given command of 257 Squadron at Northolt on July 22 1940. He claimed a Ju 88 destroyed on August 13 and was posted away on September 12 1940. He resigned his commission on December 4 1943.

PO 29.12.30   FO 29.8.32   FL 1.4.36   FL (RAFO) 29.12.36
FL 16.10.39   SL 1.6.40

THOMAS PATRICK HARNETT

41347   FO   Pilot   Canadian   219 Squadron

Harnett, of Moncton, joined the RCAF on January 3 1938 and transferred to the RAF on November 6 1938. His first posting was as a staff pilot to Penrhos.

In early July 1940 Harnett was with 219 Squadron at Catterick. He was posted back to Canada in January 1941, as an instructor. On November 11 1943 he transferred back into the RCAF (C 799).

In September 1944 Harnett went to India to form and command 435 (RCAF) Squadron, which flew Dakotas on supply drops to the 14th Army. He was awarded the DFC (19.10.45). Harnett was released from the RCAF on September 10 1946, as a Wing Commander. He died on December 19 1985.

PO 6.11.38   FO 6.6.40   FL 6.6.41

WILLIAM JOHN HARPER

40110   FO   Pilot   British   17 Squadron

Born in Calcutta on July 22 1916, Harper was educated at North Point, India and Windsor, England. He joined the RAF on a short service commission in July 1937, was posted to 6 FTS, Netheravon on September 18 and went on to the staff at RAF Leuchars on May 7 1938.

Harper was with 17 Squadron in early 1940 and over Dunkirk on May 29 he shared in probably destroying a Bf 110. After probably destroying a Bf 109 on August 15 he was shot down and crash-landed near Laurel Farm, outside Felixstowe, on a dead engine. Harper was admitted to Felixstowe Cottage Hospital with face and leg wounds.

On March 23 1941 he was posted to 57 OTU, Hawarden, to instruct. From October 1941 to March 1942 Harper commanded 453 Squadron in the Malaya/Java area, in June/July 1942 he commanded 135 Squadron at Dum Dum and from January to May 1943 he commanded 92 Squadron in North Africa.

Harper retired from the RAF on April 22 1949. He emigrated to Rhodesia and began farming but turned to mining and started an earth-moving business. In May 1958 he was elected to the Southern Rhodesian Parliment, as Member for Gatooma. Harper became President of the Dominion Party in 1959. He resigned on February 2 1962 to coordinate opposition to the United Federal Party Government. When the Rhodesian Front came to power on December 17 1962 Harper became a Cabinet Minister. On April 13 1964, when Ian Smith was elected, Harper was appointed Minister of Internal Affairs. He split with Smith on July 4 1968, resigned as an MP and left the Rhodesian Front Party. He was out of public life until February 1972, when he became one of the founders of the United Front Party. Harper was noted for his strong views on white supremacy

APO 5.9.37   PO 12.7.38   FO 12.2.40   FL 12.2.41
SL 1.3.42   SL 1.8.47

PATRICK ARTHUR HARRIS

86328   PO   Pilot   British   3 Squadron

Harris, of Ash Vale, Surrey, joined 3 Squadron at Turnhouse on September 30 1940. He was killed on June 17 1941, as a Pilot Officer with 56 Squadron.

Harris was 20. He is remembered on the Runnymede Memorial, Panel 33.

PO 31.8.40

ANTHONY ROBERT JAMES HARRISON

812347   Sgt   Air Gunner   British   219 Squadron

Joined 219 Squadron at Catterick in July 1940. He was killed on July 2 1941, as a Flight Sergeant with 149 Squadron, operating in Wellingtons from Mildenhall.

Harrison was 20. He is buried in Kerfautras Cemetery, Brest, France.

DAVID STEWART HARRISON

83290   PO   Pilot   British   238 Squadron

Born in Sidcup, Kent on June 10 1911, Harrison was at Tonbridge School from 1925 to 1927. He joined the RAFVR on January 16 1939 and was called to full-time service after the outbreak of war. Harrison was posted to 4 ITW on December 13, went to 9 FTS, Hullavington on May 11 1940, moved to 6 OTU, Sutton Bridge to convert to Hurricanes on August 17 and joined 238 Squadron at Middle Wallop on September 12.

Harrison made a forced-landing outside Padstock on the 25th, following a combat with enemy aircraft. He was shot down by Bf 109s over the Solent on September 28 1940. His Hurricane, P 3836, crashed into the sea and Harrison was reported 'Missing'.

His body was washed ashore at Brighton on October 9 and he was buried in St Andrew's churchyard, Tangmere.

PO 17.8.40

JOHN HOWARD HARRISON

75677   PO   Pilot   British   145 Squadron

Harrison was born in Mitcham, Surrey on November 11 1917. He joined 145 Squadron at Westhampnett in early August 1940. He failed to return from a combat with Ju 88s and Bf 110s south of the Isle of Wight on August 12 and was reported 'Missing'.

Harrison was 22. He is remembered on the Runnymede Memorial, Panel 8.

PO 24.12.39

FREDERICK CECIL HARROLD

42707 **PO** **Pilot** **British** **501 and 151 Squadrons**

Harrold was with 501 Squadron at Croydon in early July 1940. He went to 151 Squadron at Stapleford on August 26 but rejoined 501, then at Kenley, on September 26.

On the 28th Harrold was shot down by Bf 109s and killed. His Hurricane, P 3417, crashed at the Strawberry Plantations, College House, Ulcombe and burned out.

Harrold was 23 years old. He is buried in St Andrew's churchyard, Cherry Hinton, Cambridgeshire.

PO 20.4.40

JOHN STEWART HART

41696 **FO** **Pilot** **Canadian** **54 and 602 Squadrons**

Hart, of Sackville, New Brunswick, was at Mount Allison University and learned to fly at Halifax Flying Club. He joined the RAF on a short service commission in January 1939.

He joined 54 Squadron at Catterick in mid-September 1940 but moved soon afterwards to 602 Squadron at Westhampnett. On October 29 Hart claimed a Bf 109 destroyed and on November 13 he shared a Ju 88. In early 1941 he was with 91 Squadron at Hawkinge, went back to 602 and then went to OTU, as an instructor.

Hart commanded 67 Squadron in Burma from May to July 1943 and 112 Squadron in Italy from April to August 1945. He was awarded the DFC (22.6.45) and released from the RAF in 1946, as a Squadron Leader.

APO 4.3.39   *PO 2.10.39*   *FO 2.10.40*   *FL 2.10.41*
SL 1.7.45

KENNETH GRAHAM HART

42222 **PO** **Pilot** **British** **65 Squadron**

Hart was born in Mitcham, Surrey and educated at Heath Clark School. He joined the RAF on a short service commission in April 1939 and was with 65 Squadron at Hornchurch in March 1940.

On a patrol to Dunkirk on May 22 Hart's engine burst into flames and he crash-landed at North Foreland and burned out. On the 26th Hart claimed a Bf 109 destroyed and was himself shot down, crash-landed on a beach at Dunkirk and returned to England by ship. On June 25 he claimed a Bf 109, on July 5 shared a He 111 and on August 12 claimed another Bf 109 destroyed. He made a forced-landing on Havengore Island, Foulness on August 20, in Spitfire R 6818, after his engine was damaged by a Bf 109 in combat over the Thames Estuary. Hart probably destroyed a Bf 109 on August 24 and shared a He 111 on November 5.

He was posted to 250 Squadron in the Western Desert in mid-1941 and was awarded the DFC (20.1.42), being then credited with at least eight enemy aircraft destroyed.

Hart was killed on December 28 1944, as a Squadron Leader with 18 Squadron, operating in Bostons from Falconara, Italy. He was 23 and is buried in Coriano Ridge War Cemetery, Italy.

APO 24.6.39   *PO 27.12.39*   *FO 27.12.40*   *FL 27.12.41*

NORRIS HART

81879 **PO** **Pilot** **Canadian** **242 Squadron**

Hart was born in Montreal and brought up in Hamilton. He was posted to 242 Squadron at Coltishall on July 18 1940 but lacking Hurricane experience was sent to 5 OTU, Aston Down and rejoined 242 on August 12.

He claimed a He 111 destroyed on August 30, a Bf 109 on September 15 and two Ju 88s on the 18th. Hart did not return from a combat with Bf 109s off Sheerness on November 5 1940, in Hurricane P 2806. He was 25 and is remembered on the Runnymede Memorial, Panel 8.

PO 7.7.40

PETER McDONNELL HARTAS

41407 **FO** **Pilot** **British** **603 Squadron and 421 Flight**

Joined the RAF on a short service commission in October 1938. Hartas was posted to 603 Squadron at Hornchurch on September 24 1940. He claimed a Bf 109 destroyed on October 2.

Hartas joined 421 Flight, when it was formed at Hawkinge in October 1940. He claimed a Bf 109 destroyed over the Channel on December 1 and shared a probable Do 17 off Dover on December 18. He was killed on February 10 1941, as a Flying Officer with 91 Squadron.

Hartas was 21. He is buried in Folkestone New Cemetery.

APO 14.12.38   *PO 3.9.39*   *FO 3.9.40*

LESLIE WALTER HARVEY

176381 **Sgt** **Pilot** **British** **54 and 245 Squadrons**

Joined 54 Squadron at Hornchurch on August 22 1940 and moved to 245 Squadron at Aldergrove on September 27.

Commissioned in April 1944, Harvey was released in 1946, as a Flight Lieutenant.

PO 5.4.44   *FO 5.10.44*

DOUGLAS HASTINGS

42406 **PO** **Pilot** **British** **74 Squadron**

Hastings, of North Shields, joined 74 Squadron at Hornchurch in May 1940. He claimed a Bf 109 destroyed on August 11 and a Do 17 on the 13th.

During a flight making practice attacks over Coltishall on October 9 1940 Hastings collided with Pilot Officer Buckland and was killed when he crashed, inverted, south of Green Farm, Gillingham, in Spitfire P 7329.

Hastings was 25. He is buried in Preston Cemetery, Tynemouth, Northumberland.

PO 6.4.40

———— HATTON

No unknown **Sgt** **Aircrew** **British** **604 Squadron**

No service details traced.

RALPH EDWARD HAVERCROFT

114000 **Sgt** **Pilot** **British** **92 Squadron**

Born on June 14 1916, Havercroft joined the RAFVR in April 1937. He trained at 4 E&RFTS, Brough and had 250 hours flying by April 1939, when, being of suitable standard and experience he took the opportunity to train with the regular RAF. He was attached to 41 Squadron at Catterick from May 1 to July 10 1939 for Spitfire instruction, after which he returned to his job with a Hull cement company until called up on September 1.

Havercroft went to the 11 Group Pool at St Athan, where he converted to the Hurricane. He was then posted to 604 Squadron at North Weald on September 11, on Blenheims. His short stature made flying the Blenheim difficult and on March 14 1940 Havercroft was posted to 92 Squadron at Croydon.

On August 13 he shared in the destruction of a Ju 88. On July 15 1941 he was appointed test pilot to the Aircraft Gun Mounting Establishment at Duxford, where he flew a Beaufighter with 40 mm cannons. He was commissioned in November 1941. On January 18

RE Havercroft (continued)

1942 his unit was incorporated with the A&AEE at Boscombe Down.

Havercroft went into the Armament Testing Squadron. In April 1944 he was selected to go to the newly-formed Test Pilots' School on No 2 Course. After the war he returned to Boscombe Down, to the Performance Testing Squadron. He later went to the US as a test pilot for the British Air Commission at White Field, near Dayton, Ohio.

Havercroft held a series of appointments and commands in the post-war RAF. He was awarded the AFC (1.1.49) and retired on June 4 1963, as a Wing Commander. He then worked for Hunting Engineering until June 1981.

PO 17.11.41   FO 1.10.42   FL 17.11.43   SL 1.8.47
WC 1.1.55

JOHN KENNETH HAVILAND

82690   PO   Pilot   American   151 Squadron

Born on January 19 1921 in Mount Kisco, New York, Haviland was the son of a US Navy officer and an English mother. He spent most of his early life in England, starting school there at the age of five. Haviland went to Nottingham University at 17. He obtained his 'A' License and joined the RAFVR.

Called up at the outbreak of war, Haviland was posted to ITW at Pembroke College, Cambridge in November 1939. After completing his flying training he went to the No 1 School of Army Co-operation, Old Sarum. He volunteered for Fighter Command, was posted to 6 OTU, Sutton Bridge in August 1940 and after converting to Hurricanes joined 151 Squadron at Digby on September 23. The following day he collided with another Hurricane during formation practice and made a forced-landing in a paddock at Waddington.

After leaving 151 Haviland became an instructor. He did two further tours, on intruder and bomber support operations, and was awarded the DFC (16.2.45), as a Flight Lieutenant with 141 Squadron.

Haviland was released from the RAF on December 3 1945, completed his degree and moved to Canada, where he served in the RCAF Reserve, flying Vampires. He later became a Professor at the School of Engineering, University of Virginia, involved in aerospace projects.

PO 27.7.40   FO 27.7.41   FL 27.7.42

RICHARD HAVILAND

76571   PO   Pilot   South African   248 Squadron

Haviland was with 248 Squadron in early July 1940. On August 7 he ditched in the sea off St Abbs Head due to fuel shortage. The Blenheim was towed into land by a trawler and salvaged. Haviland and his crew were picked up from their dinghy and landed at South Shields.

He was killed in a flying accident on August 28 1940. Haviland was 27 and was cremated at Aberdeen Crematorium.

PO 6.11.39

CHARLTON HAW

117992   Sgt   Pilot   British   504 Squadron

Born on May 8 1920 in York, Haw worked as an apprentice lithographer. He joined the RAFVR in October 1938 and began his elementary flying training at 4 E&RFTS, Brough.

Called up on September 1 1939, Haw was posted to ITW at Bexhill in October and in November went to 5 FTS, Sealand. After completing the course Haw was posted to 6 OTU at Sutton Bridge, but went instead directly to 504 Squadron at Wick in late May 1940.

On September 27 Haw claimed a Bf 110 destroyed and was himself shot down in combat over Bristol and landed at Gammons Farm, Kilmington, Axminster, unhurt.

In late July 1941 'A' Flight of 504 was re-numbered 81 Squadron and posted to Leconfield. The personnel were kitted out for an unknown overseas destination. They flew to Abbotsinch in Harrows and embarked for Russia on the carrier HMS 'Argus', which carried crated Hurricanes. On September 1 the squadron flew off in sixes for Vaenga airfield, near Murmansk.

On September 12 Haw destroyed a Bf 109, on the 17th another and a third later in the month. Operations, including bomber escorts, continued until mid-November, when pilots of the squadron began converting Russian pilots on to Hurricanes. They left Russia on November 29, leaving all equipment behind and returned in HMS 'Kenya', landing at Rosyth on December 7 1941. Haw was awarded the DFM (23.1.42) and the Order of Lenin (31.3.42), one of four given by the Russians.

81 Squadron went to Turnhouse, where it received Spitfire Vbs. Commissioned in March 1942, Haw rejoined 504 for a short time but in late May was posted to 122 Squadron at Hornchurch. In February 1943 he was given command of 611 Squadron at Biggin Hill. In May Haw was sent on a tour of factories speaking to workers and in July was posted to the staff of the Fighter Leaders' School at Milfield.

In November 1943 he returned to operations, when he took command of 129 Squadron at Hornchurch, leading it until July 1944, when he returned to the Fighter Leaders' School. Haw was awarded the DFC (17.10.44). He was posted to Wittering in October 1944 to a unit, which became the Central Fighter Establishment and moved to Tangmere in December 1944.

Haw commanded 65 Squadron from 1946 to 1948. Granted a Permanent Commission in 1948, he later lost his flying category because of eyesight and retired from the RAF on September 19 1951, as a Flight Lieutenant, retaining the rank of Squadron Leader. As a holder of the Order of Lenin, Haw was invited to Moscow in 1985 to attend the celebrations marking the 40th Anniversary of the end of the war.

PO 6.3.42   FO 1.10.42   FL 17.5.43   FL 10.2.46

PETER SYDNEY HAWKE

126862   Sgt   Pilot   British   64 and 19 Squadrons

Born on August 13 1918 at Reading, Berkshire, Hawke joined the RAFVR in November 1937 and did his weekend flying at 8 E&RFTS, Woodley. Called up at the outbreak of war, he was posted to 4 ITW, Bexhill on November 22 1939 and then to 10 FTS, Tern Hill on February 1 1940.

With training completed Hawke went to 5 OTU, Aston Down on July 6 and after converting to Spitfires he joined 64 Squadron at Kenley on the 27th. He claimed a He 111 destroyed on August 18. Hawke moved to 19 Squadron at Duxford on September 20. He was posted away to CFS, Upavon on November 9 1940, for an instructor's course.

Hawke instructed at 8 EFTS, Reading from December 12 1940 until December 3 1941, when he went to 6 FIS, Staverton. Commissioned in June 1942, Hawke was posted to 2 EFTS, Worcester on July 22, moving to 29 EFTS, Clyffe Pypard on September 16. He was awarded the AFC (1.1.46). Hawke was released from the RAF in 1946, as a Flight Lieutenant. He died on May 12 1988.

PO 1.6.42   FO 1.12.42   FL 1.6.44

STANLEY NELSON HAWKE

804142   **Sgt**   **Air Gunner**   **British**   **604 Squadron**

Hawke, of Stockwell, London was with 604 Squadron at Northolt in early July 1940 and served with the squadron until his death.

On May 29 1941 Hawke went with Pilot Officer PF Jackson and an Australian pilot, who was new to the squadron, on an air-sea firing exercise at Chesil Beach. Whilst they were there the clouds came in from the sea blanketing the Dorset hills. Instead of climbing above them Jackson flew through and crashed on high ground. All three men were killed.

Hawke was 25. He is buried in Streatham Park Cemetery, Mitcham, Surrey.

REDVERS PERCIVAL HAWKINGS

748627   **Sgt**   **Pilot**   **British**   **601 Squadron**

With 601 Squadron at Tangmere in June 1940. On July 7 he shared in the destruction of a Do 17.

Hawkings was shot down in combat over the Sussex coast on August 18 1940 and killed. His Hurricane, L 1990, crashed off Summer Lane, Nyetimber, Pagham. He was 22 years old and is buried in St Peter's churchyard, Filton, Gloucestershire.

FREDERICK BERNARD HAWLEY

748286   **Sgt**   **Pilot**   **British**   **266 Squadron**

Hawley, of Coventry, was with 266 Squadron at Wittering in early July 1940. On August 15 he was reported 'Missing', following the destruction of a He 115 off Dunkirk and is believed to have crashed into the sea, in Spitfire N 3189.

Hawley was 23 and is remembered on the Runnymede Memorial, Panel 15.

JOSEPH FREDERICK JOHN HAWORTH

39734   **FO**   **Pilot**   **British**   **43 Squadron**

Haworth, of Teddington, Middlesex, joined the RAF on a short service commission in March 1937. He was posted to 2 FTS, Brize Norton on June 5 and joined 25 Squadron at Hawkinge on January 8 1938.

In June 1940 Haworth was posted to 43 Squadron at Tangmere. Whilst investigating a He 115 south of the Needles on July 20 1940 he was shot down into the sea, in Hurricane P 3964. Haworth baled out but was never found. He was 23 and is remembered on the Runnymede Memorial, Panel 5.

APO 18.5.37   *PO 15.3.38*   *FO 15.11.39*

IAN BRUCE DAVID ERROLL HAY

72483   **FO**   **Pilot**   **South African**   **611 Squadron**

Born in Johannesburg on June 4 1916, Hay was at Rugby School from 1930 to 1933. He obtained his 'A' License in 1934 and joined the Cambridge University Air Squadron in 1937, when he was at Trinity Hall. He was commissioned in the RAFVR in September 1938.

Called up in September 1939, Hay was posted to 6 FTS, Little Rissington in October and joined 611 Squadron at Digby in April 1940. He left the squadron in early 1941 and became Sector Controller at Digby and later Coltishall, Tangmere and Exeter, among others.

Hay was invalided out of the RAF in 1945, as a Wing Commander. He returned to South Africa, where he was a director of Miles Aircraft, of Rand Mines 1950-52 and Central Mining and Investment Corporation from 1952.

PO (RAFVR) 27.9.38   *PO 25.9.39*   *FO 27.3.40*   *FL 6.4.41*
SL 10.7.44

RONALD CUTHBERT HAY

Lieutenant (RM)   **Pilot**   **British**   **808 Squadron**

Hay joined the Royal Marines in 1935. He was with HMS 'Ark Royal' for the Norwegian campaign and had taken part in the evacuation of Dunkirk. In early July 1940 he was with 808 Squadron at Wick, flying Fulmars on dockyard defence. Hay served again on 'Ark Royal' in the Mediterranean in 1941 on the Malta convoys. He shared in destroying a Sm 79 on May 8, shared a Cant Z 506B on July 23 and shared another on September 28. He was awarded the DSC (25.11.41).

From August 1942 Hay commanded 809 Squadron, flying from HMS 'Victorious', and took part in Operation 'Torch', the landings in North Africa. In August 1944 Hay was appointed Wing Leader 47 Wing, operating from 'Victorious' against the Japanese in Sumatra. In December 1944 he was made Air Coordinator to 1st Aircraft Carrier Squadron and led all the strikes against oil refineries and airfields. Hay was awarded the DSO (1.5.45) for gallantry in air strikes against oil tanks at Palembang and a Bar to the DSC (31.7.45).

He returned to the Royal Marines after the war but transferred to the Royal Navy in 1947. Hay retired in November 1966, as a Commander.

2nd Lt (RM) 1.9.35   *Lt (RM) 1.10.37*   *Capt (RM) 16.11.42*
Actg Major (RM) 1944   *Actg Lt-Col (RM) 1945*   *Lt-Cdr 1.9.47*
Cdr 30.6.55

LAWRENCE HAMILTON HAYDEN

67041   **Sgt**   **Air Gunner**   **British**   **264 Squadron**

With 264 Squadron at Duxford in early July 1940. Hayden was awarded the DFM (11.2.41).

Commissioned in May 1941, he was released from the RAF in 1945, as a Flight Lieutenant.

PO 17.5.41   *FO 17.5.42*   *FL 17.5.43*

HERBERT LEONARD HAYES

20175   **SL**   **Pilot**   **British**   **242 Squadron**

Hayes was a Lieutenant Commander RN, who held an RAF commission as a Squadron Leader. He transferred to the RAF on July 26 1938, with seniority from January 1. He appeared in the Air Force List until the end of 1942.

It would appear that he must have flown at least one authorised operational sortie with 242 Squadron during the Battle of Britain period to qualify for the clasp but he was certainly not on the strength of the squadron.

THOMAS NORMAN HAYES

90095   **FL**   **Pilot**   **British**   **600 Squadron**

Joined 600 Squadron, AuxAF in 1936. Hayes was called to full-time service on August 24 1939.

On May 10 1940 Hayes flew one of six Blenheims, which attacked Rotterdam airfield in daylight. In company with the CO he shared

TN Hayes (continued)

in destroying a Ju 52 on the ground by machine gun fire. Climbing away, the Blenheims were attacked by twelve Bf 110s, which Hayes, instructed by his gunner, managed to evade. Soon afterwards he saw a Ju 52 and in spite of being harrassed by enemy aircraft and his own aircraft being damaged he attacked the Ju 52 until it was seen to go down with its port engine on fire. He then evaded his attackers and headed for home but encountered three He 115s, upon which he expended his remaining ammunition, breaking up their formation. Hayes then got safely back to base, the only Blenheim of the six which set out to do so. He was awarded the DFC (24.5.40).

From October 1942 to June 1943 Hayes commanded 256 Squadron. He was later Station Commander at West Malling and commanded 149 Wing in Europe in 1944/45. He was released from the RAF in 1945, as a Wing Commander.

Hayes rejoined the RAuxAF and commanded 600 Squadron from July 1946 to July 1948.

PO (AuxAF) 5.7.36   FO (AuxAF) 23.3.48   FO 24.8.39
FL 3.9.40   SL 1.12.41   SL (RAuxAFRO) 1.8.46

ROBERT ARTHUR HAYLOCK

120505   Sgt   Pilot   British   236 Squadron

Joined 236 Squadron in September 1940.

In September 1941 Haylock was with 272 Squadron in Malta, flying Beaufighters. On the 29th he inflicted damage on two E-boats and two Z 501 flying boats.

Commissioned in November 1941, Haylock was released from the RAF in 1946, as a Flight Lieutenant.

PO 22.11.41   FO 1.10.42   FL 22.11.43

GEOFFREY DAVID LEYBOURNE HAYSOM

39736   FL   Pilot   South African   79 Squadron

Haysom, of Durban, joined the RAF on a short service commission in March 1937. He was posted to 2 FTS, Brize Norton on June 5, went to the staff of the School of Naval Co-operation at Ford on January 8 1938 and joined 79 Squadron at Biggin Hill on November 1 1938.

Over Abbeville on June 6 1940 Haysom claimed a Bf 109 destroyed. He took temporary command of the squadron on July 7 when the CO was killed. On August 15 he claimed a Bf 110, on the 28th made a forced-landing at Appledore Station,

near Tenterden, when his glycol system was damaged in combat over Hythe, on the 30th probably destroyed a Bf 109 and on the 31st shot down another. Haysom shot down a Ju 88 on November 20 1940, which had been photographing damage caused in the Coventry raid. He was awarded the DFC (29.4.41) and commanded 79 from June to September, when he was posted to OTU, as an instructor. In the Middle East in 1942 Haysom was given command of 260 Squadron on July 19 but on the 22nd he was promoted to Acting Wing Commander to lead 239 Wing in the Western Desert. At the end of his tour he was awarded the DSO (16.2.43), being then credited with at least six enemy aircraft destroyed.

In Italy, after experience supporting the Army in the Western Desert, Haysom evolved the 'Cab Rank' system, which was later used with such success in the 1944 invasion. A squadron of fighters was airborne, generally in line astern, and was called up by a Mobile Observation Post with the forward troops to attack specific targets as required.

Haysom was released in 1946, as a Group Captain. He died in 1979.

APO 18.5.37   PO 18.3.38   FO 11.10.39   FL 11.10.40
SL 1.12.41   WC 1.1.44

JAMES CHILTON FRANCIS HAYTER

36207   FO   Pilot   New Zealander   615 and 605 Sqdns

Born in Timaru on October 18 1917, Hayter was at Nelson College from 1928 to 1934. He worked on farms and in 1936 took flying lessons at the Marlborough Aero Club.

In November 1938 Hayter joined the RNZAF on a short service commission. He was awarded his wings on April 19 1939. On May 8 Hayter was flying as an observer in a Vildebeeste, which struck a beach, wiping off the undercarriage and damaging the propellor. The pilot crash-landed at Wigram. A month later Hayter was again flying as an

observer in a Vildebeeste, flying low over Lake Ellesmere on a swan-strafing run, when the aircraft hit the water and plunged in. The crew of three came very close to drowning but escaped with minor injuries.

Hayter sailed for the UK on July 14 1939 in the 'Tamaroa' from Auckland. After arrival he was posted to 98 Squadron at Hucknall. On November 12, whilst low flying, he hit an air raid shelter and wrote off the Battle but escaped with slight injuries. Later in the month Hayter joined 103 Squadron at Plivot in France. On May 12 he was flying one of three Battles attacking roads and bridges near Sedan. Although attacked by Bf 110s they bombed a pontoon bridge from a height of 20 feet and succeeded in holding up German tanks for some hours.

On June 16 1940 Hayter was shot down by a Bf 109 as he was about to land. He was unhurt. Later that day the squadron was withdrawn to Honington, Suffolk. Hayter volunteered for Fighter Command and joined 615 Squadron at Prestwick on September 4 but moved to 605 Squadron at Croydon on the 18th. On October 26 he was shot down by a Bf 109. Hayter baled out at 25000 feet and landed in the grounds of Great Swifts, home of Major Victor Cazalet, where a cocktail party was in progress and to which he was invited. His Hurricane, V 6943, crashed at Staplehurst.

On December 1 Hayter destroyed a Bf 109. He was made a Flight Commander on February 20 1941 and was posted away on May 1 to 52 OTU, Debden, as an instructor. After crashing twice with the same pupil, on June 17 and 19, Hayter returned to operations in early July 1941, when he joined 611 Squadron at Hornchurch. On July 10 he destroyed a Bf 109 but crash-landed near Southend on the return from the sweep after his aircraft was badly damaged by flak. He was awarded the DFC (17.10.41).

On March 1 1942 Hayter was posted to the Middle East and joined 33 Squadron at Gambut in May. One day in June he was shot down by a Mc 202. As he was about to crash-land the pursuing Italian pilot overshot and Hayter fired a short burst, causing him to crash-land. The two pilots shared a bottle of whiskey in the nearby Australian lines.

On July 5 1942 Hayter was given command of 274 Squadron at LG 92. He probably destroyed a Mc 202 on July 10 and destroyed a Bf 109 on the 18th. At the end of September he was posted to Turkey to instruct Turkish pilots on Hurricanes. He went to Iran and took command of 74 Squadron at Mehrabad on April 1 1943.

In May the squadron moved to Egypt, where it began convoy patrols and taking part in Wing sweeps over Crete. In late September Hayter took nine squadron Spitfires to Antimachi airfield on Kos Island, in the Dodecanese. On the 29th Ju 88s put the airfield out of action and on October 3 the Germans invaded Kos and over-ran the airfield. Hayter and four others took to the hills. After evading enemy patrols for several days they met some men of the Special Boat Service and were taken off by boat on October 8 and put ashore on the Turkish coast. They reached Cyprus in a fishing boat on the 14th and Hayter flew back to Edku ten days later.

The squadron came together again on Christmas Day 1943 at Edku and began convoy patrols in January 1944. Hayter received a Mention in Despatches (14.1.44). 74 Squadron sailed from Port Said on April 7 for the UK and went to North Weald. Hayter received a second Mention in Despatches (8.6.44), took the squadron to France on August 19 and led 74 until December 30, when he was posted to

Milfield for a course at the Fighter Leaders' School. He was awarded a Bar to the DFC (26.1.45).

In mid-August 1945 Hayter sailed for New Zealand. He went on to the Reserve on December 28.

APO 29.11.38   PO 3.9.39   FO 3.9.40   FL 3.9.41
SL 1.7.44

DOUGLAS HAYWOOD

46222   Sgt   Pilot   British   151 and 504 Squadrons

Haywood joined the RAF on August 24 1936 as a direct-entry for training as a Sergeant Pilot. He went directly to 11 E&RFTS, Perth and then to 9 FTS, Thornaby on October 31. With training completed he was posted to the newly-formed 88 Squadron at Boscombe Down on July 1 1937.

The squadron flew its Battles to France on September 1 1939 and was heavily involved in the fighting in May 1940, suffering heavy losses. On June 13 Haywood was attacked by Bf 109s whilst he was bombing German tanks near Paris. His observer shot two down but they then had to bale out for the Battle was on fire. Haywood was wounded in the leg and his observer had an injured knee. The French took them to Sens Hospital and the next day they were evacuated in a hospital train going south. With confusion everywhere progress was slow and after five days they arrived at Bordeaux. They went to the British Consul, who directed them to the port, where a ship was waiting to take off British evacuees. They landed at Falmouth on June 21. Haywood rejoined the squadron at Belfast on August 10.

He volunteered for Fighter Command on September 3 and was flown to Digby the same afternoon to join 151 Squadron. He had one flight in a Hurricane and was at readiness the next morning at 6.00 am.

Haywood was posted to 504 Squadron at Filton on September 21. Apart from a month spent in No 2 Ferry Pool of the ATA from February 6 1941 he was with 504 until July 9 1941, when he was posted to 6 OTU, Sutton Bridge. Commissioned in July, he went to CFS, Upavon for a short instructor's course in August, then instructed at 56 OTU until September 14 1942, when he joined 41 Squadron at Llanbedr.

On April 27 1943 Haywood and another pilot were on a reconnaissance over Dieppe. They were surprised by seven FW 109s. Wounded in the left foot and with his Spitfire damaged, Haywood managed to get back across the Channel and crash-landed behind Dungeness. He was admitted to hospital in Canterbury and later moved to Halton.

Haywood rejoined the squadron in August. On a sweep over northern France on the 27th he had engine failure. He turned out over the Channel and baled out. He spent seventeen hours in his dinghy in a gale before being picked up by a French fishing boat. He was taken off by the Germans and made a PoW.

Freed in May 1945 Haywood went to 17 FTS, Coleby Grange on December 4 for a refresher course and was then posted to the School of Air Support on April 25 1946. Haywood was later grounded for high tone deafness and retired on June 1 1955, as a Squadron Leader.

PO 19.7.41   FO 19.7.42   FL 19.7.43   SL 1.8.47

FREDERICK ARTHUR PERCY HEAD

902546   Sgt   Air Gunner   British   236 Squadron

Head was with 236 Squadron in early July 1940. On the 11th he was in Blenheim L 6816, which was damaged by return fire from a He 111 engaged over Start Point but landed safely at St Eval.

On August 1 1940 Head was in Blenheim R 2774, which failed to return from a bomber escort operation. It may have been shot down by the ground defences at Querqueville aerodrome or could have been the victim of Oberleutnant Düllberg of III/JG 27.

Head was 25. He is remembered on the Runnymede Memorial, Panel 15.

GEOFFREY MONS HEAD

42224   PO   Pilot   British   219 Squadron

Head joined the RAF on a short service commission in April 1939 and was with 219 Squadron at Catterick in early July 1940.

He was killed on February 8 1941, as a Flying Officer with 219. He was cremated at St John's Crematorium, Woking, Surrey. Head was 22 years old.

APO 24.6.39   PO 16.12.39

PHILIP WILLIAM DUNSTAN HEAL

90220   FL   Pilot   British   604 Squadron

Born on January 15 1912, Heal joined 604 Squadron, AuxAF in early 1937. He was called to full-time service on September 24 1939 and served with the squadron throughout the Battle of Britain.

Heal was awarded the AFC (8.6.44), as an Acting Wing Commander. He stayed on in the RAF and retired on February 24 1962, as a Group Captain.

PO (AuxAF) 24.3.37   FO (AuxAF) 24.9.38   FO 24.8.39
FL 3.9.40   SL 1.12.41   WC 1.10.46   GC 1.1.53

TERENCE WILLIAM RICHARD HEALY

100609   Sgt   Pilot   British   41 and 611 Squadrons

Healy, of Edgware, Middlesex, was initially with 41 Squadron but moved to 611 Squadron at Tern Hill on September 29 1940.

Commissioned in June 1941, Healy was killed on March 2 1944, as a Flight Lieutenant with 266 Squadron. He was 23 and is buried in Bayeux War Cemetery, France.

PO 28.6.41   FO 28.6.42   FL 28.6.43

BARRIE HEATH

90818   FL   Pilot   British   611 Squadron

The son of the Senior Director of Rootes Motors, Heath was born on September 11 1916. He was educated at Wrekin and Pembroke College, Cambridge. He learned to fly with the University Air Squadron and was commissioned in the RAFVR in May 1937.

Heath transferred to 611 Squadron, AuxAF in June 1939 and was called to full-time service on August 29. Over Dunkirk on June 2 1940 Heath claimed a Ju 87 destroyed. He was appointed 'B' Flight Commander in November and in March 1941 was posted from 611 to take command of 64 Squadron at Hornchurch, which he did until September 1941. He was awarded the DFC (29.4.41).

In October 1942 Heath was at HQ Fighter Command, as Wing Commander Tactics, and in December he went to the Middle East. In 1944 he commanded 324 Wing in Italy and late in the year he was posted to the staff at Advanced HQ Desert Air Force.

Heath was released from the RAF in 1946, as a Wing Commander. He became a prominent industrialist, was knighted in 1978 and died on February 22 1988.

PO (RAFVR) 4.5.37   PO (AuxAF) 12.6.39   FO 29.8.39
FL 3.9.40   SL 1.12.41

GEORGE STEPHEN HEBRON

78252   PO   Observer   British   235 Squadron

Joined the RAFVR in March 1939 as a trainee observer. Called to full-time service at the outbreak of war, Hebron completed his training, was commissioned in March 1940 and joined 235 Squadron.

In March 1941 he was posted to OTU, as an instructor. Hebron joined 233 Squadron in November 1942, went to Special Operations Executive in November 1943 and was sent to RAF Staff College in September 1944 for a three month course.

In January 1945 Hebron was posted to Air Ministry on intelligence duties. He was released from the RAF in June 1946, as a Wing Commander.

PO 24.3.40   FO 24.3.41   FL 24.3.42

ALAN LINDSAY HEDGES

76578   PO   Pilot   British   245 and 257 Squadrons

Hedges was with 245 Squadron in June 1940. He was posted to 257 Squadron at Debden on September 10. He claimed a share in destroying a Do 17 on the 15th.

Hedges was released from the RAF in 1945.

PO 24.12.39   FO 24.12.40
FL 24.12.41

LEOPOLD HEIMES

1299983   Sgt   Pilot   Belgian   235 Squadron

Joined 235 Squadron on August 26 1940.

Heimes was in the RAF after the war and was gazetted as a Master Pilot on April 1 1948.

DENIS ARNOLD HELCKE

745320   Sgt   Pilot   British   504 Squadron

Helcke was born in Herne Bay. His parents took him to South Africa as a child and he was educated at King Edward VII School, Johannesburg. He returned to England in 1935 and entered the Chelsea College of Aeronautical Engineering. Helcke graduated with a diploma and passed Air Ministry examinations. He obtained his 'A' license and had done a considerable amount of flying before joining the RAFVR in 1938.

Called to full-time service on September 1 1939, Helcke was with 504 Squadron at Castletown in early July 1940. Flying from Hendon on September 7 he claimed a He 111 destroyed. On the 17th Helcke was killed, when he baled out after losing control following dummy attacks during a practice flight over Faversham. He may have struck the aircraft and he fell dead near Selling. His Hurricane, V 7529, crashed at Shepherds Hill, Selling.

Helcke was 24. He is buried in Herne Bay Cemetery, Kent.

RICHARD OWEN HELLYER

90054   FL   Pilot   British   616 Squadron

Hellyer joined 503 Squadron, AuxAF in November 1936 and was awarded his flying badge on July 3 1938. In late 1938 it was decided to disband 503 and form 616 as a new bomber squadron at Doncaster. Squadron Leader the Earl of Lincoln began forming 616 on November 1 1938 and Hellyer transferred, as a founder-member. On November 15 the squadron became part of Fighter Command.

Called to full-time service at the outbreak of war, Hellyer was shot down and wounded on May 28 1940 and landed on Dunkirk beach. He flew with the squadron until October 1 1940, when he was posted to 56 OTU, Sutton Bridge. In April 1941 he was

appointed 'A' Flight Commander.

Hellyer joined the MSFU at Speke on June 25 1941, staying with it until December 28, when he was posted to 6 FIS for an instructor's course, after which he went to 28 EFTS at Wolverhampton on May 2 1942, to instruct.

On April 25 1944 Hellyer moved to 5 (P) AFU at Hutton Cranswick. He was released from the RAF on October 24 1945, as a Flight Lieutenant. He later settled in South Africa.

PO (AuxAF) 10.11.36   FO (AuxAF) 15.5.38   FO 24.8.39
FL 15.5.40 '

JOHN ALLMAN HEMINGWAY

40702   FO   Pilot   Irish   85 Squadron

Born in Dublin on July 17 1919, Hemingway joined the RAF on a short service commission in March 1938. He was with 85 Squadron in France in early 1940 and on May 10 claimed a He 111 destroyed.

On August 18 Hemingway baled out after his Hurricane, V 7249, was damaged by return fire from a Ju 88 engaged over the Thames Estuary. He fell into the sea and was rescued by a light ship twelve miles east of Clacton. On the 26th he was shot down by a Bf 109 over Eastchurch and baled out, unhurt. His Hurricane, P 3966, crashed on Pitsea Marshes.

Hemingway was awarded the DFC (1.7.41). He commanded 43 Squadron from early April until December 1945. He retired from the RAF on September 12 1969, as a Group Captain.

APO 5.7.38   PO 7.3.39   FO 3.9.40   FL 3.9.41
SL 1.1.44   SL 1.8.47   WC 1.7.54

JAMES ALAN MacDONALD HENDERSON

74719   FO   Pilot   British   257 Squadron

Joined 257 Squadron at Hendon on July 7 1940. Henderson claimed two Bf 110s destroyed on August 31 and was then hit in the petrol tank during combat over Clacton. He baled out, injured and burned, was rescued from the sea and admitted to Brightlingsea Naval Hospital. His Hurricane, V 6601, crashed in Colne Creek, near Aldborough Point.

Henderson was released from the RAF in 1946, as a Flight Lieutenant.

PO 18.9.39   FO 18.9.40   FL 18.9.41

DAVID OSWALD HENDRY

129121   Sgt   Radar Operator   British   219 Squadron

Joined 219 Squadron at Catterick on September 2 1940. Promoted to Warrant Officer on May 1 1942, Hendry was commissioned in July 1942. He was awarded the DFC and released from the RAF in 1946.

Hendry's service record must be unique. He served with 219 Squadron continuously from September 1940 until his release in 1946, in Britain, North Africa and on the Continent.

PO 25.7.42   FO 25.1.43   FL 25.7.44

WILLIAM BRYAN HENN

137301   Sgt   Pilot   British   501 Squadron

Joined 501 Squadron at Kenley in August 1940. Henn claimed a He 111 destroyed on August 30.

Commissioned in September 1942, Henn was awarded the AFC (1.1.45) and released from the RAF in 1947. He died in 1979.

PO 16.9.42   FO 16.3.43   FL 16.9.44

ZDZISLAW KAROL HENNEBERG

P 1393   FO   Pilot   Polish   303 Squadron

Born in Warsaw on May 5 1911, Henneberg was in the PAF before the war and shared in the destruction of an enemy aircraft in September 1939. He escaped to France, joined l'Armée de l'Air and in 1940 commanded a flight of nine Bloch MB 152s defending Chateauroux airfield and the Bloch factory. He was awarded the C de G (Fr).

After the collapse of France Henneberg made his way to England and joined 303 Squadron at Northolt at its formation on August 2 1940. On August 31 he claimed a Bf 109 destroyed, on September 7 a probable Bf 109, on the 11th a He 111 and a Bf 109, on the 15th a Do 17 and a Bf 109, on the 27th another Bf 109 and on October 5 a Bf 110.

Henneberg, who was appointed 'A' Flight Commander on September 7, held temporary joint command of 303 from October 21 to November 8 1940. He was awarded the VM (5th Class)(23.12.40) and the KW and Bar (1.2.41) and took complete command of the squadron on February 20 1941.

Returning from an operation against French airfields on April 12 1941 Henneberg's Spitfire, P 8029, was damaged by enemy fire and he went down into the sea ten to thirteen miles off Dungeness. Although he was seen swimming he was not found and is presumed to have drowned. Henneberg is remembered on the Polish Air Force Memorial at Northolt. He was awarded the DFC (30.10.41).

FO 1.3.41

BERNARD HENSON

742563   Sgt   Pilot   British   32 and 257 Squadrons

Joined 32 Squadron at Biggin Hill on July 2 1940. He claimed a Ju 87 destroyed on July 19 and a Do 215 on August 18. On this day he was hit by return fire during a combat over Biggin Hill and forced-landed at Otford, with a slight wound on the face.

Henson was posted to 257 Squadron at Martlesham Heath on September 20 1940. He was reported 'Missing' on November 17 after being shot down by Adolf Galland in an action ten miles east of Harwich, in Hurricane N 2342. His body was recovered and he is buried in Wisbech Borough Cemetery, Cambridgeshire.

LAWRENCE FREDERICK HENSTOCK

37751   FL   Pilot   British   64 Squadron

Henstock joined the RAF on a short service commission in February 1936. On April 18 he was posted to 7 FTS, Peterborough and on March 22 1937 joined 72 Squadron, then being formed at Church Fenton.

In May 1940 Henstock was with 64 Squadron at Kenley. Over Dunkirk on May 29 he damaged a Bf 110.

Henstock was released from the RAF in 1946, as a Squadron Leader. He died in 1981.

APO 6.4.36   PO 10.2.37   FO 10.9.38   FL 3.9.40
SL 1.12.41

HUGH MICHAEL TURRETIN HERON

41700   PO   Pilot   British   266 and 66 Squadrons

Joined the RAF on a short service commission in December 1938. Heron was with 266 Squadron in early July 1940 and moved to 66 Squadron at Kenley on September 15. He claimed a Bf 109 destroyed on the 30th.

After leaving 66 Heron spent the remainder of his RAF service as a flying instructor. He was awarded the AFC (7.9.45) and released from the RAF in September 1946, as a Squadron Leader.

APO 4.3.39   PO 6.11.39   FO 6.11.40   FL 6.11.41

BRIAN HENRY HERRICK

42003   PO   Pilot   New Zealander   236 Squadron

Born in Hastings, New Zealand on February 1 1915, Herrick was at Wanganui Collegiate School from 1929 to 1933. He later went to England to study accountancy in London and when his interest waned he joined the RAF on a short service commission.

Herrick began his flying training at 3 E&RFTS, Hamble on March 6 1939, moved on to 12 FTS, Grantham on May 13 and joined the newly-formed 236 Squadron at Stradishall on November 6. He served with the squadron throughout the Battle of Britain.

On November 1 1940 Herrick was posted to 272 Squadron. On the 24th he took off on a convoy escort flight. At 16.20 hrs his Blenheim was seen to make a high speed stall in a turn at less than 100 feet above the sea and went straight in. A boat from the destroyer HMS 'Vesper' made a search for survivors but only a rubber dinghy and a petrol tank were found. It is believed that as the squadron returned to base it was ordered to take part in a mock dogfight at low-level, to practice actions necessary in a combat situation.

Herrick is remembered on the Runnymede Memorial, Panel 6.

APO 29.4.39   PO 6.11.39   FO 6.11.40

MICHAEL JAMES HERRICK

33566   PO   Pilot   New Zealander   25 Squadron

Born in Hastings, New Zealand on May 5 1921, Herrick was educated at Wanganui Collegiate School and whilst there he obtained his 'A' license at the Hawke's Bay and East Coast Aero Club at Hastings.

In late 1938 Herrick successfully applied for a cadetship at RAF College, Cranwell. He sailed for the UK on the RMS 'Rangitiki' on March 9 1939. He began the two year course on April 27 but with the outbreak of war it was condensed and he was granted a Permanent Commission on March 7 1940 and ten days later joined 25 Squadron at North Weald.

On September 4 Herrick, flying with Sergeant JS Pugh as his gunner, destroyed two He 111s at night, the second breaking up after a burst fired at less than thirty yards. On the 13th Herrick destroyed another and he was awarded the DFC (24.9.40). He may have destroyed another enemy aircraft in December 1940. He damaged a Ju 88 on May 9 1941 and destroyed another on June 22.

Herrick was posted from 25 in October 1941 and arrived back in New Zealand on December 23, on attachment to the RNZAF. On January 10 1942 he went to 2 FTS, Woodbourne, as an instructor, moved to 3 FTS, Ohakea in March and on June 25 was posted to 15 Squadron at Whenuapai, as a Flight Commander. It had no aircraft, its promised Kittyhawks having been diverted to the Middle East. In early October the squadron was posted to Tonga and took over P 40s and equipment of the 68th Pursuit Squadron, USAAF at Fuamotu.

The squadron moved to Santo in February 1943 and then to Fiji on March 20. Five days later the CO was killed and Herrick took command. On May 26 15 flew to Guadalcanal and began operations. Herrick destroyed a Zero fighter on June 7, shared a Val dive bomber on October 1 and shared a Zeke fighter on October 27.

His attachment finished, Herrick sailed from Auckland on January 14 1944, in charge of 300 aircrew trainees bound for Canada. He left them at Edmonton and continued to the UK. He was awarded a Bar to the DFC (10.2.44).

Herrick joined 302 Squadron at Lasham, as 'B' Flight Commander. A Polish fighter-bomber unit equipped with Mosquitos, the squadron was then carrying out mostly night operations but in May 1944 it began 'Day Rangers', which were operations flown as free-lance intrusions over enemy territory, with the primary aim of wearing out the enemy fighter force.

On June 16 Herrick took off on his first such operation. He flew in company with Wing Commander JRD Braham. They split at the Jutland coast and Herrick went towards Aalborg airfield. He was

MJ Herrick (continued)

intercepted and shot down by Leutnant Spreckels of JG 1. Herrick and his navigator, Flying Officer Turski, baled out but were too low. Herrick fell into the sea. A German search for his body was unsuccessful but it was washed up on July 4 and buried two days later in the Military Cemetery at Fredrikshavn. Nine days later Spreckels shot down Braham, who was captured.

Herrick was posthumously awarded the US Air Medal in July 1944 and it was presented to his parents in Wellington on June 14 1945. Brother to BH Herrick.

PO 7.3.40   FO 4.3.41   FL 7.3.42

VICTOR WILLIAM HESLOP

51508   Sgt   Pilot   British   56 Squadron

Born on May 9 1913, Heslop joined 56 Squadron at North Weald on September 5 1940.

Promoted to Warrant Officer on October 1 1941, Heslop was commissioned in February 1943. He left the RAF in 1948 but rejoined in June 1949 and retired on May 9 1963, as a Flight Lieutenant.

PO 10.2.43   FO 10.8.43   FL 10.2.45   FL 10.8.46
FL 11.7.48

ALEXANDER HESS

81888   SL   Pilot   Czechoslovakian   310 Squadron

Hess was born in 1899 and was one of the oldest fighter pilots in the Battle of Britain. He joined 310 Squadron as a supernumerary at its formation at Duxford on July 10 1940. On August 31 he claimed the destruction of a Do 215 and a Bf 109.

On September 15 Hess was shot down in combat with enemy fighters over the Thames Estuary and baled out, unhurt. His Hurricane, R 4085, crashed and burned out south of Billericay church.

Hess went to the USA in 1942, as Czech Air Attaché, as an Acting Group Captain. On a tour organised by the Inspectorate General of the Czech Air Force in the latter half of 1943 he accompanied the Czech ace, Karel Kuttelwascher. The object was to recruit pilots for the Czech squadrons in England.

Hess, who was awarded the DFC, went to live in America after the war. He died at his home in Florida in 1981.

SL 1.3.41

ERIK LAWSON HETHERINGTON

102091   Sgt   Pilot   British   601 Squadron

Hetherington, from Northumberland, joined 601 Squadron at Exeter on September 9 1940.

Commissioned in July 1941, Hetherington was posted to 611 Squadron at Hornchurch in the autumn. In April 1942 he was posted overseas, reached Malta in May and joined 249 Squadron. On May 10 Hetherington claimed a Bf 109 destroyed. He was appointed a Flight Commander in early July, destroyed a Mc 202 on July 11, destroyed an unidentified enemy aircraft on the 14th, shared a Mc 202 on September 2, destroyed a Bf 109 on October 13 and two Ju 88s on October 14 and 17.

Tour-expired, Hetherington was on his way back to the UK in a Liberator on October 31 1942. Attempting to land at Gibraltar the aircraft crashed into the sea and broke in half. Trapped in the rear half, Hetherington was drowned. He was 24 years old and is remembered on the Gibraltar Memorial in the North Front Cemetery there.

PO 17.7.41   FO 17.7.42

GORDON ARTHUR HEWETT

102992   Sgt   Pilot   British   607 Squadron

Hewett was with 607 Squadron at Usworth in early July 1940.

Commissioned in August 1941, Hewett does not appear in an Air Force List after May 1944 and has not been traced as a casualty, so presumably left the RAF in early 1944, as a Flight Lieutenant.

PO 9.8.41   FO 9.8.42   FL 9.8.43

DUNCAN ALEXANDER HEWITT

76579   PO   Pilot   Canadian   501 Squadron

Born in Toronto in 1920, Hewitt was with 501 Squadron at Croydon in June 1940. On July 11 he shot down a Hurricane with German markings.

Hewitt was shot down attacking a Do 17 over a convoy off Portland Bill on July 12, in Hurricane P 3084. A search by the Weymouth lifeboat failed to find him. He was 20 years old and is remembered on the Runnymede Memorial, Panel 8.

PO 24.12.39

COLIN ROY HEWLETT

69438   Sgt   Pilot   British   65 Squadron

Hewlett, of Frenchay, joined 65 Squadron at Hornchurch on August 7 1940. Commissioned in June 1941, Hewlett was still with the squadron in 1942 and was made a Flight Commander in early May. He flew on the Dieppe operation on August 19 and was awarded the DFC (3.11.42).

On December 12 1942 Hewlett was circling to land at Drem, with his speed still over 300 mph, when his Spitfire exploded. His parachute opened but he was dead when picked up, apallingly injured. Hewlett was 22 years old. He is buried in the churchyard of St John the Baptist, Frenchay, Winterbourne.

PO 26.6.41   FO 26.6.42

JOHN MINCHIN HEWSON

39083   FL   Pilot   Australian   616 Squadron

Born in England of Australian parents, Hewson was at Harrow School from 1928 to 1932. He joined the RAF on a short service commission in July 1936.

Hewson was posted to 11 FTS, Wittering on September 12 and with training completed he joined 142 Squadron at Andover on May 22 1937. The squadron changed its Hinds for Battles in March 1938 and went to France on September 2 1939 as part of the AASF. After being involved in the heavy fighting of May 1940 it was withdrawn from France on June 15. Hewson was awarded the DFC (6.8.40). He volunteered for Fighter Command and joined 616 Squadron at Leconfield on August 19.

Hewson was released from the RAF in 1946, as a Squadron Leader.

APO 31.8.36   PO 10.7.37   FO 10.2.39   FL 3.9.40
SL 1.3.42

GEORGE FRANCIS WHEATON HEYCOCK

26138   SL   Pilot   British   23 Squadron

Born on September 17 1909, Heycock was educated at Haileybury and Imperial Service College. He entered RAF College, Cranwell in January 1928 as a flight cadet. On graduation in December 1929 he was commissioned and joined 111 Squadron at Hornchurch.

Heycock went back to Cranwell on August 5 1931, as a flying instructor. In January 1933 he was appointed PA to the AOC Inland Area, Air Vice-Marshal Longmore, at Bentley Priory. On October 22 1934 Heycock was posted to CFS, Wittering, as an instructor. He joined 823 (Fleet Spotter-Reconnaissance) Squadron on August 30 1935, on HMS 'Furious' and land-based at Hal Far, Malta.

On January 14 1938 Heycock went to the Experimental Section at the RAE Farnborough, as a test pilot. He was given command of 23 Squadron at Collyweston on August 9 1940, led it until November and then commanded it again from January to March 1941.

In July 1941 Heycock took command of 141 Squadron at Ayr. From August he converted the squadron from Defiants to Beaufighters. On May 1 1942 he probably destroyed a Do 217 at night and at the end of his tour was awarded the DFC (29.9.42).

Heycock remained in the RAF after the war. He was Air Attaché in Washington in 1955, Air Attaché in Paris 1959-64, was made a CB (8.6.63) and retired on May 1 1964, as an Air Commodore. He died in 1983.

PO 14.12.29   FO 14.6.31   FL 14.6.35   SL 1.10.38
WC 1.12.40   GC 1.1.44   GC 1.7.49   AC 1.7.55

NORMAN BAGSHAW HEYWOOD

41923   PO   Pilot   British   32, 607 and 257 Squadrons

Joined the RAF on a short service commission in February 1939. Heywood was posted to 32 Squadron at Acklington in September 1940, moved to 607 Squadron at Tangmere on the 22nd and then to 257 Squadron at Martlesham Heath in early October.

On the 22nd Heywood was hit by anti-aircraft fire, whilst in combat with Bf 109s over Folkestone. His Hurricane, R 4195, crashed south of Lydd Church and he was killed.

Heywood was 22. He is buried in Stretford Cemetery, Manchester.

APO 15.4.39   PO 6.11.39

JOHN HARVEY HEYWORTH

32079   SL   Pilot   British   79 Squadron

Heyworth joined the RAF on September 11 1931 and on the 26th was posted to 5 FTS, Sealand. After training he joined 54 Squadron at Hornchurch. On November 22 1934 Heyworth went to 504 Squadron, AuxAF at Hucknall, as Flying Instructor. He went on to the RAFO in September 1936.

Recalled at the outbreak of war, Heyworth took command of 79 Squadron at Acklington on July 12 1940. He shared in the destruction of a He 111 on September 27. He was posted away in June 1941.

Heyworth was released from the RAF in 1945, as a Wing Commander. He was awarded the AFC (1.1.46) and died on September 21 1959.

PO 11.9.31   FO 11.3.33   FL 1.4.36   SL 1.3.40
WC 1.3.42

DAVID THORNHILL HICK

748104   Sgt   Pilot   British   32 Squadron

Joined 32 Squadron at Acklington in late September 1940. Believed to have left the RAF during the war, as a Warrant Officer. Hick died on July 26 1973.

WILLIAM BURLEY HIGGINS

741927   Sgt   Pilot   British   32 and 253 Squadrons

Born in 1914 at Hodthorpe, Whitwell, Derbyshire, Higgins was educated at Brunts Grammar School, Mansfield. He trained as a teacher and taught at his old junior school in Whitwell.

Higgins joined the RAFVR in 1937 and carried out his elementary flying training at Tollerton, near Nottingham. Called to full-time service on September 1 1939, he completed his training at 5 FTS, Sealand and joined 32 Squadron at Biggin Hill on July 2 1940. He shared in destroying a Do 17 on July 3, destroyed a Bf 110 on the 20th and Bf 109s on August 12 and 24.

On September 9 Higgins was posted to 253 Squadron at Kenley. He destroyed a Bf 109 on the 11th and on the 14th he was killed in combat with Bf 109s and his Hurricane, P 5184, crashed in flames on Swanton Farm, Bredgar. He is buried in St Lawrence's churchyard, Whitwell.

FREDERICK WILLIAM HIGGINSON

44630   PO   Pilot   British   56 Squadron

Born in Swansea on February 17 1913, Higginson joined the RAF in 1929 as an aircraft apprentice at Halton. He passed out in 1932 and later volunteered for pilot training.

On August 6 1935 Higginson began his elementary flying training at 4 E&RFTS, Brough and moved on to 5 FTS, Sealand on October 2. He joined 19 Squadron at Duxford on July 1 1936 but when 'C' Flight became 66 Squadron on July 20 Higginson went with it. From April 13 1937 he flew with the anti-aircraft co-operation flights at Biggin Hill and Bircham Newton.

Higginson joined 56 Squadron at North Weald on October 20 1937 and was still with it in May 1940. He went with 'B' Flight to Vitry-en-Artois, France on May 16, claimed a Do 17 and a He 111 destroyed on the 17th and a Bf 109 on the 19th. On the evening of the 18th the flight evacuated Vitry and went to Norrent Fontes. Higginson and Sergeant C Whitehead were sent back to destroy the remaining aircraft and stores. When they left the Germans were 3 to 4 miles away. Over Dunkirk on May 29 Higginson claimed a Bf 109 and on July 15 a probable Do 17. He was awarded the DFM (30.7.40).

On August 12 Higginson claimed a Do 17, on the 16th another, on the 18th a Do 215, on the 25th a Bf 110, on the 28th and 31st Bf 109s, on September 14 a Do 17 and on the 30th two Bf 110s. He was commissioned in September 1940.

On June 17 1941 Higginson was shot down over France. He evaded capture and returned to England in 1942 and rejoined 56 Squadron, then at Matlask, on October 6. He was awarded the DFC (9.2.43). From January 5 1943 he was on special duties in London and on April 1 1944 was posted to 83 Group TAF, firstly at Redhill, then Thorney Island and from August 6 on the Continent.

At the end of the war Higginson was with 11 Group, on organisation duties. He went to RAF Staff College and Army Staff College, was made an OBE and retired from the RAF on April 5 1956, as a Wing Commander. Higginson's portrait was done by Cuthbert Orde in December 1940 and Eric Kennington.

PO 18.9.40   FO 8.4.41   FL 8.4.42   SL 1.8.47
WC 1.7.53

THOMAS PETER KINGSLAND HIGGS

36165   FO   Pilot   British   111 Squadron

Higgs joined the RAF with a direct-entry Permanent Commission. He was with 111 Squadron at Croydon in June 1940. On July 10 Higgs was attacked by Oberleutnant Oesau of lll/JG 51 over the Channel off Folkestone. He collided with a Do 17 and lost a wing at 6000 feet. He baled out but was killed. The Dornier, of 3/KG 2, crashed near Dungeness Buoy.

Higgs was 23. His body was washed ashore at Noordwijk on August 15. He is buried in Noordwijk General Cemetery, Netherlands.

PO 29.10.38   FO 9.8.39

CECIL HENRY HIGHT

41924   PO   Pilot   New Zealander   234 Squadron

Born in Stratford, New Zealand on September 6 1917, Hight worked as a car salesman. He obtained his 'A' license at the Western Federated Aero Club in August 1937. Early in 1938 he worked his passage to England to join the RAF. He could not meet the educational requirements and took a cramming course in mathematics, applied again and was provisionally accepted for a short service commission.

On January 16 1939 Hight began training at 9 E&RFTS, Ansty, went to 6 FTS, Little Rissington on April 29 and after completing the course joined 234 Squadron, then reforming with Blenheims at Leconfield, on November 6. In March the squadron began to re-equip with Spitfires.

Hight was shot down near Swanage on August 15 1940. He stayed with the aircraft and was killed attempting to avoid landing in a residential area. The Spitfire, R 6988, crashed at Walsford Road, Meyrick Park, Bournemouth. He is buried in Bournemouth East Cemetery, Boscombe. Hight is remembered by having Pilot Hight Road in Bournemouth named after him.

APO 15.4.39   PO 6.11.39

ARTHUR HERBERT HILES

85008   PO   Observer   British   236 Squadron

Hiles, of Wellington, Somerset, joined 236 Squadron on September 24 1940. He was killed on March 15 1942, as a Flying Officer with 233 Squadron, operating in Hudsons.

Hiles was 25 and is remembered on the Runnymede Memorial, Panel 67.

PO 25.8.40   FO 25.8.41

CLIVE GEOFFREY HILKEN

745482   Sgt   Pilot   British   74 Squadron

Joined 74 Squadron at Wittering in August 1940. Hilken was shot down on October 20 in combat with Bf 109s over south London, baled out, wounded, and was admitted to Orpington Hospital. His Spitfire, P 7426, crashed at Cowden.

On June 27 1941 Hilken was shot down on a sweep over St Omer, in Spitfire W 3252, and captured. He was released from the RAF in 1945, as a Warrant Officer.

Hilken was commissioned in the RAFVR in March 1949.

PO (RAFVR) 3.3.49

ARCHIBALD EDMUND HILL

42125   PO   Pilot   British   248 Squadron

HIll, of Wiltshire, joined the RAF on a short service commission in March 1939. He began his ab initio course at 10 E&T FTS, Yatesbury on the 16th, was posted to 5 FTS, Sealand on May 30 and with training completed joined 248 Squadron at Hendon on November 6 1939.

He served with the squadron throughout the Battle of Britain. Hill was killed on April 15 1941, as a Flight Lieutenant with 254 Squadron.

He is buried in Rosseb churchyard, Haugesund, Norway.

APO 13.5.39   PO 6.11.39   FO 6.11.40

ARNOLD MAURICE HILL

121333   Sgt   Air Gunner   British   25 Squadron

With 25 Squadron in June 1940. Commissioned in May 1942, Hill was awarded the DFC (2.2.43), as a Pilot Officer with 25. He had then destroyed two enemy aircraft at night.

He qualified at a Specialist Armament Course and was released from the RAF in 1945, as a Flight Lieutenant.

PO 1.5.42   FO 1.11.42   FL 1.4.44

CHARLES RICHARD HILL

112518   Sgt   Air Gunner   British   141 Squadron

Hill was born on March 1 1914 and served with 141 Squadron in the Battle of Britain. In December 1940 he retrained as a Radio Observer and in mid-1941 teamed up with Flight Sergeant PS Kendall in 255 Squadron. He was commissioned in November 1941.

They went to North Africa with the squadron in November 1942. On December 29 they damaged a four-engined enemy aircraft, on January 7 1943 destroyed a Cant Z 1007, on the 15th another, on April 27 a Ju 88, on May 5 a Ju 52 and probably another and on the 25th a Ju 88. Hill was awarded the DFC (30.4.43), the citation stating that he destroyed one enemy aircraft as an air gunner as well as his later successes as a Navigator Radar.

Hill retired from the RAF on April 13 1959, as a Squadron Leader. He died on October 20 1985.

PO 24.11.41   FO 1.10.42   FL 24.11.43   SL 1.8.47

GEOFFREY HILL

61046   Sgt   Pilot   British   65 Squadron

Joined the RAFVR in 1938. Called to full-time service on September 1 1939, Hill was posted to ITW, Hastings in October. In December he went to 11 EFTS, Perth for his elementary flying training and then to 6 FTS, Little Rissington.

Hill joined 65 Squadron at Hornchurch in June 1940. Commissioned in November, he was shot down over France on February 4 1941. He was in Stalags Luft I, II and III and finished the war at Colditz. Hill was released from the RAF in 1945 and was made an MBE for distinguished service whilst a PoW.

PO 27.11.40   FO 27.11.41   FL 27.11.42

GEORGE EDWARD HILL

42126   PO   Pilot   British   245 Squadron

Hill, from Hampshire, joined the RAF on a short service commission in March 1939 and was with 245 Squadron in May 1940. Over Dunkirk on June 1 Hill claimed a Bf 109 destroyed.

He was killed on March 31 1944, as a Flight Lieutenant with 245 Squadron. Hill was 28. He is buried in Attleborough Cemetery, Nuneaton, Warwickshire.

APO 13.5.39   PO 6.11.39
FO 6.11.40   FL 6.11.41

HOWARD PERRY HILL

41847   PO   Pilot   New Zealander   92 Squadron

Born on April 17 1920 in Christchurch, Hill was at Marlborough College from 1932 to 1936. He applied for an RAF short service commission in 1938 and after being provisionally accepted he sailed for the UK on December 16 in the RMS 'Rangitata'.

On January 24 1939 Hill went to 13 E&RFTS, White Waltham to begin his elementary flying training. He moved to 13 FTS, Drem on April 17. On completion of the course Hill was posted to 8 Observers' School, Evanton on October 9, as a staff pilot. Two weeks later he joined the newly-reformed 92 Squadron at Tangmere, then equipped with Blenheims but re-equipped with Spitfires in March 1940.

On July 26 Hill shared in the destruction of a Ju 88, on September 15 he destroyed two Do 17s and damaged a third, on the 18th a Ju 88 and on the 19th a probable Bf 109.

North of Dungeness on September 20 1940 the squadron was attacked from above and behind by Bf 109s of JG 51. Hill was in the rear section and one of the first to be attacked. He was shot down in flames by Major Mölders and crashed into high tree tops at West Hougham, Kent. The Spitfire, X 4417, remained undiscovered for a month.

Hill is buried in Folkestone Cemetery and his name appears on the reredos in St George's Chapel of Remembrance at Biggin Hill.

APO 1.4.39   PO 21.10.39

JOHN HAMAR HILL

32172   SL   Pilot   British   222 Squadron

Hill was born on December 28 1912 and joined the RAF on April 1 1932. He carried out his flying training at 3 FTS, Grantham and joined 19 Squadron at Duxford on August 21 1933. He was posted to 800 (Fleet Fighter) Squadron, Upavon on September 26 1934.

Hill was posted to the Air Staff at 21 Group, Sleaford on December 1 1938. He commanded 87 Squadron in November/December 1939 and in mid-May 1940 took command of 504 Squadron in France. On the 19th he was shot

down by a Bf 110 and baled out. Within a few hundred feet of the ground he was fired at by French peasants with shotguns. After landing he managed to convince them that he was not German. As he was about to be driven away in a French Air Force car a British patrol arrived and he was arrested as a fifth columnist. Reaching for his identity card Hill was fired on by one of the British soldiers. When he ducked below the windscreen all the others fired. Hill rolled out of the car into a ditch and when firing had ceased he convinced the officer-in-charge of his identity. Having seen all this the French peasants were sure Hill was German. They attacked him savagely, rendering him unconscious, while the soldiers stood by and watched.

He came to with his head in the lap of a French Air Force Commandant, a man he had known in Rouen. The shamefaced peasants tried to make amends, the British Army re-appeared and again tried to arrest him, unsuccessfully. Hill was evacuated from Lille by ambulance train. Between Le Touquet and Boulogne Ju 87s dive-bombed it and the driver and fireman fled. Hill and another officer finally mastered the engine's controls and drove the train to Boulogne. Evacuated from Dunkirk, Hill landed at Dover and went on an ambulance train. When he asked the engine driver to change some French francs so that he could phone his wife he was arrested as a fifth columnist. Fortunately a Wing Commander he knew came along and he was released.

Hill was given command of 222 Squadron at Hornchurch on July 31 1940 and he claimed a Bf 109 destroyed on September 1.

Hill was made a CBE (1.1.46) and retired from the RAF on February 1 1960, as a Group Captain.

APO 1.4.32   PO 1.4.33   FO 1.11.34   FL 1.11.36
SL 1.4.39   WC 1.3.41   WC 1.10.46   GC 1.1.52

MICHAEL ROWLAND HILL

72467   FO   Pilot   South African   266 Squadron

Commissioned in the RAFVR in October 1938, Hill was called to full-time service in October 1939 and joined 266 Squadron at Wittering on September 28 1940.

Hill was killed on March 12 1945, as a Squadron Leader with 19 Squadron. He is remembered on the Runnymede Memorial, Panel 265.

PO (RAFVR) 18.10.38   PO 11.10.39   FO 9.8.40   FL 9.8.41
SL 1.7.43

SYDNEY JENKYN HILL

77795   PO   Pilot   British   609 Squadron

Born in April 1917, Hill, of Ferndown, Dorset, was at Uppingham School from 1931 to 1935. He joined 609 Squadron at Middle Wallop in October 1940. On the 21st he shared in the destruction of a Ju 88, 609's 100th victory.

Hill was killed on June 18 1941, as a Pilot Officer with 609. After being in combat with Bf 109s off Cap Gris Nez he got back to the English coast and was seen gliding down near Dover but he then crashed and burned out. Hill is buried in Folkestone New Cemetery.

APO 7.3.40   PO 7.9.40

RICHARD HOPE HILLARY

74677   FO   Pilot   Australian   603 Squadron

Hillary was born in Sydney on April 20 1919, the son of a government official. He went to London at the age of 3, when his father was appointed to a post at Australia House. Hillary was at Shrewsbury School from 1931 to 1937 and then went to Trinity College, Oxford. Whilst there he learned to fly with the University Air Squadron. He was sometime President of the Rugby Club and Secretary of the Boat Club.

Called to full-time service on October 3 1939, Hillary was posted to ITW at Hastings and

RH Hillary (continued)

after a course at an FTS in Scotland he went to No 1 School of Army Co-operation at Old Sarum. In early June 1940 he moved to 5 OTU, Aston Down and after converting to Spitfires joined 603 Squadron at Dyce.

The squadron moved south to Hornchurch on August 27. Hillary claimed a Bf 109 destroyed on August 29 and was himself shot down, crash-landing near Lympne, unhurt. He claimed a Bf 109 on the 31st, two Bf 109s destroyed, one probably destroyed and another damaged on September 2 and another destroyed on the 3rd. On this day he was shot down in flames into the Channel off Margate by Hauptmann Bode of ll/JG 26. Hillary baled out, grieviously burned, and was rescued by the Margate lifeboat. He spent three months in the Royal Masonic Hospital and then went to the Queen Victoria Hospital, East Grinstead, where he underwent surgery by Archie McIndoe and became a Guinea Pig.

After leaving hospital in late 1941 Hillary went to RAF Staff College, Gerrards Cross in January 1942 for a three month's course. He regained his flying category and went to 54 OTU, Charter Hall to convert to night fighters.

On January 8 1943, circling a beacon at night, his Blenheim spun into the ground and he and his navigator were killed. Hillary was cremated at Golders Green Crematorium, London.

He is remembered for his book 'The Last Enemy', published in June 1942. Hillary's portrait was done by Eric Kennington.

PO 3.10.39   FO 3.10.40   FL 3.10.41

HARRY BRYAN LILLIE HILLCOAT

90256   FO   Pilot   British   1 Squadron

Hillcoat, of Bromsgrove, Worcestershire, joined 605 Squadron, AuxAF in early 1938. He was called to full-time service on August 24 1939. He joined No 1 Squadron in France on May 10 1940 and destroyed a He 111 on June 4 but made a forced-landing with a bullet in his engine.

In late June Hillcoat was appointed 'B' Flight Commander. On August 18 he shared in destroying a Do 17, on September 1 claimed a Bf 109 and on the 2nd probably destroyed another. He failed to return from a squadron patrol on September 3 1940, in Hurricane P 3044, and was reported 'Missing'.

Hillcoat was 25. He is remembered on the Runnymede Memorial, Panel 4.

PO (AuxAF) 11.3.38   PO 24.8.39   FO 11.9.39

RALPH WALTER HILLMAN

643257   Sgt   Wop/AG   British   235 Squadron

Joined 235 Squadron on August 1 1940. He was killed on April 6 1941, as a Flight Sergeant with 22 Squadron.

Hillman is buried in Kerfautras Cemetery, Brest, France.

FRANK WILLIAM HILLOCK

C 1018   PO   Pilot   Canadian   1 (RCAF) Squadron

Hillock joined the RCAF Auxiliary on May 18 1939, in 400 Squadron, an army co-operation unit. He was called to full-time service on September 2 1939 and went with the squadron to England in February 1940, to serve with the 1st Canadian Division.

In August 1940 Hillock was posted to 5 OTU, Aston Down to convert to Hurricanes. He was then attached to 151 Squadron at Digby and later No 1 Squadron at Wittering to gain experience. He joined No 1 (RCAF) Squadron at Prestwick on October 21 1940.

Hillock was posted to Acklington on January 5 1941 to join 406 (RCAF) Squadron, as a Flight Commander. He was given command of 410 (RCAF) Squadron at Ayr on August 18 1942. The squadron converted from Beaufighters to Mosquitos in October and Hillock flew the unit's first operational Mosquito sortie on December 6. In a sortie to the Ruhr on April 15 1943 Hillock found himself in the midst of several radio masts. In climbing out he flew through antennae at Appledorn radio station. The Mosquito lost a foot off the starboard wingtip and on return to base was found to be trailing some 300 feet of thick copper cable.

In May 1943 Hillock was sent to Staff College, after which he

returned to Canada on August 23. Two months later he came back to the UK to form 143 Wing 2nd TAF at Ayr. It moved down to Hurn on April 20 1944 and across to France on June 12. A month later he was replaced by a Group Captain, when 2nd TAF was re-organised.

Hillock went on a course at the Fighter Leaders' School at Milfield and then returned to a staff job in Canada, concerned with Mosquito training. He held a series of appointments and commands at home and overseas in the post-war RCAF. He retired on November 21 1965, as a Wing Commander.

PETER HILLWOOD

120107   Sgt   Pilot   British   56 Squadron

Hillwood was with 56 Squadron at North Weald in June 1940. He claimed a Ju 87 destroyed on July 13 and was himself shot down on August 13, in a head-on attack by a Bf 110 off Sheerness. He baled out, unhurt, swam two miles towards Sheppey and was near collapse when two anti-aircraft gunners waded out and helped him in.

Commissioned in January 1942, Hillwood was awarded the DFC (24.11.44), as a Flight Commander with 127 Squadron. He was released in 1946, as a Flight Lieutenant.

Hillwood went into civil aviation. He flew as second pilot to RP Beamont on the record-breaking double crossing of the Atlantic in a Canberra on August 26 1952, which won the Royal Aero Club's Britannia Trophy for the year's best performance in the air. Hillwood died in 1966.

PO 23.1.42   FO 1.10.42   FL 23.1.44

JAROSLAV HIMR

81891   PO   Pilot   Czechoslovakian   79 and 56 Sqdns

Joined 79 Squadron at Pembrey on September 11 1940 and moved to 56 Squadron at Boscombe Down on October 8.

After the Battle of Britain Himr was posted to 601 Squadron at Exeter and remained with it throughout 1941. In June 1942 he was given command of 313 Squadron at Church Stanton.

Himr was killed on September 24 1943, as a Squadron Leader with 313. He is remembered on the Runnymede Memorial, Panel 118.

PO 12.7.40   FO 27.12.40   FL 27.12.41

FREDERICK GEORGE HINDRUP

NZ 40284   Sgt   Air Gunner   New Zealander   600 Sqdn

Born in Dannevirke on May 24 1914, the son of a teamster from Gisborne, who was killed in action in 1918. Hindrup was working for New Zealand Railways when he volunteered for the RNZAF in September 1939.

Hindrup reported to the Ground Training School at Weraroa on January 16 1940. In February he was posted to the Air Observers' School, Ohakea for a gunnery course. He sailed for the UK on June 7 in the RMS 'Rangitata'.

In early August Hindrup went to 5 OTU, Aston Down, completed his training, gained his air gunner's badge and joined 600 Squadron at Redhill on September 21. With the advent of the Beaufighter and airborne radar air gunners were doing little flying by the end of 1940. With others, Hindrup asked to go to Bomber Command and in February 1941 was posted to 11 OTU, Bassingbourn. He converted to Wellingtons and in March joined 99 Squadron at Waterbeach.

On the night of April 20 1941 Hindrup took off on his tenth operational flight but failed to return to base. His body was later recovered from the sea and he was listed as 'Killed in Action'. Hindrup is buried in Felixstowe Cemetery, Suffolk.

MERRICK HUBERT HINE

745148   Sgt   Pilot   British   65 Squadron

Hine, of Penn, Bucks, joined 65 Squadron at Hornchurch on August 19 1940. He was shot down and killed in an action near Selsey Bill on December 12 1940.

Hine was 24 and is remembered on the Runnymede Memorial, Panel 15.

LEONARD HIRD

936364   Sgt   Air Gunner   British   604 Squadron

Hird, from Yorkshire, joined 604 Squadron at Middle Wallop on August 14 1940. He was killed on June 28 1941, as a Flight Sergeant with 10 Squadron, operating in Whitleys from Leeming in Yorkshire.

Hird was 23. He is buried in Hamburg Cemetery, Ohlsdorf, Germany.

BRYAN ALBERT HAROLD HITCHINGS

41701   FO   Pilot   British   3 Squadron

Born in Bombay on February 5 1919, Hitchings returned to the UK in 1926 and was educated in Kent. He joined the RAF on a short service commission and began his elementary training at 10 E&RFTS, Yatesbury on December 28 1938.

Hitchings went to 8 FTS, Montrose on March 18 1939, completed his training at 8 ATS, Evanton and joined 76 Squadron at Upper Heyford on October 1 1939. He moved to 106 Squadron at Finningley on December 9, went to 5 Group Flight at Grantham on January 6 1940, to 20 MU, Aston Down on May 25, to 5 OTU on September 8 to convert to Hurricanes and joined 3 Squadron at Turnhouse on October 2.

Hitchings was released from the RAF on June 6 1947, as a Squadron Leader. He rejoined the RAF on December 18 1950 and retired on October 1 1963, as a Flight Lieutenant, retaining the rank of Squadron Leader.

APO 4.3.39   PO 30.9.39   FO 30.9.40   FL 30.9.41
SL 1.7.45   FL 9.10.45

ARTHUR JAMES BEAUMONT HITHERSAY

749366   Sgt   Air Gunner   British   141 Squadron

Born in 1920, Hithersay joined the RAFVR in December 1938. He was called to full-time service at the outbreak of war and posted to the newly-formed 141 Squadron at Grangemouth in October 1939. He served with the squadron throughout the Battle of Britain.

In May 1941 Hithersay shot down a He 111 at night south of Glasgow. When the squadron converted to Beaufighters in September he transferred to 4 Group Bomber Command and went into Flying Control. He was stationed at Linton-on-Ouse, responsible for airfield control for 76 and 78 Squadrons.

Hithersay later operated a satellite station at Brighton. He was released from the RAF in 1946, as a Warrant Officer.

JAROSLAV HLAVAC

787542   Sgt   Pilot   Czechoslovakian   79 and 56 Sqdns

Hlavac was born on September 11 1914. He joined 79 Squadron at Pembrey on September 11 1940 and moved to 56 Squadron at Boscombe Down on October 8.

Two days later Hlavac was shot down and killed in combat with Bf 109s over Wareham. His Hurricane, P 3421, crashed at Manor Farm, Worgret. He is buried in Holy Trinity churchyard, Warmwell.

ALOIS HLOBIL

82547   PO   Pilot   Czechoslovakian   312 Squadron

Joined 312 Squadron at Duxford on September 5 1940. No further service details traced.

PO 2.8.40   FL 1.3.41

JAMES HAMMOND HOARE-SCOTT

87673   PO   Pilot   British   601 Squadron

Hoare-Scott, of Surrey, joined 601 Squadron at Debden on September 1 1940. He was killed on November 21 1940, when his Hurricane crashed at Broadclyst, soon after taking off from Exeter.

Hoare-Scott was 29. He is buried in St Mary's churchyard, Frensham, Surrey.

APO 4.3.40   PO 17.8.40

DUDLEY ORMSTON HOBBIS

42709   PO   Pilot   British   219 Squadron

A well-known amateur tennis player, Hobbis came from Tynemouth, Northumberland. He joined the RAF on a short service commission in July 1939 and was posted to 219 Squadron at Catterick on July 13 1940.

Hobbis was awarded the DFC (8.7.41), as a Flying Officer with 219. The citation credited him with three enemy aircraft destroyed at night. From May to September 1942 Hobbis commanded 530 Squadron, a Turbinlite Havoc unit at Hunsdon.

In April 1943 Hobbis joined 488 Squadron at Ayr, as 'A' Flight Commander. On November 25 1943 he reported over the R/T that his port engine was on fire and that he had ordered his navigator to bale out. It is believed that he also baled out but his body was never recovered, although that of his navigator was washed ashore some months later.

Hobbis was 33 and is remembered on the Runnymede Memorial, Panel 118.

APO 18.9.39   PO 20.4.40   FO 20.4.41   FL 20.4.42

JOSEPH BEDO HOBBS

41926   PO   Pilot   British   3 and 232 Squadrons

Hobbs, of Folkestone, joined the RAF on a short service commission in November 1938. He was with 3 Squadron at Wick in early July 1940 and as a member of 'B' Flight went with it to Sumburgh on July 17, when it was renumbered as 232 Squadron.

In 1941 Hobbs was with 274 Squadron in the Western Desert. On June 24, on a convoy patrol, he intercepted three Sm 79s and destroyed one. He was killed on December 7 1941, as a Flight Lieutenant, shot down by Unteroffizier Grimm in an action west of El Adem.

Hobbs was 26. He is buried in Halfaya Sollum War Cemetery.

APO 15.2.39   PO 6.11.39   FO 6.11.40

SYDNEY JOHN HOBBS

742901   Sgt   Pilot   British   235 Squadron

With 235 Squadron in early July 1940. Hobbs was killed on August 14 1941, as a Sergeant with 143 Squadron, a Beaufighter coastal-reconnaissance unit.

Hobbs was 25. He is buried in Brookwood Military Cemetery, Woking.

COLIN ANTHONY HOBSON

42566   PO   Pilot   British   600 Squadron

Born on October 25 1918, Hobson was educated at Eastbourne. He joined the RAF on a short service commission in June 1939 and was with 600 Squadron at Northolt in early July 1940.

On October 3 Hobson was captain of Blenheim L 4905, which had engine failure during a routine patrol in heavy rain. He crashed into trees on high ground at Broadstone Warren, Forest Row, Sussex in the early hours of the morning. Hobson and his crew of two were all killed. He was 21 and is buried in All Saints' churchyard, Banstead, Surrey.

APO 19.8.39   PO 9.2.40

DESMOND BOGAN HOBSON

37736   FL   Pilot   British   64 Squadron

Joined the RAF on a short service commission in January 1936. Hobson was posted to 7 FTS, Peterborough on April 18 and joined 3 Squadron at Kenley on October 25 1936. He was still with the squadron at the outbreak of war but went to 64 Squadron in early 1940. Over Dunkirk on May 29 Hobson damaged a Bf 109.

He was released from the RAF in 1945, as a Squadron Leader.

APO 30.3.36   PO 3.2.37   FO 3.9.38   FL 3.9.40
SL 1.12.41

WILLIAM FRANCIS CRIPPS HOBSON

26180   SL   Pilot   British   601 Squadron

Born on December 28 1910, Hobson entered RAF College, Cranwell in January 1929 as a flight cadet. On graduation he was commissioned and joined 54 Squadron at Hornchurch on December 20 1930.

Hobson was sent to the Air Armament School, Eastchurch for a course on February 26 1934. He joined the staff at No 1 Air Defence Group, ADGB, London on September 9 1935, was posted to the staff of the Aircraft Depot, Karachi on March 14 1936 and, back in the UK, he went to a staff job at 6 Armament Training Station, Warmwell on August 16 1938.

Hobson took command of 601 Squadron at Tangmere on July 17 1940. He was posted away on August 10.

He retired from the RAF on May 23 1956, as a Wing Commander, retaining the rank of Group Captain.

PO 20.12.30   FO 20.6.32   FL 1.4.36   SL 1.12.38
WC 1.3.41   WC 1.10.46

WILLIAM HENRY HODDS

908359   Sgt   Aircrew   British   25 Squadron

No service details traced.

JOHN STEPHEN ARTHUR HODGE

812278   Sgt   Air Gunner   British   141 Squadron

Joined 141 Squadron at Dyce on August 19 1940. Hodge was killed on July 15 1942, as a Flight Sergeant with 159 Squadron, operating in Liberators from Palestine.

Hodge is remembered on the Alamein Memorial, Column 249.

ARTHUR JOHN HODGKINSON

45353   Sgt   Pilot   British   219 Squadron

Hodgkinson was with 219 Squadron at Catterick in June 1940. He claimed a Do 17 destroyed on October 25.

In January 1941 Hodgkinson teamed up with Sergeant BE Dye. They destroyed a Do 17 on March 13, a probable He 111 on April 7, a probable Ju 88 on the 10th, an unidentified enemy aircraft on the 30th, He 111s on May 1, 9 and 16, unidentified enemy aircraft on June 21 and 25 and a Ju 88 on the 27th. Hodgkinson was awarded the DFC (11.4.41) and a Bar (6.6.41).

Hodgkinson was rested from operations and was then with 264 Squadron at Colerne from March 1942. He was posted overseas in early 1943 and joined 23 Squadron at Malta in February. On March 15 he shot down a He 111 of ll/KG 26 over Catania, Sicily. On the 23rd, on a train-busting operation over Western Sicily, a bullet fired from the ground entered the cockpit of the Mosquito and killed the navigator, Warrant Officer WA Woodman. Hodgkinson destroyed two Ju 88s west of Sicily on April 26.

He was killed on July 10 1943, aged 27. Hodgkinson is buried in Beach Head War Cemetery, Anzio, Italy. He was awarded the DSO (23.7.43).

PO 19.2.41   FO 19.2.42   FL 19.2.43

WILLIAM HENRY HODGSON

36269   PO   Pilot   New Zealander   85 Squadron

Born at Frankton Junction on September 30 1920, Hodgson worked as a radio technician in Dunedin. In late October 1938 he joined the Civil Reserve of Pilots. In early 1939 he applied for a short service commission in the RNZAF and on June 26 began his elementary flying training at the Otago Aero Club, Dunedin.

On September 12 Hodgson went to No 1 FTS, Wigram, was awarded his flying badge on November 23 and sailed for the UK in early March 1940. Having transferred into the RAF he was posted to No 1 Fighter Pilot Unit at Meir in late April. Hodgson converted to Hurricanes at 6 OTU, Sutton Bridge and joined 85 Squadron at Debden on May 25 1940.

He destroyed a Bf 109 and damaged a Do 17 and a Bf 110 on August 18, shared in destroying two Do 17s on the 26th, destroyed a Bf 109 on the 28th and got a probable Bf 110 and damaged two others and a He 111 on the 30th. In combat on the 31st Hodgson damaged a Do 17 and probably destroyed a Bf 109 and was then hit himself. With damaged oil lines and glycol tank and his engine on fire Hodgson prepared to bale out but saw he was over a densely populated area and decided to attempt a forced-landing elsewhere. He kept the flames under control by side-slipping and crash-landed in a field near Shotgate, Essex, narrowly missing anti-invasion obstacles. He was awarded the DFC (25.10.40).

On December 5 1940 Hodgson claimed a Bf 109 destroyed. He then became ill and was classed as medically unfit for operational flying. The squadron began to re-equip with Havocs in February 1941 and on March 13 Hodgson went along as a passenger in one to gain air experience. Piloted by Geoffrey Allard, the Havoc took off, then suddenly appeared to lose speed, banked to the left, went into a double spin and dived to the ground. Hodgson, Allard and a second passenger, Sergeant FR Walker-Smith, were all killed. The crash was believed to have been caused by the top nose panel becoming detached and flying off to jam the rudder.

Hodgson is buried in Saffron Walden Cemetery, Essex. In Wickford, Essex a road is named Hodgson Way in his memory and a memorial was erected near to the scene of his 1940 crash.

APO (RNZAF) 12.9.39   PO 13.4.40

CLAUDE GORDON HODSON

116806   Sgt   Pilot   Rhodesian   1 Squadron

Hodson joined No 1 Squadron at Wittering in September 1940.

He was posted to the Middle East in early 1941 and on January 29 flew a Hurricane to Malta and joined 261 Squadron. When the unit was disbanded in May he went to the newly-formed 185 Squadron.

Commissioned in December 1941, Hodson served later with 242 Squadron in North Africa. He went to the Southern Rhodesian Air Force on August 26 1945.

PO 6.12.41   FO 1.10.42   FL 6.12.43

HENRY ALGERNON VICKERS HOGAN

26181   SL   Pilot   British   501 Squadron

Born on October 25 1909, Hogan was educated at Malvern College and entered RAF College, Cranwell in January 1929 as a flight cadet. He graduated in December 1930 and joined 54 Squadron at Hornchurch

In March 1932 Hogan was posted to the Fleet Air Arm at Leuchars. On November 9 he joined 404 (Fleet Fighter) Flight at Netheravon, operating at sea from HMS 'Courageous'. On May 2 1933 he moved to 800 Squadron. In July 1934 Hogan was sent to CFS,

Upavon for a course, following which he went to No 1 FTS, Leuchars, to instruct Naval and Army officers. He returned to CFS on August 31 1936 to join the staff there.

On January 3 1938 Hogan was posted to No 1 Bomber Group Long Range Development Unit and flew with the RAF Long Distance Flight to Australia in November 1938, in Wellesleys. He joined 'P' staff at the Air Ministry in January 1939, then became CFI at 15 FTS, Lossiemouth, when it was formed and moved with it to Middle Wallop in May 1940.

Hogan went to 6 OTU, Sutton Bridge in June, to convert to Hurricanes. He took command of 501 Squadron at Croydon on June 22. He claimed a Bf 109 destroyed on July 20, a Do 215 on August 27 and a Bf 109 probably destroyed on September 17. Hogan was shot down in a combat with He 111s and Bf 109s over West Malling on September 18 and baled out, unhurt. His Hurricane, V 6620, crashed near Charing. He shared a Bf 110 on the 27th, claimed another on October 5, shared a Bf 109 on the 7th and claimed Bf 109s on the 12th and 15th. Hogan was awarded the DFC (25.10.40).

On November 5 1940 he was posted to Grangemouth, to form 58 OTU but the airfield was not ready so he went to Church Fenton, to form 54 OTU, returning to Grangemouth in January. Hogan was posted to the USA in June 1941, to set up pilot training there. In August 1942 he was in Washington with the RAF Delegation and was appointed Director of Flying Training RAF in the USA, as Group Captain.

Hogan returned to the UK in late 1943 and in December was made Chief Instructor at the Empire Central Flying School, Hullavington. In April 1945 he became CO of 19 FTS, when it was formed at Cranwell. He went to RAF Staff College at Haifa in April 1946. Made a CB (1955), Hogan held a series of appointments and commands before retiring on April 29 1962, as an Air Vice-Marshal. His portrait was drawn by Cuthbert Orde in 1940.

PO 20.12.30   FO 20.6.32   FL 1.4.36   SL 1.12.38
WC 1.3.41   GC 1.1.44   GC 1.7.47   AC 1.7.53
AVM 1.7.56

DOUGLAS WILLIAM HOGG

77977   PO   Pilot   British   25 Squadron

Hogg joined 25 Squadron at Martlesham Heath on September 1 1940. He was killed on the 3rd, when he was shot down over North Weald by an RAF Hurricane. His gunner, Sergeant E Powell, baled out, unhurt. The Blenheim, L 1512, crashed near Greensted Green. Hogg was 23. He is buried in Eastwood Cemetery, Glasgow.

PO 1.2.40

EDWARD SYDNEY HOGG

70312   FL   Pilot   British   152 Squadron

Hogg joined the RAF on a short service commission in March 1937 and did his intermediate and advanced flying training at 8 FTS, Montrose. He joined 152 Squadron at Acklington at its reformation there on October 1 1939.

Hogg shared in the destruction of a Ju 88 on August 23 1940. He left the squadron in October 1940.

He was released from the RAF in 1945, as a Wing Commander, and died in 1986.

APO 9.5.37   PO 8.3.38   FO 8.9.39   FL 8.9.40
SL 1.12.41

JOHN HENRY HOGG

751642   Sgt   Pilot   British   141 Squadron

Hogg, of Wolviston, Co Durham, joined 141 Squadron at Dyce on August 21 1940. He was killed on July 23 1942, as a Flight Sergeant with 159 Squadron, operating in Liberators from Palestine.

Hogg was 22. He is remembered on the Alamein Memorial, Column 249.

RALPH VINCENT HOGG

754794   Sgt   Pilot   British   616 Squadron

Joined 616 Squadron at Kirton-in-Lindsey on October 6 1940. Returning from a routine sortie on the 14th, Hogg was unable to lower his undercarriage and crash-landed at base.

He was reported 'Missing' on December 12 1940, serving with 41 Squadron, when he failed to return from a squadron patrol, in Spitfire P 7326. Hogg was 24 and is remembered on the Runnymede Memorial, Panel 15.

RICHARD MALZARD HOGG

33486   PO   Pilot   British   152 Squadron

Hogg, of Jersey, entered RAF College, Cranwell in April 1938 as a flight cadet. The outbreak of war meant that the course had to be condensed and Hogg left in September 1939, was commissioned in October and went to the 11 Group Pool at St Athan.

He joined the newly-formed 145 Squadron at Croydon on October 30. In Blenheim K 7114 Hogg collided with another Blenheim west of Gatwick on February 10 1940. Both aircraft got safely back to base.

In early July Hogg was with 152 Squadron at Acklington. On August 12 and 21 he shared in destroying two Ju 88s. He was shot down by enemy fighters in combat over the Channel on August 25 and reported 'Missing'.

Hogg was 21 and is remembered on the Runnymede Memorial, Panel 8.

PO 23.10.39

ROBERT DUDLEY HOGG

754041   Sgt   Pilot   British   56 and 17 Squadron

In early September 1940 Hogg, of Bedford, joined 56 Squadron at North Weald. He moved to 17 Squadron at Debden on September 11.

Hogg claimed a Bf 110 destroyed on the 27th, shared a Do 17 on October 24, shared a Bf 109 on the 29th and destroyed a Ju 87 and shared another on November 8.

Following a combat with Ju 87s and Bf 109s off Burnham on November 11 Hogg crashed at Monckton, near Manston and was killed, aged 22. He is buried in Bedford Cemetery, Bedfordshire.

EUSTACE HOLDEN

37970   FL   Pilot   British   501 Squadron

Born on December 28 1912, Holden joined the RAF on a short service commission in June 1936. He was posted to 3 FTS, Grantham on August 22 and joined 56 Squadron at North Weald on April 24 1937.

In 1940 Holden was with 501 Squadron and went with it to France on May 10. He claimed a Ju 88 destroyed on the 12th and a He 111 on the 27th. The squadron was withdrawn to England on June 18 and re-assembled at Croydon on the 21st.

Holden probably destroyed a Do 17 on July 12 and was awarded the DFC (16.8.40). It is believed that he was in hospital for several weeks and did not return to the squadron until late September. On October 5, 7, 12 and 25 Holden claimed Bf 109s destroyed. He took command of the squadron on November 1 1940 and led it until mid-June 1941, when he was posted to the Middle East.

After converting to twins Holden went to Lagos, where he was OC Dispatch Flight until early 1943. He returned to the UK and was given a staff job at Air Ministry. Holden later went on a course to RAF Staff College, after which he was posted to the Far East, returning to the UK in 1947.

Holden retired from the RAF on December 28 1964, as a Wing Commander.

APO 4.8.36   PO 8.6.37   FO 8.12.38   FL 3.9.40
SL 1.12.41   WC 1.7.44   WC 1.7.49

KENNETH HOLDEN

90705   **FO**   **Pilot**   **British**   **616 Squadron**

Holden joined 616 Squadron, AuxAF in early 1939 and flew his first solo as a trainee pilot on March 26. Called to full-time service on September 4 1939, he completed his training and rejoined the squadron in April 1940.

Over Dunkirk on May 28 Holden destroyed a Bf 109 and probably a second, on June 1 he destroyed another and probably a second and on September 27 destroyed a Bf 109.

In mid-May 1941 Holden took command of 610 Squadron at Westhampnett. He destroyed a Bf 109 on June 22, destroyed a Bf 109 and shared another on July 6, probably destroyed a Bf 109 on the 10th and was awarded the DFC (15.7.41). In November 1941 he was posted to the staff at HQ 12 Group.

Holden did not return to operations. He was released from the RAF in 1945, as a Wing Commander. He rejoined the RAuxAF in 1946 and commanded 616 Squadron at Finningley from July 1946 to 1950. Holden's portrait was drawn by Cuthbert Orde.

APO (AuxAF) 15.4.39   PO 4.9.39   FO 4.9.40   FL 4.9.41
SL 6.9.42   SL (RAuxAFRO) 1.8.46

GERALD ARTHUR HOLDER

81688   **PO**   **Observer**   **British**   **236 Squadron**

Joined 236 Squadron on July 18 1940. Holder was released from the RAF in 1946, as a Flight Lieutenant.

PO 30.6.40   FO 30.6.41   FL 30.6.42

ROBERT HOLDER

391556   **Sgt**   **Pilot**   **British**   **151 Squadron**

Holder was born on April 16 1917 at Bidford-on-Avon, Warwickshire. He went to New Zealand in 1938 and was employed on a farm at Hicks Bay, Gisborne.

At the outbreak of war Holder volunteered for pilot training in the RNZAF and he reported to the Ground Training School at Weraroa on November 19 1939. In December he was posted to 2 EFTS, New Plymouth and moved to 2 FTS, Woodbourne on March 11 1940.

Holder completed his training at the end of June and was promoted to Sergeant. He sailed for the UK on July 12 in the RMS 'Rangitane'. In mid-September he was at 6 OTU, Sutton Bridge, where he converted to Hurricanes. On September 30 Holder joined 151 Squadron at Wittering.

In the evening of October 26 he was one of a group practicing night circuits and landings at Coleby Grange. The Hurricane ahead of him took off but crashed and burst into flames some 500 yards beyond the windward boundary. The Flight Commander asked Holder if he was all right and said no one would think badly of him if he preferred not to take off. Holder said he would go and the Flight Commander checked his gyro to see that it was uncaged. The Hurricane took off and shortly afterwards went into a left-hand turn and flew into the ground 800 yards beyond the first crash. Holder was killed.

He is buried in Bidford-on-Avon Cemetery.

JOHN BROWNING HOLDERNESS

SR 72329   **FL**   **Pilot**   **Rhodesian**   **1 and 229 Squadrons**

Transferred from the SRAF in May 1938 and attached to the RAF. Holderness joined 248 Squadron at Hendon, when it was reformed on October 30 1939.

He was posted to No 1 Squadron at Tangmere in August 1940. Holderness claimed a Do 215 destroyed on September 7. He moved to 229 Squadron at Northolt on October 17 and was posted away in December 1940.

Holderness returned to the SRAF on August 26 1945.

FO 12.5.38   FL 3.9.40   SL 1.12.41

ARTHUR LAWRENCE HOLLAND

05204   **SL**   **Pilot**   **British**   **501 and 65 Squadrons**

Born on May 4 1909, Holland went up to Cambridge to read Engineering in October 1928. He joined the University Air Squadron in January 1930 and trained in Avro 504s and Bristol Fighters. Later in the year he began training with the RAFO at Hatfield.

In the summer of 1931 Holland was granted a Permanent Commission, as a University Entrant. He was posted to 3 FTS, Grantham on October 24 1931 and after training joined 17 Squadron at Upavon on March 27 1932. Holland went to RAF Henlow in August 1934 for a two-year Officers' Engineering Course and was posted to RAF Gosport in August 1936 as Officer i/c Aircraft Repair Squadron. He was responsible for servicing the Torpedo Training Squadron and the FAA on board HMS 'Furious' and 'Courageous'.

In March 1938 Holland was promoted to Squadron Leader and sent to Air HQ India as Command Engineering Officer. He returned to the UK in December 1939. In January 1940 he was posted to Air Ministry on Engineering duties, firstly at Harrogate and later in London. Holland's request to be allowed to return to flying was answered in July 1940, when he was posted to 6 OTU, Sutton Bridge to convert to Hurricanes.

On August 6 Holland was attached to 501 Squadron at Gravesend, as a supernumerary to gain combat experience. He made a forced-landing outside Dover on August 12 after a combat with Bf 109s off Westgate. Holland was posted to Rochford on August 14 to command 65 Squadron. He converted himself to Spitfires, flew from Rochford until August 27 and then took the squadron to Turnhouse.

In November Holland was admitted to Edinburgh Infirmary with a suspected tumour behind the right eye. He was grounded and non-effective sick for four months. Holland was transferred to the Technical Branch and in April 1941 became Chief Technical Officer at 58 OTU, Grangemouth. He moved to 51 OTU, Cranfield in February 1942 and in July 1943 went to the Ministry of Aircraft Production.

In September 1944 Holland joined the Directing Staff at RAF Staff College, Bracknell, as an Acting Group Captain. He held a number of commands in India, the Canal Zone and the UK in the post-war RAF. Holland was made a CBE (1.1.55) and he retired on October 25 1960, as a Group Captain.

PO 24.10.31   FO 24.6.32   FL 1.4.36   SL 1.12.38
WC 1.3.41   GC 1.7.44   WC 1.10.46   GC 1.7.54

DENNIS FREDERICK HOLLAND

77269   **PO**   **Pilot**   **British**   **72 Squadron**

Born in 1917, Holland was educated at Newbury, Berkshire and had obtained his 'A' and 'B' licences by the time he was 17. He became the youngest Civil Air Guard instructor in Britain and in 1938 was instructing at the Portsmouth Aero Club. By September 1939, when he was called up as a member of the RAFVR, Holland had 3000 flying hours.

Commissioned in December 1939, he joined 72 Squadron in early 1940. On September 4 he claimed a Bf 110 destroyed, on the 5th a Bf 109 and on the 15th a He 111. Holland was shot down over Canterbury on September 20. He baled out, severely wounded, and died soon after admission to hospital. His Spitfire, X 4410, is believed to have crashed at Stiff Street, Sittingbourne.

Holland is buried in St Andrew's churchyard, Chaddlesworth, Berkshire.

PO 10.12.39

KENNETH CHRISTOPHER HOLLAND

754503   Sgt   Pilot   Australian   152 Squadron

Originally from Sydney, Holland came under the care of a guardian, who lived in Camelford in Cornwall.

He was with 152 Squadron at Acklington in early July 1940. On September 17 he shared in the destruction of a Ju 88 and on the 19th destroyed a Ju 88. On September 25 Holland attacked a He 111 and set it on fire. Seeing a parachute he went in for a closer look but was shot down by a gunner, still in the Heinkel. His Spitfire, N 3173, crashed near Church Farm, Wolverton and he was killed. The enemy aircraft also crashed at Church Farm. Four of the crew were killed. The pilot baled out and was captured.

Holland was 20 years old. He was cremated at Weymouth Crematorium.

ROBERT HUGH HOLLAND

33487   FO   Pilot   British   92 Squadron

Born in Ceylon, Holland entered RAF College, Cranwell in April 1938 as a flight cadet. The outbreak of war caused the course to be condensed and Holland left in September 1939, was commissioned in October and went to the 11 Group Pool at St Athan.

He joined the newly-reformed 92 Squadron at Tangmere at the end of October. Over France on May 23 1940 Holland claimed two Bf 110s and a Ju 88 destroyed, on the 24th a Do 17 and on June 2 a Bf 109 over Dunkirk.

Holland shared in the destruction of a Do 17 on July 8, claimed a Ju 88 on the 15th and shared another on the 25th. He was shot down in combat west of Ashford on September 15, baled out and was injured on landing. He was admitted to hospital at East Grinstead. At some time Holland was treated by Archie McIndoe and became a Guinea Pig.

On October 26 and November 1, 2, 15 and 17 he claimed Bf 109s destroyed and was awarded the DFC (26.11.40). In early 1941 Holland was posted to 91 Squadron at Hawkinge, as a Flight Commander. He claimed a Bf 109 destroyed on March 13. Rested from operations, Holland was OC 5 Squadron at 61 OTU, Heston in November 1941.

He was posted to 615 Squadron at Fairwood Common in February 1942, as a Flight Commander. In October 1942 Holland was given command of 607 Squadron at Jessore in India. He destroyed a Nakajima 'Oscar' on March 5 1943. Later in March he took command of 615 Squadron at Feni, India.

Holland was posted away in January 1944. He remained in the RAF after the war and died on November 17 1954, as a Wing Commander.

PO 23.10.39   FO 23.10.40   FL 23.10.41   SL 1.6.45

ROBERT MEREDITH HOLLAND

626982   Sgt   Aircrew   British   600 Squadron

No service details traced.

ERNEST JAMES HOLLIS

970073   Sgt   Aircrew   British   25 Squadron

Joined 25 Squadron at North Weald on September 30 1940. Promoted to Warrant Officer on July 1 1942, Hollis was awarded the DFC (12.12.44), serving with 141 Squadron.

He was released from the RAF in 1945 and died on January 27 1975.

SYDNEY VICTOR HOLLOWAY

121329   Sgt   Pilot   British   25 Squadron

Born on February 27 1918, Holloway joined the RAFVR on March 29 1938 and began his flying training at 3 E&RFTS, Hamble in mid-April. Called up after the outbreak of war, he went to No 1 ITW Cambridge on December 14 1939 and was posted to 3 FTS, South Cerney on February 1 1940.

Holloway converted to Blenheims at 5 OTU, Aston Down from June 22 to July 6, when he joined 25 Squadron at Martlesham Heath. He was credited with a He 111 destroyed on November 15 1940.

Commissioned in May 1942, Holloway was posted to 60 OTU, East Fortune on July 20, as an instructor. On January 13 1943 he was attached to 3 FIS, Castle Combe for an instructor course on Mosquitos, after which he returned to East Fortune, by then re-numbered as 132 OTU.

On August 18 1943 Holloway joined 85 Squadron at West Malling. He destroyed a Ju 88 on October 8 and flew anti-flying bomb patrols in 1944. Holloway was posted to the Ground Controlled Approach School at Honiley in September for a course. From March 1945 to August 1951 he served with GCA units on the Continent and in Britain. He was made an OBE (9.6.49) for his work with GCA at Gatow during the Berlin Airlift.

Holloway went to Air Traffic Control in August 1951. He retired on March 2 1968, as a Squadron Leader.

*PO 1.5.42   FO 1.11.42   FL 1.5.44   FL 1.11.45
SL 1.7.55*

KENNETH BRUCE HOLLOWELL

113338   Sgt   Pilot   British   25 Squadron

With 25 Squadron at Martlesham Heath in early July 1940. Commissioned in November 1941, Hollowell was awarded the AFC (8.6.44) and released from the RAF in 1945, as a Flight Lieutenant.

PO 25.11.41   FO 1.10.42   FL 25.11.43

ERIC LEONARD HOLMES

740063   Sgt   Pilot   British   248 Squadron

Holmes, of Ilford, Essex, was with 248 Squadron in early July 1940. On November 14 he attacked a 2500 ton ship in a Norwegian fjord and scored two direct hits.

On June 12 1941 Holmes was killed, as a Flight Sergeant with 248. He was 25 and is remembered on the Runnymede Memorial, Panel 36.

FREDERICK HENRY HOLMES

76583   PO   Pilot   British   152 Squadron

Holmes, of Lincolnshire, was instructing before he joined 152 Squadron at Acklington in June 1940. On July 25 he shared in the destruction of a Do 17, on August 18 he claimed a Ju 87 destroyed and on the 21st he shared a Ju 88.

On December 4 1944 Holmes was killed, as a Flight Lieutenant with 487 Squadron, aged 31. He is buried in the Reichswald Forest War Cemetery, Cleves, Germany.

PO 24.12.39   FO 24.12.40   FL 24.12.41

GEORGE HENRY HOLMES

84682　　PO　　Air Gunner　　British　　600 Squadron

Holmes was with 600 Squadron at Manston in early 1940. He flew as gunner in Flying Officer TN Hayes' Blenheim in the attack on Rotterdam aerodrome on May 10. Under intense fire and handicapped by petrol fumes from a burst tank Holmes directed Hayes in the evasive manoeuvres required to escape enemy fighters and was largely responsible for the aircraft's safe return to base, the only one of the six involved to do so. Holmes was awarded the DFM (24.5.40) and commissioned in August.

On December 20 1940 Holmes was in a Blenheim returning to Catterick after a searchlight co-operation exercise. R/T contact was lost and the aircraft crashed into the side of a hill west of Richmond, Yorkshire. The pilot was killed and Holmes died of his injuries on December 25. He is buried in Catterick Cemetery.

PO 18.8.40

RAYMOND TOWERS HOLMES

68730　　Sgt　　Pilot　　British　　504 Squadron

Holmes joined the RAFVR in February 1937 and began his flying training at 12 E&RFTS, Prestwick. He later flew at 7 E&RFTS, Desford and 17 E&RFTS, Barton. Called up at the outbreak of war, Holmes was posted to 4 ITW, Bexhill on October 29 1939. He went to 5 FTS, Sealand on December 9 and with training completed joined 504 Squadron at Wick on June 18 1940.

On September 15 1940 Holmes was involved in shooting down a Do 17 over central London. Probably the best-known German casualty in the Battle of Britain, the Dornier may have bombed Buckingham Palace and after Holmes had administered the coup de grace it broke up, a large section of wreckage falling on the forecourt of Victoria Station. Holmes aircraft was damaged by return fire and he baled out, unhurt, and landed in Hugh Street, Chelsea. His Hurricane, P 2725, crashed and burned out outside Fountain Court, Buckingham Palace Road.

Holmes was commissioned in June 1941. In late July 'A' Flight of 504 was re-numbered 81 Squadron and posted to Leconfield, where the personnel, Holmes included, were kitted out for an unknown destination. They flew to Abbotsinch in Harrows and embarked for Russia on the carrier HMS 'Argus', which carried crated Hurricanes. On September 1 the squadron flew off in sixes for Vaenga airfield, near Murmansk. Operations were flown until mid-November, when pilots of the squadron began converting Russian pilots on to Hurricanes. They left Russia on November 29, leaving all equipment behind and returned in HMS 'Kenya', landing at Rosyth on December 7 1941.

81 Squadron went to Turnhouse, where it received Spitfire Vbs. On March 1 1942 Holmes was posted to 2 FIS, Montrose for an instructor's course, after which he joined the staff at 5 (P) AFU at Tern Hill. He returned to 2 FIS on September 17 1942, as an instructor, and stayed with the unit until mid-November 1944.

After a short spell with 309 at Andrews Field in early 1945 Holmes joined 541 Squadron at Benson, a Spitfire photographic-reconnaissance unit. He became a King's Messenger for Winston Churchill, when he was preparing for the Potsdam Conference, flying mail between London and Biarritz, and Berlin and London when he was at Potsdam.

Holmes left the squadron at the end of August and was released from the RAF on October 4 1945, as a Flight Lieutenant.

PO 10.6.41　　FO 10.6.42　　FL 10.6.43

WILFRED BARWELL HOLROYD

101040　　Sgt　　Pilot　　British　　501 and 151 Squadrons

Served with 501 Squadron at Kenley and later 151 Squadron at Digby in October 1940.

Holroyd was commissioned in July 1941 and released from the RAF in 1946, as a Flight Lieutenant.

PO 12.7.41　　FO 22.3.42　　FL 22.3.43

ARTHUR GERALD VAUGHAN HOLTON

755479　　Sgt　　Air Gunner　　British　　141 Squadron

Joined 141 Squadron at Turnhouse on August 19 1940. After being posted away from the squadron Holton retrained as a Navigator Radar.

He went with 89 Squadron to the Middle East and served in Malta with a squadron detachment. In January 1943 Holton went with a detachment to Calcutta, which formed the nucleus of 176 Squadron, also equipped with Beaufighters.

Holton was released from the RAF in 1945, as a Warrant Officer.

MICHAEL GILES HOMER

33409　　PO　　Pilot　　British　　1 and 242 Squadrons

Homer, of Swanage, Dorset, was at Wellington College from 1933 to 1936. He entered RAF College, Cranwell in January 1937 as a flight cadet. On graduation he was commissioned and joined 106 Squadron at Thornaby on December 17 1938.

In early 1940 Homer was with 44 Squadron, operating in Hampdens from Waddington. On April 12 he was captain of an aircraft, which carried out a high-level bombing attack on two enemy cruisers in Christiansand Bay. He pressed home his attack in the face of intense anti-aircraft fire and attacks by enemy fighters, one of which his air gunner shot down. He then got his damaged aircraft safely back to base. For this operation Homer was awarded the DFC (26.4.40).

In August he volunteered for Fighter Command and joined No 1 Squadron at Northolt in early September 1940. On the 7th he damaged a Do 17. Homer was posted to 242 Squadron at Coltishall on September 21. He was shot down and killed on the 27th, when he crashed in flames at Bluetown, Mintching Wood, Milstead, near Sittingbourne.

Homer was 21. He is buried in Godlingston Cemetery, Swanage.

PO 17.12.38

DOUGLAS HAROLD HONE

80816　　PO　　Pilot　　British　　615 Squadron

Born on September 30 1917, Hone, from Purley, was a bank clerk. He joined the RAFVR in September 1938 and carried out his elementary training at 19 E&RFTS, Gatwick.

Called up after the outbreak of war, Hone was posted to No 1 ITW, Cambridge on November 11 1939 and on December 30 went to 12 FTS, Grantham. After completing his training Hone moved to 6 OTU, Sutton Bridge on June 8 1940, to convert to Hurricanes. He joined 615 Squadron at Kenley on July 6 and saw his first action on the 19th.

Hone shared in destroying a He 59 on July 27 and claimed a Do 17 destroyed on the 29th. He was attacked by a Hurricane on August 14 and with instruments shot away managed to land at Kenley. On the 24th he engaged Do 17s but after his glycol tank was damaged by return fire he crash-landed in a field at Meopham, uninjured. Two days later he was wounded in the leg and thigh by cannon shell splinters, in an attack by a Bf 109. Hone was admitted to Southend

Hospital. He flew again on September 29 with the squadron, then at Prestwick.

On February 26 1941 Hone was shot down by Bf 109s and crashed at Tenterden, suffering concussion and bleeding eyes. He was posted to 56 OTU, Sutton Bridge on July 9, as an instructor. He made a wheels-up landing on August 14, near the mouth of the River Nene, with a goose in the radiator, causing engine failure. After a short spell at 61 OTU, Rednal in April/May 1942 Hone joined 41 Squadron at Merston. Operating over Dieppe on August 19 he damaged a FW 190.

Hone went to 501 Squadron at Hawkinge on September 1 1943 and left on January 3 1944 to become a Controller. He was released from the RAF in April 1946, as a Flight Lieutenant, and returned to the bank. He joined the RAFVR as a controller and then rejoined the RAF in July 1950 and was granted a Permanent Commission in the Fighter Control Branch.

Hone retired on September 30 1975, as a Flight Lieutenant.

PO 9.6.40   FO 9.6.41   FL 9.6.42   FO 23.8.46
FL 7.6.51

DUDLEY SANDRY GARTON HONOR

40113   FO   Pilot   British   145 Squadron

An Anglo-Argentinian, Honor joined the RAF on a short service commission in July 1937. He was posted to 6 FTS, Netheravon on September 18 and joined 88 Squadron at Boscombe Down on March 7 1938. At the outbreak of war the squadron went to France with the AASF and suffered heavy losses in the German blitzkrieg. For his services in France Honor was awarded the DFC (5.11.40).

After 88 was withdrawn from France in June 1940 Honor volunteered for Fighter Command and was posted to 145 Squadron at Drem on August 28. On October 12 he shared in the destruction of an Arado Ar 196 floatplane. On the 27th he made a forced-landing at Hollington, near St Leonards after running out of fuel following a combat with Bf 109s. The Hurricane, V 7422, was written off.

In April 1941 Honor was posted to 274 Squadron in the Western Desert, as a Flight Commander. He joined it at Amriya on the 6th. He claimed Bf 109s destroyed on May 1 and 15 and on the 20th destroyed a Bf 110, which had just taken off from Mechili, as well as a Ju 52 on the ground. On a patrol over Crete on May 25 Honor destroyed a Ju 52 and a Sm 79. He was then shot down by a Bf 109 and swam to Crete. After hiding for several days he was picked up by a Sunderland and returned to the squadron on June 5. He was awarded a Bar to the DFC (10.6.41).

In August 1941 Honor took command of 274 and led it until November 12, when he was promoted to Acting Wing Commander to lead 258 Wing. On December 6 he destroyed a Mc 202 eight miles from Tobruk. Honor was commanding 17 Sector, Benghazi in December 1942.

He was posted as Air Attaché to Central America in 1944 and was released from the RAF in 1947, as a Group Captain. He died in Canada.

APO 5.9.37   PO 12.7.38   FO 12.1.40   FL 12.1.41
SL 1.3.41   WC 24.9.45

HILARY RICHARD LIONEL HOOD

26110   SL   Pilot   British   41 Squadron

Hood was at Tonbridge School from 1923 to 1927 and entered the RAF College, Cranwell in September 1927 as a flight cadet. He graduated in July 1929 and joined 23 Squadron at Kenley. On October 9 1931 Hood was posted to 403 (Fleet Fighter) Flight on HMS 'Hermes' in the Far East.

Back in the UK he went to CFS, Wittering for an instructor's course on August 22 1933 and afterwards joined the staff at RAF Leuchars to train FAA pilots. Hood was posted to the staff at 11 FTS, Wittering on October 1 1935, returned to 23 Squadron at Biggin Hill on October 26 1936, went to the staff at 5 FTS, Sealand on March 15 1937 and was given command of the Station Flight at Northolt on June 27 1938.

Hood took command of 41 Squadron at Catterick in April 1940. During the Dunkirk evacuation he came upon a German bomber at sea level but had no ammunition and very little fuel. He made a feint attack and the enemy aircraft dived into the sea.

On July 29 Hood claimed a Bf 109 and a Ju 87 destroyed. He was killed on September 5, when he collided with Flying Officer JT Webster, during an attack on Do 17s over the Thames Estuary. Hood's Spitfire, P 9428, is believed to have disintegrated over Wickford.

He was 32 years old and is remembered on the Runnymede Memorial, Panel 4.

PO 27.7.29   FO 27.1.31   FL 27.1.35   SL 1.8.38

ARCHIE HOOK

647887   Sgt   Air Gunner   British   248 Squadron

Hook, of Beeston, Nottinghamshire, joined 248 Squadron on September 10 1940. He was one of the crew of a Blenheim detailed to fly from Sumburgh to Wick for operations on December 13 1940. The aircraft collided with another whilst formating and crashed into the sea and sank. All three men aboard were killed.

Hook was 18. He is remembered on the Runnymede Memorial, Panel 15.

DOUGLAS NEWCOMBE HOOKWAY

82691   PO   Pilot   British   234 Squadron

Born in 1920, Hookway joined the RAFVR in February 1939 and did his flying training at 5 E&RFTS, Hanworth. Called up at the outbreak of war, he was posted to 7 EFTS, Desford in November.

Hookway moved on to 10 FTS, Tern Hill in April 1940 and on completion of the course in July he went to No 1 School of Army Co-operation at Old Sarum. The shortage of fighter pilots led to Hookway being posted to 7 OTU, Hawarden in August and he joined 234 Squadron at St Eval on September 20 1940.

In March 1941 he went to CFS, Upavon for an instructor's course and was posted in May to 9 FTS, Hullavington. In June Hookway moved to 53 OTU at Heston and in October he went to 28 EFTS at Pendeford. Apart from six months instructing at 7 EFTS, Desford from July 1942 to January 1943 Hookway remained at Pendeford until he was released from the RAF in January 1946, as a Squadron Leader. He was awarded the AFC (1.1.46) and was CFI during his final year at 28 EFTS.

PO 27.7.40   FO 27.7.41   FL 27.7.42

BERESFORD GWYNNE HOOPER

40707   FO   Pilot   British   25 Squadron

Joined the RAF on a short service commission in March 1938. In May Hooper was posted to 11 FTS, Shawbury and in December he joined 25 Squadron at Hawkinge.

On September 15 1940 Hooper was the only survivor, when Beaufighter R 2067 crashed near Biggin Hill, cause unknown. He transferred into the Administrative Branch in late 1942 and went into the Fighter Control Branch in 1945.

Hooper was released from the RAF some time after April 1951.

APO 7.5.38   PO 17.12.38   FO 3.9.40   FL 3.9.41
FL 1.9.45

Sir ARCHIBALD PHILIP HOPE

90127   FL   Pilot   British   601 Squadron

Born on March 27 1912, Hope succeeded his father as the 17th Baronet of Craighall in 1924. He was educated at Eton and Balliol College, Oxford, and learned to fly with the University Air Squadron.

Hope served in the RAFO from 1931 until joining 601 Squadron, AuxAF at Hendon in late 1934. He was called to full-time service on August 24 1939. He flew one of the six Blenheims of 601, which attacked the seaplane base at Borkum on November 28.

As 'A' Flight Commander Hope led his flight to Merville on May 16 1940. He crash-landed in a field the next day, shot down by return fire from Dorniers he was attacking. On the 27th, flying from Tangmere again, Hope was leading 601, when he was attacked by Bf 110s and shot down some five miles out from the coast between Calais and Dunkirk. He headed for land and flew as far east as possible, away from the advancing Germans. Hope crash-landed on a beach, set fire to his Hurricane and was then taken by a French farmer to Bergues, where there was a British Brigade HQ. He was taken by lorry to the Dunkirk docks, spent a night on the dunes and went aboard the destroyer HMS 'Wakeful' the next day. After landing at Dover Hope phoned 601 and a Magister picked him up at Hawkinge, still carrying his parachute.

On August 15 Hope shared in the destruction of a Ju 88 and on the 16th he claimed a Bf 110 destroyed. He was promoted to Acting Squadron Leader on August 19 and took command of the squadron. Awarded the DFC (1.10.40), Hope was posted away in December 1940.

In May 1945 he was commanding RAF Peterhead, as a Group Captain. He was released later in the year. He died in June 1987. Hope's portrait was done by Cuthbert Orde in November 1940.

PO (AuxAF) 25.1.35   FO (AuxAF) 25.7.36   FL 12.3.40
SL 1.6.41   WC 1.6.42

RALPH HOPE

90257   FO   Pilot   British   605 Squadron

Born in Birmingham on July 18 1914, Hope was related, on his mother's side, to Joseph, Austen and Neville Chamberlain. He was educated at Eton and New College, Oxford. He won his rowing blue in 1935 and rowed bow in the University Boat Race. In 1936 Hope joined the family firm of metal window manufacturers. He went to the firm's subsidiary in Jamestown, New York in September 1937. Whilst there he started flying and returned to England in 1938 with his pilot's license.

Hope joined 605 Squadron, AuxAF at Castle Bromwich soon after his return. He was called to full-time service on August 24 1939. On May 9 1940 Hope shared in destroying a Do 17 off Dunnet Head. He was shot down on September 28 by Bf 109s over Ticehurst and baled out, unhurt. His Hurricane, P 3828, crashed at Bewl Bridge, Lamberhurst.

On October 14 1940 Hope flew into the Inner Artillery Zone during a patrol. He crashed and was killed, either by striking a balloon cable or shot down by anti-aircraft fire. His Hurricane, P 3107, crashed in Tennison Road, South Norwood.

Hope was cremated at St John's Crematorium, Woking

PO (AuxAF) 12.6.38   PO 24.8.39   FO 10.12.39

JAMES HOPEWELL

516702   Sgt   Pilot   British   616 and 66 Squadrons

Hopewell, of Bingley, Yorkshire, joined 616 Squadron at Leconfield in July 1940. He claimed a Ju 88 destroyed on August 15, a Bf 109 on the 30th, a Do 215 on September 1 and a Bf 110 on the 2nd.

Posted to 66 Squadron at West Malling on October 14 1940, Hopewell remained with it until early 1941, when he went to 151 Squadron at Wittering. He was awarded the DFM (24.6.41) and was killed on January 21 1942, as a Warrant Officer, aged 27. The unit he was serving with is not known.

Hopewell is buried in Bingley Cemetery.

CHARLES LEONARD HOPGOOD

745559   Sgt   Pilot   British   64 Squadron

Hopgood, of Reading, Berkshire, joined 64 Squadron at Leconfield on September 29 1940.

He was killed on December 5 1940, aged 22. Hopgood is buried in Boulogne Eastern Cemetery, France.

WILLIAM PELHAM HOPKIN

42606   PO   Pilot   British   54 and 602 Squadrons

Born on March 15 1921, Hopkin joined the RAF on a short service commission in May 1939. He was with 54 Squadron at Rochford in early July 1940.

On August 18 he claimed a Do 17 destroyed and a Bf 110 shared and on the 22nd a Bf 110 destroyed. Hopkin was posted to 602 Squadron at Westhampnett on September 12. On the 26th he claimed a He 111, on the 27th a Bf 110 and on October 30 a probable Bf 109.

Hopkin became a Flight Commander in early 1941 and was awarded the DFC (9.9.41).

He stayed on in the RAF, in the Secretarial Branch, and retired on August 1 1967, as a Wing Commander. In the sixties he was Hon Secretary of the Battle of Britain Fighter Association.

APO 10.7.39   PO 6.4.40   FO 6.4.41   FL 6.4.42
FL 1.9.45   SL 1.1.52   WC 1.1.61

BERNARD WALTER HOPTON

745034   Sgt   Pilot   British   600, 615, 73 and 66 Sqdns

Hopton, of New Malden, Surrey, was with 600 Squadron at Northolt in early July 1940, moved to 615 at Prestwick on August 17, to 73 at Castle Camps on October 1 and to 66 at West Malling on October 23.

On November 14 Hopton probably destroyed a Bf 109. He was killed on August 6 1941, as a Sergeant with 616 Squadron. He was 21 and is buried in Ladywell Cemetery, Lewisham, London.

WILLIAM HENRY HORNBY

60513   Sgt   Pilot   British   234 Squadron

Born in 1912, Hornby was a junior civil servant before the war. He joined the AuxAF in 1936 as an aircrafthand and transferred to the RAFVR as a u/t pilot in April 1937. He did his weekend flying at 5 E&RFTS, Hanworth and later at 21 E&RFTS, Stapleford.

Mobilised on September 1 1939, Hornby was sent to 10 FTS, Tern Hill for assessment of his flying capabilities. He joined the newly-reformed 234 Squadron at Leconfield on November 6. Hornby claimed a Bf 109 destroyed on August 26 1940 and a Bf 110 on September 4. Two days later he was shot down and baled out, with facial injuries. His Spitfire, X 4183, exploded over Quickbourne Lane, Northam. After four days at the Casualty Clearing Station at Benenden Hornby was taken to Hollymoor Hospital, Birmingham. He rejoined the squadron at St Eval but did not fly operationally again until November 1.

Commissioned in January 1941, Hornby was posted to 124 Squadron at Castletown on May 23 but moved to 58 OTU, Grangemouth on August 5, as an instructor. On September 16 he was transferred to 61 OTU, Heston, remaining with it until April 22 1942, when he was sent on a course at 2 FIS, Montrose.

Hornby instructed at 7 (P) AFU at Peterborough from June 13 1942 until September 12 1944. The unit then moved to Sutton Bridge, was re-named 7 SFTS and there Hornby instructed trainee pilots of the Free French Air Force until his demobilisation in 1945.

PO 22.1.41   FO 22.1.42   FL 22.1.43

FRANK GEORGE HORNER

100034   Sgt   Pilot   British   610 Squadron

Joined 610 Squadron at Acklington on September 16 1940. Horner was commissioned in June 1941 and released from the RAF in 1947, as a Flight Lieutenant.

PO 12.6.41   FO 12.6.42   FL 12.6.43

JAMES MICHAEL HORROX

85268   PO   Pilot   British   151 Squadron

Horrox, of Keyningham, Yorkshire, was posted to 151 Squadron at Digby in October 1940.

In mid-November 1940 the carrier HMS 'Argus' sailed from Gibraltar with Hurricanes for Malta. Horrox was one of the six pilots, who flew off on November 16 in the second flight of Hurricanes, led by a FAA Skua. A series of mishaps saw the Hurrricanes run out of fuel and fall one by one into the sea, with the loss of all six pilots.

Horrox was 20. He is remembered on the Runnymede Memorial, Panel 8.

PO 22.9.40

VLADIMIR HORSKY

787554   Sgt   Pilot   Czechoslovakian   238 Squadron

Joined 238 Squadron at Middle Wallop on September 12 1940. He was shot down in combat with Bf 110s over the Solent on September 25. His Hurricane, P 3098, is presumed to have crashed into the sea.

Horsky was 26. He is remembered on the Runnymede Memorial, Panel 15.

PATRICK WILMOT HORTON

42128   PO   Pilot   New Zealander   234 Squadron

Horton was born in Dunedin on March 25 1920. He was educated at Hutchings School, Hobart and Wellington College. In 1936 he went to work for the Mines Department.

Having been provisionally accepted for an RAF short service commission Horton sailed for the UK on February 1 1939 in the RMS 'Tainui'. He began his ab initio training at 10 E&RFTS, Yatesbury on March 13 and went on to 5 FTS, Sealand on May 26. Horton joined the newly-reformed 234 Squadron at Leconfield on November 6.

The squadron began to change its Blenheims for Spitfires in May 1940. On July 28 Horton shared in the destruction of a Ju 88 thirty miles south of Plymouth, on August 16 he destroyed a Bf 109, on the 26th he claimed another Bf 109 but crash-landed himself at Middle Wallop after being damaged in combat near Portsmouth. He claimed a Bf 110 destroyed on September 4.

In October Horton volunteered for service in the Middle East. In mid-November 1940 the carrier HMS 'Argus' sailed from Gibraltar with Hurricanes for Malta. Horton was one of the six pilots, who flew off on November 16 in the second flight of Hurricanes, led by a FAA Skua. A series of mishaps saw the Hurricanes run out of fuel and fall one by one into the sea, with the loss of all six pilots.

Horton is remembered on the Runnymede Memorial, Panel 6. He received a Mention in Despatches (17.3.41).

APO 12.5.39   PO 6.11.39   FO 6.11.40

HAROLD BASIL LINCOLN HOUGH

79548   PO   Pilot   British   600 Squadron

Hough, of Finchley, London, joined 600 Squadron at Northolt in June 1940. On September 8 he became lost following R/T failure during a night patrol. When the fuel was exhausted Hough and his crew of two baled out at 6000 feet, over Basingstoke. The Blenheim, L 1111, crashed near Odiham.

Posted away from the squadron in early 1941, Hough was killed on August 16, as a Flying Officer instructor, aged 23. He was cremated at the Lawns Wood Crematorium, Leeds.

PO 2.6.40

CYRIL GEORGE HOUGHTON

84912   PO   Pilot   British   141 Squadron

Born in Bedford on October 22 1916, Houghton was educated at Bedford School and worked at St Pancras Station as a trainee clerk with LMS Hotel Services.

He joined the RAFVR in June 1939 and was called up at the outbreak of war. Houghton was posted to 141 Squadron at Dyce on August 18 1940 and served with it until October 1942, when he was posted to North Weald as a controller.

Houghton returned to operations on March 15 1943, joining 29 Squadron at West Malling. He went to 85 Squadron, also at West Malling, on August 23 1943 and stayed with it until 1945, when he was seconded to BOAC. When BEA was formed Houghton transferred. He retired in February 1962, as a Senior Captain.

He then went into partnership with Jimmy Chipperfield to build and manage Plymouth Zoo. Houghton and his family did this until May 1968, when they went to Tilburg, Holland, to build and run a Lion Park. He returned to England in October because of ill-health and died on May 22 1969.

PO 3.8.40   FO 3.8.41   FL 3.8.42

OLIVER VINCENT HOUGHTON

745437   Sgt   Pilot   British   32 and 501 Squadrons

Houghton was born at Faleshill, Coventry on January 19 1921 and worked as an aero fitter. He joined the Civil Air Guard in October 1938 and flew at Whitley aerodrome, Coventry. He joined the RAFVR on March 22 1939 and was called up on September 1.

Posted to 4 ITW, Bexhill on October 30, Houghton went to 5 FTS, Sealand on December 9. He completed his training and joined 615 Squadron at Kenley on June 18 1940, moved to 32 Squadron at Biggin Hill on July 10 and then to 501 Squadron at Kenley on August 27.

Houghton was shot down and killed in combat over Ashford on September 6. His Hurricane, V 6646, crashed into Long Beech Wood, Charing. He is buried in All Saints' churchyard extension, Allesley, Coventry.

———— HOWARD

No unknown   Sgt   Aircrew   British   235 Squadron

No service details traced.

JOHN HOWARD

86628   PO   Pilot   British   54 and 74 Squadrons

Joined 54 Squadron at Catterick in October 1940 and moved to 74 Squadron at Biggin Hill on the 24th.

Howard damaged a Bf 109 on April 7 1941. He did not return from an escort operation for Blenheims of 101 Squadron on May 6. He was 22 and is buried in Marquise Communal Cemetery, France.

PO 24.8.40

PETER IAN HOWARD-WILLIAMS

33569   PO   Pilot   British   19 Squadron

Born in Cowes on December 27 1919, Howard-Williams entered RAF College, Cranwell in April 1939 as a flight cadet. The outbreak of war caused the course to be condensed and he was commissioned in March 1940 and joined 19 Squadron at Duxford soon afterwards.

Howard-Williams served with 19 throughout the Battle of Britain. He was with 610 Squadron in early 1941 and later went to 118 Squadron at Ibsley. Awarded the DFC (4.11.41), Howard-Williams appeared briefly as himself in the film 'The First of the Few', filmed at Ibsley in late 1941. He was made a Flight Commander early in 1942 and claimed a Bf 109 destroyed on February 2 1942.

Howard-Williams retired from the RAF on June 11 1958, as a Squadron Leader, retaining the rank of Wing Commander.

PO 7.3.40   FO 7.3.41   FL 7.3.42   SL 1.6.45
SL 1.10.46

ERIC FRANCIS HOWARTH

741519   Sgt   Pilot   British   501 Squadron

Howarth was with 501 Squadron at Middle Wallop in early July 1940. On August 7 he collided with Sergeant WA Wilkinson during a landing approach at Gravesend in poor visibility. Both men were unhurt.

Howarth was killed on September 5 1941, as a Flight Sergeant with 48 Squadron. He is remembered on the Runnymede Memorial, Panel 36.

BERNARD HOWE

33427   PO   Pilot   British   25 Squadron

Howe, of Wadebridge, Cornwall, entered RAF College, Cranwell in September 1937 as a flight cadet. He graduated in July 1939 and was commissioned. He joined 25 Squadron at North Weald in September 1940.

On April 20 1941 Howe was killed, as a Flying Officer with 263 Squadron, aged 22. He is buried in All Saints' churchyard, Wittering, Northants.

PO 29.7.39   FO 29.1.41

DONALD CHARLES HOWE

78253   PO   Observer   British   235 Squadron

Howe joined 235 Squadron in March 1940 and served with it until March 1941. He was released from the RAF in 1946, as a Flight Lieutenant.

PO 24.3.40   FO 24.3.41   FL 24.3.42

FRANCIS VINCENT HOWELL

47751   Sgt   Pilot   British   87 Squadron

Born at Herne Hill, London on May 29 1915, Howell was educated at St Paul's School, Dorking and Redhill Technical College. He joined the RAF on September 1 1931, as an aircraft apprentice at Halton. After three weeks he was sent to the Electrical and Wireless School at Cranwell.

Howell passed out in September 1934 and was posted to 65 Squadron at Hornchurch, as an ACI. He became a Wop/AG on Demons, making his first flight as an air gunner on October 5 1934. He did a gunnery course at Leuchars in May 1935 and returned to the squadron on May 28 with his winged bullet on his sleeve.

In early September 1935 the squadron went by sea to Malta because Italy was on a war footing with Ethiopia. It returned to Hornchurch a year later. Howell had applied for pilot training and in May 1937 he began flying at 3 E&RFTS, Hamble. In July he went to 2 FTS, Brize Norton and in May 1938 joined 3 Squadron at Kenley, equipped with Gladiators.

On September 10 1939 Howell was coming in to land at Croydon, when he forced-landed in a field due to bad visibility. It was too small to take off again. At the end of September he was posted to 87 Squadron in France. On December 9 he forced-landed a Hurricane in Belgium in bad visibility and approaching darkness. He just managed to get back over the French frontier before the police arrived.

On May 10 1940 Howell probably destroyed two He 111s. On the 13th he was jumped by Bf 109s and badly damaged. He baled out and landed in Belgium, was taken to Brussels General Hospital and then transferred to Ghent. He rejoined the squadron at Lille on the 18th. Unfit for flying, he spent the last days of May trying to get out of France. He finally commandeered a big van from a local garage, filled it with airmen and drove to Boulogne, from where they all managed to get on a ship for Dover the next day. The squadron reformed at Church Fenton and began day and night patrols in early June. On August 25 Howell was credited with a Bf 110 probably destroyed.

In February 1941 Howell was posted to 2 Aircraft Delivery Flight and in May he was sent to CFS, Upavon for an instructor's course, after which he went to 9 FTS, Hullavington. Commissioned from Warrant Officer in January 1942, Howell was posted to 9 (P) AFU at Errol, near Dundee. He remained there until December 1944, when he volunteered for a Long Officers' Signal Course at Cranwell. He passed out in late 1946 and went to 110 Wing at Croydon, then preparing for the advent of civil airlines.

In January 1947 Howell moved to RAF Abingdon in Transport Command. In May he was offered a civilian post as an Experimental Officer at the Atomic Energy Research Establishment, Harwell, which he accepted. In late 1950 he became a Senior Experimental Officer and an established civil servant. He died on March 5 1984.

PO 26.1.42   FO 1.10.42   FL 26.1.44

FRANK JONATHAN HOWELL

39612   FL   Pilot   British   609 Squadron

Howell, from Golders Green, London, joined the RAF on a short service commission in March 1937. He was posted to 3 FTS, South Cerney on May 8 and joined 25 Squadron at Hawkinge on November 27. He joined 80 Squadron at Ismailia on March 29 1938. Howell returned to the UK and in November 1939 was posted to 609 Squadron at Drem.

Over Dunkirk on June 1 1940 he damaged a He 111 and was appointed 'A' Flight Commander on the same day. On July 18 Howell was shot down by return fire from a Ju 88 engaged five miles off Swanage. He baled out and was rescued from the sea by a Royal Navy vessel. On August 13 Howell claimed a Ju 87 destroyed, on the 15th a Ju 88, on the 25th a Bf 110, on September 7 another, on the 13th a Ju 87, on the 15th a Do 17, on October 7 a Bf 110 and on the 21st he shared a Ju 88, which was 609's 100th victory. Howell was awarded the DFC (25.10.40).

On February 20 1941 he was posted to Filton to form and command 118 Squadron. Howell destroyed a He 111 at night on July 7, the squadron's first victory. He probably destroyed a Bf 109 and shared another on October 13. He was awarded a Bar to the DFC (4.11.41). After briefly commanding 243 Squadron at Kallang in early December 1941, Howell was on the battleship 'Prince of Wales' when it was sunk on the 10th. He was captured by the Japanese trying to reach Sumatra.

After the war Howell was given command of a Vampire squadron. On May 9 1948 he was making a ciné film of Vampires taxying. He was killed when the wing of one decapitated him.

APO 3.5.37   PO 1.3.38   FO 1.9.39   FL 3.9.40
SL 1.12.41   SL 15.11.46

HAROLD NORMAN HOWES

740896   Sgt   Pilot   British   85 and 605 Squadrons

Howes, of Gillingham, Kent, was with 85 Squadron in France in May 1940. On the 20th he destroyed four Do 17s and possibly a fifth. On August 18 Howes destroyed two Bf 110s, on the 26th a Do 215 and on September 1 another. He was posted to 605 Squadron at Croydon on September 12, destroyed a Do 17 on the 15th and a Bf 109 on October 12. Howes was awarded the DFM (25.10.40).

He was shot down by a Bf 109 on December 1, in Hurricane V 6844, and crash-landed on Gravesend aerodrome. Howes was killed on December 22 1940, aged 24. He is buried in St Margaret's churchyard, Rainham, Kent.

PETER HOWES

74332   PO   Pilot   British   54 and 603 Squadrons

Howes, of Wadebridge, Cornwall, was educated at Oundle School and St John's College, Oxford, where he read Natural Science. He learned to fly with the University Air Squadron and was a friend of Richard Hillary.

Commissioned in the RAF in October 1939, Howes completed his training and was posted to No 1 School of Army Co-operation at Old Sarum. In early June 1940 he went to 5 OTU, Aston Down and joined 54 Squadron at Rochford on July 8.

Howes was posted to 603 Squadron at Hornchurch on September 11. He was shot down by Bf 109s on the 18th and killed. His Spitfire, X 4323, crashed at Kennington, near Ashford. Howes was 21. He was cremated at St John's Crematorium, Woking.

PO 6.10.39

GEOFFREY LEONARD HOWITT

81037   PO   Pilot   British   245 and 615 Squadrons

Born in Beddington, Mitcham in 1914, Howitt joined the Class F Reserve in September 1936, as a Sergeant u/t pilot, and began training at 13 E&RFTS, White Waltham. In October 1937 he transferred to the RAFVR and trained at 19 E&RFTS, Gatwick; 23 E&RFTS, Rochester and No 1 E&RFTS at Hatfield.

Called up in September 1939, Howitt was posted to 10 FTS, Tern Hill for an assessment of his flying capabilities. He joined 245 Squadron at Leconfield in November 1939 and was commissioned in April 1940.

On October 9 Howitt was posted to 615 Squadron at Prestwick. He moved to 85 Squadron at Debden on November 18 1940. He destroyed a He 111 at night on April 9 1941 and on June 11 damaged a Ju 88. In August Howitt was posted to 51 OTU, Cranfield, as an instructor. He was awarded the DFC (30.9.41).

He rejoined 85 Squadron at Hunsdon in April 1942. Howitt destroyed a Do 217 on April 12 1943 and a FW 190 on May 16. In June 1943 he was promoted to Acting Squadron Leader and made 'B' Flight Commander. On August 22 he destroyed a Me 410 and on September 7 a FW 190. Howitt was awarded a Bar to the DFC (26.10.43) and posted to 63 OTU, Honiley.

In April 1944 he joined 456 (RAAF) Squadron at Ford, as 'A' Flight Commander. On June 10 he destroyed a He 177, on August 8 a V1 and on the 12th probably another. Howitt took command of 125 Squadron at Coltishall in December 1944 and led the squadron until he was released on October 6 1945, as a Wing Commander.

PO 25.4.40   FO 25.4.41   FL 25.4.42   SL 15.3 45

ISAAC EDWARD HOWITT

47172   Sgt   Pilot   British   41 Squadron

With 41 Squadron at Catterick in early July 1940. Howitt was commissioned in October 1941 and released from the RAF in 1945, as a Flight Lieutenant.

PO 15.10.41   FO 1.10.42   FL 15.10.43

RICHARD ALEXANDER HOWLEY

41705   PO   Pilot   Newfoundlander   141 Squadron

Howley joined the RAF on a short service commission in January 1939. With training completed he joined 141 Squadron on October 6 1939, when it reformed at Turnhouse.

On the morning of July 19 1940 Howley was flying one of the nine Defiants attacked by Bf 109s of III/JG 51 off Dover. He was shot down into the Channel, in Defiant L 6995, and he and his gunner, Sergeant AG Curley, were reported 'Missing'.

Howley was 20. He is remembered on the Runnymede Memorial, Panel 27.

APO 4.3.39   PO 2.10.39

GEORGE VINCENT HOYLE

754467   Sgt   Pilot   British   232 Squadron

Joined 232 Squadron at Castletown on September 14 1940. Hoyle was killed on May 21 1941, as a Flight Sergeant with 56 Squadron.

He is remembered on the Runnymede Memorial, Panel 36.

HENRY NUTTALL HOYLE

47052   **Sgt**   **Pilot**   **British**   **32 and 257 Squadrons**

Hoyle joined the RAF as a direct-entry Sergeant Pilot on June 29 1936 and did his ab inito training at 12 E&RFTS, Prestwick. After a month on an induction course at RAF Uxbridge Hoyle went to 2 FTS, Digby on September 24. He was awarded his flying badge on January 2 1937 and joined 103 Squadron at Usworth on May 25 1937.

Hoyle was posted to 98 Squadron at Hucknall on April 8 1938 and to 226 Squadron at Harwell on September 4 1939. Nine days later he joined the squadron in France, where it was part of the AASF. It was heavily involved in the fighting of May/June 1940 and was withdrawn to England on June 15.

After two months at Sydenham, Belfast, during which time the squadron carried out some anti-submarine patrols, Hoyle volunteered for Fighter Command. On September 3 he was posted to 32 Squadron at Acklington but moved on the 16th to 257 Squadron at Debden. Hoyle went to 145 Squadron at Tangmere on December 22 1940. He was posted to 2 CFS, Cranwell on January 1 1941 for an instructor's course, after which he went to No 1 (Polish) EFTS at Hucknall, which became 25 EFTS on June 5 1941.

Hoyle was posted to Canada on September 9 1941 and was commissioned in October. He instructed at 37 FTS, Calgary until June 10 1942, when he joined 133 (RCAF) Squadron at Lethbridge. On September 10 he went to No 1 (Fighter) OTU at Bagotville, to instruct, and moved on to 31 SFTS at Kingston, Ontario on March 15 1943. After returning to the UK in late January 1944 Hoyle was posted to 107 OTU at Leicester East on May 11 1944. His final posting came on February 19 1945, when he went as Testing Officer at the Empire Central Flying School, Hullavington. He was released in January 1946, as a Flight Lieutenant.

PO 31.10.41   *FO 1.10.42*   *FL 31.10.43*

FRANTISEK HRADIL

81889   **PO**   **Pilot**   **Czechoslovakian**   **310 and 19 Sqdns**

Joined 310 Squadron at Duxford on August 28 1940 and attached to 19 Squadron at Fowlmere the next day.

Hradil was shot down in flames and killed during combat with Bf 109s over Canterbury on November 5 1940. His Spitfire, P 7545, crashed into the sea off Southend. He was 28 years old and is buried in Sutton Road Cemetery, Southend-on-Sea.

PO 12.7.40

OTAKAR HRUBY

No unknown   **PO**   **Pilot**   **Czechoslovakian**   **111 Sqdn**

Joined 111 Squadron at Dyce on October 16 1940. He later served with 310 and 313 Squadrons and was awarded the DFC in 1943. No further details traced.

JOSEF HUBACEK

60517   **Sgt**   **Pilot**   **Czechoslovakian**   **310 Squadron**

Joined 310 Squadron at Duxford on August 6 1940. Hubacek shared in attacking the Do 17, which crashed in the forecourt of Victoria Station on September 15. On this day he was shot down in combat over the Thames, baled out, slightly injured in the right foot, and was admitted to Chatham Hospital. His Hurricane, R 4087, is believed to be that which crashed and burned out north-west of the junction of the B 1011 and A 13 roads, outside Pitsea.

Hubacek left the RAF after the war, as a Flight Lieutenant.

PO 9.2.41

BRIAN FREDERICK ROBERT HUBBARD

751399   **Sgt**   **Aircrew**   **British**   **235 Squadron**

Hubbard, of Radford, Coventry, was with 235 Squadron in early July 1940. He was killed on November 9 1940 and is remembered on the Malta Memorial, Panel 1, Column 1.

THOMAS EDWARD HUBBARD

90138   **FL**   **Pilot**   **British**   **601 Squadron**

Hubbard joined 601 Squadron, AuxAF in 1937. He was called to full-time service on August 25 1939. He flew one of the six 601 Blenheims, which attacked the seaplane base at Borkum on November 28.

Over Dunkirk on May 27 1940 Hubbard claimed a Bf 110 destroyed. On July 16 he shared in the destruction of a Ju 88 off St Catherine's Point and on the 20th he shared in destroying a He 59 twenty five miles south-east of Selsey. Hubbard, together with Pilot Officers MD Doulton and T Grier had attempted to escort the floatplane back to land but it was abandoned by its crew of four, who baled out at too low a level for their parachutes to open, and the aircraft went into the sea.

Hubbard left the RAF in mid-1943, as a Squadron Leader.

PO (AuxAF) 7.5.37   *FO 25.8.39*   *FL 3.9.40*

PHILIP EDWARD HUCKIN

151056   **Sgt**   **Pilot**   **British**   **600 Squadron**

With 600 Squadron at Northolt in early July 1940. Commissioned in January 1943, Huckin was awarded the DFC (7.3.44), as a Flying Officer with 157 Squadron. He was released from the RAF in 1945, as a Flight Lieutenant.

PO 10.1.43   *FL 10.7.43*   *FL 10.1.45*

A J HUGHES

No unknown   **Sgt**   **Pilot**   **British**   **245 Squadron**

No service details traced.

DAVID ERNEST HUGHES

NZ 40920   **Sgt**   **Air Gunner**   **New Zealander**   **600 Sqdn**

Born in Dunedin on October 20 1912, Hughes worked on his father's farm. He volunteered for aircrew duties after the outbreak of war but did not report to the Ground Training School at Weraroa until April 9 1940. In early May he went on a gunnery course at the Air Observers' School, Ohakea and sailed for the UK in June in the RMS 'Rangitata'.

On July 30 Hughes was posted to No 1 (Coastal) OTU but after four days moved to 5 OTU, Aston Down, where he converted to Blenheims. He joined 600 Squadron at Redhill on September 21. He was a member of the crew of Blenheim L 4905, which crashed in heavy rain at Forest Row, Sussex in the early hours of October 3 1940 after an engagement with an enemy aircraft. All three men aboard were killed.

Hughes is buried in St Luke's churchyard, Whyteleafe, Surrey.

Obituary

Desmond Hughes

ONE of Britain's top Second World War fighter pilots Ulsterman Desmond Hughes has died aged 72.

Night fighter Air Vice Marshal "Hawk-Eye" Hughes CB, CBE, DSO, DFC two bars, AFC, was the most decorated member of the Battle of Britain Fighter Association living.

By the end of the war after service in North Africa, Sicily and Italy and still only 25 years old he was credited with shooting down 18.5 enemy aircraft, the half being a shared Ju-88.

His escapades included taking his pet mongrel Scruffy, dressed in flying overalls for warmth, on a mission in 1942. The unfortunate dog survived the flying sortie only to be run over by a WAAF truck shortly afterwards.

Born the son of a Donaghadee flour miller in 1919 Desmond Hughes was head boy of Campbell College and read law at Cambridge, joining the university air squadron in 1938 and the RAF when war broke out.

His post-war career included two years as director of air staff plans at the Ministry of Defence and ADC to the Queen 1962-64 and commandant of the RAF College, Cranwell 1970-72.

After two years as senior air staff officer at the Near East Air Force headquarters in Cyprus he retired in 1974 and was made deputy lieutenant of Lincolnshire in 1983.

A keen sportsman all his life he played wing for the London Irish RFC after the war.

Air Vice Marshal survived by his

DAVID PRICE HUGHES

37769   FL   Pilot   British   238 Squadron

Hughes, of St Annes-on-the-Sea, Lancashire, joined the RAF in February 1936 on a short service commission. He was posted to 2 FTS, Digby on May 2 and joined 16 (Army Co-operation) Squadron at Old Sarum on May 1 1937. He moved to 53 Squadron at Farnborough on June 28 and in June 1938 was posted to the staff at the School of Army Co-operation at Old Sarum.

On August 4 1940 Hughes joined 238 Squadron at Middle Wallop. He claimed a Bf 110 destroyed on August 8, a Bf 109 on the 11th and a Do 17 and two Bf 110s on the 13th. He failed to return following the interception of Ju 88s south of Tunbridge Wells on September 11 and was reported 'Missing', in Hurricane V 7240.

Hughes was 22 and is remembered on the Runnymede Memorial, Panel 4. He was awarded the DFC (9.5.41), with effect from August 21 1940.

APO 20.4.36   PO 17.2.37   FO 17.8.38   FL 17.8.40

DENNIS LAWRENCE HUGHES

84913   PO   Pilot   British   141 Squadron

Joined 141 Squadron at Dyce on August 19 1940. Hughes was awarded the DFC (8.12.44), as an Acting Squadron Leader with 239 Squadron. He was released from the RAF in 1946, as a Squadron Leader.

PO 3.8.40   FO 3.8.41   FL 3.8.42

FREDERICK DESMOND HUGHES

74706   FO   Pilot   British   264 Squadron

Born in Belfast on June 6 1919, Hughes was educated at Campbell College, Belfast and Pembroke College, Cambridge. He learned to fly with the University Air Squadron, was called to full-time service after the outbreak of war and in November went to No 1 ITW, Cambridge.

On January 1 1940 Hughes was posted to FTS, Cranwell on the second war course. He completed his flying training at 5 FTS, Sealand and was then posted to the School of Army Co-operation at Old Sarum. After a week Hughes was posted to 5 OTU, Aston Down, to convert to Defiants and he joined 264 Squadron at Duxford in mid-June 1940.

Flying with Sergeant F Gash as gunner, Hughes claimed two Do 17s destroyed on August 26, a He 111 on October 16, a probable He 111 on November 23, a He 111 on March 12 1941 and a Ju 88 on April 10. Hughes was awarded the DFC (18.4.41). In January 1942 he was posted to 125 Squadron at Colerne, as a Flight Commander. He shared in the squadron's first victory, a Ju 88 on June 27. Later in the year he teamed up with Pilot Officer L Dixon and they shared in the destruction of a Ju 88 on November 4 1942.

Hughes was posted to 600 Squadron in North Africa on January 19 1943, as a Flight Commander. Dixon went with him and on January 23 they claimed two Ju 88s destroyed and on February 12 a Cant Z 1007. Hughes was awarded a Bar to the DFC (13.4.43). On April 26 they claimed a Ju 88, on July 13 a He 111, on the 21st a Ju 88, on August 11 three Ju 88s and on the 18th a Ju 87. Hughes was awarded a second Bar to the DFC (28.9.43).

At the end of 1943 he was posted back to the UK and went to a staff job at Fighter Command. In February 1944 he was promoted to Acting Wing Commander and posted to 85 Group TAF. Hughes returned to operations on July 19 1944, when he took command of 604 Squadron at Hurn. In early August the squadron was operating from A 8, an airstrip close to the Arromanches beaches. With Dixon as his navigator Hughes destroyed a Ju 88 on August 6 and they claimed their final victory on January 14 1945, a Ju 188 over Rotterdam. Hughes was awarded the DSO (23.3.45).

He went on to a notable career in the post-war RAF. Hughes was awarded the AFC (1.1.54), made a CBE (1.1.62), a CB (1972) and retired on June 6 1974, as an Air Vice-Marshal

*PO 29.10.39   FO 29.10.40   FL 3.10.41   SL 1.7.45
SL 1.8.47   WC 1.1.53   GC 1.7.58   AC 1.1.63
AVM 1.7.67*

JOHN McCULLOCH MIDDLEMORE HUGHES

33191   FL   Pilot   British   25 Squadron

Hughes was born at Chilworth, Hampshire on February 13 1917. He was at Haileybury College from 1930 to 1934 and entered RAF College, Cranwell in September 1935 as a flight cadet. On graduation in July 1937 he joined 218 Squadron at Boscombe Down.

The squadron flew to France on September 2 1939, as part of the AASF. In the fighting in May 1940 Hughes led many bombing raids on enemy troop concentrations and lines of communication. In one operation he was attacked by Bf 109s and by skilful manoeuvring enabled his gunner to shoot one down. He was awarded the DFC (21.6.40).

Hughes volunteered for Fighter Command and joined 25 Squadron at North Weald on September 16. He was killed on December 7 1940 and is buried in Chilworth churchyard.

PO 31.7.37   FO 31.1.39   FL 3.9.40

PATERSON CLARENCE HUGHES

39461   FO   Pilot   Australian   234 Squadron

Born in Cooma, New South Wales on February 19 1917, Hughes joined the RAAF in 1935 at Point Cook, as a cadet. He trained in Australia and was commissioned. In early 1937 he went to the UK and was attached to the RAF and commissioned.

On February 27 1937 Hughes was posted to 2 FTS, Digby for an assessment of his flying capabilities and was afterwards posted to 64 Squadron at Martlesham Heath. He joined 234 Squadron at Leconfield at its reformation on October 30 1939, as a Flight Commander.

On July 8, 27 and 28 1940 Hughes shared in the destruction of three Ju 88s, on August 14 he claimed two Bf 110s destroyed, on the 16th two Bf 109s, on the 18th another two Bf 109s, on the 26th two more, on September 4 three Bf 110s, on the 5th two Bf 109s and on the 6th a Bf 109.

Hughes was shot down and killed in combat on September 7 1940. His Spitfire, X 4009, crashed at Darks Farm, Bessels Green. He is buried in St James' churchyard, Sutton, Hull. He was awarded the DFC (22.10.40), being then credited with seven enemy aircraft destroyed.

PO 19.2.37   FO 19.11.38

WILLIAM ROBERT KENT HUGHES

137124   F/Sgt   Wop/AG   British   23 Squadron

Hughes joined the RAFVR in Northampton in Spring 1939, as a trainee Wop/AG. He joined the RAF on May 12 and was called up on August 27 1939.

He went to Hamble on a wireless course on March 4 1940 and to Jurby on a gunnery course on June 22. Hughes was posted to 5 OTU, Aston Down on July 20 to convert to Blenheims and was promoted to Sergeant. On August 17 1940 he joined 23 Squadron at Wittering, as a Flight Sergeant. He was posted to 9 Squadron on November 16 but went instead to 149 Squadron at Mildenhall on the 21st, to fly in Wellingtons.

WRK Hughes (continued)

On March 11 1941 Hughes went to Malta to join 148 Squadron at Luqa but was posted to Egypt, where he joined 70 Squadron at Kabrit on April 2. With his tour completed he returned to the UK in early 1942, went to 23 OTU, Pershore in April and joined 12 Squadron at Binbrook on July 27. Commissioned from Warrant Officer in November 1942, Hughes completed his second tour and was awarded the DFC (12.3.43).

In early March 1943 he went to 28 OTU, Wymeswold, as an instructor. He was posted to CGS, Sutton Bridge for a Gunnery Leaders' course on June 15, after which he moved to 8 AGS, Evanton and then to 7 AGS, Bishopscourt, Northern Ireland as Gunnery Leader. On January 18 1944 Hughes went to 50 Squadron at Skellingthorpe on operational liaison duties. He was released from the RAF in March 1946, as a Flight Lieutenant.

PO 11.11.42   FO 11.5.43   FL 11.11.44

JOHN ANTHONY HUGHES-REES

113942   Sgt   Pilot   British   609 Squadron

Hughes-Rees, of Newport, Monmouthshire, joined 609 Squadron at Middle Wallop on September 22 1940. He claimed a Bf 110 destroyed on the 25th and then crash-landed at Glastonbury with engine trouble, in Spitfire L 1008.

Awarded the DFM (8.8.41), having then destroyed at least four enemy aircraft, Hughes-Rees was commissioned in December 1941. He was killed on April 30 1943, as a Flying Officer at 73 OTU, Abu Sueir. He was 22 and is buried in the Moascar War Cemetery, Egypt.

PO 1.12.41   FO 1.10.42

PETRUS HENDRIK HUGO

41848   FO   Pilot   South African   615 Squadron

Born at Pampoenpoort West, Cape Province on December 20 1917, Hugo studied at the Witwatersrand College of Aeronautical Engineering. He joined the RAF on a short service commission in February 1939 and did his ab initio training at 6 E&RFTS, Sywell. After completing his advanced course at 13 FTS, Drem Hugo went to the Fighter Pool at St Athan, was posted to 2 Ferry Pool at Filton and then joined 615 Squadron at Vitry, France in December 1939.

On May 20 1940 he destroyed a He 111. The squadron was withdrawn to Kenley the next day. On July 14 Hugo claimed a share in a Ju 87 destroyed, on the 20th two Bf 109s, on the 25th another Bf 109, on the 27th a shared He 59, on August 12 a Bf 109 and on the 16th he probably destroyed a He 111 but during the combat his aircraft was severely damaged by a Bf 110 and he returned to Kenley, slightly wounded in both legs. On the 18th Hugo crash-landed at Orpington after a combat with Bf 109s, in Hurricane R 4221. He was admitted to Orpington Hospital, with wounds to the face.

Hugo was awarded the DFC (23.8.40) and returned to the squadron in September. On October 14 1941 he shared a He 59, on the 27th shared another and was awarded a Bar to the DFC (25.11.41). In November 1941 Hugo was given command of 41 Squadron at Merston. On February 12 1942 he destroyed a Bf 109 and damaged another, on March 14 and 26 he destroyed Bf 109s, on April 12 he was appointed Wing Leader at Tangmere and on the 27th was shot down, baled out into the Channel and was picked up by an ASR launch, wounded. Hugo was awarded the DSO (29.5.42).

After a spell at HQ 11 Group Hugo was appointed Wing Leader at Hornchurch on July 18 1942 but stayed only until August 31, being then posted to lead 322 Wing in North Africa. On November 12 he shared a Do 217, on the 13th he probably destroyed a Ju 88, on the 15th a probable He 111, on the 16th and 18th two Bf 109s and on the 21st, 26th and 28th Bf 109s. On November 29 Hugo took temporary

command of 322 Wing when the CO was injured in an attack on the airfield. On December 2 he destroyed a Breda 88 and shared another and on the 14th he destroyed a Sm 79. Hugo was awarded a second Bar to the DFC (16.2.43) and posted to HQ North West African Coast Air Force on March 13 1943.

He took command of 322 Wing again in June 1943. On the 29th he destroyed a Bf 109, on September 2 a FW 190 and an Arado Ar 196 on November 18. Hugo continued to lead the Wing until its disbandment in November 1944, when he was posted to HQ Mediterranean Allied Air Forces. He was later seconded to Marshal Tolbukin's 2nd Ukranian Army, then moving from Roumania to Austria. After returning to the UK Hugo was posted to the Central Fighter Establishment. In addition to his other awards he received the C de G (Fr) and the DFC (US)(14.11.44). Hugo retired from the RAF on February 19 1950, as a Squadron Leader, retaining the rank of Group Captain. He died in South Africa in 1986. His portrait was drawn by Cuthbert Orde in February 1941.

APO 1.4.39   PO 21.10.39   FO 21.10.40   FL 21.10.41
SL 12.7.42   SL 1.9.45

DONALD JAMES HULBERT

176565   Sgt   Pilot   British   257 and 501 Squadrons

With 257 Squadron at Hendon in June 1940. On July 19 he shared in the destruction of a Do 17. Hulbert's Hurricane, V 7317, was severely damaged in combat over the Thames Estuary on September 7 and he made a forced-landing near Sittingbourne.

Towards the end of the Battle of Britain Hulbert was posted to 501 Squadron at Kenley.

Commissioned in April 1944, he was released in early 1946, as a Flying Officer. Hulbert joined the RAFVR in 1948 and served with it for some years.

PO 26.4.44   FO 26.10.44   FO (RAFVR) 15.12.48

FRANK HORACE RAYMOND HULBERT

123641   Sgt   Pilot   British   601 Squadron

Hulbert joined the RAFVR in December 1938 and began flying training at 14 E&RFTS, Castle Bromwich. Called to full-time service at the outbreak of war, Hulbert was posted to ITW at Hastings. In March 1940 he went to 18 EFTS, Fair Oaks, moved to 10 EFTS, Yatesbury in May and finished his training at 8 FTS, Montrose.

In early August Hulbert was posted to 5 OTU, Aston Down, converted to Hurricanes and then joined 601 Squadron at Exeter late in the month. In May 1941 he went to the Station Flight at RAF Northolt and in August was posted to 59 OTU, Crosby-on-Eden, as an instructor.

Hulbert was commissioned in May 1942. He returned to operations in February 1943, when he joined 193 Squadron at Harrowbeer. He was awarded the AFC (2.6.43). In April 1944 Hulbert was appointed CO of 10 Group Communication Flight and was posted to 11 Armament Practice Camp at Fairwood Common in August. It became No 1 Armament Practice Squadron in July 1945. Hulbert went to RAF Molesworth for 1335 Jet Conversion Course in August and in September went to his final posting, 3 Armament Practice Squadron at Hawkinge.

Demobilised in November 1945, Hulbert joined the RAFVR in March 1947 and instructed at 5 RFS, Castle Bromwich until 1953. He retired in 1957, as a Flight Lieutenant.

PO 8.5.42   FO 8.11.42   FL 8.5.44   FO (RAFVR) 11.3.48

CAESAR BARRAND HULL

| 37285 | FL | Pilot | South African | 263 and 43 Squadrons |

Hull was born in Shangani, Southern Rhodesia and brought up in South Africa. He was educated at St John's College, Johannesburg and began flying as a cadet in the SAAF Reserve.

In 1935 Hull applied for an RAF short service commission and was provisionally accepted. He began his ab initio training in July and on September 28 went to 3 FTS, Grantham. Hull joined 43 Squadron at Tangmere on August 5 1936. At the outbreak of war he was commanding 'A' Flight. On January 30 1940 he shared in the destruction of a He 111 five miles east of Coquet Island, on February 13 he destroyed a He 111 in the first raid on Scapa Flow and on March 28 shared another He 111.

On May 9 1940 Hull was posted to 263 Squadron at Scapa Flow. The squadron's Gladiators were loaded on to HMS 'Furious', which sailed for Norway on May 18. They were unloaded on the 21st and began standing patrols. On the 24th Hull shared a He 111, on the 26th he destroyed two He 111s and two Ju 52s and on the 27th he destroyed a Ju 87 but was hit by return fire and crashed, wounded in the head and knee. He was flown back to Britain in a Sunderland.

Hull was awarded the DFC (21.6.40). He returned to 43 Squadron at Tangmere on August 31, to take command after the CO was killed on the 30th. He claimed two Bf 110s probably destroyed on September 2 and claimed a Bf 109 on the 6th. In the late afternoon of the 7th the squadron was scrambled to meet a large force of Do 17s escorted by Bf 109s. Hull was last seen diving to attack the bombers. He is believed to have been shot down by a Bf 109 and killed. His Hurricane, V 6641, crashed in the grounds of Purley High School.

Hull was 27 years old. He is buried in St Andrew's churchyard, Tangmere.

APO 16.9.35   PO 16.9.36   FO 16.4.38   FL 16.4.40

JOHN BERNARD WILLIAM HUMPHERSON

| 39317 | FL | Pilot | British | 32 and 607 Squadrons |

Born in Enfield, Middlesex, Humpherson joined the RAF on a short service commission in October 1936. After his ab initio training he was posted to 10 FTS, Tern Hill on January 16 1937 and joined 32 Squadron at Church Fenton on August 7.

In September 1939 Humpherson was with 607 Squadron at Acklington. He went with the squadron when it flew its Gladiators from Croydon to Merville on November 15. He destroyed a He 111 on May 10 and was posted back to England soon afterwards to join 32 Squadron at Wittering. Using Abbeville as a forward base the squadron took part in the fighting in France. On May 20 Humpherson damaged a Bf 109 and on the 22nd destroyed one.

Flying from Biggin Hill, he claimed a Do 17 destroyed on July 10, a Ju 87 on the 20th, a Bf 109 on August 12 and a Ju 88 and a probable Bf 109 on the 15th. Humpherson was posted back to 607 Squadron on August 23 and awarded the DFC (30.8.40).

Humpherson joined 90 Squadron, when it reformed at Watton, Norfolk on May 7 1941. He was killed on June 22, as a Flight Lieutenant, operating in Flying Fortresses from Polebrook. Humpherson was 24 and is buried in St Paul's churchyard, Heslington, Yorkshire.

APO 21.12.36   PO 12.10.37   FO 12.5.39   FL 3.9.40

ANDREW HENRY HUMPHREY

| 33543 | PO | Pilot | British | 266 Squadron |

Born in Edinburgh on January 10 1921, Humphrey was educated at Bradfield College and entered RAF College, Cranwell on January 12 1939 as a flight cadet. The course was shortened because of the war and he was granted a Permanent Commission at the end of April 1940

and on May 4 was posted to 9 BGS, Penrhos, as a staff pilot.

Humphrey went to 7 OTU, Hawarden on September 3 and joined 266 Squadron at Wittering on the 16th. He destroyed a He 111 at night on December 4, another on May 9 1941 and on the 11th he destroyed a Bf 110 and a He 111. He was awarded the DFC (30.5.41). In July Humphrey was posted to 452 Squadron at Kenley and on the 24th he claimed a Bf 109. With his tour completed he went to 58 OTU, Grangemouth, as an instructor.

In April 1942 Humphrey joined the newly-formed 175 Squadron at Warmwell and on May 19 claimed two Bf 109s destroyed. In July he returned to 58 OTU and on September 2 went to 2 FIS for a course. Humphrey later served in the Middle East. He was awarded the AFC (1.1.43) and Bar (1.1.45). He had a long and distinguished career in the RAF and became a Marshal of the RAF in August 1976. He was made an OBE (1.1.51), was awarded a second Bar to the AFC (9.6.55) and made a GCB (1974)(KCB 1968; CB 1959).

Humphrey was Chief of the Air Staff 1974 to 1976 and Air ADC to the Queen. He died on January 24 1977.

PO 30.4.40	*FO 1.5.41*	*FL 1.5.42*	*SL 20.2.45*
WC 1.7.51	*GC 1.7.57*	*AC 1.7.62*	*AVM 1.1.65*
AM 1.1.69	*ACM 1.12.70*	*MRAF 6.8.76*	

JACK DAVID HUMPHREYS

| 41419 | FO | Pilot | British | 29 Squadron |

Humphreys was born in October 1919 and was at Uppingham School from 1933 to 1935. He joined the RAF on a short service commission in October 1938.

He was with 29 Squadron at Debden in September 1939. His was one of the Blenheims attacked by Hurricanes of 312 Squadron on October 13 1940. Although damaged, he returned to base at Tern Hill. In late July 1941 he attacked and probably destroyed a He 111 over the east coast. Humphreys was awarded the DFC (21.10.41) and posted to 51 OTU at Cranfield, as an instructor.

Humphreys was killed on August 2 1942, as an Acting Squadron Leader with 605 Squadron. He is buried in Putney Vale Cemetery, Wandsworth, London.

APO 14.12.38   PO 3.9.39   FO 3.9.40   FL 3.9.41

JAMES SAMUEL HUMPHREYS

| 41928 | PO | Pilot | New Zealander | 605 Squadron |

Born in Greymouth on November 13 1918, Humphreys was at Christ's College, Christchurch from 1932 to 1935. In 1936 he went to work in the Government Audit Office in Wellington. After joining the Civil Reserve of Pilots in February 1938 Humphreys applied for a short service commission in the RAF. Provisionally accepted, he sailed for the UK on November 19 in the RMS 'Rangitiki'.

Humphreys began his ab initio course at 9 E&RFTS, Ansty on December 28. He went to 6 FTS, Little Rissington on April 29 1939 and began his intermediate training on Ansons. With the advanced term of the course completed he joined the newly-formed 245 Squadron at Leconfield on November 6. In early May 1940 Humphreys volunteered for France and on the 11th joined 607 Squadron at Vitry-en-Artois. After a period of hectic fighting and high losses the squadron withdrew to Croydon on May 21. Humphreys was posted to 605 Squadron at Hawkinge a week later.

He took part in the action of August 15, when the Germans sent a force of He 111s, escorted by Bf 110s, from Norway to attack the Newcastle area. They were intercepted out to sea and heavy losses inflicted. Flying from Croydon on September 9 Humphreys was shot down and baled out with a badly wounded hand. Falling from 12000 feet he pulled his ripcord at 3000. As he drifted across the Canadian Army Camp at Bordon he was fired on, one bullet going through the left breast pocket of his tunic, leaving a weal on the left side of his

JS Humphreys (continued)

body. Humphreys landed just outside the camp, was picked up by Canadians, relieved of his buttons, maps and flying boots and then taken to Cambridge Military Hospital at Aldershot. He ultimately lost his little finger.

Humphreys rejoined the squadron on November 28 and two weeks later was posted to 15 FTS, Oxford, as a staff pilot, having been classified as A2 flying category. Throughout 1941 and 1942 he served at various training schools, as a staff pilot. In late December 1942 Humphreys returned to operations, joining 486 Squadron at Tangmere as a supernumerary. He went to 609 Squadron at Manston in mid-February 1943, did a ground-attack course, specialising in rocket projectiles, and in early May was posted to the Middle East.

After three weeks practice flying at 71 OTU, Ismailia Humphreys joined 6 Squadron at Ben Gardane as special instructor on rockets. On September 25 he went to 127 Squadron at St Jean in Palestine, as a Flight Commander. In January 1944 he was posted to HQ Air Command South East Asia at Calcutta, on staff duties. He joined 42 Squadron at Tulihal on July 23, as supernumerary, moving in late October to 11 Squadron at Imphal, as a Flight Commander. He was given command of 60 Squadron at Kangla on December 6. Humphreys fell sick with hepatitis on April 22 1945 and he was taken to Calcutta, relinquishing his command on May 23. Fully-recovered, he took command of 8 Squadron, IAF. The squadron worked up for six weeks and then moved to Mingaladon on July 15 and began fighter-bomber attacks against the Japanese. On August 26 it escorted the Japanese generals into Rangoon for the formal surrender. Humphreys was posted away on November 15 1945, when the IAF became Royal and the personnel became completely Indian.

He took command of 20 Squadron at Bangkok, left it in mid-February 1946, returned to the UK in May and was released from the RAF on July 12 1946, as a Squadron Leader. Humphreys married in England and remained there until June 1951, when he returned to New Zealand. He died in Wanganui in 1986.

APO 15.4.39   PO 6.11.39   FO 6.11.40   FL 6.11.41

PETER CECIL HUMPHREYS

85272   PO   Pilot   British   32 Squadron

Commissioned in September 1940, Humphreys joined 32 Squadron at Acklington on October 18. He was posted to 73 Squadron on November 5 and went with it to the Middle East.

Humphreys was released from the RAF in 1945, as a Flight Lieutenant. He later went to live in Spain.

PO 22.9.40   FO 22.9.41   FL 22.9.42

PETER HARRY HUMPHREYS

84961   PO   Pilot   British   152 Squadron

Humphreys, of Lymington, joined 152 Squadron at Warmwell on September 29 1940. He was posted to 92 Squadron at Biggin Hill in the spring of 1941. On November 3 he flew to the Middle East in a Sunderland and joined 112 Squadron at Sidi Heneish, as a Flight Commander.

On April 24 1942 Humphreys was posted to the Fighter School at El Ballah, as an instructor. He returned to operations in early 1943, when he joined 92 Squadron at Castel Benito, as a Flight Commander. He destroyed a Bf 109 on March 7. Humphreys took command of the squadron on May 6 and led it to Malta in June and then on to Sicily and Italy. He was awarded the DFC (1.10.43), being then credited with two enemy aircraft destroyed whilst with the squadron.

Posted away in November 1943, Humphreys was given command of 111 Squadron at Lago, Italy in April 1944. He returned to the UK in November 1944. He was Station Commander at RAF Castle Bromwich in 1946 and afterwards served on the staff of HQ 12 Group, Nottingham. On November 11 1947 Humphreys went as a passenger in a Lincoln during fighter affiliation exercises, to observe mock attacks. A Hornet, making a head-on attack, misjudged the breakaway and collided with the Lincoln. All in the bomber and the fighter were killed.

Humphreys was 27. He was cremated at Bournemouth Crematorium.

PO 7.9.40   FO 7.9.41   FL 7.9.42   SL 20.6.45
SL 1.9.45

DOUGLAS ALFRED CHARLES HUNT

111976   Sgt   Pilot   British   66 Squadron

Born on June 1 1918, Hunt was educated at Kingswood Grammar School, Bristol. He started as an apprentice at the Bristol Aeroplane Co in September 1934 in aero engine fitting and testing and got his technical qualifications over a five year period at the Merchant Venturers Technical College, Bristol.

In August 1937 Hunt joined the RAFVR, carried out his flying training at 2 E&RFTS, Filton and was awarded his flying badge in November 1938. He was called to full-time service on September 3 1939 and attached to the FAA at Donibristle, where he did a deck-landing course with Gladiators on the carrier HMS 'Furious'.

In November 1939 Hunt went to 5 OTU, Aston Down, converted to Spitfires and joined 66 Squadron at Duxford in December. On June 2 1940 on an early morning patrol over Dunkirk Hunt was hit by return fire from a Ju 88 and baled out. He was taken to Dunkirk by the French, handed over to the British and taken out by launch to a destroyer, which arrived in Dover at 2.00 am the next morning.

On August 31 1940 Hunt shared in destroying a Do 215, on December 2 shared a He 111, on the 11th shared an unidentified enemy aircraft and on the 15th claimed a He 111.

In October 1941 Hunt was sent to CFS, Upavon, for an instructor's course. Commissioned in November 1941, he was on the staff of a number of flying schools, 5 FTS Tern Hill, CFS Upavon, 7 FIS Upavon, 3 FIS Castle Coombe and Lulsgate Bottom. In January 1946 he did a four months course at the Empire Test Pilots' School at Cranfield and was then posted to the RAE at Farnborough, as a test pilot.

Hunt retired from the RAF on October 1 1958, as a Squadron Leader, retaining the rank of Wing Commander.

PO 11.11.41   FO 1.10.42   FL 10.11.43   FL 1.9.45
SL 1.1.51

DAVID WALTER HUNT

42754   PO   Pilot   British   257 Squadron

Born at Chapel Ash, Wolverhampton on August 26 1919, Hunt joined the RAF on a short service commission and began his elementary flying at 12 E&RFTS, Prestwick on August 1 1939. He went to ITW, Hastings on October 6 and on the 25th was posted to 11 FTS, Shawbury.

Hunt joined 257 Squadron, then reforming at Hendon, on May 20 1940. He was shot down by enemy fighters on September 3 and baled out, severely burned, landing near Brook Farm, Margretting. Taken to Billericay Hospital, Hunt later went to the Queen Victoria Hospital, East Grinstead, where he underwent plastic surgery by Archie McIndoe and became a Guinea Pig.

After nearly a year Hunt was posted as Officer i/c Hornchurch Detachment of 11 Group Flight. The unit had a Hurricane, which he flew, a Lysander and a Blenheim. It was engaged on calibration of radar, searchlights and anti-aircraft defences, which involved flying on set courses at known heights and speeds to co-ordinate the defence systems.

Hunt was posted away in October 1943 and appointed Station Adjutant at RAF, Aberporth. He was released from the RAF in September 1945, as a Flight Lieutenant.

APO 9.10.39   PO 11.5.40   FO 11.5.41   FL 11.5.42

HENRY NORMAN HUNT

82656   PO   Pilot   British   504 Squadron

Hunt, of Harrow, Middlesex, was with 263 Squadron in June 1940. He was posted to 504 Squadron at Castletown on July 11.

He was killed on May 13 1941, still with 504. Hunt was 22 and is remembered on the Runnymede Memorial, Panel 33.

PO 9.6.40

ALASTAIR STUART HUNTER

90222   FL   Pilot   British   604 Squadron

Hunter joined 604 Squadron, AuxAF in 1937 and was called to full-time service on August 24 1939.

He shot a He 115 down into the sea near Dunkirk on June 18 1940. It was 604's first night victory. Hunter took off in the dark in a Beaufighter for a belated air test on February 6 1941. He spun in as he approached to land and both he and his radar operator, Pilot Officer T Genney, were killed.

Hunter was 24. He is buried in St Andrew's churchyard, Hatfield Peverel, Essex.

PO (AuxAF) 17.4.37   FO (AuxAF) 17.10.38   FO 24.8.39
FL 3.9.40

DOUGLAS JOHN HUNTER

101027   Sgt   Air Gunner   British   29 Squadron

With 29 Squadron at Digby in June 1940. Commissioned in June 1941, Hunter was released from the RAF in 1947, as a Flight Lieutenant. He died in July 1984.

PO 24.6.41   FO 24.6.42   FL 24.6.43

PHILIP ALGERNON HUNTER

32081   SL   Pilot   British   264 Squadron

Hunter, of Chesham, Bucks, joined the RAF in September 1931. He carried out his flying training at 5 FTS, Sealand and then joined 25 Squadron at Hawkinge on August 29 1932.

He was posted to Ismailia on February 28 1933, to join 6 Squadron. Back in the UK in 1936 Hunter was posted to the staff at RAF College, Cranwell on November 9. He moved to the staff of CFS, Upavon on March 24 1937. In March 1940 Hunter took command of 264 Squadron at Martlesham Heath. With LAC FH King as his gunner he had a run of successes in May 1940. On the 12th they destroyed a Ju 88, on the 27th a Bf 109 and a shared He 111, on the 28th two Bf 109s, on the 29th a Bf 109, a Bf 110 and a Ju 87 and on the 31st a Bf 109, a He 111 and another damaged. Hunter was awarded the DSO (14.6.40).

On August 24 1940 Hunter's Defiant, N 1535, was last seen in pursuit of Ju 88s following an attack on Manston. He was 27 years old and is remembered on the Runnymede Memorial, Panel 4.

PO 11.9.31   FO 11.4.33   FL 11.4.36   SL 1.12.38

JOHN HUNTER HUNTER-TOD

77424   FO   British   23 Squadron

Born on August 21 1917, Hunter-Tod was educated at Marlborough College and Trinity College, Cambridge, where he obtained a degree in Mathematics. He was commissioned in the RAF in January 1940 and in early July was serving with 23 Squadron at Collyweston, as a Technical Officer. Part of his duties was to train AI operators, during the course of which he flew on night operations and scrambles, thus qualifying him for the Battle of Britain clasp.

Hunter-Tod served in the Middle East later in the war. He held a series of technical appointments and commands in the post-war RAF. He was created a KBE (1.1.71)(OBE 1957), a CB (14.6.69) and retired on April 30 1973, as an Air Marshal.

PO 30.1.40   FO 1.9.40   FL 1.3.42   SL 1.7.45
SL 1.8.47   WC 1.7.52   GC 1.1.58   AC 1.7.63
AVM 1.1.68   AM 1.1.71

CHARLES ALEXANDER LYALL HURRY

48324   Sgt   Pilot   British   43 and 46 Squadrons

Born on March 24 1916, Hurry joined the RAF in late 1931, as an aircraft apprentice. Whilst in Aden in 1936 he volunteered for pilot training and was selected in 1938. He did his ab initio course at 2 E&RFTS, Filton and then went on to 6 FTS, Little Rissington.

In 1939, with training completed, Hurry was posted to the Air Observers' School at Acklington, as a staff pilot at the Gunnery School. After the war started he did a gunnery course at Warmwell, passed through the Fighter Combat Unit at St Athan and then joined 43 Squadron at Acklington in January 1940.

On September 5 and 6 Hurry claimed Bf 109s destroyed. On the 10th he was posted to 46 Squadron at Stapleford. He claimed a share in a Do 215 destroyed on the 15th and three days later he was shot down and baled out, with bullet wounds in the leg and burned on the face and hands. Hurry was admitted to Chatham Hospital and afterwards went to Queen Victoria Hospital, East Grinstead, where he became a Guinea Pig.

Fit again, Hurry was posted to Brough for an Air Traffic Contoller's course, after which he went to North Weald, as Duty Pilot. Later in 1941 he did an instructor's course at Perth and was posted to EFTS, Wolverhampton, moving later to EFTS, Carlisle. Commissioned in March 1942, Hurry joined the Communications Squadron at Northolt and flew as personal pilot to Air Marshal Sir Roderic Hill until the end of the war. He was awarded the AFC (1.1.46).

Hurry was released in January 1946, as a Flight Lieutenant. After running his own businesses in Britain he went to live in Canada in 1970.

PO 7.3.42   FO 1.10.42   FL 7.3.44

PETER RICHARD SCOTT HURST

41421   PO   Pilot   British   600 Squadron

Hurst, of Hampshire, joined the RAF on a short service commission in October 1938. He joined 600 Squadron at Redhill in September 1940.

During a practice flight through cloud on October 23 Hurst crashed into a hillside at Kirkby Malzeard, Yorkshire, in Blenheim L 1272, and was killed. He was 20 and is buried in Catterick Cemetery.

APO 14.12.38   PO 3.9.39

IAIN HUTCHINSON

102960   Sgt   Pilot   British   222 Squadron

Born on November 13 1918, Hutchinson was with 222 Squadron at Hornchurch in early July 1940. His aircraft was damaged in combat on August 30 and he made a forced-landing at Damyns Hall Farm, Rainham, unhurt.

Hutchinson claimed Bf 109s destroyed on September 6, 7 and 14. After this last combat he forced-landed at Detling, following damage by Bf 109s. On the 18th Hutchinson baled out, slightly wounded, after a combat over Canterbury and landed at Molash. His Spitfire, R 6772, crashed and burned out at Clock House Farm, Challock. Following an action over south-west London on the 30th, Hutchinson again forced-landed, this time at Denham, wounded.

Commissioned in August 1941, he was released from the RAF in 1946 but rejoined in 1947. Hutchinson retired on December 1 1957, as a Squadron Leader.

PO 5.8.41   FO 5.8.42   FL 5.8.43   FO 11.1.47
FL 5.4.48   SL 1.1.55

DAVID ALEXANDER HUTCHISON

Sub-Lieutenant (FAA)   Pilot   British   74 and 804 Sqdns

Hutchison was loaned to the RAF in late June 1940 and joined 74 Squadron at Hornchurch on July 6. He was posted to 804 Squadron at Hatston on July 20, flying Gladiators on dockyard defence.

On December 9 1940 Hutchison joined 802 Squadron, then forming at Donibristle for the escort carrier HMS 'Audacity'. He was awarded the DSC (10.3.42), serving with 802 for convoy HG 76. Hutchison was killed on November 15 1942 in HMS 'Avenger', sunk whilst returning from the landings in North Africa. He was 23 and is remembered on the Fleet Air Arm Memorial at Lee-on-Solent.

Midshipman 11.9.39   Sub-Lt 14.3.40   Lt 1.3.42

RICHARD RALPH HUTLEY

84323   PO   Pilot   British   32 and 213 Squadrons

Joined 32 Squadron at Acklington in late September 1940. Hutley moved to 213 Squadron at Tangmere in October.

On the 29th he was shot down in combat off Selsey, in Hurricane V 7622. Hutley baled out and was picked up, unconscious, by the Selsey lifeboat. All efforts to revive him failed. He was 22 and is buried in St Andrew's churchyard, Tangmere.

PO 24.8.40

ROBERT SCOTT HUTTON

754874   Sgt   Pilot   British   85 Squadron

Hutton, of Shirehampton, Bristol, joined 85 Squadron at Castle Camps on September 16 1940. He was killed on December 12 1940, when he crashed at night at Tilbury Docks during an electrical storm, in Hurricane V 6674.

Hutton was 25. He is buried in St Mary Redcliffe Cemetery, Bristol.

JOSEF EMIL HYBLER

82551   PO   Pilot   Czechoslovakian   310 Squadron

Born on September 18 1913 in Prague, Hybler joined the Czech Air Force at Prostejov on September 29 1932 and trained as an observer, serving in 2/1 and 1/1 Squadrons from June 1 1933 to September 1935. He then went to the Military Academy until the end of July 1937. He had his civilian flying license before he began military pilot training on August 1 1937.

In March 1938 he was posted to III/4 Fighter Squadron of the 4th Regiment, at Pardubice. Hybler escaped to Cracow, Poland in June 1939 and in mid-August he arrived in France. After joining l'Armée de l'Air he was posted to Chartres on October 10 to train on French aircraft.

On May 10 1940 Hybler joined Groupe de Chasse II/2 at Laon. The unit retreated via Paris and Chateaudun and ended up at Chissey. After the French collapse Hybler flew south. He left his aircraft at Montpellier and on June 20 went on a coach to Port Vendres and boarded a ship for Oran. He went by train to Casablanca, got on a ship to Gibraltar and then sailed in a convoy to Liverpool, arriving there on July 12.

Hybler went to a reception centre at RAF Cosford and on September 28 was posted to 6 OTU, Sutton Bridge, to convert to Hurricanes. He joined 310 Squadron at Duxford on October 15. He stayed with the squadron until April 28 1942, when he was posted to 234 Squadron at Portreath. Hybler moved to 286 Squadron on September 14 and then went to 57 OTU, Eshott, as an instructor. He was posted to RAF Coltishall on Flying Control on January 10 1944.

Hybler remained on control duties, at Fairwood Common, Castle Camps and other stations before his release in August 1945, when he returned to Czechoslovakia. He rejoined the Czech Air Force but was dismissed in the 1948 Communist putsch. Arrested in 1949, Hybler was tried and sentenced to 20 years imprisonment. He was released in 1960 and was allowed to do only menial jobs until 1966, when he became a teacher of languages.

In 1968 Hybler went to England. The Russians marched into Czechoslovakia and he did not go back. He settled in England and became a technical author for Lucas Industries. He died on January 9 1984.

PO 2.8.40   FO 27.12.40   FL 27.12.41

GEORGE GORDON HYDE

C 948   FO   Pilot   Canadian   1 (RCAF) Squadron

Born on February 11 1914 in Montreal, Hyde joined the RCAF on September 1 1938. He was with No 1 (RCAF) Squadron, when it arrived in the UK on June 20 1940.

Hyde was shot down in combat with Bf 109s on August 31 and baled out, with burns. His Hurricane, P 2971, crashed near Staplehurst.

He was killed in a flying accident on May 17 1941, as a Flight Lieutenant with 402 Squadron at Digby. Hyde is buried in Scopwick Burial Ground, Lincolnshire.

JOHN WOOLARD HYDE

104766   Sgt   Pilot   British   229 Squadron

Born in 1913, Hyde was with 229 Squadron at Wittering in early July 1940. He claimed a Do 215 destroyed on September 11.

Commissioned in April 1941, Hyde later transferred to the Administrative Branch and was released in early 1946, as a Flying Officer.

PO 16.8.41   FO 16.8.42

REGINALD JACK HYDE

2440   Sgt   Pilot   New Zealander   66 Squadron

Hyde was born in Islington, Canterbury on December 21 1912. He trained as an electrician and in 1936 went to the UK to gain further experience. He began taking flying lessons at the Cambridge Aero Club and on July 23 1938 he joined the RAFVR and trained at the weekends at 15 E&RFTS, Redhill.

In May 1939 Hyde was accepted for full-time service and at the outbreak of war had almost completed his training. He was posted on loan to 769 (FAA) Squadron at Donibristle, where he flew Gladiators and Swordfishes and practiced carrier landings on HMS 'Furious'. Hyde was posted to 66 Squadron at Duxford in October 1939. On July 18 1940 he reported to RAF Uxbridge and joined a group of pilots, which ultimately became 418 Flight. They collected Hurricanes from the MU at Hullavington and flew them to Abbotsinch. The wings were removed and the aircraft were loaded on to the carrier HMS 'Argus', which sailed on July 23. They flew off for Malta on August 2 and landed safely at Luqa, with the exception of one which crashed on landing. On the 16th 418 Flight was incorporated into the newly-formed 261 Squadron. Hyde was in 'B' Flight.

On September 5 he is believed to have destroyed a CR 42, in the period January 16 to 19 1941 he is believed to have claimed enemy aircraft destroyed and on April 22 1941 is believed to have claimed a Bf 109 and damaged another. Records in Malta over this period are virtually non-existent. When 261 Squadron added an Intelligence Officer to its establishment he went through the scrappy paperwork done prior to his arrival. Hyde was credited with five enemy aircraft destroyed, seven probably destroyed and others damaged. As well as flying Hurricanes he also flew in the three Gladiators, 'Faith', 'Hope' and 'Charity'.

When 261 was disbanded in early May Hyde returned to the UK and was posted to 58 OTU, Grangemouth, as an instructor. Promoted to Warrant Officer on October 1, he was recommended for the DFM but instead received a Mention in Despatches (1.1.42). Commissioned in January 1942, Hyde moved to 55 OTU, Aston Down in April. He returned to operations in early December, joining the newly-formed 197 Squadron at Drem. He left the squadron in October 1943 and then spent three months flying Gladiators for the film 'Signed with their Honour', set in Greece in 1941.

In February 1944 Hyde went to CGS, Sutton Bridge on a course, at the end of which he was posted to 3 Tactical Exercise Unit at Annan. He was appointed OC Gunnery and Rocket Squadron at 62 OTU, Newcastle in July 1944, as an Acting Wing Commander. He was awarded the AFC (1.1.45) and in February transferred to the RNZAF.

Hyde was posted to 59 OTU, Acklington as OC Flying in early March 1945 and recommended for an OBE but instead received a second Mention in Despatches (1.6.45). In June he went as OC Flying to the Tactical Exercise Unit at Milfield. He returned to New Zealand on September 17 and went on to the Reserve at the end of December 1945.

Hyde started an electrical business in Christchurch and ran it for many years. He died on March 23 1985.

PO 18.1.42   FO 1.10.42   FL 19.1.44   SL 29.12.45

NORMAN LANCELOT IEVERS

37812   FL   Pilot   Irish   312 Squadron

Ievers joined the RAF on a short service commission in March 1936. He was posted to 10 FTS, Tern Hill on May 14 and joined 56 Squadron at North Weald on December 25.

He was posted away to 6 FTS, Netheravon on April 24 1939, as an instructor, moved to 15 FTS, Lossiemouth on September 16 and was at No 1 FTS from September 17 1940 until October 19, when he joined 312 Squadron at Speke, as a Flight Commander.

Ievers was posted away on November 3 1940 and later in the month went to the High Altitude Flight at the A&AEE, Boscombe Down. On July 28 1941 he joined 257 Squadron at Coltishall, moved to 19 Squadron at Matlask on September 9 and was posted to the Middle East on November 3. Ievers was given command of 80 Squadron in the Western Desert on the 13th.

He was posted to the Air Staff HQ Middle East on January 23 1942 and sailed for the Far East in mid-February in the SS 'Orestes', acting as OC Troops. Ievers served on the staffs at 221, 222 and 224 Groups and on August 20 1942 was made Acting Station Commander at RAF Kanchrapara. He was posted to 320 MU, Karachi on February 20 1943.

Ievers returned to the UK later in the year and was released from the RAF in 1944, as a Squadron Leader.

APO 4.5.36   PO 9.3.37   FO 9.10.38   FL 3.9.40
SL 1.12.41

CHARLES PATRICK IGGLESDEN

39086   FO   Pilot   British   234 Squadron

Born on March 9 1918, Igglesden joined the RAF on a short service commission in June 1936. He was posted to 8 FTS, Montrose on September 5 and joined 23 Squadron at Wittering on April 24 1937.

Igglesden was with 234 Squadron at St Eval in early July 1940. He was taken off flying duties on August 7, resigned his commission on September 27 1941 and joined the Royal Navy, as an Able Seaman. Commissioned in February 1943, Igglesden was released in Australia on March 30 1946 from HMS 'Golden Hind', having served as a Fighter Director Officer.

APO 24.8.36   PO 29.6.37   FO 24.10.39
Acting Sub-Lt 19.2.43   Sub-Lt 19.8.43   Lt 30.12.43

HORACE STANLEY IMRAY

751235   Sgt   Air Gunner   British   600 Squadron

With 600 Squadron at Northolt in early July 1940. No further service details traced.

ALEC INGLE

83980   PO   Pilot   British   605 Squadron

Born on February 8 1916, Ingle joined the RAFVR in 1937 and did his flying training at 4 E&RFTS, Brough. Called up at the outbreak of war, he completed ITW and was posted to 14 FTS, Kinloss on February 5 1940.

Ingle finished the course in mid-June 1940, was commissioned and joined 605 Squadron at Drem. In early September the squadron moved to Croydon. On the 8th Ingle probably destroyed a Do 17, on October 12 he destroyed a Bf 109 and on the 26th and 27th he claimed two more. On the 27th he was damaged in combat with Bf 109s and forced-landed at Sewells Farm, Barcombe, with cuts to the face. On November 8 Ingle damaged a Bf 109 and on the 11th he claimed one as destroyed.

During November he was appointed 'B' Flight Commander and on December 1 1940 was shot down and baled out at Hollingbourne, wounded, from Hurricane V 7609. In July 1941 Ingle was posted to 59 OTU, Crosby-on-Eden, as an instructor. He was awarded the AFC (1.1.43) and returned to operations on May 5 1943, when he took command of 609 Squadron at Manston.

Awarded the DFC (17.8.43), Ingle was promoted to lead 124 Wing on August 18. He was shot down near Oumal, France on September 11 1943. His Typhoon blew up in combat with a FW 190. Ingle could not get out but the aircraft disintegrated within 300 feet of the ground, he was flung out and his parachute opened only just in time. Although burned, he stayed free for a few hours but was forced to give himself up to get medical attention. Ingle was in Stalag Luft III.

Freed in May 1945, Ingle stayed on in the RAF. He retired on May 6 1966, as a Group Captain.

PO 18.6.40   FO 21.1.41   FL 21.1.42   SL 19.11.43
SL 1.9.45   WC 1.1.52   GC 1.7.60

MICHAEL ROSCOE INGLE-FINCH

84328   PO   Pilot   British   151, 607 and 56 Squadrons

Born at St Helens, Isle of Wight on June 17 1919, Ingle-Finch was at Harrow School from 1933 to 1937. He was posted to 151 Squadron at Digby on September 18 1940, moved to 607 Squadron at Tangmere on October 3 and to 56 Squadron at Boscombe Down on the 13th.

On a flight to Kidlington in the squadron Magister on November 16 1940 Ingle-Finch was injured when it crashed near Tidworth. He was admitted to Tidworth Hospital.

At some time he was a test pilot at Short Bros and Harland and was awarded the AFC (1.1.43). In September 1943 Ingle-Finch was given command of 175 Squadron at Lydd, a Typhoon fighter-bomber unit. He was awarded the DFC (25.7.44). He completed his tour with the squadron in November 1944 and was awarded a Bar to the DFC (23.1.45).

Ingle-Finch was released from the RAF in 1946, as a Wing Commander.

PO 24.8.40   FO 24.8.41   FL 24.8.42

ROBERT ALEXANDER INNES

63784   Sgt   Pilot   British   253 Squadron

Born on June 15 1918, Innes was with 253 Squadron at Prestwick in August 1940. On the 30th he claimed a Bf 110 destroyed and on September 15 he shot down a Do 17 of 8/KG 2.

Innes crashed in Hurricane V 6736 on September 20, following an attack by Bf 109s over Maidstone. He crashed again during an interception patrol on October 11, in Hurricane L 1666, from an unknown cause. He probably destroyed a Bf 109 off the coast of Essex on November 11.

Commissioned in March 1941, Innes retired from the RAF on August 31 1961, as a Squadron Leader.

PO 5.3.41   FO 5.3.42   FL 5.3.43   SL 1.8.47

RICHARD FREDERICK INNESS

41292 FO Pilot British 152 Squadron

Educated at Eton, Inness joined the RAF on a short service commission in August 1938. He was with 152 Squadron at Warmwell in July 1940. He claimed a Ju 88 destroyed on September 26 and a Bf 109 on the 27th.

In early 1941 Inness was posted to 53 OTU, Heston, as an instructor. He commanded 130 Squadron from October 1943 to February 1944 and then 222 Squadron until June 1944. Inness was released from the RAF in 1946, as a Squadron Leader.

APO 29.10.38   PO 29.8.39   FO 3.9.40   FL 3.9.41
SL 1.7.44

AUBREY RICHARD de LISLE INNISS

42005 PO Pilot British 236 Squadron

Inniss was born on November 21 1916 and joined the RAF on a short service commission in January 1939. He was posted to 236 Squadron on September 3 1939. He destroyed a He 111, which was out on a weather reconnaissance over the Atlantic on September 23 1940.

Posted away from 236 on July 21 1941, Inniss joined 248 Squadron in 1942. On January 29 1943 he destroyed a Ju 88 and on March 10 another. Awarded the DFC (9.7.43), he later commanded the squadron, as a Wing Commander.

Inniss retired from the RAF on December 18 1957, as a Squadron Leader, retaining the rank of Wing Commander.

APO 6.3.39   PO 6.11.39   FO 6.11.40   FL 6.11.41
SL 15.9.44   SL 1.9.45

MAURICE MILNE IRVING

90277 FO Pilot British 607 Squadron

Irving, of Jesmond, Northumberland, joined 607 Squadron, AuxAF in 1934, having already obtained his 'A' license. He was called to full-time service on August 24 1939 and flew with the squadron to Merville on November 15.

Irving claimed a share in the destruction of a Ju 88 on September 14 1940. He was shot down in combat with Bf 109s east of Selsey on September 28. His Hurricane, R 4189, crashed into the Channel and Irving was reported 'Missing'. He was 29 and is remembered on the Runnymede Memorial, Panel 4.

PO (AuxAF) 10.3.34   FO (AuxAF) 10.9.35   FO 24.8.39

LEWIS REGINALD ISAAC

748158 Sgt Pilot British 64 Squadron

Isaac, of Llanelly, Wales, was a member of the RAFVR. Called to full-time service at the outbreak of war he completed his training and joined 64 Squadron at Kenley in late July 1940.

He failed to return from a squadron sortie, after a surprise attack by enemy fighters over the Channel on August 5, in Spitfire L 1029. Isaac was 24. He is remembered on the Runnymede Memorial, Panel 15.

DONALD WILLIAM ISHERWOOD

808410 Sgt Air Gunner British 29 Squadron

Enlisted on May 21 1939 in 608 Squadron, AuxAF at Thornaby, as an air gunner. Called to full-time service on August 24 1939 Isherwood began flying on convoy patrols in the squadron's Ansons.

In early May 1940 he was posted to 29 Squadron at Digby and later promoted to Sergeant. Isherwood retrained as a Radio Observer, when the squadron changed over to Beaufighters. On the night of May 8/9 1941 his aircraft was engaged in an action over Cap Gris Nez and he was severely wounded in one leg, resulting in its eventual amputation. Isherwood was discharged from the RAF on November 21 1941, as a Flight Sergeant.

THOMAS CLIFFORD IVESON

128539 Sgt Pilot British 616 Squadron

Born on September 11 1919, Iveson joined 616 Squadron at Kenley on September 2 1940. He ditched in the North Sea 20 miles north of Cromer on the 16th, after running out of fuel pursuing a Ju 88, in Spitfire L 1036. He was picked up by an MTB and landed at Yarmouth.

Commissioned in May 1942, Iveson did his second operational tour with Bomber Command. He was awarded the DFC (16.3.45), as an Acting Squadron Leader with 617 Squadron.

Iveson retired from the RAF on July 12 1949, as a Flight Lieutenant.

PO 1.5.42   FO 1.11.42   FL 1.5.44   FL 11.4.48

REGINALD IVEY

122762 Sgt Pilot British 248 and 616 Squadrons

Ivey was posted to 248 Squadron in July 1940 but moved to 616 Squadron at Kirton-in-Lindsey on October 6. He severely damaged Spitfire N 3066 on the 18th, when he made a forced-landing at Broughton, having run out of fuel through inexperience of the aircraft.

Promoted to Warrant Officer on January 1 1942, Ivey was with 252 Squadron operating in Beaufighters in the Western Desert. He destroyed two Ju 52s and damaged another on May 12.

Commissioned in May 1942, Ivey was later with 143 Squadron and was awarded the DFC (19.5.44). He was released in 1946, as a Flight Lieutenant.

PO 2.5.42   FO 2.11.42   FL 2.5.44

DONALD MacFARLANE JACK

90170 FL Pilot British 602 Squadron

Jack joined 602 Squadron, AuxAF in 1936. He was called to full-time service on September 4 1939.

He damaged a Ju 88 on July 9 1940, claimed a Bf 110 destroyed on August 25 and a Bf 109 on the 26th. Jack was posted to the Air Staff at HQ 13 Group on December 27 1940.

In May 1941 he went to RAF Turnhouse to form and command 123 Squadron. It flew convoy and shipping patrols in the Firth of Forth area and trained pilots from OTU before they were posted to squadrons in the south. On April 11 1942 the squadron went to the Middle East and having no aircraft was attached initially to ADU in June and then to 274 Squadron in the Western Desert from early July. Part of 123 went to Iraq and the rest merged with 80 Squadron. Jack took command of 80 Squadron at El Bassa, Palestine on September 17 1942.

The squadron moved to the Western Desert on October 12. Jack was posted away in February 1943 to the Air Staff of Air HQ Air Defence Eastern Mediterranean in Cairo. He was appointed Squadron Leader Flying 243 Wing to take part in a proposed landing on Rhodes. In October 1943 he was appointed SASO at HQ 209 Group at Haifa.

Jack took command of HQ 12 Sector at Port Said on August 19 1944. He returned to the UK in March 1945 and became Station Commander at RAF High Ercall in May. He was released from the RAF in September 1945, as a Wing Commander. Jack rejoined 602

Squadron in September 1946, as Adjutant, and served with it until March 1948.

PO (AuxAF) 8.11.36   FO (AuxAF) 13.6.38   FO 4.9.39
FL 3.9.40   SL 1.12.41   FL (RAuxAFRO) 14.10.46

ARTHUR JACKSON

1050666   AC 2   Radar Operator   British   29 Squadron

Joined 29 Squadron at Digby on August 10 1940. Jackson was one of the crew of Blenheim L 6637, which was attacked in error by Hurricanes of 312 Squadron on October 13 1940. It crashed in flames off the Point of Aire, near the Morecambe Light. All three men on board were lost.

Jackson was 29. He is buried in Mexborough Cemetery, Yorkshire.

PETER FREDERIC JACKSON

63790   Sgt   Pilot   British   604 Squadron

Jackson, of West Norwood, London, joined 604 Squadron at Northolt in late June 1940. He damaged a Ju 88 caught in searchlights on December 6 1940. When about to attack a Ju 88 on December 22 Jackson was fired on by its rear gunner and badly cut about the head and face. He ordered his AI operator to bale out and in spite of his face being covered in blood and only being able to see with one eye he returned to Middle Wallop without wireless aid and in poor visibility and crash-landed, in Beaufighter R 2091.

Awarded the DFM (14.1.41), Jackson was commissioned in April 1941. On May 29 he went on an air-sea firing exercise to Chesil Beach, with Sergeant SN Hawke and a new Australian pilot. While in progress clouds came in from the sea and blanketed the Dorset hills. Instead of climbing above them Jackson flew through and crashed into high ground. All three men were killed.

Jackson was 22. He was cremated at Golders Green Crematorium, Hendon.

PO 11.4.41

HENRY JACOBS

78685   PO   Air Gunner   British   219 and 600 Sqdns

Born on April 15 1907, Jacobs joined 219 Squadron at Catterick in September 1940. He moved to 600 Squadron, also at Catterick, in October. With the advent of the Beaufighter and AI he retrained as a Radio Observer and in early 1942 was Chief AI Instructor at 51 OTU, Cranfield.

Jacobs flew with JRD Braham, when the latter's operator was away. In August 1942 he assisted Braham in the destruction of two enemy aircraft and was awarded the DFC (9.10.42). In August 1943 Jacobs left Cranfield to join Braham in 141 Squadron at Wittering. Before Braham was posted to Army Staff College in October they had destroyed three enemy aircraft at night and damaged another. Jacobs was awarded a Bar to the DFC (5.11.43).

In February 1944 he was transferred to 2 Group at Braham's request, to assist in the work of night interdiction.

Jacobs was awarded the AFC (3.4.45). He retired from the RAF on December 29 1958, as a Squadron Leader. He died on October 9 1978.

APO 29.3.40   PO 29.5.40   FO 29.5.41   FL 29.5.42
FL 1.9.45   SL 1.7.52

NORMAN JACOBSON

1050704   AC 2   Radar Operator   British   29 Squadron

Jacobson, of Grimsby, joined 29 Squadron at Digby on August 25 1940. In the late evening of that same day he was a member of the crew of Blenheim L 1330, which crashed into the sea, believed shot down in combat over Wainfleet. Jacobson and the pilot, Pilot Officer RA Rhodes, were reported 'Missing' and the gunner, Sergeant RA Gouldstone, was killed.

Jacobson was 18 and is remembered on the Runnymede Memorial, Panel 27. However his body is known to have been picked up by the trawler 'Alfredian' near the Inner Dowsing and buried at sea on August 27 1940.

RICHARD HARWOOD JAMES

116678   Sgt   Aircrew   British   29 Squadron

James joined 29 Squadron at Digby on October 20 1940.

One night in March 1941 he was in a Beaufighter, which attacked a He 111 flying towards the Humber. After the first burst the cannons jammed and the enemy aircraft climbed to 15000 feet. Although without oxygen, James struggled for at least forty minutes, changing ammunition pans. When finished he collapsed, exhausted. With the one cannon successfully cleared the pilot was able to destroy the He 111. James was awarded the DFM (2.9.41), having assisted in the destruction of three enemy aircraft and damaged another.

Commissioned in February 1942, James was released from the RAF in 1945, as a Flight Lieutenant.

PO 10.2.42   FO 10.2.43   FL 10.2.44

ROBERT STUART SEYMOUR JAMES

581456   Sgt   Observer   British   248 Squadron

James was with 248 Squadron in early July 1940. He was killed on May 29 1942, as a Flight Sergeant with 228 Squadron. He is remembered on the Runnymede Memorial, Panel 74.

PATRICK GERAINT JAMESON

37813   FL   Pilot   New Zealander   266 Squadron

Jameson was born in Wellington on November 10 1912. After leaving school he was employed as an assurance clerk. In 1933 he learned to fly privately at Wellington Aero Club at Rongotai. On January 7 1936 Jameson left for the UK at his own expense in the SS 'Aorangi'. On arrival he applied for an RAF short service commission and was provisionally accepted.

He began his elementary flying on March 12 at No 1 E&RFTS at Hatfield, moved on to 8 FTS, Montrose on May 28 and with training completed joined 46 Squadron at Kenley in January 1937. He became a Flight Commander in March 1939. In April 1940 the squadron prepared to go to France but was suddenly issued with Arctic clothing and sent to Scotland. Its Hurricanes were loaded on to the carrier HMS 'Glorious' and they sailed for Norway on May 18, in company with HMS 'Furious', carrying 263 Squadron. The airfield at Skaanland was not able to take the Hurricanes until the 26th so 46 Squadron returned in the carrier to Scapa Flow. On May 24 it sailed again and on the 26th the first flight took off but the surface at Skaanland was still too soft and two aircraft crashed on landing. Already airborne, Jameson was ordered to lead the rest of the squadron to Bardufoss.

On May 28 he shared in destroying two Do 26s, moored in Rombaks Fiord, and on the 29th he destroyed a Ju 88. On June 7 263 Squadron flew its Gladiators on to the 'Glorious'. It was considered impossible for the Hurricanes to land on without arrester gear and they were ordered to be destroyed. Having obtained naval permission three Hurricanes, with sandbags fix under their tailplanes, were led by Jameson and made successful deck landings. The squadron's other seven aircraft followed and landed safely.

The following day the 'Glorious' met the German battleships 'Scharnhorst' and 'Gneisenau' and was sunk by shell fire. Jameson and 46's CO, Squadron Leader KBB Cross, found themselves on a Carley float with thirty other survivors. Over the next three days the majority died from exposure and when finally picked up by a small Norwegian ship only Jameson, Cross and five others were still alive, of whom two died after being taken to the Faroe Islands.

After a week they returned to the UK in a destroyer. Jameson spent six weeks at the Gleneagles Hotel, then a wartime hospital, followed by six weeks sick leave, some of which he spent with relatives in Ireland. He was awarded the DFC (19.7.40). He was given command of 266 Squadron at Wittering on September 17 1940.

PG Jameson (continued)

Jameson destroyed a He 111 at night over Coventry on April 9 1941 and another He 111 at night on the 10th. In early June he was made Wing Commander Flying at Wittering, destroyed a Bf 109 on June 23 and a Bf 110 on September 5. He was awarded a Bar to the DFC (7.10.41) and received a Mention in Despatches (1.1.42). He destroyed a FW 190 over Dieppe on August 19 1942. In December Jameson was posted to North Weald to lead the Norwegian Spitfire Wing. On February 15 he destroyed two FW 190s and on March 8 probably destroyed another. He was awarded the DSO (10.3.43) and in May was posted to HQ 11 Group, as Wing Commander Training. He was awarded the Norwegian War Cross (1.10.43) and in November became Group Captain Plans at 11 Group.

In late July 1944 Jameson took command of 122 Wing 83 Group, in Normandy. He led it until its disbandment at Flensburg on September 7 1945. He was made Station Commander at Schleswigland and later at Wunsdorf. In March 1946 Jameson went to RAF Staff College, Haifa. He stayed on in the RAF and retired on August 6 1960, as Group Captain, retaining the rank of Air Commodore. He returned to New Zealand to live.

As well as his other wartime awards Jameson received the Silver Star (US) and the Order of Orange-Nassau.

APO 9.3.36   PO 9.3.37   FO 9.9.38   FL 3.9.40
SL 9.9.41   WC 1.1.44   WC 1.10.46   GC 1.1.52

ZBIGNIEW JANICKI

76694   PO   Pilot   Polish   32 Squadron

Born on February 5 1917, Janicki trained in Britain and joined 32 Squadron at Acklington on October 12 1940. He was posted to 213 Squadron at Leconfield in late 1940.

On April 23 1941 Janicki joined 307 Squadron at Exeter but on May 3 he moved to 302 Squadron at Kenley and stayed with it until December 14 1941, when he was posted to 317 Squadron at Exeter. On the 18th he claimed a Bf 109 destroyed.

Janicki was rested on April 12 1942 and went to 116 Squadron, engaged on radar calibration duties. He was awarded the KW (5.5.42) and returned to operations on June 12, when he rejoined 317. He was awarded a Bar to the KW (20.8.42) and a second Bar (20.10.43), when his tour with 317 ended and he was posted to HQ 9 Group.

On May 12 1944 Janicki was attached to the US 56th Fighter Group. He was killed on June 13 1944, flying a Thunderbolt with 61 Squadron, USAAF. On an operational flight over France he reported his engine malfunctioning. Janicki either baled out or was killed trying to land near Le Mans. German sources reported that he was shot down. He is buried in Le Mans Cemetery.

PO 24.1.40   PO (PAF) 1.3.41   FO 1.3.42   FL 1.3.43

JERZY JANKIEWICZ

83698   PO   Pilot   Polish   601 and 303 Squadrons

Born on July 15 1913, Jankiewicz joined 601 Squadron at Debden on August 18 1940. He claimed a Bf 110 probably destroyed on September 4 in combat over Worthing. His Hurricane, R 4214, was damaged and Jankiewicz made a forced-landing near Goring, slightly wounded. On September 25 he claimed a Bf 109 destroyed.

Jankiewicz was posted to 303 Squadron at Leconfield on October 22 1940. Awarded the KW and Bar (1.2.41), he was rested with Operations Room duties from February 8 1941 until he was appointed 'A' Flight Commander on April 13. He shared in the destruction of a Ju 52 on May 15 and became 'B' Flight Commander, destroyed a Bf 109 on June 22 and shared a probable Bf 109 on July 6.

Jankiewicz took command of the squadron on July 9, was awarded a second Bar to the KW (15.7.41), the VM (5th Class) (10.9.41), the DFC (30.10.41), came off operations on November 20 and went as a Flying Control Officer. On May 22 1942 Jankiewicz joined 222 Squadron at North Weald, as a Flight Commander. Three days later he failed to return from an operation over France and was probably shot down west of Dunkirk, in Spitfire AD 233. With no known grave he is remembered on the Polish Air Force Memorial at Northolt.

PO 13.6.40   FO 1.3.41

SVATOPLUK JANOUCH

81892   PO   Pilot   Czechoslovakian   310 Squadron

Joined 310 Squadron at Duxford at its formation on July 10 1940. Janouch claimed a Bf 110 destroyed on September 7 and shared a Do 215 on the 18th.

He was released from the RAF as a Squadron Leader and is believed to have settled in the USA.

PO 12.7.40   FO 27.12.40

WOJCIECH JANUSZEWICZ

P 1385   FO   Pilot   Polish   303 Squadron

Born on April 30 1911, Januszewicz was in the PAF before the war and destroyed at least two enemy aircraft in September 1939.

He escaped to France and in May 1940 was with a Dewoitine fighter squadron at Meaux. After the collapse he made his way to North Africa and then reached England, via Gibraltar.

Januszewicz joined 303 Squadron at Northolt at its formation on August 2 1940. He was shot down by a Bf 109 on September 6 and crash-landed near Lenham, in Hurricane P 3089. On the 26th he was damaged in combat over Southampton and forced-landed between Charity and Wyton Farms, near Fareham, in Hurricane P 3544.

He was killed on October 5 1940, when he was shot down by Bf 109s and crashed in flames at Stowting, in Hurricane P 3892. Januszewicz is buried in Northwood Cemetery, Middlesex and is remembered on the Polish Air Force Memorial at Northolt. He was awarded the VM (5th Class)(23.12.40).

RAYMOND WALTER EMLYN JARRETT

56779   Sgt   Pilot   British   245 and 501 Squadrons

Born at Aberconyn, Wales on November 26 1911, Jarrett joined the RAF in 1926, as an aircraft apprentice. He later volunteered for pilot training and in May 1940 went to France with 'A' Flight, 245 Squadron. He escaped from Amiens back to England in a Lysander.

Jarrett was posted to 501 Squadron at Kenley in September 1940. On October 15 his Hurricane was damaged by Bf 109s in a combat over Sheppey and he forced-landed at Rochford, wounded.

Commissioned from Warrant Officer in April 1945, Jarrett retired from the RAF on April 17 1946, as a Flying Officer. He was commissioned in the RAFVR in March 1950 and in the

RAuxAF Regiment in August 1950. Jarrett later went to live in South Africa and he died in Durban on August 10 1984.

FO 6.4.45   FO (RAFVR) 7.3.50   FO (RAuxAF Regt) 26.8.50

JOSEF ANTONIN JASKE

83226   PO   Pilot   Czechoslovakian   312 Squadron

Born on January 30 1913, Jaske was in the Czech Air Force from 1933 until escaping to France in 1939. He was in l'Armée de l'Air and after the collapse of France he made his way to North Africa and left Casablanca in a British cruiser for Gibraltar. From there he sailed to Cardiff and after arrival there on August 5 1940 Jaske went to a reception centre at RAF Cosford.

On September 5 he joined the newly-formed 312 Squadron at Duxford. He became a Flight Commander on May 6 1941 and on the 27th was posted to Catterick to form and take joint command of 313 Squadron. Jaske went to HQ 10 Group on December 15 1941, as Czech Liaison Officer. He was posted to HQ Fighter Command on September 1 1942, as Deputy Liaison Officer.

Jaske was flying on November 26 and crashed into the sea after striking a balloon cable south of Penarth, Cardiff. He was taken to St Athan Hospital and was non-effective sick until May 27 1943, when he was posted to Ottawa as Liaison Officer with the United Kingdom Air Liaison Mission. On March 16 1945 Jaske went on a course at the Command and General Staff School at Fort Leavenworth, Kansas. He returned to the UK in June and was posted to Manston on MoD duties in connection with repatriation.

Jaske was released from the RAF in September 1945. He rejoined the Czech Air Force on staff duties and served until 1948. He later escaped with his family to Britain and rejoined the RAF in December 1949. He held a series of appointments in the UK and overseas, latterly in Aircraft Control. Jaske retired on May 31 1968, as a Flight Lieutenant, retaining the rank of Squadron Leader.

PO 17.8.40   FO 27.12.40   FL 1.3.41   FL 15.12.49

FRANCISZEK JASTRZEBSKI

P 1296   FL   Pilot   Polish   302 Squadron

Born on November 10 1905, Jastrzebski trained as a teacher. He joined the Army Reserve and went to the Officer Cadet School to train as an infantry officer. He transferred to the PAF and went to the Officers' School, Deblin and was commissioned as a 2nd Lieutenant in 1928.

Jastrzebski was posted to the 5th Air Force Regiment, Lida in 1929, joined the 4th Air Force Regiment, Torun in 1931 and from 1935 to 1937 was an instructor on the advanced course of Bombing and Gunnery at Grudziadz. In 1938 he was CO of 132 Squadron of III/3 Fighter Dyon, Posnan. In the fighting in September 1939 Jastrzebski claimed at least two victories. He was released by the High Command on September 16 and went to Warsaw, where he was wounded and in hospital. He escaped and made his way through Hungary and Yugoslavia and reached Lyons, France in January 1940.

Jastrzebski joined l'Armee de l'Air and from May 19 1940 he led a flight of six pilots in II/1 Groupe de Chasse, defending the Chateaudun area. He claimed one enemy aircraft destroyed and shared another. After the collapse he got to England and joined 302 Squadron at Leconfield on July 23 1940, as a Flight Commander.

On September 15 Jastrzebski shared in the destruction of a Do 17 and on the 18th probably destroyed another. He failed to return from a patrol over the Channel on October 25 1940 and was last seen gliding towards the enemy coast. Jastrzebski is buried in Kiel War Cemetery, Germany and is remembered on the Polish Air Force Memorial at Northolt.

He was awarded the VM (5th Class)(1.2.41), the KW (20.10.43), the C de G (Fr) and three Bars to the KW (31.10.47).

LUCIEN LEON GUSTAV JAVAUX

84284   PO   Observer   Belgian   235 Squadron

Joined 235 Squadron on August 5 1940. Javaux was killed on October 18 1943, aged 32, as a Flight Lieutenant with 681 Squadron, a photographic-reconnaissance unit in the Far East. His remains were repatriated to Belgium after the war.

PO 18.8.40

DUDLEY TREVOR JAY

42063   PO   Pilot   British   87 Squadron

Born in London, Jay joined the RAF on a short service commission in March 1939. He was with 87 Squadron in France in early 1940 and on May 10 destroyed a He 111.

On July 10 Jay claimed a He 111 destroyed, on the 11th a Bf 110, on August 13 shared a Ju 88, on the 15th destroyed two Ju 87s and a Bf 109. On this day he was damaged by Bf 109s in combat over Portland and forced-landed at Field Barn Farm, Radipole, in Hurricane R 2687. Jay shared a He 111 on September 15.

He collided with Flying Officer JR Cock during a routine patrol on October 24 and baled out but may have struck the aircraft as he did so because he did not pull his ripcord and was killed. His Hurricane, P 3404, crashed and burned out.

Jay was 19 years old. He is buried in Exeter Higher Cemetery, Heavitree, Exeter.

APO 27.5.39   PO 18.11.39

MICHAEL JEBB

72449   FO   Pilot   British   504 Squadron

Jebb was commissioned in the RAFVR in September 1938. He was posted to 504 Squadron at Castletown in July 1940.

He crashed near Dartford on September 15, following a combat near south-east London, in Hurricane N 2705. Jebb was admitted to Dartford Hospital with burns and died of his injuries on the 19th, aged 22. He was cremated at Hendon Crematorium.

PO (RAFVR) 13.9.38   FO 13.3.40

ROBERT VOASE JEFF

39285   FO   Pilot   British   87 Squadron

Jeff, of Tenby, Pembrokeshire, was born on March 31 1913 at Kuala Lumpur, Federated Malay States. He was at Cheltenham College from May 1927 to July 1930. He joined the RAF on a short service commission in October 1936.

Jeff was posted to 3 FTS, Grantham on January 11 1937 and on August 7 joined 87 Squadron at Debden. He went with the squadron to France at the outbreak of war. On November 2 1939 he destroyed a He 111, the first enemy aircraft to fall on French soil in the war. For this action he was awarded the C de G (Fr), which was presented to him by General Vuillemin in early February 1940. Jeff was also awarded the DFC (8.3.40).

On May 10 1940 he destroyed a Do 17 and on the 20th a Bf 109. He was awarded a Bar to the DFC (4.6.40), being then credited with

RV Jeff (continued)

five enemy aircraft destroyed.

Jeff was reported 'Missing' on August 11 1940. He was last seen diving to attack enemy aircraft off Portland Bill, in Hurricane V 7231. He is remembered on the Runnymede Memorial, Panel 4.

APO 21.12.36   PO 12.10.37   FO 12.4.39

HARRY JEFFREY JEFFCOAT

79240   PO   Air Gunner   British   236 Squadron

With 236 Squadron in early July 1940. Jeffcoat was posted away on August 1. He was killed on December 13 1941, as a Flying Officer with 44 Squadron, operating in Hampdens from Waddington.

Jeffcoat is remembered on the Runnymede Memorial, Panel 30.

PO 15.6.40   FO 15.6.41

JERRARD JEFFERIES

39286   FL   Pilot   British   85 and 310 Squadrons

Jefferies joined the RAF on a short service commission in October 1936. He was posted to 3 FTS, Grantham on January 11 1937 and joined 17 Squadron at Kenley on August 7.

He was with 85 Squadron in France in early 1940 and on May 11 he destroyed a Hs 126. On July 12 Jefferies was posted as a Flight Commander to 310 Squadron, then forming with Czech pilots at Duxford. On August 31 he claimed a Do 17 destroyed, on September 3 a Bf 110, on the 15th a Bf 109 and three shared Do 17s and on the 18th another Do 17. Jefferies was awarded the DFC (1.10.40) and the Czech Military Cross (24.12.40).

In January 1941 he took command of the squadron. About this time Jefferies changed his name to Latimer by deed poll. On April 9 he probably destroyed a Ju 88. Latimer left 310 in June 1941 and on July 7 went to Tangmere to form and command 1455 Flight, a Turbinlite Havoc unit. He led the Flight until January 1942.

Latimer was killed on April 5 1943, as a Squadron Leader with 106 Squadron, operating in Lancasters from Syerston. He is buried in Sauviller-Mongiual Communal Cemetery, France.

APO 21.12.36   PO 12.10.37   FO 12.4.39   FL 3.9.40
SL 1.6.42

GEORGE JEFFERSON

134187   Sgt   Pilot   British   43 Squadron

Joined 43 Squadron at Tangmere in August 1940. Promoted to Warrant Officer on February 1 1941, Jefferson was commissioned in August 1942 and released from the RAF in 1946, as a Flight Lieutenant.

PO 12.8.42   FO 12.2.43   FL 12.8.44

STANLEY FRANCIS JEFFERSON

85009   PO   Observer   British   248 Squadron

Served with 248 Squadron from September 30 1940 to June 15 1941. Jefferson was released from the RAF in 1945, as a Flight Lieutenant.

PO 25.8.40   FO 25.8.41   FL 25.8.42

HUGH RONALD JEFFERY-CRIDGE

154490   Sgt   Aircrew   British   236 Squadron

Jeffery-Cridge was born in 1921. He joined 236 Squadron on September 26 1940. Commissioned in November 1943, he was released from the RAF in 1946, as a Flight Lieutenant.

PO 26.11.43   FO 26.5.44   FL 26.11.45

GEORGE WILLIAM JEFFERYS

754867   Sgt   Pilot   British   43 and 46 Squadrons

Born in Hemel Hempstead in 1920, Jefferys was in the RAFVR before the war. He joined 43 Squadron at Tangmere in August 1940.

On September 2 he destroyed a Bf 109, on the 4th a Bf 110 and on the 6th a Bf 109. He was posted to 46 Squadron on September 15 and on that day shared a Do 17.

Jefferys was shot down in combat over Clacton on September 18 1940, in Hurricane V 7442. He baled out but was killed when his parachute failed to open. He was 20 years old and is buried in St Michael's churchyard, near his home in Winterbourne, Wiltshire.

ALISTAIR JOHN OSWALD JEFFREY

39740   FO   Pilot   British   64 Squadron

Joined the RAF on a short service commission in March 1937. He was posted to 2 FTS, Brize Norton on June 5 and joined the staff of SHQ RAF Church Fenton on June 10 1938.

In early 1940 Jeffrey was with 64 Squadron at Church Fenton. Over Dunkirk on June 1 he destroyed a Ju 87 in the air and three more and a Ju 86 on the ground.

On July 7 he claimed a Bf 110 destroyed and on the 19th a He 115 floatplane. Jeffrey failed to return from a combat with enemy aircraft near Dover on July 25 1940. His Spitfire, P 9421, crashed into the sea. His body was later recovered by the Germans and he is buried in Vlissingen Northern Cemetery, Netherlands. He was 22 years old. Jeffrey was awarded the DFC (13.8.40).

APO 18.5.37   PO 15.3.38   FO 15.10.39

CHARLES GORDON St DAVID JEFFRIES

41929   PO   Pilot   British   3 and 232 Squadrons

Born on March 1 1920, Jeffries joined the RAF on a short service commission in February 1939. He did his ab initio course at 11 E&RFTS, Perth and in June went to 2 FTS, Brize Norton.

Jeffries was with 3 Squadron in France in May 1940 and at Wick in early July. He went to Sumburgh on the 17th, when 'B' Flight was re-numbered as 232 Squadron. On August 23 he shared in the destruction of a He 111 off Fair Isle, the squadron's first victory.

On April 27 1941 Jeffries flew off HMS 'Ark Royal' to Hal Far, Malta and joined 261 at Ta Kali. On May 5 he shared a Ju 88. When 'C' Flight 261 was incorporated into a newly-reformed 185 Squadron at Hal Far on May 12 Jeffries was appointed 'A' Flight Commander. On July 4 he destroyed a Mc 200 and damaged another, on the 9th he took part in a strafing attack on Syracuse seaplane base, in which a number of aircraft were destroyed, on the 11th he claimed a Mc 200 and another damaged and on September 4 he claimed another Mc 200. Jeffries was awarded the DFC (26.9.41).

He was posted to the Middle East in October 1941. Jeffries commanded 155 Squadron in India and Burma from November 1942 to November 1943. He was awarded a Bar to the DFC (25.1.44). He stayed in the RAF after the war and was awarded a second Bar to the DFC (22.3.55) for operations in Kenya. Jeffries retired on October 1 1967, as a Wing Commander, and died in January 1985.

APO 15.4.39   PO 6.11.39   FO 6.11.40   FL 6.11.41
SL 1.7.45   SL 1.8.47   WC 1.1.55

JOZEF JEKA

P 1654   Sgt   Pilot   Polish   238 Squadron

Born on April 6 1917, Jeka joined 238 Squadron at St Eval on September 2 1940. On the 15th he claimed a Bf 110 destroyed, on the 26th two He 111s, on the 27th a shared Bf 110 and on October 7 a Ju 88. He was shot down by Bf 109s over Bournemouth on November 5 and baled out over Wimborne. His Hurricane, V 7535, crashed at East Farm, Tarrant Monkton. Jeka was awarded the KW and two Bars (1.2.41).

In 1941 he was posted to 306 Squadron at Tern Hill. On June 17 he claimed a Bf 109 destroyed and on August 16 another. Jeka was awarded the VM (5th Class)(10.9.41). Commissioned in November 1941, he was posted to 58 OTU, Grangemouth on December 2, as an instructor. He was awarded the DFM (19.2.42).

Jeka returned to operations on May 29 1942, rejoining 306 Squadron, then at Kirton-in-Lindsey. Awarded a third Bar to the KW (12.5.43), he went to 308 Squadron at Church Fenton on May 24 1943 and moved to 316 Squadron at Northolt on August 11. He claimed a FW 190 destroyed on August 19. Jeka was posted to 18 APC on December 18 and joined 308 Squadron at Northolt on March 30 1944. He was shot down on May 21 and did not return to operations until September 11.

Jeka moved to 306 Squadron at Andrews Field, Essex on November 24 1944, was appointed Flight Commander on December 6 and took command of the squadron on May 25 1945. He was awarded the Silver Cross of Merit, with Swords (15.6.45). On May 4 1946 Jeka was posted to Coltishall. He was released from the PAF in January 1947, as a Flight Lieutenant.

PO 1.11.41   FO 1.11.42   FL 1.11.43

DAVID NICHOLAS OWEN JENKINS

41930   PO   Pilot   British   253 Squadron

Jenkins was born on May 13 1919 and was at Marlborough College from 1933 to 1937. He joined the RAF on a short service commission in February 1939 and did his elementary flying training at 11 E&RFTS, Perth. In June he went to 2 FTS, Brize Norton and on November 6 1939 joined the newly-formed 253 Squadron at Manston.

Flying from Turnhouse on August 7 Jenkins got into difficulties whilst flying in cloud at night. He decided to bale out and landed at Fail Mains Farm, a half-mile from where his Hurricane, P 3457, crashed, five miles east of Prestwick.

On August 30 Jenkins was shot down in combat over Redhill. He baled out but was killed by enemy fighters. His Hurricane, P 3921, crashed at Butlers Dene Road, Woldingham.

Jenkins is buried in St Margaret's churchyard, Bagendon, Gloucestershire.

APO 15.4.39   PO 6.11.39

BERNARD JAMES JENNINGS

47706   Sgt   Pilot   British   19 Squadron

Born on March 21 1915, Jennings joined the RAF on May 1 1933. After training he was posted to the Parachute Flight, Hendon and was standby member of the Parachute Pull-Off team for the Air Display in 1934, which involved standing on the wingtip of a Vickers Virginia.

In 1934 Jennings went to Farnborough for a photographic course and in 1935 was posted to 33 Squadron at Upper Heyford as a photographer/air gunner. The squadron went to the Middle East in October 1935. Having volunteered for pilot training, Jennings returned to the UK in late 1937 and did his ab initio course at 11 E&RFTS, Perth. In March 1938 he was posted to 10 FTS, Tern Hill and in November went as a staff pilot in the Signals Squadron at RAF Cranwell.

In August 1939 Jennings joined 19 Squadron at Duxford. Over Dunkirk on May 27 1940 he shared in a probable Do 17 and on June 1 destroyed two Bf 110s and damaged a Do 215 on a later patrol.

He claimed a Bf 110 destroyed and a He 111 probably destroyed on September 11 and a Bf 109 destroyed on the 29th. He was awarded the DFM (4.4.41).

Jennings went to CFS, Upavon on April 12 1941 for an instructor's course, after which he was posted to 5 FTS, Tern Hill in May but returned to Upavon in September, as an instructor. Commissioned in December 1941, he remained at CFS until March 1943, when he was posted to 3 (P) AFU at South Cerney.

To prepare for a return to operations Jennings went to 41 OTU, Hawarden in May 1944 and in August joined 168 Squadron, a tactical reconnaissance unit with Mustangs and later Typhoons. After the squadron disbanded at Eindhoven on February 26 1945 Jennings was appointed CO of 83 GSU Ferry Flight.

He retired from the RAF on March 21 1962, as a Wing Commander. From 1963 until 1980 he was with the Ministry of Defence.

PO 30.12.41   FO 1.10.42   FL 30.12.43   SL 1.8.47
WC 1.7.54

DENNIS MAYVORE JERAM

Sub-Lieutenant (FAA)   Pilot   British   213 Squadron

Loaned to the RAF in mid-June 1940, Jeram joined 213 Squadron at Exeter on July 5.

He claimed a Ju 88 destroyed on August 11, Bf 110s on the 12th and 15th and a Do 17 on September 15. After the Battle of Britain Jeram returned to the FAA and in December 1941 he was posted to 888 Squadron. From February 1942 until the end of 1943 the squadron was in the carrier HMS 'Formidable'. During the operations in North Africa Jeram shot down a Vichy French Bloch 175 on November 6 1942. It was searching for an Allied convoy, which had been reported as it passed through the Straits of Gibraltar on its way to North Africa. Three days later Jeram shared in destroying a Ju 88 near Algiers. It had Italian markings and a German crew. He also took part in the invasion of Sicily and the Salerno landings.

Jeram retired in 1954, as a Lieutenant-Commander. He died on March 24 1977.

Actg Sub-Lt 16.3.39   Sub-Lt 14.3.40   Lt 1.2.42
Lt-Cdr 1.2.50

EDMUND WINCENTY JERECZEK

76664   PO   Pilot   Polish   43 and 229 Squadrons

Jereczek was born on August 14 1904. He joined 43 Squadron at Usworth in September 1940 and later moved to 229 Squadron at Northolt.

In 1941 he was posted to 25 EFTS, Hucknall, as an instructor. He went on courses at FIS, Woodley and 5 FIS, Perth in the second half of 1942, after which he returned to Hucknall. Jereczek was awarded the AFC (26.5.45).

He was posted to 16 FTS, Newton on November 13 1945, as an instructor. Jereczek was released from the PAF in December 1946 and settled in England. He died on August 26 1984.

FO 1.3.41   FL 1.9.42

ERNEST ROBERT JESSOP

742987   Sgt   Pilot   British   257, 43 and 253 Sqdns

Posted to 257 Squadron at Debden on September 1 1940, moved to 43 Squadron at Usworth on the 10th and then to 253 Squadron on the 28th.

Jessop joined 242 Squadron at Martlesham Heath in February 1941. He was posted away on March 11 and on April 3 took off in a Hurricane from HMS 'Ark Royal', as part of a batch of reinforcements for Malta.

Jessop joined 261 Squadron at Ta Kali. On May 12 1941 the squadron disbanded. 'C' Flight became part of a new squadron, 185, at Hal Far. The remainder of 261's pilots went to the Middle East, Jessop among them, and became part of a new 261, when it was reformed at Habbaniya on July 12 1941.

Jessop was killed in a flying accident on November 15 1941, as a Flight Sergeant. He is buried in Khayat Beach War Cemetery, Israel.

VACLAV JICHA

78567   PO   Pilot   Czechoslovakian   1 Squadron

An aerobatics champion in Czechoslovakia before the war, Jicha joined No 1 Squadron in September 1940. He shared in the destruction of a Ju 88 on October 30.

Jicha was awarded the DFC and the AFC but no details have been traced. He was killed in a flying accident on February 1 1945, aged 31. He is buried in Haddington Roman Catholic Graveyard, East Lothian, Scotland.

MIROSLAV JIROUDEK

78745   F/Sgt   Pilot   Czechoslovakian   310 Squadron

Jiroudek was in the Czech Air Force in the thirties. He escaped to Poland on the night of June 14/15 1939 and eventually went to France.

He joined 310 Squadron at Duxford in mid-August 1940 and shared in the destruction of a Do 215 on September 18. After being hit by anti-aircraft fire over Faversham on November 5 Jiroudek baled out. His Hurricane, V 7588, crashed at Graveney, Sittingbourne.

Jiroudek returned to Czechoslovakia after the war.

PO 12.4.42   FO 12.4.43   FL 12.4.44

GEORGE BINMORE JOHNS

45543   Sgt   Pilot   British   229 Squadron

Born on March 24 1917, Johns joined the RAF on January 9 1934, as an aircraft apprentice at No 1 S of TT, Halton. He passed out in January 1937 as an LAC Fitter II and was posted to 4 Squadron at Farnborough.

Johns volunteered for pilot training and was selected in March 1939. He did his ab initio course at 4 E&RFTS, Brough and the intermediate and advanced training at 3 FTS, Grantham. He was promoted to Corporal and awarded his flying badge on August 19 1939.

In November Johns joined the newly-reformed 229 Squadron at Digby, as a Sergeant-Pilot. The squadron exchanged its Blenheims for Hurricanes in March 1940 and on May 16 Johns went to France with a squadron detachment. After suffering losses it returned to Digby on the 22nd. Johns took part in operations over Dunkirk and in the Battle of Britain from September.

Commissioned in March 1941, Johns embarked with the squadron in May in the carrier HMS 'Furious', bound for the Middle East. The Hurricanes flew off to Malta on May 21, refuelled there and then flew on to Mersa Matruh. Johns was attached to 73 Squadron for operations. He destroyed a Ju 87 on July 15, a Ju 88 on the night of August 8 and a He 111 by day on the 9th. In early September he flew down to Takoradi to collect a Hurricane IIc, with which the squadron once again came together as a unit.

In March 1942 Johns was posted to 71 OTU, Gordon's Tree, Sudan, as an instructor. He was awarded the DFC (7.4.42). He returned to the Western Desert in January 1943 and took command of 250 Squadron on February 2. After the invasion of Sicily Johns was posted to Middle East Staff College in September and in December went on staff duties.

He returned to the Desert Air Force in May 1944 and took command of 260 Squadron in Italy. With his tour completed Johns was awarded the DSO (29.12.44) and posted to Sector Operations duties. He returned to the UK in May 1945 and went on to staff duties at Air Ministry.

Johns was awarded the AFC (2.1.56). He held a series of appointments and commands in the UK and overseas prior to his retirement on March 24 1972, as a Group Captain. From then until June 1977 he was RAF Regional Liaison Officer for Scotland, a civilian post.

PO 26.3.41   FO 12.12.41   FL 12.12.42   SL 15.3.45
SL 1.9.45   WC 1.7.52   GC 1.7.61

ALFRED ERNEST JOHNSON

123312   Sgt   Air Gunner   British   23 Squadron

With 23 Squadron at Collyweston in early July 1940. Commissioned in the Technical Branch (Armament) in July 1942, Johnson was released from the RAF in 1945, as a Flying Officer. He died on October 23 1959.

PO 29.7.42   FO 29.1.43

ALLAN EVERITT JOHNSON

41425   PO   Pilot   British   46 Squadron

Johnson, of Kenton, Middlesex, joined the RAF on a short service commission in October 1938. He was with 46 Squadron at Digby in early July 1940.

On September 5 he claimed a Bf 109 destroyed, on the 15th a Ju 88 and on the 27th a Bf 110.

Johnson reformed and then commanded 243 Squadron at Ouston and in North Africa from June 1 1942 until February 1943. He returned to the UK and was killed on July 4 1943, as a Squadron Leader. The unit he was serving with is not known. Johnson was 22 and is buried in the Kirton-in-Lindsey Burial Ground, Lincolnshire.

APO 14.12.38   PO 3.9.39   FO 3.12.40   FL 3.12.41

CHARLES ALEXANDER JOHNSON

161484   Sgt   Air Gunner   British   25 Squadron

Joined 25 Squadron at North Weald on September 26 1940. Commissioned in November 1943, Johnson was reported to have died on May 5 1945 but no trace has been found to confirm this.

PO 15.11.43   FO 15.5.44

CHARLES EDWARD JOHNSON

79241   PO   Air Gunner   British   264 Squadron

Joined 264 Squadron at Kirton-in-Lindsey in mid-August 1940. Johnson was gunner in Defiant L 7026, shot down in combat by Bf 109s of JG 26 over Thanet on August 28. The aircraft crashed in flames on Sillibourne Farm, Hinxhill. Both Johnson and the pilot, Pilot Officer PL Kenner, were killed.

Johnson was 35 and is buried in Folkestone New Cemetery, Kent.

PO 27.7.40

GERALD BRUCE JOHNSON

| 391859 | Sgt | Air Gunner | New Zealander | 23 Squadron |

Born in Auckland on September 4 1919, Johnson worked as an assistant in a clothing shop. He volunteered for aircrew duties in September 1939 and began his training at Weraroa on December 18.

In mid-January 1940 he went to the Air Observers' School, Ohakea for a gunnery course and air experience. Johnson sailed for the UK on March 23 in the SS 'Akaroa'. He was posted to 5 OTU at Aston Down on May 29 to convert to Blenheims, was awarded his air gunner's badge and Sergeant's stripes on July 5 and joined 23 Squadron at Collyweston the next day.

From late December 1940 the squadron, flying from Ford, was carrying out night-intruder sorties over enemy-occupied France and in March 1941 began receiving Havocs. On May 28 Johnson was a member of the crew in one of these aircraft on a training flight. It crashed near Manston and all aboard were killed.

Johnson is buried in Clymping churchyard, Sussex.

JAMES EDGAR JOHNSON

| 83267 | PO | Pilot | British | 616 Squadron |

Born in Loughborough, Leicestershire on March 9 1915, Johnson qualified as a civil engineer in 1937 at Nottingham University. He was in the RAFVR and did some flying training at 21 E&RFTS, Stapleford before being called to full-time service at the outbreak of war.

Johnson went to ITW at Jesus College, Cambridge, completed his ab initio flying at 22 EFTS, Cambridge and did his intermediate and advanced at 5 FTS, Sealand. He was posted to 7 OTU, Hawarden in August 1940, joined 19 Squadron at the end of the month and moved to 616 Squadron at Kenley on September 5.

Johnson's first victory came on June 26 1941, a Bf 109. On July 6 and 14 he destroyed Bf 109s and on September 21 two more. He was awarded the DFC (30.9.41) and made a Flight Commander. He was awarded a Bar to the DFC (26.6.42). In July 1942 Johnson was given command of 610 Squadron at Ludham. Over Dieppe on August 19 he destroyed a FW 190 and on February 13 probably destroyed another.

In March 1943 Johnson was posted to Kenley to lead the Canadian Wing. Between April 3 and September 4 1943 he destroyed ten FW 190s and shared another, destroyed four Bf 109s and shared three more and shared a Bf 110. He was awarded the DSO (4.6.43) and a Bar (24.9.43). Johnson was posted to the Planning Staff at 11 Group in September and returned to operations in March 1944, when he was posted to Digby to lead 144 Wing. Between April 25 and September 27 1944 he destroyed eight FW 190s and five Bf 109s. He was awarded a second Bar to the DSO (7.7.44).

The Wing was disbanded in October 1944 and Johnson was posted to lead 127 Wing. On April 6 1945 he was promoted to Acting Group Captain and given command of 125 Wing.

Johnson ended the war as the top-scoring Allied pilot, with thirty-eight confirmed victories. He received the DFC (US)(18.1.44), the Order of Leopold (Belg)(1947) and the C de G (Belg)(1947). He remained in the RAF and in 1950 was attached to the USAF, serving in the US and Korea. He was awarded the Air Medal (US) in December 1950 and the Legion of Merit (US) in October 1951.

Johnson retired on March 15 1966, as an Air Vice-Marshal. He was made a CBE (1.1.60) and a CB (1.1.65).

PO 10.8.40	FO 10.8.41	FL 10.8.42	SL 16.6.43
WC 4.10.45	WC 1.7.47	GC 1.1.55	AC 1.7.60
AVM 1.1.63			

JOSEPH INKERMAN JOHNSON

| 520406 | Sgt | Pilot | British | 222 Squadron |

A pre-war airman pilot, Johnson was with 222 Squadron at Hornchurch in early July 1940. He was shot down and killed by Bf 109s on August 30. His Spitfire, R 6628, crashed and burned out at Longhampark Lodge, Bishopsbourne.

Johnson was 26. He is buried in Towcester Cemetery, Northamptonshire.

REGINALD BERNARD JOHNSON

| 126859 | Sgt | Pilot | British | 222 Squadron |

Joined the RAFVR in 1938 and did his elementary flying training at 22 E&RFTS, Cambridge. Called up at the outbreak of war, Johnson did his intermediate and advanced flying at 10 FTS, Tern Hill, was awarded his flying badge in January 1940 and joined 222 Squadron at Duxford in April.

On September 3 Johnson baled out over Burnham, having developed a glycol leak on a routine patrol. His Spitfire, L 1010, crashed at Lower Raypits, Canewdon. He baled out again on September 14 after being damaged in combat with Bf 109s. His Spitfire, X 4249, crashed south of Cockhide Farm, Avely.

In February 1941 Johnson was posted to 52 OTU, Debden, as an instructor. He went on a course at CFS, Upavon in July 1941. Commissioned from Warrant Officer in June 1942, Johnson instructed at 9 FTS, Hullavington; 22 EFTS, Cambridge; RAF Watchfield and 3 EFTS, Shellingford. He was released from the RAF in 1945, as a Flight Lieutenant.

| PO 29.6.42 | FO 29.12.42 | FL 29.6.44 |

RICHARD KENNETH HOWARD JOHNSON

| 102084 | Sgt | Pilot | British | 235 Squadron |

Johnson, of Belper, Derbyshire, joined 235 Squadron in mid-October 1940. He was commissioned in July 1941 and awarded the DFC (7.7.44), as an Acting Squadron Leader with 272 Squadron.

Johnson was killed on January 31 1945, aged 25, as an Acting Wing Commander with 272. He is remembered on the Malta Memorial, Panel 18, Column 1.

| PO 12.7.41 | FO 12.7.42 | FL 12.7.43 |

RONALD ARTHUR JOHNSON

| 116721 | Sgt | Pilot | British | 43 Squadron |

Joined 43 Squadron at Usworth on October 12 1940. Commissioned in January 1942, Johnson was awarded the DFC (25.7.44), as a Flight Lieutenant with 144 Squadron.

He was released from the RAF in 1946, as a Flight Lieutenant.

| PO 12.1.42 | FO 1.10.42 | FL 12.1.44 |

SYDNEY FREDERICK FARQUHAR JOHNSON

| 91005 | PO | Pilot | British | 600 Squadron |

Johnson, of Chelsea, London, joined 600 Squadron, AuxAF in 1939. He was called to full-time service on August 24. He rejoined 600 Squadron at Northolt in June 1940.

Johnson was killed on February 26 1941, as a Flight Lieutenant with 256 Squadron, operating in Defiants from Colerne. He was 25 and is buried in Cliveden War Cemetery, Taplow, Buckinghamshire.

| APO 24.8.39 | PO 4.5.40 |

WILLIAM JOHN JOHNSON

115410   Sgt   Pilot   British   85 and 145 Squadrons

Born on July 15 1919, Johnson was posted to 85 Squadron at Church Fenton in early October 1940 and moved on the 18th to 145 Squadron at Tangmere. On January 26 1941 he destroyed a Bf 109.

Commissioned in January 1942, Johnson was posted to 611 Squadron at Drem. In April he joined 126 Squadron at Ta Kali, Malta. On August 14 he destroyed two Mc 202s and on October 5 a Bf 109. He was awarded the DFC (22.1.43) and returned to the UK.

In July 1944 Johnson was given command of 257 Squadron, operating in France with Typhoons. He was posted away in October and awarded a Bar to the DFC (1.12.44).

Johnson retired from the RAF on February 6 1959, as a Squadron Leader.

PO 7.1.42   FO 1.10.42   FL 7.1.44   FL 1.9.45
SL 1.1.54

JAMES THOMAS JOHNSTON

43037   PO   Pilot   Canadian   151 Squadron

After completing his flying training at 2 FTS, Brize Norton, Johnston was posted direct to 151 Squadron at Martlesham Heath on July 13 1940. Having bypassed OTU he was converted on the Station Flight Master by Barry Sutton of 56 Squadron, then non-operational, sick.

On August 15 Johnston was shot down by Bf 109s and crashed into the Channel off Dymchurch, in Hurricane P 3941. He was dead when picked up. He was 26 years old and is buried in Folkestone New Cemetery, Kent.

APO 23.3.40   PO 13.7.40

ALEXANDER VALLANCE RIDDELL JOHNSTONE

90163   SL   Pilot   British   602 Squadron

Johnstone was born on June 2 1916 and educated at Kelvinside Academy, Glasgow. He was working for a footwear firm in Edinburgh when he joined 602 Squadron, AuxAF in late 1934.

In early 1938 Johnstone went to work for Scottish Aviation Ltd as a navigation instructor at 12 E&RFTS and No 1 Civil Air Navigation School at Prestwick. Under the aegis of 602 Squadron he went to RAF Manston in August 1938 for a service navigation course.

Johnstone was called to full-time service with 602 on August 24 1939. He shot down a He 111 at night on June 26 1940 and took command of the squadron on July 12 1940. On August 13 it went south to Westhampnett. Johnstone shared in destroying a Ju 88 on the 19th, destroyed a Bf 110 and a Bf 109 on the 25th, a He 111, a Ju 88 and a Bf 109 on September 7, shared a Do 17 on the 9th and destroyed a Ju 88 on the 30th. He was awarded the DFC (1.10.40).

He left the squadron in mid-April 1941, became Controller at Turnhouse and in September was posted to the Middle East, going to HQ 263 Group, Beirut to help establish an air defensive organisation in the Levant. Johnstone was given command of Sector Headquarters at Haifa in April 1942. In September he went to Malta, firstly as Deputy Station Commander at Luqa, then to Valetta as Fighter Controller and on January 27 1943 he was appointed Wing Commander Flying at Krendi.

Johnstone returned to the UK on March 19 1943 and was posted to RAF Staff College at Gerrards Cross on May 24. He went to 56 OTU, Tealing on September 1 for a refresher course and conversion to Typhoons. On November 11 1943 Johnstone was appointed Sector Commander at Fairwood Common. He was promoted to Acting Group Captain on May 29 1944 and posted to HQ Allied Expeditionary Air Force at Bentley Priory as Ops 1. He moved across to Jouloville in France on August 31 but returned to Stanmore in mid-October.

In early January 1945 Johnstone went to the USA to join the RAF Delegation in Washington. He returned to the UK in late June, was posted to a staff job at HQ 12 Group and then in January 1946 was appointed Air Attaché in Dublin.

Johnstone retired from the RAF on December 14 1968, as an Air Vice-Marshal. He was made a CB (1966).

PO (AuxAF) 3.5.35   FO (AuxAF) 3.11.36   FL 24.8.39
SL 1.9.40   WC 1.3.42   WC 1.7.47   GC 1.1.54
AC 1.1.61   AVM 1.7.65

IAN KENNETH SEFTON JOLL

90951   PO   Pilot   British   604 Squadron

Joll joined 604 Squadron, AuxAF in 1939. He was called to full-time service on August 24 1939. With training completed he rejoined the squadron in April 1940.

On May 10 the squadron provided an escort for Blenheims detailed to bomb German transport aircraft on the beach at Wassenaar, Holland. After the bombing Joll decided to have a low-level strafe of the beach. His port propellor came off, either shot off by ground fire or by striking the ground. The Blenheim crash-landed on the beach but did not catch fire and Joll and his gunner were not badly hurt. With the help of Dutch people they managed to get on the SS 'Dotterel' on the 13th and return to England.

Joll was on a night patrol on May 1 1941. He was closing in to attack an enemy aircraft, when a burst of return fire severely wounded his radar operator and damaged the Beaufighter. With the wounded man's help he flew the aircraft safely back to base. On May 6 Joll destroyed a Ju 88 and on July 4 a He 111.

In late 1941 Joll was posted to 153 Squadron, recently reformed at Ballyhalbert. He returned to 604 Squadron, then at Middle Wallop, in October 1942. He destroyed a Do 217 on September 21 1943 and was awarded the DFC (29.10.43).

Joll was released from the RAF in 1946, as a Squadron Leader.

APO 24.8.39   PO 17.3.40   FO 2.12.40   FL 2.12.41

CYRIL ARTHUR TREVOR JONES

43693   PO   Pilot   British   611 and 616 Squadrons

Joined 611 in April 1940. Jones probably destroyed a Bf 109 over Dunkirk on June 2. He was posted to 616 Squadron at Kenley on September 4.

Jones was badly wounded in the right elbow by return fire from a He 111 engaged off Spurn Head on November 5 1940. He returned safely to Kirton-in-Lindsey and was admitted to Scunthorpe Hospital. The enemy aircraft crashed into the Humber.

From February 1942 until February 1944 Jones commanded 79 Squadron, mostly in India. He was awarded the DFC (14.4.44) and was released from the RAF in 1946, as a Wing Commander. He later went to Australia.

PO 1.4.40   FO 24.12.40   FL 1.6.41   SL 1.5.44

DENYS ALLAN EVAN JONES

40119   FO   Pilot   British   3 and 501 Squadrons

Jones joined the RAF on a short service commission in July 1937. He was posted to 11 FTS, Wittering on September 18 and on May 7 1938 went as a staff pilot to 8 Armament Training Station, Evanton, Ross-shire.

In early July 1940 Jones was with 3 Squadron at Wick. On July 25 he claimed a share in destroying a He 111 off Pentland Firth. He was posted to 501 Squadron at Kenley on September 26, as a Flight Commander.

Two days later Jones crashed on landing following a combat with Bf 109s over Deal. On October 4 he made a forced-landing at Great Bentley Farm, Cuckfield because of deteriorating weather during a routine patrol.

Jones destroyed a Bf 109 on November 8. He was posted away to instruct in January 1941. No trace of Jones as a casualty has been found. He disappears from the Air Force List after January 1943.

APO 5.9.37   PO 12.7.38   FO 12.2.40   FL 12.2.41

EDWIN JONES

523574   Sgt   Air Gunner   British   29 Squadron

Jones, of Askam-in-Furness, was in the RAF before the war. He was with 29 Squadron at Digby in early July 1940.

On December 19 1940 Jones was one of four men in an aircraft, probably a Blenheim, which crashed two miles south-west of Digby, possibly after striking a tree. All aboard were killed.

Jones was 27 and is buried in Barrow-in-Furness Cemetery, Lancashire.

HERBERT DANIEL BAYNTON JONES

517897   Sgt   Pilot   British   504 and 85 Squadrons

A pre-war airman pilot, Jones was with 504 Squadron in early July 1940. On September 27 he destroyed a Bf 110, which crashed at Haydon, near Radstock, Somerset and on the 30th he claimed two He 111s destroyed.

Jones was posted to 85 Squadron at Kirton-in-Lindsey on October 16.

He was killed on July 6 1941, aged 25. He is buried in St Philip's churchyard, Pennfields, Wolverhampton.

JOHN FERDINAND READ JONES

128559   Sgt   Aircrew   British   25 Squadron

Served with 25 Squadron in the Battle of Britain. Promoted to Warrant Officer on October 1 1941, Jones was commissioned in July 1942 and released from the RAF in 1946, as a Flight Lieutenant.

PO 25.7.42   FO 25.1.43   FL 25.7.44

JOHN SINCLAIR BUCKNALL JONES

33467   PO   Pilot   British   152 Squadron

Jones, of Marlborough, Wiltshire, entered RAF College, Cranwell in January 1938 as a flight cadet. He graduated in October 1939 and was with 152 Squadron at Acklington in early July 1940.

Later in the month the squadron moved south to Warmwell. On August 11 Jones was shot down in combat with Bf 109s in mid-Channel, in Spitfire R 6614. He baled out but was killed, aged 21. He is buried in Sainte Marie Cemetery, Le Havre, France.

PO 1.10.39

JOSEPH TREVOR JONES

78855   PO   Pilot   British   264 Squadron

Jones was posted to 264 Squadron at Duxford in early July 1940. He failed to return from a combat with Ju 88s and Bf 109s over the Channel off Thanet on August 24, in Defiant L 6966. Jones and his gunner, Pilot Officer WA Ponting, were both reported 'Missing', believed shot down by Major Lützow of JG 3.

Jones was 21. He is remembered on the Runnymede Memorial, Panel 8.

PO 28.4.40

KENNETH HAROLD JONES

745153   Sgt   Pilot   British   85 and 605 Squadrons

Joined 85 Squadron at Church Fenton on September 14 1940. He moved to 605 Squadron at Croydon on October 19.

Jones was shot down on February 2 1941 and captured. He was freed on May 9 1945. No further details traced.

RICHARD LEOLINE JONES

81362   PO   Pilot   British   64 and 19 Squadrons

Jones joined 64 Squadron at Kenley in late July 1940 and moved to 19 Squadron at Fowlmere in October.

He was released from the RAF in 1946, as a Flight Lieutenant. He joined the RAFVR in January 1948.

PO 6.7.40   FO 6.7.41   FL 6.7.42   FO (RAFVR) 1.1.48

ROBERT ERIC JONES

83981   PO   Pilot   British   605 Squadron

Joined 605 Squadron at Drem in June 1940. Jones claimed a He 111 destroyed on August 15 and shared another on September 11. Four days later he was shot down during an engagement with Do 17s and Bf 109s over Croydon and baled out, slightly injured. His Hurricane, L 2122, crashed at Drux Farm, Plaxtol.

Jones was shot down by Bf 109s over North Foreland on November 15, in Hurricane P 2560. He baled out, unhurt. He was posted away in April 1941 but served again with 605 from March 1943 to March 1944. He was released from the RAF in 1945, as a Flight Lieutenant.

PO 18.6.40   FO 18.6.41   FL 18.6.42

WILLIAM ROSS JONES

44635   PO   Pilot   British   266 and 602 Squadrons

Born on November 22 1911, Jones was with 266 Squadron at Wittering in early July 1940. He shared in the destruction of a He 115 floatplane on August 15. Jones was commissioned in early September 1940 and posted to 602 Squadron at Westhampnett on the 13th.

He was given the task on September 2 1944 of forming and then commanding the Special Duties Flight for communication duties in support of 2nd TAF and 21 Army Group on the Continent. Jones later went to the Air Staff at Technical Training Command and carried out many special flights to Southern France, Belgium, Germany and Holland, carrying many important passengers. He was awarded the AFC (1.1.46).

Jones was in the Fighter Control Branch after the war and retired from the RAF on January 28 1959, as a Flight Lieutenant, retaining the rank of Squadron Leader.

PO 2.9.40   FO 2.9.41   FL 2.9.42   FL 1.9.45

ALEXIS RENE ISIDORE GHISLAIN JOTTARD

82515   PO   Pilot   Belgian   145 Squadron

Jottard was in the Belgian Air Force before the war and when Belgium was over-run he escaped to France and flew with l'Armée de l'Air. In June 1940 he was one of a group of Belgian pilots on aerodrome defence at Chartres.

On June 20 he and Jean Offenberg took two Caudron Simouns and flew to Corsica, then to Phillipeville, Algeria, then to Oujda, where Belgians had set up a training school. Finding morale there to be low the two took a train to Casablanca. Here they met some other Belgians, who were trainee pilots, and some Poles. The Poles had permission to sail that evening in a cargo boat for Gibraltar. The Belgians and some French airmen slipped aboard with them. They transferred to a British ship at Gibraltar and disembarked at Liverpool on July 16 1940.

Jottard went to 6 OTU, Sutton Bridge on the 30th and on August 17 he joined 145 Squadron at Westhampnett. He was shot down on October 27 by a Bf 109 five miles south-east of the Isle of Wight, in

ARIG Jottard (continued)

Hurricane P 3167, and reported 'Missing'. Jottard was 28. He is remembered on the Runnymede Memorial, Panel 8 and has a memorial grave in the Pelouse d'Honneur Cemetery of Brussels at Evere.

PO 30.7.40

CHARLES CECIL OLIVER JOUBERT

81618   PO   Pilot   British   56 Squadron

Joubert joined 56 Squadron at North Weald on July 15 1940. In an action over Sheppey on August 13 his radiator exploded following an attack by a Bf 110. He baled out, slightly injured, from Hurricane P 3479 and landed at Capton Farm, Faversham.

Later in the war Joubert transferred to the Administrative Branch. He was released from the RAF in 1946, as a Flight Lieutenant.

PO 29.6.40   FO 29.6.41   FL 1.1.44

LEONARD JOWITT

562160   Sgt   Pilot   British   85 Squadron

Jowitt, of Thornton, Lancashire, was born in 1912. He joined the RAF in 1928 as an aircraft apprentice and trained as a Fitter Engines/Airframes. He served in India in 1932/33 and received the Mohmand 1933 clasp to the India General Service Medal. Jowitt volunteered for pilot training, was selected and began his ab initio course in mid-1937.

On June 1 1938 he joined 85 Squadron, then being formed at Debden. Jowitt went to France with the squadron on September 9 1939 and was with it until it was withdrawn to Debden on May 22 1940.

During an attack on a He 111 on July 12 Jowitt was shot down and killed. His Hurricane, P 2557, crashed into the sea and he was reported 'Missing'. Jowitt was 28. He is remembered on the Runnymede Memorial, Panel 16.

JOHN RUSHWORTH JULEFF

82717   PO   Air Gunner   British   600 Squadron

Joined 600 Squadron at Manston on July 11 1940. Juleff was released from the RAF in 1946, as a Squadron Leader. He died in 1977.

PO 9.5.40   FO 9.5.41   FL 9.5.42

ARTHUR HAROLD EVANS KAHN

85010   PO   Observer   British   248 Squadron

Kahn, of Sutton, Surrey, joined 248 Squadron on September 29 1940. He was killed on June 15 1944, as a Flight Lieutenant with 172 Squadron, aged 25. He is remembered on the Runnymede Memorial, Panel 202.

PO 23.8.40   FO 23.8.41   FL 25.8.42

TERENCE MICHAEL KANE

41185   FO   Pilot   British   234 Squadron

Kane, of Hove, Sussex, was born on September 9 1920. He joined the RAF on a short service commission in July 1938. He began his ab initio course at 3 EFTS, Hamble on the 25th and went on to 5 FTS, Sealand. Whilst there he was injured in an Audax crash and admitted to hospital. Kane finished his advanced training at 10 FTS, Tern Hill.

On completion of the advanced term he was posted to CFS, Upavon, for an instructor's course, after which he joined the staff at 14 FTS, Kinloss and later Cranfield. Kane went to 7 OTU,

Hawarden in July 1940, converted to Spitfires and joined 234 Squadron at St Eval on September 14. He shared a Ju 88 on the 22nd.

The next day Kane failed to return from a routine section patrol. His Spitfire, R 6896, crashed into the Channel off the French coast. He baled out at 6000 feet and was picked up from the sea by the Germans. Before being shot down Kane destroyed a Bf 109.

Freed in May 1945, Kane stayed in the RAF until 1950, when he went on to the RAFO. He rejoined in April 1954, in the Fighter Control Branch, and retired on May 29 1974, as a Wing Commander.

APO 17.9.38   PO 25.7.39   FO 3.9.40   FL 3.9.41
SL 1.7.44   FL 1.12.42   SL 1.7.63   WC 1.7.69

JOSEF KANIA

794087   F/Sgt   Pilot   Polish   303 Squadron

Born in Krupina, Czechoslovakia, Kania was a member of the PAF. He joined 303 Squadron at Northolt on August 21 1940.

Kania was posted to 315 Squadron at Acklington at its formation on January 21 1941. He came off operations on April 22, going to 4 Ferry Pilots' Pool, Kemble. He was awarded the KW (15.8.41).

On January 5 1942 Kania was posted to No 1 AACU. He went to 587 Squadron on attachment on June 5 1944. He was released from the PAF in 1946, as a Warrant Officer.

LAURENCE ROBERT KARASEK

581460   Sgt   Observer   British   23 Squadron

Joined 23 Squadron at Collyweston on July 30 1940. Karasek was a member of the crew of Blenheim L 8369, which stalled and crashed manoeuvring to land, with flaps and undercarriage lowered, at Middle Wallop on September 25 1940. The aircraft fell at Broughton, near Stourbridge and all three men aboard were killed. Karasek was 23 and is buried in St Peter's churchyard, Over Wallop, Hampshire.

STANISLAW KARUBIN

793420   Sgt   Pilot   Polish   303 Squadron

Karubin was born on October 29 1915. He was in the PAF before the war and was credited with one German aircraft destroyed in the September 1939 fighting. He joined 303 Squadron at Northolt at its formation on August 2 1940.

He claimed a Bf 109 destroyed on August 31 and two more on September 5. On the 6th Karubin claimed a He 111 but was himself shot down by return fire and crashed at Fletchers Farm, Pembury, in Hurricane V 7290. He was slightly injured and admitted to Farnborough Hospital. On September 30 and October 5 he destroyed two more Bf 109s.

Karubin was awarded the VM (5th Class)(23.12.40) and the KW (23.12.40). He was posted to 58 OTU, Grangemouth on March 7 1941, as an instructor, and moved later to 55 OTU at Usworth.

On August 12 1941 Karubin was killed when he crashed on Horn Crag, Eskdale, Cumberland, breaking through clouds to land. He is buried in Castletown Cemetery, near Sunderland. He was awarded the DFM (30.10.41) and two Bars to the KW (31.10.47).

WLODZIMIERZ EUGENIUSZ KARWOWSKI

P 1284   PO   Pilot   Polish   302 Squadron

Karwowski was born on September 13 1912 at Kielce. He enlisted in the PAF there in 1934 and was commissioned as a pilot in 1937.

He was immediately in action, when the Germans invaded on September 1 1939. When Poland surrendered, after the Russians invaded, Karwowski was in Roumania taking delivery of an aircraft. With fellow pilots he escaped to France on foot, posing as a student.

He joined l'Armée de l'Air and after the French collapse made his way south and boarded a ship for England, arriving in early July. Karwowski was posted to 302 Squadron at Leconfield. He first flew in a Hurricane on July 28 and the squadron became operational on August 19. He claimed a Ju 88 destroyed on September 18. Karwowski was awarded the KW (23.12.40) and Bar (1.2.41).

He was appointed 'A' Flight Commander in January 1942, went to a course at CGS, Sutton Bridge in April and in mid-June was posted to 58 OTU, Balado Bridge, as an instructor. He had carried out 197 operational sorties with 302.

On December 12 1942 Karwowski joined 316 Squadron at Hutton Cranswick, as 'B' Flight Commander. He was posted as CO to 306 Squadron at Northolt on March 4 1943 and was awarded a second Bar to the KW (7.7.43). He flew 51 'Ramrods' with 306.

Karwowski left the squadron on January 1 1944 and was posted to Northolt. He went to HQ 12 Group at Hucknall on April 27 and moved to 84 GSU, Aston Down on June 17 1944. He was posted to CGS, Catfoss on July 18 1945, for a Gunnery Leaders' course. Karwowski flew only five times in 1946 and twice in 1947. He was released from the PAF on December 23 1947, as a Squadron Leader. He held the C de G (Fr).

He married a WAAF officer in March 1944 and they emigrated to New Zealand in 1948 and Karwowski went farming. He died on May 29 1978. His eldest son, Stefan (born 4.6.45) was a brilliant stunt pilot and served in the RAF and RNZAF. He crashed in his Pitts Special at Beacon Point, Wanaka, New Zealand on April 25 1985 and died in Christchurch two days later of his injuries.

FO 1.3.41

JAN KAUCKY

117615   Sgt   Pilot   Czechoslovakian   310 Squadron

Joined 310 Squadron at Duxford in late August 1940. Kaucky shared in the destruction of two Do 17s on September 15, one of which crashed on to the forecourt of Victoria Station.

In 1941 Kaucky was instructing at 52 OTU, Debden. Commissioned in March 1942, he was released from the RAF in 1946, as a Flight Lieutenant. He returned to Czechoslovakia and became a pilot with Czech Airlines. In 1950 Kaucky escaped to England with his family and two other Czech airline pilots, Rechka and Prchal, and their families.

Kaucky died in Britain in the early seventies.

PO 11.3.42   FO 11.3.43   FL 11.3.44

TADEUSZ WILHELM KAWALECKI

76698   PO   Pilot   Polish   151 Squadron

Born on March 12 1915, Kawalecki arrived in England in late 1939. He did his ab initio training at 15 EFTS, Redhill and his intermediate and advanced at 5 FTS, Perth and 4 FTS, Cambridge.

Kawalecki joined 151 Squadron at Martlesham Heath on August 8 1940. After the Battle of Britain he served with 145 Squadron at Tangmere. In early 1941 he was posted to 2 AACU at Farnborough. In 1942 Kawalecki instructed at 15 EFTS, Carlisle and 25 EFTS, Hucknall. He went on a course to the PAF Staff College on April 17 1943 and on January 16 1944 was posted to HQ 84 Group. He returned to the Staff College on June 11 1945, as an instructor.

Kawalecki was released from the PAF in May 1946, as a Squadron Leader.

PO 24.1.40   FO 1.3.41   FL 1.9.42

ARCHIBALD KAY

647610   Sgt   Air Gunner   British   248 Squadron

Joined 248 Squadron in mid-July 1940. On August 7 Kay was one

of the crew of a Blenheim, which ditched in the sea off St Abbs Head due to fuel shortage. The aircraft was towed into land by a trawler and salvaged. The crew were picked up from their dinghy and landed at South Shields.

Kay's Blenheim failed to return from a reconnaissance of the Feje-Stadlandet sector of the Norwegian coast on September 13 1940. The pilot, Sergeant WJ Garfield, was killed and Kay and the observer, Sergeant BW Mesner, were reported 'Missing'.

Kay was 24. He is remembered on the Runnymede Memorial, Panel 16.

DESMOND HAYWARD SIDLEY KAY

42006   PO   Pilot   British   264 Squadron

Kay, of Thurlestone, Devon, joined the RAF on a short service commission in February 1939. He was posted to 264 Squadron on October 30 1939 at its reformation at Sutton Bridge.

In mid-May 1940 Kay made a forced-landing at Zoute in Holland, with a petrol tank holed by return fire. On the 29th Kay's Defiant was badly damaged over Dunkirk. He ordered his gunner, LAC EJ Jones, to bale out and he then managed to get the aircraft back to base. Jones drowned and his body was washed up on the French coast. He is buried in Dunkirk Cemetery. Kay was awarded the DFC (14.6.40), being then credited with two Ju 87s probably destroyed and a share in the destruction of four other enemy aircraft.

Kay was awarded a Bar to the DFC (13.10.44), as an Acting Squadron Leader with 109 Squadron, operating in Mosquitos from Little Staughton, Huntingdonshire. He was killed on October 19 1944 and is buried in Adinkerke Military Cemetery, Belgium.

APO 29.4.39   PO 6.11.39   FO 6.11.40   FL 6.11.41

JACK KININMONTH KAY

83730   PO   Pilot   British   111 and 257 Squadron

Born on January 10 1920 at Leith, Kay was educated at Burramuir College, Edinburgh and worked for a firm of stockbrokers there. He joined the RAFVR in 1939. Called up at the outbreak of war, Kay went to No 1 ITW, Cambridge. He did his elementary flying training at No 1 EFTS, Hatfield and then moved on to 10 FTS, Tern Hill.

With training completed Kay was posted to 6 OTU, Sutton Bridge and joined 111 Squadron at Drem on September 12 1940. He moved to 257 Squadron at Martlesham Heath on the 28th. Kay claimed a Ju 87 destroyed and a Bf 109 and another Ju 87 damaged on November 11. On a later sortie on the same day he destroyed a BR 20.

On May 1 1941 Kay was posted to 46 Squadron at Sherburn-in-Elmet. It was preparing to leave for the Middle East. Some pilots and the groundcrews went to Egypt, via the Cape but Kay was among those who embarked with their Hurricanes on the carrier HMS 'Argus'. They reached Gibraltar at the end of May and the aircraft were transferred on to HMS 'Ark Royal'. They flew off to Hal Far, Malta on June 6 1941. Both the pilots and the Hurricanes then moved to Ta Kali and on June 28 became 126 Squadron. During his time in Malta Kay damaged a number of enemy aircraft.

On February 20 1942 he flew to Cairo in a Hudson. He then went by flying boat in stages to South Africa, arriving at Vaal Dam on March 6. Kay was posted to 25 Air School, Standerton, as an instructor. He met his future wife soon after arriving and they married in September 1943. Kay remained instructing until June 1945, when he returned to the UK. He was released in 1946, as a Flight Lieutenant. He returned to South Africa and settled there. He died in Johannesburg on September 18 1981.

PO 17.8.40   FO 17.8.41   FL 17.8.42

JOSEPH ROBERT KAYLL

90276   **SL**   **Pilot**   **British**   **615 Squadron**

Born in Sunderland in 1916, Kayll obtained his 'A' license in 1934 and joined 607 Squadron, AuxAF. Appointed a Flight Commander in early 1939, he was called to full-time service with 607 on August 24 1939. Kayll flew from Croydon to Merville with the squadron on November 15 1939.

In March 1940 he took command of 615 Squadron at Vitry. On May 15 Kayll destroyed two Bf 110s and on the 20th a He 111. He was given the double award of the DSO and DFC (31.5.40), being then credited with nine enemy aircraft destroyed. Kayll was decorated by the King on June 27 at Kenley. He probably destroyed a He 111 on June 22.

Kayll claimed a He 59 destroyed on July 27, a He 111 on August 16, a Do 17 on the 20th, shared a He 111 on the 24th and claimed a probable Do 17 on the 28th.

In December 1940 Kayll was posted to HQ Fighter Command. He returned to operations on June 2 1941, when he was appointed Wing Leader at Hornchurch. He was shot down near St Omer in July and captured. Firstly at Oflag IX A/H, Kayll was moved to Wartburg in October 1941. He escaped in a mass breakout in September 1942 and with a companion walked for seven days, covering 90 kilometres before being captured by a forester south of Fulda. Kayll was transferred to Stalag Luft III in May 1943 and was in charge of the Escape Committee for the East Compound. Escape activities involved a very high proportion of the camp and its direction was both arduous and dangerous. Kayll was unsparing in his efforts in this work and also organised the whole of the security and intelligence section.

Freed in May 1945, Kayll was released from the RAF later in the year, as a Wing Commander. He received a Mention in Despatches (28.12.45) and was made an OBE (26.6.46). His portrait was done by Eric Kennington in 1941.

PO (AuxAF) 9.3.34   *FO (AuxAF) 9.9.35*   *FL (AuxAF) 7.1.39*
FL 24.8.39   *SL 1.9.40*

JOHN ALEXANDER KEARD

827000   **PO**   **Pilot**   **British**   **235 Squadron**

Keard, of Sidcup, Kent, joined 235 Squadron on September 27 1940. He was killed on May 4 1944, as a Flight Lieutenant with 101 Squadron, operating in Lancasters from Ludford Magna, Lincolnshire.

Keard was 23. He is buried in the Canadian War Cemetery, Janval Cemetery, Dieppe.

PO 27.7.40   *FO 27.7.41*   *FL 27.7.42*

ALBERT WALLACE KEARSEY

60518   **Sgt**   **Pilot**   **British**   **152 Squadron**

Prior to the Battle of Britain Kearsey was a staff pilot at 10 BGS, Warmwell. He joined 152 Squadron at Warmwell in August 1940. He claimed a Bf 110 destroyed on September 30 and shared in the destruction of a Ju 88 west of Shaftesbury on November 14 1940.

Commissioned in January 1941, Kearsey was released from the RAF in 1946, as a Flight Lieutenant. He joined the RAFVR in April 1948.

PO 22.1.41   *FO 22.1.42*   *FL 22.1.43*   *FO (RAFVR) 22.4.48*

PHILIP JAMES KEARSEY

85239   **PO**   **Pilot**   **British**   **607 and 213 Squadrons**

Kearsey, of Cheltenham, Gloucestershire, joined 607 Squadron at Turnhouse on October 9 1940 and moved to 213 Squadron at Tangmere on the 26th.

He went to the Middle East in late 1940 and on January 29 1941 flew a Hurricane to Malta and joined 261 Squadron there. Kearsey was shot down and killed on February 26 defending Luqa airfield against a bombing attack.

He was 20 and is remembered on the Malta Memorial, Panel 1, Column 1.

PO 7.9.40

FRANCIS JOHN KEAST

801399   **Sgt**   **Air Gunner**   **British**   **600 Squadron**

Keast, of Swalecliffe, Whitstable, was with 600 Squadron at Northolt in early July 1940.

On August 8 he was a member of the crew of Blenheim L 8665, which was shot down in flames by Oberleutnant Sprick of III/JG 26. The pilot, Flying Officer DN Grice, stayed at the controls of the burning aircraft, guiding it clear of Ramsgate before crashing into the sea. All three men on board were killed.

Keast was 32. He is buried in Whitstable Cemetery.

JOHN KEATINGS

519611   **Sgt**   **Air Gunner**   **British**   **219 Squadron**

Joined the RAF as an Aircrafthand in early 1935 and after initial training at Uxbridge was posted to Northolt. In September 1935 Keatings joined 45 Squadron at Helwan, Egypt and started training as an Armourer/Air Gunner, making his first flight on October 11. Keatings' Flight was posted to 6 Squadron at Ismailia and then detached to Palestine, where it operated against terrorists.

In December 1936 Keatings returned to the UK and was posted to 21 Squadron at Lympne, flying in Hinds. He took part in the 1937 Hendon Air Display, in the mass formation of 250 aircraft. He went to No 1 Air Armament School at Eastchurch in November 1937, to convert to Fitter-Armourer.

Keatings joined 269 Squadron in March 1939, a general reconnaissance unit with Ansons, on armament and flying duties. At the outbreak of war he was recalled from a hydraulic turret course at Bristol Aircraft, Filton to rejoin the squadron, which had moved to Montrose to carry out anti-U-boat patrols. In October 1939 Keatings was posted to 219 Squadron, then reforming as a night-fighter unit at Catterick.

He was sent on a Gunnery Leaders' course to CGS, Warmwell in January 1940 and rejoined the squadron in March. He then combined operational flying and training air gunners, which he did throughout the Battle of Britain.

Keatings did not fly operationally after the end of 1940 and became a Senior Armament Instructor. He was released from the RAF in 1945, as a Warrant Officer.

ERNEST HENRY CLARKE KEE

69441   Sgt   Pilot   British   253 Squadron

Kee, of Co Donegal, was with 253 Squadron at Kirton-in-Lindsey in early July 1940. He crashed at Dunton Green on October 15, unhurt, after his aircraft was severely damaged in combat.

In February 1941 Kee was posted to 242 Squadron at Martlesham Heath. He was commissioned in June 1941. The squadron was declared non-operational on October 1, to prepare for overseas. It sailed in the carrier HMS 'Argus' at the end of the month, arrived in Gibraltar on November 5 and sailed into the Mediterranean on the 7th. The Hurricanes flew off for Malta on the 11th and the pilots remained on the island, flying with 185 and 249 Squadrons.

Kee was killed on April 20 1944, as an Acting Squadron Leader with 241 Squadron, a reconnaissance unit. He is buried in Belgrade War Cemetery, Yugoslavia. He was awarded the DFC (21.12.45), back-dated to the day before his death.

PO 10.6.41   FO 6.4.42   FL 6.4.43

GEORGE ERNEST KEEL

751079   Sgt   Wop/AG   British   235 Squadron

Joined 235 Squadron on August 13 1940. Keel was one of the crew of Blenheim N 3530, which failed to return from combat with enemy fighters over the Channel on October 9 1940. Keel and the observer, Pilot Officer RC Thomas, were killed and the pilot, Pilot Officer JC Kirkpatrick, was reported 'Missing'.

Keel was 20. He is buried in Highland Road Cemetery, Eastney, Hampshire.

ROB ROY GIBBONS KEELER

126143   Sgt   Air Gunner   British   236 Squadron

Joined 236 Squadron on September 20 1940. Commissioned in May 1942, Keeler was released from the RAF in 1946, as a Flight Lieutenant.

PO 14.5.42   FO 14.11.42   FL 14.5.44

GEOFFREY KEIGHLEY

90677   FO   Pilot   British   610 Squadron

A manager at Harrods before the war, Keighley joined 610 Squadron, AuxAF in early 1939. Called to full-time service after the outbreak of war, he completed his training and rejoined 610 Squadron at Biggin Hill in May 1940.

On May 31 Keighley was shot down by return fire from a Do 215 and baled out into the Channel, from Spitfire R 6629. He was picked up by a trawler and taken to Ramsgate by the Royal Navy.

Keighley baled out again on July 20, when his tail was shot away by Oberfeldwebel Schmid of I/JG 51 in combat over Hawkinge. He landed at Lydden, slightly wounded. His Spitfire, N 3201, crashed at Wootton.

Made an OBE (1.1.45), Keighley was released from the RAF in 1946, as a Wing Commander.

APO (AuxAF) 21.3.39   PO 16.12.39   FO 17.9.40
FL 4.6.41   SL 15.2.44

MICHAEL KELLETT

86630   PO   Pilot   British   111 Squadron

Born on September 25 1917, Kellett joined 111 Squadron at Drem on October 2 1940.

He commanded 504 Squadron from October 1944 until August 1945, the second squadron to receive Meteors. Kellett was awarded the DFC (21.11.44). He retired from the RAF on June 19 1956, as a Squadron Leader, retaining the rank of Wing Commander. He died on August 28 1975.

PO 7.9.40   FO 7.9.41   FL 7.9.42   SL 20.6.45
SL 1.9.45

RONALD GUSTAVE KELLETT

90082   SL   Pilot   British   249 and 303 Squadrons

Kellett, of Tadcaster, joined 600 Squadron, AuxAF in 1934. He transferred to 616 Squadron on January 30 1939, as a Flight Commander, and was called to full-time service on August 25.

In May 1940 Kellett was posted to 249 Squadron, then forming at Church Fenton, as a Flight Commander. He went to RAF Northolt on July 19 to form and command 303 Squadron. On August 21 and September 5 he claimed Bf 109s destroyed, on the 15th a Bf 110 and on the 26th another Bf 109. Kellett was awarded the DFC (1.10.40), the DSO (25.10.40) and the VM (5th Class)(24.12.40).

He was posted to Cranage in December 1940, to form 96 Squadron from 422 Flight. He commanded the squadron until March 1941, when he was appointed Wing Leader at North Weald. Kellett came off operations later in the year.

He was released from the RAF in 1945, as a Wing Commander. Kellett commanded 615 Squadron, RAuxAF from July 1946 to 1949.

PO (AuxAF) 20.3.34   FO (AuxAF) 20.9.35
FL (AuxAF) 1.7.38   FL 25.8.39   SL 1.6.40
WC 1.12.41   SL (RAuxAFRO) 1.8.46

WILLIAM HENRY KELLITT

122985   Sgt   Aircrew   British   236 Squadron

Joined 236 Squadron on September 3 1940. Kellitt was commissioned in May 1942 and released from the RAF in 1945, as a Flight Lieutenant. He died in January 1984.

PO 1.5.42   FO 1.11.42   FL 1.5.44

RAYMOND ALAN KELLOW

39615   FL   Pilot   British   213 Squadron

Kellow joined the RAF on a short service commission in March 1937. He did his flying training at 3 FTS, South Cerney and joined 213 Squadron at Church Fenton on December 6 1937.

Still with the squadron in 1940, Kellow claimed Bf 110s destroyed on September 11, 28 and 30. He was posted away on December 7 1940. His name disappears from the Air Force List after January 1943.

APO 3.5.37   PO 1.3.38   FO 1.10.39   FL 1.10.40

LIONEL GEORGE HOSFORD KELLS

70806   FO   Pilot   British   29 Squadron

Joined the RAFO in November 1937. Kells was posted to 8 FTS, Montrose on January 6 1938 and joined 29 Squadron at Debden on July 9.

He was still with 29 in early July 1940. Kells was killed on February 21 1941, as a Flying Officer with 248 Squadron. He is remembered on the Runnymede Memorial, Panel 30.

APO (RAFO) 24.11.37   PO (RAFO) 23.9.38   FO 22.8.40

DILLON PIERS DENIS GERARD KELLY

33168   SL   Pilot   British   74 Squadron

Born on August 4 1915, Kelly was educated at Beaumont College, Windsor and entered the RAF College, Cranwell in September 1933 as a flight cadet. He graduated in July 1935 and joined 4 (Army Co-operation) Squadron at Farnborough. He was appointed 'B' Flight Commander in August 1938.

At the outbreak of war Kelly was posted to HQ British Air Forces in France. After the German offensive in May 1940 he attached himself to No 1 Squadron and flew with it until its withdrawal to England on June 18.

Kelly went to 7 OTU, Hawarden, where he converted to Spitfires and then joined 74 Squadron at Hornchurch on July 15 1940. He was made 'B' Flight Commander on the 23rd, claimed a Bf 109 destroyed on the 28th and was posted away to 6 OTU, Sutton Bridge on September 8, as an instructor.

In late January 1941 Kelly went to 604 Squadron at Middle Wallop, he moved to 93 Squadron, also at Middle Wallop, in April and in late November joined 125 Squadron at Fairwood Common. Kelly was given command of 255 Squadron at Coltishall in December 1941. He led the squadron to North Africa in November 1942 and on December 17 he destroyed a Ju 88.

In late March 1943 Kelly was posted to HQ North Africa Air Forces i/c night operations. He was awarded the DFC (21.5.43) and returned to the UK in January 1944. After the war Kelly was RAF representative on the Allied Control Commission in Finland until August 1948, when he was posted to Germany. Kelly retired on October 7 1961, as a Group Captain. He died on February 11 1987.

PO 27.7.35   FO 27.1.37   FL 27.1.39   SL 1.9.40
WC 1.12.41   WC 1.7.47   GC 1.7.55

ERIC NORMAN KELSEY

741557   Sgt   Pilot   British   611 Squadron

Kelsey, of Wyken, Coventry, was in the RAFVR before the war. In September 1939 the FAA was short of pilots and after Kelsey was called up he was posted to Donibristle and joined the Torpedo-Spotter-Reconnaissance Flight. He was later posted to 770 Squadron for deck-landing training on HMS 'Argus' in the Western Mediterranean. He was offered a transfer to the FAA but declined and was posted to 3 BGS, Aldergrove, as a staff pilot.

On May 4 1940 Kelsey was recalled to the FAA and joined 759 (T) Squadron at Eastleigh for a refresher deck-landing course. He was later posted to 804 Squadron at Hatston. By mid-June the RAF was short of pilots and Kelsey was recalled and posted to 7 OTU, Hawarden and after converting to Spitfires he was posted to 611 Squadron at Digby on July 1.

Within three weeks Kelsey was told to report to Uxbridge and became one of a group of nine sergeants and one officer. They were flown to Hullavington, picked up Hurricanes, flew them to Abbotsinch and then embarked on the carrier HMS 'Argus', where they were joined by four officers. They were told their destination was Malta and that they were now 418 Flight.

The 'Argus' sailed on July 23, arrived at Gibraltar and sailed for Malta on July 31. At dawn on August 2 they flew off to Luqa. 418 Flight and the Malta Fighter Flight were amalgamated into 261 Squadron on August 16 1940.

Kelsey was last seen chasing a Ju 87 on January 19 1941, in Hurricane P 2629. He was 20 years old and is remembered on the Malta Memorial, Panel 1, Column 2.

JOHN LESLIE KEMP

70862   FO   Pilot   British   54 Squadron

Kemp began his ab initio course at 11 E&RFTS, Perth in January 1938. He was commissioned in the class 'A' Reserve at Uxbridge in March 1938 and posted to 10 FTS, Tern Hill. On completion of his training Kemp joined 64 Squadron at Church Fenton late in 1938. With his one year of service terminated Kemp returned to civilian life in January 1939.

Called up on September 2 1939, Kemp was posted to 609 Squadron at Catterick. He joined 54 Squadron at Hornchurch in May 1940. On July 4 Kemp's aircraft was damaged in combat with Bf 109s near Manston. During a convoy patrol on the 27th, in Spitfire N 3184,

his engine failed 15 miles east of Clacton. He baled out and was rescued by a destroyer. After an action with Bf 109s off Dover on August 12 he made a forced-landing at Lympne.

Kemp was posted away from 54 in October 1940 and did not fly any more. He went on to Fighter Control duties and landed in Normandy with a small mobile radar control unit soon after D Day and by VE Day had reached the Baltic. He was released from the RAF in 1946, as a Flight Lieutenant.

APO (RAFO) 26.3.38   PO 2.9.39   FO 17.7.40   FL 1.6.42

JOHN RICHARD KEMP

41850   PO   Pilot   New Zealander   141 Squadron

The son of a police inspector, Kemp was born in Napier on August 14 1914. He was educated at Wellington College and afterwards employed as a clerk. In February 1938 he applied for an RAF short service commission and after being provisionally accepted later in the year he sailed for the UK on December 15 in the RMS 'Rangitata'.

On January 23 1939 Kemp began his ab initio training at 13 E&RFTS, White Waltham and on April 15 was posted to 13 FTS, Drem. He joined the newly-reformed 141 Squadron at Grangemouth on October 21. The squadron became operational with Defiants on June 3 1940.

With no operational experience 141 flew south to West Malling on July 12. Shortly after 09.00 hrs on the 19th twelve Defiants moved to the forward airfield at Hawkinge. At 12.23 hrs they were ordered off to carry out an offensive patrol twenty miles south of Folkestone. Three were left behind with engine trouble. During the patrol the nine Defiants were surprised by a force of Bf 109s of III/JG 51 and in less than a minute four were shot down into the sea, three in flames, one of which was Kemp's, L 6974.

He and his gunner, Sergeant R Crombie, were never seen again. Their names appear on the reredos in St George's Chapel of Remembrance at Biggin Hill. Kemp is remembered on the Runnymede Memorial, Panel 8.

APO 1.4.39   PO 21.10.39

NIGEL LESLIE DIGBY KEMP

84941   PO   Pilot   British   85 and 242 Squadrons

Born on July 24 1919, Kemp joined 85 Squadron at Church Fenton on September 29 1940. He moved to 242 Squadron at Coltishall on October 18.

Kemp claimed a Bf 109 probably destroyed on a bomber escort to Bethune on June 17 1941. He was awarded the DFC (7.10.41), having been very successful in attacks on enemy shipping. He went with 242 to Malta in November 1941.

Kemp was released from the RAF in 1946 and rejoined in 1948. He retired on August 31 1966, as a Flight Lieutenant. Kemp was CFI at the Southampton School of Flying, Eastleigh in the seventies.

PO 7.9.40   FO 7.9.41   FL 7.9.42   FL 25.9.48

JOHN BEDFORD KENDAL

83268 PO Pilot British 66 Squadron

Kendal, of Chepstow, was born on September 29 1920 and educated at Ardingly. A member of the RAFVR before the war, he joined 66 Squadron at Gravesend on September 29 1940, his 20th birthday. He claimed a Bf 109 destroyed on October 2. Kendal was himself shot down three days later in combat with Bf 109s over Tenterden. He is believed to have made a forced-landing at Detling, slightly injured, and to have been admitted to Preston Hall Hospital.

In 1941 Kendal volunteered for the MSFU. He was in the first Camship to sail in a Russian convoy, the 'Empire Morn'. Convoy PQ 15 sailed from Hvalfjord, Iceland on April 26 1942 and arrived at Murmansk on May 6, having lost three ships to He 111 torpedo-bombers. The convoy, now numbered QP 12, sailed from Murmansk on May 21. Four days later Kendal was launched to attack enemy aircraft around the convoy. He destroyed a Ju 88. Later, at the limit of his fuel, Kendal baled out but his parachute did not function properly and he sustained serious injuries when he struck the sea. He was quickly picked up from the icy water but died soon afterwards. Kendal was the first MSFU pilot to destroy an enemy aircraft and he was the only one to die after an operational launching. His final action had been to radio the position of the dinghy of the Ju 88 crew.

Kendal was buried at sea. He is remembered on the Runnymede Memorial, Panel 67. He received a Mention in Despatches.

PO 10.8.40   FO 10.8.41

HUGH CHARLES KENNARD

40396 FO Pilot British 66 Squadron

Joined the RAF on a short service commission on October 25 1937. Kennard did his ab initio course at 12 E&RFTS, Prestwick. He was posted to 11 FTS, Shawbury on January 9 1938 and joined 66 Squadron at Duxford in August 1938.

Kennard moved to 610 Squadron at Wittering in October 1939 but went back to 66 Squadron in March 1940. He claimed a share in the destruction of a Bf 110 on August 20. He was posted away on the 29th to 306 Squadron, then forming at Church Fenton, as a Flight Commander.

On May 14 1941 Kennard went to 121 Squadron, then reforming at Kirton-in-Lindsey, as a Flight Commander. He took command of the squadron in mid-January 1942 and was awarded the DFC (30.6.42). He was shot down over the Channel and wounded on July 31, leading the squadron on a bomber-escort operation. Kennard relinquished command in September 1942 and was posted to HQ 11 Group on Operations Planning.

From February to April 1943 Kennard was Air Adviser to the Vice-Admiral, Dover. He then went to Air Ministry, in the Directorate of Fighter Operations until October 1944, when he was posted to command troopships, the 'Orduna' on the Bombay route and the 'Queen Mary' on the Atlantic route.

In May 1945 Kennard was given command of 74 Squadron at Colerne. From September he commanded RAF Hawkinge and later Charter Hall. He left the RAF in June 1946, as a Wing Commander,

and formed his own civilian aviation business. Kennard commanded 500 Squadron, RAuxAF from January 1949 until September 1952.

APO 9.1.38   PO 25.10.38   FO 25.7.40   FL 25.7.41
SL 1.7.43   SL (RAuxAF) 14.1.49

PETER FRANK KENNARD-DAVIS

42348 PO Pilot British 64 Squadron

Joined the Royal Navy at the age of 16 but went into the RAF on a short service commission in May 1939.

Kennard-Davis was posted to 7 OTU, Hawarden in July 1940 and after converting to Spitfires he joined 64 Squadron at Kenley on August 3. Five days later his aircraft caught fire during combat with Bf 109s north of Dover and Kennard-Davis baled out, seriously wounded. He was admitted to Royal Victoria Hospital and died there on August 10. The Spitfire, L 1039, crashed and burned out near West Langdon.

Kennard-Davis was 19. He is buried in Brookwood Cemetery, Surrey.

APO 22.7.39   PO 13.1.40

JOHN CONNELLY KENNEDY

40052 FO Pilot Australian 238 Squadron

Kennedy, of Sydney, trained in Australia with the RAAF. He transferred to the RAF in August 1937 and was posted to No 1 FTS, Leuchars for a short course. On December 19 he joined 65 Squadron at Hornchurch.

In early July 1940 Kennedy was with 238 Squadron at Middle Wallop. He shared in the destruction of a Do 17 over Chesil Beach on July 13. It is believed that he was wounded by return fire during the action. Kennedy stalled and crashed at Southdown, Littlemore trying to avoid HT cables whilst landing and was killed.

He was 23 years old and is buried in Holy Trinity churchyard, Warmwell.

PO 26.8.37   FO 26.5.39

RONALD WILLIAM KENNEDY

162542 Sgt Air Gunner British 604 Squadron

Kennedy, of East Dulwich, London was with 604 Squadron in June 1940. He retrained as a Radio Observer after the arrival of Beaufighters.

In May 1941 Kennedy was posted to 109 Squadron. This unit was formed from the Wireless Intelligence Development Unit at Boscombe Down and was concerned with the development of radio countermeasures and new radar aids.

Commissioned in October 1943, Kennedy was killed on March 26 1944, as a Pilot Officer with 192 Squadron. He was 29 and is buried in the Wierhuizen Protestant Cemetery, Eenrum, Netherlands.

PO 25.10.43

PETER LEWIS KENNER

73032 PO Pilot British 264 Squadron

Joined 264 Squadron at Kirton-in-Lindsey in mid-August 1940. The squadron went to Hornchurch on August 21. Kenner was shot down in combat with Bf 109s of JG 26 over Thanet on the 28th. He and his gunner, Pilot Officer CE Johnson, were both killed when their Defiant, L 7206, crashed in flames on Sillibourne Farm, Hinxhill.

Kenner was 21. He is buried in London Road Cemetery, Brentwood, Essex.

PO (RAFVR) 20.6.39

PETER KENNETT

82685　PO　Pilot　British　3 and 605 Squadrons

Kennett, of Bexhill-on-Sea, joined 3 Squadron at Wick in early September 1940. He moved to 605 Squadron at Croydon on the 30th.

In late March 1941 Kennett sailed in HMS 'Ark Royal' for Malta. He flew off the carrier on April 3 and joined 261 Squadron. Eight days later he and Sergeant PH Waghorn intercepted a Ju 88 and may have shot it down. They were then jumped by Bf 109s and both shot down into the sea. Kennett got out of his Hurricane, Z 3036, and was seen swimming but by the time the rescue launch reached him he was dead.

Kennett was 21. He is buried in Capuccini Naval Cemetery, Malta.

PO 27.7.40

GEORGE KENSALL

1052337　Sgt　Air Gunner　British　25 Squadron

Kensall, of Blyth, joined 25 Squadron at North Weald in early October 1940.

He was killed on December 20 1943, as a Sergeant with 428 Squadron, operating in Halifaxes from Middleton St George, Co Durham.

Kensall was 22. He is buried in Rheinburg War Cemetery, Germany.

JOHN ALEXANDER KENT

37106　FL　Pilot　Canadian　303 and 92 Squadrons

Born in Winnipeg on June 23 1914, Kent learned to fly at the Winnipeg Flying Club and got his license in November 1931. He joined the Northwest Aero Marine Company in 1932, obtained his commercial license in June 1933 and became the youngest commercial pilot in Canada.

Kent joined the RAF on a short service commission in January 1935. He was posted to 5 FTS, Sealand on March 15 and went to 19 Squadron at Duxford on February 29 1936. He moved to the Experimental Section, RAE, Farnborough on October 19 1937, in the Instrument, Armament and Defence Flight. Kent was awarded the AFC (2.1.39) for his work on balloon cable research. Whilst at RAE he carried out 300 collisions.

On May 13 1940 Kent was posted to the Photographic Development Unit at Heston. In early July he went to 7 OTU, Hawarden and after converting to Hurricanes he joined 303 Squadron at Northolt at its formation on August 2 1940, as a Flight Commander. On September 9 Kent claimed a Bf 110 destroyed and a Ju 88 probably destroyed, on the 14th and 23rd Bf 109s destroyed, on the 27th a Ju 88 and on October 1 a Bf 109 and probably another. He was awarded the DFC (25.10.40) and on the 26th posted to command 92 Squadron at Biggin Hill.

Kent claimed a Bf 109 destroyed on November 1 and two Bf 109s and another probable on the 2nd. He was awarded the VM (5th Class)(24.12.40) for his work with 303 Squadron. On March 5 1941 he was posted to 53 OTU, then about to be formed at Heston, to organise the Training Wing, as Wing Commander Flying. In early June Kent went to Northolt to lead the Polish Wing. On June 21 and July 3 he destroyed Bf 109s and on the 20th he destroyed another and probably a second.

On August 2 1941 Kent was appointed to lead the Kenley Wing. He destroyed Bf 109s on August 7 and 16. In mid-October he was posted back to 53 OTU, then at Llandow, and was awarded a Bar to the DFC (21.10.41). Late in 1941 Kent was sent on a lecture tour of Canada and the US. In June 1942 he was made Station Commander at RAF Church Stanton and in October he went to HQ Fighter Command as Wing Commander Training.

Kent was posted to the Middle East in December 1942 and took command of 17 Sector, Benghazi. In August 1943 he was made Command Training Inspector at Air HQ Air Defences Eastern Mediterranean. In mid-March 1944 Kent returned to the UK and was posted to CFS, Upavon for an instructor's course, after which he took command of a satellite station of the AFU at South Cerney.

In late August 1945 Kent went on a course at RAF Staff College and was then posted to Air HQ British Air Forces of Occupation as Wing Commander Operations Plans. In late 1946 he became Personal Staff Officer to Sholto Douglas, the Commander-in-Chief and Military Governor of the British Zone of occupied Germany.

Kent retired from the RAF on December 1 1956, as a Group Captain. He died on October 7 1985. His portrait was done by Cuthbert Orde in 1940.

APO 15.3.35　　PO 15.3.36　　FO 15.9.37　　FL 15.9.39
SL 1.12.40　　WC 1.3.42　　WC 1.7.47　　GC 1.7.52

RAYMOND DUGDALE KENT

77358　PO　Air Gunner　British　235 Squadron

Born in 1905, Kent was commissioned in February 1940 and joined 235 Squadron on July 11. He was released from the RAF in 1945, as a Flight Lieutenant.

APO 3.2.40　　PO 16.3.40　　FO 16.3.41　　FL 16.3.42

VERNON CHARLES KEOUGH

81630　PO　Pilot　American　609 Squadron

Keough, of Brooklyn, New York, was a former professional parachutist and had made more than 500 jumps at shows and fairs in the US. With fellow Americans, Mamedoff and Tobin, he volunteered for flying in Finland and when that country fell they were told they could fly in France with l'Armée de l'Air.

They went to Paris, via Canada. The blitzkrieg of May had already started and they were virtually ignored. They joined two Czech pilots in an attempt to steal two Potez bombers to fly to England. It failed and the two Czechs were killed by French guards. The three Americans then made their way to St Jean de Luz, boarded a ship and eventually reached London. After some initial problems they were accepted by the RAF and on July 5 they went to 7 OTU, Hawarden to convert to Spitfires.

Keough joined 609 Squadron at Middle Wallop on August 8 and he shared in the destruction of a Do 215 on September 15. At 4 feet 10 inches tall he sat on cushions to fly a Spitfire.

On September 19 Keough was posted to Church Fenton to join 71 Squadron, then forming there with American volunteers. He, Tobin and Mamedoff, all from 609, were the first pilots to arrive.

Keough failed to return from a scramble on February 15 1941 and was reported 'Missing'. He was 29 and is remembered on the Runnymede Memorial, Panel 33.

JOSEF KEPRT

787695　Sgt　Pilot　Czechoslovakian　312 Squadron

Joined 312 Squadron at Duxford on September 5 1940. On the 10th Keprt baled out, unhurt, cause unknown. His Hurricane, L 1644, crashed and burned out south of Cambridge.

Commissioned in May 1941, Keprt was later awarded the DFC and released from the RAF, as a Flying Officer. He died in Czechoslovakia in the mid-seventies.

PO 25.5.41

ROBERT GERALD KER-RAMSAY

37321   FL   Pilot   British   25 Squadron and FIU

Ker-Ramsay joined the RAF on a short service commission in August 1935. He was posted to 5 FTS, Sealand on October 19 and joined 17 Squadron at Kenley on June 28 1936. He moved to the staff of the Home Aircraft Depot, Henlow on February 11 1937 and then joined the staff at 8 FTS, Montrose on May 30 1938.

In early July 1940 Ker-Ramsay was with 25 Squadron at Martlesham Heath. He was posted to FIU at Shoreham on the 13th.

He was captain of a Blenheim, which failed to return from an operational patrol on the night of September 13. Ker-Ramsay and his crew of two baled out and were captured. The Blenheim, Z 5721, crashed into the Channel off Calais.

In 1941 Ker-Ramsay was on the Escape Committee at Stalag Luft 1 and worked on two tunnels, which were discovered before completion. Whilst in Stalag Luft III he worked on the three simultaneous tunnels, Tom, Dick and Harry. He organised and controlled the exit during the mass breakout in March 1944 and unselfishly sacrificed chances of his own escape. In April he was appointed Camp Security Officer and it was largely through his efforts that the camp had a reliable news service. He was also in charge of the radio at Westortimke from February to April 1945.

Ker-Ramsay was made an MBE (28.6.46) for services as a PoW. He retired from the RAF in 1948, as a Squadron Leader.

APO 30.9.35   PO 6.8.36   FO 6.4.38   FL 6.4.40
SL 1.3.41   WC 1.6.42   SL 1.6.44

ANTHONY KERSHAW

91191   PO   Pilot   British   1 Squadron

Kershaw, of Macclesfield, joined the AuxAF before the war. He was called to full-time service on August 26 1939 and after training was posted to No 1 Squadron at Wittering on September 20 1940.

With two other pilots, Kershaw went on the squadron's first offensive operation, on January 1 1941, strafing German installations between Calais and Boulogne.

On a convoy patrol on March 19 1941 Kershaw was shot down by a Bf 109. He baled out but was too low. His body was picked up and landed at Newhaven the next day. He was 21 and was cremated at Manchester Crematorium.

APO 26.8.39   PO 13.7.40

BASIL VIRGIL KERWIN

42580   PO   Pilot   Canadian   1 (RCAF) Squadron

Born on May 10 1914, Kerwin joined the RAF on a short service commission in July 1939. He was posted to No 1 (RCAF) Squadron in August 1940. On the 31st he claimed a Do 215 destroyed and on September 1 a Bf 110 and a Do 215. In this action Kerwin was shot down and baled out, with burns. His Hurricane, P 3963, crashed and burned out at Shipbourne.

Kerwin stayed on in the RAF after the war. He was awarded the DFC (11.10.55) for distinguished service in Malaya. He retired on January 1 1958, as a Squadron Leader.

APO 28.8.39   PO 24.3.40   FO 24.3.41   FL 24.3.42
SL 1.8.47

IAN HERBERT KESTIN

Sub-Lieutenant (FAA)   Pilot   British   145 Squadron

Kestin, of Hatfield, Hertfordshire, was born on July 24 1917. Before the war he was an instructor at the London Aero Club. He joined the Navy on September 15 1939 and after further flying training at HMS 'Daedalus' and 'Raven' he joined 758 Squadron.

In early 1940 Kestin volunteered for a fighter course and on May 27 was sent on one at 'Raven'. He was loaned to the RAF in mid-June and posted to 7 OTU, Hawarden and after converting to Hurricanes he joined 145 Squadron at Tangmere on July 1.

Kestin attacked a Hs 126 ten miles south of Hastings on August 1 1940. His Hurricane, P 3155, was hit by return fire and crashed into the Channel. He was reported 'Missing'. He was 23 and is remembered on the Fleet Air Arm Memorial at Lee-on-Solent.

Sub-Lt 26.10.39

OLDRICH KESTLER

787527   Sgt   Pilot   Czechoslovakian   111 Squadron

Kestler joined 111 Squadron at Dyce on October 19 1940. He was killed on April 7 1941, still with 111, aged 28. He is buried in Market Drayton Cemetery, Shropshire.

Kestler was awarded the Czech Military Cross (15.7.41).

MICHAEL KEYMER

748504   Sgt   Pilot   British   65 Squadron

Keymer was born at Eastleigh Vicarage on May 21 1916. His father, the vicar, was serving in France as a padre with the Leicestershire Regiment at that time. He was educated at Pinewood, Farnborough and Blundell's at Twerton, Devon.

After leaving school he worked on a chicken farm in Sussex. Keymer learned to fly with the Civil Air Guard at Hamble. He was a car salesman in Bournemouth in September 1939.

Keymer joined 65 Squadron at Hornchurch on August 7 1940. He shared in the destruction of a Bf 109 on the 14th. He was shot down and killed in combat with Bf 109s over the sea off Dover on August 22, in Spitfire K 9909. He is buried in Bazinghen churchyard, France.

JOHN DOUGLAS KEYNES

88419   Sgt   Pilot   British   236 Squadron

Keynes, of Thornton Heath, Surrey, joined 236 Squadron on September 27 1940. He was commissioned in November.

He was captain of a Blenheim damaged by return fire from a BV 138 floatplane engaged over south-west Ireland on November 30 1940. Keynes returned to St Eval and he and his observer, Sergeant JE Symonds, were admitted to Truro Hospital with splinter wounds.

Keynes was killed on June 4 1943, as a Flight Lieutenant with 126 Squadron, aged 29. He is remembered on the Malta Memorial, Panel 6, Column 1.

PO 27.11.40   FO 27.11.41   FL 27.11.42

RUDAL KIDSON

41297   PO   Pilot   New Zealander   141 Squadron

Kidson was born in Wellington on May 7 1914. In 1931 he was a sapper in the 2nd Battalion, New Zealand Engineers, a territorial unit. He spent three years sheep-farming in the Marlborough district.

In 1937 Kidson joined the Auckland Aero Club and obtained his 'A' license in February 1938. He sailed to the UK at his own expense and applied for a short service commission. He was provisionally accepted and began his elementary flying training at No 1 E&RFTS, Hatfield on August 29 1938.

Kidson was posted to 3 FTS, Shellingford on November 12 and with his training completed he went to 3 Air Observers' School, Aldergrove on June 10 1939, as a staff pilot.

On October 4 he joined 141 Squadron, then reforming at Turnhouse. In April 1940 the squadron began to be equipped with Defiants and became operational on June 3. With no operational experience it flew south to West Malling on July 12. Shortly after 09.00 hrs on the 19th twelve Defiants moved to the forward airfield at Hawkinge. At 12.23 hrs they were ordered off to carry out an offensive patrol twenty miles south of Folkestone. Three were left behind with engine trouble. During the patrol the nine Defiants were surprised by a force of Bf 109s of III/JG 51 and in less than a minute four were shot down, three in flames, one of them Kidson's L 7015.

He and his gunner, Sergeant FPJ Atkins, were never seen again. Their names appear on the reredos in St George's Chapel of Remembrance at Biggin Hill. Kidson is remembered on the Runnymede Memorial, Panel 9.

APO 29.10.38   PO 28.10.39

PETER KILLICK

144792   **Sgt**   **Pilot**   **British**   **245 Squadron**

Born on September 27 1919, Killick was posted to 245 Squadron at Aldergrove on July 17 1940. He stalled and crashed on the 28th, in Hurricane N 2593, cause unknown. He was seriously injured and the aircraft was written off.

Killick retired from the RAF on September 27 1970, as a Squadron Leader. He died in the early eighties.

PO 31.3.43   FO 30.12.43   FL 30.9.46   SL 1.10.54

FREDERICK WILLIAM GEORGE KILLINGBACK

46560   **Sgt**   **Pilot**   **British**   **249 Squadron**

With 249 Squadron at Leconfield in early July 1940. Killingback was shot down by Bf 109s over Maidstone on September 7 and baled out, wounded. His Hurricane, R 4230, is believed to have crashed at Eastling.

Commissioned in August 1941, Killingback was released from the RAF in 1948, as a Flight Lieutenant.

PO 21.8.41   FO 21.8.42   FL 21.8.43   FL 1.1.43

JOHN IGNATIUS KILMARTIN

39793   **FO**   **Pilot**   **Irish**   **43 Squadron**

Born in Dundalk, Ireland on July 8 1913, Kilmartin worked on a cattle ranch in Australia and as a bank clerk in Shanghai, where he was a professional jockey in his spare time. He joined the RAF on a short service commission in February 1937. He was posted to 6 FTS, Netheravon on June 5 1937 and joined 43 Squadron at Tangmere on January 8 1938.

Kilmartin was posted to No 1 Squadron in France on November 3 1939. He claimed a Do 17 destroyed on the 23rd. In early April 1940 he claimed a Bf 109, on the 20th a Ju 88 and a He 111, on May 10 he shared a Do 17, on the 11th destroyed two Bf 110s, on the 12th a Bf 109, on the 14th two Bf 109s and on the 15th another Bf 110.

At the request of the CO the tired pilots of No 1 were withdrawn to England on May 24, to be replaced by new men. Kilmartin was posted to Aston Down, to instruct at 5 OTU. On September 4 he rejoined 43 Squadron at Tangmere, claimed a Bf 110 destroyed on the 6th and a Bf 109 on the 7th. The squadron went north to Usworth on the 8th. Kilmartin was awarded the DFC (8.10.40).

He was given command of 602 Squadron at Ayr in April 1941. He was posted away on May 10 to form 313 Squadron at Catterick but the posting was changed and he went instead to West Africa. Kilmartin took command of 128 Squadron at Hastings, Sierra Leone in March 1942 and led it until August, when he returned to the UK. In November he went to 504 Squadron at Middle Wallop, as supernumerary Squadron Leader. He took command of the squadron in January 1943 and on March 30 was promoted to lead the Hornchurch Wing, which he did until May 30.

In 1944 Kilmartin led the TAF Typhoon Wing. He was made an OBE (1.1.45) and retired from the RAF on July 8 1958, as a Wing Commander. His portrait was drawn by Cuthbert Orde in January 1941.

APO 5.4.37   PO 5.4.38   FO 5.11.39   FL 5.11.40
SL 1.12.41   SL 1.1.45   WC 1.1.53

JOSEPH RICHARD KILNER

63783   **Sgt**   **Pilot**   **British**   **65 Squadron**

Kilner was a pre-war airman pilot and joined 65 Squadron at Hornchurch on May 1 1939.

Over Dunkirk on May 28 1940 Kilner shared in the probable destruction of a Do 17. On July 5 he claimed a share in the destruction of a He 111, on August 8, 12 and 13 he claimed Bf 109s probably destroyed, on the 16th he claimed two Bf 109s destroyed and on the 20th two more and probably a Do 17.

Commissioned in April 1941, Kilner was with 21 Squadron in 1944, operating from Thorney Island in Mosquitos. He was awarded the DFC (5.9.44), being then credited with seven enemy aircraft destroyed and four shared.

Kilner was released from the RAF in 1946, as a Squadron Leader. He died on May 11 1986.

PO 2.4.41   FO 2.4.42   FL 2.4.43

DOUGLAS STEELE KINDER

42611   **PO**   **Pilot**   **British**   **615 and 73 Squadrons**

Joined the RAF on a short service commission in July 1939. Kinder was posted to 615 Squadron at Prestwick on September 4 1940 and moved to 73 Squadron at Castle Camps on the 15th.

Kinder crashed near Lightship 93 following an attack by Bf 109s on September 23, in Hurricane P 3226. He was rescued from the Thames Estuary and admitted to the Royal Naval Hospital, Chatham, with severe burns.

Kinder was awarded the DFC (7.12.43), as a Flight Lieutenant with 166 Squadron, operating in Lancasters from Kirmington, Lincolnshire. He was released from the RAF in 1947, as a Flight Lieutenant.

APO 2.9.39   PO 24.3.40   FO 24.3.41   FL 24.3.42

MAURICE CRAIG KINDER

40836   **FO**   **Pilot**   **New Zealander**   **85, 607 and 92 Sqdns**

The son of a surgeon, Kinder was born in Parnell, Auckland on May 29 1913. He made his first flight in 1931, to attend his grandmother's funeral. In 1933 he was one of six people selected from three thousand for a scholarship at the Auckland Aero Club for lessons up to 'A' license. He built and flew a Flying Flea in 1935 but his plan to build the aircraft for sale in New Zealand did not eventuate.

Kinder applied for a short service commission in the RAF and after initial failure he was provisionally accepted in December 1937. He sailed for the UK in February 1938 in the RMS 'Remuera'. He began his ab initio training at No 1 E&RFTS, Hatfield on April 4 and moved on to 5 FTS, Sealand on June 18. Kinder was posted to No 1 Air Armament School, Manby on May 13 1939, as a staff pilot. He moved to 5 Air Observers' School, Jurby on September 7 and carried out staff pilot duties until June 4 1940, when he went to 4 (Continental) Ferry Pool, Kemble, flying aircraft and passengers to and from France.

On September 6 Kinder was posted to 7 OTU, Hawarden and after converting to Spitfires he joined 85 Squadron at Church Fenton on September 14. He moved to 607 Squadron at Tangmere on the 29th. He was posted to 92 Squadron at Biggin Hill on October 13. Kinder destroyed two Ju 87s on November 1 but was himself shot down by Bf 109s. Wounded and weak from loss of blood, he managed to crash-land beside the Ramsgate-Canterbury road. Some Australian soldiers came up and, thinking him dead, took his helmet, gloves and buttons as souvenirs. They were somewhat surprised when Kinder came to and swore at them. Too weak to climb out of the cockpit he waited until an ambulance came to take him to Chartham Military Hospital. He was transferred to the RAF Uxbridge Hospital and after convalescence at Torquay he rejoined 92, then at Manston.

On February 5 1941 Kinder was posted to 91 Squadron at Hawkinge, in mid-March he went to HQ Fighter Command, on April 7 to 58 OTU, Grangemouth, as an instructor and on July 7 he was posted to CFS, Upavon for an instructor's course. Kinder went to 61 OTU, Heston on September 18.

On December 5 1941 he was posted to No 1 Beam Approach School, Watchfield for a course and on the 22nd went to Drem to help form 1528 VHF Beam Approach Training Flight. Eager to return to operations the CO there later arranged for Kinder to take command, which he officially did on June 21 1942. He was posted to Hunsdon on November 11 1942 to form and command 1530 BAT Flight, which was visited by the King.

Kinder went to a staff job at HQ ADGB, Bentley Priory on November 13 1943, transferred to the RNZAF on December 15 and was awarded the AFC (1.1.44). He was posted to HQ 83 Group on May 21 1944, moved to HQ 2nd TAF on June 23 and went to Brussels on October 21, on 85 Group Air Movements.

After returning to England in early March 1945 Kinder was posted to 59 OTU, Acklington, as CGI. He returned to New Zealand on June 30 1946 and went on to the Reserve on October 18.

APO 4.6.38   PO 13.5.39   FO 3.9.40   FL 3.9.41
SL 1.1.44

ANTHONY THOMAS JAMES KINDERSLEY

Lieutenant (FAA)   Pilot   British   808 Squadron

Kindersley, of Yarmouth, joined the Navy in 1933. In early July 1940 he was with 808 Squadron at Wick, flying Fulmars on dockyard defence. He was with the squadron when it embarked on HMS 'Ark Royal' on October 22 1940.

In 1941 the carrier was in the Mediterranean, protecting convoys to Malta. On May 8 Kindersley shared in destroying a Sm 79 bomber. He was killed on July 25 1941, shot down by return fire whilst attacking a formation of Sm 79s.

Kindersley was 26. He is remembered on the Fleet Air Arm Memorial at Lee-on-Solent.

Midshipman 1.5.33   Actg Sub-Lt 1.9.35   Sub-Lt 16.1.36
Lt 16.1.38

ERIC BRUCE KING

32199   SL   Pilot   British   253, 249 and 151 Squadrons

King joined the RAF in 1933 and was posted to 26 (Army Co-operation) Squadron at Catterick on August 20. He went to 31 Squadron at Karachi on February 15 1934, returned to the UK in 1936 and was sent to the Home Aircraft Depot, Henlow on August 12 for an Officers' Engineering Course.

On June 15 1937 King joined the staff at 2 FTS, Brize Norton and on September 12 1938 he was appointed to the staff of 612 Squadron, AuxAF.

King was posted as supernumerary Squadron Leader to 253 Squadron at Turnhouse on July 17 1940 and moved in the same capacity to 249 Squadron at Church Fenton on August 5. His aircraft was damaged in combat over Southampton on the 16th. King was given command of 151 Squadron at Stapleford on the 21st. He had his airscrew shot off in combat with Bf 110s over North Weald on the 24th but landed safely.

During a routine patrol on August 30 1940 King was killed, when his Hurricane, V 7369, crashed and burned out in Temple Street, Strood, from an unknown cause. He was 29 and is buried in Highgate Cemetery, St Pancras.

PO 12.8.33   FO 12.3.35   FL 12.3.37   SL 1.8.39

FREDERICK HARRY KING

43845   PO   Air Gunner   British   264 Squadron

King flew as gunner with 264's CO, Squadron Leader PA Hunter. He was commissioned from LAC in early May 1940. They were a very successful team.

On May 12 they destroyed a Ju 88. Over Dunkirk on May 27 they destroyed a Bf 109 and shared a He 111, on the 28th two Bf 109s, on the 29th a Bf 109, a Bf 110 and a Ju 87 and on the 31st a Bf 109, a He 111 and another damaged. King was awarded the DFM (14.6.40).

King and Hunter were last seen in pursuit of a Ju 88 after an attack on Manston on August 24 1940, in Defiant N 1535. King was 24 years old. He is remembered on the Runnymede Memorial, Panel 9.

PO 9.5.40

LEONARD FRANK DOUGLAS KING

42612   PO   Pilot   British   64 Squadron

King of Windsor, Berkshire, was with 64 Squadron at Kenley in early July 1940.

He was killed on March 19 1945, as a Squadron Leader with 105 Squadron, operating in Mosquitos from Bourn in Cambridgeshire. He was 26 and is remembered on the Runnymede Memorial, Panel 265.

APO 2.9.39   PO 10.4.40   FO 10.4.41   FL 10.4.42

MARTYN AUREL KING

42845   PO   Pilot   British   249 Squadron

With 249 Squadron at Leconfield in early July 1940. King was shot down by enemy fighters over Southampton on August 16. He baled out but was killed when his parachute collapsed during descent. His Hurricane, P 3616, is believed to be that which crashed at Toothill, near Lee.

King was 19. He is buried in All Saints' churchyard, Fawley, Hampshire.

PO 23.10.39

PETER JAMES CHRISTOPHER KING

41298   PO   Pilot   British   66 Squadron

King, of Farnborough, Warwickshire, joined the RAF on a short service commission in September 1938. He was with 66 Squadron at Coltishall in early July 1940.

He claimed a Bf 109 destroyed on September 4 but although his aircraft was badly damaged in the combat over Dover he returned safely to Kenley. King was shot down on September 5 by Bf 109s over the Medway, in Spitfire N 3060. He baled out but was killed when his parachute failed.

He was 19 and is buried in St Botolph's churchyard, Farnborough.

APO 29.10.38   PO 29.8.39

WILLIAM LAURENCE KING

77359   PO   Pilot   British   236 Squadron

King, of Watford, was with 236 Squadron in early July 1940.

He was killed on January 22 1943, as a Flight Lieutenant with 264 Squadron, aged 31. He is buried in St Paul's churchyard, Langleybury, Abbots Langley.

PO 16.3.40   FO 16.3.41   FL 16.3.42

DONALD ERNEST KINGABY

112406   Sgt   Pilot   British   266 and 92 Squadrons

Born in Islington, London on January 7 1920, Kingaby was educated at King's School, Ely and afterwards worked in an insurance office in Cambridge. He joined the RAFVR in April 1939, was called up at the outbreak of war and after his training was completed he joined 266 Squadron at Wittering in June 1940.

Kingaby was posted to 92 Squadron at Biggin Hill on September 25. On October 12 and 15 he claimed Bf 109s destroyed, on the 20th he shared a Bf 110 and on the 24th a Do 17. Between November 1 1940 and July 2 1941 Kingaby destroyed twelve Bf 109s. He was awarded the DFM (6.12.40) and Bar (29.7.41) and was described in the newspapers as 'the 109 Specialist'. On August 9, October 1 and 3 he destroyed three more Bf 109s and was awarded a second Bar to the

DE Kingaby (continued)

DFM (11.11.41), the only man to be so honoured during the war.

In early November 1941 Kingaby went to 58 OTU, Grangemouth, as an instructor. Commissioned in November, he returned to operations in March 1942, with a posting to 111 Squadron at Debden. Kingaby moved to 64 Squadron at Hornchurch in April and on July 30 he destroyed a FW 190. He joined 122 Squadron at Hornchurch in early August 1942, as a Flight Commander, and over Dieppe on the 19th he claimed a Do 217 destroyed.

Kingaby took command of the squadron in November, destroyed a Bf 109 on January 20 1943 and FW 190s on January 21 and March 8. He was awarded the DSO (9.3.43) and promoted to Acting Wing Commander in April to lead the Hornchurch Wing. In September 1943 Kingaby was posted to a staff job at HQ Fighter Command.

In April 1944 he was posted to lead a Spitfire Wing, which would provide low-level cover for the invasion forces. He claimed his final victory on June 30 1944, when he shared in the destruction of a Bf 109. In addition to his British awards Kingaby received the C de G (Belg) in October 1944 and the DFC (US)(15.5.45).

He was granted a Permanent Commission after the war, was awarded the AFC (5.6.52) and retired from the RAF on September 29 1958, as a Squadron Leader, retaining the rank of Wing Commander.

*PO 15.11.41   FO 30.6.42   FL 30.6.43   SL 24.7.44
SL 1.1.49*

CHARLES BRIAN FABRIS KINGCOME

33319   FO   Pilot   British   92 Squadron

Born in Calcutta on May 31 1917, Kingcome was educated at Bedford and entered RAF College, Cranwell in January 1936 as a flight cadet. He joined 65 Squadron at Hornchurch on July 30 1938 and was still with it in 1940. He shared in the destruction of a Do 17 on May 25 over Dunkirk. Two days later he was posted to 92 Squadron at Northolt, as a Flight Commander.

Kingcome damaged two He 111s on June 2, shared Ju 88s on July 10 and 24, claimed a Bf 110 probably destroyed on September 9, a He 111 destroyed on the 11th, shared a Ju 88 on the 18th, claimed a Bf 109 on the 23rd, a Ju 88 on the 27th and Bf 109s on October 11, 12 and 13. On October 15 Kingcome was shot down in combat with Bf 109s. He baled out, wounded, and was admitted to the Royal Naval Hospital at Chatham. His Spitfire, X 4418, crashed at Wyborne's Farm, High Halstow. Kingcome was awarded the DFC (25.10.40).

On June 16 1941 he probably destroyed a Bf 109 and on July 24 destroyed another. Kingcome was posted away in August to 61 OTU, as a Flight Commander. He returned to operations in February 1942, taking command of 72 Squadron at Gravesend. He destroyed a Bf 109 on May 28 and in late June was promoted to lead the Kenley Wing. He was posted away in late 1942 to Charmy Down, where the Fighter Leaders' School was being formed. He was awarded the DSO (15.12.42).

In May 1943 Kingcome was posted to Malta to lead 244 Wing, which flew in support of the Eighth Army in Sicily and Italy. After the invasion of Italy he was promoted to Acting Group Captain.

Kingcome went on a course to the RAF Staff College, Haifa in October 1944 and in March 1945 became SASO at 205 (Heavy Bomber) Group. He remained in Italy after the end of the war, then moved to Egypt, where he was mostly concerned with repatriating troops to the UK. In mid-1946 Kingcome was posted to command 324 Spitfire Wing at Zeltweg, Austria.

He held various staff appointments and instructed at RAF Staff College before being invalided out of the RAF on January 26 1954, as a Wing Commander, retaining the rank of Group Captain. His portrait was drawn by Cuthbert Orde.

*PO 30.7.38   FO 30.1.40   FL 30.1.41   SL 1.3.41
WC 8.1.44   WC 1.1.50*

ROBERT AUSTIN KINGS

82953   PO   Pilot   British   238 Squadron

Born on October 22 1914, Kings joined the RAFVR in early 1938 and began his flying training at 29 E&RFTS at Luton in August. Called up after the outbreak of war, he was posted to 3 ITW, Hastings on December 13 1939 and moved on to 14 FTS, Kinloss on March 12 1940, later moving to Cranfield.

Kings went to 6 OTU, Sutton Bridge on August 8 and after converting to Hurricanes he joined 238 Squadron at St Eval on the 27th. He was shot down by a Bf 110 in combat over the Isle of Wight on September 26 and baled out, unhurt. His Hurricane, P 3830, is believed to have crashed on Coleman's Farm, Porchfield. Four days later he baled out again after colliding with Pilot Officer VC Simmonds during a routine patrol. Kings was injured in a heavy landing because of a damaged parachute and admitted to hospital. His Hurricane, L 1702, crashed near Shaftesbury.

238 Squadron embarked on HMS 'Victorious' on May 17 1941 en route for the Middle East but was delayed when the carrier was involved in chasing the 'Bismarck'. After returning to Scotland to refuel it set off again for the Mediterranean. On June 14 Kings flew off south of Majorca for Malta. Refuelled, the squadron flew to Egypt the next day and on the 19th was attached to 274 Squadron in the Western Desert.

On September 16 1941 the 238 pilots were flown to Takoradi to fly back Hurricane 11cs. On November 26 Kings was shot down in a sweep over Sidi Rezegh and forced-landed in the desert. He was picked up by members of the 22nd Armoured Brigade and finished up in Tobruk. He rejoined the squadron on December 6.

Kings was posted to the ADU in the Delta on April 30 1942 and remained with it until May 17 1945, when he was repatriated to the UK. In November 1945 he was posted to India and served at RAF Poona and Calcutta before returning to the UK in November 1947. Subsequently trained in Air Traffic Control and Radar duties, King retired from the RAF on October 27 1964, as a Flight Lieutenant, retaining the rank of Squadron Leader.

PO 3.8.40   FO 3.8.41   FL 3.8.42   FL 1.9.45

THOMAS BRIAN KIRK

808416   Sgt   Pilot   British   74 Squadron

Kirk joined 74 Squadron at Kirton-in-Lindsey on August 26 1940. He claimed a Bf 110 destroyed on September 11.

He was shot down in combat with enemy fighters over Maidstone on October 20. Kirk baled out, severely wounded, and was admitted to Preston Hall Hospital, Maidstone. His Spitfire, P 7370, crashed at Coxheath.

Kirk died of his wounds on July 22 1941, aged 22. He is buried in St Oswald's churchyard, East Harlsey, Yorkshire.

JAMES CHARLES KIRKPATRICK

81630   **PO**   **Pilot**   **Belgian**   **235 Squadron**

Kirkpatrick joined 235 Squadron on August 5 1940. He was reported 'Missing' following a combat with enemy aircraft over the Channel on October 9 1940, in Blenheim N 3530. The bodies of the two members of his crew, Pilot Officer RC Thomas and Sergeant GE Keel, were recovered.

Kirkpatrick was 25. He is remembered on the Runnymede Memorial, Panel 9 and with a memorial grave in Pelouse d'Honneur Cemetery of Brussels at Evere.

MARK TYZACK KIRKWOOD

39287   **FL**   **Pilot**   **British**   **610 Squadron**

Joined the RAF on a short service commission in October 1936. Kirkwood was posted to 10 FTS, Tern Hill on January 16 1937 and joined the staff at 3 Armament Training Station at Sutton Bridge on May 4 1938.

Kirkwood went to 610 Squadron at Acklington on September 22 1940. He was reported 'Missing' on November 8, serving with 603 Squadron at Hornchurch. He failed to return from a combat with Ju 87s and Bf 109s east of Deal, in Spitfire P 7285.

Kirkwood is remembered on the Runnymede Memorial, Panel 4.

APO 21.12.36   PO 12.10.37   FO 12.7.39   FL 3.9.40

DAVID IAN KIRTON

550500   **Sgt**   **Pilot**   **British**   **65 Squadron**

Kirton, of Dover, was in the pre-war RAF. He was posted to 22 E&RFTS, Cambridge in May and qualified as a pilot in June 1940. He joined 65 Squadron at Hornchurch in July.

On August 8 Kirton was killed, when he was shot down in flames in combat with Bf 109s over Manston, in Spitfire K 9911. He was 21 years old and is buried in St James' Cemetery, Dover.

SZYMON KITA

P 781003   **Sgt**   **Pilot**   **Polish**   **85 and 253 Squadrons**

Kita was born in 1916. He was posted to 85 Squadron at Castle Camps on September 12 1940 and moved to 253 Squadron at Kenley on the 30th. He was shot down in combat on December 1 and crash-landed at Falmer, in Hurricane P 3678, injured.

Kita later served with 287 Squadron, an anti-aircraft co-operation unit. On April 9 1942 he went to RAF Lyneham and flew to the Middle East to join No 1 ADU. He returned to the UK in March 1944 and went to 25 EFTS on June 10, as a staff pilot. On November 1 Kita was posted to 16 FTS for a refresher course and moved to 3 (P) AFU for advanced flying training on March 20 1945.

In September 1945 Kita went to the PAF Depot, Blackpool and was released in March 1946 as a Flight Sergeant. He was awarded the KW and Bar (31.10.47).

THOMAS ROY KITSON

41934   **PO**   **Pilot**   **British**   **245 Squadron**

Kitson joined the RAF on a short service commission in February 1939. He was with 245 Squadron at Aldergrove during the period of the Battle of Britain.

On March 10 1941 Kitson flew a Blenheim to Blackpool for weekend leave. Flying back to Aldergrove on the 13th he crashed and both he and his passenger, another pilot from 245, were killed.

Kitson was cremated at Carleton Crematorium, Blackpool.

APO 15.4.39   PO 6.11.39   FO 6.11.40

STEFAN KLECZKOWSKI

76717   **PO**   **Pilot**   **Polish**   **302 Squadron**

Kleczkowski was born on September 2 1917. He converted to Hurricanes at 6 OTU, Sutton Bridge and joined 302 Squadron at Leconfield on September 23 1940. He was with the squadron until February 9 1941, when he was posted as a staff pilot to 10 BGS.

Kleczkowski later instructed at 16 FTS, Newton. He returned to operations on October 7 1944, joining 303 Squadron at Coltishall. He was awarded the KW (27.9.45), went to RAF Hethel on June 5 1946 and was released from the PAF in December 1946.

PO 1.3.41   FO 1.3.42   FL 1.3.43

ZYGMUNT KLEIN

780685   **Sgt**   **Pilot**   **Polish**   **234 and 152 Squadrons**

Klein was born on August 24 1918. He joined 234 Squadron at St Eval on August 6 1940. He claimed a Bf 109 destroyed on the 7th.

Klein was posted to 152 Squadron at Warmwell on October 5 1940 and damaged a Bf 110 on the 7th. He crash-landed near Torquay on November 26, having run out of petrol. Klein was reported 'Missing' two days later, believed shot down into the Channel by Bf 109s in the Isle of Wight area, in Spitfire P 9427. He is remembered on the Polish Air Force Memorial at Northolt.

WOJCIECH KLOZINSKI

780465   Sgt   Pilot   Polish   54 Squadron

Born on February 26 1915 at Kaznad, Germany, Klozinski entered the PAF NCOs Training School at Bydgoszcz in 1931. He passed out in 1934 as an aircraft mechanic and with some elementary flying training. He completed training as a bomber pilot at Sadkow and was posted to an Air Force Regiment.

Klozinski returned to Bydgoszcz as an instructor. In September 1939 he was evacuated with student pilots from Krosno to Roumania. He reached France on November 12 and then moved on to England on February 9 1940. After training Klozinski joined 54 Squadron at Catterick on June 2.

He claimed a Bf 109 destroyed on August 12. Three days later he crashed at Hythe during combat with Bf 109s over Dover, in Spitfire R 7015. Severely wounded, Klozinski was admitted to Ashford Hospital. He did not recover from his injuries until October 1942, when a medical board suspended him from flying.

Klozinski was posted to 58 OTU, Grangemouth on November 5 1942, as a Link Trainer instructor. He went to 61 OTU on October 15 1943 on the same duties and to 14 Base at RAF Faldingworth on January 12 1945. Klozinski went to Canada on August 24 1945 and later changed his name to VK Stewart. He was awarded the KW and Bar (15.7.41).

ROLAND ANTHONY LEE KNIGHT

37772   FL   Pilot   British   23 Squadron

Joined the RAF on a short service commission in February 1936. Knight was posted to 2 FTS, Digby on May 2 and joined 23 Squadron at Northolt on January 10 1937. He was still with the squadron in 1940 and served with it throughout the Battle of Britain.

In February 1941 Knight was posted to 91 Squadron at Hawkinge, as 'B' Flight Commander. He claimed Bf 109s destroyed on April 7 and May 5 and 18. In June 1941 he joined 610 Squadron at Westhampnett. He claimed a Bf 109 destroyed on June 17, a Bf 109 and another probably destroyed on the 21st, a Bf 109 damaged on the 26th, another shared on July 3 and two more destroyed on the 8th and 14th. Knight was awarded the DFC (5.8.41).

On August 21 1941 he was posted to Hornchurch to take command of 403 Squadron. Knight was killed on September 27 1941, aged 24. He is buried in Dunkirk Town Cemetery, France.

APO 20.4.36   PO 17.2.37   FO 17.11.38   FL 3.9.40

WILLIAM RODNEY ALEXANDER KNOCKER

74333   FO   Pilot   British   264 Squadron

Knocker was at Wellington College from 1933 to 1938 and then St John's College, Oxford. He went to No 1 ITW, Cambridge in November 1939 and was posted to FTS, Cranwell on January 1 1940, on the second war course. He finished his training at 5 FTS, Sealand and then went to the School of Army Co-operation at Old Sarum.

After a week Knocker was posted to 5 OTU, Aston Down and after converting to Defiants he joined 264 Squadron at Duxford in mid-June 1940. In the squadron's last spell of day-fighting he claimed a Ju 88 destroyed on August 24.

Knocker was flying Defiant N 1547 on November 15 1940, when it caught fire. On an emergency approach he hit a tree and crashed and burned out on Rochford golf course. He was unhurt but his gunner, Pilot Officer FA Toombs, was badly burned and later died of his injuries.

In May 1941 Knocker was shot down over London by anti-aircraft fire and baled out.

Knocker was released from the RAF in 1946, as a Wing Commander. He later went to live in Kenya.

PO 14.10.39   FO 26.9.40   FL 26.9.41   SL 8.12.44

LENNERT AXEL KOMAROFF

118438   Sgt   Air Gunner   British   141 Squadron

Komaroff was with 141 Squadron at Turnhouse in early July 1940. He later trained as a Navigator Radar, was commissioned in March 1942 and killed on September 19 1944, as a Flight Lieutenant with 29 Squadron, operating in Mosquitos from Hunsdon.

Komaroff was 26. He is buried in Bergen-op-Zoom Cemetery, Netherlands.

PO 11.3.42   FO 1.10.42   FL 11.3.44

JOSEF KOMINEK

787980   F/Sgt   Pilot   Czechoslovakian   310 Squadron

Joined 310 Squadron at Duxford at its formation on July 10 1940. He destroyed a Do 17 on September 15 and claimed a Bf 109 on the 27th.

Kominek was on patrol in Hurricane L 1842 on November 2, when it caught fire. He baled out, unhurt, and the aircraft crashed on to a bungalow at Warden, Sheppey.

Kominek was killed in a flying accident on June 8 1941, aged 27. He is buried in Brookwood Military Cemetery. He was awarded the Czech Military Cross (15.7.41).

VACLAV AUGUST KOPECKY

87620   Sgt   Pilot   Czechoslovakian   111 and 253 Sqdns

Joined 111 Squadron at Croydon on September 12 1940 and moved to 253 Squadron at Kenley on the 25th.

Commissioned in March 1941, Kopecky was posted to No 1 Squadron at Croydon. He destroyed a Bf 109 on June 16. Five days later he shot down another Bf 109. Watching it go down he was jumped by two others. Wounded in the hand and with his glycol tank punctured, Kopecky ditched in the sea near Folkestone and was picked up by an ASR launch. He was awarded the Czech Military Cross (15.7.41).

Later in 1941 Kopecky was instructing at 52 OTU, Debden and later Aston Down. He left the RAF as a Flight Lieutenant and returned to Czechoslovakia. He died there in the seventies.

PO 1.3.41   FO 1.3.42   FL 1.3.43

JOSEF KOPRIVA

104395   Sgt   Pilot   Czechoslovakian   310 Squadron

Joined 310 Squadron at Duxford at its formation on July 10 1940. Kopriva was shot down during an attack on Bf 110s on September 3, in Hurricane P 8811. He baled out, unhurt.

Commissioned in August 1941, Kopriva was released from the RAF as a Flight Lieutenant. He died in Czechoslovakia.

PO 20.8.41   FO 20.8.42   FL 20.8.43

KAREL KORBER

787699   Sgt   Pilot   Czechoslovakian   32 Squadron

Joined 32 Squadron at Acklington on October 14 1940. Korber was killed on May 3 1943, as a Warrant Officer with 310 Squadron. He is remembered on the Runnymede Memorial, Panel 134.

FRANTISEK KORDULA

82156   PO   Pilot   Czechoslovakian   1 and 17 Sqdns

Kordula joined No 1 Squadron at Northolt in late August 1940 and moved to 17 Squadron at Debden on September 25. He shared in the destruction of a Bf 110 and damaged another on November 17.

Kordula is believed to have re-enlisted in the RAF on September 3 1949, as an AC 2. He died later in Britain.

PO 12.7.40   FL 1.3.41

WILHELM KOSARZ

780828   Sgt   Pilot   Polish   302 Squadron

Kosarz was born on June 20 1908. He joined 302 Squadron at Leconfield on August 20 1940.

He hit a balloon cable at Langley in bad visibility on October 15, losing 14 inches from his starboard wing. He landed safely at Heston.

Kosarz was shot down in flames by a Bf 109 over Maidstone on November 8 1940. He baled out but fell dead at Mayfield, after his parachute caught fire. His Hurricane, P 3538, crashed, inverted, and burned out at Pennybridge Farm, Mayfield Xavierian College. He is buried in Northwood Cemetery. Kosarz was awarded the KW (31.10.47).

BRONISLAW KAZIMIERZ KOSINSKI

P 0298   FL   Pilot   Polish   32 Squadron

Born on August 26 1907, Kosinski escaped to France after the fall of Poland and in June 1940 was commanding a flight of Curtis Hawk 75As, operating from Bourges and providing cover for an aircraft factory there. He arrived in England on July 7 1940.

Kosinski was posted to 307 Squadron on September 10, then forming at Kirton-in-Lindsey, as a Flight Commander. He was posted away to Old Sarum on October 9 and then joined 32 Squadron at Acklington on the 22nd. Kosinski moved to 308

Squadron at Baginton on December 22. He was awarded the KW (1.2.41).

On July 24 1941 Kosinski was posted to 72 Squadron at Biggin Hill and was awarded a Bar to the KW (30.10.41). He went to 302 Squadron at Harrowbeer on November 29, as a Flight Commander.

Kosinski was killed on January 26 1942. His Spitfire, AA 747, was one of four in the region of Brest. He disappeared after an attack by enemy fighters and was not seen again, probably lost in the sea. Kosinski is remembered on the Polish Air Force Memorial at Northolt. He was awarded the VM (5th Class)(5.5.42).

JOSEF KOUKAL

120764   Sgt   Pilot   Czechoslovakian   310 Squadron

Koukal joined 310 Squadron at Duxford in July 1940. He was shot down over the Thames Estuary on September 7 and baled out, grievously burned, at 22000 feet. He made a delayed drop to 11000 feet to extinguish his burning clothes. When he landed they blazed again and he suffered 70 per cent burns. His Hurricane, V 7437, crashed near Capel Fleet, Harty Marshes, Sheppey.

Koukal was one of the first of Archie McIndoe's patients at the Queen Victoria Hospital, East Grinstead and an early member of the Guinea Pig Club. When the site of his crash was excavated in 1972 Koukal went to England and met the widow of the man who tore off his burning clothes.

Awarded the Czech Military Cross (15.7.41), Koukal was later commissioned and left the RAF as a Flight Lieutenant. He became State Test Pilot in Czechoslovakia. He died in Luze, Czechoslovakia on February 23 1980.

JAN KOWALSKI

P 1909   Sgt   Pilot   Polish   303 Squadron

Born at Mircze on November 19 1916, Kowalski entered the PAF NCOs Training School at Bydgoszcz in 1932. He qualified as an aircraft mechanic in 1935. He was then posted to the Air Force Officers Training Centre at Sadkow for pilot training, which he completed at the Advanced Pilots' Training Centre at Grudziadz. Kowalski then joined 112 Fighter Squadron of the 1st Air Force Regiment, Warsaw.

In 1937 he returned to the NCOs School, as an instructor. He was evacuated with the student pilots to Roumania in

September 1939 and reached Marseilles on October 31. Kowalski joined l'Armée de l'Air and in Spring 1940 was posted to Rennes, as an instructor on multi-engined aircraft. After France collapsed he went to England, arriving on June 22 1940.

Kowalski joined 303 Squadron at Northolt on August 21 and claimed a Bf 109 destroyed on September 25. He was posted to 315 Squadron at Acklington at its formation on January 21 1941, was awarded the KW (1.2.41) and a Bar (19.2.42). Commissioned in June 1942, he was posted away to 58 OTU, Grangemouth on December 5, as an instructor.

On February 13 1943 Kowalski joined the Polish Fighting Team at West Kirby. They flew to the Middle East in a C 47, arriving on March 13. They were attached to 145 Squadron and operated in the Western Desert from March 17 to May 12 and downed 30 enemy aircraft. Back in the UK he joined 316 Squadron at Northolt on July 21 and was with it until October 20, when he was posted to HQ 131 Wing. Kowalski was awarded a second Bar to the KW (20.12.43).

On April 28 1944 he joined 317 Squadron at Chailey. He went to the PAF Depot, Blackpool on May 1 1945, was awarded the VM (5th Class)(1.6.45) and on November 9 was attached to HQ 131 Wing and posted to the Enemy Aircraft Salvage and Service Unit at Hamburg-Fühlsbuttel.

Kowalski was awarded the DFC (10.4.46) and released from the PAF in December 1948, as a Flight Lieutenant. He settled in Britain.

PO 1.6.42   FO 1.6.43   FL 1.6.44

JULIAN KOWALSKI

P 1400 FO Pilot Polish 302 Squadron

Born at Nagornik, Kielce on July 10 1910, Kowalski joined the PAF in 1932. He was posted to 302 Squadron at Leconfield on July 26 1940. On September 15 he claimed a Do 17 destroyed and another two probably destroyed, on the 18th he got a probable Do 17, on the 19th destroyed a Ju 88 and on the 26th a Bf 109.

Kowalski was awarded the KW (23.12.40) and a Bar (1.2.41). He was given command of the squadron in February 1942, awarded a second Bar to the KW (19.2.42), a third Bar (20.8.42) and the VM (5th Class)(20.8.42). On August 25 1942 Kowalski was posted to HQ 10 Group, as Polish Liaison Officer. He moved to HQ 81 Group on November 11 to do the same job. He was awarded the DFC (15.11.42).

On June 20 1943 Kowalski went to 58 OTU, Grangemouth, as an instructor. He moved to 18 Sector HQ on February 15 1944 and on April 12 was given command of No 1 Polish Wing at Northolt. He probably destroyed a FW 190 on June 20.

Kowalski was posted to HQ 11 Group on October 10 1944, moved to RAF Coltishall on February 25 1945 and to Andrews Field, Essex on August 8 1945, as OC Polish personnel. He was released from the PAF in January 1947, as a Wing Commander, and settled in Britain.

FO 1.3.41   FL 1.3.42   SL 1.9.42   WC 20.6.43

FRANCISZEK KOZLOWSKI

76729 PO Pilot Polish 501 Squadron

Born on April 14 1917, Kozlowski arrived in Britain in late 1939. He was commissioned in January 1940 and after completing his flying training he joined 501 Squadron at Gravesend on August 7.

Kozlowski was shot down in combat over Canterbury on August 18 and seriously injured, when he crashed at Rayham's Farm, near Whitstable, in Hurricane P 3815.

On February 25 1941 Kozlowski joined 316 Squadron, then being formed at Pembrey. He was awarded the KW (19.2.42) and a Bar (20.8.42). He was appointed a Flight Commander on October 4 1942 and killed on March 13 1943. Kozlowski was shot down by enemy fighters at Fesques, near Neufchatel, in Spitfire EN 171. He is buried in Hautot-sur-Mer Cemetery, France.

Kozlowski was awarded a second Bar to the KW (29.5.43) and a third Bar (31.10.47).

PO 27.1.40   FO 1.3.41   FL 1.3.42

MARCUS KRAMER

77345 PO Air Gunner British 600 Squadron

A pharmacist of Thorpe Bay, Essex, Kramer joined 600 Squadron at Manston in March 1940. On May 10 he flew as gunner with Pilot Officer RC Haine in one of six Blenheims detailed for an afternoon attack on Waalhaven aerodrome, Rotterdam, which had been captured by German paratroops that morning. After the attack the Blenheims were jumped by Bf 110s and five were shot down. Kramer, Haine and the CO's navigator, Sergeant Davis, evaded capture and

were evacuated by the Royal Navy.

Kramer was awarded the DFC (9.7.40). He was killed on May 21 1941, as a Flight Lieutenant with 29 Squadron, aged 29. He is remembered on the Runnymede Memorial, Panel 29.

PO 4.2.40   FO 4.2.41

ZDZISLAW KRASNODEBSKI

P 1505 FL Pilot Polish 303 Squadron

Born in Wola Osowinska, near Lukow, on August 10 1904, Krasnodebski joined the PAF in 1928. He shared in the destruction of an enemy aircraft in September 1939, when he was in command of III/1 Dyon.

Krasnodebski was joint CO of 303 Squadron at Northolt from its formation on August 2 1940. He was shot down in combat with Bf 109s on September 6 and baled out, badly burned. His Hurricane, P 3974, crashed between Hextable and Wilmington. Krasnodebski was admitted to Farnborough Hospital and later went to Queen Victoria Hospital, East Grinstead, where he underwent plastic surgery by Archie McIndoe and became a Guinea Pig.

Awarded the VM (5th Class)(23.12.40), Krasnodebski returned to duty on June 2 1941 and was posted to Canada. Back in the UK, he commanded RAF Heston from April 1 to October 14 1943, when he was posted to command 131 Airfield, Northolt, which he did until February 17 1944. Krasnodebski went to Staff College for a course on January 2 1945, after which he commanded RAF Newton from October 15 until he was released from the PAF in December 1946, as a Group Captain. He was awarded the KW (31.10.47).

Krasnodebski settled in Canada and died in Toronto in 1980.

SL 3.5.40   WC 1.9.44

BEDRICH KRATKORUKY

110669 Sgt Pilot Czechoslovakian 1 Squadron

Kratkoruky escaped from Czechoslovakia to France and joined l'Armée de l'Air. He trained at the Fighter Training School at Chartres and on May 18 1940 was posted to III/3 Pursuit Squadron. On the 19th he shared in the destruction of a Bf 109 and on the 20th he destroyed a Do 17 and then made a forced-landing, when he was shot down himself.

After reaching England Kratkoruky joined No 1 Squadron at Wittering on October 4 1940. On May 11 1941 he intercepted a He 111 over Canvey Island in the early hours of the morning. He chased it to Southend and attacked it. When last seen the enemy aircraft was at 2000 feet, losing height, with both engines smoking. Coastguards at Southend later reported that it crashed into the sea off Shoeburyness. On May 25 Kratkoruky destroyed a Bf 109.

He was commissioned in November 1941 and in early 1942 was posted away to 61 OTU, Rednal, as an instructor. Later in the year he joined 313 Squadron at Church Stanton.

On January 16 1943 he was flying in Spitfire AR 546 with the Czech Wing, escorting Bostons to bomb the docks at Cherbourg. Ten miles north of Cap de la Hague he turned into the sun and collided with Flight Sergeant Blaha. Neither pilot baled out. Kratkoruky ditched successfully ten to fifteen miles south of Portland but his aircraft sank nose down and he was lost. He is remembered on the Runnymede Memorial, Panel 125.

PO 1.11.41   FO 1.11.42

MIROSLAV KREDBA

81895 PO Pilot Czechoslovakian 310 Squadron

Joined 310 Squadron at Duxford at its formation on July 10 1940. Kredba was shot down by Bf 109s over the Thames Estuary on August 31, in Hurricane P 8814. He baled out, unhurt.

He was killed on February 14 1942, as a Flight Lieutenant. His unit at the time of his death is not known. Kredba is buried in St Illogan's churchyard, Illogan, Redruth, Cornwall.

PO 12.7.40   FO 27.12.40   FL 27.12.41

WALENTY KREPSKI

76755   PO   Pilot   Polish   54 Squadron

Joined 54 Squadron at Hornchurch on August 23 1940. Krepski failed to return from an operational sortie over the Flamborough area on September 7. It is believed he lost his bearings due to R/T failure and crashed into the sea, in Spitfire R 6901.

Krepski was 23. He is remembered on the Polish Air Force Memorial at Northolt.

WACLAW SZCZEPAN KROL

P 1299   FO   Pilot   Polish   302 Squadron

Born in Sandomierz on December 25 1915, Krol joined the PAF in 1937. He shared in the destruction of an enemy aircraft in September 1939 and claimed two destroyed and another probably destroyed in the fighting in France in May/June 1940, serving with l'Armée de l'Air. He was awarded the C de G (Fr).

Krol arrived in Britain on July 16 1940 and joined 302 Squadron at Leconfield on August 21. He claimed a Bf 109 destroyed on October 15. Awarded the KW and Bar (1.2.41), he was appointed 'B' Flight Commander on May 29 1941 and posted to 58 OTU, Grangemouth on November 22, as an instructor. He was awarded a second Bar to the KW (10.9.41).

A return to operations came on May 24 1942, when Krol went to 316 Squadron at Heston, as a Flight Commander. He claimed a FW 190 destroyed on June 5 and was awarded the VM (5th Class)(20.8.42). On December 1 1942 Krol was posted to 315 Squadron's Operations Room.

He went to West Kirby on February 13 1943 to prepare for overseas and on March 13 arrived in the Middle East in a C 47 with other Polish pilots, to form the Polish Fighting Team, otherwise known as 'Skalski's Circus'. They were attached to 145 Squadron and operated in the Western Desert from March 17 to May 12 and downed 30 enemy aircraft. Krol claimed Bf 109s on April 4 and 21 and a Mc 202 on April 20.

Back in the UK Krol joined 303 Squadron at Ballyhalbert on July 25 1943. He took command of 302 Squadron at Northolt on October 18, was awarded a third Bar to his KW (20.12.43), the DFC (15.2.44) and led the squadron until June 5 1944, when he was posted to HQ 11 Group.

Krol went to 61 OTU on October 1, as CFI, moved to HQ 84 Group on January 30 1945 and was posted to RAF Coltishall to lead the Wing on April 18. He was appointed to lead 133 Wing on July 24 and then 131 Wing on August 15.

After the war Krol was released from the PAF as a Wing Commander and returned to Poland.

FO 1.3.41   FL 1.9.42

TOMAS KRUML

83229   PO   Pilot   Czechoslovakian   312 Squadron

Served with 312 Squadron in the Battle of Britain.

Kruml was later posted to 53 OTU, as a Flight Commander. In mid-1942 he joined 66 Squadron at Ibsley and served with it into 1943. He later served as a Flight Commander in both 131 and 122 Squadrons.

After the war Kruml was repatriated to Czechoslovakia.

JAROSLAV KUCERA

787665   Sgt   Pilot   Czechoslovakian   245 Squadron

Kucera served with 245 Squadron in the Battle of Britain. He was killed on December 19 1941, when he collided with another Czech pilot. His unit at the time of his death is not known.

Kucera is buried in Ayr Cemetery, Scotland.

JIRI KUCERA

787568   Sgt   Pilot   Czechoslovakian   238 Squadron

Kucera escaped from Czechoslovakia to France in 1938 and joined l'Armée de l'Air. He shot down three German aircraft in May/June 1940. When France fell he went to England.

On September 12 1940 Kucera joined 238 Squadron at Middle Wallop. He claimed a Bf 110 destroyed and two others damaged on the 26th and a He 111 destroyed on the 30th.

Kucera was commissioned in August 1941. He returned to Czechoslovakia after the war and died there on January 24 1980.

PO 13.8.41

OTMAR KUCERA

No unknown   Sgt   Pilot   Czechoslovakian   111 Sqdn

Joined 111 Squadron at Drem on October 6 1940. Kucera claimed a share in the destruction of a He 111 on November 13.

In 1941 he was posted to 312 Squadron at Speke. He claimed a Bf 109 probably destroyed on June 8, destroyed Bf 109s on July 3 and 9 and a Ju 88 on February 16 1942. Commissioned in early 1942 Kucera was posted to 313 Squadron at Hornchurch in April and claimed a FW 190 destroyed and another probably destroyed on May 5.

Kucera was appointed a Flight Commander in early 1943, he claimed a FW 190 on September 27 1943 and was awarded the DFC. He took command of 313 Squadron, then at North Weald, in November 1944 and led it until August 1945, when he returned to Czechoslovakia.

TADEUSZ LEON KUMIEGA

76700   PO   Pilot   Polish   17 Squadron

Kumiega was born on October 16 1916. He reached England in late 1939 and was commissioned in January 1940. With his training completed he was posted to 6 OTU, Sutton Bridge on August 1 and joined 17 Squadron at Tangmere on September 1.

Kumiega shared in destroying a Bf 109 on October 29. He was posted to 317 Squadron at Acklington at its formation on February 22 1941. He claimed a Bf 109 destroyed on December 18, was awarded the KW (5.5.42), was posted away to RAF Northolt on July 6 1942 and received a Bar to the KW (20.8.42).

On September 16 1942 Kumiega went as Liaison Officer to RAF Matlask. He was posted to HQ ADGB on June 30 1944 for staff duties, as an Acting Squadron Leader. On August 21 1946 he went to RAF Coltishall, as a supernumerary for flying duties.

Kumiega stayed on in the RAF, in the Secretarial Branch. He retired on June 1 1966, as a Flight Lieutenant.

PO 24.1.40   FO 1.3.41   FL 1.9.42   FL 1.3.47

ZBIGNIEW KUSTRZYNSKI

76718   FO   Pilot   Polish   607 Squadron

Born in Moscow on September 18 1911, Kustrzynski joined the PAF in 1934. He went to 607 Squadron at Usworth on September 1 1940 and was posted to 303 Squadron at Leconfield on November 12.

The squadron combined with 316 and 317 on April 4 1942 to provide an escort for twelve Bostons detailed to attack St Omer railway station. Near Boulogne they were intercepted by Bf 109s and FW 190s and a combat ensued. Kustrzynski sent out a distress signal, in Hurricane AB 824. He forced-landed in France and was captured. He was awarded the KW (20.8.42).

On February 1 1945 he escaped from a PoW farm working party, in company with Stanford Tuck. They were found by the Russians two weeks later and spent some time fighting alongside them. They made their way into Poland, then into Russia and reached the British Embassy at Moscow. Kustrzynski and Tuck boarded a ship at Odessa for Southampton.

Kustrzynski was posted to HQ 11 Group on November 20 1945, as an Operations Room Controller. He was released from the PAF in January 1947 and went to live in Canada.

FO 1.3.41   FL 1.9.42

KAREL MIROSLAV KUTTELWASCHER

111519   Sgt   Pilot   Czechoslovakian   1 Squadron

Born in Svaty Kriz on September 23 1916, Kuttelwascher left secondary school, did three years at a commercial school and at 17 went to work as a clerk at a flour-milling company near Prague. He joined the Czech Air Force on October 1 1934 and after finishing his training in March 1937 he was posted to No 1 Flying Regiment.

Kuttelwascher escaped from Czechoslovakia on the night of June 13/14 1939 to Poland. He took a train from Cracow to Gdynia on July 25 and boarded a Swedish ship for France, arriving at Calais on August 1. The only unit open to foreigners was the Foreign Legion and Kuttelwascher sailed from Marseilles to Oran and went by train to Sidi-bel-Abbes. In October he was back in France, seconded from the Foreign Legion, and joined l'Armée de l'Air. After training at the Fighter Training School at Chartres he joined III/3 Groupe de Chasse on May 18 1940.

Kuttelwascher claimed to have destroyed six German aircraft during the May/June fighting. When France collapsed he flew an aircraft to Algiers and then with nine other Czechs he took a train for Casablanca on July 5 1940. They were taken to Gibraltar in a British cruiser and sailed from there to Cardiff, arriving on August 5. He became a Sergeant-Pilot on September 14 and was posted to 5 OTU, Aston Down.

On October 3 Kuttelwascher joined No 1 Squadron at Wittering. He claimed a Bf 109 probably destroyed on February 2 1941 and destroyed three more on April 8, May 21 and June 27. Kuttelwascher was promoted to Acting Flight Lieutenant and appointed 'A' Flight Commander on February 14 1942. No 1 Squadron began night intruder operations on April 1 and on that night Kuttelwascher destroyed a Ju 88 as it took off from Melun. He claimed Do 217s on April 16 and 26, another Do 17 and a He 111 on the 30th, three He 111s on the 4/5th, a Do 217 on June 2/3, a He 111 and a Do 217 on

the 3/4th, a Ju 88 on the 22nd, a Do 217 on the 28/29th and two Do 217s on July 1/2. Kuttelwascher was awarded the DFC (20.5.42) and Bar (1.7.42).

On July 9 he was posted to 23 Squadron at Ford. He began flying Mosquitos on night intruder operations but without success. He was awarded the Czech Military Cross (11.8.42). Kuttelwascher went to 42 Group, Maintenance Command on October 1 1942, to act as liaison with the Czech Inspectorate General. He was posted to special duties with the Inspectorate on June 10 1943 and was sent to the USA to recruit Czechs for the RAF, to lecture and to liaise with the USAAF.

Kuttelwascher returned to the UK on December 12 and was posted to 32 MU, St Athan as a member of the Test Flight on January 24 1944. He flew back to Czechoslovakia on August 18 1945, was given the rank of Staff Captain and based in the military section of Prague airport. On May 21 1946 Kuttelwascher resigned from the Czech Air Force and five days later flew back to the UK in an RAF Dakota. He qualified for a commercial license and joined BEA in November 1946. He flew as First Officer on Vickers Vikings and in 1951 was promoted to Captain.

Kuttelwascher was taken ill on August 13 1959, whilst on holiday in Cornwall, and he died of a heart attack just before midnight on the 17th. He is buried in Uxbridge Cemetery.

PO 7.10.41   FO 7.11.42   FL 17.5.43

JOSEF KWIECINSKI

780691   F/Sgt   Pilot   Polish   145 Squadron

Kwiecinski was born on May 4 1917. He joined 145 Squadron at Westhampnett on August 4 1940. He failed to return from a combat south of the Isle of Wight on the 12th, in Hurricane P 3391, and was reported 'Missing'. Kwiecinski is remembered on the Polish Air Force Memorial at Northolt.

EDWARD RICHARD LACEY

134518   Sgt   Pilot   British   219 Squadron

Lacey was born on August 18 1920. He joined 219 Squadron at Catterick on July 20 1940.

Commissioned from Flight Sergeant in October 1942, Lacey was awarded the DSO (20.4.43), as a Pilot Officer with 90 Squadron, operating in Stirlings from Ridgewell, Essex.

He remained in the RAF, was made an OBE (13.6.70) and retired on August 18 1975, as a Wing Commander. Lacey died on March 10 1980.

PO 30.10.42   FO 30.4.43   FL 30.10.44   FL 30.10.47
SL 1.7.58   WC 1.1.66

JAMES HARRY LACEY

60321   Sgt   Pilot   British   501 Squadron

Born at Wetherby, Yorkshire on February 1 1917, Lacey was educated at King James' Grammar School, Knaresborough. He left school in 1933 and became an apprentice pharmacist. Lacey joined the RAFVR in 1937 and was on the first course of Sergeant u/t pilots at 11 E&RFTS, Perth. He was the first to solo and afterwards continued to fly at 4 E&RFTS, Brough at weekends. In late January 1939 Lacey went on a six weeks' attachment to No 1 Squadron at Tangmere.

Called up at the outbreak of war, Lacey joined 501 Squadron at Filton. He went to France with the squadron on May 10 1940. He destroyed a Bf 109, a He 111 and a Bf 110 on the 13th and two He 111s on the 27th. Lacey returned to England, when the squadron was withdrawn on June 19. He had received the C de G (Fr) and a Mention in Despatches.

Lacey destroyed a Bf 109 and shared another on July 20, destroyed a Bf 110 and a Ju 87 on August 12, a Ju 88 on the 24th, a Bf 109 on the 29th, a He 111 on the 30th, a Bf 109 on the 31st, two Bf 109s on September 2 and two more on the 5th. In an engagement on the 13th Lacey destroyed a He 111 but had his own radiator shot off by one of his victim's gunners. He baled out, with slight burns, and his Hurricane, P 2793, is believed to have crashed at Abbey Farm, Leeds. On the 15th Lacey destroyed two Bf 109s and a He 111. He was shot down over Ashford on the 17th and baled out, unhurt. His Hurricane, V 7357, is believed to have crashed at Winstead Court.

On September 27 Lacey destroyed a Bf 109 and on October 12, 26 and 30 three more. He was awarded the DFM (23.8.40) and Bar (26.11.40).

Commissioned in January 1941, he was promoted to Acting Flight Lieutenant on June 26 and appointed 'A' Flight Commander. Lacey destroyed a Bf 109 on July 10, a He 59 on the 17th and two more Bf 109s on the 24th. He was posted away to 57 OTU, Hawarden on August 18 1941, as an instructor.

Lacey joined 602 Squadron at Kenley on March 10 1942 and was posted to HQ 81 Group on May 7, as Tactics Officer. He went to the A&AEE, Boscombe Down on September 28 1942 to do research on rocket armament. He moved to No 1 Special Attack Instructors' School at Milfield on November 30, as Chief Instructor.

Posted overseas on March 26 1943, Lacey arrived in India in June and was posted to 20 Squadron at Kalyan to convert it from Lysanders to Hurricanes. On July 6 1943 he went to 1572 Gunnery Flight to convert Blenheim bomber squadrons on to Hurricanes and later Hurricanes to Thunderbolts. Lacey was posted to 155 Squadron, to command, on November 6 1944 but moved on the 23rd to take over 17 Squadron at Palel. He destroyed a Nakajima 'Oscar' on February 19 1945.

In March 1946 Lacey led the squadron to Japan. He was posted back to the UK in May. Granted a Permanent Commission in December 1948, Lacey retired from the RAF on March 5 1967, as a Flight Lieutenant, retaining the rank of Squadron Leader. Lacey's portrait was done by both Eric Kennington and Cuthbert Orde.

PO 15.1.41   FO 22.9.41   FL 27.8.42   FL 1.9.45

WILLIAM LECKIE LACKIE

507102   Sgt   Air Gunner   British   141 Squadron

Joined 141 Squadron at West Malling on August 20 1940. No further service details traced.

HENRI G LAFONT

FR 2886   Adjudant   Pilot   French   245 and 615 Sqdns

Born in Cahors on August 10 1920, Lafont joined l'Armée de l'Air on November 4 1938. During the first half of 1940 he was stationed in Oran and escaped from there to Gibraltar with Mouchotte on June 30 in a stolen plane.

They sailed for Britain on July 3, were at St Athan on the 25th and went to 6 OTU, Sutton Bridge on August 19. Lafont joined 245 Squadron at Aldergrove on September 11 but a week later he was posted to 615 Squadron at Prestwick.

On October 29 Lafont had engine failure after a glycol leak and crashed amongst trees force-landing at Teston, near West Malling, in Hurricane V 7383. He was unhurt. On February 26 1941 he destroyed a Bf 109, the first by a Free French pilot, and on March 15 he probably destroyed another.

In 1941 Lafont was instructing French pilots at 59 OTU, Crosby-on-Eden. Late in the year he was posted to the Middle East and joined Groupe de Chasse 1. This unit operated in the Western Desert as the Free French Flight, attached to various RAF squadrons there. It was disbanded in 1942 and went to the UK, where it was expanded to squadron strength and re-numbered as 341 Squadron at Turnhouse

on January 1 1943. Lafont, who was the youngest Free French pilot, was in the squadron.

He survived the war. Lafont was a Companion de l'Ordre de Liberation and a Commander of the Légion d'Honneur. He was the last survivor of the French pilots, who took part in the Battle of Britain.

PIOTR LAGUNA

P 1287   FL   Pilot   Polish   302 Squadron

Born on November 11 1905, Laguna was in the PAF before the war. After Poland fell he escaped to France and in early May 1940 he was in the Groupe de Chasse Polonaise de Varsovie I/145, flying Morane-Saulnier MS 406s.

When the blitzkrieg started on May 10 the unit was at Lyons-Bron airfield. After being bombed it moved to Mions, to defend the Lyons district and on June 6 moved to Dreux, with Caudron C 714s. On the 8th five Polish pilots attacked a formation of Bf 110s over Rouen and destroyed five

without loss. On the 9th three enemy aircraft were destroyed but three Caudrons were lost and on the 10th three more enemy aircraft were shot down but the Polish CO was seriously wounded.

Laguna took command, the unit moved to Semaises on the 11th and received some Bloch MB 152s. Eight of the pilots were sent to Groupe de Chasse I/1. For the rest a move to Chateauroux was made on the 13th, for airfield and local protection, and on the 17th to Rochefort to defend the airfield there. On the 19th the Poles abandoned their aircraft and went to La Rochelle to sail for England.

Laguna was posted to the newly-formed 302 Squadron at Leconfield on July 23 1940, as 'A' Flight Commander. He was awarded the KW (23.12.40) and on December 31 took command of the squadron. Laguna was again promoted on May 27 1941 and appointed to lead the Northolt Wing.

On June 27 1941 Laguna led the Wing over France. At low-level he was shot down by ground fire near Coquelles, in the Calais area, in Spitfire P 8331. He was reported 'Missing, presumed killed'. Laguna is buried in Pihen-les-Guines Cemetery. He was awarded the VM (5th Class) (15.7.41).

FL 1.3.41

ALAN LAING

52759   Sgt   Pilot   British   151 Squadron

Laing was born on December 16 1914. He joined 151 Squadron at Digby on September 30 1940.

Commissioned in the Technical Branch (Armament) in November 1943, Laing retired on May 8 1955, as a Flight Lieutenant.

PO 9.11.43   FO 9.5.44   FL 9.5.47

ALEXANDER JAMES ALAN LAING

39993   FO   Pilot   British   64 Squadron

Laing joined the RAF on a short service commission in May 1937. He was posted to 10 FTS, Tern Hill on August 21 and joined the staff of the School of Naval Co-operation at Ford on March 26 1938. He was with 64 Squadron at Kenley in early July 1940.

No further service details traced.

*APO 9.8.37   PO 24.5.38   FO 24.12.39   FL 24.12.40
SL 1.3.42*

DONALD MILLAR LAKE

42234   PO   Pilot   British   219 Squadron

Lake, of Harrow, Middlesex, joined the RAF on a short service commission in April 1939. He was with 219 Squadron at Catterick

DM Lake (continued)

in early July 1940.

He was killed on September 4 1941, as a Flying Officer. His unit at the time of his death is unknown. Lake was 20. He is buried in St Andrew's churchyard, Tangmere.

APO 24.6.39   PO 16.12.39   FO 16.12.40

ALBERT LAMB

1003621   Sgt   Aircrew   British   25 Squadron

Joined 25 Squadron at North Weald in early October 1940. No other service details traced. Lamb died on January 5 1948.

OWEN EDWARD LAMB

42411   PO   Pilot   New Zealander   151 Squadron

Lamb was born in Auckland on May 10 1917. Early in 1939 he applied for an RAF short service commission, was provisionally accepted and sailed for the UK on May 6 in the RMS 'Rangitane'.

On June 12 1939 Lamb began his elementary flying training at 10 E&RFTS, Yatesbury and in late August moved to 2 FTS, Brize Norton. With training completed Lamb was posted to 7 AGS, Newton Down in February 1940 for a gunnery course, after which he went to 6 OTU, Sutton Bridge to convert to Hurricanes.

On April 13 Lamb began a Specialist Armament Officers' Course at No 1 Air Armament School at Manby. He was posted to 5 OTU, Aston Down on August 31 for a Hurricane refresher course and then joined 151 Squadron at Digby in mid-September.

Lamb volunteered for overseas service in early November and joined 73 Squadron at Castle Camps. The squadron embarked on HMS 'Furious' on November 6, en route for the Middle East. They flew their Hurricanes off to Takoradi on the 29th and then flew in easy stages to Heliopolis, via Lagos, Accra, Kano, Maidugari, Khartoum, Wadi Halfa and Abu Sueir. On arrival the squadron was attached to 274 Squadron in the Western Desert. 73 Squadron became operational on its own account at Sidi Heneish in early January 1941.

The Luftwaffe mounted a heavy attack against Tobruk on April 14 1941, with a force of more than ninety fighters and bombers. 73 Squadron was operating from within the perimeter defences that day and took off to engage the enemy. After the action Lamb failed to return to base and his body was later found and buried in an isolated grave near the Tobruk-Bardia road.

After the war Lamb's remains were re-interred in the Knightsbridge War Cemetery, Acroma, Libya.

APO 5.8.39   PO 28.2.40

PETER GILBERT LAMB

90349   FL   Pilot   British   610 Squadron

Joined 610 Squadron, AuxAF in early 1938. Lamb was called to full-time service with the squadron in late October 1939.

On August 24 and 26 1940 he claimed Bf 109s destroyed, on the 29th a Bf 110 and on the 30th a He 111. Lamb was posted away from the squadron on October 28 1940.

He was awarded the AFC (26.10.43) and released from the RAF in 1945, as a Squadron Leader. In June 1946 he began to reform 610 Squadron at Hooton Park, its having been disbanded at Warmwell on March 3 1945.

Lamb commanded the squadron from July 31 1946 to March 1950.

PO (AuxAF) 25.4.38   FO 25.10.39   FL 25.10.40
SL 1.12.41   SL (RAuxAFRO) 1.8.46

ROBERT LIONEL LAMB

82718   PO   Air Gunner   British   600 Squadron

Lamb joined 600 Squadron at Manston on July 17 1940. He was later with 35 (Pathfinder) Squadron, operating in Halifaxes from Graveley.

After 23 operations Lamb was shot down and captured in February 1944 and was a PoW in Stalag Luft III.

He was released from the RAF in 1947, as a Squadron Leader.

PO 9.5.40   FO 9.5.41   FL 9.5.42

RODERICK RUSSELL LAMB

Sub-Lieutenant (FAA)   Pilot   British   804 Squadron

Lamb was with 804 Squadron at Hatston in early July 1940, flying Gladiators on dockyard defence.

On December 9 1940 he was posted to 802 Squadron, then forming at Donibristle for HMS 'Audacity'. Lamb joined 881 Squadron for HMS 'Illustrious' on February 25 1942. He was killed on August 24 1942 in a flying accident, when his aircraft spun into the ground.

Lamb was 22. He is buried in Mbaraki Cemetery, Mombasa, Kenya.

' 'idshipman 4.7.38   Actg Sub-Lt 14.3.40

HUGH MICHAEL STANFORD LAMBERT

39419   FO   Pilot   British   25 Squadron

Lambert joined the RAF on a short service commission in November 1936. He was posted to 2 FTS, Digby on February 6 1937 and joined 25 Squadron at Hawkinge on September 4.

Lambert was killed on September 15 1940, possibly in a collision between a Blenheim and a Beaufighter near Biggin Hill. He was 22 and was cremated at Henley Road Crematorium, Reading.

APO 28.1.37   PO 16.11.37   FO 16.8.39

WILLIAM GAVIN MEIN LAMBIE

42235   PO   Pilot   British   219 Squadron

Lambie, of Edinburgh, joined the RAF on a short service commission in April 1939. He was with 219 Squadron at Catterick in early July 1940.

On November 15 Lambie was killed in Beaufighter R 2084, which crashed near Kenley, cause unknown. He is buried in Nutfield Cemetery, Surrey.

APO 24.6.39   PO 16.10.39

ALFRED LAMMER

81940   PO   Air Gunner   British   141 Squadron

Lammer was born in Linz, Austria on November 28 1909. In 1934 he went to London to work for the Austrian Travel Service. When Germany invaded Austria in 1938 he was offered German citizenship but being bitterly anti-Nazi he declined and was declared stateless as a consequence. Lammer lost his job and for a year he lived on his savings and studied photography.

At the outbreak of war he volunteered for the RAF but did not hold out much hope of being accepted but he was granted an Emergency Commission in March 1940, for training as an Air Gunner.

After initial ground training at Loughborough Lammer went on a gunnery course at 9 BGS, Penrhos on April 8. He joined 254 Squadron at Bircham Newton on May 4 and was immediately attached to 206 Squadron, flying in Hudsons on convoy escorts. In early July Lammer was posted to 5 OTU, Aston Down, where he converted to Defiants before joining 141 Squadron at Prestwick.

On August 10 he was sent to Warmwell for a Gunnery Leaders' course and then rejoined 141. Lammer retrained on Beaufighters and was posted to 409 (RCAF) Squadron at Coleby Grange on November 1 1941. He went to 255 Squadron at Coltishall on February 5 1942, as Navigation Leader.

The squadron flew to Gibraltar on November 14 and landed at Maison Blanche, Algiers the next day. Lammer went with a detachment to Souk-el-Arba on December 5. He assisted in the destruction of a He 111 and two Cant 1007s on the 6th, flying with Squadron Leader JH Player, on December 15 and 17 two Ju 88s were destroyed with Wing Commander DPDG Kelly. Lammer was awarded the DFC (16.2.43).

On June 25, flying again with Player, Lammer assisted in destroying a Cant 1007. The detachment at Souk-el-Arba ended on July 31. With his tour completed Lammer returned to the UK and was posted as Squadron Leader i/c Radar and Navigation at 62 OTU, Ouston on September 21 1943. He was awarded a Bar to the DFC (29.10.43).

Lammer went to 54 OTU, Charter Hall as Senior Navigator Radar Instructor on June 5 1945. He received a Mention in Despatches (14.6.45) and was released on November 7 1945, as a Squadron Leader. He went into photography and had his own studio, specialising in photographing children. Lammer later taught at Guildford and the London School of Art.

APO 15.3.40   PO 4.5.40   FO 4.5.41   FL 4.5.42

LESLIE NINIAN LANDELS

84695   PO   Pilot   British   32, 3 and 615 Squadrons

Joined 32 Squadron at Acklington on September 19 1940, moved to 3 Squadron at Turnhouse on the 27th and to 615 Squadron at Northolt in October.

After destroying a Bf 109 on November 8 1940 Landels was shot down over Maidstone and crash-landed at Challock, in Hurricane V 7652, slightly injured.

In late 1941 Landels was in the Far East. He commanded 232 Squadron briefly in January 1942, before being killed on the 20th, as an Acting Flight Lieutenant.

Landels is remembered on the Singapore Memorial, Column 411.

PO 24.8.40   FO 17.8.41

JOHN LANDESDELL

740990   Sgt   Pilot   British   607 Squadron

Landesdell was an Associate Fellow of the Royal Aeronautical Society and had a First Class Honours Diploma in Aeronautics. He was with 607 Squadron at Usworth in early July 1940. Landesdell was shot down and killed by a Bf 109 on September 17. His Hurricane, P 3860, crashed at The Bell at Beltring.

He was 23 and is buried in St Margaret's churchyard, Hempnall, Norfolk.

BRIAN JOHN EDWARD LANE

37859   FL   Pilot   British   19 Squadron

Born in 1917, Lane was educated at St Paul's School. In 1935 he lost his job as a supervisor in an electric bulb factory and applied for a short service commission in the RAF. Provisionally accepted, he began his ab initio training at 3 E&RFTS, Hamble on March 22 1936, went on to 11 FTS, Wittering on June 1 and then joined 66 Squadron at Duxford on January 8 1937.

Lane was posted to 213 Squadron on March 8 1937 at its reformation at Northolt. He was with the squadron up to the outbreak of war, when he joined 19 Squadron at Duxford, as a Flight Commander. When the CO was killed over Dunkirk on May 25 1940 Lane took temporary command. On the 26th he destroyed a Ju 87 and two Bf 109s and on

June 1 probably destroyed a Bf 110. He was awarded the DFC (30.7.40).

Lane claimed a Bf 110 destroyed on August 24. He took command of the squadron on September 5 when the CO was killed. Lane claimed Bf 110s destroyed on September 5 and 11, probably a Bf 109 on the 15th and shared a Bf 110 on November 15.

In early July 1941 he went to HQ 12 Group at Hucknall, on staff duties. Lane was posted to the Middle East in November. He was at Air HQ Western Desert until February 1942 and then at HQ Middle East until June, when he returned to the UK and was posted to 61 OTU at Montford Bridge.

On December 9 1942 Lane was given command of 167 Squadron at Ludham. Four days later he took off with three other pilots for a 'Rhubarb' operation over Holland. They got into combat with FW 190s. When searched for afterwards Lane had disappeared, never to be seen again. He is remembered on the Runnymede Memorial, Panel 65. Lane wrote a book, 'Spitfire', published under the pseudonym of BJ Ellan in 1942.

APO 18.5.36   PO 23.3.37   FO 23.12.38   FL 3.9.40
SL 1.12.41

ROY LANE

41028   PO   Pilot   British   43 Squadron

Lane, of Southampton, joined the RAF on a short service commission in June 1938. He joined 43 Squadron at Tangmere on July 13 1940 and claimed a Ju 87 destroyed on August 18.

In combat with He 111s over Portsmouth on August 26 Lane was shot down, in Hurricane P 3220, and is believed to have crashed at Wittering, Sussex. Wounded and badly burned, Lane was admitted to the West Sussex Hospital, Brighton and then went to the Queen Victoria Hospital, East Grinstead, where he underwent plastic surgery by Archie McIndoe and became a Guinea Pig.

After leaving hospital Lane was sent on a speaking tour of the aircraft factories. In 1942 he was with the MSFU at Speke. On May 21 he sailed from Iceland in convoy PQ 16 to set up and command the MSFU Pool at Archangel. Lane returned to the UK in November 1942 in convoy QP 15, as pilot on the 'Empire Moon'. From the beginning of 1943 Camships were no longer used on Russian convoys, replaced by auxiliary carriers.

Lane was posted to India in late 1943. He volunteered to go into Burma and operate with the Chindits, as air liaison officer to Brigadier Bernard Fergusson. When the Chindits reached their area of operations in Japanese-occupied territory they built an airstrip and a Hurricane was flown in for Lane to use. Returning to the strip after a liaison trip to India the aircraft had engine trouble and Lane forced-landed in the jungle twenty miles east of the Chindwin River. The RAF dropped supplies and information to him but Lane was captured by the Japanese and is believed to have been killed by them on June 20 1944. He was 24 and is buried in Taukkyan War Cemetery, Rangoon, Burma.

APO 20.8.38   PO 27.6.39   FO 3.12.40   FL 3.12.41

CHARLES EDWARD LANGDON

43705   PO   Pilot   New Zealander   43 Squadron

Born at Hawera on August 21 1918, Langdon was educated at the High School there. After leaving he was employed as a costing clerk.

Langdon applied for an RAF short service commission in February 1939 and was accepted for training in New Zealand. He reported to the Ground Training School at Rongotai on September 20, began his elementary flying training at No 1 EFTS, Taieri on October 21 and moved on to No 1 FTS, Wigram on December 19. Langdon was awarded his flying badge on February 13 1940 and at the end of the course was graded as a future light-bomber pilot.

CE Langdon (continued)

He sailed for the UK on April 26 in the RMS 'Rangitiki' and after arrival went to RAF Depot, Uxbridge, where he transferred into the RAF. Langdon went to 4 Ferry Pilots' Pool, Kemble for a short refresher course on June 17. He soloed on Ansons, was posted to 12 OTU, Benson on the 30th, to convert to Battles and then joined 142 Squadron at Eastchurch on August 24.

Langdon probably volunteered for Fighter Command in response to a call for pilots. He joined 43 Squadron at Usworth on September 21 and having bypassed OTU he had to be converted to Hurricanes. He flew five operational sorties with 43 before he was posted away to the Air Gunners' School at Newton Downs, as a staff pilot on Whitleys, on November 3 1940. After only two days he went to 145 Squadron at Tangmere and shot down a Bf 109 on November 15.

In early December Langdon was posted away and embarked on HMS 'Furious' on the 17th, for an unknown destination. There were 25 Hurricanes aboard, with wings unattached. On January 9 1941 Langdon flew off the carrier to Takoradi and then flew north in easy stages, via Lagos, Kano, Maidugari, Khartoum, Wadi Halfa and arrived at Abu Sueir on January 14. He flew to LG 2 on the 22nd and then flew to Hal Far, Malta, via Gazala, on the 29th.

Langdon joined 261 Squadron at Ta Kali on the 30th and flew his first operational patrol the next day. He failed to return from an interception patrol on February 26 1941, in Hurricane V 7474. He is remembered on the Malta Memorial, Panel 1, Column 1.

APO 20.9.39   PO 8.6.40

NEVILLE CHARLES LANGHAM-HOBART

77792   PO   Pilot   British   73 Squadron

In August 1939 Langham-Hobart joined 607 Squadron, AuxAF, as an LAC u/t pilot. Called up at the outbreak of war, he was posted to 7 FTS, Peterborough for further training.

In March 1940 Langham-Hobart joined 611 Squadron at Digby but soon afterwards was posted to 73 Squadron in France. After the French collapse the squadron was finally withdrawn on June 17, to Church Fenton.

On September 7 1940 Langham-Hobart claimed a Bf 110 destroyed. He was shot down over the Thames Estuary on September 23, in Hurricane L 2036. Severely burned, he was rescued from the sea by the Navy and admitted to the Royal Naval Hospital, Chatham. Langham-Hobart later moved to the Queen Victoria Hospital, East Grinstead, where he had skin grafts on face and legs, becoming a Guinea Pig.

In 1941 he was posted to the Ministry of Aircraft Production and visited munition factories, speaking to the workers. He later went to Canada, where, after doing a specialist navigation course at Goderich, Ontario, he instructed at Charlotte Town, Prince Edward Island.

Back in the UK Langham-Hobart went to the Air Ministry and later moved to HQ 13 Group, Newcastle, as Navigation Officer. He was posted to HQ Cairo and given the job of setting up mobile light beacons between Tripoli and Algiers. With this completed he was appointed CGI at Abu Sueir.

Langham-Hobart returned to the UK, did an intensive course on radar systems at RAF Shawbury and then returned to Air HQ, Cairo. His final posting was as CO of RAF Port Reitz at Mombasa. He returned to the UK and was released from the RAF in September 1945, as a Squadron Leader.

PO 7.3.40   FO 7.3.41   FL 7.3.42

GERALD ARCHIBALD LANGLEY

81641   PO   Pilot   British   41 Squadron

Born at Stony Stratford, Langley was educated at Wolverton Grammar School. In 1936 the family moved to Northampton and he went to work for the Prudential Assurance Co.

Langley joined the RAFVR in March 1939 and was with 41 Squadron at Catterick in early September 1940. On the 11th he was shot down by return fire from a Ju 88 over Sevenoaks, in Spitfire X 4325, and baled out, unhurt.

On September 15 Langley was shot down and killed in combat with Bf 109s. His Spitfire, P 9324, is believed to be that which crashed and burned out at Wick House, Bulphan.

Langley was 24. He is buried in Sts Peter and Paul churchyard, Abington, Northamptonshire.

PO 18.6.40

LEONARD LANGLEY

101648   Sgt   Air Gunner   British   23 Squadron

Langley joined 23 Squadron at Collyweston on July 9 1940. He was awarded the DFM (30.5.41), the squadron's first, being then credited with assisting in the destruction of three enemy aircraft at night.

Commissioned in July 1941, Langley was released from the RAF in 1946 but rejoined in 1947. He died on September 26 1953, whilst still serving.

PO 12.7.41   FO 12.7.42
FL 12.7.43   FL 23.10.47

FRANCIS CHARLES ANTHONY LANNING

79580   PO   Air Gunner   British   141 Squadron

Born on February 28 1907, Lanning was commissioned in the RAF in May 1940. He joined 141 Squadron at Turnhouse in June.   He was awarded the DFC (6.6.41) for assisting in the destruction of a He 111 and a Ju 88 on the same night in May 1941.

Lanning was posted to 410 Squadron at its formation at Ayr on June 30 1941. He moved to 289 at Turnhouse, when it was formed there on November 20 1941, for anti-aircraft co-operation duties. In January 1944 he was appointed Air-to-Ground Range Officer at RAF Predannack.

In August 1945 Lanning became OC HQ 701 Air Disarmament Wing at Graz, Austria and his final posting was as Camp Commandant at RAF Klagenfurt, Austria on June 18 1946. He was released from the RAF on November 2 1946, as a Flight Lieutenant.

APO 18.5.40   PO 15.6.40   FO 15.6.41   FL 15.6.42

STANISLAW LAPKA

76702   PO   Pilot   Polish   302 Squadron

Born in Borzyny, Warsaw on August 15 1915, Lapka joined the PAF in 1936. He was posted to 302 Squadron at Leconfield at its formation on July 13 1940.

Lapka shared in destroying a Ju 88 on March 28 1941. He was awarded the KW (10.9.41), became 'B' Flight Commander on January 7 1942, received a Bar to the KW (5.5.42) and became 'A' Flight Commander on June 21 1942. He got a second Bar to the KW (20.8.42) and took command of 302 Squadron on August 26 1942. Lapka probably destroyed a FW 190 on September 7.

He was posted away to a course for squadron COs on January 14 1943, after which he was appointed as Liaison Officer at HQ 11 Group. Lapka was awarded the VM (5th Class) (29.5.43). He returned to operations on January 1 1944 when he took command of 306 Squadron at Llanbedr. Lapka destroyed a Bf 109 and was reported

'Missing' on June 7. He did not return to the squadron but went to the PAF Depot on August 26 1944.

Lapka was posted to HQ ADGB as Squadron Leader Tactics and Organisation on October 20. He went to a course at PAF Staff College on September 17 1945 and then held various administrative appointments prior to his release from the PAF in 1947, as a Squadron Leader. Lapka settled in England and died in 1978.

FO 1.3.41   FL 1.3.42

WACLAW LAPKOWSKI

P 1506   PO   Pilot   Polish   303 Squadron

Born on November 6 1913, Lapkowski was in the PAF before the war and was credited with destroying one German aircraft and sharing another in the September 1939 fighting in Poland.

Lapkowski joined 303 Squadron at its formation at Northolt on August 2 1940. He claimed a Ju 88 destroyed on September 5. On that day he was himself shot down by a Bf 109 in combat over Gillingham. He baled out, with a broken leg and burns, landed at Hawkwell and was admitted to Rochford Hospital. His Hurricane, P 2985, crashed at Bonvill's Farm, North Benfleet.

Awarded the VM (5th Class)(23.12.40), Lapkowski did not return to the squadron until January 6 1941. He returned from a sweep over France on the 22nd with 25 yards of telephone wire round his engine. Lapkowski was awarded the KW (1.4.41) and was wounded on April 13 1941 and admitted to hospital. On May 5 he took command of 303 Squadron, on June 4 he damaged a Bf 109, on the 8th he destroyed one, on the 22nd two more, on the 24th another and on the 27th he damaged another.

On July 2 1941 Lapkowski was leading 303, in Spitfire B 8596, flying with the Polish Wing, escorting Blenheims to Lille. They were attacked in mid-Channel by fifty Bf 109s coming down from a higher altitude. Lapkowski was shot down. His body was washed ashore and he is buried in Lombardsijde Communal Cemetery, Belgium. He was awarded a Bar to the KW (10.4.46) and two more Bars (31.10.47).

BASIL DOUGLAS LARBALESTIER

84706   PO   Air Gunner   British   600 Squadron

Joined 600 Squadron, AuxAF in March 1934, as a Wireless Operator (Air). In August 1936 the squadron was transferred to Fighter Command and Larbalestier remustered as an air gunner. He flew with 600 until January 1941, when he was posted to 200 Squadron, Coastal Command at Oban.

In April 1942 Larbalestier went to the Coastal OTU at Cranwell, as an instructor. He was posted to Canada in May 1943, returned to the UK in June 1944 and joined 75 Squadron, operating in Lancasters from Mepal, Cambridgeshire, still as an air gunner.

Larbalestier was released from the RAF on September 2 1945, as a Flight Lieutenant.

PO 8.8.40   FO 8.8.41   FL 8.8.42

JOSEPH EMILE PAUL LARICHELIERE

42849   PO   Pilot   Canadian   213 Squadron

Laricheliere, of Montreal, joined 213 Squadron at Biggin Hill on May 25 1940.

He claimed two Bf 110s and a Bf 109 destroyed on August 13 and two Bf 110s and a Ju 87 on the 15th. He failed to return from a combat off Portland on August 16. Laricheliere was 27 and is remembered on the Runnymede Memorial, Panel 9.

APO 23.10.40   PO 18.5.40

H G LASCOT

No unknown   PO   Pilot   Belgian   236 Squadron

Joined 236 Squadron on August 5 1940 and posted away on September 15. No further service details traced but it is known that he survived the war.

JOHN BLANDFORD LATTA

42008   PO   Pilot   Canadian   242 Squadron

Latta, of Victoria, British Columbia, was a salmon fisherman before joining the RAF on a short service commission in February 1939. With his training completed he was posted to the newly-reformed 242 Squadron at Church Fenton on November 6 1939.

On patrol between Dunkirk and Nieuport on May 29 1940 Latta probably destroyed a Bf 109 and on the 31st claimed the destruction of another. He flew with 242 to France, when they were there between June 8 and 18 covering the Army's rearguard actions towards the Atlantic ports.

On August 21 1940 Latta shared a Do 215, on September 9 and 15 he destroyed two Bf 109s and on the 27th two more. He was awarded the DFC (8.11.40).

Latta was reported 'Missing' after a patrol over the Dutch coast on January 12 1941, in Hurricane V 7203. He was 27 and is remembered on the Runnymede Memorial, Panel 33.

ARNOLD JOHN LAUDER

48822   Sgt   Pilot   British   264 Squadron

Born in March 1916, Lauder joined the RAF in September 1931, as an aircraft apprentice at Halton. He did a three year course and passed out as an LAC Fitter Aero Engines in September 1934 and was posted to RAF Gosport, maintaining aircraft used for training pilots for service on carriers.

At the time of the Abyssinia scare in 1936 Lauder was posted to the MU at Aboukir but returned in 1937 to Gosport. He went to RAF Henlow for a Fitter 1 Course and on passing out was promoted to Corporal and posted to 87 Squadron at Debden. Lauder was in 'A' Flight and on June 1 1938 this was re-numbered as 85 Squadron.

Lauder volunteered for pilot training and late in 1938 he was posted to 4 E&RFTS, Brough to begin his ab initio course. He moved on to 3 FTS, Grantham, completed the course in late August 1939 and was promoted to Sergeant-Pilot. Lauder joined 264 Squadron on October 30, when it reformed at Sutton Bridge.

Over Dunkirk on May 29 1940 he destroyed a Ju 87 and probably a second. Lauder also took part in 264's final bout of day-fighting in August. On the 28th he had his petrol tank holed by return fire during an attack on a He 111 over Folkestone. He and his gunner were unhurt and returned safely to Hornchurch.

AJ Lauder` (continued)

Commissioned in May 1942, Lauder was posted to 54 OTU, Charter Hall on April 14 1943, as an instructor. He returned to 264 Squadron, then at Coleby Grange, on November 12 1943 and stayed with it until the end of the war.

Lauder later went as a supernumerary Engineering Officer with a Spitfire squadron. He was released from the RAF in 1947, as a Flight Lieutenant. He became a partner in a motor engineering firm in Surrey.

PO 1.5.42   FO 1.11.42   FL 1.5.44

JOHN HAMILTON LAUGHLIN

39995   FO   Pilot   British   235 Squadron

Joined the RAF on a short service commission in June 1937. Laughlin was posted to 3 FTS, South Cerney on August 21 and after completing the course he went to RAF Gosport on March 26 1938, under instruction. Laughlin was posted to the FAA Pool at Gosport on October 10 1938. He joined 235 Squadron, when it was reformed in October 1939.

On August 3 1940 he destroyed a He 115 over the North Sea. In September an aircraft of the squadron, carrying a full load of bombs, crashed among other aircraft and burst into flames. Laughlin, Pilot Officer J Coggins and another officer immediately ran to these aircraft, started the engines and taxied them away. During this time two of the bombs exploded. Three aircraft were taken to safety without damage and a fourth with only minor damage. Laughlin and Coggins received the MBE (21.1.41).

Laughlin was awarded the DSO (23.3.45), as a Squadron Leader with 149 Squadron, operating in Lancasters from Methwold. He was released from the RAF in 1946.

*APO 9.8.37   PO 24.5.38   FO 24.12.39   FL 24.12.40
SL 1.3.42*

GEORGE LAURENCE

47392   Sgt   Pilot   British   141 Squadron

With 141 Squadron at Turnhouse in early July 1940. Flying with a detachment at Biggin Hill Laurence destroyed a Ju 88 at night on September 17.

In May 1941 he destroyed another enemy aircraft at night. He was awarded the DFM (30.5.41), still with 141 Squadron.

Commissioned from Warrant Officer in December 1941, Laurence was killed on November 9 1944, as a Flight Lieutenant with 219 Squadron. He is buried in Massicault War Cemetery, Tunisia.

FO 1.12.41   FL 1.12.42

DEREK NAPIER LAWFORD

113266   Sgt   Pilot   British   247 Squadron

Lawford joined the RAFVR in July 1939 and began elementary flying training at No 1 E&RFTS, Hatfield. Called up at the outbreak of war, he was posted to 3 ITW, Hastings, moved to 6 EFTS, Sywell on November 27 to complete his ab initio flying and went to 8 FTS, Montrose on April 10 1940.

With training completed Lawford went to 5 OTU, Aston Down on August 3, served very briefly with 609 Squadron at Middle Wallop, then went to 7 OTU, Hawarden and was posted to 247 Squadron at Roborough on September 6, flying Gladiators in defence of Plymouth.

Commissioned in October 1941, Lawford embarked on HMS 'Prince of Wales' on October 24 and landed at Freetown, then went

by troopship to Takoradi. He went up to the Middle East and spent brief periods with 250 Squadron at Port Said and 73 Squadron in the Western Desert before joining the ADU at Cairo on May 14 1942.

Lawford returned to the UK in June 1944 and after a course at 3 (P) AFU at South Cerney joined Transport Command. He served with 511, 233 and 575 Squadrons prior to his release from the RAF on October 4 1945, as a Flight Lieutenant. He went to live in the USA, moving in 1985 to Canada.

PO 23.10.41   FO 1.10.42   FL 23.10.43

EDGAR STANLEY LAWLER

182840   Sgt   Air Gunner   British   604 Squadron

With 604 Squadron at Middle Wallop in July 1940. Lawler was commissioned from Warrant Officer in July 1944 and released from the RAF in 1945, as a Flying Officer. He died in 1984.

PO 27.7.44   FO 27.1.45

JOHN THORNETT LAWRENCE

104428   Sgt   Pilot   British   235 Squadron

Joined 235 Squadron on October 5 1940. Commissioned in August 1941, Lawrence was awarded the AFC (14.6.45). He was released from the RAF in 1946, as a Flight Lieutenant.

PO 5.8.41   FO 5.8.42   FL 5.8.43

KEITH ASHLEY LAWRENCE

42133   PO   Pilot   New Zealander   234, 603 Sqdns, 421 Flt

Born in Waitara on November 25 1919, Lawrence was at Southland Boys' High School from 1933 to 1936 and then went to work as a bank clerk in Invercargill.

He enrolled in the Civil Reserve of Pilots in February 1938 and in June successfully applied for a short service commission in the RAF. Lawrence left for the UK on February 1 1939 in the RMS 'Tainui'. He went to 10 E&RFTS, Yatesbury on March 13, moved to 5 FTS, Sealand on May 28 and joined the newly-reformed 234 Squadron at Leconfield on November 6. The squadron then had Blenheims but began to receive Spitfires in March 1940.

Lawrence shared in the destruction of a Ju 88 on July 8, the squadron's first victory. On August 24 he damaged a Bf 110 and on September 7 claimed a Bf 109 destroyed and damaged a Do 17. Two days later Lawrence was posted to 603 Squadron at Hornchurch and on the 15th he claimed a Bf 109 destroyed and two more damaged.

On October 8 Lawrence was posted to 421 Flight, then forming at Hawkinge. On a weather reconnaissance over Ramsgate on November 26 he was shot down by Bf 109s. The Spitfire disintegrated and Lawrence found himself falling. He got his parachute open, went into the sea and burst a dye sachet, colouring the water. He was picked up by a minesweeper and taken to Ramsgate, where he was admitted to hospital, with his right arm dislocated and his right leg broken.

After convalescence at Torquay Lawrence rejoined his unit, by then re-numbered as 91 Squadron, on December 4 1941. He was sent to 52 OTU, Aston Down for a refresher course on Spitfires, rejoined the squadron on January 10 1942 but soon afterwards was posted to HQ RAF Mediterranean at Valetta, Malta. Lawrence joined 185 Squadron at Hal Far on February 17.

Lawrence shared a He 111 on March 23, destroyed Ju 87s on May 9 and 10 and on the 19th damaged a Bf 109. He was promoted on May 28 1942 and took command of 185, leading it until he returned to the UK in early August. Lawrence was posted to 52 OTU at Aston Down but moved on September 4 to 57 OTU, Hawarden. He was awarded the DFC (12.9.42).

In early July 1943 Lawrence went to Duxford for liaison duties with the USAF. On October 27 he was posted to 56 OTU, Sutton Bridge on the Pilot Gunnery Instructors' Training Wing. In late May 1944 Lawrence went to 28 OTU, Wymeswold, where he flew Hurricanes by day and night against Wellingtons, training air gunners.

Lawrence returned to operations on February 5 1945, when he joined 124 Squadron at Manston, flying Spitfire IXs.

On July 15 1945 Lawrence transferred to the RNZAF. He returned to New Zealand in late May 1946 and went on to the Reserve on September 2. He later returned to Britain and settled there.

APO 13.5.39   PO 6.11.39   FO 6.11.40   FL 6.11.41

NORMAN ANTHONY LAWRENCE

88855   Sgt   Pilot   British   54 Squadron

With 54 Squadron in early July 1940. Lawrence claimed a Bf 109 destroyed on July 9 and three Ju 87s on August 15. After the destruction of the dive bombers Lawrence was shot down by a Bf 109 and crashed into the sea off Dover, in Spitfire N 3097. He was rescued by the Navy and admitted to Dover Hospital with shock.

Commissioned in December 1940, Lawrence left the RAF in mid-1943, as a Flying Officer. He died on August 22 1958.

PO 4.12.40   FO 4.12.41

ADRIAN FRANCIS LAWS

45092   PO   Pilot   British   64 Squadron

Laws, of East Dereham, Norfolk, was a pre-war airman pilot. He was with 64 Squadron in early 1940.

On June 12 Laws shared a He 111, on July 29 he claimed a Bf 109 destroyed, on August 11 he damaged a Bf 109, on the 13th damaged a Do 17, on the 15th claimed a Bf 109 destroyed and on the 18th a Bf 110 and shared a He 111.

Laws' commission was gazetted on September 27 1940. He was killed on the 30th, when he was in collision with another Spitfire during a routine patrol. The tail unit of his Spitfire, P 9564, was sheared off and he spiralled into the ground. Laws was 28. He is buried in Wells-next-the-Sea Cemetery, Norfolk. He was awarded the DFM (1.10.40).

PO 27.9.40

GEORGE GODFREY STONE LAWS

745649   Sgt   Pilot   British   151 and 501 Squadrons

Laws, of Gwersylt, joined 151 Squadron at Digby on September 28 1940. In October he moved to 501 Squadron at Kenley.

He was killed on March 28 1941, still with 501. Laws was 21. He is buried in St Meugan's churchyard, Llanrhydd, Llanbedr.

RICHARD CHESTER LAWSON

43006   PO   Pilot   British   601 Squadron

Lawson was the son of Admiral RN Lawson CB and before joining the RAF was an officer in the Royal Tank Regiment.

He was posted to 601 Squadron at Exeter on September 9 1940. Lawson was killed on February 10 1941, still with 601, aged 21. He is remembered on the Runnymede Memorial, Panel 33.

PO 7.3.40

WALTER JOHN LAWSON

43419   PO   Pilot   British   19 Squadron

Lawson was born in Tunbridge Wells, Kent. He joined 19 Squadron at Duxford in April 1940.

On September 5 he was promoted to Acting Flight Lieutenant and made a Flight Commander. On September 9 Lawson claimed a Bf 110 destroyed, on the 11th a He 111, on the 15th a probable Do 17, on the 18th he shared a Ju 88, on the 27th claimed a Bf 109 and on November 5 two Bf 109s and probably another. Lawson was awarded the DFC (26.11.40).

On June 27 1941 he claimed a Bf 109 destroyed and probably two more. Lawson took command of 19 Squadron in early July and he was killed on August 28 1941, aged 28. He is remembered on the Runnymede Memorial, Panel 28.

PO 1.4.40   FO 6.12.40

JOHN LAWSON-BROWN

82692   PO   Pilot   British   64 Squadron

Lawson-Brown, of Leeds, joined 64 Squadron at Leconfield on September 14 1940.

He was killed on May 12 1941, still with 64, aged 28. He was cremated at Lawns Wood Crematorium, Leeds, Yorkshire.

PO 27.7.40

PHILIP CHARLES FENNER LAWTON

90217   FL   Pilot   British   604 Squadron

Born in London in 1912, Lawton joined 604 Squadron, AuxAF in 1936. He was called to full-time service on August 24 1939.

Lawton served with 604 throughout the Battle of Britain. He received a Mention in Despatches in March 1941.

On April 4 the weather clamped down whilst he was on a night patrol in a Beaufighter. With no airfield in range open for landings, he baled out.

Awarded the DFC (11.11.41), Lawton was then credited with two Ju 88s destroyed and probably a He 111.

Lawton was released from the RAF in 1945, as a Group Captain. He became an executive with British European Airways.

PO (AuxAF) 4.7.36   FO (AuxAF) 4.3.38   FO 24.8.39
FL 3.9.40   SL 1.12.41   WC 6.9.44

———— LAYCOCK

No unknown   FO   Pilot   British   87 Squadron

No service details traced.

HERBERT KEITH LAYCOCK

40925   FO   Pilot   British   79 and 56 Squadrons

Laycock, of Walton-on-Thames, joined the RAF on a short service commission in May 1938. He was with 616 Squadron in May 1940 and on June 1 damaged a He 111 over Dunkirk.

He joined 79 Squadron at Acklington on July 27 and moved to 56 Squadron at Boscombe Down on October 8 1940.

Laycock was killed on August 26 1943, as a Squadron Leader with 603 Squadron, aged 24. He is buried in Phaleron War Cemetery, Athens.

APO 9.7.38   PO 16.5.39   FO 3.9.40

WLODZIMIERZ LAZORYK

P 1000   FO   Pilot   Polish   607 Squadron

Born on August 27 1904, Lazoryk was in the PAF before the war. In September 1939 he was CO of 152 Fighter Squadron. He escaped to France and after the French collapse he made his way to England, arriving there on June 23 1940.

Lazoryk joined 607 Squadron at Turnhouse on October 9 1940. He was posted to 308 Squadron at Baginton on February 15 1941 and served with it until November 30 1941, when he was posted to 3 FTS, South Cerney for a conversion course. Lazoryk went to 18 OTU, Bramcote on January 9 1942 and then joined 301 Squadron, operating in Wellingtons from Hemswell, on June 15 1942. He was awarded the KW and Bar (20.8.42) and a second Bar (15.11.42).

On February 18 1943 Lazoryk was posted to 305 Squadron, also flying Wellingtons from Hemswell. He was awarded the VM (5th Class)(20.2.43). Lazoryk was attached to HQ 9th Troop Carrier Command, USAAF on July 22 1945, as Polish Liaison Officer. He was sent on a course to PAF Staff College on January 1 1945 and after a spell at HQ PAF he returned to Staff College on February 1 1946, as an instructor.

Lazoryk was released from the PAF in May 1946, as a Squadron Leader.

FO 1.3.41

DAVID COOPER LEARY

42756   PO   Pilot   British   17 Squadron

Leary was born in London. He was with 17 Squadron when it was operating from Le Mans in early June 1940. On the 12th he destroyed a He 111. The squadron returned to Debden in mid-June.

On August 25 Leary claimed a Bf 109 destroyed, on September 3 he probably destroyed a Bf 110 and shared another and a Do 17, on the 27th he probably destroyed another Bf 110, on November 8 he claimed two Ju 87s destroyed and another shared and on the 13th he damaged a Do 17.

Leary was awarded the DFC (26.11.40). He was killed on December 28 1940, when he crashed near Debden in fog and low cloud, in Hurricane V 6791. He was 19 and is buried in Ipswich Cemetery, Suffolk.

APO 9.10.39   PO 11.5.40

ERNEST GEORGE CUTHBERT LEATHEM

78087   PO   Observer   British   248 Squadron

With 248 Squadron in early July 1940.

Leathem was awarded the DFC (25.5.43), as a Flight Lieutenant with 544 Squadron, for photographic-reconnaissance work in Mosquitos. He was released from the RAF in 1945, as a Flight Lieutenant, but rejoined later, serving for several years.

PO 10.3.40   FO 10.3.41   FL 10.3.42   FL 1.9.45

JAMES ANTHONY LEATHART

39625   FL   Pilot   British   54 Squadron

Born in London on January 5 1915, Leathart was educated at St Edward's, Oxford and graduated from Liverpool University as an electrical engineer. Whilst there he joined 610 Squadron, AuxAF on May 2 1936, as one of its founder-members. He qualified to wings and operational standard on Harts.

Leathart transferred to the RAF on May 8 1937 and was posted to 3 FTS, Grantham, later moving with it to South Cerney. On November 27 1937 he joined 54 Squadron at Hornchurch. He was appointed a Flight Commander in November 1939.

Over Dunkirk on May 21 Leathart probably destroyed a He 111. The next day he flew a Master to Calais-Marck aerodrome to pick up the CO of 74 Squadron, who had been shot down and could not get back. With cover provided by two Spitfires of 54 the operation, although extremely hazardous, was carried out successfully.

On May 24 Leathart claimed a Bf 109, on the 25th a probable Bf 110 and on the 26th two Bf 110s and a Ju 88. On this day he took command of 54 Squadron. On the 27th he shared a Ju 88, was awarded the DSO (11.6.40) and on June 17 damaged two Ju 88s.

On August 18 1940 Leathart claimed a Bf 109 probably destroyed, on the 28th a Do 17, on September 2 a Bf 109 and on the 3rd probably another. He was posted to Air Ministry on October 18 1940, to the Deputy Directorate of Air Tactics. Leathart went to HQ Fighter Command on March 3 1941, as Ops 2 Night Fighters. He was loaned to the RCAF on May 10 to form and command 406 Squadron at Acklington and did so until the CO post was upgraded to Wing Commander.

On November 8 1941 Leathart went to HQ RAF Middle East as Wing Commander Air Tactics. He was given command of 89 Squadron on October 16 1942. He destroyed a Cant Z 1007 on February 23 1943. Leathart returned to the UK on July 5 and was posted to HQ 84 Group to prepare for the invasion of Europe. He was appointed personal Staff Officer and pilot to Air Chief Marshal T Leigh-Mallory, C-in-C Allied European Air Force.

On May 30 1944 Leathart volunteered to take in light Warning Radar in a Jeep to control night fighters on D Day and was landed on J Beach in France at H hours plus 5.

Leathart was posted from 85 Group to command 148 Wing, Mosquito night fighters, on March 7 1945. He went on to the Directing Staff at RAF Staff College on July 10 1945. In the post-war RAF Leathart held a series of appointments and commands. He was made a CB (11.6.60) and retired at his own request on July 24 1962, as an Air Commodore.

APO 10.5.37   PO 1.1.38   FO 1.9.39   FL 24.8.40
SL 1.12.41   WC 1.7.44   WC 1.7.47   GC 1.7.55
AC 1.7.60

WILLIAM JOHNSON LEATHER

90355   FL   Pilot   British   611 Squadron

Leather joined 611 Squadron, AuxAF in May 1936, one of the first two volunteers for pilot training. He was called to full-time service with the squadron on August 26 1939.

He claimed a share in the destruction of a Do 17 on July 2 1940, claimed a Do 17 destroyed and another shared on September 15 and on October 11 shared in destroying two Do 17s. Leather was awarded the DFC (8.10.40). He shared Ju 88s on November 13 and December 7.

In January 1941 Leather was given command of 145 Squadron at Tangmere, which he led until April 1941.

At the end of the war Leather was in the Far East. He was released in 1945, as a Group Captain. When 611 Squadron, RAuxAF was reformed on May 10 1946 Leather was appointed to command and did so until 1949. He died in 1965.

PO (AuxAF) 14.5.36   FO (AuxAF) 1.1.38   FO 26.8.39
FL 1.1.40   SL 1.3.41   WC 1.6.42   SL (RAuxAFRO) 1.8.46

JERROLD le CHEMINANT

126148   Sgt   Pilot   British   616 Squadron

Le Cheminant was born on April 24 1918. He was posted to 616 Squadron at Kirton-in-Lindsey on October 14 1940. He claimed a Bf 109 probably destroyed on June 23 1941 and another destroyed on August 9.

Commissioned in May 1942, le Cheminant joined 72 Squadron at Biggin Hill in early August and went with it to North Africa in November. On December 2 1942 he was shot down by a FW 190 flown by Oberleutnant Bühlingen of II/JG 2. Le Cheminant crash-landed at Tebourba and was picked up by French troops, who returned him to his squadron. On December 4 he shot down a Bf 109, on January 6 and March 1 he damaged Bf 109s, on March 2 he chased one to ground level and it crashed into a hill and on April 24 he destroyed another. Le Cheminant was posted away to 232 Squadron at Souk-el-Khemis on April 26 and was awarded the DFC (21.5.43).

He stayed on in the RAF, in the Fighter Control Branch. He was made an OBE (13.6.70) and retired on November 1 1972, as a Wing Commander.

PO 9.5.42   FO 9.11.42   FL 9.5.44   FL 9.11.45
SL 1.7.63   WC 1.1.70

PHILLIP HOWARD LECKRONE

84655   PO   Pilot   American   616 Squadron

Leckrone came from Salem, Illinois. He joined 616 Squadron at Kenley on September 2 1940 and was posted to 71 Squadron at Church Fenton on October 12, to join other American volunteers in the first 'Eagle' squadron.

On January 5 1941 Leckrone was killed on a formation practice, when he collided with Pilot Officer EE Orbison. He was the squadron's first fatality. He is buried in Kirton-in-Lindsey Burial Ground.

JOHN GAGE LECKY

33570   PO   Pilot   British   610 and 41 Squadrons

Lecky was born in Yokohama, Japan. His father was Language Officer at the British Embassy. He was educated at Highfield Preparatory School, Liphook and Wrekin College, Shropshire. Lecky entered RAF College, Cranwell in April 1939 as a flight cadet. The course was shortened because of the war and he was commissioned in March 1940.

His first posting was to an army co-operation squadron and he joined 610 Squadron at Biggin Hill in August. Lecky moved to 41 Squadron at Hornchurch on October 1 1940. He was shot down in combat with Bf 109s on the 11th and baled out but was killed. His Spitfire, P 9447, crashed at Preston Hall, Maidstone.

Lecky was 19 years old. He is buried in All Saints' churchyard, Tilford, Surrey.

PO 7.3.40

EDGAR FRANCIS le CONTE

149330   Sgt   Radar Operator   British   FIU

Le Conte was born on March 8 1920. He was serving with FIU at Tangmere in early July 1940.

Commissioned from Warrant Officer in June 1943, Le Conte was then with 604 Squadron at Scorton. He assisted in damaging a Do 17 over the Humber on July 17. At the end of 1943 Le Conte was with 108 Squadron at Luqa, Malta. From then until July 1944 he flew many sorties with the CO, Wing Commander AJ Banham.

Le Conte stayed on in the RAF, was made an OBE (1.1.72) and retired on March 8 1975, as a Wing Commander. He died on May 4 1981.

PO 24.6.43   FO 24.12.43   FL 24.6.45   FL 21.2.49
SL 1.7.54   WC 1.1.67

LESLIE LEDGER

56339   Sgt   Air Gunner   British   236 Squadron

Joined 236 Squadron on July 19 1940. Ledger was awarded the DFM (12.1.43), as a Flight Sergeant with 35 Squadron, operating in Halifaxes from Graveley, Huntingdonshire.

Commissioned in November 1944, Ledger was released from the RAF in 1946, as a Flying Officer.

PO 8.11.44   FO 8.5.45

TERRY le DONG

613302   Sgt   Wop/AG   British   219 Squadron

Le Dong, of Swansea, joined 219 Squadron at Catterick on September 1 1940. He was killed on February 8 1941, with 219, aged 20.

Le Dong is buried in St Andrew's churchyard, Tangmere.

KENNETH NORMAN THOMSON LEE

72998   FO   Pilot   British   501 Squadron

Born in Birmingham, Lee joined the RAFVR on January 25 1937. His number (740004) was the fourth to be issued. He was sent to 11 E&RFTS, Perth for a two months ab initio course, after which he returned to his job, flying at weekends at 9 E&RFTS, Ansty.

In January 1939 Lee was released by his employer to spend six months with the regular RAF. He joined 111 Squadron at Northolt and in late March he was commissioned and went to 43 Squadron at Tangmere. Lee did not return to his job and on September 4 1939 he was posted to 501 Squadron at Filton.

The squadron went to France on May 10 1940. On the 12th Lee destroyed a Do 17, on the 13th a Bf 109 and on the 27th a He 111. He was then wounded and did not rejoin the squadron until July, at Middle Wallop. On August 12 Lee claimed a Ju 87 destroyed and on the 18th he was shot down by Oberleutnant Schöpfel of JG 26 over Canterbury, in Hurricane P 3059. He was admitted to hospital with leg wounds and was non-effective until October. Lee was awarded the DFC (22.10.40).

He was then posted to 52 OTU, Crosby-on-Eden. In December 1941 he went to the Middle East and served in the Western Desert with 112 Squadron, as a Flight Commander. On September 18 1942 Lee went to 260 Squadron, again as a Flight Commander. He took command of 123 Squadron at Abadan, Persia in March 1943. The squadron went to the Western Desert in May and on July 27 1943 Lee was shot down and captured on a dawn raid on Crete. He spent the duration of the war in Stalag Luft III.

Lee was released from the RAF in 1945, as a Squadron Leader.

PO (RAFVR) 29.3.39   PO 1.9.39   FO 3.9.40   FL 3.9.41

MAURICE ALEXANDER WILLIAM LEE

742796   Sgt   Pilot   British   72 Squadron, 421 Flight

Lee, of Ridgeway, Somerset, joined 72 Squadron at Croydon on September 15 1940. He claimed a He 111 destroyed on the 27th.

He was posted to 421 Flight on October 3, then forming at Hawkinge. On the 15th Lee's Spitfire, P 7444, was damaged by Bf 109s and he was wounded. He crashed attempting a forced-landing at Blackham Farm, Broadoak and was admitted to hospital.

On December 12 Lee was again damaged in combat and made a forced-landing. Later the same day the weather deteriorated and he could not return to Hawkinge and he wrecked his Spitfire trying to make an emergency landing at Lingfield.

Lee was sent out in thick morning mist on the 22nd looking for some Wellingtons that were lost. He found two and escorted them in over the Sussex coast. One crashed, killing the crew, and the other made a forced-landing. Lee's own fuel was by then exhausted and he had to glide down through dense cloud to make a belly-landing behind the downs.

On December 31 1940 Lee was killed, when he crashed near Biggin Hill attempting to land in bad weather and burned out. He was 21 years old and is buried in St Mary Cray Cemetery, Orpington, Kent.

RICHARD HUGH ANTONY LEE

33208   FO   Pilot   British   85 Squadron

Lee entered RAF College, Cranwell in September 1935 as a flight cadet, and graduated in July 1937. On June 1 1938 he joined 85 Squadron, then reforming at Debden. He went to France with the squadron at the outbreak of war.

On November 21 1939 Lee destroyed a He 111 over Boulogne, 85's first victory. He was awarded the DFC (8.3.40). On May 10 1940 he shared a Ju 86 and damaged a Ju 88 and on the 11th after shooting down two enemy aircraft he was himself shot down by flak and captured. Lee escaped and made his way back to the squadron.

On May 22 85 withdrew to Debden. Flying with 56 Squadron over Dunkirk on May 27 Lee was shot down into the sea and was picked up after an hour. He was awarded the DSO (31.5.40).

Back with 85 Squadron, Lee was last seen in pursuit of an enemy formation thirty miles off the east coast on August 18 1940. He was 23 and is remembered on the Runnymede Memorial, Panel 6. Lee is believed to have destroyed at least nine enemy aircraft.

PO 31.7.37   FO 19.5.39

ALAN FARQUHAR YOUNG LEES

81681   PO   Pilot   British   236 Squadron

Joined the RAFVR in 1938 and did his weekend flying at 12 E&RFTS, Prestwick. Lees was called up on September 1 1939 and in November went to ITW at Hastings. In January 1940 he was posted to 3 EFTS, Hamble and in March went to 14 FTS, Kinloss and later Cranfield.

In July 1940 Lees converted to Blenheims at 5 OTU, Aston Down and joined 236 Squadron at Thorney Island on August 11. He was awarded the DFC (27.10.41). On December 27 1941 he flew a Beaufighter in the Maaloy/Vaagso commando raid and shot down a He 111, his second victory. In June 1942 Lees was posted to staff duties at HQ Coastal Command.

In July he was a passenger in a Walrus, which landed on Gareloch, Scotland with its wheels down. The aircraft crashed, one crew member was killed and Lees suffered severe concussion. He was in a head-injuries hospital in Oxford for several months and did not return to operations. In 1943 and 1944 he instructed at RAF Leuchars and East Fortune.

In 1945 Lees suffered severe back pains and it was found that he had received broken vertebrae in the Walrus crash. He had an operation in December and was invalided out of the RAF in 1946, as a Flight Lieutenant. Lees died on October 27 1987.

PO 11.7.40   FO 11.7.41   FL 11.7.42

RONALD BERESFORD LEES

29257   SL   Pilot   Australian   72 Squadron

Born on April 27 1910 in Broken Hill, Sydney, Lees was educated at St Peter's College, Adelaide and joined the RAAF in the late twenties. He transferred to the RAF in March 1931 and on the 27th joined 29 Squadron at North Weald.

Lees was posted to 4 FTS, Abu Sueir on May 10 1935, as an instructor. Back in the UK, he took command of 72 Squadron at Church Fenton on December 8 1938.

Over Dunkirk on June 2 1940 Lees destroyed a Ju 87. He was posted away from 72 on July 26 1940. He was attached to the squadron on August 31 and on September 2 his Spitfire, K 9840, was severely damaged in combat south of Dungeness. He crashed on return to Hawkinge, wounded.

In October 1940 Lees became Station Commander RAF Coltishall. He was awarded the DFC (22.10.40), as an Acting Wing Commander, and a Bar (26.12.41). In October 1942 he was commanding 324 Wing as part of the Allied forces about to invade North Africa. On November 25 he shot down a SM 79. In 1943 Lees was SASO HQ 242 Group, was made a CBE (2.6.43) and in 1943/45 was on the staff at HQ Mediterranean Allied Tactical Air Force. He was made a CB (1.1.46).

Lees was ADC to the King from 1949 to 1952 and then to the Queen in 1952/53. He was knighted in 1961, KCB (10.6.61) and he retired from the RAF on February 3 1966, as an Air Marshal. Lees returned to live in Australia.

PO 18.3.31   FO 13.10.31   FL 13.10.35   SL 1.10.38
WC 1.12.40   GC 1.7.43   GC 1.7.47   AC 1.1.53
AVM 1.7.55   AM 1.1.61

PETER WILLIAM LEFEVRE

40719   **FO**   **Pilot**   **British**   **46 Squadron**

Born in 1918, Lefevre was educated at Tonbridge School and spent two years at Pembroke College, Cambridge. He joined the RAF on a short service commission in March 1938 and did his elementary flying training at 4 E&RFTS, Brough. On May 21 he was posted to 6 FTS, Netheravon, finished at Little Rissington and joined 46 Squadron at Digby in December 1938. Lefevre destroyed a He 115 floatplane on October 21 1939.

On May 9 1940 the squadron flew to Abbotsinch and later embarked in the carrier HMS 'Glorious' for Norway. Lefevre took off with the CO on May 28 to make the first exploratory landing. On June 7 he shared in damaging a He 111. When the squadron left Norway by flying its Hurricanes back on to the 'Glorious' Lefevre remained behind to destroy stores and equipment. As a consequence he was one of the very few 46 Squadron pilots to be at Digby when it reformed there on June 15 1940.

On September 3 Lefevre claimed a Ju 88 destroyed and returned to Stapleford badly damaged by a Bf 109. He was shot down in combat over Chatham on the 18th and baled out with minor injuries. His Hurricane, V 6554, is believed to have crashed at Chesnut Avenue, Walderslade. Lefevre shared a Do 17 on November 3.

On May 22 1941 46 Squadron sailed in HMS 'Argus' for the Middle East. It transferred its Hurricanes and pilots on to HMS 'Ark Royal' at Gibraltar on May 29 and on June 6 they flew off to Malta and were retained there, to become 126 Squadron on July 15 1941. Lefevre, who had been a Flight Commander with 46, carried on as one in the new squadron. On June 12 he had destroyed a Mc 200, on July 27 he attacked and damaged an Italian MTB and on August 19 and September 4 he destroyed Mc 200s. Lefevre took command of 126 Squadron on October 8 1941, was awarded the DFC (12.12.41) and was posted back to the UK in late December.

He was posted to 'X' Air Firing Squadron at 52 OTU, Aston Down in late March 1942. In early 1943 Lefevre spent a short time with 129 Squadron at Ibsley and was then posted in early April to command 616 Squadron, also at Ibsley. On April 16 the squadron was acting as top cover for Venturas attacking Brest. Lefevre was shot down by flak. Found by the French Resistance he spent many weeks hiding and moving around before crossing the border into Spain. The British Ambassador got him to Gibraltar and he flew back to England on July 13 1943 and rejoined 616 on August 11. A few days later he took command of 266 Squadron at Exeter.

On January 21 1944 Lefevre destroyed a Bf 109 and on the 23rd he shared a FW 190. The squadron was detailed to attack anti-aircraft guns at Aber-Wrach on February 6 1944. Lefevre went into a shallow dive from 1000 feet into intense fire. He was seen to leave his Typhoon as it went out of control but was too low for his parachute to open properly.

Lefevre was reported 'Missing'. He is remembered on the Runnymede Memorial, Panel 200.

APO 7.5.38   PO 7.3.39   FO 3.9.40   FL 3.9.41

RICHARD JAMES LEGG

22166   **WC**   **Pilot**   **British**   **601 Squadron**

Born on May 14 1903, Legg joined the RAF in March 1926. He trained at 5 FTS, Sealand and on July 14 1927 was posted to the School of Army Co-operation at Old Sarum. He moved to the staff of RAF College, Cranwell on December 20 1927 and was appointed Flying Instructor with 604 Squadron, AuxAF at Hendon on May 19 1930.

Legg went to 603 Squadron, AuxAF on September 9 1931, as Flying Instructor and Adjutant. He was posted to Iraq on February 26 1934 to join 30 Squadron at Mosul. Back in the UK, he went on to the staff at CFS, Upavon on August 6 1936 and on April 18 1937 was posted to 8 FTS, Montrose.

In the Battle of Britain Legg must have flown one operational sortie with 601 Squadron to qualify for the clasp, probably on October 16 1940. He was not on the strength of the squadron and his status at that time is not known. He retired from the RAF on November 4 1953, as a Group Captain, retaining the rank of Air Commodore. He died in 1959.

PO 13.3.26   FO 13.9.27   FL 30.6.31   SL 1.4.37
WC 1.3.40   GC 1.3.42   GC 1.10.46

PERCIVAL GRAHAM LEGGETT

86329   **PO**   **Pilot**   **British**   **615, 245 and 46 Squadrons**

Leggett was born on February 24 1921. He joined 615 Squadron at Prestwick in early September 1940, moved to 245 Squadron at Aldergrove on the 28th and then to 46 Squadron at Stapleford on October 18.

He claimed a Fiat BR 20 probably destroyed and shared in the destruction of another on November 11.

In late June 1941 Leggett joined 249 Squadron in Malta. He claimed a Mc 200 destroyed on July 17. He was shot down by enemy fighters on December 21 1941, baled out and was admitted to hospital with slight abrasions.

Leggett retired from the RAF on May 23 1958, as a Squadron Leader.

PO 31.8.40   FO 31.8.41   FL 1.12.42   FL 1.9.45
SL 1.7.49

ARTHUR CHARLES LEIGH

111975   **Sgt**   **Pilot**   **British**   **64 and 72 Squadrons**

The son of a regular soldier, Leigh was born in London in 1920. He was working as an assistant in a clothing shop in Cambridge, when he joined the RAFVR in June 1939. He did his weekend flying at 22 E&RFTS, Cambridge.

Called up at the outbreak of war, Leigh went to No 1 ITW, Cambridge. In January 1940 he returned to Cambridge to complete his ab initio training and in April was posted to 15 FTS, Middle Wallop and finished on Masters and Harvards at Chipping Norton.

Leigh was posted to 7 OTU, Hawarden on August 31 1940 and after converting to Spitfires he joined 64 Squadron at Leconfield. He moved to 72 Squadron at Biggin Hill on October 11 and then to 611 Squadron at Acklington on November 8 1940.

Awarded the DFM (9.9.41), Leigh had then completed fifty sweeps, had destroyed two Bf 109s, probably destroyed another four and shared in the destruction of a Do 17. He was commissioned in early October and on the 21st posted to CFS, Upavon, for an instructor's course. Leigh went to 8 FTS, Montrose in December 1941, to instruct on Masters. He moved to 17 (P) AFU, Watton in February 1942 and then to 56 OTU, Tealing in February 1943.

Leigh was posted to Gibraltar in April 1943, from where he ferried Hurricanes to Cairo. In early August he returned to the UK and joined 56 Squadron at Manston on the 6th. He was shot down

AC Leigh (continued)

on his first sweep by flak, near Calais. Leigh baled out into the Channel and was picked up by an ASR launch. In late 1943 he was posted to 129 Squadron at Hornchurch, awarded the DFC (19.9.44) and on completing his second tour in December Leigh went on a gunnery course to Catfoss and afterwards became an instructor.

In December 1945 Leigh was released from the RAF. He later started a successful builders/hardware business in Norwich.

PO 10.11.41   FO 1.10.42   FL 10.11.43

RUPERT HENRY ARCHIBALD LEIGH

26237   SL   Pilot   British   66 Squadron

Born on May 14 1912, Leigh was educated at Cheltenham College. He entered RAF College, Cranwell in January 1930, as a flight cadet. On graduation in December 1931 he was posted to 57 Squadron at Netheravon. On September 4 1932 Leigh went to RAF Gosport, under instruction, and on May 8 1933 he joined 810 (Fleet Torpedo-Bomber) Squadron, based at Gosport and on HMS 'Courageous'.

Leigh went as an instructor to No 1 FTS, Leuchars on July 13 1936 and joined the staff at CFS, Upavon on August 16 1937. He was a Flight Commander there in October 1939 and tested Bader on the 18th, when he was trying to get back on flying duties.

In April 1940 Leigh was given command of 66 Squadron at Duxford. He claimed a He 111 destroyed on September 9 and shared in the destruction of an enemy aircraft on the 11th. Leigh was posted to HQ 12 Group on October 18 1940, as Wing Commander Training. He returned to operations in May 1941, taking command of 23 Squadron at Ford. He was posted away in December.

Leigh retired from the RAF on December 7 1954, as a Group Captain, retaining the rank of Air Commodore. During the war years he received five Mentions in Despatches.

PO 19.12.31   FO 19.6.33   FL 16.9.36   SL 1.2.39
WC 1.3.41   GC 1.7.44   GC 1.1.50

O G LEJEUNE

No unknown   Sgt   Pilot   Belgian   235 Squadron

Joined 235 Squadron on August 5 1940. Lejeune was posted away at the end of October to join the recently-reformed 272 Squadron, on anti-shipping operations.

In mid-1941 the squadron was in Egypt and flew across to operate from Malta on July 19. It flew out to Malta again on September 24 1941 and on the way Lejeune and two other Belgian pilots saw and damaged two Ju 52 transports over the Gulf of Bomba.

Commissioned in May 1942, Lejeune died on April 10 1947.

PO 25.5.42

JOHN DESMOND LENAHAN

41302   PO   Pilot   British   607 Squadron

Lenahan, of Hayes, Kent, joined the RAF on a short service commission in August 1938. He was posted to 607 Squadron at Usworth on August 12 1940.

Flying from Tangmere on September 9 Lenahan was killed when he crashed at Mount Ephraim, Cranbrook following a combat over Mayfield, in Hurricane P 3117. He was 20 years old and is buried in Cranbrook Cemetery, Kent.

APO 20.10.38   PO 20.4.40

MAURICE EQUITY LENG

67035   Sgt   Pilot   British   73 Squadron

Joined the RAFVR in September 1938. Leng did his weekend flying at 21 E&RFTS, Stapleford Tawney. Called to full-time service after the outbreak of war, he was posted to 12 FTS, Grantham in October 1939 to complete his training.

In January 1940 Leng went to 4 BGS, West Freugh, as a staff pilot. He joined 4 Continental Ferry Unit at Cardiff in May and later in the month was posted to 73 Squadron in France. The squadron was withdrawn to Church Fenton in mid-June 1940.

On August 25 Leng was shot down by British anti-aircraft defences whilst on a night patrol and baled out, unhurt. His Hurricane, P 3758, crashed west of Beverley. On September 23 he was shot down by Bf 109s over Sheppey and baled out. He was injured in a heavy landing and admitted to Chatham Hospital. His Hurricane, P 8812, crashed at Ludgate, Lynstead, near Rodmersham.

73 Squadron was posted to the Middle East in November. It embarked on HMS 'Furious' on the 10th and flew off to Takoradi on the 29th. It then flew in easy stages to Heliopolis, via Lagos, Accra, Kano, Maidugari, Khartoum, Wadi Halfa and Abu Sueir. The pilots were attached to 274 Squadron in the Western Desert in December. The squadron began to operate on its own account in early January 1941.

Leng was posted back to Takoradi on April 9 1941, to the Ferry Pool. He was commissioned later in the month and on October 6 1941 went to 71 OTU, Gordon's Tree, Sudan, as an instructor. Two weeks later he joined 335 Squadron, a Greek fighter unit at Aqir, Palestine. Leng went to the RHAF Training Flight, also at Aqir on January 17 1942. He returned to Egypt in July 1942 and was posted to 2 PRU, Heliopolis on August 2.

Leng was shot down on September 30 1942 and captured. He was held in captivity at Sagan in Germany from October 20 1942 until May 2 1945. He was released from the RAF in March 1946 and joined the RAFVR in September 1947. Leng retired in September 1962, as a Flight Lieutenant.

PO 26.4.41   FO 26.4.42   FL 26.4.43   FO (RAFVR) 30.9.47

PAUL LEONARD LENNARD

Midshipman (FAA)   Pilot   British   501 Squadron

Lennard, of Eltham, joined 501 Squadron at Croydon on July 8 1940. He was posted away on July 20 and embarked on HMS 'Ark Royal' on October 22, with 808 Squadron.

In April 1941 Lennard was at Worthy Down. He was killed on March 26 1942, aged 20, serving with HMS 'Kestrel'. He was cremated at West Norwood Crematorium, Lambeth, London.

Midshipman 20.1.39   Actg Sub-Lt 21.12.40

EDWIN CLAUDE LENTON

41187   FO   Pilot   British   56 Squadron

Joined the RAF on a short service commission in July 1938. Lenton was posted to 56 Squadron at North Weald on August 5 1940 and left the squadron on September 7.

Lenton was released from the RAF in 1947, as a Squadron Leader.

APO 17.9.38   PO 25.7.39   FO 3.9.40   FL 3.9.41
SL 1.7.45

STANLEY PAUL le ROUGETEL

70392   FL   Pilot   British   600 Squadron

Le Rougetel was born on May 18 1912. He was commissioned in the RAFO in May 1937 and learned to fly in his year's term of service. He was recalled to full-time service on August 26 1939 and posted to 600 Squadron at Northolt.

During night operations on August 9 1940 le Rougetel's Blenheim, L 8679, had engine failure and came under fire from British anti-aircraft defences. He baled out and was rescued by the Margate lifeboat. His gunner, Sergeant EC Smith, baled out and swam ashore at Westgate.

Le Rougetel was released from the RAF in 1946 and rejoined in 1947. He retired on February 11 1958, as a Squadron Leader, retaining the rank of Wing Commander.

APO (RAFO) 9.5.37   PO (RAFO) 8.3.38   PO 26.8.39
FO 8.9.39   FL 8.9.40   SL 1.12.41   SL 1.8.47

DANIEL ALBERT RAYMOND GEORGES le ROY du VIVIER

82159   PO   Pilot   Belgian   43 Squadron

Le Roy du Vivier was born on January 13 1915 at Amersfoort. He did his military service in the Guides and in 1937 entered l'Aéronautique Militaire, carrying out his flying training at Wevelghem, where he gained his wings on March 15 1938.

He was posted to Tirlemont on November 29 1939, as a Sergeant-Pilot. Commissioned on March 1 1940, le Roy du Vivier joined 4/IIe Groupe de Chasse at Nivelles, flying Fiat CR 42s and Fairey Fireflies. On May 11 he was shot down in a Firefly, baled out and was taken prisoner by the Belgians, mistaken for a German paratrooper.

On May 15 le Roy du Vivier's unit was posted to France. On June 21 the French signed an Armistice with the Germans and the Belgians were told to stay put. With other pilots le Roy du Vivier reached Port Vendres, where with the help of a British destroyer and the support of the Belgian Embassy in London they caught a passing convoy and embarked on the SS 'Apapa' on the 24th. They arrived in Liverpool on July 7.

Le Roy du Vivier was posted as a deserter by the French. He was commissioned in the RAF, went to 5 OTU, Aston Down to convert to Hurricanes and then joined 43 Squadron at Tangmere on August 4. He claimed a Ju 87 destroyed on August 16, baled out on September 2 following a combat with Bf 109s and was admitted to the casualty clearing station at Benenden, suffering from leg wounds. His Hurricane, P 3903, crashed at Bell Corner, near Old Romney.

On October 22 le Roy du Vivier returned to the squadron. He was made a Flight Commander on April 14 1941. He shared Ju 88s on May 6 and 7 and destroyed a Ju 88 on May 25. He was awarded the C de G (Belg)(21.7.41). Le Roy du Vivier took command of 43 Squadron on January 15 1942 and was awarded the DFC (30.1.42). He destroyed a Ju 88 on April 25, was awarded a Bar to the DFC (15.9.42) and on September 22 was posted to HQ 13 Group on staff duties.

Le Roy du Vivier went to the Middle East in April 1943 and was posted to lead 324 Wing in Italy on July 19. He went to RAF Staff College at Haifa for a course and rejoined the Wing on December 24. He returned to England in July 1944 and took command of 53 OTU on August 14.

In April 1946 le Roy du Vivier took command of 160 Belgian Wing in Germany. He left the Air Force on September 16 1946 and joined Sabena Airlines, as a pilot. He was killed in a road accident in the USA on September 2 1981.

PO 20.7.40   FO 20.12.40   FL 14.4.41

FREDERICK THOMAS LERWAY

142495   Sgt   Wop/AG   British   236 Squadron

Joined the RAFVR in May 1939. Lerway was called up at the outbreak of war. He joined 236 Squadron on September 3 1940 and stayed with the squadron until September 1941, when he was posted to OTU, as an instructor.

Commissioned in January 1943, Lerway went to 53 Squadron, Coastal Command in April. He moved to 279 Squadron in May 1943, an ASR unit with Hudsons. In January 1944 Lerway was posted to 281, another ASR unit, with Warwicks.

He went to Air Ministry in September 1945, dealing with the demobilisation of RAF personnel. Lerway was released from the RAF in January 1946, as a Flight Lieutenant. He emigrated to Canada in 1951.

PO 15.1.43   FO 15.7.43   FL 15.1.45

GEORGE MENNIE LESLIE

1002658   Sgt   Wop/AG   British   219 Squadron

Leslie, of Aberdeen, joined 219 Squadron at Catterick on August 2 1940. He was killed on December 17 1940, when the aircraft he was in crashed on its landing approach.

Leslie was 29. He is buried in Saffron Walden Cemetery, Essex.

STEPHEN AUSTIN LEVENSON

745292   Sgt   Pilot   British   611 Squadron

Levenson, of Taynuilt, was with 611 Squadron at Digby in early July 1940.

He claimed a Ju 88 destroyed on September 11. On that day Levenson's Spitfire, P 7321, was severely damaged by return fire from a He 111 engaged over Croydon. He crashed on a dead engine at Pendall Court, Bletchingley, unhurt. On the 15th he claimed a Do 17 destroyed.

Levenson was killed on September 17 1942, as a Warrant Officer with 214 Squadron, operating in Stirlings from Stradishall. He is buried in Heverlee War Cemetery, Belgium.

ALBERT GERALD LEWIS

41303   PO   Pilot   South African   85 and 249 Sqdns

Born in Kimberley in 1918, Lewis was educated at the High School there. He joined the RAF on a short service commission in August 1938.

Lewis was with 616 Squadron in 1939 and went to 504 Squadron at Debden in March 1940. He joined 85 Squadron in France in early April. On May 19 he shot down five enemy aircraft before he was himself shot down over Lille. He was awarded the DFC (25.6.40).

On August 18 1940 Lewis probably destroyed a Bf 110, on the 31st a Bf 109, on September 15 a He 111, on the 18th a Bf 109 and on the 27th three Bf 109s, two Bf 110s and a Ju 88. He was shot down during a combat over Faversham on September 28, baled out, badly burned, and was admitted to Faversham Cottage Hospital. His Hurricane, V 6617, crashed at Blackett's Farm, Tonge. He was awarded a Bar to the DFC (22.10.40).

In May 1941 Lewis was posted to 52 OTU, Debden and became CO of 'C' Squadron there. He took command of 261 Squadron at China Bay, Ceylon in March 1942. Lewis led the squadron against a Japanese carrier-based aircraft attack on Trincomalee on April 9 1942. He was wounded and did not return to the squadron.

Lewis returned to the UK in June 1942. He was released from the RAF in 1946, as a Squadron Leader. His portrait was done by Eric Kennington.

APO 29.10.38   PO 29.11.38   FO 29.11.40   FL 29.11.41

CHARLES SYDNEY LEWIS

182072   Sgt   Air Gunner   British   600 Squadron

With 600 Squadron in early July 1940. Lewis was commissioned in October 1944 in the Administrative Branch. He was released from the RAF in 1945, as a Flying Officer. He died in 1954.

PO 19.10.44   FO 19.4.45

RAYMOND GRANT LEWIS

41852   **FO**   **Pilot**   **Canadian**   **1 Squadron**

Lewis joined the RAF on a short service commission in February 1939. He was posted to No 1 Squadron at Wittering on October 21 1940. On the 30th he shared in the destruction of a Ju 88. He went on No 1's first offensive operation, on January 1 1941. With two other pilots he strafed German installations between Calais and Boulogne.

On February 5 1941 Lewis' engine was set on fire in an attack by Bf 109s and he baled out into the Channel. He was not seen again and is remembered on the Runnymede Memorial, Panel 30.

APO 1.4.39   PO 23.10.39   FO 23.10.40

WILLIAM GEORGE LEWIS

967100   **Sgt**   **Air Gunner**   **British**   **25 Squadron**

Joined 25 Squadron at North Weald at the end of September 1940. Lewis was killed on July 14 1941, as a Flight Sergeant with 214 Squadron, operating in Wellingtons from Stradishall. He is buried in Mynydd Bach Congregational Chapelyard, Llwchwr.

REGINALD HARRY LEYLAND

52003   **Sgt**   **Radar Operator**   **British**   **FIU**

Leyland was with the FIU in early July 1940. On the night of July 22/23 he was a member of the crew of an AI-equipped Blenheim, which shot down a Do 17 of 2/KG3 . It crashed into the sea off the Sussex coast and its crew of four were rescued, wounded, from the sea.

Commissioned in March 1943, Leyland was released from the RAF in 1946, as a Flying Officer.

PO 21.3.43   FO 21.9.43

P LILLE

No unknown   **Sgt**   **Air Gunner**   **British**   **264 Squadron**

No service details traced.

ROBERT LILLEY

801556   **Sgt**   **Air Gunner**   **British**   **29 Squadron**

Lilley was with 29 Squadron at Digby in early July 1940. With the advent of the Beaufighter he retrained as a Radio Observer.

In 1943 Lilley was with 89 Squadron in the Middle East and was awarded the DFC (3.9.43), as a Warrant Officer. He was killed on April 28 1944, serving with 141 Squadron, operating in Mosquitos from West Raynham. Lilley is buried in Heverlee War Cemetery, Belgium.

ERIC RONALD LIMPENNY

189635   **Sgt**   **Pilot**   **British**   **64 Squadron**

Joined 64 Squadron at Leconfield at the end of September 1940. Commissioned in January 1945, Limpenny was released from the RAF in 1946, as a Flying Officer.

PO 5.1.45   FO 5.7.45

ALEC IAN LINDSAY

83982   **PO**   **Pilot**   **British**   **72 Squadron**

Lindsay was educated at King's School, Bruton, Somerset. He was a member of the RAFVR and did his weekend flying at 6 E&RFTS, Sywell.

Called to full-time service at the outbreak of war, Lindsay joined 72 Squadron at Croydon on September 11 1940. In early 1941 he was posted to 58 OTU, Grangemouth, as an instructor. Lindsay went to MSFU, Speke in July.

He joined 185 Squadron in Malta in August 1942 and was killed in action on October 23, as a Flight Lieutenant. Lindsay is buried in the Naval Cemetery, Capuccini, Malta.

PO 21.7.40   FO 21.7.41   FL 21.7.42

ARTHUR PETER LINES

39742   **FO**   **Pilot**   **British**   **17 Squadron**

Lines joined the RAF on a short service commission in March 1937 and did his intermediate and advanced training at 2 FTS, Brize Norton.

He joined 17 Squadron at Debden on July 9 1940 and was posted away on August 21. Lines was released from the RAF in 1947, as a Flight Lieutenant.

APO 18.5.37   PO 15.3.38   FO 15.12.39   FL 15.12.40
FL (RAFRO) 1.9.45

JOHN GRANVILLE LINGARD

44774   **PO**   **Pilot**   **British**   **25 and 219 Squadrons**

Born on September 1 1914, Lingard was a pre-war airman pilot. He was posted to 25 Squadron in 1937. Commissioned in October 1940, he joined 219 Squadron at Redhill on October 24.

In early 1942 Lingard was with 272 Squadron in the Western Desert and on May 11 he shared in destroying a He 111. He was a Flight Commander with 143 Squadron in 1944 and was awarded the DFC (25.7.44) for attacks on shipping.

Lingard retired from the RAF on March 31 1958, as a Wing Commander.

PO 4.10.40   FO 24.12.40   FL 24.12.41   SL 7.11.44
SL 15.4.46   WC 1.7.47

ANTHONY STUART LINNEY

41717   **FO**   **Pilot**   **British**   **229 Squadron**

Linney joined the RAF on a short service commission in January 1939. He was posted to 229 Squadron on October 6 1939, when it reformed at Digby.

Over Dunkirk on May 29 1940 Linney was shot down and baled out, returning safely to the squadron. He was posted away in October and in July 1941 was with the MSFU at Speke. After completing his catapult training Linney was posted to Canada as a back-up pilot, to replace any pilot fired off on a voyage from the UK and killed or injured. He remained at Dartmouth, Nova Scotia for nine months i/c MSFU Pool.

Linney was made an OBE (2.6.43) and was released from the RAF in 1945, as a Wing Commander. He died in 1983.

APO 4.3.39   PO 3.10.39   FO 3.10.40   FL 3.10.41
SL 4.10.43

ALFRED JOHN LIPSCOMBE

759213   **Sgt**   **Wop/AG**   **British**   **600 Squadron**

Lipscombe, of Edgware, joined 600 Squadron at Catterick on October 8 1940. He retrained as a radar operator and teamed up with Flying Officer RS Woodward.

In late April 1941 they destroyed a Ju 88 near Shepton Mallet. On the night of May 9/10 their aircraft was set on fire a long way out to sea, in an attack by another night fighter, probably of 604 Squadron. Woodward managed to fly it back over land and then he and Lipscombe baled out safely. On July 9 they shot down a He 111 near Abergavenny.

They were flying on September 20 1941, when their Beaufighter went into a spin. Woodward ordered Lipscombe to bale out. He did so and was killed. Woodward got away with a broken leg.

Lipscombe was 22. He is buried in Hendon Cemetery.

ROBERT CHARLES FRANKLIN LISTER

33118   **SL**   **Pilot**   **British**   **41 and 92 Squadrons**

Born on August 23 1913, Lister was at Cheltenham College from 1927 to 1932. He entered RAF College, Cranwell in September 1932 as a flight cadet. He won the Graves Memorial Prize in 1934 and after graduating joined 13 (Army Co-operation) Squadron at Netheravon on July 28 1934.

Lister was posted to 20 (Army Co-operation) Squadron at Peshawar on February 28 1935. In 1937 he was involved in close support with Army columns operating in the mountains of Waziristan, against tribesmen led by the Fakir of Ipi. Lister was awarded the DFC (16.8.38) for gallant and distinguished services in operations in Waziristan from September 16 to December 15 1937.

Back in the UK Lister was posted to CFS, Upavon for an instructor's course, after which he went to 10 FTS, Tern Hill. On January 2 1939 he was appointed Adjutant of 614 Squadron, AuxAF at Cardiff. In late 1939 Lister crashed during take-off with engine failure and fractured his spine. He was in plaster for nine months and had a temporary job at Air Ministry.

Lister was cleared for flying duties in August 1940 and asked for fighters. He was posted to 7 OTU, Hawarden, converted to Spitfires and then took temporary command of 41 Squadron at Hornchurch on September 8. He was shot down on the 14th whilst flying at the rear of a squadron formation, by a Bf 109 out of the evening sun, whom no one spotted. Lister baled out, slightly wounded in the arm. On September 22 he was attached to 92 Squadron at Biggin Hill, as a supernumerary. Shortly after Lister's arrival the CO was burned and he took command.

On September 24 92 was scrambled to be part of a 'Big Wing' of three squadrons. Time was wasted and it met a formation of nine Ju 88s with a one hundred plus Bf 109 escort, head-on and slightly below. After a general break Lister found himself alone and being circled by some nine Bf 109s. He was eventually hit by a cannon shell in the bottom of the cockpit and wounded in both legs. He went into a spin, managed to get back to Biggin Hill but had only one flap working, causing him to go out of control into a skidding diving turn. Lister regained control, made a landing without flaps and stopped ten yards short of a wood at the end of the airfield.

After long hospital treatment Lister was declared medically unfit for flying duties in June 1941 and posted to Operations Room duties, as Controller at Biggin Hill. In April 1942 he was SASO at HQ 219 Group at Alexandria and in October 1943 became CO 209 Group at Haifa. From September 1944 until July 1945 Lister was on the staff at Air HQ Eastern Mediterranean, after which he commanded RAF Amman, Jordan until March 1946, when he was posted back to the UK.

Lister retired from the RAF on October 31 1954, as a Wing Commander, retaining the rank of Group Captain.

PO 28.7.34   FO 28.1.36   FL 28.1.38   SL 1.1.40
WC 1.12.41   WC 1.10.46

PETER LITCHFIELD

76461   PO   Pilot   British   610 Squadron

With 610 Squadron at Digby in early July 1940. On the 14th Litchfield severely damaged a Bf 109 in an action off Dover. The pilot baled out, wounded, and the aircraft crashed near Boulogne.

On July 18 1940 Litchfield was shot down over the Channel north of Calais by Hauptmann Tietzen of II/JG 51, in Spitfire P 9452. He was reported 'Missing', aged 25. He is remembered on the Runnymede Memorial, Panel 9.

PO 18.11.39

FREDERICK WILLIAM RONALD LITSON

145432   Sgt   Air Gunner   British   141 Squadron

Litson was with 141 Squadron in early July 1940. Commissioned in May 1943, he was released from the RAF in 1946, as a Flight Lieutenant. He later rejoined.

PO 4.5.43   FO 4.11.43   FL 4.5.45   FL (RAFRO) 23.12.46

ARTHUR GUTHRIE LITTLE

78546   PO   Air Gunner   British   235 Squadron

Joined 235 Squadron in May 1940. Little was released from the RAF in 1945, as a Flight Lieutenant.

APO 15.3.40   PO 4.5.40   FO 4.5.41   FL 4.5.42

BERNARD WILLIAMSON LITTLE

90326   FL   Pilot   British   609 Squadron

Little joined 609 Squadron, AuxAF in 1937. He was then a solicitor in Wakefield. He was called to full-time service with the squadron on August 24 1939.

He damaged a Ju 87 on July 11 1940. In early August Little was out of action with appendicitis and was then posted away to 7 OTU, Hawarden, as an instructor. At some time later he was in hospital for six months with frozen joints.

Little was released from the RAF in 1945, as a Squadron Leader, and was made an OBE (1.1.46). He died in 1986.

PO (AuxAF) 12.7 37   FO 24.8.39   FL 3.9.40   SL 1.12.41

JAMES HAYWARD LITTLE

90125   FL   Pilot   British   219 Squadron

Educated at Eton, Little joined 601 Squadron, AuxAF in 1934. He transferred to 611 Squadron, AuxAF on September 25 1936.

Little was called to full-time service with the squadron at the outbreak of war. He was given command of 219 Squadron at Catterick in May 1940 and led it until February 1941, when he was posted away, tour-expired, and awarded the DFC (18.3.41), being then credited with a Do 17 destroyed.

In December 1942 Little took command of 418 Squadron, operating in Bostons from Bradwell Bay. He was killed on June 12 1943, as a Wing Commander, aged 31. He is buried in Grange Cemetery, Hoylake.

PO (AuxAF) 25.7.34   FO (AuxAF) 15.3.36   FL 3.9.39
SL 1.12.40   WC 1.3.42

RONALD LITTLE

754893   Sgt   Pilot   British   238 Squadron

Little, of Armathwaite, Cumberland, was with 238 Squadron at Middle Wallop in early July 1940.

On August 13 he was shot down in combat over Portland and crashed at Bredy Farm, Burton Bradstock, unhurt. Little was shot down into the sea during combat with Bf 109s over the Isle of Wight on September 28, in Hurricane N 2400. He was reported 'Missing', aged 22, and is remembered on the Runnymede Memorial, Panel 16.

THOMAS BURGESS LITTLE

C 1117   FO   Pilot   Canadian   1 (RCAF) Squadron

Born in Montreal on September 9 1917, Little joined the RCAF on August 16 1939. He was with No 1 (RCAF) Squadron, when it arrived in the UK on June 20 1940.

Little was shot down on September 11, during an attack on He 111s over Tunbridge Wells. He baled out, wounded in the leg and with burns to face and side of body, landed at Rotherfield and was admitted to the Kent and Sussex Hospital, Tunbridge Wells. His Hurricane, P 3534, crashed at Lakestreet Manor, Mayfield.

On August 27 1941 Little was reported 'Missing', as a Flight Lieutenant with 402 Squadron, aged 24. He is remembered on the Runnymede Memorial, Panel 59.

ARTHUR JOHN ALEXANDER LLEWELLIN

39998   FO   Pilot   British   29 Squadron

Llewellin, of Woodford Wells, joined the RAF on a short service commission in June 1937. He was posted to 10 FTS, Tern Hill on August 21 and joined 19 Squadron at Duxford on November 7 1938.

AJA Llewellin (continued)

He was with 29 Squadron at Digby in early July 1940.

In October 1941 Llewellin was given command of 232 Squadron and in November the squadron left the UK for Singapore, arriving on January 13 1942. He left the squadron for other duties and was killed on February 7 1942, when he struck a wireless mast taking off from Kallang. Llewellin is remembered on the Singapore Memorial, Column 41.

APO 9.8.37   PO 24.5.38   FO 24.3.40   FL 24.3.41

REGINALD THOMAS LLEWELLYN

47380   Sgt   Pilot   British   213 Squadron

Born in Bristol on March 25 1914, Llewellyn enlisted in the RAF on January 13 1930 as an aircraft apprentice at Halton. He served in Iraq from 1934 to 1937 and with 27 Squadron in India in 1938. Llewellyn returned to the UK in late 1938 for pilot training. As a Sergeant-Pilot he joined 263 Squadron when it was reformed at Filton on October 2 1939.

Llewellyn was posted to 41 Squadron at Catterick in January 1940 and moved to 213 Squadron at Wittering in March. Over Dunkirk on May 29 he destroyed a Bf 109, probably another and probably a He 111.

On August 11 Llewellyn claimed a Bf 109 destroyed, on the 13th a Ju 88, on the 15th three Bf 110s, on the 19th and 20th Ju 88s, on the 25th a Bf 110 and a shared Bf 109 and on September 11 two Bf 110s. Llewellyn was shot down in combat with Bf 110s over Hawkhurst on the 15th. He baled out, severely wounded in the right arm and was admitted to the casualty clearing station at Benenden. He was awarded the DFM (22.10.40), credited with twelve enemy aircraft destroyed.

Commissioned in November 1941, Llewellyn did not fly operationally again. In 1943 he was a Specialist Weapons Officer. He joined 74 Squadron at Colerne in 1945, as a Flight Commander and took command in September.

In January 1946 Llewellyn was posted to Palestine, as OC 208 Squadron. He took command of 87 Squadron at Treviso, Italy in August 1946. He held a series of staff appointments and commands prior to retiring from the RAF on March 24 1957, as a Flight Lieutenant.

PO 11.11.41   FO 1.10.42   FL 11.11.43   FL 11.5.45

———— LLOYD

No unknown   Sgt   Aircrew   British   29 Squadron

No service details traced.

DAVID EDWARD LLOYD

115061   Sgt   Pilot   British   19 and 64 Squadrons

Lloyd, of Wanstead, was with 19 Squadron at Fowlmere in mid-August 1940. He was posted to 64 Squadron at Leconfield on August 28.

He shared in the destruction of a Ju 88 on September 18. Lloyd went to 92 Squadron at Biggin Hill in November and on December 1 he damaged a Bf 109.

Commissioned in January 1942, Lloyd was killed on March 17, aged 22. The unit he was serving with is not known. He is buried in St Mary's churchyard, Wanstead, Essex.

PO 13.1.42

JOHN PHILLIP LLOYD

83983   PO   Pilot   British   64 and 72 Squadrons

Lloyd was with 64 Squadron in early August 1940 and claimed a Bf 109 destroyed on the 14th. He was posted to 72 Squadron at Croydon on September 11. His Spitfire, P 9368, was seriously damaged in combat with Bf 109s on the 18th and Lloyd made a forced-landing at Martin Mill, Dover, seriously wounded.

Awarded the AFC (1.1.43), Lloyd was released from the RAF in 1945, as a Squadron Leader. He died in 1971.

PO 21.7.40   FO 21.7.41   FL 21.7.42

PHILIP DAVID LLOYD

745794   Sgt   Pilot.   British   41 Squadron

Born in Loughton, Essex, Lloyd worked for the Chigwell Urban District Council. He joined the RAFVR in September 1938 and did his weekend flying at 21 E&RFTS, Stapleford Tawney.

Called to full-time service at the outbreak of war, Lloyd completed his training and joined 41 Squadron at Catterick in early September 1940. Lloyd was shot down and killed in a surprise attack by Hauptmann Fözö of 4/JG 51 on October 15. His Spitfire, X 4178, crashed into the Channel. His body was washed ashore near Kings Hall, Herne Bay twelve days later.

Lloyd was 23. He is buried in the Holy Innocents' churchyard, High Beach, Essex.

PETER WILLIAM LOCHNAN

C 997   FO   Pilot   Canadian   1 (RCAF) Squadron

Lochnan, of Ottawa, was born there on August 3 1913. He joined the RCAF on June 5 1939 and went to the UK with an Army Co-operation Reserve Unit. He was posted to No 1 (RCAF) Squadron on August 30 1940.

Following an engagement with He 111s over Tunbridge Wells on September 11 Lochnan crashed near Romney and his Hurricane, V 6670, burned out. He was unhurt. On the 15th he claimed a He 111 destroyed, on the 27th he shared a Bf 110 and on October 7 he claimed a Bf 109.

Lochnan was killed in a flying accident on May 21 1941, as a Flying Officer with 400 Squadron, aged 27. He is buried in Brookwood Military Cemetery, Woking.

ERIC STANLEY LOCK

81642   PO   Pilot   British   41 Squadron

Born at Bayston Hill, Shrewsbury in 1920, Lock was educated at Prestfelde School and went into the family farming and quarrying business. He joined the RAFVR in 1939 and was called up at the beginning of the war.

Lock joined 41 Squadron at Hornchurch in early August 1940. On August 15 he claimed a Bf 110 destroyed, on September 5 two Bf 109s and two He 111s, on the 6th a Ju 88, on the 9th two Bf 109s, on the 11th a Ju 88 and a Bf 110, on the 14th two Bf 109s, on the 15th a Bf 109 and a shared Do 17, on the 18th a Bf 109, on the 20th a Bf 109 and a Hs 126, on October 5, 9, 11 and 20 Bf 109s and on November 17 two Bf 109s. In this last combat Lock was jumped by a Bf 109 and wounded in the right arm and both legs. He managed to crash-land on Martlesham Heath. Unable to move he sat in the cockpit for two hours before being found by two soldiers, who carried him for two miles on a makeshift stretcher, made of rifles and a greatcoat.

Lock was awarded the DFC (1.10.40) and Bar (22.10.40) and the DSO (17.12.40). He was in hospital until May 1941 and had fifteen operations for removal of splinters. In June he went on a flying refresher course and in early July was posted to 611 Squadron at Hornchurch, as a Flight Commander.

He claimed Bf 109s destroyed on July 6 and 8. On a sweep over France on August 3 1941 Lock saw some German soldiers on a road near Calais. He dived to attack them and was not seen again.

Lock is remembered on the Runnymede Memorial, Panel 29. His portrait was drawn by Cuthbert Orde in July 1941.

PO 18.6.40   FO 18.6.41

JAMES LOCKHART

74708   FO   Pilot   British   85 and 213 Squadrons

Lockhart, of London, was with 85 Squadron at Martlesham Heath in early July 1940 and moved to 213 Squadron at Tangmere on September 16. He commanded 213 from November 1941 to January 1942.

Lockhart was killed on April 5 1942, as a Flight Lieutenant with 258 Squadron, aged 26. He is buried in Kanatte Cemetery, Colombo, Sri Lanka.

PO 8.11.39   FO 3.10.40   FL 3.10.41

ERIC EDWARD LOCKTON

740005   Sgt   Pilot   British   236 Squadron

Lockton, of Ashby-de-la-Zouche, joined the RAFVR in March 1937. He was posted to 236 Squadron on July 3 1940. Whilst flying on an escort mission on July 20 he was shot down by Hauptmann Neumann of JG 27 and crashed into the Channel off Cherbourg, in Blenheim L 1300. Both he and his gunner, Sergeant H Corcoran, were reported 'Missing'.

Lockton was 22 and is remembered on the Runnymede Memorial, Panel 16.

JOSEPH CHARLES LOCKWOOD

754820   Sgt   Pilot   British   54 Squadron

Lockwood, of Purley, Surrey, joined 54 Squadron at Hornchurch on August 22 1940. He was killed on March 3 1941, still with 54, aged 22. He is buried in Bandon Hill Cemetery, Beddington, Surrey.

KEITH TEMPLE LOFTS

90483   FO   Pilot   British   615 and 249 Squadrons

Born on February 8 1918, Lofts was at Haileybury College from 1932 to 1935. He joined 615 Squadron, AuxAF in 1938 and was called to full-time service on August 24 1939.

Lofts flew from Croydon to Merville with the squadron on November 15 and is believed to have destroyed three enemy aircraft whilst in France. The squadron was withdrawn to Kenley on May 21st 1940 and was operational again a month later. On a patrol over France on June 22 Lofts damaged a Ju 52.

On August 14 1940 he claimed a Ju 87 destroyed, on the 15th shared a Bf 109, on the 16th destroyed a He 111, on the 20th two Bf 109s and on the 24th a probable Bf 109. Lofts was posted to 249 Squadron at North Weald on September 10. He crash-landed at West Malling on the 15th, when his Hurricane was severely damaged by a Bf 109 following the destruction of a He 111 south-east of London. He claimed a Bf 110 destroyed on the 27th.

Lofts was hit by return fire from a Do 215 engaged over Kent on October 16. He made a forced-landing at Rolvenden, near Tenterden, in Hurricane V 6878. His aircraft was damaged in a bombing attack on October 29, as he was taking off from North Weald. He was awarded the DFC (22.10.40).

In February 1941 Lofts was posted to 52 OTU, Debden, as an instructor, and left there on July 30. He was posted to Turnhouse later

in the year to form and command 340 Squadron. Lofts commanded 134 Squadron at Eglinton and later Baginton from February to April 1942. He took command of 66 Squadron at Skeabrae in May 1943. On October 8 he damaged a Bf 110, on the 13th shared a Ju 88 and on May 19 1944 damaged a Bf 109. He was posted away in late May 1944 and awarded a Bar to the DFC (26.1.45).

Lofts was released from the RAF in 1946, as a Wing Commander. He rejoined the RAuxAF in January 1948 and commanded 604 Squadron from 1948 until he was killed in a flying accident in a Vampire on May 20 1951, at Swiss Park, Cranbrook.

PO (AuxAF) 22.4 39   PO 24.8.39   FO 3.9.40   FL 3.9.41
SL 1.7.44   SL (RAuxAF) 1.1.48

COLIN LOGAN

44178   PO   Pilot   British   266 Squadron

Logan, of Bedhampton, joined 266 Squadron at Hornchurch on August 20 1940.

He was killed on March 27 1941, as a Pilot Officer with 222 Squadron, aged 29.

Logan is buried in Brookwood Military Cemetery, Woking.

PO 25.4.40

ORMONDE ARTHUR LOGIE

77360   PO   Air Gunner   British   29 Squadron

With 29 Squadron at Digby in early July 1940. Logie relinquished his commission because of ill-health on April 30 1941.

APO 3.2.40   PO 16.3.40

WITOLD LOKUCIEWSKI

P 1492   PO   Pilot   Polish   303 Squadron

Born in Russia on February 1 1917, Lokuciewski joined the PAF in 1936. He graduated from the Officers' School, Deblin in 1938 and joined 112 Fighter Squadron in III/1 Dyon, Warsaw. During the fighting in September 1939 he destroyed one German aircraft and probably another.

Lokuciewski joined 303 Squadron at Northolt at its formation on August 2 1940. He claimed a Do 17 destroyed and probably another on September 7, a Do 17 and a Bf 109 on the 11th and a Bf 109 on the 15th. On this day he was wounded in the leg in combat with Bf 109s over the Kent coast. He was awarded the VM (5th Class)(23.12.40) and the KW (1.2.41).

On April 24 1941 Lokuciewski destroyed a Bf 109, on June 18 a Bf 109, on the 22nd a Bf 109 and another probable and on July 11 another probable. He was awarded a Bar to the KW (10.9.41) and the DFC (30.10.41). Lokuciewski was appointed a Flight Commander on November 21 1941 and was shot down and captured on March 13 1942.

Lokuciewski was held in Stalag Luft III, took part in the Great Escape and was recaptured. He was freed in late April 1945. On September 22 1945 he went to Andrews Field for a flying refresher

W Lokuciewski (continued)

course and was posted to 303 Squadron there on November 29. Lokuciewski commanded the squadron from February 1 to December 11 1946, when it was disbanded.

He returned to Poland in 1947 and was later imprisoned for five years. He rejoined the PAF in 1957, was Polish Military Naval and Air Attaché in London from 1969 to 1972 and retired in 1974.

———— LONG

No unknown **Sgt** **Aircrew** **British** **236 Squadron**

Believed to have flown one sortie with 236 on July 22 1940. No service details traced.

JOHN LONSDALE

81682 **PO** **Pilot** **British** **3 Squadron**

Lonsdale, of Stockton-on-Tees, joined 3 Squadron at Wick in early July 1940. He shared in the destruction of a He 111 on July 25, shot down into the sea off Pentland Firth during a weather reconnaissance sortie.

Lonsdale was killed on November 26, as a Flight Lieutenant and still with 3 Squadron, aged 28. He is buried in Durham Road Cemetery, Stockton-on-Tees.

PO 29.6.40   FO 29.6.41   FL 29.6.42

ROBERT HENRY LONSDALE

919410 **Sgt** **Pilot** **British** **46, 242 and 501 Squadrons**

With 46 Squadron at Digby in early July 1940. He went to 242 Squadron at Coltishall on July 20. Lonsdale claimed a He 111 destroyed on August 30 and a Do 17 on September 9. He was hit by return fire in this engagement and baled out, unhurt, landing at Caterham. His Hurricane, P 2831, crashed at Ninehams Road, Kenley.

Lonsdale joined 501 Squadron at Kenley on October 12 1940. He was promoted to Warrant Officer on October 1 1941. Nothing further known.

DAVID JOHN LOOKER

90607 **FO** **Pilot** **British** **615 Squadron**

Looker joined 615 Squadron, AuxAF in 1938 and was called to full-time service on August 24. He flew from Croydon to Merville with the squadron on November 15, in a Gladiator.

On May 15 1940 Looker shot down a Hs 126 but his own aircraft was damaged by return fire. He made a forced-landing near Brussels and was sent back to hospital in England with leg wounds.

Looker's Hurricane, L 1592, was severely damaged by Bf 109s over Sevenoaks on August 18 1940. He was fired on by the ground defences whilst making a forced-landing at Croydon and was admitted to hospital with severe shock and concussion.

In December 1940 Looker was posted to Canada, as a staff pilot at a training school. He was released from the RAF in 1945, as a Flight Lieutenant.

PO (AuxAF) 24.7.39   PO 24.8.39   FO 3.9.40   FL 3.9.41

MALCOLM JOHN LOUDON

37293 **FL** **Pilot** **British** **141 Squadron**

Joined the RAF on a short service commission in July 1935. Loudon was posted to 3 FTS, Grantham on September 22 and joined 23 Squadron at Northolt on August 5 1936.

In June 1940 Loudon was with 141 Squadron at Turnhouse, as a Flight Commander. The squadron flew south to West Malling on July 12. Shortly after 09.00 hrs on the 19th twelve Defiants moved to the forward airfield at Hawkinge. At 12.23 hrs they were ordered off to carry out an offensive patrol twenty miles south of Folkestone. Three were left behind with engine trouble. During the patrol the nine Defiants were surprised by a force of Bf 109s of III/JG 51. Loudon's aircraft, L 7001, was badly damaged. He ordered his gunner to bale out and he was rescued, uninjured from the sea. Loudon crashed near Hawkinge, after his engine failed. He was admitted to Canterbury Hospital, with an arm wound.

In early April 1941 Loudon was posted to 242 Squadron at Martlesham Heath, as 'A' Flight Commander. On July 4 he shot down a Bf 109 on a bomber-escort operation to Bethune. He left 242 on July 23 to take command of 603 Squadron at Hornchurch. In October 1941 Loudon was sent to the Middle East, ostensibly for three weeks, to brief Desert Air Force squadrons on current Fighter Command tactics. He remained out there and was given command of a Wing. He was awarded the DFC (26.12.41).

Loudon later went on to the staff of HQ Desert Air Force. In January 1944 he was appointed Wing Leader 324 Wing in Italy. Soon afterwards he was shot down on a fighter sweep north of Rome and baled out. He dislocated both shoulders on landing and was captured.

Freed in May 1945, Loudon was released from the RAF in 1946, as a Wing Commander.

APO 16.9.35   PO 16.9.36   FO 16.6.38   FL 16.6.40
SL 1.9.41   WC 1.7.43

ANTHONY DESMOND JOSEPH LOVELL ⚴

40402 **FO** **Pilot** **British** **41 Squadron**

Born in Ceylon, Lovell joined the RAF on a short service commission in November 1937. He was posted to 6 FTS, Netheravon on January 6 1938. In late 1938 he joined 41 Squadron at Catterick and was a Flight Commander in early 1940. Over Dunkirk on May 31 Lovell claimed a He 111 destroyed and on June 1 he shared another.

On July 8 he claimed a Ju 88. In combat off Dover on the 28th he was attacked by Major Mölders of JG 51 and crashed on landing at Manston. He was admitted to Margate Hospital, wounded in the thigh. On August 15 Lovell claimed a Bf 110. He was shot down over the Thames Estuary on September 5 and baled out, unhurt. His Spitfire, R 6885, crashed and burned out in Kimberley Road, South Benfleet.

On September 6 Lovell claimed a Bf 110, on the 15th and October 20 Bf 109s and on November 17 and 27 two more. He was awarded the DFC (26.11.40). He claimed a Ju 88 on March 30 1941.

Lovell was given command of 145 Squadron in October 1941. He claimed a Ju 88 on November 11 and another on January 19 1942.

He was awarded a Bar to the DFC (10.2.42). In May Lovell was posted to Malta to join 603 Squadron. He shared a Ju 88 on July 28. When the squadron was disbanded on August 3 and partly incorporated into 1435 Flight to form 1435 Squadron Lovell was given command of the new unit.

On August 13 he claimed a Ju 88 and a SM 84, on the 14th shared a Ju 87, on October 12 destroyed a Ju 88, on December 7 shared a Ju 88 and on the 17th destroyed a SM 79. Lovell was awarded the DSO (3.11.42).

He was promoted on March 31 1943 and appointed to lead the Malta Spitfire Wing. Lovell led 244 Wing during the invasion of Italy. He destroyed FW 190s on May 3 and 15 1944 and was awarded a Bar to the DSO (23.2.45) and the DFC (US)(14.11.44).

and Lovell was killed on August 17 1945 when he crashed into a field adjoining Old Sarum airfield whilst doing aerobatics in a Spitfire. He was 26 years old and is buried in Portrush Cemetery, Co Antrim, near his home.

APO 9.1.38   PO 25.10.38   FO 25.5.40   FL 25.5.41
SL 1.6.42

TERENCE GUNION LOVELL GREGG

29244   SL   Pilot   New Zealander   87 Squadron

The son of a doctor, Lovell Gregg was born in Wanganui on September 19 1912 and was educated at Nelson College. He was a brilliant scholar and intended to enter Otago University to study medicine but was held back because of his youth. He took flying lessons and became the youngest qualified pilot in Australasia.

He applied for a short service commission in the RAF in July 1930 but was considered 'too weak' and advised to take up rugby. Lovell Gregg travelled to England at his own expense in October 1930 and successfully applied. He went to the RAF Depot, Uxbridge on March 13 1931 and two weeks later was posted to 5 FTS, Sealand. With training completed he joined 41 Squadron at Northolt on March 8 1932.

Lovell Gregg went to CFS, Wittering for an instructor's course on September 26 1932 but on February 28 1933 he was posted to 30 Squadron, operating in Wapitis from Mosul, Iraq. He returned to the UK in February 1935 and after a Floatplane Conversion Course at Calshot he returned to CFS, then at Upavon, for another instructor's course. In February 1936 Lovell Gregg was posted to 3 FTS, Grantham, on the instructing staff.

On September 16 1938 he went on Flying Examining Officer duties at HQ 26 Group at Hendon. Shortly after the outbreak of war Lovell Gregg went to 15 FTS, Lossiemouth, as an instructor. On December 21 1939 he went on Operations Room duties to RAF Finningley, moving in early January 1940 to the Operations Room at HQ 5 Group.

Lovell Gregg was posted to 6 OTU, Sutton Bridge on May 26 1940 and after converting to Hurricanes he joined 87 Squadron at Church Fenton on June 15, as a supernumerary. He took command on July 12 when the CO was posted away. Aware of his lack of operational experience Lovell Gregg allowed the experienced Flight Commanders to lead the squadron until he felt able to do so.

On August 15 1940 the squadron was scrambled at 17.30 hrs to intercept forty Ju 87s, escorted by twenty Bf 110s and sixty Bf 109s. Lovell Gregg led the squadron out of the sun in line-astern, straight at the Bf 110s. His Hurricane was hit and caught fire. He came down from 15000 feet, apparently under control and heading for Warmwell. Eye-witnesses said that the pilot appeared to change his mind and he circled the Abbotsbury area, skimmed low across a wood and a ploughed field and crashed in a copse, striking a large oak tree. Lovell Gregg was thrown clear but was already dead when reached. He is buried in Holy Trinity churchyard, Warmwell.

PO 13.3.31   FO 30.10.32   FL 30.12.36   SL 1.1.40

JOHN ERIC LOVERSEED

907964   Sgt   Pilot   British   501 Squadron

Joined 501 Squadron at Middle Wallop on July 19 1940. Loverseed was awarded the AFC (1.1.43), as a Warrant Officer.

In 1943 he became the first Common Wealth Party Member of Parliament.

REGINALD ERIC LOVETT

37543   FL   Pilot   British   73 Squadron

Lovett, of Golders Green, joined the RAF on a short service commission in November 1935. He was posted to 8 FTS, Montrose on February 8 1936 and joined 66 Squadron at Duxford on August 16.

In early September 1939 Lovett was a Flight Commander with 73 Squadron in France. He shot down a French Potez 63 in error for a Do 17 on December 18 and the crew of two were killed. On March 22 1940 he destroyed a Bf 109, on the 26th a Do 17 and another enemy aircraft and on April 21 a Bf 110. Lovett was shot down on May 10. He was unable to bale out and crash-landed badly burned. He was awarded the DFC (16.7.40).

On July 23 Lovett rejoined 73, then at Church Fenton. On August 15 he claimed a Ju 88 destroyed and probably another. In combat over Burnham on September 5 Lovett was shot down, in Hurricane P 3204, and baled out, unhurt.

Two days later he was shot down and killed in combat. His Hurricane, P 3234, crashed on Fritze Farm, Stock, near Billericay. Lovett was 26 and is buried in Hendon Cemetery.

APO 20.1.36   PO 25.11.36   FO 25.5.38   FL 25.5.40

JOSEPH LOWE

541411   Sgt   Air Gunner   British   236 Squadron

A pre-war regular airman, Lowe was with 236 Squadron in June 1940.

He was awarded the DFM (22.9.42), as a Flight Sergeant with 218 Squadron, operating in Stirlings from Downham Market, Norfolk. Lowe was a member of the Guinea Pig Club, having undergone plastic surgery at the Queen Victoria Hospital, East Grinstead. He died in 1973.

PHILLIP ANTHONY LOWETH

42242   PO   Pilot   British   249 Squadron

Joined the RAF on a short service commission in April 1939. Loweth was with 249 Squadron at Leconfield in early July 1940. He was released from the RAF in 1950, as a Flight Lieutenant.

APO 24.6.39   PO 11.5.40   FO 11.5.41   FL 11.5.42
FL 1.9.45

WALTER LOWTHER

1050690   Sgt   Aircrew   British   219 Squadron

No service details traced.

WILFRED WILLIAM LOXTON

36032   SL   Pilot   British   25 Squadron

Born on January 20 1909, Loxton joined the RAF on January 20 1925 as an aircraft apprentice. He applied for pilot training, was duly selected and began his ab initio course at Sealand in April 1930.

With training completed, Loxton joined 32 Squadron at Kenley in February 1931, as a Sergeant-Pilot. He was commissioned in April 1935 and posted to 43 Squadron at Tangmere on July 14. He moved to 822 (Fleet Spotter-Reconnaissance) Squadron on January 21 1936, based at Manston and on HMS 'Furious'. On January 28 1939 Loxton was posted to 5 FTS, Sealand, as an instructor.

Loxton commanded 25 Squadron at North Weald from June 1 to September 24 1940. In December he was posted to Canada for flying training duties. He returned to the UK in September 1943, was awarded the AFC (1.1.45) and retired from the RAF on May 31 1957, as a Wing Commander.

PO 30.4.35   FO 30.10.36   FL 30.10.38   SL 1.6.40
WC 1.12.41   WC 1.10.46

ROBIN MORTON McTAGGART DELIGHT LUCAS

42853   PO   Pilot   British   141 Squadron

Lucas joined the RAF on a short service commission in July 1939 and began his elementary flying training at 10 E&RFTS, Yatesbury on the 24th. He went to 3 ITW, Hastings on October 22 1939 and then to 6 FTS, Little Rissington on November 7.

With training completed Lucas was posted to 5 OTU, Aston Down and after converting to Defiants he joined 141 Squadron at Prestwick on August 19 1940. He was with the squadron until June 17 1941. Lucas went to 410 (RCAF) Squadron on July 10, then forming at Ayr with Defiants.

In mid-January 1942 Lucas was posted to 61 OTU, East Fortune and was later with 132 OTU there. In the second half of 1943 he was at 8 OTU, Dyce and later with 6 (P) AFU, Little Rissington on November 30, as an instructor.

Lucas was posted to a staff job at Air Ministry on November 14 1944. He went to India in May 1945 and returned to the UK for release in February 1946.

APO 23.10.39   PO 3.8.40   FO 3.8.41   FL 3.8.42
FL 1.9.45

SIDNEY EDWARD LUCAS

171647   Sgt   Pilot   British   32 and 257 Squadrons

Joined 32 Squadron at Acklington in mid-September 1940. Lucas moved to 257 Squadron at North Weald on October 15 and claimed a Fiat CR 42 destroyed on November 11.

Commissioned in February 1944, Lucas was awarded the DFC (8.8.44), as a Pilot Officer with 149 Squadron, operating in Stirlings from Methwold, Norfolk. One night in June 1944 Lucas was captain of an aircraft detailed for a mine-laying operation. When nearing the target the aircraft was illuminated in a cone of searchlights and came under heavy anti-aircraft fire. Lucas flew on and released his mines in the designated area. The aircraft was hit in many places and the flight engineer seriously wounded. In order to escape the barrage Lucas dived, almost to sea level. As the course was set for home the engineer asked to return to his instrument panel but collapsed immediately, the crew only then becoming aware of the extent of his injuries. Eventually Lucas reached an airfield. On landing the brake pressure failed, the aircraft overshot the runway, crashed and caught fire. The petrol tanks exploded and Lucas was hurled backwards for some distance. He quickly recovered and assisted in rescuing the wounded engineer from the burning aircraft.

Lucas was released from the RAF in 1946, as a Flying Officer.

PO 9.2.44   FO 9.8.44

KAZIMIERZ LUKASZEWICZ

76761   FO   Pilot   Polish   303 and 501 Squadrons

Converted to Hurricanes at 6 OTU, Sutton Bridge and joined 303 Squadron at Northolt on July 26 1940.

Lukaszewicz moved to 501 Squadron at Gravesend on August 7. On the 12th he was reported 'Missing', following a combat with enemy fighters west of Ramsgate, in Hurricane P 3803. He was 27 and is remembered on the Polish Air Force Memorial at Northolt. Lukaszewicz was awarded the KW (1.2.41).

DUGALD THOMAS MOORE LUMSDEN

33545   PO   Pilot   British   236 Squadron

Born on June 27 1920, Lumsden entered RAF College, Cranwell in January 1939 as a flight cadet. The course was shortened because of the war and Lumsden was commissioned in December 1939 and joined the recently-reformed 236 Squadron at Martlesham Heath on January 4 1940.

After operating with Fighter Command in July 1940 the squadron moved to St Eval in early August and went into Coastal Command. In July 1941 Lumsden was posted to 2 (Coastal) OTU at Catfoss, as an instructor. Whilst there he converted to Beaufighters and in late May 1942 joined 248 Squadron at Dyce. On July 11 1942 Lumsden was shot down by Bf 109s off Trondheim and captured.

Freed in May 1945, he joined 254 Squadron in September, flying Beaufighters from RAF Chivenor. Lumsden stayed on in the RAF, was made an MBE (1.6.53) and retired on May 16 1964, as a Wing Commander.

PO 23.12.39   FO 23.12.40   FL 23.12.41   SL 1.8.47
WC 1.7.53

JOHN CLAPPERTON LUMSDEN

972078   Sgt   Wop/AG   British   248 Squadron

Born in 1919, Lumsden joined the RAF in September 1939. After basic training at Padgate he was posted to Yatesbury for a wireless course and then to Manby for gunnery training.

Lumsden went to No 1 (Coastal) OTU at Silloth, converted to Blenheims and then joined 248 Squadron on October 5 1940. He later served with 53 Squadron at Bircham Newton, in Hudsons. He was discharged from the RAF in 1942.

JOHN WILFRED LUND

74334   PO   Pilot   British   611 and 92 Squadrons

Lund, of Biggleswade, Bedfordshire, was at Oriel College, Oxford, where he read Mediaeval History. He was a member of the University Air Squadron and was called to full-time service in November 1939.

On January 1 1940 Lund was posted to FTS, Cranwell, on the second war course. After completing this he went to No 1 School of Army Co-operation at Old Sarum for further training on June 2 1940. Eight days later Lund was posted to 5 OTU, Aston Down and after converting to Spitfires he joined 611 Squadron at Digby.

On July 2 he shared in the destruction of a Do 17 and shared another on August 21. Lund was posted to 92 Squadron at Biggin Hill on October 2 1940. He was shot down by Bf 109s on the 15th and crashed into the sea off Bee Ness Jetty, Kent Reach, in Spitfire R 6642. He was rescued from the sea by HMS 'Nysan'.

Lund damaged a Bf 109 on December 1. He was killed on October 2 1941, as a Flight Lieutenant with 92 Squadron, aged 22. He is remembered on the Runnymede Memorial, Panel 29.

PO 18.11.39   FO 26.11.40

HAROLD STEWART LUSK

72539   **FO**   **Pilot**   **New Zealander**   **25 Squadron**

Born in Auckland on August 7 1918, Lusk was educated at King's School and King's College. In 1937 he went to the UK to study at Merton College, Oxford. He joined the University Air Squadron in 1938 and was commissioned in the RAFVR in January 1939.

Called to full-time service on September 9 1939, Lusk was posted to FTS, Cranwell, where he trained on Oxfords. He was selected for bombers and converted to Blenheims but an attack of jaundice resulted in a changed posting and he joined 25 Squadron at North Weald instead.

Lusk served with the squadron until August 1941, when he was posted to RAF Valley, as Senior Flying Control Officer. After an airfield control course at Prestwick he returned to Valley as Airfield Controller. In February 1943 Lusk joined 285 Squadron at Woodvale, an anti-aircraft co-operation unit. He was given command of 291 Squadron at Hutton Cranswick, on similar duties, in December 1943.

On January 1 1944 Lusk transferred to the RNZAF and at the end of the year he left 291 Squadron to resume his studies at Oxford, retaining the rank of Squadron Leader. After qualifying in late 1945 Lusk returned to the RNZAF and was repatriated to New Zealand, disembarking on January 10 1946. He went on to the Reserve soon afterwards and joined a law firm in Auckland.

Lusk was appointed QC on October 23 1973.

PO (RAFVR) 10.1.39   PO 9.9.39   FO 10.10.40
FL 10.10.41

KENNETH ROY LUSTY

66502   **Sgt**   **Air Gunner**   **British**   **25 Squadron**

Lusty was with 25 Squadron at Martlesham Heath in June 1940. Commissioned in May 1941, he was released from the RAF in 1947, as a Squadron Leader.

PO 16.5.41   FO 16.5.42   FL 16.5.43

ALASTAIR McLAREN LYALL

39289   **FL**   **Pilot**   **British**   **25 Squadron**

Joined the RAF on a short service commission in October 1936. Lyall was posted to 10 FTS, Tern Hill on January 16 1937 and joined 25 Squadron at Hawkinge on August 7 1937.

Still with the squadron in July 1940, Lyall was posted away on September 14. He was released from the RAF in 1946.

APO 21.12.36   PO 12.10.37   FO 12.7.39   FL 3.9.40

ARCHIBALD LYALL

81047   **PO**   **Pilot**   **British**   **602 Squadron**

The son of an officer of the HLI, killed in action in France in July 1916, Lyall came from Glasgow. He joined 602 Squadron at Drem in March 1940, as a Sergeant-Pilot, and was commissioned in April.

On September 9 Lyall claimed a Bf 109 and a Do 17 destroyed, on the 15th a Do 17, on the 21st shared a Ju 88, on October 29 a Bf 109 and on November 6 probably another.

Lyall was shot down over the Isle of Wight on November 28 1940. He baled out too low and was killed. His Spitfire, N 3242, crashed at Whiteley

Bank, Isle of Wight. He was 27 and was cremated at Woodvale Crematorium, Brighton.

PO 25.4.40

JAMES LYNCH

910937   **Sgt**   **Air Gunner**   **British**   **25 Squadron**

Lynch, of Hetton-le-Hole, Durham, joined 25 Squadron at North Weald in late September 1940.

He was killed on January 22 1944, as a Sergeant with 166 Squadron, operating in Lancasters from Kirmington, Lincolnshire. Lynch was 23. He is remembered on the Runnymede Memorial, Panel 233.

EMANUEL BARNETT LYONS

83269   **PO**   **Pilot**   **British**   **65 Squadron**

Joined 65 Squadron at Turnhouse on September 2 1940.

Lyons commanded 222 Squadron on the Continent from January to May 1945. He was awarded the DFC (8.5.45) and released from the RAF in 1946.

PO 10.8.40   FO 10.8.41   FL 10.8.42

ANTONI LYSEK

P 1911   **Sgt**   **Pilot**   **Polish**   **302 Squadron**

Born on January 25 1917, Lysek joined 302 Squadron at Leconfield on August 20 1940. He was awarded the KW (10.9.41).

Commissioned in May 1942, Lysek was killed on June 5, as a Pilot Officer with 302. The squadron was providing high cover in the area of Le Havre. Lysek was lost in the sea, in Spitfire AD 257, probably through damage causing engine failure. He is remembered on the Polish Air Force Memorial at Northolt. Lysek was awarded a Bar to the KW (20.8.42).

PO 31.5.42

★ JOHN McADAM

748076   **Sgt**   **Pilot**   **British**   **41 Squadron**

Born in Gillingham, Kent on March 21 1919, McAdam joined the RAFVR on April 28 1939. He was called to full-time service at the outbreak of war, went to 4 ITW, Bexhill on October 30 and moved on to 6 FTS, Little Rissington on December 9.

With the course completed McAdam was posted to 6 OTU, Sutton Bridge on June 19 1940. After converting to Spitfires he joined 41 Squadron at Catterick on the 22nd.

McAdam claimed a Do 17 destroyed on September 7. On this day he crashed at Leonard Drive, Drakes Farm, Rayleigh after a combat over Hornchurch, in Spitfire P 9430. The aircraft partly burned out and was written off. McAdam was unhurt.

On the 23rd he was shot down during a squadron patrol off Dover, in Spitfire N 3118. McAdam baled out, was rescued from the sea and admitted to Dover Hospital. He crashed at Globe Road, Hornchurch on October 12 after his engine cut on take-off.

On the 25th McAdam claimed a Bf 109 destroyed. He was shot down by Major Molders on February 20 1941 over Dover, in Spitfire P 7302. He baled out but was picked up dead from the sea.

McAdam is buried in Ballyharry Cemetery, Island Magee, Co Antrim.

WILLIAM DAVID McADAM

519802   **Sgt**   **Air Gunner**   **British**   **23 Squadron**

A pre-war regular airman, McAdam, of Grangemouth, Stirlingshire, was with 23 Squadron at Collyweston in early July 1940.

McAdam was killed on September 1 1941, as a Flight Sergeant with 23 Squadron. He was 26 and is buried in Zeebrugge Communal Cemetery, Bruges, Belgium.

P J McALLISTER

1005245   **Sgt**   **Aircrew**   **British**   **23 and 29 Squadrons**

No service details traced.

JAMES HENRY GORDON McARTHUR

37925 **FL** **Pilot** **British** **238 and 609 Squadrons**

A civil pilot in the thirties, McArthur held the London-Baghdad record. He joined the RAF on a short service commission in May 1936. McArthur was posted to 9 FTS, Thornaby on July 18 and after completing his training joined the Station Flight at Aldergrove on January 14 1937. He went to the Experimental Section at RAE, Farnborough on October 1 1938, as a test pilot.

After being with 238 Squadron at Middle Wallop in 1940 McArthur was posted to 609 Squadron there on August 1, as 'B' Flight Commander. On the 8th he claimed two Ju 87s destroyed, on the 11th a Bf 110, on the 15th two more, on the 25th another, on September 7 a Do 17 and on the 25th another Bf 110.

On September 15 McArthur's oxygen supply failed at 25000 feet. He lost consciousness and came to in a high-speed dive and very near the ground. Regaining control, he pulled out but his ears were badly damaged. In late September he handed over command of his flight to John Dundas and went to hospital. McArthur lost his operational category and was not allowed to fly above 5000 feet. He was awarded the DFC (22.10.40). His portrait was done by Cuthbert Orde in November 1940.

McArthur was released from the RAF in 1947, as a Wing Commander. He later joined the RCAF and held the UN Korea Medal and Canadian Forces Decoration. He was killed in a flying accident at Las Vegas in May 1961.

APO 6.7.36   PO 11.10.36   FO 11.5.38   FL 11.5.40
SL 1.9.41   WC 1.1.44

MALCOLM ROBERT MacARTHUR

70416 **FL** **Pilot** **British** **236 Squadron**

MacArthur learned to fly with the RAFO and was commissioned in April 1934. He transferred to the RAFVR in September 1938 and was called to full-time service in 1939.

He was with 236 Squadron in early July 1940 and was awarded the DFC (25.4.41). MacArthur was released in 1946, as a Group Captain.

PO (RAFO) 1.9.34   FO (RAFO) 1.3.36   FO 9.9.39
FL 9.9.40   SL 1.5.43   WC 5.10.44

S V McCALL

No unknown **PO** **Pilot** **British** **607 Squadron**

No service details traced.

THOMAS ANDREW McCANN ✷

116980 **Sgt** **Pilot** **British** **601 Squadron**

McCann, of Co Down, joined 601 Squadron at Exeter on September 9 1940. Commissioned in February 1942, he died in the Middle East on July 27 1942, as a Pilot Officer with 134 Squadron, aged 23.

He is buried in El Alamein War Cemetery.

PO 19.2.42

JAMES PATRICK McCARTHY

542137 **Sgt** **Aircrew** **British** **235 Squadron**

No service details traced.

THOMAS FRANCIS McCARTHY

751520 **Sgt** **Aircrew** **British** **235 Squadron**

McCarthy, of West Hartlepool, was with 235 Squadron in early July 1940. He was killed on October 6 1942, as a Flight Sergeant with 404 Squadron, aged 29.

He is remembered on the Runnymede Memorial, Panel 75.

JOHN PATRICK McCAUL

1050678 **AC 2** **Radar Operator** **British** **219 Squadron**

McCaul joined 219 Squadron at Catterick on August 16 1940. He was one of a number of airmen in the Battle of Britain, who had been given a rudimentary course on radar and then flew operationally in Blenheims without rank or flying badge, using the primitive AI equipment.

On September 30 McCaul was one of the crew of Blenheim L 1261 on a routine night patrol. With the pilot and the gunner he was killed when the aircraft disintegrated and crashed, from an unknown cause.

McCaul was 28. He is buried in Leigh Cemetery, Lancashire.

DEREK CHARLES McCAW

36139 **FO** **Pilot** **British** **238 Squadron**

Born on August 27 1915, McCaw was at Marlborough College from 1929 to 1934 and then King's College, Cambridge. He entered the RAF in June 1938 on a direct-entry Permanent Commission, one of the few offered in competition each year to graduates of British and Commonwealth universities.

McCaw was with 238 Squadron at Middle Wallop in early July 1940. He was shot down in combat over convoy 'Peewit' south of the Isle of Wight on August 8 and crashed into the Channel, in Hurricane P 3617. He was 24 and is buried in Sennerville-sur-Fécamp churchyard, France.

PO 4.6.38   FO 4.9.38

ROBERT IAN McCHESNEY

62434 **Sgt** **Air Gunner** **New Zealander** **236 Squadron**

Born in Auckland on October 4 1913, McChesney worked as a bricklayer. At the outbreak of war he volunteered for aircrew duties and was accepted as a trainee air gunner.

McChesney went to the Ground Training School at Weraroa on January 15 1940 and moved on to the Air Observers' School, Ohakea on February 9 for a Lewis gunnery course and air experience. He sailed for the UK on March 23 in the SS 'Akaroa'.

Initially McChesney was attached to 264 Squadron at Duxford and had three flights in Defiants the nine days he was there. On June 13 1940 he was posted to 5 OTU, Aston Down, where he converted to Blenheims. He was promoted to Sergeant and awarded his air gunner's badge on July 5 and the next day joined 236 Squadron at Thorney Island.

With thirty-one operational flights carried out McChesney was posted to the newly-reformed 255 Squadron at Kirton-in-Lindsey on December 4 1940. Flying with Pilot Officer Wright on May 9 1941 McChesney shot down a Ju 88, first sighted over Hull and then chased thirty miles out over the North Sea.

McChesney was commissioned in June 1941. When the squadron began to convert to Beaufighters he began retraining as a Radio Observer and on October 20 he qualified. He was posted to 488 Squadron at Church Fenton on July 26 1942. The squadron moved north to Ayr in September for further training.

On December 6 some Beaufighters of 488 were taking part in an exercise at Ayr. As it was concluded McChesney's aircraft collided with another and all four men were killed.

McChesney is buried in Ayr Cemetery.

PO 10.6.41   FO 10.6.42

JOHN ARTHUR PETER McCLINTOCK

91064 **PO** **Pilot** **British** **615 Squadron**

Joined 615 Squadron, AuxAF in 1939. McClintock was called to full-time service on August 24 1939. He was with 615 at Kenley in early July 1940.

On August 24 he shared in destroying a He 111 and two days later was himself shot down into the sea off Sheerness, in Hurricane R 4121. He baled out, unhurt.

McClintock was killed on November 25 1940. He and Pilot Officer AJA Truran were flying in the squadron Magister, when a wing fell off at 200 feet. It crashed at Sunningdale and both men were killed. They were cremated at St John's Crematorium, Woking.

APO 24.8.39   PO 13.7.40

JAMES ELLIS McCOMB

90352   SL   Pilot   British   611 Squadron

McComb was born in 1909 and educated at Stowe. He trained as a solicitor and worked for the Legal Department of the Lancashire County Council. In early 1934 he joined 600 Squadron, AuxAF and transferred to 611 Squadron, AuxAF on September 25 1936.

In 1938 McComb became a Flight Commander. In March 1939, on a visit to 611, Leigh-Mallory told him that in the event of war he would have command of the squadron. 611 went to summer camp at Duxford on August 4 1939 and learned on the 24th that the squadron had been embodied into the RAF for the duration. As promised, McComb was given command on September 3 1939.

Over Dunkirk on June 2 McComb claimed a Bf 109 and a He 111 as probably destroyed. On August 21 he claimed a Do 17 destroyed and shared another and on September 15 he claimed a Do 17. He was posted away for a rest on October 19 and awarded the DFC (22.11.40).

McComb was released from the RAF in 1945, as a Wing Commander. He died in August 1982. His portrait was drawn by Cuthbert Orde.

PO (AuxAF) 7.2.34   FO (AuxAF) 8.8.35   FL (AuxAF) 29.1.38
FL 26.8.39   SL 1.3.40   WC 1.9.41

JOHN McCONNELL

136316   Sgt   Pilot   British   145 Squadron

Born on May 18 1918, McConnell joined 145 Squadron at Drem on September 11 1940.

He was shot down by a Bf 109 of JG 2 on November 7, baled out, slightly injured, and landed at Earnley Mill. His Hurricane, P 8816, crashed at Birdham, south-west of Chichester.

Commissioned in October 1942, McConnell retired from the RAF on January 29 1958, as a Flight Lieutenant. He died in 1965.

PO 17.10.42   FO 17.4.43   FL 17.10.44   FL 17.4.46

WILLIAM WINDER McCONNELL ★

81643   PO   Pilot   Irish   245, 607 and 249 Squadrons

McConnell was posted to 245 Squadron at Aldergrove on July 6 1940. He joined 607 Squadron at Tangmere on September 24 and moved to 249 Squadron at North Weald on October 16. He shared in destroying a Ju 88 on the 28th.

Near Dover on January 10 1941 McConnell was shot down by Bf 109s. He baled out and broke a leg on landing. His Hurricane went head-on into the Dover cliffs. Wing Commander FV Beamish destroyed the Bf 109 which shot him down.

On March 3 1942 McConnell joined 174 Squadron, then forming at Manston, as a Flight Commander. He was awarded the DFC (30.6.42) and given command of the squadron when the CO was killed over Dieppe on August 19 1942. He was awarded a Bar to the DFC (22.9.42).

McConnell led 174 until February 1944, when he was shot down in a Typhoon and captured. He was released from the RAF in 1945, as a Squadron Leader.

PO 18.6.40   FO 18.6.41   FL 18.6.42

JOHN BERNARD McCORMACK ★

50661   Sgt   Air Gunner   British   25 Squadron

McCormack, of Brosna, Co Kerry, was with 25 Squadron at Martlesham Heath in early July 1940.

He later went to Bomber Command and was commissioned from Flight Sergeant in May 1942. McCormack failed to return from operations on September 10 1942 and was reported 'Missing', aged 23. He was serving with 102 Squadron, operating in Halifaxes from Pocklington. McCormack is remembered on the Runnymede Memorial, Panel 70.

PO 23.5.42

JOHN ALEXANDER McDERMOTT

NZ 40610   Sgt   Air Gunner   New Zealander   23 Sqdn

Born in Gourock, Scotland on April 11 1915, McDermott was taken to New Zealand in 1923. He was educated in Wellington and worked in the Public Service there.

In January 1940 McDermott volunteered for aircrew duties and was accepted as a trainee air gunner. He reported to the Ground Training School at Weraroa in mid-February and moved to the Air Observers' School at Ohakea on March 10 for a Lewis gunnery course and air experience.

McDermott sailed for the UK on April 26 in the RMS 'Rangitiki'. He was posted to 5 OTU, Aston Down on July 17, where he converted to Blenheims, was awarded his air gunner's badge and promoted to Sergeant. He joined 23 Squadron at Ford on September 24.

In late February 1941 McDermott damaged two German bombers during a night intruder operation over Lille aerodrome. In early March, landing after a patrol, a bomb stuck in the rack exploded, setting the aircraft on fire. The navigator was killed but McDermott and the pilot were unhurt. On May 5 1941 he shared in destroying a He 111.

McDermott was posted to 116 Squadron at Hendon on March 11 1942, on radar calibration duties in Lysanders. In May he went to 1653 Conversion Unit at Polebrook for crewing-up and conversion to Liberators. On July 1 McDermott's crew took off in a Liberator of 159 Squadron for India. After arrival at Fayid, Egypt his was one of the five Liberators kept there for operations in the Middle East.

The squadron operated initially from St Jean in Palestine, and later Aqir but after merging with 160 Squadron in September 1942 the combined unit moved to Shandur in Egypt. Commissioned in November 1942, McDermott returned to the UK and was posted to 21 OTU on January 8 1943, as an instructor.

In mid-April he flew out to India, via Gibraltar, and rejoined 159 Squadron, then based at Digri, the first four-engined heavy bomber unit in India. McDermott left the squadron on February 2 1944, returned to the UK and was later repatriated to New Zealand, arriving there on July 28. He went on to the Reserve on November 22 1944.

McDermott rejoined the Public Service. He died on January 2 1970.

PO 19.11.42   FO 19.5.43

ALEXANDER STEWART MacDONALD

741080   Sgt   Pilot   British   601 Squadron

No service details traced.

DONALD KENNEDY MacDONALD

74679   PO   Pilot   British   603 Squadron

Born on August 20 1918, MacDonald came from Murrayfield, Edinburgh. He was at Marlborough College from 1932 to 1936 and

DK MacDonald (continued)

later at Cambridge. Whilst an undergraduate he was a member of the University Air Squadron.

MacDonald was called to full-time service in November 1939 and was with 603 Squadron at Dyce in early July 1940. He failed to return from a combat with Bf 109s over Dover on August 28, in Spitfire L 1046. He is remembered on the Runnymede Memorial, Panel 9. Younger brother of HK MacDonald.

PO 8.11.39

DUNCAN STUART MacDONALD

37451   FL   Pilot   British   213 Squadron

Born on March 15 1912, MacDonald joined the RAF on a short service commission in September 1935. He was posted to 4 FTS, Abu Sueir on November 23 and joined 41 Squadron at Catterick on April 24 1936. He became a Flight Commander in 1938 and left the squadron in 1939.

MacDonald was posted to 213 Squadron at Exeter on August 28 1940, to command. He was awarded the DFC (17.12.40), credited with at least three enemy aircraft destroyed. In May 1941 213 embarked on HMS 'Furious' for the Middle East and MacDonald continued in command until October.

In July 1944 he formed and then commanded 283 Wing of the Balkan Air Force in Italy until its disbandment in May 1945. He returned to the UK and was awarded the DSO (21.8.45).

In the post-war RAF MacDonald held various appointments, his last being Air Attaché in Stockholm until he retired on July 6 1963, as a Group Captain. After 1948 he changed his name to Wilson-MacDonald.

APO 6.11.35   PO 24.4.36   FO 24.10.37   FL 24.10.39
SL 1.12.40   WC 1.3.42   WC 1.10.46   GC 1.1.54

HAROLD KENNEDY MacDONALD

90193   FL   Pilot   British   603 Squadron

Joined 603 Squadron, AuxAF in early 1935. MacDonald was called to full-time service on August 24 1939.

During a night patrol off the Firth of Forth on June 26 1940 MacDonald saw anti-aircraft fire, flew towards it and shot down a He 111 caught in the searchlights. On August 31, September 18 and 27 he claimed Bf 109s destroyed.

On September 28 MacDonald was jumped by Bf 109s over Gillingham. He was shot down and his Spitfire, L 1076, crashed on to Brompton Barracks. MacDonald was killed, aged 28. He was cremated at Warriston Crematorium, Edinburgh. Elder brother of DK MacDonald.

PO (AuxAF) 4.3.35   FO (AuxAF) 4.9.36   FO 24.8.39
FL 12.3.40

AENEAS RANALD DONALD MacDONNELL

33120   SL   Pilot   British   64 Squadron

The Hereditary 22nd Chief of Glengarry, MacDonnell was born on November 15 1913. He was educated at Hurstpierpoint College and entered RAF College, Cranwell in September 1932 as a flight cadet. He graduated in July 1934 and joined 54 Squadron at Hornchurch.

On May 17 1936 MacDonnell was posted to 802 (Fleet Fighter) Squadron, based on shore at Hal Far, Malta and at sea on HMS 'Glorious'. He left the squadron in January 1938 and went to RAF Gosport, as an instructor. MacDonnell was posted to CFS, Upavon on January 22 1939 for a course. He was at Air Ministry later in the year and in mid-July 1940 was posted to Kenley to take command of 64 Squadron.

On July 25 MacDonnell claimed a Ju 87 destroyed, on the 29th a Ju 87 and a Bf 109, between August 5 and 15 six more Bf 109s and on the 16th a Bf 109 and a shared He 111. On this day he was shot down by a Bf 109 as he returned to Kenley from Hawkinge and baled out, unhurt, landing at Possingworth Park. His Spitfire, P 9554, crashed at Blackboy, Uckfield. MacDonnell destroyed a Bf 110 on August 18 and was awarded the DFC (6.9.40).

In March 1941 MacDonnell was shot down on a sweep over France, baled out and was captured. Freed in April 1945, he received a Mention in Despatches (28.12.45) for distinguished services while a PoW.

MacDonnell was made a CB (1.1.64) and retired from the RAF on November 15 1964, as an Air Commodore. His portrait was drawn by Cuthbert Orde in 1940.

PO 28.7.34   FO 28.1.36   FL 28.1.38   SL 1.8.39
WC 1.9.41   WC 1.10.46   GC 1.7.54   AC 1.1.60

BRYAN MARTIN McDONOUGH

42137   PO   Pilot   Australian   236 Squadron

McDonough joined the RAF on a short service commission in March 1939. With training completed he was posted to the newly-reformed 236 Squadron in early November 1939.

During a bomber escort mission on August 1 1940 he was shot down, in Blenheim R 2774, either by the ground defences of Querqueville aerodrome or by Oberleutnant Düllberg of III/JG 27. Both McDonough and his gunner, Sergeant FAP Head, were reported 'Missing'.

McDonough was 23. He is remembered on the Runnymede Memorial, Panel 9.

APO 13.5.39   PO 6.11.39

CHARLES WHITE MacDOUGAL

811002   Sgt   Pilot   British   111 Squadron

MacDougal, of Garston, Liverpool was with 111 Squadron at Croydon in early July 1940.

He went to the Middle East in late 1940 and on January 29 1941 he flew to Malta, where he joined 261 Squadron. MacDougal destroyed a Ju 87 on March 5 1941 and was then himself shot down and killed by a Bf 109, in Hurricane V 7102.

MacDougal was 24. He is buried in Capuccini Naval Cemetery, Malta.

IAN NEIL MacDOUGALL

33491   FO   Pilot   British   141 Squadron

Born on June 11 1920, MacDougall was educated at Morrison's Academy, Crieff. He entered RAF College, Cranwell in April 1938 as a flight cadet. The course was shortened because of the war and MacDougall was commissioned in October 1939 and he joined 141 Squadron, then reforming at Turnhouse.

The squadron flew south to West Malling on July 12 1940. Shortly after 09.00 hrs on the 19th twelve Defiants moved to the forward airfield at Hawkinge. At 12.23 hrs they were ordered to carry out an offensive patrol twenty miles south of Folkestone. Three were left behind with engine trouble. During the patrol the nine Defiants were surprised by a force of Bf 109s of III/JG 51. MacDougall's aircraft, L 6983, was hit in the engine. He ordered his gunner, Sergeant JF Wise, to bale out. He then managed to get the aircraft back to West Malling. Wise was reported 'Missing' and no trace of him was ever found.

MacDougall was a Flight Commander with 260 Squadron in the Middle East in late 1941/early 1942. He was awarded the DFC (15.5.42). He commanded 94 Squadron in the Western Desert from

260

February to May 1942, commanded 185 Squadron in Malta from June 1943 to January 1944 and then 131 Squadron in the UK from May to October 1944.

He retired from the RAF on December 27 1969, as an Air Commodore. MacDougall died in August 1987.

PO 21.10.39 FO 21.10.40 FL 21.10.41 SL 1.7.45
WC 1.7.51 GC 1.7.58 AC 1.7.64

RALPH IAN GEORGE MacDOUGALL

29041 SL Pilot British 17 Squadron

Born on August 8 1911, MacDougall joined the RAF in March 1930. He carried out his flying training at 5 FTS, Sealand and then joined 43 Squadron at Tangmere on March 8 1931. He commanded the squadron from August 1936 until February 4 1937, when he was posted to the Experimental Section, RAE, Farnborough, to command the Instrument, Armament and Defence Flight.

In October 1939 MacDougall formed and then commanded 235 Squadron. He took command of 17 Squadron at Debden in June 1940 and was posted away on July 18, going as a Fighter Controller to HQ 9 Group and later RAF Catterick.

From 1942 to 1944 MacDougall was Station Commander at Hal Far, Ramleh, Haifa and Ramat David. He returned to the UK in 1945 and was Station Commander at RAF Andover until 1947, when he went on to the Reserve. MacDougall returned to full-time service in 1948 and finally retired from August 9 1966, as a Flight Lieutenant, retaining the rank of Wing Commander.

PO 14.3.30 FO 14.9.31 FL 14.9.35 SL 1.10.38
WC 1.6.41

ROY McDOUGALL

82706 PO Pilot British 3 and 232 Squadrons

McDougall joined 3 Squadron at Wick on August 20 1940. He was posted to 232 Squadron at Castletown on September 8.

In February 1941 McDougall was posted to the Middle East, to join 73 Squadron at Gazala West. On July 15 he destroyed two Ju 87s, on August 8 probably destroyed a Bf 109, on January 8 1942 probably destroyed another and on May 28 he destroyed a Ju 88.

McDougall was released from the RAF in 1946, as a Flight Lieutenant.

PO 27.7.40 FO 27.7.41 FL 27.7.42

ANDREW McDOWALL

89299 Sgt Pilot British 602 Squadron

Born in 1913 at Kirkinner, Wigtownshire, Scotland, McDowall was working as an engineer on Clydeside before the war. He trained with the RAFVR and joined 602 Squadron in mid-1939, as a Sergeant-Pilot. He was called to full-time service at the outbreak of war.

On July 24 1940 McDowall attacked a He 111 caught in searchlights. It jettisoned two parachute mines and although his attack had no apparent result the enemy aircraft was later reported to have crashed in the sea. On August 18 he claimed a Bf 109 destroyed, on the 26th a He 111, on September 9 a Bf 109, on the 11th a Bf 110, on the 30th two Ju 88s, on October 27 another Ju 88, on the 29th two Bf 109s, on the 30th a Bf 109 and on November 6 two Bf 109s. He was awarded the DFM (8.10.40) and Bar (17.12.40).

Commissioned in November 1940, McDowall was posted to 245 Squadron at Aldergrove on April 15 1941, as a Flight Commander. In July he was OC 'B' Squadron at 52 OTU, Debden. On April 10 1942 McDowall took command of 232 Squadron, when it reformed

at Atcham. He was posted away to a staff job at HQ 13 Group in September.

In July 1944 McDowall was given command of 616 Squadron at Manston. He left the squadron in May 1945 and was released from the RAF later in the year, as a Wing Commander. He went to work for Gloster's, testing Meteors being sold to foreign air forces.

McDowall died in 1981. His portrait was drawn by Cuthbert Orde in 1940.

PO 29.11.40 FO 2.5.41 FL 2.5.42 SL 5.10.43

AUBREY McFADDEN

42510 PO Pilot British 73 Squadron

Joined the RAF on a short service commission in June 1939. McFadden was with 73 Squadron in France in May 1940. He was shot down on the 10th but was unhurt.

On September 27 McFadden claimed a Bf 110 destroyed. At the beginning of April 1942 he was with 258 Squadron, operating from Racecourse airfield in Ceylon. He was killed on April 5 when the Japanese made a carrier-based aircraft attack on Colombo. 258 was scrambled and destroyed four of the attacking bombers but it was then jumped by Zeros and nine of its Hurricanes were destroyed, McFadden's amongst them. He was 24 years old and is remembered on the Singapore Memorial, Column 412.

APO 19.8.39 PO 28.2.40 FO 23.2.41

COLIN HAMILTON MacFIE

90657 FO Pilot British 611 and 616 Squadrons

Born at Cheltenham on June 12 1920, MacFie joined 611 Squadron, AuxAF in early 1939. He was called to full-time service with the squadron on August 26.

MacFie was congratulated by the AOC for carrying out a convoy patrol in terrible visibility on February 28 1940, from which one of the three pilots involved failed to return.

Over Dunkirk on June 2 MacFie destroyed a Ju 87. He was posted to 616 Squadron at Coltishall on September 7, as a Flight Commander.

On a sweep over France on July 5 1941 MacFie was forced down and captured. He was awarded the DFC (8.8.41), being then credited with two enemy aircraft destroyed and three damaged.

MacFie commanded No 1 Squadron from October 1946 to July 1947 and then 3 Squadron until November 1949. He retired from the RAF on October 18 1963, as a Squadron Leader, and died in 1982.

APO (AuxAF) 12.3.39 PO 26.8.39 FO 3.9.40 FL 3.9.41
FL 1.12.42 SL 1.7.44 SL 1.1.52

CHARLES ALEXANDER McGAW

42414 PO Pilot British 73 and 66 Squadrons

McGaw, of Paisley, Renfrewshire, joined the RAF on a short service commission in June 1939. He was with 73 Squadron at Church Fenton in early July 1940 and moved to 66 Squadron at West Malling on October 23.

McGaw was killed on October 1 1943, as a Flight Lieutenant with 18 Squadron, operating in Bostons from Gerbini, Sicily. He was 23 and is remembered on the Malta Memorial, Panel 6, Column 1.

APO 5.8.39 PO 6.4.40 FO 6.4.41 FL 6.4.42

JAMES McGIBBON

84016   **PO**   **Pilot**   **British**   **615 Squadron**

McGibbon, of Shandon, Dumbartonshire, joined 615 Squadron at Prestwick on September 23 1940.

During a practice flight on the 29th McGibbon dived into the ground from 7000 feet, in Hurricane V 7312, from causes unknown. He was killed, aged 25. He is buried in Faslane Cemetery, Rhu, Dumbartonshire.

PO 24.8.40

KENNETH BUTTERWORTH McGLASHAN

42138   **PO**   **Pilot**   **British**   **245 Squadron**

McGlashan was born on August 28 1920 and joined the RAF on a short service commission in January 1939. He was posted to 245 Squadron on November 6, soon after its reformation at Leconfield.

On May 31 1940 McGlashan was shot down over Dunkirk and returned to England by ship. He served with 245 throughout the Battle of Britain.

Awarded the AFC (8.6.50), McGlashan retired from the RAF on August 29 1958, as a Squadron Leader. He later settled in Australia.

APO 13.3.39   PO 6.11.39   FO 6.11.40   FL 6.11.41
FL 1.9.45   SL 1.1.49

HERBERT WALTER McGOWAN

78935   **PO**   **Pilot**   **British**   **92 Squadron**

Joined 92 Squadron at Pembrey in late August 1940. McGowan was shot down by Bf 109s on September 14, baled out, wounded, and was admitted to Faversham Hospital. His Spitfire, R 6624, crashed at Sale Street House, Faversham.

McGowan later transferred to the Administrative Branch and was released from the RAF in late 1944, as a Flight Lieutenant.

PO 1.5.40   FO 1.5.41   FL 1.6.42

ROY ANDREW McGOWAN

73001   **FO**   **Pilot**   **British**   **46 Squadron**

McGowan joined the newly-formed RAFVR in March 1937. He began training at 2 E&RFTS, Filton and soloed in April. At the request of Air Ministry McGowan's employers released him for six months from December 1938 for continuous training with the regular RAF. He joined 66 Squadron at Duxford, was commissioned in late March 1939 and posted to 46 Squadron at Digby.

With war looking more likely McGowan's attachment, due to end in June, was extended and he was still with 46

at the outbreak of war. In November 1939 he moved to 610 Squadron at Wittering. Due to return to 46 in March 1940, McGowan was diverted to ferry Gladiators to Turnhouse, where they were picked up by 263 Squadron for eventual use in Norway.

McGowan returned to Digby and found 46 was also destined for Norway. He and other pilots of the squadron sailed from Aberdeen to Harstad, whilst 46 flew its Hurricanes off to Bardufoss. Soon after McGowan's arrival the decision to evacuate Norway was made and he returned to the UK, without having done any flying.

Reformed at Digby in June 1940, the squadron supported 11 Group and joined 12 Group formations. The squadron moved south to Stapleford Tawney on September 1. McGowan was shot down on the 15th and baled out, with burns. He received skin grafts and other treatment at the Queen Victoria Hospital at East Grinstead, making him a Guinea Pig.

In May 1941 McGowan was back on limited flying and was posted to Martlesham Heath i/c Airfield Control. He later instructed at 57 OTU, Hawarden. McGowan was loaned to the RNZAF in June 1942 and was based in Wellington as Ops II to assist in the formation of Kittyhawk squadrons and setting up Fighter Operations Control. He returned to the UK in late 1943 and was posted to CGS, Sutton Bridge for a Spitfire course at the Fighter Wing.

McGowan was then given command of the Fighter Armament Practice Camp at Peterhead, later moving to 53 OTU, Kirton-in-Lindsey, in command of 3 (Gunnery) Squadron there. In December 1944 McGowan was posted to Italy and joined 8 (SAAF) Wing, as supernumerary Squadron Leader, and flew operationally in Spitfires until the end of the war. He was then posted to 239 Wing in Italy as Squadron Leader Admin and returned from there to the UK for demobilization in November 1945.

PO (RAFVR) 29.3.39   PO 30.10.39   FO 3.9.40   FL 3.9.41
SL 1.7.44

JOHN KESWICK ULICK BLAKE McGRATH

90967   **PO**   **Pilot**   **British**   **601 Squadron**

Born in Tonbridge, Kent on November 19 1919, McGrath was at Harrow School from 1933 to 1937. He joined 601 Squadron, AuxAF in 1939 and was called to full-time service on August 25.

McGrath flew to France with 'A' Flight of 601 on May 16 1940, to reinforce 3 Squadron. On the 22nd he destroyed a Bf 109 over Arras. The squadron was withdrawn to Tangmere and over Dunkirk on the 27th McGrath destroyed a Bf 110 and probably another.

On July 11 he probably destroyed a He 111, on August 8 two Bf 109s, on August 11 two Bf 110s and on the 13th a Ju 88 and a Bf 109. He was awarded the DFC (27.8.40).

McGrath was released from the RAF in 1946, as a Squadron Leader.

APO 25.8.39   PO 4.5.40   FO 9.12.40   FL 9.12.41

ALAN JAMES McGREGOR

81919   **PO**   **Pilot**   **British**   **504 Squadron**

Born on November 23 1920, McGregor was with 504 Squadron at Castletown in early July 1940.

In late July 1941 'A' Flight of 504, McGregor's, was re-numbered 81 Squadron and posted to Leconfield, where the personnel were kitted out for an unknown destination overseas. They flew to Abbotsinch in Harrows and embarked for Russia on the carrier HMS 'Argus', which carried crated Hurricanes. On September 1 the squadron flew off in sixes for Vaenga airfield, near Murmansk. Operations, including bomber escorts, continued until mid-November, when 81's pilots began converting Russian pilots on to Hurricanes. They left Russia on November 29, leaving all aircraft and equipment behind and returned in HMS 'Kenya', landing at Rosyth on December 7 1941.

McGregor commanded 123 Squadron in the Far East, with Spitfires and later Thunderbolts, from July 1943 until its disbandment in June 1945. He then commanded 81 Squadron briefly in July. He was awarded the DSO (19.10.45).

Released from the RAF in 1946, McGregor rejoined later and retired on November 23 1976, as a Wing Commander.

PO 18.6.40   FO 18.6.41   FL 18.6.42   FL 1.10.52
SL 1.1.65   WC 1.1.71

ALEXANDER NOEL MacGREGOR

109895   Sgt   Pilot   British   266 and 19 Squadrons

MacGregor joined 602 Squadron, AuxAF on January 12 1936 as a trainee air gunner. He transferred to the RAFVR for pilot training on September 29 1937 and began flying at 12 E&RFTS, Prestwick.

Called to full-time service at the outbreak of war, MacGregor was posted to 4 AOS, West Freugh, as a staff pilot. He went to 7 OTU, Hawarden on September 2 1940, converted to Spitfires, joined 266 Squadron at Wittering on the 14th and moved to 19 Squadron at Duxford on the 27th.

MacGregor was posted away to 46 Squadron at Sherburn-in-Elmet on May 5 1941. Later in the month the squadron pilots and aircraft sailed in HMS 'Argus' for Gibraltar, where they transferred to the 'Ark Royal' and sailed into the Mediterranean. They flew off to Malta on June 6 1941.

MacGregor damaged a SM 79 on the 11th. 46 Squadron was re-numbered 126 Squadron at Ta Kali on July 15. MacGregor probably destroyed a Mc 200 on August 19, another on the 26th, another on September 4 and damaged a Mc 202 on November 22. He was wounded in the foot on December 23 and made a forced-landing in Hurricane Z 5118.

MacGregor was commissioned in October 1941. He was posted away from 126 in March 1942 and went to 33 FIS at Salisbury, Southern Rhodesia, for an instructor's course, after which he instructed at 28 EFTS, Mount Hampden.

On February 19 1944 MacGregor sailed from Durban for the UK. He was posted to 1 TEU, Tealing to convert to Typhoons, went to GSU, Cranfield on May 22 and then to 3 TEU, Aston Down on August 14. MacGregor was posted to the Middle East in late November 1944 and was in various units before returning to the UK on September 2 1945. He was released later in the year, as a Flight Lieutenant. MacGregor rejoined the RAFVR and instructed at 18 RFS, Fair Oaks and later 11 RFS, Perth until October 30 1952.

PO 8.10.41   FO 1.10.42   FL 1.10.43
FO (RAFVR) 31.10.47

GORDON ROY McGREGOR

C 936   FL   Pilot   Canadian   1 (RCAF) Squadron

Born in Montreal on September 26 1901, McGregor was educated at St Andrew's College, Toronto and McGill University, Montreal. He was the winner in 1935, 1936 and 1938 of the Webster Trophy, open to non-professional airmen and awarded for airmanship and navigation.

McGregor was commissioned in October 1938, serving with the RCAF Auxiliary, in 115 Squadron. At the outbreak of war pilots of the squadron and pilots of No 1 Squadron of the regular RCAF formed No 1 (RCAF)

Squadron. McGregor was with this squadron when it arrived in the UK on June 20 1940, as a Flight Commander.

He claimed a Do 17 destroyed on August 26, a He 111 on September 11 and Bf 109s on September 30 and October 5. He was awarded the DFC (25.10.40). McGregor commanded his squadron in November/December 1940. In January 1941 he was given command of 2 (RCAF) Squadron at Digby, which was re-numbered 402 Squadron on March 1.

McGregor was promoted on April 14 to lead the Canadian Wing at Digby. He came off operations on August 31 1941 and returned to Canada but was back in London in October. He was appointed Director of Air Staff at HQ RCAF, London on December 5 and did this job until April 17 1942, when he again returned to Canada.

He formed and then commanded a Wing to give air support to the Americans in Alaska. McGregor was made an OBE (1.1.43), promoted to Group Captain and posted back to Canada in late February 1943. On April 1 he took command at Patricia Bay, from where its squadrons served on defence of the west coast of Canada.

McGregor returned to England on February 23 1944, spent four months at HQ 83 Group and in mid-July was given command of 126 (RCAF) Wing. He still flew occasional sorties, one of his last being on March 28 1945, when he destroyed a locomotive. Said to be the oldest Canadian fighter pilot to see action in the war, McGregor left the Wing on September 27, returned to Canada and was released from the RCAF on November 27 1945. He was awarded the C de G (Fr) in 1947, the Czech Military Cross and was made a Commander of the Order of Orange-Nassau with Swords.

From 1948 to 1969 McGregor was with Trans-Canada Airlines and Air Canada, becoming President of the Company. He died in Montreal on March 8 1971.

HECTOR DOUGLAS McGREGOR

27031   SL   Pilot   New Zealander   213 Squadron

Born at Wairoa on February 15 1910, McGregor was educated at Napier Boys' High School. He went to the UK early in 1928 and joined the RAF on a short service commission.

McGregor was posted to 3 FTS, Grantham on April 28 and after training he joined 111 Squadron at Hornchurch on April 2 1929. He went to 407 (Fleet Fighter) Flight on HMS 'Courageous' on January 20 1931 but moved to the Home Aircraft Depot on August 5 1931, for a specialist engineering course. McGregor was posted to the School of Naval Co-operation, Lee-on-Solent on July 24 1933 and then to HQ Coastal Command, Engineer Section on August 2 1934.

He was at Air Ministry, in the Directorate of Repair and Maintenance, from April 30 1936 until posted to Egypt in September 1938, to take command of 33 Squadron at Heliopolis. In March 1939 the squadron began policing duties at Lydda, with small detachments at strategic points. They assisted ground forces to round up armed tribesmen, who were terrorising certain areas. The tactics were successful and order was restored by June. For his leadership in the operations McGregor was awarded the DSO.

In early 1940 McGregor returned to the UK and in early June took command of 213 Squadron at Biggin Hill. On May 31, as CO designate, he went on a patrol over Dunkirk and was shot down. He baled out, was rescued from the sea by a destroyer and put ashore at Dunkirk, eventually returning in a ship to Dover.

McGregor claimed a Ju 88 destroyed on August 11 1940 and a Bf 110 on the 12th. He was quoted as saying that he destroyed six enemy aircraft in the Battle of Britain, three Ju 88s, two Bf 109s and a Bf 110. He was posted away from 213 in September 1940.

In 1941 McGregor commanded RAF Ballyhalbert, from 1942 to mid-1943 RAF Tangmere and in June 1943 he was appointed Group Captain Ops at Mediterranean Air Command, on the staff of Air Chief Marshal Tedder.

In April 1944 McGregor became Allied Deputy Director of Operations, Intelligence Plans, North Africa and Italy. He took an important part in negotiations at the time of the Italian Armistice, concerning the handing over of the Italian Air Force. He was awarded the US Legion of Merit in April 1944 and was made a CBE in June 1945.

McGregor went on to a most distinguished post-war career in the RAF. He retired from the RAF on September 27 1964, as an Air Marshal KCB. He died on April 11 1973.

PO 13.4.28   FO 13.10.29   FL 1.6.34   SL 1.2.38
WC 1.9.40   GC 1.9.42   GC 1.10.46   AC 1.7.53
AVM 1.7.55   AM 1.1.60

PETER REGINALD McGREGOR

73002   FO   Pilot   British   46 Squadron

McGregor joined the RAFVR in Bristol on May 22 1937 and did his flying training at 2 E&RFTS, Filton. In February 1939 he went on six months continuous training with the regular RAF and was attached to 66 Squadron at Duxford from February 27.

Commissioned in June 1939, McGregor was posted to 46 Squadron at Digby on June 13. The attachment period was extended and he remained with 46 after the outbreak of war. On May 11 1940 he embarked with the squadron on HMS 'Glorious' for Norway. The airfield at Skaanland was not considered suitable for the Hurricanes and the carrier returned to Scapa Flow. It sailed again on the 24th and they flew off to Bardufoss on the 26th. McGregor left Norway on June 7 and was with 46, when it reformed at Digby on the 15th.

The squadron went south to Stapleford on September 1 and on the 18th McGregor was shot down by a Bf 109. He crash-landed at Meopham Green, in Hurricane P 3053, unhurt. On the 11th he was shot down in combat over the Thames Estuary, baled out, injured, and was admitted to hospital. His Hurricane, P 3094, crashed and burned out in West Lordine Wood, Staplecross.

On May 22 1941 46 Squadron pilots and aircraft sailed in HMS 'Argus' for Gibraltar, where they transferred to the 'Ark Royal' and sailed into the Mediterranean. They flew off to Hal Far, Malta on June 6. McGregor shared in destroying a SM 79 on the 11th. 46 Squadron was re-numbered 126 Squadron on July 15. On an early morning strafe of Syracuse seaplane base on August 17 McGregor damaged at least four aircraft. He joined 185 Squadron at Hal Far on January 1 1942, staying with it until March 2, when he was posted back to the UK.

McGregor went to 53 OTU, Llandow on April 5 1942. He did a course at the Pilot Gunnery Instructors Training Wing at CGS, Sutton Bridge and then returned to 53 OTU. Further gunnery courses followed at Valley, Llanbedr and Exeter before he joined 611 Squadron at Coltishall on October 25 1943, as a Flight Commander. McGregor took command of the squadron in August 1944 and led it until January 29 1945, when he was posted to No 1 CTC, Bombay for combined operations.

On October 20 1945 McGregor took command of 11 Squadron at Seletar, Singapore. He led it to Japan in April 1946 and returned to the UK in early November. He was released from the RAF on December 15 1946, as a Squadron Leader. McGregor joined 501 Squadron, RAuxAF in January 1948 and served until January 1951.

PO (RAFVR) 29.3.39   PO 31.10.39   FO 3.9.40   FL 3.9.41
SL 1.7.44   FO (RAuxAF) 26.1.48   FL (RAuxAF) 1.9.49

ROBERT McGUGAN

115801   Sgt   Air Gunner   British   141 Squadron

Born on May 17 1920, McGugan was with 141 Squadron at Turnhouse in early July 1940. Commissioned in January 1942, he retired from the RAF on May 17 1969, as a Squadron Leader.

PO 5.1.42   FO 1.10.42   FL 5.1.44   FL 1.9.45
SL 1.1.55

JIRI MACHACEK

82560   PO   Pilot   Czechoslovakian   310 and 145 Sqdns

Machacek joined 310 Squadron at Duxford on August 6 1940 and moved to 145 Squadron at Drem on September 11.

Flying from Tangmere on October 15 Machacek was attacked by Bf 109s over Christchurch, baled out, wounded in the leg, and admitted to Lymington Hospital. His Hurricane, V 7337, was abandoned over Milton and presumably crashed into the sea.

Machacek was killed on July 8 1941, as a Flying Officer with 145 Squadron. He is remembered on the Runnymede Memorial, Panel 30.

FO 27.12.40

DONALD BALLANTINE HARDY McHARDY

40928   FO   Pilot   British   229 Squadron

Born on January 10 1918, McHardy was at Cheltenham College from September 1931 to December 1932. In 1937 he was a 2nd Lieutenant in the 4th Battalion Welch Regiment (TA). He joined the RAF on a short service commission in May 1938.

McHardy was with 229 Squadron at Wittering in early July 1940.

He claimed a He 111 destroyed on September 27. Patrolling the Croydon area on October 26 the squadron sighted a number of Bf 109s, which they pursued to the coast of France but then lost. A section, composed of Flying Officer GM Simpson, Sergeant RJ Ommaney and McHardy, went down to attack a He 59 floatplane flying low off the coast near Boulogne. The enemy aircraft alighted on the sea, damaged, and the three Hurricanes were attacked by Bf 109s and gunfire from the shore. Ommaney got back to base but Simpson and McHardy failed to return. McHardy was later reported to be a prisoner of war.

McHardy was released from the RAF in 1946, as a Flight Lieutenant. He joined the RAFVR in 1949 and died in 1967.

APO 9.7.38   PO 16.5.39   FO 3.9.40   FL 3.9.41
FL (RAFRO) 1.12.42   FO (RAFVR) 22.11.47

EDRIC HARTGILL McHARDY

42139   PO   Pilot   New Zealander   248 Squadron

Born in Palmerston North on June 24 1920, McHardy was at Wanganui Collegiate School from 1935 to 1937, after which he farmed with his parents at Waipawa. In June 1938 he went to Wellington to apply for entrance into the Navy but was too late to sit the examinations. McHardy applied for an RAF short service commission and after provisional acceptance he sailed for the UK on February 1 1939 in the RMS 'Tainui'.

McHardy began his ab initio course at 10 E&RFTS, Yatesbury on March 16, moved on to 5 FTS, Sealand on May 30 and after high-dive bombing and low-level bombing exercises at Aldergrove he joined 248 Squadron at Hendon.

In February 1940 the squadron was transferred to Coastal Command and moved to North Coates. On May 18, on a trawler escort off Zeebrugge, McHardy destroyed a Bf 110 and shared a He 111.

248 Squadron did most of its work over the Norwegian coast. On July 27 McHardy flew to Trondheim to photograph the 'Gneisenau' in the harbour there. He had to go below cloud, at 10000 feet, and encountered heavy flak. Reconnaissances of the fjords, searching for German ships, were extremely hazardous and often carried out in adverse weather conditions.

On November 3 McHardy damaged a He 111. Awarded the DFC (10.3.41), he was posted to 404 (RCAF) Squadron at Skitten on July 21, as 'B' Flight Commander. On December 21 1941 McHardy was RAF representative and fighter controller on the combined operations raid on Vaagso. He was flown to Scapa Flow and embarked on the cruiser HMS 'Kenya'. After entering the fjord at dawn the commandos landed under cover of a barrage from ships and a smoke screen. McHardy directed the fighters by R/T from the bridge of the 'Kenya'.

McHardy probably destroyed a He 115 on January 16 1942 and on April 22 he damaged a Ju 88. On May 17 404 escorted Beauforts to attack the German battleship 'Prinz Eugen' off Norway. As the squadron withdrew McHardy saw a Beaufighter ditch and its crew surface without a dinghy. He circled and dropped his own. This incident led to his being awarded the C de G (Fr) in 1949, the ditched crew having been members of the Free French Air Force.

Awarded a Bar to the DFC (15.6.42), McHardy took command of 404 Squadron on July 14. Then, with his tour completed, he was posted away to RAF Ferry Command at Prestwick on October 17 1942. He began flying Liberators to and from West Africa. He received a Mention in Despatches (1.1.43) and was sent to Brazil to establish a staging post at Para Belem, on the Amazon. In August 1943 McHardy took command of the South Atlantic Ferry Service at Nassau.

He returned to operations on November 20 1943, when he took command of 143 Squadron at Portreath, as a Wing Commander. On December 12 he destroyed two Ju 88s over the Bay of Biscay. McHardy was awarded the DSO (22.8.44). With his third tour of operations completed he went to RAF Staff College at Gerrards Cross on January 8 1945. He was posted to HQ 46 Transport Command

Group on July 9 for staff duties.

McHardy retired from the RAF at his own request on May 7 1958, as a Squadron Leader, retaining the rank of Wing Commander. He returned to New Zealand to live.

APO 12.5.39   PO 6.11.39   FO 6.11.40   FL 6.11.41
SL 14.10.42   FL 1.9.45   SL 1.1.49

WILLIAM HOWARD MACHIN

968717   Sgt   Air Gunner   British   264 Squadron

Machin, of Handsworth, Birmingham, joined 264 Squadron at Hornchurch on August 22 1940. He was gunner in Defiant L 6965, which was shot down by Bf 109s of JG 51 over Hornchurch on the 24th.

Machin died of his wounds, aged 20. He is buried in Handsworth Cemetery.

MICHAL MACIEJOWSKI

P 1912   Sgt   Pilot   Polish   249 Squadron

Born on October 29 1913, Maciejowski joined 249 Squadron at North Weald in October 1940.

He claimed Bf 109s destroyed on October 29, November 7, December 5, January 10 1941 and February 10. Maciejowski was posted to 317 Squadron at Acklington at its formation on February 22 1941. He claimed a probable Ju 52 on May 22. He was awarded the KW and Bar (1.4.41), a second Bar (15.7.41) and the DFM (30.10.41). Maciejowski claimed two Bf 109s destroyed on December 30. He was awarded the VM (5th Class)(5.5.42), commissioned in June, claimed a Ju 88 and a FW 190 destroyed and shared a Do 17 over Dieppe on August 19 and was posted away from 317 on August 25 to 58 OTU, Grangemouth, as an instructor.

Maciejowski was awarded a third Bar to the KW (15.11.42) and the DFC (15.11.42). He returned to operations on March 23 1943, when he joined 316 Squadron at Northolt. He probably destroyed a FW 190 on May 4 and destroyed a Bf 109 on June 11. Maciejowski was shot down on August 9 1943 and captured. He returned to duty on June 1 1945.

After a refresher course at 16 FTS, Newton from August 21, Maciejowski was posted to 309 Squadron at Coltishall on November 11. He remained with the squadron until its disbandment on January 6 1947. Maciejowski was then released from the PAF, as a Flight Lieutenant. He settled in England and changed his name to Manson.

PO 1.6.42   FO 1.6.43   FL 1.6.44

ARCHIBALD McINNES

84920   PO   Pilot   British   601 and 238 Squadrons

McInnes was born in 1913. He joined 601 Squadron at Exeter on September 17 1940 and moved to 238 Squadron at Chilbolton on October 8.

McInnes was released from the RAF in 1946, as a Flight Lieutenant.

PO 31.8.40   FO 31.8.41   FL 31.8.42

JANUSZ MACINSKI

76721   PO   Pilot   Polish   111 Squadron

Joined 111 Squadron at Debden on August 31 1940. Macinski was shot down during combat with Bf 109s on September 4 and baled out. His Hurricane, Z 2309, is presumed to have crashed in the Channel five miles east of Folkestone.

Macinski was reported 'Missing' and is remembered on the Polish Air Force Memorial at Northolt. He was 24. One report stated that he was killed by German fighters as he floated down. Macinski was awarded the KW (31.10.47).

PETER ROY CHARLES McINTOSH

745004   Sgt   Pilot   British   151 and 605 Squadrons

Born at Crofton Park, Brockley on August 9 1920, McIntosh was educated at Woodside Primary School and Whitgift Middle School. He worked for the Eagle Star Insurance Co and joined the RAFVR on February 7 1939.

Called to full-time service on September 11 1939, McIntosh went to ITW and began flying training on January 1 1940. He was awarded his flying badge on May 21 and joined 151 Squadron at Martlesham Heath on July 7.

McIntosh was posted to 605 Squadron on September 13. He was shot down and killed in action against Bf 109s over the Channel off Dungeness on October 12 1940. His Hurricane, P 3022, crashed by Littlestone golf course. McIntosh is buried in St John's churchyard, Shirley, Croydon.

ATHOL GORDON McINTYRE

36257   PO   Pilot   New Zealander   111 Squadron

Born in Auckland on January 4 1917, McIntyre was educated at New Plymouth Boys' High School. He went to work for an insurance company in Wellington.

In August 1938 McIntyre applied for an RNZAF short service commission but with no immediate vacancies he did not begin his elementary flying training at the Wellington Aero Club until June 26 1939. McIntyre was posted to No 1 FTS, Wigram on September 12, awarded his flying badge on November 23 and sailed for the UK in early March 1940 in the SS 'Remuera'.

McIntyre transferred to the RAF at Uxbridge and went to 12 OTU, Benson in May, to convert to Battles. On June 3 he was carrying out a night cross-country exercise. At one point he was engaged by searchlights and fired on by anti-aircraft guns, in spite of having given correct code signals for the day. Later on the same flight he ran out of fuel and baled out, landing safely but suffering concussion.

In June McIntyre moved to 7 OTU, Hawarden to convert to Spitfires and joined 111 Squadron at Croydon in the middle of July. On August 13 he shared a Do 17 and on the 15th he was shot down by a Bf 110 over Thorney Island. His Hurricane, P 3595, was severely damaged and he landed at Hawkinge, slightly wounded.

On March 1 1941 McIntyre was posted to 485 Squadron, then being formed at Driffield. With his tour completed he went to 51 OTU, Cranfield in August 1941, as an instructor and did not return to operations until November 1942, when he joined 488 Squadron at Ayr. McIntyre was made a Flight Commander in February 1943 and in May went on attachment to Rolls Royce at Derby, where he became Senior

AG McIntyre (continued)

Service Instructor on the Fighter Pilots' Engine-Handling Course.

McIntyre was posted away in October 1944 and in January 1945 went to 83 GSU, Aston Down, to convert to Typhoons and Tempests. He joined 3 Squadron at Volkel in March 1945 and was with it until July, when he was posted to RAF Sealand, as a maintenance test pilot. McIntyre was awarded the AFC (1.1.58) and retired from the RAF on January 30 1959, as a Squadron Leader. He went to work for Rolls Royce and eventually became Military Representative in the Aero Division. He retired in 1981.

APO 12.9.39   PO 13.4.40   FO 13.4.41   FL 13.4.42
FL 1.9.45   SL 1.7.56

DONALD ALISTAIR STEWART McKAY

113322   Sgt   Pilot   British   501 Squadron & 421 Flight

Born in 1917 at Pontefract, Yorkshire, McKay joined the RAFVR in April 1937 and trained at 5 E&RFTS, Hanworth. On February 6 1939 he began a six month attachment for continuous training with the regular RAF and joined 43 Squadron at Tangmere. On June 13 he moved to 111 Squadron at Northolt and with war looking to be imminent his attachment was extended and he was officially called up at the outbreak of war.

On September 6 1939 McKay was posted to 501 Squadron at Filton and went to France with the squadron on May 10 1940. He claimed a He 111 destroyed on the 12th and another and probably a second on the 25th. The squadron was withdrawn from France on June 18 and re-assembled at Croydon on the 21st.

McKay claimed a probable Ju 87 on July 29 and destroyed two more on August 15. Three days later he was shot down over Canterbury by Oberleutnant Schöpfel of JG 26 and baled out over Dargate, slightly burned, from Hurricane N 2617. He claimed a Do 17 on October 12 and on the 22nd he was posted to the newly-formed 421 Flight at Hawkinge. McKay claimed a Bf 109 on November 27 and a Ju 88 on December 17.

He was awarded the DFM (7.1.41), claimed a Bf 109 on February 4 1941, was awarded a Bar to the DFM (18.3.41) and destroyed Bf 109s on April 21 and May 11. McKay was posted to 55 OTU on June 20, as an instructor. Commissioned in October 1941, he joined 234 Squadron at Ibsley on January 16 1942 and on February 12 he destroyed two Bf 109s. He was posted to 130 Squadron at Perranporth on the 24th, as a Flight Commander. McKay's stay was a short one and he left for service in the Middle East on April 7 1942.

McKay may have joined 213 Squadron on arrival. He went to 33 Squadron at Edku on August 23 1942 and then to 274 Squadron at LG 37 on November 1. Tour-expired, he was posted to a communications flight and later an MU. On January 25 1944 McKay went south to Rhodesia, as an instructor. He departed for the UK on July 16 1945 and went to 7 EFTS, Desford on October 1, as an instructor. McKay was released from the RAF in 1947, as a Flight Lieutenant. He joined the RAFVR and continued as an instructor at Desford until June 30 1953. He died on September 30 1959.

PO 7.10.41   FO 15.4.42   FL 15.4.43
FO (RAFVR) 10.12.47

RONALD MacKAY

91227   PO   Pilot   British   234 Squadron

Born on April 13 1910, MacKay was in the AuxAF before the war. He was called to full-time service in late August 1939 and after completing his training he joined 234 Squadron at Middle Wallop on September 9 1940.

Returning to St Eval from a routine sortie on September 25 he baled out and was seriously injured. His Spitfire, X 4182, crashed near St Mawgan.

MacKay was released from the RAF in January 1946, as a Flight Lieutenant.

PO 17.8.40   FO 20.6.41   FL 20.6.42

ARCHIBALD ASHMORE McKELLAR

90168   FL   Pilot   British   605 Squadron

Born in Paisley in 1912, McKellar was educated at Shawlands Academy, Glasgow. He worked in the family plastering business. After gaining his 'A' license at the Scottish Flying Club McKellar joined 602 Squadron, AuxAF in 1936.

Called to full-time service with the squadron on August 24 1939, McKellar shared in shooting down a He 111 on October 28. It crashed at Kidlaw, the first enemy aircraft to fall on British soil in the war.

McKellar was posted to 605 Squadron at Drem on June 21 1940, as a Flight Commander. On August 15 he claimed three He 111s destroyed, on September 9 three He 111s and a Bf 109, on the 11th a shared He 111, on the 15th two Bf 109s and a Do 17 and on the 16th a He 111. On September 29 McKellar took command of 605. On October 7 he claimed five Bf 109s destroyed and on October 20, 26 and 27 three more.

McKellar was shot down and killed on November 1 1940. His Hurricane, V 6879, crashed at Woodlands, Adisham. He is buried in New Eastwood Cemetery, Glasgow. McKellar was awarded the DFC (13.9.40), a Bar (8.10.40) and the DSO (26.11.40). His portrait was drawn by Cuthbert Orde in October 1940.

PO (AuxAF) 8.11.36   FO (AuxAF) 8.5.38   FO 24.8.39
FL 1.6.40

DONALD CARR MACKENZIE

43706   PO   Pilot   New Zealander   56 Squadron

Born in Wellington on August 26 1921 Mackenzie was educated at Wellington College and went to work for an insurance company. He served as a gunner in the 22nd Anti-Aircraft Territorial Battery.

In late July 1939 Mackenzie applied for a short service commission in the RNZAF and was accepted for the last course, beginning his ground training on September 20. He was posted to No 1 EFTS, Taieri on October 21 and then to No 1 FTS, Wigram on December 16. Awarded his flying badge on February 13 1940, Mackenzie completed his training and sailed for the UK on April 26 in the RMS 'Rangitiki'.

Mackenzie was posted to 4 Ferry Pilots' Pool at Kemble on June 17, flying Wellingtons for further air experience. On July 18 he went to 12 OTU, Benson to convert to Battles. He then joined 142 Squadron at Eastchurch and flew one operation over enemy territory before volunteering for Fighter Command. Mackenzie joined 56 Squadron at Boscombe Down on September 5. Before being posted away to CFS, Upavon on January 1 1941 Mackenzie had taken part in twenty-three operational sorties and was credited with one Bf 109 destroyed.

After completing his instructor's course Mackenzie went to 2 FTS, Brize Norton. In March 1942 he was posted to RAF Hucknall, as a test pilot for Rolls Royce. In preparation for a return to operations Mackenzie went to 1654 Conversion Unit at Wigsley, to crew-up and convert to Wellingtons. He then joined 467 (RAAF) Squadron, being formed at Scampton.

In early April 1943 Mackenzie was promoted and appointed a Flight Commander. In the late evening of June 11 he took off in a Lancaster to attack Düsseldorf. He failed to return and he and his crew were reported 'Missing'. They are buried in a collective grave at Rheinberg Military Cemetery, Germany.

Mackenzie was awarded the DFC (20.7.43). It was presented to his parents by the Governor General in Wellington on January 9 1945.

APO 20.9.39   PO 8.6.40   FO 8.6.41   FL 8.6.42

JOHN NOBLE MACKENZIE

40547   FO   Pilot   New Zealander   41 Squadron

Mackenzie was born at Goodwood, Otago on August 11 1914, the grandson of a former Prime Minister of New Zealand. He was educated at Timaru and Otago Boys' High Schools and after leaving went farming in partnership with his father.

In April 1937 Mackenzie applied for an RAF short service commission and after provisional acceptance he sailed for the UK on October 23 in the RMS 'Remuera'. He began his ab initio course at 7 E&RFTS, Desford on December 16 and was posted to 9 FTS, Hullavington on March 5 1938.

Mackenzie joined 41 Squadron at Catterick on September 6. He was still with the squadron at the start of the Battle of Britain. On July 29 Mackenzie's Hurricane, N 3112, was badly damaged by Bf 109s over Dover. He could not bale out because his hood was jammed but he evaded the enemy fighters and made a forced-landing at Ringwould, near Deal. On August 15 Mackenzie claimed a Ju 88 destroyed, on September 6 a Bf 109, on the 11th a He 111, on October 5 and 30 and November 17 and 27 Bf 109s. He was awarded the DFC (15.11.40).

On January 16 1941 Mackenzie was made a Flight Commander. He was decorated by the King in March and posted away in April to be a Fighter Controller at Catterick. During his time with 41 Mackenzie had flown 245 operational sorties.

On September 3 1941 Mackenzie was posted to Singapore to join 488 (NZ) Squadron, as a Flight Commander. The squadron was formed in New Zealand and received its Buffalos at Kallang, when it arrived in November. It was not fully operational when the Japanese attacked and fought its first action on January 12 1942, suffering heavy losses then and during the next few days. Nine Hurricanes arrived on the 25th to reinforce the badly-depleted squadron but Japanese bombing of Kallang airfield made it almost impossible to continue operations. The remaining aircraft were evacuated to Sumatra on January 31 but by February 23 1942 it was all over and most of the pilots, Mackenzie among them, sailed in the 'Deucalion' for Fremantle. Six pilots remained behind to strengthen 605 Squadron.

Mackenzie arrived in New Zealand in April and was given command of 14 (RNZAF) Squadron, then forming at Ohakea. In August 1942 he was made CO of the Fighter OCU at Ohakea. He returned to the UK in June 1943. After a course at CGS, Sutton Bridge Mackenzie was posted to 61 OTU, Rednal as OC Bombing and Gunnery Squadron.

In April 1944 he took command of 64 Squadron at Deanland. He was now officially in the RNZAF and in September 1944 was posted away from 64 and repatriated to New Zealand. In mid-February 1945 he did a Corsair conversion course but it was decided that the RNZAF would not move north of the Solomons and the squadrons were withdrawn. Mackenzie was then posted to the Fighter Leaders' School at Ohakea on March 5. In August he left the RNZAF at his own request, in early 1946 returned to the UK and in July was granted an Extended Service Commission in the RAF. This became a Permanent Commission in 1948.

Mackenzie retired on December 18 1957, as a Squadron Leader, and returned to New Zealand.

APO 19.2.38   PO 6.12.38   FO 3.9.40   FL 3.9.41
SL 1.1.44   SL 1.8.47

JOHN WOFFENDEN McKENZIE

33461   PO   Pilot   British   111 Squadron

McKenzie, of Johannesburg, entered RAF College, Cranwell in April

1938 as a flight cadet. On graduation in September 1939 he was commissioned and joined 111 Squadron at Northolt.

On August 11 1940 McKenzie is believed to have been shot down by Bf 109s during a combat off Margate. His Hurricane, P 3922, crashed into the sea and he was reported 'Missing'.

McKenzie was 20. He is remembered on the Runnymede Memorial, Panel 9.

PO 1.10.39

KENNETH WILLIAM MACKENZIE

84017   PO   Pilot   British   43 and 501 Squadrons

Born in Belfast on June 8 1916, Mackenzie was educated at the Methodist College there and started an engineering apprenticeship at Harland and Wolff. He studied for an engineering degree at Queen's University, Belfast.

In 1935 Mackenzie learned to fly at the North of Ireland Aero Club at Newtownards and in early 1939 joined the RAFVR and did his flying training at 24 E&RFTS at Sydenham. Called up at the outbreak of war, Mackenzie went to 1 ITW, Hastings on December 28 1939. He moved to 5 EFTS, Hanworth on February 25 1940 and then to 3 FTS, South Cerney on May 25.

With his training completed Mackenzie was posted to 6 OTU, Sutton Bridge on August 30, to convert to Hurricanes. He joined 43 Squadron at Usworth on September 21. After sixteen training flights and two operational patrols Mackenzie was posted to 501 Squadron at Kenley on the 29th.

He shared in the destruction of a Ju 88 on October 4, claimed a Bf 109 destroyed on the 5th and another destroyed and a second shared on the 7th. The Bf 109 destroyed on this day was attacked by Mackenzie with no apparent result. He followed it down to almost sea level and when it did not ditch he struck the tailplane with his wing and the enemy fighter crashed into the sea. Mackenzie then made a forced-landing outside Folkestone, in Hurricane V 6799, with slight facial injuries.

On October 25 Mackenzie claimed a Bf 109 destroyed and another shared. In a later patrol that day he collided with Pilot Officer V Göth of 501 as he manoeuvred his section to attack a formation of Bf 109s. Mackenzie was awarded the DFC (25.10.40). On October 27, 29 and 30 he claimed Bf 109s destroyed, on November 15 a Bf 109 and another damaged, on the 23rd a Ju 88 shared and on the 28th a Bf 109 destroyed.

Mackenzie was posted to 247 Squadron at Predannack on June 19 1941, as a Flight Commander. He destroyed a Ju 88 at night on July 7 and a He 111 at night over a convoy on September 13. He flew from Predannack at dusk on September 29 to attack Lannion airfield in Brittany. Mackenzie was hit by heavy flak from the ground defences and ditched in the sea. He took to his dinghy, paddled to the shore and was captured. He was in various camps before finishing up at Stalag Luft III, Sagan.

Mackenzie was repatriated to the UK in October 1944, arriving at Liverpool on the 10th. He was posted to 53 OTU, Kirton-in-Lindsey on December 19, as an instructor. On June 17 1945 Mackenzie went to 61 OTU, Keevil, as a Flight Commander.

Awarded the AFC (1.1.53), Mackenzie retired from the RAF on July 1 1967, as a Wing Commander.

PO 24.8.40   FO 24.8.41   FL 24.8.42   SL 1.8.47
WC 1.1.54

ERNEST JOHN McKIE

120195   Sgt   Air Gunner   British   248 Squadron

Joined 248 Squadron on September 4 1940. McKie was commissioned in April 1942 and released from the RAF in 1945, as a Flight Lieutenant. He died in 1981.

PO 8.4.42   FO 8.10.42   FL 8.4.44

ADAM McLEOD MacKINNON

Lieutenant (FAA)   **Pilot**   **British**   **804 Squadron**

Joined the RAF on a short service commission in December 1936. MacKinnon was posted to 9 FTS, Hullavington on March 20 1937 and joined 51 Squadron at Linton-on-Ouse on October 23.

MacKinnon transferred to the FAA in 1938. He was with 804 Squadron at Hatston in early July 1940, flying Sea Gladiators on dockyard defence.

He later served in 808 and 821 Squadrons and flew from HMS 'Furious', 'Courageous', 'Ark Royal', 'Illustrious' and 'Attacker'.

MacKinnon retired in 1958, as a Lieutenant Commander.

APO 8.3.37   *PO 21.12.37*   *Sub-Lt 21.10.37*   *Lt 21.8.39*
Lt-Cdr 21.8.47

DONALD DUNCAN MacKINNON

745928   **Sgt**   **Air Gunner**   **British**   **236 Squadron**

With 236 Squadron in early July 1940. MacKinnon was one of the crew of Blenheim L 6639, lost during a photo-reconnaissance operation over Le Havre on July 18. The weather was bad and intense anti-aircraft fire was encountered over Cap de la Hague. The Blenheim is believed to be that claimed by Oberfeldwebel Schnell of II/JG 2.

MacKinnon was 21. He is buried in Villerville Communal Cemetery, France.

WILLIAM LIDSTONE McKNIGHT

41937   **PO**   **Pilot**   **Canadian**   **242 Squadron**

Born in Edmonton, Alberta in 1918, McKnight was educated at Crescent Heights High School and the University of Alberta. He was a medical student before joining the RAF on a short service commission in February 1939.

McKnight joined the newly-reformed 242 Squadron at Church Fenton on November 6 1939. He went to France on May 14 1940, on attachment to 607 Squadron. After moving to 615 Squadron on the 16th he shot down a Bf 109 near Cambrai on the 17th. McKnight returned to England two days later.

Over Dunkirk on May 28 McKnight destroyed a Bf 109, on the 29th a Bf 109, a Do 17 and a probable Bf 109, on the 31st two Bf 110s and a Bf 109 and on June 1 two Ju 87s and two more damaged. He was awarded an immediate DFC on June 4 and decorated by the King three days later.

242 Squadron flew to Le Mans on June 8 1940 to reinforce the hard-pressed squadrons in France and support the Army in its rearguard actions back to the Atlantic ports. On June 14 McKnight destroyed two Bf 109s. The squadron returned to England on the 18th.

McKnight claimed three Bf 110s destroyed on August 30, two Bf 109s on September 9 and a Do 17 and a shared Ju 88 on the 18th. He was awarded a Bar to the DFC (8.10.40) and on November 5 he claimed his final victory, a Bf 109 over Gravesend.

On January 12 1941 McKnight, in company with Pilot Officer MK Brown, was on a 'Rhubarb' operation. They crossed the coast near Gravelines and strafed enemy troops. As they turned to make a second attack a Bf 109 was seen, at 500 feet. Brown attacked the

troops but when he looked for McKnight he had vanished. He did not return to base and either fell to the flak or the Bf 109.

McKnight is remembered on the Runnymede Memorial, Panel 30 and also by a commemorative plaque at Calgary Airport.

APO 15.4.39   *PO 6.11.39*   *FO 6.11.40*

ALAN MONCRIEFF MacLACHLAN

90085   **SL**   **Pilot**   **British**   **92 Squadron**

MacLachlan joined 600 Squadron, AuxAF in early 1935. He was called to full-time service on August 24 1939 and commanded 92 Squadron at Biggin Hill from September 26 to October 25 1940.

He was released from the RAF in 1945, as a Wing Commander.

PO (AuxAF) 28.4.35   *FO (AuxAF) 28.10.36*
FL (AuxAF) 15.1.39   *FL 24.8.39*   *SL 1.9.40*
WC 1.3.42

JAMES ARCHIBALD FINDLAY MacLACHLAN

39639   **FL**   **Pilot**   **British**   **73 and 145 Squadrons**

Born in 1919 at Styal, Cheshire, MacLachlan joined the RAF on a short service commission in March 1939. He was posted to 3 FTS, South Cerney on May 8 and joined 88 Squadron at Boscombe Down on November 27. Then equipped with Hinds, the squadron soon afterwards received Fairey Battles and took them to France at the outbreak of war. The squadron was withdrawn to England in June 1940.

MacLachlan volunteered for Fighter Command and was posted to 73 Squadron at Church Fenton in late June 1940. He was awarded the DFC (16.7.40). On August 20 MacLachlan joined 145 Squadron at Drem but returned to 73 on September 28. He was posted away on October 19 and on November 17 he led six Hurricanes off HMS 'Argus' for Malta, where they joined 261 Squadron at Ta Kali.

On January 9 1941 MacLachlan claimed two Mc 200s destroyed, on the 19th a Z 506B, a Ju 88, two Ju 87s and another probable and on February 8 a He 111. He was awarded a Bar to the DFC (11.2.41).

In combat on February 16 1941 MacLachlan was hit by a Bf 109 and severely wounded in the left arm. He baled out and landed on Malta. After three days in hospital his arm was amputated below the elbow. MacLachlan returned to the UK and went to the Limb Centre at Roehampton, who designed a special detachable forearm and hand, suitable for use in a Hurricane. He returned to operations on November 4 1941, when he took command of No 1 Squadron at Redhill.

The squadron began night intruder operations over France. On April 27 1942 MacLachlan destroyed a Do 17 and damaged another, on May 3/4 destroyed a Do 17 and a He 111 and on June 3/4 two Do 217s. He was awarded the DSO (29.5.42) and on July 31 was posted to 59 OTU, Crosby-on-Eden, as an instructor. Later in the year MacLachlan was sent on a lecture tour of the USA.

In June 1943 he went to the Air Fighting Development Unit at Wittering. On June 29 MacLachlan, in company with Geoffrey Page, flew a Mustang on a daylight sortie, in the course of which he destroyed three Hs 126s, a Ju 88 and shared a second with Page, who also destroyed a Hs 126. They went again on July 18 but as they crossed the French coast MacLachlan was hit by machine gun fire. He forced-landed in a field and ploughed through an orchard. He survived the crash but was taken, as a prisoner, to a German field hospital. MacLachlan died there on July 31 1943. He is buried in Route de Caen Communal Cemetery, Pont L'Eveque, France. He was awarded a second Bar to the DFC (30.7.43). MacLachlan's portrait was drawn by Eric Kennington.

APO 3.5.37   *PO 1.3.38*   *FO 1.10.39*   *FL 1.10.40*
SL 1.12.41

JAMES ROBERT MacLACHLAN

36005   SL   Pilot   British   46 Squadron

Born on February 27 1911, MacLachlan joined the RAF in May 1934, on a direct-entry Permanent Commission. He was posted to 3 FTS, Grantham on the 26th and joined 19 Squadron at Duxford on March 4 1935. He moved to the newly-reformed 213 Squadron at Church Fenton on March 23 1937, as a Flight Commander.

MacLachlan went to the RAF School of Aeronautical Engineering at Henlow on January 3 1938 for a course. He took command of 46 Squadron at Digby in June 1940 and was posted away on October 6. MacLachlan transferred to the Technical Branch later in 1940.

He retired from the RAF on September 1 1956, as a Group Captain.

PO 26.5.34   FO 26.11.34   FL 1.10.36   SL 1.4.39
WC 1.3.41   WC 1.7.47   GC 1.1.54

ARCHIBALD COLIN MacLAREN

90950   PO   Pilot   British   604 Squadron

MacLaren was born in 1913 and educated at Eton. He joined 604 Squadron, AuxAF in 1939. He was called to full-time service on August 24 and was with the squadron in early July 1940.

MacLaren was released from the RAF in 1946, as a Flight Lieutenant. He died on March 21 1971.

APO 24.8.39   PO 4.5.40   FO 2.12.40   FL 2.12.41

JOHN WILLIAM McLAUGHLIN

146149   Sgt   Pilot   British   238 Squadron

Joined 238 Squadron at Middle Wallop in September 1940. McLaughlin was shot down by Bf 109s on October 5, in Hurricane P 3611. He baled out, with multiple burns, and was admitted to Shaftesbury Hospital.

McLaughlin later went to Queen Victoria Hospital, East Grinstead for skin grafts, becoming a Guinea Pig. Commissioned in April 1943, he was released from the RAF in 1946, as a Flight Lieutenant, and later settled in Australia.

PO 22.4.43   FO 22.10.43   FL 22.4.45

CHARLES HECTOR MacLEAN

90166   FL   Pilot   British   602 Squadron

MacLean joined 602 Squadron, AuxAF in 1936. He was called to full-time service on August 24 1939 and on December 22 shared in the destruction of a He 111, which was laying mines fifteen miles east of the Isle of May.

On July 7 1940 MacLean shared a Ju 88. He was shot down on August 26, seriously wounded. He crash-landed at Tangmere and was admitted to hospital, where his right leg was amputated.

It is believed that MacLean remained in the RAF and was released in 1945, as a Wing Commander.

PO (AuxAF) 16.5.36   FO (AuxAF) 16.11.37   FO 24.8.39
FL 3.9.40

GEORGE SUTHERLAND MURRAY MacLEOD

553787   Sgt   Aircrew   British   235 Squadron

MacLeod, of Dornoch, Sutherlandshire, joined 235 Squadron on September 26 1940. He was killed with the squadron on March 23 1941, aged 18. He is remembered on the Runnymede Memorial, Panel 47.

ANDREW CRAWFORD RANKIN McLURE

82167   PO   Pilot   British   87 Squadron

McLure, of Craigmillar, Edinburgh, was with 87 Squadron in early July 1940. In an action with Bf 109s off Portland Bill on August 11 he claimed one destroyed and then forced-landed near Warmwell, wounded in one leg. Back with the squadron, he claimed a Bf 110 destroyed on September 30.

McLure was killed on July 20 1942, as a Flight Lieutenant with 605 Squadron, aged 24. He is buried in Littlehampton Cemetery, Sussex.

PO 18.6.40   FO 18.6.41   FL 18.6.42

JOHN REGINALD McMAHON

49290   Sgt   Air Gunner   British   235 Squadron

With 235 Squadron in early July 1940. Commissioned in June 1942, McMahon was released in 1946, as a Flight Lieutenant.

PO 27.6.42   FO 27.12.42   FL 27.6.44

DESMOND ANNESLEY PETER McMULLEN

40002   FO   Pilot   British   54 and 222 Squadrons

Born at Godstone, Reigate on December 6 1917, McMullen was at Cheltenham College from 1928 to 1931. He joined the RAF on a short service commission in June 1937 and was posted to 6 FTS, Netheravon on September 18.

McMullen was posted to No 1 Air Armament School at Manby on July 9 1938 and joined 54 Squadron at Hornchurch in September 1939. Over Dunkirk on May 24 1940 he probably destroyed a Bf 109, on the 25th a probable Bf 110 and on the 26th a Bf 110.

On July 4 McMullen's Spitfire was damaged by Bf 109s near Manston and three days later he made a forced-landing at Manston after a combat with Bf 109s near Deal. On July 24 McMullen claimed a Bf 109 destroyed, on August 15 a probable Bf 109, on the 16th, 24th and 26th Bf 109s, on the 30th he shared a Do 17 and on September 2 a Do 215. On the 11th McMullen was posted to 222 Squadron at Hornchurch and claimed Bf 109s on the 14th and 15th. He was awarded the DFC (1.10.40). On October 15 McMullen shared a Bf 109, on the 17th he claimed a Bf 109 destroyed, on the 20th he shared a Bf 110 and on October 25, 28 and November 8 claimed Bf 109s.

In December 1940 McMullen was posted to 151 Squadron at Wittering. He probably destroyed a Ju 88 on January 15 1941. The squadron converted to Defiants and McMullen teamed up with Sergeant Fairweather. He was awarded a Bar to the DFC (7.3.41). On April 8 and 9 the team destroyed He 111s and on May 10 a Ju 88.

In July 1941 McMullen joined 266 Squadron at Wittering. On August 19 he destroyed a He 111, on September 12 probably another, on October 13 a Bf 109 and on the 25th a Bf 110. In late November McMullen was posted to 55 OTU, as an instructor and awarded a second Bar to the DFC (12.12.41). He returned to operations in early May 1942 and was briefly attached to 602 Squadron at Redhill before joining 124 Squadron at Gravesend. He damaged two FW 190s on May 24.

In June 1942 McMullen was posted to 64 Squadron at Hornchurch, as supernumerary Squadron Leader. He was given

DAP McMullen (continued)

command of 65 Squadron at Gravesend in July and over Dieppe on August 19 he damaged a Do 217. McMullen left the squadron in September and in November he briefly led 324 Wing in North Africa before being given a staff job.

McMullen retired from the RAF on December 16 1957, as a Squadron Leader, retaining the rank of Wing Commander. He died on July 1 1985. His portrait was drawn by Cuthbert Orde.

APO 9.8.37   PO 9.7.38   FO 9.2.40   FL 9.2.41
SL 1.3.42   SL 1.9.45

ERNEST ARCHIBALD McNAB

C 134   SL   Pilot   Canadian   1 (RCAF) and 111 Sqdns

Born in 1905, McNab joined the RCAF in 1926. Before the war he had flown more than 2000 hours and apart from normal service duties he had carried mails to Ottawa and made a photographic survey of the Hudson Bay area. In September 1937 McNab was appointed a Flight Commander in 46 Squadron at Kenley. He was on an exchange attachment from the RCAF and was still in England when the war started.

McNab returned to Canada and took command of No 1 (RCAF) Squadron at St Hubert in November 1939. He was leading the squadron when it arrived in the UK on June 20 1940. To gain operational experience he flew occasional sorties with 111 Squadron, when both squadrons were based at Croydon. On August 15 he claimed a Do 215 destroyed, flying with 111. On August 26 McNab claimed a Do 215 destroyed, on September 7 and 9 probable Bf 109s, on the 15th a He 111 and on the 27th a Bf 110 and a shared Ju 88. He was awarded the DFC (22.10.40).

In November 1940 McNab returned to Canada and in June 1941 he was given command of 118 Squadron and took it to Dartmouth, Nova Scotia for east coast defence.

McNab was made an OBE in 1946 and also held the Czech Military Cross. He retired from the RCAF in October 1957, as a Group Captain, and settled in Vancouver. He died on January 10 1977.

ROBIN JOHN McNAIR

112522   Sgt   Pilot   British   3 and 249 Squadrons

McNair joined the RAFVR in early 1939 and began his flying training at 16 E&RFTS, Shoreham. Called up at the outbreak of war, he completed his training and was posted to 5 OTU, Aston Down. After converting to Spitfires he joined 3 Squadron at Wick in late July 1940, to fly Hurricanes.

On September 27 McNair was posted to 249 Squadron at North Weald. He went to 96 Squadron, when it was formed at Cranage on December 18 1940. He destroyed a He 111 over Liverpool on March 12 1941. With his tour completed McNair was posted to a night-fighter OTU, as an instructor. He was commissioned in November 1941.

In early 1942 McNair joined 87 Squadron at Charmy Down and flew with the squadron in the Dieppe operation on August 19. He was awarded the DFC (22.9.42). In October he was posted to 245 Squadron at Middle Wallop and became a Flight Commander in early 1943.

McNair was given command of 247 Squadron at Merston in January 1944 and led the squadron to Normandy in June. Whilst

leading it on an armed reconnaissance in July his Typhoon was hit by flak and his engine failed. McNair glided over enemy lines through intense fire and landed in a field. He was posted away in August, became CFI at 55 OTU, Aston Down and was awarded a Bar to the DFC (26.9.44).

In 1945 McNair converted to Meteors and was in command of 74 Squadron when he was released from the RAF in January 1946.

PO 26.11.41   FO 1.10.42   FL 26.11.43

BRIAN RADLEY MacNAMARA

25123   FO   Pilot   British   603 Squadron

Born on June 2 1915, MacNamara was seconded to the RAF from the Royal Tank Corps on November 8 1938. After completing his flying training he was posted in September 1939 to the School of Army Co-operation at Old Sarum.

In October 1939 MacNamara joined 614 Squadron at Odiham, flying Lysanders. He volunteered for Fighter Command in August 1940 and on the 22nd went to 7 OTU, Hawarden. After converting to Spitfires MacNamara was posted to 603 Squadron at Hornchurch on September 1. He shared in the destruction of a He 111 on the 7th and destroyed a Bf 109 on the 14th.

MacNamara returned to 614 Squadron at Macmerry on February 1 1941 and stayed with it until August 5 1942, when he was posted to 296 Squadron at Hurn, a Whitley squadron for moving troops in Horsa gliders. On March 8 1943 he took command of 295 Squadron, on similar duties. MacNamara towed the glider carrying General Gale, GOC 6th Airborne Division, to Normandy on D Day.

In early 1945 MacNamara went to RAF Staff College, after which he was posted to the Far East. He took command of 31 Squadron at Akyab, Burma on September 15 1945.

MacNamara was awarded the DSO (4.6.46) and was made a CBE (13.6.57) for distinguished services in operations in the Near East in October to December 1956. He retired on June 4 1965, as an Air Commodore.

FO 8.11.38   FL 8.11.40   SL 1.12.41   WC 1.7.47
GC 1.1.56   AC 1.1.61

ALEXANDER LOGAN McNAY

741569   Sgt   Pilot   British   73 Squadron

McNay, of Shawlands, Glasgow joined 73 Squadron at Church Fenton on July 21 1940. He claimed two Ju 88s destroyed on August 15 and two more the next day.

After a combat over Burnham on September 5 McNay's Hurricane, P 3224, crashed and burned out at White House Farm, North Fambridge. He was reported 'Missing', aged 22. He is remembered on the Runnymede Memorial, Panel 17.

ALFRED RIPPON DUKE MACONOCHIE

47418   Sgt   Air Gunner   British   235 Squadron

Maconochie was born on May 12 1916. He joined 235 Squadron on July 16 1940.

Commissioned in October 1941, Maconochie stayed on in the RAF, in the Aircraft Control Branch. He retired on March 2 1960, as a Flight Lieutenant, retaining the rank of Squadron Leader.

PO 27.10.41   FO 1.10.42   FL 27.10.43   FL 1.9.45

JAMES FREDERICK JOHN MacPHAIL

42014   PO   Pilot   British   603 Squadron

MacPhail joined the RAF on a short service commission in February 1939. He was posted to 603 Squadron at Hornchurch on August 31 1940. MacPhail claimed a He 111 destroyed on September 11 and a Bf 109 on the 15th.

He received plastic surgery treatment at some time at the Queen Victoria Hospital, East Grinstead and was a Guinea Pig. MacPhail was released from the RAF in 1945, as a Flight Lieutenant. He died in 1963.

APO 29.4.39   PO 6.11.39   FO 6.11.40   FL 6.11.41

JAMES McPHEE

146128 **Sgt** **Pilot** **British** **151 and 249 Squadrons**

Born on August 3 1919, McPhee joined the RAFVR in November 1938 and had carried out some flying training before being called up at the outbreak of war. After ITW he was posted to 10 EFTS, Yatesbury on May 1 1940, went to 2 FTS, Brize Norton on June 1 and then to 5 OTU, Aston Down, where he converted to Hurricanes.

On September 17 McPhee joined 151 Squadron at Digby. On the 24th he collided with Pilot Officer JK Haviland during a formation practice and the tail of his Hurricane, P 3306, was knocked off. McPhee baled out, unhurt. On September 29 he was posted to 249 Squadron at North Weald and then to 17 Squadron at Martlesham Heath on November 21.

McPhee was sent to CFS, Upavon on January 21 1941, for an instructor's course, after which he went to 8 FTS, Montrose. He was posted to South Africa on July 29, where he instructed at 24 Air School until May 18 1942 and then 27 Air School after that. Commissioned from Warrant Officer in October 1942, McPhee was awarded the AFC (1.1.43) and posted back to the UK on July 24 1944.

He went to 13 OTU, Harwell on October 17 and then joined 45 Squadron in the Far East on February 19 1945 and served with it until November 27, when he returned to the UK for release. McPhee rejoined the RAF on July 24 1951 and served at home and overseas prior to his retirement on June 1 1968, as a Flight Lieutenant.

PO 16.10.42   FO 16.4.43   FL 16.10.44   FO 13.2.49
FL 4.12.52

ROBERT REID MacPHERSON

45459 **F/Sgt** **Pilot** **British** **65 Squadron**

A pre-war airman pilot, MacPherson came from Dinas Powis, Glamorgan. He was with 65 Squadron at the outbreak of war. Over Dunkirk on May 27 1940 he destroyed a Do 17.

MacPherson claimed a Bf 109 destroyed on August 12, shared one on the 14th and claimed another destroyed on the 20th. Commissioned in November 1940, MacPherson was killed on October 13 1941, as a Flight Lieutenant with 129 Squadron, aged 27. He is remembered on the Runnymede Memorial, Panel 29.

PO 27.11.40   FO 19.9.41

IAN NICHOLSON MacRAE

565633 **Sgt** **Aircrew** **British** **FIU**

No service details traced.

HARRY IAN MacRORY

801456 **Sgt** **Aircrew** **British** **23 Squadron**

MacRory, of Penge, Kent, joined 23 Squadron at Collyweston on August 5 1940. He was killed on January 3 1941, still with 23, aged 21. He is remembered on the Runnymede Memorial, Panel 48.

SYDNEY JAMES MADLE

86323 **PO** **Pilot** **British** **615 and 605 Squadrons**

Born at Strood, Kent on January 13 1921, Madle was educated at St Joseph Williamson's Mathematical School and afterwards worked for South Eastern Electricity at Rochester. He joined the RAFVR in 1939 and learned to fly at 23 E&RFTS at Rochester.

Called to full-time service on September 2 1939, Madle completed his training and joined 615 Squadron at Kenley in June 1940. On August 28 the engine of his Hurricane, R 4116, was hit by return fire from a Do 17 over Sandwich. He forced-landed at Snoadstreet Farm, Throwley and was admitted, injured, to Hothfield Hospital.

In late 1940 Madle was posted to the Middle East. He later served in Burma. Madle was released from the RAF in 1947. He flew as a Captain with Dan Air, BEA and BOAC and was later Chief Pilot and Operations Manager with Gulf Aviation, Bahrein. He finished his flying career as Manager of Air Freight at Lympne. Madle suffered from ill-health and had two heart bypass operations. He died on January 31 1984.

PO 18.6.40   FO 18.6.41   FL 18.6.42

GERALD HAMILTON MAFFETT

80814 **PO** **Pilot** **British** **257 Squadron**

Maffett joined 257 Squadron at Hendon on July 7 1940. He was shot down and killed in combat with Bf 110s over Clacton on August 31 1940. His Hurricane, P 3175, crashed at Walton-on-the-Naze.

Maffett was 24. He is buried in Windsor Road Cemetery, Bray, Berkshire.

PO 9.6.40

MERVYN HENRY MAGGS

79359 **PO** **Air Gunner** **British** **264 Squadron**

Born at Axbridge in October 1899, Maggs served in an infantry regiment in the Great War before transferring to the RFC and becoming a Camel pilot.

Maggs joined the RAFVR in June 1939 and after being called up at the outbreak of war he served in the Operations Room at 11 Group. In November he volunteered for aircrew duties and after training as an air gunner he was posted to 78 Squadron, operating in Whitleys from Linton-on-Ouse.

On May 3 1940 Maggs joined 264 Squadron at Kirton-in-Lindsey. He remained with the squadron until October 1942, when he joined 605 Squadron at Ford, flying in Bostons. Maggs was awarded the DFC (9.3.43), as a Flight Lieutenant with 605 Squadron. The citation stated 'During a long career he has displayed exceptional keenness and unswerving devotion to duty. He has destroyed two enemy aircraft at night'.

Maggs was released from the RAF in 1945. He died in November 1987, the oldest survivor of those who flew with the RAF in the Battle of Britain.

PO 7.4.40   FO 7.4.41   FL 7.4.42

HAROLD JOHN MAGUIRE ✏

34048   SL   Pilot   British   229 Squadron

Born in Ireland on April 12 1912, Maguire was educated at Wesley College, Dublin and Dublin University. He joined the RAF in March 1933 and on April 4 was posted to 3 FTS, Grantham. On March 11 1934 he went on a course to RAF Calshot and on December 1 joined 230 (Flying Boat) Squadron at Pembroke Dock and served with it in Egypt and the Far East.

Back in the UK, Maguire was posted to CFS, Upavon on January 22 1939 for an instructor's course. He reformed and commanded 229 Squadron at Digby from October 6 1939. Over Dunkirk on May 28 1940 Maguire damaged a Do 17. He was posted away from the squadron on September 8.

In 1941 Maguire was an instructor at 56 OTU, Sutton Bridge. Late in the year he was posted to Singapore, as Wing Commander Flying of the proposed 266 Wing. After the fall of Singapore the RAF went to Sumatra but the speed of the Japanese advance made it impossible for any organised aerial defence. In mid-February 1942 Maguire led the ground defence of P1 Airfield against Japanese paratroops but he was eventually captured by the Japanese and was a PoW until August 1945.

Maguire was awarded the DSO (1.10.46), was made an OBE (2.1.50), a CB (1958) and was created KCB (1966). He retired from the RAF on September 28 1968, as an Air Marshal. From then until 1972 he was Director-General of Intelligence at the Ministry of Defence.

APO 24.3.33   PO 24.3.34   FO 24.9.35   FL 24.9.37
SL 1.6.39   WC 1.6.41   WC 1.10.46   GC 1.1.52
AC 1.1.58   AVM 1.1.60   AM 1.1.66

TIMOTHY JOSEPH MAHONEY

Petty Officer (FAA)   Pilot   British   804 Squadron

In early July 1940 Mahoney was in 804 Squadron at Hatston, flying Gladiators on dockyard defence. Commissioned after the war, he retired in 1958, as a Lieutenant Commander, and died on August 1 1977.

Lt 1.1.46

ALISTAIR DAVID WILLIAM MAIN

748115   Sgt   Pilot   British   249 Squadron

Main was with 249 Squadron at Leconfield in early July 1940. On the 8th he shared in the destruction of a Ju 88 off Hornsea. Taking off on July 16 Main's engine failed and he was killed, when his Hurricane, P 2995, crashed and burned out in Copmanthorpe Wood. He was 22 and was cremated at Dundee Crematorium.

HEDLEY RONALD MAIN

751420   Sgt   Aircrew   British   25 Squadron

Joined 25 Squadron at Martlesham Heath in August 1940. Main was killed on August 27 1941, as a Flight Sergeant with 109 Squadron. This unit was flying in Ansons and Wellingtons from Boscombe Down, developing radio counter-measures and radar aids.

Main is remembered on the Runnymede Memorial, Panel 37.

WILFORD HUGH MAITLAND-WALKER

70707   FL   Pilot   British   65 Squadron

Born on June 15 1909, Maitland-Walker was commissioned in the RAFO in August 1934. He transferred to the RAFVR in January 1938 and was called to full-time service on September 18 1939.

Maitland-Walker was with 65 Squadron at Hornchurch in early July 1940. He was posted away on September 19.

He retired from the RAF on June 15 1956, as a Wing Commander, retaining the rank of Group Captain. He died in 1969.

PO (RAFO) 13.8.34   FO (RAFO) 13.2.36
FO (RAFVR) 1.1.38   FO 18.9.39   FL 3.9.40
SL 1.12.41   WC 1.8.44   WC 1.10.46

———— MAKINS

No unknown   Sgt   Pilot   British   247 Squadron

No service details traced.

ADOLPH GYSBERT MALAN

37604   FL   Pilot   South African   74 Squadron

Malan was born in Wellington, South Africa on October 3 1910. In February 1924 he became a cadet on the training ship 'General Botha' and joined the Union Castle Steamship Line in 1927.

In 1935 Malan applied for a short service commission in the RAF, was accepted and began his elementary flying training at 2 E&RFTS, Filton on January 6 1936. He went on to 3 FTS, Grantham on March 14 and joined 74 Squadron at Hornchurch on December 20 1936. Malan was made a Flight Commander in late 1937.

Near Dunkirk on May 21 1940 he destroyed a Ju 88, probably a He 111 and damaged a second Ju 88, on the 22nd he shared a Ju 88, on the 24th shared a Do 17 and destroyed a He 111, on the 27th a Bf 109 and probably a Do 17. He was awarded the DFC (11.6.40). On June 19 Malan destroyed two He 111s at night, on July 12 shared another, on the 19th a probable Bf 109 and on the 28th a Bf 109. Malan took command of 74 Squadron on August 8. On the 11th he destroyed two more Bf 109s and on the 13th a Do 17 and another probable. He was awarded a Bar to the DFC (13.8.40).

Malan destroyed a Ju 88 on September 11, a probable Bf 109 on October 17 and destroyed Bf 109s on October 22, November 23, 27 (2) and December 2. He was awarded the DSO (24.12.40). He destroyed a Bf 109 on February 2 1941, shared a Do 215 on the 5th and on March 10 1941 was posted away to lead the Biggin Hill Wing.

Between June 17 and July 6 1941 Malan destroyed twelve Bf 109s and shared two more. He was awarded a Bar to the DSO (22.7.41) and in mid-August was appointed CFI at 58 OTU, Grangemouth. Two months later Malan was sent to the USA with five other pilots to lecture and to liaise with the US Army Air Corps.

Back in the UK in late 1941 Malan was posted to Sutton Bridge, to command the CGS. On January 1 1943 he was appointed Station Commander Biggin Hill. He often flew on operations over the next few months but scored no further victories. Biggin Hill Sector claimed its 1000th victory on May 15 1943. Malan was posted away on October 7 and after sick leave took command of 19 Fighter Wing 2nd TAF on November 1. In March 1944 he took command of 145 Wing at Merston, composed of three French squadrons, 329, 340 and 341. He flew a Ramrod sortie on D Day, leading Yellow Section of 340 Squadron, escorting Albemarles towing Horsa gliders.

Malan was made CO of the Advanced Gunnery School at Catfoss in July 1944. He did a course at RAF Staff College in 1945 but decided not to stay in the RAF. He was released in 1946, as a Group Captain, and returned with his family to South Africa. He died there on September 17 1963. As well as his British awards Malan received the C de G (Belg)(4.11.41), the C de G (Fr), the French Légion d'Honneur and the Czech Military Cross. His portrait was done by Eric Kennington and Cuthbert Orde.

APO 2.3.36   PO 6.1.37   FO 6.7.38   FL 6.7.40
SL 10.6.41   WC 1.9.42

ROGER MALENGREAU

82160   PO   Pilot   Belgian   87 Squadron

Born in Brussels on August 1 1914, Malengreau entered the Royal Military Academy in 1934. He graduated in November 1936, was commissioned and joined the Belgian Air Force. He was at the School of Navigation in 1937 and qualified as a pilot in 1938.

Malengreau joined an Army Co-operation Squadron, equipped with Fairey Foxes. The squadron moved to an advanced airfield near Liege on May 10 1940 but was completely wiped out by enemy action, mostly on the ground on the 12th. The pilots escaped to France but no replacement aircraft were found for them.

On June 21 the French signed an Armistice with the Germans and the Belgians were told to stay put. With other pilots Malengreau reached Port Vendres, where with the help of a British destroyer and the support of the Belgian Embassy in London they caught a passing convoy and embarked on the SS 'Apapa' on the 24th. After arriving in Liverpool on July 7 Malengreau was commissioned in the RAF on the 19th.

He was posted to 7 OTU, Hawarden on the 30th and after converting to Hurricanes he joined 87 Squadron at Exeter on August 12 and flew his first interception patrol the next day.

Malengreau was posted to 56 Squadron at North Weald on December 8 and flew in the early sweeps over Northern France. He moved to 609 Squadron at Biggin Hill on April 7 1941 and on June 30 shared a probable Bf 109 with Paul Richey, on a Blenheim escort to Lens.

In October 1942 Malengreau left 609, having then carried out 178 operational sorties. He was offered the job of forming a new Belgian squadron, 349. After acceptance he found that its base was to be in Lagos, Nigeria. Malengreau arrived in West Africa on January 1 1943. On the voyage from the UK the planes on the ship's deck were smashed by severe gales. At his request the squadron was recalled to the UK in June 1943 and Malengreau relinquished his command and went on sick leave.

In October 1943 he was posted to HQ Fighter Command. In May 1944 he was on a twin-engine conversion course but was recalled to Bentley Priory for D Day. Malengreau asked for special service and was detached in July to the 12th US Army Group, with which he witnessed the liberation of Paris and Brussels. When Belgium was completely liberated Malengreau became a liaison officer between SHAFE and the Belgian Ministry of Foreign Affairs.

Malengreau began a career in the Belgian Foreign Service in August 1945, during the course of which he served in China and Africa and was Ambassador to Malaysia, Singapore and later Chile. He was made a CBE by the British Government.

PO 19.7.40   FO 19.7.41   FL 19.7.42

ERNEST EDWARD MALES

82661   PO   Pilot   British   72 Squadron

Males, of Southgate, London, joined 72 Squadron at Acklington on June 19 1940.

He claimed a Bf 109 destroyed on September 2. Two days later Males baled out of Spitfire R 6971, when it was set alight during combat with Bf 110s. It crashed on Culvers Farm, Hartfield. Males shared in the destruction of a Do 215 on September 10 but was hit by return fire and then his Spitfire, K 9841, was further damaged when his undercarriage collapsed in a forced-landing at Little Hitchings Farm,

Etchingham.

Males claimed a Bf 109 destroyed on September 14. He was shot down and killed in combat with Bf 109s over Sevenoaks on the 27th. His Spitfire, X 4340, crashed at Shadwell Dock, Stepney, London.

He was 20 years old and is buried in Great Northern London Cemetery.

PO 18.6.40

BRONISLAW MALINOWSKI

P 3036   Sgt   Pilot   Polish   43 Squadron

Malinowski was born on February 12 1912. He arrived in the UK on July 13 1940 and his first posting was to 307 Squadron on September 10. The squadron was to be the first Polish night-fighter squadron but training ceased when the pilots were posted away to day-fighter squadrons. Malinowski converted to Hurricanes and joined 43 Squadron at Usworth on October 25.

In December 1940 he was posted to 501 Squadron at Drem and on April 11 1941 joined 302 Squadron at Westhampnett. Malinowski probably destroyed a Bf 109 on December 30 1941. He was awarded the KW (20.2.42) and with his tour completed he went to 58 OTU, Grangemouth on May 6, as an instructor.

Malinowski returned to 302 Squadron, then at Heston, on November 10 1942. He went to West Kirby on February 13 1943 to prepare for overseas and on March 13 arrived in the Middle East in a C 47 with other Polish pilots to form the Polish Fighting Team, otherwise known as 'Skalski's Circus'. They were attached to 145 Squadron and operated in the Western Desert from March 17 to May 12 and destroyed 30 enemy aircraft. Malinowski destroyed a Bf 109 on April 7.

Back in the UK, he rejoined 302 Squadron on July 22 1943. Over France on September 8 he destroyed two Bf 109s and was then shot down and crashed, with leg injuries. Malinowski evaded capture and returned to England in December, rejoining 302 on the 13th. He was awarded two Bars to the KW (20.12.43).

On March 25 1944 Malinowski went to No 1 ADU, Croydon and returned to 302, at Chailey, on June 29. He was awarded the DFC (25.9.44), the VM (5th Class)(25.9.44) and a third Bar to the KW (30.12.44). He joined 133 Wing on the Continent on March 18 1945. Malinowski was commissioned from Warrant Officer in June 1945 and was released from the PAF in January 1947, as a Flight Lieutenant. In addition to his other awards he also held the C de G (Fr). He died in May 1982.

PO 9.6.45   FO 9.12.45

JAN MALINSKI

P 1286   PO   Pilot   Polish   302 Squadron

Born on March 1 1917, Malinski was in the PAF before the war. In the September 1939 fighting he destroyed at least two enemy aircraft, flying with 132 Squadron.

Malinski arrived in England on June 27 1940 and joined 302 Squadron at Leconfield on August 20. He destroyed a Ju 88 on March 3 1941. He was posted to the 307 Squadron Operations Room on June 28, moved to the Operations Room at RAF Exeter on May 20 1942 and returned to 307 Squadron Operations Room on December 1 1943.

Malinski returned to flying duties with 307 on September 16 1944. He was awarded the KW (27.9.45). In September 1945 he was posted to Transport Command and was released late in 1946, as a Flight Lieutenant.

PO 1.3.41   FO 1.3.42   FL 1.3.43

RONALD SPENCER MALLETT

158594   Sgt   Air Gunner   British   29 Squadron

Mallett was with 29 Squadron at Digby in early July 1940. After the introduction of airborne radar he retrained as a Radio Observer.

Commissioned in October 1943, Mallett was awarded the DFC (9.6.44), as a Flying Officer with 141 Squadron, operating in Mosquitos from West Raynham. He was credited with assisting in the destruction of two enemy aircraft at night.

Mallett was killed on June 28 1944. He is buried in Woensel General Cemetery, Eindhoven, Netherlands.

PO 1.10.43   FO 2.4.44

JAROSLAV MARIA MALY

81909   PO   Pilot   Czechoslovakian   310 Squadron

Maly joined 310 Squadron at Duxford at its formation on July 10 1940. He claimed a Bf 109 destroyed on August 31 and returned to base damaged after the combat over the Thames Estuary.

On October 29 Maly collided with Pilot Officer E Fechtner, whilst formating for a wing patrol. He forced-landed near Duxford, injured. Fechtner was killed.

Maly died on June 5 1941 and is buried in Brookwood Military Cemetery. The circumstances are not known.

PO 13.7.40   FL 1.3.41

ANDREW MAMEDOFF

81621   PO   Pilot   American   609 Squadron

Born on August 24 1912, Mamedoff grew up in Thompson, Connecticut. He learned to fly and performed at air shows. He bought his own aeroplane and tried to develop a charter service in the Miami area, later moving it to Southern California.

In late 1939 Mamedoff volunteered for flying in the war in Finland. When that war ended he was told he would fly with l'Armée de l'Air. With fellow Americans, VC Keough and EQ Tobin, he went to Paris, via Canada. The May 1940 blitzkrieg had already started when they arrived and the three men were virtually ignored. They joined two Czech pilots in an attempt to steal two Potez bombers to fly to England but the scheme failed and the Czechs were killed by French guards.

The Americans made their way to St Jean de Luz, where they managed to get a ship. They eventually reached London and after some initial problems were accepted by the RAF. They went to 7 OTU, Hawarden on July 7 1940 and joined 609 Squadron at Middle Wallop on August 8.

Still together, the three were posted to Church Fenton on September 19 to become the first three members of 71 Squadron, about to be formed with American volunteers.

Mamedoff was posted to Coltishall on August 1 1941, to be a Flight Commander in 133 Squadron, the second American volunteer unit. In a squadron move from Fowlmere to Eglinton, Northern Ireland on October 8 1941 fifteen pilots took off. They landed at Sealand to refuel and then headed for Andreas, in the Isle of Man. Four failed to arrive, one of whom was Mamedoff. His body was recovered and he is buried in Brookwood Military Cemetery, Woking.

KENNETH MANGER

70867   PO   Pilot   British   17 Squadron

Manger was born at Halifax, Yorkshire in 1917. He joined the RAF on a short service commission in February 1938. He was posted to 3 FTS, South Cerney on April 9 and on October 29 joined 17 Squadron at Kenley.

Still with the squadron Manger destroyed a Ju 87 over France on May 17 1940. Over Dunkirk on May 26 he damaged a Do 17, on the 28th he destroyed a Do 215 and damaged another, on the 31st he destroyed a Bf 109 and probably a second. Manger was shot down on June 1 and baled out into the sea. He was picked up by a French boat, returned to England in a British troopship and was back with the squadron the next day.

On June 7 17 Squadron was ordered to France, to the airfield at Le Mans. Manger destroyed a Bf 109 on this day. The squadron was withdrawn to England on the 17th. Manger was awarded the DFC (25.6.40).

He shared He 111s on July 9 and 12. He was reported 'Missing' after a combat with Bf 110s off the east coast on August 11 1940, in Hurricane P 3760. Manger was 23. He is remembered on the Runnymede Memorial, Panel 9.

APO 26.3.38   PO 17.1.39

HAROLD JOHN MANN

42247   PO   Pilot   British   1 Squadron

Joined the RAF on a short service commission in April 1939. Mann was with No 1 Squadron at Tangmere in early July 1940. He claimed a Bf 109 destroyed over Martlesham Heath on August 15 and two Bf 110s damaged on August 30.

Mann was released from the RAF in 1950, as a Flight Lieutenant.

APO 10.6.39   PO 16.12.39   FO 16.12.40   FL 16.12.41
FL 1.9.45

JACK MANN

127025   Sgt   Pilot   British   64 and 92 Squadrons

Mann was with 64 Squadron at Kenley in early July 1940. On the 25th he claimed a Bf 109 destroyed and on August 5, 8 and 12 Bf 109s. He was posted to 92 Squadron at Pembrey at the end of the month.

With 91 Squadron on March 31 1941 Mann destroyed a Bf 109. His aircraft was severely damaged and he was badly burned when he crash-landed. He underwent plastic surgery at the Queen Victoria Hospital, East Grinstead and became a Guinea Pig.

Mann was awarded the DFM (25.4.41). Commissioned from Warrant Officer in July 1942, he was released from the RAF in 1946, as a Flight Lieutenant.

PO 23.7.42   FO 23.1.43   FL 23.7.44   DIED 11·11·95

JOHN MANSEL-LEWIS

42248   PO   Pilot   British   92 Squadron

Mansel-Lewis, of Pembrey, Carmarthenshire, joined the RAF on a short service commission in April 1939. He was posted to 92 Squadron at Biggin Hill on September 16 1940. He claimed a Do 17 destroyed on the 27th and a Bf 109 on December 1.

In early March 1941 Mansel-Lewis joined 243 Squadron, then forming at Kallang, Singapore. On April 4 he was a passenger in a Blenheim of 27 Squadron, on a formation practice flight. The aircraft flicked over and dived into the sea. Mansel-Lewis baled out but was struck by the propellor and killed. The pilot and gunner were killed when the aircraft went into the sea. Mansel-Lewis was 20. He is buried in Kranji War Cemetery, Singapore.

APO 24.6.39   PO 9.12.39   FO 9.12.40

MIROSLAV JAN MANSFELD

69453   Sgt   Pilot   Czechoslovakian   111 Squadron

Born on December 14 1912, Mansfeld was in the Czech Air Force. When the Germans came he escaped to France and joined the French Foreign Legion, the only unit open to foreigners. He was seconded to l'Armée de l'Air and in 1940 flew Bloch 210 bombers.

Mansfeld escaped to England and eventually joined 111 Squadron at Drem on October 6 1940. He shared in destroying a He 111 on November 13. Commissioned in June 1941, he was posted to 68 Squadron at High Ercall. On October 13 Mansfeld destroyed two Ju 88s and damaged two more and on April 30 1942 two He 111s and a shared Do 17. He was awarded the DFC (10.7.42).

On December 10 1942 Mansfeld destroyed a Do 217, on March 15 1943 a Ju 88 and on May 14 two Do 217s. He was posted away from the squadron for a rest but rejoined later, as a Flight Commander. He destroyed two V1s.

Mansfeld was awarded the DSO (21.5.45). He later rejoined the RAF, was awarded the AFC (1.1.53) and retired on September 30 1958, as a Squadron Leader.

PO 9.6.41   FO 9.6.42   FL 9.6.43   SL 1.1.57

BERNARD MARTIN MANSFIELD

749519   Sgt   Aircrew   British   236 Squadron

Mansfield, of Dagenham, Essex, joined 236 Squadron in late September 1940. He was killed on February 25 1941, aged 21. He is remembered on the Runnymede Memorial, Panel 48.

DAVID ERNEST MANSFIELD

102106   Sgt   Wop/AG   British   236 Squadron

Born on March 18 1920, Mansfield joined the RAFVR on June 8 1939. Called up on September 2 1939 he was posted to No 1 Electrical and Wireless School, Cranwell in early 1940.

Mansfield went to 5 BGS for a gunnery course on July 26 1940 and joined 236 Squadron on August 24. He carried out fifty operational sorties with the squadron before his tour finished in early April 1941. On May 24 Mansfield was posted to 2 OTU to convert to Sunderlands before joining 228 Squadron on December 23. He left the squadron on August 5 1942.

Mansfield went to 14 ITW for instruction on December 12 and on March 1 1943 was posted to the Empire Air Gunnery School, as an instructor. He went on a Ground Control Interception Course at Fullarton on July 12 1944, after which he was posted as Controller at 21 Sector and later HQ 11 Group.

In February 1945 Mansfield was posted to the Far East and went into the Operations Room of 909 Wing. He returned to the UK in February 1946 and was released from the RAF, as a Flight Lieutenant. Mansfield joined the RAuxAF in January 1950 in the Fighter Control Branch, with 3513 Fighter Control Unit.

PO 31.7.41   FO 31.7.42   FO (RAuxAF) 9.1.50

EDWARD MANTON

810081   Sgt   Pilot   British   610 Squadron

Manton, of Bebington, Cheshire joined 610 Squadron, AuxAF before the war and was selected for pilot training. Called up in late August 1939, he completed his flying training and rejoined 610 Squadron, then at Biggin Hill, on July 27 1940. Having had no experience of Spitfires he was sent to 7 OTU, Hawarden for three weeks for a conversion course.

On August 29 1940 Manton was shot down and killed in combat over Mayfield. His Spitfire, R 6629, crashed at Great Wigsell Estate, Hurst Green. He was 25 years old and is buried in Hawkhurst Cemetery, Kent.

GRAHAM ASHLEY LEONARD MANTON

32050   SL   Pilot   British   56 Squadron

Born on June 18 1910, Manton joined the RAF in June 1931. He was posted to 2 FTS, Digby on July 13 and after training joined 111 Squadron at Hornchurch on June 20 1932.

Manton went to 605 Squadron, AuxAF on March 29 1934, as Assistant Adjutant and Instructor. After qualifying as a flying instructor he was posted to 607 Squadron, AuxAF on July 17 1936, as Adjutant. On January 1 1937 Manton went to Air Ministry for duty in the Directorate of Flying Training to deal with AuxAF, VR and University Air Squadron training.

After a refresher flying course he was posted to command 56 Squadron at North Weald in early July 1940. On the 13th Manton destroyed a Ju 87, on the 18th a Bf 110 and on the 24th a Bf 109. In early September he was promoted to Wing Commander and posted to command RAF Manston. In March 1941 Manton was appointed Wing Leader at Northolt. He was shot down on April 16, in Hurricane Z 2492, crash-landing between New Romney and Dymchurch.

Manton was wounded in May and after a period of limited duty at Colerne he was posted to Fighter HQ at Belfast. In 1942 he was promoted to Acting Group Captain and appointed SASO HQ 82 Group and later at HQ RAF Northern Ireland. Manton commanded RAF Church Fenton and RAF Coltishall in 1943 and then became Group Captain Operations at HQ 12 Group, Watnall.

Having volunteered for overseas Manton was posted in September 1944 to command 907 Fighter-Bomber Wing in Burma. He returned to the UK in 1946 and went as SASO to HQ 13 Group, Inverness.

Manton retired from the RAF on June 26 1960, as a Group Captain. He settled in Australia.

PO 26.6.31   FO 26.12.32   FL 1.4.36   SL 1.12.38
WC 1.3.41   GC 1.7.44   GC 1.1.49

ROY ACHILLE MARCHAND

42070   PO   Pilot   British   73 Squadron

Marchand was born on August 24 1918 at Beckenham, Kent. He was educated at Abbey Preparatory School and Westminster School. He studied for two years at London University Faculty of Medicine.

In March 1939 Marchand joined the RAF on a short service commission. He did his elementary flying at 30 E&RFTS and then moved to 15 FTS, Lossiemouth, where he was awarded his flying badge in August 1939. Marchand was posted to 73 Squadron in France in late December.

On May 13 1940 he was wounded in the shoulder and beneath the left eye. After recovering he went on leave and got married. He and his wife were injured in a car accident whilst on honeymoon and spent three weeks in hospital. Marchand returned to 73 Squadron on July 6.

He claimed a Bf 109 destroyed on September 6, ten miles north of Maidstone. Marchand was shot down and killed on the 15th, in combat over Maidstone. His Hurricane, P 3865, crashed at Nouds Farm, Teynham.

Marchand is buried in Bromley Hill Cemetery, Lewisham. Over his grave was a magnificent granite memorial. His father removed it in the early seventies and gifted it to the London Air Museum. In 1982 it was acquired by the Tangmere Military Aviation Museum. Marchand's grave had by this time been marked by the Commonwealth War Graves Commission. Tangmere arranged for the memorial to be erected near the site of Marchand's crash. A ceremony of dedication was held on September 15 1985.

APO 27.5.39   PO 18.11.39

MIECZYSLAW MARCINKOWSKI

780491   Sgt   Pilot   Polish   501 Squadron

Marcinkowski was born on February 24 1919. He joined 501 Squadron at Kenley in October 1940. He was reported 'Missing' after a squadron patrol on November 1 1940 and was last seen over the Channel, heading for the French coast, in Hurricane V 7405.

Marcinkowski is remembered on the Polish Air Force Memorial at Northolt.

FRANTISEK MAREK

1299985   Sgt   Pilot   Czechoslovakian   310 and 19 Sqdns

Marek was born on January 30 1913. He joined 310 Squadron at Duxford on August 6 1940 and went on attachment to 19 Squadron at Fowlmere on the 29th.

Marek was killed on September 14, when he crashed near Horndon-on-the-Hill, Orsett during a routine patrol, in Spitfire R 6625. The cause of the crash is unknown but is presumed to have been Marek's losing consciousness because of oxygen failure.

He is buried in Eastbrookend Cemetery, Barking, Essex.

ANTONI MARKIEWICZ

793546   Sgt   Pilot   Polish   302 Squadron

Born on January 13 1915. Markiewicz joined 302 Squadron at Leconfield on August 6 1940. He claimed a Bf 109 as probably destroyed on October 26.

Awarded the KW (23.12.40), Markiewicz was posted to No 1 ADU at Croydon on February 2 1941. He went to 2 FIS, Montrose for an instructor's course on July 29 1942 and then was posted to 16 FTS, Newton, where he remained until being released from the PAF in late November 1945, as a Warrant Officer.

Markiewicz was awarded a Bar to the KW (20.8.42) and a second Bar (31.10.47).

RAINFORD GENT MARLAND

62657   Sgt   Pilot   British   222 Squadron

Marland, of Preston, Lancashire, joined 222 Squadron at Hornchurch on September 1 1940. He claimed a Bf 109 destroyed on the 7th, a Ju 88 on the 11th, a Bf 110 on the 14th, two probable Bf 109s on the 30th and another probable on October 25.

He shared a probable Ju 88 on February 17 1941 and shared another on March 8. Marland was commissioned in March 1941. He claimed a Do 17 destroyed on April 7 and a Bf 109 and two others damaged on July 9.

Marland was killed on December 17 1941, as a Pilot Officer with 229 Squadron, aged 25. He is buried in Halfaya Sollum War Cemetery, Egypt.

PO 19.3.41

ROY MARPLES

70868   FO   Pilot   British   616 Squadron

Marples, of Manchester, joined the RAF on a short service commission in January 1938. He was posted to 8 FTS, Montrose on April 9 and joined 19 Squadron at Duxford on October 29.

In May 1940 Marples was with 616 Squadron at Rochford. Over Dunkirk on June 1 he damaged a He 111. On the 30th he shot down a He 111 at night, near Hornsea. Marples shared in destroying a Ju

88 on August 15 and was himself shot down on the 26th. He made a forced-landing near Adisham and was admitted to Kent and Canterbury Hospital, with cannon shell splinter wounds in the leg.

On May 5 1941 Marples damaged a Ju 88 at dusk and on June 22 he destroyed a Bf 109. In July he went to 41 Squadron at Merston, as a Flight Commander. On August 12 he shared a Bf 109 and on September 18 shared a Ju 52. He was posted away later in the month and awarded the DFC (17.10.41).

Marples joined 127 Squadron in the Western Desert on June 9 1942, as a Flight Commander. He shared a Bf 109 on July 8, was given command of 238 Squadron on July 20, probably destroyed a Ju 87 on October 30 and then took command of 145 Squadron in the Desert on November 25. Marples was awarded a Bar to the DFC (5.1.43). He shot down a Mc 202 on January 12 1943. After this action his own engine failed and he ditched on the sea. Two soldiers swam out from shore and helped him to land. He was posted away from 145 on January 26 1943.

In April 1944 Marples was leading 145 Wing at Merston, made up of 329, 340 and 341 Free French Squadrons. He was killed on April 26, when he collided with a pilot of 329 over Washington, Sussex. He was 24 years old and is buried in Chichester Cemetery.

APO 26.3.38   PO 8.5.39   FO 3.9.40   FL 3.9.41
SL 1.1.44

ERIC SIMCOX MARRS

33572   PO   Pilot   British   152 Squadron

Born in Dover on July 9 1921, Marrs entered RAF College, Cranwell in April 1939 as a flight cadet. He was granted a Permanent Commission on March 7 1940 and joined 152 Squadron at Acklington ten days later.

On August 13 Marrs claimed a Bf 110 destroyed, on the 16th a probable He 111, on the 18th a Ju 87, on the 22nd a shared Do 17, on the 25th a Bf 110, on September 17 a shared Ju 88, on the 27th a Ju 88, on November 14 a shared Ju 88 and on the 28th a Bf 109.

Marrs destroyed a Do 17 north of Warmwell on January 4 1941. He was awarded the DFC (7.1.41) and became a Flight Commander in April. He shared a He 111 over the Scilly Isles on July 18. The squadron provided close escort for Hampdens detailed to bomb the 'Scharnhorst' and 'Gneisenau' at Brest on July 24 1941. Heavy flak was encountered over the target and Marrs was shot down and killed. He is buried in Kerfautras Cemetery, Brest, France. His portrait was drawn by Cuthbert Orde.

PO 7.3.40   FO 7.3.41

ALAN EDWARD MARSH

Lieutenant (RM/FAA)   Pilot   British   804 Squadron

Marsh was commissioned in the Royal Marines in January 1935. In early July 1940 he was with 804 Squadron at Hatston, flying Sea Gladiators on dockyard defence.

On November 22 1940 he transferred to 802 Squadron, HMS 'Audacity' but rejoined 804 on March 24 1941 for Fighter Catapult ships, as Senior Pilot. Marsh commanded the squadron from February 9 to October 30 1942, after which he was at Combined Operations HQ as FAA Planner.

Marsh held a series of appointments as Lieutenant Commander Flying, on HMS 'Rajah' from January 3 to December 16 1944, on HMS 'Khedive' from December 31 1944 to June 11 1945 and at RNAS Trincomalee from June 12 to November 21 1945. He returned to the Royal Marines in January 1946 and served in 42 Commando in Malta. Marsh retired at his own request on September 30 1953.

2nd Lt 1.1.35   Lt 21.5.37   Capt 13.1.41   Capt 13.1.47

EDWARD HOWARD MARSH

156314   Sgt   Pilot   British   152 Squadron

Marsh joined the RAFVR in July 1939 and flew a few times at 14 E&RFTS, Castle Bromwich before being called to full-time service on September 1 1939. In early October Marsh was posted to ITW, St Leonards. He did a Link Trainer course at Derby in December, returned to ITW and moved on to 22 EFTS, Cambridge on April 12 1940.

After completing his flying training at 5 FTS, Sealand Marsh went to 7 OTU, Hawarden on September 18, converted to Spitfires and joined 152 Squadron at Warmwell on the 28th. In March 1941 he destroyed a Ju 88 off Portland, on July 18 shared a He 111, on August 28 damaged a Bf 109 and on September 7 destroyed another.

Marsh was posted to CFS, Upavon on October 4 1941, for an instructor's course, after which he went to 10 FTS, Tern Hill. He later instructed at 2 FIS, Montrose and 3 FIS, Hullavington, Babdown Farm, Castle Combe and Lulsgate Bottom. Commissioned in July 1943, Marsh was released from the RAF in 1945, as a Flight Lieutenant. He worked for Wolverhampton Aviation, obtained his private and commercial licenses and flew until 1953, when bad hearing forced him to give up.

PO 22.7.43   FO 22.1.44   FL 22.7.45   FO (RAFVR) 30.7.47

HENRY JAMES MARSH

762584   Sgt   Pilot   British   238 Squadron

Joined the RAF at Halton at the age of 18. Marsh later volunteered for pilot training and when he was posted to 11 E&RFTS, Perth in February 1939 he was a Sergeant Observer.

Marsh went to 2 FTS, Brize Norton in May. He was with 238 Squadron at Middle Wallop in early July 1940. On August 11 Marsh claimed a He 111 destroyed. In combat over Portland on August 13 he destroyed a Bf 110 but failed to return to Middle Wallop, probably shot down by Bf 109s, in Hurricane P 3177.

Marsh was 27. He is remembered on the Runnymede Memorial, Panel 17.

WILLIAM CHARLES MARSH

119521   Sgt   Air Gunner   British   236 Squadron

Joined 236 Squadron on July 19 1940. Commissioned in March 1942, Marsh was released from the RAF in 1945, as a Flight Lieutenant.

PO 26.3.42   FO 1.10.42   FL 26.3.44

ALFRED ERNEST MARSHALL

47124   Sgt   Pilot   British   73 Squadron

Marshall, of Hitchin, Hertfordshire joined 73 Squadron in France in May 1940. He shared a He 111 on the 19th and destroyed a Do 17 on June 11. The squadron was withdrawn to England on June 17. Marshall probably destroyed a Bf 110 on September 7 but his Hurricane, P 3863, was severely damaged in combat and he made a forced-landing near Dammerwick Farm, Burnham Marshes after his engine failed. He was slightly injured.

In early November 1940 73 Squadron was posted to the Middle East. It sailed on HMS 'Furious' and flew off at Takoradi on the 29th. It then flew in easy stages to Heliopolis, via Lagos, Accra, Kano, Maidugari, Khartoum, Wadi Halfa and Abu Sueir. During December the pilots were attached to 274 Squadron in the Western Desert. Marshall shot down two SM 79s on December 16, on an offensive patrol over Bardia.

On January 3 1941 Marshall found five SM 79s bombing HMS 'Terror' nine miles north-east of Bardia. He shot two down, forced a third to crash-land in the sea and damaged a fourth. His ammunition was all gone. The same afternoon he joined the CO and Flying Officer JE Storrar in destroying eight enemy aircraft on a landing ground. On January 5 Marshall shot down a SM 79, on February 5 he joined the CO and Storrar in destroying another eight enemy aircraft on the ground, this time at Benina. On April 23 after destroying a Ju 87 Marshall landed to refuel and was shot up on the ground and wounded.

Marshall left the squadron in May and was awarded the DFM (6.6.41). Commissioned in August 1941, he returned to operations in April 1942, joining 250 Squadron at Sidi Heneish. On July 5 he destroyed a Bf 109 and a Mc 202 and on the 8th another Bf 109. Marshall was rested from operations on August 1 1942 and returned to the UK. He was awarded the DFC (6.10.42).

He was posted to 51 OTU, Cranfield, as an instructor. He joined 25 Squadron at Coltishall in July 1944. On November 27 Marshall was killed, as a Flight Lieutenant, aged 29. He is buried in Hitchin Cemetery.

PO 11.8.41   FO 12.8.42   FL 12.8.43

JAMES EGLINGTON MARSHALL

70809   FO   Pilot   British   85 Squadron

Marshall, of Dover, was brought up in West Africa. He was with 85 Squadron in early July 1940.

On August 18 Marshall claimed a He 111 destroyed. On this day he collided with a He 111 in combat over the Thames Estuary and returned to Debden minus his starboard wingtip. On the 29th Marshall claimed a Bf 109 and the next day was shot down attacking He 111s. He baled out, unhurt. His Hurricane, V 6624, crashed at Langley Farm, Smarden. On October 27 he claimed a He 111 destroyed.

Marshall was awarded the DFC (29.4.41). He was given command of 1452 Flight at West Malling at its formation on July 7 1941, with Turbinlite Havocs. He was killed on April 18 1942, aged 23. He was returning to West Malling with two passengers, when his aircraft crashed at Widford and all three men were killed. Marshall is buried in Maidstone Cemetery, Kent.

PO (RAFO) 30.10.38   PO 23.6.39   FO 3.9.40   FL 3.9.41

JOHN VICTOR MARSHALL

83286   PO   Pilot   British   232 Squadron

Marshall was born on November 11 1918. He joined 232 Squadron at Castletown on September 14 1940. He served with 152 Squadron in India and Burma in 1943 and was awarded the DFC (18.2.43).

He commanded 81 Squadron in Burma from March to October 1944. Marshall retired from the RAF on September 3 1970, as a Group Captain. He died on June 24 1984.

PO 17.8.40   FO 17.8.41   FL 17.8.42   SL 1.8.47
WC 1.1.55   GC 1.1.63

THOMAS BRIAN MARSHALL

102085   Sgt   Pilot   British   235 Squadron

Joined 235 Squadron on September 19 1940.

Commissioned in July 1941, Marshall was awarded the DFC (20.4.45), as an Acting Squadron Leader with 39 Squadron, operating in Marauders from Biferno, Italy.

Marshall was released from the RAF in 1945.

PO 12.7.41   FO 12.7.42   FL 12.7.43

THOMAS ROBSON MARSHALL

611372   Sgt   Air Gunner   British   219 Squadron

Joined 219 Squadron at Catterick in August 1940. Marshall was killed on June 29 1941, as a Flight Sergeant with 218 Squadron, operating in Wellingtons from Marham, Norfolk. He is buried in Becklingen War Cemetery, Soltau, Germany.

GUY MARSLAND

41940 **PO** **Pilot** **British** **245 and 253 Squadrons**

Born on November 5 1919, Marsland joined the RAF on a short service commission in December 1938. After completing his flying training he joined 245 Squadron at Leconfield in early November 1939.

Posted to 253 Squadron at Kenley on September 24 1940, Marsland claimed a Bf 110 destroyed on October 29.

He retired from the RAF on October 1 1958, as a Squadron Leader, retaining the rank of Wing Commander. Marsland became a successful antique dealer. He died in 1983.

APO 6.2.39   PO 6.11.39
FO 6.11.40   FL 6.11.41   SL 1.7.45   SL 1.8.47

KENNETH JOHN MARSTON

83715 **PO** **Pilot** **British** **56 Squadron**

Marston was born in Coventry on October 26 1918. He was educated at Bablake School there and was apprenticed to the Coventry City Transport Department. He joined the RAFVR in early 1939.

Called up at the outbreak of war, Marston did his flying training at 6 EFTS, Sywell and 8 FTS, Montrose. After converting to Hurricanes Marston joined 56 Squadron at North Weald on July 28 1940.

Marston claimed a Bf 109 destroyed on August 24, two more on the 26th and a Bf 110 on September 25. He was shot down during a combat with Bf 109s and Bf 110s over Bournemouth on September 30. He crashed at East Knighton in Hurricane P 2866, with shrapnel wounds and abrasions.

On December 12 1940 Pilot Officer Z Nosowicz had overshot landing at Middle Wallop and as he climbed away his propellor hit the tail of Marton's Hurricane, V 7510, as he was circling to land. Marston crashed one mile north-west of the aerodrome and was killed. He is buried in St James' churchyard, Stivichall, Coventry, Warwickshire.

PO 21.7.40

LUDWIK MARTEL

76812 **PO** **Pilot** **Polish** **54 and 603 Squadrons**

Martel was born on March 5 1919. He joined 54 Squadron at Catterick in mid-September 1940 and moved to 603 Squadron at Hornchurch on the 28th. He claimed a Bf 109 destroyed on October 5.

Martel was posted to 317 Squadron at Acklington on March 19 1941. He was awarded the KW (1.4.41) and was rested on January 28 1942, going to 58 OTU, Grangemouth as an instructor. Martel returned to 317 on August 25.

He went to West Kirby on February 13 1943 to prepare for

overseas and on March 13 arrived in the Middle East in a C 47 with other Polish pilots to form the Polish Fighting Team, otherwise known as 'Skalski's Circus'. They were attached to 145 Squadron and operated in the Western Desert from March 17 to May 12 and destroyed 30 enemy aircraft. Martel damaged a FW 190 on April 4 and destroyed a Bf 109 and damaged a Mc 200 on the 20th.

Back in the UK Martel returned to 317 on July 22 1943. He was posted to 16 FTS, Newton on August 20 but went back to 317 on November 4, as a Flight Commander. Martel was awarded two Bars to the KW (20.12.43). Tour-expired, he was posted to HQ PAF on September 12 1944 and awarded the VM (5th Class)(25.9.44).

Martel was attached to the School of Air Support at Old Sarum on March 4 1945, for a course. He went to HQ BAFO in January 1946 for Operations Room duties and served with 131 Wing from October 14 1946 until released from the PAF in January 1947, as a Flight Lieutenant.

FO 1.3.41   FL 1.9.43

A MARTIN

No unknown **Sgt** **Air Gunner** **British** **264 Squadron**

No service details traced.

ALLAN WILLIAM MARTIN

78254 **PO** **Observer** **British** **235 Squadron**

Martin was born in 1914. He was with 235 Squadron in early July 1940.

Awarded the DFC (7.12.43), as a Flight Lieutenant with 502 Squadron. Martin was released from the RAF in 1945, as a Squadron Leader. He joined the RAFVR in May 1948.

PO 24.3.40   FO 24.3.41   FL 24.3.42   FO (RAFVR) 24.5.48

JOHN CLAVERLY MARTIN

40313 **FO** **Pilot** **New Zealander** **257 Squadron**

Born in Timaru on May 6 1914, Martin was at the High School there from January 1929 to December 1932. He applied for an RAF short service commission in April 1937 and after provisional acceptance sailed for the UK on August 14 1937 in the RMS 'Arawa'.

Martin began his flying training at 9 E&RFTS, Ansty on September 27. He was posted to 10 FTS, Tern Hill on December 11 and joined 63 Squadron at Upwood on July 9 1938. The squadron was disbanded into 12 OTU in early April 1940 and Martin was posted to 98 Squadron, AASF in France, flying Battles. After the fall of France the squadron was withdrawn to England in June and Martin was posted to 226 Squadron at Thirsk, Yorkshire.

In August 1940 Martin volunteered for Fighter Command and joined 3 Squadron at Acklington in early September. He moved to 257 Squadron at Martlesham Heath on the 17th. Martin was with the squadron until March 7 1941, when he joined 485 Squadron, the first all-New Zealand fighter squadron, then forming at Driffield. He was made a Flight Commander.

On June 20 1941 Martin was attached to 222 Squadron at North Weald, as a Flight Commander. He claimed two enemy aircraft destroyed on August 19. The squadron was ordered to escort nine Blenheims to bomb targets in the Lille area on August 27 1941. On the return journey German fighters made numerous rear and side attacks. Martin is known to have reached the Channel. A collision occurred, in which at least two British aircraft were involved. As no one saw Martin attacked by the fighters or hit by flak it is assumed that his was one of the aircraft involved in the collision, when he failed to return to base.

Martin is remembered on the Runnymede Memorial, Panel 29.

APO 28.11.37   PO 30.9.38   FO 27.5.40

RICHARD MAURICE SCOTT MARTIN

Sub-Lieutenant (FAA) **Pilot** **British** **808 Squadron**

Martin joined the FAA in 1939. He was with 808 Squadron at Wick in early July 1940, flying Fulmars on dockyard defence.

He embarked with the squadron on HMS 'Ark Royal' on October 22 and was killed on November 27 1940. Martin is remembered on the Fleet Air Arm Memorial at Lee-on-Solent.

Midshipman 20.1.39   Actg Sub-Lt 8.4.40

THOMAS ARTHUR MASLEN

615059   **Sgt**   **Wop/AG**   **British**   **235 Squadron**

Maslen, of Bath, was with 235 Squadron in early July 1940. He was killed on October 25 1941, aged 25. The unit he was serving with at that time is not known.

Maslen is buried in Haycombe Cemetery, Englishcombe, Somerset.

WILLIAM MASON

745149   **Sgt**   **Pilot**   **British**   **235 Squadron**

Mason, of York, joined 235 Squadron on October 2 1940. He was killed on February 14 1941, as a Sergeant with 235, aged 24. He is buried in York Cemetery.

KENNETH MASSEY

115600   **Sgt**   **Aircrew**   **British**   **248 Squadron**

Joined 248 Squadron on September 25 1940. Commissioned in January 1942, Massey was released from the RAF in 1946, as a Flight Lieutenant. He joined the RAFVR in June 1948.

PO 24.1.42   *FO 1.10.42*   *FL 24.1.44*   *FO (RAFVR) 7.6.48*

JOHN ROMNEY MATHER

78976   **PO**   **Pilot**   **British**   **66 Squadron**

Mather was born at Blackheath in 1915 and educated at Dulwich College. His father worked for the Tata Iron and Steel Co in India and Mather worked for Stewarts and Lloyds at Glasgow and Corby.

He joined the RAFVR in 1937 and was called to full-time service at the outbreak of war. Mather was with 66 Squadron in June 1940. On July 10 he shared in the destruction of a Do 17 and on September 2 shared a He 111. He was shot down in combat over the Thames Estuary on September 18 and baled out, unhurt. His Spitfire, R 6925, is believed to have crashed near Coldred.

On October 27 1940 Mather was killed when his Spitfire, P 7539, crashed and burned out at Half Moon Lane, Hildenborough. The cause of the crash is unknown but he may have been the victim of anoxia. Mather is buried in St. Margaret's churchyard, Ifield, Sussex.

PO 1.4.40

JAMES W MATHERS

1003686   **Sgt**   **Aircrew**   **British**   **23 and 29 Squadrons**

Joined 23 Squadron at Middle Wallop on September 26 1940 and moved to 29 Squadron at Digby in October. No further service details traced.

GEOFFREY CHARLES MATHESON

39363   **FL**   **Pilot**   **British**   **222 Squadron**

Joined the RAF on a short service commission in October 1936. Matheson was posted to 10 FTS, Tern Hill on January 16 1937 and joined 41 Squadron at Catterick on August 7.

Matheson was with 222 Squadron at Hornchurch in early July 1940. He claimed a Bf 109 destroyed on August 30 but was shot down himself and crash-landed near Sittingbourne, in Spitfire P 9443, seriously injured. On September 30 he was again shot down, crash-landing near Sittingbourne. The aircraft later exploded but he was unhurt.

On August 24 1943 Matheson was killed, as a Squadron Leader with 418 Squadron, operating in Mosquitos from Ford. He is remembered on the Runnymede Memorial, Panel 118.

APO 6.1.37   *PO 12.10.37*   *FO 12.7.39*   *FL 3.9.40*
SL 1.12.41

KENNETH MATHEWS

82954   **PO**   **Pilot**   **British**   **23 Squadron**

Mathews, of Middleton-on-Sea, Sussex, joined 23 Squadron at Wittering in late August 1940.

He commanded 534 Squadron at Tangmere from September 1942 until its disbandment on January 25 1943. Mathews was killed on October 20 1943, as a Squadron Leader with 25 Squadron, aged 27. He is buried in Sneek General Cemetery, Netherlands.

PO 21.7.40   *FO 21.7.41*   *FL 21.7.42*

HENRY GEORGE MATTHEWS

49220   **Sgt**   **Wop/AG**   **British**   **236 Squadron**

Matthews was born on January 30 1920. He joined 236 Squadron on September 3 1940 and was awarded the DFM (25.11.41). Commissioned in June 1942, Matthews stayed on in the RAF, in the Secretarial Branch. He retired on January 30 1969, as a Squadron Leader.

P0 4.6.42   *FO 4.12.42*   *FL 4.6.44*   *FL 4.12.46*
SL 1.1.54

HENRY KEY FIELDING MATTHEWS

40551   **FO**   **Pilot**   **British**   **54 and 603 Squadrons**

Joined the RAF on a short service commission in November 1937. Matthews was posted to 9 FTS, Hullavington on March 5 1938 and joined 64 Squadron at Church Fenton on September 17.

In June 1940 Matthews was with 54 Squadron at Hornchurch. On July 9 he shared in the destruction of a He 59 and on August 25 claimed a Bf 109 destroyed. On September 30 Matthews was posted to 603 Squadron at Hornchurch.

He was shot down and killed in combat with Bf 109s on October 7 1940. His Spitfire, N 3109, crashed at Hurst Farm, Godmersham. Matthews was 28 years old and is buried in Crystal Palace District Cemetery.

APO 19.2.38   *PO 29.11.38*   *FO 15.3.40*

IAN WALTER MATTHEWS

102092   **Sgt**   **Pilot**   **British**   **64 Squadron**

Matthews, of Eltham, London, joined 64 Squadron at Leconfield on September 22 1940.

Commissioned in July 1941, Matthews was with 238 Squadron in the Western Desert in 1942. On September 1 he was attacked by two Bf 109s and shot down and killed, south of El Imayid.

Matthews was 21. He is buried in the El Alamein War Cemetery.

PO 17.7.41

PETER GERALD HUGH MATTHEWS

40247   **FO**   **Pilot**   **British**   **1 Squadron**

Born in Liverpool on May 8 1919, Matthews was the son of a veterinary surgeon. He planned to follow his father and was scheduled to go to Liverpool University in 1941.

Matthews joined the RAF on a short service commission on August 14 1937 and began his ab initio course at 6 E&RFTS, Sywell. He was posted to 5 FTS, Sealand on October 24 1937 and on June 6 1938 joined the staff at No 1 Air Armament School at Manby, on drogue-towing duties. On August 20 1939 Matthews was posted to No 1 Squadron at Tangmere. He went to France with the squadron at the outbreak of war.

PGH Matthews (continued)

On December 7 1939 Matthews wrote off a Hurricane, when he made a forced-landing at St Dizier after his engine seized. Matthews destroyed a Bf 110 on May 16 1940 and a He 111 on June 4. The squadron returned to Tangmere on June 17.

Matthews claimed a Bf 110 destroyed on August 16. He was appointed 'B' Flight Commander on November 10 and on April 29 1941 was posted to 52 OTU, Debden, as 'C' Flight Commander. He was awarded the DFC (13.5.41). Matthews was given command of 74 Squadron at Llanbedr on November 3 1941, took it to the Middle East in April 1942 and led it until July 10. He took command of 145 Squadron in the Western Desert on August 30 1942. Matthews probably destroyed a Mc 202 on September 3, destroyed a Mc 202 on the 11th, shared in a probable Ju 52 on the 29th, probably destroyed a Bf 109 on October 23 and shared another on the 27th.

During an engagement with Bf 109s and Stukas on November 3 Matthews was shot down and baled out into the Mediterranean. After four hours in his dinghy he was picked up by an ASR launch. At the end of the month Matthews went to HQ ME, in the Delta, and was posted as CGI to 71 OTU, Carthago, south of Port Sudan. In April 1943 the unit moved to Ismailia.

Matthews returned to operations on August 15 1943, taking command of 111 Squadron at Panebianco, Sicily. He destroyed a Fiesler Storch on December 2. Matthews was injured in a motor accident in December, was taken to hospital in North Africa and afterwards returned to the UK, where he was posted to Bentley Priory as Tactics 2.

In the post-war years Matthews was Air Attaché in Prague for three years and Permanent President Courts Martial for two. He retired from the RAF on May 8 1966, as a Wing Commander, retaining the rank of Group Captain.

APO 24.10.37   PO 23.8.38   FO 23.3.40   FL 23.3.41
SL 1.6.42   SL 1.8.46   WC 1.7.53

DAVID ALEXANDER MAXWELL

84962   PO   Pilot   British   611 and 603 Squadrons

Joined 611 Squadron at Tern Hill on September 29 1940 and moved to 603 Squadron at Hornchurch in October.

Maxwell was killed on February 14 1941, as a Pilot Officer with 66 Squadron, aged 24. He is remembered on the Runnymede Memorial, Panel 33.

PO 7.9.40

HUGH LOCKHART MAXWELL

25046   SL   Pilot   British   600 Squadron

Born on December 21 1908, Maxwell was a lieutenant in the Northamptonshire Regiment when he transferred to the RAF in September 1935. He was posted to No 1 FTS, Leuchars on the 23rd and joined 26 (Army Co-operation) Squadron at Catterick on April 27 1936.

Maxwell was later with a bomber squadron. He was posted to command 600 Squadron at Catterick on September 15 1940, which he did until November, when he went to HQ 13 Group, Newcastle as a Controller. Maxwell was awarded the DSO (22.11.40).

He was Station Commander at Hornchurch from July 20 to October 28 1943 and at Biggin Hill from November 1943 to February 1945. Maxwell was made a CBE (1.1.45). He retired from the RAF on June 10 1956, as a Group Captain, retaining the rank of Air Commodore.

FO 23.9.35   FL 16.9.37   SL 1.3.40   WC 1.9.41
GC 1.1.46   GC 1.7.47

WALTER MAXWELL

967872   Sgt   Air Gunner   British   264 Squadron

Maxwell, of Meols, Cheshire, joined 264 Squadron at Kirton-in-Lindsey on August 4 1940.

In an action with Bf 109s on August 26 Maxwell was gunner in Defiant L 7025, shot down into the sea two miles off Herne Bay. The pilot, Flying Officer IR Stephenson, baled out and was rescued from the sea. Maxwell was reported 'Missing'. He was 23 and is remembered on the Runnymede Memorial, Panel 17.

HOWARD CLIVE MAYERS

77976   PO   Pilot   Australian   601 Squadron

Mayers was born in Sydney on January 9 1910. He lived in London before the war and was Managing Director of a company.

He joined 601 Squadron at Tangmere on August 2 1940. Mayers claimed a Bf 109 destroyed on August 8 and a Ju 88 on the 13th. On this day he was shot down by enemy fighters off Portland. He baled out, was picked up by an MTB and treated for slight shrapnel wounds at Portland Hospital. His Hurricane, P 2690, crashed in the Channel off Whitnose, Weymouth. Mayers claimed two Ju 87s destroyed on August 16, Do 17s on the 31st and September 4 and a Bf 110 on the 25th. He was awarded the DFC (1.10.40). He made a forced-landing south of Axminster on October 7 after glycol tank damage during a combat with Bf 110s over Portland. Mayers was slightly injured and the Hurricane, R 4218, was written off.

He took command of 94 Squadron at Ismailia, Egypt in July 1941 and shared in destroying a Ju 88 on September 11. In December 1941 Mayers was leading an attack on an enemy column. He saw one of his pilots shot down by flak. He landed near the crashed aircraft and although enemy vehicles were approaching he let the pilot into his seat, got in on top and took off, safely reaching his base.

In January 1942 Mayers was promoted to lead a Hurricane Wing and awarded a Bar to the DFC (13.2.42). On April 26 he became Wing Leader 239 Wing, with Kittyhawks. He claimed two Ju 52s destroyed and another damaged on May 12 and a Bf 109 destroyed on July 8.

Leading the Wing on July 20, Mayers radioed that he was making a forced-landing in the Qattara Depression, with engine trouble. His aircraft was found and there being no trace of him it was presumed that he had been captured. He was never heard of again and may have been lost in a Ju 52, which was shot down whilst ferrying PoWs to Germany. He was awarded the DSO (28.7.42).

Mayers is remembered on the Alamein Memorial, Column 247.

PO 11.3.40   FO 29.12.40   FL 1.10.41

PAUL FRANCIS MAYHEW

74336   FO   Pilot   British   79 Squadron

Mayhew, of Felthorpe, Norfolk, was a member of the Oxford University Air Squadron when he was an undergraduate at Christ Church College.

He was called to full-time service in September 1939 and with training completed he joined 79 Squadron at Acklington in August 1940. Mayhew shared a He 59 on August 28, claimed a He 111 on the 30th and a Do 17 on September 1. He made a forced-landing at Enniscorthy, Co Wexford, Ireland on September 29, lost and low on fuel following an interception of He 111s over the Irish Sea. His Hurricane, P 5178, was impounded.

Mayhew was killed on February 19 1942, still with 79, aged 22. He was cremated at Perry Bar Crematorium, Birmingham.

PO 26.9.39   FO 26.9.40   FL 26.9.41

ERNEST MAYNE

46329   WO   Pilot   British   74 Squadron

Born on January 2 1901, Mayne was in the RFC in the Great War. As an airman pilot he was with 74 Squadron at its reformation in September 1935. He was promoted to Warrant Officer on May 15 1940.

Over Dunkirk on May 26 he shared in the destruction of a Hs 126 and on the 27th he destroyed a Bf 109. Mayne used to wear his RFC badge on his cap. On July 15 he left his cap at Manston to go on patrol. Instead of returning there he was ordered to Hornchurch. He never saw his cap again and was said to be heartbroken at the loss of his badge.

Mayne shared in the destruction of two Bf 110s on August 11 1940. It was his final operation. He had flown 2000 hours in fighters. He was posted to 5 OTU, Aston Down on September 17, as an instructor.

Commissioned in August 1941, Mayne was awarded the AFC (1.1.42). In June 1945 he was posted to Manston as Station Gunnery Officer. Mayne retired on December 4 1945, as a Flight Lieutenant, retaining the rank of Squadron Leader. He died on March 24 1978.

FO 21.8.41   FL 21.8.42

JAMES REGINALD BRYAN MEAKER ✠

42514 PO Pilot British 249 Squadron

Meaker was born in Kinsale, Co Cork. He joined the RAF on a short service commission in June 1939. After completing his training he was posted to 46 Squadron at Digby. Meaker was with 263 Squadron, when it embarked on HMS 'Furious' for Norway on April 21. The Gladiators landed on frozen Lake Lesjakog on the 24th but the few left were withdrawn on the 27th, the rest having been destroyed by the Germans on the ice.

Meaker joined 249 Squadron at Leconfield in May 1940. He claimed a Bf 110 destroyed on August 15, a Bf 109 on the 24th, shared a Do 17 and a Bf 110 on September 2, destroyed two Do 17s on the 15th and shared a Bf 110 on the 27th. Meaker was shot down by return fire from a Ju 88 on this day. He baled out but fell dead at Warren Field, Brightling Park. His Hurricane, P 3834, crashed at Brake Field, Giffords Farm, Dallington.

He was 21 years old and is buried in West Dean Cemetery, Sussex. Meaker was awarded the DFC (8.10.40).

APO 19.8.39   PO 24.2.40

STANLEY THOMAS MEARES

37683 FL Pilot British 54 Squadron

Born in Sidcup, Kent in 1916, Meares joined the RAF on a short service commission in January 1936. He was posted to 9 FTS, Thornaby on April 4 and joined 74 Squadron at Hornchurch on January 4 1937.

In late 1939 Meares was posted to HQ Fighter Command. He was not on the strength of 54 during the Battle of Britain but is believed to have flown one operational sortie with the squadron from Hornchurch on August 12 1940, qualifying him for the clasp.

In May 1941 Meares joined 611 Squadron at Westhampnett, as a Flight Commander. He was given command of 74 Squadron at Gravesend on June 30 1941 and awarded the DFC (22.7.41), being then credited with two Bf 109s destroyed and two more damaged.

Meares was posted to command 71 Squadron at North Weald on August 24 1941. On a training flight on November 15 he collided with Pilot Officer RO Scarborough. Both men were killed. Meares was 25 and is buried in Brookwood Military Cemetery, Woking.

APO 23.3.36   PO 27.1.37   FO 27.10.38   FL 5.4.40

WILLIAM EDWARD GEOFFREY MEASURES

33198 FL Pilot British 74 and 238 Squadrons

Born on August 7 1916, Measures entered RAF College, Cranwell in September 1935 as a flight cadet. After graduation in July 1937 he joined 74 Squadron at Hornchurch.

Over Dunkirk on May 21 1940 he probably destroyed a He 111, on the 23rd he shared a Hs 126 and on the 24th and 27th shared Do 17s. He was appointed 'B' Flight Commander on June 15. Measures destroyed a He 111 on July 6 and shared another on the 8th.

He was posted away to 7 OTU, Hawarden on July 24, as an instructor. Measures joined 238 Squadron at Chilbolton on October 12 1940.

He took command of 87 Squadron in September 1942 and led it to North Africa in November. He left the squadron in June 1943.

Awarded the AFC (1.9.44), Measures retired from the RAF on November 23 1957, as a Squadron Leader, retaining the rank of Wing Commander.

PO 31.7.37   FO 31.3.39   FL 3.9.40   SL 1.6.43

JOHN CHARLES OSWALD MEDWORTH

146294 Sgt Aircrew British 25 Squadron

Joined 25 Squadron at North Weald in late September 1940. Commissioned in April 1943, Medworth was released from the RAF in 1946, as a Flight Lieutenant.

PO 25.4.43   FO 25.10.43   FL 25.4.45

CHARLES VICTOR MEESON

748697 Sgt Pilot British 56 Squadron

Meeson, of Loughton, Essex, joined the RAF at the outbreak of war. He was posted to 56 Squadron at North Weald in late August 1940.

He was killed on September 20 1940 in a flying accident during a formation practice. Meeson crashed in Hurricane L 1595 west of Bulford Camp, near Amesbury. He was 21 and is buried in Loughton Burial Ground.

JAMES COSMO MELVILL

74681 FO Pilot British 264 Squadron

Born on April 12 1920, Melvill was educated at Winchester School and Trinity College, Cambridge. He learned to fly with the University Air Squadron and as a member of the RAFVR he was called to full-time service at the outbreak of war.

Melvill joined 264 Squadron at Kirton-in-Lindsey on September 1 1940. After being damaged in an engagement at night over London on March 8 1941 Melvill landed back at Luton. Instead of turning off the flarepath he taxied down it and was struck by a Defiant taking off. Both he and his gunner, Sergeant WL Butler, were injured. At some time Melvill was treated at Queen Victoria Hospital, East Grinstead and was a Guinea Pig.

From May 1942 until August 1943 Melvill commanded 247 Squadron. He was instructing in 1944 and received the AFC (1.9.44). He commanded 174 Squadron from August 1944 until January 1945. Melvill was released in 1946, as a Squadron Leader.

PO 8.11.39   FO 3.10.40   FL 3.10.41

GEORGE HOLMES MELVILLE-JACKSON

80842 PO Pilot British 236 Squadron

Born on November 23 1919, Melville-Jackson joined the RAF at the outbreak of war. With his training completed he was posted to 236 Squadron on July 9 1940.

In August 1941 Melville-Jackson was with 272 Squadron in Malta. He was awarded the DFC (20.4.43), as a Flight Lieutenant with 248 Squadron. The citation credited him with at least four enemy aircraft destroyed.

Melville-Jackson was released from the RAF in 1946, joined the RAFVR in 1949 and rejoined the RAF later. He retired on September 29 1968, as a Wing Commander.

PO 22.6.40   FO 22.6.41   FL 22.6.42   SL 14.1.46
FL (RAFVR) 18.11.49   WC 1.1.58

THOMAS NATHAN MENAGE

518613 Sgt Air Gunner British 29 Squadron

A pre-war airman, Menage joined 29 Squadron at Digby in September 1940. He was killed on May 10 1941, as a Sergeant with 149 Squadron, operating in Wellingtons from Mildenhall.

Menage is remembered on the Runnymede Memorial, Panel 48.

ROBERT TURNER DEIGHTON MERCER

748316 Sgt Pilot British 609 Squadron

Mercer, of Broadstairs, Kent, joined 609 Squadron at Middle Wallop on October 26 1940.

He was killed on May 9 1941 whilst trying to make a forced-landing on the beach at St Margaret's Bay. Mercer was still with 609. He was 24 years old and is buried in Folkestone New Cemetery.

HENRY JAMES MERCHANT

108856   **Sgt**   **Pilot**   **British**   **1 Squadron**

With No 1 Squadron in early July 1940. He ran out of fuel on a night patrol on August 23 and crashed at Hunt's Farm, Withyham, in Hurricane P 2980.

On August 30 he claimed a He 111 destroyed and on the 31st a Bf 110 and another damaged. In the combat over Chelmsford his aircraft was set alight and Merchant baled out and was admitted to Halstead Cottage Hospital, with burns. His Hurricane, V 7375, crashed and burned out on Ovington Hall Farm, Halstead.

Commissioned in August 1941, Merchant was released from the RAF in 1945, as a Flight Lieutenant.

PO 13.8.41   *FO 13.8.42*   *FL 13.8.43*

ARTHUR DOUGLAS MEREDITH

62651   **Sgt**   **Pilot**   **British**   **242 and 141 Squadrons**

Meredith joined the RAFVR in May 1938 and trained at 9 E&RFTS, Ansty on Avro Cadets and Hawker Harts. He was posted to 8 FTS, Montrose on December 19 1939 and after completing the course there he joined 17 Squadron at Hawkinge on May 10 1940.

With no Hurricane experience, Meredith went to 6 OTU, Sutton Bridge on May 27 to convert, after which he was posted to No 1 Squadron on June 7. He then joined 242 Squadron in France on the 13th.

Meredith moved to 141 Squadron at Grangemouth on August 10. Commissioned in March 1941 he remained with the squadron until June 25 1942, when he was posted to 1530 (BAT) Flight at Hunsdon, as an instructor. He was awarded the AFC (8.6.44). From September 4 1944 to June 18 1945, Meredith was on anti-aircraft co-operation duties, serving with 288, 597, and 598 Squadrons.

He was released from the RAF on October 16 1945, as a Flight Lieutenant.

PO 12.3.41   *FO 12.3.42*   *FL 12.3.43*

HERBERT WALDEMAR MERMAGEN

29097   **SL**   **Pilot**   **British**   **222 and 266 Squadrons**

Born on February 1 1912, Mermagen was educated at Brighton College. He joined the RAF on a short service commission in June 1930. He was posted to 2 FTS, Digby on July 12 and soloed in an Avro 504K on August 1. He joined 43 Squadron at Tangmere on June 23 1931.

Mermagen was posted to CFS, Upavon in February 1934, for an instructor's course. He became Flying Instructor with the Oxford University Air Squadron in May and on April 1 1935 joined the staff at 6 FTS, Netheravon. Mermagen went to the staff at CFS on August 17 1936. He led the Inverted Flying Formation at the 1937 Hendon Air Display and performed individual aerobatics before the King on May 9 1938. As i/c Handling Flight at CFS he flew all the new prototype fighters and bombers before they were in squadron use.

In October 1939 Mermagen formed and then commanded 222 Squadron at Duxford, initially with Blenheims but Spitfires from March 1940. Over Dunkirk on June 1 he destroyed a Bf 110 and on the 19th probably destroyed a He 111 at night over Hull. He was awarded the AFC (11.7.40).

Mermagen was posted from 222 in late July. He temporarily commanded 266 Squadron at Wittering from September 12 to 17 1940. He formed and commanded new fighter stations at Speke and Valley from September 1940 to May 1941. Mermagen was posted to the Middle East in June, where he commanded the Fighter Sector Station at Port Said and then 259 Wing in Cyprus. Whilst serving as Service Training Officer at HQ Middle East Mermagen flew a Spitfire VBS floatplane from Lake Timsor, one of the few RAF pilots to do so.

In July 1944 Mermagen returned to the UK and served on the staff of HQ AEAF and later SHAEF at Versailles until July 1945, when he was posted to Berlin as AOC British Air Command.

Mermagen held various appointments and commands at home and overseas before retiring from the RAF on November 14 1960, as an Air Commodore. He was made a CBE (1.1.45)(OBE 24.9.41) and a CB (11.6.60). He was a Commander Legion of Merit (US)(1946), was awarded the Medal for Distinguished Services (USSR)(28.8.45) and was made a Chevalier Légion d'Honneur (Fr)(1951).

PO 27.6.30   *FO 27.1.32*   *FL 27.1.36*   *SL 1.10.38*
WC 1.12.40   *GC 1.1.44*   *WC 1.10.46*   *GC 1.1.49*
AC 1.7.55

JOHN CHARLES MERRETT

104441   **Sgt**   **Observer**   **British**   **235 Squadron**

Born in 1919, Merrett joined the RAFVR in 1938. He carried out navigation exercises at Luton Airport in Ansons. At the outbreak of war he was called to full-time service and posted to the School of Navigation at Staverton, as an LAC. Following a course at BGS, West Freugh Merrett joined 235 Squadron at North Coates on April 1 1940, as a Sergeant.

The squadron served with Fighter Command during the Battle of Britain. When it was over 235 returned to its coastal work. Merrett was commissioned in August 1941 and on the 6th was posted away to Cranage for an instructor's course, after which he went to 5 OTU, Chivenor and later RAF Turnberry.

In November 1942 Merrett joined 612 Squadron at Wick, operating in Whitleys on long-range patrols over the sea. At the end of the year the squadron was searching for the 'Gneisenau' and 'Scharnhorst' but unsuccessfully. In March 1943 Merrett's flight was re-numbered as 179 Squadron, equipped with Leigh Light Wellingtons for anti-submarine operations. It operated from Gibraltar.

On January 3 1944 Merrett was posted to 6 OTU, Silloth, as a navigation instructor. He moved to 4 RFU, Mullage Moor, Northern Ireland in October, training on radar/sonar for anti-submarine work. In February 1945 Merrett was posted to 3 School of General Reconnaissance, as an instructor. He later moved to RAF Leuchars.

Merrett was seconded to BOAC but did not take up the appointment. He was released from the RAF in 1946, as a Flight Lieutenant.

PO 19.8.41   *FO 19.8.42*   *FL 19.8.43*

CLAUDE MERRICK

83256   **PO**   **Pilot**   **British**   **610 Squadron**

Merrick joined 610 Squadron at Biggin Hill on July 27 1940. He was shot down on August 24 by Bf 109s over the Thames Estuary and crash-landed at Fyfield. He was admitted to Ongar Hospital, slightly wounded.

On the night of June 5 1944 Merrick was pilot of an Albemarle detailed to drop paratroops in Northern France. They were to prepare and light a landing zone for the use of airborne forces, spearheading the invasion. On the success of this vital operation depended the success of later parachute and glider landings in the Caen area. In spite of bad weather Merrick executed his mission faultlessly. He was awarded the DFC (14.7.44), as an Acting Squadron Leader with 295 Squadron.

Merrick also received the Bronze Star (US)(30.10.45). He was released from the RAF in 1946, as a Wing Commander. He died in 1984.

PO 21.7.40   *FO 27.1.42*   *FL 27.1.43*

SYDNEY WILLIAM MERRYWEATHER

517691   **Sgt**   **Pilot**   **British**   **229 Squadron**

A pre-war airman pilot, Merryweather joined 229 Squadron at its formation at Digby in early October 1939.

He was posted to France with a 229 detachment in May 1940 and destroyed a Bf 109 there. Over Dunkirk during the evacuation he destroyed another.

After a combat with Bf 110s over Southampton on September 26 1940 Merryweather made a forced-landing at Hambledon, in Hurricane V 6745. He was wounded and slightly burned.

He was killed on June 5 1942, as a Warrant Officer with 174 Squadron, operating in Hurricanes from Manston. Merryweather was 27 and is remembered on the Runnymede Memorial, Panel 72. He was awarded the DFM (26.6.42).

BERTRAM WILLIAM MESNER

745987   **Sgt**   **Observer**   **British**   **248 Squadron**

Mesner, of Forest Gate, Essex, was with 248 Squadron in early July 1940. He was one of the crew of a Blenheim, which failed to return from a reconnaissance of the Fye-Stadlandet sector of the Norwegian coast on September 13 1940. The pilot, Sergeant WJ Garfield, was killed and the gunner, Sergeant A Kay, and Mesner were reported 'Missing'.

He was 29 and is remembered on the Runnymede Memorial, Panel 17.

ARTHUR CHARLES METCALFE

800630   **Sgt**   **Aircrew**   **British**   **604 Squadron**

No service details traced.

JAMES METHAM

47370   **Sgt**   **Pilot**   **British**   **253 Squadron**

Metham, of Blackpool, was with 253 Squadron at Kirton-in-Lindsey in early July 1940. He was shot down by Bf 109s in combat over Thanet on September 2 1940. His Hurricane, P 2946, is believed to be that which crashed at Longport, Crundale. He was slightly injured.

Commissioned in October 1941, Metham was killed on September 21 1942, as a Flight Lieutenant flying instructor. His unit at the time of his death is not known. He was 28 and was cremated at Carleton Crematorium, Poulton-le-Fylde, Blackpool.

PO 29.10.41

REGINALD HENRY ROWE MEYER

100613   **Sgt**   **Pilot**   **British**   **236 Squadron**

Meyer, of Holborn, London, joined 236 Squadron on October 20 1940.

Commissioned in July 1941, he was killed on February 9 1944, as a Flight Lieutenant with 252 Squadron, aged 23. He is buried in Phaleron War Cemetery, Athens.

PO 3.7.41   FO 3.7.42   FL 3.7.43

ALBERT CHARLES ANTOINE MICHIELS

141761   **Sgt**   **Observer**   **Belgian**   **235 Squadron**

Michiels, of Brussels, joined 235 Squadron on September 26 1940. Commissioned in January 1943, Michiels died on July 16 1944. The unit he was serving with is not known. His remains were repatriated to Belgium after the war.

PO 9.1.43

WILLIAM MIDDLEMISS

970668   **Sgt**   **Aircrew**   **British**   **235 Squadron**

Joined 235 Squadron on September 26 1940. Middlemiss was awarded the AFC (1.1.46), as a Warrant Officer. He was gazetted as a Master Signaller on September 1 1947.

WILLIAM ARTHUR MIDDLETON

39928   **PO**   **Pilot**   **New Zealander**   **266 Squadron**

Middleton was born in Auckland on December 31 1918 and educated at Auckland Grammar School. He was accepted for a short service commission in the RNZAF in June 1939 but the scheme lapsed on the outbreak of war. Middleton then volunteered for flying duties and was on the first course at the Ground Training School at Weraroa on October 26 1939.

In late November Middleton was posted to 2 EFTS, New Plymouth and on January 15 1940 moved to 2 FTS, Woodbourne. He was awarded his flying badge on April 23, completed the course and sailed for the UK in the RMS 'Rangitata' on June 7. Middleton went to 7 OTU, Hawarden on August 4 and joined 266 Squadron at Wittering on the 26th.

When he was posted to 485 Squadron, then forming at Driffield, on March 8 1941 Middleton had flown 57 operational sorties with 266. On May 4 he collided with a crashed Whitley whilst taking off on a night exercise. He was injured and admitted to York Military Hospital and did not rejoin the squadron, then stationed at Redhill, until August 23.

Four days later Middleton took off for a sweep over France. He failed to return and was reported 'Missing'. He is buried in Dunkirk Communal Cemetery.

APO 26.10.39   PO 28.5.40   FO 28.5.41

BOGUSLAW MIERZWA

P 1389   **PO**   **Pilot**   **Polish**   **303 Squadron**

Born in Warsaw on March 14 1918, Mierzwa was in the PAF before the war and was in action against the Luftwaffe in September 1939. He joined 303 Squadron at Northolt on August 21 1940.

Mierzwa landed at a decoy aerodrome at Borstal, Chatham after a combat with Bf 109s on October 7, in Hurricane P 3089. He crashed and caught fire taking off again. He was unhurt.

On April 16 1941 303 and 601 Squadrons escorted six Blenheims of 21 Squadron detailed to bomb the fighter airfield at Berck-sur-Mer. As they turned for home 303 was jumped by Bf 109s over the Channel. Mierzwa and another pilot, who were acting as weavers, were shot down. He was killed, when he crashed and burned out on the shore at Dungeness, in Spitfire P 7819. He is buried in Northwood Cemetery. An unknown person erected a wooden memorial cross at the crash site.

Mierzwa was awarded the KW (1.2.41) and Bar (31.10.47).

PO 1.3.41

WLODZIMIERZ MIKSA

P 0286   **PO**   **Pilot**   **Polish**   **303 Squadron**

Born at Lodz on September 27 1915, Miksa joined the PAF in 1936. In the September 1939 fighting in Poland he destroyed two German aircraft and damaged another.

Miksa arrived in England on July 16 1940. He was posted to 5 OTU, Aston Down on September 25, to convert to Hurricanes, and then joined 303 Squadron at Leconfield on October 23. He moved to 315 Squadron at Acklington at its formation on January 21 1941. Miksa destroyed a Bf 109, probably destroyed another and damaged a third on October 21.

He was awarded the KW (20.1.42) and appointed a Flight Commander on June 20 1942.

W Miksa (continued)

Miksa was posted to 58 OTU, Grangemouth on April 5 1943 and was awarded a Bar to the KW (12.5.43) and a second Bar (7.7.43). After going to 61 OTU, Rednal on October 4 1943 he joined 302 Squadron at Northolt on the 18th. Miksa was given command of 317 Squadron, also at Northolt, on January 1 1944. He was posted away on August 25, for liaison duties at HQ 12 Group.

Awarded the VM (5th Class)(7.9.44), Miksa went to HQ Fighter Command on Ops duty on May 15 1945. He was awarded the DFC (26.5.45). He was released from the PAF in February 1946 and awarded a third Bar to the KW (31.10.47). Miksa settled in England and changed his name to Pilkington-Miksa.

PO 1.3.41   FO 1.3.42   FL 1.3.43

REGINALD ALAN MILBURN

742926   Sgt   Pilot   British   601 and 87 Squadrons

Joined 601 Squadron at Exeter in early October 1940 and moved to 87 Squadron at Church Fenton on the 31st. No further service details traced. Milburn died on December 19 1983.

PETER RAYMOND MILDREN

42864   PO   Pilot   British   54 and 66 Squadrons

Joined 54 Squadron at Catterick in early October 1940 and moved to 66 Squadron at West Malling on the 14th.

Mildren was killed on a sweep over France on February 11 1941, still serving with 66 Squadron. He is buried in Boulogne Eastern Cemetery, France.

APO 23.10.39   PO 31.8.40

DENYS EDGAR MILEHAM

77678   PO   Pilot   British   610 and 41 Squadrons

Mileham, of Boxmoor, Hertfordshire, joined 610 Squadron at Westhampnett on September 3 1940. He moved to 41 Squadron at Hornchurch on the 29th and claimed a Bf 109 destroyed on October 5.

He was killed on April 15 1942, as a Flight Lieutenant with 234 Squadron, aged 22. Mileham is remembered on the Runnymede Memorial, Panel 66.

PO 1.2.40   FO 1.2.41

ERNEST EDWIN MILES

747829   Sgt   Aircrew   British   236 Squadron

Joined 236 Squadron in late September 1940. No further service details traced.

STANLEY FREDERICK MILES

53720   Sgt   Air Gunner   British   23 Squadron

With 23 Squadron at Collyweston in early July 1940. Commissioned in November 1942, Miles stayed on in the RAF until May 1950, on an Extended Service Commission.

PO 25.11.42   FO 25.5.43   FL 25.11.44   FL (RAFRO) 25.5.46

MILES JOHN MILEY

33345   FO   Pilot   British   25 Squadron

Miley entered RAF College, Cranwell in September 1936 as a flight cadet. On graduation he joined 25 Squadron at Hawkinge on July 30 1938.

He was killed on September 15 1940, when Beaufighter R 2067 crashed near Biggin Hill. Circumstances are unknown. Miley was 22 and is buried in St Andrew's churchyard, North Weald Bassett, Essex.

PO 30.7.38   FO 30.1.40

WILLIAM BRUCE MacDOUGAL MILLAR

C 892   FO   Pilot   Canadian   1 (RCAF) Squadron

Millar was born at Penticton, British Columbia on December 14 1914. He joined the RCAF on November 7 1938. He was posted to No 1 (RCAF) Squadron on August 30 1940.

Millar was shot down by enemy fighters south of Northolt on September 9 1940 and baled out, wounded and burned.

He retired from the RCAF on July 10 1964, as a Wing Commander. He died on January 8 1969.

JOCELYN GEORGE POWER MILLARD

83999   PO   Pilot   British   1 and 242 Squadrons

Millard enlisted in the RAFVR in August 1939. He was called to full-time service on September 1. He did his ab initio course at 9 EFTS, Ansty and then moved to 12 FTS, Grantham.

With training completed in mid-August 1940 Millard was commissioned and posted to the School of Army Co-operation at Old Sarum. In early September he went to OTU and after converting to Hurricanes joined No 1 Squadron at Wittering in early October. On the 17th Millard was posted to 242 Squadron at Coltishall. He moved to 615 Squadron at Northolt on November 3 1940.

In early March 1941 Millard was sent to CFS, Upavon, for an instructor's course, and in mid-April went to FTS, Cranwell, staying there until July, when he was posted to Canada. Millard instructed at 35 SFTS there from September 1941 to mid-May 1944, serving as Flying Instructor, Flight Commander, Examining Officer and Squadron Commander.

Back in the UK, Millard went to Technical Training Command for flying and administrative duties. He was released from the RAF in 1947, as a Squadron Leader.

PO 18.8.40   FO 18.8.41   FL 18.8.42

ALFRED JOHN MILLER

1003598   Sgt   Aircrew   British   23 Squadron

Joined 23 Squadron at Middle Wallop on October 4 1940. No other service details traced.

ANTHONY GARFORTH MILLER

90088   SL   Pilot   British   FIU and 17 Squadron

Born in Calcutta in 1912, Miller joined 600 Squadron, AuxAF in June 1937. During the Munich crisis in September 1938 the squadron was embodied in the RAF. It proceeded to its War Station at Kenley but was stood down after two weeks.

On August 24 1939 Miller was called to full-time service and became a Flight Commander with 600. In March 1940 he was posted to HQ 11 Group, Uxbridge for Operations Room duties. He joined the Fighter Interception Unit at Tangmere at its formation in April, as a Flight Commander.

On August 29 1940 Miller took command of 17 Squadron at Tangmere. Following an attack by a Bf 110 he made a forced-landing at North Weald on September 3, unhurt. Miller commanded the squadron until July 1941, when he was posted to Leconfield to form and command 134 Squadron.

The squadron embarked on HMS 'Argus' on August 12 for Russia and flew off on September 6 to the airfield at Vaenga, near Murmansk. It was mainly involved in bomber-escort flights. In October 134 began converting Russian pilots to the Hurricane and on the 28th all aircraft and equipment was handed over to the Russians and in November the squadron personnel returned to the UK. Miller was awarded the DFC (3.3.42) and the Order of Lenin (31.3.42).

In February 1942 he was attached to FIU, Ford for a night-fighter refresher course and in April was posted to command 600 Squadron at Predannack, as a Wing Commander. In September Miller was appointed OC Training Wing at 54 OTU, remaining there until June 1943, when he became Station Commander RAF High Ercall. In July he took command at RAF Honiley.

Miller was posted to HQ 9 Group in January 1944, for staff duties. He was made Station Commander at Middle Wallop in July, went to HQ Fighter Command in March 1945, took up staff duties at Air Ministry in October and was released from the RAF in August 1946, as a Group Captain.

PO (AuxAF) 18.7.35   FO (AuxAF) 18.1.37   FL 24.8.39
SL 1.9.40   WC 1.3.42

ARTHUR CHARLES MILLER

119169   Sgt   Air Gunner   British   604 Squadron

Miller was born in 1909. He was with 604 Squadron at Northolt in early July 1940.

Commissioned in March 1942, Miller was awarded the DFC (26.2.43), as an Acting Flight Lieutenant with 13 Squadron, serving as Gunnery Leader in Blenheims in North Africa. He was released from the RAF in 1945, as a Squadron Leader.

PO 21.3.42   FO 1.10.42   FL 21.3.44

ROBERT MILLER

36143   FL   Pilot   British   3 Squadron

Joined the RAF on a direct-entry Permanent Commission. Miller was posted to 72 Squadron at Church Fenton on January 14 1939. He was later with 616 Squadron and damaged two Ju 88s over Dunkirk on June 1 1940. He joined 3 Squadron at Wick in mid-August.

Miller took command of 122 Squadron at Catterick in August 1941 and was killed on April 24 1942. He is remembered on the Runnymede Memorial, Panel 65.

APO 4.4.36   PO 4.9.36   FO 4.3.38   FL 4.3.40
SL 1.9.41

ROGERS FREEMAN GARLAND MILLER

42419   PO   Pilot   British   609 Squadron

Miller, of Radford Semele, joined the RAF on a short service commission in June 1939 and was posted to 609 Squadron at Northolt on June 11 1940.

He damaged a Do 17 on July 13 and claimed a Ju 87 destroyed over Lyme Bay on August 13. Miller was killed on September 27 1940, when he collided with a Bf 110 over Chesilbourne, near Kingscombe. His Spitfire, X 4107, exploded and the main wreckage fell east of Doles Ash.

Miller was 20 years old. He is buried in St Nicholas' churchyard, Radford Semele, Warwickshire.

PO 6.4.40

THOMAS HENRY MILLER

624065   Sgt   Aircrew   British   25 Squadron

Miller, of East Grinstead, Sussex, joined 25 Squadron at North Weald in early October 1940. He was killed on December 17 1942, as a Flight Sergeant. The unit he was serving with is not known.

Miller was 22. He is remembered on the Runnymede Memorial, Panel 75.

WILLIAM HENRY MILLINGTON

42720   PO   Pilot   Australian   79 and 249 Squadrons

Millington, from Edwardston, South Australia, joined the RAF on a short service commission in July 1939. He joined 79 Squadron at Biggin Hill in May 1940.

On July 9 Millington claimed a Bf 109 destroyed, on August 15 three He 111s, on the 30th another and on the 31st two Bf 109s and

a Do 17. On this day his Hurricane, P 3050, was set alight in combat with Bf 109s over Romney. Millington crash-landed on Conghurst Farm, Hawkhurst, wounded in the left thigh and badly burned. He was admitted to Croydon Hospital. He could have baled out but chose to steer his aircraft away from a village. He got out just before the petrol tanks exploded. He was awarded the DFC (1.10.40).

Millington was posted to 249 Squadron at North Weald on September 19. He claimed a Ju 88 destroyed and another shared on the 27th, probable Bf 109s on October 7 and 25, a shared Ju 88 on the 28th and another probable Bf 109 on the 29th.

Following an action with enemy fighters over the Channel on October 30 Millington failed to return and was reported 'Missing'. He was 23 years old and is remembered on the Runnymede Memorial, Panel 9.

APO 18.9.39   PO 20.4.40

KENNETH MILTON MILLIST

42420   PO   Pilot   British   615 and 73 Squadrons

Joined the RAF on a short service commission in June 1939. Millist joined 615 Squadron at Prestwick on September 3 1940 and moved to 73 Squadron at Castle Camps on the 18th. On his first flight with the squadron he smashed his propellor and damaged his port wing in a heavy landing.

Millist went to the Middle East with 73 in November 1940. On February 4 1941 he was shot down in combat with CR 42s over Barce and crash-landed ten miles north-east of Benina. He evaded capture and after three days met Australian troops. He then hitch-hiked to Derna and rejoined his squadron.

On April 5 Millist shot down a Ju 87. Two days later he was killed, circumstances unknown. He was 22 years old and is remembered on the Alamein Memorial, Column 241.

Millist was awarded the DFC (4.11.41), with effect from March 15 1941.

APO 5.8.39   PO 24.3.40

JACK BAILLIE MILLS

629563   Sgt   Aircrew   British   23 Squadron

Joined 23 Squadron at Middle Wallop on October 1 1940. No other service details traced.

JACK PERCIVAL MILLS

64890   Sgt   Pilot   British   43 and 249 Squadrons

Mills joined 43 Squadron at Tangmere in early July 1940. He claimed a Bf 109 destroyed on August 13, a Ju 87 on the 18th and another Bf 109 on September 6. He was posted to 249 Squadron at North Weald on the 13th and shared in destroying a Ju 88 on the 27th.

Commissioned in April 1941, Mills went with the squadron to Malta in May. It flew off 'Ark Royal' on the 21st, in two groups. On August 5 Mills joined the Malta Night Fighter Unit, then being formed at Ta Kali. On December 2 the Unit became 1435 (Night Fighter) Flight.

Mills was awarded the DFC (7.4.44), as a Flight Lieutenant with 73 Squadron. He was released from the RAF in 1947, as a Squadron Leader.

PO 24.4.41   FO 24.4.42   FL 24.4.43

RANDOLPH STUART MILLS

36067   FL   Pilot   British   263 and 87 Squadrons

Born on October 20 1909, Mills joined the RAF on a direct-entry Permanent Commission in May 1936. He was posted to 17 Squadron at Kenley on June 3 and moved to the Station Flight at Northolt on February 1 1937.

Mills joined 263 Squadron at its formation at Filton on October 20 1939, as a Flight Commander. He went with the squadron to Norway in April 1940 and shared a He 111 and damaged another enemy aircraft. He was awarded the DFC (10.5.40). In Norway again in May Mills was wounded and in hospital when 263's pilots embarked on HMS 'Glorious' on June 6 to return to the UK. They were all lost when the carrier was sunk by the 'Scharnhorst' on the 8th.

RS Mills (continued)

The squadron reformed at Drem. Mills was promoted on August 24 1940 and took command of 87 Squadron at Church Fenton. He was posted away in December to the USA, as Assistant Air Attaché, to develop British training facilities. The RAF eventually had six schools there. Mills personally briefed Mr Roosevelt at the White House on European operations.

He did not return to the UK until 1945. Mills retired from the RAF on October 20 1956, as a Wing Commander, retaining the rank of Group Captain.

PO 21.5.36   FO 21.11.37   FL 21.11.39   SL 1.12.40
WC 1.6.42   WC 1.10.46

JOHN ARCHIBALD MILNE

42758   PO   Pilot   Canadian   605 Squadron

Milne obtained his private pilot's license in 1935 and served in the RCAF as an aero engine fitter. He went to England in June 1939 and later joined the RAF in August, on a short service commission.

With training completed Milne joined 605 Squadron at Drem in 1940. He claimed a Bf 110 destroyed on September 27. He was shot down on October 22 by Bf 109s over Croydon and crash-landed near Dorking, in Hurricane V 6783. Milne was slightly wounded in the action but fractured his hip on landing and was admitted to hospital. He later married his nurse.

In April 1941 Milne went to 52 OTU, Crosby-on-Eden, as an instructor. He was posted to Aden in November 1941 and in early 1942 joined 112 Squadron in the Western Desert. Milne returned to the UK in November 1942, later commanded 10 Group Communications Flight and in 1944 went to Assam as Chief Test Pilot.

Milne was released from the RAF in July 1946 and returned to Canada.

APO 9.10.39   PO 21.5.40   FO 21.5.41   FL 21.5.42

RICHARD MAXWELL MILNE

40129   FO   Pilot   British   151 Squadron

Born in Edinburgh on July 8 1919, Milne was at Cheltenham College from September 1931 to December 1935. He joined the RAF in July 1937, on a short service commission. On September 18 he was posted to 11 FTS, Wittering and on May 7 1938 he joined the staff at 8 Armament Training Station at Evanton.

Milne went to 151 Squadron at North Weald on January 26 1939. In May 1940 the squadron used Vitry, in France, as an advanced landing ground. On the 17th Milne destroyed a Ju 87, on the 18th a Bf 110 and on the 22nd another Ju 87.

On July 9 he claimed a Bf 109 destroyed, on August 13 two Do 17s, on the 15th a Bf 109 and on the 18th a He 111. Milne was awarded the DFC (30.8.40). In mid-1941 he joined 92 Squadron at Biggin Hill, as a Flight Commander, and in September took command. On the 27th he probably destroyed a Bf 109 and on October 13 claimed three more. Milne was awarded a Bar to the DFC (11.11.41).

On January 19 1942 he took command of 222 Squadron at North Weald and led it until May, when he was rested from operations. In early January 1943 Milne was appointed Wing Leader at Biggin Hill. On the 20th he destroyed two FW 190s.

Milne was shot down and captured on March 14 1943, leading the Wing on a sweep over France. Freed in May 1945, he was released from the RAF in 1946, as a Wing Commander.

APO 5.9.37   PO 12.7.38   FO 12.1.40   FL 12.1.41
SL 1.3.42

AMBROSE HENRY MILNES

101001   Sgt   Pilot   British   32 Squadron

Born on May 24 1912, Milnes trained as a Sergeant-Pilot with the Class F Reserve from 1935 to 1937. He then acted as a flying instructor in the RAFVR until the outbreak of war, when he was called up and posted to the Instructor Pool at Brough, Yorkshire.

In November 1939 Milnes was sent to CFS, Upavon, for an instructor's course, after which he went on instructional duties to 8 FTS, Montrose. In May 1940 he was posted to 12 OTU, Benson, to convert to Battles. Milnes joined 12 Squadron at Finningley in June, volunteered for Fighter Command in August and went to 6 OTU, Sutton Bridge, to convert to Hurricanes. He joined 32 Squadron at Acklington in late September 1940 and in November moved to 615 Squadron at Northolt.

On September 18 1941, escorting Blenheims to attack a motor vessel at Blankenburghe, Milnes was shot down, baled out and was rescued from the sea. Later in the month he was posted to 258 Squadron at Martlesham Heath. The squadron flew to Debden on October 3 to prepare for overseas. Leaving their Hurricanes behind the twenty-two pilots went to Abbotsinch on the 30th and two days later sailed in the HMS 'Athene' for Gibraltar, with wing-detached Hurricanes on board. After arriving on the 21st the aircraft were to be unloaded, to be taken by 'Ark Royal' to Malta later. However the carrier was sunk returning to Gibraltar so other plans were made for the 258 pilots.

They left on Christmas Eve 1941, on the 'Athene'. They berthed at Takoradi on January 1 1942, disembarked and the 'Athene' left, taking their Hurricanes with her. On the 3rd they flew on the ferry route to the Middle East in a DC 3, arrived at Port Sudan, from where they sailed in the carrier HMS 'Indomitable' on the 9th, with Hurricanes aboard. They flew off on the 28th and later in the morning arrived at Airfield P2 at Palembang, Sumatra. In the afternoon they flew off to Seletar airfield, Singapore and flew their first operation on January 31st.

On February 10 1942 the three surviving Hurricanes of 258 were withdrawn to Palembang. Of the fifteen surviving pilots six were required to remain behind there to fly with a reformed 605 Squadron. One was nominated, two volunteered and the other three were selected by cutting cards. Milnes was one of the nine who were evacuated from Java to Ceylon in the SS 'Kota Gede'. 258 Squadron was reformed at Ratmalana on March 1 1942. Milnes rejoined it on the 7th.

In September 1942 he was posted to 273 Squadron at China Bay, Ceylon. He stayed with it until September 1943, when he was posted to flying instructor duties at Bangalore, India. In December Milnes joined the staff at 224 Group, Chittagong, in the Accidents Branch. He returned to instructor duties in February 1944, this time at Peshawar.

Milnes joined 84 Squadron at Quetta in September, operating in Vultee Vengeances. He returned briefly to instructor duties in August 1945 and was repatriated to the UK in October. He retired from the RAF on April 24 1958, as a Squadron Leader.

PO 5.7.41   FO 5.7.42   FL 5.7.43   SL 1.8.47
SL 1.7.56

GEORGE MITCHELL

46210   Sgt   Air Gunner   British   23 Squadron

Mitchell was born on February 18 1917. He joined 23 Squadron at Collyweston in early July 1940.

Commissioned in July 1941, Mitchell retired from the RAF on October 3 1953, as a Flight Lieutenant. He died in 1969.

PO 12.7.41   FO 12.7.42   FL 12.7.43   FL 1.9.45

GORDON THOMAS MANNERS MITCHELL

90484   PO   Pilot   British   609 Squadron

Born on September 24 1910, Mitchell was a hockey blue at Cambridge University. He joined 609 Squadron, AuxAF in 1938 and was called to full-time service on August 24 1939.

Mitchell was posted to 6 FTS, Little Rissington on October 7 1939 and with training completed he rejoined 609, then at Northolt, in May

1940. He was shot down in combat over a convoy off Portland on July 11, in Spitfire L 1095, and reported 'Missing'. His body was washed ashore near Newport, Isle of Wight. Mitchell is buried in All Saints' churchyard, Letchworth, Hertfordshire.

APO (AuxAF) 10.11.38   PO 24.8.39

HARRY THORNE MITCHELL

41447   PO   Pilot   Canadian   87 Squadron

Born in Port Hope, Ontario in 1920, Mitchell moved to England with his family and went to King's College, London. He joined the RAF on a short service commission in October 1938 and was with 87 Squadron in France in early 1940.

On May 10 he claimed a Do 17 destroyed and on the 11th another Do 17 and a Ju 87. The squadron was withdrawn to Debden on May 22. Mitchell claimed a Ju 87 destroyed on August 14, a Bf 110 on the 15th and a Bf 109 on the 25th.

In early 1941 he was posted away to be an instructor and was awarded the DFC (11.2.41). In 1942 Mitchell was posted to Canada and served in the Aleutians with RCAF fighter squadrons. He returned to the UK in February 1943 for a second operational tour.

Mitchell was released from the RAF in 1946, as a Squadron Leader.

APO 14.12.38   PO 6.1.40   FO 6.1.41   FL 6.1.42

HENRY MAYNARD MITCHELL

90246   SL   Pilot   British   25 Squadron

Mitchell was born on April 16 1914. He was educated at Harrow School and Birmingham University. In 1935 he joined 605 Squadron, AuxAF and in 1936 entered the family firm of Mitchells and Butlers, Brewers.

He was called to full-time service on August 25 1939 and served in Norway in 1940. Mitchell took command of 25 Squadron at North Weald on September 25 1940 and was awarded the DFC (22.10.40). He left the squadron in January 1941 and then formed and commanded 125 Squadron at Colerne from June to December 1941.

Mitchell later served in the Middle East. He was released from the RAF in 1946, as a Wing Commander.

PO (AuxAF) 26.7.35   FO (AuxAF) 26.1.37
FL (AuxAF) 26.1.39   FL 25.8.39   SL 1.9.40
WC 1.1.43

HERBERT ROBERT MITCHELL

391843   Sgt   Pilot   New Zealander   3 Squadron

Mitchell was born at Havelock, Marlborough on March 13 1917. He worked in the Public Works Department and afterwards as a stonemason in Greymouth.

In late March 1939 Mitchell applied to join the Civil Reserve of Pilots and began training at the West Coast United Aero Club in June. He volunteered for the RNZAF at the outbreak of war and reported to the Ground Training School at Weraroa on December 17 1939. He went to No 1 EFTS, Taieri on January 16 1940 and then to No 1 FTS, Wigram on March 11.

After completing his training Mitchell sailed for the UK on July 12 1940 in the RMS 'Rangitane'. He was posted to 6 OTU, Sutton Bridge on September 10 and after converting to Hurricanes he joined 3 Squadron at Turnhouse on October 4. Mitchell moved to 615 Squadron at Northolt on November 20, joined 260 Squadron at Skitten on December 1 and after eighteen operational sorties moved to 41 Squadron at Catterick on May 15 1941.

Commissioned in early January 1942, Mitchell was posted to 603 Squadron at Abbotsinch in early April. The pilots of the squadron embarked on the carrier USS 'Wasp' soon afterwards and flew their Spitfires off for Malta on April 20, landing at Luqa.

Mitchell shared in destroying two Bf 109s on May 9 and damaged another. On the 12th he took off from Ta Kali on an interception patrol. He failed to return and was seen to crash into the sea. Mitchell was reported 'Missing' and was later presumed to have lost his life at sea. He is remembered on the Malta Memorial, Panel 5, Column 1.

PO 5.1.42

LANCELOT ROBERT GEORGE MITCHELL

70469   FO   Pilot   British   257 Squadron

Mitchell, of Keith, Banffshire, joined the RAF on a short service commission in June 1937. He went to 8 FTS, Montrose on August 21 and was posted to 85 Squadron at Debden on July 27 1938.

Mitchell was posted to 257 Squadron at Hendon at its reformation on May 17 1940. He shared in the destruction of a Do 17 on July 19 and claimed a Bf 110 destroyed on August 31. Appointed 'B' Flight Commander on August 8, Mitchell was shot down in an action over the Thames Estuary on September 7, in Hurricane V 7254. He was believed to have crashed into the sea and was reported 'Missing'.

He was 24 and is remembered on the Runnymede Memorial, Panel 6.

APO 9.8.37   PO 27.7.38   FO 27.2.40

PETER MITCHELL

932483   Sgt   Pilot   British   65 Squadron

Mitchell, of West Norwood, London, joined 65 Squadron at Hornchurch on August 19 1940.

He was killed on July 26 1942, serving as a Flight Sergeant with 79 Squadron in India.

Mitchell is buried in Bhowanipore Cemetery, Calcutta.

PHILLIP HENRY GURREY MITCHELL

42252   PO   Pilot   British   266 Squadron

Joined the RAF on a short service commission in April 1939. Mitchell was with 266 Squadron at Wittering in early July 1940. He was released from the RAF in 1948, as a Flight Lieutenant.

APO 24.6.39   PO 9.12.39   FO 9.12.40   FL 9.3.42
FL (RAFRO) 1.9.45

RICHARD RONALD MITCHELL

45093   Sgt   Pilot   British   229 Squadron

Born at Perranporth, Cornwall on April 24 1914, Mitchell joined the RAF on September 9 1930, as an aircraft apprentice at Halton. He qualified as a Metal Rigger in September 1933 and was posted to 10 Squadron at Boscombe Down. Whilst with the squadron Mitchell became an air gunner, firstly on Virginias and then Heyfords.

In 1936 he served with 31 (Army Co-operation) Squadron on the North-West Frontier, as a Metal Rigger and as an air gunner in Wapitis. Mitchell had applied for pilot training and in late 1938 he returned to the UK and was posted to 2 E&RFTS, Filton for an ab

RR Mitchell (continued)

initio course. He chose to go on twin-engine aircraft and continued his training at 11 FTS, Shawbury, on Oxfords. Mitchell was promoted to Corporal and then to Sergeant in October 1939, when he joined 229 Squadron, then reforming at Digby with Blenheims.

The squadron re-equipped with Hurricanes in February 1940. It took part in operations over France and Dunkirk in May/June. Commissioned in November 1940, Mitchell went with the 229 pilots to the Middle East in May 1941. They embarked on HMS 'Furious' on the 10th and arrived in Gibraltar during the night of 18/19th. There was a delay whilst the Navy dealt with the 'Bismarck' and it was not until June 6 that 229 flew off to Malta. After refuelling they flew on to Mersa Matruh the next day and began operations in the Western Desert, attached to 73 and 274 Squadrons. Mitchell destroyed a Ju 87 on June 17 1941. The ground crews arrived in late August and 229 began operating as a unit on September 1.

Mitchell was made a Flight Commander. In March 1942 he was posted to 71 OTU, Khartoum, as a Flight Commander. He was given command of 250 Squadron in January 1943 but fell sick and was sent to hospital in Cairo. Mitchell was appointed Chief Test Pilot at 107 MU, Kasfereet in April. He was posted to 80 Squadron in June 1943, to command a special flight of stripped Spitfire IXs, to combat high-flying enemy reconnaissance aircraft.

In September 1943 Mitchell took command of 33 Squadron at Bersis. He led the squadron back to the UK in April 1944 and it took part in operations over France and after D Day. He was posted away in August, awarded the DFC (19.9.44) and given a 'P' staff job at HQ 12 Group, becoming SPSO in 1945.

Mitchell was made an MBE (1.1.46) and retired from the RAF on April 24 1961, as a Wing Commander.

PO 29.11.40   FO 29.11.41   FL 29.11.42   SL 1.8.47
WC 1.1.55

GEORGE EDWARD MOBERLEY

90332   FO   Pilot   British   616 Squadron

Moberley was born in Bombay on December 23 1914. He was educated at Ampleforth School, Yorkshire and learned to fly at Ipswich in 1937. He joined 609 Squadron, AuxAF in the summer of 1938 but transferred to 616 Squadron when the Earl of Lincoln began to form it on November 1 1938 and was one of the first two officers to join.

Called to full-time service on August 24 1939, Moberley was in action over Dunkirk. On May 28 he claimed two Bf 109s destroyed and on June 1 a Ju 88.

On July 3 Moberley shared a Do 17. He was shot down and killed in combat off Dover on August 26 1940. His Spitfire, N 3275, crashed into the Channel. Moberley's body was recovered and he is buried in Caterham and Warlingham Burial Ground, Surrey.

PO (AuxAF) 19.7.38   PO 24.8.39   FO 19.1.40

HARTLAND de MONTARVILLE MOLSON

C 1226   FO   Pilot   Canadian   1 (RCAF) Squadron

Born in Montreal on May 29 1907, Molson was educated at Bishop's College School, Lennoxville, Quebec and Charterhouse, England. He served in the Canadian Militia from 1928 to 1933, in the 27th Field Battery.

Molson joined the RCAF in 1939 and was with No 1 (RCAF) Squadron, when it arrived in the UK on June 20 1940. He damaged a Do 215 on August 26, damaged two Bf 110s on September 4 and claimed a He 111 destroyed on September 11. He was shot down during combat with enemy fighters over Canterbury on October 5, baled out, wounded, and was admitted to Chartham Hospital. His Hurricane, P 3873, crashed at Deering Farm, Smarden.

Molson returned to Canada in early 1941. He commanded 118 (Auxiliary) Squadron at Dartmouth, Nova Scotia from July 23 1941 to June 14 1942, operating Kittyhawks in defence of Canada's east coast. From June 15 to September 6 1942 he commanded 126 (RCAF) Squadron on similar duties, with Hurricanes.

In 1945 Molson retired from the RCAF, as a Group Captain. He was made an OBE (1.1.46). Very prominent in Canadian business circles, he was appointed a Senator, Dominion of Canada in July 1955.

DENIS AUBREY MONK

142560   Sgt   Aircrew   British   236 Squadron

Joined 236 Squadron in early September 1940. Commissioned from Warrant Officer in February 1943, Monk was released from the RAF in 1946, as a Flight Lieutenant.

PO 9.2.43   FO 9.8.43   FL 9.2.45

ERNEST WILLIAM JOHN MONK

44403   PO   Pilot   British   25 Squadron

Joined 25 Squadron at Martlesham Heath on August 12 1940. Monk was killed on November 21, when he crashed into the sea shortly after taking off. His gunner, Sergeant E Powell, was also lost.

Monk was 26. He is remembered on the Runnymede Memorial, Panel 9.

PO 7.8.40

GEORGE WROUGHTON MONTAGU

26241   SL   Pilot   British   236 Squadron

Montagu entered RAF College, Cranwell in January 1930 as a flight cadet. After graduating in December 1931 he joined 40 Squadron at Abingdon.

On September 7 1933 Montagu was posted to 822 Squadron, on HMS 'Furious'. He joined the staff at 10 FTS, Tern Hill on November 9 1936 and went to 2 AACU at Lee-on-Solent on June 13 1938.

Montagu took command of 236 Squadron on August 15 1940. He failed to return from a reconnaissance sortie over Brest on December 12 1940 and he and his crew of two were reported 'Missing'. Montagu is buried in Bayeux War Cemetery, France.

PO 19.12.31   FO 11.7.33   FL 11.7.36   SL 1.4.39

ARTHUR MONTAGU-SMITH

37128 FL Pilot British 264 Squadron

Born on July 17 1915, Montagu-Smith joined the RAF on a short service commission in January 1935. He was posted to 5 FTS, Sealand on March 30 1935 and joined 99 Squadron at Mildenhall on February 29 1936. He was appointed Adjutant in 1938. The squadron was the first to receive Wellingtons and Montagu-Smith flew on 99's first sortie to the German coast in October 1939, in search of enemy naval units.

In November he was posted to the Special Duty Flight at the A&AEE, Boscombe Down. Montagu-Smith went to CGS, Warmwell in April 1940, as a Flight Commander. He joined 264 Squadron at Kirton-in-Lindsey on September 11, as 'A' Flight Commander. In December 1940 Montagu-Smith was promoted to Squadron Leader and posted to 221 Squadron, as a Flight Commander. He carried out the first Coastal Command Wellington attack on a German U-boat in the Atlantic in May 1941.

Montagu-Smith went to a staff job at HQ 18 Group in October 1941. A year later he took command of 248 Squadron, operating Beaufighters in long-range fighter patrols between the UK and Gibraltar. Before he was posted away in August 1943 to HQ 19 Group the squadron had destroyed twenty-five enemy aircraft.

In February 1944 Montagu-Smith joined the RAF Delegation in Washington, as Deputy Director RAF Operational Training USA. He returned to the UK and in July 1945 was appointed OC 104 Wing in France, with PR Mosquitos.

Montagu-Smith held a series of appointments at home and overseas in the post-war RAF. He retired on January 1 1961, as a Wing Commander, retaining the rank of Group Captain.

APO 15.3.35   PO 15.3.36   FO 15.10.37   FL 15.10.39
SL 1.12.40   WC 1.3.42   WC 1.7.47

CECIL ROBERT MONTGOMERY

42421 PO Pilot British 615 Squadron

Joined the RAF on a short service commission in June 1939. Montgomery was with 615 Squadron at Kenley in early July 1940. He was reported 'Missing' after a combat over the Channel off Dover on August 14. His Hurricane, P 3160, crashed into the sea.

Montgomery was 26. He is buried in Oye-Plage Communal Cemetery, France.

APO 5.8.39   PO 24.2.40

HERBERT FRANCIS MONTGOMERY

741305 Sgt Pilot British 43 Squadron

Joined 43 Squadron at Northolt from 6 OTU, Sutton Bridge on August 3 1940. Montgomery failed to return from an interception of a He 111 forty miles south of Beachy Head on August 14. His Hurricane, L 1739, crashed into the sea.

Montgomery was 26. He is buried in Senneville-sur-Fécamp churchyard, France.

DENNIS GEORGE MOODY

118929 Sgt Aircrew British 604 Squadron

With 604 Squadron at Northolt in early July 1940. Commissioned in March 1942, Moody was released from the RAF in 1945, as a Flight Lieutenant.

PO 20.3.42   FO 1.10.42   FL 20.3.44

HENRY WOLLASTON MOODY

81046 PO Pilot British 602 Squadron

Moody joined 602 Squadron at Drem in March 1940, as a Sergeant-Pilot. Later in the month he broke a collar bone, when he slipped whilst climbing into a Spitfire. He was commissioned in April 1940.

On August 18 Moody claimed a Ju 87 destroyed. The next day his aircraft was set alight by return fire from a Ju 88 engaged off Bognor. He baled out, with burned hands, and landed outside Arundel. The Spitfire crashed and burned out on Colworth Farm, Toad Hall, North Berstead.

Moody claimed a Do 17 destroyed on September 4. He failed to return from combat over the Biggin Hill area on the 7th and was reported 'Missing'. Moody was 30 years old. He is remembered on the Runnymede Memorial, Panel 9.

PO 25.4.40

ARTHUR ROBERT MOORE

102100 Sgt Pilot British 615, 245 and 3 Squadrons

Moore was initially with 615 Squadron at Prestwick. He was posted to 245 Squadron at Aldergrove on September 28 1940 and moved to 3 Squadron at Castletown in October.

Commissioned in July 1941, Moore was awarded the DFC (21.7.44), as a Flight Lieutenant with 3 Squadron. He was credited with destroying a Bf 109 and twenty V1s, with another shared. He was released from the RAF in 1946, as a Squadron Leader. Moore joined the RAFVR in 1950.

He died in 1989.

PO 18.7.41   FO 18.7.42   FL 18.7.43   FO (RAFVR) 11.3.50

PETER JOHN MOORE

112401 Sgt Pilot British 253 Squadron

Moore, of Melbourne, Australia, joined 253 Squadron at Kenley in October 1940. He crash-landed at Newbarn Farm, Southfleet on the 30th in Hurricane V 7301, after a combat with Bf 109s.

Commissioned in November 1941, Moore was killed on June 3 1942, as a Pilot Officer with 616 Squadron, aged 22. He is buried in Etaples Military Cemetery, France.

PO 8.11.41

WILLIAM ROY MOORE

77947   PO   Air Gunner   British   264 Squadron

Joined 264 Squadron at Kirton-in-Lindsey in mid-July 1940.

Moore served with the squadron until May 1941.

He was released from the RAF in 1945, as a Flight Lieutenant. He died in 1984.

APO 9.3.40   PO 15.6.40
FO 15.6.41   FL 15.6.42

WILLIAM STOREY MOORE

40007   FO   Pilot   British   236 Squadron

Moore, of Melbourne, Australia, joined the RAF on a short service commission in June 1937. He was posted to 10 FTS, Tern Hill on August 21 and after completing his training he went to the FAA Pool at Gosport on October 10 1938.

In early July 1940 Moore was with 236 Squadron. He was killed on December 24 1943, as a Squadron Leader with 143 Squadron, aged 27. He is remembered on the Runnymede Memorial, Panel 118.

APO 9.8.37   PO 24.5.38   FO 12.12.39   FL 3.12.40
SL 1.3.42

JAMES WINTER CARMICHAEL MORE

26161   SL   Pilot   British   73 Squadron

More entered RAF College, Cranwell in September 1928 as a flight cadet. On graduation in July 1930 he joined 54 Squadron at Hornchurch. On February 12 1932 he was posted to 403 (Fleet Fighter) Flight, on HMS 'Hermes' in the Far East. More returned to the UK and joined the staff at RAF College, Cranwell on October 22 1934.

In mid-April 1935 More was posted to 43 Squadron at Tangmere and was appointed 'B' Flight Commander in January 1936. He returned to the FAA in December 1936, joining 800 (Fleet Fighter) Squadron, based at Southampton and on HMS 'Courageous'. In this aircraft carrier before the war there was a plaque on the flight deck to commemorate More landing on in a Fury, a feat which amazed the Navy.

On October 24 1938 More went to SHQ RAF Cottesmore. He was given command of 73 Squadron in France in April 1940. On the 21st he destroyed a Bf 109 and probably a Bf 110, on May 10 a He 111 and another shared, on the 13th a He 111, on the 14th a Ju 87, on the 15th another He 111, on the 17th another Ju 87 and on the 21st he destroyed six enemy aircraft, one each on six sorties. More was awarded the DFC (30.7.40).

He was promoted to Acting Wing Commander on August 8 1940 and posted away to HQ 9 Group. More was a sector commander in 1941 and in July was badly injured when he crashed in a Beaufighter. He was made an OBE (1.1.42).

More was posted to the Far East in late 1941 and was captured by the Japanese at Singapore. In 1944, after making a nuisance of himself, he was sent away by sea to Japan. On the way his ship was torpedoed and sunk by an Allied submarine. More is believed to have lost his life on September 12 1944, as a Group Captain, aged 34. He is remembered on the Singapore Memorial, Column 431.

PO 26.7.30   FO 26.1.32   FL 26.1.36   SL 1.10.38
WC 1.12.40

ROGER EDWARD GUY MOREWOOD

37978   FL   Pilot   British   248 Squadron

Morewood joined the RAF in September 1935 as a direct-entry for training as a Sergeant-Pilot. He was at 4 E&RFTS, Brough from September 30 to November 24. He was posted to 7 E&RFTS, Desford on January 20 1936 for further training and left there on August 4 to go to RAF Depot, Uxbridge, where he became an Acting Pilot Officer, with a short service commission.

On August 22 1936 Morewood was posted to 3 FTS, Grantham and he joined 56 Squadron at North Weald on April 24 1937. He left the squadron on October 1 1939 to help form 248 Squadron at Hendon. The squadron transferred to Coastal Command in February 1940 but was seconded back to Fighter Command for the Battle of Britain.

Morewood served with 248 until early July 1942. On the 29th he went to 9 OTU, Aldergrove. After a week he was sent to 3 FIS, Hullavington, for an instructor's course, after which he returned to 9 OTU. On May 17 1944 Morewood was appointed Wing Commander Flying at Bircham Newton. He moved to Langham on August 12, in the same capacity.

On October 23 Morewood went to HQ Transport Command, was made OC Flying at Castel Benito on November 29 and in early March 1945 he took command of 65 Staging Post at Pommigliano. After a six month period of sickness and sick leave from mid-July 1945 until the end of January 1946 Morewood became Station Commander at RAF Dalcross. He went to HQ 64 Group, Norton in May 1946, as SASO, and was released from the RAF in July 1947, as a Wing Commander. During the war years he received two Mentions in Despatches.

Morewood rejoined the RAF in November 1951 and after a refresher course at South Cerney and instruction at CFS, Little Rissington he was posted to 8 AFTS, Dalcross on April 28 1952. He instructed at the Edinburgh University Air Squadron from October 21 1953 to August 22 1955 and then at Glasgow University Air Squadron until September 1957, when he retired for a second time, as a Wing Commander.

APO 4.8.36   PO 8.6.37   FO 8.3.39   FL 3.9.40
SL 1.12.41   WC 1.7.45   FL 7.11.51

PERCY FREDERICK MORFILL

47655   F/Sgt   Pilot   British   501 Squadron

Morfill was born at Gosport on December 11 1914. He joined the RAF on September 3 1930, as an aircraft apprentice at Halton. After passing out as a Metal Rigger in September 1933 he was posted to FAA Gosport. Morfill volunteered for pilot training, was selected and began his flying at 3 E&RFTS, Hamble in early January 1936.

He went to 6 FTS, Netheravon in March and in January 1937 joined 65 Squadron at Hornchurch. In early 1940 Morfill was posted to 501 Squadron at Tangmere. He went with the squadron to France on May 10, destroyed a Bf 109 on the 11th and a He 111 on the 12th. The squadron was withdrawn to England on June 18 and re-assembled at Croydon on the 21st.

Morfill claimed Bf 109s destroyed on July 29 and August 24, a He 111 on the 30th, damaged a Do 17 on September 2, shared a He

111 on the 11th and destroyed a Do 17 on the 15th. He was awarded the DFM (22.10.40).

In June 1941 Morfill was posted to 58 OTU, Grangemouth. He was sent to CFS, Upavon for an instructor's course and then returned to 58 OTU. He was posted to CFS, as an instructor, in late 1941 and was commissioned from Warrant Officer in January 1942. Morfill later instructed at 3 FIS, Hullavington and was then posted to Norton, Southern Rhodesia, where he stayed until the end of the war.

On return to the UK he went to Air Ministry, later going to the Ministry of Aircraft Production, on Bomber Research and Development. Morfill stayed on in the RAF on an Extended Service Commission. He retired on February 4 1958, as a Squadron Leader. His portrait was done by Eric Kennington.

PO 15.1.42   FO 1.10.42   FL 15.1.44   FL 1.1.43
SL 1.7.53

PETER JACQUES MORGAN

42992   PO   Pilot   British   79 and 238 Squadron

Morgan was a 2nd lieutenant in the 3rd Hussars before transferring to the RAF.

He joined 79 Squadron at Pembrey on September 17 1940 and moved to 238 Squadron at Chilbolton on October 5.

Morgan was released from the RAF in 1946, as a Flight Lieutenant. He died in 1977.

PO 7.3.40   FO 7.3.41   FL 7.3.42

THOMAS FREDERICK DALTON MORGAN

37415   FL   Pilot   British   43 Squadron

Born in Cardiff. Morgan joined the RAF on a short service commission in August 1935. He was posted to 11 FTS, Wittering on November 2 and joined 22 (Torpedo Bomber) Squadron at Donibristle on November 2 1936.

Morgan went to Air Ministry on May 29 1939, on the staff of the Directorate of Training. He was posted to 43 Squadron at Tangmere in June 1940, as 'B' Flight Commander. On July 12 Morgan shared in the destruction of a He 111, on the 21st he claimed a Bf 109 destroyed, on August 8 a Ju 87 and a Bf 109 and on the 13th a He 111. In this combat Morgan's Hurricane, P 3972, was damaged by cross-fire from He 111s over Petworth and he baled out, slightly wounded. On September 4 Morgan claimed two Bf 110s destroyed and on the 6th a Bf 109. On this day he crashed at Tangmere after an engagement with Bf 109s over Dungeness, in Hurricane V 6542, wounded in the knee. He was awarded the DFC (6.9.40).

On September 16 1940 Morgan was promoted to Acting Squadron Leader and took command of 43 Squadron. He destroyed two enemy bombers at night on May 5 1941 and a Ju 88 at night off St Abb's Head on the 6th. He was awarded a Bar to the DFC (30.5.41). On June 8 he destroyed a Ju 88 at night, on the 11th a He 111 and on July 24 he shared a Ju 88. Immediately afterwards his own engine failed and he landed on the sea, losing two front teeth on impact with the reflector sight in the process. Morgan got into his dinghy, was picked up by HMS 'Ludlow', transferred to a trawler and taken to hospital at Aberdeen. His final victory was another Ju 88 at night on October 2.

In January 1942 Morgan was posted away to controller duties at Turnhouse. He returned to operations in November 1942, taking command of 16 Squadron, a Mustang reconnaissance unit. He was awarded the DSO (25.5.43) and later made an OBE (14.6.45).

Morgan resigned his commission on November 4 1952. His portrait was drawn by Cuthbert Orde in January 1941.

APO 21.10.35   PO 26.8.36   FO 26.4.38   FL 26.4.40
SL 1.6.41   WC 1.6.42   WC 1.7.47

HUGH MORGAN-GRAY

40556   FO   Pilot   British   46 Squadron

Joined the RAF on a short service commission in December 1937. Morgan-Gray was posted to 7 FTS, Peterborough on March 5 1938 and joined 29 Squadron at Debden on September 17.

In early July 1940 Morgan-Gray was with 46 Squadron at Digby. On September 3 his aircraft was set alight by return fire from a Do 215 over Rochford and he baled out, wounded. The Hurricane, P 3063, crashed at Apton Hall Farm, Canewdon.

Still with 46 Squadron, Morgan-Gray was killed on February 22 1941, aged 22. He is buried in Scopwick Church Burial Ground, Lincolnshire.

APO 19.2.38   PO 29.11.38   FO 29.8.40

EDWARD JAMES MORRIS

40132   FO   Pilot   South African   79 Squadron

Born on April 6 1915, Morris was educated at Michaelhouse, Natal. He joined the RAF on a short service commission in June 1937. He was posted to 6 FTS, Netheravon on September 18 and on completion of the course was posted to the Home Aircraft Depot at Henlow on May 7 1938, as a pilot in the Parachute Test Flight.

In January 1939 Morris joined 79 Squadron at Biggin Hill. Still with the squadron in 1940, he shared in the destruction of a He 59 on August 28 and destroyed a He 111 by ramming on the 30th.

The Heinkel was on its way to attack Farnborough, when Morris engaged it over Reigate. They collided. Morris baled out, unhurt, landing at Dorking. His Hurricane, P 3203, crashed on Lodge Farm, South Holmwood, Brockham. The Heinkel crashed at Swires Farm, Capel and exploded. The next day Morris was wounded and crashed on landing at Biggin Hill, after being damaged by a Bf 109 during an attack on Do 17s over base.

Morris was posted to 238 Squadron at Chilbolton in January 1941, as a Flight Commander. He shared in destroying a Ju 88 on March 23. In May the squadron went to the Middle East and in September Morris was posted to 250 Squadron, to command. He shared a Bf 110 on January 22 1942. He was posted to HQ Desert Air Force in March and awarded the DSO (7.4.42).

In late 1942 Morris was appointed Chief Instructor at 71 OTU, then in the Sudan but later Egypt. He became Wing Leader 251 Wing Desert Air Force in Italy in mid-1943. On June 8 1944 he shared a Ju 88 and on the 14th destroyed a Bf 109. Morris was awarded the DFC (14.11.44) and was posted away at the end of the year to HQ MAAF, as Wing Commander Air Plans. He was awarded the DFC (US) in 1945.

Morris was granted a Permanent Commission in May 1945 and went to RAF Staff College. He held a series of appointments and commands in the post-war years. He was made a CBE (1.1.59), a CB (1.1.66) and retired from the RAF on July 16 1968, as an Air Commodore.

APO 5.9.37   PO 12.7.38   FO 12.1.40   FL 12.1.41
SL 1.3.42   WC 1.7.47   GC 1.1.56   AC 1.1.62

GEOFFREY EDWARD MORRIS

78464   PO   Observer   British   FIU

Morris was born on April 22 1917. He joined the FIU at Tangmere in April 1940. He was a member of the crew of an AI-equipped Blenheim which destroyed a Do 17 off the Sussex coast on the night of July 22/23.

He later transferred to the Administrative Branch and stayed on in the RAF after the war, in the Aircraft Control Branch. Morris retired on May 29 1970, as a Wing Commander.

PO 7.4.40   FO 7.4.41   FL 7.4.42   FL 1.9.45
SL 1.7.50   WC 1.7.53

JOHN MORRIS

78088   PO   Pilot   British   248 Squadron

Joined 248 Squadron in late October 1940. Morris was released from the RAF in 1946, as a Squadron Leader.

PO 10.3.40   FO 10.3.41   FL 1.6.42

JOSEPH PEARSON MORRISON

754728   Sgt   Pilot   British   43 and 46 Squadrons

Initially with 43 Squadron, Morrison joined 46 Squadron at Stapleford Tawney on September 17 1940.

He was shot down and killed in combat with enemy fighters over Dungeness on October 22. His Hurricane, R 4074, crashed near Newchurch church.

Morrison was 25. He is buried in St Andrew's and Jesmond Cemetery, Newcastle-upon-Tyne.

NEIL MORRISON

740636   Sgt   Pilot   British   54, 72 and 74 Squadrons

Morrison joined 54 Squadron at Catterick in late September 1940, moved to 72 Squadron at Biggin Hill on October 4 and then to 74 Squadron also at Biggin Hill, on the 26th.

Morrison destroyed a Bf 109 between Dover and Calais on November 1 and shared in the destruction of a Bf 110 on February 22 1941. He was killed two days later, aged 26, and is buried in Eastwood Cemetery, Glasgow.

OLIVER BERTRAM MORROGH-RYAN

40970   FO   Pilot   British   41 Squadron

Morrogh-Ryan, of Bretton-by-Manor, joined the RAF on a short service commission in June 1938. He was with 41 Squadron at Hornchurch in May 1940 and over Dunkirk on June 1 he shared in destroying a He 111.

On September 5 he claimed a Bf 109 and two days later made a forced-landing in Kemsley's Field, Star Lane, Brickfields, Great Wakering after a combat over Hornchurch, in Spitfire X 4318.

Morrogh-Ryan was killed on July 26 1941, as a Flying Officer with 68 Squadron, operating in Beaufighters from High Ercall. He was 22 and is buried in St Cuthbert's churchyard, Barton, Yorkshire.

APO 20.8.38   PO 27.6.39   FO 3.9.40

PERCIVAL ALEXANDER MORTIMER

87382   PO   Pilot   British   257 Squadron

Mortimer, of Wrexham, Denbighshire, joined 85 Squadron at Croydon on September 4 1940 and moved to 257 Squadron at Debden on the 11th.

He shared in destroying a Do 17 and a He 111 on September 15 and a Fiat BR 20 on November 11. Mortimer was slightly wounded in the left hand by a cannon shell splinter on November 17, in combat with Bf 109s over a convoy off Harwich.

In December 1940 Mortimer sailed in HMS 'Furious' for the Middle East. On January 9 1941 he flew off with other Hurricanes at Takoradi but crashed on landing. Mortimer eventually went into the Pilots' Pool at Ismailia. He flew a Hurricane to Malta on March 5 and joined 261 Squadron. On April 11 he crash-landed after a combat with Bf 109s, in Hurricane V 7116.

Mortimer was killed in a flying accident on November 7 1942, as a Flight Lieutenant, aged 28. His unit at the time of his death is not known. He is buried in West Road Cemetery, Newcastle-upon-Tyne.

PO 17.8.40   FO 17.8.41   FL 17.8.42

EDWARD BRIAN MORTIMER-ROSE

41944   PO   Pilot   British   234 Squadron

Born at Littleport, Cambridgeshire, Mortimer-Rose was educated at Haileybury. He joined the RAF on a short service commission in February 1939 and was posted to 234 Squadron at Leconfield on November 6 1939, soon after its reformation.

On August 15 1940 Mortimer-Rose claimed a Bf 110 destroyed, on the 18th a Bf 109, on the 26th another and on October 9 he shared a Ju 88. He shared a Bf 110 on March 11 1941, probably destroyed a Ju 88 on April 2 and destroyed two Bf 109s on May 19. Mortimer-Rose was awarded the DFC (6.6.41). On June 17 he shared a Bf 109, on July 14 destroyed another, on October 26 probably destroyed a Ju 88 and on November 24 shared a Do 17. This was his last victory with 234.

Mortimer-Rose went to HQ Middle East at the end of November and on December 6 arrived in Malta to take command of 249 Squadron. He was awarded a Bar to the DFC (12.12.41). On December 24 he shared in destroying a Ju 88. Two days later he crash-landed at Luqa, with a bullet wound in his heel.

In February 1942 Mortimer-Rose joined 185 Squadron, as a Flight Commander. He destroyed two Bf 110s on March 21. After a rest from operations he was posted to 111 Squadron at Souk-el-Khemis in December 1942.

Mortimer-Rose was killed on January 28 1943 when he collided with Wing Commander GK Gilroy over Khemis and spun in. He was 22 and is buried in Medjez-el-Bab War Cemetery, Tunisia.

APO 15.4.39   PO 6.11.39   FO 6.11.40   FL 6.11.41

JAMES STORRS MORTON

90727   FO   Pilot   British   603 Squadron

Joined 603 Squadron, AuxAF in 1939. Morton was called to full-time service on August 24. He shared in the destruction of a He 111 over the Firth of Forth on October 16, the first enemy aircraft to be destroyed over British territory since 1918. Later the same day he shared another He 111 and damaged a second. He received a Mention in Despatches in February 1940.

On July 15 and 16 1940 Morton shared in destroying two He 111s, on August 28 he destroyed a Bf 109, on the 31st a Do 17, on September 1 a Bf 109, on the 7th a probable He 111, on the 28th a probable Bf 109 and on the 30th a Bf 109 and a second shared. Morton was himself shot down in combat with Bf 109s over Dover on October 5 and baled out, burned. His Spitfire, K 9807, crashed near Chilham.

Morton was awarded the DFC. He was posted from 603 in August 1941, to train as a fighter controller. In October he joined 54 Squadron at Hornchurch, as a Flight Commander. Morton was posted to a night-fighter OTU in December and in March 1942 took command of 539 Squadron at Acklington, a Turbinlite Havoc unit. He was with 539 until its disbandment on January 25 1943. He was then posted to 219 Squadron at Scorton, as a Flight Commander. On March 14 1943 he destroyed a Do 217 but baled out after being hit by return fire.

The squadron went to North Africa in May. Morton destroyed a He 111 on August 16. Tour-expired, he returned to the UK in October 1943 and was awarded a Bar to the DFC (30.11.43). He was on instructional duties until being released from the RAF in 1946, as a Wing Commander. Morton rejoined the RAuxAF and commanded 613 Squadron from its reformation on November 1 1946 until March 1951. He died in 1982.

APO (AuxAF) 23.5.39   PO 24.8.39   FO 3.9.40   FL 3.9.41
SL 8.3.44   SL (AuxAFRO) 1.8.46

RAYMOND CHRISTOPHER MOSS

174241   Sgt   Air Gunner   British   29 Squadron

Joined 29 Squadron at Digby on July 1 1940. After the Battle of Britain Moss retrained as a Radio Observer and in 1942 he was with 89 Squadron in the Middle East, operating in Beaufighters.

In January 1943 a detachment of the squadron went to Calcutta, Moss with it, to form the nucleus of 176 Squadron. On January 19 Moss and his pilot, Flying Officer CA Crombie, destroyed two Mitsubishi Sallys. One engine of their Beaufighter was hit by return fire and set alight and Crombie ordered Moss to bale out. He stayed to damage a third Sally and then baled out himself.

Moss was awarded the DFC (19.2.43), as a Warrant Officer. The citation stated that he and Crombie had flown together in the UK, Middle East and India and had destroyed eight enemy aircraft and damaged another.

Commissioned in March 1944, Moss was released from theRAF in 1946, as a Flight Lieutenant.

PO 29.3.44   FO 29.9.44   FL 29.3.46

WILLIAM JAMES MARCH MOSS

Sub-Lieutenant (FAA)   Pilot   British   213 Squadron

Born on October 31 1917, Moss joined the FAA on July 3 1939 and did his ground training at HMS 'President', 'Frobisher' and 'St Vincent'. On October 9 1939 he began his ab initio flying course at 14 EFTS, Castle Bromwich and then moved on December 11 to 7 FTS, Peterborough, where he was awarded his wings on March 17 1940.

After completing the course on May 26 Moss was loaned to the RAF and on June 15 was posted to 7 OTU, Hawarden, where he converted to Hurricanes. Moss joined 213 Squadron at Exeter on July 1 1940. He was killed on August 27, when he lost control and crashed into the sea during a routine patrol, in Hurricane N 2336.

Moss is remembered on the Fleet Air Arm Memorial at Lee-on-Solent.

Midshipman 3.7.39   Actg Sub-Lt 13.8.39   Sub-Lt 14.3.40

WALTER HENRY MOTT

139388   Sgt   Air Gunner   British   141 Squadron

Born on April 4 1910. Mott was posted to 141 Squadron at Turnhouse on August 21 1940.

Commissioned in December 1942, Mott retired from the RAF on May 30 1964, as a Squadron Leader.

PO 14.12.42   FO 14.6.43   FL 14.12.44   FL 14.12.48
SL 1.7.58

ROY MOTTRAM

42870   PO   Pilot   British   92 Squadron

Mottram joined the RAF on a short service commission in August 1939 and was with 92 Squadron at Pembrey in June 1940.

On September 15 he claimed a He 111 destroyed. Three days later he crashed after a combat with Bf 109s. His Spitfire burned out. Mottram was admitted to Orpington Hospital, with slight burns. On October 20 he claimed a Bf 110 destroyed.

Mottram was killed on August 31 1941, as a Flight Lieutenant with 54 Squadron. He is buried in Merville Communal Cemetery Extension, France.

APO 23.10.39   PO 20.4.40   FO 20.4.41

RENE GASTON OCTAVE JEAN MOUCHOTTE

FL 30661   Adjudant   Pilot   French   245 and 615 Sqdns

Born at Saint Mande on August 21 1914, Mouchotte was in l'Armée de l'Air before the war. In early June 1940 he was ordered back to Algeria, as an instructor, and went to Oran.

On June 30 Mouchotte took a Renault Goeland and flew to Gibraltar with five other Frenchmen. He sailed for the UK on July 3 and on the 25th was at RAF St Athan. Five days later he went to Old Sarum and then on August 19 he was posted to 6 OTU, Sutton Bridge, as a Sergeant-Pilot.

Having converted to Hurricanes Mouchotte was posted to 245 Squadron at Aldergrove on September 11, went to 615 Squadron at Prestwick on the 18th and was promoted to Adjudant. Commissioned in February 1941, Mouchotte was temporarily

commanding 'B' Flight from March 4, when Flight Lieutenant CN Foxley-Norris went into hospital. Mouchotte was awarded the C de G (Fr)(2.7.41) and on July 29 was made a Flight Commander.

Mouchotte destroyed a Ju 88 on August 26 and on November 10 was posted to Turnhouse as Deputy 'A' Flight Commander with 340 Squadron, then forming there. He was promoted to Captain in March 1942 and awarded the DFC (1.9.42). On January 18 1943 Mouchotte returned to Turnhouse to form and command 341 Squadron. He was awarded the Croix de la Liberation (8.5.43). He destroyed a Bf 109 on May 17. In July the squadron was at Biggin Hill and on the 15th excitement was running high as to who would claim the sector's 1000th victory. Mouchotte destroyed a FW 190, apparently simultaneously with Squadron Leader EFJ Charles destroying one. It being impossible to decide whose had been first to fall the two pilots shared the honour and the cash sweepstake, getting ninety pounds each.

On August 27 1943 Mouchotte failed to return from a sweep over St Omer and was reported 'Missing'. After the war evidence showed that his body was washed up on the beach at Middelkerke, Belgium on September 3 and that he was buried there.

Mouchotte was awarded the Croix de la Légion d'Honneur (20.10.43). His body was exhumed in October 1949 and returned to France. In a ceremony at Pere-Lachaise Cemetery, Paris on November 3 1949 he was buried in the family vault.

Sous-Lt 17.2.41   Lt 5.8.41   Capt 15.3.42

EDWARD ANTHONY MOULD

67599   Sgt   Pilot   British   74 Squadron

Mould, of Mill Hill, Middlesex, was with 74 Squadron at Leconfield in May 1940. On the 22nd he shared in destroying a Ju 88 and after being shot down over the French coast on the 24th he returned to England by boat.

On July 8 Mould destroyed a Bf 109. He was shot down by Bf 109s in combat off Dover on the 28th and baled out, wounded. He was admitted to Dover Military Hospital. His Spitfire, P 9336, crashed on to the roof at Buckland Mill, north of Dover.

Commissioned in May 1941, Mould was killed on January 20 1943, as a Flying Officer with 85 Squadron, aged 26. He is buried in Brookwood Military Cemetery, Woking.

PO 22.5.41   FO 22.5.42

ERIC WALTER MOULTON

630470   Sgt   Aircrew   British   600 Squadron

Joined 600 Squadron at Manston on July 20 1940. No other service details traced.

MAURICE HEWLETT MOUNSDON

42871   PO   Pilot   British   56 Squadron

Mounsdon joined the RAF on a short service commission. On August 24 1939 he began his elementary flying training at 3 E&RFTS, Burnaston Hall, Derby and on October 20 moved to 3 ITW, Hastings. He was posted to 14 FTS, Kinloss on November 2, later moving to Cranfield in April 1940.

With training completed, Mounsdon spent a few days at No 1 Flying Practice Unit at Meir before joining 66 Squadron at Duxford on May 19. He went to 56 Squadron at North Weald on June 3. Mounsdon claimed a Ju 87 destroyed on July 25, a Bf 110 on August 13, shared another on the 18th and claimed a Bf 109 destroyed on the 26th.

Mounsdon was shot down by enemy fighters over Colchester on August 31. He spent the next nine months in various hospitals and became a Guinea Pig after a stay at Queen Victoria Hospital, East Grinstead. On June 4 1941 Mounsdon returned to duty on the staff at SHQ North Weald. He was posted to 4 FIS, Cambridge on April 4 1942 and afterwards instructed at 22 EFTS, Cambridge from June 9 1942 until December 18 1943 and then at 21 EFTS, Booker until April 14 1945, when he was posted to 8303 Air Disarmament Wing in Germany.

Mounsdon was released from the RAF on February 22 1946, as a Flight Lieutenant.

APO 23.10.39   PO 17.5.40   FO 17.5.41   FL 17.5.42

CHRISTOPHER JOHN MOUNT

36162 FL Pilot British 602 Squadron

Born on December 14 1913, Mount was educated at Eton and Trinity College, Oxford, where he read Law. Whilst there Mount was in the University Air Squadron. He joined 600 Squadron, AuxAF in 1935 and entered the RAF in June 1938, with a direct-entry Permanent Commission with a special seniority, which varied according to the entrant's university degree. In Mount's case this was eighteen months.

He was posted to 23 Squadron at Hawkinge. In May 1939 Mount was appointed Personal Assistant to Air Vice-Marshal RE Saul at HQ 13 Group, Newcastle.

Mount joined 602 Squadron at Drem in late June 1940. He claimed a Bf 109 destroyed on October 29 and was awarded the DFC (26.11.40), being then credited with two enemy aircraft destroyed and three others damaged. In January 1941 Mount was posted to Acklington, to form and command 317 Squadron. He took command of 260 Squadron at Drem in April 1941.

In May the squadron embarked on HMS 'Victorious' at Scapa Flow, which carried Hurricanes, with wings detached. At Gibraltar the aircraft were transferred to the 'Ark Royal' and the aircraft were put on the flight deck and their wings were re-attached. They flew off to Malta on June 14 1941, refuelled there and then flew on to Egypt two days later.

In August Mount went down with a burst appendix and was in hospital for several months. He took command of 238 Squadron in the Western Desert on March 1 1942 and led it until July 1. Later in the year Mount went on a Wellington conversion course and then joined 70 Squadron, as a supernumerary Flight Commander. He was posted to 104 Squadron in Egypt in early 1943. When the CO fell ill Mount took command of the squadron.

After completing his tour he was awarded the DSO (1.10.43) and became operations officer for a Liberator/Halifax Wing, later serving as a staff officer at HQ Middle East. Mount went to RAF Staff College, Haifa in 1945. He was made a CBE (2.1.56) and retired from the RAF on December 26 1966, as an Air Commodore. After a six month refresher course on law he joined a law firm in Berkshire and became a partner in 1970. His portrait was drawn by Cuthbert Orde.

PO 26.6.38 (Seny 26.12.36)   FO 26.8.38   FL 26.6.40
SL 1.9.41   WC 1.7.43   WC 1.10.46   GC 1.7.51
AC 1.1.58

NOEL JOSEPH MOWAT

41725 FO Pilot New Zealander 245 Squadron

Mowat was born on September 18 1914 at Clydevale, Otago and was educated at St Kevin's College, Oamaru. He went to work on his father's farm and later was employed by the Public Works Department on survey and construction work.

In April 1938 Mowat applied for an RAF short service commission, was accepted and sailed for the UK on November 19 in the RMS 'Rangitiki'. The day after arrival he went to 9 E&RFTS, Ansty, as a pupil pilot. Mowat was posted to 10 FTS, Tern Hill on March 4 1939, completed his training at 6 FTS, Little Rissington and on November 6 joined 245 Squadron, then forming at Leconfield.

Mowat was made a Flight Commander on April 18 1940. Near Dunkirk on June 1 he probably destroyed a Bf 109. The squadron made a successful low-level attack on the airfield at Rouen-Boos on June 20 and Mowat led the second section of three Hurricanes. Considerable damage was done to the fifty aircraft on the ground. He received a Mention in Despatches (1.1.41).

On March 17 1941 Mowat was posted to 607 Squadron at Drem, as a Flight Commander. He was given command of the squadron on December 3. He led 607 in the operations against the 'Scharnhorst' and 'Gneisenau' on February 12 1942 and was personally responsible for the destruction of a vessel in the convoy. Mowat was awarded the DSO (16.3.42).

On March 21 the squadron sailed from Liverpool in the 'Empress of Russia' for India and by June 20 was at Alipore, receiving Hurricane 11cs. In mid-July it moved to Jessore, Burma to begin operations against the Japanese along the Irrawaddy. On October 1 1942 Mowat was posted to lead 166 Wing at Chittagong but again took command of 607 on March 5 1943. In April he was posted away and began a series of staff jobs.

Mowat served at Air HQ Bengal, 3rd TAF Air Command South East Asia, Air HQ India and Base HQ Bombay. He returned to the UK in August 1944 and went to the Fighter Leaders' School at Milfield. On December 2 Mowat was appointed Station Commander at RAF Peterhead. After a further series of staff jobs in 1945 he was posted to HQ 2nd TAF on April 1 1946 and on June 24 he was given command of 4 Squadron at Gutersloh, Germany.

He was a passenger in an Anson, which struck a high chimney and crashed near Hamm on November 7 1946. The crew and passengers were all killed. Mowat is buried in Lazanette Cemetery, Munster.

APO 20.2.39   PO 6.11.39   FO 18.7.40   FL 18.7.41
SL 21.6.43

ROBERT INNES MOWAT

974191 Sgt Wop/AG British 248 Squadron

Joined the RAF on December 8 1939. After completing his training Mowat was posted to 248 Squadron at Sumburgh. On July 10 1941 he joined 53 Squadron at Bircham Newton and on December 11 went to a Hudson ferrying unit for service in India.

Mowat joined 353 Squadron at its formation at Dum Dum on June 1 1942 and served with it in India and Burma until March 1944. He then went to 294 Squadron, an ASR unit operating in Wellingtons and Walruses along the coast of North Africa, Egypt, Palestine, Cyprus and Greece.

After returning to the UK in February 1945 Mowat's final posting was as a flying controller in the Orkneys. He was released from the RAF on October 30 1945, as a Warrant Officer.

HAROLD FREDERICK JOHN MOYNHAM

634201 Sgt Aircrew British 248 Squadron

Moynham, of Tooting, London, joined 248 Squadron in late July 1940. He was killed on November 3 1940, still serving with 248, aged 21. He is remembered on the Runnymede Memorial, Panel 17.

KARL MRAZEK

82561 PO Pilot Czechoslovakian 43 and 46 Sqdns

Mrazek was posted to 43 Squadron at Usworth on September 10 1940 and moved to 46 Squadron at Stapleford Tawney on the 17th.

He made a forced-landing at Rochester on the 27th, after his Hurricane's engine was damaged in combat with enemy aircraft over North Kent. On November 11 he shot a CR 42 down into the sea.

In December 1941 Mrazek took command of 313 Squadron at Hornchurch. On March 28 1942 he destroyed a Bf 109. He was posted away in June.

Mrazek was awarded the DSO and DFC. He was released from the RAF after the war as a Group Captain and returned to Czechoslovakia.

PO 2.8.40   FO 27.12.40   FL 27.12.41

KONRAD ANTONI MUCHOWSKI

P 2208   Sgt   Pilot   Polish   85 and 501 Squadrons

Born on July 3 1918. Muchowski completed his flying training and was posted to 5 OTU, Aston Down on August 19 1940. He joined 85 Squadron at Castle Camps on September 10 and moved to 501 Squadron at Kenley on October 23.

Muchowski was posted to 308 Squadron at Baginton on March 9 1941. He was rested on June 25 and went to CGS, Warmwell, as a staff pilot. On July 22 1942 Muchowski was sent to 4 FIS for an instructor's course and went to 25 EFTS, Hucknall on October 23. Commissioned in April 1943, he instructed there until January 2 1946. He was then posted to 16 FTS, Newton and was there until his release from the PAF in November 1946, as a Flight Lieutenant.

Muchowski died in 1988.

PO 15.4.43   FO 15.10.43   FL 15.4.45

MICHAEL ROBERT MUDIE

42073   PO   Pilot   British   615 Squadron

Joined the RAF on a short service commission in March 1939. Mudie was with 615 Squadron at Kenley in June 1940. He was shot down by Bf 109s in combat over a convoy off Dover on July 14, in Hurricane L 1584. He baled out, badly wounded, and was rescued from the sea by the Navy and admitted to Dover Hospital.

Mudie died the next day, aged 24. He is buried in Esher Cemetery, East Molesey, Surrey.

APO 27.5.39   PO 18.11.39

WLODZIMIERZ MUDRY

780416   Sgt   Pilot   Polish   79 Squadron

Born in 1917. Mudry joined 79 Squadron at Pembrey on September 11 1940. He was posted to the newly-formed 316 Squadron, also at Pembrey, on February 23 1941.

Mudry went to 286 Squadron on March 4 1942, an anti-aircraft co-operation unit. He joined the staff at 16 FTS, Newton on June 24 1944, later did an instructor's course there and began instructing on November 17. He was released from the PAF in January 1946.

Mudry joined the RAF and was gazetted as a Master Pilot on August 1 1948.

IAN JAMES MUIRHEAD

43362   PO   Pilot   British   605 Squadron

Muirhead was born in West Ham, London and his family later moved to Carlisle. He was an airman pilot before the war and served as a Flight Sergeant with 151 Squadron before being commissioned in April 1940 and posted to 605 Squadron.

On April 10 Muirhead damaged an enemy reconnaissance aircraft, on May 22 he destroyed a He 111 and on the 25th a Hs 126 and two Ju 87s. He was shot down patrolling Dunkirk on the 26th, probably by Royal Navy anti-aircraft gunners, baled out, was rescued from the sea and rejoined his squadron. Muirhead was awarded the DFC (28.6.40), 605's first decoration.

He claimed a He 111 destroyed on August 15 and shared a Do 17 on September 24. Muirhead was shot down in combat with Bf 109s over South London on October 7 and baled out, unhurt. His Hurricane, V 7305, crashed and burned out at Bexley.

Muirhead was shot down and killed by Bf 109s over Maidstone on October 15 1940. His Hurricane, N 2546, crashed at Spekes Bottom, Darland, near Gillingham. He was 27 and is buried in St Mary's churchyard, Holme Cultram, Cumberland.

PO 1.4.40

MIECZYSLAW MUMLER

P 1288   SL   Pilot   Polish   302 Squadron

Born on December 10 1899, Mümler was a Major in the PAF in September 1939, commanding III/3 Dyon, made up of 131 and 132 Squadrons. He is said to have destroyed two German aircraft and shared another at that time.

Mümler escaped to France and in May 1940 was commanding 2e Groupe de Chasse Polonaise, with Morane Ms 406s. In June he went to England and was appointed joint CO of 302 Squadron at Leconfield on July 23 1940. Mümler claimed a Do 17 destroyed on September 18.

He was posted to CFS, Upavon on December 15, for an instructor's course. Awarded the VM (5th Class)(1.2.41), he was posted to 58 OTU, Grangemouth on February 24 1941 and instructed there until August 25 1942. Mümler was made Station Commander at Northolt a month later. He continued to fly occasional sorties. On February 3 1943 he was flying with 308 Squadron on a Ventura escort to Courtrai and damaged a FW 190. Mümler was awarded the KW (7.7.43).

On October 24 1943 he was posted to HQ 84 Group, as Polish Liaison Officer, was awarded a Bar to the KW (15.2.44) and made a CBE (9.2.45). Mümler was posted to HQ Fighter Command on June 19 1945 and returned to 84 Group on February 21 1946. He was released from the PAF later in the year, as a Group Captain. He also held the C de G (Fr). Mümler died in England in 1985.

SL 1.3.41   WC 1.3.43

JOHN COLIN MUNGO-PARK

40008   FO   Pilot   British   74 Squadron

Born in Wallasey in 1918, Mungo-Park was educated at Liverpool College and joined the RAF on a short service commission in June 1937. He was posted to 10 FTS, Tern Hill on August 21, went to 2 AACU at Lee-on-Solent on March 26 1938 and then to the Fleet Requirements Unit, HMS 'Argus' on August 22 1938.

Mungo-Park joined 74 Squadron at Hornchurch on September 4 1939. Over Dunkirk on May 24 1940 he shared two Do 17s and a Hs 126.

On July 10 Mungo-Park claimed a Do 17 destroyed, on August 11 a Bf 109 and a Bf 110, on the 13th a probable Do 17, on September 11 a He 111, on the 14th a Bf 110, on October 20 a Bf 109, on the 22nd a shared Bf 109, on the 29th two Bf 109s, on November 14 a Ju 87 and on the 30th shared another Bf 109, Biggin Hill's 600th victory. Mungo-Park was awarded the DFC (15.11.40), as an Acting Flight Lieutenant. He had been commanding 'B' Flight from September 8.

Mungo-Park took command of 74 Squadron on March 10 1941. He was attacked by six Bf 109s over the French coast on June 16 and shot down two but his Spitfire's glycol system was damaged and after his engine seized he glided back across the coast and crash-landed near Hawkinge.

On a sweep over France on June 27 1941 Mungo-Park was shot down and killed. He is buried in Adinkerke Military Cemetery, Belgium. He was awarded a Bar to the DFC (11.7.41). His portrait was done by both Cuthbert Orde and Eric Kennington in 1940.

APO 9.8.37   PO 31.5.38   FO 31.12.39   FL 31.12.40

WELLESLEY SPENCER MUNN

45255   F/Sgt   Pilot   British   29 Squadron

Born on November 20 1911, Munn was a pre-war airman pilot. He joined 29 Squadron at North Weald in April 1937 and served with it throughout the Battle of Britain.

Munn was awarded the DFM (17.1.41), 29 Squadron's first. He was decorated by the King in a ceremony at Waddington. Commissioned in January 1941, Munn stayed on in the RAF after the war, in the Aircraft Control Branch. He retired on February 29 1960, as a Squadron Leader. He died in 1982.

PO 22.1.41   FO 22.1.42   FL 16.12.42   FL 1.9.45
SL 1.1.51

LEONARD CHARLES MURCH

41946   PO   Pilot   British   253 Squadron

Murch, of Plymstock, Devon, joined the RAF on a short service commission in February 1939. He did his ab initio course at 11 E&RFTS, Perth and then went to 2 FTS, Brize Norton.

On November 6 1939 Murch joined the newly-reformed 253 Squadron at Manston. During a squadron sortie on September 3 1940 he crashed into a wood at Nonnington, in Hurricane P 3610, and escaped unhurt. Murch claimed a He 111 destroyed on the 7th and on October 6 he shared a Do 17. He was shot down in a combat over Tunbridge Wells on October 11, baled out of Hurricane V 6570, injured, and was admitted to hospital with a broken arm.

In early July 1941 Murch joined 185 Squadron in Malta. He was killed on September 16 1943, as a Flight Lieutenant with 680 Squadron, a photographic-reconnaissance unit. He was 22 and is buried in Benghazi War Cemetery, Libya.

APO 15.4.39   PO 6.11.39   FO 6.11.40   FL 6.11.41

WILLIAM JOHN MURLAND

391867   Sgt   Air Gunner   New Zealander   264 Sqdn

Born in New Plymouth on November 14 1917, Murland went farming after leaving school and later became a carpenter. In October 1939 he volunteered for aircrew duties and went to the Ground Training School at Weraroa on December 18. He moved to the Air Observers' School, Ohakea in mid-January 1940 for a Lewis gunnery course and air experience and then sailed for the UK on March 23 in the SS 'Akaroa'.

Murland joined 264 Squadron at Duxford and continued training. Before being posted away to 5 OTU, Aston Down on July 27 he must have flown at least one authorised operational sortie after July 10 to qualify for the clasp. Murland was awarded his air gunner's badge and promoted to Sergeant at Aston Down. On November 4 he joined 75 Squadron, operating in Wellingtons from Feltwell. He moved to 214 Squadron at Stradishall on February 6 1941 and a month later was posted to 148 Squadron at Luqa, Malta. The squadron moved soon afterwards to Kabrit, Egypt.

Murland left 148 for the Middle East Pool on September 10 1941 and returned to the UK on November 16. He was posted to 1622 Flight

at Gosport on March 23 1942, on anti-aircraft co-operation duties. He joined 140 Squadron on March 15 1943, a photographic-reconnaissance unit with Blenheims. He was promoted to Warrant Officer on April 1. On October 31 Murland went to 13 OTU, to convert to Mitchells. He then joined 98 Squadron at Dunsfold on December 14.

In early May 1944 Murland was posted away for repatriation to New Zealand. He was recommended for a Medical Discharge and went on to the Reserve on November 3 1944. After several years of failing health Murland died in Porirua Hospital on November 15 1978. He is buried in the Whenua Tapu Cemetery.

ALAN DUNCAN MURRAY

34168   SL   Pilot   British   46, 501 and 73 Squadrons

Born on July 10 1915, Murray joined the RAF on a short service commission in January 1934. He was posted to 3 FTS, Grantham on April 3 and joined 18 Squadron at Upper Heyford on March 4 1935, flying Hart light bombers. In late 1935 Murray went to Leuchars for catapult training, then Calshot for floatplane training and finally Gosport for deck-landing and torpedo training, after which he was detached to HMS 'Malaya' in the Mediterranean on Swordfish catapult duty.

On May 30 1936 Murray was posted to 812 (Fleet Torpedo-Bomber) Squadron, based at Hal Far, Malta and on HMS 'Glorious'. In early 1939 he went to the A&AEE, Martlesham Heath. The Establishment moved to Boscombe Down on September 5 1939. Murray converted to Hurricanes at 6 OTU, Sutton Bridge in June 1940 and joined 46 Squadron at Digby. After a month he returned to Boscombe Down. He spent a week attached to 501 Squadron at Kenley in September, to gain operational experience, and was then posted to 73 Squadron at Castle Camps on September 21, to command.

Murray took the squadron to the Middle East in November and the pilots began operating in the Western Desert in December, attached to 274 Squadron. On January 1 the squadron began operating as a unit and on the 3rd Murray shared in destroying eight enemy aircraft on a landing ground. On the 21st he shot down a Fiat G50 over Tobruk, on February 1 destroyed a Caproni Ghibli on Apollonia airfield, on the 5th shared in destroying eight enemy bombers on the ground at Benina and on the 20th shot down a Ju 88 whilst flying with 3 (RAAF) Squadron. Murray was awarded the DFC (28.3.41) and in April was posted to Cairo, as Controller at Heliopolis.

He later had the job of locating possible new airfields in the Desert, then went to Group HQ, Cairo and was afterwards posted to command the Fighter Sector at Abadan, Iran. Murray returned to the UK in March 1944 and took command of a unit at Hurn, servicing fighters for France. He later moved with it to Tangmere. From September 1944 until September 1945 Murray commanded RAF Manston, as an Acting Group Captain. He retired from the RAF on January 15 1958, as a Wing Commander, retaining the rank of Group Captain.

APO 16.3.34   PO 16.3.35   FO 16.9.36   FL 16.9.38
SL 1.9.40   WC 1.12.41   WC 1.7.47

JAMES MURRAY

519400   Sgt   Pilot   British   610 and 74 Squadrons

Joined 610 Squadron at Acklington on September 16 1940 and moved to 74 Squadron at Biggin Hill on October 28. Murray was killed in the Middle East on April 3 1943, as a Warrant Officer. The unit he was serving with is not known. He is remembered on the Alamein Memorial, Column 269.

PATRICK HATTON MURRAY

968359   Sgt   Air Gunner   British   23 Squadron

Murray, of Hartley, Plymouth, joined 23 Squadron at Collyweston on July 9 1940. He was killed on December 8 1942, as a Flight Sergeant with 149 Squadron, operating in Stirlings from Lakenheath.

Murray was 24. He is buried in Kiel War Cemetery, Germany.

THOMAS BURNLEY MURRAY

90991   PO   Pilot   British   616 Squadron

A member of the AuxAF before the war, Murray was called to full-time service on August 24 1939. He was with 616 Squadron at Leconfield in June 1940. On August 15 he claimed two Ju 88s destroyed.

Murray was released from the RAF in 1946, as a Flight Lieutenant. He was awarded the AFC (13.6.46) and died in 1984.

APO 24.8.39   PO 6.4.40   FO 3.12.40   FL 3.12.41

KENNETH EDWARD NAISH

45447   Sgt   Pilot   British   235 Squadron

Naish joined 235 Squadron in June 1940. On August 28 his Blenheim, Z 5736, was attacked by Hurricanes of 1 (RCAF) Squadron over Thorney Island and badly damaged. He crashed on landing but he and his gunner, Sergeant WG Owen, were unhurt.

Commissioned in February 1941, Naish was posted away from 235 in July. He was awarded the DFC (19.5.44), as a Flight Lieutenant with 236 Squadron. In April 1944 he had taken part in an attack on a convoy off the Dutch coast. His aircraft was hit by flak and one engine set alight but he pressed home his attack. Whilst putting out the flames he was heavily engaged by ship and shore flak batteries. Naish got back to base and successfully crash-landed.

Naish was released in 1945, as a Squadron Leader. He rejoined the RAF in 1946 and served for some years in the Fighter Control Branch.

PO 19.2.41   FO 19.2.42   FL 1.11.42   FO 7.12.46

ALEKSANDER RYSZARD NARUCKI

P 0146   PO   Pilot   Polish   607 Squadron

Narucki was born on January 1 1916. He arrived in England from France on July 16 1940 and after converting to Hurricanes joined 607 Squadron at Turnhouse on October 9.

Narucki was posted to 302 Squadron at Northolt on November 13 1940. He was killed on May 11 1941, when he crashed after touching another Hurricane with his wing on a training flight, in Hurricane BZ 3433. Narucki is buried in Northwood Cemetery.

PO 1.3.41

HAROLD THOMAS NAUGHTIN

754002   Sgt   Aircrew   British   235 Squadron

Joined 235 Squadron on August 5 1940. Naughtin was killed on May 28 1941, as a Flight Sergeant with 235. He was 21 years old and is remembered on the Runnymede Memorial, Panel 37.

N NEER

No unknown   Sgt   Aircrew   British   29 Squadron

Joined 29 Squadron in July 1940. No other service details traced.

THOMAS FRANCIS NEIL

71968   PO   Pilot   British   249 Squadron

Neil was born in Bootle on July 14 1920. He joined the RAFVR on October 17 1938 and began his flying training at 17 E&RFTS, Barton, Manchester. Called up on September 2 1939, Neil went to ITW at Bexhill in early November.

On December 1 he was posted to 8 FTS, Montrose and on completion of the course he was commissioned and joined 249 Squadron on May 15 1940 at its reformation at Church Fenton. Flying from North Weald on September 7 Neil claimed a Bf 109 destroyed, on the 11th a He 111, on the 15th two Do 17s and on the 27th a Bf 110, a Ju 88 and another shared. He was awarded the DFC (8.10.40). On October 25 Neil claimed a Bf 109 destroyed, on the 27th a probable Do 17, on the 28th he shared a Ju 88 and on November 7 he claimed a Ju 87 and two Bf 109s destroyed. On this day Neil collided with Wing Commander FV Beamish during a patrol and lost his tail. He baled out of Hurricane V 7676, unhurt. Neil was awarded a Bar to the DFC (26.11.40) and made a Flight Commander in December.

In May 1941 249 went to Malta. The squadron flew off 'Ark Royal' on the 21st, Neil leading the second group of Hurricanes. After a series of mishaps and misadventures they all reached Malta safely. On June 11 1941 Neil destroyed a Mc 200. He left Malta on December 26 1941 and returned to the UK via the Middle East, South Africa, West Africa and Canada, finally arriving at Liverpool in early March 1942.

Neil was posted to 81 Group as Tactics Officer. He went to 56 OTU in mid-June and on September 1 1942 took command of 41 Squadron at Llanbedr. In July 1943 he was posted to 53 OTU, Kirton-in-Lindsey, as an instructor. He later went to the 9th US Air Force, as Flying Liaison Officer with the 100th Fighter Wing. After D Day Neil did some operational flying in France, as a supernumerary.

In January 1945 he was posted to the School of Land/Air Warfare at Old Sarum, instructing and lecturing. Neil went to Burma in March 1945, investigating. Whilst there he flew some operational sorties with No 1 Indian Wing. He returned to Old Sarum in April, leaving there in January 1946 to go on an Empire Test Pilots' course at Cranfield.

Neil was awarded the Bronze Star (US)(2.8.49) and the AFC (2.1.56). He retired from the RAF in 1964, as a Wing Commander.

PO 12.5.40   FO 3.3.41   FL 3.3.42   FL 1.9.45
SL 1.1.51   WC 1.1.57

DICK NELSON

47651   F/Sgt   Pilot   British   235 Squadron

Born on January 16 1915, Nelson was a pre-war airman pilot. He was with 235 Squadron in June 1940.

Commissioned in January 1942, he transferred to the Technical Branch in 1945 and retired from the RAF on February 26 1967, as a Wing Commander. He died on June 26 1972.

PO 5.1.42   FO 1.10.42   FL 5.1.44   FL 1.9.45
SL 1.7.51   WC 1.1.57

WILLIAM HENRY NELSON

39675   FO   Pilot   Canadian   74 Squadron

Nelson, of Montreal, joined the RAF on a short service commission in March 1937. He was posted to 8 FTS, Montrose on May 9 and joined 10 Squadron at Dishforth on November 27 1937.

The squadron's first operational sortie in the war was made on the night of 8/9 September 1939, when eight of its Whitleys dropped leaflets and made a reconnaissance of north-west Germany. Nelson took part and was later awarded the DFC (4.6.40) for his services with the squadron.

WH Nelson (continued)

On July 20 1940 Nelson joined 74 Squadron at Hornchurch. He claimed a Bf 109 and a Bf 110 destroyed on August 11 and Bf 109s on October 15, 17, 27 and 29. He was killed on November 1 1940, shot down in a surprise attack by Bf 109s over Dover and is believed to have crashed into the Channel, in Spitfire P 7312.

Nelson was 25 years old. He is remembered on the Runnymede Memorial, Panel 4.

APO 9.5.37   PO 8.3.38   FO 8.9.39

GEORGE HASSALL NELSON-EDWARDS

74355   FO   Pilot   British   79 Squadron

Born on March 8 1918, Nelson-Edwards was educated at Shrewsbury School and Brasenose College, Oxford. He learned to fly with the University Air Squadron and was called to full-time service in September 1939.

Nelson-Edwards joined 79 Squadron at Acklington on August 1 1940. He shared in the destruction of a He 59 on the 28th. Three days later he crashed at The Grange, Water Lane, Limpsfield following a combat over Biggin Hill, in Hurricane N 2345, slightly injured. On September 27 Nelson-Edwards was hit by return fire from a He 111 engaged off the Welsh coast. He baled out over the Irish sea and was picked up by the SS 'Dartford' and landed at Milford Haven, unhurt.

On June 1 1942 Nelson-Edwards took command of 93 Squadron, then forming at Andreas. In October it went overseas, to take part in the Anglo-American invasion of North Africa and landed at Algiers on November 13. Nelson-Edwards probably destroyed a Ju 88 on November 26 1942 and had another confirmed on December 4. He was posted away in February 1943 and awarded the DFC (26.2.43).

In 1944 Nelson-Edwards was Liaison Officer with the US 9th Air Force North-West Europe. He retired from the RAF on September 30 1960, as a Wing Commander.

PO 26.9.39   FO 26.9.40   FL 26.9.41   SL 7.6.44
SL 1.9.45   WC 1.7.53

ARTHUR DEANE NESBITT

C 1327   FO   Pilot   Canadian   1 (RCAF) Squadron

Nesbitt was born in Montreal in 1904. He was with No 1 (RCAF) Squadron when it arrived in the UK on June 20 1940.

He claimed a Bf 110 destroyed on September 4 and a Bf 109 on the 15th. On this day Nesbitt was attacked by Bf 109s and shot down over Tunbridge Wells, in Hurricane P 3080. He baled out, wounded, and was admitted to hospital. Back in action on October 7 Nesbitt's Hurricane, P 2993, was badly damaged in combat with a Bf 109. He landed at Biggin Hill, unhurt.

In March 1941 he took command of the squadron, now re-numbered 401, and led it until September. Nesbitt was awarded the DFC (23.9.41). He was made an OBE (1.1.46) and released from the RCAF in 1946, as a Wing Commander. He died in 1979.

WILLIAM JOHN NEVILLE

741783   Sgt   Pilot   British   610 Squadron

Neville, of Shepperton, Middlesex, joined 610 Squadron at Biggin Hill on July 27 1940. He made a forced-landing at Potmans Heath Marsh, Wittersham on August 8, in Spitfire L 1045. The aircraft overturned but Neville was unhurt.

Three days later he was reported 'Missing', following a patrol off Calais, in Spitfire R 6603. Neville was 26. He is remembered on the Runnymede Memorial, Panel 17.

JOHN CHARLES NEWBERY

70497   FO   Pilot   British   609 Squadron

Newbery learned to fly with the RAFO and was called to full-time service in September 1939. He joined 609 Squadron at Middle Wallop on July 8 1940.

Following a combat on September 25 Newbery pulled out of a power dive in such a way as to strain the Spitfire's wings, pulling his seat off its fixings and sending him to hospital with severe internal injuries.

Newbery was released from the RAF in 1945, as a Wing Commander.

PO (RAFO) 22.12.36   FO (RAFO) 1.9.38   FO 25.9.39
FL 15.5.41   SL 1.7.44

EDWARD ARNOLD NEWHAM

159832   Sgt   Aircrew   British   235 Squadron

Joined 235 Squadron on September 23 1940. Newham was commissioned in November 1943, in the Administrative Branch, and was released from the RAF in 1944, as a Flying Officer. He died on February 14 1976.

APO 18.11.43   PO 13.1.44

MICHAEL ALAN NEWLING

41867   FO   Pilot   British   145 Squadron

Newling joined the RAF on a short service commission in February 1939. He carried out his intermediate and advanced flying training at 11 FTS, Shawbury and then went to the newly-reformed 145 Squadron at Croydon on October 23 1939.

Newling was shot down east of Brussels on May 18 1940. He baled out and rejoined his squadron two days later. Over Dunkirk on May 31 he shared a Bf 109 and on June 1 destroyed a Bf 110.

On July 19 Newling shared in destroying a He 111 but his Hurricane, P 2770, was hit in the glycol tank and hydraulic system. He made a forced-landing on Shoreham aerodrome, slightly concussed, and was admitted to Shoreham Hospital. Newling wrote off Hurricane V 6856 when he overshot the runway landing at Tangmere on October 18. He hit a stationary aircraft but escaped unhurt.

Newling was awarded the DFC (4.2.41). He shared a Ju 88 on March 1 1941 and probably destroyed a Bf 109 on June 27. He was killed on July 6 1941, on a Circus operation over the Lille area. Newling is remembered on the Runnymede Memorial, Panel 29.

APO 1.4.39   PO 23.10.39   FO 23.10.40

DOUGLAS VICTOR NEWPORT

615682   Sgt   Air Gunner   British   235 Squadron

With 235 Squadron in early July 1940. No other service details traced.

EDWIN FRANK NEWTON

614682   **Sgt**   **Aircrew**   **British**   **29 Squadron**

Joined 29 Squadron at Digby on September 13 1940. No other service details traced.

HARRY SNOW NEWTON

134750   **Sgt**   **Pilot**   **British**   **111 Squadron**

Newton was born on July 13 1920. He joined 504 Squadron, AuxAF and served as an AC2 photographer. In April 1939 he joined the RAFVR, as a Sergeant u/t pilot, and began flying training at 27 E&RFTS, Tollerton.

Called to full-time service in September 1939, Newton was posted to 8 FTS, Montrose. With training completed he joined 111 Squadron at Croydon in April 1940.

On August 11 Newton crash-landed on the marshes at Boyton, near Martlesham Heath, in Hurricane P 3548, having run out of fuel after combat with enemy aircraft over Thanet. He claimed a Do 17 destroyed on August 16 and another on the 18th. In this engagement Newton's Hurricane, P 3943, was set alight by return fire and he baled out over Botley.

In February 1941 Newton was posted to the Air Navigation School at Staverton, as a staff pilot. He moved to 8 BGS, Jurby in April on similar duties. Commissioned from Flight Sergeant in August 1942, Newton later flew as a staff pilot at 11 Air Gunners' School, Andreas. He was awarded the AFC (1.9.44) and released from the RAF in June 1946, as a Flight Lieutenant. He rejoined later the same year and retired on July 13 1975, as a Squadron Leader. Over a long flying career Newton logged 10,000 hours.

PO 30.8.42   *FO 2.3.43*   *FL 30.8.44*   *FL 5.11.46*
SL 1.1.67

JOHN BEVILLE HOWARD NICHOLAS

39798   **FO**   **Pilot**   **British**   **65 Squadron**

Joined the RAF on a short service commission in April 1937. Nicholas began his flying training at 12 E&RFTS, Prestwick, went to 6 FTS, Netheravon on May 30 and joined 65 Squadron at Hornchurch on December 31 1937.

Over Dunkirk on May 26 1940 Nicholas destroyed two Bf 109s and damaged a Bf 110. During the Battle of Britain he shared a Do 17 and damaged several other enemy aircraft. Nicholas was posted away to 2 CFS, Cranwell on December 9 1940, for an instructor's course, after which he went to 9 EFTS, Ansty, as a Flight Commander.

On April 14 1943 he was posted to Cranwell for a refresher course, went to 61 OTU, Rednal on June 15 and moved to 2 TEU, Grangemouth on October 8.

Nicholas was posted to Australia in 1944. After a month at 2 OTU, Mildura he took command of 54 Squadron at Darwin in June. He led the squadron until its disbandment on October 31 1945. Nicholas returned to the UK and on February 5 1946 went to a staff job at HQ 11 Group. He stayed on in the RAF on an Extended Service Commission and resigned in July 1949, as a Flight Lieutenant.

APO 31.5.37   *PO 5.4.38*   *FO 5.1.40*   *FL 5.1.41*
SL 1.7.45   *FL 1.12.42*

DOUGLAS BENJAMIN FLETCHER NICHOLLS

114121   **Sgt**   **Pilot**   **British**   **85,242 and 151 Sqdns**

Nicholls joined the RAFVR in September 1938, as a Sergeant u/t pilot. Called to full-time service at the outbreak of war he completed his elementary flying training at 6 EFTS, Sywell and then moved on to 8 FTS, Montrose.

In June 1940 Nicholls converted to Hurricanes at 7 OTU, Hawarden. After brief stays with 85 and 242 Squadrons he joined 151 Squadron at Digby in September. On the 30th he shared in the destruction of a Ju 88 and returned to Digby with his Hurricane, P 5182, severely damaged by return fire.

In August 1941 Nicholls was posted to 258 Squadron at Martlesham Heath. The squadron flew to Debden on October 3 to prepare for overseas. Leaving their Hurricanes behind the twenty-two pilots went to Abbotsinch on the 30th and two days later sailed in HMS 'Athene' for Gibraltar, with wing-detached Hurricanes on

board. After arriving on the 21st the aircraft were to be unloaded, to be taken by 'Ark Royal' to Malta later. However the carrier was sunk returning to Gibraltar so other plans were made for the 258 pilots.

They left on Christmas Eve 1941, on the 'Athene'. They berthed at Takoradi on January 1 1942, disembarked, and the 'Athene' left, taking their Hurricanes with her. On the 3rd they flew on the ferry route to the Middle East in a DC3, arrived at Port Sudan, from where they sailed in HMS 'Indomitable' on the 9th, with Hurricanes aboard. They flew off on the 28th and later in the morning arrived at Airfield P2 at Palembang, Sumatra. In the afternoon they went on to Seletar airfield, Singapore and flew their first operation on January 31.

On February 10 1942 the three surviving Hurricanes of 258 were withdrawn to Palembang. Of the fifteen surviving pilots six were required to remain behind there to fly with a reformed 605 Squadron. One was nominated, two volunteered and the other three were selected by cutting cards. Nicholls was one of the nine evacuated from Java to Ceylon in the SS 'Kota Gede'. 258 Squadron was reformed at Ratmalana on March 1 1942. Nicholls rejoined it on March 7.

Commissioned in December 1941, Nicholls was awarded the DFC (19.5.44) and remained with 258 until August 1944, when he was posted to HQ 224 Group, Burma, as Squadron Leader Tactics. He returned to the UK in October 1945 and was released from the RAF in March 1946, as a Squadron Leader. Nicholls rejoined the RAFVR in 1949.

PO 17.12.41   *FO 24.10.42*   *FL 17.12.43*
FO (RAFVR) 4.5.49

THOMAS GEORGE FRANK NICHOLLS

532244   **Sgt**   **Air Gunner**   **British**   **23 Squadron**

Nicholls, of Upper Tooting, London, served with 23 Squadron throughout the Battle of Britain. He was killed on April 10 1941, still with 23, aged 26. He is buried in Ennetières Communal Cemetery, Avelin, France.

DENNIS HUGH NICHOLS

118094   **Sgt**   **Pilot**   **British**   **56 Squadron**

Nichols joined the RAFVR in 1938 and had carried out some elementary flying training at 6 E&RFTS, Sywell before being called to full-time service in September 1939.

After a spell at 3 ITW, Hastings Nichols completed his ab initio course at 5 EFTS, Hanworth and then moved on to 8 FTS, Montrose. After converting to Hurricanes Nichols joined 56 Squadron at Boscombe Down on September 15 1940.

He was shot down in combat with enemy aircraft south of Yeovil on October 7, in Hurricane P 3514. Nichols baled out but his parachute failed to open fully and he broke his back in a heavy landing. He left hospital in 1941 and was posted to 286 Squadron, an anti-aircraft co-operation unit.

Commissioned in March 1942, Nichols eventually regained his operational category and went to 54 OTU, Charter Hall in 1943, for night-fighter training. He joined 255 Squadron in North Africa and later went with it to Sicily and Italy. In 1945 Nichols was seconded to BOAC. After release from the RAF in 1946 he joined BEA.

PO 10.3.42   *FO 1.10.42*   *FL 10.3.44*

JAMES BRINDLEY NICOLSON

39329   **FL**   **Pilot**   **British**   **249 Squadron**

Born in Hampstead on April 29 1917, Nicolson went to Tonbridge School from 1930 to 1934. He joined the RAF on a short service commission and began his elementary flying training at 13 E&RFTS, White Waltham on October 12 1936.

Nicolson was posted to 10 FTS, Tern Hill on January 16 1937 and joined 72 Squadron at Church Fenton on August 7. He went to 249 Squadron, then reforming at Church Fenton, on May 15 1940, as a Flight Commander.

On August 16 Nicolson was shot down in a surprise attack by Bf 109s over Southampton. Wounded in the left foot and with a perspex splinter through his left eyelid Nicolson prepared to abandon his burning Hurricane, P 3576. As he did so a Bf 110 appeared in front of him. Nicolson slid back into his seat and fired at the enemy fighter. His cockpit was now a mass of flames and he was being burned but he continued firing until it became impossible to remain and he baled out, at 12000 feet. Nicolson's hands were severely burned, parts of his face also, his eyelid was all but severed and his wounded foot was becoming ever more painful. Near the ground he was fired on by LDV volunteers and wounded in the buttock by shotgun pellets.

Nicolson was taken to Southampton Hospital and three weeks later moved to the RAF Hospital, Halton and in early November was convalescing at Torquay. He was awarded the VC (15.11.40), the only one given to Fighter Command. Nicolson was decorated by the King at Buckingham Palace on November 25.

He was posted to 54 OTU on February 24, as an instructor. He regained his operational category and on September 22 1941 was given command of 1459 Flight at Hibaldstow, a Turbinlite Havoc unit. Nicolson was posted to India in early 1942 and on March 17 began a staff job at HQ 293 Wing, Alipore, moving in December to Air HQ, Bengal.

On August 4 1943 Nicolson was given command of 27 Squadron, operating in Mosquitos from Agartala, Burma. He was posted away to HQ 3rd TAF, Comilla, Bengal on August 11 1944 and awarded the DFC (11.8.44), as a Wing Commander.

In April 1945 Nicolson was on the staff of HQ RAF Burma. On May 2 he went on a bombing sortie with a Liberator of 355 Squadron, as an observer. After taking off from Salbani the aircraft was 130 miles south of Calcutta, when one engine caught fire. The Liberator crashed into the sea and there were only two NCO survivors.

Nicolson is remembered on the Singapore Memorial, Column 445.

APO 21.12.36   PO 21.10.37   FO 12.5.39   FL 3.9.40
SL 1.12.41

PETER BETHUNE NICOLSON

740866   **Sgt**   **Pilot**   **British**   **232 Squadron**

Nicolson, of Glasgow, joined 232 Squadron at Sumburgh at its reformation on July 17 1940. He was killed over Crete on May 29 1941, as a Flight Sergeant with 274 Squadron. He is remembered on the Alamein Memorial, Column 242.

PAWEL NIEMIEC

76748   **PO**   **Pilot**   **Polish**   **17 Squadron**

Born in Cieszyn on November 25 1913, Niemiec joined the PAF in 1933. After arriving in England in late 1939 he was commissioned in January 1940 and joined 17 Squadron at Tangmere on September 1.

Niemiec destroyed a Ju 87 on November 8 and shared a Bf 110 on the 17th. He was posted to 317 Squadron's Operations Room on February 26 1941 and later began flying with the squadron. Awarded the KW (1.4.41) and Bar (10.9.41), Niemiec was appointed a Flight Commander with 317 on March 1 1942. He was given command of 308 Squadron at Northolt on March 5 1943 and led it until May 15. He was posted to 316 Squadron, also at Northolt, on August 17 and took command on September 15.

Niemiec was awarded a second Bar to the KW (20.10.43). He took command of 306 Squadron on June 26 1944 and was posted away to HQ PAF on September 25 and attached to 13 Group. On March 11 1945 Niemiec was attached to the School of Air Support at Old Sarum for a course and then joined 84 GSU on April 18 for flying duties. He took command of 317 Squadron at Warelbusch, Germany on May 17 1945.

Awarded the VM (5th Class)(1.6.45), Niemiec returned to 316 Squadron, then at Andrews Field, on October 12 1945, to command. He was released from the PAF in December 1946, as a Squadron Leader. Niemiec was credited with two enemy aircraft destroyed, two more damaged and he shared in destroying a V1. He later settled in Argentina.

PO 27.1.40   FO 1.3.41   FL 1.9.42   SL 13.9.43

FREDERICK GEORGE NIGHTINGALE

44979   **PO**   **Pilot**   **British**   **219 Squadron**

Nightingale was a pre-war airman pilot and was with 219 Squadron at Catterick in June 1940. Commissioned from Sergeant in October, he was killed on December 17 1940 when his Beaufighter crashed during a landing approach, cause unknown. His radar operator, Sergeant GM Leslie, was also killed.

Nightingale was 26. He is buried in Saffron Walden Cemetery, Essex.

PO 9.10.40

HUGH GLEN NIVEN

91226   **PO**   **Pilot**   **Canadian**   **601 and 602 Squadrons**

Born in Canada in 1919, Niven went to Scotland in June 1937. He joined 602 Squadron, AuxAF at Abbotsinch on May 7 1939 and began his flying training in Avro Tutors.

Called to full-time service at the outbreak of war, Niven was posted to 11 EFTS, Perth on October 25 1939. He went to 15 FTS, Lossiemouth on March 23 1940 and with the course completed moved to 5 OTU, Aston Down on August 17, where he converted to Hurricanes.

Niven rejoined 602 Squadron, then at

Westhampnett, on September 1 1940 but having no Spitfire experience he was posted to 601 Squadron at Debden three days later. After much complaining he rejoined 602 Squadron on September 21. His Spitfire, X 4603, was damaged in combat with Bf 109s over Maidstone on October 29.

Apart from a few days with 603 Squadron in late July 1941 Niven was with 602 until September 23 1941. He was admitted to Horton Emergency Hospital on the 24th, suffering from tuberculosis. He was invalided out on March 12 1942, as a Flying Officer. When 602 Squadron was reformed in June 1946 Niven rejoined as a civilian clerk.

APO 23.3.40   PO 17.8.40   FO 20.6.41

WILLIAM NIXON

152339   Sgt   Pilot   British   23 Squadron

Nixon, of Sheffield, joined 23 Squadron at Middle Wallop on September 24 1940.

Commissioned in May 1943, he was killed on August 30 1944, as a Flying Officer with 103 Squadron, operating in Lancasters from Elsham Wolds, Lincolnshire. Nixon was 23. He is buried in Kiel War Cemetery, Germany.

PO 28.5.43   FO 28.11.43

BRIAN ROBERT NOBLE

81043   PO   Pilot   British   79 Squadron

Born on August 26 1916, Noble joined 79 Squadron at Biggin Hill in June 1940. He claimed a share in destroying a He 59 on August 28.

Noble was shot down in combat with Bf 109s over Biggin Hill on September 1. He baled out, wounded, landing at Marley Lake, Riverhead and was admitted to Sevenoaks Hospital. His Hurricane, L 2062, crashed in Court Road Orchard, Chelsfield. Noble later went to Queen Victoria Hospital, East Grinstead for plastic surgery and became a Guinea Pig.

He was released from the RAF in 1946 but later rejoined, in the Fighter Control Branch. Noble retired on May 1 1969, as a Wing Commander.

PO 15.6.40   FO 15.6.41   FL 15.6.42   FL 4.7.49
SL 1.1.56   WC 1.7.63

DENNIS NOBLE

742128   Sgt   Pilot   British   43 Squadron

Noble, of East Retford, Nottinghamshire, was posted to 6 OTU, Sutton Bridge in July 1940. He joined 43 Squadron at Northolt on August 3.

Following an operational sortie on the 13th Noble made an emergency landing at Tangmere with damage to glycol system and radiator. On the 16th he claimed a Ju 87 destroyed. Noble was shot down and killed by a Bf 109 off the Sussex coast on August 30. His Hurricane, P 3179, crashed near the junction of Portland and Woodhouse Roads, Hove. Noble was 20 years old. He is buried in East Retford Cemetery.

WILLIAM JOHN NOBLE

112500   Sgt   Pilot   British   54 Squadron

Joined 54 Squadron at Catterick on September 22 1940. Commissioned in November 1941, Noble was released from the RAF in 1946, as a Flight Lieutenant. He died in 1979.

PO 17.11.41   FO 1.10.42   FL 17.11.43

BENJAMIN NOKES-COOPER

77362   PO   Air Gunner   British   236 Squadron

Nokes-Cooper was with 236 Squadron in early July 1940. He was killed as a member of the crew of Blenheim N 3601, shot down during a bomber escort operation to attack Quequerville aerodrome, either by ground defences or possibly Oberleutnant Adolph of III/JG 27. The captain of the Blenheim, Squadron Leader PE Drew, was also killed.

Nokes-Cooper was 32. He is buried in Bayeux War Cemetery, France.

APO 3.2.40   PO 16.3.40

NORMAN ROBERT NORFOLK

44929   PO   Pilot   British   72 Squadron

Norfolk was with 72 Squadron in early July 1940 and was commissioned in August. Following a combat with Bf 109s off Dungeness on September 1 Norfolk returned to Croydon with a severely damaged tail unit. The next day he was shot down in combat over Herne Bay, in Spitfire K 9938, which crashed and burned out at Garrington Farm, near Bekesbourne emergency landing ground. Norfolk baled out, unhurt.

On September 7 and 11 he claimed Do 17s destroyed and a Bf 110 on October 25. Norfolk was awarded the DFC (7.1.41), credited with at least four enemy aircraft destroyed.

He was released from the RAF in 1945, as a Flight Lieutenant.

PO 21.8.40   FO 21.8.41   FL 21.8.42

PHILIP PURCHALL NORRIS

740810   Sgt   Pilot   British   213 Squadron

Born in Burgess Hill, Sussex in 1918. Norris was with 213 Squadron at Exeter in early July 1940. He failed to return from an action over Portland on August 13, in Hurricane P 3348.

Norris' body was later washed ashore on the French coast and he is buried in Etaples Military Cemetery.

ROBERT WILSON NORRIS

C 994   FO   Pilot   Canadian   1 (RCAF) Squadron

Norris, of Toronto, joined the RCAF on June 12 1939 and after training went to 112 Squadron, flying Lysanders. The squadron was posted to the UK and arrived at Highpost, near Salisbury on June 17 1940.

From July 15 to August 8 Norris was at Old Sarum on an Army Co-operation course. Responding to a call for volunteers for Fighter Command Norris was posted to a Hurricane OTU and then joined No 1 (RCAF) Squadron at Northolt on August 17. He claimed a Bf 109 probably destroyed on September 15 and a He 111 and a Bf 110 damaged on the 27th.

Norris was posted to 400 Squadron on January 30 1941, flying Tomahawks from Odiham on photographic-reconnaissance duties across the Channel. He was repatriated to Canada in March 1942 and commanded 125 (RCAF) Squadron from June 3 1942, flying Hurricanes from Sydney, Nova Scotia on east coast defence.

In January 1944 he took his squadron to the UK but lost his command to a more experienced fighter pilot on February 8. Norris

RW Norris (continued)

refused a posting back to Canada and went to Bomber Command, eventually taking command of 424 Squadron on March 27 1945, operating in Lancasters from Skipton-on-Swale. After the war's end the squadron airlifted British and Canadian troops back from Italy to the UK. He was posted away on September 30 and released from the RCAF on November 28 1945, as a Wing Commander.

On May 26 1951 Norris rejoined the RCAF and served in Transport Command. He retired on November 6 1963, as a Flight Lieutenant.

STANLEY CHARLES NORRIS

40561   FO   Pilot   British   610 Squadron

Born in Tooting, London in 1919, Norris joined the RAF on a short service commission in December 1937. He did his ab initio course at 8 E&RFTS, Woodley, moved on to 9 FTS, Hullavington on March 5 1938 and was awarded his flying badge on June 1.

Norris joined 29 Squadron at Debden on September 17 1938. He was posted to 66 Squadron at Duxford on September 18 1939 and moved on to 610 Squadron at Wittering in November. Over Dunkirk on May 29 1940 Norris claimed a Bf 109 destroyed.

On July 25 he claimed two Bf 109s, on August 14 two Ju 87s, on the 24th a Bf 109 and on the 29th probably another. Norris was awarded the DFC (24.9.40). He took part in the squadron's first sweep on January 9 1941, shared in destroying a Ju 88 on April 3 and then next day was posted to 55 OTU at Debden, as an instructor.

In August 1941 Norris joined 485 Squadron at Redhill, as a Flight Commander. He destroyed a Bf 109 on the 29th. In mid-December 1941 he went to Malta to command 126 Squadron at Ta Kali. Norris shared a Ju 88 on the 19th, destroyed another on January 9 1942 and shared another on March 10.

Norris was posted to Abadan, Persia on April 4 1942 for a staff job concerned with building up defences of the oilfields. In October he was made Squadron Leader Flying 243 Wing but took command of 33 Squadron in the Western Desert on November 20. Norris was rested in February 1943 and went to West Africa, returning to the Middle East in June. He was posted to India in August and in September took command of 11 Squadron. It had just returned to the fighter role, exchanging its Blenheim bombers for Hurricane 11cs. The squadron became operational in December 1943 and took part in operations at Imphal.

In March 1944 Norris was promoted to Wing Commander Flying of a Fighter Wing there. He was awarded a Bar to the DFC (23.5.44) and returned to the UK in early 1945. In May 1945 Norris took command of RAF Aston Down. He was released from the RAF in September 1947, as a Wing Commander. He became a King's, and later a Queen's Messenger, serving as such until 1976.

APO 19.2.38   PO 29.11.38   FO 29.8.40   FL 29.8.41
SL 1.7.43

GERALD NORTH

83719   PO   Pilot   British   85 and 257 Squadrons

North, of Penrith, was posted to 85 Squadron at Croydon on September 2 1940 but moved to 257 Squadron at Martlesham Heath on the 11th.

Following combat with Bf 109s over the Thames Estuary on October 15 North made a forced-landing at Hawkinge, unhurt, in Hurricane V 7351. He claimed a Bf 109 and an Italian aircraft destroyed on November 11 1940.

In Autumn 1941 North was a pilot with the MSFU, on Atlantic convoys. It became customary for pilots on this duty to bring back things in short supply, such as cigarettes, liquor and silk stockings. North was fired off from a ship, which arrived in convoy off Anglesey on October 6 1941, the idea being to land at some airfield without customs officers, rather than go to the MSFU base at Speke, where they abounded. Visibility over Wales was bad and after failing to find Valley North finally made a crash-landing in a field near Bangor.

North was killed on February 10 1943, as a Flight Lieutenant with 232 Squadron, aged 22. He is buried in Bone War Cemetery, Annaba, Algeria.

PO 3.8.40   FO 3.8.41   FL 3.8.42

HAROLD LESLIE NORTH

41608   FO   Pilot   New Zealander   43 Squadron

North was born in Dunedin on October 31 1919. After leaving Otago Boys' High School he went to Wellington College and was then employed as a law clerk. He applied for an RAF short service commission in early 1938 and after provisional acceptance he sailed for the UK on September 22 in the RMS 'Rangitane'.

On October 31 North began his elementary flying training at 12 E&RFTS, Prestwick. He was posted to 9 FTS, Hullavington on January 28 1939 and with training completed he went to the 11 Group Pool on September 9. North joined 43 Squadron at Acklington on November 20 and was still with the squadron in early July 1940.

On August 18 he claimed a Ju 87 destroyed and probably another and on the 26th he claimed a He 111 and probably a second. In this action North's Hurricane, V 7259, was badly damaged and he baled out, landed at Birdham and was admitted to the Royal Sussex Hospital, Chichester, with shell splinter wounds. He returned to the squadron on September 10.

North was posted to 96 Squadron on December 17 1940, then forming as a night-fighter unit at Cranage. He was rested on April 7 1941 and joined 3 ADU. A return to operational flying came on June 23 1941, when North joined the newly-formed 457 (RAAF) Squadron at Baginton, as a Flight Commander.

He claimed a FW 190 destroyed on March 26 1942, damaged two more on the 28th and April 4, destroyed a FW 190 on the 16th and damaged another on the 27th. The squadron was detailed to act as high cover for bombers attacking the shell factory at Marquise on May 1 1942. North was last seen diving on an enemy aircraft from 17000 feet, ten miles inland from the French coast. He was not seen again and is believed to have been killed in action. He is remembered on the Runnymede Memorial, Panel 66.

North's health was never good and he suffered from kidney trouble but he continued to fly operationally in spite of it. He was awarded the DFC (15.6.42), the citation crediting him with at least five enemy aircraft destroyed.

APO 13.1.39   PO 3.9.39   FO 3.9.40   FL 3.9.41

DAVID JOHN NORTH-BOMFORD

742833   Sgt   Pilot   British   229, 17 and 111 Squadrons

North-Bomford joined the RAF in March 1934, was posted to 5 FTS, Sealand on the 16th and joined 111 Squadron at Northolt on March 3 1935. He joined the staff of the Electrical and Wireless School at Cranwell on January 27 1936 and was posted to Hinaidi, Iraq on December 19 to join 55 Squadron there.

On April 20 1937 North-Bomford resigned his commission. He rejoined the RAF after the outbreak of war and in early July 1940 was with 229 Squadron at Wittering. He moved to 17 Squadron at Debden on July 29 and then to 111 Squadron, also at Debden, on August 28.

Promoted to Warrant Officer on October 1 1941, North-Bomford was released from the RAF in 1947, still with the same rank.

APO 16.3.34   PO 16.3.35   FO 16.10.36

JOHN KING NORWELL

129717   Sgt   Pilot   British   54 and 41 Squadrons

Norwell was with 54 Squadron in early 1940. Over Dunkirk on May 24 he claimed a Bf 109 and on the 25th shared another.

He shared a Do 17 on July 3, shared a Bf 110 on August 18, claimed a Bf 109 destroyed on the 22nd, another probably destroyed on the 28th and shared another on the 31st. Norwell was posted to 41 Squadron at Catterick in early September and on the 27th he claimed a Bf 109. He wrote off Spitfire X 4545 when he collided with a stationary aircraft taking off on October 2.

Soon afterwards Norwell volunteered for Malta and in early November sailed in HMS 'Argus' for the Mediterranean. On the 17th he was in the first flight of six Hurricanes to take off, led by Flight Lieutenant JAF MacLachlan. Two were lost en route, when their fuel gave out. Norwell landed with two gallons left. He joined 261 Squadron at Ta Kali and was posted away on April 7 1941, flying to the Middle East as a passenger in a Wellington. Norwell ferried a Hurricane to Greece and then went to ADU, Takoradi.

He did not fly operationally again. Commissioned in July 1942, Norwell was awarded the AFC (1.1.45) and released from the RAF in 1946, as a Flight Lieutenant. He joined the RAFVR in 1947.

PO 2.7.42   FO 2.1.43   FL 2.7.44   FO (RAFVR) 8.9.47

ROBIN KEITH COLLEN NORWOOD

85232   PO   Pilot   British   65 Squadron

Joined 65 Squadron at Turnhouse on September 2 1940. Norwood was released from the RAF in 1946, as a Flight Lieutenant. He died on April 2 1970.

PO 17.8.40   FO 17.8.41   FL 17.8.42

ZBIGNIEW NOSOWICZ

76703   PO   Pilot   Polish   56 Squadron

Nosowicz was born on January 2 1914. He joined 56 Squadron at North Weald on August 31 1940. He claimed a Do 17 probably destroyed and a Bf 110 damaged on October 7.

Having overshot on landing on December 12 1940 Nosowicz climbed and his propeller hit Flying Officer KH Marston's tail. Both aircraft crashed on Middle Wallop aerodrome. Marston was killed and Nosowicz was injured.

On February 23 1941 he was posted to 316 Squadron's Operations Room and later flew with the squadron, becoming a Flight Commander on January 12 1942. He became unfit for flying and came off operations on February 10 and was posted to the staff at RAF Northolt. Nosowicz was awarded the KW (14.3.42) and invalided out in 1946.

FO 1.3.41

TADEUSZ NOWAK

76704   PO   Pilot   Polish   253 Squadron

Nowak was born on June 2 1914. He joined 253 Squadron at Kirton-in-Lindsey on July 10 1940.

He claimed a He 111 destroyed on August 31 and a Bf 110 on September 4. Nowak crashed at Gains Hill, Yalding on October 17, in Hurricane P 3537, due to engine failure. He claimed a Do 17 destroyed on the 29th. Nowak was posted to 303 Squadron at Leconfield on November 13 and moved to 315 Squadron at Acklington at its formation on January 21 1941. He was awarded the VM (5th Class)(1.2.41).

On August 19 Nowak destroyed a Bf 109. The squadron was flying as part of the Polish Wing on September 21 1941, on a circus operation covering bombers to Gosnay. The Spitfires met Bf 109s and a combat developed over Fruges and moved over the Channel towards Dover. Nowak was shot down, in Spitfire AB 927, and went into the sea near Dover. All efforts to save him failed and he was drowned. His body was later washed up near Dieppe and buried in Quiberville Communal Cemetery, France.

Nowak was awarded the KW and Bar (30.10.41) and a second Bar (31.10.47).

FO 1.3.41

EUGENIUSZ JAN ADAM NOWAKIEWICZ

P 1913   Sgt   Pilot   Polish   302 Squadron

Born in Jasle on January 2 1919, Nowakiewicz entered the PAF NCOs Training School at Bydgoszcz in 1936. He qualified as a pilot at Krosno in 1939, was posted to the 2nd Air Force Regiment at Cracow and joined 123 Fighter Squadron. After the September fighting Nowakiewicz flew his aircraft to Roumania. He reached France, joined l'Armée de l'Air and served in Vll/2 Groupe de Chasse. After the French collapse he made his way to North Africa and arrived in the UK on July 16 1940.

Nowakiewicz joined 302 Squadron at Leconfield on August 20 1940. He probably destroyed a Ju 88 on October 18 and on November 8 made a forced-landing at Detling, slightly wounded after being damaged in combat with Bf 109s. Nowakiewicz was awarded the VM (5th Class)(21.12.40) and the KW and Bar (10.9.41). He destroyed a Bf 109 on May 8 1941.

Commissioned in June 1942, he failed to return from operations on July 23 1942, after being shot down by flak at Pont de Brique, near Boulogne. Nowakiewicz was hidden by the Resistance and it was later arranged that he would fly a stolen Ju 88 to Britain but the day before it was to happen he was captured by the Gestapo. After seven months in Fresnes Prison Nowakiewicz was sent to a PoW camp at Szubin, Poland. Two months later he was moved to Stalag Luft III at Sagan. He was on the long march in the winter of 1944/5 and was freed on March 2 1945, near Lubeck.

Nowakiewicz went to 17 FTS on January 1 1946 for a flying refresher course and was released from the PAF in 1947, as a Flight Lieutenant.

PO 1.6.42   FO 1.6.43   FL 1.6.44

WILLIAM RONALD NOWELL

Sub-Lieutenant (FAA)   Pilot   British   804 Squadron

With 804 Squadron at Hatston in early July 1940, flying Sea Gladiators on dockyard defence.

On July 23 HMS 'Argus' sailed from Greenock with twelve Hurricanes and two Skuas aboard, heading for Gibraltar. On the 31st the carrier sailed for Malta, heavily escorted. At dawn on August 2 the Hurricanes took off in two groups of six, each led by a Skua, flown by an RAF pilot and navigated by, in one case, a marine pilot and in the other by a naval pilot, Nowell. His Skua crashed on landing at Luqa but both he and his pilot were unhurt.

Nowell and the marine pilot, Captain KL Ford, were attached to 431 Flight to crew the undamaged Skua on reconnaissance sorties but it proved unsuitable for the task. Nowell returned to Gibraltar in mid-November and led another six Hurricanes off the 'Argus' on the 17th, again in a Skua but this time as pilot. Two of the Hurricanes were lost en route when their fuel ran out.

In 1943 Nowell was with 820 Squadron, in 1950 he was SO (Air) at HMS 'Daedalus', in 1953 was in HMS 'Eagle' and in 1954 was in 750 Squadron at Culdrose. He retired on July 29 1958, as a Lieutenant-Commander. Nowell died on December 2 1976.

Actg Sub-Lt 13.3.39   Sub-Lt 14.3.40   Lt 13.9.41
Actg Lt-Cdr 1944   Lt-Cdr 13.9.49

TADEUSZ NOWIERSKI

76803   FO   Pilot   Polish   609 Squadron

Nowierski joined the PAF in 1929. He entered the RAF in March 1940. After converting to Spitfires he joined 609 Squadron at Middle Wallop on August 5 1940.

He claimed a Bf 109 destroyed on the 13th, a probable Do 17 on September 7, a He 111 on the 25th and a Bf 109 on the 30th. Nowierski baled out of Spitfire N 3223 over Salisbury Plain on October 5 due to undercarriage failure following a routine patrol. On the 10th he claimed a Bf 109 destroyed and on December 2 shared a Bf 110 and a Do 17.

Nowierski was awarded the KW and two Bars (1.2.41) and posted away to 316 Squadron at Pembrey on March 21 1941. He was awarded the VM (5th Class)(15.7.41) and appointed 'B' Flight Commander on August 10. He was awarded the DFC (30.10.41). From January 9 to April 30 1942 Nowierski commanded 308 Squadron at Woodvale. He then became Squadron Leader Flying of the Northolt Wing. He was awarded a third Bar to the KW (20.8.42).

On December 1 1942 Nowierski was posted to HQ 11 Group as Polish Liaison Officer, on February 15 1943 he went to an OTU, as an instructor, and on June 20 he was appointed Wing Commander Flying 2 Polish Wing. Nowierski commanded 133 Airfield from October 20 1943 to February 17 1945, when he was sent to a course at the Command and General Staff School, Fort Leavenworth, Kansas. In July Nowierski went to the Central Fighter Establishment and in 1946 he commanded RAF Dunholme Lodge, as a Group Captain. He returned to Poland on June 8 1947 and died there on April 2 1983.

FO 1.3.41   FL 1.3.42   SL 1.9.42   WC 1.9.44

STANLEY GEORGE NUNN

81935   PO   Pilot   British   236 Squadron

Born on July 25 1920, Nunn joined the RAFVR on June 23 1939, made his first flight at 3 E&RFTS, Hamble on the 25th and soloed on July 5. He was called to full-time service on September 3 and with flying training completed he joined 236 Squadron at Thorney Island in July 1940.

Tour-expired, Nunn was posted to CFS, Upavon in early 1941 for an instructor's course, after which he went to 2 (Coastal) OTU at Catfoss. In December 1943 he joined 248 Squadron at Predannack. One day in July 1944 Nunn was captain of an aircraft, leading a section escorting a naval force. He engaged a He 177 and set its port engine alight. Nunn and his navigator were both wounded and their aircraft damaged but he flew back safely to base. For this action and the completion of many sorties he was awarded the DFC (5.9.44).

In December 1944 Nunn went to the USA for a course at the Command and General Staff School at Fort Leavenworth, Kansas. He returned to the UK in May 1945 and was posted to Air Ministry, in the Accidents Branch.

Nunn held a series of appointments and commands in a long post-war career. He was made an OBE (1.1.67), received the Queen's Commendation for Services in the Air in 1968 and was ADC to Her Majesty from 1973 to 1975. Nunn retired on July 25 1975, as a Group Captain. His younger son, a Royal Marine helicopter pilot, was killed in the Falklands on May 28 1982. He was awarded the DFC.

PO 11.7.40   FO 11.7.41   FL 11.7.42   FL 1.9.45
SL 1.7.53   WC 1.7.64   GC 1.1.70

ROMILLY RONALD JAMES NUTE

523120   Sgt   Air Gunner   British   23 Squadron

With 23 Squadron at Collyweston in early July 1940. Nute was killed on March 10 1941, still with 23. He is buried in St Pierre Cemetery, Amiens, France.

REGINALD CHARLES NUTTER

108855   Sgt   Pilot   British   257 Squadron

Nutter joined the RAFVR in March 1939 and began his flying training at 3 E&RFTS, Hamble. In July he moved to 46 E&RFTS, Portsmouth for more advanced training. Called up at the outbreak of war, he was posted to 3 ITW, Hastings, moving on to 5 FTS, Sealand in October.

Awarded his flying badge in April 1940, Nutter was posted to 601 Squadron at Tangmere in May but went soon afterwards to 257 Squadron, then reforming at Hendon. He served with the squadron throughout the Battle of Britain.

In December 1940 Nutter was posted to 9 FTS, Hullavington, as an instructor. He went to Canada in February 1941 and began instructing at 34 SFTS, Medicine Hat. Commissioned in June 1941, Nutter was posted to 36 SFTS, Penhold, Alberta in November and then joined 133 (RCAF) Squadron at Lethbridge, Alberta in June 1942. He was posted to No 1 (Fighter) OTU at Bagotville, Quebec in September, as an instructor. In June 1943 Nutter went to 31 SFTS, Kingston, Ontario, to instruct FAA pupil-pilots.

He returned to the UK in February 1944 and was attached to HQ ADGB. In April Nutter was posted to 61 OTU, Rednal for a refresher course on Spitfires and in May he joined 175 Squadron, 83 Group 2nd TAF, on Typhoons. In August he went to Aston Down for a conversion course on Typhoons and then joined 245 Squadron at Antwerp. Nutter was posted back to 175 Squadron in February 1945, as 'B' Flight Commander.

In April 1945 he worked on the ground with the 7th Armoured Division, advancing from the Rhine to Lübeck. He was in a tank, equipped with nine radios, directing aircraft overhead on to specific targets or to carry out reconnaissances.

Nutter was awarded the DFC (14.9.45). He led the squadron back to Dunsfold for disbandment on September 29 1945. His final posting was to HQ 83 Group in October, as a staff officer investigating aircraft accidents within the group. He was released from the RAF in April 1946 and emigrated to Canada in June.

PO 21.6.41   FO 21.6.42   FL 21.6.43

TREVOR WALTER OAKS

391870   Sgt   Observer   New Zealander   235 Squadron

Born in Gisborne on October 17 1915, Oaks received his secondary education at Wellington Technical College and then went to work for a motor company. He volunteered for aircrew duties in early October 1939 and began training as an air gunner but in March 1940 remustered as a trainee observer.

Oaks carried out his navigation training at the Air Observers' School, Ohakea and was awarded his observers' badge and promoted to Sergeant on May 28. He sailed for the UK on June 7 in the RMS 'Rangitata'.

On July 30 Oaks was posted to 17 OTU, Upwood and after converting to Blenheims he joined 106 Squadron at Finningley on October 3 but on the 12th moved to 235 Squadron at Bircham Newton. Oaks went to 69 Squadron in Malta on May 5 1941, for general reconnaissance duties over the Mediterranean. He was posted to the Sea Rescue Flight, Middle East on December 1, operating from Benghazi and later Alexandria.

Oaks went to 294 Squadron on September 24 1943, on ASR duties, and on November 8 was posted to 76 OTU, Aqir, Palestine, as an instructor. Commissioned in April 1944, he returned to New Zealand in November and was released from the RNZAF on February 6 1945, as a Flying Officer.

PO 9.4.44   FO 9.10.44

PETER GEOFFREY St GEORGE O'BRIAN

33329   FL   Pilot   Canadian   152 and 247 Squadrons

O'Brian was born in Toronto on September 16 1917, He entered RAF College, Cranwell in January 1936 as a flight cadet. He was awarded the Sword of Honour in December 1937, when he graduated.

On December 18 O'Brian joined 26 (Army Co-operation) Squadron at Catterick. In August 1940 he volunteered for Fighter Command and joined 152 Squadron at Warmwell. On the 27th he shared in the destruction of a He 111 and on September 17 shared a Ju 88. O'Brian took command of the newly-reformed 247 Squadron at Roborough on September 24 1940. He was awarded the DFC (2.12.41) and led the squadron until May 1942.

O'Brian was awarded a Bar to the DFC (6.8.43). He stayed on after the war, was made an OBE (1.1.54) and retired on July 18 1959, as a Group Captain. He was ADC to the Queen in 1958.

PO 18.2.37   FO 18.6.39   FL 16.2.40   SL 1.12.41
WC 1.7.44   WC 1.1.49   GC 1.7.56

JOSEPH SOMERTON O'BRIEN

34171   SL   Pilot   British   92 and 234 Squadrons

The son of a major killed in France in 1917, O'Brien trained on HMS 'Conway' for a career in the Merchant Navy. He spent several years at sea before joining the RAF on a short service commission in January 1934.

After carrying out his flying training at 3 FTS, Grantham O'Brien joined 3 Squadron at Kenley on March 16 1935. He was posted to 23 Squadron at Wittering on July 9 1936.

O'Brien went to RAF Pembrey on June 9 1940 to take charge of the Operations Room. He joined 92 Squadron there on July 1, as a supernumerary Squadron Leader. He was awarded the DFC (30.7.40). On August 17 he took command of 234 Squadron at St Eval. O'Brien shared a Ju 88 on the 21st, a Bf 109 on the 24th and two more on September 6. He was shot down and killed in combat over St Mary Cray on September 7 1940. His Spitfire, P 9466, crashed near Biggin Hill.

O'Brien was 28. He is buried in St Mary Cray Cemetery, Orpington.

APO 16.3.34   PO 16.3.35   FO 16.10.36   FL 16.10.38
SL 1.6.40

PETER O'BYRNE

740334   Sgt   Pilot   British   73 and 501 Squadrons

Joined 73 Squadron at Church Fenton on June 19 1940. O'Byrne made a forced-landing near Staffhurst Wood, Limpsfield on September 27, in Hurricane P 3209, after the engine was damaged in combat with Bf 110s over Kenley.

On October 25 O'Byrne was posted to 501 Squadron at Kenley and four days later crashed near Leatherhead during a routine patrol, in Hurricane V 7595, unhurt.

O'Byrne was promoted to Warrant Officer on October 1 1941. No further service details traced.

ANTHONY O'CONNELL

43260   PO   Air Gunner   British   264 Squadron

O'Connell was born on July 9 1911. He was with 264 Squadron at Duxford in early July 1940.

His Defiant was damaged in collision with another aircraft during a scramble from Hornchurch on August 24. O'Connell was injured on October 7, when his Defiant, N 1578, crashed on take-off. Both he and his pilot were admitted to hospital.

O'Connell retired from the RAF on September 9 1958, as a Flight Lieutenant. He died on December 17 1976.

PO 7.4.40   FO 7.4.41   FL 1.4.42   FL 1.9.45

NORMAN CYRIL ODBERT

24213   SL   Pilot   British   64 Squadron

Born on June 6 1909, Odbert joined the RAF in December 1927. He was posted to 2 FTS, Digby on January 14 1928 and in early 1929 joined 26 (Army Co-operation) Squadron at Catterick. After a course at the School of Army Co-operation at Old Sarum Odbert was posted to the Middle East on September 13 1929 to 208 (Army Co-operation) Squadron at Heliopolis.

Back in the UK, Odbert went to CFS, Wittering in September 1932, for an instructor's course, following which he was posted to the staff of 504 Squadron, AuxAF, as Flying Instructor and Adjutant. He moved later to 601 Squadron, AuxAF and on February 10 1936 went to the staff of 609 Squadron, AuxAF, when it was formed at Yeadon. Odbert left the squadron in 1938 and after a spell instructing at Cranwell he was posted to Air Ministry on the staff of the Directorate, AuxAF.

In late 1939 Odbert was on the staff of 54 Group. He went to 6 OTU, Sutton Bridge in June 1940 and after converting to Spitfires took command of 64 Squadron at Kenley. He was posted away in late July to 23 WSU, Northern Ireland, remaining there until October 1941, when he went to Air Ministry, as Deputy Director, Directorate of Operational Requirements.

Odbert did this job until December 1945. He was made an OBE (13.6.46) and held a series of appointments and commands at home and overseas prior to his retirement on January 29 1957, as a Group Captain.

PO 30.12.27   FO 9.7.29   FL 1.12.33   SL 1.10.38
WC 1.12.40   GC 1.1.44   GC 1.7.47

JOHANNES ROELOF STEPHANUS OELOFSE

42519   PO   Pilot   South African   43 Squadron

Oelofse joined the RAF on a short service commission in June 1939. He was posted to 43 Squadron at Wick in February 1940.

On August 8 1940 Oelofse was shot down and killed in combat with enemy aircraft ten miles south of the Isle of Wight, in Hurricane P 3468. His body was later recovered. Oelofse was 23 years old. He is buried in St Andrew's churchyard, Tangmere.

APO 19.8.39   PO 1.2.40

JEAN HENRI MARIE OFFENBERG

82517   PO   Pilot   Belgian   145 Squadron

Offenberg was born at Laeken on July 3 1916. When the Germans invaded Belgium he was a pilot in 2 Group, 4th Squadron, 2nd Regiment d'Aéronautique. He destroyed a Do 17 on May 10. After the country was over-run he flew with other pilots and their Fiat CR 42s to France. At the request of the French the Belgians were put on aerodrome defence at Chartres.

Offenberg and fellow-Belgian, ARIG Jottard took two Caudron Simouns on June 20 and flew to Corsica, then to Phillipeville, Algeria, then to Oujda, where Belgians had set up a training school. Finding morale there to be low the two took a train to Casablanca. Here they met some other Belgians, who were trainee pilots, and some Poles. The Poles had permission to sail that evening in a cargo boat for Gibraltar. The Belgians and some French airmen slipped aboard with them. They transferred to a British ship at Gibraltar and disembarked at Liverpool on July 16 1940.

Offenberg went to 6 OTU, Sutton Bridge on the 30th and on August 17 he joined 145 Squadron at Westhampnett. He claimed Bf 109s destroyed on November 1 and 6, a He 111 on December 11 and a He 60 and a Bf 109 on May 5. Offenberg was appointed 'B' Flight Commander on May 21 1941. He was awarded the DFC in June, the first Belgian to receive one.

On June 17 Offenberg was posted to 609 Squadron at Biggin Hill. He destroyed a Bf 109 on July 7, was awarded the C de G (Belg) on the 21st and became 'B' Flight Commander on the 27th.

Whilst training a new pilot on January 22 1942, Offenberg was subjected to a mock attack by a pilot of 92 Squadron. This resulted in a collision and the tail unit of Offenberg's aircraft was cut off. He was only at 1000 feet, went into a vertical dive and was killed in the crash. He was buried with full military honours on January 26, in Scopwick Church Burial Ground, Lincolnshire. As well as his seven confirmed victories Offenberg was credited with five enemy aircraft probably destroyed and seven others damaged.

PO 30.7.40   FO 30.7.41

ALFRED KEITH OGILVIE

42872   PO   Pilot   Canadian   609 Squadron

Born in Ottawa in 1915, Ogilvie joined the RAF on a short service commission on August 11 1939. He did his ab initio course at No 1 E&RFTS, Hatfield and was posted to 9 FTS, Hullavington on November 6. After completing the course Ogilvie went to No 1 Flying Practice Unit, Meir, Staffordshire on May 16 1940, for further training. He was sent to CFS, Upavon on June 6 for an instructor's course but was then posted to 7 OTU, Hawarden, to convert to Spitfires.

Ogilvie joined 609 Squadron at Middle Wallop on August 20. He claimed a Bf 109 destroyed on September 7, shared a Do 17 on the 15th, probably destroyed Do 17s on the 24th and 25th and destroyed a Bf 110 on the 27th.

In 1941 Ogilvie destroyed a Bf 109 on May 16, shared in probably destroying a Ju 52 on the 22nd and destroyed Bf 109s on June 17 and 21. The squadron escorted bombers to Lille on July 4 1941. Ogilvie's aircraft was damaged by a Bf 109 and he was wounded, in the arm

and shoulder. He lost consciousness but came to and baled out, landing in a field. Weak from loss of blood he was unable to take up offers of French people to help him escape. Ogilvie was in hospital in Lille and Brussels for nine months and was then sent to Stalag Luft III, Sagan.

He took part part in the Great Escape but was recaptured after two days. Interrogated by the Gestapo, he was returned to the camp whilst others were shot. He insisted he was a career officer.

After the war Ogilvie transferred to the RCAF and retired on September 14 1962. He was awarded the DFC (11.7.41) and his portrait was done by Cuthbert Orde in June 1941.

APO 23.10.39   PO 25.5.40   FO 25.5.41   FL 25.5.42

DONALD BRUCE OGILVIE

83287   PO   Pilot   British   601 Squadron

Ogilvie joined 601 Squadron at Debden on August 31 1940. Landing after a training flight on September 24 he overshot the runway and overturned. He was slightly injured and admitted to hospital.

In May 1941 Ogilvie was appointed a Flight Commander. He was posted away in October to the Fighter Leaders' School, as an instructor. In January 1942 he went to the Westland Aircraft Co as Liaison Test Pilot on Whirlwinds and then joined 137 Squadron, operating in these aircraft from Matlask. Ogilvie was posted to No 1 (Fighter) Group USAAF in May 1942, as Liaison Officer, moving later to 82 (Fighter) Group. He returned to operations with Whirlwinds, when he joined 263 Squadron at Warmwell in October.

In February 1943 Ogilvie went to No 1 Specialised Low Attack Instructors' School at Berwick and in April took a Close Support Unit to the Middle East and joined 6 Squadron in the Close Support (Anti-Tank) Group at Derna. Ogilvie was posted to HQ Eastern Mediterranean in July 1943, as Squadron Leader Ops and Air Support Officer for SAS operations.

He was Senior Air Officer in the invasion of the Dodecanese Islands in November 1943 and was captured in the German counter-attack. After being held in Athens Ogilvie was transferred to Germany and was in various PoW camps, the last being at Vogelgesand, from where he was released by the Russians.

Ogilvie returned to England in May 1945 and was invalided out of the RAF in July. He received two Mentions in Despatches and was awarded the US Silver Star and the Air Medal with Oak Leaves.

PO 17.8.40   FO 17.8.41   FL 17.8.42

TREVOR GUEST OLDFIELD

819030   Sgt   Pilot   British   64 and 92 Squadrons

Joined 64 Squadron at Leconfield in early September 1940 and moved soon afterwards to 92 Squadron at Biggin Hill. Oldfield was shot down and killed by enemy aircraft on September 27. His Spitfire, R 6622, crashed at Fullers House, Hesketh Park, Dartford and exploded on impact.

Oldfield was 21 years old. He is buried in St Stephen's Church Burial Ground, Chertsey, Surrey.

ARTHUR ALEXANDER O'LEARY

54654   LAC   Radar Operator   British   604 Squadron

At the outbreak of war O'Leary was under training as an air gunner with 217 Squadron, a general reconnaissance unit at St Eval. In early March 1940 he joined a Blenheim squadron in France, as a Wireless Operator (Air).

Back in England after the French collapse O'Leary volunteered for aircrew duties of a secret nature. In June 1940 he went to Yatesbury for a short radar course and was then posted to 604 Squadron at Northolt on July 1.

In an engagement at night on December 20 O'Leary baled out, wounded in the leg, after his aircraft was hit by return fire. He was admitted to hospital. O'Leary was again wounded on May 1 1941. The pilot, Flying Officer IKS Joll, closed in to attack an enemy aircraft and O'Leary was severely wounded by return fire, having five bullet wounds in the leg. In spite of his wounds he rendered valuable assistance to Joll, enabling him to get the aircraft safely back to base. O'Leary was awarded the DFM (30.5.41).

In July 1941 he was posted away to 89 Squadron, then forming at Colerne for service in the Middle East. O'Leary was awarded the DFC (16.2.43), having then assisted in the destruction of at least seven enemy aircraft. On February 20 1943 he assisted in destroying a Ju 88 and damaging a second and on the 26th he assisted in destroying another. He was awarded a Bar to the DFC (14.5.43), credited with assisting in the destruction of fourteen enemy aircraft at night.

O'Leary flew back to the UK in July 1943 and was posted to 62 OTU, Ouston, as an instructor. He returned to operations on February 5 1944, joining 239 Squadron at West Raynham, operating in Mosquitos on bomber support duties. Commissioned in April 1944, O'Leary was awarded a second Bar to the DFC (14.11.44) and posted away to a GCA Development Unit on November 29 1944.

He was released from the RAF in 1946, as a Flying Officer.

PO 9.4.44   FO 9.10.44

WILFRID PALLASEN OLESEN

42570   PO   Pilot   British   607 Squadron

Olesen joined the RAF on a short service commission in June 1939 and was posted to 607 Squadron in France in March 1940.

He transferred to the Technical Branch (Armament) in early 1941 and continued with it until he died on July 6 1950, as a Wing Commander.

APO 19.8.39   PO 28.2.40   FO 28.2.41   FL 28.2.42
SL 1.9.45   WC 1.1.49

ZBIGNIEW OLENSKI

76617   FO   Pilot   Polish   234 and 609 Squadrons

Born on November 13 1907, Olenski graduated from Warsaw University with a Diploma in Engineering and then worked for the Aeronautical Technical Institute.

Olenski was in charge of scientific research into aeroplane performance and was a test pilot, specialising in fighters, and was a pilot in the PAF Reserve. After the collapse of Poland in September 1939 he went to France, via Roumania. Olenski was selected for service in Britain and arrived at Eastchurch in December 1939.

He joined 234 Squadron at Middle Wallop on August 14 1940. He claimed a Bf 109 probably destroyed on the 24th and a Bf 110 destroyed on September 4. Olenski was posted to 609 Squadron, also at Middle Wallop, on the 5th. He submitted a report on the shortcomings of the Spitfire MK 1 and suggested modifications, which were accepted and implemented. On the basis of this report Olenski was attached to the RAE, Farnborough on March 28 1941. He worked in the Aerodynamics Department and reached the position of Senior Aerodynamicist. On July 1 1942 he was attached to 316 Squadron at Heston for two weeks.

On October 29 1945 Olenski was attached to the Central Fighter Establishment and from June 4 1946 to HQ Fighter Command. He was released in March 1947, as a Flight Lieutenant. He joined AV Roe in Manchester, as an aerodynamicist, and worked on several projects, including the Vulcan bomber.

Olenski suffered a stroke in 1960 and died on June 20 1970.

FO 1.3.41   FL 1.9.41

BOLESLAW OLEWINSKI

780695   Sgt   Pilot   Polish   111 Squadron

Born in Jersey City, USA on October 26 1919, Olewinski entered the PAF NCOs Training School at Bydgoszcz in 1936. He qualified as a pilot at Krosno in 1939, was posted to the 1st Air Force Regiment, Warsaw and joined 114 Fighter Squadron.

Olewinski was shot down and wounded on September 1 1939. He was evacuated with other hospital patients to Roumania. After eventually reaching France he went on to England, arriving on February 20 1940. He continued training and then joined 111 Squadron at Dyce on October 19. He was killed on November 3 1940, when he was shot down by return fire from a He 111 engaged thirty miles east of Rock Point. His Hurricane, V 6560, crashed into the sea.

Olewinski is remembered on the Polish Air Force Memorial at Northolt.

CHARLES GORDON CHALONER OLIVE

39469   FL   Pilot   Australian   65 Squadron

Born in Bardon, Queensland on July 3 1916, Olive trained with the RAAF in 1935/36. He transferred into the RAF in February 1937 and after a three months course at 2 FTS, Digby he joined 65 Squadron at Hornchurch.

Over Dunkirk on May 26 1940 Olive probably destroyed a Bf 109. He claimed a Bf 109 destroyed on July 20, probably another on August 12, two more destroyed on the 13th, another probably destroyed on the 14th, a probable Ju 88 on the 16th, a probable Bf 109 on the 24th and a Bf 110 on the 26th. Olive was awarded the DFC (24.9.40). He destroyed a Bf 110 on December 9.

In June 1941 Olive was given the job of forming and then commanding 456 Squadron at Valley, initially with Defiants but later Beaufighters. After being posted away from the squadron in March 1942 Olive returned to Australia later in the year. In 1944 he was at Air Defence HQ, Sydney and in 1945 at Air Defence HQ, Morotai.

Olive died in Australia in 1987.

PO 19.2.37   FO 19.8.38 FL 19.8.40   SL 1.9.41

GEORGE DIXON OLIVER

936196   Sgt   Air Gunner   British   23 Squadron

Oliver, of Gosforth, was with 23 Squadron at Collyweston in early July 1940. He was killed with the squadron on September 8 1941, as a Flight Sergeant. He was 26 and is buried in Kerfautras Cemetery, Brest.

PETER OLVER

84963   PO   Pilot   British   603 Squadron

Olver joined 603 Squadron at Hornchurch in October 1940. On the 25th he was shot down by Bf 109s over Hastings and baled out, wounded, landing at Westfield. His Spitfire, P 7309, landed at Pickdick Farm, Brede.

On November 11 1940 Olver probably destroyed a Ju 87 and during the month is believed to have shared a Bf 110 and a Do 17.

P Olver (continued)

He was posted to 66 Squadron at Biggin Hill in December 1940. Olver shared a He 111 on May 27 and probably destroyed a Bf 109 on August 20.

In June 1942 he was posted to the Middle East and joined 238 Squadron in the Western Desert on July 2, as a Flight Commander. Olver went to 213 Squadron on October 13, as supernumerary Squadron Leader. He destroyed a Ju 87, probably another and damaged a third on November 2 and destroyed three CR 42s on the ground at Agedabia on the 14th. Olver took command of 213 on the 24th but was given command of No 1 (SAAF) Squadron on December 27. He was awarded the DFC (5.1.43), destroyed a Mc 202 on January 21 1943 and was posted to 244 Wing on February 5, as Squadron Leader Flying.

After Wing Commander IR Gleed was killed on April 16 Olver took over temporarily. He shared a Mc 205 on the 17th. He was promoted on May 2 1943 and his appointment as Wing Commander Flying 244 Wing was confirmed. Over Italy on July 11 1943 Olver destroyed two Bf 109s but was then himself shot down and captured.

He was released from the RAF in 1947, as a Squadron Leader. Olver lived in Kenya for some time but later returned to the UK.

PO 7.9.40   FO 7.9.41   FL 7.9.42   SL 17.7.43

DEREK KEPPEL COLERIDGE O'MALLEY

72475   FO   Pilot   British   264 Squadron

A pre-war member of the RAFVR, O'Malley was with 264 Squadron in early July 1940. On August 24 his Defiant was damaged in collision with another aircraft during a scramble from Hornchurch. O'Malley and his gunner were unhurt.

In the evening of September 4 1940 he was the pilot of Defiant N 1628, ordered to take off on an interception patrol. The aircraft crashed shortly after taking off and O'Malley and his gunner, Sergeant LAW Rasmussen were both killed.

O'Malley was 29. He is buried in Kirton-in-Lindsey Burial Ground, Lincolnshire.

PO (RAFVR) 11.10.38   PO 18.9.39   FO 1.5.40

JAMES JOSEPH O'MEARA

40844   FO   Pilot   British   64 and 72 Sqdns, 421 Flight

O'Meara was born in Barnsley, Yorkshire on February 20 1919. He joined the RAF on a short service commission on April 3 1938. He was posted to 9 FTS, Hullavington on June 18 and joined 64 Squadron at Church Fenton on January 14 1939.

Over Dunkirk on May 31 1940 he destroyed a Bf 109. On July 19 he claimed a Bf 109 destroyed, on August 11 a probable Bf 109, on the 15th a Bf 109 and on the 18th a Ju 88 and shared another. O'Meara was posted to 72 Squadron at Biggin Hill on September 20 and awarded the DFC (24.9.40). He claimed a Do 17 destroyed on the 27th and then joined 421 Flight on October 3 at its formation at Hawkinge.

Flying a high performance blue-painted Spitfire on November 26 O'Meara shot down a He 59 into the Channel. He destroyed a Bf 109 that was attacking a minesweeper on December 5 and damaged another. He was awarded a Bar to the DFC (18.3.41) and on April 9 he destroyed another He 59. Later in the month O'Meara rejoined 64 Squadron, as a Flight Commander.

In April 1943 he was given command of 131 Squadron at Castletown and remained with it until May 1944. He was awarded the DSO (27.10.44), being then credited with twelve enemy aircraft destroyed.

O'Meara retired from the RAF on July 31 1959, as a Squadron Leader.

*APO 3.4.38   PO 4.4.39   FO 3.9.40   FL 3.9.41
SL 1.1.44   FL 21.1.45   SL 1.7.53*

RUPERT JOHN OMMANEY

742538   Sgt   Pilot   British   229 Squadron

With 229 Squadron at Wittering in early July 1940. Ommaney claimed a Bf 110 destroyed and a Do 215 shared on September 15.

He was one of a section of three Hurricanes, which attacked a He 59 floatplane flying low off the coast in the vicinity of Boulogne on October 26. The enemy aircraft alighted on the sea with three of its crew of four killed. The Hurricanes were then attacked from the rear by Bf 109s and fired on by guns from the shore. Ommaney made off at low level across the Channel and reached his base. The section-leader, Flying Officer GM Simpson, was never heard of again and the third pilot, Flying Officer DBH McHardy, was later reported captured.

Ommaney was killed on February 12 1942, as a Warrant Officer with 607 Squadron. He was 26 and is remembered on the Runnymede Memorial, Panel 72.

DESMOND HUGH O'NEILL

40638   FO   Pilot   British   611 and 41 Squadrons

O'Neill joined the RAF on a short service commission in January 1938. He was posted to 10 FTS, Tern Hill on April 9 and joined 2 AACU at Lee-on-Solent on October 29 1938.

He went to 611 Squadron at Digby on August 20 1940 and moved to 41 Squadron at Hornchurch on September 29. O'Neill was involved in a collision with Sergeant LR Carter during a battle climb to engage Bf 109s. He baled out but was killed when his parachute failed to open. His Spitfire, X 4042, crashed near the Crooked Billet, Ash.

O'Neill was 25. He is buried in Streatham Park Cemetery, Mitcham.

APO 26.3.38   PO 17.1.39   FO 17.8.40

JOHN ANTHONY O'NEILL

37117   FL   Pilot   British   601 and 238 Squadrons

Born on October 7 1915, O'Neill joined the RAF on a short service commission on March 15 1935. He was posted to 5 FTS, Sealand on April 1 and joined 99 Squadron at Mildenhall on February 29 1936. From early February until mid-July 1937 O'Neill was off flying with a wrist injury. He was posted to 58 Squadron at Boscombe Down on July 16 1937.

O'Neill took part in the first incursion into Germany of the war, when Whitleys of 58 Squadron made a leaflet raid on the night of September 3/4 1939. He operated with the squadron until June 22 1940, when he was posted away to be OC Flying at the Central Landing School at Ringway. O'Neill was awarded the DFC (30.7.40) for his work with 58.

On October 4 he joined 601 Squadron at Exeter to convert to Hurricanes, after which he was posted to 238 Squadron at Chilbolton, as a Flight Commander. O'Neill rejoined 601 Squadron at Northolt on December 14 1940, to command. He shot down a Bf 109 on April 16 1941 and was then himself shot down, ditching in the sea off Dungeness, with leg wounds.

After hospital and convalescence O'Neill rejoined 238 Squadron at Tangmere on June 13, as a Flight Commander. He was posted away on November 24, to become OC Flying at 60 OTU, East Fortune. On February 5 1942 O'Neill was appointed Wing Commander Training at HQ 10 Group, Rudloe Manor. He was posted to India in August 1942. He commanded 293 Wing at Alipore until January 15 1943, when he took command of 176 Squadron, then forming at Dum Dum from a detachment of 89 Squadron. When the squadron moved to Baigachi in February O'Neill also became Station Commander there. He left the squadron on July 23 1943 and was invalided home at the end of the year.

From February 1 1944 until June 23 1945 O'Neill was Station Commander at West Malling and later Bradwell Bay. He retired from the RAF on November 29 1957, as a Wing Commander, retaining the rank of Group Captain.

*APO 15.3.35   PO 15.3.36   FO 15.10.37   FL 15.10.39
SL 1.12.40   WC 14.8.42   WC 1.7.47*

HAROLD CHARLES ORCHARD

523288   Sgt   Pilot   British   65 Squadron

A pre-war airman pilot, Orchard was with 65 Squadron at Hornchurch in early July 1940.

He served with 65 throughout the Battle of Britain and was killed with the squadron on February 5 1941. Orchard was 24. He is buried in Neufchatel New Cemetery, Neufchatel-Hardelot, France.

ERIC ORGIAS

36272   PO   Pilot   New Zealander   23 Squadron

Orgias was born in Palmerston North on November 23 1914. After leaving High School there he worked for a local farmer before going to Massey Agricultural College, where he obtained a diploma in sheep farming in 1936.

In February 1938 Orgias joined the Civil Reserve of Pilots and did his required forty hours of flying at the Middle Districts Aero Club. He applied for an RNZAF short service commission in March 1939 but did not report to the Ground Training School at Rongotai until September 20, in the last intake of the short service scheme.

On October 24 Orgias was posted to No 1 FTS, Wigram. He was awarded his flying badge in January 1940 and sailed for the UK in early March on the SS 'Remuera'. On arrival at the RAF Depot at Uxbridge on April 13 Orgias relinquished his RNZAF commission and transferred to the RAF.

He was posted to 5 OTU, Aston Down on May 5 1940, converted to Blenheims and then joined 23 Squadron at Collyweston on June 12. During a night patrol on September 25 Orgias reported that he was returning with one engine running badly. He reached his base area at Middle Wallop but crashed near Broughton, Hampshire. Orgias and his crew of two were killed. As he was preparing to land it is believed that he stalled after turning away to make a wide approach into wind, possibly due to the failure of the port engine.

Orgias is buried in Over Wallop churchyard.

APO 20.9.39   PO 13.4.40

VICTOR ORTMANS

82161   PO   Pilot   Belgian   229 Squadron

Ortmans was a pilot in the Belgian Air Force. He was in 7/IIIe, an army co-operation squadron equipped with Fairey Foxes. The squadron moved to an advanced airfield near Liège on May 10 1940 but was completely wiped out by enemy action, mostly on the ground on the 12th. The pilots escaped to France but no replacement aircraft were found for them.

On June 21 the French signed an Armistice with the Germans and the Belgians were told to stay put. With other pilots Ortmans reached Port Vendres, from where with the help of a British destroyer and the support of the Belgian Embassy in London they caught a passing convoy and embarked on the SS 'Apapa' on the 24th. After arriving in Liverpool on July 7 Ortmans was commissioned in the RAF on the 19th.

He was posted to 7 OTU, Hawarden on the 30th and after converting to Hurricanes joined 229 Squadron at Wittering on August 10. Ortmans claimed a share in the destruction of a Do 17 on September 15, a He 111 destroyed on the 27th and a Do 17 destroyed and a Bf 109 probably destroyed on the 30th. On this day he was hit by return fire from a Do 17 and made a forced-landing on the beach at Lydd.

On April 7 1941 Ortmans was posted to 609 Squadron at Biggin Hill. He shared a Bf 109 on May 21 and destroyed Bf 109s on June 4 and 30, July 3 and August 18. The one shot down in July was flown by Hauptmann Wilhem Balthasar, an ace of JG 2. Ortmans was awarded the C de G (Belg)(21.7.41).

On an escort operation on August 19 he crashed into the sea and was picked up by an ASR launch. Towards the end of the month he was again down in the sea and was rescued by the same launch. Ortmans was awarded the DFC in September. He was shot down in combat with Bf 109s and FW 190s on a sortie to Boulogne on October 21 1941. He baled out, badly wounded, and spent two days and a night in his dinghy before being picked up by the Germans and becoming a PoW.

Ortmans was killed in 1948 in a flying accident in a training aircraft.

PO 19.7.40   FO 19.7.41   FL 19.7.42

JERZY ORZECHOWSKI

76825   FL   Pilot   Polish   615 and 607 Squadrons

Born on May 12 1905. Orzechowski was initially posted to 303 Squadron at Northolt on September 16 1940 and went to 6 OTU, Sutton Bridge on the 21st. After converting to Hurricanes he joined 615 Squadron at Prestwick on October 3 and then moved to 607 Squadron at Turnhouse on the 16th. A series of squadron moves followed; to 306 on the 22nd, to 245 on November 15, back to 615 on the 29th and to 308 Squadron at Baginton on December 5, as supernumerary Squadron Leader.

Orzechowski took command of the squadron on the 8th and led it until June 23 1941, when he was posted to RAF Middle Wallop. On July 23 he went to HQ 81 Group, as Polish Liaison Officer. Preparing for a return to operations, Orzechowski was posted to 51 OTU, Cranfield on August 13 1942 for night-fighter training. He joined 23 Squadron at Bradwell Bay on September 25. Orzechowski was given command of 307 Squadron at Exeter on April 1 1943. He was awarded the KW and two Bars (7.7.43). On September 11 he probably destroyed a Bf 110 and damaged three others. He was awarded the VM (5th Class)(20.10.43) and posted away to the PAF Staff College on November 7 1943 for a course.

Awarded the DFC (15.5.44), Orzechowski went to HQ Fighter Command on October 20 1944 and was Polish Air Attaché in Paris from May 1945 until returning to HQ Fighter Command on September 10 for liaison duties.

Orzechowski was released from the PAF in January 1947, as a Wing Commander. He settled in Canada and died there in 1988.

FL 3.5.40   SL 1.3.43   WC 1.9.44

ALEXANDER GORDON OSMAND

79169   PO   Pilot   British   213 and 3 Squadrons

Osmand, of London, was with 213 Squadron at Exeter in early July 1940. On August 11 the hydraulic system of his Hurricane, N 2708, was damaged by return fire from a Ju 88 engaged over Portland. He crashed on landing back at base. Two days later Osmand claimed a Bf 109 destroyed.

He was killed on October 20 1943, as a Flight Lieutenant with 261 Squadron, operating in Hurricane IIcs in Burma. Osmand was 28. He is buried in Chittagong War Cemetery.

PO 12.5.40   FO 12.5.41   FL 12.5.42

PIOTR OSTASZEWSKI-OSTOJA

76741   FO   Pilot   Polish   609 Squadron

Ostaszewski-Ostoja was born on May 19 1910. After converting to Hurricanes at 5 OTU, Aston Down he joined 609 Squadron at Middle Wallop on August 5 1940. He claimed two Ju 87s probably destroyed on the 13th and a Bf 110 destroyed two days later.

On August 25 Ostaszewski-Ostoja returned to Warmwell in Spitfire R 6986, badly damaged by cannon fire from a Bf 110 engaged over Swanage. With flaps damaged he overshot the runway and crashed through the boundary hedge, slightly wounded in one arm. He was awarded the KW (1.2.41). Ostaszewski-Ostoja was posted away on March 7 1941 to the Operations Room of 317 Squadron at Acklington. He continued on Operations Room duties until September 16 1942, firstly at 303 Squadron and then at 302. He was then posted to 308 Squadron at Heston for flying duties.

Ostaszewski-Ostoja went to 306 Squadron at Catterick on June 1 1943. He was posted to 12 (P) AFU at Grantham on August 17, for conversion to Blenheims, after which he went to 51 OTU, Cranfield for night-fighter training. On February 8 1944 Ostaszewski-Ostoja joined 85 Squadron at West Malling, flying Mosquitos. A number of squadron postings followed; to 125 Squadron on April 30, to 501 Squadron on August 15 and to 307 Squadron at Church Fenton on September 25. Ostaszewski-Ostoja was awarded a Bar to the KW (30.12.44).

On April 23 he was posted to HQ 12 Group, as Ops Night, a Wing Commander post. After being attached to HQ 11 Group from May 28 1945 Ostaszewski-Ostoja went to HQ 229 Group South-East Asia. He was with 78 Squadron from December 12 1945, on transport duties. He was awarded a second Bar to the KW (5.1.46). He returned to the UK in July 1946 and then served with 301 Squadron on transport work from October 26 until its disbandment on December 10 1946. Ostaszewski-Ostoja was released at the end of the year, as a Wing Commander. He settled in England and changed his name to Raymond.

FO 1.3.41   FL 1.9.42

ANTONI OSTOWICZ

76705   FO   Pilot   Polish   145 Squadron

Joined 145 Squadron at Tangmere on July 16 1940. Ostowicz shared in destroying a He 111 on the 19th.

He was shot down in combat with enemy fighters on August 11 1940, in Hurricane V 7294, which is believed to have crashed on the Isle of Wight. Ostowicz was reported 'Missing', aged 29. He was awarded the KW and Bar (1.2.41) and is remembered on the Polish Air Force Memorial at Northolt.

CHARLES NEVIL OVERTON

40639   FO   Pilot   British   609 Squadron

Overton joined the RAF on a short service commission in January 1938. He did his elementary flying at 13 E&RFTS, White Waltham, moved to 8 FTS, Montrose on April 9 and with the course completed he was posted to the School of Naval Co-operation at Ford on October 29.

In late September 1939 Overton joined 17 Squadron at Debden. He moved to 609 Squadron at Drem in late November. Over Dunkirk on May 31 1940 he destroyed a Bf 109 and shared a He 111. Overton claimed a Bf 109 destroyed on August 12 and two Ju 87s on the 13th. He was appointed 'A' Flight Commander on February 22 1941 and soon afterwards was posted to 59 OTU, Crosby-on-Eden, as an instructor.

In December 1941 Overton joined 145 Squadron at Catterick, as a Flight Commander. He went with it to the Middle East in February 1942 and took command in April at Helwan. It became operational in early June, the first Spitfire squadron in the Western Desert. On June 3 Overton damaged a Bf 109 and on the 10th he destroyed one.

He was posted away to 239 Wing Desert Air Force in August 1942 and was awarded the DFC (6.10.42). After leaving the Wing Overton was at HQ Desert Air Force, as Wing Commander Ops. In late 1944 he was posted to Malta on officer training.

Overton returned to the UK in September 1945 and was released from the RAF in June 1946, as a Wing Commander.

APO 26.3.38   PO 17.1.39   FO 3.9.40   FL 3.9.41
SL 1.1.44

ARTHUR EDWARD OWEN

1163347   Sgt   Air Gunner   British   600 Squadron

Owen, of Birmingham, joined 600 Squadron at Manston on July 19 1940. He was killed on July 24 1941, as a Sergeant with 103 Squadron, operating in Wellingtons from Elsham Wolds. He was 25 and is remembered on the Runnymede Memorial, Panel 49.

HENRY OWEN

56204   Sgt   Wop/AG   British   219 and 235 Sqdns

Born in Durham on June 4 1921, Owen joined the RAF in 1938, as a boy entrant. He went to No 1 Electrical and Wireless School at Cranwell and passed out as AC 1 in September 1939. After qualifying as an air gunner at No 1 Air Armament School at Manby in October he joined 219 Squadron at Catterick.

Owen was promoted to LAC in February 1940 and to Sergeant in May. He was posted to 235 Squadron when 219 converted to Beaufighters in September. Owen left 235 in July 1941 and was sent on a flying boat conversion course. He joined 413 (RCAF) Squadron in October, to fly in Catalinas.

In February 1942 Owen went to 240 Squadron and operated in Catalinas in the Mediterranean and later South-East Asia. He was rested in December and posted to the Communications Flight at Air HQ Bangalore. He later became a Wop/AG instructor on Vengeances at Peshawar, moving in May 1943 to instruct at the Gunnery School at Bhopal.

Owen was commissioned from Warrant Officer and went on a Liberator conversion course in September 1944 and then joined 356 Squadron. He flew operationally in Burma, Malaya and Siam until May 1945. He went to Air HQ Burma in August and returned to the UK in March 1946. Owen retired from the RAF on July 15 1955, as a Flight Lieutenant. He worked in the UK on Flight Simulators and then emigrated to New Zealand in 1962.

PO 20.9.44   FO 20.3.45   FO 20.9.45   FL 4.1.51

WILLIAM GETHIN OWEN

103386   Sgt   Air Gunner   British   235 Squadron

Joined 235 Squadron in March 1940. Owen was flying in Blenheim Z 5736 on August 24, when it was attacked by Hurricanes of No 1 (RCAF) Squadron over Thorney Island. The aircraft was badly damaged and crashed on landing. Owen and his pilot, Sergeant KE Naish, were unhurt.

Posted away from 235 in December 1940, Owen was commissioned in July 1941. He was awarded the DFC (20.7.45), as a Flight Lieutenant with 48 Squadron. He was released from the RAF in 1946, as a Flight Lieutenant.

PO 31.7.41   FO 31.7.42   FL 31.7.43

ROBERT WARDLOW OXSPRING

40743   FO   Pilot   British   66 Squadron

The son of a 1914-18 war fighter ace, Oxspring was born in Sheffield on May 22 1919. He joined the RAF on a short service commission in March 1938. After completing his ab initio course at 4 E&RFTS, Brough Oxspring went to 2 FTS, Brize Norton on May 21. He joined 66 Squadron at Duxford on December 17.

He was still with 66 in early July 1940. On the 29th Oxspring shared in destroying a He 111, on September 11 claimed a He 111 destroyed, on the 15th a Do 17, on the 18th a Bf 109, on the 24th a He 111, on the 27th a Bf 110, on the 30th a Bf 109 and two more on October 5 and 13. Oxspring was shot down by Bf 109s over Tunbridge Wells on the 25th and baled out, slightly injured. His Spitfire, X 4170, crashed into an orchard near Capel. He was awarded the DFC (8.11.40).

Oxspring, who had been appointed a Flight Commander in September, was posted away to 59 OTU, Crosby-on-Eden in April 1941, as an instructor and Flight Commander. He returned to operations in September, joining 616 Squadron at Westhampnett but after only a week moved to 41 Squadron at Merston, as a Flight Commander. In January 1942 Oxspring took command of 91 Squadron at Hawkinge. He was given command of 72 Squadron at Biggin Hill in July 1942 and on the 26th he probably destroyed a Bf 109. He was detached temporarily to command 222 Squadron at Winfield in August and took part in operations over Dieppe. Awarded a Bar to the DFC (18.9.42), Oxspring led 72 Squadron to Gibraltar in November and on the 16th it flew into Algiers, beginning patrols the next day.

On the 22nd Oxspring was shot down and made a forced-landing eight miles east of Beja. He probably destroyed a Bf 109 on the 25th, destroyed a Bf 109 on December 5, a FW 190 on the 22nd and probably destroyed a Bf 109 on January 2 1943. Oxspring was awarded a second Bar to the DFC (16.2.43). He shared a Bf 109 on March 1 and destroyed another on April 11. Later in the month he was posted to HQ 242 Group, situated in caravans and tents at Medjez, coordinating Army requests for air support.

Late in 1943 Oxspring returned to the UK and went to HQ Fighter Command in the Tactics and Training Branch. He was promoted in March 1944 and appointed Wing Leader 24 Wing. Between June 23 and July 16 Oxspring destroyed 4 V1s over London and Kent. In September 1944 he went to lead 141 Wing at Deanland and when it was disbanded he was made leader of the Detling Wing.

In May 1945 Oxspring was posted to CFE, Tangmere and later in the year he was sent for a course to the Command and General Staff School at Fort Leavenworth, Kansas. Oxspring was awarded the AFC (1.1.49) and retired from the RAF on February 29 1968, as a Group Captain.

APO 7.5.38   PO 7.3.39   FO 3.9.40   FL 3.9.41
SL 1.1.44   SL 1.8.47   WC 1.1.53   GC 1.1.60

ALAN GEOFFREY PAGE

74709   FO   Pilot   British   56 Squadron

Page was born at Boxmoor, Hertfordshire on May 16 1920. He was educated at Cheltenham College and London University, where he was doing an engineering course. Whilst there he learned to fly at Northolt, with the University Air Squadron.

Called to full-time service in mid-September 1939, Page was posted to ITW, Hastings in October. He went to FTS, Cranwell in mid-November. At the end of the course in May 1940 he was posted to No 1 Fighter Pilot Unit at Meir for further training. A few days later he joined 66 Squadron but on June 6 moved to 56 Squadron at Digby.

On July 13 Page claimed a Bf 109 destroyed, on the 20th he shared a Ju 88 and on the 25th he shared a Ju 87. During an attack on Do 17s ten miles north of Margate on August 12 Page was shot down and baled out, badly burned. He was rescued by tender and transferred to the Margate lifeboat. His Hurricane, P 2970, crashed in flames two miles off Epple Bay.

Page was in hospital for over two years. He underwent plastic surgery at Queen Victoria Hospital, East Grinstead and was a founder-member of the Guinea Pig Club. In late 1942, with a limited flying category, he was posted to an army co-operation squadron in Wales. After three months Page applied for another medical board and was given an A1B category.

He was posted to 132 Squadron at Hornchurch in early 1943, as supernumerary Flight Lieutenant. He volunteered for service in North Africa but after three months there the heat of the sun was too much for his grafted skin. Page returned to England and was posted to AFDU at Wittering. On June 29 1943, in company with Squadron Leader JAF MacLachlan, he flew a Mustang on a daylight sortie, in the course of which he destroyed a Hs 126 and shared a Ju 88. On

a second sortie on July 18 MacLachlan failed to return. Page was awarded the DFC (30.7.43).

After a further spell at East Grinstead he was posted to 122 Squadron, as a Flight Commander. In January 1944 Page was given command of 132 Squadron at Detling. He took the squadron to France in June and on July 7 was promoted and became leader of a Wing of four squadrons.

In September Page crashed on landing, injured his face on his gunsight and fractured his back. He was flown back to England and taken to the Queen Victoria Hospital at East Grinstead. He was awarded the DSO (29.12.44), being then credited with fifteen enemy aircraft destroyed. In January 1945 Page was sent on a lecture tour to the USA. He returned to the UK in April and went into hospital to have a piece of cannon shell removed from his leg that had been there since August 1940. Fit again, Page was attached to Vickers-Armstrong at Weybridge, as a test pilot.

Granted a Permanent Commission in 1946, Page was selected for a course at the Empire Test Pilots' School. It was postponed and after a Senior Officers Administration Course he was posted as PA to the senior RAF Officer on the Military Staff Commission at the UN in New York. He retired from the RAF on December 1 1948, as a Squadron Leader, and joined Vickers-Armstrong as a sales executive.

PO 8.11.39   FO 3.10.40   FL 3.10.41   SL 12.10.44
SL 1.8.47

ANTHONY DURRANT PAGE

745566   Sgt   Pilot   British   111 and 257 Squadrons

Page joined 111 Squadron at Debden on August 31 1940 and moved to 257 Squadron at Martlesham Heath on September 28. He was killed on November 8 1940, when his Hurricane, V 6870, crashed and burned out in Day's Cornfield, Stelling Minnis during a squadron patrol.

Page was 21 years old and is buried in Folkestone New Cemetery, Hawkinge.

ARTHUR JOHN PAGE

745411   Sgt   Pilot   British   257 Squadron

Page, of Horton Kirby, Kent, joined 257 Squadron at Debden on September 1 1940. He was killed on October 24 1941, as a Flight Sergeant with 101 Squadron, operating in Wellingtons from Oakington.

Page was 25. He is buried in Ostende Communal Cemetery, Belgium.

CYRIL LESLIE PAGE

37205   FL   Pilot   British   234 and 145 Squadrons

Joined the RAF on a short service commission in April 1935. Page was posted to 2 FTS, Digby on May 7 and on completion of the course he joined the staff at the School of Army Co-operation at Old Sarum. Page went to 16 (Army Co-operation) Squadron there on June 21 1938.

He was with 234 Squadron at St Eval in early July 1940, went to 145 Squadron on the 31st but rejoined 234, then at Middle Wallop, on August 19.

Page commanded 174 Squadron at Manston and Fowlmere from May to August 1942. He was released from the RAF in 1947, as a Squadron Leader.

APO 16.4.35   PO 16.4.36   FO 16.1.38   FL 16.1.40
SL 1.3.42

VERNON DOUGLAS PAGE

65502   Sgt   Pilot   British   601 and 610 Squadrons

Initially with 601 Squadron, Page joined 610 Squadron at Acklington on October 17 1940.

Commissioned in April 1941, he was awarded the DFC (19.5.44), as a Flight Lieutenant with 11 Squadron, operating in Hurricane IIcs in Burma. Page received a Bar to the DFC (3.4.45), still with 11 Squadron. He was released from the RAF in 1946, as a Squadron Leader. He served in the RAuxAF after the war.

PO 9.4.41   FO 9.4.42   FL 9.4.43   FL (RAuxAF) 14.11.48

WILFRID THOMAS PAGE

65992   Sgt   Pilot   British   1 Squadron

Page, of Epsom, Surrey, joined No 1 Squadron at Wittering on October 1 1940. In an engagement with a Do 17 on the 29th, in Hurricane P 3318, the glycol system was damaged by return fire and Page made a forced-landing at Orton, near Peterborough, writing the aircraft off.

Commissioned in May 1941, Page was killed on November 16 1943, as a Squadron Leader with 126 Squadron, operating in Spitfires from Grottaglie, Italy. He was 29 and is remembered on the Malta Memorial, Panel 6, Column 1.

PO 1.5.41   FO 18.3.42   FL 5.8.42

JOHN FRANCIS PAIN

43291   PO   Pilot   Australian   32 Squadron

Joined 32 Squadron at Biggin Hill on August 2 1940. Pain claimed a Ju 88 destroyed on the 16th and a Do 17 on the 18th. On this day his Hurricane, P 3147, was set alight in combat over Biggin Hill. Pain baled out, slightly wounded, landed at Horsmonden and was admitted to hospital.

On January 16 1941 Pain arrived at Abu Sueir, Egypt. He had flown off HMS 'Furious' to Takoradi and then flown up to Egypt in stages. He flew a Hurricane to Malta on January 29 and joined 261 Squadron. On February 1 he damaged a Ju 88, on the 12th he probably destroyed a Bf 109, on the 25th claimed a probable Do 215, on March 5 shared a Bf 110, on the 18th a CR 42 destroyed and probably a second, on April 20 a CR 42 and probably another and on May 15 a SM 79.

Pain returned to the Middle East in early May 1941 and was posted to ADU at Takoradi. He was with 73 Squadron in the Western Desert in 1942, commanded 26 AACU in 1943 and later in the year was at 20 MU. Pain was released from the RAF in early 1944 and returned to Australia. He died there on September 12 1980.

APO 10.4.40   PO 14.7.40   FO 14.7.41   FL 14.1.43

FREDERICK GEORGE PAISEY

78753   PO   Pilot   British   235 Squadron

With 235 Squadron in early July 1940, Paisey served with the squadron throughout the Battle of Britain.

He was awarded the DFC (17.7.45), as an Acting Wing Commander with 354 Squadron. The citation stated that he had shown great skill and courage in low-level attacks on enemy shipping and had been responsible for the destruction of two of the six ships sunk by the squadron.

Paisey was released from the RAF in 1947, as a Wing Commander.

APO 12.4.40   PO 1.6.40   FO 1.6.41   FL 1.6.42
SL 20.6.45

JAN PALAK

793341   Sgt   Pilot   Polish   302 and 303 Squadrons

Born on February 12 1911. Palak was posted to 302 Squadron at Leconfield on July 24 1940. He claimed a Bf 109 probably destroyed and shared a Do 17 on September 15. He moved to 303 Squadron at Northolt on the 23rd and claimed a Bf 109 destroyed on October 5.

Palak was awarded the KW (1.2.41) and Bar (10.9.41). On January 25 1942 he went to 58 OTU, Grangemouth, as an instructor. A return to operations came on June 29 1942, when he rejoined 303 Squadron at Kirton-in-

Lindsey. Promoted to Warrant Officer on September 1 1942, Palak went to the squadron's Operations Room on September 11 1943. He was awarded a second Bar to the KW (20.10.43).

He moved to the Northolt Operations Room on November 23 and remained there until April 18 1944, when he rejoined 302 Squadron, then at Deanland. Palak was posted to 411 Repair and Salvage Unit on March 18 1945, as a test pilot. He was awarded the VM (5th Class)(1.6.45) and the DFC (10.4.46).

GEORGE CHARLES CALDER PALLISER

64891   Sgt   Pilot   British   17, 43 and 249 Squadrons

Joined the RAFVR in June 1939 at West Hartlepool and did a small amount of flying at 32 E&RFTS there before being called to full-time service at the outbreak of war.

Palliser was posted to 3 ITW, Hastings, moved to 11 EFTS, Perth on December 5 and went to 6 FTS, Little Rissington in April 1940. After converting to Hurricanes at 6 OTU, Sutton Bridge in July Palliser joined 17 Squadron at Debden on August 3. He moved to 43 Squadron at Tangmere on the 18th and joined 249 Squadron at North Weald on September 14.

Palliser shared in destroying a Do 17 on the 15th, damaged a Do 17 on the 21st, destroyed two Bf 110s on the 27th, damaged a Do 215 on October 21, shared a Bf 110 on November 11 and destroyed a Bf 109 on the 15th. He was shot down on December 5 by Bf 109s at the end of a long patrol and crashed with no fuel left.

On February 10 1941 Palliser probably destroyed a Bf 109, on a Blenheim escort to Dunkirk. He was commissioned in April. 249 Squadron embarked on HMS 'Furious' on May 10 and sailed for Gibraltar, where it transferred to HMS 'Ark Royal'. The squadron flew off on the 21st to Ta Kali, Malta.

Palliser shared in the destruction of a Cant Z 506B on June 12 and a Mc 200 on the 18th. On a long range patrol on October 19 he shared in destroying a SM 81 south of Lampedusa, on December 20 destroyed a Ju 88 and damaged a Bf 109 and on the 24th shared in destroying two Ju 88s.

On January 8 1942 Palliser joined 605 Squadron at Hal Far, as a Flight Commander. He was awarded the DFC (30.1.42) and posted from Malta on February 26, arriving at 25 Air School, Standerton, South Africa on March 28, to be an instructor. Palliser was posted to 62 CFS, Bloemfontein on July 17, to 2 EFTS, Randfontein on October 19 and then to 4 EFTS, Benoni on September 27 1943. He was admitted to Baragwanath Military Hospital in Johannesburg on January 21 1944 and remained there until leaving for the UK on May 24.

From September 2 Palliser instructed at 15 EFTS, Carlisle. He moved to 10 FTS, Woodley on September 19 1945, instructed there until March 16 1946, going then to CFS, South Cerney. In October Palliser was posted to instruct at the flying school at Heany, Southern Rhodesia.

In October 1947 Palliser left the RAF and settled with his family in South Africa, moving later to Australia.

PO 24.4.41   FO 24.4.42   FL 24.4.43   FL 1.9.45

NORMAN NELSON PALMER

748710   Sgt   Aircrew   British   248 Squadron

Joined 248 Squadron in mid-September 1940. Palmer was killed on February 8 1942, as a Flight Sergeant with 407 (RCAF) Squadron, a Hudson maritime-reconnaissance unit.

He was 21 and is remembered on the Runnymede Memorial, Panel 75.

JERZY HIPOLIT PALUSINSKI

P 1388   PO   Pilot   Polish   303 Squadron

Palusinski was born on August 13 1912 and was in the PAF before the war. He joined 303 Squadron at Northolt on August 21 1940. He went on short attachments to 308 Squadron at Woodvale on February 19 1942 and 306 Squadron at Kirton-in-Lindsey on May 25 but otherwise stayed with 303 until September 21 1943, when he was posted to 316 Squadron's Operations Room.

In early November 1943 Palusinski went on to Administration and Special Duties. He was posted to HQ 84 Group on September 7 1945 and was released from the PAF in January 1947. He was awarded the VM (5th Class)(31.10.47). Palusinski settled in England and took up pig-farming. He died in 1984.

FO 1.3.41   FL 1.9.42

WILHELM PANKRATZ

76662   FL   Pilot   Polish   145 Squadron

Pankratz was born on October 1 1903. He joined 145 Squadron at Tangmere on July 16 1940. He was reported 'Missing' after a combat with enemy aircraft south of the Isle of Wight on August 12, in Hurricane R 4176.

Pankratz is remembered on the Polish Air Force Memorial at Northolt. He was awarded the KW (1.2.41).

GEOFFREY CHARLES RUSSELL PANNELL

391856   Sgt   Pilot   New Zealander   3 Squadron

Pannell was born in Christchurch on August 22 1913. After leaving Waitaki Boys' High School he went farming with his father. He was accepted for a short service commission in late March 1939 but the scheme lapsed at the outbreak of war.

On December 17 Pannell went to the Ground Training School at Weraroa. He was posted to No 1 EFTS, Taieri on January 15 1940 and moved on to No 1 FTS, Wigram on March 11. After completing his training and being promoted to Sergeant on June 28 Pannell sailed for the UK on July 12, on the RMS 'Rangitane'.

He was posted to 6 OTU, Sutton Bridge on September 10 and after converting to Hurricanes went to 3 Squadron at Turnhouse on the 29th. Pannell joined the newly-reformed 260 Squadron at Castletown on December 6 1940 and on May 16 1941 was posted to 41 Squadron at Catterick.

Pannell went to 91 Squadron at Hawkinge on July 16 1941 and was to serve with it on and off over the next two years. Commissioned in August, he went on a six weeks' attachment to 111 Squadron at North Weald on the 31st. He was rested on April 20 1942 and posted as a test pilot to Morris Motors at Cowley, flying rebuilt Spitfires, new Tiger Moths and Masters. Pannell was awarded the DFC (29.6.42), being then credited with two enemy aircraft destroyed and several more damaged.

On September 26 1942 Pannell rejoined 91. He was awarded the C de G (Fr)(20.1.43), for distinguished services to Free French pilots in operations. He was posted to Cowley on July 12 1943, to organise the 84 Group Communications Squadron there. The expansion of the unit to twelve aircraft led to Pannell's being promoted to Acting Squadron Leader and taking formal command on March 1 1944. He went to 33 Squadron at Carpiquet on August 20, as supernumerary Flight Lieutenant, moved to 222 Squadron in the same capacity on September 12 and was then posted to the Communications Squadron at Northolt on November 25, as a Flight Commander.

Pannell was posted away on July 5 1945 for repatriation to New Zealand. He disembarked at Lyttelton on October 22 and went on to the Reserve on January 25 1946, as a Flight Lieutenant. He died on May 3 1980. Pannell's service career is unusual, in as much as he never had a posting or course of a non-flying nature. By the end of the war he had five confirmed victories, four more enemy aircraft probably destroyed and five damaged.

PO 17.8.41   FO 1.4.42   FL 1.5.43

THOMAS ROBERT VERNER PARKE

Sub-Lieutenant (FAA)   Pilot   British   804 Squadron

Joined the FAA in early 1939. Parke was with 804 Squadron at Hatston in early July 1940, flying Sea Gladiators on dockyard defence. He remained with the squadron when it reformed for service on the Fighter Catapult Ships in March 1941.

In the early days many difficulties were experienced with launchings. On July 7 1941 Parke was launched in a Fulmar from HMS 'Pegasus'. It was a day of low cloud, poor visibility and rain and no enemy aircraft was engaged. Parke failed to return to land. Later in the day it was learned that he had crashed into high ground south of Campbeltown, on the Mull of Kintyre. Both he and his gunner were killed.

Parke was 21. He is buried in Kilnerran Cemetery, Campbeltown.

Midshipman 1.5.39   Actg Sub-Lt 2.7.40

DENIS KEITH PARKER

128987   Sgt   Pilot   British   616 and 66 Squadrons

Parker joined the RAFVR in June 1939 and was called to full-time service at the outbreak of war. After completing his training and converting to Spitfires he joined 616 Squadron at Kirton-in-Lindsey on September 20 1940. He moved to 66 Squadron at Gravesend ten days later.

On January 30 1941 Parker was posted to 57 OTU, Hawarden, as an instructor. He left there on an overseas posting on October 23 1941 and landed at Aden on January 4 1942. Parker joined 229 Squadron in the Western Desert and went with it to Malta in March 1942. In May he was transferred to 185 Squadron at Hal Far and was commissioned in July.

Parker returned to the UK in August 1942 and was posted to 53 OTU, Llandow, as an instructor on Spitfires. He went to CFS, Montrose for a course in April 1943 and from August on he was training Free French pilots in intermediate and advanced flying up to OTU standard.

He was released from the RAF in November 1945, as a Flight Lieutenant.

PO 7.7.42   FO 7.1.43   FL 7.7.44

IAN ROBERTSON PARKER

90335   WC   Pilot   British   611 Squadron

Parker was educated at Eton and learned to fly with the RAFO in the early thirties. When 610 Squadron, AuxAF was formed at Hooton Park on February 10 1936 he was given command. The squadron was then a light bomber unit, with Harts. On January 1 1939 it was transferred to Fighter Command and Parker continued in command until January 7 1940, when he was promoted and posted away to be Station Commander at RAF Digby.

When 611 Squadron was at Digby in August 1940 Parker flew an operational sortie with it on the 21st and qualified for the Battle of Britain clasp.

Parker was released from the RAF in 1945, as a Group Captain, and made an OBE (1.1.46). In December 1947 he was appointed Honorary Air Commodore in the RAuxAF.

PO (RAFO) 9.10.31   FO (RAFO) 9.4.33   SL (AuxAF) 10.2.36
SL 24.8.39   WC 1.1.40   GC 1.7.43
Hon AC (RAuxAF) 8.12.47

KENNETH BRUCE PARKER

742267   **Sgt**   **Pilot**   **British**   **64 and 92 Squadrons**

Joined 64 Squadron at Leconfield in mid-September 1940 and moved to 92 Squadron at Biggin Hill on the 24th.

Parker was shot down and killed in combat with Bf 109s over the Thames Estuary on October 15 1940 and his Spitfire, R 6838, is believed to have crashed into the sea off Hoo Marina. Parker was 25. He is buried in Terschelling General Cemetery, Netherlands.

THOMAS CAMPBELL PARKER

70812   **FO**   **Pilot**   **British**   **79 Squadron**

Parker was born on September 1 1915 and commissioned in the RAFO in November 1937. He was posted to 8 FTS, Montrose on December 11 and joined 29 Squadron at Debden on July 9 1938. When his training year was up he returned to civilian life and was then called to full-time service at the outbreak of war.

Parker was posted to 79 Squadron in late 1939. Over Abbeville on June 7 1940 he claimed two Bf 109s destroyed. On August 28 he shared in the destruction of a He 59.

From April to September 1942 Parker commanded 242 Squadron and from July 1943 to August 1944 67 Squadron, in India. He was released from the RAF in 1945, as a Wing Commander, and was made an OBE (1.1.46).

APO (RAFO) 24.11.37   *PO (RAFO) 23.9.38*   *PO 1.9.39*
FO 3.9.40   *FL 3.9.41*   *SL 1.7.44*

VINCENT PARKER

42356   **PO**   **Pilot**   **Australian**   **234 Squadron**

Joined the RAF on a short service commission in May 1939. Parker was with 234 Squadron at St Eval in early July 1940.

On August 15 1940 Parker failed to return after a combat with enemy fighters off Swanage. He is believed to have crashed into the Channel, in Spitfire R 6985. Parker was rescued by the Germans and made a PoW.

He was killed in a flying accident on January 29 1946, as a Flight Lieutenant. His unit at the time of his death is not known. Parker was 27 years old. He is buried in Stonefall Cemetery, Harrogate, Yorkshire.

APO 22.7.39   *PO 10.4.40*   *FO 10.4.41*   *FL 10.4.42*

WILLIAM BERT PARKES

143727   **Sgt**   **Pilot**   **British**   **74 Squadron**

Born on April 27 1919, Parkes joined the RAFVR on July 23 1939 and began his elementary flying training at 9 E&RFTS, Ansty. Called to full-time service on September 13 he later went to ITW at Hastings, moved on to 15 EFTS, Redhill on November 22 and was posted for intermediate and advanced training to 5 FTS, Sealand on April 27 1940.

Parkes went to 5 OTU, Aston Down on August 6 and after converting to Spitfires he joined 74 Squadron at Wittering on the 17th. He remained with the squadron until April 16 1941, when he was posted to SHQ Manston. On September 30 Parkes joined 11 Group Flight at Croydon, engaged on calibration of radar, searchlights and anti-aircraft defences.

On December 11 1942 Parkes went to AFDU at Duxford and was commissioned in February 1943. He was posted to 2 FIS, Montrose on December 9 1943 and then went to 14 (P) AFU at Banff, as an instructor, moving to 5 (P) AFU at Tern Hill on August 16 1944. Granted a Permanent Commission, Parkes joined 613 Squadron RAuxAF on May 17 1946, as Flying Instructor and Adjutant. He resigned his commission on May 3 1950.

PO 18.2.43   *FO 18.8.43*   *FL 18.2.45*   *FL 18.8.46*

ERIC GORDON PARKIN

79734   **PO**   **Pilot**   **British**   **501 Squadron**

Born on April 21 1917, Parkin joined the RAFVR on September 13 1938 and began his elementary flying training at 8 E&RFTS, Woodley.

Called to full-time service on September 3 1939, he went to ITW at Bexhill in November and in February 1940 was posted to 8 FTS, Montrose.

In May 1940 Parkin completed the course and went to 6 OTU, Sutton Bridge, converted to Hurricanes and then joined 501 Squadron in France at the end of the month. In mid-June the squadron prepared to evacuate France. Parkin was flown to Caen, then to Dinard and two days later to Jersey, from where he sailed in a coal boat with Pilot Officer RS Don to Weymouth, arriving on the 17th. The squadron re-assembled at Croydon on the 21st.

The squadron took off from Hawkinge to return to Gravesend in the late evening of July 31 1940. Parkin's aircraft had a starting problem and he took off later, arriving at Gravesend in failing light. He undershot the runway and touched coiled barbed wire on the boundary. The Hurricane inverted and Parkin was injured. He was admitted to Gravesend Hospital, later transferred to Halton and did not rejoin 501 until February 5 1941.

With a non-operational category he was posted away for an instructor's course on April 16 1941 and was instructing until the end of the war. Parkin was released from the RAF in 1946, joined the RAFVR in 1947 and then rejoined the RAF in December 1953. He retired on April 21 1972, as a Flight Lieutenant.

PO 26.5.40   *FO 26.5.41*   *FL 26.5.42*
FO (RAFVR) 30.6.47   *FL 23.12.54*

CECIL PARKINSON

741376   **Sgt**   **Pilot**   **British**   **238 Squadron**

Parkinson, of Counden, Coventry, was with 238 Squadron at Middle Wallop in early July 1940. On the 13th he shared in the destruction of a Do 17, which crashed into the sea off Chesil Beach.

On July 20 1940 Parkinson was shot down in flames in combat over the Channel fifteen miles south of Swanage, in Hurricane P 3766. He baled out, was picked up by HMS 'Acheron' but died of his injuries the next day. Parkinson was 25. He is buried in St Michael's churchyard, Stoke, Coventry.

DENIS GEACH PARNALL

70522   **FO**   **Pilot**   **British**   **249 Squadron**

Parnall was commissioned in the RAFO in December 1936 and transferred to the RAFVR in January 1938. He was with 249 Squadron at Leconfield in June 1940.

On July 8 Parnall shared a Ju 88, on August 15 and September 2 he claimed Bf 110s destroyed and shared He 111s on September 7 and 11. He was shot down and killed during a patrol over Gravesend on September 18 1940. His Hurricane, V 6685, crashed and burned out by the A 12 road, near Furness Farm, Furze Hill, Margretting, Essex.

Parnall was 25. He is buried in St Genesius' churchyard, St Gennys, Cornwall.

PO (RAFO) 3.12.36   *PO (RAFVR) 1.1.38*
FO (RAFVR) 3.12.38

STUART BOYD PARNALL

90844   PO   Pilot   British   607 Squadron

May 14 1940.

APO 24.8.39   PO 23.3.40

Parnall, of Walthamstow, Essex, was in the AuxAF before the war. He was called to full-time service on August 24 1939 and was with 607 Squadron at Usworth in early July 1940.

On September 9 1940 Parnall was shot down and killed over Mayfield, in combat with Do 17s and Bf 109s. His Hurricane, P 3574, crashed at Lime Trees Farm, Goudhurst. He was 30 years old and was cremated at Golders Green Crematorium, Hendon, where his name appears on a bronze panel. Parnall's brother, James, was killed as a pilot in France on

DOUGLAS JOHN PARR

751383   Sgt   Aircrew   British   29 Squadron

Parr, of Macclesfield, Cheshire, joined 29 Squadron in early October 1940. He was killed on November 7 1941, as a Flight Sergeant and still with 29. He was 22 and is remembered on the Runnymede Memorial, Panel 37.

LESLIE ALFRED PARR

67605   Sgt   Pilot   British   79 Squadron

Born on March 14 1914. Parr was posted to 79 Squadron at Biggin Hill on July 6 1940 and on August 30 he shared in the destruction of a He 111. He remained with the squadron until August 25 1941.

Commissioned in May 1941, Parr stayed on in the RAF and qualified in Fighter Control. He retired on March 14 1969, as a Wing Commander, and died in 1986.

PO 25.5.41   FO 29.5.42
FL 29.5.43   FL 1.9.45
SL 1.7.51   WC 1.7.54

DENNIS THOMAS PARROTT

40211   FO   Pilot   British   19 Squadron, 421 Flight

Joined the RAF on a short service commission in June 1937. Parrott was posted to 8 FTS, Montrose on August 21 and with training completed he joined 9 Squadron at Stradishall on June 11 1938.

Parrott was posted to 19 Squadron at Fowlmere on July 31 1940 and on September 27 claimed a Bf 109 destroyed. In early October he joined the newly-formed 421 Flight at Hawkinge. He was slightly injured on the 19th, when he made a forced-landing at Clement Street, Old Swanley in Hurricane Z 2352, cause unknown.

On June 22 1941 Parrott was killed, as a Flight Lieutenant with 29 Squadron. He was 24 and is buried in Maidstone Cemetery, Kent.

APO 9.8.37   PO 31.5.38   FO 29.2.40

PETER LAWRENCE PARROTT

41054   FO   Pilot   British   145 and 605 Squadrons

Born at Aylesbury on June 28 1920, Parrott joined the RAF on a short service commission on June 27 1938 and began his ab initio course at No 1 E&RFTS, Hatfield. He was posted to 11 FTS, Shawbury on September 3 and after completing his training went as a staff pilot to No 1 Armament Training School at Catfoss on March 30 1939, towing targets.

On September 27 1939 Parrott went to No 1 Air Armament School, Manby, as a staff pilot. He was posted to the Pilot Pool at St Athan on December 23 1939, converted to Hurricanes and then joined 607 Squadron in France on January 23 1940. Parrott claimed two He 111s destroyed and another two damaged on May 10 and shared another on the 11th. He was jumped by Bf 109s near Louvain on the 13th and had his radio shot to pieces.

Parrott went on leave on the 17th and at home on the 19th he received a telegram posting him to 145 Squadron at Tangmere. Over Arras on the 22nd he damaged a Bf 110 and on the 26th, over Dunkirk, he damaged a He 111 but was hit by return fire. Heading home, his engine seized as he crossed the coast and he crash-landed in a field at Great Mongeham, near Deal.

On July 18 1940 Parrott shared a He 111, on August 8 claimed a Bf 109 and a Ju 87 destroyed and on the 12th a Ju 88 destroyed. He was posted to 605 Squadron at Croydon on September 27 and awarded the DFC (22.10.40). Acting as weaver on December 1 Parrott was jumped by a Bf 109 and his Hurricane, Z 2323, damaged. He dived to 3000 feet and fearing fire he baled out over East Hoathly, landed in a field and was found by a farm labourer.

Parrott was posted to CFS, Upavon on April 12 1941, for an instructor's course, after which he went to 9 FTS, Hullavington on May 26. He moved to 5 (P) AFU, Tern Hill on March 22 1942 to instruct and joined the Handling Squadron at Hullavington on September 1, to prepare pilots notes.

As a preliminary for a return to operations Parrott went to 57 OTU, Eshott on May 11 1943, for air-firing practice and up-to-date procedures. He joined 501 Squadron at Martlesham Heath on June 1. Parrott was posted overseas on July 16 1943, arrived at Safi, Malta on August 1 and then joined 72 Squadron at Pachino, Sicily on the 10th, as a supernumerary. Eight days later he went to 111 Squadron, also at Pachino, as a Flight Commander.

Parrott destroyed a Mc 202 on September 4. He was given command of 43 Squadron at Capodichino, Naples on October 13 1943 and led the squadron until March 6 1944, when he was posted to the Middle East. After a course at the Air Bombing and Gunnery School at El Ballah in April Parrott was appointed OC Gunnery at 73 OTU, Abu Sueir on May 2.

He returned to Italy in early November 1944 and took command of 72 Squadron at Rimini on the 11th. He was posted away to HQ Desert Air Force, Italy on February 15 1945 and was awarded a Bar to the DFC (20.3.45). Parrott became Group Training Inspector, Fighters and later Wing Commander Ops. He returned to the UK in June 1946.

Parrott was awarded the AFC (1.1.52) and retired from the RAF on July 10 1965, as a Wing Commander.

APO 27.6.38   PO 27.6.39   FO 3.9.40   FL 3.9.41
SL 1.7.44   SL 1.8.47   WC 1.1.54

REGINALD JAMES PARROTT

748634   Sgt   Pilot   British   32 Squadron

Parrott joined 32 Squadron at Acklington in late September 1940. He was with 257 Squadron at North Weald in November and on the 11th he shot a Fiat BR 20 down into the sea.

On May 5 1941 Parrott was killed, as a Sergeant with 257. He was 25 and is buried in the churchyard of St Mary and St Andrew, Whittlesford, Cambridgeshire.

EMLYN PARRY

137569 Sgt Wop/AG British 23 Squadron

Parry, of Beaumaris, joined 23 Squadron at Middle Wallop on October 6 1940. Commissioned in November 1942, he was killed on April 4 1944, as a Flying Officer with 10 Squadron, operating in Halifaxes from Melbourne, Yorkshire.

Parry was 26. He is buried in the Reichswald Forest War Cemetery, Germany.

PO 28.11.42   FO 28.5.43

MONTAGUE EDWARD PARRY

743083 Sgt Aircrew British 604 Squadron

Joined 604 Squadron at Middle Wallop on September 4 1940. No other service details traced.

CLAUDE ARTHUR PARSONS

748043 Sgt Pilot British 610 and 66 Squadrons

Parsons, of Halterworth, Romsey, Hampshire, was with 610 Squadron at Gravesend in early July 1940. He claimed an unidentified aircraft shot down on August 18. He was posted to 66 Squadron at Kenley on September 10.

Parsons claimed a He 111 destroyed on the 15th and a Ju 88 on the 27th. He was killed on November 8 1941, as a Flight Sergeant with 66 Squadron. He was 27 years old and is remembered on the Runnymede Memorial, Panel 37.

EDWIN ERNEST PARSONS

NZ 40627 Sgt Air Gunner New Zealander 23 Sqdn

Parsons was born in Auckland on December 26 1913. After leaving school he was employed as a bookbinder in Napier. He volunteered for aircrew duties in late 1939 and reported to the Ground Training School at Weraroa on February 13 1940, as a trainee air gunner. In mid-March Parsons went to the Air Observers' School, Ohakea for a Lewis gunnery course and air experience. He sailed for the UK on April 26 in the RMS 'Rangitiki'.

On July 17 Parsons was posted to 5 OTU, Aston Down and promoted to Sergeant. After converting to Blenheims he was awarded his air gunner's badge and then joined 23 Squadron at Ford on September 24, with a total of 28 hours and 55 minutes in his flying logbook. After months of unsuccessful night patrols the squadron began night intruder operations in late December 1940. On one such operation to Merville aerodrome on February 25 1941 the Blenheim, in which Parsons was gunner, probably destroyed two He 111s.

Parsons left 23 Squadron on March 2 1942 and joined 116 Squadron at Hendon on radar calibration duties. On May 11 he was posted to 1653 Conversion Unit at Polebrook, to crew-up and convert to Liberators. His crew reported to 1445 Flight, Lyneham on July 3 to pick up an aircraft and then fly overseas. They left for Gibraltar on the 15th, reached Fayid, Egypt on the 16th and were at St Jean, Palestine on the 17th and joined 160 Squadron.

On the 21st Parsons flew on his first long-range operational flight, a daylight raid on Heraklion, Crete. On January 15 1943 the squadron was disbanded into 178 Squadron. Parsons' crew flew their thirtieth and final operation on the 17th. He left Shandur on February 23 and using ferry aircraft he eventually arrived at Freetown and sailed from there to the UK on March 27. Soon after arrival at West Kirby Parsons was repatriated to New Zealand. After an attachment to the Air Department he went on to the Reserve on October 16 1943, as a Warrant Officer.

Parsons died in Auckland on October 4 1977.

JOHN GRAHAM PARSONS

143773 Sgt Observer British 235 Squadron

Joined the RAFVR on April 14 1939, as an AC 2 Air Observer and regraded LAC on the 15th. This procedure ensured that demotion could take place in the event of disciplinary action being required.

Parsons was mobilised on September 3 1939, posted to 8 Civil Air Navigation School at Sywell on October 16, moved to 9 Air Observer Navigation School at Squires Gate on November 25 and then completed his training at 3 BGS, Aldergrove. He was awarded his brevet, promoted to Acting Sergeant and then joined 235 Squadron at Bircham Newton. Parsons served with the squadron throughout the Battle of Britain, operating in Blenheims on bomber-escort, long-range fighter patrols or reconnaissance sweeps along the English Channel.

On April 5 1941 Parsons was posted to 2 BGS, Millom, as an armament instructor. He was promoted to Warrant Officer on April 1 1942. Commissioned in January 1943, he was appointed Bombing Leader in April and on December 6 posted to No 1 Staff Pilots Training Unit at Cark. Parsons was released from the RAF on January 26, as a Flight Lieutenant. He rejoined the RAFVR in February 1950 and served with it until February 1955.

PO 26.1.43   FO 26.7.43   FL 26.1.45   FO (RAFVR) 21.2.50

PHILLIP TREVOR PARSONS

90491 FO Pilot British 504 Squadron

Parsons, of Exeter, joined 504 Squadron, AuxAF in 1938. He was called to full-time service on August 26 1939.

He was with 504 Squadron at Castletown in early July 1940. On September 15 Parsons claimed a Do 17 destroyed and shared a He 111.

Parsons was killed on October 2 1942, as a Squadron Leader with 264 Squadron, aged 25. He is buried in the churchyard of St John the Baptist, Colerne, Wiltshire.

APO (AuxAF) 31.10.38   PO 26.8.39   FO 3.9.40   FL 3.9.41

CYRIL WOOLRICH PASSY

72028 FO Pilot British 605 Squadron

Born on February 27 1917, Passy was at Marlborough College from 1930 to 1935 and won a School Scholarship to Trinity College, Cambridge, where he obtained a BA in Modern Languages. He was commissioned in the RAFVR in November 1937 and was called to full-time service in October 1939.

In early July 1940 Passy was with 605 Squadron at Drem. On August 15 he made a forced-landing one mile from Usworth after a combat off the east coast, in Hurricane P 3827, unhurt. Passy shared in destroying a Bf 109 on October 7 and on the 26th he forced-landed at Town Row Green, Marks Cross in Hurricane P 3737, after being damaged in combat with Bf 109s.

He was shot down by a Bf 109 on December 1 and baled out, wounded. He was posted to RAF Cranage on the 18th, for night-flying duties. In 1942 Passy was with 89 Squadron in the Middle East and later North Africa. On December 20 1942 he destroyed a Do 217 and a Ju 88. He was awarded the DFC (12.2.43).

Passy was made an OBE (14.6.45) and retired from the RAF on June 4 1947, as a Squadron Leader, retaining the rank of Wing Commander. He died in 1971.

PO (RAFVR) 16.11.37   FO 10.10.39   FL 24.3.41
SL 1.6.42   SL 1.9.45

LUDWIK WITOLD PASZKIEWICZ

P 0042   FO   Pilot   Polish   303 Squadron

Born on October 28 1907, Paszkiewicz was in the PAF before the war. After the fall of Poland he escaped to France, where he flew with l'Armée de l'Air in Groupe de Chasse III/2.

Paszkiewicz joined 303 Squadron at Northolt at its formation on August 2 1940. On the 9th he wrecked Hurricane P 3645 in a taxying accident. He destroyed a Do 17 on the 30th. This enemy aircraft was shot down whilst Paszkiewicz was on a training flight. He broke away from the squadron formation to attack it. Back at Northolt he was reprimanded and then congratulated.

On September 7 Paszkiewicz claimed two Do 17s destroyed, on the 11th a Bf 110, on the 15th a Bf 109 and on the 26th a He 111. He was shot down and killed on the 27th. His Hurricane, L 1696, crashed at Crowhurst Farm, Borough Green.

Paszkiewicz is buried in Northwood Cemetery and remembered on the Polish Air Force Memorial at Northolt. He was awarded the VM (5th Class)(23.12.40), the KW (1.2.41) and the DFC (30.10.41).

EDWARD PATEREK

793342   Sgt   Pilot   Polish   302 and 303 Squadrons

Paterek was born on May 30 1910. He joined 302 Squadron at Leconfield on July 23 1940. He claimed a He 111 probably destroyed on September 15 and a Ju 88 on the 18th. It is believed that his aircraft was hit by debris from this enemy aircraft, causing him to make a crash-landing in Hurricane P 3086 at Sandon Lodge Farm, Danbury, unhurt.

On September 23 Paterek was posted to 303 Squadron at Northolt. He went to 315 Squadron at Acklington at its formation on January 21 1941. He was awarded the KW (1.2.41).

On a training flight on March 28 1941 Paterek collided with another aircraft and crashed into the sea near Bar Lightship, in Hurricane V 7187. He was never found and is presumed to have drowned. He is remembered on the Polish Air Force Memorial at Northolt.

BRIAN PATERSON

Lieutenant (FAA)   Pilot   British   804 Squadron

Paterson joined the RAF on a short service commission in May 1937. He was posted to 7 FTS, Peterborough on July 17 and joined 46 Squadron at Digby on February 19 1938. He transferred to the FAA in early 1939.

In September Paterson was with 803 Squadron but in December 1939 he joined 804 Squadron at Hatston and in early July 1940 he was flying Sea Gladiators from there, on dockyard defence.

Paterson later served with 885 Squadron and in HMS 'Argus', 'Ark Royal', 'Victorious', 'Eagle' and 'Dasher'. After the war he converted to helicopters. He was made an MBE (16.2.54) for Greek earthquake relief operations and awarded the DFC (31.5.55) for operations in Malaya with the Royal Marine Commandos and the SAS. He retired in 1959, as a Lieutenant Commander.

APO 5.7.37   PO 10.5.38   Sub-Lt 10.5.38   Lt 10.1.40
Lt-Cdr 10.1.48

JAMES ALFRED PATERSON

36193   FO   Pilot   New Zealander   92 Squadron

Born at Chatton, near Gore on October 16 1919, Paterson worked on his father's farm. He was a trooper in the Otago Mounted Rifles, Territorial Army. In December 1937 he applied for an RNZAF short service commission and after acceptance he began flying training at the Otago Aero Club, gaining his 'A' License on August 15 1938. Paterson was posted to No 1 FTS, Wigram on September 6, was awarded his flying badge on December 17, completed his training and sailed for the UK on the 'Waimarama' from Auckland on April 17 1939.

Paterson was posted to 82 Squadron at Cranfield on June 3. At the outbreak of war he went to 71 Wing in France, flying in Magisters on reconnaissance patrols and observation flights for the BEF. In late 1939 Paterson joined 226 Squadron at Rheims. In May 1940 he was detached to special duties to supply hard-pressed squadrons with mail, medical supplies, petrol and despatches.

After the French collapse in June Paterson went with 226 Squadron to Northern Ireland. He volunteered for Fighter Command and after converting to Spitfires at 7 OTU, Hawarden he joined 92 Squadron at Pembrey. On July 24 Paterson shared in the destruction of a Ju 88. He shared another on August 19 and destroyed a Bf 110 on September 11. Later the same day he was shot down by Bf 109s and baled out, with clothes on fire and badly burned about the face. His Spitfire, R 6613, crashed north-east of Ashford.

Paterson insisted on flying again before he could see properly. On September 27 he took off with other Spitfires of 92 to intercept enemy aircraft. He was shot down in flames by Bf 109s near Maidstone and fellow-pilots saw him struggling to escape from his cockpit but he failed to do so and was killed. His Spitfire, X 4422, crashed and burned out at Sparepenny Lane, Farningham. Paterson is buried in Star Lane Cemetery, Orpington, Kent.

He was made an MBE (1.1.41) for his outstanding services in France in May 1940.

APO 13.9.38   PO 20.5.39   FO 20.5.40

LEON FRED PATRICK

123303   Sgt   Pilot   British   222 Squadron

Joined 222 Squadron at Hornchurch in late August 1940. Patrick was commissioned from Warrant Officer in May 1942 and was released from the RAF in 1946, as a Flight Lieutenant. He joined the RAFVR in 1947 and served until 1951.

Patrick died on October 23 1985.

PO 1.5.42   FO 1.11.42
FL 1.5.44
FO (RAFVR) 3.10.47

ARTHUR GEORGE PATSTON

103000   LAC   Radar Operator   British   604 Squadron

Patston was in France with the AASF as a ground radio operator. Back in England in June 1940 he volunteered for aircrew duties of a secret nature and went to RAF Yatesbury for a short radar course.

AG Patston (continued)

He joined 604 Squadron at Gravesend on July 10. During the Battle of Britain Patston flew with the squadron without flying brevet or rank. Eventually he was promoted to Sergeant. He retrained with the squadron, qualified as a Radio Observer and flew in Beaufighters. On April 4 1941 the weather clamped down and there being no airfield in range open for landings Patston and his pilot baled out.

In July 1941 Patston was commissioned and posted away to 54 OTU at Church Fenton, as an instructor. In 1943 he joined 85 Squadron and served with it until the end of the war. He was awarded the DFC (9.11.43), having then assisted in the destruction of three enemy aircraft at night. Patston was Senior Navigation Officer with 85 in May 1945. He was released from the RAF later in the year, as a Flight Lieutenant.

PO 14.7.41   FO 14.7.42   FL 14.7.43

HUBERT PAUL FREDERICK PATTEN

40423   FO   Pilot   British   64 Squadron

Patten was born on October 15 1917. He joined the RAF on a short service commission in October 1937. He carried out his elementary flying training at No 1 E&RFTS Hatfield, was posted to 2 FTS, Brize Norton on January 9 1938 and joined 79 Squadron at Biggin Hill on August 20.

In October 1938 Patten went to CFS, Upavon for an instructor's course but became ill and did not graduate. After three months supernumerary sick at Uxbridge he was posted to 64 Squadron at Church Fenton in April 1939. Over Dunkirk on May 31 1940 Patten claimed a Bf 110 destroyed and flying from Kenley on July 10 he claimed another.

On September 15 1940 he joined the newly-formed 307 Squadron at Kirton-in-Lindsey, a Polish night-fighter unit with Defiants. In May 1941 Patten moved to 604 Squadron at Middle Wallop, remaining with it until October, when he went to Exminster as a GCI Controller.

Patten was posted to 52 OTU, Aston Down in February 1943 for a Spitfire refresher course. In May he joined 276 (ASR) Squadron at Harrowbeer as a supernumerary Squadron Leader but was then posted to Air HQ Malta in June, where he served as Staff Officer Night Ops. In December 1943 Patten was attached to 108 Squadron at Luqa, a Beaufighter night-fighter unit, then went to HQ 242 Group, Taranto later in the month as a staff officer on Fighter Operations.

In April and May 1944 Patten was with 1435 Squadron at Rimini, as a supernumerary Squadron Leader, before joining 255 Squadron at Foggia, as a Flight Commander. He returned to the UK in January 1945, was at Air Ministry until September and then after a short spell on Mustangs at 61 OTU, Keevil he was released from the RAF in October 1945. He worked in the International Civil Aviation Organisation in Montreal and Paris from December 1945 until June 1949. Patten then rejoined the RAF, in the Fighter Control Branch. He retired early on May 28 1964, as a Flight Lieutenant, retaining the rank of Squadron Leader. From October 1964 until April 1980 he worked as a civilian with NATO in France and Belgium.

APO 9.1.38   PO 25.10.38   FO 25.5.40   FL 25.5.41
SL 1.6.42   FL 22.6.47

LEONARD JOHN PATTERSON

741219   Sgt   Pilot   British   501 Squadron

Patterson, of Freeland, Oxfordshire, joined 501 Squadron at Kenley on September 2 1940. He was shot down and killed by Bf 109s east of Hastings on November 28 1940. His Hurricane, P 5189, is believed to have crashed into the sea.

Patterson was 23. He is remembered on the Runnymede Memorial, Panel 18.

NORRIS HENRY PATTERSON

Sub-Lieutenant (FAA)   Pilot   British   804 Squadron

With 804 Squadron at Hatston in early July 1940, flying Sea Gladiators on dockyard defence. Patterson later transferred to 802 Squadron, then forming for HMS 'Audacity'.

He was killed on December 22 1941 when the carrier was sunk. Patterson is remembered on the Fleet Air Arm Memorial at Lee-on-Solent.

Midshipman 1.5.39   Actg Sub-Lt 14.3.40   Sub-Lt 25.12.40

PETER JOHN PATTERSON

Midshipman (FAA)   Pilot   British   242 Squadron

Loaned to the RAF in mid-June 1940, Patterson converted to Hurricanes and then joined 242 Squadron at Coltishall on July 1. He was killed on August 20 1940, when his Hurricane, P 2967, dived vertically into the sea and exploded five miles north-east of Winterton during a squadron patrol, cause unknown.

Patterson was 19. He is remembered on the Fleet Air Arm Memorial at Lee-on-Solent.

Midshipman 1.7.39

ROBERT LAWSON PATTERSON

77529   PO   Pilot   British   235 Squadron

Patterson, of Wormit, Fife, was with 235 Squadron in June 1940. He was captain of Blenheim N 3541, which failed to return from an operational sortie on July 18 1940. He and his crew of two, Sergeants RY Tucker and LHM Reece, were reported 'Missing'.

Patterson was 26. He is remembered on the Runnymede Memorial, Panel 9.

PO 18.11.39

ABERCONWAY JOHN SEFTON PATTINSON

40563   PO   Pilot   British   23 and 92 Squadrons

Born in Chelsea, London, Pattinson joined the RAF on a short service commission in December 1937. He was posted to 5 FTS, Sealand on March 5 1938 and joined 25 Squadron at Hawkinge on September 17.

In early July 1940 Pattinson was with 23 Squadron at Collyweston. He was posted to 92 Squadron at Pembrey on September 5 and was shot down and killed by a Bf 109 over Hawkinge on October 12. His Spitfire, X 4591, crashed and burned out in Bartholomews Wood, Postling Wents.

Pattinson was 21 years old. He is buried in Parkestone Cemetery, Poole, Dorset.

APO 19.2.38   PO 29.11.38

JOHN DAVID PATTISON

C 957   FO   Pilot   Canadian   1 (RCAF) Squadron

Joined the RCAF on December 13 1938. Pattison was posted to No 1 (RCAF) Squadron at Northolt on August 30 1940.

He was with 419 (RCAF) Squadron in 1942 and was awarded the DFC (6.11.42), as an Acting Squadron Leader. Pattison returned later to Canada and commanded 145 (RCAF) Squadron at Dartmouth, Nova Scotia, from March 1 to June 30 1945, when it was disbanded.

Pattison was released from the RCAF on September 5 1945, as a Wing Commander.

JOHN GORDON PATTISON

39931   PO   Pilot   New Zealander   266 and 92 Sqdns

Pattison was born at Waipawa on January 27 1917 and after leaving Wanganui Collegiate School he went farming with his father. In January 1939 he enrolled in the Civil Reserve of Pilots and learned to fly at Bridge Pa, Hastings. At the outbreak of war Pattison volunteered for the RNZAF and went to the Ground Training School, Weraroa on October 26 1939.

He was posted to 2 EFTS, New Plymouth on November 20 and then to 2 FTS, Woodbourne on January 15 1940. Pattison was awarded his flying badge on April 23, completed the course on May 28 and sailed for the UK on June 7 in the RMS 'Rangitata'. On August 4 Pattison was posted to 7 OTU, Hawarden and then joined 266 Squadron at Wittering on August 27 1940. On his first operational patrol he became lost, ran out of fuel and crash-landed in a field bristling with anti-invasion obstacles, to be greeted by farmworkers with pitchforks, who thought him a German.

On September 14 Pattison was posted to 92 Squadron at Biggin Hill. He was shot down by a Bf 109 on the 23rd, severely wounded in the thigh by a cannon shell. He was admitted to Preston Hall Hospital, Maidstone, spent the next eight months in various hospitals and did not rejoin 92 until June 1 1941. Pattison was posted away to 61 OTU, Llandow on July 4, as an instructor.

On April 13 1942 Pattison joined 485 Squadron at Kenley. On a Hurri-bomber escort on the 26th 485 was jumped by a large force of FW 190s. Pattison's engine was hit and his cockpit filled with smoke. He managed to glide back across the Channel, baled out near Dungeness and was picked up by an ASR launch.

Pattison was rested on June 1 1943 and on July 7 was appointed CFI at 56 OTU, Kinell. He returned to operations on March 3 1944 as supernumerary Flight Lieutenant with 66 Squadron at North Weald. Awarded the DFC (16.5.44), Pattison stayed with the squadron until September 8, when he took command of 485 Squadron at Caen-Carpiquet. In February 1945 the squadron was withdrawn to Predannack to convert to Tempests. Pattison, tour-expired, was posted to a staff job at HQ 84 Group. He was awarded the DSO (20.3.45), the citation stating that within recent months he had destroyed many enemy vehicles and two enemy aircraft.

After the war's end Pattison was based at Hanover. He was repatriated to New Zealand in January 1946 and released from the RNZAF, as a Squadron Leader.

APO 26.10.39   PO 28.5.40   FO 28.5.41   FL 28.5.42

KENNETH CLIFTON PATTISON

742457   Sgt   Pilot   British   611 Squadron

Pattison was posted to 611 Squadron at Tern Hill on September 26 1940. In the evening of October 11 some Spitfires of 611 intercepted Do 17s attacking Liverpool. Pattison shot one down but was hit by return fire and damaged. He crashed at Cooksey Green, near Kidderminster, in Spitfire P 7323. Critically injured, he was admitted to Barnsley Hall Hospital, Bromsgrove, where he died two days later.

Pattison was 27. He is buried in Nottingham Southern Cemetery, West Bridgeford.

WILLIAM BLAIR PATTULLO

43379   PO   Pilot   British   46, 151 and 249 Squadrons

With 46 Squadron at Digby in early July 1940. Pattullo joined 151 Squadron at Stapleford Tawney on August 26 and on the 31st he claimed a Do 17 destroyed.

On September 10 Pattullo was posted to 249 Squadron at North Weald and on the 11th he shared in destroying a He 111. He returned to 46 Squadron, then at Stapleford Tawney, on September 15 and on that day claimed a Do 17 destroyed. On the 27th he claimed a Bf 110 destroyed and shared a Bf 109.

After a routine patrol on October 25 1940 Pattullo crashed on to a house in Woodstock Avenue, Romford, in Hurricane V 6804. He was rescued from the wreckage and admitted to Oldchurch Hospital, where he died from his injuries the next day.

Pattullo was 21 years old. He is buried in St Andrew's churchyard, North Weald Bassett, Essex.

APO 27.4.40   PO 10.8.40

FRANCIS DAWSON PAUL

Sub-Lieutenant (FAA)   Pilot   British   64 Squadron

Paul was born in Chelsea, London on February 18 1916. He entered the FAA on September 26 1939 and trained with 758 Squadron at HMS 'Raven' at Eastleigh. After a short Fighter Course there from May 27 1940 he was loaned to the RAF on June 15 and went to 7 OTU, Hawarden, where he converted to Spitfires.

On July 1 Paul joined 64 Squadron at Kenley. On the evening of this day he shared in destroying a Do 17 south of Beachy Head. He claimed a Bf 109 destroyed on the 5th in combat over Rouen and made a forced-landing at Hawkinge on the way back. Paul claimed a Bf 110 destroyed on the 7th, two more and probably a third on the 10th, a Bf 109 on the 13th and a Do 17 on the 24th.

Paul destroyed another Bf 109 on the 25th. On this day he was shot down into the Channel off the south coast, in Spitfire L 1035. He was picked up by a German E boat, severely wounded. Paul died five days later. He is buried in Hardinghen churchyard, France.

Sub-Lt 26.9.39

HAROLD JOHN PAVITT

50901   Sgt   Aircrew   British   235 Squadron

Pavitt was born on February 9 1917. He joined 235 Squadron on September 18 1940. Commissioned from Flight Sergeant in September 1942, he stayed on in the RAF and retired on January 10 1958, as a Squadron Leader. He died in 1972.

PO 16.9.42   FO 15.3.43   FL 19.12.44   FL 21.3.46
SL 1.7.52

OTTO PAVLU

117614   Sgt   Pilot   Czechoslovakian   1 Squadron

Joined No 1 Squadron at Wittering on October 4 1940. Commissioned in March 1942, Pavlu was killed on April 28 1943, as a Flying Officer with 310 Squadron. He was flying Spitfire EE 635 on an anti-shipping strike. A convoy was attacked at mast height, heavy flak was encountered and Pavlu was hit and crashed into the sea.

He is remembered on the Runnymede Memorial, Panel 128.

PO 3.3.42   FO 3.9.42

ALEC DAWSON PAYNE

745798   F/Sgt   Pilot   British   501 and 610 Sqdns

Payne was with 501 Squadron in France in May 1940. On the 11th, 12th and 14th he destroyed He 111s and on the 15th a Do 17.

He was posted to 610 Squadron at Acklington on September 23 1940 and later in the year he joined 74 Squadron at Biggin Hill. Payne shot down a Bf 109 over Boulogne during a sweep on February 2 1941.

No further service details traced.

ROY AINLEY PAYNE

77789   PO   Pilot   British   602 Squadron

Payne joined 602 Squadron at Westhampnett on September 3 1940, from an army co-operation Lysander squadron.

His name last appears in the January 1944 Air Force List but no trace has been found of him as a casualty.

PO 7.3.40   FO 7.6.41   FL 7.6.42

REGINALD IRVING PAYNE

1052320   AC 2   Wop/AG   British   23 Squadron

Born in Rotherham. Payne was posted to 23 Squadron at Middle Wallop on September 23 1940. Two days later he was a member of the crew of Blenheim L 8369 on a night patrol. The pilot, Pilot Officer E Orgias, reported that he was returning, with one engine running badly. He reached his base area at Middle Wallop but crashed near Broughton, Hampshire. Payne, Orgias and the observer, Sergeant LR Karasek, were all killed. As Orgias was preparing to land it is believed that he stalled after turning away to make a wide approach into wind, possibly due to the failure of the port engine.

Payne was 31. He is buried in St Helen's churchyard extension, Treeton, Yorkshire. According to AMO 416 dated June 27 1940 Payne should have held the rank of Temporary Sergeant but had apparently not been given his due. There were eight cases of such an oversight among air gunners, observers and Wop/AGs killed in the Battle of Britain.

CHARLES BARTON GOWER PEACHMENT

42022 PO Pilot British 236 Squadron

Joined the RAF on a short service commission in February 1939. Peachment was posted to the newly-reformed 236 Squadron on November 6.

On August 8 1940 he landed at Ford with severe damage to the oil system of Blenheim L 8684, following an attack by fighters off Le Havre.

Peachment was released from the RAF in 1947, as a Squadron Leader. He died in 1979.

APO 29.4.39   PO 6.11.39   FO 6.11.40   FL 6.11.41
SL 1.7.45

DENIS CHARLES PEACOCK

754649 Sgt Pilot British 605 Squadron

Served with 605 Squadron during the Battle of Britain. Peacock was killed on September 15 1942, as a Warrant Officer, aged 21. His unit at the time of his death is not known.

Peacock is buried in Stanton Cemetery, Hartlepool, Durham.

REGINALD JOHN PEACOCK

40257 FO Pilot British 235 Squadron

Peacock, of London, joined the RAF on a short service commission in August 1937. After completing his training at No 1 FTS, Leuchars he was posted to the FAA Pool at RAF Gosport.

He served with 235 Squadron in the Battle of Britain. On August 20 1942 the squadron became 227 Squadron at Luqa, Malta. Peacock was killed on February 5 1943, as a Squadron Leader with 227, aged 25. He is buried in Tobruk War Cemetery, Libya.

APO 24.10.37   PO 23.8.38   FO 23.9.40   FL 23.9.41

WILLIAM ALBERT PEACOCK

808268 Sgt Pilot British 46 Squadron

Peacock, of Middlesborough, Yorkshire, was with 46 Squadron at Digby in early July 1940.

On September 8 he claimed a Bf 109 destroyed. Three days later Peacock failed to return from combat over the Thames Estuary, in Hurricane V 7232. He was presumed to have crashed into the sea and was reported 'Missing'. Peacock was 20 years old. He is remembered on the Runnymede Memorial, Panel 18.

SPENCER RITCHIE PEACOCK-EDWARDS

40747 FO Pilot British 615 and 253 Squadrons

Born on May 27 1915, Peacock-Edwards joined the RAF on a short service commission in March 1938. He was posted to 2 FTS, Brize Norton on May 21 and joined 150 Squadron at Boscombe Down on December 17.

From the outbreak of war he served in France with the squadron, flying Fairey Battles. After returning to England in June 1940 Peacock-Edwards volunteered for Fighter Command and joined 615 Squadron at Kenley on July 10. He moved to 253 Squadron, also at Kenley, on September 15.

Peacock-Edwards arrived in Malta on January 30 1941, in a Sunderland from the Middle East. He joined 261 Squadron at Hal Far, claimed a Ju 88 destroyed on February 1 and was appointed 'A' Flight Commander on the 16th. He claimed two Ju 87s destroyed on March 23, damaged a Bf 109 on April 13 and then crash-landed at Hal Far, in his badly-damaged Hurricane, V 7472.

In May 1941 Peacock-Edwards returned to the Middle East. He was instructing in South Africa later in the year and in March 1942 he joined 258 Squadron in Ceylon. On April 5 he scrambled with the squadron, when Japanese carrier-based aircraft attacked Colombo. He destroyed at least one enemy aircraft. Peacock-Edwards was awarded the DFC (29.12.42).

From February 1943 to May 1944 he commanded 30 Squadron in Ceylon. Peacock-Edwards retired from the RAF on February 14 1958, as a Squadron Leader. He went to live in South Africa and died there in 1983.

APO 7.5.38   PO 7.3.39   FO 3.9.40   FL 3.9.41
SL 1.1.44   FL 1.12.42   SL 1.1.54

LEONARD HILARY BORLASE PEARCE

741920 Sgt Pilot British 32, 249 and 46 Squadrons

Pearce, of Harrogate, was with 32 Squadron at Biggin Hill in early July 1940. He shared a Do 17 destroyed on August 15. Three days later he was shot down in combat over Canterbury and baled out, slightly wounded. His Hurricane, R 4106, crashed at Rose Garden Cottage, Chartham Hatch.

On September 18 Pearce was posted to 249 Squadron at North Weald. In October he was with 46 Squadron at Stapleford Tawney and on the 13th he made a forced-landing at Biggin Hill after being attacked by Bf 109s over Dungeness, wounded.

Pearce was killed on April 9 1941, as a Flight Sergeant with 46 Squadron. He was 27 and is buried in the churchyard extension of St John the Baptist at Kirby Wharfe.

PETER GRIFFIN PEARCE

916157 Sgt Aircrew British 600 Squadron

With 600 Squadron at Northolt in early July 1940. Pearce was killed on December 15 1941, as a Flight Sergeant with 600. He is remembered on the Runnymede Memorial, Panel 37.

ROY PEARCE

143995 Sgt Air Gunner British 29 Squadron

Joined 29 Squadron at Digby in early October 1940.

Commissioned in January 1943, Pearce was released from the RAF in 1946, as a Flight Lieutenant.

PO 17.1.43   FO 17.7.43   FL 17.1.45

WILLIAM JOHN PEARCE

755517 Sgt Aircrew British 236 Squadron

Pearce, of Headington, Oxfordshire, joined 236 Squadron on September 24 1940. He was killed on November 5 1941, as a Flight Sergeant with 404 (RCAF) Squadron, aged 19.

He is remembered on the Runnymede Memorial, Panel 37.

DENNIS JACK PEARCY

903249 Sgt Air Gunner British 219 Squadron

Pearcy served with 219 Squadron in the Battle of Britain. He was in Beaufighter R 2048, which crashed near Kenley on November 15 1940, cause unknown. He and his pilot, Pilot Officer WGM Lambie, were both killed.

Pearcy was 25. He is buried in Yeovil Cemetery, Somerset.

STANLEY JAMES PEARMAIN

78767 PO Air Gunner British 141 Squadron

With 141 Squadron at Turnhouse in early July 1940. He was released from the RAF in 1947, as a Flight Lieutenant.

APO 20.4.40   PO 15.5.40   FO 15.5.41   FL 15.5.42

LESLIE LEWIS PEARSE

142916 Sgt Aircrew British 236 Squadron

Joined 236 Squadron on October 10 1940. Commissioned in November 1942, Pearse was awarded the DFC (21.9.45), as a Flight Lieutenant with 460 (RCAF) Squadron.

He was released from the RAF in 1945, as a Flight Lieutenant.

PO 9.11.42   FO 9.5.43   FL 9.11.44

DENNIS EDWARD PEARSON

581471 Sgt Aircrew British 236 Squadron

A pre-war regular airman, Pearson joined 236 Squadron on July 21 1940. He was a member of the crew of a Blenheim, which was hit by flak after destroying a Do 24 flying boat twenty miles north-west of Brest on November 6 1940. Pearson was wounded in one eye and one arm.

No further service details traced.

GEOFFREY WILBERFORCE PEARSON

742740   Sgt   Pilot   British   501 Squadron

Joined 501 Squadron at Kenley in late August 1940. Pearson failed to return from combat over the Ashford area on September 6. His Hurricane, P 3516, crashed at Cowleas Farm, near Kempton Manor, Hothfield and he was killed.

Pearson was 21 years old. He is buried in St Stephen's churchyard, Lympne, Kent.

PHILIP PEARSON

119010   Sgt   Pilot   British   238 Squadron

Pearson, of Saffron Walden, Essex, joined 238 Squadron at Chilbolton in mid-October 1940. After being damaged by Bf 109s over Bournemouth on November 5 Pearson made a forced-landing at Sturminster, in Hurricane P 2983. He was slightly injured and was admitted to Shaftesbury Hospital.

The squadron went to the Middle East in May 1941 and became fully operational with Hurricane IIcs in October. On November 29 Pearson probably destroyed a Fiat G 50 and shared another. He was commissioned in January 1942 and posted to 80 Squadron at El Adem.

Pearson was killed on May 29 1942, aged 21. He is remembered on the Alamein Memorial, Column 249.

PO 21.1.42

ARTHUR PETER PEASE

72447   FO   Pilot   British   603 Squadron

The son of Sir Richard and Lady Pease of Richmond, Yorkshire, Pease learned to fly with the Cambridge University Air Squadron and was commissioned in the RAFVR in September 1938.

Called to full-time service in October 1939, Pease completed his flying training and was posted to No 1 School of Army Co-operation at Old Sarum in late May 1940. He met Richard Hillary there and they became friends. They went to 5 OTU, Aston Down in early June and after converting to Spitfires they joined 603 Squadron at Dyce on July 6.

Pease shared in destroying a He 111 on the 30th. He was hit by return fire but returned to Montrose, unhurt. On September 3 he claimed a Bf 109 destroyed and on the 7th made a belly-landing back at Hornchurch in Spitfire L 1057, after being damaged in combat over London.

On September 15 1940 Pease was shot down and killed in combat. His Spitfire, X 4324, crashed at Kingswood, near Chartway Street, Kent. He was 22 years old and is buried in the churchyard of St Michael and All Angels, Middleton Tyas, Yorkshire.

PO (RAFVR) 6.9.38   PO 5.10.39   FO 30.3.40

WILLIAM PEEBLES

755887   Sgt   Aircrew   British   235 Squadron

With 235 Squadron in early July 1940. Peebles was killed on May 7 1941, as a Flight Sergeant with 240 Squadron. He is remembered on the Runnymede Memorial, Panel 37.

CHARLES DAVID PEEL

90199   FO   Pilot   British   603 Squadron

Peel was born on May 3 1919 and was at Cheltenham College from September 1932 to July 1937. He joined 603 Squadron, AuxAF in early 1938.

Called to full-time service on August 25 1939, he was still with the squadron in June 1940. On July 17 Peel was reported 'Missing', after failing to return from an operational sortie, in Spitfire K 9916. He was 21 years old and is remembered on the Runnymede Memorial, Panel 6.

PO (AuxAF) 25.2.38   FO 25.8.39

JOHN RALPH ALEXANDER PEEL

33011   SL   Pilot   British   145 Squadron

Born at Boscombe on October 17 1911, Peel was educated at Clifton and entered RAF College, Cranwell in September 1930 as a flight cadet. He graduated in July 1932 and joined 19 Squadron at Duxford. On January 5 1934 Peel was posted to 801 (Fleet Fighter) Squadron, based at Upavon and on HMS 'Furious'.

He joined the staff of 601 Squadron, AuxAF on September 21 1935, as Flying Instructor. Peel went to the staff of RAF College, Cranwell on July 13 1936 but returned to 601 Squadron on September 23 1937.

In early 1940 Peel was at Air Ministry, in the Postings Section. He was given command of 145 Squadron at Tangmere in July 1940. On July 7 he shared in destroying a Do 17. Peel was shot down over the Channel on the 11th and ditched off Selsey Bill, in Hurricane P 3400. He was rescued, semi-conscious, by the Selsey lifeboat. On the 17th he returned to Tangmere, damaged by return fire from a Ju 88 engaged near St Catherine's Point.

Peel shared a Do 17 on the 19th, shared a Ju 88 on the 29th and claimed two Ju 87s and a Bf 109 destroyed on August 8. He made a forced-landing on the Isle of Wight on the 11th, after being damaged by enemy fighters south of Swanage, slightly injured. He was awarded the DFC (13.8.40).

On September 16 Peel left the squadron but returned to command again on November 18. In January 1941 he was posted away and in March was appointed Wing Leader at Kenley. On April 7 he destroyed two Bf 109s as they prepared to take off from Berck airfield.

Peel was shot down into the channel off the French coast in July 1941 but was picked up and led the Wing the next morning. He was posted away in early August and awarded the DSO (5.8.41).

Peel retired from the RAF on January 20 1948, as a Wing Commander, retaining the rank of Group Captain.

PO 23.7.32   FO 23.1.34   FL 1.10.36   SL 1.4.39
WC 1.3.41   WC 1.10.46

CONSTANTINE OLIVER JOSEPH PEGGE

41317   FO   Pilot   British   610 Squadron

Pegge was born in Slough, Middlesex. He joined the RAF on a short service commission in August 1938. He was with 610 Squadron at Gravesend in June 1940.

On July 8 Pegge claimed a Bf 109 destroyed, on August 12 two more and on the 18th a Bf 109 and a He 111. On the return to Biggin Hill his Spitfire, R 6694, was damaged by a Bf 109 and then further damaged by running into a bomb crater on landing. Pegge was unhurt. On August 24 he probably destroyed a Bf 109, claimed another destroyed on the 28th and a He 111 on the 30th. He was awarded the DFC (22.10.40).

Pegge commanded 610 from December 1941 until February 1942, when he was posted overseas. On June 9 he was given command of 127 Squadron in the Western Desert. Pegge destroyed a Bf 109 on July 8 and two Ju 87s on September 2. He left the squadron in April 1943, returned to the UK and became an instructor at 56 OTU.

In September 1944 Pegge went to 126 Squadron at Bradwell Bay, as supernumerary Squadron Leader. He took command of 131 Squadron at Friston in October and led it until June 1945. He was then posted to command 607 Squadron in Burma, which he did until its disbandment at Mingaladon on August 19 1945.

Pegge was awarded a Bar to the DFC (29.1.46). He died on May 9 1950, serving as a Squadron Leader.

APO 29.10.38   PO 29.8.39   FO 3.9.40   FL 3.9.41
SL 1.7.44   SL 1.8.47

DAVID ALWYNE PEMBERTON

33036   SL   Pilot   British   1 Squadron

Pemberton entered RAF College, Cranwell in January 1930 as a flight cadet. On graduation in December 1932 he joined 99 Squadron at Upper Heyford. In March 1934 Pemberton was posted to HQ Palestine and Transjordan at Jerusalem. He returned to the UK in September 1936 and was supernumerary at No 1 RAF Depot, Uxbridge until posted to the staff of 601 Squadron, AuxAF on July 22 1937.

Pemberton was appointed a Flying Examining Officer at 26 (Training) Group on September 16 1938. In 1940 he was with HQ 67 Wing in France and on May 23 took command of No 1 Squadron. The squadron was withdrawn to Tangmere on June 17 1940.

On August 16 Pemberton claimed a He 111 destroyed. His Hurricane, P 2751, was set alight by return fire in this engagement but he returned safely to Northolt. On the 18th Pemberton destroyed a Bf 109. He was awarded the DFC (1.10.40).

At dawn on November 3 1940 Pemberton was flying back from Collyweston to Wittering. He was killed when he slow-rolled and flew into the ground. Pemberton was 28. He is buried in the new churchyard of St Eadburgh at Broadway, Worcestershire.

PO 17.12.32   FO 17.6.34   FL 1.10.36   SL 1.4.39

PAUL ERIC PENFOLD

77684   PO   Air Gunner   British   29 Squadron

Penfold served with 29 Squadron from 1939 to 1941. He was released from the RAF in 1945, as a Squadron Leader.

PO 1.2.40   FO 1.2.41   FL 1.8.42

WILLIAM DAVID PENFOLD

115753   Sgt   Aircrew   British   236 Squadron

Joined 236 Squadron on October 12 1940. Commissioned in January 1942, Penfold was released from the RAF in 1947, as a Squadron Leader MBE.

PO 26.1.42   FO 1.10.42   FL 26.1.43   SL 1.5.45

VERNON WILLIAM FOX PENFORD

52434   F/Sgt   Pilot   British   23 Squadron

Born on August 26 1909, Penford was a pre-war airman pilot and was with 23 Squadron at Collyweston in early July 1940.

Commissioned from Warrant Officer in February 1943, he retired from the RAF on September 1 1950, as a Flight Lieutenant, retaining the rank of Squadron Leader. Penford died in 1976.

PO 22.2.43   FO 22.8.43   FL 22.2.45   FL 22.8.46

DENIS ARTHUR PENNINGTON

41949   PO   Pilot   British   245 and 253 Squadrons

Pennington joined the RAF on a short service commission in February 1939. He was with 245 Squadron in early 1940 and over Dunkirk on May 30 he shared in probably destroying a Do 17.

On October 13 1940 Pennington was posted to 253 Squadron at Kenley.

He was awarded the DFC (5.3.43), as an Acting Squadron Leader with 151 Squadron, operating in Mosquitos from Wittering. The citation credited him with three enemy aircraft destroyed. Pennington was released from the RAF in 1946, as a Squadron Leader.

APO 15.4.39   PO 6.11.39   FO 6.11.40   FL 6.11.41

ALAN WILLIAM PENNINGTON-LEGH

37687   FL   Pilot   British   248 and 232 Squadrons

Pennington-Legh joined the RAF on a short service commission in January 1936. He was posted to 9 FTS, Thornaby on April 4 and with training completed he joined 43 Squadron at Tangmere on October 11.

When 248 Squadron was reformed at Hendon in October 1939 Pennington-Legh joined it as a Flight Commander. He took command of 232 Squadron at Skitten on October 1 1940 and led it until May 1941. He returned to the squadron in July and commanded it until October 1941.

In early 1942 Pennington-Legh was commanding 11 Squadron, operating in Blenheims in the Western Desert. He took the squadron to Ceylon in March 1942. He was killed with the squadron on June 1 1943, as a Wing Commander.

Pennington-Legh was 28. He is remembered on the Singapore Memorial, Column 423.

APO 23.3.36   PO 27.1.37   FO 27.10.38   FL 3.9.40
SL 1.12.41

BRUCE PENNYCUICK

122315   **Sgt**   **Observer**   **British**   **236 Squadron**

Joined the RAFVR in April 1939 as a trainee Wop/AG. Pennycuick later trained as an observer and joined 236 Squadron in late September 1940.

At the end of the year Pennycuick was posted to 59 Squadron at Thorney Island, operating in Hudsons on anti-shipping duties. He was commissioned in May 1942. On the night of June 25/26 1942 the squadron took part in the third 1000-bomber raid, flying from North Coates and with Bremen as the target.

After a staff job at HQ 16 Group Pennycuick was posted to 279 (ASR) Squadron at Thornaby-on-Tees, operating in Warwicks which had airborne lifeboats attached.

Pennycuick's final posting was as Station Commander RAF Beccles, a satellite of RAF Langham. He was released in 1946, as a Squadron Leader.

PO 1.5.42   FO 1.11.42   FL 1.5.44

HUGH HAROLD PERCY

74688   **FO**   **Pilot**   **British**   **264 Squadron**

Percy, of Chwilog, Caernarvonshire, learned to fly with the Cambridge University Air Squadron and was called to full-time service soon after the outbreak of war. He went to ITW, Cambridge in November 1939 and was then posted to FTS, Cranwell on No 2 War Course. After completing his training at 5 FTS, Sealand Percy went to the No 1 School of Army Co-operation at Old Sarum.

After a few days he was posted to 5 OTU, Aston Down, where he converted to Defiants. Percy joined 264 Squadron at Duxford in mid-June 1940.

He was killed on May 22 1944, as a Flight Lieutenant with 610 Squadron. Percy was 24 years old and is remembered on the Runnymede Memorial, Panel 203.

PO 8.11.39   FO 3.10.40   FL 3.10.41

FREDERICK STANLEY PERKIN

104446   **Sgt**   **Pilot**   **British**   **600, 615, 73 Sqdns, 421 Flt**

Perkin was born in 1920 and joined the RAFVR in April 1939, beginning his elementary flying training at 15 E&RFTS, Redhill in June. Called to full-time service at the outbreak of war he went to No 1 ITW, Cambridge and on October 25 1939 to 22 EFTS, Cambridge on No 1 War Course.

On April 12 1940 Perkin was posted to 11 FTS, Shawbury, moving on to 5 OTU, Aston Down on July 28, to convert to Blenheims, after which he joined 600 Squadron at Manston on August 16. The squadron moved to Hornchurch on the 21st, Perkin made one flight with 600, on the 24th and then next day went to 615 Squadron at Kenley.

The squadron was withdrawn to Prestwick on the 28th and there Perkin converted to Hurricanes. On September 15 1940 he was posted to 73 Squadron at Castle Camps. He was shot down in flames over London on the 23rd, baled out, unhurt, and landed in the sea east of Sheppey. His Hurricane, V 7445, crashed in the Swale, Elmley.

Perkin joined 421 Flight at Gravesend on October 25. It was expanded to squadron strength and re-numbered 91 Squadron at Hawkinge on January 12 1941. Commissioned in August, Perkin was posted to 58 OTU, Grangemouth on September 12, moving soon afterwards to 61 OTU, Heston and later Rednal. From July 12 1942 he was attached to the 52nd Pursuit Group USAAF at Eglinton, Northern Ireland, instructing on Spitfires. He rejoined 91 Squadron on August 24 but moved on to 111 Squadron at Kenley on September 15.

The squadron was posted to North Africa later in the month and embarked on the SS 'Christiaan Huygens' for Gibraltar. It flew into Maison Blanche, Algiers on November 11 1942. Perkin served with 111 until May 13 1943, when he returned to the UK. He instructed at 55 OTU, Annan from July 1 1943 until January 1944 and then spent the remainder of the war controlling on long-range radar sets from Hythe, directing Spitfires and Tempests intercepting V1 flying bombs.

Perkin was released from the RAF in May 1946, as a Flight Lieutenant. He died in 1988.

PO 21.8.41   FO 21.8.42   FL 21.8.43

GEORGES CAMILLE PERRIN

No unknown   **Adjudant**   **Pilot**   **French**   **615 and 249 Sqdns**

Perrin was born in Huriel, France on August 5 1917. He was posted to 6 OTU, Sutton Bridge on August 19 1940 and joined 615 Squadron at Prestwick on September 19.

He moved to 249 Squadron at North Weald on October 1 and on the 12th was shot down in combat with Bf 109s over Eastchurch, in Hurricane V 7313. Perrin baled out, slightly wounded, and was admitted to hospital.

After being wounded in 1941 he was grounded. He was a trained engineer and was posted to an RAF School for further training, after which he specialised in radio.

In the post-war years Perrin owned a radio and TV business in Bourges. He died in 1981.

HENRY THOMAS PERRY

770435   **Sgt**   **Radar Operator**   **British**   **23 Squadron**

Perry, of Saffron Walden, joined 23 Squadron at Collyweston on July 18 1940. He was one of the crew of Blenheim L 6721, which crashed at Orchard Way Road, South Berstead on October 30 1940, killing all three men on board. The aircraft's R/T had failed and weather conditions had seriously deteriorated when it returned from a night patrol, looking for its base at Ford.

Perry was 23. He is buried in Saffron Walden Cemetery, Essex.

GEORGE CHARLES BOYCE PETERS

40593   **FO**   **Pilot**   **British**   **79 Squadron**

Joined the RAF on a short service commission in January 1938. Peters was posted to 3 FTS, South Cerney on April 9 and after completing his training he went to the staff of 2 School of Technical Training at Cosford on December 23 1938.

Peters joined 79 Squadron at Biggin Hill in early August 1940. On the 15th he claimed a Bf 110 destroyed, on the 30th a He 111 and on September 4 another Bf 110. He failed to return from intercepting He 111s over the Irish Sea on September 29. His Hurricane, P 5177, crashed into the sea and his body was recovered on the Irish coast. Peters was 27 years old. He is buried in Rathnew Cemetery, Co Wicklow.

OTTO JOHN PETERSON

C 900   **PO**   **Pilot**   **American**   **1 (RCAF) Squadron**

Born in Eckville, Atlanta on March 14 1915, Peterson joined the RCAF on November 7 1938 and was with No 1 (RCAF) Squadron when it arrived in the UK on June 20 1940.

He claimed a Bf 109 destroyed on September 9 and shared a Do 17 on the 25th. Peterson was shot down and killed in combat with Ju 88s and Bf 110s over North Kent on September 27. His Hurricane, P 3647, crashed at Hever.

Peterson was 24. He is buried in Brookwood Military Cemetery, Woking.

ALEXANDER HENRY PETTET

85011   **PO**   **Observer**   **British**   **248 Squadron**

Pettet, of Hassocks, Essex, joined 248 Squadron on September 29 1940. He was one of the crew of a Blenheim detailed to fly from Sumburgh to Wick for operations on December 13 1940. The aircraft collided with another whilst formating, crashed into the sea and sank.

Pettet was 28. He is remembered on the Runnymede Memorial, Panel 9.

PO 25.8.40

HENRY WILLIAM PETTIT

745645   **Sgt**   **Pilot**   **British**   **1 and 605 Squadrons**

Pettit, of Chingford, Essex, joined No 1 Squadron at Wittering in September 1940. He moved to 605 Squadron at Croydon on October 20.

He was killed on February 2 1941, as a Sergeant with 605. Pettit was 20 years old. He is remembered on the Runnymede Memorial, Panel 50.

RICHARD DUNNING PEXTON

72150   **FL**   **Pilot**   **British**   **615 Squadron**

Born in Yorkshire and brought up in Alberta, Canada, Pexton was commissioned in the RAFVR in January 1938. He was called to full-time service at the outbreak of war and joined 615 Squadron at Croydon. He flew to Merville on November 15 1939, in a squadron Gladiator.

Shot down in France in June 1940, Pexton was reported 'Missing' but he turned up in a hospital in England, with leg wounds. He served with 615 throughout the Battle of Britain.

Pexton was awarded the AFC (26.10.43) and the DFC (16.2.45). He was then an Acting Wing Commander with 61 Squadron, operating in Lancasters from Skellingthorpe.

He was released from the RAF in 1945, as a Wing Commander.

PO (RAFVR) 26.1.38   *FO 15.9.39*   *FL 15.9.40*   *SL 1.12.41*

JAN PIOTR PFEIFFER

76728   **PO**   **Pilot**   **Polish**   **32 and 257 Squadrons**

Pfeiffer was born on November 25 1909. He joined 32 Squadron at Biggin Hill on August 18 1940. He crashed on landing at Hawkinge on the 22nd, unhurt. The next day he again crashed at Hawkinge, landing on one wheel after his Hurricane, P 2795, was damaged in combat.

On September 16 Pfeiffer moved to 257 Squadron at Martlesham Heath but was posted away to 5 BGS on the 28th, as a staff pilot. He was later instructing at 12 (P) AFU at Grantham. To prepare for a return to operations Pfeiffer went to 54 OTU, Charter Hall on July 13 1943. He joined 307 Squadron at Predannack on October 12 and

was killed on December 20, on a training flight from Sumburgh. His Mosquito, X 648, crashed into the sea, cause unknown. Both Pfeiffer and his navigator, Pilot Officer KE Kesicki, were lost.

PO 1.3.41   *FO 1.3.42*   *FL 1.3.43*

JACQUES ARTHUR LAURENT PHILIPPART

81628   **PO**   **Pilot**   **Belgian**   **213 Squadron**

Philippart was in the Belgian Air Force in early 1940 and flew Fairey Foxes. After the blitzkrieg of May 1940 he went to France and was employed in ferrying aircraft for l'Armée de l'Air. In June he flew to Bayonne and sailed in a Dutch cargo ship for England, arriving at Southampton on June 23.

After converting to Hurricanes Philippart joined 213 Squadron at Exeter on July 23. He claimed a Ju 88 destroyed on August 11, three Bf 110s on the 15th and a Ju 88 on the 22nd. Philippart claimed another Ju 88 on August 25 but was himself shot down in combat off Portland by Hauptmann Mayer of I/JG 53. He baled out but was killed, his body being washed ashore three days later.

Philippart was 31. He was buried in Exeter Higher Cemetery, Heavitree but on October 20 1949 his remains were exhumed and re-buried in the Pelouse d'Honneur Cemetery of Brussels at Evere. Philippart was the first Belgian ace of the war.

JAMES PHILLIP

751714   **Sgt**   **Aircrew**   **British**   **25 Squadron**

Joined 25 Squadron at North Weald in early October 1940. Phillip was killed on May 17 1942, as a Flight Sergeant with 48 Squadron.

He was 21 years old and is remembered on the Runnymede Memorial, Panel 75.

AUSTIN PHILLIPS

525665   **Sgt**   **Aircrew**   **British**   **604 Squadron**

A pre-war regular airman, Phillips joined 604 Squadron at Middle Wallop on October 12 1940.

No other service details traced.

ERNEST RUSSELL PHILLIPS

83293   **PO**   **Pilot**   **British**   **235 Squadron**

Phillips joined 235 Squadron on August 14 1940. He was killed on February 14 1941, still with the squadron. He was 28 years old and is buried in St Mary's churchyard, Great Bircham, Norfolk.

PO 28.7.40

NORMAN TAYLOR PHILLIPS

365324   **F/Sgt**   **Pilot**   **British**   **65 Squadron**

Born in Gillingham, Kent in 1909, Phillips joined the RAF as a direct-entry apprentice in 1924. He later volunteered for pilot training and passed out as a Sergeant-Pilot in 1931.

He was with 65 Squadron at Northolt in early 1940. Over Dunkirk on May 27 Phillips destroyed a Do 17. On July 7 he claimed a Bf 109 destroyed. He was shot down and killed during an action with Bf 109s over Manston on August 8 1940, probably by Oberleutnant Müncheberg of III/JG 26. His Spitfire, K 9905, crashed and burned out.

Phillips is buried in Chatham Cemetery, Kent.

RANDALL FREDERICK PRENTER PHILLIPS

116899   Sgt   Pilot   British   602 Squadron

Joined 602 Squadron, AuxAF at Abbotsinch in June 1937 as a trainee air gunner. In April 1939 a scheme was brought in for the AuxAF to have NCO pilots. Phillips was probably the first man accepted for training as such.

He was called to full-time service in late August 1939 and posted to 7 FTS, Peterborough to complete his flying training. Phillips rejoined 602 at Drem in March 1940, as a Sergeant-Pilot. In March 1941 he went to CFS, Upavon for an instructor's course, after which he was posted to 6 FTS, Little Rissington. Commissioned in February 1942, Phillips moved to 3 (P) AFU at Lulsgate Bottom in June, later moving with the unit to South Cerney.

Phillips returned to Lulsgate Bottom in October 1943, when he became an instructor at 7 FIS. He was released from the RAF in September 1945, as a Flight Lieutenant.

PO 16.2.42   FO 1.10.42   FL 16.2.44

JOHN ROSS PHILLIPSON

650678   LAC   Radar Operator   British   604 Squadron

Phillipson, of Nottinghamshire, was in France with the AASF, as a ground radio operator. Back in England in early June 1940 he volunteered for aircrew duties of a secret nature. After a short radar course at Yatesbury he was posted to 604 Squadron at Gravesend on July 10.

Flying with John Cunningham on November 19 1940 Phillipson assisted in the destruction of a Ju 88, Cunningham's first victory. On December 23 and January 3 1941 he assisted in destroying He 111s, both times with Cunningham.

In 1942 Phillipson was with 89 Squadron in the Middle East. He was killed on January 5 1943, in a flying accident, as a Warrant Officer. The award of the DFC (19.2.43) was gazetted after his death. The citation stated that he had recently taken part in the destruction of three enemy aircraft.

Phillipson is buried in Moascar War Cemetery, Egypt.

ROBERT FERGUSON PHILO

42433   PO   Pilot   British   151 Squadron

Philo joined the RAF on a short service commission in June 1939. He was posted to 151 Squadron at Digby on September 18 1940. He was released from the RAF in 1945, as a Flight Lieutenant.

APO 5.8.39   PO 28.4.40   FO 28.4.41   FL 28.4.42

STANISLAW PIATKOWSKI

76618   PO   Pilot   Polish   79 Squadron

Joined 79 Squadron at Biggin Hill on September 11 1940. Piatkowski was killed on October 25 when he crashed near Carew Cheriton after a routine patrol, in Hurricane N 2708.

Piatkowski was 28. He is buried in St Illtyd's churchyard, Pembrey, Carmarthenshire. He is also remembered on the Polish Air Force Memorial at Northolt. He was awarded the KW (30.10.41).

JAMES PICKERING

117397   Sgt   Pilot   British   64 Squadron

Pickering was in the RAFVR before the war. In September 1939 the FAA was short of pilots and after Pickering was called up he was posted to Donibristle and joined the Torpedo-Spotter-Reconnaissance Flight. He was later posted to deck-landing training on HMS 'Argus' in the Western Mediterranean. Offered a transfer to the FAA, he declined and was posted to 3 BGS, Aldergrove, as a staff pilot.

On May 4 1940 Pickering was recalled to the FAA and joined 759 (T) Squadron at Eastleigh for a refresher deck-landing course. He was later posted to 804 Squadron at Hatston. By mid-June the RAF was short of pilots and Pickering was recalled and posted to 7 OTU, Hawarden. After converting to Spitfires he joined 64 Squadron at Kenley in early July.

Within two weeks Pickering was told to report to Uxbridge and became one of a group of nine sergeants and one officer. They were flown to Hullavington, picked up Hurricanes, flew them to Abbotsinch and were embarked on HMS 'Argus', where they were joined by four more officers. They were told their destination was Malta and they were now 418 Flight.

The 'Argus' sailed on July 23, arrived at Gibraltar and sailed for Malta on the 31st. At dawn on August 2 they flew off to Luqa. 418 Flight and the Malta Fighter Flight were amalgamated into 261 Squadron on August 16 1940.

Pickering damaged a Ju 87, a Ju 88 and a Cant Z 506B on January 19 1941. He left Malta on April 7, flying to Egypt as a passenger in a Wellington. He ferried a Hurricane to Greece then joined the ADU at Takoradi. Commissioned in January 1942, Pickering was then with 80 Squadron in the Western Desert. Later in the year he joined 145 Squadron there.

In 1944/45 Pickering was in Belgium, commanding 511 FRU. He was released from the RAF in 1945, as a Flight Lieutenant, and was awarded the AFC (1.1.46). Pickering served in the RAFVR from 1947.

PO 29.1.42   FO 1.10.42   FL 29.1.44   FO (RAFVR) 17.7.47

JOHN HARCOURT PICKERING

80821   PO   Pilot   British   66 Squadron

Pickering, of Reading, Berkshire, was with 66 Squadron at Coltishall in early July 1940. On the 29th he shared a He 111 and on August 30 shared another. On this day Pickering was shot down into the sea during an attack on a Do 17 twenty miles east of Aldeburgh. He was rescued by the crew of a lightship, unhurt.

On September 24 Pickering claimed a Bf 109 destroyed. He was shot down by Major Mölders of JG 51 in combat over Canterbury on October 11. His Spitfire, X 4562, crashed and burned out in Covert Wood, Elham. Pickering was injured and was admitted to the Kent and Canterbury Hospital.

He was posted away from 66 in April 1941 to be an instructor. He was killed on February 15 1942, aged 21. The unit he was serving with at the time of his death is not known. Pickering is buried in Llanwit Major Cemetery, Glamorganshire.

PO 10.6.40   FO 10.6.41

TONY GARFORTH PICKERING

114471   Sgt   Pilot   British   32 and 501 Squadrons

Joined the RAFVR on July 30 1939 and began flying training at 9 E&RFTS, Ansty. Pickering was called up in mid-September 1939 and posted to 3 ITW, Hastings. He went to 15 EFTS, Redhill on November 23 and moved on to 5 FTS, Sealand on April 27 1940.

Pickering was posted from Sealand direct to 32 Squadron at Biggin Hill on July 27. The CO, Squadron Leader J Worrall, would have none of this and he, with two other new arrivals, was sent to 6 OTU, Sutton Bridge. Having converted to Hurricanes, Pickering rejoined 32 on August 25. Two days later the squadron was sent north to Acklington for a rest. The CO said that Pickering was not in need of a rest and he went to 501 Squadron at Gravesend on August 28.

In an action with Bf 109s over Maidstone on September 11 Pickering was shot down, in Hurricane P 5200. He baled out, unhurt. He claimed a Bf 109 destroyed on October 29. Pickering was posted to 601 Squadron at Northolt on December 20. He was posted away to 57 OTU, Hawarden on February 14 1941, as a test pilot for the MU there. Commissioned in December 1941, Pickering became an instructor at 57 OTU on the 20th of the month.

He returned to operations on February 19 1943, when he joined 131 Squadron at Castletown, as a Flight Commander. Pickering served with the squadron until January 7 1944. From then on he held

TG Pickering (continued)

various appointments in the Exeter Sector, as Controller and Gunnery Officer among other things.

On February 11 1945 Pickering was posted to the Middle East and became Squadron Commander at the BGS, El Ballah. He returned to the UK in December 1945 and was released later in the month, as a Squadron Leader.

PO 13.12.41   FO 1.10.42   FL 13.12.43

JAMES THOMAS PICKFORD

175421   Sgt   Air Gunner   British   604 Squadron

Born on September 1 1917, Pickford joined the RAFVR in February 1939 as a trainee Wop/AG. He did his gunnery instruction at Store Street, Westminster and flew in Harts and Hinds at Gravesend on Sundays.

Mobilised on September 1 1939, Pickford was posted to 604 Squadron at North Weald. He went to Evanton on November 6 and after a month-long course passed out as an LAC Air Gunner and returned to 604.

On May 10 1940 the squadron provided an escort for Blenheims detailed to bomb German transport aircraft on the beach at Wassenaar, Holland. After the bombing Pickford's pilot, Pilot Officer IKS Joll, decided to have a low-level strafe of the beach. The port propellor came off, either shot off by ground fire or by striking the ground. The Blenheim crash-landed on the beach but did not catch fire and the two men were not badly hurt. With the help of Dutch people they managed to get on the SS 'Dotterel' on the 13th and return to England.

In late December 1940 Pickford was posted to 207 Squadron at Waddington, equipped with Manchesters and later Lancasters. He did two tours, flying 53 operations and was awarded the DFM (29.12.42), as a Flight Sergeant.

Commissioned from Warrant Officer in February 1944, Pickford was released from the RAF on June 23 1946, as a Flying Officer.

PO 15.2.44   FO 15.8.44

LESLIE PIDD

742636   Sgt   Pilot   British   238 Squadron

Pidd, of Dunswell, Yorkshire, was born in 1918. A pre-war member of the RAFVR, he was called to full-time service at the outbreak of war.

He joined 238 Squadron at Middle Wallop on July 18 1940. Pidd claimed a Bf 109 destroyed on August 11, returning to base with his starboard wing and glycol system damaged following the combat two miles east of Weymouth, slightly injured.

On September 15 Pidd was shot down and killed in combat with He 111s and Bf 110s over Kenley. His Hurricane, P 2836, crashed into an oak tree at Kent College, Pembrey.

Pidd is buried in St Peter's churchyard, Woodmansey, Yorkshire.

OSWALD St JOHN PIGG

39678   FO   Pilot   British   72 Squadron

Born in 1918, Pigg was educated at the Royal Grammar School, Newcastle-upon-Tyne. He joined the RAF on a short service commission in March 1937, was posted to 10 FTS, Tern Hill on May 9 and joined 72 Squadron at Church Fenton on November 27 1937.

Over Dunkirk on June 2 1940 Pigg destroyed a Ju 87. His aircraft was damaged by machine-gun fire from another Stuka and he made a belly landing at Gravesend, slightly wounded in the leg.

On August 15 Pigg claimed a Bf 109 destroyed. He was shot down

and killed in combat with Bf 109s on September 1 1940. His Spitfire, P 9458, crashed and burned out on Elvey Farm, Pluckley. Pigg is buried in St Oswald's Burial Ground, Durham.

APO 9.5.37   PO 8.3.38   FO 8.10.39

EDWARD ROMAN PILCH

76706   PO   Pilot   Polish   302 Squadron

Pilch was born on February 25 1915. He joined 302 Squadron at Leconfield on July 16 1940. He claimed a Do 17 destroyed on September 15 and a Ju 88 on the 19th.

Awarded the KW and Bar (1.2.41), Pilch shared in destroying a Ju 88 on February 16 1941. On a training flight from Westhampnett four days later Pilch crashed in flames at Arundel, cause unknown, and was killed. He is buried in Chichester Cemetery, Sussex. He was awarded the VM (5th Class)(19.2.42).

PO 24.1.40

ALFRED PILKINGTON

1052307   Sgt   Aircrew   British   23 Squadron

Joined 23 Squadron at Middle Wallop on September 20 1940. No other service details traced.

DAVID JOHN COLIN PINCKNEY

72520   FO   Pilot   British   603 Squadron

Pinckney, of Hungerford, Berkshire, was educated at Eton and learned to fly with the Cambridge University Air Squadron. He was commissioned in the RAFVR in December 1938.

Called to full-time service in early October 1939, Pinckney completed his flying training and was posted to No 1 School of Army Co-operation at Old Sarum in late May 1940. He went to 5 OTU, Aston Down in early June and after converting to Spitfires joined 603 Squadron at Dyce on July 6.

Pinckney claimed a Bf 109 shot down on August 29 but he was himself shot down, baled out, slightly burned, and was admitted to hospital. His Spitfire, R 6753, crashed at St Mary's Road, Dymchurch. On September 27 Pinckney probably destroyed a Bf 109, on October 17 and 19 he claimed two more destroyed, on November 11 and 17 probably two more and on the 23rd a CR 42 destroyed.

In December 1940 Pinckney was posted to the Far East and in March 1941 he was in charge of the initial formation of 67 Squadron at Kallang. When the squadron was fully formed with Buffalo IIs he was appointed a Flight Commander. During actions fought against the Japanese in December 1941 and early January 1942 Pinckney destroyed three Japanese aircraft.

He was killed on January 23 1942, as a Flight Lieutenant with 67 Squadron, aged 24. He is remembered on the Singapore Memorial, Column 412. Pinckney was awarded the DFC (8.5.42).

PO (RAFVR) 6.12.38   PO 2.10.39   FO 6.6.40   FL 6.6.41

HERBERT MORETON PINFOLD

37021   SL   Pilot   British   56 Squadron

Born on February 5 1913, Pinfold joined the RAF on a short service commission in mid-September 1934. On the 29th he was posted to 5 FTS, Sealand and with training completed he went to 6 Squadron at Ismailia, Egypt on September 5 1935. Back in the UK, Pinfold was posted to 64 Squadron at Martlesham Heath on March 19 1936 and on July 16 1938 he joined 502 Squadron, AuxAF at Aldergrove, as Flying Instructor and Adjutant.

Pinfold was instructing at 8 FTS, Montrose when he was posted to command 56 Squadron at North Weald on August 25 1940. He left the squadron in January 1941.

In September 1945 Pinfold was a Wing Commander on the staff at Air HQ Kandy. He retired from the RAF on October 1 1958, as a Group Captain.

APO 14.9.34   PO 14.9.35   FO 14.3.37   FL 14.3.39
SL 1.9.40   WC 1.9.42   WC 1.10.46   GC 1.7.53

PHILIP CAMPBELL PINKHAM

37208   FL   Pilot   British   19 Squadron

Joined the RAF on a short service commission in April 1935. Pinkham was posted to 6 FTS, Netheravon on May 7 and joined 17 Squadron at Kenley on February 17 1936. He moved to the Station Flight at Mildenhall on August 16 1937.

Pinkham took command of 19 Squadron at Duxford on June 5 1940. He was awarded the AFC (11.7.40). On September 5 he was shot down and killed in combat with Bf 109s over the Thames Estuary. His Spitfire, P 9422, is believed to have crashed in Whitehorse Wood, Birling, Kent. Pinkham was 25. He is buried in St Andrew's churchyard, Kingsbury, Middlesex.

APO 16.4.35   PO 16.4.36   FO 16.10.37   FL 16.10.39

JOSEF PIPA

145101   Sgt   Pilot   Czechoslovakian   43 Squadron

Began flying in 1935. When the Germans moved into Czechoslovakia Pipa went to Poland. In September 1939 he travelled to Roumania and eventually reached France, where he joined l'Armée de l'Air. He was awarded the Czech Military Cross and the C de G (Fr) in 1940.

After the collapse of France Pipa escaped to Morocco, reached Gibraltar and finally arrived in England. He joined 43 Squadron at Usworth on October 4 1940.

One day in October 1941 Pipa's No 2 ditched in the sea after his engine failed. Pipa made sure the pilot was out of his aircraft and obtained a fix for ASR. In the cramped space of his cockpit he removed his Sutton harness and parachute, extracted his dinghy, inflated it and then dropped it within fifty yards of the pilot in the water. For this action he was commended by the AOC and given a Bar to the Czech Military Cross. Later in 1941 Pipa shared a Ju 88 with his Flight Commander.

Commissioned in February 1943, Pipa was released from the RAF as a Flight Lieutenant. He died in Britain in 1977.

PO 2.2.43   FO 2.8.43   FL 2.2.45

ARTHUR HOWARD PIPER

68149   Sgt   Air Gunner   British   236 Squadron

Joined the RAFVR as a u/t pilot but was invalided out in 1938 with high blood pressure. Piper rejoined as an air gunner in 1939.

Called to full-time service at the outbreak of war, he completed his training and joined 236 Squadron in January 1940. On August 8 Piper was gunner in Blenheim N 3603, which returned to Thorney Island with severe damage to its tail caused by flak during ground attack on Querqueville aerodrome. The aircraft was possibly also attacked by Oberfeldwebel Richter of III/JG 27. Piper and his pilot, Sergeant RC Smith, were unhurt.

In October 1940 Piper was posted to 7 Squadron, operating in Stirlings from Oakington. He left the squadron in March 1941 and was commissioned in June. Piper joined 218 Squadron in August 1943, again with Stirlings and operating from Downham Market. On one occasion he was rear gunner of an aircraft detailed for a mine-laying operation. Near the target the aircraft was attacked by a fighter. At the outset Piper's turret was hit and his guns put out of action. He skilfully directed his captain's manoeuvres so that eight attacks were frustrated and the enemy aircraft driven off. Piper was awarded the DFC (10.3.44).

He took a pilot's course in 1948 and later qualified as an A 2 Instructor at CFS. Piper retired from the RAF on January 24 1958, as a Squadron Leader.

PO 5.6.41   FO 31.3.42   FL 31.3.43   SL 1.8.47

HAROLD ALFRED PIPPARD

77365   PO   Air Gunner   British   29 Squadron

Born on June 15 1909, Pippard joined the RAF with a direct-entry commission as an air gunner in early 1940. He joined 29 Squadron at Digby in July.

Pippard was released from the RAF in 1946 but rejoined in 1947. He retired on September 5 1958, as a Squadron Leader.

APO 3.2.40   PO 16.3.40   FO 16.3.41   FL 16.3.42
SL 1.8.47

JOHN GILBERT PIPPET

86347   PO   Pilot   British   64 Squadron

Pippet, of Hull, joined 64 Squadron at Biggin Hill on October 16 1940. He was killed on February 23 1941, still with 64.

He was 21 years old and is remembered on the Runnymede Memorial, Panel 34.

PO 21.9.40

MARIAN PISAREK

P 1381   FO   Pilot   Polish   303 Squadron

Born on January 3 1912, Pisarek was in the PAF before the war. In the fighting in September 1939 he destroyed two enemy aircraft and shared another, flying with 141 Squadron.

Pisarek arrived in England on June 23 1940. He was posted to 303 Squadron at Northolt on August 21. He claimed a Bf 109 destroyed on September 7. On this day Pisarek was himself shot down by a Bf 109 and baled out, unhurt. His Hurricane, R 4173, crashed into the back garden of 40 Roding Road, Loughton, Essex, killing three people in an air raid shelter.

On September 15 Pisarek claimed a Bf 109 destroyed, on October 5 a Bf 110 and on the 7th another Bf 109. He was awarded the VM (5th Class)(23.12.40). Pisarek was posted to 315 Squadron at Acklington at its formation on January 21 1941. He was awarded the KW (1.2.41).

On March 30 Pisarek was posted to 308 Squadron at Baginton, as a Flight Commander. He took command of the squadron on June 23 1941. He destroyed a Bf 109 on July 2, shared one on the 17th, probably destroyed one on the 22nd and destroyed another four Bf 109s on August 14, September 20 and 21 and October 13. Pisarek was awarded three Bars to the KW and the DFC (30.10.41).

He was posted away to HQ 11 Group on December 8 1941, as Polish Liaison Officer. Pisarek was appointed Wing Leader of the Northolt Polish Wing on April 17 1942. He was killed on April 29, leading the Wing over France, in Spitfire MB 307. He probably crashed into the sea.

Pisarek is remembered on the Polish Air Force Memorial at Northolt. He was awarded the VM (4th Class)(31.10.47). His portrait was done by Eric Kennington and Cuthbert Orde.

FO 1.3.41   FL 1.9.41

PAUL BROOKS PITCHER

C 615   FO   Pilot   Canadian   1 (RCAF) Squadron

Born in Montreal on August 5 1913, Pitcher was educated in Canada and the Institut Sillig at Vevey, Switzerland. He graduated from the McGill University Law Faculty in 1938 and joined a law firm.

In December 1935 Pitcher had joined the RCAF Auxiliary and served with 115 (F) Squadron, Montreal. He was with 1 (RCAF) Squadron when it arrived in the UK on June 20 1940.

Pitcher damaged a He 111 on September 15, damaged a Do 17 on the 27th and claimed a Bf 109 destroyed and a Bf 110

PB Pitcher (continued)

damaged on October 5. He took command of the squadron on December 13 1940. It was re-numbered 401 Squadron on March 1. Pitcher commanded until the 11th, when he was posted away. He later formed 411 Squadron at Digby and commanded the squadron from June 16 to December 16 1941.

After leave in Canada Pitcher took command of the recently-formed 417 Squadron at Tain on March 28 1942. He led the squadron to the Middle East in April and served with it until November 17, when he was repatriated to Canada. Pitcher served as SASO at Western Air Command, Vancouver and temporarily commanded RCAF 'X' Wing at Anchorage, Alaska for nine months. He then attended RCAF Air Staff College and afterwards served at Air Force HQ, Ottawa until late March 1944.

Pitcher then went back overseas, to 83 Group 2nd TAF. He returned to Canada in early September and was released on November 28 1944, as a Wing Commander.

GEOFFREY EDWARD PITTMAN

41614   FO   Pilot   British   17 Squadron

Joined the RAF on a short service commission in October 1938. Pittman did his ab initio course at No 1 E&RFTS, Hatfield, moved on to 5 FTS, Sealand on January 28 1939 and then joined 17 Squadron at Croydon on September 3.

From June 8 to 16 1940 the squadron used Le Mans, Dreux, Beaumont and Dinard as forward bases until withdrawn to Jersey and then Debden. After a week's leave the squadron was operational again. On July 12 Pittman shared a He 111 and on August 11 and 25 he shared in destroying Bf 110s. He destroyed a Ju 87 on November 11.

Pittman was posted to CFS, Upavon on November 15, for an instructor's course. He was then at 8 FTS, Montrose from December 18 1940 to March 9 1941, when he went to Southern Rhodesia, serving as an instructor at 22 SFTS, Thornhill from April 24 1941 to February 20 1944.

On his return to the UK Pittman went to 57 OTU, Eshott for a Spitfire refresher course, then to 83 GSU, Redhill on May 26, to convert to Mustang IIIs. He joined 122 Squadron at Funtington on June 5 and moved with it to Normandy on the 25th. The squadron returned to England on September 29 and began escorting RAF heavy bombers on daylight saturation raids on German targets, flying from Andrews Field, Essex.

In January 1945 Pittman was posted to No 1 Radio School at Cranwell for a Specialist Signals Officer Course. He was appointed Station Signals Officer at RAF Valley in November and was released from the RAF in January 1946, as a Squadron Leader. Pittman emigrated to Australia in 1957.

APO 14.1.39   PO 3.9.39   FO 3.9.40   FL 3.9.41
SL 1.7.45

RONALD ERIC PLANT

748027   Sgt   Pilot   British   72 and 611 Squadrons

Plant, of Coventry, joined 72 Squadron at Acklington on July 15 1940 and moved to 611 Squadron at Tern Hill on October 10.

In November Plant was with 603 Squadron at Hornchurch. He collided with a He 111 over Faversham on November 21, baled out but fell dead near Teynham. His Spitfire, P 7387, crashed and burned out at Buckland Farm, Widdenham.

Plant was 21 years old. He is buried in St Michael's churchyard, Stoke, Coventry.

GEOFFREY FRANK COLMAN PLEDGER

79216   PO   Air Gunner   British   141 Squadron

Pledger, of Westcliff-on-Sea, Essex, joined 141 Squadron at Turnhouse in June 1940. He teamed up with Flying Officer DC Williams and they flew together until they were killed on April 4 1941.

Pledger was 35. He is buried in Sutton Road Cemetery, Southend-on-Sea, Essex.

PO 15.6.40

ROBERT PLENDERLEITH

139411   Sgt   Pilot   British   73 Squadron

Plenderleith was a trainee in aeronautical engineering at Supermarine Aviation, Southampton when he joined the RAFVR on May 29 1937. He carried out his flying training at 3 E&RFTS, Hamble and being of a sufficiently high standard he was selected for six months training with the regular RAF, which he began at 11 Group Pool at Andover on April 1 1939.

On August 25 Plenderleith joined 43 Squadron at Tangmere and remained with it until May 16 1940, when he was posted to 73 Squadron in France. After the French collapse 73 was withdrawn to Church Fenton on June 18.

Plenderleith claimed a Bf 110 destroyed on September 27 and returned, damaged, to Kenley, in Hurricane P 3785. Whilst acting as weaver on October 11 he was shot down and baled out, slightly burned. His Hurricane, V 6676, crashed at Dillywood, Frindsbury. Plenderleith was admitted to Chatham Hospital and transferred three days later to the Royal Naval Auxiliary Hospital at Newton Abbot. Discharged in December, he was posted to SHQ Debden on Duty Pilot and Aerodrome Control Pilot duties.

On March 9 1941 Plenderleith went to 17 Squadron at Martlesham Heath but a month later was posted to 59 OTU, Crosby-on-Eden as an instructor. He was there until September 25, leaving then for overseas. Plenderleith began instructing at 71 OTU, Khartoum, Sudan on October 31st 1941. He rejoined 73 Squadron, then in the Western Desert, on October 27 1942 and was commissioned from Warrant Officer in November.

Plenderleith joined 253 Squadron at La Sebala on October 4 1943, as 'B' Flight Commander. The squadron moved to Italy later in the month. He was posted back to the UK on May 19 1944 and awarded the DFC (7.7.44). He was on ground duties at 26 OTU from July to September, on a basic engineering course at RAF Henlow from September to November and on an armament course at the Empire Air Armament School at RAF Manby from November 1944 to February 1945.

From March 14 1945 until released from the RAF on July 21 1947 Plenderleith served at 9 MU, Cosford and RAF Leconfield, Polebrook and Henlow, on test pilot and ferrying duties. He was employed as a civilian test pilot by de Havilland's until June 1964, when he retired from active flying. Plenderleith also served in the RAFVR from May 27 1949 to August 1951, on flying duties.

PO 21.11.42   FO 21.5.43   FL 21.11.44
FO (RAFVR) 27.5.49

RICHARD PRYER PLUMMER

39753   FO   Pilot   British   46 Squadron

Born on August 2 1912 at Haywards Heath, Plummer was educated at Hill Crest Preparatory School and Cranleigh School. He joined the RAF on a short service commission in March 1937, was posted to 5 FTS, Sealand on August 3 and joined 46 Squadron at Digby on February 19 1938.

Plummer was shot down in combat with enemy fighters on September 4. He baled out, landing at Stambridge, with extensive burns to both legs, hands and face, and was admitted to Rochford Hospital.

His Hurricane, P 3052, crashed and burned out on the railway line at Rectory Road, Hawkwell.

After Rochford Hospital was bombed, Plummer was transferred to Bradford Hospital in Yorkshire. He died there on September 14. He is buried in Western Road Cemetery, Haywards Heath.

APO 18.5.37   PO 15.3.38   FO 15.10.39

STANISLAW PLZAK

102595   Sgt   Pilot   Czechoslovakian   310 and 19 Sqdns

Joined 310 Squadron at Duxford at its formation on July 10 1940. Plzak was attached to 19 Squadron at Fowlmere on August 29 and on September 18 claimed a He 111 destroyed and on the 27th a Bf 109.

Gazetted as a Pilot Officer on August 6 1941, Plzak was reported 'Missing' on the 7th, still with 19 Squadron. He is remembered on the Runnymede Memorial, Panel 34.

PO 6.8.41

KAROL PNIAK

76707   PO   Pilot   Polish   32 and 257 Squadrons

Born at Jaworzno, Cracow on January 26 1910, Pniak joined the PAF in 1932. In the fighting in September 1939 he served in 142 Squadron, claiming two German aircraft destroyed, two others shared and two damaged.

Pniak was commissioned in January 1940 and was posted from 6 OTU, Sutton Bridge to 32 Squadron at Biggin Hill on August 8. He claimed Bf 109s destroyed on the 12th and 15th, two more on the 18th and another probably destroyed on the 24th. The next day Pniak was shot down in combat with Bf 109s over Folkestone, baled out, injured his ankle and knee in a heavy landing and was admitted to hospital. His Hurricane, V 6572, crashed at Rhodes Minnis, near Lyminge.

On September 16 Pniak was posted to 257 Squadron at Martlesham Heath. He claimed a Fiat BR 20 destroyed on November 11 and shared a second. He was posted to 306 Squadron at Tern Hill on the 23rd. Pniak was awarded the VM (5th Class)(1.2.41) and the KW (1.4.41). He was posted away to the AFDU at Duxford on November 18 1941 and on January 30 1942 he returned to 306 for duties in the Operations Room. He was awarded the DFC (1.6.42).

Pniak returned to operations with 306 on December 1 1942, as a Flight Commander. He went to West Kirby on February 13 1943 to prepare for overseas and on March 13 arrived in the Middle East in a C47 with other Polish pilots to form the Polish Fighting Team, otherwise known as 'Skalski's Circus'. They were attached to 145 Squadron and operated in the Western Desert from March 17 to May 12 and destroyed thirty enemy aircraft.

After returning to the UK Pniak went to 3 Wing on ground duties, moved to 58 OTU, Grangemouth on September 24 1943 as an instructor, and was posted to the Northolt Operations Room on November 23. He was awarded two Bars to the KW (20.12.43). Pniak then went to 61 OTU, Rednal on March 12 1944. He was posted to 84 Group on September 25 and on November 28 returned to operations, taking command of 308 Squadron at Ghent.

Pniak led the squadron until June 30 1945. He then went to HQ PAF, Blackpool and relinquished his acting rank. After an attachment to HQ 131 Wing from November 9 1945 Pniak rejoined 308 as a supernumerary on August 16 1946. He had received a third Bar to the KW (8.3.46). He was released from the PAF in December 1946 and repatriated to Poland on February 24 1947. He died there in 1980.

PO 24.1.40   FO 1.3.41   FL 1.9.42

MAURICE HENRY POCOCK

124960   Sgt   Pilot   British   72 Squadron

Born on August 1 1920, Pocock joined the RAFVR on July 21 1938. Having achieved a high standard and the required number of flying hours he was selected for six months training with the regular RAF and joined 72 Squadron at Church Fenton on June 1 1939. He was still with the squadron in early July 1940.

On September 1 Pocock's Spitfire, L 1056, was severely damaged in combat with a Bf 109 over Beachy Head. He made a belly-landing at West Malling, wounded in the left leg and wrist and was admitted to Preston Hall Hospital, Maidstone. Recovered, Pocock rejoined 72 and stayed with it until November 19 1941, when he went to 58 OTU, Grangemouth as an instructor.

Commissioned from Warrant Officer in May 1942, Pocock was posted to 93 Squadron at Wansford on September 24. It left for North Africa on October 20 1942 and landed at Algiers on November 13. Pocock was posted away to 152 Squadron at Souk-el-Khemis on April 23 1943, as a Flight Commander. The next day his Spitfire was damaged by flak and he made a forced-landing, returning to the squadron on foot on the 25th.

Pocock left the squadron on June 13 1943, returned to the UK and went to HQ Fighter Command on July 1. He went to the Middle East on October 5 to join 108 Squadron, operating in Beaufighters. Posted away on January 19 1944, Pocock returned again to the UK and went to 21 (P) AFU on April 7, as an instructor.

He received a Mention in Despatches (8.6.44) and was released from the RAF on December 19 1946, as a Flight Lieutenant.

PO 16.5.42   FO 16.11.42   FL 16.5.44

JOSEPH KENNETH POLLARD

740815   Sgt   Pilot   British   232 Squadron

Joined 232 Squadron at Sumburgh at its formation on July 17 1940. Pollard was killed on December 12 1941, as a Flight Sergeant. The unit he was serving with at that time is not known.

Pollard is remembered on the Runnymede Memorial, Panel 37.

PHILIP SELWYN COVEY POLLARD

41462   FO   Pilot   British   611 Squadron

Pollard, of Kingston, Surrey, joined the RAF on a short service commission in September 1938. He was with 611 Squadron at Digby in early July 1940.

On September 15 Pollard shared in destroying a Do 17 and on October 11 he shared in the destruction of two more.

611 Squadron acted as high cover for bombers attacking the marshalling yards at Hazebrouck on June 22 1941. In an engagement with Bf 109s Pollard was shot down and killed. He was 21 and is buried in Dunkirk Town Cemetery, France.

APO 14.12.38   PO 3.9.39   FO 3.9.40

ARTHUR HERBERT DORRIEN POND

51845   F/Sgt   Pilot   British   601 Squadron

Born on December 15 1914, Pond joined the RAF in January 1931 as an aircraft apprentice at Halton. He passed out as an LAC Metal Rigger in December 1933 and was posted to 41 Squadron at Northolt. He later went to 6 FTS, Netheravon.

Having volunteered for pilot training, Pond was selected and in July 1936 was posted to 5 E&RFTS, Hanworth, after which he moved to 6 FTS, Tern Hill. With training completed Pond joined 80 Squadron at Henlow in May 1937, to fly Gladiators. In April 1938 he was posted to No 1 AACU, then at Biggin Hill but later at Weston Zoyland and Farnborough.

Pond went to 6 OTU, Sutton Bridge on May 28 1940, converted to Hurricanes and then joined 601 Squadron at Middle Wallop on June 9. He claimed a Ju 87 destroyed on August 18. On this day his Hurricane, V 7305, was hit in the oil system by a Bf 109 of 4/JG 27 during an attack on Ju 87s over Selsey. The engine seized over the Tangmere boundary, causing Pond to crash on landing, unhurt. He received a Mention in Despatches (29.9.40). With hearing problems, he lost his operational flying category in December 1940.

AHD Pond (continued)

In March 1941 he was posted to 1403 Met Flight at St Eval, moving soon afterwards to 1404 Met Flight at Tangmere. In May Pond became an air-firing instructor at 2 (Coastal) OTU, Millom. He went to 1401 Met Flight at Bircham Newton in February 1942, became a staff pilot at 1447 Flight at Hooton Park in May 1942 and later moved to 10 Radio School at Carew Cheriton.

Commissioned from Warrant Officer in December 1942, Pond was given command of the HQ Technical Training Command Flight at White Watham in April 1944, which appointment he held until October 1945. Pond was awarded the AFC (1.1.46). He was granted a Permanent Commission in February 1949, in the Secretarial Branch, and retired on December 17 1963, as a Squadron Leader.

PO 1.12.42   FO 1.6.43   FL 1.12.44   FL 1.6.47
SL 1.7.53

WILLIAM ALAN PONTING

79216   PO   Air Gunner   British   264 Squadron

Ponting, of Whetstone, Middlesex, joined 264 Squadron at Duxford on July 9 1940.

Following a combat with Ju 88s and Bf 109s over the Channel off Thanet on August 24 Ponting and his pilot, Pilot Officer JT Jones were reported 'Missing'. Their Defiant, L 6966, is believed to have been shot down into the sea by Major Lützow of JG 3.

Ponting was 30. He is remembered on the Runnymede Memorial, Panel 9.

PO 15.6.40

PETER DESMOND POOL

83281   PO   Pilot   British   266 and 72 Squadrons

Born on July 21 1916, Pool was at Cheltenham College from 1930 to 1934. He joined 266 Squadron at Wittering on August 26 1940 and moved to 72 Squadron at Biggin Hill on October 3. Pool was shot down in flames by a Bf 109 during combat over a convoy off Deal on the 11th and baled out, wounded. His Spitfire, K 9870, crashed at Milton Regis, Sittingbourne.

Pool was killed on August 19 1942, as a Flight Lieutenant with 610 Squadron. He is remembered on the Runnymede Memorial, Panel 66.

PO 4.8.40   FO 4.8.41   FL 4.8.42

ERIC LEONARD RONALD POOLE

53222   Sgt   Pilot   British   604 Squadron

Joined 604 Squadron at Gravesend on July 15 1940. Poole was commissioned from Warrant Officer in July 1943 and released in 1947, as a Flying Officer.

PO 30.7.43   FO 30.1.44

JERZY POPLAWSKI

76751   PO   Pilot   Polish   111 and 229 Squadrons

Born in Model, Warsaw on September 21 1919, Poplawski joined the PAF in 1938.

He converted to Hurricanes at 5 OTU, Aston Down and then joined 111 Squadron at Croydon on September 10 1940, moving to 229 Squadron at Northolt on the 26th. He was injured on November 6, when he made a forced-landing at Streatley, in Hurricane P 3898, having lost the squadron in cloud and run out of fuel.

Poplawski was posted to 308 Squadron at Baginton on March 16 1941. He destroyed Bf 109s on September 4, 16, 21 and 27 and October 13. He was awarded the KW and Bar (30.10.41), a second Bar (19.2.42) and the VM (5th Class)(4.3.42). Poplawski was appointed a Flight Commander on April 30 1942 and posted away on September 1 to 58 OTU, Grangemouth, as an instructor. He went to Hullavington on September 29 for a course and returned to 58 OTU on January 28 1943.

Poplawski was given command of 315 Squadron at Hutton Cranswick on April 16. He was awarded a third Bar to the KW (20.10.43) and remained with the squadron until February 15 1944, being then posted to the Inspectorate at the PAF Staff College. He went to HQ Fighter Command on February 28 1944 and was released from the PAF in February 1947.

FO 1.3.41   FL 1.3.43

EDWARD FRANCIS PORTER

542209   Sgt   Air Gunner   British   141 Squadron

Porter, of Glasgow, joined 141 Squadron at Turnhouse on August 20 1940. He was killed on July 2 1941, as a Flight Sergeant with 12 Squadron, operating in Wellingtons from Binbrook, Lincolnshire.

Porter was 21. He is remembered on the Runnymede Memorial, Panel 37.

JOHN ANTHONY PORTER

116148   Sgt   Pilot   British   242 and 615 Squadrons

Joined 242 Squadron at Coltishall in late June 1940. Porter was posted to 615 Squadron at Kenley on August 10 and claimed a Ju 87 destroyed and shared a second on the 14th. He was posted away on September 23.

Commissioned in November 1941, Porter was released from the RAF in 1947, as a Flight Lieutenant.

PO 19.11.41   FO 1.10.42   FL 19.11.43

OWEN WELLS PORTER

146316   Sgt   Pilot   British   111 Squadron

Porter, of Alberta, Canada, joined 111 Squadron at Debden on August 31 1940.

Commissioned in February 1943, he was killed on July 31 1944, as a Flying Officer with 21 Squadron, operating in Mosquitos from Thorney Island. Porter was 23. He is buried in Morgny-la-Pommeraye churchyard, France.

PO 1.2.43   FO 1.8.43

FREDERICK HYAM POSENER

41735   PO   Pilot   South African   152 Squadron

Joined the RAF on a short service commission in December 1938.

Posener was with 152 Squadron at Warmwell in early July 1940. On the 27th he was shot down by Oberleutnant Homuth of 3/JG 27 over the Channel off Swanage, in Spitfire K 9880.

Posener was 23 years old. He is remembered on the Runnymede Memorial, Panel 9.

APO 4.3.39   PO 23.9.39

JOHN ALFRED POTTER

580179   Sgt   Pilot   British   19 Squadron

A pre-war airman pilot, Potter, of Wallasey, was with 19 Squadron in early 1940.

Over Dunkirk on May 26 he destroyed a Bf 109. On June 1 his Spitfire was severely damaged in combat over Dunkirk and the engine seized at 4000 feet, still fifteen miles from the English coast. Potter saw a small boat, glided down and landed on the sea. The French fishing boat picked him up and took him back towards Dunkirk. As they approached the port a destroyer, HMS 'Basilisk', was seen, stopped. Its engines were out of action through bombing. The French crew agreed to tow the destroyer further out, away from the bombers. In the course of all this German bombers appeared, attacked without result and were driven off by Spitfires of 19 Squadron. Towing began again. Ju 87s then appeared and their bombs set the destroyer sinking. The fishing boat took off 200 men and another destroyer arrived to pick up more survivors. Potter eventually landed at Dover, having been transferred to a coastal patrol boat.

Potter claimed Bf 110s destroyed on August 16 and 18. He failed to return from combat with enemy fighters on September 15 1940, in Spitfire X 4070. It is believed that he ditched off the French coast with severe aircraft damage and wounded. Potter's capture by the Germans was confirmed on October 4.

He was released from the RAF as a Warrant Officer and died in 1977.

HARRY ROBERT GODFREY POULTON

84925   PO   Pilot   British   616 and 64 Squadrons

Born on September 19 1918, Poulton joined the RAFVR in 1938 and began his elementary flying training at 18 E&RFTS, Fair Oaks. Called up at the outbreak of war, he was posted to No 1 ITW, Cambridge, went to 22 EFTS Cambridge in January 1940 and then to 15 FTS, Middle Wallop in May 1940.

Poulton completed his training at 15 FTS, Chipping Norton and in August was posted to 7 OTU, Hawarden to convert to Spitfires. He then joined 616 Squadron at Kirton-in-Lindsey on September 23, moving to 64 Squadron at Leconfield on October 12.

During a routine patrol on the 28th Poulton made a forced-landing near Horsford in Spitfire N 3293, cause unknown. In November 1940 he was posted to 74 Squadron at Biggin Hill. He destroyed a Bf 109 over North Foreland on May 7 1941.

In August Poulton went to 53 OTU, Llandow to instruct on Spitfires. He was posted to 611 Squadron at Drem in March 1942 but rejoined 64 Squadron at Kenley in September. Awarded the DFC (25.5.43), Poulton was captured by the Germans in January 1944. His engine failed near Dieppe, he baled out and broke his leg on landing. After two months in hospital at Amiens Poulton was sent to Dulag Luft at Frankfurt, moving soon afterwards to Stalag Luft l at Barth.

In January 1945 he was repatriated in an exchange of wounded prisoners and went into RAF Hospital, Weeton. Poulton was released from the RAF in September 1946. He rejoined in September 1951, in the Aircraft Control Branch.

Poulton retired on September 19 1968, as a Flight Lieutenant.

PO 31.8.40   FO 24.8.41   FL 30.11.42   FL 4.12.52

REGINALD ROBERT CHARLES POUND

910960   Sgt   Aircrew   British   25 Squadron

Joined 25 Squadron at North Weald in early October 1940.
No other service details traced.

EDWIN POWELL

548940   Sgt   Air Gunner   British   25 Squadron

Joined 25 Squadron at Martlesham Heath in September 1940.

Powell was killed on November 21 1940. The aircraft he was in crashed into the sea shortly after taking off. The pilot, Pilot Officer EWJ Monk, was also killed.

Powell is remembered on the Runnymede Memorial, Panel 18.

RONALD JAMES POWELL

84324   PO   Pilot   British   248 Squadron

Powell, of Finchley, Middlesex, joined 248 Squadron on September 29 1940. He was killed on July 2 1941, still with 248, aged 28.

He is remembered on the Runnymede Memorial, Panel 34.

PO 24.8.40

ROBIN PETER REGINALD POWELL

33278   FL   Pilot   British   111 Squadron

Born on September 30 1916, Powell entered RAF College, Cranwell in September 1934 as a flight cadet. On graduation he joined 111 Squadron at Northolt on August 1 1936.

At the outbreak of war Powell was a flight commander. On January 13 1940 he shared in destroying a He 111 and on April 10 shared another. During the May blitzkrieg 111 Squadron flew patrols over France from Northolt, its pre-war station. Powell destroyed an enemy aircraft on May 10, two more on the 11th and damaged two Bf 110s on the 18th. He was awarded the DFC (31.5.40).

Over Dunkirk on May 31 Powell's oxygen failed at 19000 feet and he fell to 5000 feet before regaining consciousness. On June 2 he destroyed a Bf 109 and two more on the 7th.

Powell served with 111 Squadron throughout the Battle of Britain. He formed and then took command of 121 Squadron at Kirton-in-Lindsey on May 14 1941, the second of three Eagle squadrons. He probably destroyed a Bf 109 on August 18.

Promoted to Acting Wing Commander on January 17 1942, Powell was appointed leader of the Hornchurch Wing. On a sweep over the French coast in June he was wounded in the neck and head, fracturing the base of his skull. He did not return to the Wing and was awarded a Bar to the DFC (24.7.42).

Powell later served in Tunisia. He retired from the RAF on November 6 1963, as a Group Captain. He died on January 28 1970.

PO 1.8.36   FO 1.2.38   FL 1.2.40   SL 1.3.41
WC 1.6.42   WC 1.1.49   GC 1.7.58

SYDNEY WILLIAM MARTIN POWELL

68136   Sgt   Air Gunner   British   141 Squadron

With 141 Squadron at Turnhouse in early July 1940. In the ill-fated patrol from Hawkinge on the 19th Powell was flying with Pilot Officer HN Tamblyn. They claimed a Bf 109 destroyed in the one-sided battle and returned safely to Hawkinge, one of only four Defiants to do so.

Commissioned in May 1941, Powell was released from the RAF in 1946, as a Flight Lieutenant. He joined the RAuxAF in May 1949, in the Fighter Control Branch. He died in 1979.

PO 16.5.41   FO 16.5.42   FL 16.5.43
FO (RAuxAFRO) 12.5.49

GEORGE ffOLLIOTT POWELL-SHEDDEN

33277   FL   Pilot   British   242 Squadron

Born on April 1 1916, Powell-Shedden was at Wellington College from 1929 to 1933. He was at the Royal Military Academy, Woolwich in 1934 but transferred to the RAF and entered RAF College, Cranwell in January 1935. After graduation Powell-Shedden was posted to 47 Squadron at Khartoum on January 11 1937.

In September 1939 he was a flight commander with 33 Squadron at Mersa Matruh. Powell-Shedden returned to the UK in June 1940 and in early July joined 242 Squadron at Coltishall. On August 21 he shared a Do 17, on September 7 destroyed a Bf 109, on the 9th a Do 17 and on the 15th destroyed a Do 17 and shared another. Following this engagement he was shot down by Bf 109s over Rye, baled out and was admitted to Rye Hospital, with a dislocated left shoulder. His Hurricane, P 2884, crashed at Church Field, Udimore.

Powell-Shedden was posted to 258 Squadron on November 22 1940, as a Flight Commander. He took command of 615 Squadron at Valley in April 1941. On July 19 he arrived in Malta with orders to form a new squadron. At the end of the month the Malta Night Fighter Unit came into being at Ta Kali, with Hurricanes. On August 11 Powell-Shedden damaged a Fiat BR 20, on the 26th shared in damaging two BR 20s and on September 8 destroyed a Cant Z 1007.

The MNFU was re-named 1435 (Night Fighter) Flight on December 2 1941 and Powell-Shedden handed over command. He was promoted to Acting Wing Commander and appointed commander of Ta Kali. He was awarded the DFC (12.12.41) and left for the Middle East shortly afterwards.

In January 1944 Powell-Shedden joined 96 Squadron at West Malling, as a supernumerary. He took command of 29 Squadron at Ford in March 1944, left in April and re-assumed command in July, leading the squadron until December 1944. He was awarded the DSO (27.4.45).

Powell-Shedden retired from the RAF on March 20 1961, as a Group Captain.

PO 19.12.36   FO 19.6.38   FL 19.6.40   SL 1.9.41
WC 1.7.43   WC 1.7.47   GC 1.1.54

RICHARD MAURICE POWER

39471   FL   Pilot   Australian   236 Squadron

Power trained as a pilot with the RAAF and transferred to the RAF in February 1937. On the 28th he was posted to 11 FTS, Wittering and on May 22 joined 66 Squadron at Duxford.

In late 1939 Power went to 504 Squadron at Debden. In early July 1940 he was with 236 Squadron. On the 26th he crashed at Carew Cheriton, in Blenheim R 2777, during bad weather. He and his crew were injured and the aircraft written off.

Power was released from the RAF in 1946, as a Wing Commander, and returned to Australia.

PO 19.2.37   FO 19.11.38   FL 3.9.40   SL 1.12.41

EDWARD MAXIMILIAN PRCHAL

112323   Sgt   Pilot   Czechoslovakian   310 Squadron

Born on January 1 1911 in Dolni Brezany, north of Prague. Prchal joined the Czech Air Force in 1929. He qualified as a pilot and served until 1936. From 1936 to 1939 he flew as a pilot for the Bata Co in Czechoslovakia, on international trips. In June 1939 he escaped from his Nazi-occupied country to Poland, then went to France, later joining l'Armée de l'Air.

After the French collapse Prchal escaped to England. He joined 310 Squadron at Duxford at its formation on July 10 1940. He claimed a Do 17 destroyed on August 26 and on this day his Hurricane, P 3157, was severely damaged in combat over the Thames Estuary and he made a forced-landing near Upminster, slightly wounded.

Commissioned in December 1941, Prchal served with 68 Squadron, a night-fighter unit with many Czech pilots and radar operators. He was later posted to 511 Squadron, Transport Command and flew VIPs to and from the Middle East and ferried aircraft from Canada to the Middle East. On July 4 1943 Prchal was pilot of a Liberator going from Gibraltar to London with General Sikorski and members of his staff on board, as well as other VIPs. Soon after taking

off the aircraft crashed into the sea and Prchal was the sole survivor. He was taken from the water badly injured and unconscious. He returned to 511 after recovering from his injuries.

After the war Prchal returned to Czechoslovakia with his wife and daughter. He was in the Czech Air Force until January 1946, when he joined Czech Airlines as a Senior Captain. In 1950 he escaped to England with his family and two other Czech airline pilots, Kaucky and Rechka, and their families. Prchal went to the USA in 1951 and became Czech language instructor at the US Army Language School at Monterey, California. He retired in 1978.

Prchal died at St Helena, California on December 12 1984. His ashes were taken to England. Part of them was scattered over the Channel and the remainder buried in Brookwood Military Cemetery.

PO 20.12.41   FO 20.12.42   FL 20.12.43

STANLEY GEORGE PREATER

581299   Sgt   Aircrew   British   235 Squadron

Joined 235 Squadron on July 13 1940. Preater was promoted to Warrant Officer on October 1 1941.

No other service details traced.

LEON PREVOT

84285   PO   Pilot   Belgian   235 Squadron

Joined 235 Squadron on September 26 1940. Prevot destroyed a He 59 off Cherbourg on October 8 whilst on a reconnaissance operation to the French coast.

Awarded the C de G (Belg)(21.7.41), Prevot was with 64 Squadron in March 1942, commanding 'A' Flight. He was given command of 122 Squadron at Hornchurch in May. On the 17th he claimed a FW 190 destroyed and on July 30 he claimed another but was himself shot down over France. Evading capture, he escaped through Spain and returned to England.

Prevot commanded 197 Squadron from its formation at Drem on November 21 1942 until June 1943 and 350 Squadron at Hornchurch from January to March 1944. He survived the war, one of nine Belgians to do so of the twenty-nine who took part in the Battle of Britain. He was awarded the DFC.

ARTHUR OWEN PRICE

77366   PO   Air Gunner   British   236 Squadron

With 236 Squadron in early July 1940.

Price was awarded the DFC (15.9.44), as an Acting Squadron Leader with 7 Squadron, operating in Lancasters from Oakington. He was released from the RAF in 1945, as a Squadron Leader. He died in 1982.

APO 3.2.40   PO 16.3.40   FO 16.3.41   FL 16.3.42

JAMES PRICE

130054   Sgt   Air Gunner   British   29 Squadron

Price, of Cartref, Glamorgan, was born on July 12 1919. He joined 29 Squadron at Digby on September 14 1940.

Commissioned in April 1942, Price was awarded the DFM (6.10.42) for service as a Flight Sergeant with 38 Squadron in the Middle East. He was released from the RAF in 1946, rejoined in 1956 and retired on July 12 1974, as a Flight Lieutenant. Price died on March 16 1988.

PO 12.4.42   FO 12.10.42   FL 12.4.44   FL 17.5.56

NORMAN ALBERT JOSEPH PRICE

745229   Sgt   Pilot   British   236 Squadron

Price, of Reading, Berkshire, joined the RAFVR in early 1939 and began his elementary flying training at 8 E&RFTS, Woodley. Called to full-time service in September, he went to ITW, Bexhill, moved on to 6 E&RFTS, Sywell, then to 8 FTS, Montrose. The course was split and Price was selected for twin-engined aircraft.

He converted to Blenheims at No 1 (Coastal) OTU, Silloth and joined 236 Squadron at St Eval in early September 1940. The squadron's duties included escorting FAA torpedo aircraft attacking Channel shipping, reconnaissances of submarine bases and Channel ports, looking for FW Condors harrassing convoys and escorting convoys in the Atlantic.

In April 1941 Price converted to Beaufighters at RAF Chivenor and joined 272 Squadron. In May five aircraft of the squadron departed for the Middle East, via Gibraltar and Malta. Only two arrived safely at Gibraltar, Price's and the CO's. Initially based at Abu Sueir 272 moved later to Mersa Matruh, where its main duty was to strafe enemy airfields. It also covered Tobruk convoys and made occasional operational visits to Malta.

In late November 1941 Price was shot down by flak near Agedabia. He made a belly-landing on fire and was then unable to get out because his hatch was jammed. His navigator, Sergeant Southern, forced it open and Price got out, badly burned. They were captured and Price was taken to an Italian field hospital for treatment. He later went in a hospital ship to Caserta, near Naples, for further, but limited, treatment. After a year at Parma he went before a Red Cross tribunal and was passed for repatriation, returning to England in April 1943.

After skin-grafting operations Price was posted to White Waltham, to assist the ATA. As he was not flying he asked to be medically-boarded out of the RAF. He was discharged in October 1945, as a Warrant Officer.

ROBERT BUCKTON PRICE

532196   Sgt   Pilot   British   245, 73 and 222 Squadrons

Price, of Acomb, Yorkshire, joined 245 Squadron at Aldergrove on September 27 1940, moved to 73 Squadron at Castle Camps on October 14 and then to 222 Squadron at Hornchurch on the 23rd.

He was killed on November 15 1941, as a Flight Sergeant with 33 Squadron. Price was 24. He is remembered on the Alamein Memorial, Column 242.

JOHN SINCLAIR PRIESTLEY

NZ 39934   PO   Pilot   New Zealander   235 Squadron

Born in Wellington on August 15 1913, Priestley left Wellington College in 1930 and was then employed as a clerk. He applied for an RNZAF short service commission in March 1939, was accepted but the scheme lapsed and he was not called.

Priestley volunteered for flying duties at the outbreak of war and entered the Ground Training School, Weraroa on October 26 1939. He was posted to No 1 EFTS, Taieri on November 21 and moved to No 1 FTS, Wigram on January 16 1940. Priestley was awarded his flying badge on March 21 and later passed out as a Sergeant-Pilot. He was commissioned later, with effect from May 4.

In late May Priestley sailed for the UK in the SS 'Mataroa'. He was posted to No 1 (Coastal) OTU, Silloth on July 27 1940 and joined 235 Squadron at Bircham Newton on August 22. He took part in two operations, both convoy escorts. Priestley took off in a Blenheim on a non-operational flight on August 30. He crashed at Barwick Farm, near Bircham Newton after going into a sustained spin and failing to recover. He and his gunner were both killed.

Priestly is buried in St Mary's churchyard, Bircham Newton.

PO 4.5.40

JOSEF PRIHODA

110307   Sgt   Pilot   Czechoslovakian   1 Squadron

Joined No 1 Squadron at Wittering on October 5 1940. Prihoda probably destroyed a Bf 109 over the channel on April 21 1941. On the 28th he was jumped by a Bf 109 near Dungeness and shot down. He baled out, landing safely in a marsh at New Romney.

Prihoda destroyed a Bf 109 on June 16 1941 and probably another two on the 21st. Commissioned in 1941, he was awarded the DFC. He later joined 313 Squadron. On a Ramrod operation on March 6 1943 Prihoda was engaged in combat with German fighters over Brest. He was never seen again and is believed to have crashed into the sea, in Spitfire BP 862. Prihoda is remembered on the Runnymede Memorial, Panel 129.

CHARLES ARTHUR PRITCHARD

90092   FL   Pilot   Australian   600 Squadron

Born in Manildra, New South Wales, Pritchard joined 600 Squadron AuxAF in 1936. Called to full-time service on August 24 1939, he took part in the squadron's attack on Rotterdam aerodrome on May 10 1940.

Pritchard destroyed a Ju 88 on the night of September 15/16. The enemy aircraft was caught in searchlights and was shot down into the sea off Bexhill. Pritchard commanded 600 from November 1940. In early May 1941 he destroyed a He 111 over Sherborne and his own aircraft was damaged by return fire. On May 16 he was about to open fire on a Ju 88 when searchlights suddenly illuminated his Beaufighter, blinding him. The enemy aircraft opened fire, shooting Pritchard down. He and his radar operator baled out.

Awarded the DFC (24.6.41), Pritchard was promoted and posted away in September 1941 to be Wing Commander Flying at 51 OTU, Cranfield. He was released from the RAF in 1945, as an Acting Wing Commander.

PO (AuxAF) 19.5.36   FO (AuxAF) 18.11.37   FO 24.8.39
FL 3.9.40   SL 1.12.41

JACK PROCTOR

741471   Sgt   Pilot   British   602 Squadron

Proctor, of Coventry, joined 602 Squadron at Drem on June 21 1940.

He claimed a Ju 88 destroyed on August 31, a Bf 109 on September 6 and Bf 110s on the 7th and 11th.

Proctor was killed on April 18 1941, aged 24. He is buried in St Michael's churchyard, Stoke, Coventry.

JOHN ERNEST PROCTOR

44131   PO   Pilot   British   32 Squadron

Born on July 15 1913, Proctor was a pre-war airman pilot. He went to France with 501 Squadron on May 10 1940. He claimed a Bf 110 and a Do 17 destroyed on the 12th, two He 111s on the 14th and a Bf 110 on the 15th. The squadron was withdrawn on June 19 and re-assembled at Croydon on the 21st.

Proctor was commissioned from Sergeant in early July and joined 32 Squadron at Biggin Hill on the 10th. He claimed a Bf 110 destroyed and shared another on July 20 and claimed Bf 109s on August 12 and 24. He was awarded the DFC (18.3.41), being then credited with at least eleven enemy aircraft destroyed, seven of them in the fighting in France.

On May 18 1942 Proctor took command of 33 Squadron in the Western Desert and three days later made a forced-landing after being

JE Proctor (continued)

hit by flak. He commanded 352 Squadron from its formation at Benina on April 22 1944 until September 1944. This was the first Yugoslav operational unit in the RAF.

Proctor, who was also awarded a Bar to the DFC, stayed on in the RAF and retired on October 15 1957, as a Wing Commander.

PO 8.7.40   FO 24.11.40   FL 24.11.41   SL 16.3.44
SL 1.9.45   WC 1.1.52

PERCY ROLLO PROSSER

755800   Sgt   Air Gunner   British   235 Squadron

Prosser, of Quinton, Birmingham, was with 235 Squadron in early July 1940.

He was killed on December 16 1940, when the Blenheim he was in crashed into the sea during a minesweeper escort operation. All three men on board were lost.

Prosser is remembered on the Runnymede Memorial, Panel 18.

DOUGLAS HARRY PROUDMAN

635790   Sgt   Wop/AG   British   248 Squadron

Proudman, of Devizes, joined 248 Squadron in mid-July 1940. He died on April 27 1941 and is buried in Devizes Cemetery.

HARRY ARTHUR ROBIN PROWSE

42358   PO   Pilot   British   266 and 603 Squadrons

Joined the RAF on a short service commission in May 1939. Prowse began his ab initio course at 8 E&RFTS, Woodley on May 30, moved to 13 FTS, Drem on August 11 and finished training at 15 FTS, Lossiemouth.

On January 6 1940 Prowse was posted to 9 BGS, Penrhos, as as staff pilot. He went to 4 Ferry Pilots Pool on May 16. In June he was shot down near Lille by flak. He forced-landed his Hurricane in a field and returned to England by ship from Cherbourg, just before France fell. Prowse went to 7 OTU, Hawarden on September 5 and after converting to Spitfires he joined 266 Squadron at Wittering on the 16th, moving to 603 Squadron at Hornchurch on October 20. He probably destroyed a Bf 109 on November 11.

Prowse destroyed two Bf 109s over St Omer on July 4 1941 and was then himself shot down by flak. He crash-landed in a field and set his Spitfire alight with his Verey pistol before being captured. Prowse was freed on May 2 1945 and returned to England on the 8th.

After a long leave he did a flying refresher course at 5 (P) AFU at Atcham on Harvards, from October 16 1945 to January 23 1946. Prowse was released from the RAF but decided to return to flying duties for a year. He went to 61 OTU, Keevil on June 18 for a refresher course on Spitfires and from July 18 1946 until released again on June 6 1947 he instructed at Keevil.

In September 1947 Prowse and his wife sailed for Brazil, where he managed a 17000 acre farm until his retirement in December 1983.

APO 22.7.39   PO 6.1.40   FO 6.1.41   FL 1.6.42

RUDOLF PTACEK

787434   Sgt   Pilot   Czechoslovakian   43 Squadron

Joined 43 Squadron at Usworth on October 4 1940. In November Ptacek was with 615 Squadron at Northolt.

He was killed on March 28 1942, as a Warrant Officer with 602 Squadron. He was shot down into the sea during an engagement with FW 190s over Le Havre.

Ptacek is remembered on the Runnymede Memorial, Panel 73.

RAIMUND PUDA

69458   Sgt   Pilot   Czechoslovakian   310 and 605 Sqdns

Joined 310 Squadron at Duxford in August 1940. Puda shared in the destruction of Do 17s on September 15 and 18. He was posted to 605 Squadron at Croydon on October 19 and on November 5 he baled out of Hurricane V 6619 after being attacked by Bf 109s over the Thames Estuary and having his oxygen system damaged.

Commissioned in June 1941, Puda was released from the RAF as a Flight Lieutenant. He settled in England.

PO 24.6.41   FO 24.6.42   FL 24.6.43

GEOFFREY BRUCE PUDNEY

Sub-Lieutenant (FAA)   Pilot   British   64 Squadron

Pudney, joined the FAA in 1939, was loaned to the RAF in mid-June 1940 and after converting to Spitfires at 7 OTU, Hawarden he was posted to 64 Squadron at Kenley on July 1.

He was killed on August 26 1941, serving on HMS 'Grebe' but no details have been traced. Pudney is remembered on the Fleet Air Arm Memorial at Lee-on-Solent.

Midshipman 1.7.39   Sub-Lt 14.3.40

JOHN STEWART PUGH

120329   Sgt   Air Gunner   British   29 Squadron

With 29 Squadron at Digby in early July 1940. On September 4, flying as gunner with Pilot Officer MJ Herrick, Pugh shot down two He 111s at night, the second one falling in pieces after a burst fired at less than thirty yards. They destroyed another He 111 on the night of the 15th.

Commissioned in March 1942, Pugh was awarded the DFC (21.9.45), as a Flight Lieutenant with 149 Squadron, operating in Lancasters from Methwold. He stayed on in the RAF, in the Physical Fitness Branch. His name does not appear in the Air Force list after July 1954.

13.3.42   FO 1.10.42   FL 13.3.44   FL (RAFRO) 13.9.46

THOMAS PATRICK PUGH

49137   FO   Pilot   British   263 Squadron

Pugh, of Farnborough, Hampshire, joined the RAF on a short service commission in July 1937. He was posted to 11 FTS, Wittering on September 18 and after completing his training he joined 103 Squadron at Abingdon.

In early July 1940 Pugh was with 263 Squadron at Grangemouth. He commanded the squadron from August 1941 until February 1942 and was awarded the DFC (21.10.41), being then credited with two Ju 88s and a Bf 109 destroyed on the ground.

Pugh formed and then commanded 182 Squadron at Martlesham Heath from September 1 1942. He was killed on August 2 1943, as an Acting Wing Commander with 182. He was 23 and is remembered on the Runnymede Memorial, Panel 64.

APO 5.9.37   PO 12.7.38   FO 12.2.40   FL 12.2.41
SL 1.3.42

GEORGE RUPERT PUSHMAN

42260   PO   Pilot   Canadian   23 Squadron

Joined the RAF on a short service commission in April 1939. Pushman was posted to 23 Squadron at Collyweston on June 24 1940 and remained with it until August 4 1941.

Pushman was awarded the DFC (17.10.44), as an Acting Squadron Leader with 88 Squadron, operating in Bostons from Blackbushe. The citation mentioned his laying of smoke screens on D Day and after. Pushman transferred to the RCAF in March 1945.

APO 24.6.39   PO 16.6.40   FO 16.6.41   FL 16.6.42

ALAN ROBERT PUTT

37519   FL   Pilot   British   501 Squadron

Joined the RAF on a short service commission in November 1935. Putt was posted to 10 FTS, Tern Hill on February 1 1936 and then joined 65 Squadron at Hornchurch on August 10. He went to the Electrical and Wireless School at Cranwell on August 30 1937, as a staff pilot on the Signals Squadron.

Putt joined 501 Squadron at Gravesend on August 5 1940. He was shot down on the 15th during an engagement with Ju 87s over Hawkinge and baled out, unhurt, from Hurricane P 3040.

Putt was released from the RAF in 1946, as a Wing Commander. He died in 1977.

APO 20.1.36   PO 25.11.36   FO 25.6.38   FL 25.6.40
SL 1.9.44   WC 1.1.44

WILLIAM GEORGE VERNON PUXLEY

117933   Sgt   Air Gunner   British   236 Squadron

Joined 236 Squadron on September 20 1940.

Commissioned in March 1942, Puxley was released from the RAF in 1946, as a Flight Lieutenant. He joined the RAFVR in 1950 and died in 1984.

PO 7.3.42   FO 1.10.42   FL 7.3.44   FO (RAFVR) 17.10.50

JOHN WALTER PYE

66503   Sgt   Air Gunner   New Zealander   25 Squadron

Pye was born at Aldbourne, England on November 15 1917. He was taken to New Zealand at the age of six. He sailed from New Zealand with his parents on March 9 1939 for a holiday in England. They planned to return on September 29 but war came and they were unable to return and spent the war years in Salisbury.

Pye joined the RAF on September 11, did his initial training at North Coates, followed by a gunnery course at Jurby, Isle of Man. He qualified on March 2 1940 and was posted to 236 Squadron as an AC Air Gunner. In May Pye joined 25 Squadron at North Weald and was promoted to Sergeant on the 27th.

After the arrival of airborne radar Pye remustered as a Radio Observer and retrained with the squadron. Commissioned in May 1941, Pye was posted to 1453 Flight on July 17, operating in Turbinlite Havocs from Wittering. He moved to 1451 Flight at Hunsdon on February 24 1942 and then to 1452 Flight at West Malling on May 3.

In September 1942 Pye finished flying duties and was posted to No 1 Air Armament School, Manby for a Specialist Armament Officers' course, after which he went to Gravesend as Station Armament Officer. On January 31 1944 he went as Wing Armament Officer to 146 Wing at Tangmere, then forming with four squadrons of Typhoons. He went to the Continent with the Wing on July 19.

Pye was posted away in May 1945 for repatriation to New Zealand. He arrived there on October 22 and went on to the Reserve on January 28 1946, as a Flight Lieutenant.

PO 16.5.41   FO 16.5.42   FL 16.5.43

LAURENCE LEE PYMAN

72586   FO   Pilot   British   65 Squadron

Commissioned in the RAFVR in January 1939, Pyman joined 65 Squadron at Hornchurch on July 20 1940.

He claimed a Bf 109 destroyed on August 14 but his own aircraft was severely damaged in combat over the Channel and he forced-landed at Manston.

Pyman failed to return from an action over the Channel on August 16 1940. His Spitfire, K 9915, crashed into the sea and he was killed. He was 23 and is buried in Calais Southern Cemetery, France.

PO (RAFVR) 13.1.39   PO 18.9.39   FO 31.7.40

COLIN CAMPBELL PYNE

39972   Sgt   Air Gunner   New Zealander   219 Squadron

Pyne was born in Wellington on March 12 1921 and after leaving Wellington Boys' College he was employed as a clerk. He volunteered for aircrew duties at the outbreak of war and reported to the Ground Training School, Weraroa on October 26 1939.

Posted to No 1 Air Gunners' School, Ohakea on November 20, Pyne qualified on December 18 and then carried out further navigation training in January 1940. He sailed for the UK on March 23 in the SS 'Akaroa'. Pyne was posted to 5 OTU, Aston Down on May 29 and trained in Defiants and Blenheims. He was awarded his air gunner's badge and promoted to Sergeant on July 5 and joined 219 Squadron at Catterick the next day.

Pyne qualified as a Radio Operator on August 5 and flew his first night operational sortie on the 7th. In February 1941 the squadron became fully operational with Beaufighters. On the 17th Pyne assisted in the destruction of a Do 17 and on June 1 an unidentified enemy bomber. He qualified as a Radio Observer on July 6 1941.

In early September Pyne was posted to 51 OTU for an instructor's course and then began instructing pupils there. He returned to 219 Squadron in early November and resumed operations. Pyne joined the Telecommunications Flying Unit at Hurn in early March 1942, carrying out flying trials on new radar developments. Promoted to Warrant Officer on April 1 1942, he was posted to 157 Squadron at Castle Camps at the end of the month, operating in Mosquitos at night. He assisted in intercepting and damaging a Do 217 on July 30.

Pyne was involved in an accident on September 7 1942. He was knocked from his bicycle and suffered spine and head injuries. He was unconscious for three days and in bed for nearly three months. Pyne returned to the squadron in December for a medical board. He was repatriated to New Zealand in January 1943, graded unfit for aircrew duties in February and was released from the RNZAF on July 27 1943. He died on February 19 1975 after many years of ill-health.

BASIL HERBERT QUELCH

115130   Sgt   Pilot   British   235 Squadron

With 235 Squadron in early July 1940.

Commissioned in December 1941, Quelch was awarded the DFC (6.2.45), as a Flight Lieutenant with 235. He was released from the RAF in 1946 and joined the RAFVR in 1947.

PO 30.12.41   FO 1.10.42   FL 30.12.43
FO (RAFVR) 27.5.47

JEFFERY KINDERSLEY QUILL

32110   FO   Pilot   British   65 Squadron

Born in 1913, Quill was educated at Lancing College. He joined the RAF on a short service commission in October 1931. He was posted to 3 FTS, Grantham on the 24th and joined 17 Squadron at Upavon on September 18 1932. He went to the Station Flight at Duxford on December 11 1933.

In November 1935 Quill was offered the post of assistant to the chief test pilot at Vickers (Aviation). He left the RAF and went on to the Reserve. He was initially involved with testing the Wellesley and from March

JK Quill (continued)

1936 the Spitfire. Quill was awarded the AFC (23.6.36).

In 1940 Quill was determined to do some operational flying and in early August he managed to go on an attachment to 65 Squadron at Hornchurch. He claimed a Bf 109 destroyed on the 16th. Quill had said that operational experience would help in his job and when he returned to Vickers he submitted a long report detailing suggested improvements, particularly cannon armament.

Quill continued test-flying throughout the war, particularly with the many marks of Spitfire. After sixteen years of flying fighter aircraft he became very tired and in 1947 took a period of enforced leave. He began to fly again in 1950, on a private pilot's license, and also made some overseas deliveries of Spitfires. Quill flew Spitfire AB 910 at air shows and RAF Open Days until 1965, nearly thirty years after his first test flight on the prototype.

His work with Vickers was concerned solely with military aircraft and as Head of the Military Aircraft Office at Weybridge he was involved with the development of the TSR 2, Jaguar and Tornado. Quill retired in December 1978.

PO 9.10.31   FO 9.4.33   FO (RAFO) 31.12.35

JAMES QUINN

118425   Sgt   Pilot   British   236 Squadron

Born on June 14 1919. Quinn joined 236 Squadron on October 10 1940.

Commissioned in December 1941, he was awarded the DFC (1.9.42), as a Pilot Officer with 204 Squadron, operating in Sunderlands. He was later awarded a Bar to the DFC.

Quinn retired from the RAF on October 20 1969, as a Group Captain.

PO 28.12.41   FO 1.10.42   FL 28.12.43   FL 1.9.45
SL 1.1.49   WC 1.7.55   GC 1.1.64

ALEXANDER COULTATE RABAGLIATI

37209   FL   Pilot   British   46 Squadron

Born in Durban, South Africa in 1914, Rabagliati joined the RAF on a short service commission in April 1935. He was posted to 2 FTS, Digby on May 7 and joined No 1 Squadron at Tangmere on March 4 1936.

Rabagliati was posted to 27 Squadron in India on December 15 1936. He joined 46 Squadron at Digby in early July 1940. He claimed a Bf 110 destroyed on August 18, Bf 109s on September 5 and 14 and a Bf 110 and a Ju 88 on the 27th. Rabagliati was awarded the DFC (22.10.40). On October 29 he claimed a Bf 109 destroyed and on November 8 another, off Dover.

In December 1940 Rabagliati took command of 46 Squadron. On May 22 1941 the squadron pilots and aircraft sailed in HMS 'Argus' for Gibraltar, where they transferred to the 'Ark Royal' and then sailed into the Mediterranean. They flew off to Hal Far, Malta on June 6. On the 11th Rabagliati shared in destroying a SM 79 and later in the day destroyed a CR 42, on the 22nd he damaged a Mc 200, on the 23rd he probably destroyed a Sm 79 and on the 27th he destroyed a Mc 200 and damaged a Sm 79. 46 Squadron was re-numbered 126 Squadron on July 15.

Rabagliati destroyed a Z 506B on August 10, claimed a Mc 200 on the 26th and another on September 4. He was promoted on October 8 1941 and appointed Wing Commander Flying at Ta Kali. He was awarded a Bar to the DFC (31.10.41). Rabagliati was posted to Air HQ Mediterranean on December 2 1941. He claimed a Mc 200 destroyed and a second probably destroyed on the 21st.

Flying from Ludham, Norfolk on July 6 1943, Rabagliati was leading 195 Squadron on a shipping strike when he was shot down into the sea, possibly by flak, and killed. He is remembered on the Runnymede Memorial, Panel 118.

APO 16.4.35   PO 16.4.36   FO 16.1.38   FL 16.1.40
SL 1.3.41   WC 1.6.42

JOHN HENRY MICHAEL RABONE

90226   FL   Pilot   British   604 Squadron

Joined 604 Squadron, AuxAF in early 1938. Called to full-time service at the outbreak of war, Rabone was with the squadron at Northolt in early July 1940.

On September 24 1940 he was posted to CFS, Upavon, for an instructor's course. Rabone served in Flying Training Command until released from the RAF in 1945, as a Flight Lieutenant.

PO (AuxAF) 7.3.38   FO 7.9.39   FL 7.9.40

PAUL WATTLING RABONE

36179   FO   Pilot   New Zealander   145 Sqdn, 422 Flt

Rabone was born in Salisbury, England on March 2 1918 and was taken to New Zealand as a child. From September 1935 until June 1936 he served in the 7th Field Battery, Territorial Army. In April 1938 Rabone was accepted for the Civil Reserve of Pilots and carried out his flying training at Middle Districts and Auckland Aero Clubs, obtaining his 'A' License on May 18.

Having applied for a short service commission earlier in the year, Rabone was now accepted and he reported to No 1 FTS, Wigram on July 4 1938, as an Acting Pilot Officer. He was awarded his flying badge on October 13 and completed the course two months later. Rabone sailed for the UK on February 1 1939 and on arrival at RAF Depot, Uxbridge he transferred into the RAF.

On April 17 Rabone joined 88 Squadron at Boscombe Down. The squadron went to France on September 2. In May 1940, returning from a raid on the Maastricht bridges Rabone's aircraft was severely damaged by flak and he and his crew baled out, landing behind enemy lines. They acquired civilian clothes, joined a refugee column and after five days reached Dieppe. From here they flew back to England and rejoined the squadron in France three days later. Rabone was shot down by a Bf 109 on June 12 during an attack on a Seine bridge. He and his crew again baled out and rejoined the squadron, which was withdrawn to Driffield, Yorkshire on the 15th.

In August 1940 Rabone volunteered for Fighter Command and on the 19th he joined 145 Squadron at Drem. He shot down a Bf 109 on October 12, which went down into the sea off Dungeness. On the 28th Rabone was posted to 422 Flight and on November 6 he destroyed a Bf 109.

The Flight was re-numbered 96 Squadron on December 18 and assigned to the night defence of Liverpool, Manchester and Birmingham, based at Cranage. Rabone destroyed an enemy bomber on December 22, which went into the sea off Blackpool. In March 1941 the squadron began to receive Defiants and it was from one of these that Rabone and his gunner, Flying Officer Ritchie, baled out over the Peak District on April 13. The aircraft crashed at Rowlee Pasture.

Rabone was posted to 85 Squadron at Hunsdon on May 2 1941. He left on July 7 to take command of 1451 Flight, also at Hunsdon, a Turbinlite Havoc unit. He was rested from operations on November 2 and posted to Kenley for controller training, attached to 485 Squadron. In mid-December Rabone was given command of 1528 Beam Approach Training Flight at Drem. He joined 256 Squadron at Squires Gate on May 12 1942, went on a seven week attachment to 29 Squadron at West Malling and was then posted to 488 Squadron at Church Fenton, as a Flight Commander.

On April 24 1943 Rabone went to 51 OTU, then on to 60 OTU. He flew a Mosquito from Lyneham in early June and joined 23 Squadron at Luqa, Malta. He was made a Flight Commander in July. He borrowed a Spitfire on August 15 to fly spare parts from Malta to a squadron detachment at Palermo. On the way back he met a Ju 88 fifteen miles west of Trapani airfield and after a ten mile chase he shot it down into the sea.

The squadron moved to Sigonella, Sicily in early September and on the 8th Rabone led an intruder raid on Grosseto airfield. During the operation he shot down a Ju 88, a He 111 and damaged a second He 111. In mid-November 1943 Rabone returned to the UK and was posted to 60 OTU, as an instructor. He was awarded the DFC (25.1.44).

On March 16 1944 Rabone transferred to the RNZAF and was posted to 515 Squadron, operating in Mosquitos from Little Snoring. On June 21 he destroyed a Bf 110 in daylight and on the 30th a He 111 and a Ju 34. Rabone rejoined 23 Squadron in mid-July, also based at Little Snoring.

He took off to attack a target in north-west Germany on July 24 1944 and failed to return. His body was washed ashore at Heligoland Island three months later and buried there.

After the war Rabone's remains were re-interred in Hotten British Military Cemetery, Belgium.

APO 4.7.38   PO 15.3.39   FO 3.9.40   FL 3.9.41

JERZY RADOMSKI

P 1427   PO   Pilot   Polish   303 Squadron

Radomski was born on July 18 1915. He joined 303 Squadron at Northolt on August 21 1940. He shared a Do 17 destroyed on September 30 and on this day his Hurricane, P 3663, was severely damaged by Bf 109s over mid-Channel and Radomski crash-landed on a beach near Lydd, unhurt. He was awarded the KW (23.12.40) and Bar (1.2.41).

On April 14 1941 he went to 58 OTU, Grangemouth, as an instructor. Radomski rejoined 303 Squadron, again at Northolt, on November 19 1941 but moved to 316 Squadron there on December 14. He shared a FW 190 destroyed on May 6 1942 and was awarded a second Bar to the KW (20.8.42).

Radomski was posted to 222 Squadron at Drem on August 27 1942. He once again rejoined 303 Squadron, then at Kirton-in-Lindsey, on December 8. He moved to 317 Squadron at Perranporth on June 28 1943, was appointed a Flight Commander on September 2 and claimed a Bf 109 destroyed on the 8th. Radomski was awarded the C de G (Fr)(7.7.43) and the VM (5th Class)(20.12.43).

Rested from operations, Radomski went to HQ PAF, Blackpool on April 14 1944, was posted to PAF Staff College on January 2 1945 and afterwards served at HQ 46 Group on administrative duties. He was released from the PAF in November 1946 and awarded a third Bar to the KW (31.10.47).

Radomski joined the RAF in 1951, (No 501702), in the Catering Branch. He retired on July 18 1973, as a Flight Lieutenant, retaining the rank of Squadron Leader. He died in 1978.

PO 1.3.41   FO 1.3.42   FL 1.3.43   FL 26.2.51

GUSTAW RADWANSKI

76708   PO   Pilot   Polish   56 Squadron

Born on May 2 1913, Radwanski was a trained psychologist in Poland before the war. He arrived in Britain on June 27 1940 and joined 56 Squadron at Boscombe Down on September 15.

Radwanski was posted to 302 Squadron at Jurby on May 21 1941. He moved to 316 Squadron at Northolt on December 16 1941. He collided with Sergeant Musial on February 13 1942. Radwanski baled out and was slightly injured and Musial was killed. Awarded the KW (19.2.42), Radwanski was posted away on April 16 to Northolt and later went to Croydon.

On July 4 1942 he was sent to 16 FTS, Newton, as an instructor. After a course at 2 FIS, Montrose Radwanski instructed at Newton until April 15 1944, when he was posted to HQ PAF, Blackpool. After a series of moves he went to 61 OTU, Rednal on January 8 1945 for a refresher course. He joined 84 GSU on February 28 and was posted to 317 Squadron in Holland on March 11 1945 for operations. Radwanski was awarded two Bars to the KW (20.6.45) and was released from the PAF in late 1946, as a Flight Lieutenant.

PO 1.3.41   FO 1.3.42   FL 1.3.43

WILLIAM PEARCE HAUGHTON RAFTER

42572   PO   Pilot   British   603 Squadron

Rafter, of Birmingham, was at Shrewsbury School in 1935/36. He joined the RAF on a short service commission in June 1939 and was posted to 603 Squadron at Hornchurch on August 31 1940.

During an action over the Biggin Hill area on September 5 Rafter is believed to have been shot down by Bf 109s, crashing at Marden in Spitfire X 4264. He was admitted to West Kent Hospital, Maidstone, wounded. On November 29 1940 Rafter was killed, when he crashed at East Sutton, near Broomfield, in Spitfire P 7449, cause unknown.

Rafter was 19. He is buried in St Peter's churchyard, Harborne, Birmingham. His brother, Charles, was killed in a flying accident at Stradishall on October 11 1940, serving as a pilot with 214 Squadron.

APO 19.8.39   PO 1.2.40

WOODROW RAINE

745118   Sgt   Pilot   British   610 Squadron

Raine, of Cumberland, joined 610 Squadron at Acklington on October 5 1940.

He was killed on August 21 1941, as a Sergeant with 610. Raine was 22. He is buried in Longuenesse Souvenir Cemetery, St Omer, France.

DOUGLAS NORMAN RAINS

641910   Sgt   Wop/AG   British   248 Squadron

Rains, of Poynton, Cheshire, joined 248 Squadron in mid-July 1940.

He was killed on August 12 1942, as a Flight Sergeant, aged 22. The unit he was serving with is not known. He is buried in St George's churchyard, Poynton.

LESLIE FRANCIS RALLS

48668   Sgt   Pilot   British   605 Squadron

Born on December 20 1916. Ralls was with 605 Squadron at Drem in early July 1940.

Commissioned from Warrant Officer in the Administrative Branch in May 1942, he was made an OBE (1.1.71) and retired from the RAF on December 20 1972, as a Wing Commander. Ralls died in 1976.

PO 13.5.42   FO 13.1.43   FL 13.11.46   SL 1.1.55 WC 1.7.64

JOHN BASIL RAMSAY

41204   PO   Pilot   British   151 Squadron

Ramsay, of Lilliput, Dorset, joined the RAF on a short service commission in July 1938. He did his ab initio course at 10 E&RFTS, Yatesbury, moved on to 9 FTS, Hullavington on October 1, went to 6 ATS, Warmwell on April 11 1939, returned to Hullavington on May 5 and joined 24 (Communications) Squadron at Hendon on May 14 1939.

The squadron moved to France on January 23 1940 and was finally withdrawn to Hendon on May 29. Ramsay was posted to 7 OTU, Hawarden and after converting to Hurricanes he joined 151 Squadron at North Weald on July 29 1940.

Ramsay failed to return from an engagement with enemy aircraft over Chelmsford on August 18, in Hurricane R 4181, and was reported 'Missing'. His name appears on the Runnymede Memorial, Panel 9. However, a post-war excavation of a Hurricane at Deal Hall Farm, Holiwell Point, Essex proved it to be Ramsay's and his remains were still in the cockpit.

Aged 21 at the time of his death, Ramsay was buried with full military honours at Brookwood Military Cemetery on October 25 1983.

APO 17.9.38   PO 25.7.39

JOHN STRACHAN RAMSAY

968956   Sgt   Aircrew   British   235 Squadron

Joined 235 Squadron on August 18 1940. Ramsay was killed on April 27 1941, as a Sergeant with 22 Squadron, aged 28.

He is remembered on the Runnymede Memorial, Panel 51.

NORMAN HUGH DONALD RAMSAY

62658   **Sgt**   **Pilot**   **British**   **610 and 222 Squadrons**

Born on July 29 1919 at Eastcote, Middlesex, Ramsay joined the RAFVR in 1938. At that time he was an apprentice at Vickers Supermarine at Southampton.

Ramsay began his elementary flying training at 3 E&RFTS, Hamble and had soloed on the Avro Cadet before he was called to full-time service at the outbreak of war. After ITW, Hastings Ramsay was posted to 10 FTS, Tern Hill on November 5 1939 and on completion of his training he joined 92 Squadron at Croydon on May 12 1940. He moved to 610 Squadron at Gravesend in June and on August 14 claimed a Bf 110.

On September 15 1940 Ramsay joined 222 Squadron at Hornchurch. He was attacked by a Do 17 over Coltishall on February 10 1941, whilst on a night training flight. He took violent evasive action, escaped undamaged and the enemy aircraft was driven off by Sergeant RG Marland of 222 and Sergeant LD Barnes of 257.

Commissioned in March 1941, Ramsay was posted away to 61 OTU, Rednal on October 22, as an instructor. He went to West Kirby for overseas on December 17 1942 and on January 11 1943 joined 1435 Squadron at Luqa, Malta. Ramsay was posted back to the UK on July 29 1943 and awarded the DFC (28.9.43).

He held a series of staff appointments until August 20 1946, when he was posted to 61 OTU for a refresher course before joining No 1 Squadron at Tangmere on September 11. Ramsay retired from the RAF on July 29 1962, as a Flight Lieutenant.

PO 19.3.41   *FO 19.3.42*   *FL 19.3.43*   *FL 1.9.45*

JOHN WILLIAM RAMSHAW

740175   **Sgt**   **Pilot**   **British**   **222 Squadron**

Born in Beverley, Yorkshire, Ramshaw was educated at the Grammar School there. In 1934 he began work as a clerk with the Halifax Building Society. He took private flying lessons and later joined the RAFVR.

Called to full-time service at the outbreak of war, Ramshaw was with 222 Squadron at Hornchurch in early July 1940. He crashed at Mockbeggar, Collier Street, near Yalding on September 4, after being shot down by Bf 109s, in Spitfire K 9962. Severely injured, Ramshaw was taken to West Kent Hospital but was dead on arrival.

He was 24 and is buried in Queensgate Cemetery, Beverley.

LAURITZ ANDREW WOODNEY RASMUSSEN

391868   **Sgt**   **Air Gunner**   **New Zealander**   **264 Sqdn**

Rasmussen was born in Auckland on September 10 1921 and educated at Auckland Grammar School. In early 1939 he joined the 3rd Auckland Regiment as a territorial soldier.

At the outbreak of war Rasmussen volunteered for aircrew duties. He reported to the Ground Training School, Weraroa on December 18 and moved to the Air Observers' School, Ohakea in mid-January 1940, for a gunnery course. Rasmussen sailed for the UK on April 26 in the RMS 'Rangitiki'.

On July 17 he was posted to 5 OTU, Aston Down and after being awarded his air gunner's badge he joined 264 Squadron at Kirton-in-Lindsey on August 29. In the evening of September 4 1940

Rasmussen was the gunner in a Defiant ordered off on an interception patrol. The aircraft crashed shortly after taking off and he and the pilot, Flying Officer DKC O'Malley, were killed.

Rasmussen is buried in Kirton-in-Lindsey Burial Ground. He was the youngest of the New Zealanders who took part in the Battle of Britain and had only 19 hours as an Air Gunner at the time of his death.

MALCOLM RAVENHILL

40750   **PO**   **Pilot**   **British**   **229 Squadron**

Ravenhill, of Sheffield, joined the RAF on a short service commission in March 1938. He was posted to 4 FTS, Abu Sueir on June 3.

He was with 229 Squadron at Wittering in early July 1940. On September 11 Ravenhill was shot down in combat over Biggin Hill, in Hurricane P 3038. He baled out and was admitted to Shorncliffe Hospital, suffering from shock.

On September 30 1940 Ravenhill was shot down and killed by Bf 109s. His Hurricane, P 2815, crashed and burned out at Church Road, Ightham. Ravenhill was 27 years old. He is buried in City Road Cemetery, Sheffield. His portrait was done by Cuthbert Orde in 1940.

APO 7.5.38   *PO 13.5.39*

ANTHONY JAMES RAWLENCE

90106   **FO**   **Pilot**   **British**   **600 Squadron**

Joined 600 Squadron, AuxAF in 1938. Rawlence was called to full-time service on August 25 1939.

He was released from the RAF in late 1945, as a Squadron Leader.

PO (AuxAF) 18.7.38   *PO 25.8.39*   *FO 18.1.40*   *FL 18.1.41*
SL 1.3.42

CECIL FREDERICK RAWNSLEY

102089   **Sgt**   **Air Gunner**   **British**   **604 Squadron**

Born in London in March 1904, Rawnsley was an electrical engineer, concerned with supply to Hendon, Golders Green and Mill Hill. He joined 604 Squadron in late 1936, as an aircraftsman for ground duties. In September 1937 he was accepted for training as an air gunner and crewed-up with John Cunningham.

In the first half of 1938 Rawnsley passed his air gunner's board at Eastchurch and was promoted to LAC. He was called to full-time service on August 28 1939 and promoted to Sergeant in May 1940.

Rawnsley was given the chance to retrain as a Radio Observer with the squadron and he and Cunningham became one of the most successful and certainly the best known of the night-fighting partnerships. They had their first victory on February 15 1941, a He 111. Rawnsley was awarded the DFM (4.4.41), having assisted in the destruction of two enemy aircraft. Then came a Bar to the DFM (23.5.41), for seven enemy aircraft destroyed.

Commissioned in July 1941, Rawnsley was awarded the DFC (19.9.41). In July 1942 Cunningham was posted to HQ 81 Group, to direct the work of night-fighter OTUs. Rawnsley went with him to assist. In January 1943 Cunningham was given command of 85 Squadron at Hunsdon and Rawnsley again went with him, as Navigation Leader. He was awarded the DSO (26.10.43) and had then assisted in the destruction of seventeen enemy aircraft, sixteen at night.

In March 1944 Rawnsley stood down as Navigation Leader when Cunningham was posted to HQ 11 Group, as Group Captain Night Ops. Rawnsley went to the Fighter Interception Unit but soon afterwards he joined Cunningham, to help with preparations for the invasion of Europe.

Rawnsley was released in 1946, as a Squadron Leader. He was awarded the DFC (US)(14.6.46). He served in the RAuxAF from 1946, in the Secretarial Branch, and died on February 12 1965.

PO 14.7.41   FO 14.4.42   FL 14.7.43
FO (RAuxAFRO) 30.10.46

RONALD WILFRED RAY

742754   Sgt   Pilot   British   56 Squadron

Joined 56 Squadron at North Weald on September 5 1940. On the 30th Ray crashed in Hurricane P 3655, following an engagement with Bf 109s and Bf 110s over Bournemouth. He was wounded and suffered a broken arm.

A Warrant Officer Ray was flying with 604 Squadron in 1943. He destroyed a Dornier over the Humber on July 13 and shared a Ju 88 on the 27th.

Ray was released in 1946, as a Warrant Officer. He died in 1985.

RODERICK MALACHI SEABURNE RAYNER

40138   FO   Pilot   British   87 Squadron

Joined the RAF on a short service commission in July 1937. Rayner was posted to 6 FTS, Netheravon on September 18 and joined 87 Squadron at Debden on September 17 1938.

The squadron went to France at the outbreak of war. Rayner destroyed a Bf 110 on May 17 1940, a Bf 109, a He 111 and a Do 17 on the 19th and a Bf 109 and a Bf 110 on the 20th.

He claimed a Bf 110 destroyed on August 15. Rayner baled out of Hurricane V 7204 on December 23 1940 in bad weather, near Brize Norton.

In January 1941 Rayner was appointed 'A' Flight Commander and awarded the DFC (11.2.41).

He was released from the RAF in 1946, as a Wing Commander. Rayner died in 1982.

APO 5.9.37   PO 16.9.38   FO 16.5.40   FL 16.5.41
SL 1.6.42

WILLIAM ALBERT ALEXANDER READ

80822   PO   Pilot   British   603 Squadron

Born on August 11 1918 in Palmers Green, London, Read joined the RAFVR in July 1938. He began his elementary flying training at 21 E&RFTS, Stapleford Tawney and by the time he reported for full-time service at the outbreak of war he had logged 46 hrs 40 mins flying time.

Read went to ITW at Selwyn College, Cambridge in November 1939 and moved to 15 FTS, Lossiemouth at the end of December. After completing the course in late May 1940 he did a bombing course at Middle Wallop. In early June Read was posted to 5 OTU, Aston Down and after converting to Spitfires he joined 263 Squadron at Grangemouth on June 26 but went to 603 Squadron at Dyce on July 7.

Off Aberdeen on the 24th Read shared in damaging a He 111. Its port engine was stopped but it regained its base on the other. On March 4 1941 Read was posted to 53 OTU, Heston as an instructor, later moving with the unit to Llandow. In September 1941 he went to West Kirby for embarkation to Russia. Read sailed in the 'River Aston' to Archangel, with crated Hurricanes. At Kineshma, on the Volga, the aircraft were assembled by RAF men and test-flown by Read and another pilot. The first flight was made on November 3 1941 and the last on January 13 1942. Read formed five Russian squadrons

and instructed the pilots.

After returning to the UK he was posted to 51 OTU, Cranfield in early April 1942. Read was awarded the AFC (11.6.42). He was decorated by the King, who asked him questions about his work in Russia.

In March 1943 Read was posted to 29 Squadron at West Malling, on Beaufighters and from May on Mosquitos from Bradwell Bay. He moved to the Intensive Flying Development Flight at Boscombe Down in September 1943, testing the Westland Welkin. In early February 1944 Read went to the AFDU at Wittering and flew various aircraft in developing rocket projectiles.

He was seconded to BOAC in July 1944 and posted to Cairo. Read flew as First Officer on Lodestars to Istanbul and Nairobi and later on Ensigns to Calcutta. He was released from the RAF in March 1946 and eventually joined BOAC as a Junior Captain, at £ 600 per year.

In 1949 Read began flying Constellations on the London-Sydney run and later Comets. He retired from BOAC in 1963 and went farming.

PO 10.6.40   FO 10.6.41   FL 10.6.42

CHARLES ALFRED REAM

741907   Sgt   Pilot   British   235 Squadron

Joined 235 Squadron on September 22 1940.
No other service details traced. Ream died in 1947.

JOHN REARDON-PARKER

Sub-Lieutenant (FAA)   Pilot   British   804 Squadron

Reardon-Parker was with 804 Squadron at Hatston in early July 1940, flying Gladiators on dockyard defence. He was later with 757 Squadron at Worthy Down and in April 1941 he joined 752 Squadron at Piarco, Trinidad.

On November 28 1941 Reardon-Parker's commission was terminated. In France on June 7 1944, the day after D Day, a Lance-Corporal John Reardon-Parker of 591 Parachute Squadron (14550031) was killed in action. He was 26 years old, came from Chadwell Heath and is buried in the Ranville War Cemetery, France. It is not known whether he was the man who took part in the Battle of Britain.

Midshipman 21.2.39   Sub-Lt 7.5.40

JOSEPH RECHKA

No unknown   Sgt   Pilot   Czechoslovakian   310 Sqdn

Joined 310 Squadron at Duxford at its formation on July 10 1940. On September 15 Rechka shared in destroying a He 111.

He returned to Czechoslovakia after the war and became a pilot with Czech Airlines. In 1950 Rechka escaped to England with his family and two other Czech airline pilots, Kaucky and Prchal, and their families.

Rechka died in Britain in 1984.

LESLIE ARTHUR EDWIN REDDINGTON

742516   Sgt   Pilot   British   152 Squadron

Reddington, of Allesley, Warwickshire, served an apprenticeship at the Daimler Engineering Co at Coventry and later taught mathematics and technical drawing at Coventry Technical College in the evenings.

In 1938 Reddington joined the RAFVR and began his flying training at 9 E&RFTS, Ansty. He was called up at the outbreak of war and after completing his training he joined 152 Squadron at Warmwell in August 1940. During combat over Portland on September 30 Reddington

LAE Reddington (continued)

was shot down, in Spitfire L 1072, and is believed to have crashed into the sea. He was 26 years old and is remembered on the Runnymede Memorial, Panel 18.

Reddington was married and had a daughter, born in 1936. His widow had their second daughter in February 1941 and named her Lesley, after her father.

ERIC ARTHUR REDFERN

754694   **Sgt**   **Pilot**   **British**   **607 and 232 Squadrons**

Redfern, of Suffolk, was with 607 Squadron at Usworth in early July 1940 and moved to 232 Squadron at Castletown on August 27.

He was posted to 242 Squadron at Martlesham Heath on January 29 1941. Redfern claimed a Bf 109 probably destroyed on a bomber escort to Bethune on June 17, damaged a Bf 109 on the 23rd, and damaged another on a Stirling escort to Lille on July 8.

242 provided low-level escort for Blenheims sent to attack enemy supply vessels at Le Touquet on August 17 1941. The bombers turned away in the face of intense opposition and did not bomb. Redfern was one of two 242 pilots shot down and killed.

Aged 27, he was a Flight Sergeant at the time of his death. He is buried in Etaples Military Cemetery, France.

JOHN REDMAN

41952   **PO**   **Pilot**   **British**   **245, 43 and 257 Squadrons**

Joined the RAF on a short service commission in February 1939. Redman joined the newly-formed 245 Squadron at Leconfield on November 6.

Over Dunkirk on June 1 1940 he claimed a Bf 109 destroyed. On September 16 Redman was posted to 43 Squadron at Usworth and moved soon afterwards to 257 Squadron at Martlesham Heath. He crashed at Saffrey Farm, Owens Court, Selling on October 12, after a combat with Bf 109s over Deal, unhurt.

Redman was killed on April 20 1943, as a Flight Lieutenant with 224 Group. He is remembered on the Singapore Memorial, Column 423.

APO 15.4.39   *PO 6.11.39*   *FO 6.11.40*   *FL 6.11.41*

LAWRENCE HUGH MURRELL REECE

747825   **Sgt**   **Observer**   **British**   **235 Squadron**

With 235 Squadron in June 1940. Reece was a member of the crew of Blenheim N 3541, which failed to return from an operational sortie on July 18. All three men aboard were reported ' Missing'.

Reece was 26. He is remembered on the Runnymede Memorial, Panel 18.

HORACE REED

1001998   **Sgt**   **Radar Operator**   **British**   **600 Squadron**

Reed joined the RAF on March 31 1940. After basic training he volunteered for aircrew duties and went to Yatesbury for a short radar course.

He joined 600 Squadron at Manston on July 11. After failing to qualify as a Radio Observer he came off aircrew duties, losing his rank of Sergeant.

Reed remustered as a firefighter and after training joined 45 Squadron, serving with it in the Middle East and later India from November 11 1941 to September 13 1945. He was released from the RAF on May 2 1946, as a Corporal.

BRIAN VICTOR REES

40942   **FO**   **Pilot**   **British**   **610 Squadron**

Rees joined the RAF on a short service commission in May 1938 and was with 610 Squadron at Gravesend in early July 1940. He claimed a Bf 109 destroyed on August 12 and a Do 17 and a Bf 109 on the 18th.

His name does not appear on an Air Force List after January 1944 so presumably he left the service. Rees died in 1979.

APO 9.7.38   *PO 16.8.39*   *FO 3.9.40*   *FL 3.9.41*

J A REES

No unknown   **Sgt**   **Pilot**   **British**   **601 Squadron**

Joined 601 Squadron on September 11 1940.
No other service details traced.

ROBERT REID

80836   **PO**   **Pilot**   **British**   **46 Squadron**

Joined 46 Squadron at Digby in June 1940. Reid claimed Bf 109s destroyed on September 18 and October 15.

He was killed on March 23 1945, as a Squadron Leader with 235 Squadron. Reid is remembered on the Runnymede Memorial, Panel 265.

PO 17.6.40   *FO 25.4.41*   *FL 25.4.42*

HUGH WILLIAM REILLEY

43043   **PO**   **Pilot**   **American**   **64 and 66 Squadrons**

Reilley was born in Detroit, Michigan of a Scottish mother an an American father. His parents died in the late twenties and he was brought up by an uncle and aunt.

Before going to England and joining the RAF Reilley lived in London, Ontario. He was posted to 64 Squadron at Leconfield in early September 1940, moved to 66 Squadron at Gravesend on the 15th and claimed a Bf 109 destroyed on the 27th.

Reilley was shot down and killed by Major Mölders of JG 51 in combat over Westerham on October 17 1940. His Spitfire, R 6800, crashed and burned out at Crockham Hall, Sevenoaks. Reilley was 22 years old. He is buried in Gravesend Cemetery, Kent.

PO 23.3.40

CHARLES CHRISTOPHER REILLY

NZ 40626   **Sgt**   **Air Gunner**   **New Zealander**   **23 Sqdn**

Born in Auckland on May 15 1913, Reilly went to Te Awamutu District High School and afterwards worked as a hardware assistant. He volunteered for aircrew duties in late September 1939.

Reilly reported to the Ground Training School, Weraroa on February 13 1940, going a month later to the Air Observers' School, Ohakea for a gunnery course. He sailed for the UK in the RMS 'Rangitiki' on April 26. After a period at Uxbridge Reilly was posted to 5 OTU, Aston Down, where he was awarded his air gunner's badge after further training. He joined 23 Squadron at Ford on September 21 1940.

Reilly was with the squadron until early March 1942, when he was posted to 116 Squadron at Hooton Park, flying in Lysanders on radar calibration duties. In May he went to 1653 Conversion Unit, Polebrook for crewing-up and conversion to Liberators. Commissioned in June, Reilly joined 1445 Flight, Ferry Command at Lyneham and he flew in a Liberator on a delivery flight to Egypt, returning as a passenger in various civil aircraft, including a Boeing Clipper.

On October 16 1942 Reilly left the UK to join 160 Squadron at Aqir, Palestine, flying in a Liberator intended for squadron use. He arrived on the 19th and on the 27th took off on an operational flight to Crete, from which the aircraft failed to return. Radio contact was lost in the early hours of October 28 and the crew is officially presumed to have been lost on that date.

Another member of the crew was a New Zealander, Pilot Officer CR Durrant. He and Reilly had been together from the day they joined up. After the war Reilly's remains were re-interred in the Suda Bay Military Cemetery, Crete.

PO 10.6.42

JAMES VERDUN RENVOIZE

110352   Sgt   Pilot   British   247 Squadron

Renvoize applied to join the RAFVR in 1938 but was advised to take a six months course in mathematics and aircraft engineering at Chelsea Aeronautical College. After doing so he applied again and was attested on May 4 1939.

Before being called up at the outbreak of war Renvoize had done some weekend flying at 13 E&RFTS, White Waltham. He went to No 1 ITW, Cambridge in October 1939, moved to 10 EFTS, Yatesbury on December 5 and then to 3 FTS, South Cerney on April 28 1940.

With training completed Renvoize was posted to 5 OTU, Aston Down on August 4, where he converted to short-nose Blenheims. He joined the newly-reformed 247 Squadron at Roborough on August 14, to fly Gladiators on defence of the Devonport Naval Dockyard. The squadron began to receive Hurricanes in December 1940 and later began intruder raids over France.

Commissioned in October 1941, Renvoize was posted to 276 (ASR) Squadron at Warmwell on February 10 1942, as 'A' Flight Commander. He was still with the squadron when it went to France in September 1944. He was posted away to 2 FIS, Montrose on February 7 1945 for an instructor's course.

From May 28 Renvoize was at 7 (P) AFU, Peterborough, as assistant to the Wing Commander Flying. He was released from the RAF in January 1946, as a Flight Lieutenant.

PO 23.10.41   FO 1.10.42   FL 23.10.43

RICHARD CAREW REYNELL

32091   FL   Pilot   Australian   43 Squadron

Born in 1911, Reynell went to Balliol College, Oxford. In 1929 he joined the University Air Squadron there and in September 1931 went into the RAF on a short service commission.

Reynell was posted to 5 FTS, Sealand on September 28 and joined 43 Squadron at Tangmere on March 8 1932. He flew one of three Furies of the squadron which performed at the International Air Meeting at Brussels on June 11 1933. Reynell went to the Station Flight at Duxford on December 6 1934 and then joined the instructing staff at 8 FTS, Montrose on May 4 1936. He went on to the RAFO on January 15 1937 and became a test pilot at Hawker's.

At the outbreak of war Reynell was recalled to the RAF but was seconded to Hawker's to continue his test pilot duties. On August 26 1940 he was attached to 43 Squadron at Tangmere, for operational experience. On September 2 he claimed a Bf 109 destroyed. Reynell was shot down on the 7th in combat with Bf 109s over South London. He baled out, wounded, but his parachute failed to open and he fell dead near Greyladies. His Hurricane, V 7257, crashed at Crown Point, Blackheath.

Reynell is buried in Brookwood Cemetery, Surrey.

PO 28.9.31   FO 28.3.33   FL 1.4.36   FL (RAFO) 15.1.37

EDWIN MICHAEL REYNO

C 806   FL   Pilot   Canadian   1 (RCAF) Squadron

Born in Halifax, Nova Scotia in 1917, Reyno graduated from St Mary's University in 1936. He joined the RCAF on January 3 1938 and was with No 1 (RCAF) Squadron when it arrived in the UK on June 20 1940.

Reyno was posted to 2 (RCAF) Squadron on January 1 1941, as a Flight Commander. He returned to Canada later in the year and served at RCAF stations at Rockliffe, Ontario and Mossbank, Saskatchewan. In 1942 Reyno was appointed Chief Instructor at No 1 (Fighter) OTU at Bagotville, Quebec. He was awarded the AFC (8.6.44).

In 1944 Reyno was Station Commander at Greenwood, Nova Scotia and in 1946 was appointed Senior Personnel Officer at Western Air Command, Vancouver.

He retired on October 30 1972, as a Lieutenant General, Canadian Forces. Reyno died on February 10 1982.

RICHARD ARTHUR RHODES

42529   PO   Pilot   British   29 Squadron

Joined the RAF on a short service commission in June 1939. Rhodes was with 29 Squadron at Digby in early July 1940. On a night patrol on August 18 Rhodes, flying with Sergeant WJ Gregory as his gunner, destroyed a He 111 off Spurn Head in the early hours of the morning.

On August 25 Rhodes failed to return and is believed to have been shot down in combat over Wainfleet, crashing into the sea in Blenheim L 1330. He and his crew of two were reported 'Missing'. Rhodes was 19 and is remembered on the Runnymede Memorial, Panel 9.

APO 19.8.39   PO 10.2.40

WILLIAM HENRY RHODES-MOORHOUSE

90140   FO   Pilot   British   601 Squadron

Born in Brompton Square, London in January 1914, Rhodes-Moorhouse was the only son of WB Rhodes-Moorhouse, who won the first VC ever given for supreme valour in aerial operations. He bombed Courtrai rail junction on April 26 1915 and although he regained his airfield he was mortally wounded and died on the 27th.

Rhodes-Moorhouse the younger was educated at Eton and obtained his pilot's license at Heston when he was seventeen. He joined 601 Squadron, AuxAF in 1937. He was a keen skier and took part in the Winter Games of 1937/38.

Called to full-time service on August 26 1939, Rhodes-Moorhouse flew one of the six 601 Blenheims, which attacked the German seaplane base at Borkum on November 27 1939 in company with six of 25 Squadron.

On May 16 1940 Rhodes-Moorhouse went with 'A' Flight of 601 to Merville. He shot down a He 111 east of Brussels on the 18th and destroyed a Bf 109 on the 22nd.

Rhodes-Moorhouse shared Do 17s on July 7 and 11 and destroyed a Ju 88 on the 16th. He was awarded the DFC (30.7.40). On August 11 he claimed two Bf 109s destroyed, on the 18th another, on the 30th he shared a He 111, on the 31st probably destroyed two Bf 109s and on September 4 claimed a Do 17.

WH Rhodes-Moorhouse (continued)

On September 6 Rhodes-Moorhouse was shot down and killed in combat over Tunbridge Wells. His Hurricane, P 8818, crashed near High Brooms Viaduct, Southborough. He is buried in the private cemetery of his family home, Parnham, Beaminster, Dorset.

PO (AuxAF) 28.7.37   FO (AuxAF) 29.1.39   FO 26.8.39

ALAN LESLIE RICALTON

70872   FO   Pilot   British   74 Squadron

Ricalton, of Gosforth, Newcastle-upon-Tyne, joined the RAF on a short service commission in January 1938. He was posted to 8 FTS, Montrose on April 9 and went to 142 Squadron at Andover on October 29 1938.

The squadron took its Battles to France at the outbreak of war, as part of the AASF. On May 10 1940 the squadron was the first to bomb the advancing Germans. After heavy losses it was withdrawn to Waddington in June 1940.

Ricalton volunteered for Fighter Command in August and joined 74 Squadron at Kirton-in-Lindsey on the 21st. He was shot down and killed in combat with Bf 109s over Maidstone on October 17 1940. His Spitfire, P 7360, crashed near Hollingbourne. Ricalton was 26 years old. He is buried in Sittingbourne Cemetery, Kent. He received a Mention in Despatches.

APO 26.3.38   PO 17.1.39   FO 17.8.40

PETER GEOFFREY RICH

939496   Sgt   Aircrew   British   25 Squadron

Joined 25 Squadron at North Weald in early October 1940.
No other service details traced.

DUNCAN HAMILTON RICHARDS

Sub-Lieutenant (FAA)   Pilot   British   111 Squadron

Joined 111 Squadron at Drem on September 22 1940.

Richards was later with 803 Squadron at Dekheila, Egypt, flying Hurricanes in the Naval Fighter Wing in the Western Desert. In late 1942 he returned to the UK and joined 784 Squadron at Donibristle.

After some time at the Air Warfare Training Division Richards was given command of 809 Squadron and later led 781 Squadron. He died on September 2 1955, still serving.

*Midshipman 11.9.39   Actg Sub-Lt 14.3.40   Sub-Lt 9.1.41
Lt 14.9.42   Actg Lt Cdr 1949   Lt Cdr 14.9.50*

WILLIAM CHARLES RICHARDS

102978   Sgt   Pilot   British   235 Squadron

Joined 235 Squadron in early October 1940.

Commissioned in July 1941, Richards was killed on August 11 1941, as a Pilot Officer with 235. He is remembered on the Runnymede Memorial, Panel 34.

PO 5.7.41

ERIC RICHARDSON

45464   Sgt   Pilot   British   242 Squadron

Richardson was born on December 4 1912. He was posted to 242 Squadron at Biggin Hill on June 6 1940. The squadron moved to France on the 8th to help cover the retreat of British troops to the Atlantic ports. It was withdrawn on the 18th. Richardson flew back with no maps and after running out of fuel he landed on a beach near Minehead.

He claimed a Ju 88 destroyed on August 1 and a Do 17 on September 9. Richardson was posted away from 242 on the 18th.

Commissioned in February 1941, he served with 258 Squadron and was awarded the DFC (9.9.41), as an Acting Flight Lieutenant.

Richardson retired from the RAF on October 1 1958, as a Squadron Leader. He died on September 2 1973.

*PO 19.2.41   FO 19.10.41   FL 19.10.42   FL 1.9.45
SL 1.1.49*

RONALD WILLIAM RICHARDSON

52460   Sgt   Air Gunner   British   141 Squadron

With 141 Squadron at Turnhouse in June 1940.

Commissioned in September 1943 in the Administrative Branch, Richardson was released from the RAF in 1946, as a Flying Officer. He died in December 1970.

PO 9.9.43   FO 9.3.44

ROLAND WHARRIER RICHARDSON

113339   Sgt   Pilot   British   610 Squadron

Born on May 2 1920, Richardson joined the RAFVR in May 1939. Called to full-time service at the outbreak of war, he carried out his elementary flying training at 6 EFTS, Sywell and 9 EFTS, Ansty and then went to 5 FTS, Sealand.

In September 1940 Richardson was posted to 7 OTU, Hawarden and after converting to Spitfires he joined 610 Squadron at Acklington on October 14. Tour-expired in December 1941, he was commissioned and volunteered for the Middle East.

Richardson joined 80 Squadron in the Western Desert in February 1942, was appointed 'A' Flight Commander in April and posted away to 71 OTU, Abu Sueir in June. On May 5 1943 he joined 92 Squadron in Tunisia, moved with it to Malta on June 19 and then to Sicily on July 14. Six days later he was posted to 93 Squadron at Comiso, Sicily.

On February 18 1944 Richardson's tour ended and in April he returned to the UK and was posted to CGS, Catfoss on June 10, as an instructor. In September he was sent to the USA, as Gunnery and Attack Adviser to the British FTSs there.

Richardson returned to the UK in September 1945. He was awarded the AFC (13.6.59) and retired from the RAF on May 2 1963, as a Squadron Leader. He died on November 18 1988.

*PO 3.12.41   FO 3.8.42   FL 3.8.43   FL 1.9.45
SL 1.10.55*

WILLIAM ARTHUR RICHARDSON

29047   SL   Pilot   British   141 Squadron

Born on July 19 1903, Richardson joined the RAF in March 1930. He was posted to 5 FTS, Sealand on the 29th and joined 23 Squadron at Kenley on March 8 1931. He went to SHQ Hal Far, Malta on July 31 1936 and transferred to 3 AACU there on August 16 1937.

Richardson returned to the UK in early 1938 and on March 19 he was posted to 9 FTS, Hullavington, as an instructor. When 141 Squadron was reformed at Turnhouse on October 4 1939 Richardson was given command. He was posted away in September 1940.

He retired from the RAF on July 19 1955, as a Wing Commander. Richardson died in 1970.

*PO 14.3.30   FO 14.9.31   FL 14.9.35   SL 1.10.38
WC 1.6.41   WC 1.10.46*

HERBERT WAIN RICKETTS

54692   Sgt   Air Gunner   British   235 Squadron

Ricketts, of Rowsley, was with 235 Squadron in June 1940 and served with the squadron throughout the Battle of Britain.

Commissioned in March 1944, Ricketts was killed on March 31 1945, as a Flying Officer, Navigator with 229 Squadron, aged 26. He is buried in Indre churchyard, Sondeled, Norway.

PO 21.3.44   FO 21.9.44

VICTOR ANTHONY RICKETTS

77341　PO　Pilot　British　248 Squadron

Before the war Ricketts was Air Correspondent for the London Daily Express. In December 1937 he approached AE Clouston (qv) with a proposition that he would arrange backing for a record-breaking attempt to Australia and back in a Comet if Clouston would take him along as second pilot.

It was arranged and they took off at 4 am on February 2 1938 but came to grief in Turkey, damaging the port undercarriage leg as they took off. They returned to England and a second attempt was planned on a revised route. They took off from Gravesend during the night of March 15 1938 and landed back at Croydon 10 days 21 hrs and 22 mins later, having established eleven records, including the first direct round trip England-New Zealand-England.

Ricketts was probably in the RAFVR and after passing out as a Sergeant-Pilot he was commissioned in February 1940 and joined 248 Squadron, which was formed as a night-fighter squadron but transferred to Coastal Command soon after Ricketts' arrival. The squadron served with Fighter Command during the Battle of Britain.

In 1942 Ricketts was with No 1 PRU. On March 4 he was detailed to photograph the Renault works near Paris, attacked the previous night. Despite bad weather, low cloud and poor visibility he succeeded in obtaining valuable photographs. For this operation he was awarded the DFC (2.6.42).

Ricketts failed to return from a photographic sortie to Strasbourg and Ingolstadt on July 12 1942. He was 29 and is buried in the Calais Canadian War Cemetery.

PO 1.2.40　FO 1.2.41　FL 1.2.42

LEO PATRICK VINCENT JOHN RICKS

552653　Sgt　Wop/AG　Canadian　235 Squadron

Ricks was born on December 20 1921 in Calgary, Alberta. He went to England in 1938 to join the Royal Navy but a defect in his left eye made him unacceptable and he joined the RAF instead, on September 26 1938.

He joined 235 Squadron on April 24 1940 and served with it until February 2 1941, when he went to 3 (Coastal) OTU, as an instructor. From November 27 1941 until May 15 1942 Ricks was with 2 AACU. He then went to 7 (Coastal) OTU until March 9 1943, when he joined 86 Squadron, a general reconnaissance unit.

After serving with a GCA unit from August 1944 Ricks transferred to the RCAF on February 14 1945 and was repatriated to Canada in May. He was later commissioned and retired from the RCAF in 1964, as a Flying Officer.

Ricks went to Ireland to live in January 1969 and died there on January 8 1985.

JOHN DERRICK RIDDELL-HANNAM

54784　Sgt　Wop/AG　British　236 Squadron

Born in 1921, Riddell-Hannam enlisted in the RAF in July 1939 as an ACH u/t Wireless Operator for six years regular service. He completed his training in May 1940 and in June volunteered for air crew duties.

After air gunnery training and conversion at a Blenheim OTU Riddell-Hannam joined 236 Squadron on September 16 1940. In July 1941 he was posted to 86 Squadron, operating in Beauforts but in March 1942 he was categorised as permanently unfit for aircrew, the result of a head injury sustained in the second of three aircraft crashes in which he had been involved.

In January 1943 Riddell-Hannam volunteered for Combined Operations and he served with 105 Wing in the Mediterranean, taking part in the invasions of Pantelleria, Sicily and Italy. He was commissioned in the RAF Regiment in June 1944, served with 2837

Squadron and later 2739 Squadron in the Far East.

Riddell-Hannam stayed on in the RAF, serving at home and overseas until his retirement in January 1955, as a Flight Lieutenant. He later changed his name to Hannam.

PO 13.6.44　FO 13.6.45　FL 4.1.51

CHRISTOPHER JOHN HENRY RIDDLE

90143　FL　Pilot　British　601 Squadron

Born on April 4 1914, Riddle was at Harrow School from 1928 to 1931. He joined 601 Squadron, AuxAF in early 1938 and was called to full-time service in October 1939.

Over Dunkirk on May 27 1940 Riddle probably destroyed a Bf 110. He shared in destroying a Do 17 on September 4. He was posted away from 601 in 1941.

Riddle was released from the RAF in 1946, as a Squadron Leader. Brother of HJ Riddle.

PO (AuxAF) 14.4.38　FO 14.10.39　FL 14.10.40　SL 1.12.41

HUGH JOSEPH RIDDLE

90141　FL　Pilot　British　601 Squadron

Born on May 24 1912, Riddle was at Harrow School from 1926 to 1930 and then Magdalene College, Oxford. He joined 601 Squadron, AuxAF in 1937 and was called to full-time service on August 25 1939.

Riddle shared in destroying a Bf 110 on July 11 1940, with Wing Commander JS Dewar of 87 and Green Section of 238.

He was released from the RAF in 1945, as a Squadron Leader. Brother of CJH Riddle.

PO (AuxAF) 31.7.37　FO (AuxAF) 31.3.39　FO 25.8.39 FL 3.9.40　SL 1.12.41

MARMADUKE RIDLEY

565201　Sgt　Pilot　British　616 Squadron

Ridley, of Benwell, Newcastle-upon-Tyne, joined 616 Squadron at Leconfield in early 1940. Over Dunkirk on May 28 his Spitfire was badly damaged in what was the squadron's first real action of the war and he suffered a slight head wound.

On August 26 1940 Ridley was shot down and killed in combat over Dover, possibly by Hauptmann Fözö of 4/JG 51. He was 24 years old and is buried in Folkestone New Cemetery, Kent.

ROBERT HAROLD RIGBY

42149　PO　Pilot　British　236 Squadron

Joined the RAF on a short service commission in March 1939. Rigby did his ab initio course at 10 E&RFTS, Yatesbury, moved to 5 FTS, Sealand on May 30 and joined 236 Squadron at Stradishall on November 6 1939.

He failed to return from a photographic-reconnaissance operation over Le Havre on July 18 1940, in Blenheim L 6690. The weather was bad and intense flak was encountered over Cap de la Hague.

Rigby was 24. He is buried in Ste Marie Cemetery, Le Havre, France.

APO 13.5.39　PO 6.11.39

FREDERICK RILEY

42024　PO　Pilot　British　236 Squadron

Riley, of Manchester, joined the RAF on a short service commission in February 1939. After training he was posted to 236 Squadron at Stradishall on November 6 1939 and served with the squadron throughout the Battle of Britain.

Riley was killed on December 7 1942, as a Flight Lieutenant with 542 Squadron, a photographic-reconnaissance Spitfire unit. He was 30 years old and is buried in Boulogne Eastern Cemetery, France.

APO 29.4.39　PO 6.11.39　FO 6.11.40　FL 6.11.41

WILLIAM RILEY

37422   FL   Pilot   British   263, 302 and 145 Sqdns

Riley, of Manorhamilton, Co Leitrim, joined the RAF on a short service commission in August 1935. He was posted to 11 FTS, Wittering on November 2 and joined 54 Squadron at Hornchurch on May 11 1936. He went to the Electrical and Wireless School, Cranwell on February 9 1937, as a staff pilot on the Signals Squadron. On December 16 1938 Riley was posted to HQ RAF Far East, Singapore, on organisation duties on the administrative staff.

Back in the UK, Riley was with 263 Squadron at Grangemouth in early July 1940. He was posted to 302 Squadron at Leconfield at its formation on July 13, as a Flight Commander. On August 21 Riley claimed a Ju 88 probably destroyed, on September 18 a Ju 88 destroyed and probably a second and on October 15 a Bf 109 destroyed. He went to 145 Squadron at Tangmere on October 30.

In early 1941 Riley joined 252 Squadron and on April 16 he shot down a FW Condor, the squadron's first victory. He was awarded the DFC (31.10.41). In April 1942 Riley went to Malta, ostensibly to form 227 Squadron but delays resulted in his flying with 272 Squadron in the Middle East. On April 14 whilst escorting Beauforts on a convoy attack Riley destroyed two Bf 110s, on May 1 he destroyed a Ju 52 and on June 26 was himself shot down by flak but returned to the squadron the next day.

Riley was killed on July 16 1942, as a Wing Commander with 272 Squadron. He collided with another Beaufighter soon after taking off and crashed into the sea. He was 25 and is remembered on the Alamein Memorial, Column 247.

APO 21.10.35   PO 26.8.36   FO 26.4.38   FL 26.4.40
SL 1.6.41   WC 1.6.42

REGINALD FRANK RIMMER

39683   FO   Pilot   British   229 Squadron

Rimmer, of Meols, Cheshire, joined the RAF on a short service commission in March 1937. He was posted to 10 FTS, Tern Hill on May 9 and joined 66 Squadron at Duxford on November 27 1937.

Over Dunkirk on June 2 1940 Rimmer damaged a He 111. He was posted to 229 Squadron at Wittering later in the month. On September 15 Rimmer claimed a Do 17 destroyed and shared a He 111. He was shot down and killed in combat with Bf 109s on the 27th. His Hurricane, V 6782, exploded over Franchise Manor Farm, Burwash.

Rimmer was 21 years old. He is buried in Grange Cemetery, Hoylake, Cheshire and is remembered on a memorial plaque at the farm, near the crash site.

APO 9.5.37   PO 8.3.38   FO 8.11.39

ERIC ALFRED RINGWOOD

629710   Sgt   Observer   British   248 Squadron

Joined 248 Squadron in mid-July 1940. Ringwood was one of the crew of a Blenheim, which failed to return from a reconnaissance sortie to the south Norwegian coast on August 27 1940 and is known to have crashed into the sea.

He and the pilot, Pilot Officer CJ Arthur, were reported 'Missing' and the gunner, Sergeant RCR Cox, was known to be killed.

Ringwood was 20 years old. He is remembered on the Runnymede Memorial, Panel 18.

WILLIAM GEORGE RIPLEY

139951   Sgt   Wop/AG   British   604 Squadron

Ripley, of Emsworth, Hampshire, joined 604 Squadron at Middle Wallop on August 20 1940. He later trained as a Radio Observer and flew with Flying Officer RA Chisholm.

On March 13 1941 they destroyed two He 111s at night, on April 9 another two, on the 11th a He 111 and probably a Ju 88, on the 29th a He 111 and on July 8 another He 111 and a second damaged. Ripley was awarded the DFM (13.5.41).

Promoted to Warrant Officer on March 1 1942, he was commissioned in January 1943. Ripley died on November 16 1943, of injuries received on active service, as a Flight Lieutenant with 141 Squadron. He was 30 and is buried in Warblington Cemetery, Havant.

PO 12.1.43   FO 12.7.43

ANTHONY JOHN RIPPON

42262   PO   Pilot   British   601 Squadron

Joined the RAF on a short service commission in June 1939. Rippon was posted to 601 Squadron at Exeter on September 26 1940.

Rippon arrived in Malta in a Sunderland from the Middle East on January 30 1941 and joined 261 Squadron at Hal Far. On March 5 he destroyed a Ju 87 and shared a Bf 110, on the 9th he shared in damaging a Ju 88, on the 23rd he destroyed two Ju 87s and on April 29 he shared a Ju 88. Rippon returned to the Middle East in May 1941 and later served at the ADU, Takoradi.

He was killed on August 25 1944, as a Flight Lieutenant with 107 Squadron, operating in Mosquitos from Lasham. He is buried in Ouroux-sur-Saone Communal Cemetery, France. An award of the DFC (5.9.44) was gazetted after his death. The citation credited him with the destruction of five enemy aircraft.

APO 10.6.39   PO 18.11.39   FO 18.11.40   FL 18.2.42

ARTHUR HARRY RISELEY

106080   Sgt   Air Gunner   British   600 Squadron

Born on June 7 1914 at Rotherhithe, London, Riseley went into a hotel-work apprenticeship. He joined 600 Squadron, AuxAF at Hendon in 1934, as a trainee Fitter (Aero Engine). After a year of evening classes at Armoury House Riseley took a trade test, passed and was promoted to LAC.

He later remustered as a u/t air gunner, flying in Harts and Demons from Hendon. After qualifying Riseley was promoted to Corporal. He was called to full-time service on August 24 1939 and later promoted to Sergeant. After making many applications for pilot training Riseley was selected and early in 1941 he went to ITW at Downing College, Cambridge, then to 22 EFTS, Cambridge for his ab initio course. He moved on to FTS, Kidlington and was commissioned in September 1941 at the end of the course.

Riseley asked for night fighters and was posted to 51 OTU, Cranfield. He converted to Bostons and joined 418 (RCAF) Squadron at Debden at its formation on November 15 1941. The British crews were gradually replaced by Canadians and at the end of 1942 Riseley was posted to 88 Squadron at Oulton, on daylight Bostons.

On August 16 1943 the squadron went to raid the marshalling yards at Valenciennes. Riseley's aircraft was hit by flak before reaching the target and he had lost one engine. After bombing he went down to low-level for the return flight and was shot down by Bf 109s in the Pas de Calais area. He crash-landed in a field, with his crew of two injured. They managed to reach a small wood. Riseley left them and went to a farmhouse, where he was given civilian clothes and sent on. French people went out to the injured crew.

Riseley evaded capture, lived on roots and was given food at a farmhouse. After a few days he met an expatriate Englishman, who had stayed on in 1918 and owned a café. Riseley was taken to a miliner's shop, where he was joined by his gunner. The navigator had been captured. They hid at the shop for several weeks, eventually went to Amiens station and took a train to Paris. From there they went south, returned to Paris, and then took a train to Vannes and ended up in Brest, where they were nearly caught.

They eventually got away in a fishing boat and after thirty-six hours at sea reached Penzance on October 25 1943. Riseley rejoined the squadron at Swanton Morley. In December he was posted to HQ 2 Group at Wallingford, as an Operations Controller. He was awarded the DSO (14.1.44).

Riseley went to 2nd TAF, Brussels later in 1944, moved to Osnabruck in 1945 and finally to Gutersloh, to prepare for the arrival of the RAF. He was released from the RAF on April 1 1946, as a Squadron Leader. During his service Riseley received a Mention in Despatches.

PO 3.9.41   FO 3.9.42   FL 3.9.43

GEOFFREY LOUIS RITCHER

41209　**FO**　**Pilot**　**British**　**234 Squadron**

Joined the RAF on a short service commission in July 1938. Ritcher was posted to 234 Squadron at St Eval in mid-September 1940 and claimed a Do 17 destroyed on November 29.

Ritcher was posted away to 53 OTU, Heston in December 1940, as an instructor. He was released from the RAF in 1946, as a Squadron Leader.

APO 17.9.38　PO 25.7.39　FO 3.9.40　FL 3.9.41
SL 1.7.44

IAN SMALL RITCHIE

90198　**FL**　**Pilot**　**British**　**603 Squadron**

Joined 603 Squadron, AuxAF in early 1938. Ritchie was called to full-time service on August 23 1939.

He shared in destroying a Ju 88 on July 3 and shared a He 111 on the 16th. Ritchie was wounded in combat with Bf 109s off Dover on August 28 and returned to Hornchurch in his severely-damaged Spitfire, R 6989. He was admitted to Oldchurch Hospital, Romford and returned to the squadron on September 5.

Ritchie was released from the RAF in 1945, as a Wing Commander.

PO (AuxAF) 15.2.38　FO 23.8.39　FL 3.9.40　SL 1.12.41

JOHN MILLAR RITCHIE

79193　**PO**　**Air Gunner**　**British**　**141 Squadron**

Born on May 19 1911. Ritchie was with 141 Squadron at Turnhouse in early July 1940. He was posted away on August 30 1940.

Ritchie retired from the RAF on January 20 1959, as a Squadron Leader.

APO 20.4.40　PO 13.5.40　FO 13.5.41　FL 13.5.42
SL 1.8.47

JAMES RITCHIE RITCHIE

41781　**PO**　**Pilot**　**British**　**600, 111 and 72 Sqdns**

Born on June 4 1920, Ritchie joined the RAF on a short service commission in February 1939.

He was posted to 600 Squadron at Northolt on July 1 1940, moved to 111 Squadron at Debden on August 28 and then to 72 Squadron at Biggin Hill.

Ritchie commanded 132 Squadron from May 1942 to August 1943. He instructed at 58 OTU, Grangemouth and later went to a staff post in India. He was awarded the AFC (13.6.46). Ritchie retired from the RAF on June 3 1972, as a Squadron Leader, retaining the rank of Wing Commander.

APO 1.4.39　PO 6.11.39　FO 6.11.40　FL 1.3.42
SL 1.7.45　FL 1.12.42　SL 1.7.53　SL 1.1.68

ROBERT DOUGLAS RITCHIE

745702　**Sgt**　**Pilot**　**British**　**605 Squadron**

Ritchie was born in Fife and was a pre-war member of the RAFVR. He was with 605 Squadron at Drem in early July 1940.

During a section patrol off the east coast on August 9 1940 Ritchie called up, reporting that he had a glycol leak and the fumes were making him drowsy. He crashed into the sea one mile off Dunbar, East Lothian, in Hurricane L 2103, breaking his neck. The body was picked up by the 'Eunmara'.

Ritchie was 24. He is buried in Leslie Cemetery, Fife.

THOMAS GLYN FINLAYSON RITCHIE

73010　**PO**　**Pilot**　**British**　**602 Squadron**

Ritchie, of Dunbartonshire, was commissioned in the RAFVR in March 1939. Called to full-time service at the outbreak of war, he joined 602 Squadron at Abbotsinch in September 1939.

On August 19 1940 Ritchie shared in destroying a Ju 88. On the 23rd he returned to Westhampnett with damage caused by colliding with another RAF fighter in cloud. Ritchie claimed a Bf 110 destroyed on August 25 and on September 6 he was wounded in the legs in combat with Bf 109s over Hailsham and was admitted to Chichester Hospital.

In March 1941 Ritchie was commanding 'A' Flight. On July 21 the squadron escorted three Stirlings to attack a target at Lille. On the way in they were jumped by Bf 109s and Ritchie was shot down and killed. He is buried in Reninghelst churchyard extension, Belgium.

PO (RAFVR) 29.3.39　PO 1.9.39　FO 26.11.40

ROBERT JAMES BAIN ROACH

42263　**PO**　**Pilot**　**British**　**266 Squadron**

Born on October 25 1919. Roach joined the RAF on a short service commission in March 1939 and was with 266 Squadron at Wittering in early July 1940.

He shared in destroying a He 115 floatplane on August 15 and shared a Do 17 on September 7. After being hit by return fire from a He 111 on the 11th Roach baled out over Billericay from Spitfire N 3244, unhurt.

He retired from the RAF on October 25 1965, as a Flight Lieutenant, retaining the rank of Squadron Leader.

APO 1.5.39　PO 9.3.40　FO 9.3.41　FL 9.3.42
FL 1.9.45

ROBERT ANDREW LINDSAY ROBB

86626　**PO**　**Pilot**　**British**　**236 Squadron**

Joined 236 Squadron on September 26 1940. Robb's name does not appear in the Air Force List after October 1942 and he has not been traced as a casualty.

PO 24.8.40

ROBERT HORLEY ROBBINS

161726　**Sgt**　**Pilot**　**British**　**54 and 66 Squadrons**

Robbins was born in 1915. He was with 54 Squadron at Rochford in early July 1940 and was posted to 66 Squadron at Kenley on September 11. Robbins was shot down in combat over Maidstone on the 14th, in Spitfire X 4327. He was admitted to Leeds Castle Hospital, seriously injured.

Commissioned in October 1943, Robbins was released from the RAF in 1947, as a Flight Lieutenant.

PO 24.10.43　FO 24.4.44　FL 24.4.45

ARTHUR JOHN ALAN ROBERTS

45717　**Sgt**　**Pilot**　**British**　**29 Squadron**

Born on December 23 1915. Roberts was with 29 Squadron at Digby in early July 1940. On August 22 his Blenheim was struck by lightning during an RDF trial flight. He and Pilot Officer PA Tomlinson returned to Digby, unhurt.

On October 29 Roberts struck a tree, taking off in Blenheim L 1503. He was again unhurt.

AJA Roberts (continued)

Commissioned in April 1941, Roberts was with 600 Squadron in 1943. He shot a SM 84 down into the sea four miles north of Monastir on April 26. He was awarded the DFC (20.8.43), as a Flying Officer with 600. The citation credited him with three enemy aircraft destroyed.

Roberts retired from the RAF on December 23 1957, as a Squadron Leader.

PO 24.4.41   FO 24.4.42   FL 24.4.43   SL 1.8.47

DAVID FRANCIS ROBERTS

965482   Sgt   Wop/AG   British   25 Squadron

Roberts, of Penylan, joined 25 Squadron at Martlesham Heath in August 1940. He was killed on April 3 1941, still with 25. He was 32 years old and is buried in All Saints' churchyard, Wittering, Northamptonshire.

DAVID NEAL ROBERTS

16229   WC   Pilot   British   609 and 238 Squadrons

Born on June 4 1906, Roberts entered RAF College, Cranwell in September 1924 as a flight cadet. On graduation he joined 39 Squadron at Grantham on July 30 1926, to fly DH9s and Westland Wapitis. Roberts was sent to CFS, Wittering in September 1928 and joined the instructing staff at 2 FTS, Digby on December 19.

He was posted to 504 Squadron, AuxAF at Hucknall on August 18 1930 as Flying Instructor. On October 5 1931 Roberts went to King's College, London University for a Russian language course, followed by a special language leave for one year in Estonia. Passed out as a Russian interpreter.

After a refresher course at CFS, Wittering in early 1933 Roberts joined 41 Squadron at Northolt on March 17, as 'A' Flight Commander. In early 1935 he was posted to RAF Amman as Station Adjutant and on July 24 went to 4 FTS, Abu Sueir as Flying Instructor and Flight Commander. He was awarded the AFC (9.6.38).

Whilst on leave from Egypt in 1938 Roberts was posted to the Air Staff at HQ Fighter Command. In June 1940 he was given the job of forming and then commanding the Fighter Station and Sector at Middle Wallop. During the period of the Battle of Britain he flew occasional sorties with 609 and 238 Squadrons, thus qualifying for the Battle of Britain clasp.

Made an OBE (24.9.41) Roberts was posted overseas in November to command a fighter wing for special operations in North Africa. When the war with Japan started he was diverted to the Dutch East Indies. Roberts was evacuated to India in early 1942, where he commanded the fighter defences for Calcutta and Eastern India. He later commanded RAF Assam.

In 1943 Roberts was posted to Moscow as Air Attaché and Head of the UK Air Mission. He returned to the UK in 1945 and was appointed Assistant SASO at HQ Transport Command. Later in the year he went to 45 Group, Dorval, Canada.

Roberts was made a CBE (1.1.54) and retired from the RAF on May 29 1958, as an Air Commodore.

PO 30.7.26   FO 30.1.28   FL 30.6.31   SL 1.4.37
WC 1.3.40   GC 1.6.42   GC 1.10.46   AC 1.1.51

ELWYN COOPER ROBERTS

52544   Sgt   Wop/AG   British   23 Squadron

Roberts joined the RAF in May 1939 and after training was posted to a Battle squadron at RAF Benson in November. In May 1940 he went to 23 Squadron at Wittering and was promoted to Sergeant.

In October 1940 Roberts was posted to 99 Squadron, operating in Wellingtons from Newmarket. With his tour completed in June 1941 he went to 27 OTU, Lichfield, as an instructor.

Commissioned in February 1942, Roberts was posted as a signals instructor to RAF Wigtown, later becoming Chief Signals Instructor. He was seconded to BOAC in 1945 and resigned his commission in 1947 to join the Corporation.

PO 4.2.42   FO 4.8.42   FL 4.2.44

GEORGE WILLIAM ROBERTS

Midshipman (FAA)   Pilot   British   808 Squadron

Roberts, of Woking, was with 808 Squadron at Wick in early July 1940, flying Fulmars on dockyard defence. He embarked with the squadron in HMS 'Ark Royal' on October 22 1940 and served with it in the actions in the Mediterranean in 1941.

On October 11 1941 Roberts was posted to 800 Squadron in HMS 'Indomitable'. He later served at Macrihanish and then went to HMS 'Khedive' on December 31 1943, for air gunnery duties.

Roberts was killed on May 30 1946, whilst serving with HMS 'Vulture'. He was 25 and is buried in St Merryn churchyard, Cornwall.

Midshipman 1.5.39   Actg Sub-Lt 20.11.40   Sub-Lt 7.11.41
Lt 20.5.43

RALPH ROBERTS

90897   FO   Pilot   British   615 and 64 Squadrons

In March 1939 Roberts joined 616 Squadron, AuxAF at Doncaster. He was accepted for pilot training.

Roberts was called to full-time service on August 24 and was awarded his wings in September. He was posted to the Fighter Pool at St Athan, where he converted to Hurricanes. He then joined the Ferry Pilots Pool at Filton, pending a squadron posting, meanwhile ferrying a Hurricane to a front-line squadron in France.

In late December Roberts was posted to 615 Squadron in France and arrived at Vitry on January 1 1940. He informed the CO that he had expected to go to 616 Squadron and was told that it would be arranged but that it would take time.

Roberts flew Gladiators in France until operations ceased there and then he flew one back to Lympne. He did patrols over Dunkirk in Gladiators, operating from Manston. The squadron, which had lost its new Hurricanes in France, was re-equipped with replacements at Kenley in June and Roberts continued to fly with 615 until the end of July. He was then informed that his posting to 616 had finally come through but pending ratification from Group he was asked to fly with 64 Squadron, also at Kenley, which was short of pilots.

On August 13 Roberts claimed a Do 17 destroyed. Two days later he was shot down over Calais Marck and captured. Freed in May 1945, Roberts was released from the RAF on March 9 1946, as a Flight Lieutenant.

APO 24.8.39   PO 4.9.39   FO 4.9.40   FL 4.9.41

BASIL LIONEL ROBERTSON

748333   Sgt   Pilot   British   54 Squadron

Robertson, of Portslade, Sussex, joined 54 Squadron at Hornchurch on August 22 1940.

He was killed on February 12 1942, as a Warrant Officer with 137 Squadron, operating in Whirlwinds from Matlask. Robertson was 20 years old. He is remembered on the Runnymede Memorial, Panel 73.

FREDERICK NEAL ROBERTSON

119881   Sgt   Pilot   British   66 Squadron

Robertson, of Lockerly, was in the RAFVR. Mobilised on September 2, he was then posted on loan to 769 (FAA) Squadron at Donibristle, where he flew Gladiators and Swordfishes and practiced carrier landings on HMS 'Furious'.

In October 1939 Robertson was posted to 66 Squadron at Duxford. Over Dunkirk on June 2 1940 he probably destroyed a Ju 88. Immediately afterwards his Spitfire was hit by flak, making it uncontrollable. Robertson baled out and landed on a beach five miles west of Dunkirk. He managed to get on one of the last boats to leave.

Robertson shared in destroying a Do 17 on July 10. He was posted away on July 18 to join a group of pilots at Uxbridge. They were flown to Hullavington, picked up Hurricanes, flew them to Abbotsinch and there embarked in the carrier HMS 'Argus', where they were joined by four more officers. They were told their destination was Malta and they were now 418 Flight.

The 'Argus' sailed on July 23, arrived in Gibraltar and sailed for Malta on July 31. At dawn on August 2 they flew off to Luqa. On the 16th 418 Flight combined with the Malta Fighter Flight, becoming 261 Squadron. Robertson damaged a CR 42 on the 20th, probably destroyed a Mc 200 on September 25, damaged a Mc 200 on October 4, damaged a CR 42 on November 23, destroyed a SM 79 on the 28th, destroyed a SM 79 at night on December 18, destroyed a Ju 87, a CR 42 and probably two others on January 19, destroyed a CR 42 and damaged a SM 79 on February 1, destroyed a Ju 88 on the 3rd and a Ju 88 and a Bf 109 on March 5. Robertson was awarded the DFM (18.3.41). He destroyed two Ju 87s on March 23 but was hit by return fire and set alight. He baled out and landed in a field near Luqa.

Robertson was rested at the end of April 1941 and returned to the UK, via Cairo. He instructed at 60 OTU and 54 OTU. Commissioned in March 1942, he was posted to 219 Squadron at Tangmere. Robertson later served with 153 Squadron at Portreath. In April 1943 he joined 96 Squadron at Honiley.

He was killed on August 31 1943, as a Flying Officer with 96. Robertson collided with a B 17 at night near Norwich. He was 25 and is buried in Cambridge City Cemetery.

PO 30.3.42   FO 1.10.42

ANDREW IAN ROBINSON

39569   FL   Pilot   British   222 Squadron

Joined the RAF on a short service commission in December 1936. After completing his training Robinson joined 19 Squadron at Duxford on October 23 1937.

In early 1940 Robinson was with 222 Squadron at Duxford. Over Dunkirk on June 1 he shared in probably destroying a He 111. He claimed Bf 109s destroyed on August 31 and September 2. On this day Robinson forced-landed back at Hornchurch, wounded in the leg, after a head-on attack on a Bf 110.

Robinson was released from the RAF in 1946, as a Squadron Leader. He died in 1958.

APO 8.3.37   PO 21.12.37   FO 21.6.39   FL 3.9.40
SL 1.12.41

DENIS NORMAN ROBINSON

60515   Sgt   Pilot   British   152 Squadron

Joined the RAFVR in March 1938. Robinson began his flying training at 21 E&RFTS, Stapleford, later continuing at 26 E&RFTS, Oxford and 22 E&RFTS, Cambridge.

Called to full-time service in October 1939 Robinson had completed his training and was posted to CFS, Upavon for an instructor's course. He then went to 14 FTS, Kinloss on November 15, moved to 14 FTS, Cranfield on April 19 1940, to 6 EFTS, Sywell on May 24 and finally to 11 EFTS, Perth on June 11.

Robinson was posted to 152 Squadron at Acklington on June 21 1940. He probably destroyed a Bf 109 on July 25 and destroyed another on August 5. He was shot down by Bf 109s of II/JG 53 off Swanage on the 8th, in Spitfire K 9894. Robinson decided against baling out and crash-landed in a field near Wareham. He was unhurt but the aircraft was a write-off. On August 15 he claimed a Bf 109 destroyed, on the 17th a Ju 87 and on September 4 a Ju 88.

On September 26 1940 Robinson was posted away to CFS, Upavon and from October 7 he was instructing at 6 FTS, Little Rissington. Commissioned in January 1941, he remained there until November 17 1941, when he was sent to instruct in Canada, firstly at 39 SFTS, Swift Current, then briefly at 35 SFTS, North Battleford and finally at 32 OTU, Patricia Bay until June 19 1944, when he was posted away to return to the UK.

Robinson went to 109 OTU, Crosby on August 27 to convert to transport aircraft and on March 1 1945 he was seconded to BOAC

at Whitchurch. He was released from the RAF in 1946, as a Flight Lieutenant. Robinson then joined BOAC, later flying for British Caledonian and British Island Airways before retiring in 1978.

PO 15.1.41   FO 1.11.41   FL 1.11.42

GERALD ROBINSON

43261   PO   Air Gunner   British   264 Squadron

Robinson was with 264 Squadron at Duxford in early July 1940. The squadron went to Hornchurch on August 21 for what was to be its final spell of day-fighting.

On the 24th Robinson was gunner in Defiant L 7013, which was attacked by Bf 109s over Thanet and badly damaged. The pilot, Flight Lieutenant EW Campbell-Colquhoun, made a forced-landing at Manston after Verey cartridges exploded in the cockpit. Both men were unhurt.

Robinson later flew as an air gunner with 78 and 307 Squadrons and after retraining, as a Navigator Radar with 85 and 141 Squadrons. He was made an MBE (1.1.45) and released from the RAF in 1945, as a Flight Lieutenant.

PO 7.4.40   FO 7.4.41   FL 7.7.42

JAMES ROBINSON

47845   Sgt   Pilot   British   111 Squadron

With 111 Squadron in early 1940. Over Dunkirk on May 31 Robinson destroyed a Ju 88 but was wounded in the ankle and made a forced-landing at Manston.

He rejoined the squadron on July 18 and on the 28th shared in destroying a He 59, shot down into the Channel whilst on a search and rescue operation.

Commissioned in January 1942, Robinson was awarded the AFC (8.6.44) and released from the RAF in 1945, as a Flight Lieutenant. He died on July 2 1956.

PO 2.1.42   FO 2.8.42   FL 2.1.44

JAMES CLIFTON EDMESTON ROBINSON

74710   FO   Pilot   British   1 Squadron

Robinson, of Colwyn Bay, joined No 1 Squadron at Wittering in late September 1940. He claimed a Do 17 destroyed on October 29.

He damaged a Bf 109 over Maidstone on April 21 1941 and on May 11 intercepted a He 111 over Redhill, silenced the gunner and claimed the enemy bomber as probably destroyed.

On May 21 1941 Robinson was reported 'Missing'. He was attacked by two Bf 109s over the Channel and never seen again. He was 23 and is remembered on the Runnymede Memorial, Panel 30. Robinson's portrait was drawn by Cuthbert Orde.

PO 8.11.39   FO 3.10.40

MARCUS ROBINSON

90161   SL   Pilot   British   616 Squadron

Born on May 27 1912, Robinson joined 602 Squadron, AuxAF in September 1933. He was appointed a Flight Commander in June 1938 and was called to full-time service on August 24 1939.

Robinson engaged and fired on Ju 88s over the Firth of Forth on October 16 and shared in destroying a He 111 on January 13 1940. He was promoted to Squadron Leader on May 1 and given command of 616 Squadron at Leconfield. The squadron went south to Rochford on the 27th and over Dunkirk the next day

M Robinson (continued)

Robinson's aircraft was severely damaged by a Bf 109 and he made a forced-landing at Manston, writing the aircraft off. He damaged a Bf 109 in the vicinity of Dunkirk on June 1.

In mid-September 1940 Robinson was posted away to No 6 FTS, Netheravon, as an instructor. He was awarded the AFC (30.9.41). In March 1942 he was promoted to Wing Commander and posted as Chief Instructor to 15 (P) AFU, Leconfield. Awarded a Bar to the AFC (1.1.44), Robinson was promoted to Group Captain in January 1945 and appointed CO of the unit. He went to RAF Church Lawford in April as Station Commander and CO 20 and 21 FTSs. Robinson moved to HQ 23 Group in August, as SASO, Group Captain Postings. He was released from the RAF in February 1946.

In September 1946 Robinson re-formed 602 Squadron, RAuxAF and commanded it until September 1 1951. He was created a CB (31.5.56).

PO (AuxAF) 8.5.34   FO (AuxAF) 8.11.35   FL (AuxAF) 5.2.38
FL 24.8.39   SL 1.6.40   WC 1.3.42   SL (RAuxAF) 1.8.46

MICHAEL LISTER ROBINSON

37300   FL   Pilot   British   601, 238 and 609 Sqdns

Born in Chelsea, London in 1917, Robinson was the son of Sir Roy, later Lord, Robinson. He joined the RAF on a short service commission in September 1935. On the 28th he was posted to 3 FTS, Grantham and joined 111 Squadron at Northolt on August 3 1936.

In early 1940 Robinson joined 87 Squadron in France. On May 8 he was involved in a crash, sustaining a hand injury which sent him back to England. Fit again, he was posted to 601 Squadron at Tangmere on August 16, as a Flight Commander. On the 31st

he claimed a Bf 109, on September 4 shared a probable Bf 110 and on the 6th claimed another Bf 109.

Robinson went to 238 Squadron at Chilbolton on September 28 and claimed two Bf 110s destroyed and a Bf 109 probably destroyed on the 30th. He was posted to command 609 Squadron at Middle Wallop on October 4. Robinson claimed two Bf 110s destroyed on the 7th. He was awarded the DFC (26.11.40).

Between May 8 and July 24 1941 he claimed eight Bf 109s destroyed and another probably destroyed. Robinson was awarded the DSO (5.8.41), the C de G (Belg)(22.8.41) and posted away to lead the Biggin Hill Wing. On August 19 Ortmans of 609 went down into the sea during a Blenheim escort operation. Robinson circled him until his fuel ran very low, by which time an ASR launch was well on the way. He just managed to make it back to Manston, where he crash-landed. On August 24 Robinson destroyed a Bf 109 off Dunkirk and on the 27th another over Gravelines.

In September 1941 Robinson was rested and commanded RAF Manston until October, when he was appointed as aide to the Inspector General of the RAF. Back on operations, Robinson was appointed to lead the Tangmere Wing on January 1 1942. He failed to return from a sweep on April 10 whilst leading the Wing at the head of 340 Squadron.

Robinson is remembered on the Runnymede Memorial, Panel 64. His portrait was done by Cuthbert Orde.

APO 16.9.35   PO 16.9.36   FO 16.4.38   FL 16.4.40
SL 1.6.41

MAURICE WILBRAHAM SANDFORD ROBINSON

26189   SL   Pilot   British   73 Squadron

Born on September 20 1910, Robinson entered RAF College, Cranwell in January 1929. On graduation he joined 111 Squadron at Hornchurch on December 20 1930. He was posted to 60 Squadron at Kohat, India on April 4 1932 and after returning to the UK joined the staff at 3 FTS, Grantham on October 22 1934.

Robinson went to 24 (Communications) Squadron at Hendon on April 22 1936 and he rejoined 111 Squadron at Northolt on September 28 1938, as a Flight Commander. Promoted to Squadron Leader, he commanded 29 Squadron at Debden from December 1938 until February 1939.

On August 8 1940 Robinson took command of 73 Squadron at Church Fenton. On September 5 he made a forced-landing at Wallasea Yacht Club after his Hurricane, P 2815, sustained damage in combat over Burnham. Two days later Robinson claimed a Bf 110 destroyed, on the 11th another and on the 14th he was shot down during a combat over the Tonbridge area. He baled out, wounded, and was admitted to the Kent and Sussex Hospital. Robinson was posted away from the squadron on September 26 1940.

In mid-1942 he was SASO at HQ 81 Group and he commanded Biggin Hill from April to June 1945. Robinson was awarded the KW (10.3.44) and made a CBE (1.1.46). He retired from the RAF on March 1 1958, as an Air Commodore. He died in 1977.

PO 20.12.30   FO 20.6.32   FL 1.4.36   SL 1.12.38
WC 1.3.41   GC 1.1.44   GC 1.1.49   AC 1.1.55

PETER BEVERLEY ROBINSON

90462   FO   Pilot   British   601 Squadron

Robinson joined 601 Squadron, AuxAF in 1934 and went on to the Reserve when he left the country in 1938. He was in the USA at the outbreak of war and returned to rejoin 601.

Over Dunkirk on May 27 Robinson claimed a Bf 110 destroyed. On September 6 he claimed a Bf 109 and on the 25th a Bf 110.

Robinson was released from the RAF in 1945, as a Wing Commander.

PO (AuxAF) 5.8.34   FO (AuxAF) 5.2.36
FO (AuxAFRO) 11.7.38   FO 8.12.39   FL 8.12.40
SL 1.3.42

PETER ETHELBERT MERRICK ROBINSON

100584   Sgt   Pilot   British   56 Squadron

Robinson, of Harrow, joined 56 Squadron at North Weald on July 25 1940. He destroyed a Bf 110 on August 18. It crashed and burned out at Pluckley.

Commissioned in June 1941, Robinson was killed on the 17th of the month, still with 56 Squadron. He was 27 and is buried in St Andrew's churchyard, North Weald Bassett, Essex.

PO 5.6.41

PETER TREVOR ROBINSON

742005   Sgt   Pilot   British   257 Squadron

Joined 257 Squadron at Northolt on August 3 1940. Robinson returned to Debden with damage sustained in combat over the Thames Estuary on September 7 in Hurricane P 3709, unhurt.

No further service details traced. Robinson died on October 3 1975.

FREDERICK ASPINALL ROBSHAW

42441   PO   Pilot   British   85 and 229 Squadrons

Joined the RAF on a short service commission in June 1939. Robshaw was posted to 85 Squadron at Castle Camps on September 16 1940 and moved to 229 Squadron at Northolt on the 27th.

Robshaw's Hurricane, P 3227, was damaged in combat with Bf 109s over North Kent on September 30. He crash-landed west of Ash, slightly wounded.

He was released from the RAF in 1946, as a Flight Lieutenant.

APO 5.8.39   PO 24.3.40   FO 24.3.41   FL 24.3.42

NORMAN CHARLES HAROLD ROBSON

70874   FO   Pilot   British   72 Squadron

Joined the RAF on a short service commission in January 1938. Robson was posted to 10 FTS, Tern Hill on April 9 and joined 72 Squadron at Church Fenton on January 17 1939.

Still with the squadron in early July 1940, he claimed a He 111 destroyed on August 15 and shared Do 17s on September 10 and 27.

Robson stayed on in the RAF and was killed in a flying accident on January 18 1954, as a Squadron Leader.

APO 26.3.38   PO 17.1.39   FO 17.8.40   FL 17.8.41
SL 1.7.43   SL 1.8.46

HENRY ADRIAN CHARLES RODEN

740410   Sgt   Pilot   British   19 Squadron

With 19 Squadron at Fowlmere in early July 1940. Roden crashed on landing at Duxford on the 28th after an attack on a Ju 88, unhurt.

He crash-landed on September 15 in Spitfire P 9431, after his glycol tank was damaged in an action with Bf 109s, slightly injured. The aircraft was written off.

Roden hit a tree whilst attempting a forced-landing in bad visibility following an action against Bf 110s off Harwich on November 15 1940, in Spitfire P 7420. He died of his injuries the next day. Roden is buried in Linlithgow Cemetery, West Lothian.

BERNARD JOHN ROFE

40751   FO   Pilot   British   25 Squadron

Rofe, of Douglas, Isle of Man, joined the RAF on a short service commission in March 1938. He was posted to 2 FTS, Brize Norton on May 21 and joined 25 Squadron at Hawkinge on December 17 1938.

During an attack on an enemy aircraft at night on September 4 1940 Rofe's Blenheim was hit by anti-aircraft fire and the tail unit badly damaged. On the 18th he returned to North Weald with his aircraft damaged by return fire from an enemy aircraft intercepted during a night patrol.

Rofe was killed on January 12 1942, as a Flight Lieutenant with 31 (GR) Squadron. He was 21 years old and is buried in Sherwood Cemetery, Charlottetown, Canada.

APO 7.5.38   PO 7.3.39   FO 1.9.40   FL 3.9.41

BRUCE ARTHUR ROGERS

72088   FO   Pilot   British   85 and 242 Squadrons

Rogers was commissioned in the RAFVR in February 1938 and called to full-time service in October 1939. He joined 85 Squadron at Castle Camps on September 15 1940 and moved to 242 Squadron at Coltishall on the 28th.

On a squadron escort for Blenheims detailed to bomb the Chocques chemical works at Bethune on June 17 1941 Rogers was shot down and killed. He was 23 and is buried in Ambleteuse Communal Cemetery, France.

PO (RAFVR) 1.2.38   PO 7.10.39   FO 7.1.40   FL 7.1.41

EVERETT BRYAN ROGERS

81373   PO   Pilot   British   615 and 501 Squadrons

Joined 615 Squadron at Kenley on August 4 1940 and moved to 501 Squadron there on September 13.

Rogers claimed a Do 17 destroyed on the 15th and on the 29th he was shot down by Bf 109s over Deal, baling out, unhurt. His Hurricane, V 7497, crashed and burned out at Chartway Street, East Sutton.

Later in the war Rogers was with Bomber Command. He was awarded the DFC (27.3.45), as an Acting Squadron Leader with 640 Squadron, operating in Halifaxes from Leconfield. The citation mentioned an occasion when a shell burst beneath the tailplane of his aircraft as it approached Sterkrada. The Halifax turned completely

on to its back and fell towards the ground, out of control. Rogers eventually righted it, assured himself that the crew was unharmed and then went on to bomb the target, afterwards safely regaining his base. On another operation flak damaged his controls on the way to Chemnitz and only the trimming tabs could be used to control the aircraft. He continued on and successfully bombed the target.

Rogers was released from the RAF in 1945, as a Squadron Leader. He died in 1960.

PO 6.7.40   FO 6.7.41   FL 6.6.42

GEORGE WADE ROGERS

741720   Sgt   British   234 Squadron

Rogers, of Falmouth, Cornwall, was posted to 234 Squadron at St Eval in mid-September 1940.

He was killed on January 16 1941, aged 24. He is remembered on the Runnymede Memorial, Panel 51.

JAN ALEKSANDER ROGOWSKI

781018   Sgt   Pilot   Polish   303 Squadron

Born on January 3 1920. After completing his training and converting to Hurricanes Rogowski joined 303 Squadron at Northolt on August 19 1940 and claimed a Bf 109 destroyed on September 2. He was awarded the KW (23.12.40).

On February 7 1941 Rogowski was posted to 74 Squadron at Biggin Hill. He destroyed a Bf 109 on April 10. With his tour completed he went to 15 EFTS, Carlisle for an instructor's course. On July 5 Rogowski was posted to 8 FTS, Montrose for a further course, after which he went to No 1 AGS, Pembrey as a staff pilot.

On April 14 1942 he was sent to 58 OTU, Grangemouth and then joined 306 Squadron at Northolt on June 15. Rogowski was posted to 41 Squadron at Llanbedr on December 28 and he joined 315 Squadron at Northolt on April 14 1943.

Rogowski was shot down and killed by a Bf 109 over Bergues on May 28 1943 in Spitfire BR 624, as a Flight Sergeant. He is buried in Pihen-les-Guines Cemetery, Calais, France. Rogowski was awarded two Bars to the KW (20.10.43) and the VM (5th Class)(25.6.45).

RUDOLF BOHUMIL ROHACEK

81910   PO   Pilot   Czechoslovakian   238 and 601 Sqdns

Joined 238 Squadron at St Eval in August 1940. Rohacek was posted to 601 Squadron at Exeter on September 9 but rejoined 238, then at Chilbolton, on October 8.

Rohacek was attacked by Bf 109s over Bournemouth on November 5, in Hurricane P 3618. His radiator was damaged and he made a forced-landing at Blandford, unhurt.

On April 27 1942 Rohacek was killed, as a Flight Lieutenant, aged 21. The unit he was serving with is not known. He is buried in St Hilary of Poictiers' Cemetery, Killay, Swansea.

PO 13.7.40   FO 27.12.40   FL 27.12.41

WILLIAM THOMAS EDWARD ROLLS

116492   Sgt   Pilot   British   72 Squadron

Rolls was born in Lower Edmonton, London on August 6 1914. He won a scholarship to Higher Latymer Secondary School in 1925. He joined the RAFVR in March 1939 and did the long course at 19 E&RFTS, Gatwick, completing it on June 29 1939.

Called up at the outbreak of war, Rolls completed his training at 3 FTS, South Cerney and after passing out on June 14 1940 he joined 72 Squadron at Acklington on the 19th. The squadron went south to Biggin Hill on August 31. Rolls claimed a Bf 110 and a Do 17

WTE Rolls (continued)

destroyed on September 2, two Ju 88s on the 4th, a Do 17 and another probably destroyed on the 8th, a Bf 109 and another probably destroyed on the 14th and a Bf 109 on the 20th.

Rolls was awarded the DFM (8.11.40) and posted to 58 OTU, Grangemouth in January 1941, as an instructor. He moved to 61 OTU, Heston in July. He returned to operations on October 23 1941, joining 122 Squadron at Scorton and was commissioned in January 1942. The squadron went to Hornchurch on April 2 1942. Rolls destroyed a FW 190 on May 5, destroyed another and probably a second on the 17th and probably destroyed a FW 190 and shared another on June 2.

In July 1942 Rolls was posted to Debden, then flew a Spitfire to Abbotsinch and embarked in HMS 'Furious' at Greenock. With others he flew off in early August to Luqa, Malta, where he joined 126 Squadron. Rolls was appointed a Flight Commander. On August 13 he destroyed a Ju 88, on September 19 a Do 24, on October 12 a Ju 88 and two Mc 202s, on November 11 a Reg 2001 and damaged another, on the 13th and 16th Ju 88s and on the 20th a Bf 109.

Soon afterwards Rolls broke a leg and was admitted to hospital. He was flown to Gibraltar in a Hudson and then took off for Portsmouth in a Catalina. Strong headwinds caused fuel to run low, necessitating a forced-landing off the Welsh coast and the flying boat was towed in by a destroyer. Rolls was taken to the Royal Naval Hospital, Swansea. He was awarded the DFC (4.12.42).

In early 1943 he was posted to the Publicity Branch, Air Ministry, to lecture and talk at 'Wings for Victory' functions. Rolls was sent to the Air Armament School at Manby in September 1943 for a six months course, after which he was posted to HQ 12 Group, as a Specialist Armament Officer.

In November 1944 Rolls was attached to the Bombing Analysis Unit and went to France with it in June 1945. He was later attached to the US Air Evaluation Board. He was released from the RAF in January 1946, as a Flight Lieutenant.

Rolls went to work at the Ministry of Works and was later with the Department of Scientific and Industrial Research. In 1960 he became a Senior Information Officer at Air Ministry and took over production of RAF Training Films. He was appointed Director of the Directorate of Training Films Requirements (RAF) in 1968. Rolls retired in 1975 and died in July 1988.

PO 6.1.42   FO 1.10.42   FL 6.1.44

CHARLES L ROMAN

81634   PO   Pilot   Belgian   236 Squadron

Joined 236 Squadron on August 5 1940.

It is known that Roman was with 272 Squadron in the Middle East in September 1941. He destroyed a Bf 109 in 1942 and shared a Ju 52 with two other pilots in July 1943. He was awarded the DSO and DFC and was released from the RAF after the war as a Squadron Leader.

Roman died in 1951.

ANDREW LUNN ROMANIS

751715   Sgt   Wop/AG   British   25 Squadron

Romanis, of Edinburgh, joined 25 Squadron at Debden in October 1940. He was a member of the crew of a Blenheim, which crashed near Ingatestone during a night patrol on November 16 1940. All three men on board were killed.

Romanis was 24. He is buried in Saffron Walden Cemetery, Essex.

ANTHONY HARTWELL ROOK

90071   FL   Pilot   British   504 Squadron

Joined 504 Squadron, AuxAF in early 1937. Rook was called to full-time service on August 24 1939 and was with 504 in France from May 10 to 22 1940, when it reinforced squadrons there.

He claimed a Bf 110 destroyed on September 27 1940. In late July 1941 'A' Flight of 504 went to Leconfield and was expanded to squadron strength and re-numbered 81 Squadron, with Rook as CO. The squadron embarked in HMS 'Argus' on August 12, bound for Russia. It flew its Hurricanes off on September 1 to Vaenga, near Murmansk.

The squadron operated with 134 Squadron, forming 151 Wing. Its operations, including bomber escorts, continued until mid-November, when pilots of 81 began converting Russian pilots on to Hurricanes. They left Russia on November 29, leaving all equipment behind and returned in HMS 'Kenya', landing at Rosyth on December 7 1941.

The squadron then went to Turnhouse to re-equip. Rook was posted away in January 1942. He was awarded the DFC (3.3.42) and the Order of Lenin (31.3.42), one of four given by the Russians.

Rook was awarded the AFC (8.6.44) for services at 57 OTU. He was released from the RAF in 1945, as a Wing Commander. When 504 was reformed as a RAuxAF squadron in May 1946 Rook was given command and led it until 1948. He died in 1976.

PO (AuxAF) 23.6.37   FO (AuxAF) 23.12.38   FO 24.8.39
FL 3.9.40   SL 1.12.41   SL (RAuxAFRO) 1.8.46

MICHAEL ROOK

90077   FO   Pilot   British   504 Squadron

Born in October 1915, Rook was at Uppingham School from 1929 to 1933. He joined 504 Squadron, AuxAF in 1938. Called to full-time service on August 24 1939, Rook was with the squadron in France from May 10 1940 until it was withdrawn twelve days later.

On September 15 1940 Rook shared in the destruction of a Do 17 and on the 27th he claimed a Bf 110 destroyed and probably a second. From March 1941 he commanded 504 Squadron until posted away in July to 134 Squadron, then forming at Leconfield, as a Flight Commander.

The squadron embarked in HMS 'Argus' on August 12, bound for Russia. It flew its Hurricanes off on September 1 to Vaenga, near Murmansk. The squadron operated with 81 Squadron, forming 151 Wing. Rook destroyed a Bf 109 on September 27. The Wing cotinued its operations, including bomber escorts, until mid-November, when pilots of 134 began converting Russian pilots on to Hurricanes. The squadrons left Russia on November 29, leaving all equipment behind and returned in HMS 'Kenya', landing at Rosyth on December 7 1941. The squadron then went to Catterick to re-equip.

Rook took command of 43 Squadron at Kirton-in-Lindsey in September 1942. On October 19 the pilots went to Greenock and sailed in the SS 'Ashland' for Gibraltar, from where at dawn on November 8 they took off for North Africa, landing soon after 10 am at Maison Blanche, the first RAF aircraft to land there.

Awarded the DFC (16.2.43), Rook was posted away on August 9 1943 to a staff job in Egypt. Some sources say he destroyed three enemy aircraft in the Mediterranean area.

He was released from the RAF in 1946 as a Wing Commander. Rook was killed in a flying accident on March 13 1948. At one time he was the tallest pilot in the RAF.

PO (AuxAF) 8.8.38   PO 24.8.39   FO 8.8.40
FL 8.8.41   SL 1.7.43

GEOFFREY LAWRENCE ROSCOE

42900   PO   Pilot   British   79 and 87 Squadrons

Roscoe, of Stoke-on-Trent, was commissioned in the Royal Engineers (Territorial Army). He transferred to the RAF and after completing his flying training he joined 79 Squadron at Pembrey on September 17 1940, moving on October 8 to 87 Squadron at Church Fenton.

Roscoe was killed on February 24 1942, as a Flight Lieutenant with 87 Squadron, aged 25. He was cremated at the Stoke-on-Trent Crematorium, Staffordshire.

PO 7.3.40   FO 7.3.41

JACK ROSE

41472   FO   Pilot   British   3 and 32 Squadrons

Joined the RAF on a short service commission in October 1938. Rose was with 3 Squadron from the outbreak of war and went with it to France, when it was attached to 63 Wing for ten days during the fighting in May 1940. Whilst there he destroyed three enemy aircraft.

On August 20 1940 Rose was posted to 32 Squadron at Biggin Hill. He was shot down over the Channel by a Bf 109 on the 25th, in Hurricane V 6547. He baled out and was rescued from the sea.

Rose was awarded the DFC (9.10.42). He commanded 184 Squadron from its formation at Colerne on December 1 1942 until August 1944 and 113 Squadron in Burma from November 1944 to May 1945. Rose was released from the RAF in 1946, as a Wing Commander. He was later made an MBE and a CMG.

APO 14.12.38   PO 3.9.39   FO 3.9.40   FL 3.9.41
SL 1.7.44

JAMES STANLEY ROSE

566059   Sgt   Pilot   British   23 Squadron

Rose, of Featherstone, Yorkshire, was with 23 Squadron at Collyweston in early July 1940.

He was killed on March 4 1941, aged 25, still with 23 Squadron. He is buried in Guines Communal Cemetery, France.

STUART NIGEL ROSE

81920   PO   Pilot   British   602 Squadron

Born on June 21 1918, Rose was a trainee quantity surveyor when he joined the RAFVR at Southampton in March 1939. He began his flying training at 3 E&RFTS, Hamble and had logged 87 hours before being called up at the outbreak of war.

On November 22 1939 Rose went to No 1 ITW, Cambridge and was posted to 14 FTS, Kinloss on February 3 1940, moving to 14 FTS, Cranfield on April 19. With training completed on June 17 he joined 602 Squadron at Drem the next day.

Rose claimed a Bf 110 destroyed on August 25 and a Bf 109 on October 29. He was posted to 54 Squadron at Hornchurch on September 2 1941. Tour-expired, he went to 57 OTU, Hawarden on November 12, as an instructor. Rose was sent to CFS, Hullavington on November 11 1942 for a course, returning to 57 OTU, then at Eshott, on February 11 1943. He went to CGS, Sutton Bridge on June 2 for a gunnery instructor's course and returned to 57 OTU on July 1.

Rose was posted to 15 APC, Peterhead on January 10 1944, moving later to 14 APC, Ayr. He went to the Middle East on July 1, to BGS, El Ballah. Rose returned to the UK in late May 1945 for a gunnery instructor's course at CGS, Catfoss. He went back to El Ballah in July but returned again to the UK in December and was released from the RAF in February 1946, as a Squadron Leader. Rose qualified as a Chartered Quantity Surveyor in June 1948.

PO 18.6.40   FO 18.6.41   FL 18.6.42

ARTHUR THOMAS ROSE-PRICE

39762   FO   Pilot   British   501 Squadron

Born in Concepcion, Chile on April 28 1919, Rose-Price was at Tonbridge School from February 1934 to February 1936. He joined the RAF on a short service commission on March 15 1937 and did his ab initio course at CFS, Upavon.

On June 5 1937 Rose-Price was posted to 11 FTS, Wittering and joined 38 Squadron at Marham on January 8 1938. He was appointed a Flight Commander in early January 1940. Rose-Price became an instructor at 10 FTS, Tern Hill in mid-April.

He joined 501 Squadron at Kenley on September 2 1940. After arriving in the morning he flew one patrol and on the second one, in the afternoon, he failed to return from a combat over Dungeness, in Hurricane L 1578.

Rose-Price is remembered on the Runnymede Memorial, Panel 6. He was the brother of Dennis Price, the well-known actor.

APO 18.5.37   PO 15.3.38   FO 15.10.39

FREDERICK ERNEST ROSIER

37425   FL   Pilot   British   229 Squadron

Born on October 13 1915, Rosier was educated at Grove Park School, Wrexham. He joined the RAF on a short service commission in August 1935, was posted to 11 FTS, Wittering on November 2 and joined 43 Squadron at Tangmere on May 11 1936. Rosier later became 'B' Flight Commander.

He was posted away in 1939 and when 229 Squadron was formed at Digby on October 6 he joined it, as a Flight Commander. On May 16 1940 he led a 229 Squadron detachment to France. Two days later he was shot down and baled out, badly burned, near Vitry. Rosier was sent back to England on the 23rd, via Dieppe. He later rejoined the squadron and on October 19 1940 he took command after the CO was shot down.

He was posted away to the Middle East in October 1941 to lead a Fighter Wing. He was awarded the DSO (13.2.42). The citation mentioned one occasion when Rosier saw a pilot forced to land in enemy territory. In an attempt to rescue he landed to pick the man up but was unable to take off again because of the closeness of the enemy. Both pilots eventually got away and after some narrow escapes regained their base after three days.

Rosier was made an OBE (2.6.43) and a Commander, Order of Orange Nassau (1947). He held a series of appointments and commands in the post-war RAF. He was made a CBE (1.1.55), a CB (31.12.60), a KCB (11.6.61) and a GCB (3.6.72). Rosier was Air ADC to the Queen in 1972/73 and retired from the RAF on September 3 1973, as an Air Chief Marshal.

APO 21.10.35   PO 26.8.36   FO 26.4.38   FL 26.4.40
SL 1.6.41   WC 1.6.42   WC 1.7.47   GC 1.1.53
AC 1.1.59   AVM 1.7.61   AM 1.7.66   ACM 1.3.70

ALEXANDER RICHARD ROSS

84922   PO   Pilot   British   610 Squadron

Ross, of Surbiton, joined 610 Squadron at Acklington on September 22 1940.

He was shot down by return fire from a Ju 88 engaged over Portsmouth on April 15 1941. Ross crashed into the sea in Spitfire P 7684 and was drowned. He was 21 and is buried in Surbiton Cemetery, Surrey.

PO 31.8.40

JACK KENNETH ROSS

79163   PO   Pilot   British   17 Squadron

Ross joined 17 Squadron at Kenley in May 1940. He flew in France when the squadron was using Le Mans and Dinard as forward bases in June and probably destroyed a Bf 109 on the 14th.

On October 2 1940 Ross shared in destroying a Do 17 but had to make a forced-landing when he ran out of fuel. On October 6 he shared in destroying another Do 17 and on the 13th he was shot down by anti-aircraft fire during a squadron patrol over Chatham, baled out, wounded, and was admitted to Gravesend Hospital. His Hurricane, P 3536, crashed at Rochester. Ross claimed a Do 17 destroyed on October 27 and a Ju 87 destroyed and probably a second on November 11.

When 134 Squadron was formed at Leconfield on July 31 1941 from 17 Squadron personnel Ross was promoted and went to the new unit as a Flight Commander. He served in Russia with the squadron and was awarded the DFC (25.11.41). After a short stay at Catterick following its return to the UK in December 1941 the squadron was posted to Eglinton, in Northern Ireland. On January 6 1942 Ross had to ditch in the Irish Sea because of engine failure. Extensive searches failed to find him.

He is remembered on the Runnymede Memorial, Panel 66.

PO 12.5.40   FO 12.5.41

JOHN HEDLEY ROTHWELL

33576   PO   Pilot   British   601, 32 and 605 Squadrons

Rothwell, of Brighton, entered RAF College, Cranwell in April 1939 as a flight cadet. The normal course was shortened because of the outbreak of war and he passed out in March 1940.

On August 28 Rothwell joined 601 Squadron at Debden, moved to 32 Squadron at Acklington on September 24 and then to 605 Squadron at Croydon on October 12.

He was killed on February 22 1941, with 605, aged 20. Rothwell is buried in Poynings Cemetery, Sussex.

PO 7.3.40

JAMES HENRY ROUND

740667   Sgt   Pilot   British   248 Squadron

Round, of Netherton Dudley, Warwickshire, was with 248 Squadron in early July 1940.

On August 3 he made a forced-landing in a cornfield at Tranent, cause unknown, unhurt. Round was captain of a Blenheim which failed to return from a reconnaissance of the south Norwegian coast on August 19 1940. He and his crew, Sergeants WH Want and MP Digby-Worsley were reported 'Missing'.

Round was 27. He is remembered on the Runnymede Memorial, Panel 19.

JOHN ROURKE

56988   Sgt   Air Gunner   British   248 Squadron

Served with 248 Squadron in the Battle of Britain.

Commissioned from Warrant Officer in January 1945, Rourke was released from the RAF in 1946, as a Flying Officer. He died in 1966.

PO 26.1.45   FO 26.7.45

GEOFFREY WALTER ROUSE

132337   Sgt   Pilot   British   236 Squadron

Joined 236 Squadron on September 12 1940.

Commissioned from Warrant Officer in August 1942, Rouse was awarded the DFC (5.12.44), as a Flight Lieutenant with 235 Squadron. He was released from the RAF in 1946, as a Flight Lieutenant.

PO 12.8.42   FO 12.2.43   FL 12.8.44

JOHN HAMPTON ROWDEN

83249   PO   Pilot   British

Joined 616 Squadron at Kenley on Se[...]
64 Squadron at Biggin Hill on Octob[...]

Rowden was killed on April 9 1941[...] a richer Cemetery, France.

PO 21.7.40

PETER ARCHIBALD ROWEL[...]

115449   Sgt   Pilot   British

With 249 Squadron at Leconfield i[...]
Hurricane, V 6635, was damaged by a[...]
September 3 Rowell crashed on landing[...] income you concussed.

Commissioned in January 1942[...]
(1.1.47). Rowell retired from the RA[...]n't hesitate.
Lieutenant.

PO 6.1.42   FO 1.10.42   FL 6.1[...]

RICHARD MICHAEL BERNARD ROWL[...]

90142   FL   Pilot   British   145 Squadron

Rowley joined the AuxAF in 1937. He was called to full-time service on August 25 1939 and was with 145 Squadron at Tangmere in early July 1940.

One source states that Rowley was killed in late 1941 but no trace has been found of him as a casualty.

PO (AuxAF) 11.2.38   FO 25.8.39   FL 3.9.40

MICHAEL ELLIOTT APPELBEE ROYCE

90076   FO   Pilot   British   504 Squadron

Born on September 23 1919, Royce was at Rugby School from 1933 to 1936. He joined 504 Squadron, AuxAF in 1938 and reported for full-time service in December 1939.

On September 15 1940 Royce shared in the destruction of a Do 17 and destroyed a Bf 110 on September 27.

In June 1941 Royce was OC 'B' Flight at 55 OTU, He was released from the RAF in 1946, as a Squadron Leader. Brother of WB Royce.

PO (AuxAF) 28.8.38   FO 28.12.39   FL 28.12.40   SL 1.7.43

WILLIAM BARRINGTON ROYCE

90062   FL   Pilot   British   504 Squadron

Royce learned to fly with the RAFO and was commissioned in June 1932 serving in 504 Squadron, a Special Reserve Unit.

He was called to full-time service on August 24 1939 and was with the squadron when it operated in France from May 10 to 22 1940. Royce assumed temporary command of the squadron there when the CO was lost. He destroyed four enemy aircraft during the twelve day period and was awarded the DFC (31.5.40).

In December 1940 Royce was posted away to command the newly-reformed 260 Squadron at Skitten. He led it until April 1941. In November 1941 Royce was on HMS 'Ark Royal', directing Hurricanes taking off for Malta.

He was released from the RAF in 1945, as a Wing Commander. Royce died in 1979.

PO (RAFO) 4.6.32   FO (AuxAF) 4.12.33   FO 24.8.39
FL 24.8.40   SL 1.12.40   WC 1.3.42

MIECZYSLAW ROZWADOWSKI

76720   PO   Pilot   Polish   151 Squadron

Joined 151 Squadron at Martlesham Heath on August 8 1940. Rozwadowski failed to return from a combat with Bf 109s over the Channel off Dover on August 15. He was reported 'Missing', aged 25 years.

He is remembered on the Polish Air Force Memorial at Northolt. Rozwadowski was awarded the KW (10.9.41) and Bar (31.10.47).

PO 24.1.40

WLADYSLAW ROZYCKI

76762   PO   Pilot   Polish   238 Squadron

Born on August 11 1907. Rozycki joined 238 Squadron at St Eval on August 19 1940. He claimed He 111s destroyed on September 11 and 25 and a Bf 110 on the 28th.

Rozycki was posted to 306 Squadron at Tern Hill on November 20 1940. He was awarded the KW (23.12.40) and Bar (1.2.41). On May 3 1941 he went to 23 Squadron at Ford. He was awarded the VM (5th Class)(10.9.41). On April 23 1942 Rozycki joined 307 Squadron at Exeter. He was awarded a second Bar to the KW (20.8.42) and the DFC (15.11.42).

Tour-expired, he was posted to HQ 10 Group on November 11 1942 as Polish Liaison Officer, remaining there until May 28 1943, when he went to 54 OTU as an instructor. Rozycki rejoined 23 Squadron, then at Sigonella, Italy, on October 4. The squadron returned to the UK in June 1944 and began bomber-support operations.

Rozycki was posted to 5 Ferry Unit on August 22 1945. He was released from the PAF in September 1946 and repatriated to Poland. He was awarded a third Bar to the KW (31.10.47).

PO 27.1.40   FO 1.3.41   FL 1.9.42

WILFRED SHEPHERD RUDDOCK

753197   Sgt   Aircrew   British   23 Squadron

Joined 23 Squadron at Collyweston on July 18 1940.

Ruddock left the RAF before 1945, as a Warrant Officer. He died on November 6 1980.

CLIFFORD PERCIVAL RUDLAND

65998   Sgt   Pilot   British   263 Squadron

Rudland was born in 1915, joined the RAFVR in March 1939 and began his elementary flying training at 3 E&RFTS, Hamble. Called up at the outbreak of war, he was posted to 15 EFTS, Redhill in November, moved on to 5 FTS, Sealand in April 1940 and joined 263 Squadron at Drem in June.

Commissioned in May 1941, Rudland destroyed a Bf 109 on August 6, as it was taking off. He was appointed a Flight Commander later in 1941 and awarded the DFC (19.9.41). Rudland was posted to 19 Squadron at Perranporth in September 1942, as a Flight Commander. He was detached to Vickers-Supermarine, Southampton in December and flew on test-pilot duties until October 1943.

Rudland joined 131 Squadron at Church Stanton in November, as a Flight Commander. He was promoted in August 1944 and given command of 64 Squadron at Harrowbeer. He was posted away in March 1945 to be Wing Commander Flying at Andrews Field, Essex. Rudland was awarded a Bar to the DFC (15.5.45) and the DFC (US)(15.5.45).

He served as a Planning Officer at HQ 11 Group from May to August 1945 and was then sent on a course at the Command and General Staff School at Fort Leavenworth, Kansas. Rudland returned to the UK in November 1945 and was released from the RAF later in the month, as a Wing Commander. He served in the RAFVR from 1946 to 1951.

PO 8.5.41   FO 9.12.41   FL 9.12.42   SL 4.6.45
FL (RAFVR) 28.4.48

FREDERICK WILLIAM RUSHMER

90192   FL   Pilot   British   603 Squadron

Born in Sisland, Norfolk on April 12 1910, Rushmer joined 603 Squadron, AuxAF in 1934. He was called to full-time service with the squadron on August 23 1939 and was appointed leader of Red Section.

On July 30 1940 Rushmer shared in destroying a He 111 south-east of Montrose and his aircraft was hit by return fire. On August 29 he made a forced-landing at Bossingham in Spitfire P 9459, after a combat over Deal, slightly wounded.

Rushmer failed to return from a combat with Do 17s and Bf 109s over Biggin Hill on September 5 1940. His Spitfire, X 4261, could be that which crashed at Buckmans Green Farm, Smarden. The pilot from this aircraft was buried as 'unknown' in All Saints' churchyard, Staplehurst on September 11. An investigation of the crash site in 1970 failed to establish the pilots' identity. Rushmer was reported 'Missing' and is remembered on the Runnymede Memorial, Panel 4.   CEREMONY OF DEDICATION Sunday 6.9.98

PO (AuxAF) 19.10.34   FO (AuxAF) 19.4.36   FO 23.8.39
FL 12.3.40

BLAIR DALZEL RUSSEL

C 1319   FO   Pilot   Canadian   1 (RCAF) Squadron

Born in Toronto on December 9 1917, Russel was educated at Selwyn House, Montreal and Trinity College School, Port Hope, Ontario. He worked for the Dominion Steel and Coal Co in Toronto. He learned to fly in 1938, joined up at the outbreak of war and was commissioned into 115 (Auxiliary) Squadron in mid-September 1939.

Russel continued flying training in November at Trenton, moving later to Camp Borden, on Harvards. 115 Squadron was augmented by some regular pilots from No 1 peacetime squadron and became No 1 (RCAF) Squadron. It sailed for the UK on June 11 1940, arriving on the 20th. It trained at Middle Wallop for six weeks and its Hurricanes were modified to UK standards. It then moved to Croydon and flew each day to Northolt for instruction with 111 Squadron, under the supervision of the AFDU. No 1 (RCAF) Squadron was declared operational on August 17.

Russel shared in destroying a Do 17 on the 26th, claimed a Do 17 probably destroyed on September 4, probably destroyed a He 111 on the 15th, shared Do 17s on the 21st and 25th and destroyed a Bf 110, a Bf 109 and shared another on the 27th. He was awarded the DFC (25.10.40), one of the first two to be awarded to the RCAF in the war. Russel was repatriated to Canada on February 15 1941 and joined 118 (RCAF) Squadron at Rockliffe on March 26. He was promoted and took command of 14 (RCAF) Squadron, also at Rockliffe, on January 1 1942.

He was posted away on November 27 and reported to HQ RCAF, London on December 21. Russel went to 402 Squadron at Kenley as a supernumerary, moving later to 416 Squadron. On April 16 1943 he took command of 411 Squadron at Redhill. Russel was promoted on July 9 1943 to lead 126 (Canadian) Wing at Redhill. He completed his tour on October 15, was posted to HQ 83 Group as Wing Commander Tactics and awarded a Bar to the DFC (16.11.43).

Russel dropped a rank to take command of 442 Squadron at

BD Russel (continued)

Westhampnett on April 28 1944. He was sent to land on the first Allied airfield in Normandy on June 10, the first Spitfire pilot to land in France after the invasion. Russel shared in destroying a FW 190 on the 22nd. He was re-promoted on July 8 and again took command of 126 Wing. He was awarded the DSO (3.10.44). Russel led the Wing until his third tour ended on January 26 1945. He flew home to Canada on March 12 and left the RCAF on July 3.

PO 15.9.39   FO 1.8.40   FL 1.8.41   SL 1.1.43

————— RUSSELL

No unknown   PO   Pilot   British   141 Squadron

Joined 141 Squadron at Drem on October 2 1940.
    No other service details traced.

ANTHONY GERALD RUSSELL

120491   Sgt   Pilot   British   43 Squadron

Joined 43 Squadron at Usworth on September 28 1940.
    Commissioned in April 1942, Russell was released from the RAF in 1946, as a Flight Lieutenant. He later served in the RAFVR.

*PO 13.4.42   FO 13.10.42   FL 13.4.44
FO (RAFVR) 15.6.48*

GODFREY FREDERICK RUSSELL

Lieutenant (FAA)   Pilot   British   804 Squadron

Russell, of Ewshott, was with 804 Squadron at Hatston in early July 1940, flying Sea Gladiators on dockyard defence.
    In December 1940 he was posted to 802 Squadron, forming at Donibristle for HMS 'Audacity'. On a collection flight from Abbotsinch to Donibristle on December 13 Russell crashed into Ben Lomond and was killed.
    He was 23 and is buried in Douglas Bank Cemetery, Dunfermline, Scotland.

Midshipman 1.5.35   Sub-Lt 16.1.38   Lt 1.5.39

GRAHAM HERBERT RUSSELL

42025   PO   Pilot   British   236 Squadron

Joined the RAF on a short service commission in February 1939. Russell was with 236 Squadron in early July 1940.
    On November 6 his Blenheim was hit by anti-aircraft fire following the destruction of a Do 24 twenty miles north-west of Brest. Russell returned to St Eval with one member of his crew wounded in the eye and arm. He was awarded the DFC (26.11.40). On December 12 Russell's Blenheim, L 3602, was damaged by a He 115 floatplane. He crash-landed on return to St Eval.
    Russell left the RAF on August 31 1942, as a Flight Lieutenant. He died in 1981.

APO 29.4.39   PO 16.12.39   FO 16.12.40   FL 16.12.41

HUMPHREY a'BECKETT RUSSELL

37692   FL   Pilot   British   32 Squadron

Born on September 1 1913, Russell was at Marlborough College from 1927 to 1931 and joined the RAF on a short service commission in January 1936. He was posted to 9 FTS, Thornaby on April 4 and joined 32 Squadron at Biggin Hill on October 11 1936.
    Russell went to SHQ RAF Biggin Hill on July 13 1938. He rejoined 32 Squadron at Biggin Hill on August 17 1940. He claimed a Bf 110 destroyed on the 18th. During the combat over Biggin Hill a cannon shell exploded in his cockpit. Russell baled out, seriously wounded in

the leg and was admitted to Edenbridge Hospital. His Hurricane, V 7363, crashed at Skeynes Park Farm, Edenbridge.
    In April 1941 Russell took command of the squadron. He was posted to 118 Squadron at Ibsley in October 1941, to command, and led it until January 1942. Russell commanded 128 Squadron at Hastings, Sierra Leone from August 1942 to March 8 1943.
    Back in the UK, he took command of 164 Squadron at Fairlop. Russell was shot down in May 1944 and became a PoW. He was awarded the DFC (19.5.44).
    Russell retired from the RAF on February 17 1958, as a Wing Commander. He died on February 15 1983.

*APO 23.3.36   PO 27.1.37   FO 27.10.38   FL 10.5.40
SL 1.12.41   WC 5.10.45   WC 1.10.46*

LESLIE PLIMMER RUSSELL

NZ 40209   Sgt   Air Gunner   New Zealander   264 Sqdn

Russell was born in Marton on August 18 1916 and educated at the High School there. He first applied to join the RNZAF in April 1936 but after repeated further applications was unsuccessful until late 1939, when he was accepted as a trainee air gunner.
    On January 15 1940 Russell went to the Ground Training School at Weraroa. He moved to the Air Observers' School at Ohakea on February 9 for a Lewis gunnery course. Russell sailed for the UK on March 23 in the SS 'Akaroa'. He joined 264 Squadron at Duxford on June 4 and continued his training.
    Russell was awarded his air gunner's badge on July 26 and promoted to Sergeant the next day. On August 21 the squadron went down to Hornchurch for what proved to be its final spell of day-fighting. On the 24th Russell and his pilot, Pilot Officer MH Young, damaged a Ju 88 and on a later patrol destroyed a He 111. After suffering severe losses the squadron withdrew to Kirton-in-Lindsey to resume night patrols. On an intruder patrol to Lille on the night of May 8 1941 Russell, again flying with Young, shot down a Bf 110.
    In early November 1941 Russell was posted to a Conversion Unit at Waterbeach. After crewing-up and converting to Halifaxes he joined 35 Squadron at Linton-on-Ouse in mid-December. Russell was rear gunner of a Halifax, which took off to raid Mannheim on the evening of May 19 1942, his ninth operation. The aircraft failed to return and the crew were reported 'Missing'. The International Red Cross later reported that Russell had been killed. He is buried in the Central Cemetery, Mannheim.

CHARLES ALAN RUST

905074   Sgt   Pilot   British   85 and 249 Squadrons

Rust was with 85 Squadron at Martlesham Heath in early July 1940 and moved to 249 Squadron at North Weald on September 11.
    No other service details traced.

PAUL RUSTON

37291   FL   Pilot   British   604 Squadron

Commissioned in the RAF Special Reserve in January 1934 and joined 503 (Special Reserve) Squadron at Waddington. Flying a Handley Page Hinaidi in late 1934 Ruston reached a height of 18500 feet.
    In September 1935 Ruston entered the RAF. On October 7 he was posted to 215 Squadron at Worthy Down, equipped with Vickers Virginias. He joined the staff of 604 Squadron, AuxAF on August 13 1936 and moved to the instructing staff at 9 FTS, Hullavington on August 16 1937.
    Ruston was posted to 604 Squadron at Northolt on July 12 1940 and served with the squadron throughout the Battle of Britain.

He was released from the RAF in 1945, as a Wing Commander. He died on January 11 1954.

PO (Special Reserve) 30.1.34   PO 16.9.35   FO 13.4.37
FL 13.4.39   SL 1.12.40   WC 1.7.43

ROBERT DURHAM RUTTER

42574   PO   Pilot   British   73 Squadron

Rutter joined the RAF on a short service commission on June 26 1939 and did his ab initio course at 9 E&RFTS, Ansty. He was posted to 14 FTS, Kinloss on September 1 and on completion of the course went to 6 OTU, Sutton Bridge on February 28 1940.

After converting to Hurricanes Rutter was posted to 73 Squadron in France on May 11 and flew there until the squadron was withdrawn to Church Fenton on June 18. He received a Mention in Despatches.

On September 5 1940 Rutter was shot down in a surprise attack by Bf 109s whilst intercepting a Ju 88. He baled out and was admitted to Billericay Hospital with a bullet in the ankle. His Hurricane, P 3110, crashed at Seaman's Lane, West Hanningfield.

Rutter was posted to 17 Squadron at Croydon on March 3 1941, staying until June 26. He was with the Defence Flight at Takoradi from July 22 1941 until November 4 1942, when he left for the UK, going to 56 OTU, Tealing on January 13 1943 as Chief Flying Instructor.

After three weeks at the Fighter Leaders' School at Aston Down Rutter joined 195 Squadron at Fairlop on December 2 1943, as a Flight Commander. When the squadron was disbanded on February 18 1944 he went to 183 Squadron at Tangmere. Rutter was given command of 263 Squadron at Harrowbeer on April 9. He led the squadron to France on August 6 1944 and was awarded the DFC (1.9.44) and the C de G (Fr).

On January 3 1945 Rutter was posted to the Directing Staff at the School of Air Support at Old Sarum. He went into RAF Hospital, Wraughton on February 5 1946 and remained there until late December. Rutter, who had been granted a Permanent Commission in 1946, was invalided out in 1947, as a Squadron Leader.

APO 19.8.39   PO 28.2.40   FO 28.2.41   FL 28.2.42

DERRICK LANG RYALLS

44601   PO   Aircrew   British   29 Squadron, FIU

Ryalls, of West Kirby, was with 29 Squadron at Digby in early July 1940, as a Sergeant. He was commissioned in August and posted to the Fighter Interception Unit.

Ryalls was killed on December 26 1944, as an Acting Squadron Leader with 219 Squadron, operating from Amiens-Glisy in Mosquitos. He was 32 and is buried in Brussels Town Cemetery.

PO 26.8.40   FO 26.8.41   FL 26.8.42

EDGAR NORMAN RYDER

39193   FL   Pilot   British   41 Squadron

Born in Risalpur, India on November 28 1914, Ryder returned to England as a boy of ten. He joined the Royal Fusiliers at Hounslow in 1931 and served until 1934, then becoming a mathematics master at Tredennick School, Worcester.

Ryder joined the RAF on a short service commission in August 1936. He was posted to 9 FTS, Thornaby on October 31 and joined 41 Squadron at Catterick on June 30 1937.

Still with the squadron, Ryder took off alone on April 1 1940, in bad visibility and low cloud to investigate an enemy aircraft. He sighted a He 111 and shot it down into the sea. His own aircraft was losing power and he came down on the sea, his aircraft sinking immediately. At considerable depth he extricated himself, struggled to the surface and was picked up by a trawler. He was awarded the DFC (18.4.40).

On September 5 and 6 1940 Ryder claimed Bf 109s destroyed and on the 15th he shared a Do 17. Ryder was shot down by Bf 109s during a squadron patrol on September 27 and baled out, unhurt. His Spitfire, R 6755, crashed and burned out at East Malling. He destroyed Bf 109s on October 30 and November 27.

In January 1941 Ryder was given command of 56 Squadron at North Weald. He was appointed to lead the Kenley Wing in June and was awarded a Bar to the DFC (29.7.41). Ryder was shot down by flak in October, leading an escort for Hurricanes on a low-level shipping strike, and captured. He escaped from his prison camp and reached Poland but was recaptured in 1943. Ryder received a Mention in Despatches (28.12.45) for distinguished service whilst a PoW.

He was made a member of the Order of Orange-Nassau and a CBE (1.1.58). Ryder retired from the RAF on October 28 1960, as a Group Captain. His portrait was drawn by Cuthbert Orde in January 1941.

APO 24.8.36   PO 24.8.37   FO 24.2.39   FL 3.9.40
SL 22.9.41   WC 1.7.47   GC 1.7.56

FRANTISEK RYPL

81900   PO   Pilot   Czechoslovakian   310 Squadron

Joined 310 Squadron at its formation at Duxford on July 10 1940.

Rypl crash-landed at Oxted on September 9 in Hurricane P 3142, following a combat with Bf 109s.

He was repatriated to Czechoslovakia after the war.

PO 12.7.40   FO 1.12.40
FL 1.3.41

HERBERT SAMUEL SADLER

44825   PO   Pilot   British   611 and 92 Squadrons

A pre-war airman pilot, Sadler was with 611 Squadron at Digby in early 1940 and destroyed a Bf 110 over Dunkirk on June 2.

He was posted to 92 Squadron at Pembrey on September 5, claimed a Bf 110 destroyed on the 11th and shared a Do 17 on the 15th. Sadler rejoined 611 Squadron, then at Tern Hill, on September 26.

Commissioned in late October, he was killed on February 5 1941, with 611, aged 24. His aircraft was badly damaged on a sortie over the French coast. Losing height rapidly, with his engine on fire, Sadler seemed unable to get out of the cockpit. He finally slumped over the controls and the Spitfire went into a steep dive into the sea.

Sadler is remembered on the Runnymede Memorial, Panel 34.

PO 30.10.40

NORMAN ALFRED SADLER

82732   PO   Observer   British   235 Squadron

Joined 235 Squadron on September 6 1940.

Sadler was killed on December 16 1940 when the Blenheim he was in crashed into the sea during a minesweeper escort operation. All three men on board were lost.

Sadler is remembered on the Runnymede Memorial, Panel 18.

PO 28.7.40

EDWARD FITZROY St AUBYN

90055   FL   Pilot   British   616 Squadron

St Aubyn was educated at Eton and was said to be an ex-Guards officer when he joined 503 Squadron, AuxAF in 1937. In late 1938 it was decided to disband 503 and from it form a new squadron, 616, at Doncaster. Squadron Leader the Earl of Lincoln began formation on November 1 1938 and St Aubyn transferred from 503, being one of the first two officers in 616.

Called to full-time service on August 24 1939, he completed his training and rejoined 616, then at Leconfield, in early August 1940. On the 26th his Spitfire, R 7018, was damaged by a Bf 109 over Dungeness and St Aubyn crash-landed on the perimeter of Eastchurch aerodrome, where it burned out. He was admitted to Minster County Hospital, with burns.

St Aubyn was killed on May 27 1943, as a Squadron Leader with 170 Squadron, operating with Mustangs as an army co-operation squadron. He is remembered on the Runnymede Memorial, Panel 119.

PO (AuxAF) 1.7.37   FO (AuxAF) 1.1.39   FO 24.8.39
FL 3.9.40   SL 1.3.42

RONALD GODFREY St JAMES-SMITH

551203   Sgt   Air Gunner   British   600 Squadron

Joined 600 Squadron at Redhill in September 1940.

St James-Smith was killed on April 13 1941, as a Flight Sergeant with 18 Squadron, operating in Blenheims from Great Massingham, Norfolk. He is remembered on the Runnymede Memorial, Panel 37.

PETER CAPE BEAUCHAMP St JOHN

40320   FO   Pilot   British   74 Squadron

Joined the RAF on a short service commission in September 1937. St John was posted to 3 FTS, South Cerney on December 11 and joined 87 Squadron at Debden on July 9 1938.

St John was with 74 Squadron in May 1940 and over Dunkirk on the 27th he shared in destroying a Do 17.

On July 28 St John claimed a Bf 109 destroyed, on September 11 a He 111, and Bf 109s on October 15 and 17. He was shot down and killed in combat with Bf 109s on October 22. His Spitfire, P 7431, crashed at South Nutfield, Surrey.

St John was 23. He is buried in St Mary's churchyard, Amersham, Buckinghamshire.

APO 28.11.37   PO 27.9.38   FO 27.6.40

HAROLD NIGEL EGERTON SALMON

70586   FO   Pilot   British   1 and 229 Squadrons

Salmon learned to fly with the RAFO. He was called to full-time service on September 10 1939 and was with No 1 Squadron at Tangmere in early July 1940.

He claimed a Bf 109 probably destroyed on July 25 and a Bf 110 destroyed on August 16. Salmon was posted to 229 Squadron at Northolt in October.

Salmon transferred to the ATA in late 1942, with the rank of Captain. On December 6 1943 he took off from Dorval, Montreal in Mitchell FW 159, bound for Reykjavik, Iceland. When he failed to arrive a search was made but no trace of aircraft or crew was ever found.

Salmon was 36 years old. He is remembered on the Ottawa Memorial, Panel 3, Column 2.

PO (RAFO) 8.6.33   FO (RAFO) 8.12.34   FO 10.9.39
FL 1.12.41

WILLIAM NOEL COMPTON SALMOND

40947   PO   Pilot   British   64 Squadron

Salmond was born on December 19 1916. He served in the Royal Corps of Signals in the early thirties and was awarded the Palestine Medal. On May 16 1938 Salmond transferred to the RAF on a short service commission. He did his ab initio course at 3 E&RFTS, Hamble, moving to 3 FTS, South Cerney on July 23.

With training completed Salmond was posted to CFS, Upavon on March 6 1939 for an instructor's course, after which he went to 2 FTS, Brize Norton. On December 12 he was posted to 5 BGS, Jurby, as a staff pilot. From May 26 1940 Salmond was attached to various MUs. He went to 7 OTU, Hawarden on October 6 and joined 64 Squadron at Coltishall on the 26th. During a formation practice on the 30th Salmond's section was vectored on to a Bf 110, which was intercepted and damaged, changing the flight into an authorised operational sortie and qualifying him for the Battle of Britain clasp.

On January 29 1941 Salmond was posted to No 1 FTS, Netheravon, as an instructor. He returned to operations on May 16, joining 611 Squadron at Hornchurch. He went to 11 Group Flight there on July 21 1941. Salmond later commanded a Defiant unit. He was released from the RAF in 1946 and died on September 26 1985.

APO 9.7.38   PO 15.3.39   FO 3.9.40   FL 3.12.41

ERNEST SALWAY

749368   Sgt   Air Gunner   British   141 Squadron

Salway, of North Wingfield, was with 141 Squadron at Turnhouse in early July 1940.

He was killed on June 21 1942, as a Flight Sergeant with 76 Squadron, operating in Halifaxes from Middleton St George. Salway was 22. He is buried in Ulrum Cemetery, Netherlands.

WLODZIMIERZ MICHAL CZECH SAMOLINSKI

76709   PO   Pilot   Polish   253 Squadron

Born on October 14 1916. Samolinski was posted from 6 OTU, Sutton Bridge to 253 Squadron at Turnhouse on July 16 1940.

He claimed Bf 110s destroyed on August 30 and September 4. Samolinski failed to return from combat over the Channel on September 26 1940. He was believed to have crashed into the sea and was reported 'Missing'.

Samolinski is remembered on the Polish Air Force Memorial at Northolt. He was awarded the VM (5th Class) (1.2.41).

JOHN SAMPLE

90278   SL   Pilot   British   504 Squadron

Sample, of Morpeth, was an estate agent in civilian life. He joined 607 Squadron, AuxAF in 1934. He was appointed a Flight Commander in early 1939 and called to full-time service on August 24.

Leading a section of three Gladiators on October 16 Sample sighted and attacked a Do 18 flying boat twenty-five miles out to sea. Severely damaged, the enemy aircraft crashed into the sea fifty miles out and the crew were captured by a trawler.

On November 13 the squadron flew south from Acklington to Croydon and two days later flew on to Merville in France. During the fighting in May 1940 Sample destroyed two enemy aircraft and was shot down himself, baling out safely. The squadron was withdrawn from France on May 21.

Sample was given command of 504 Squadron at Wick in late May 1940. He was awarded the DFC (4.6.40). On September 15 he claimed a Do 17 destroyed and a He 111 shared.

In March 1941 Sample was posted away from 504. He was given the job of forming 137 Squadron at Charmy Down in September 1941 and commanded the squadron until October 28, when he was killed in a flying accident.

Sample was 28. He is buried in St Andrew's churchyard, Bothal, Ashington, Northumberland.

PO (AuxAF) 27.4.34   FO (AuxAF) 27.10.35
FL (AuxAF) 10.1.39   FL 24.8.39   SL 1.9.40

ARTHUR SAMPSON

522757   Sgt   Air Gunner   British   23 Squadron

Joined the RAF on August 13 1935 and trained as a Fitter I. Before the war Sampson served with 204 Squadron at Mount Batten, Plymouth and 217 Squadron at Wittering. He had done part-time duty as an air gunner and at the outbreak of war he went on permanent duty as such.

Sampson was with 23 Squadron at Ford during the Battle of Britain. He later served with 40 Squadron at Wyton and at No 1 Air Armament School at Manby.

He received a Mention in Despatches (11.6.42) and was awarded the BEM, whilst stationed at 21 OTU, Moreton-in-the-Marsh, for his efforts in maintaining maximum serviceability during the 1000 bomber raids.

Sampson was released from the RAF in October 1946, as a Flight Sergeant.

JAMES GILBERT SANDERS

37510   FL   Pilot   British   615 Squadron

Joined the RAF on a short service commission in January 1936. Sanders was posted to 10 FTS, Tern Hill on February 1 and joined 111 Squadron at Northolt on August 10.

In October 1939 Sanders joined 615 Squadron at Croydon, as a Flight Commander. On November 15 he led his flight when 615's Gladiators flew to Merville in company with those of 607. Sanders was flying a weather test on December 29 1939 when he sighted a He 111. Having chased it up to 23000 feet and used up all his ammunition he lost it in cloud. So ended 615 Squadron's first encounter with the Luftwaffe.

On May 17 1940 Sanders destroyed a Ju 88 near Lille, one of three enemy aircraft he claimed whilst in France. The squadron withdrew to Kenley on the 21st. Sanders was awarded the DFC (4.6.40), destroyed a Bf 110 on June 22, was decorated by the King at Kenley on the 27th and shot down a Bf 109 on the 30th.

Sanders destroyed a Ju 88 at night near Hastings in the early hours of August 25. In early 1941 he was with 255 Squadron at Kirton-in-Lindsey, as a Flight Commander. He probably destroyed a He 111 on March 13.

Sanders was released from the RAF in 1947, as a Wing Commander.

APO 20.1.36   PO 25.11.36   FO 25.8.38   FL 25.8.40
SL 1.9.41   WC 1.7.44

PHILLIP JAMES SANDERS

36057   SL   Pilot   British   92 Squadron

Born on May 1 1911, Sanders was educated at Cheltenham College and Balliol College, Oxford. He joined the RAF with a direct-entry Permanent Commission in March 1936, carried out his flying training at 5 FTS, Sealand and joined No 1 Squadron at Tangmere on October 11 1936.

Sanders took command of 92 Squadron at Northolt on May 27 1940. Over Dunkirk on June 2 he destroyed a He 111. On September 11 he claimed a He 111 and a Bf 109 destroyed and on the 15th a Do 17. On the 20th Sanders landed back at Biggin Hill after destroying a Bf 109 near Dover. His aircraft was damaged in the action and his clothes were soaked in petrol. He lit a cigarette and set himself on fire, suffering serious burns and did not return to the squadron. He was awarded the DFC (8.11.40).

From June to December 1941 Sanders commanded 264 Squadron at Colerne.

He retired from the RAF on April 3 1962, as a Group Captain, retaining the rank of Air Commodore. He died in 1989.

PO 3.3.36   FO 3.6.36   FL 3.6.38   SL 1.6.40
WC 1.12.41   WC 1.10.46   GC 1.1.52

ALFRED KEMP SANDIFER

156361   Sgt   Air Gunner   British   604 Squadron

Joined 604 Squadron at Gravesend in July 1940. With the advent of the Beaufighter Sandifer retrained as a Radio Observer. On December 12 1940, flying with Flight Lieutenant H Speke, he assisted in damaging a He 111.

In May 1941 Sandifer was posted away to 109 Squadron, which was formed from the Wireless Intelligence Development Unit at Boscombe Down, concerned with the development of radio counter-measures and new radar aids.

Commissioned in July 1943, Sandifer was released from the RAF in 1945, as a Flight Lieutenant.

PO 27.7.43   FO 27.1.44   FL 27.7.45

ROBERT EDWARD BUTLER SARGENT

122024   Sgt   Pilot   British   219 Squadron

Joined 219 Squadron at Catterick on July 20 1940.

Commissioned in May 1942, Sargent was awarded the AFC (3.4.45). He was released from the RAF in 1945, as a Flight Lieutenant. He served with the RAFVR after the war.

PO 1.5.42   FO 1.11.42   FL 1.5.44   FO (RAFVR) 11.2.48

ALFRED RICHARD SARRE

197053   Sgt   Pilot   British   603 Squadron

Joined 603 Squadron at Montrose in August 1940. Sarre claimed a Bf 109 destroyed on the 30th and had his aircraft's tail shot off in combat. He baled out, unhurt. His Spitfire, R 7021, crashed at Addington Park, near West Malling.

On September 4 he made a forced-landing at Elstead, near Ashford after his engine failed. Sarre was shot down in combat over the Thames on the 7th and baled out, slightly wounded, from Spitfire P 9467.

Commissioned from Warrant Officer in February 1945, Sarre was released from the RAF in 1946, as a Flying Officer. He died in 1980.

PO 25.2.45   FO 25.8.45

WILHELM SASAK

781267   Sgt   Pilot   Polish   32 Squadron

Sasak was born on October 11 1916. He joined 32 Squadron at Acklington in late September 1940.

On November 30 1940 Sasak was returning from a squadron patrol. His engine caught fire and he broke from the formation but did not bale out, possibly overcome by fumes from the engine. His Hurricane, P 3704, crashed at Donnington, south of Chichester.

Sasak is buried in the Roman Catholic Cemetery, Chichester.

WILLIAM ARTHUR JOHN SATCHELL

29048   SL   Pilot   British   302 Squadron

Born on February 2 1908, Satchell joined the RAF in March 1930. He was posted to 5 FTS, Sealand on the 29th and joined 54 Squadron at Hornchurch on March 8 1931.

Satchell went to the School of Naval Co-operation at Lee-on-Solent on December 16 1932. He was posted to 204 (GR) Squadron at Mount Batten, Plymouth on June 5 1937 and went on to the SHQ staff there on October 10 1938.

After taking command of 234 Squadron at Leconfield at its reformation on October 30 1939 Satchell was injured in a motor car accident three days later and posted away. In early 1940 he went to France as Fighter Controller at Merville. During the retreat in May 1940 Satchell left Merville as the Germans were coming in. He walked forty miles to Boulogne, hiding during the day.

Satchell was given command of 302 Squadron at Leconfield at its formation on July 13 1940. It became operational on August 19 and Satchell shot down a Ju 88 on the 20th, the squadron's first victory. He claimed a Bf 109 probably destroyed on September 14 and Do 17s destroyed on the 15th and 18th. Satchell made a forced-landing at Slough on October 15 after his Hurricane, P 3812, was damaged in combat over the Thames Estuary. He claimed a Bf 109 probably destroyed on the 26th.

WAJ Satchell (continued)

In January 1941 Satchell was posted away. Later in the year he was on HMS 'Ark Royal' directing Hurricanes flying off to Malta. He arrived in Ta Kali on December 20 1941 to be Station Commander there. Satchell destroyed a Ju 88 and a Bf 109 during January 1942 and a Bf 109 on February 15. He also shot down a Bf 109 from a ground defence post.

In April 1942 Satchell went to Air HQ Malta. He was awarded the DSO (6.10.42) and took no further part in operations. He retired from the RAF on July 1 1956, as a Group Captain. Satchell died in March 1986.

PO 14.3.30   FO 14.9.31   FL 1.1.36   SL 1.10.38
WC 1.3.41   GC 1.1.44   GC 1.7.47

CECIL HENRY SAUNDERS

42893   PO   Pilot   British   92 Squadron

Born on July 7 1911, Saunders joined the RAF on a short service commission on August 24 1939. He did his ab initio course at the Civil Training School at Derby and then moved on to 14 FTS, Kinloss.

Saunders joined 92 Squadron at Croydon in April 1940. He claimed a He 111 destroyed, probably a second and shared another on July 4. After a combat with enemy aircraft over Biggin Hill on September 9 Saunders crash-landed at Midley, near Rye, in Spitfire L 1077. He was admitted to the RAMC Hospital at Brookland, with shrapnel wounds in the leg. On October 29 Saunders claimed a Bf 109 destroyed and on November 1 he probably destroyed a Ju 87. In this action he was damaged by a Bf 109 and crash-landed three miles east of Eastchurch in Spitfire X 4555, unhurt.

On February 1 1941 Saunders claimed a Bf 109 destroyed. In May 1941 he was posted to 74 Squadron, as a Flight Commander. The squadron went to the Middle East in April 1942 but had no aircraft after its arrival in Palestine. Saunders joined 145 Squadron in the Western Desert in late July 1942, as a Flight Commander. On August 3 he probably destroyed a Bf 109, on September 11 destroyed a Mc 202 and on October 25 claimed another Bf 109. He was posted away from 145 in November 1942.

Awarded the DFC (4.12.42), Saunders was posted to 71 OTU, Port Sudan, which later moved up to Abu Sueir, Egypt. For the invasion of Sicily on July 10 1943 Saunders was on a Fighter Direction ship. He took command of 154 Squadron at Lentini East in August. The squadron moved on to Italy and in February 1944 went to Corsica to cover the American invasion of southern France.

Saunders commanded the squadron until October 1944. He also commanded 145 Squadron in July/August 1945. He retired from the RAF on May 5 1958, as a Wing Commander.

APO 23.10.39   PO 20.4.40   FO 20.4.41   FL 20.4.42
SL 1.7.44   SL 1.8.47   WC 1.1.52

GERALD ALFRED WELLESLEY SAUNDERS

37482   FL   Pilot   British   65 Squadron

Joined the RAF on a short service commission in October 1935. Saunders was posted to 7 FTS, Peterborough on January 4 1936 and joined 65 Squadron at Hornchurch on July 13. He was still with the squadron in 1940 and over Dunkirk on May 26 he damaged a Ju 88 and probably destroyed a Do 17 on the 27th.

Saunders claimed Bf 109s destroyed on July 7 and 9 and shared a Do 17 on August 26. He took command of the squadron on October 30 1940, was awarded the DFC (4.4.41) and posted away in September 1941.

Saunders was released from the RAF in 1945, as a Wing Commander.

APO 23.12.35   PO 28.10.36   FO 12.7.38   FL 28.7.40
SL 1.9.41   WC 1.7.45

THOMAS WOOD SAVAGE

105167   Sgt   Pilot   British   64 Squadron

Savage, of Porthill, Stoke-on-Trent, joined 64 Squadron at Leconfield on October 14 1940.

Commissioned in August 1941, he was killed on July 10 1943, as a Flight Lieutenant with 92 Squadron, aged 23. Savage is remembered on the Malta Memorial, Panel 6, Column 1.

PO 2.8.41   FO 2.8.42

JOSEPH ERNEST SAVILL

740971   Sgt   Pilot   British   151, 242 and 501 Sqdns

With 151 Squadron at Martlesham Heath in early July 1940. Savill claimed a Do 17 destroyed on August 13. He was posted to 242 Squadron at Coltishall on September 21 and moved to 501 Squadron at Kenley on October 12.

Savill was promoted to Warrant Officer on October 1 1941. No other service details traced.

CYRIL JOSEPH SAWARD

137927   Sgt   Pilot   British   615 and 501 Squadrons

Joined the RAFVR in Coventry in June 1939. Saward began his flying training at 9 E&RFTS, Ansty. Called up at the outbreak of war, he went to ITW, Hastings in September, moved to 6 EFTS, Sywell in October and then to 8 FTS, Montrose in February 1940.

Saward joined 615 Squadron at Kenley on July 30 1940 and moved to 501 Squadron there on September 13. Five days later he was shot down by Bf 109s in combat over Tonbridge and baled out, unhurt. His Hurricane, V 6600, crashed near Clapper Lane, Staplehurst.

In November 1940 Saward was posted to 4 Ferry Pilots Pool, Kemble. He went to 2 CFS, Cranwell in May 1941 for an instructor's course, after which he became an instructor on Oxfords at 6 FTS, Little Rissington.

Saward was posted to Canada in January 1942. He instructed at 39 SFTS, Swift Current until September 1942, was commissioned in October and then instructed at 37 SFTS, Calgary until March 1944, when he returned to the UK. Saward joined 577 Squadron at Wrexham in April 1944, flying Hurricanes on army co-operation duties. He did a blind-flying course at CFS, Montrose from November 1944 and then instructed at 20 (P) AFU, Wheaton Aston from February to September 1945.

Saward's final posting was to RAF Perton, as OC Flying. He was released from the RAF in March 1946, as a Flight Lieutenant. He returned to the motor car industry and worked for Daimler, Humber, British Leyland, Standard and Triumph, as a designer. He became Principle Engineer with Jaguar Cars and retired in 1983. Saward died in 1988.

PO 19.10.42   FO 19.4.43   FL 19.10.44

TADEUSZ SAWICZ

P 0596   FO   Pilot   Polish   303 Squadron

Born in Warsaw on February 13 1914, Sawicz joined the PAF in 1934. During the fighting in Poland in September 1939 he destroyed two German aircraft and damaged three more.

Sawicz arrived in Britain on July 17 1940. After converting to Hurricanes at 5 OTU, Aston Down he joined 303 Squadron at Leconfield on October 20. Sawicz was posted to the newly-formed 316 Squadron at Pembrey on February 22 1941 and he shot a He 111 down into the sea on April 10, the squadron's first confirmed victory. He was awarded the KW and Bar (15.7.41) and appointed a Flight Commander on November 14.

Tour-expired, Sawicz was posted to 58 OTU, Grangemouth on June 6 1942 as an instructor. He was awarded a second Bar to the KW (20.8.42). He returned to operations on September 25 1942, taking command of 315 Squadron at Northolt. Sawicz was appointed Squadron Leader Flying at Northolt on April 16 1943 and was awarded the VM (5th Class)(12.5.43). He was posted to HQ 12 Group on July 3 as Polish Liaison Officer and on October 18 he went to 61 OTU, as an instructor.

Sawicz was awarded the DFC (20.10.43). On March 3 1944 he was attached to the US 9th Air Force and later to 61 Squadron, USAF. He was later awarded the DFC (US) and the Air Medal (US). Sawicz led No 1 Polish Wing from October 11 1944 to August 8 1945. He was awarded a third Bar to the KW (15.6.45). After a series of short postings Sawicz was released from the PAF in January 1947, as a Wing Commander, and returned to Poland.

FO 1.3.41   FL 1.12.42   SL 1.9.44

HENRY CECIL SAWYER

33144   SL   Pilot   British   65 Squadron

Sawyer entered RAF College, Cranwell in January 1933 as a flight cadet. After graduation in December 1934 he joined 142 Squadron at Andover. He was posted to the staff of the Electrical and Wireless School at Cranwell on May 30 1936 and moved to the staff of RAF College there on July 16 1938.

Sawyer was posted to 65 Squadron at Hornchurch on July 2 1940 and took command on the 8th. He was killed on August 2 when he crashed on take-off from Hornchurch on a night patrol, in Spitfire R 6799, which burned out. Sawyer was 25. He was cremated at the City of London Crematorium, East Ham.

PO 15.12.34   FO 15.6.36   FL 15.6.38   SL 1.6.40

JAMES EDWARD SAYERS

560204   F/Sgt   Pilot   British   41 Squadron

Born on April 10 1910, Sayers joined the RAF straight from school in January 1926 as an aircraft apprentice. He passed out in January 1929 as a Fitter Airframe/Engines and was posted to 2 (Army Co-operation) Squadron at Manston.

Sayers did an air gunnery course in April 1930 and became an AG/FAE. He later volunteered for pilot training, was selected and on April 4 1934 he was posted to 3 FTS, Grantham. On passing out as a Sergeant-Pilot on February 27 1935 he joined 65 Squadron at Hornchurch but moved to 41 Squadron at Northolt in September. The squadron was posted to Aden in October and returned to Catterick in August 1936.

Sayers was still with 41 Squadron in early July 1940 and served with it until October 3 1940, when he reverted to his basic trade of Fitter Airframe/Engines. Promoted to Warrant Officer on November 1 1941, he became a Fitter 2E on September 3 1942. Sayers was discharged from the RAF on January 5 1953, as a Warrant Officer.

KENNITH SCHADTLER-LAW

42267   PO   Pilot   British   605 Squadron

Born on December 12 1916, Schadtler-Law joined the RAF on a short service commission in April 1939. After completing his training he was posted to 605 Squadron at Tangmere in November 1939.

On March 28 1940 Schadtler-Law was flying in Yellow Section when a He 111 was sighted entering cloud at 6000 feet. The section-leader fired two short bursts, setting the enemy aircraft on fire. The bomber was attacked and finished off by 43 Squadron at 1000 feet and the victory was shared. It was 605's first encounter with the Luftwaffe.

On August 15 Schadtler-Law made a forced-landing near Hartley railway station after a combat near Newcastle, in Hurricane P 2717. He was badly injured and admitted to West Hartlepool Hospital.

Schadtler-Law retired from the RAF on July 1 1968, as a Wing Commander. He later changed his name to Law. He died in 1986.

APO 24.6.39   PO 27.12.39   FO 27.12.40   FL 27.12.41
FL 1.9.45   SL 1.1.52   WC 1.7.59

EDWARD CRANSTON SCHOLLAR

78256   PO   Observer   British   248 Squadron

Joined 248 Squadron in April 1940. Schollar served with the squadron throughout the Battle of Britain.

He was released from the RAF in 1945, as a Squadron Leader.

PO 24.3.40   FO 24.3.41   FL 24.3.42

FRANCIS HERBERT SCHUMER

84970   PO   Pilot   British   600 Squadron

Schumer was at Worcester College, Oxford and was a member of the University Air Squadron.

He joined 600 Squadron at Redhill on September 24 1940. He was killed on July 12 1941, with 600. Schumer was 22. He was

cremated at Golders Green Crematorium, Hendon.

PO 7.9.40

LIONEL HAROLD SCHWIND

37870   FO   Pilot   British   257, 43 and 213 Squadrons

Joined the RAF on a short service commission in March 1936. Schwind was posted to 11FTS, Wittering on June 2 and joined the staff of the Aircraft Depot, Dhibban, Iraq on April 3 1937.

Schwind went to 257 Squadron at Debden on September 1 1940, moved to 43 Squadron at Usworth on the 10th and came south again to 213 Squadron at Exeter on the 20th. He was shot down and killed in combat with enemy fighters over Gatwick on September 27 1940. His Hurricane, N 2401, crashed on to Wildernesse Golf Course, Seal, near Sevenoaks.

Schwind was 27. He is buried in Crowborough Burial Ground, Sussex. In 1980 Bill Terry arranged for the erection of a memorial plaque at the site of the crash.

APO 18.5.36   PO 23.3.37   FO 9.7.39

KIRKPATRICK MacLURE SCLANDERS

37301   PO   Pilot   Canadian   242 Squadron

Born in Saskatoon, Saskatchewan, Sclanders was brought up in St John's, Newfoundland. He learned to fly at 15 but could not get a license until he was 17. He took part in air shows as a Boy Scout, who accidentally started an aircraft engine and then performed aerobatics. Sclanders went to England in 1935 and joined the RAF on a short service commission in September.

He was posted to 3 FTS, Grantham on September 28 and joined 25 Squadron at Hawkinge on August 5 1936. Sclanders resigned his commission in September 1937 because of ill-health and returned to Canada. He became a reporter, underwent surgery and regained his fitness but was unsuccessful when he tried to get into the RCAF.

Sclanders applied to fly in the Russo-Finnish war but it finished and he went to France to try for the French Air Force. He was there when the collapse came and escaped from southern France by boat with Polish refugees. Sclanders reached England and rejoined the RAF.

Posted to 242 Squadron at Coltishall on August 26 1940, Sclanders was shot down and killed in combat with Do 17s and Bf 110s over Thames Haven on September 9. His Hurricane, P 3087, crashed at Marden Park Farm, Caterham. He was 24 and is buried in St Luke's churchyard, Whyteleafe, Surrey.

APO 16.9.35   PO 16.9.36   PO 25.7.40

ALEC MAXTONE WRIGHT SCOTT

76023   PO   Pilot   British   3, 607 and 605 Squadrons

Scott, of Glasgow, was at Brasenose College, Oxford and learned to fly with the University Air Squadron. Called to full-time service in November 1939 he completed his training and joined 3 Squadron at Wick in late June 1940.

On September 27 Scott was posted to 607 Squadron at Tangmere and moved to 605 Squadron at Croydon on October 15. He was killed on January 2 1941, as a Pilot Officer with 605. Scott was 29 and is buried in St Mary's churchyard, Black Bourton, Oxfordshire.

APO 30.11.39   PO 22.6.40

ALFRED ENOCH SCOTT

117308   Sgt   Pilot   British   73 Squadron, 422 Flight

Scott, of Nottingham, was with 73 Squadron at Church Fenton in early July 1940 and moved to 422 Flight at Shoreham on October 17.

Commissioned in February 1942, Scott was killed on August 19 1942, as a Pilot Officer with 245 Squadron. He was 25 and is remembered on the Runnymede Memorial, Panel 71.

PO 26.2.42

DONALD STUART SCOTT

40569   FO   Pilot   British   73 Squadron

Joined the RAF on a short service commission on November 29 1937 and did his elementary flying training at 10 E&RFTS, Yatesbury.

DS Scott (continued)

In February 1938 Scott was posted to 7 FTS, Peterborough and moved to 6 FTS, Netheravon on May 21. He was non-effective, sick at Uxbridge from August 1938 to January 1939. Scott finished his training at 6 FTS, Little Rissington and was posted to 2 AOS, Acklington in May 1939, as a staff pilot. He went to 10 BGS, Warmwell on September 5, again as a staff pilot.

On January 1 1940 Scott was posted to 11 Group Pool at St Athan, moving in February to 6 OTU, Sutton Bridge. He converted to Hurricanes and joined 73 Squadron at Rouvres in France in late February 1940. Scott was with 73 throughout the fighting in May and June and after many squadron moves he flew back to Church Fenton on June 18.

He claimed a Ju 88 destroyed on August 15 and a Bf 109 on September 15. He was awarded the DFC (24.9.40), being then credited with five enemy aircraft destroyed.

73 Squadron moved to Castle Camps in September and left there on November 11 1940 for overseas. It embarked on HMS 'Furious' on the 16th, with its aircraft, and flew off to Takoradi on the 29th. The squadron then flew in easy stages to Heliopolis, via Lagos, Accra, Kano, Maidugari, Khartoum, Wadi Halfa and Abu Sueir. During December the pilots were attached to 274 Squadron in the Western Desert. 73 began operating on its own account in early January 1941.

Scott was posted away in June to instruct at 71 OTU, Ismailia, which later moved to Gordon's Tree, Sudan. He returned to operations in the Western Desert on March 16 1942, taking command of 94 Squadron at LG 115. He was seconded to the Turkish Air Force at Izmir on November 29 as a liaison officer and instructor.

In June 1943 Scott returned to the UK. On October 14 he was posted to 2 FIS, Montrose for an instructor's course. He was at 7 (P) AFU, Peterborough from January to April 1944, at 9 (P) AFU, Findo Gask from April to October and at 5 (P) AFU, Tern Hill from October 1944 to June 1945.

Scott was released from the RAF in late 1945, as a Squadron Leader.

APO 19.2.38   PO 15.4.39   FO 3.9.40   FL 3.9.41
SL 1.1.44

DOUGLAS REGINALD SCOTT

90246   SL   Pilot   British   605 Squadron

Joined 605 Squadron, AuxAF in 1935. Called to full-time service on August 24 1939, Scott was with 605 as a Flight Commander until August 29 1940.

He was then posted away to form and command 306 Squadron at Church Fenton, remaining with it until December 1940.

Scott was appointed Wing Leader at Kirton-in-Lindsey in October 1941. He was killed leading 616 Squadron on a Wing patrol of the Dunkirk area on November 8 1941. He was shot down by FW 190s, the first time they had ever been seen by 616 pilots.

Scott was 33. He is buried in Dunkirk Town Cemetery. He was awarded the AFC (15.1.43), with effect from October 9 1941.

PO (AuxAF) 1.8.35   FO (AuxAF) 25.4.37
FL (AuxAF) 25.4.39   FL 24.8.39   SL 1.9.40

ERNEST SCOTT

525152   Sgt   Pilot   British   222 Squadron

Scott, of Mansfield, Nottinghamshire, was a pre-war regular airman. He was with 222 Squadron at Hornchurch in early July 1940.

On September 3 Scott claimed a Do 17 and Bf 109 destroyed, on the 5th a Bf 110 and a probable Bf 109, on the 7th a Bf 110 and on the 11th a He 111. From this engagement he returned to Hornchurch with his hood shattered after being attacked by a Bf 109. On September 27 Scott claimed a Bf 109 destroyed but he himself failed to return from an operational sortie in the

afternoon and was reported 'Missing'. His Spitfire, P 9364, may be that which crashed at Greenway Court, Hollingbourne, possibly shot down by Major Mölders of JG 51.

Scott is remembered on the Runnymede Memorial, Panel 19.

GEORGE WARDROP SCOTT

62257   Sgt   Pilot   British   64 and 19 Squadrons

Initially with 64 Squadron, Scott was posted to 19 Squadron at Fowlmere on September 25 1940.

Commissioned in March 1941, Scott was awarded the AFC (8.6.44). He commanded 124 Squadron from September 1944 to June 1945 and was released from the RAF in 1945, as a Squadron Leader.

Scott joined the RAuxAF in 1948 and was made an MBE (1.6.53). He later settled in Canada and died there in 1986.

PO 5.3.41   FO 5.3.42   FL 5.3.43   FO (RAuxAF) 22.3.48
FL (RAuxAF) 1.4.50

JOHN ALAN SCOTT

745385   Sgt   Pilot   British   611 and 74 Squadrons

Joined 611 Squadron at Tern Hill on September 27 1940 and moved to 74 Squadron at Biggin Hill on October 23.

Scott was shot down and killed in combat with Bf 109s over Maidstone on October 27 1940. His Spitfire, P 7526, crashed and exploded at Dundas Farm, Elsted.

He was 22 years old and is buried in the Alperton Burial Ground, Wembley, Middlesex.

RONALD HAMILTON SCOTT

90221   FL   Pilot   British   604 Squadron

Scott joined 604 Squadron, AuxAF at Hendon in early 1937. He was called to full-time service on August 24 1939 and served with the squadron throughout the Battle of Britain.

He was released from the RAF in 1945, as a Wing Commander. Scott rejoined the RAuxAF in 1948.

PO (AuxAF) 10.4.37   FO (AuxAF) 16.10.38   FO 24.8.39
FL 3.9.40   SL 1.12.41   WC 1.1.45
WC (RAuxAF) 16.12.48

WILLIAM JACK SCOTT

46285   Sgt   Air Gunner   New Zealander   264 Squadron

Born in Auckland on May 19 1918, Scott was a seaman with the Union Steamship Co when he volunteered for aircrew duties at the outbreak of war.

Scott reported to the Ground Training School at Weraroa on January 18 1940 and on February 9 moved to the Air Observers' School, Ohakea for a Lewis gunnery course and air experience. On March 23 he sailed for the UK in the SS 'Akaroa'.

On June 3 Scott was posted to 264 Squadron at Duxford for further training. He was sent for a course to a gunnery school in North Wales and after gaining his air gunner's brevet he rejoined 264 Squadron and was promoted to Sergeant on September 5.

Scott was posted away to the No 1 School of Army Co-operation at Old Sarum on October 19 1940 for a course, after which he joined 268 Squadron, flying in Lysanders from Bury St Edmunds. In November Scott's aircraft crashed from 300 feet and he sustained a fracture at the base of the spine. After five weeks in hospital he was posted to 256 Squadron at Pembrey on January 8 1941, a night-fighter unit.

Flying with Flight Lieutenant EC Deansely on April 10 Scott shot down a He 111 over Smethwick. On May 3 they destroyed a Do 17 and a Ju 88 and on the 7th shot down a He 111 over Manchester. Scott was awarded the DFM (29.5.41), which he received from the King in October. Commissioned in November 1941, Scott was posted away on May 11 1942 to 17 AGS, Stormy Down as an instructor. In March 1943 he went to HQ 19 Group, Plymouth for staff duties.

Scott moved to HQ RNZAF, London in May and was repatriated to New Zealand in November. He became a gunnery instructor at Ohakea and moved to Rongotai in mid-June 1944. He was transferred to the Reserve on July 31 1944.

PO 24.11.41   FO 1.10.42

WILLIAM JOHN MOIR SCOTT

70611   FO   Pilot   British   41 Squadron

Scott, of Dundee, was born on June 14 1915. He was commissioned in the RAFVR in March 1937 and called to full-time service on September 12 1939.

In early July 1940 Scott was with 41 Squadron at Catterick. He destroyed a Bf 109 on September 7, shooting it down into the Channel off Folkestone. The next day Scott was shot down and killed during a squadron patrol off Dover, possibly the victim of a surprise attack by Bf 109s. His Spitfire, R 6756, crashed in flames.

Scott was 25. He is buried in Dundee Western Cemetery, Angus.

PO (RAFVR) 16.3.37   FO 12.9.39

FRANCIS DAVID STEPHEN SCOTT-MALDEN

74690   FO   Pilot   British   611 and 603 Squadrons

Born on December 26 1919, Scott-Malden was educated at Winchester College and King's College, Cambridge, where he won the Sir William Browne Medal for Greek Verse in 1939.

Scott-Malden joined the University Air Squadron in November 1938 and was called to full-time service in October 1939. On January 1 1940 he was posted to FTS, Cranwell and after completing his flying training he went to No 1 School of Army Co-operation at Old Sarum for a course in late May 1940. A week later Scott-Malden was sent to 7 OTU, Hawarden and then joined 611 Squadron at Digby in June.

On October 3 1940 Scott-Malden was posted to 603 Squadron at Hornchurch and probably destroyed a Bf 109 on the 12th. He became a Flight Commander in May 1941. On May 28 he probably destroyed a Bf 109, on August 17, 19 and 26 he destroyed Bf 109s and on September 18 probably another. Scott-Malden was awarded the DFC (19.8.41) and in late September he was promoted and given command of 54 Squadron at Hornchurch. On November 4 he destroyed another Bf 109.

In late November 1941 Scott-Malden was posted to HQ 14 Group, Inverness on staff duties. He was appointed to lead the North Weald Wing in March 1942. Scott-Malden was awarded a Bar to the DFC (5.6.42). On June 19 and 29 he shared in destroying FW 190s. He was awarded the DSO (11.9.42), the Norwegian War Cross (6.10.42), posted away for a rest and then sent on a speaking tour of American universities.

Scott-Malden commanded RAF Hornchurch from October 28 1943 to February 6 1944, when he was posted to a mobile GCU in 2nd TAF, preparing for the invasion of Europe. After D Day the unit moved to Normandy. In August 1944 Scott-Malden was promoted to Group Captain and took command of 126 Wing. He was posted to Air Ministry in April 1945 to work on redeployment of Air Forces from Europe to the Far East. He was made a Commander, Order of Orange Nassau in 1945.

Scott-Malden went on to a distinguished post-war career in the RAF. He retired on September 25 1966, as an Air Vice-Marshal. His portrait was done by Eric Kennington in 1941.

PO 10.10.39   FO 3.10.40   FL 3.10.41   SL 12.6.42
SL 1.8.46   WC 1.7.53   GC 1.7.58   AC 1.7.62
AVM 6.4.64

GEORGE EDWARD THOMAS SCRASE

90675   FO   Pilot   British   600 Squadron

Joined 600 Squadron, AuxAF in late 1938. Scrase was called to full-time service in October 1939 and after completing his flying training he rejoined 600 at Manston in April 1940.

Scrase served with the squadron throughout the Battle of Britain. He was killed on September 28 1941, as an Acting Squadron Leader, Flight Commander with 600. Whilst testing the stalling speed of a Beaufighter MK V he went into a spin and crashed near Acton Turville. His Radio Observer, Sergeant Ladymore, baled out to safety.

Scrase was cremated at Golders Green Crematorium, Hendon.

APO (AuxAF) 24.2.39   PO 7.10.39   FO 7.4.40   FL 7.4.41

ERIC WILLIAM SEABOURNE

105162   Sgt   Pilot   British   238 Squadron

Seabourne was born on August 26 1919 and joined 601 Squadron, AuxAF in June 1935 as an air gunner. In January 1938 he applied to join the RAFVR for pilot training and was accepted.

In August 1938 he went to 15 E&RFTS, Redhill, training on DH 60s, Magisters, Harts and Audaxes. Seabourne had been awarded his flying badge at Redhill and after being called to full-time service at the outbreak of war he was posted to 9 FTS, Hullavington in December 1939 to do the course again.

Seabourne was posted direct from FTS to 151 Squadron at Martlesham Heath in May 1940. He had no experience in Hurricanes and did not fly with the squadron before being posted away to 238 Squadron at Tangmere in June. Seabourne had three hours on Masters and then went solo on the Hurricane. After seven hours he was declared operational, without ever having fired the guns.

On July 13 Seabourne shared in destroying a Bf 110 and damaged two more in his first encounter with the Luftwaffe. On August 8 he got a confirmed Bf 109 and on the 13th two more. In this engagement Seabourne was shot down himself. His engine seized up after a cannon shell hit the radiator. He was then attacked by three Bf 109s and set on fire. He prepared to bale out but his hood jammed, then the aircraft turned on its back and Seabourne fell out, taking the hood with him. After a delayed drop of 16000 feet he opened his parachute, blew up his Mae West and went into the sea about seven miles south of the Isle of Wight. He was picked up by a destroyer, HMS 'Bulldog' and taken to the Royal Naval Hospital at Haslar. After a week Seabourne was moved to Park Prewitt Hospital at Basingstoke, where he remained for seven months undergoing plastic surgery by Harold Gillies.

In May 1941 Seabourne was posted to 2 Delivery Flight at Colerne. He was commissioned in August and in October joined 276 (ASR) Squadron, as a Flight Commander. He was awarded the DFC (23.6.42). In December 1942 Seabourne was given command of 275 (ASR) Squadron at RAF Valley and led it until February 1945, when it was disbanded. From then to June 1945 he was at HQ 10 Group as Ops 1.

Seabourne retired from the RAF on December 2 1960, as a Squadron Leader.

PO 12.8.41   FO 12.8.42   FL 12.8.43   SL 1.8.47

LIONEL ARGENT SEARS

42895   PO   Pilot   British   145 Squadron

Sears, of Cambridge, was with 145 Squadron at Tangmere in June 1940. On July 1 he shared a Do 17.

On August 8 he failed to return from combat with enemy aircraft over the Channel south of the Isle of Wight, in Hurricane P 2955. He was possibly shot down by Unteroffizier Sippel of 1/JG 27.

Sears was 19 years old. He is remembered on the Runnymede Memorial, Panel 10.

PO 21.5.40

DENNIS SECRETAN

41746   FO   Pilot   British   54 and 72 Squadrons

Joined the RAF on a short service commission in January 1939. Secretan was posted to 54 Squadron at Catterick on September 3 1940 and moved to 72 Squadron at Biggin Hill on the 27th.

Secretan damaged a Bf 110 on October 27. He received a Mention in Despatches (1.1.41) and probably destroyed a Bf 109 on September 17 1941. He was given command of 242 Squadron at Digby in September 1942 and took the squadron to North Africa in November.

On January 1 1943 Secretan damaged a FW 190 and on the 2nd destroyed a Ju 87. He was then attacked by two Bf 109s just as his ammunition was exhausted. His Spitfire was damaged and Secretan made a forced-landing seven miles north of Morris. The Bf 109s dived on the Spitfire but waited until he got out before machine-gunning it.

Secretan was awarded the DFC (26.2.43) and left 242 in March 1943. After returning to the UK he served with Transport Command. He was released from the RAF in 1946, as a Wing Commander.

APO 4.3.39   PO 23.9.39   FO 23.9.40   FL 23.9.41
SL 28.9.43

KAREL SEDA

121182   Sgt   Pilot   Czechoslovakian   310 Squadron

Joined 310 Squadron at Duxford in August 1940.

Seda was later commissioned and was released from the RAF as a Flight Lieutenant. He was repatriated to Czechoslovakia on August 17 1945.

WILFRID JOHN SEDDON

74711   FO   Pilot   British   601 Squadron

Seddon, of Kingston-upon-Thames, Surrey, joined 601 Squadron at Exeter on October 1 1940.

He was killed on March 31 1941, still with 601. Whilst ferrying a new Hurricane from Carlisle to Duxford he crashed near Keswick in a snowstorm.

Seddon was 23. He is buried in Painswick Cemetery, Gloucestershire.

PO 3.10.39   FO 3.10.40

EUGENE GEORGE ACHILLES SEGHERS

82162   PO   Pilot   Belgian   46 and 32 Squadrons

Seghers was a pilot in the Belgian Air Force. In May 1940 he went to France. On June 21 the French signed an Armistice with the Germans and Belgians in the country were told to stay where they were.

At the time Seghers was at Montpellier. With five other Belgian pilots he reached Port Vendres, from where with the help of a British destroyer and the support of the Belgian embassy in London they caught a passing convoy and embarked on the SS 'Apapa' on the 24th. After arriving in Liverpool on July 7 Seghers was commissioned in the RAF on the 19th.

He was posted to 7 OTU, Hawarden on the 30th and after converting to Hurricanes he joined 46 Squadron at Digby on August 10 but moved to 32 Squadron at Biggin Hill a few days later. Seghers was shot down by Bf 109s on August 24 and baled out into the sea, unhurt. His Hurricane, V 6567, crashed at Tedders Leas, near Eltham.

In early April 1941 Seghers was posted to 609 Squadron at Biggin Hill. He destroyed a Bf 109 on July 11 and was awarded the C de G (Belg)(21.7.41). From March to June 1943 Seghers commanded 165 Squadron at Peterhead.

He was killed on July 26 1944, as a Flight Lieutenant attached to 91 Squadron at Deanland. He was attacking a V1 over Uckfield and struck it, causing it to explode. After the war his remains were exhumed and repatriated to Belgium. At some time Seghers was awarded the DFC.

PO 19.7.40   FO 19.7.41   FL 19.7.42

RAYMOND FREDERICK SELLERS

111224   Sgt   Pilot   British   111 and 46 Squadrons

Born in London on October 9 1919, Sellers joined the RAFVR in August 1939. He was called up at the outbreak of war, went to 3 ITW, Hastings on September 18, to 6 EFTS, Sywell on November 26 and then to 8 FTS, Montrose on April 9 1940.

Sellers completed his training on July 25 and was posted to 6 OTU, Sutton Bridge. After converting to Hurricanes he joined 111 Squadron at Croydon on August 17. Following a combat with enemy aircraft over Essex on the 26th Sellers crashed near Brightwell Church, Martlesham Heath in Hurricane R 4096. He was slightly injured and admitted to hospital with shock.

On September 15 1940 Sellers joined 46 Squadron at Stapleford and claimed a share in the destruction of a Bf 110 on the 27th. He was posted away to 2 CFS, Cranwell on January 13 1941 for an instructor's course, after which he went to 5 EFTS, Meir on March 23.

Sellers was instructing for the rest of the war. He was posted to Church Lawford and served with three different units there; with 2 CFS from September 12 1941 to June 28 1942, with No 1 FIS from July 5 to October 26 1942 and with 18 (P) AFU from October 27 to December 6 1942. Sellers then went to 3 FIS, serving with it from December 7 1942 until July 15 1944. Initially at Castle Camps, the unit moved to Lulsgate Bottom on October 1 1943. He was commissioned in October 1941 and awarded the AFC (8.6.44).

The final posting for Sellers was to 7 FIS, Upavon. He was there from July 15 1944 to December 9 1945. He was released from the RAF on the 10th, as a Flight Lieutenant. Sellers served in the RAFVR at Fair Oaks from 1946 to 1951.

PO 29.10.41   FO 1.10.42   FL 29.10.43
FO (RAFVR) 17.1.48

JOHN BARRY SELWAY

90219   FO   Pilot   British   604 Squadron

Selway learned to fly with the Cambridge University Air Squadron and joined 604 Squadron, AuxAF at Hendon on May 5 1936. In early 1939 he was working in the Department of Civil Aviation. He was called to full-time service on August 24 1939 and served with 604 throughout the Battle of Britain.

In late October 1941 Selway destroyed a Do 17 at night off the French coast and damaged another off Plymouth four nights later. When he left 604 in the latter half of 1942 Selway was the last of the squadron's pre-war Auxiliary pilots.

In early November 1943 he was posted to 85 Squadron at West Malling, as a Flight Commander. On the night of 6/7th, on his first operational patrol with the squadron, Selway shot down a FW 190. Shortly afterwards he chased a Ju 88. His Mosquito was hit by return fire and Selway was wounded. He managed to get back to base and underwent an emergency operation to remove the nose of a bullet from his liver. He was awarded the DFC (31.12.43).

Selway did not return to operations. He was released from the RAF in 1946, as a Wing Commander.

PO (AuxAF) 5.5.36   PO 24.8.39   FO 1.2.40   FL 1.2.41

BENJAMIN SENIOR

1002640   Sgt   Aircrew   British   600 Squadron

No service details traced.

JOHN NORMAN SENIOR

748662   Sgt   Pilot   British   23 Squadron

Senior, of Maidenhead, Berkshire, joined 23 Squadron at Wittering in late August 1940.

He was killed on March 21 1941, probably still with 23. Senior was 20 years old. He is buried in Maidenhead Cemetery.

ANTONI SEREDYN

780958   Sgt   Pilot   Polish   32 Squadron

Seredyn was born on April 10 1920. He arrived in England on June 27 1940 and was posted to 32 Squadron at Acklington on October 12.

After the Battle of Britain Seredyn was at Turnhouse with the 13 Group Flight. On July 2 1941 he was posted to 285 Squadron at Woodvale, on anti-aircraft co-operation duties. Seredyn was promoted to Warrant Officer on September 1 1943 and joined 286 Squadron on the 14th, again on anti-aircraft co-operation duties.

On May 9 1944 Seredyn was posted to 61 OTU. He moved to 3 TEU on August 29 and was posted to 315 Squadron at Brenzett on September 24 to fly Mustangs. Seredyn was awarded the KW (17.8.45) and left the squadron on November 29 1945.

ARTHUR SERVICE

749347   Sgt   Wop/AG   British   29 Squadron

Joined 29 Squadron at Digby in late September 1940.

Service was killed on October 15 1941, as a Sergeant with 75 Squadron, operating in Wellingtons from Feltwell. He is buried in Rheinburg War Cemetery, Germany.

DONALD ALEC SEWELL

47397   Sgt   Pilot   British   17 Squadron

Sewell, of Hall Green, Birmingham is believed to have been with 73 Squadron in France in 1940. At the time of Dunkirk he was with 17 Squadron at Kenley and went with it to France in June.

On August 25 1940 Sewell claimed a Bf 109 destroyed and on November 8 he probably destroyed two Ju 87s.

Commissioned in November 1941, Sewell was killed on March 19 1944, as a Squadron Leader with 166 Squadron, operating in Lancasters from Kirmington, Lincolnshire. He was 28 and is remembered on the Runnymede Memorial, Panel 201.

PO 25.11.41   FO 1.10.42   FL 25.11.43

MARTIN MICHAEL SHANAHAN

741263   Sgt   Pilot   British   1 Squadron

Shanahan, of Seven Kings, Essex, joined No 1 Squadron at Tangmere on August 5 1940.

He was reported 'Missing' on the 15th after a combat with enemy fighters off Harwich, in Hurricane P 3043.

Shanahan was 25 and is remembered on the Runnymede Memorial, Panel 19.

MICHAEL MORAY SHAND

391368   PO   Pilot   New Zealander   54 Squadron

Born in Wellington on February 20 1915, Shand was at Nelson College from 1929 to 1932. In early 1939 he applied for a short service commission in the RNZAF and was provisionally accepted in July.

Shand reported to the Ground Training School at Weraroa on November 19 1939, moving a month later to No 1 EFTS, Taieri. In mid-February 1940 he was posted to No 1 FTS, Wigram, was awarded his flying badge on April 26 and after completing the course in late May Shand sailed for the UK in the RMS 'Rangitiki' on June 7.

He was posted to 7 OTU, Hawarden on August 4 and after converting to Spitfires joined 54 Squadron at Hornchurch on the 22nd. Shand flew as Alan Deere's No 2 on his first operational sortie. On August 25, on his second sortie, he was shot down by Bf 109s and made a forced-landing near Manston, badly wounded. After several months in hospital Shand was posted to Exeter for Operations Room duties.

He returned to operations on October 21 1941, when he joined 485 Squadron at Kenley. In May 1942 he was appointed a Flight Commander and later awarded the DFC (16.9.42), having completed sixty sorties over northern France. On November 28 Shand was leading six Spitfires on a low-level sweep across the Dutch coast, seeking targets of opportunity. They successfully attacked a tanker-barge on a canal and as they returned Shand and Sergeant Tucker went down to shoot up a train. They were attacked by two FW 190s and Shand was shot down and taken prisoner.

He was held in Stalag Luft III, was released in early May 1945 and returned to New Zealand on September 23. Shand went on to the Reserve on April 10 1946 and then took up farming. He retired in 1978.

APO 19.11.39   PO 28.5.40   FO 28.5.41   FL 28.5.42

HERBERT RONALD SHARMAN

78257   PO   Observer   British   248 Squadron

Joined the RAFVR in February 1939 at the age of 31, as an LAC u/t Observer. Sharman was called up at the outbreak of war and sent to Blackpool for further navigation training. He later went to Jurby for a bombing and gunnery course.

Sharman passed out and was commissioned in March 1940 and joined 248 Squadron at North Coates. The squadron served with Fighter Command in the Battle of Britain on fighter/reconnaissance duties.

HR Sharman (continued)

In March 1941 Sharman was posted to 31 Air Navigation School, Port Albert, Ontario, Canada for a Specialist Navigation Course, after which he was posted to 33 ANS at Mount Hope, Ontario as an instructor. Sharman returned to the UK in February 1943 and spent some months going round to operational squadrons instructing pilots and navigators in the use of new navigational aids.

Sharman then joined 297 Squadron, flying in Whitleys engaged in dropping secret agents into enemy-occupied territory. In September 1943 he was posted to 511 Squadron, Transport Command at Lyneham. He flew to many countries, carrying VIPs to the various theatres of war and conferences, including those at Casablanca, Teheran and Yalta. Sharman also made a number of Atlantic crossings, ferrying Liberators from Montreal to the Near and Far East.

In March 1944 Sharman went to HQ Transport Command as Deputy Chief Navigation Officer. He made a number of special flights, including over the Himalayas into China, as well as to India, Ceylon and Africa. He was awarded the AFC (7.9.45).

Sharman was released from the RAF in September 1945, as a Squadron Leader. He had been on flying duties for the whole six years of service.

PO 24.3.40   FO 24.3.41   FL 24.3.42

BRUCE ROBERTSON SHARP

628218   Sgt   Air Gunner   British   235 Squadron

With 235 Squadron in early July 1940. Sharp was one of the crew of a Blenheim which failed to return from an escort operation for FAA Albacores attacking Calais on September 11. The aircraft is presumed to have been shot down into the sea by Bf 109s. All three men on board were lost.

Sharp was 27. He is remembered on the Runnymede Memorial, Panel 19.

LESLIE MARK SHARP

85241   PO   Pilot   British   111 Squadron

Sharp, of Belfast, joined 111 Squadron at Drem on October 2 1940.

He was killed on December 28 1940, as a Pilot Officer with 96 Squadron. His Hurricane, P 3899, crashed into the sea after taking off from Squires Gate. Sharp was 23. He is buried in Carnmoney Jewish Cemetery, Co Antrim.

PO 7.9.40

RONALD JAMES SHARP

49537   Sgt   Pilot   British   236 Squadron

With 236 Squadron in early July 1940.

Commissioned in July 1942, Sharp was released from the RAF in 1945, as a Flight Lieutenant.

PO 10.7.42   FO 10.1.43   FL 10.7.44

HUGH SHARPLEY

742802   Sgt   Pilot   British   234 Squadron

With 234 Squadron at St Eval in early July 1940. On October 19 Sharpley claimed a Ju 88 destroyed.

He was killed on November 16 1940, still with 234, when he crashed into the sea off Porth in Spitfire X 4027.

Sharpley is remembered on the Runnymede Memorial, Panel 19.

WILLIAM GORDON SHARRATT

970537   Sgt   Aircrew   British   248 Squadron

Sharratt, of Blackpool, Lancashire, joined 248 Squadron on October 5 1940.

He was killed on July 2 1941, as a Flight Sergeant with 248. Sharratt was 26. He is remembered on the Runnymede Memorial, Panel 37.

FREDERICK JAMES SHAW

FAA/FX 79970   Petty Officer   Pilot   British   804 Sqdn

Shaw, of Brixton, London, was with 804 Squadron at Hatston in early July 1940, flying Sea Gladiators on dockyard defence.

On January 11 1941 a Fulmar, piloted by Shaw, was catapulted from HMS 'Pegasus' to chase a FW Condor which was attacking a ship five miles away. The ship had been hit and the Condor was making for cloud cover by the time the Fulmar arrived at the scene. An unsuccessful pursuit showed the Fulmar to be too slow for the job. This action took place 250 miles off the Irish coast and Shaw was able to land safely at Aldergrove.

Shaw was launched in a Fulmar from the 'Springbank' on June 10 1941 to chase a Condor, 250 miles out in the Atlantic. He fired at the enemy aircraft from long range but the Condor escaped. Shaw again managed to reach Aldergrove but only just, with five gallons of petrol left.

Shaw's third launch, again from the 'Springbank', came on September 25 1941, one day out from Gibraltar on the way home. Again the Condor was lost. Shaw returned safely to Gibraltar but the 'Springbank' was torpedoed by a U boat. She floated for more than eighteen hours and was finally sunk by one of the escort.

On August 2 1942 Shaw was killed in a deck-landing accident on HMS 'Illustrious'. He was 28 and is remembered on the Fleet Air Arm Memorial at Lee-on-Solent.

IAN GARSTIN SHAW

40265   FO   Pilot   British   264 Squadron

Joined the RAF on a short service commission in August 1937. Shaw was posted to 7 FTS, Peterborough on October 24 and on completion of the course he joined the SHQ staff at RAF Gosport.

Shaw was posted to 264 Squadron at Kirton-in-Lindsey in July 1940. On August 21 the squadron went south to Hornchurch for what was to be its last spell of day-fighting. Shaw failed to return from combat with Bf 109s off Manston on the 24th, in Defiant L 7027. He may have been shot down by Major Lützow of JG 3.

Shaw is remembered on the Runnymede Memorial, Panel 6.

APO 24.10.37   PO 23.8.38   FO 23.3.40

ROBERT HENRY SHAW

77465   PO   Pilot   British   1 Squadron

Born at Astley Bridge, Bolton on July 28 1916, Shaw joined the RAFVR on October 1 1937. He reported for full-time service at the Manchester Transit Centre on September 2 1939.

Shaw was posted to 5 FTS, Sealand on the 9th. He was commissioned and posted to the 11 Group Pool at St Athan on February 1 1940. After converting to Hurricanes Shaw joined No 1 Squadron in France on March 11. The squadron was withdrawn from Nantes to Tangmere on June 18.

After being attacked by a British fighter over the Sussex coast on August 11 Shaw made a forced-landing back at Tangmere with damaged aileron controls. He failed to return from a patrol on September 3 1940, in Hurricane P 3782.

Shaw is remembered on the Runnymede Memorial, Panel 10.

PO 1.2.40

HAROLD FREDERICK WILLIAM SHEAD

147535   Sgt   Pilot   British   32 and 257 Squadrons

Born in Bow, London on May 24 1920, Shead worked as a law clerk for a practice in Holborn. He joined the RAFVR early in 1939 and carried out his elementary flying training at 21 E&RFTS, Stapleford Tawney.

Called up at the outbreak of war, Shead went to ITW, Hastings on October 2 1939, was posted to 5 EFTS, Hanworth on December 4 and finished his ab initio course at 10 EFTS, Yatesbury on May 25 1940. Shead then went to 3 FTS, South Cerney until August 23 and arrived at 6 OTU, Sutton Bridge on the 31st. After converting to Hurricanes he joined 32 Squadron at Acklington on September 23, moving to 257 Squadron at North Weald on October 15.

Shead was attached to 46 Squadron at Digby on December 28 and posted to 615 Squadron at Kenley on February 20 1941. He went to the recently-reformed 68 Squadron at High Ercall on May 14 but with no twin-engine experience he was sent to 54 OTU and after converting to Beaufighters Shead joined 25 Squadron at Wittering on July 18 1941.

In May 1942 Shead was posted to the Middle East. After a short spell at 9 ADU, Takoradi he joined 89 Squadron at Abu Sueir on July 25, as a Warrant Officer. Shead teamed up with Flight Sergeant FW Curtis and they flew together for the first time on October 16 1942. On a scramble on December 21 they destroyed a He 111, a Ju 88 and probably another, on January 8 1943 a He 111, on the 21st they damaged a Ju 88 and on March 16 destroyed another.

Shead was commissioned in March 1943. He crashed in the desert on June 8, was badly injured and in hospital in Tripoli until August 18. Awarded the DFC (3.9.43), he left 89 Squadron on October 2 and was posted back to England on November 4 1943. Shead was sent on a Pilot Gunnery Instructor course on December 23 and posted to instruct at 551 Squadron at Twinwoods.

He went on a flying instructor's course at 2 FIS, Montrose on October 4 1944, was posted to 15 (P) AFU, Babdown on January 3 1945 and moved to 20 FTS, Church Lawford on May 3.

Shead was released from the RAF in October 1945, as a Flight Lieutenant. He returned to his old firm and started a three year law course, qualifying at the end of 1948. He remained with the firm, becoming first a junior partner and later a senior one. He died in 1981.

PO 3.3.43   FO 3.9.43   FL 3.3.45

HORACE SHEARD

638019   Sgt   Aircrew   British   236 Squadron

Sheard, of Dewsbury, Yorkshire, joined 236 Squadron on July 24 1940.

He was killed on March 21 1941, still with 236. Sheard was 20. He is remembered on the Runnymede Memorial, Panel 52.

DESMOND FREDERICK BURT SHEEN

39474   FL   Pilot   Australian   72 Squadron

Born in Sydney on October 2 1917, Sheen joined the RAAF in January 1936 and did his flying training in Australia. He transferred to the RAF in February 1937, was posted to 9 FTS, Thornaby on March 20 and joined 72 Squadron at Church Fenton on June 30 1937.

Still with 72 at the outbreak of war, Sheen destroyed a He 115 over the North Sea on October 21 1939, shared another in November and shared a He 111 on December 7.

In April 1940 Sheen was posted to 212 Squadron, which was part of the Photographic Development Unit at Heston. He was awarded the DFC (7.5.40). In May 1940 212 was disbanded and its pilots transferred to the PRU. Sheen rejoined 72 Squadron, then at Acklington, in late July as a Flight Commander.

On August 15 he claimed a Ju 88 and a Bf 110 destroyed. Sheen

was shot down on September 1 and baled out, unhurt. His Spitfire, X 4109, crashed at Court Lodge Farm, Ham Street. On the 4th he claimed a probable Bf 110. He was shot down in flames the next day by a Bf 109 over Hawkinge and baled out, wounded. His Spitfire, X 4034, crashed at Wildage Farm, Bladbean.

In April 1941 Sheen was given command of 72 Squadron and led it until October. He was awarded a Bar to the DFC (21.10.41). He commanded RAF Manston from November 10 1942 to April 18 1943, then commanded at Skeabrae and later Drem.

In 1944/45 Sheen commanded HQ 148 Airfield. He was released from the RAF in 1946 but rejoined in 1950. He retired from the RAF on January 2 1971, as a Group Captain.

PO 19.2.37   FO 19.9.38   FL 3.9.40   SL 1.12.41
WC 1.7.44   SL 1.1.50   WC 1.1.56   GC 1.1.64

FRANCIS WILLIAM SHEPHERD

139477   Sgt   Wop/AG   British   264 Squadron

Shepherd, of Leyland, Lancashire was with 264 Squadron at Duxford in early July 1940.

Commissioned in January 1943, he was killed on July 27 1944, as a Flying Officer with 31 Squadron. Shepherd was 28 and is buried in Bari War Cemetery, Italy.

PO 8.1.43   FO 8.7.43

FREDERICK ERNEST RICHARD SHEPHERD

811129   Sgt   Pilot   British   611 Squadron

Joined 611 Squadron at Digby on August 17 1940.

Shepherd made a forced-landing near Henlow on September 9, out of fuel during a routine flight from Fowlmere. On the 11th his aircraft was set alight during a combat over Croydon. He baled out, with parachute in flames, and fell dead at Frylands Wood, Farleigh. His Spitfire, P 7298, crashed into Nos 49 and 51 Hartland Way, Shirley.

Shepherd was 22. He is buried in St Luke's churchyard, Whyteleafe, Surrey.

JOHN BEAN SHEPHERD

104447   Sgt   Pilot   British   234 Squadron

Shepherd, of Edinburgh, joined 234 Squadron at Middle Wallop on September 13 1940.

He damaged a Ju 88 on March 23 1941 and shared a Bf 109 on June 17. Commissioned in August 1941, Shepherd destroyed a Bf 109 on October 15.

In early 1942 he was posted to 118 Squadron at Predannack. Shepherd shared a Do 217 over Dieppe on August 19 and was awarded the DFC (22.9.42). He was then a Flight Commander. On July 18 1943 he destroyed a Bf 109 and shared another. Tour-expired, he was awarded a Bar to the DFC (27.8.43) and posted away.

In June 1944 Shepherd joined 610 Squadron. He destroyed seven V1s in the latter half of the year. The squadron went to Armament Practice Camp at Warmwell in February 1945 and Shepherd took temporary command. Whilst there the squadron was informed that it was being disbanded on March 3.

Shepherd took command of 41 Squadron at Eindhoven in early April 1945. On the 14th he shot down a Bf 110 towing a Me 163 rocket fighter, on the 16th a FW 190, on the 20th a FW 190 and shared another, on the 30th a Bf 109 and a FW 190 and on May 1 he shared another FW 190. He was awarded a second Bar to the DFC.

On January 22 1946 Shepherd was killed in a flying accident. He was 26 and is buried in Hamburg Cemetery, Ohlsdorf, Germany.

PO 21.8.41   FO 8.2.42   FL 8.2.43

DOUGLAS CLAYTON SHEPLEY

33464   PO   Pilot   British   152 Squadron

Shepley was born at Carlton-in-Lindrick in 1918, the youngest of five brothers. He was at Oundle School from September 1931 until 1935, when he left to join his father's business.

In January 1938 Shepley entered RAF College, Cranwell as a flight cadet. On graduating in September 1939 he was posted to 152 Squadron, then reforming at Acklington.

On August 8 and 11 1940 Shepley claimed Bf 109s destroyed. He was reported 'Missing' on the 12th after an attack on Ju 88s south of the Isle of Wight, in Spitfire K 9999.

He is remembered on the Runnymede Memorial, Panel 10.

After Shepley's death his mother and his widow raised 5700 in north Derbyshire and south Yorkshire to buy a Spitfire. The aircraft, W 3649, a MK Vb, was named 'Shepley' and issued to 602 Squadron on August 16 1941. It was taken over by Group Captain FV Beamish for his personal use and carried the code FV-B. He was flying it when he and Wing Commander RF Boyd spotted the 'Scharnhorst' and 'Gneisenau'. The Spitfire was lost in action on March 28 1942 when Beamish was shot down and killed.

In the winter of 1979 a public house at Totley, Yorkshire, called 'The Shepley Spitfire', was declared open by Shepley's only surviving brother, Seymour.

PO 1.10.39

WALTER JOHN PATRICK SHEPPARD

747895   Sgt   Observer   British   236 Squadron

Sheppard, of Cottingham, East Yorkshire, joined 236 Squadron on October 4 1940. He became a PoW on December 4 1940.

After being freed in 1945 Sheppard stayed on in the RAF and became a Master Navigator on April 11 1953. He was released from the RAF in the mid-sixties.

EDMUND ERIC SHEPPERD

566529   Sgt   Pilot   British   152 Squadron

Shepperd was born at Binstead, Isle of Wight in 1917. His father died on April 8 1919 of wounds received in the Great War.

In the mid-thirties Shepperd joined the RAF and was a pre-war airman pilot. He joined 152 Squadron at Acklington at its reformation on October 1 1939.

Shepperd claimed a Bf 109 destroyed on July 25 1940, a Ju 88 on August 12, a Ju 87 on the 18th and another Ju 88 on October 7. He was killed on October 18 when his Spitfire, R 6607, crashed at Tadnoll Mill, near Dorchester, cause unknown.

He was 23 years old and is buried in Binstead Cemetery.

GEORGE EDWARD SHEPPERD

523887   Sgt   Air Gunner   British   219 Squadron

Shepperd, of Sidcup, Kent, was a pre-war regular airman. He was with 219 Squadron at Catterick in early July 1940.

On September 30 he was a member of the crew of Blenheim L 1261 which disintegrated and crashed during a routine night patrol, cause unknown. All three men on board were killed.

Shepperd was 23. He is buried in Catterick Cemetery, Yorkshire.

STEPHEN SHERIDAN

644861   Sgt   Wop/AG   British   236 Squadron

Joined the RAF in May 1939 and trained as a wireless operator. At the outbreak of war Sheridan volunteered for aircrew duties, as a Wop/AG.

After training he joined 236 Squadron at St Eval in July 1940. Sheridan remained with the squadron until March 18 1942, when he was posted to 280 (ASR) Squadron at Detling.

In June 1944 Sheridan went to 53 Squadron at St Eval, operating in Liberators on anti-submarine patrols. The squadron also operated from Iceland.

Sheridan was released in January 1946, as a Warrant Officer.

THOMAS BALDWIN ALOYSIUS SHERRINGTON

42082   PO   Pilot   British   92 Squadron

Joined the RAF on a short service commission in March 1939. After completing his training Sherrington was posted to 92 Squadron at Croydon in March 1940.

On September 27 he shared in the destruction of a Ju 88 and on October 25 destroyed a Bf 109.

Sherrington was posted away to 53 OTU, Heston in February 1941 and in August 1941 was OC 4 Squadron at 61 OTU.

He was released from the RAF in 1947, as a Flight Lieutenant.

APO 27.5.39   PO 18.11.39   FO 18.11.40   FL 18.11.41

———— SHEWEL

No unknown   Sgt   Aircrew   British   236 Squadron

Joined 236 Squadron on September 3 1940.
No other service details traced.

EDWARD ANDREW SHIPMAN

43364   PO   Pilot   British   41 Squadron

Born on December 9 1909, Shipman joined the RAF on May 26 1930 on an eight-year engagement. He remustered as a driver on January 1 1931 and on March 17 1933 as a Fitter Aero Engine. Shipman later volunteered for pilot training, was selected and began his ab initio course at 4 E&RFTS, Brough on January 27 1936. He went to 9 FTS, Thornaby on April 5, was awarded his flying badge on June 27, completed the course on October 10 and joined 41 Squadron at Catterick.

At the outbreak of war Shipman was still with 41. He shared in the destruction of a He 111 twenty-five miles east of Whitby on October 17 1939. He was commissioned in April 1940. On August 15 Shipman claimed a Bf 110 destroyed and on the 21st a He 111.

On October 21 1940 Shipman was posted to CFS, Upavon for a flying instructor's course, after which he went to 8 FTS, Montrose. In 1941 he was back at CFS, Upavon as an instructor and later a Flight Commander. Shipman was recategorised as an A2 flying instructor in late 1941 and then served at 3 FIS, Castle Combe. In 1942 he did a course at ECFS, Hullavington, was recategorised A1 and posted to CFS, Norton, Southern Rhodesia in 1943, as an instructor. He later became CFI and then CO at Norton.

Shipman was awarded the AFC (1.1.45). He returned to the UK in 1945 and went to ECFS, Hullavington as a staff tutor.

He retired from the RAF on December 9 1959, as a Squadron Leader, retaining the rank of Wing Commander.

PO 1.4.40   FO 1.4.41   FL 1.4.42   FL 1.9.45
SL 1.7.51

SIDNEY HARRY JAMES SHIRLEY

804422   Sgt   Air Gunner   British   604 Squadron

Shirley, of Wembley, joined 604 Squadron at Northolt in early July 1940. On August 24 he was one of the crew of a Blenheim which crashed near Odiham during a night patrol, cause unknown. Shirley and his pilot, Flying Officer H Speke, were both unhurt.

After the advent of the Beaufighter Shirley retrained as a Radio Observer. He was posted away from 604 in May 1941 to join 35 Squadron, operating in Halifaxes from Linton-on-Ouse, as an air gunner.

Shirley failed to return from operations on July 27 1941. He was then a Flight Sergeant, aged 32. He is buried in Angles Communal Cemetery, France.

NORMAN BASIL SHORROCKS

78265   PO   Observer   British   235 Squadron

With 235 Squadron in early July 1940. Shorrocks was a member of the crew of a Blenheim which failed to return from an escort operation for FAA Albacores attacking Calais on September 11 1940. It was presumed to have been shot down into the sea by Bf 109s. All three men on board were reported 'Missing'.

Shorrocks was 29. He is remembered on the Runnymede Memorial, Panel 10.

PO 24.3.40

Lord SHUTTLEWORTH

70356   FO   Pilot   British   145 Squadron

Richard Ughtred Paul Kay-Shuttleworth was born on October 30 1913, the son of Lawrence Ughtred Kay-Shuttleworth, barrister-at-law, killed in action on March 30 1917, whilst serving as a captain in the Royal Field Artillery.

Kay-Shuttleworth was educated at Eton and Balliol College, Oxford and was a JP and County Councillor for Lancashire. A member of the RAFO, Kay-Shuttleworth succeeded his grandfather in 1939, becoming the 2nd Baron.

Called to full-time service at the outbreak of war, he completed his training and joined 145 Squadron at Tangmere in June 1940.

On July 11 Shuttleworth shared in the destruction of a He 111 and on the 27th he shared a Ju 88. He failed to return from a combat with Ju 87s and Bf 110s over a convoy south of the Isle of Wight on August 8, in Hurricane P 3163. Shuttleworth was reported 'Missing'. He is remembered on the Runnymede Memorial, Panel 6.

PO (RAFO) 27.7.37   PO 25.9.39   FO 15.12.39

FREDERICK ALBERT SIBLEY

758073   Sgt   Pilot   British   238 Squadron

Joined 238 Squadron at Middle Wallop on August 19 1940.

Sibley made a forced-landing at Charmy Down on September 25 after an action with He 111s and Bf 110s south of Yeovil. He was unhurt but his Hurricane, N 2597, was written off.

He was reported 'Missing' after combat with enemy fighters over Poole Harbour on October 1 1940 in Hurricane P 3599. Sibley was 26. He is remembered on the Runnymede Memorial, Panel 19.

JAROSLAV SIKA

158967   Sgt   Pilot   Czechoslovakian   43 Squadron

Joined 43 Squadron at Usworth on October 6 1940.

Sika was awarded the Czech Military Cross and the C de G (Fr) in 1940. He was commissioned in July 1943, returned to Czechoslovakia after the war and died there.

PO 23.7.43

FRANK HARRY SILK

111979   Sgt   Pilot   British   111 Squadron

Silk was born on May 12 1917. He joined 111 Squadron at Croydon in early August 1940. On September 5 he made a forced-landing near Lullingstone Castle after a combat with Bf 109s over North Kent, slightly wounded.

On September 24 1940 he was posted away. Silk was commissioned in November 1941 and in early 1942 was a Flight Commander in 91 Squadron at Hawkinge. Later in the year he went on the Special Duties List, as a test pilot at Hawkers on production testing.

Silk was awarded the DFC (10.4.45), as a Flight Lieutenant with 4 Squadron, a photographic-reconnaissance unit.

He retired from the RAF on February 25 1958, as a Flight Lieutenant. He died on August 25 1970.

PO 21.11.41   FO 15.5.42   FL 15.5.43   FL 1.9.45

WILLIAM GERALD SILVER

563391   Sgt   Pilot   British   152 Squadron

A pre-war airman pilot, Silver was with 152 Squadron at Acklington in early July 1940.

On September 25 he failed to return from a combat over the Portsmouth area and is believed to have been shot down by enemy aircraft, in Spitfire P 9463.

Silver was 27. He is buried in Milton Road Cemetery, Portsmouth.

GEORGE FREDERICK SILVESTER

113838   Sgt   Pilot   British   245 and 229 Squadrons

Silvester was born in Gravesend on November 9 1920 and educated at the Grammar School there. He began training as a Quantity Surveyor. He joined the RAFVR in 1939 and began flying in the weekends at 20 E&RFTS, Gravesend.

Called to full-time service at the outbreak of war, Silvester was posted to 3 ITW, Hastings on October 3 1939. He went to 5 EFTS, Hanworth on December 4 and moved on to 10 EFTS, Yatesbury on April 29 1940. Silvester did his intermediate and advanced training at 2 FTS, Brize Norton, from May 25. After completing the course he went to 5 OTU, Aston Down on August 31.

Silvester joined 245 Squadron at Aldergrove on September 28 and moved to 229 Squadron at Northolt on October 16. He was posted to 145 Squadron at Tangmere on January 21 1941, was commissioned in early December and left on the 24th to go to 52 OTU, Aston Down as an instructor. In mid-March 1942 Silvester was sent to CFS, Upavon for an instructor's course. He returned to Aston Down and on July

GF Silvester (continued)

10 1942 he was posted to the 52nd Pursuit Group USAAF at Eglinton to instruct American pilots on Spitfires.

On September 29 Silvester joined 154 Squadron at Wellingore. He went with the squadron to North Africa in November 1942. He was posted to 242 Squadron at Souk-el-Khemis on March 13 1943, as a Flight Commander. Tour-expired, Silvester left the squadron at the end of July 1943 and went to 73 OTU, Abu Sueir on August 19 as an instructor. He moved to 76 OTU, Aqir on December 1.

Silvester returned to operations on July 12 1944, when he was given command of 32 Squadron at Foggia. He was awarded the DFC (17.10.44) and led the squadron until April 19 1946, when he returned to the UK. He went on to the Reserve in January 1950.

PO 4.12.41   FO 1.10.42   FL 4.12.43   FL 1.9.45

ROBERT BLACK SIM

742609   Sgt   Pilot   British   111 Squadron

Sim, of Stewarton, Ayrshire, was born in Kilmarnock in 1917. He joined 111 Squadron at Croydon in early July 1940.

On August 11 Sim failed to return from combat with Bf 109s engaged off Margate. His Hurricane, P 3942, is presumed to have crashed into the Channel.

Sim is remembered on the Runnymede Memorial, Panel 19.

VERNON CHURCHILL SIMMONDS

42653   PO   Pilot   British   238 Squadron

Joined the RAF on a short service commission in June 1939. Simmonds did his elementary flying training at 12 E&RFTS, Prestwick. He went on to 9 FTS, Hullavington and completed his course at 15 FTS, Lossiemouth. He was then posted to a Specialist Armament Officers Course at RAF Manby.

In early July 1940 Simmonds went to 7 OTU, Hawarden and after converting to Hurricanes he joined 238 Squadron at Middle Wallop on the 29th. Simmonds claimed a Bf 110 destroyed on August 13,

He 111s on September 15 and 25 and another Bf 110 on the 26th. He landed at Andover on the 28th, out of fuel following a combat over the Isle of Wight, and died attempting to take off. On the 30th Simmonds baled out after colliding with Pilot Officer RA Kings. His Hurricane, N 2474, crashed near Shaftesbury.

In May 1941 Simmonds joined 118 Squadron at Ibsley as 'B' Flight Commander. He went to 10 BGS, Warmwell in November for gunnery training and in December was appointed OC Gunnery Training Flight at 52 OTU, Aston Down. In 1942 Simmonds became CGI at the Fighter Gunnery Instructors Wing at CGS, Sutton Bridge. He returned to operations in 1943, firstly with 118 Squadron at Coltishall and later with 333 Squadron at Ludham and Tangmere.

In late 1944 Simmonds was at HQ Fighter Command as Armament Training Staff Officer. He commanded the Armament Wing at A&AEE, Boscombe Down in 1945. Simmonds was released from the RAF in early 1946, as a Squadron Leader.

APO 2.9.39   PO 2.3.40   FO 2.3.41   FL 2.3.42

GEOFFREY MERVYN SIMPSON

41481   PO   Pilot   New Zealander   229 Squadron

Born in Christchurch on June 22 1919, Simpson was at Christ's College there from 1933 to 1935. He was employed as a clerk and joined the territorials in February 1936, serving in the 1st Canterbury Regiment. In mid-June 1938 Simpson was provisionally accepted for an RAF short service commission and sailed for the UK in the RMS 'Rangitata' on August 25.

Simpson began his ab initio course at 9 E&RFTS, Ansty in early October, then, after a short spell at Uxbridge he went to 6 FTS, Little Rissington on December 28. He was awarded his flying badge on May 6 1939 and after completing his senior term he was posted in August to 8 ATS, Lossiemouth for advanced training on Wallace and Henley aircraft.

On November 6 Simpson joined 229 Squadron, newly-reformed at Digby with Blenheims. In March 1940 these were replaced by Hurricanes. On May 16 Flight Lieutenant FE Rosier led 'A' Flight to France, Simpson included. On the 18th he destroyed a Bf 110 and on the 21st two more. It was his last sortie in France and Simpson returned to Digby the next day.

229 Squadron took part in operations over Dunkirk, based at Biggin Hill and using Manston as a forward base. After being sent to Digby on June 5 it moved to Wittering at the end of the month to build up again to operational strength. The squadron moved south to Biggin Hill on September 10. On the 15th Simpson shared in destroying a He 111.

On October 26 1940 229 took off to patrol the Croydon area, in company with 302 Squadron. A number of Bf 109s were seen and 302, followed by 229, gave chase, pursuing the enemy fighters to the French coast. They lost them and turned for home. Simpson, leading Blue Section, saw a He 59 flying low off the coast in the vicinity of Boulogne. He went down, accompanied by Sergeant Ommaney and Pilot Officer DBH McHardy. After two bursts from Ommaney the floatplane alighted on the sea, with three of its crew of four killed. The Hurricanes were then attacked from the rear by Bf 109s and ground fire from the shore. Ommaney made off at low-level across the Channel and reached his base. Simpson and McHardy were last seen heavily engaged by Bf 109s and failed to return. McHardy was later reported to be a PoW but Simpson was not heard of again. He was in Hurricane W 6669.

He is remembered on the Runnymede Memorial, Panel 6 and his name appears on the reredos in St George's Chapel of Rememberance at Biggin Hill.

APO 14.12.38   PO 6.10.39

JOHN WILLIAM CHARLES SIMPSON

37642   FL   Pilot   British   43 Squadron

Simpson was born at Ramsey St Mary's, Huntingdonshire in 1913. He joined the RAF on a short service commission in January 1936 and did his ab initio course at 9 E&RFTS, Ansty. Simpson was posted to 5 FTS, Sealand on March 21 and joined 43 Squadron at Tangmere on October 11 1936. In December he became squadron adjutant.

Still with 43, Simpson shared in probably destroying a He 111 on February 3 1940 and on the 13th destroyed another. On May 9 he was appointed a Flight Commander and on this day he shared in the destruction of a Do 17. Over Dunkirk on June 1 Simpson destroyed two Bf 109s and on the 2nd two Bf 109s and a Bf 110 over France. He was awarded the DFC (25.6.40).

Simpson claimed a Bf 109 destroyed on July 19. He was then shot down himself and baled out, landing in a cucumber frame at Worthing and suffering a broken collar bone and wounded in the ankle. His Hurricane, P 3140, crashed into the Channel off Felpham. Simpson returned to 43 in October and in late November destroyed a Ju 88, which crashed into the sea.

In early December 1940 Simpson was given command of 245 Squadron at Aldergrove. On April 8 1941 he destroyed a He 111 at night over Belfast, the first German aircraft to fall on Northern Ireland, and on May 6 he shot down another He 111 at night. He was awarded a Bar to the DFC (30.5.41). In mid-June 1941 Simpson was posted away to a staff job.

In November 1942 he was in Gibraltar, as a Wing Commander, and in January 1943 he was in North Africa, as a Group Captain. Still serving in the RAF, Simpson died on August 12 1949. He is buried in St Andrew's churchyard, Tangmere. His portrait was done by Eric Kennington and Cuthbert Orde.

APO 9.3.36   PO 6.1.37   FO 6.7.38   FL 6.7.40
SL 1.9.41   WC 9.5.43   WC 1.10.46

LESLIE WILLIAM SIMPSON

76471   PO   Air Gunner   British   264 and 141 Sqdns

Simpson was posted to 264 Squadron at Kirton-in-Lindsey on July 12 1940 and moved to 141 Squadron at Grangemouth on the 29th.

He was released in 1945, as a Flight Lieutenant.

APO 10.12.39   PO 6.2.40   FO 20.1.41   FL 20.1.42

PETER JAMES SIMPSON

41875   FO   Pilot   British   111 and 64 Squadrons

Born on March 5 1921, Simpson joined the RAF on a short service commission in January 1939. After completing his training he joined 111 Squadron at Acklington in November 1939.

Over Dunkirk on June 2 1940 Simpson probably destroyed a Bf 110. He claimed a Bf 109 destroyed on July 19. He was posted to 64 Squadron at Kenley in early August. Simpson claimed a Bf 109 destroyed and shared a He 111 on August 16. In this engagement his Spitfire, L 1068, was severely damaged by cannon fire.

Simpson returned to 111 Squadron, then at Debden, on August 17. The next day he probably destroyed a Do 17, receiving such damage himself as to necessitate a forced-landing on Woodcote Park golf course, Epsom Downs. He shared another Do 17 on August 26, destroyed a Bf 109 on September 4 and shared a He 111 on November 13. Simpson was awarded the DFC (17.12.40).

In May 1941 Simpson was posted away for a rest. He joined 66 Squadron at Portreath in December, as a Flight Commander. He commanded 130 Squadron from July 1942 to January 1943 and 504 Squadron from July to October 1943. Simpson was appointed Wing Leader at Hornchurch on December 18 1943, the last of a long line. The fighter squadrons were withdrawn in February 1944 so that Hornchurch could prepare for D Day.

In June 1944 Simpson led the Portreath Wing over Normandy. He was awarded a Bar to the DFC (29.8.44).

He retired from the RAF on March 5 1968, as a Wing Commander, retaining the rank of Group Captain. He died in 1987.

APO 1.4.39   PO 23.10.39   FO 23.10.40   FL 23.10.41
SL 28.12.43   SL 1.8.47   WC 1.1.54

IVOR REGINALD SIMS

120223   Sgt   Observer   British   248 Squadron

Sims, of Gloucester, was with 248 Squadron in early July 1940. He flew with Flying Officer EH McHardy from September 1940 until July 1941, when 248 converted to Beaufighters.

In 1942 Sims was with 604 Squadron. Commissioned in April, he was awarded the DFM (22.9.42) for services as a Flight Sergeant.

Sims was killed on January 13 1945, as a Flight Lieutenant. The unit he was serving with is not known. He was 34 and is buried in Coney Hill Cemetery, Gloucester.

PO 8.4.42   FO 8.10.42   FL 8.4.44

JAMES AYSCOUGH SIMS

43944   PO   Pilot   British   3 and 232 Squadrons

Born on October 2 1912, Sims was with 3 Squadron at Biggin Hill at the outbreak of war.

Commissioned in April 1940, he was in 'B' Flight when it was renumbered as 232 Squadron at Sumburgh on July 17 1940. He served with the squadron throughout the Battle of Britain.

Sims retired from the RAF on March 25 1959, as a Flight Lieutenant, retaining the rank of Squadron Leader. He died in 1977.

PO 25.4.40   FO 25.4.41   FL 25.4.42   FL 1.9.45

GORDON LEONARD SINCLAIR

39644   FL   Pilot   British   310 Squadron

Born on August 15 1916, Sinclair joined the RAF on a short service commission on March 1 1937 and began his elementary flying training at 9 E&RFTS, Ansty. He was posted to 3 FTS, South Cerney on May 8 and joined 19 Squadron at Duxford on November 27 1937.

Sinclair was still with 19 in 1940. Over Dunkirk on May 26 he destroyed a Bf 109 and probably another, on June 1 he destroyed two Bf 109s and on a later patrol the same day damaged a He 111 and a Do 17. He was awarded the DFC (25.6.40).

In late June Sinclair was posted to Duxford, to be 'A' Flight Commander in 310 (Czech) Squadron, then about to be formed. It became operational on August 17. Sinclair claimed a Do 17 destroyed on August 31, on September 3 a Do 17 and a Bf 110 and on the 9th another Do 17. On this day he collided with Flying Officer JE Boulton and baled out, spraining his ankle landing in a wood at Caterham. His Hurricane, R 4084, crashed off Purley Way, Wallington. On September 29 Sinclair was shot down by a Bf 109 in an engagement over Thanet. He baled out, unhurt, landing at Chilham. His Hurricane, V 6608, is believed to have crashed on Woodsdale Farm, Godmersham. He was awarded the Czech Military Cross (24.12.40).

In January 1941 Sinclair was posted to HQ 12 Group, Hucknall, on staff duties. He was given the task of forming and then commanding 313 Squadron at Catterick in May 1941. He took command of 79 Squadron at Fairwood Common in September and led it until posted to Air Ministry in December, in the Directorate of Fighter Operations.

GL Sinclair (continued)

From March to September 1943 Sinclair was attached to various squadrons, awaiting re-appointment. He was given command of 56 Squadron at Bradwell Bay in October 1943. Sinclair was promoted to Wing Commander in May 1944 and joined the staff at HQ 84 Group. In January 1945 he returned to Air Ministry, in the Directorate of Fighter Operations and in October was appointed Personal Air Secretary to the Secretary of State for Air, holding the post until November 1947.

Sinclair retired from the RAF on December 23 1957, as a Wing Commander.

APO 3.5.37   PO 1.3.38   FO 1.10.39   FL 1.10.40
SL 1.12.41   SL 1.9.45   WC 1.1.51

JOHN SINCLAIR

81346   PO   Pilot   British   219 Squadron

Sinclair was born on November 13 1919. He joined 219 Squadron at Catterick on July 7 1940.

He retired on August 4 1961, as a Flight Lieutenant.

PO 22.6.40   FO 22.6.41   FL 22.6.42   FL 6.11.45

JOHN ERIC JAMES SING

37429   FL   Pilot   British   213 Squadron

Born in Bristol on October 21 1916, Sing joined the RAF on a short service commission in October 1935. He was posted to 2 FTS, Digby on November 2 and joined 213 Squadron at Northolt at its formation on March 8 1937.

Sing was still with the squadron in early July 1940. He claimed a Bf 109 destroyed on August 8, two Bf 110s on the 12th, a Bf 109 on the 13th and a Bf 110 and two Ju 87s on the 15th. During a combat over Selsey Bill on September 11 Sing's aircraft was damaged in a surprise attack and he baled out, unhurt. His Hurricane, P 3780, crashed into the sea. On the 15th he claimed a Do 17 destroyed and on the 27th shared a Bf 110. He was awarded the DFC (22.10.40).

In October 1941 Sing reformed 153 Squadron at Ballyhalbert from 'A' Flight of 256, with Defiants. He left the squadron in March 1942, went to 501 Squadron at Ibsley in June 1942 as a supernumerary Squadron Leader and was given command of 152 Squadron at Wittering in September. Sing took the squadron to North Africa in November 1942 and on the 25th he damaged a FW 190. He led 152 until April 1943.

Sing retired from the RAF on October 23 1962, as a Wing Commander.

APO 21.10.35   PO 21.10.36   FO 21.7.38   FL 21.7.40
SL 1.9.41   WC 13.12.43   SL 1.6.44   WC 1.1.52

ANTONI SIUDAK

P 5128   Sgt   Pilot   Polish   302 and 303 Squadrons

Born on April 1 1909. Siudak joined 302 Squadron at Leconfield on July 23 1940. He shared in the destruction of a Do 17 on September 15.

Siudak was posted to 303 Squadron at Northolt on September 23. He claimed two Bf 109s destroyed and a Bf 110 shared on October 5. The next day a lone raider struck at Northolt just after mid-day and killed Siudak, bombing his Hurricane, P 3120, as he was taxying.

He is buried in Northwood Cemetery, Middlesex and is remembered on the Polish Air Force Memorial at Northolt. Siudak was awarded the VM (5th Class)(1.2.41).

WILFRED MAX SIZER

40758   FO   Pilot   British   213 Squadron

Born in Chelmsford on February 23 1920, Sizer joined the RAF on a short service commission in March 1938. He was serving with 213 Squadron at Wittering at the outbreak of war.

On May 17 1940 the squadron flew to Merville to support squadrons in France. During a five day period Sizer destroyed one enemy aircraft and shared in destroying four others. On his final patrol Sizer was attacked by five Bf 109s and shot down. He landed two miles from La Panne, swam across a canal and was taken to a casualty clearing station, with facial wounds. He was taken back to England and rejoined the squadron soon after.

Over Dunkirk on May 28 Sizer destroyed a Bf 109, on the 29th he damaged a He 111 and on the 31st he destroyed another Bf 109 and damaged a second but was shot down himself. Sizer crash-landed south of Dunkirk and returned to England by ship.

On August 11 Sizer claimed a Ju 88 destroyed, on the 12th a Bf 110 and on the 15th two Ju 87s. He was awarded the DFC (8.11.40). In late April Sizer was posted to No 1 Squadron at Kenley, as a Flight Commander.

In 1942 Sizer was with 152 Squadron and on August 23 he shared a Ju 88. The squadron went to North Africa in November. Sizer damaged a Mc 202 on November 25 and damaged a Ju 88 on December 28. He was given command of 93 Squadron at Souk-el-Khemis in February 1943. He damaged a Bf 109 on July 12 and destroyed a Mc 202 the next day.

Sizer was released from the RAF in 1946, as a Wing Commander. He rejoined later and retired on February 23 1963, as a Squadron Leader, retaining the rank of Wing Commander. His portrait was done by Cuthbert Orde in October 1940.

APO 7.5.38   PO 7.3.39   FO 3.9.40   FL 3.9.41
SL 1.1.44   SL 1.1.50

STANISLAW SKALSKI

76710   PO   Pilot   Polish   302 and 501 Squadrons

Skalski was born in Kodyn, Russia on November 27 1915. He joined the PAF on January 1 1936 and after qualifying as a pilot he joined 142 Squadron, the 'Wild Ducks'. In the September 1939 fighting in Poland Skalski shot down two Do 17s on the 2nd and two other enemy aircraft, with another shared, before he escaped from his country.

He made his way to the Mediterranean and boarded a ship for England. Skalski was commissioned in the RAF in January 1940. He joined 302 Squadron at Leconfield on August 3 but moved to 501 Squadron at Gravesend on the 12th. Skalski claimed a He 111 destroyed on the 30th, a Bf 109 on the 31st and two Bf 109s on September 2. He was shot down by Bf 109s over Canterbury on the 5th, in Hurricane V 6644. He was injured and admitted to Herne Bay Hospital, where he remained for several weeks. Back with 501 Skalski shared a Bf 109 on November 8.

Awarded the VM (5th Class)(1.2.41), he was posted to 306 Squadron at Tern Hill on February 25 1941. Skalski destroyed Bf 109s on July 24 and August 19 and shared another on the 21st. He was appointed a Flight Commander on August 15, awarded the KW and Bar (10.9.41) and destroyed two more Bf 109s on September 17.

In October Skalski was posted to 58 OTU, Grangemouth as an instructor. He was awarded two more Bars to the KW (30.10.41) and the DFC (19.2.42). On March 1 1942 Skalski joined 316 Squadron at Northolt, as 'B' Flight Commander. He destroyed a FW 190 on April 10 and probably another on May 3. He was given command of 317 Squadron, also at Northolt, on June 11 1942. Skalski was awarded a Bar to the DFC (15.11.42) and posted away on November 2 to 58 OTU, Balado Bridge as CFI.

Skalski went to West Kirby on February 13 1943 to prepare for overseas and on March 13 arrived in the Middle East in a C 47 with other Polish pilots to form the Polish Fighting Team, otherwise known as 'Skalski's Circus'. They were attached to 145 Squadron and operated in the Western Desert from March 17. On the 28th Skalski destroyed a Ju 88 and on April 2 and 4 Bf 109s. The Team, led by Skalski, operated until May 12 and by that time had destroyed thirty enemy aircraft.

In mid-July Skalski took command of 601 Squadron at Luqa, Malta. Shortly afterwards the squadron moved to Sicily. Skalski left 601 in early October to return to the UK. He was awarded a second Bar to the DFC (20.10.43) and appointed Wing Leader of 131 Wing at Northolt on December 13. Skalski moved to lead 133 Wing on April 11 1944, with three Polish Mustang Squadrons. He destroyed two Bf 109s on June 24.

Skalski left the Wing on July 12, was awarded the VM (4th Class)(25.9.44) and went on a course to the Command and General Staff School at Fort Leavenworth, Kansas on October 4. He returned to the UK in late January 1945 and was posted to HQ 11 Group, as Wing Commander Ops. He was awarded the DSO (26.5.45).

In January 1947 Skalski returned to Poland and was given command of Fighter Command of the Polish Air Force. He was later imprisoned by the Russians and not released until October 1956. Skalski was later put in charge of aero clubs in Poland.

PO 24.1.40   FO 1.3.41   FL 1.9.42   SL 1.9.43

VICTOR HALL SKILLEN

745460   Sgt   Pilot   British   29 Squadron

Skillen, of Northern Ireland, joined 29 Squadron at Digby in July 1940.

He was killed on March 11 1941, as a Sergeant with 23 Squadron. Skillen was 24. He is buried in St Pierre Cemetery, Amiens, France.

CHARLES DAVID EVELYN SKINNER

90225   FL   Pilot   British   604 Squadron

Skinner, of West Byfleet, Surrey, was born on July 17 1916. He was at Cheltenham College from 1931 to 1934 and became an engineering apprentice at Simms Motor Units in 1935. He joined 604 Squadron, AuxAF in early 1938.

Called to full-time service on September 28 1939, Skinner served with 604 throughout the Battle of Britain.

He became a Legionaire of the Legion of Merit (US) (9.10.45), as an Acting Wing Commander. He was released from the RAF in 1946 and went to work for Rotax Ltd. Skinner was later a director of Joseph Lucas Export Ltd. He rejoined the RAuxAF.

PO (AuxAF) 28.3.38   FO 28.9.39   FL 28.9.40   SL 1.12.41
FO (RAuxAF) 29.12.47

STANLEY HEWITT SKINNER

90210   FL   Pilot   British   604 Squadron

Skinner joined 604 Squadron, AuxAF in 1934. He was called to full-time service on August 25 1939 and served with 604 throughout the Battle of Britain.

On August 19 1942 Skinner was killed whilst acting as an observer with naval forces during the Dieppe raid, as an Acting Wing Commander. He was 30 years old and is remembered on the Runnymede Memorial, Panel 64.

PO (AuxAF) 24.7.34   FO (AuxAF) 16.3.36   FO 25.8.39
FL 12.3.40   SL 1.6.41

WILFRED MALCOLM SKINNER

68722   Sgt   Pilot   British   74 Squadron

Born in Gloucester, Skinner was in the RAFVR. He had sufficient flying hours and had reached the standard required to be recommended for a full-time training period with the regular RAF. On June 10 1939 he went from 5 E&RFTS, Hanworth to 74 Squadron at Hornchurch.

After the outbreak of war Skinner remained with the squadron. Over Dunkirk on May 24 he damaged a He 111 and on the 27th destroyed a Do 17. Skinner shared in the destruction of a He 111 on July 8, claimed a Bf 109 on July 31, claimed a Bf 110 and shared two others on August 11 and a Do 17 destroyed on the 13th. During a routine patrol on the 30th Skinner collided with Pilot Officer EWG Churches and baled out, unhurt. His Spitfire, X 4022, crashed and burned out.

On October 27 and November 1 Skinner destroyed Bf 109s, on November 14 a Ju 87 and on the 15th another Bf 109. He was awarded the DFM (24.12.40). In March 1941 Skinner was posted to 59 OTU, Crosby-on-Eden as an instructor. He was commissioned in May and rejoined 74 Squadron, then at Rochford, on June 10 1941.

Skinner was shot down on July 6 1941, during a Roadstead operation to attack shipping near Gravelines. He was later reported to be a PoW. He was 74's longest-serving member. Skinner was released from the RAF in 1946, as a Flight Lieutenant. He later rejoined the RAFVR.

PO 17.5.41   FO 17.5.42   FL 17.5.43
FO (RAFVR) 21.10.47

HENRYK SKOWRON

781283   Sgt   Pilot   Polish   303 Squadron

Skowron was born on May 26 1916. He joined 303 Squadron at Leconfield on October 23 1940.

He was posted to 151 Squadron at Wittering on February 1 1941 and went to 10 BGS, Dumfries on April 8 as a staff pilot. Skowron was killed on July 18 1941 whilst target towing. His Battle, L 5775, crashed at Blackshaw Bank, Solway Firth.

Skowron is buried in St Andrew's Catholic Cemetery, Dumfries.

JOHN WILLIAM SLADE

101518   Sgt   Pilot   British   64 Squadron

Slade, of Weston-super-Mare, joined 64 Squadron at Leconfield in mid-September 1940.

Commissioned in July 1941, Slade was awarded the DFC (22.1.43), as an Acting Flight Lieutenant with 126 Squadron. He commanded 94 Squadron in Greece from November 1944 until the squadron was disbanded at Sedes on April 26 1945.

Slade was killed on September 19 1945, as a Squadron Leader with 337 Wing. He was 28 and is buried in Phaleron War Cemetery, Athens.

PO 17.7.41   FO 17.7.42   FL 17.7.43

DUDLEY MALINS SLATTER

44597   PO   Air Gunner   British   141 Squadron

Slatter, of Southsea, joined 141 Squadron at Turnhouse on July 10 1940.

With no operational experience the squadron flew south to West Malling on July 12. Shortly after 09.00 hrs on the 19th twelve Defiants moved to the forward airfield at Hawkinge. At 12.23 hrs they were ordered off to carry out an offensive patrol twenty miles south of Folkestone. Three were left behind with engine trouble. During the patrol the nine Defiants were surprised by a force of Bf 109s of III/JG 51 and in less than a minute four were shot down.

Slatter was flying with Pilot Officer JR Gard'ner, in Defiant L 7016. Theirs was one of the four rear victims immediately shot down. Unlike the other three victims their aircraft did not catch fire and Gard'ner landed on the sea four miles off Dover. The Defiant sank, the pilot managed to extricate himself but Slatter was not seen again.

He was 26 and is remembered on the Runnymede Memorial, Panel 10.

PO 9.5.40

JAMES WALLACE SLEIGH

Lieutenant (FAA)   Pilot   British   804 Squadron

Sleigh, of Finsbury Park, London, was with 804 Squadron at Hatston in early July 1940, flying Sea Gladiators on dockyard defence. He was injured in a crash on November 11 after the engine of his Martlet failed.

In late 1940 Sleigh joined 802 Squadron, then forming at Donibristle for HMS 'Audacity'. He was awarded the DSC (10.3.42). In June 1942 he formed 890 Squadron, which took part in the Salerno landings operating from HMS 'Illustrious'.

Sleigh was awarded the DSO (30.5.44) for leading a Wing of three squadrons to attack the 'Tirpitz' on April 3 1944. He was made an OBE (6.11.53) for services on HMS 'Glory' during the Korean War. Sleigh retired on January 29 1958, as a Commander. He later went to live in South Africa.

Sub-Lt 14.3.38   Lt 14.3.40   Lt-Cdr 14.3.48   Cdr 31.12.50

VACLAV SLOUF

112547   Sgt   Pilot   Czechoslovakian   312 Squadron

After escaping from Czechoslovakia Slouf made his way to France and joined l'Armée de l'Air. In May 1940 he was a Corporal-Pilot in Groupe de Chasse III/3.

On May 19 his Morane-Saulnier MS 406 was hit by return fire from a Do 17 and set alight. Slouf baled out. For his service in France he was awarded the Medaille Militare, the C de G (Fr) with five palms and the Czech Military Cross.

Slouf went to England and joined 312 Squadron at Duxford on September 5 1940. Commissioned in November 1941, he commanded 312 Squadron from November 1944 to April 1945 and was awarded the DFC.

Slouf was released from the RAF, as a Squadron Leader.

PO 26.11.41   FO 26.11.42   FL 26.11.43

OSWALD KENNETH SLY

759093   Sgt   Air Gunner   British   29 Squadron

Sly, of Weston-super-Mare, joined 29 Squadron at Digby on August 7 1940. He was a member of the crew of a Blenheim shot down in error by Hurricanes of 312 Squadron on October 13 1940. The aircraft, L 6637, crashed in flames off the Point of Aire, near the Morecambe Light. All three men on board were lost.

Sly was 20. He is remembered on the Runnymede Memorial, Panel 23.

JAMES SMALLMAN

627873   AC2   Radar Operator   British   236 and 23 Sqdns

Born on August 3 1919, Smallman joined the RAF in November 1938. At the outbreak of war he was on an electrician's course. In October 1939 he was posted to Martlesham Heath for an AI course.

Smallman was posted to 604 Squadron at Northolt in December and moved to 600 Squadron at Manston in February 1940. He returned to Martlesham Heath in late May for further AI training. In late June Smallman joined 236 Squadron at Middle Wallop, moving later to Thorney Island and then St Eval. He was posted to 23 Squadron at Wittering in early September, moving to Ford on the 12th.

On December 6 1940 Smallman made his final flight with 23. With other radar operators, he was posted away in early 1941. In mid-1942 Smallman went on a course for motor boat crew and spent the rest of his service in marine craft and ASR launches, including a tour in West Africa. He was released from the RAF in February 1946.

THOMAS SMART

40324   FO   Pilot   British   65 Squadron

Smart was born in Broughton-in-Furness. He joined the RAF on a short service commission in September 1937. He was posted to 10 FTS, Tern Hill on December 11 and after completing his training he joined the staff at No 1 Air Armament School, Manby.

In early 1940 Smart was with 65 Squadron at Northolt. Over France on May 22 he damaged a Ju 88, on the 24th shared a Hs 126, over Dunkirk on the 26th destroyed a Bf 110, on the 27th two Do 17s and on June 25 a probable Bf 109. Smart claimed a Bf 109 destroyed on August 13 and destroyed a Do 17 and probably destroyed another on the 26th.

Smart destroyed a bomber at night on January 10 1941, was awarded the DFC (4.2.41), destroyed a Bf 109 on July 8 and was posted away from 65 in October to be an instructor.

He was given command of 229 Squadron at Ta Kali, Malta in November 1942 and led it until he was killed on April 12 1943. Smart is remembered on the Malta Memorial, Panel 6, Column 1. He was awarded a Bar to the DFC (18.9.45), with effect from April 11 1943.

APO 28.11.37   PO 27.9.38   FO 27.6.40   FL 27.6.41

ALEXANDER SMITH

1050686   Sgt   Aircrew   British   600 Squadron

With 600 Squadron at Northolt in early July 1940. Smith was one of the crew of a Blenheim which became lost following R/T failure during a night patrol. The crew of three baled out over Basingstoke when the petrol was exhausted. The aircraft, L 1111, crashed near Odiham.

Smith was killed on August 22 1941, as a Sergeant with 600. He is remembered on the Runnymede Memorial, Panel 52.

ANDREW THOMAS SMITH

90337   FL   Pilot   British   610 Squadron

Smith, of Fulwood Park, Liverpool, was born in 1906. He was at Oundle School from 1921 to 1924, when he left to go to St Catherine's College, Cambridge. He later worked for a flour-milling company and became manager.

In 1936 Smith joined 610 Squadron, AuxAF. He was called to full-time service on August 24 1939 and appointed a Flight Commander in October. Over Dunkirk on May 27 1940 Smith destroyed a Bf 110 and probably another. He took command of 610 on the 29th when the CO was killed.

On July 10 Smith crashed on landing at Hawkinge after being damaged in combat over Dover. He was killed on July 25 1940, when he stalled attempting to land at Hawkinge after an action with Bf 109s over the Channel. His Spitfire, R 6693, crashed and burned out in a disused engine-testing shed.

Smith is buried in St Peter's churchyard, Delamere, Cheshire.

PO (AuxAF) 9.4.36   FO (AuxAF) 9.10.37   FO 24.8.39
FL 9.10.39

ARTHUR DUMBELL SMITH

580153   Sgt   Pilot   British   66 Squadron

With 66 Squadron at Coltishall in early July 1940. On the 24th Smith is believed to have crashed into the sea during a routine patrol in Spitfire N 3041, cause unknown, unhurt. On August 30 Smith shared in the destruction of a Do 17.

He was shot down in combat over Ashford on September 4 and baled out, seriously wounded. He was admitted to No 7 Casualty Clearing Station, Benenden and died of his wounds on the 6th. His Spitfire, N 3048 crashed near Mersham.

Smith was 22. He is buried in St Luke's churchyard, Whyteleafe, Surrey.

ARTHUR JOSEPH SMITH

42657   **PO**   **Pilot**   **British**   **74 Squadron**

Joined the RAF on a short service commission in June 1939. Smith joined 74 Squadron at Coltishall on September 30 1940 and was posted away on October 29 1940.

Smith was released from the RAF in 1946, as a Flight Lieutenant.

APO 2.9.39   *PO 13.4.40*   *FO 13.4.41*   *FL 13.4.42*

ARTHUR WILLIAM SMITH

41073   **FO**   **Pilot**   **Canadian**   **141 Squadron**

Born in Southport, Florida, Smith was brought up in Summerland, British Columbia. He joined the RAF on a short service commission in June 1938.

Smith was posted to 141 Squadron at Turnhouse at its reformation on October 4 1939 and served with the squadron throughout the Battle of Britain. He joined 242 Squadron at Duxford on November 4 1940.

Patrolling over Clacton on March 28 1941 Smith's turbo charger cut out. He spun in at Bradfield St George and was killed. He was 26 and is buried in Ipswich Cemetery, Suffolk.

APO 20.8.38   *PO 27.6.39*   *FO 3.9.40*

CHRISTOPHER DERMONT SALMOND SMITH

33287   **FL**   **Pilot**   **British**   **25 Squadron**

Smith of Overy Staithe, Norfolk, entered RAF College, Cranwell in September 1934, as a flight cadet. After graduating in July 1936 he was posted to the School of Air Navigation, Manston for a course. He joined 220 (GR) Squadron at Bircham Newton on November 29 1936.

Smith went to the A&AEE, Martlesham Heath on June 1 1938. He flew operationally after the outbreak of war, being awarded the DFC (7.5.40). He joined 25 Squadron at North Weald on September 20 1940.

In November 1941 Smith took command of 79 Squadron at Fairwood Common. He was killed on December 22 1941, aged 25. He is remembered on the Runnymede Memorial, Panel 28.

PO 1.8.36   *FO 1.2.38*   *FL 1.2.40*   *SL 1.3.41*

DENIS NORMAN EVELYN SMITH

79524   **PO**   **Pilot**   **British**   **74 Squadron**

An ex-transport pilot, Smith is reputed to have fought in the Spanish Civil War. He was posted to 74 Squadron at Hornchurch on July 20 1940.

He failed to return from combat with Bf 110s over convoy 'Booty' thirty miles east of Harwich on August 11. Smith crashed into the sea in Spitfire R 6962 and was killed.

He was 24 years old and is buried in Ostende New Communal Cemetery, Belgium.

PO 1.6.40

DONALD SYDNEY SMITH

40859   **PO**   **Pilot**   **British**   **616 Squadron**

Smith, of Highley, Shropshire, was educated at Bridgnorth Grammar School and later Winchester College. He became Geography Master at Droxford School and later at Highley School, where his father was headmaster.

In April 1938 Smith joined the RAF on a short service commission. After completing his training he was posted to the FAA. In early 1940 Smith was with 616 Squadron at Leconfield. Over Dunkirk on June 1 he damaged a Ju 88. He destroyed a He 111 soon after midnight on June 27.

During a night-flying practice on August 7 Smith's Spitfire, R 6696, crashed and exploded three miles from Leconfield. He is believed to have baled out, unhurt. On the 15th Smith shared in the destruction of a Ju 88 and on the 30th he claimed a Bf 109 destroyed.

On September 27 Smith was shot down by Bf 109s whilst acting as a weaver. It is believed that he crashed in Spitfire R 6702 at Workhouse Cottage, Throwley, near Faversham, seriously wounded. Smith was admitted to Faversham Cottage Hospital, where he died the next day. He is buried in St Mary's churchyard, Highley.

APO 4.6.38   *PO 4.4.39*

EDWARD BRIAN BRETHERTON SMITH

90340   **FL**   **Pilot**   **British**   **610 Squadron**

Smith was born in Formby, Lancashire. He joined 610 Squadron, AuxAF in 1936. He was called to full time service on August 24 1939. Over Dunkirk on May 27 1940 he destroyed a He 111.

He claimed Bf 109s destroyed on July 24 and 25 and damaged a He 59 floatplane off Calais on August 11. The following day Smith was shot down in flames in a combat over New Romney. He baled out, was rescued from the sea and admitted to Dover Hospital with burns. Smith was awarded the DFC (30.8.40), credited with the destruction of six enemy aircraft.

He was released from the RAF in 1946, as a Squadron Leader.

PO (AuxAF) 22.9.36   *FO (AuxAF) 22.3.38*   *FO 24.8.39*
FL 3.9.40   *SL 1.12.41*

EDWARD STANLEY SMITH

90093   **FL**   **Pilot**   **British**   **600 Squadron**

Joined 600 Squadron, AuxAF in 1936. Smith was called to full-time service on August 25 1939 and was with the squadron at Northolt in early July 1940.

Smith was awarded the AFC (2.6.43). He commanded 264 Squadron from April 1944 to June 1945. He was awarded the DFC (2.10.45) and released in 1945, as an Acting Wing Commander.

PO (AuxAF) 10.7.36   *FO (AuxAF) 10.1.38*   *FO 25.8.39*
FL 3.9.40   *SL 1.12.41*

ERIC CLAUD SMITH

197580   **Sgt**   **Air Gunner**   **British**   **600 Squadron**

Born on February 16 1920, Smith joined 600 Squadron, AuxAF on November 5 1938. He was called to full-time service at the outbreak of war and was still with 600 in July 1940.

On August 9 Smith was gunner in a Blenheim which developed engine failure during night operations. He and the pilot, Flying Officer SP le Rougetel, baled out. Smith swam ashore at Westgate. The aircraft, L 8679, crashed near Westgate.

Smith was posted to 256 Squadron at Colerne on February 24 1941. Commissioned from Warrant Officer in April 1945, he retired from the RAF on June 3 1966, as a Flight Lieutenant.

PO 27.4.45   *FO 27.10.45*   *FO 28.4.48*   *FL 4.6.53*

ERIC LEIGH SMITH

77346   **PO**   **Air Gunner**   **British**   **604 Squadron**

With 604 Squadron at Northolt in early July 1940.

Smith was released from the RAF in 1945, as a Flight Lieutenant. He died on November 5 1978.

PO 4.2.40   *FO 4.2.41*   *FL 4.2.42*

FORGRAVE MARSHALL SMITH

37613   **FL**   **Pilot**   **Canadian**   **72 Squadron**

Born in Edmonton, Alberta on August 17 1913, Smith learned to fly at the Edmonton Aero Club. He joined the RAF on a short service commission in January 1936.

FM Smith (continued)

Smith was posted to 3 FTS, Grantham on March 14 and joined 72 Squadron at Church Fenton on March 22 1937. Still with the squadron in 1940, Smith shared in destroying a Do 17 on June 29. He claimed a He 111 destroyed on August 15 and was himself shot down on the 31st during a combat over Dungeness. He baled out, wounded and badly burned. His Spitfire, P 9438, crashed near New Romney.

After three months in hospital Smith returned to 72. He was promoted and posted to command 603 Squadron at Drem on April 1 1941. He destroyed Bf 109s on June 12 and 14. Smith left the squadron on July 24 and on August 14 went to 52 OTU, Debden as CFI.

Smith formed and then commanded 175 Squadron briefly from March 3 1942. He was posted to India, as CFI at Risalpur. After a course at RAF Staff College, Haifa he returned to India and became Wing Commander Ops at Air HQ, New Delhi. Smith returned to the UK for a course at the Fighter Leaders' School and again returned to India, this time to command 902 Wing. He was detached from the Wing to be Joint Assault Commander for the invasion of Ramree Island on the Arakan coast. In May 1945 Smith was detached for the invasion of Rangoon, with the task of establishing an airfield. He remained with 902 Wing until late 1945. He was awarded the DFC (30.10.45).

Smith retired from the RAF on October 13 1957, as a Wing Commander.

APO 2.3.36   PO 6.1.37   FO 6.8.38   FL 6.8.40
SL 1.9.41   WC 1.1.44   WC 1.10.46

FRANCIS ALAN SMITH

Sub-Lieutenant (FAA)   Pilot   British   145 Squadron

Born on June 24 1920, Smith joined the FAA on July 3 1939. He trained at HMS 'Frobisher' and 'St Vincent' and on October 9 went to 14 EFTS, Castle Bromwich, moving on to 7 FTS, Peterborough on December 11.

Smith was awarded his wings on March 17 1940. He completed the course on May 26 and went on loan to the RAF in mid-June, then being sent to 7 OTU, Hawarden to convert to Hurricanes.

On July 2 Smith joined 145 Squadron at Tangmere. He overturned attempting a forced-landing north-west of Ringwood during a routine patrol on the 12th. The Hurricane, N 2703, was a write-off.

Smith was reported 'Missing' following a combat south of the Isle of Wight on August 8 1940. His Hurricane, P 3545, crashed into the sea. Smith is remembered on the Fleet Air Arm Memorial at Lee-on-Solent, Bay 1, Panel 3.

Midshipman 1.7.39   Actg Sub-Lt 24.6.40

FRANK SMITH

994288   AC 2   Radar Operator   British   604 Squadron

Joined the RAF in 1940. In late June Smith was at Yatesbury for what he expected to be the start of a Wop/AG course. Instead he found himself learning about airborne radar and in late July he was posted to 604 Squadron at Gravesend, never having flown.

Smith flew operationally with 604, firstly in Blenheims and then Beaufighters, until December 1940, when he was posted back to Yatesbury for another radar course. In these five months Smith flew without rank or brevet, receiving three shillings per day, which included one shilling flying pay.

In January 1941 Smith was posted to a radar station at Saligo, Islay, Scotland. He later returned to flying duties and was killed on March 6 1942, as a Sergeant with 12 Squadron, operating in Wellingtons from Binbrook.

Smith is remembered on the Runnymede Memorial, Panel 93.

GODFREY ERNEST SMITH

122301   Sgt   Air Gunner   British   264 Squadron

Joined 264 Squadron at Kirton-in-Lindsey in early October 1940.

Commissioned in May 1942, Smith was released from the RAF in 1946, as a Flight Lieutenant. He died in 1980.

PO 1.5.42   FO 1.11.42   FL 1.5.44

IRVING STANLEY SMITH

43048   PO   Pilot   New Zealander   151 Squadron

Born in Invercargill on May 21 1917, Smith was educated in Whangarei and Auckland. He applied for a short service commission in the RNZAF, was accepted in January 1939 and opted to train in New Zealand. He began flying training at Mangere in May but was then asked if he would volunteer to train in England, which he did, sailing for the UK in the RMS 'Rangitiki' on July 27.

Smith went to Jesus College, Oxford on September 11 1939 for lectures and ground studies. He was posted to 10 EFTS, Yatesbury on the 21st and moved on to 2 FTS, Brize Norton on March 24 1940. Smith completed the course on July 11 and two days later was posted direct to 151 Squadron at North Weald.

On August 15 he claimed two Bf 109s destroyed and a third damaged, on the 24th a He 111 destroyed, on the 30th shared a Bf 109, on the 31st a Do 17 destroyed and another damaged and on October 2 a He 111 which ditched just off the beach at Chapel St Leonards, ten miles north of Skegness.

151 Squadron went over to night-fighting in November 1940 and began to convert to Defiants in December but still retained some Hurricanes. These made up 'C' Flight, which Smith commanded. He was awarded the DFC (7.3.41) and destroyed a He 111 at night on May 10 1941. 'C' Flight was merged with 'B' in July and Smith took command of the combined flight, equipped solely with Defiants.

On February 19 1942 Smith took command of 151 Squadron. At dusk the same day, on a convoy patrol, he shot down a Do 17 and damaged another and a Ju 88. The squadron began to receive Mosquitos in April 1942 and Smith, then an Acting Wing Commander, gained 151's first victories with the aircraft on June 24, destroying a Do 217, a He 111 and probably another. He was awarded a Bar to the DFC (16.7.42).

Smith was posted away for staff duties at HQ Fighter Command in March 1943. He asked to return to operations and was posted to command 488 Squadron but this was over-ridden by Basil Embry, who wanted him at HQ 2 Group. Smith went there in September 1943 on staff duties concerned with Mosquito training.

In early February 1944 he was given command of 487 Squadron at Hunsdon. Soon after his arrival the squadron took part in the historic raid on Amiens prison. After much preparation and planning it took place on February 18. Smith led the raiding force, made up of six Mosquitos each from 487, 464 and 21 Squadrons. Much has been written on the rights and wrongs of the attack but there is no doubt about the bravery of the crews who took part in the operation, the prime purpose of which was to save life and therefore considered to be very worthwhile. From later reports it is known that 258 of the 700 prisoners escaped, including half of those awaiting execution. Casualties were heavy inside the prison, some of the escapees were recaptured and some civilians outside the walls were killed.

In early August Smith led 487 to bomb the barracks at Poictiers, where German troops were assembling prior to attacking the Maquis. The raid was particularly successful. A few weeks later 487 attacked the SS HQ at Vincey, near Metz.

In October 1944 Smith was posted to 13 OTU, High Ercall as Chief Instructor. He was granted a Permanent Commission in June 1945 and went on a course at RAF Staff College, Haifa in February 1946.

Smith received a Mention in Despatches in 1945, a Commendation for Services in 1946, was made an OBE in 1953 and a CBE in 1960. He retired from the RAF on February 2 1966, as a Group Captain.

APO 11.9.39   PO 13.7.40   FO 13.7.41   FL 18.5.42
SL 16.7.42   SL 1.9.45   WC 1.7.52   GC 1.1.59

JAMES DUNCAN SMITH

40325   PO   Pilot   Canadian   73 Squadron

Smith, of Winnipeg, joined the RAF on a short service commission in September 1937. He was posted to 10 FTS, Tern Hill on December 11 and joined 87 Squadron at Debden on July 9 1938. Smith was with 87 in France from the outbreak of war until posted to 73 Squadron in May 1940.

On June 5 he shared in destroying a Do 17. The squadron was withdrawn from France on June 17. Smith claimed a Bf 110 destroyed on September 11 and a Bf 109 on the 15th.

73 Squadron moved to Castle Camps in September and left there on November 11 for overseas. It embarked on HMS 'Furious' on the 16th, with its aircraft, and flew off to Takoradi on the 29th. The squadron then flew in easy stages to Heliopolis, via Lagos, Accra, Kano, Maidugari, Khartoum, Wadi Halfa and Abu Sueir. During December the pilots were attached to 274 Squadron in the Western Desert. On the 14th, 16th and 18th Smith destroyed Sm 79s.

In early January 1941 73 Squadron began operating on its own account. On April 14 the squadron took off to intercept CR 42 and G 50 fighters attacking Tobruk. Smith single-handedly attacked five G 50s and shot down two and damaged a third before being shot down and killed. He was 27 and is buried in Knightsbridge War Cemetery, Acroma, Libya. His portrait was done by Cuthbert Orde in 1940.

APO 28.11.37   PO 27.9.38   FO 27.4.40

KENNETH BARTON SMITH

754895   Sgt   Pilot   British   257 Squadron

Smith, of Grimsby, Lincolnshire, was with 257 Squadron at Hendon in early July 1940.

He failed to return from an action off St Catherine's Point on August 8, in Hurricane R 4904. Smith was 21. He is remembered on the Runnymede Memorial, Panel 19.

LAURENCE EDWARD SMITH

112251   Sgt   Pilot   British   234 Squadron

Born in 1918, Smith joined the RAFVR at Kidlington on November 11 1938 and was called to full-time service in early September 1939. He was posted to ITW, Hastings in December, moved to 4 EFTS, Brough on March 3 1940 and completed his training at 14 FTS, Cranfield from May 12 to September 28.

Smith was posted to 7 OTU, Hawarden on the 29th and after converting to Spitfires he joined 234 Squadron at St Eval on October 15 1940. He was posted away to 53 OTU, Llandow on July 8 1941, was commissioned in October, attached to CFS, Upavon for an instructor's course for three weeks from November 17 and then returned to Llandow.

On March 10 1942 Smith moved to 59 OTU at Crosby-on-Eden, remaining there until August 11, when he was posted to 559 Squadron, Brunton. He continued instucting at various units and specialised in refresher flying training. Smith had Wing Commander RRS Tuck as a pupil after the latter's return from PoW camp.

Smith was released from the RAF in late 1945, as a Flight Lieutenant. He rejoined the RAFVR in May 1947 and was instructing at Nottingham University Air Squadron. When the RAFVR ceased Smith joined the RAuxAF, with a fighter control unit, serving until November 1963. He later changed his name to Hooper-Smith.

PO 17.10.41   FO 1.10.42   FL 22.10.43
FO (RAFVR) 27.5.47   FO (RAuxAF) 17.8.53

LEONARD SMITH

129976   AC 2   Radar Operator   British   219 Squadron

Smith was called up for service in the RAF on June 7 1940. During basic training at West Kirby he volunteered for aircrew duties and after selection was sent to Yatesbury for a short radar course.

On July 21 1940 Smith joined 219 Squadron at Catterick. In October the squadron began to receive Beaufighters. Many radar operators were posted away in late 1940 but Smith remained and in November he was promoted to Sergeant, with rank and pay back-dated. He crewed up with Pilot Officer Styles and they were to stay

together until September 1943. They damaged a He 111 on March 4 1941.

In July 1941 Smith was posted to 2 School of Air Navigation at Cranage for a course, after which he returned to 219. He joined 153 Squadron at Ballyhalbert on February 14 1942 and was commissioned in June. The squadron flew in stages to Maison Blanche, Algiers in December and became operational on the 25th.

Smith and Styles destroyed a Ju 88 on January 21 1943 and a Sm 79 on June 25 1943. Smith left for the UK on September 6, escorting a German PoW, Leutnant Hoelzel. He went on an instructor's course at 62 OTU, Ouston in October and was afterwards posted to 54 OTU, Winfield to instruct on AI.

On March 24 1944 Smith joined 264 Squadron at Church Fenton, flying in Mosquitos with Flight Lieutenant Burke as pilot. They covered the invasion and moved across to France in August. Smith was posted away in April 1945 and in June went to a GCA unit, as a controller. He was released from the RAF on November 16 1946, as a Flight Lieutenant.

PO 24.6.42   FO 24.12.42   FL 24.6.44

NORMAN HENRY JACKSON SMITH

42270   PO   Pilot   British   235 Squadron

Born on April 15 1918, Smith joined the RAF on a short service commission in March 1939. He was with 235 Squadron in early July 1940.

He was awarded the DFC (27.5.41), as a Flying Officer with 235. On December 26 1944 Smith was leader of a strike force of Mosquitos of 235 Squadron, which attacked two motor vessels in Leitvik harbour, leaving one sinking and the second blazing. One enemy fighter was shot down and one Mosquito lost.

Smith retired from the RAF on March 29 1958, as a Flight Lieutenant, retaining the rank of Wing Commander. He later changed his name to Jackson-Smith.

APO 1.5.39   PO 27.12.39   FO 27.12.40   FL 27.12.41
SL 24.6.45   FL 1.9.45

PERCY RONALD SMITH

581477   Sgt   Pilot   British   236 Squadron

Smith, of Streatham, was a pre-war airman pilot. He was with 236 Squadron in early July 1940.

He was killed on November 24 1940, as a Sergeant with 272 Squadron, aged 25. Smith is remembered on the Runnymede Memorial, Panel 19.

PHILLIP RICHARD SMITH

45352   Sgt   Pilot   British   25 Squadron

Smith was with 25 Squadron in early July 1940.

Commissioned in December 1940, he was killed on April 4 1943, as a Flight Lieutenant with 278 Squadron, an ASR unit. He is remembered on the Runnymede Memorial, Panel 121.

PO 18.12.40   FO 18.12.41   FL 18.12.42

REGINALD CYRIL SMITH

565965   Sgt   Pilot   British   236 Squadron

Smith, of Chichester, was with 236 Squadron in early July 1940. On August 1 he was captain of Blenheim N 3603, which returned to Thorney Island with severe damage to its tail caused by anti-aircraft fire during a low-level attack on Querqueville aerodrome.

On July 19 1941 Smith was killed, as a Flight Sergeant with 143 Squadron, a Beaufighter coastal-reconnaissance unit. He was 25 and is remembered on the Runnymede Memorial, Panel 37.

RODDICK LEE SMITH

37129   FL   Pilot   British   151 Squadron

Born on June 23 1915, Smith joined the RAF on a short service commission on March 15 1935. He was posted to 3 FTS, Grantham on the 30th and in February 1936 joined 19 Squadron at Duxford.

In June 1936 Smith was seconded to the FAA. He flew floatplanes at Calshot, went to No 1 FTS, Leuchars for training on Nimrods and Ospreys and in August was attached to 19 Squadron for the Sassoon Trophy, which the squadron won.

Smith joined 801 (Fleet Fighter) Squadron on September 22 1936, based at Southampton and on HMS 'Furious'. On January 26 1937 he was posted to the Pilots Pool at Gosport, where he remained until January 3 1938 when he joined 802 (Fleet Fighter) Squadron, based at Hal Far, Malta and on HMS 'Glorious' in the Mediterranean.

In June 1939 Smith went to 13 FTS, Drem as a Flight Commander. He moved to 12 Group Pool, Aston Down in November as an instructor. Smith was posted to 151 Squadron at North Weald on June 10 1940, as 'B' Flight Commander.

On August 13 he claimed a Do 17 destroyed. During his time with 151 Smith probably destroyed two enemy aircraft and damaged two more. He was posted away to Kirton-in-Lindsey on November 24 1940 to form and then command 255 Squadron. Smith destroyed a Ju 88 at night on May 5 1941 and later destroyed another enemy aircraft.

He was sent to 54 OTU, Church Fenton on June 14 for a course, after which he was posted to 60 OTU, East Fortune to instruct on Defiants. Smith took command of 32 Squadron at Manston on December 12 1941 and led the squadron until promoted to Wing Commander in April 1942 to go to HQ Fighter Command as Permanent President, Courts of Enquiry into accidents. He was also ASR Staff Officer.

In July 1943 Smith did a Spitfire refresher course at Aston Down. In August he was attached to Charmy Down for a Day Fighter Leader course. From September to November he was attached in turn to 129, 403 and 421 Squadrons. Smith was appointed Deputy SPSO at HQ Fighter Command in December 1943 and in March 1944 he went on the 2nd course at the Empire Test Pilots' School at Cranfield. He was attached to Hawkers at Langley in November 1944 and posted to Napiers at Luton in January 1945 as an experimental test pilot on Tempests. He later moved to Percivals at Luton to test Mosquitos. In June Smith was appointed OC 'D' Squadron at Boscombe Down. On June 3 1946 he went to the Empire Test Pilots' School at Cranfield as OC Flying for the 5th Course.

In the post-war RAF Smith held a series of appointments and commands in Britain and Germany. He was made an OBE (12.6 58) and retired from the RAF on June 23 1962, as a Wing Commander.

APO 15.3.35   PO 15.3.36   FO 15.9.37   FL 15.9.39
SL 1.2.40   WC 1.3.42   WC 1.7.54

ROBERT RUTHERFORD SMITH

40952   FO   Pilot   Canadian   229 Squadron

Smith, of London, Ontario, joined the RAF on a short service commission in May 1938. He joined 229 Squadron when it was reformed at Digby on October 6 1939.

Over Dunkirk on May 29 1940 Smith probably destroyed a Bf 109 and on June 1 a Ju 87 and probably another. He claimed a He 111 probably destroyed on September 11 and on the 15th he was shot down in an attack on Do 17s and Bf 110s over Sevenoaks and baled out, with leg wounds, from Hurricane V 6616.

From September 1942 Smith served with 112 Squadron in the Western Desert. On the 1st he probably destroyed a Bf 109, on the 22nd he destroyed another, on the 31st a Ju 87 and on December 10 a Bf 109 and a Mc 202.

Smith was awarded the DFC (23.2.43). On March 10 1943 112 Squadron was covering Kittyhawks of 250 and 260 Squadrons strafing Axis positions north-west of the Fuma and Tatauin area. In this operation Smith was shot down by Major Müncheberg, Kommodore of JG 27, and captured.

Smith was released from the RAF in 1945, as a Flight Lieutenant. He died in the early sixties.

APO 9.7.38   PO 16.5.39   FO 3.9.40   FL 3.9.41

WILLIAM ALEXANDER SMITH

40026   FO   Pilot   British   229 Squadron

Born on November 18 1915, Smith joined the RAF on a short service commission in June 1937. He was posted to 3 FTS, South Cerney on August 21 and went to 2 AACU at Lee-on-Solent on March 26 1938.

Smith joined 66 Squadron at Duxford on January 31 1939. He was posted to 229 Squadron at Digby in late May 1940. Over Dunkirk on June 2 he damaged a Bf 109.

On September 11 Smith claimed a He 111 destroyed and on the 26th probably another. The next day his Hurricane, P 3603, was hit by cross fire from Ju 88s and he made a forced-landing at Lingfield, writing the aircraft off. On October 6 Smith crash-landed near Leatherhead after a routine patrol, out of fuel and with the radio not working.

In May 1941 229 Squadron went to the Middle East. It flew its Hurricanes off HMS 'Furious' to Malta on the 21st, refuelled and flew on to Mersa Matruh. The pilots were attached to 73 and 274 Squadrons in the Western Desert. On July 15 Smith destroyed a Ju 87 and probably another. On September 1 the squadron began to operate on its own account and in October Smith took command. On December 14 he destroyed a Bf 109, on the 23rd a Ju 87 and probably another and on the 27th a Ju 88.

Smith was shot down and wounded on January 9 1942. He rejoined the squadron on February 7 and was posted away at the end of the month. He was awarded the DFC (17.3.42).

He retired from the RAF on November 24 1962, as a Wing Commander.

APO 9.8.37   PO 24.5.38   FO 24.12.39   FL 24.12.40
SL 1.3.42   SL 1.9.45   WC 1.1.53

WILLIAM BRUCE SMITH

742002   Sgt   Pilot   British   602 Squadron

Joined 602 Squadron at Westhampnett on October 6 1940. Smith claimed a Bf 109 destroyed on the 29th. He was shot down in a surprise attack by Bf 109s the next day and crash-landed on the foreshore at Greetstone, near Lydd, wounded. His Spitfire, X 4542, was written off.

Smith did not fly again, being medically unfit. He died on June 17 1975.

WYNFORD ORMONDE LEONI SMITH

37366   FL   Pilot   British   263 Squadron

Smith, of Worthing, joined the RAF on a short service commission in October 1935. He was posted to 6 FTS, Netheravon on October 19 and with training completed he went to the School of Army Co-operation at Old Sarum for a course. On February 11 1937 Smith was posted to the Aircraft Depot, Karachi, moving soon afterwards to 5 (Army Co-operation) Squadron at Risalpur.

In early July 1940 Smith was with 263 Squadron at Grangemouth. On the 13th he was involved in a night flying accident, crashing at Carstairs Junction Public School, Lanark, attempting to land in a built-up area. Smith was unhurt, although the Hurricane, P 2991, was written off.

He was killed on December 29 1940 when he crashed near Bovey Tracey in Whirlwind P 6975. Smith was then a Flight Lieutenant, aged 25. He is buried in Exeter High Cemetery, Devon.

APO 7.10.35   PO 7.10.36   FO 7.5.38   FL 7.5.40

ROSS SMITHER

| C 1594 | FO | Pilot | Canadian | 1 (RCAF) Squadron |

Born in London, Ontario on November 12 1912, Smither joined the RCAF on September 10 1930. He was with No 1 (RCAF) Squadron when it arrived in the UK on June 20 1940.

Smither claimed a Bf 110 destroyed on September 4. He was shot down and killed by Bf 109s over Tunbridge Wells on the 15th, in Hurricane P 3876. He is buried in Brookwood Military Cemetery.

JULIAN LANGLEY SMITHERS

| 90540 | PO | Pilot | British | 601 Squadron |

Smithers, of Knockholt, Kent, entered the City when he went to work in his father's stockbroking firm. He became a member of the Stock Exchange in early 1940.

In 1938 Smithers had joined 601 Squadron, AuxAF. He was called to full-time service on August 24 1939. After completing his training Smithers rejoined 601 in June 1940.

On August 11 he was shot down and killed during a combat off Portland and crashed into the sea, in Hurricane P 3885. Smithers was 24 years old and is buried in Ste Marie Cemetery, Le Havre, France.

APO 24.8.39   PO 4.5.40

RICHARD SMITHSON

| 46174 | Sgt | Pilot | British | 249 Squadron |

Smithson, of South Hetton, was with 249 Squadron at Leconfield in early July 1940. He crashed at Eastchurch after a combat with Bf 109s over Maidstone on September 7, in Hurricane V 6574. He was wounded and did not return to the squadron until October 13.

Commissioned in July 1941, Smithson was killed on the 22nd of the month, as a Pilot Officer with 96 Squadron, aged 25. He is buried in Holy Trinity churchyard, South Hetton, Durham.

PO 17.7.41

RONALD HENRY SMYTH

| 103514 | Sgt | Pilot | British | 111 and 249 Squadrons |

Joined the RAFVR on May 8 1939. Smyth was called to full-time service at the outbreak of war, posted to No 1 ITW, Cambridge on September 7, moved to 10 EFTS, Yatesbury on December 5 and then to 3 FTS, South Cerney on April 27 1940.

After completing his course Smyth was posted to 5 OTU, Aston Down to convert to Hurricanes. He joined 111 Squadron at Debden on August 21 but five days later went back to 5 OTU and rejoined 111 Squadron, then at Drem, on September 19. Smyth was posted to 249 Squadron at North Weald on October 2 and moved to 615 Squadron at Northolt on November 19.

Smyth was sent to CFS, Upavon on May 8 1941 for an instructor's course. On June 13 he joined the staff at 9 FTS, Hullavington and was commissioned in August. In October he was posted to No 1 Glider Training Squadron at Thame, to train Army glider pilots on Hotspurs. Smyth did this job until April 1943. He then went to 3 School of General Reconnaissance at Squire's Gate, moving to 8 (Coastal) OTU, Dyce on June 22. Smyth qualified for his 2nd Class Navigator's License in July.

He went to Benson in mid-September 1943 for training on photographic-reconnaissance duties and on December 19 he joined 541 Squadron there. Smyth commanded the squadron PRU in Gibraltar from March 9 to September 12 1944. He was awarded the DFC (27.7.45), left 541 in September 1945 and was released from the RAF in January 1946, as a Flight Lieutenant.

PO 5.8.41   FO 5.8 42   FL 5.8.43

DEREK MYLES ALTAMONT SMYTHE

| 79196 | PO | Air Gunner | British | 264 Squadron |

Smythe was born on June 26 1914. He joined the RAF on a direct commission in April 1940. He carried out his gunnery training at No 1 Air Armament School at Manby from April 21 to May 12. A week later he joined 98 Squadron in France, operating in Fairey Battles.

In early June Smythe returned to England and on the 18th he was posted to 5 OTU, Aston Down to convert to Defiants. He joined 264 Squadron at Duxford on July 12 1940. Apart from a short Gunnery Leaders' course at Warmwell in late December 1940 Smythe stayed with 264 until June 30 1942, when the squadron was re-equipped with Mosquitos.

In July 1942 Smythe joined 515 Squadron, then forming at Northolt with Defiants. The squadron aircraft were equipped with special equipment to jam German radar. They flew out over the Channel ahead of Bomber Command to confuse the enemy as to the bombers' destination. Smythe was posted away in July 1943.

He joined 223 Squadron on January 20 1944, operating in Baltimores from Celone, Italy, as Gunnery Leader. Smythe left the squadron on September 18 and was awarded the DFC (14.11.44). From April 9 1945 to February 3 1946 he was with 45 Group Transport Command at Dorval, Montreal, as Group Accidents Investigator.

Smythe was released from the RAF in March 1946, as a Flight Lieutenant.

APO 20.4.40   PO 12.6.40   FO 12.6.41   FL 14.5.42

GEORGE SMYTHE

| 47752 | Sgt | Pilot | British | 56 Squadron |

Born in Westminster, London on June 10 1915. Smythe was a pre-war airman pilot and joined 56 Squadron at North Weald in September 1939.

Over Dunkirk on May 27 1940 Smythe probably destroyed a Bf 110 and on the 29th destroyed a Ju 87 and probably a Bf 109. On June 7 and 30 he claimed Bf 109s destroyed, on July 13 a Ju 87, on August 12 a Bf 109 and on the 16th a probable Bf 109.

Smythe wrecked Hurricane P 3473 in a forced-landing at Courtsend, Foulness on the 26th, after a combat with Bf 109s. On the 28th he destroyed a Bf 109 and was then shot down himself by another. He baled out, unhurt. The Hurricane, N 2524, crashed in flames at Ladwood Farm, Acrise. Smythe was awarded the DFM (30.8.40).

Commissioned in January 1942, Smythe was at HQ Kandy in September 1945, as a Squadron Leader on staff duties. He was made an MBE (13.6.46) and retired from the RAF on November 24 1961, as a Wing Commander.

PO 27.1.42   FO 1.10.42   FL 1.10.43   SL 1.8.47
WC 1.7.54

RUPERT FREDERICK SMYTHE

| 40436 | FO | Pilot | British | 32 Squadron |

Smythe was born in Killiney, Co Dublin. He joined the RAF on a short service commission in October 1937. He was posted to 11 FTS, Wittering in January 1938 and joined 29 Squadron at Debden on October 24.

In September 1939 Smythe was posted to 504 Squadron at Digby. He moved to 32 Squadron at Wittering in May 1940. Over Dunkirk on June 2 he destroyed a Ju 88 and damaged a Bf 109. In a patrol over France on June 12 Smythe destroyed a Hs 126.

He claimed two Bf 109s destroyed on July 4, another on the 19th, a Do 17 on August 12 and another Bf 109 on the 14th. Smythe was shot down in combat with Bf 109s over Folkestone on August 24 and crashed at Lyminge, in Hurricane V 6568, wounded. He was taken to the Royal Masonic Hospital at Hammersmith.

Smythe did not return to operational flying. He was released from the RAF in 1946, as a Flight Lieutenant.

APO 9.1.38   PO 25.10.38   FO 25.7.40   FL 25.7.41

WILLIAM GEORGE SNAPE

50692   WO   Air Gunner   British   25 Squadron

Snape was with 25 Squadron at Northolt at the outbreak of war and was promoted to Warrant Officer on January 12 1940. He served with the squadron throughout the Battle of Britain.

Commissioned in the Technical Branch (Signals) in July 1942, Snape was released from the RAF in 1946, as a Flying Officer. He died on August 22 1955.

PO 14.7.42   FO 14.1.43

VIVIAN ROBERT SNELL

41485   FO   Pilot   British   151 and 501 Squadrons

Snell was born in Swansea, the son of a music publisher. He joined the RAF on a short service commission in October 1938.

He was posted to 151 Squadron at Stapleford on September 5 1940 and moved to 501 Squadron at Kenley on the 26th. Snell destroyed a Bf 109 on October 25 and was then shot down himself over Cranbrook, in Hurricane N 2438.

Snell commanded 125 Squadron at Stradishall from October 1945 until it was disbanded on November 20. He was released from the RAF in 1946, as a Wing Commander.

APO 14.12.38   PO 3.9.39   FO 3.9.40   FL 3.9.41
SL 1.7.44

WILLIAM GEORGE SNOW

84678   PO   Pilot   British   236 Squadron

Joined 236 Squadron in September 1940.

Snow was released from the RAF in 1945, as a Flight Lieutenant.

PO 10.8.40   FO 10.8.41   FL 10.8.42

ERNEST GEORGE SNOWDEN

101031   Sgt   Pilot   British   213 Squadron

With 213 Squadron at Exeter in early July 1940.

Snowden destroyed a Bf 110 over Portland on August 11. His engine was set alight by return fire and he made a forced-landing on Lulworth range, in Hurricane P 3585, unhurt. He claimed a Ju 88 destroyed on August 25, a Bf 110 on September 15 and another Ju 88 on October 9.

Commissioned in June 1941, Snowden was released from the RAF in 1946, as a Flight Lieutenant. He died on November 20 1947.

PO 28.6.41   FO 28.6.42   FL 28.6.43

HAROLD JOHN SOARS

134228   Sgt   Pilot   British   74 Squadron

Joined 74 Squadron at Kirton-in-Lindsey on August 20 1940. On November 1 Soars was shot down in a surprise attack by Bf 109s during a patrol over Dover, in Spitfire P 7523, wounded. He was admitted to Victoria Hospital, Folkestone.

Soars was promoted to Warrant Officer on May 1 1942 and commissioned in October. He was released from the RAF in 1947, as a Flight Lieutenant. Soars served in the RAFVR from 1947 to 1955. He died in 1975.

PO 5.10.42   FO 5.4.43   FL 5.10.44   FO (RAFVR) 11.9.47

PHILIP ALFRED SOBEY

904838   Sgt   Air Gunner   British   235 Squadron

Joined 235 Squadron on August 22 1940.

Sobey was killed on November 9 1940, as a Sergeant with 69 Squadron, aged 22. He is remembered on the Runnymede Memorial, Panel 17.

JOHN FLEWELLING SODEN

42903   PO   Pilot   British   266 and 603 Squadrons

Soden joined the RAF on a short service commission in August 1939. He was with 266 Squadron at Wittering in early July 1940.

On August 15 Soden shared in destroying a He 115 floatplane. In combat with Bf 109s over Canterbury the next day his Spitfire, K 9864, was severely damaged and he made a forced-landing near Oare, Faversham, slightly wounded in the legs.

On September 16 Soden was posted to 603 Squadron at Hornchurch. He claimed Bf 109s destroyed on September 30 and October 10. Following a combat with Bf 109s over the Sussex coast on the 25th Soden baled out and injured his right leg landing at Perryfields. He was admitted to East Sussex Hospital, Hastings. His Spitfire, P 7325, crashed at Stonelink Farm, Brede.

Soden was lost in the troopship, SS 'Laconia', sunk on September 12 1942. He is remembered on the Alamein Memorial, Column 247.

APO 23.10.39   PO 2.6.40   FO 2.6.41   FL 2.6.42

JERZY JAKUB SOLAK

76766   PO   Pilot   Polish   151 and 249 Squadrons

Solak was born on August 22 1910. He joined 151 Squadron at Stapleford on August 28 1940 and moved to 249 Squadron at North Weald on September 27.

He was posted to 317 Squadron at Acklington at its formation on February 22 1941. Solak was awarded the KW (30.10.41) and posted away to 164 Squadron at Skeabrae on June 9 1942. He moved to 609 Squadron at Duxford on August 8, leaving the squadron on February 4 1943 to go to AFDU, also at Duxford.

On April 9 1943 Solak joined 41 Squadron at Hawkinge and on June 4 he destroyed a FW 190. He was posted away to HQ Fighter Command on October 12 1943 as Polish Liaison Officer. Solak was awarded two Bars to the KW (20.10.43). On April 4 1944 he went to HQ PAF and from May until August was flying with the 48th Fighter-Bomber Squadron, USAF.

Solak was posted to HQ 84 Group on May 29 1945, was awarded the VM (5th Class)(25.6.45) and released from the PAF in late 1946. He later went to live in the USA.

FO 1.3.41   FL 1.9.42

NEVILLE DAVID SOLOMON

79731   PO   Pilot   British   17 Squadron

Solomon was posted to 17 Squadron at Debden on July 19 1940. His experience was not considered suitable and he returned to 5 OTU, Aston Down on the 25th.

He returned to 17 on August 15 and was reported 'Missing' three days later, after an action with Bf 109s off Dover. His Hurricane, L 1921, crashed into the sea. Solomon was 26. He is buried in Pihen-les-Guines Cemetery, France.

PO 26.5.40

LAWRENCE CHARLES SONES

127803   **Sgt**   **Pilot**   **British**   **605 Squadron**

In 1932 Sones was a civil servant, when he enlisted in 601 Squadron, AuxAF as a wireless operator. When the RAFVR came into being in 1937 Sones left 601 to join it, as a Sergeant u/t pilot.

He did his flying training at 18 E&RFTS, Fair Oaks and had just been awarded his flying badge when war was declared. He was called to full-time service and after some weeks billeted at home Sones went to 4 EFTS, Brough for a flying instructor's course. He failed this and was sent to 3 ITW, Hastings.

On February 5 1940 Sones was posted to 14 FTS, Kinloss, to requalify as a pilot on low wing monoplanes. At the end of the course he went on leave with instructions to report to 5 OTU, Aston Down. When he arrived home a telegram was waiting, cancelling his leave and ordering him to report to 605 Squadron at Drem. Sones joined the squadron on June 18 1940.

By the end of October he was credited with one Bf 109 probably destroyed, another damaged and a Ju 88 shared. In December 1940 Sones was posted to 96 Squadron, then forming at Cranage. He was later with 258, 403 and 111 Squadrons. In April 1942 he went to 52 OTU, Aston Down as an air firing instructor and was commissioned from Warrant Officer in July. He joined 65 Squadron at Drem in October. In January 1943 the squadron was on HMS 'Argus', practicing deck landings and seeing how the RAF would cope on aircraft carriers. The experiment was not successful.

In May 1943 Sones went to North Africa and joined 93 Squadron at Souk-el-Khemis. He was later with 74 Squadron in Cyprus and Egypt. He returned to the UK in February 1944 and later went into Maintenance Command as a test pilot.

Sones was released from the RAF on September 13 1945, as a Flight Lieutenant. He returned to the Civil Service.

PO 11.7.42   FO 11.1.43   FL 11.7.44

GEORGE SOUTHALL

938291   **Sgt**   **Air Gunner**   **British**   **23 Squadron**

Southall, of Wolverhampton, joined 23 Squadron at Ford on October 5 1940.

He was a member of the crew of a Blenheim, which ran out of fuel returning from an offensive night patrol over France on December 22 and crashed into the Channel off the Isle of Wight. The three men on board baled out.

Southall landed in the sea and was drowned. His body was washed ashore on the Isle of Wight. He was 20 and is buried in St Philip's churchyard, Pennfields, Wolverhampton.

GEORGE ALBERT SOUTHORN

149124   **Sgt**   **Observer**   **British**   **235 Squadron**

Born on August 21 1911, Southorn joined the RAFVR on April 4 1939 as a trainee observer. He was called up on September 1 and after training he joined 235 Squadron at Bircham Newton on August 18 1940.

Southorn was posted to 272 Squadron at Aldergrove on November 20. He went to the Overseas Aircraft Delivery Flight at Kemble on January 18 1941 and flew from Tangmere on his way to join 69 Squadron in Malta on March 12.

Tour-expired, Southorn went as an instructor to 223 Squadron at Shandur, Egypt on October 4 1941, then operating as an OTU. He went down to South Africa on January 27 1942 to instruct at 45 Air School, Oudtshoorn. On September 12 he went to 65 Air School, Capetown for a Senior Armament Instructor's course, after which he returned to Oudtshoorn. He was promoted to Warrant Officer on October 1 1942.

Commissioned in April 1943, Southorn was sent to HQ 25

Group, Port Elizabeth on November 1, to the Central Examination Board to take charge of all examinations on bombing and gunnery. In mid-May 1944 Southorn was posted back to the UK, arriving in mid-August. He was posted to the Empire Air Armanent School at Manby for a Specialist Armament Officer's course and sat the final examination the day after the war finished.

Southorn was released from the RAF later in 1945, as a Flight Lieutenant.

PO 24.4.43   FO 24.10.43   FL 24.4.45

JOHN SYDNEY SOUTHWELL

41959   **PO**   **Pilot**   **British**   **245 Squadron**

Joined the RAF on a short service commission in February 1939. After completing his training Southwell joined the newly-reformed 245 Squadron at Leconfield on November 6 1939.

Over Dunkirk on May 30 1940 Southwell probably destroyed a Do 17 and on June 1 he destroyed two Bf 109s.

In early 1941 Southwell was with 274 Squadron in the Western Desert. On March 17 a flight of the squadron was detached to Malta to reinforce 261 Squadron.

On March 22 eight Hurricanes of 261 took off to meet ten Ju 88s approaching Grand Harbour with a Bf 109 escort. In the ensuing engagement five of the Hurricanes were shot down, including V 7799, flown by Southwell. All five pilots were lost.

Southwell is buried in Capuccini Naval Cemetery, Malta.

APO 15.4.39   PO 6.11.39   FO 6.11.40

ARTHUR WILLIAM PETER SPEARS

50686   **Sgt**   **Pilot**   **British**   **222 Squadron, 421 Flight**

Spears was born on December 13 1915, a nephew of James McCudden VC. He joined the RAF in January 1932 as an aircraft apprentice. He wanted to be a Fitter Aero Engine but instead became a Metal Rigger. After qualifying at the end of 1934 Spears was posted to 3 Squadron at Kenley, as a Fitter II.

In October 1935 Spears went with the squadron to Khartoum, returning to Kenley in August 1936. He was promoted to LAC after passing a trade test in early 1937. Spears volunteered for pilot training, was selected and in June 1939 he was posted to 13 E&RFTS, White Waltham for his ab initio course. In August Spears went to Uxbridge to await a posting and on September 2 he was sent to 12 FTS, Grantham, where he flew Harts and later Ansons. In February 1940 he was posted to Jurby for a bombing course, after which he returned to Grantham.

In March 1940 Spears went to the Pilots Pool at Aston Down, the forerunner of 5 OTU. He converted to Blenheims and then joined 222 Squadron at Duxford on March 31. The squadron was then re-equipping with Spitfires. Spears flew one for the first time after a short reading of the Pilot's Notes.

On August 30 he was shot down in combat with Bf 109s. He baled out and was taken by the Army to Eastchurch. His Spitfire, P 9323, crashed at South Lees Farm, Minster, Sheppey. Spears was bombed at Eastchurch the next morning. He made his way back to Hornchurch by Underground, via Charing Cross.

On October 4 Spears was posted to 421 Flight at Hawkinge and remained with it when it was renumbered 91 Squadron on January 11 1941. Spears was shot down by Adolf Galland over Kent on April 4 1941, his 58th victory. He was admitted to hospital in Deal with shell splinters in the right arm and bullets in the leg. Spears lost his flying category and was attached to Redhill in September 1941 as Duty Pilot, on flying control. After a week he was posted to Croydon, in the Control Tower.

Spears regained his category and was attached to the ADF at Croydon. He was commissioned from Warrant Officer in October 1942. A year later he went to Heston to command the Station Flight.

AWP Spears (continued)

In July 1944 Spears was posted to the Communications Squadron, Allied Expeditionary Forces. He flew VIPs around and later became personal pilot to Air Vice-Marshal HEP Wigglesworth.

After the war Spears transferred to the Engineer Branch. He retired on December 13 1970, as a Squadron Leader.

PO 16.10.42   FO 16.4.43   FL 16.10.44   FL 16.4.46
SL 1.7.54

HUGH SPEKE

90223   FL   Pilot   British   604 Squadron

Joined 604 Squadron, AuxAF in 1937. Speke was called to full-time service on August 24 1939 and was with 604 at Northolt in early July 1940.

On August 24 he was captain of a Blenheim which crashed near Odiham during a night patrol, cause unknown. Speke and his gunner, Sergeant HJS Shirley, were both unhurt.

On December 12 Speke, flying with Sergeant AK Sandifer, damaged a He 111 at night. He received a Mention in Despatches in March 1941. On July 7 he destroyed a Ju 88, one of a force raiding Middle Wallop by night and on the 8th he destroyed another enemy aircraft.

Speke was killed on July 26 1941, when he crashed near Upavon, Wiltshire. He was 27 and is buried in St Andrew's churchyard, Dowlish Wake, Somerset. Speke was awarded the DFC (29.7.41), credited with destroying four and damaging at least two enemy aircraft by night.

PO (AuxAF) 10.7.37   FO 24.8.39   FL 3.9.40

DOUGLAS JAMES SPENCE

42445   PO   Pilot   New Zealander   245 Squadron

Born in Christchurch on August 26 1920, Spence worked for an insurance company. In early 1939 he applied for a short service commission in the RAF and after provisional acceptance he sailed for the UK in the RMS 'Rangitane' on May 6.

Spence began his ab initio course at 10 E&RFTS, Yatesbury on June 12 1939. After a short induction course at Uxbridge he was posted to 2 FTS, Brize Norton on August 19, joined an ADU in February 1940 and began ferrying aircraft to France.

On April 6 Spence was posted to 245 Squadron at Leconfield. The squadron became operational with Hurricanes in May and moved soon afterwards to Drem. Later in the month 245 was detached to Hawkinge and began patrols over France and the Channel. After Dunkirk it went north to Turnhouse for a rest. In June it returned to Hawkinge and on the 20th Spence took part in a low-level attack on Rouen aerodrome, which left many enemy aircraft destroyed or damaged on the ground. In July 245 moved to Aldergrove, for the defence of Belfast, and remained there throughout the Battle of Britain.

In December 1940 Spence was posted to the Middle East and joined 274 Squadron in the Western Desert. On April 11 he shared in shooting down a Cant Z 1007 into the sea, on the 19th he destroyed a Ju 88 and a Bf 109 and on the 21st another Bf 109. In this combat Spence got so close that he collided with the enemy fighter. He managed to glide his damaged Hurricane back to the British lines and then returned to his squadron in a Blenheim. It is believed that the two Bf 109s shot down by Spence were flown by the same pilot, Leutnant Schroer.

On April 30 1941 274 Squadron carried out ground strafing operations and during one of these Spence was shot down and killed by Oberleutnant Redlich of 1/JG 27 whilst he was making a low-level attack on enemy columns between Gazala and Sollum.

Spence is buried in Tobruk War Cemetery.

APO 5.8.39   PO 6.4.40   FO 6.4.41

DESMOND GERARD HEATH SPENCER

34114   SL   Pilot   British   266 Squadron

Born in London on March 18 1912, Spencer was educated at Harrow. In 1932 he was commissioned as a 2nd Lieutenant in the Supplementary Reserve of the Duke of Cornwall's Light Infantry. He was in Gibraltar with the 2nd Battalion in 1933.

Spencer transferred to the RAF on a short service commission in September 1933. On October 10 he was posted to 3 FTS, Grantham and with training completed joined 16 (Army Co-operation) Squadron at Old Sarum on September 2 1934. Spencer was posted to 5 (Army Co-operation) Squadron at Chaklala, Rawalpindi on March 14 1935. The squadron was at Quetta when the earthquake came and Spencer was buried for a short time. Some 60 RAF men were killed and about 60 invalided home. At Risalpur the squadron took part in the Mohmand operations in 1935 and later the Hazara operations. Spencer was awarded the old India General Service medal and clasp. After operating from Miranshah in Waziristan he was awarded the new India General Service Medal and clasp.

On May 16 1937 Spencer was posted to the Air Staff at HQ RAF India. He went to No 1 (Indian) Group at Peshawar, controlling further frontier operations. He was made an MBE (1.1.40). In August 1939 Spencer returned to the UK and joined the staff at 6 FTS, Little Rissington. He was appointed to the Air Staff at HQ British Air Forces in France at Coulomiers in January 1940.

Spencer returned to England on June 13. He was attached to 266 Squadron at Wittering on July 25, took command on August 18 and was posted away in mid-September.

From 1942 to 1944 Spencer was at Air HQ Eastern Mediterranean as Group Captain Ops and in 1945 was SASO in Jerusalem. He was made a CBE (1.1.65) and retired from the RAF on March 22 1967, as a Group Captain.

APO 22.9.33   PO 22.9.34   FO 22.4.36   FL 22.4.38
SL 1.3.40   WC 1.3.42   WC 1.10.46   GC 1.7.61

GORDON HAMILTON SPENCER

54684   Sgt   Pilot   British   504 Squadron

Posted from 46 Squadron to 504 Squadron at Digby in September 1940.

Spencer served with the squadron throughout the Battle of Britain. He was promoted to Warrant Officer on October 1 1941 and commissioned in March 1944. Spencer was released from the RAF in 1947, as a Flight Lieutenant.

PO 18.3.44   FO 18.9.44   FL 18.3.46

AUBREY SPIERS

749478   Sgt   Aircrew   British   236 Squadron

Served with 236 Squadron from May to October 1940.

Spiers was released from the RAF as a Warrant Officer. He died in 1988.

JOHN HENRY SPIRES

121239   Sgt   Aircrew   British   235 Squadron

With 235 Squadron in early July 1940.

Spires was awarded the DFM (17.6.41), as a Sergeant with 69 Squadron. Commissioned in May 1942, he was awarded the DFC (7.11.44), as a Flight Lieutenant. He was released from the RAF in 1946 and commissioned in the RAFVR. Spires was released in 1947.

PO 1.5.42   FO 1.11.42   FL 1.5.44   PO (RAFVR) 1.7.46

HENRY ARNOLD SPRAGUE

C 1365   PO   Pilot   Canadian   3 Squadron

Sprague, of Port Nelson, British Columbia, joined the RCAF on November 6 1939. He did his elementary flying training at EFTS, Calgary, moved to 1 FTS, Camp Borden on February 1 1940 and then to ATS at Trenton on May 21.

Sprague was posted to the UK and joined 112 (RCAF) Squadron at High Post on September 10 1940. He left the squadron on the 19th and four days later was at 6 OTU, Sutton Bridge to convert to Hurricanes, after which he joined 3 Squadron at Castletown on October 10.

He was posted away to Squires Gate on December 27 to join the newly-formed 96 Squadron. On February 6 1941 Sprague went to No 1 (RCAF) Squadron at Castletown, later re-numbered 401 Squadron. On July 31 he moved to 56 Squadron at Duxford.

After rejoining 401 Squadron at Biggin Hill on September 19 1941 Sprague was shot down on November 22 and captured. He was freed in May 1945, returned to Canada and was released from the RCAF on August 23, as a Flight Lieutenant.

MERVYN HERBERT SPRAGUE

741141   Sgt   Pilot   British   602 Squadron

Born on May 27 1910 in Richmond, Surrey, Sprague served in the RAF 'F' Reserve from May 13 1935 until May 14 1938 when he joined the RAFVR as a u/t pilot.

Called to full-time service at the outbreak of war, Sprague was posted to 4 EFTS, Brough on October 7 1939. He went to 3 ITW, Hastings on November 6 and then to 14 FTS, Kinloss on February 5 1940, moving to Cranfield on April 18.

Sprague joined 602 Squadron at Drem on June 18. He was shot down in combat with enemy fighters on August 25. He baled out, unhurt, and was rescued from the sea. His Spitfire, N 3226, crashed into the sea off Portland.

On September 11 Sprague was shot down and killed in combat with Bf 110s south of Selsey Bill. His Spitfire, N 3282, crashed into the Channel. Sprague's body was washed ashore at Brighton on October 10. He is buried in St Andrew's churchyard, Tangmere.

WILLIAM PATERSON SPRENGER

C 895   FO   Pilot   Canadian   1 (RCAF) Squadron

Sprenger was born at North Bay, Ontario on July 13 1911. He joined the RCAF on October 1 1938 and was with No 1 (RCAF) Squadron when it arrived in the UK on June 20 1940.

On August 31 Sprenger was shot down by Bf 109s in combat over Cranbrook. He baled out, unhurt, and landed at Little Bay Court, Ulcombe. His Hurricane, P 3858, crashed and burned out at Upper Street, Broomfield. On September 27 he made a forced-landing at Kenley after his aircraft was damaged in combat over north Kent.

Sprenger was killed on November 26 1940 when he crashed beside Loch Lomond during an anti-aircraft co-operation flight, cause unknown.

He is buried in Vale of Leven Cemetery, Bonhill, Dumbarton, Scotland.

ROBERT LAWRENCE SPURDLE

44230   PO   Pilot   New Zealander   74 Squadron

Born in Wanganui on March 3 1918, Spurdle was at Wanganui Collegiate School from 1932 to 1934. In early 1939 he applied for a short service commission in the RNZAF, was provisionally accepted in July and reported to Rongotai for ground training on September 20. He was on the 11th Short Service Course, the last one of the scheme.

Spurdle went to No 1 EFTS, Taieri for his ab initio course on October 21 and moved on to No 1 FTS, Wigram on December 18. He was selected for training as a light bomber pilot but was held back because of sickness and completed his training with No 13 (War) Course.

On June 7 1940 Spurdle sailed for the UK in the RMS 'Rangitata'. He was posted to 7 OTU, Hawarden on August 4 and after converting to Spitfires joined 74 Squadron at Kirton-in-Lindsey on the 21st. Spurdle damaged a He 111 on September 14. Whilst chasing a Bf 109 on October 22 Spurdle's Spitfire broke up in a high speed dive and he baled out, unhurt. Although attacked by enemy aircraft during the descent he landed safely. The Spitfire, P 7364, crashed at Hadlow Place, near Tonbridge.

On October 31 1940 Spurdle claimed a Bf 109 as probably destroyed, on November 2 a Bf 109 destroyed, on the 14th a Ju 87 probably destroyed and two others damaged, on December 5 a Bf 109 destroyed, on March 3 1941 two Bf 109s destroyed and one damaged, on the 24th he shared in probably destroying a Ju 88 and on April 6 he claimed a Bf 110 probably destroyed and a Bf 109 damaged.

On April 14 1941 Spurdle was posted to 91 Squadron at Hawkinge. He probably destroyed a Bf 109 on May 7 and damaged another on the 18th. He left 91 on May 23 to join the MSFU at Speke. During his time with the unit Spurdle made two trips to the USA, in the Camships, 'Novelist' and 'Eastern City'.

In February 1942 Spurdle rejoined 91 Squadron and was appointed 'A' Flight Commander in April. He destroyed a Bf 109 on July 25 and shot a FW 190 down into the sea on the 26th. He was awarded the DFC (14.8.42) and posted to Malta but was found to be 'operationally tired' and went instead to 116 Squadron at Heston on anti-aircraft co-operation duties.

In November 1942 Spurdle sailed for New Zealand, via the USA, for attachment to the RNZAF. He was posted to Ohakea, where he started the Camera Gun Assessing School at 2 Observers' Training School. In late May 1943 Spurdle was appointed 'A' Flight Commander in 16 Squadron, then preparing for its first overseas tour at Woodbourne.

On June 19 the squadron was flown to Santo, in the New Hebrides, in transport aircraft and began operations under American Interceptor Command. It moved to the Solomons in mid-July and began operations from Guadalcanal. On August 13 Spurdle destroyed a 'Hap' and on the 26th a 'Zeke'. The squadron was relieved in mid-September and returned to New Zealand.

Spurdle left for the UK in December, in the 'Umgeni', going via Melbourne, Ceylon, the Suez Canal and Gibraltar. He disembarked on March 26 1944. His attachment to the RNZAF ceased and he joined the newly-reformed 130 Squadron at Lympne on April 13. Three weeks later he was posted to 80 Squadron at Hornchurch. Spurdle was appointed a Flight Commander on May 25 and took command of the squadron on July 20.

At the end of September 1944 the squadron crossed to the Continent and on October 8 it joined 122 Wing at Volkel, in Holland. On an offensive patrol on December 8 Spurdle damaged two Ju 188s, his final aerial encounter with the Luftwaffe. He was posted to HQ 83 Group on January 15 1945 and awarded a Bar to the DFC (26.1.45).

Spurdle was given training in radio work and on March 24 flew across the Rhine in a glider in the second airborne crossing, as OC three RAF radio teams. The gliders landed at Wesel with serious casualties and were relieved by the Army after five days. Spurdle was later with the 11th Armoured Division, working in a radio tank

RL Spurdle (continued)

controlling 'cab rank' fighter support. He was on the Elbe river when the war ended.

On July 18 1945 Spurdle was posted to CGS, Catfoss for a Pilot Attack Instructor's course. On the 21st he transferred to the RNZAF, relinquishing his RAF commission. He sailed for New Zealand in late September in the RMS 'Rangitata', the same ship which had taken him to the UK five years earlier. Spurdle went on to the Reserve on April 18 1946, as a Squadron Leader.

APO 20.9.39   PO 20.7.40   FO 20.10.41   FL 20.10.42

RICHARD ALFRED SPYER

745513   Sgt   Pilot   British   607 Squadron

Spyer, of Worcester Park, Surrey, was with 607 Squadron at Usworth in early July 1940.

On September 9 Spyer crashed at Stilstead Farm, East Peckham during a combat with Do 17s and Bf 109s, in Hurricane P 2680, slightly wounded.

In early November 1940 Spyer sailed in HMS 'Argus' for the Mediterranean. On the 17th he was in the first flight of six Hurricanes to take off for Malta, led by Flight Lieutenant JAF MacLachlan. Spyer's Hurricane, V 7413, ran out of fuel and he baled out into the sea. MacLachlan called in the Sunderland, which was leading them to Malta, and it landed and picked up Spyer.

He joined 261 Squadron at Ta Kali. On March 22 1941 eight Hurricanes of 261 took off to meet ten Ju 88s approaching Grand Harbour with a Bf 109 escort. In the ensuing engagement five of the Hurricanes were shot down, including V 7672, flown by Spyer. All five pilots were lost.

Spyer was 23. He is remembered on the Malta Memorial, Panel 2, Column 1.

JOHN WILLIAM COPOUS SQUIER

125762   Sgt   Pilot   British   64 Squadron

Joined the RAFVR at Southend on April 19 1939. Squier carried out his week-end flying at 34 E&RFTS, Rochford. Called to full-time service at the outbreak of war, he was posted to 4 ITW, Bexhill on October 30 1939.

Squier went to 10 FTS, Tern Hill on December 9 and completed the course there on June 30 1940. He was then posted to 5 OTU, Aston Down on July 6 and after converting to Spitfires joined 64 Squadron at Kenley on the 28th.

Squier made a forced-landing at Couldham, Capel-le-Ferne on August 8, possibly the victim of a surprise attack by Hauptmann Trautloft of lll/JG 51. He was admitted to Canterbury Hospital, severely injured. Transferred to Queen Victoria Hospital, East Grinstead on August 15, Squier underwent plastic surgery there, becoming a Guinea Pig.

He was discharged from hospital on November 14 and rejoined 64 Squadron, then at Hornchurch. Squier was posted to 72 Squadron at Coltishall on the 22nd, joined 603 Squadron at Drem on December 20 and moved to 141 Squadron at Gravesend on the 30th.

Squier left 141 on February 27 1941 to become a test pilot. He was at 5 MU, Kemble until April 3, at 33 OTU, Lyneham until March 20 1942 and at 48 MU, Hawarden until May 12 1943. Whilst there he was commissioned from Warrant Officer in June 1942. Squier was at 51 MU, Lichfield from August 12 1945 until August 30 1946, when he was released from the RAF, as a Flight Lieutenant.

On September 1 1946 he became a test pilot with English Electric and later BAC. He ejected from the first two-seater Lightning on October 1 1959 at 1.7 Mach at 40000 feet, the first supersonic ejectee. Squier stopped test flying on December 31 1966 and retired from BAC and British Aerospace on December 31 1983.

PO 15.6.42   FO 15.12.42   FL 15.6.44
FO (RAFVR) 23.9.45

NOEL MIZPAH STANGER

NZ 39943   Sgt   Observer   New Zealander   235 Sqdn

Stanger was born in Herbert, North Otago on December 24 1916. After leaving school he was employed by a sheep farmer in Oamaru.

He was provisionally accepted for a short service commission in the RNZAF in April 1939 but the scheme was allowed to lapse and he was not called. Stanger volunteered for aircrew duties at the outbreak of war and reported as a trainee pilot to the Ground Training School at Weraroa on October 26 1939. He went to No 1 EFTS, Taieri on November 21 and moved on to No 1 FTS, Wigram on January 15 1940.

Things did not go well and Stanger ceased pilot training and remustered as a u/t Observer. On February 13 he began a course at the Air Observers' School, Ohakea, was awarded his brevet at the end of May, promoted to Sergeant and on June 7 he sailed in the RMS 'Rangitata' for the UK.

Stanger was posted to 17 OTU, Upwood on July 30 and he joined 106 Squadron at Finningley on October 2 but nine days later moved to 235 Squadron at Bircham Newton. On February 14 1941 Stanger was a member of the crew of a Blenheim which took off on a non-operational flight. The aircraft was under control but with engines misfiring badly and finally cutting out altogether. It did a gliding turn, straightened out, then lost height and crashed one mile north of Croxton. It had apparently run out of fuel. All three men on board were killed.

Stanger is buried in Bilton St Mark's churchyard, Rugby.

DONALD ARTHUR STANLEY

83271   PO   Pilot   British   64 Squadron

Stanley, of Muswell Hill, Middlesex, joined 64 squadron at Leconfield in late September 1940.

He was killed on February 25 1941, as a Pilot Officer with 611 Squadron, aged 19. Stanley is remembered on the Runnymede Memorial, Panel 34.

PO 10.8.40

DOUGLAS OWEN STANLEY

NZ 39944   Sgt   Pilot   New Zealander   151 Squadron

Stanley was born in Tirau on July 12 1916. He learned to fly privately in 1938 and in March 1939 enrolled in the Civil Reserve of Pilots, carrying out the required training at the Waikato Aero Club, Hamilton.

At the outbreak of war Stanley volunteered for service and reported to the Ground Training School, Weraroa on October 20 1939. A month later he was posted to 2 EFTS, New Plymouth, moving on to 2 FTS, Woodbourne on January 15 1940.

Awarded his flying badge on April 23, Stanley completed the course at the end of June and sailed for the UK in the RMS 'Rangitane' on July 12. He was posted to 6 OTU, Sutton Bridge on September 11 and after converting to Hurricanes he joined 151 Squadron at Wittering on the 30th.

In the evening of October 26 1940 Stanley was one of a group of pilots practising night circuits and landings at Coleby Grange, a satellite of Digby. At 20.40 hrs he took off and crashed 500 yards beyond the windward boundary of the airfield. The Hurricane, V 7434, caught fire. Stanley was taken from the wreckage and admitted to Lincoln County Hospital, where he died the same night.

Stanley is buried in Scopwick Burial Ground, Lincolnshire. A local remembrance of him is to be found at Achilles Point, Auckland, New Zealand. A seat there bears the inscription, 'Presented to the citizens of Auckland by Private JE (Ted) Scherer in memory of his friend Sergeant-Pilot Douglas O Stanley, of Matamata, who lost his life in England 26 October 1940'. A second seat there had this inscription, 'AH Scherer Esq. In fulfillment of his son's wish. Private JE (Ted) Scherer Killed in action in Italy 10 April 1945.'

NOEL KARL STANSFELD

42272   PO   Pilot   Canadian   242 and 229 Squadrons

Born in Edmonton, Alberta in 1915, Stansfeld joined the RAF on a short service commission in April 1939. He did his ab initio course at 3 E&RFTS, Brough and his intermediate and advanced flying at 8 FTS, Montrose.

Stansfeld was posted to 242 Squadron at Church Fenton on February 3 1940. On a patrol over France on May 22 he shared in the destruction of a Hs 126. Over Dunkirk on May 31 he destroyed a Bf 110 and on June 1 probably destroyed a Ju 87. Stansfeld went to France with the squadron on June 8 and on the day it was withdrawn, the 18th, he destroyed a He 111.

On August 30 he shared a He 111, on September 7 claimed a Do 17 destroyed, on the 15th another Do 17 and a He 111 and on the 27th a Ju 88 probably destroyed. Stansfeld was posted to 229 Squadron on September 29. He was shot down the next day in combat with Bf 109s over Edenbridge and baled out, wounded. His Hurricane, N 2652, crashed at Ightham Place.

Stansfeld was awarded the DFC (8.10.40). He returned to Canada to be a flying instructor. He was back in the UK in 1943 and 1944, transferred to the RCAF on February 12 1945 and served in RAF Transport Command, ferrying troops to and from India.

After the war Stansfeld contracted tuberculosis and was invalided out of the RCAF in 1947.

APO 24.6.39   PO 27.12.39   FO 27.12.40   FL 27.12.41

LIONEL STAPLES

117410   Sgt   Pilot   British   151 Squadron

Joined 151 Squadron at Digby in October 1940.

Commissioned in February 1942, Staples was released from the RAF in 1945, as a Flight Lieutenant. He joined the RAFVR in 1947.

PO 28.2.42   FO 1.10.42   FL 28.2.44   FO (RAFVR) 13.8.47

MICHAEL EDMUND STAPLES

83242   PO   Pilot   British   609 Squadron

Staples, of Kent, joined 609 Squadron at Middle Wallop on July 8 1940. On August 12 he claimed a Bf 110 destroyed, on the 13th a Ju 87, on September 7 a probable Bf 110, on the 15th a shared Do 17, on the 24th a Do 17, on the 25th a probable Bf 110 and on the 29th and 30th Bf 109s.

On October 7 Staples was shot down in flames in a surprise attack by enemy fighters over Yeovil. He baled out, wounded, and was admitted to Blandford Hospital. His Spitfire, N 3231, crashed at Shotcombe Farm, Wynford Eagle. He did not return to 609.

Staples was killed on November 9 1941, as a Flying Officer with 604 Squadron. He crashed coming in to land at night at Colerne. He was 24 and is buried in Brookwood Military Cemetery, Woking.

PO 16.6.40   FO 16.6.41

ROBERT CHARLES JOHN STAPLES

48471   Sgt   Pilot   British   72 Squadron

Born on March 13 1914, Staples joined the RAF as a direct-entry for training as a Sergeant-Pilot. He began his elementary flying course at 6 E&RFTS, Sywell on October 17 1936, moved on to 6 FTS, Netheravon on February 6 1937 and with training completed he joined 72 Squadron at Church Fenton on September 4 1937.

Staples was still with the squadron in early July 1940. On August 6 he crashed on landing from a routine patrol, writing off Spitfire L 1078, cause unknown. Staples was involved in a mid-air collision

with Pilot Officer N Sutton on October 5. He managed to return to base but Sutton was killed.

On March 26 1941 Staples was posted to 58 OTU, Grangemouth as an instructor. He was with 65 Squadron at Westhampnett briefly in November 1941 but was then sent to 2 CFS, Dalcross on November 23 for an instructor's course. Staples was commissioned in January 1942 and posted to 2 FTS, Brize Norton on the 21st. He moved to 3 (P) AFU, Long Newton on July 29. From May 10 1943 he was with 1539 BAT Flight at South Cerney, and later Bibury.

On June 19 1944 Staples went to 1533 BAT Flight at Church Lawford and stayed there until October. He transferred to the Administrative and Special Duties Branch and became involved with mechanical transport. Staples was posted to Singapore in late 1945 and remained in the Far East until returning to the UK to retire from the RAF on March 26 1948, as a Flight Lieutenant. He died in 1986.

PO 12.1.42   FO 1.10.42   FL 12.1.44   FL 1.9.45

BASIL GERALD STAPLETON

41879   FO   Pilot   South African   603 Squadron

Joined the RAF on a short service commission in January 1939. Stapleton was with 603 Squadron from October 1939.

On July 3 1940 he shared in the destruction of a Ju 88, on the 20th shared a Do 17, on August 28 probably destroyed two Bf 109s, on the 31st probably destroyed another, on September 3 claimed a Do 17 destroyed and on the 5th a Bf 109. Stapleton made a forced-landed at Sutton Valence on the 7th, after a combat with enemy fighters over South London, unhurt.

On September 11 Stapleton claimed a Bf 110 probably destroyed, on the 15th a Do 17, on the 17th and 20th probable Bf 109s and on November 11 another Bf 109 probably destroyed. He was awarded the DFC (15.11.40).

Stapleton was posted away to HQ Fighter Command in March 1941, was with 257 in 1942, as a Flight Commander and in 1943 served with 2 ADF, Colerne.

From August to December 1944 Stapleton commanded 247 Squadron, operating on the Continent with Typhoons. He was released from the RAF in 1946, as a Squadron Leader, and returned to South Africa. His portrait was done by Cuthbert Orde in February 1941.

APO 1.4.39   PO 21.10.39   FO 21.10.40   FL 21.10.41

———— STARLL

No unknown   Sgt   Pilot   British   601 Squadron

No service details traced.

HAROLD MORLEY STARR

34181   SL   Pilot   British   245 and 253 Squadrons

Starr joined the RAF on a short service commission in March 1934. He was posted to 5 FTS, Sealand on April 3 and joined 13 (Army Co-operation) Squadron at Old Sarum on March 4 1935. He moved to 59 Squadron, also at Old Sarum, on June 28 1937 and then to 2 Squadron at Hawkinge on January 19 1938.

From July 21 1940 Starr was attached to 245 Squadron at Aldergrove. On August 8 he took command of 253 Squadron at Prestwick. The squadron moved south to Kenley on the 29th and the next day Starr's aircraft was damaged in combat over Redhill. He returned to Kenley, unhurt.

On August 31 Starr was shot down by enemy fighters during an interception patrol. He baled out and was machine-gunned by a Bf 109 on his way down. He fell dead at Hammill Brickworks, near

HM Starr (continued)

Eastry. His Hurricane, L 1830, is believed to have crashed near Grove Ferry.

Starr was 25. He is buried in Radnor Street Cemetery, Swindon, Wiltshire.

APO 16.3.34   PO 16.3.35   FO 16.10.36   FL 16.10.38
SL 1.6.40

CHARLES MICHAEL STAVERT

42538   PO   Pilot   British   1 and 504 Squadrons

Joined the RAF on a short service commission in June 1939. In early May 1940 Stavert joined No 1 Squadron in France. On the 18th he destroyed a Do 17 and a He 111, then ran out of fuel and made a forced-landing in a ploughed field. He returned to England when the squadron was withdrawn on June 17. On August 16 Stavert claimed a He 111 destroyed, on the 18th a shared Do 17, on September 5 a Ju 88 and on the 6th a probable Bf 109. He was posted to 504 Squadron at Hendon in mid-September.

Stavert was awarded the AFC (1.6.53) and retired from the RAF on August 10 1964, as a Squadron Leader.

APO 19.8.39   PO 28.2.40   FO 28.2.41   FL 28.2.42
FL 1.9.45   SL 1.7.53

DENNIS JAMES STEADMAN

62661   Sgt   Pilot   British   54 and 245 Squadrons

Steadman joined 54 Squadron at Hornchurch on August 22 1940 and was posted to 245 Squadron at Aldergrove on September 27.

Commissioned in March 1941, Steadman was released from the RAF in 1946, as a Flight Lieutenant.

PO 12.3.41   FO 12.3.42   FL 12.3.43

MICHAL JAN STEBOROWSKI

76794   FO   Pilot   Polish   238 Squadron

Joined 238 Squadron at Middle Wallop on August 5 1940. Steborowski claimed a Bf 110 destroyed on the 8th. He was shot down and killed on the 11th. His Hurricane, P 3819, crashed into the sea off Portland.

Steborowski was 31. He is remembered on the Polish Air Force Memorial at Northolt. He was awarded the KW (10.9.41).

RODNEY MURREY STEELE

139199   Sgt   Air Gunner   British   235 Squadron

Joined 235 Squadron on September 4 1940.

Commissioned in December 1942, Steele was released from the RAF in 1946, as a Flight Lieutenant. He died on February 8 1986.

PO 15.2.42   FO 15.6.43   FL 15.12.44

HARRY STEERE

46016   F/Sgt   Pilot   British   19 Squadron

Steere joined the RAF at Halton in 1930 as an aircraft apprentice. He later trained as a pilot and was with 19 Squadron before the war. On May 11 1940 he shared in the destruction of a Ju 88, the squadron's first victory.

Over Dunkirk on May 26 Steere destroyed a Ju 87, on the 27th probably destroyed a Do 17, on the 28th destroyed a Bf 109 and on June 1 a Bf 109 and a He 111. He was awarded the DFM (25.6.40).

On August 19 Steere shared a Bf 110, on September 9 he claimed a Bf 110 destroyed, on the 15th a Do 17, on the 18th a shared He 111 and a shared Ju 88, on the 27th a Bf 109 and on November 28 a Bf 110.

In late 1940 Steere was posted to 8 FTS, Montrose as an instructor. Commissioned in June 1941, he joined 627 Squadron at Oakington at its formation on November 12 1943, to operate in Mosquitos on Pathfinder duties.

Steere was killed on June 9 1944, as a Flight Lieutenant with 627, aged 30. He was shot down over Rennes and is buried in St Erblon Communal Cemetery, France. An award of the DFC (23.6.44) was gazetted after his death. Younger brother of J Steere.

PO 26.6.41   FO 1.4.42   FL 1.4.43

JACK STEERE

47746   F/Sgt   Pilot   British   72 Squadron

Born on January 16 1911, Steere joined the RAF at Halton in 1927 as an aircraft apprentice. After passing out in 1930, as a Rigger, he was posted to RAF Felixstowe. In 1932 Steere served with the FAA in HMS 'Glorious'.

He volunteered for pilot training and in 1934 was posted to 4 FTS, Abu Sueir. With the course completed he joined 23 Squadron at Biggin Hill in 1935. Steere served with 41 Squadron at Sheik Othman, Aden in 1936 and joined 72 Squadron at Tangmere at its formation on March 22 1937.

He took part in squadron operations over Dunkirk and throughout the Battle of Britain. He shared in destroying a He 111 on November 9. In 1941 Steere was posted away for an instructor's course. He was promoted to Warrant Officer on April 1 1941 and commissioned in January 1942. He instructed at CFS until 1946 and was awarded the AFC (13.6.46).

Steere retired from the RAF on July 16 1961, as a Squadron Leader. Elder brother of H Steere.

PO 5.1.42   FO 1.10.42   FL 5.1.44   FL 1.9.45
SL 1.7.54

JAN STEFAN

184904   Sgt   Pilot   Czechoslovakian   1 Squadron

Joined No 1 Squadron at Wittering on October 6 1940.

On April 7 1941 Stefan destroyed a Bf 109 as it prepared to take off from Berck airfield.

Commissioned in October 1944, Stefan was released from the RAF after the war as a Flying Officer.

PO 16.10.44   FO 16.2.45

STEFAN STEGMAN

76711   PO   Pilot   Polish   229 Squadron

Born on October 15 1910. Stegman joined 229 Squadron at Northolt on September 26 1940. He was posted to the newly-formed 316 Squadron at Pembrey on March 22 1941.

Tour-expired, Stegman went to 58 OTU, Grangemouth on November 28 1941 as an instructor. He rejoined 316, then at Heston, on May 15 1942. He was awarded the KW (15.11.42). Stegman was appointed a Flight Commander on March 14 1943.

He was shot down in a combat over the sea near the Belgian coast on June 17 1943, in Spitfire BR 143. His body was washed up on July 3 and he is buried in Ostende Communal Cemetery. Stegman was awarded a Bar to the KW (20.10.43).

PO 1.3.41   FO 1.3.42   FL 1.3.43

JOSEF STEHLIK

104693   Sgt   Pilot   Czechoslovakian   312 Squadron

Stehlik was a Sergeant-Chef in III/3 Groupe de Chasse in l'Armée de l'Air. He was credited with eight victories in the fighting in France in 1940.

He joined the newly-formed 312 Squadron at Duxford on September 5 1940 and on October 8 shared in the destruction of a Ju 88.

Commissioned in August 1941, Stehlik was released from the RAF after the war, as a Flight Lieutenant.

PO 6.8.41   FO 6.8.42   FL 6.8.43

DAVID STEIN

84299   PO   Pilot   British   263 Squadron

Joined 263 Squadron at Grangemouth on August 1 1940. Stein was on a routine night training flight on the 24th when his aircraft caught fire. He baled out over Grangemouth Docks and was arrested on landing but later released. His Hurricane, L 1803, crashed and burned out.

Stein was killed on October 30 1941, as a Flying Officer with 263. He is remembered on the Runnymede Memorial, Panel 30.

PO 27.7.40   FO 27.7.41

HARBOURNE MACKAY STEPHEN

78851   PO   Pilot   British   74 Squadron

Stephen was born in Elgin on April 18 1916 and educated at Shrewsbury. His first job was copy boy with Allied Newspapers and later he moved to the advertising staff of the Evening Standard. Stephen joined the RAFVR in 1937 and learned to fly at 13 E&RFTS, White Waltham. Having achieved the required standard and number of flying hours Stephen was offered the chance to train with the regular RAF for six months and was given six months leave of absence from his job.

He began training at 11 Group Fighter Pool at St Athan, the forerunner of OTU, and finished the course as war broke out. He was posted to 605 Squadron at Tangmere, as a Sergeant Pilot. On March 28 1940 Stephen was flying in Yellow Section when an He 111 was sighted, 605's first encounter with the Luftwaffe. The section leader damaged the enemy bomber and 43 Squadron later shot it down.

Commissioned in early April, Stephen was posted to 74 Squadron at Hornchurch on the 10th. Over Dunkirk on May 24 he shared in destroying a Hs 126 and a Do 17, on the 26th shared another Hs 126 and on the 27th destroyed a Bf 109 and a Do 17.

Stephen claimed a Bf 109 destroyed on July 28, two Bf 110s, three Bf 109s and another probable on August 11 and a probable Do 17 on the 13th. He was awarded the DFC (27.8.40). On September 11 he claimed a Ju 88, on October 5 a shared Do 17, on October 20 and 27 Bf 109s and on November 14 three Ju 87s. Stephen was awarded a Bar to the DFC (15.11.40). He shared Bf 109s on November 17 and 30, probably destroyed a Bf 109 on December 2 and destroyed another Bf 109 and shared a second on the 5th. He was awarded the DSO (24.12.40).

On January 11 1941 Stephen was posted away to 59 OTU, Turnhouse as CFI but this was altered to secondment to the RAE, Farnborough. In June 1941 Stephen was posted to Portreath to help form 130 Squadron. He took command of 234 Squadron at Warmwell in late July and led the squadron until early 1942, when he was posted to the Far East.

Stephen was Wing Leader at Dum Dum and then Jessore, he later commanded 166 Fighter Wing, went to HQ 224 Group, Fighter Ops and then to Air Command South East Asia, as Ops A. He was released from the RAF in 1945, as a Wing Commander.

He returned to newspapers, becoming General Manager Sunday Express in 1958, General Manager Sunday Graphic 1960 and Managing Director Daily Telegraph and Sunday Telegraph in 1963. Stephen commanded 602 Squadron, RAuxAF from 1950 to 1952. His portrait was done by Eric Kennington and Cuthbert Orde.

PO 1.4.40   FO 1.4.41   FL 7.11.41   SL 14.7.43
SL (RAuxAF) 1.9.50

CYRIL STEPHENS

531100   Sgt   Air Gunner   British   23 Squadron

Stephens, of Pencoed, was with 23 Squadron in early July 1940. On August 8 he was in Blenheim L 1448 which crashed near Peterborough on a night patrol, cause unknown but believed to be loss of control. Both men on board were killed.

Stephens was 24. He is buried in St Gallo churchyard, Coychurch Lower, Glamorganshire.

MAURICE MICHAEL STEPHENS

33522   FO   Pilot   British   3 and 232 Squadrons

Born at Ranchi, India on October 20 1919, Stephens was educated at Mayfield College, Sussex. He entered RAF College, Cranwell in September 1938. The course was shortened because of the war and Stephens graduated in December 1939 and joined 3 Squadron at Hawkinge in January 1940.

On May 10 the squadron went to France. Stephens destroyed two Ju 87s on the 12th, a Ju 87 and a Bf 109 on the 14th, was appointed a Flight Commander on the 18th and destroyed a Do 17 on the 20th. The squadron was withdrawn to Kenley on the 25th and went north to Wick. Stephens was awarded the DFC and Bar (31.5.40).

In July 1940 Stephens' flight moved to Sumburgh and was renumbered 232 Squadron on the 17th and he was promoted to take command. On August 23 he shared in destroying a He 111 eight miles west of Fair Isle, the squadron's first victory. Stephens was posted away on September 30 1940. In December he volunteered for Greece and embarked on HMS 'Furious'. On arrival in the Middle East he was diverted to the Western Desert and attached to 274 Squadron on February 5 1941. After a while Stephens was posted to Turkey and flew with a Turkish Hurricane Squadron near the Bulgarian border.

He returned to the Western Desert in November 1941, to command 80 Squadron. On December 9 Stephens was shot down in flames, wounded in both feet. He was about to bale out when the aircraft who had attacked him, probably an Mc 202, flew past. Stephens slipped back into the cockpit and shot it down. He then baled out and was picked up by Polish troops, who took him to Tobruk. Stephens was awarded the DSO (20.1.42).

Fit again in March 1942, he was posted to HQ RAF East Africa at Nairobi. In August 1942 he returned to the Middle East and was attached to the US 57th Pursuit Group, training on P40s in Palestine. Stephens volunteered for Malta and was posted to 249 Squadron at Ta Kali in early October. He probably destroyed a Bf 109 on the 10th, destroyed another and shared a second on the 12th and destroyed a Ju 88, a Mc 202 and shared another on the 13th.

Stephens took command of 229 Squadron on the 14th and on that day claimed a Reggiane 2001 destroyed and on the 15th a Bf 109 and a Ju 88. He was awarded a second Bar to the DFC (3.11.42). In November 1942 Stephens took command of the Hal Far Wing. He returned to the UK in June 1943 and went on a course at the Empire Central Flying School, Hullavington, after which he was appointed CFI at 3 OTU in January 1944. Stephens went to the USA in April 1945 on liaison duties.

He retired from the RAF on November 10 1960, as a Group Captain.

PO 23.12.39   FO 20.8.40   FL 1.7.41   SL 6.2.43
SL 1.7.43   WC 1.7.50   GC 1.7.58

IAN RAITT STEPHENSON

72010   FO   Pilot   British   264 Squadron

Stephenson, of South Croydon, Surrey, was commissioned in the RAFVR in November 1937. He was called to full-time service in September 1939 and was with 264 Squadron in early July 1940.

On August 26 Stephenson was shot down by Bf 109s and baled out. He was rescued from the sea, injured, landed at Herne Bay and admitted to Canterbury Hospital. The Defiant, L 7025, crashed into the sea two miles off Herne Bay. The gunner, Sergeant W Maxwell, was not seen again.

Stephenson commanded 406 Squadron at Kenley from March to August 1943. He took command of 153 Squadron at Reghaia, Italy in September. Stephenson was killed on November 26 1943, as a Wing Commander, aged 26. He is remembered on the Malta Memorial, Panel 6, Column 1.

PO (RAFVR) 9.11.37   FO 11.9.39   FL 20.4.41   SL 1.6.42

PATRICK JOSEPH THOMAS STEPHENSON

81343   PO   Pilot   British   607 Squadron

Stephenson was born on August 25 1918. He joined 607 Squadron at Usworth in early July 1940.

On September 15 he collided with a Do 17 over Appledore. Stephenson baled out, slightly wounded by return fire. The Do 17 crashed and exploded at Combwell Wood, Kilndown, near Goudhurst.

In June 1941 Stephenson was instructing at 53 OTU, Heston. He commanded 607 Squadron in India and Burma from April 1943 to March 1944. He was awarded the DFC (10.9.43).

Stephenson retired from the RAF on July 31 1955, as a Squadron Leader.

PO 18.6.40   FO 18.6.41   FL 18.6.42   SL 1.9.45

STANLEY PHILIP STEPHENSON

40439   FO   Pilot   British   85 Squadron

Joined the RAF on a short service commission in November 1937. Stephenson was posted to 2 FTS, Brize Norton on January 9 1938 and joined 85 Squadron at Debden on August 20.

Stephenson was still with the squadron at the start of the Battle of Britain and was posted away on August 4 1940. He was released from the RAF in 1947, as a Squadron Leader.

APO 9.1.38   PO 25.10.38   FO 25.5.40   FL 25.5.41
SL 1.7.44

JAROSLAV STERBACEK

81901   PO   Pilot   Czechoslovakian   310 Squadron

Born on February 12 1913. Sterbacek joined 310 Squadron at Duxford on August 31 1940. He was shot down the same day by Bf 109s whilst he was attacking Do 17s over the Thames Estuary, in Hurricane P 3159.

Sterbacek was reported 'Missing'. He was 26 and is remembered on the Runnymede Memorial, Panel 10.

ELDRED JOHN STEVENS

82660   PO   Pilot   British   141 Squadron

Joined 141 Squadron at Grangemouth on July 24 1940.

Stevens was released from the RAF in 1946, as a Squadron Leader.

PO 16.6.40   FO 16.6.41   FL 16.6.42

GEOFFREY STEVENS

137305   Sgt   Pilot   British   151 and 213 Squadrons

Born on August 21 1917, Stevens joined the RAFVR on July 5 1937. He did his elementary flying at 13 E&RFTS, White Waltham and later at 5 E&RFTS, Hanworth and 19 E&RFTS, Gatwick. Called to full-time service on September 1 1939, Stevens was posted to 8 EFTS, Woodley for an instructor's course.

In November he went to ITW, Hastings and in mid-February moved to 15 FTS, Lossiemouth for a course on Harvards. At the end of July Stevens was posted to 6 OTU, Sutton Bridge and after converting to Hurricanes he joined 151 Squadron at North Weald in late August. The squadron was about to move to Digby for a rest and Stevens volunteered for a squadron in the south. He was sent to Tangmere to join 213 Squadron.

Stevens was shot down on October 17 and crashed just outside Ashford, in Hurricane V 6866, unhurt. In January 1941 213 was posted overseas but Stevens remained on the staff at RAF Castletown. He later went to No 1 AACU at Western Zoyland and then 2 AACU at Aberporth. In September 1942 he was posted to 59 OTU, Milfield as an instructor. Two months later he joined 609 Squadron.

In January 1943 Stevens was commissioned from Warrant Officer. He went to North Africa in April and joined 253 Squadron at Jemappes. He was promoted and appointed 'A' Flight Commander. Stevens took command of 87 Squadron in Italy in September 1943. He was posted away in July 1944 and went to Egypt in October, eventually taking over the Fighter Affiliation Flight at Abu Sueir.

Stevens returned to the UK in December 1945 and was released from the RAF. He rejoined and was posted to 61 OTU, Keevil in March 1946. He was invalided out on May 4 1968, as a Flight Lieutenant.

PO 16.1.43   FO 16.7.43   FL 23.12.43   FL 16.7.46
FL 16.1.49

LEONARD WALTER STEVENS

41753   PO   Pilot   British   17 Squadron

Stevens, of Hindhead, Surrey, joined the RAF on a short service commission in January 1939.

He was with 17 Squadron at Debden in early July 1940. On August 11 Stevens claimed a Bf 110 destroyed and on October 2 he shared a Do 17.

On March 30 1941 Stevens joined 145 Squadron at Tangmere as 'B' Flight Commander. As the squadron was returning from a patrol on May 21 Stevens collided with his No 2 over Tangmere. The two aircraft spun in and crashed a few yards from each other at the edge of the aerodrome. Both pilots were killed.

Stevens is buried in St Alban's churchyard, Hindhead.

APO 4.3.39   PO 23.9.39

ROBERT EDWARD STEVENS

742992   Sgt   Pilot   British   29 Squadron

Stevens, of Croydon, was born in April 1920 and educated at Winton House School, Croydon and Dover College. He joined the RAFVR in 1938.

He was posted to 29 Squadron at Digby in mid-July 1940. On October 13 Stevens was captain of Blenheim L 6637, shot down in error by Hurricanes of 312 Squadron. The aircraft crashed in flames off the Point of Aire, near the Morecambe Light. All three men on board were lost.

Stevens is remembered on the Runnymede Memorial, Panel 19.

RICHARD PLAYNE STEVENS

87639   PO   Pilot   British   151 Squadron

Stevens is one of the few near-legendary figures of Fighter Command. He was born in Tonbridge, Kent in 1909 and educated at Hurstpierpoint College, Hassocks, Sussex. Before joining the RAF Stevens had flown some 3000 hours as a civil pilot. For a long period he flew the early morning mail to and from Paris. All this, in spite of an early medical report, which described him as 'too excitable to fly'.

On September 4 1940 Stevens joined 151 Squadron at Stapleford, as a Sergeant Pilot. He was commissioned in late October, with seniority back-dated to January 4. Stevens claimed his, and the squadron's, first night victories on January 15 1941, when he destroyed a Do 17 and a He 111. He was awarded the DFC (4.2.41). The citation stated that he chased both these aircraft for over 100 miles before destroying them and in one instance followed his victim to almost ground level from 30000 feet.

Ear trouble kept Stevens off operations until early April 1941. On the 8th he destroyed two He 111s, on the 10th a Ju 88 and a He 111 and on the 19th another He 111. He was awarded a Bar to the DFC (2.5.41). On May 7 Stevens destroyed two He 111s, on the 10th a He 111 and probably a second, on June 13 a He 111, on the 22nd he damaged a He 111, on July 3 he destroyed a Ju 88. Stevens is believed to have destroyed one further enemy aircraft before he destroyed a Ju 88 on October 22, his fourteenth victory. In this engagement he intercepted the enemy aircraft at sea level off the coast of East Anglia. It turned and flew back towards the Continent at high speed. Stevens gave chase and slowly overhauled it. The 88 then opened fire and began to drop its bombs, singly. Columns of water shot up and Stevens swerved round them. He closed in to short range and shot the enemy aircraft down.

In November 1941 Stevens was posted to 253 Squadron at Hibaldstow. He was awarded the DSO (12.12.41). On the night of December 15/16 he was killed when he crashed at Hulte, near Gilze in Holland, in Hurricane Z 3456. The story goes that his wife and children were killed in a bombing raid on Manchester and from then on he flew with complete disregard for his own life. He specialised in solo night operations, flying towards concentrations of anti-aircraft shell-bursts to seek out German aircraft. Stevens always attacked at extremely close range and another story says that an exploding bomber sprayed his wings with blood, which he refused to have removed. Whatever the truth may be Stevens was an outstanding night-fighter pilot.

His portrait was done by Eric Kennington and Cuthbert Orde.

PO 30.10.40

WILLIAM RONALD STEVENS

615438　**Sgt**　**Air Gunner**　**British**　**23 Squadron**

Joined 23 Squadron at Collyweston on July 23 1940.

Stevens was later awarded the DFM and left the RAF as a Flight Sergeant but no further details have been traced.

PETER CHARLES FASKEN STEVENSON

33521　**PO**　**Pilot**　**British**　**74 Squadron**

Stevenson, from Billinghay, Lincolnshire, entered RAF College, Cranwell in September 1938 as a flight cadet. The normal course there was cut short after the outbreak of war and Stevenson graduated in December 1939.

He joined 74 Squadron at Rochford on February 15 1940. Over Dunkirk on May 22 Stevenson shared a Ju 88 and on the 27th he destroyed a Bf 109. On this day he was hit by return fire from a Do 17 and made a forced-landing on the beach at Dunkirk. He returned to the squadron on the 31st.

On July 8 and 10 Stevenson destroyed Bf 109s, on the 12th he shared a He 111 and on the 19th and 28th destroyed Bf 109s. On the 28th he was attacked by Oberleutnant Leppla whilst pursuing Major Mölders over the Channel and landed at Manston with his engine seized, unhurt.

On August 11 Stevenson was shot down into the Channel one mile off Dover following a solo attack on twelve Bf 109s, one of which he destroyed. He baled out of Spitfire P 9393 and was rescued from the sea by an MTB, after drifting eleven miles out. He attracted the MTB's attention by firing his revolver.

Stevenson was awarded the DFC (27.8.40) and posted away on September 20 1940 to 5 OTU, Aston Down as an instructor. He was killed on February 13 1943, as a Flight Lieutenant with 64 Squadron.

He is remembered on the Runnymede Memorial, Panel 121.

PO 23.12.39　　*FO 23.12.40*　　*FL 23.12.41*

GEORGE ARTHUR STEWARD

45375　**Sgt**　**Pilot**　**British**　**17 Squadron**

Steward, of Bromeswell, was with 17 Squadron in the operations over Dunkirk. On May 27 he damaged a Do 17.

On July 27 Steward claimed a Bf 110 destroyed, on November 8 claimed a Ju 87 destroyed and on the 11th shared a Bf 109 and probably another. He was awarded the DFM (17.12.40).

Commissioned in February 1941, Steward was killed on October 23 1941, as a Flight Lieutenant with 17. He was 26 and is buried in St Edmund's churchyard, Bromeswell, Suffolk.

PO 19.2.41

CHARLES STEWART

44231　**PO**　**Pilot**　**New Zealander**　**54 and 222 Sqdns**

Born in Wellington on November 22 1916, Stewart was educated at Wellington College and later worked as an accounts clerk. He applied for an RNZAF short service commission in March 1939, was accepted in June and reported to the Ground Training School at Rongotai on September 20.

Stewart was posted to No 1 EFTS, Taieri on October 21 and moved on to No 1 FTS, Wigram on February 12 1940. He was awarded his flying badge on April 15 and after completing the course in late May he sailed for the UK in the

RMS 'Rangitata' on June 7. Stewart was posted to 7 OTU, Hawarden on August 4 and after converting to Spitfires he joined 54 Squadron at Hornchurch on the 22nd.

Two days later Stewart was shot down by Bf 109s off Dover. He baled out at 20000 feet, opened his parachute at 10000 and went into the Channel. After fifteen minutes he saw an ASR launch but it failed to spot him and turned away. Stewart later described this as one of the worst moments of his life. Another launch appeared in forty-five minutes and picked him up. As the craft neared Dover it was machine-gunned by a Bf 109, without damage. Stewart was admitted to hospital suffering from shock and exposure. His Spitfire, P 9389, crashed at School Lane, Kingsdown.

He rejoined the squadron on September 3 and was posted to 222 Squadron at Hornchurch on October 1. He was with the squadron for over five months and took part in ninety operational sorties. Stewart joined the newly-formed 485 Squadron on March 12 1941. He destroyed a Bf 109 on July 8. Three days later he was flying one of eleven Spitfires on an offensive patrol. At 23000 feet in the vicinity of Gravelines they were attacked by six Bf 109s. Stewart was last seen in the ensuing engagement. He failed to return to base and a search by the squadron in the Straits of Dover was unsuccessful.

Stewart is remembered on the Runnymede Memorial, Panel 34.

APO 20.9.39　　*PO 28.5.40*

CHARLES NOEL DOUGLAS STEWART

800061　**Sgt**　**Air Gunner**　**British**　**604 Squadron**

With 604 Squadron at Northolt in early July 1940.

Stewart was killed on May 31 1942, as a Flight Sergeant with 9 Squadron, operating in Wellingtons from Honington.

He is buried in Woensel General Cemetery, Eindhoven, Netherlands.

DONALD GEORGE ALEXANDER STEWART

41624　**FO**　**Pilot**　**British**　**615 Squadron**

Stewart, of Hatfield Broad Oak, Hertfordshire joined the RAF on a short service commission in November 1938.

He was with 615 Squadron at Kenley in early July 1940. Stewart was killed on a sweep over Belgium on February 15 1941, as a Flying Officer with 615. He was 27 and is buried in Zeebrugge Communal Cemetery, Belgium.

APO 14.1.39　　*PO 3.9.39*
FO 3.9.40

DUDLEY STEWART-CLARK

78535 PO Pilot British 603 Squadron

Stewart-Clark, of West Lothian, was educated at Eton. He was with 603 Squadron at Dyce in June 1940.

On July 3 Stewart-Clark shared in the destruction of a Ju 88, on the 6th he shared a Do 17 and on the 15th and 16th he shared He 111s. He was shot down by Hauptmann Böde of II/JG 26 over the Channel off Margate on September 3, in Spitfire X 4185. Stewart-Clark baled out, wounded, and was admitted to Chelmsford Hospital.

He was killed on September 19 1941, as a Flight Lieutenant with 72 Squadron. He is buried in Pihen-les-Guines Communal Cemetery, France.

PO 17.4.40   FO 17.4.41

PHILLIP AMBROSE MEYNELL STICKNEY

37216 FL Pilot British 235 Squadron

Joined the RAF on a short service commission in April 1935. Stickney was posted to 6 FTS, Netheravon on May 7 and went to 9 Squadron at Scampton on February 17 1936. He moved to the staff of No 1 Armament Training Camp at Catfoss on June 22 1937.

Stickney joined 235 Squadron on July 28 1940. He was released from the RAF in 1947, as a Flight Lieutenant.

APO 16.4.35   PO 16.4.36   FO 16.1.38   FL 16.1.40

RONALD LESLIE STILLWELL

126839 Sgt Pilot British 65 Squadron

Stillwell joined the RAFVR on February 8 1939 and did his weekend flying at 13 E&RFTS, White Waltham. He was called to full-time service at the outbreak of war and posted to No 1 ITW, Cambridge on October 2.

From November 7 1939 to April 7 1940 Stillwell was at 7 EFTS, Desford. He moved to 10 FTS, Tern Hill and finished the course there on July 23. Stillwell was posted to 5 OTU, Aston Down on August 5 and after converting to Spitfires he joined 65 Squadron at Hornchurch on August 19 1940.

Stillwell was promoted to Warrant Officer on May 1 1942, commissioned in June and awarded the DFC (16.6.42). The citation stated that in August 1941 he sighted a bomber crew in the sea fifteen miles off the Dutch coast and his information enabled them to be rescued. In April 1942, returning from a sweep, he sighted a pilot in the sea without a dinghy and although short of fuel he managed to drop his own dinghy 25 yards from the spot. The pilot was later found to be dead.

On October 15 Stillwell was posted away from 65 and spent a month with the 97th Squadron, USAAC at Maydown, on Lightnings. He went to 57 OTU, Eshott on November 16 as an instructor on Spitfires. On June 7 1943 Stillwell rejoined 65 Squadron, then at Selsey. In October he was appointed 'B' Flight Commander. On July 9 1944 he was given command of 122 Squadron at Martragny in France. The signal posting Stillwell as CO of 65 was cancelled by the AOC, who considered 'promotion within the unit was bad for discipline'.

Stillwell was posted to 3 TEU, Aston Down on October 20 1944 as CGI. He was awarded the DFC (17.11.44), being then credited with three enemy aircraft destroyed and others damaged. He went to Hutton Cranswick on June 5 1945 as Senior Admin Officer. Stillwell was selected for a Permanent Commission in November 1945 but a medical showed tuberculosis in both lungs. He was eventually invalided from the RAF on September 15 1947, as a Squadron Leader.

PO 25.6.42   FO 25.12.42   FL 25.6 44

ERIC STOCK

1050677 AC 2 Radar Operator British 604 Squadron

Joined 604 Squadron at Gravesend on July 10 1940.
No further service details traced.

NORMAN JAMES STOCKS

552636 Sgt Air Gunner British 248 Squadron

Joined 248 Squadron in late July 1940.

Stocks was a member of the crew of Blenheim L 9453 which failed to return from a reconnaissance sortie over the Norwegian coast on October 20 1940. It had been searching for a Blenheim of 248 which had been lost earlier in the day.

Stocks is remembered on the Runnymede Memorial, Panel 12.

WILLIAM ERIC JOHN STOCKWELL

Petty Officer (FAA) Pilot British 804 Squadron

In early July 1940 he was with 804 Squadron at Hatston, flying Sea Gladiators on dockyard defence.

On November 15 1940 the carrier HMS 'Argus' sailed from Gibraltar with twelve Hurricanes and two Skuas aboard, destined for Malta. At dawn on the 17th, four hundred sea miles from Malta, the first flight of six Hurricanes took off, with an FAA Skua acting as a navigating leader.

One hour later the second flight of six took off and the navigating Skua was flown by Stockwell. Things went wrong. The Sunderland scheduled to escort them in failed to take off from Gibraltar. They missed their landfall, failed to meet the bomber sent out to meet them and became lost. The Skua navigator radioed for help but his set was faulty and unable to receive replies. Stockwell searched for somewhere to land, as the Hurricanes ran out of fuel one by one and fell into the sea, with the loss of all six pilots.

Just as the Skua was about to run out of fuel Stockwell sighted land, south-western Sicily. The aircraft was almost immediately fired on by Italian anti-aircraft defences and crash-landed on the beach at Punta Palo on the Isola delle Correnti, near Syracuse. Stockwell and his navigator were captured.

Stockwell became a Commissioned Pilot in 1945. He later served in 771 and 779 Squadrons. He retired on December 9 1950.

Commissioned Pilot 18.2.45

KENNETH MAXWELL STODDART

90358 FL Pilot British 611 Squadron

Stoddart joined 611 Squadron, AuxAF in 1936. He qualified as a pilot at the end of 1937 and was a Flight Commander when called to full-time service on August 26 1939.

He served with 611 throughout the Battle of Britain and was posted away from the squadron in November 1940. Stoddart was released from the RAF in 1945, as a Wing Commander.

PO (AuxAF) 18.12.36   FO (AuxAF) 1.9.38   FO 26.8.39
FL 3.9.40   SL 1.12.41

RICHARD WILLIAM STOKES

42027 PO Pilot British 264 Squadron

Stokes, of Acton, London, joined the RAF on a short service commission in February 1939.

He was posted to the newly-reformed 264 Squadron at Sutton Bridge on November 6 1939 and served with it throughout the Battle of Britain.

In 1942 Stokes was a flying instructor at 23 SFTS, Southern Rhodesia. He was killed on May 29, aged 21. He is buried in Bulawayo Cemetery, Zimbabwe.

APO 29.4.39   PO 6.11.39   FO 6.11.40   FL 6.11.41

JACK STOKOE

60512   Sgt   Pilot   British   603 Squadron

The son of a coal-miner, Stokoe was born at West Cornforth, Co Durham on February 1 1920. He joined the RAFVR in June 1939 and did his weekend flying at 26 E&RFTS, Oxford.

Called to full-time service at the outbreak of war, Stokoe was sent to No 1 ITW, Cambridge, based at Magdalene College. On January 1 1940 he was posted to 15 FTS, Lossiemouth and after completing the course on June 8 he went to 5 OTU, Aston Down and converted to Spitfires.

Stokoe joined 263 Squadron at Drem on June 26. The squadron was then converting to Whirlwinds and when given the option Stokoe chose to remain on single-engine fighters and was posted to 603 Squadron at Dyce on July 3 1940. He claimed a Bf 109 probably destroyed on August 28 and Bf 109s destroyed on the 31st and September 1. On the 2nd Stokoe damaged two Ju 88s but was himself shot down in flames. He baled out, wounded and spent six weeks in hospital with severe burns on hands and face.

On November 8 and 17 Stokoe destroyed two more Bf 109s. Commissioned in January 1941, he was posted away to 54 Squadron at Catterick on February 11. On March 5 Stokoe destroyed a Bf 109 and on April 20 destroyed a Bf 110 but was himself shot down. He baled out safely into the sea and was picked up. Stokoe probably destroyed another Bf 109 on June 7 and had another confirmed on the 24th.

He was posted to 74 Squadron at Gravesend on June 27 1941 but the stay was a short one and he went to 59 OTU, Crosby-on-Eden as an instructor. Stokoe moved to 60 OTU, East Fortune on July 17 1941. This unit was re-numbered 132 OTU in November 1942.

Stokoe went to 1692 (R/D) Flight at Drem on October 3 1943 to instruct on specialised airborne radar equipment. He was awarded the DFC (6.6.44). In late 1945 he became Senior Admin Officer at Great Massingham, later becoming Station Commander. He was released from the RAF on August 21 1946, as a Squadron Leader. He rejoined the RAFVR in July 1947, flying Tiger Moths and Chipmunks until June 1952 at 24 RFS, Rochester.

PO 26.1.41   FO 15.1.42   FL 15.1.43   FO (RAFVR) 14.7.47

SYDNEY STOKOE

754855   Sgt   Pilot   British   29 Squadron

Stokoe, of Gateshead, joined 29 Squadron at Digby in mid-September 1940.

He was killed on December 19 1940 when the Blenheim he was in, L 6612, crashed south-west of Digby aerodrome, possibly after hitting a tree during low flying. The two members of the crew were also killed.

Stokoe was 25. He is buried in St Mary's churchyard, Heworth, Co Durham.

CEDRIC ARTHUR CUTHBERT STONE

39424   FL   Pilot   British   263 and 245 Squadrons

Joined the RAF on a short service commission in November 1936. Stone was posted to 2 FTS, Digby on February 2 1937 and after his training was completed he joined 3 Squadron at Kenley on February 2 1938.

Stone went to France with the squadron on May 10 1940. On the 12th he destroyed a Hs 126 and shared in destroying two others and on the 14th he destroyed a Ju 87 and a Bf 109. The squadron was withdrawn to Kenley on the 25th and then went north to Wick. Stone was awarded the DFC (31.5.40).

On June 10 he was posted to 263 Squadron at Drem when it was

reformed after the Norwegian campaign. Stone went to 245 Squadron at Aldergrove on July 13, as a Flight Commander. In December 1940 he joined 607 Squadron and in July 1941 took command of 17 Squadron at Elgin. The squadron left for the Far East in November and in January 1942 was operational at Mingaladon in Burma. Stone destroyed Mitsubishi 'Sallys' on the 24th and 27th and later destroyed a Nakajima 'Nate'. He was awarded a Bar to the DFC (10.4.42).

From November 1943 until March 1944 Stone commanded 135 Squadron in India. He was released from the RAF in 1946, as a Wing Commander.

APO 28.1.37   PO 9.2.38   FO 19.9.39   FL 19.9.40
SL 1.12.41

DONALD WILLIAM ALFRED STONES

42276   PO   Pilot   British   79 Squadron

Stones joined the RAF on a short service commission on May 2 1939. He did his ab initio course at 13 E&RFTS, White Waltham, went to 10 FTS, Tern Hill on July 19 and after training was completed he was posted to the 11 Group Fighter Pool at St Athan to convert to Hurricanes.

On February 5 1940 Stone joined 32 Squadron at Biggin Hill and moved to 79 Squadron, also at Biggin Hill, on March 18. The squadron went to France on May 10 to reinforce the squadrons there. On the 14th Stones destroyed a Hs 126, a Do 17 and a Bf 110, on the 18th another Bf 110 and on the 20th a Hs 126 and another shared. The squadron was withdrawn on the 20th. Stones was awarded the DFC (4.6.40), which he received from the King at a special ceremony at Biggin Hill on the 27th. On this day Stones destroyed a Bf 110 and probably a second, on June 7 a Bf 109 and on the 8th a He 111.

Stones claimed a Bf 109 destroyed on July 9, a Do 17 and probably another on August 31, a probable Do 17 on September 1, a probable Bf 110 on the 4th and a probable Do 17 and a share in a probable Ju 88 on the 7th. On this day Stones was slightly wounded in combat and landed at West Malling. He destroyed a He 111 on September 29.

He was posted away to CFS, Upavon on December 15 1940 for an instructor's course, after which he went to 8 EFTS, Woodley on January 21 1941. Two months later Stones moved to 59 OTU, Crosby-on-Eden to instruct on Hurricanes. He rejoined 79 Squadron, then at Pembrey, on May 26 but left on July 15 to join 249 Squadron in Malta. He arrived as a passenger in a Blenheim from Gibraltar on the 19th. Stones joined the Malta Night Fighter Flight at Ta Kali on the 30th.

He shared a Cant Z 1007 in the early hours of September 5. He baled out at 500 feet on the night of November 9 because of engine trouble. Stones was awarded a Bar to the DFC (10.4.42) and posted on April 22 1942 to the OTU at El Ballah, Egypt as an instructor.

His stay was short and he took command of 155 Squadron on May 10, newly-formed at Peshawar, India, with Curtiss Mohawks. Stones led the squadron until October 30. After a rest he was given command of 67 Squadron at Alipore, India on February 1 1943. He was with 67 until May 15 1943, when he was wounded during an attack on the Japanese airstrip at Kangaung in Burma.

Stones became a test pilot at the Test Unit, Bombay on July 1 and was with the T&D Unit at Drigh Road, Karachi from September 3 1943 until September 3 1944, when he was posted back to the UK. He joined RT&D, 218 MU, Colerne on November 15 and remained with it until March 29 1945. Stones was seconded as a test pilot to Vickers Armstrong at Weybridge on April 4 and was grounded in September when he lost an eye.

In October 1945 Stones was posted to Air Ministry. He was released from the RAF in August 1946, as a Squadron Leader, to take up an appointment as a District Officer in the Colonial Service.

APO 24.6.39   PO 27.12.39   FO 27.12.40   FL 27.12.41

GEORGE EDWARD BOWES STONEY

28119   FL   Pilot   British   501 Squadron

Stoney joined the RAF in August 1929. He was posted to No 1 FTS, Netheravon on September 8 and joined the staff at 502 (Special Reserve) Squadron on August 13 1930, as Flying Instructor. On May 2 1932 Stoney went to 4 (Army Co-operation) Squadron at Farnborough. He went on to the Reserve in July 1934 and was recalled at the outbreak of war.

In early July 1940 Stoney was a Flight Commander with 501 Squadron at Croydon. On the 29th he claimed a Ju 87 destroyed and another on August 11. Four days later he was shot down and killed in combat with Bf 110s over the Thames Estuary. His Hurricane, P 2549, crashed near Stile Farm, Chilham.

Stoney was 29. He is buried in St Helen's churchyard, Sefton, Lancashire.

PO 15.8.29   FO 15.2.31   FO (RAFO) 14.7.34   FL 2.9.39

DONALD RAYMOND STOODLEY

754215   Sgt   Pilot   British   43 Squadron

Stoodley, of Southampton, joined 43 Squadron at Usworth on September 29 1940. He was killed in a flying accident at Usworth at dusk on October 24. After making several attempts to make a cross-wind landing he stalled and crashed from 250 feet in Hurricane V 7303.

Stoodley was 21. He is buried in London Road Cemetery, Salisbury.

JOHN MUNRO STORIE

84941   PO   Pilot   British   615 and 607 Squadrons

Joined 615 Squadron at Prestwick on September 30 1940 and moved to 607 Squadron at Tangmere on October 7.

Storie was released from the RAF in 1946, as a Flight Lieutenant. He joined the RAFVR in 1948.

PO 7.9.40   FO 6.9.41   FL 6.9.42   FO (RAFVR) 7.6.48

JAMES ERIC STORRAR

41881   FO   Pilot   British   145 and 73 Sqdns, 421 Flight

Joined the RAF on a short service commission in October 1938 and did his ab initio course at No 1 E&RFTS, Hatfield. He was posted to 11 FTS, Shawbury in January 1939, went to the Blenheim Conversion Flight in August and joined 145 Squadron at Croydon on October 23, soon after its reformation.

Over Dunkirk on May 27 Storrar destroyed a Bf 110. On June 11 he claimed a He 111 destroyed, on July 15 probably destroyed a Do 17, on the 16th and 18th shared He 111s, on the 20th destroyed a He 111, on the 21st shared a Do 17, on the 22nd destroyed a Bf 109, on the 29th shared a Ju 88, on the 30th claimed a Bf 109 destroyed, on August 8 a Ju 87 and on the 12th a Bf 110. Storrar was awarded the DFC (20.8.40).

On September 28 he was posted to 73 Squadron at Castle Camps. The squadron left on November 11 for overseas. It embarked on HMS 'Furious' on the 16th, with its aircraft, and flew off to Takoradi on the 29th. The squadron then flew in easy stages to Heliopolis, via Lagos, Accra, Kano, Maidugari, Khartoum, Wadi Halfa, and Abu Sueir. During December the pilots were attached to 274 Squadron in the Western Desert.

In early January 73 Squadron began operating on its own account. On the 3rd Storrar joined Squadron Leader AD Murray and Sergeant AE Marshall in destroying eight enemy aircraft on a landing ground, on the 6th he shot down a CR 42 in the Tobruk area, on February 1 he destroyed a Caproni Ghibli on Apollonia airfield and on the 5th, again with Murray and Marshall, he strafed Benina airfield, destroying some eight enemy aircraft on the ground between them.

On April 4 1941 Storrar shot down a Ju 87 near Derna. He later saw a Lockheed Lodestar forced-landed in the desert. He landed and found it to be General Wavell's personal aircraft. The pilot managed to take off again but Storrar could not restart his own engine and had to return to Tobruk on foot.

In Takoradi for a rest, Storrar and four other pilots were ordered to fly a Blenheim and two Hurricanes to Freetown on June 21 1941. Forced by bad weather to make a forced-landing in the jungle the pilots had no way of taking off again and they walked 72 miles in two days and three nights, arriving at the Firestone Rubber Plantation, 35 miles from Monrovia, Liberia.

Storrar returned to the UK in November 1941 and was posted to 55 OTU, Annan, as OC Gunnery Training Squadron. In January 1943 he took command of 65 Squadron at Drem. On June 29 he probably destroyed a FW 190, was awarded a Bar to the DFC (29.10.43) and posted away to 53 OTU in December 1943.

From April to October 1944 Storrar was in 1697 ADLS Flight, engaged on communications duties to and from the Continent. He commanded 64 Squadron in October/November, 165 Squadron from November to January 1945 and 234 Squadron from January to March 1945.

Storrar was Wing Commander Flying successively at Hunsdon, Digby and Molesworth from March to August 1945. He then went to a staff job at HQ 12 Group until January 1946, when he went to 239 Wing, Desert Air Force in Italy, leading it until April 1947, when he was released from the RAF, as a Wing Commander.

In June 1949 Storrar joined 603 Squadron, RAuxAF and served with it until March 1952. He then went to 610 Squadron, which he commanded from 1954 until its disbandment on March 10 1957. Storrar was then a veterinary surgeon in Chester.

APO 1.4.39   PO 23.10.39   FO 23.10.40   FL 23.10.41
SL 21.7.45   FL (RAuxAF) 25.7.49

ALEXANDER JAMES STORRIE

43641   PO   Air Gunner   British   264 Squadron

Storrie, of Colchester, joined 264 Squadron at Martlesham Heath in March 1940.

He was killed on November 20 1940, when Defiant N 1626 crashed soon after taking off from Rochford, at Blatches Farm. The pilot, Pilot Officer GH Hackwood, was also killed.

Storrie was 24. He is buried in St Leonard's churchyard, Lexden, Colchester.

PO 21.2.40

WHITNEY WILLARD STRAIGHT

90680   FO   Pilot   British   601 Squadron

Straight was born in New York on November 6 1912, the son of Major Willard Straight, an Oriental expert. After her husband's death in 1918 Straight's mother, one of the wealthy Whitney family, married again and went to England, where she and her husband founded the educational, artistic and agricultural community at Dartington Hall.

Straight went to England in 1925 and after education at Dartington Hall he went to Trinity College, Cambridge, where he took Moral Sciences

Tripos. At that time he flew his own aeroplane and was a well-known racing driver, in his black-and-silver Maserati.

In 1935 Straight married, became a British subject, gave up racing and settled down to business. He founded the Straight Corporation, which later took over Western Airways, which had the highest frequency of any airline in the world, with 58 services a day.

Straight joined 601 Squadron, AuxAF in early 1939 and was called to full-time service on August 24. He sailed with a naval force to Norway on April 15 1940, with the temporary rank of Squadron Leader. His job was to find frozen lakes from which aircraft could operate. After landing on the 17th he found and organised the clearing of Lake Lesjaskog in time for 263 Squadron to arrive on the 24th. The Germans bombed the lake on the 25th and destroyed most of the Gladiators. Straight was injured in the attack and evacuated to Britain by the Navy. He was temporarily deaf and grounded. He was appointed ADC to the Duke of Kent.

On August 28 1940 Straight went to HQ Flying Training Command on supernumerary flying duties. He regained his operational category and rejoined 601 Squadron at Exeter on September 28 and destroyed a He 111 on December 12. For his work in Norway Straight was awarded the MC (1.1.41). He was appointed a Flight Commander in early 1941 and destroyed a Bf 109 over the Channel on February 2. He was posted away on April 23 to command 242 Squadron at Stapleford Tawney. Straight destroyed a Bf 110 on a night intruder operation over Merville airfield on June 12, he shared a Bf 109 on a Blenheim escort to St Omer on the 21st and probably destroyed two Bf 109s on July 27. He was awarded the DFC (8.8.41).

During an attack on a destroyer at Fécamp on July 31 1941 Straight was shot down by light flak. He made a forced-landing in a field, unsuccessfully tried to fire the aircraft and first ran and then walked as far and fast as he could from the scene. He was prepared for a landing in enemy-occupied territory, with a special jacket, boots, money and a pistol. Straight slept in a barn and caught a train for Paris the next day. He went to the American Embassy but it was closed. He managed to obtain 12000 francs from the caretaker.

Straight crossed into Vichy France and was eventually imprisoned, posing as a British Army officer. He was interned until escaping on June 22 1942. With the help of the Resistance he reached a beach near Perpignan, from where he was rowed out to a trawler, which took him and other fugitives to Gibraltar. Straight reached No 1 Depot, Uxbridge on July 21 1942.

He was posted to the Middle East on September 10, as an Acting Air Commodore, going to HQ 216 Group as AOC. Straight returned to the UK in June 1945 and was appointed AOC 46 Group, Transport Command. He was released from the RAF in November 1945, as a Group Captain, retaining the rank of Air Commodore.

Straight was awarded the Norwegian War Cross (18.12.42), received a Mention in Despatches (1.1.43), was made a CBE (8.6.44) and an Officer of the US Legion of Merit (15.3.46). He became Managing Director of BOAC in 1947. Straight died on April 5 1979.

APO (AuxAF) 9.3.39   PO (AuxAF) 27.7.39   PO 24.8.39
FO 3.9.40   FL 25.6.41   GC 10.3.43

JOHN TALBOT STRANG

40861   FO   Pilot   New Zealander   253 Squadron

Born in Invercargill on January 25 1914, Strang was educated at Timaru Boys' High School. He obtained his 'A' license privately at the Canterbury Aero Club.

In March 1937 Strang applied for a short service commission in the RAF. He was provisionally accepted and sailed for the UK in the RMS 'Remuera' on February 17 1938. Strang began his ab initio course at No 1 E&RFTS, Hatfield on April 4. After a short induction course at Uxbridge he was posted to 5 FTS, Sealand on June 18. Strang joined the staff at 7 AOS on August 1 1939, as a staff pilot.

He was posted to 92 Squadron at Croydon on December 10 1939.

Strang moved to 253 Squadron at Northolt on February 22 1940. In May the squadron began ferrying Hurricanes to France and 'A' Flight was detached there, based at Poix. Strang was in this flight and took part in the actions fought there following the German invasion of France. After suffering heavy losses the flight was withdrawn on May 24 to Kirton-in-Lindsey to rejoin the squadron.

Strang was posted away from 253 on December 13 1940 to CFS, Upavon for an instructor's course. He went to 6 FTS, Little Rissington on February 11 1941, remaining there until July 26, when he was sent to instruct in South Africa. Strang was initially at 21 Air School and then at 25 Air School. He was posted to Middle East Command on February 28 1942 but his time there was short and he went on to India on March 23.

It is not known what he was doing up until April 16 1943, when he was appointed to command 23 Ferry Control. He became CGI at No 1 EFTS at Secunderbad in 1944, transferred to the RNZAF on May 5 and left India on January 4 1945.

Strang returned to the UK and in late April he was repatriated to New Zealand. He was posted to 42 Squadron at Rongotai as a supernumerary and transferred to the Reserve on November 3 1945. Strang died on July 17 1979.

APO 4.6.38   PO 4.4.39   FO 3.9.40   FL 3.9.41
SL 1.1.44

VICTOR CHARLES FREDERICK STREATFEILD

27151   SL   Pilot   British   248 Squadron

Joined the RAF in September 1928. Streatfeild was posted to 5 FTS, Sealand on October 1 and joined 3 Squadron at Upavon on September 15 1930. He joined the staff at 4 FTS, Abu Sueir on September 26 1933 and moved to 45 Squadron at Helwan on September 7 1935.

Streatfeild was posted to 223 Squadron at Nairobi on December 15 1936 and returned to 4 FTS, Abu Sueir on November 9 1937. Back in the UK he was given command of No 1 Coast Artillery Co-operation Unit, Gosport on December 5 1938. In early July 1940 Streatfeild was in command of 248 Squadron.

He was made an OBE (29.10.48) for distinguished services in Palestine. Streatfeild was released from the RAF in 1950, as a Squadron Leader.

PO 14.9.28   FO 14.4.31   FL 14.4.35   SL 1.10.38
WC 1.12.40   SL 1.10.38

REGINALD ROBERT STRETCH

747953   Sgt   Wop/AG   British   235 Squadron

Born in Southampton on June 1 1920, Stretch joined the RAFVR on May 13 1939. He was called up on September 1, as a Wop/AG. He carried out wireless instruction at Air Service Training at Hamble and No 1 Wireless School, Cranwell until the end of June 1940.

Stretch was then posted to the Gunnery School at Jurby. He joined 235 Squadron in August. When the squadron converted to Beaufighters in July 1941 Stretch joined 86 Squadron, operating in Beauforts on anti-shipping strikes.

In July 1942 he went to 8 OTU as a gunnery instructor. In December he joined 2 AACU, target-towing in Defiants and flying in Oxfords in night co-operation with anti-aircraft units and searchlights. Stretch remustered to Wireless Operator Mechanic/Air Gunner in April 1944 and was posted to Cranwell. On completion of the course in December he joined 502 Squadron at Stornaway, operating in Halifaxes on night shipping attacks.

In June 1945 Stretch was posted to 279 (ASR) Squadron, with Sea Otters and Warwicks. He was released from the RAF on December 18 1945, as a Warrant Officer. During his operational service Stretch shot down a Bf 109 and a Ju 88, both confirmed, and three other enemy aircraft, unconfirmed and not claimed.

CLAUD DOBREE STRICKLAND

91220   PO   Pilot   British   615 Squadron

Strickland joined the AuxAF in 1939. He was called to full-time service on September 1.

After completing his training he joined 615 Squadron at Prestwick in September 1940. Strickland was killed on October 27 1941, as a Flying Officer with 615. He was shot down by flak during

CD Strickland (continued)

an attack on targets along the Dutch/Belgian coast. He is buried in Bredene churchyard, Belgium.

APO 1.9.39   PO 17.8.40   FO 27.6.41

JAMES MURRAY STRICKLAND

39581   FL   Pilot   British   213 Squadron

Strickland of Ivybridge, Devon, was born in Iloilo, Philippines. He joined the RAF on a short service commission in January 1937. Strickland was posted to 5 FTS, Sealand on March 20 and joined 213 Squadron at Church Fenton on October 23 1937.

He was still with 213 in early July 1940. On August 11 Strickland claimed a Ju 88 destroyed, on the 12th a Bf 109, on the 15th a Bf 110 and a Ju 87, on the 25th a Bf 109 and on September 27 he shared a Bf 110. In this engagement his Hurricane, P 3979, was damaged by return fire and he crash-landed at Horne, near Redhill, unhurt.

Strickland crash-landed again on October 15, after a combat with a Bf 109 over the Swanage area, unhurt. He was awarded the DFC (22.10.40).

On August 14 1941 Strickland was killed in a flying accident, as a Flight Lieutenant with 130 Squadron, operating with Spitfires from Portreath. He was 22 and is buried in Ivybridge Cemetery.

APO 8.3.37   PO 21.12.37   FO 21.9.39   FL 21.9.40

JAROMIR STRIHAVKA

121736   F/Sgt   Pilot   Czechoslovakian   310 Squadron

Served with 310 Squadron during the Battle of Britain.

Commissioned in January 1943, Strihavka was released from the RAF after the war as a Flight Lieutenant. He later changed his name to Scott.

PO 5.1.43   FO 5.1.44   FL 5.1.45

GEORGE ALFRED STROUD

141736   Sgt   Pilot   British   504, 32 and 249 Sqdns

Joined the RAFVR in April 1939 and did his weekend flying at 25 E&RFTS, Rochester. Stroud was called to full-time service at the outbreak of war and completed his flying training at 15 FTS, Lossiemouth. He was then posted to 10 OTU at Bassingbourn, moved to 11 OTU, Benson and joined 150 Squadron at Newton in July 1940, to fly Battles.

With the shortage of fighter pilots Stroud was posted to 504 Squadron at Catterick, moved to 32 Squadron at Acklington and finally joined 249 Squadron at North Weald in September.

On December 5 Stroud was shot down in flames by Bf 109s over the south coast, in Hurricane V 7677. He baled out and was admitted to Rye Hospital with burns. Stroud later went to Queen Victoria Hospital, East Grinstead for plastic surgery and became a Guinea Pig.

During his time with 249 Stroud probably destroyed one enemy aircraft and shared another. He was posted away in mid-1941 to go to the Middle East. He landed at Takoradi and made his way north in stages, eventually joining 33 Squadron at Amriya on August 12.

Stroud served with 33 in the Western Desert until January 6 1942, when he was posted to 73 OTU, Sheik Othman, Aden. He destroyed a Fiat G 50 whilst in the Western Desert. Stroud joined the Aden Defence Flight at Khormaksar on October 1 1942. Commissioned from Warrant Officer in January 1943, he returned to 73 OTU, then at Abu Sueir, on February 27. He was posted away on April 2 and joined 274 Squadron at Mellaha on May 22.

Stroud moved with the squadron to Italy in early March 1944 and returned to the UK with it in April, arriving at Hornchurch on the 22nd. He was attached to CGS, Catfoss on July 19, went to 53 OTU, Kirton-in-Lindsey on September 4 and remained there until November 29 1945. Stroud was sent to 2 FIS, Montrose for an instructor's course on December 6, after which he was posted to 17 FTS, Spitalgate on July 6 1946.

He was released from the RAF in late January 1947, as a Flight Lieutenant. Stroud joined the flying staff at Short Bros, Rochester and instructed in the RAFVR at 24 RFS. He was awarded the AEA and Bar.

PO 5.1.43   FO 5.7.43   FL 5.1.45   FO (RAFVR) 10.7.47

MICHAEL STUART

902627   AC   Air Gunner   British   23 Squadron

Stuart joined the RAF on September 11 1939 and was posted to 23 Squadron at Ford on October 7 1940, as a fitter. He volunteered to fly as an air gunner for a short period and took part in three patrols over the Channel but saw no action. He thus qualified for the Battle of Britain clasp.

In 1943 Stuart was in Iraq. He volunteered for aircrew and in October was posted to 24 BG&NS, Moffat, Rhodesia for a gunnery course. He qualified and was promoted to Sergeant. Stuart returned to the UK and in January 1945 he went to 3 AGS, Castle Kennedy, on fighter affiliation duties.

Stuart was posted to 26 OTU, Wing in June and was released from the RAF on November 13 1945, as a Flight Sergeant.

SYDNEY GEORGE STUCKEY

516338   Sgt   Pilot   British   213 Squadron

Stuckey, of Bristol, was a pre-war airman pilot and was serving with 73 Squadron at the outbreak of war.

He was with the squadron in France and was posted to 213 Squadron in early July 1940. Stuckey failed to return from an action over the Channel off Bognor on August 12, in Hurricane P 2802. He was 26 and is remembered on the Runnymede Memorial, Panel 20.

JOHN ALNOD PETER STUDD

41491   PO   Pilot   British   66 Squadron

Studd, of Paignton, Devon, joined the RAF on a short service commission in October 1938. After completing his training he was posted as pilot and PA to the AOC 12 Group, Air Vice-Marshal T Leigh-Mallory.

In early July 1940 Studd was with 66 Squadron at Coltishall and on the 29th he shared in shooting down a He 111 into the sea off Lowestoft.

On August 19 Studd was shot down by return fire from a He 111 and baled out into the sea. He was picked up by the Aldeburgh lifeboat but failed to regain consciousness. His Spitfire, N 3182, crashed into the sea three miles south of Orfordness.

Studd was 22. He is buried in Holy Trinity churchyard, Touchen End, Berkshire.

APO 14.12.38   PO 3.9.39

JOHN EDWARD SULMAN

81344   PO   Pilot   British   607 Squadron

Sulman, of Hertfordshire, was with 607 Squadron at Usworth in early July 1940. He claimed a Do 17 destroyed on September 15.

In June 1941 Sulman was an instructor at 53 OTU, Heston. He was killed on November 23 1941, as a Flying Officer with 238 Squadron in the Western Desert. He failed to return from a sweep over the El Adem area.

Sulman was 25. He is buried in the Knightsbridge War Cemetery, Acroma, Libya. His portrait was done by Cuthbert Orde.

PO 18.6.40   FO 18.6.41

RICHARD GORDON BATTENSBY SUMMERS

49629   Sgt   Observer   British   219 Squadron

Born on October 18 1921, Summers joined the RAF in mid-1939. On June 26 he went to the Bristol Flying School, Yatesbury for basic navigation training, moved to BGS Warmwell on September 30 and completed his training with an astro-navigation course at St Athan in November.

On December 4 1939 Summers was posted to Church Fenton to join 242 Squadron, then equipped with Blenheims. He went to 219 Squadron at Catterick on April 16 1940. Summers left the squadron on September 28 to go to the Ferry Pool and Defence Flight at Takoradi, in West Africa.

He was awarded the AFM (1.1.42), commissioned in May 1942 and posted back to the UK, where he was appointed Bombing Leader on Hudsons at No 1 (Coastal) OTU, Silloth on October 12. Summers was posted to 48 Squadron at Gibraltar on May 22 1943, as Bombing Leader. He returned to the UK and on March 1 1944 became Bombing Leader at No 1 APC, Aldergrove.

Summers went on a Specialist Armament Course on April 19, firstly at 2 S of TT, Cosford and from late June at the Empire Air Armament School at Manby. He was appointed Armament Staff Officer at HQ 15 Group, Liverpool on November 17 1944 and moved to RAF Lossiemouth on August 7 1945, as Station Armament Officer.

From August 1953 until January 1956 Summers was Deputy Station Commander at RAF East Leigh, Kenya, during the Mau Mau Emergency. He was made an OBE (6.3.56), for 'gallant and distinguished services in Kenya'.

Summers retired from the RAF on October 18 1968, as a Wing Commander.

PO 1.5.42   FO 1.11.42   FL 1.5.44   FL 1.11.45
SL 1.7.51   WC 1.1.58

FRANK SUMNER

327457   Sgt   Air Gunner   British   23 Squadron

A pre-war regular airman, Sumner joined 23 Squadron at Collyweston on July 23 1940.

He was killed on November 30 1941, as a Flight Sergeant with 142 Squadron, operating in Wellingtons from Waltham, Lincolnshire. Sumner is buried in Kiel War Cemetery, Germany.

CLAUDE HARRY SIDNEY SUMPTER

645776   Sgt   Aircrew   British   604 Squadron

No service details traced.

FRANCISZEK SURMA

76713   PO   Pilot   Polish   151, 607 and 257 Sqdns

Born on July 1 1916. Surma was posted to 151 Squadron at Stapleford in August 1940. On the 30th he probably destroyed a He 111. He moved to 607 Squadron at Tangmere on September 11 and claimed a Bf 109 destroyed on the 26th.

Surma joined 257 Squadron at North Weald on October 20. He claimed a He 111 damaged on the 28th and was shot down on the 29th by Bf 109s and baled out, unhurt. Not surprisingly he was mistaken for a German, as he was wearing a Luftwaffe jacket, with badges, taken from a wrecked bomber in Poland in September 1939.

On December 12 1940 Surma was posted to 242 Squadron at Martlesham Heath. He left on March 13 1941 to join 308 Squadron at Baginton. On March 26 he shared in probably destroying a Bf 109, on July 22 and September 16 destroyed Bf 109s, on the 20th destroyed

another and probably a second, on the 27th probably another and on October 12 claimed another. Surma was awarded the KW and Bar (10.9.41), a second Bar (30.10.41) and the VM (5th Class)(30.10.41).

On November 8 1941 the squadron provided cover for bombers over France. Surma failed to return, probably shot down by flak near Dunkirk. He is remembered on the Polish Air Force Memorial at Northolt.

PO 24.1.40   FO 1.3.41

WILLIAM ALFRED SUTCLIFFE

565302   Sgt   Pilot   British   610 Squadron

A pre-war airman pilot, Sutcliffe joined 610 Squadron at Acklington on September 23 1940.

He was killed on December 17 1940, as a Flight Sergeant, aged 25. He is buried in St Wyllow's churchyard. Lanteglos-By-Fowey, Cornwall.

IAN WELSH SUTHERLAND

72508   PO   Pilot   British   19 Squadron

Sutherland, of Liverpool, was at Magdalene College, Oxford and learned to fly with the University Air Squadron. He was commissioned in the RAFVR in November 1938 and called to full-time service in September 1939.

In early July 1940 Sutherland was with 19 Squadron at Duxford. He was killed on active service on August 4 1940, aged 21. He is buried in St Michael's churchyard, Halton, Buckinghamshire.

PO (RAFVR) 8.11.38   PO 25.9.39

FRASER BARTON SUTTON

41962   FO   Pilot   British   56 Squadron

Born in Witney, Oxfordshire on January 28 1919. Sutton's first job was as a reporter on a Northampton evening newspaper. He joined the RAFVR in 1937 and began his weekend flying at 6 E&RFTS, Sywell. When he went to work for a Nottingham newspaper he continued at 27 E&RFTS, Tollerton.

Sutton joined the RAF on a short service commission in February 1939. After completing his training at 2 FTS Brize Norton he joined 56 Squadron at North Weald in September. On May 16 1940 'B' Flight of 56, Sutton included, flew to Vitry-en-Artois in France. He shared a Do 17 on the 18th and later on this day he was jumped by a Bf 109 soon after taking off and wounded in the foot. Sutton managed to return to Vitry. He returned to England on May 23.

Fit again, Sutton claimed a Ju 87 destroyed on July 25, a Bf 110 on August 13, a Bf 109 on the 16th and another Bf 110 on the 26th. He was shot down, possibly by a Spitfire, in combat over the Thames Estuary on August 28 1940 and baled out, seriously burned, from Hurricane R 4198. Sutton was admitted to Canterbury Hospital and later transferred to the RAF Hospital at Halton.

After a year in hospital Sutton was posted to the Middle East. He waited in Cairo for a posting and in November 1941 set out for Burma. He flew with a group of Hurricanes, led by a Blenheim, the first leg being from Cairo to Lydda. They then flew by easy stages to Mingaladon, Burma, where they joined 135 Squadron. Sutton took command of the squadron in February 1942. It was ordered to withdraw on March 5, firstly to Akyab and then to Dum Dum.

In mid-April 1942 Sutton was posted to Air HQ Bengal as a staff officer. He went to the Air Fighting Training Unit at Amarda Road in early 1943 as CFI, remaining there until November, when he was posted to Command HQ, Delhi as Chief Tactics Officer. Sutton was appointed to lead a Spitfire Wing in Bengal in April 1944 and at the end of June he became Wing Leader of a Hurricane/Spitfire Wing in the Imphal Valley.

Sutton returned to the UK in 1945. He was awarded the DFC (17.8.45). After the war he held a series of appointments and commands at home and overseas. He retired from the RAF on April 23 1966, as a Group Captain. Sutton died on March 16 1988.

APO 15.4.39   PO 3.9.39   FO 3.9.40   FL 3.9.41
SL 17.1.44   SL 1.8.47   WC 1.1.53   GC 1.1.59

FREDERICK CHARLES SUTTON

79197   PO   Air Gunner   British   264 Squadron

Joined the RAF in April 1940. After gunnery training Sutton was posted to 264 Squadron at Kirton-in-Lindsey on July 13 1940.

He was gunner in a Defiant shot down by Bf 109s of JG 26 on August 28 1940. In the engagement he claimed one Bf 109 destroyed and two more damaged.

Sutton shot down He 111s at night on April 8 and May 11 1941. He was posted away from 264 on May 16 1942 and went to Canada on October 1, as a gunnery instructor. He was released from the RAF in 1945, as a Flight Lieutenant. Sutton died in 1981.

APO 20.4.40   PO 15.5.40   FO 15.5.41   FL 15.5.42

HAROLD ROBERT SUTTON

49294   Sgt   Pilot   British   235 Squadron

Born on June 10 1914, Sutton joined the RAF on September 1 1931 as an aircraft apprentice. He qualified as a Metal Rigger at No 1 S of TT in September 1934 and was posted to 111 Squadron at Northolt. In October 1935 Sutton went with 41 Squadron to Aden, at the time of the Abyssinian crisis. The squadron returned to the UK in August 1936 and Sutton was posted to the Oxford University Air Squadron at Abingdon, as a Rigger.

Sutton went to Henlow for a Fitter 1 course, after which he joined 75 Squadron at Honington as an LAC. In September 1938 he was posted to the Long Range Development Unit. His long-submitted application for pilot training was approved and on February 6 1939 Sutton began his ab initio course at 11 E&RFTS, Perth. On May 1 he moved to 2 FTS, Brize Norton and with training completed he joined 235 Squadron at Manston on November 5 1939, soon after its reformation, as a Sergeant-Pilot.

Still with the squadron in 1940, Sutton was on a submarine escort operation on October 16 when he sighted and destroyed a He 60 floatplane. In mid-March 1941 Sutton was posted to 24 (Communications) Squadron at Hendon, was commissioned in June 1942 and remained with the squadron until September 1944, then going to 109 OTU, a Dakota conversion unit. During his time with 24 Squadron Sutton flew Lord Trenchard thirty-five times.

In December 1945 he went to HQ 47 Group, Hendon and in February 1946 went to India, as Engineering Officer at Jiwani. Sutton stayed in the RAF on an extended commission, retiring on November 28 1953, as a Flight Lieutenant.

PO 15.6.42   FO 15.12.42   FL 15.6.44   FL 15.12.45

JAMES RONALD GABERT SUTTON

90758   PO   Pilot   British   611 Squadron

Sutton, of Devon, joined 611 Squadron, AuxAF in early 1939. He was called to full-time service on August 24 and after completing his training he rejoined 611 Squadron, then at Digby, in May 1940.

On July 2 Sutton shared in destroying a Do 17. He crashed on landing at Tern Hill on September 28 and suffered slight facial injuries.

The Spitfire, P 7369, was written off. Sutton shared in destroying two more Do 17s on October 11.

He was killed on a sweep over France on July 23 1941, as a Flying Officer with 611, aged 21. Sutton was the last of the pre-war auxiliary officers. He is buried in St Pol War Cemetery, France.

APO (AuxAF) 12.3.39   APO 24.8.39   PO 6.4.40   FO 11.1.41

KENWYN ROLAND SUTTON

36182   FO   Pilot   New Zealander   264 Squadron

Born in Wellington on May 18 1919, Sutton enrolled in the Civil Reserve of Pilots in October 1937. He applied for a short service commission in the RNZAF later in the year, was accepted and began his elementary flying training at the Wellington Aero Club at Rongotai on April 1 1938.

Sutton was posted to Wigram on June 6 and after completing the course in mid-December he sailed for the UK in the RMS 'Tainui' on February 1 1939. He joined 105 Squadron at Harwell on March 28 but when the squadron went to France on September 2 Sutton and several other pilots were left behind because of over-establishment. He was posted to CGS, Warmwell as a staff pilot.

In early April 1940 Sutton joined 98 Squadron at Finningley. It moved to France on the 19th. When the blitzkrieg started on May 10 Sutton was posted to 142 Squadron at Berry-au-Bac. He took part in attacks on German lines of communication, bridges, pontoons and motor transport. On one sortie in a chase at treetop level, Sutton's gunner shot down one enemy aircraft and damaged another. Sutton crash-landed the damaged Battle near Dreux. He received a Mention in Despatches and the gunner was awarded the DFM.

The squadron was withdrawn to Waddington on June 15 1940 and Sutton was posted to 264 Squadron at Kirton-in-Lindsey on August 15. He was sent to 5 OTU, Aston Down for Defiant training, returned to 264 on September 3 and began flying night patrols. Sutton went to 23 Squadron at Ford on May 1 1941, to operate in Havocs on night intruder sorties against enemy airfields in France.

Sutton was appointed a Flight Commander in September 1941 and remained with 23 until February 11 1942, when he was posted for a rest to 287 Squadron at Croydon on anti-aircraft co-operation duties. He was awarded the DFC (27.3.42).

On July 17 Sutton joined 605 Squadron at Ford, as a Flight Commander. In the Dieppe raid on August 19 Sutton led a pre-dawn attack on gun positions covering the harbour. At the end of January 1943 he was attached to 85 Squadron at Hunsdon on special duties, plotting long and short range German radar and making daylight intruder sorties over France. He was later posted to the squadron.

Returning from a daylight operation on April 2 1943 Sutton was shot down by Canadian anti-aircraft gunners over Hove. He crashed on a railway line south of Hove Cemetery, with severe injuries, which resulted in the loss of his lower left leg and left arm. On June 19 he was posted to HQ Fighter Command on staff duties.

In August 1943 Sutton became Station Commander at Llanbedr. He received a Mention in Despatches (14.1.44). Using a special arm attachment he flew Magisters and Oxfords. Sutton transferred to the RNZAF on March 16 1944. He was posted from Llanbedr in November 1945 to be Squadron Leader Admin at Hutton Cranswick. On July 1 1946 he went to 61 OTU, Keevil in a similar job.

Sutton sailed for New Zealand in April 1947 and was released from the RNZAF on August 1. In 1950 he joined the National Airways Corporation and retired in 1980.

APO 20.6.38   PO 15.3.39   FO 3.9.40   FL 3.9.41   SL 1.1.44

NORMAN SUTTON

84033   **PO**   **Pilot**   **British**   **611 and 72 Squadrons**

Joined 611 Squadron at Digby on September 9 1940 and moved to 72 Squadron at Biggin Hill on the 29th.

Sutton was killed on October 5 1940. He collided with Sergeant RCJ Staples shortly after taking off from Biggin Hill and his Spitfire, K 9989, crashed and burned out.

Sutton was 26 years old. He is buried in St Helen's Cemetery, Lancashire.

PO 11.8.40

———— SWANWICK

No unknown   **Sgt**   **Air Gunner**   **British**   **141 Squadron**

No service details traced.

GEORGE WILLIAM SWANWICK

118533   **Sgt**   **Pilot**   **British**   **54 Squadron**

Born on November 10 1915, Swanwick was in 504 (Special Reserve) Squadron at Hucknall, Nottingham in the mid-thirties. He qualified as an air gunner in Westland Wallaces and later flew in Hinds.

In May 1936 504 became part of the AuxAF and in October 1938 converted to a fighter unit, with Gauntlets. The air gunners began to leave but some were persuaded to stay, to train as NCO pilots. Swanwick was one of these and was awarded his flying badge in August 1939 and promoted to Sergeant.

He was called to full-time service at the outbreak of war and after completing his training he was posted to 7 BGS in May 1940, as a staff pilot. Swanwick joined 54 Squadron at Catterick on September 7 and left in December 1940, to join 41 Squadron at Hornchurch.

Commissioned in October 1941, Swanwick was posted to 222 Squadron at North Weald in April 1942, as a Flight Commander. In July he joined 603 Squadron in Malta, as a Flight Commander. Swanwick went to 71 OTU at Port Sudan in September 1942, again as Flight Commander.

In July 1943 he joined 81 Squadron in Malta, as a supernumerary. Swanwick was invalided to the UK in August and after he was discharged from hospital in March 1944 he held various staff appointments until the end of the war.

Swanwick was granted a Permanent Commission in 1949 and retired on April 30 1970, as a Wing Commander.

PO 7.10.41   *FO 10.7.42*   *FL 10.7.43*   *SL 1.8.47*
WC 1.1.60

LEON SWITON

780519   **Sgt**   **Pilot**   **Polish**   **54 and 303 Squadrons**

Born on October 10 1915. Switon joined 54 Squadron at Hornchurch on August 9 1940 and moved to 303 Squadron at Northolt on the 16th.

Switon was posted away on August 2 1941 and later served in Canada at No 1 GRS. He returned to the UK in December 1944, went to 60 OTU for advanced flying training, flew as a staff pilot at 16 FTS, Newton and later instructed there. Switon was released in 1946, as a Warrant Officer.

ALBERT THOMAS SWORD-DANIELS

77127   **PO**   **Air Gunner**   **British**   **25 Squadron**

With 25 Squadron in early July 1940.

Sword-Daniels was released from the RAF in 1947, as a Squadron Leader.

PO 2.3.40   *FO 2.3.41*   *FL 2.3.42*

CHARLES SYDNEY

564940   **F/Sgt**   **Pilot**   **British**   **19, 266 and 92 Sqdns**

Sydney, of St Mary Cray, joined the RAF in 1931 as an aircraft apprentice. He later volunteered for pilot training and was a pre-war airman pilot.

Sydney joined 19 Squadron at Fowlmere on August 18 1940, moved to 266 Squadron at Wittering on the 24th and then to 92

Squadron at Biggin Hill on September 10. Sydney was shot down and killed on the 27th, crashing at Kingston-on-Thames in Spitfire R 6767. He was 25 and is buried in St Mary Cray Cemetery, Orpington, Kent.

DUNCAN BROADFORD SYKES

748418   **Sgt**   **Pilot**   **British**   **145 Squadron**

Joined 145 Squadron at Drem on August 20 1940. Sykes is believed to have made a forced-landing at Holmer Green, near Amersham on October 27, after a combat with Bf 109s. His Hurricane, N 2494, was a write-off.

On November 7 1940 Sykes was shot down by a Bf 109 of JG 2. He crash-landed near Ventnor, slightly injured, in Hurricane P 2924.

Promoted to Warrant Officer on January 1 1942, Sykes was released from the RAF in 1946.

JOHN HUMPHREY CHARLESWORTH SYKES

Sub-Lieutenant (FAA)   **Pilot**   **British**   **64 Squadron**

Joined 64 Squadron at Kenley on July 8 1940.

Back with the FAA, he was posted to Dekheila, Egypt in November 1940 and operated in the Western Desert.

Sykes was later with 806 Squadron in Ceylon and took part in the Madagascar landings in HMS 'Indomitable'. He served as an Air Gunnery Officer at Coimbatore, India in 1944, at RANAS, Nowra in 1948, at the RAN Carrier School at HMAS 'Albatross' in 1949, at Yeovilton in 1952 and finally at HMS 'Centaur'.

Sykes retired on July 29 1958, as a Lieutenant Commander.

Midshipman 1.7.39   *Sub-Lt 20.5.40*   *Lt 14.9.42*
Lt-Cdr 14.9.50

EDMUND JOHN HILARY SYLVESTER

90556   **PO**   **Pilot**   **British**   **501 Squadron**

Born at Trowbridge, Wiltshire on January 13 1914, Sylvester was at Harrow School from 1928 to 1930. He was commissioned in 501 Squadron, AuxAF in January 1939 and called to full-time service on August 29.

Sylvester went to France with 501 on May 10 1940. He shared a Do 17 with Sergeant PCP Farnes on the 12th. Sylvester failed to return from a patrol on the 25th and was last seen attacking a gun post. He turned up the next day, having made a forced-landing after his aircraft was damaged by return fire from a Do 17 and flak.

The squadron returned to England on June 19. Sylvester was shot down on July 20 by Leutnant Zirkenbach of I/JG 27 over the Channel off Cherbourg. He was reported 'Missing'. Sylvester was 26. He is remembered on the Runnymede Memorial, Panel 10.

APO (AuxAF) 5.1.39   *PO 29.8.39*

JOHN EDWARD SYMONDS

103539   **Sgt**   **Observer**   **British**   **236 Squadron**

Joined 236 Squadron in September 1940. Symonds was a member of the crew of a Blenheim damaged by return fire from a BV 138 engaged off south-west Ireland on November 30. After returning to St Eval Symonds and the pilot, Sergeant JD Keynes, were admitted to Truro Hospital with shell splinter wounds.

Commissioned in August 1941, Symonds was released from the RAF in 1947, as a Flight Lieutenant. He later joined the RAFVR.

PO 19.8.41   *FO 19.8.42*   *FL 19.8.43*   *FO (RAFVR) 26.5.49*

WILHELM SZAFRANIEC

781312   **Sgt**   **Pilot**   **Polish**   **151, 607 and 56 Sqdns**

Born on December 1 1915. Szafraniec joined 151 Squadron at Digby on September 12 1940, moved to 607 Squadron at Tangmere on the 29th and then to 56 Squadron at Boscombe Down on October 14.

He was killed on November 23 1940, after colliding with Pilot Officer TF Guest during a formation practice near Middle Wallop. Szafraniec was in Hurricane V 7569. He is buried in Amesbury Cemetery, Wiltshire.

EUGENIUSZ SZAPOSZNIKOW

P 1653   Sgt   Pilot   Polish   303 Squadron

Born on July 17 1916. Szaposznikow joined 303 Squadron at Northolt at its formation on August 2 1940. He claimed a Bf 109 destroyed on the 31st, a Do 17 and another Bf 109 on September 7, two Bf 110s on the 11th and Bf 109s on the 23rd, 27th and October 7. Szaposznikow was awarded the KW and the VM (5th Class)(23.12.40) and a Bar to the KW (1.2.41).

On May 14 1941 he was posted to 8 FTS, Montrose as an instructor. Szaposznikow was awarded the DFM (30.10.41) and commissioned in November. On January 4 1942 he was sent to the FIS, Church Lawford for an instructor's course, after which he went to 16 FTS, Newton.

Szaposznikow returned to operations on December 14 1943. He joined 316 Squadron at Acklington but moved to 303 Squadron at Ballyhalbert on the 21st. He was appointed a Flight Commander on July 6 1944 and was posted away to the PAF Depot at Blackpool on October 17. Szaposznikow returned to 16 FTS on November 15. He was awarded a second Bar to the KW (30.12.44).

He was released from the PAF in late 1946, as a Flight Lieutenant. Szaposznikow was awarded a third Bar to the KW (31.10.47) and the Silver Cross of Merit (16.5.48). He settled in Britain and changed his name to Sharman.

PO 1.11.41   FO 1.11.42   FL 1.11.44

HENRYK SZCZESNY

76781   PO   Pilot   Polish   74 Squadron

Born in Ruszkow, Warsaw on March 27 1910. Szczesny joined the PAF in 1931. He went to the Cadet School at Deblin and was commissioned in 1933, joining the 5th Air Force Regiment and later moving to the 3rd Air Force Regiment, as a fighter pilot. In the fighting in Poland in September 1939 Szczesny destroyed two German aircraft and was wounded in the left leg.

Evacuated to Roumania, he was in hospital in Bucharest and later escaped on a Greek ship, which took him to Malta. Szczesny went to France and then to England. He was at RAF Eastchurch in February 1940 and in May was at Manston, in charge of a platoon of Polish cadets. Szczesny was posted to 5 OTU, Aston Down in July and joined 74 Squadron at Hornchurch on August 6.

He claimed a Do 17 destroyed on the 13th, a Bf 110 on September 11, shared a Do 17 on October 5 and claimed Bf 109s destroyed on December 1 and 5. Szczesny was posted to 257 Squadron at North Weald on the 12th but moved to 302 Squadron's Operations Room on the 19th.

Awarded the KW and Bar (1.2.41), Szczesny returned to operations on February 24 1941, when he joined 317 Squadron at its formation at Acklington. He was awarded two more Bars to the KW (1.4.41), shared a Bf 109 destroyed on July 10, shared a Ju 88 on the 14th and took command of the squadron on August 18 1941. Szczesny was awarded the VM (5th Class)(15.9.41) and the DFC (30.10.41). He was posted away on March 7 1942 to be Polish Liaison Officer at HQ 10 Group, moving to HQ 12 Group on May 12.

Szczesny was appointed Squadron Leader Flying of the Polish Wing at Northolt on December 28 1942. He was leading the Wing on

April 4 1943, escorting American bombers detailed to attack the Renault factory near Paris. On the way back they were attacked by FW 190s. Szczesny shot one down and collided with another. He baled out and was captured by a German patrol, awaiting his landing. At some time later he was in Stalag Luft III.

After being freed in late April 1945 Szczesny returned to the UK. He was later posted to RAF Coltishall and attached to HQ 12 Group for liaison duties. In late 1946 he did a course at the School of Administration and Accountancy at Hereford and then went to 4 RU, East Wretham as Senior Admin Officer.

Szczesny stayed on in the RAF, in the Fighter Control Branch. He retired on March 27 1965, as a Flight Lieutenant, retaining the rank of Squadron Leader.

PO 20.2.40   FO 1.3.41   FL 1.9.42   FL 1.7.46

JOZEF SZLAGOWSKI

780712   Sgt   Pilot   Polish   234 and 152 Squadrons

Born at Koscierzyna in 1914, the son of the local stationmaster. After leaving school Szlagowski became an apprentice electrician. He joined the PAF in March 1934 and after completing his training at Torun he was posted to a fighter squadron.

In 1937 Szlagowski was appointed an instructor at the Officer Cadet School at Deblin. He was there at the outbreak of war and later escaped to Roumania in a light aircraft, with his mechanic. They boarded a boat for Beirut, then got on to another heading for Marseilles. On February 16 1940 Szlagowski joined l'Armée de l'Air. He was sent to England for a course on March 9 and did not return to France.

Szlagowski went to 5 OTU, Aston Down in early July and joined 234 Squadron at St Eval on August 3. After running out of petrol during a routine patrol on the 8th he made a forced-landing at Pensilva, wrecking Spitfire N 3278. Szlagowski claimed a Bf 110 and a Do 17 destroyed on September 4. He was posted to 152 Squadron at Warmwell on October 21 1940 and moved to 303 Squadron at Northolt on February 23 1941. He was awarded the KW (1.2.41).

On a Blenheim escort to Holland on March 13 the tailplane and rudder of Szlagowski's aircraft were severely damaged in collision with another Spitfire. He managed to get back to Northolt. On June 23 1941 he probably destroyed a Bf 109 and two days later was posted away to No 1 AGS, Manby as a staff pilot.

On December 23 1941 Szlagowski was sent to CFS, Upavon for an instructor's course. He joined the staff at 16 FTS, Newton on February 2 1942 and became Airfield Controller there on July 22 1943. He went on a twin-engine refresher course at Newton on September 14 1944 and then became a staff pilot there.

Szlagowski was released from the PAF in November 1946, as a Warrant Officer. He married an English lady, settled in Britain and worked for Wilkinson Sword.

WLADYSLAW SZULKOWSKI

76747   PO   Pilot   Polish   65 Squadron

Born on November 6 1909. Szulkowski arrived in Britain in late 1939 and was commissioned in January 1940. He went to 5 OTU, Aston Down in early July and after converting to Spitfires he joined 65 Squadron at Hornchurch on August 5. Szulkowski claimed a Bf 109 destroyed on the 22nd.

He was posted to 315 Squadron at Acklington at its formation on January 21 1941. He was awarded the KW (1.2.41). Szulkowski was killed in action on March 27 1941, in Hurricane V 7188, as a Flight Lieutenant. He is buried in West Derby Cemetery, Liverpool.

PO 27.1.40   FO 1.3.41

GEORGE WILLIAM TABOR

754844   Sgt   Pilot   British   65 and 152 Squadrons

Tabor, of Essex, joined 65 Squadron at Turnhouse on September 2 1940 and moved to 152 Squadron at Warmwell on October 9. His Spitfire, N 3176, was damaged in a surprise attack by Bf 109s over Portland on November 10 and Tabor landed back at base on a burst tyre, unhurt.

He was killed on July 23 1941, as a Flight Sergeant with 603 Squadron. Tabor was 21 years old. He is buried in Longuenesse Souvenir Cemetery, St Omer, France.

KENNETH WILLIAM TAIT

40441   FO   Pilot   New Zealander   87 Squadron

Tait was born in Wellington on November 19 1918. Provisionally accepted for a short service commission in the RAF, he sailed for the UK on September 22 1937. He began his ab initio training at 13 E&RFTS, White Waltham on October 28 and went to 6 FTS, Little Rissington on January 21 1938.

With training completed Tait joined 87 Squadron at Debden on August 20. He went on a short gas defence course in December and a parachute course in early February 1939. 87 Squadron was posted to France on September 9. At that time Tait was serving as squadron adjutant, continuing to do so until November, when he returned to flying duties.

In late April 1940 Tait crashed over the Maginot Line in thick fog and spent two weeks in hospital, after which he had a short convalescence in his tent on the airfield. The squadron was withdrawn to Debden on May 22. Tait had resumed flying a few days before this and destroyed three German aircraft in the final days in France, certainly sharing a Ju 88 on May 20. A newspaper report stated that Tait had piloted a Dutch plane back, wearing an old uniform, scarf, flying boots and no shirt, having lost all his belongings in the retreat.

On August 15 1940 Tait claimed a Bf 110 destroyed and two others damaged and on the 25th a Bf 109 and a Bf 110. He was posted away from 87 on December 3 1940, going then to 56 OTU, Sutton Bridge as an instructor. He was awarded the DFC (4.2.41) and received a Mention in Despatches (17.3.41).

Tait joined 257 Squadron at Coltishall on July 6 1941, as a Flight Commander. On August 4 he failed to return from an operational reconnaissance over the North Sea. It is believed that he was detailed to attack E-boats and was shot down whilst doing so.

Tait is remembered on the Runnymede Memorial, Panel 29.

APO 9.1.38   PO 28.10.38   FO 28.5.40   FL 28.5.41

JAMES MacGILL TALMAN

77101   PO   Pilot   British   213 and 145 Squadrons

Talman, of Bearsden, Dumbartonshire, took part in the fighting in France in May 1940, possibly with a Battle Squadron and was awarded the DFC (16.8.40). He joined 213 Squadron at Tangmere in September. On the 28th his aircraft was hit by return fire from a Bf 110 engaged over the Isle of Wight. He baled out, unhurt, and was rescued by the Bembridge lifeboat, which landed him at Ryde. The Hurricane, L 1770, crashed into the sea off Culver Cliffs, Bembridge. Talman was posted to 145 Squadron, also at Tangmere, on October 30.

He was killed on July 10 1944, as a Flight Lieutenant with 144 Squadron, operating with Coastal Command in Beaufighters. Talman was 26 and is remembered on the Runnymede Memorial, Panel 203. His portrait was done by Cuthbert Orde in 1940.

PO 6.11.39   FO 6.11.40   FL 6.11.41

HUGH NORMAN TAMBLYN

40862   FO   Pilot   Canadian   141 and 242 Squadrons

Tamblyn, of Watrous, Saskatchewan, learned to fly whilst working as an aircraft mechanic in Saskatoon. He joined the RAF on a short service commission in April 1938.

He joined 141 Squadron, when it was reformed at Turnhouse on October 4 1939. Tamblyn was with the squadron when it flew south to West Malling on July 12 1940. Shortly after 09.00 hrs on the 19th twelve Defiants moved to the forward airfield at Hawkinge. At 12.23 hrs they were ordered off to carry out an offensive patrol twenty miles south of Folkestone. Three were left behind with engine trouble. During the patrol the nine Defiants were surprised by Bf 109s of III/JG 51. Tamblyn was one of the only two pilots to regain his base. His gunner, Sergeant SWM Powell, claimed a Bf 109 destroyed.

On August 8 1940 Tamblyn was posted to 242 Squadron at Coltishall. He claimed a Bf 110 destroyed on September 7, two more on the 9th, a shared Do 17 on the 15th and another destroyed on the 18th. Tamblyn was awarded the DFC (7.1.41) and decorated by the King at Buckingham Palace on April 1 1941.

Two days later Tamblyn was shot down into the sea by return fire from a Do 17, whilst on convoy duty east of Felixstowe. He radioed that his aircraft was on fire. A search found his body, unwounded. He died from exposure and cold.

Tamblyn was 23. He is buried in Ipswich Cemetery, Suffolk.

APO 4.6.38   PO 6.4.39   FO 3.9.40

JOHN HENRY TANNER

565125   F/Sgt   Pilot   British   610 Squadron

A pre-war airman pilot, Tanner was with 610 Squadron at Gravesend in early July 1940.

He failed to return from a patrol over the Channel off Calais on August 11.

Tanner was 25 years old. He is buried in Calais Southern Cemetery, France.

────── TATE

No unknown   Sgt   Aircrew   British   604 Squadron

No service details traced.

REGINALD FREDERICK TATNELL

748556   Sgt   Pilot   British   235 Squadron

Joined 235 Squadron on September 20 1940.

Tatnell was killed on May 18 1941, as a Sergeant with 272 Squadron, aged 25. He is buried in St Augustine's churchyard, Heanton Punchardon, Devon.

DENNIS EDWARD TAYLOR

Petty Officer (FAA)   **Pilot**   **British**   **808 Squadron**

With 808 Squadron at Wick in early July 1940, flying Fulmars on dockyard defence.

Taylor embarked in HMS 'Ark Royal' on October 22 1940 for service in the Mediterranean. On April 3 1941 he destroyed a Cant Z 506B and on the 23rd shared a SM 79. Returning to the carrier on August 23 Taylor became lost and ditched when he ran out of fuel. He and his gunner were picked up by a patrolling Sunderland.

Taylor was later with 807 Squadron. He was commissioned in May 1943 and retired after the war as a Lieutenant. He was killed on October 7 1978, when he crashed in a Piper aircraft near Honiton, Devon after his engine failed.

Sub-Lt 1.5.43   *Lt 1.5.44*

DONALD MURRAY TAYLOR

40153   **FO**   **Pilot**   **British**   **64 Squadron**

Taylor was born on September 26 1917 and was at Oundle School from 1931 to 1934. He joined the RAF on a short service commission in July 1937. He was posted to 11 FTS, Wittering on September 18 and joined the staff at 5 Armament Training Station at Penrhos on May 7 1938.

In early 1940 Taylor was with 64 Squadron at Church Fenton. Over Dunkirk on May 31 he destroyed a Bf 110. He shared in the destruction of a Do 17 on July 1 and damaged a Bf 110 on the 10th. Taylor was shot down on the 17th in a surprise attack by Leutnant Wick of l/JG 2. He crashed at Hempstead Lane, Hailsham, in Spitfire P 9507, wounded, and was admitted to Eastbourne Hospital.

Taylor commanded 195 Squadron from its formation at Duxford on November 16 1942 until January 1944 and then 197 Squadron from January to July 1944. He was awarded the DFC (5.9.44). Taylor commanded 193 Squadron from April 1945 until its disbandment at Hildersheim on August 31 1945.

Taylor retired from the RAF on October 29 1957, as a Squadron Leader, retaining the rank of Wing Commander. He died in 1977.

APO 5.9.37   *PO 12.7.38*   *FO 12.2.40*   *FL 9.2.41*
SL 1.3.42   *SL 1.8.47*

EDGAR FRANCIS TAYLOR

910959   **Sgt**   **Air Gunner**   **British**   **29 and 600 Sqdns**

With 29 Squadron at Digby in early July 1940. Taylor moved to 600 Squadron at Catterick in late September.

He was killed on October 22 1943, as a Flight Sergeant with 57 Squadron, operating in Lancasters from East Kirkby. Taylor is buried in Hanover War Cemetery, Germany.

GEORGE STRINGER TAYLOR

391849   **Sgt**   **Pilot**   **New Zealander**   **3 Squadron**

Born in Oamaru on July 20 1918, Taylor was educated at Waitaki High School. In October 1938 he joined the Civil Reserve of Pilots and carried out his flying training at the Southland Aero Club. Taylor volunteered for war service in October 1939 and reported to the Ground Training School at Weraroa on December 17.

Taylor went to No 1 EFTS, Taieri on January 15 1940 and moved on to No 1 FTS, Wigram on March 10. He was awarded his flying badge in late May and promoted to Sergeant a month later. On July 12 Taylor sailed for the UK in the RMS 'Rangitane'.

He was posted to 6 OTU, Sutton Bridge on September 11 and after converting to Hurricanes joined 3 Squadron at Turnhouse on the 29th. Taylor was posted to the recently-reformed 96 Squadron at Cranage on January 20 1941. Patrolling over the Liverpool area in a Defiant on the night of May 8/9 Taylor destroyed a He 111.

Commissioned in May 1941, Taylor was still with 96 Squadron in early 1943. On February 9 he crashed in a Beaufighter near Turweston. He was admitted to Horton General Hospital, Banbury, where he died of his injuries the next day.

Taylor is buried in Weaverham Parish churchyard, Cheshire.

PO 22.5.41   *FO 22.5.42*

GRAHAM NEVILLE TAYLOR

61013   **Sgt**   **Observer**   **British**   **236 Squadron**

Joined 236 Squadron on July 21 1940.

Commissioned in February 1941, Taylor was released from the RAF in 1946, as a Flight Lieutenant.

PO 12.2.41   *FO 12.2.42*   *FL 12.2.43*

KENNETH TAYLOR

54655   **Sgt**   **Aircrew**   **British**   **29 Squadron**

Taylor was born on June 3 1920. He was with 29 Squadron at Digby in early July 1940.

Commissioned in April 1944, he was awarded the DFC (1.6.45), as a Pilot Officer with 307 Squadron, operating in Mosquitos from Castle Camps.

Taylor retired from the RAF on June 7 1971, as a Squadron Leader.

PO 3.4.44   *FO 3.10.44*   *FL 3.4.46*   *FL 30.6.48*
SL 1.7.53

NORMAN TAYLOR

101500   **Sgt**   **Pilot**   **British**   **601 Squadron**

Born in 1919, Taylor was an aircraft industry apprentice before the war. He joined 601 Squadron at Tangmere on August 7 1940. Taylor claimed a Ju 87 destroyed on the 18th and shared a He 111 on the 30th. He destroyed a Bf 109 on the 31st. His own aircraft was then hit in the gravity petrol tank. Taylor baled out, unhurt. His Hurricane, P 3735, crashed and burned out.

On May 25 1941 he destroyed a Bf 109 and probably another and on June 13 destroyed two more Bf 109s. Commissioned in June, Taylor was posted away in July and awarded the DFM (29.7.41).

In 1942 he was with the MSFU. On November 1 he was launched from the Camship 'Empire Heath', to engage a FW Condor. He intercepted it and drove it off before it could attack any of the ships. In the face of strong return fire he shot it down from close range. After orbiting the convoy to make sure a second Condor was not there he baled out and was picked up by a corvette. For this action Taylor was awarded the DFC (15.12.42).

In 1943 he became a test pilot, achieving an ambition held since his pre-war apprentice days. Taylor stayed on in the RAF and was killed in a flying accident on April 29 1948, as a Flight Lieutenant.

PO 19.6.41   *FO 19.6.42*   *FL 19.6.43*

REGINALD TAYLOR

82733   **PO**   **Observer**   **British**   **235 Squadron**

Joined 235 Squadron on August 14 1940.

Taylor was released from the RAF in 1947, as a Flight Lieutenant. He died on June 10 1950.

PO 28.7.40   *FO 28.7.41*   *FL 1.9.42*

RONALD HENRY WILLIAM TAYLOR

804401   **Sgt**   **Air Gunner**   **British**   **604 Squadron**

A pre-war member of the AuxAF, Taylor was with 604 Squadron at Northolt in early July 1940.

On October 10 Taylor was in Blenheim L 8373, which lost an airscrew during a night patrol over Salisbury. It crashed on landing at Middle Wallop, with undercarriage failure.

Taylor was killed on November 26, when his Blenheim, L 6728, crashed at night at Danebury Hill. The pilot, Pilot Officer NR Wheatcroft, was also killed. Taylor is buried in Hampstead Cemetery, London.

EDWARD WINCHESTER TOLLEMACHE TAYLOUR

Lieutenant (FAA)   **Pilot**   **British**   **808 Squadron**

Taylour was flying Skuas with 800 Squadron in early 1940. He took part in the sinking of the German cruiser 'Konigsberg' by aerial attack at Bergen, Norway on April 10 1940.

In early July Taylour was with 808 Squadron at Wick, flying Fulmars on dockyard defence. He was awarded the DSC and Bar (9.10.40), both awards for actions in Norway.

On October 22 808 Squadron embarked in HMS 'Ark Royal' for service in the Mediterranean. On November 27 Taylour shared in destroying a Cant Z 506B ten miles north of Bone, Algeria, on February 2 1941 he shared a Cant Z 1007, on May 5 he destroyed a Ju 87 and probably destroyed a CR 42, on September 27 he shared a SM 84 and on the 28th shared a Cant Z 506B.

Taylour was given command of 802 Squadron on April 7 1942 and on September 3 the squadron embarked in HMS 'Avenger' for the protection of Convoy PQ 18, bound for Russia. The convoy was heavily attacked on September 13 and in an action with BV 138s m Taylour was shot down in flames by return fire and killed.

He is remembered on the Fleet Air Arm Memorial at Lee-on-Solent.

Midshipman 1.1.33   Sub-Lt 16.1.36   Actg Lt 1.3.38

FRANCIS JOSEPH TEARLE

123198   Sgt   Air Gunner   British   600 Squadron

Joined 600 Squadron at Northolt on July 1 1940.

Commissioned from Flight Sergeant in May 1943, Tearle was then with 89 Squadron in the Middle East. He had retrained as a Radio Observer and was teamed with Pilot Officer RA Miller. They were both awarded the DFC (19.2.43), being then credited with four enemy aircraft destroyed.

Tearle was released from the RAF in 1947, as a Flight Lieutenant.

PO 28.5.42   FO 28.11.42   FL 28.5.44

CYRIL BERNARD TEMLETT

33530   PO   Pilot   British   3 Squadron

Entered RAF College, Cranwell in September 1938. The outbreak of war caused the course to be shortened and Temlett graduated in December 1939. He joined a Battle Squadron in France and served with it in the fighting in May 1940. The squadron was withdrawn in June.

Temlett was awarded the DFC (6.8.40). He volunteered for Fighter Command and joined 3 Squadron at Turnhouse on September 27.

In May 1941 Temlett was with 213 Squadron on board HMS 'Furious' in the Mediterranean. The squadron flew off to Malta on the 21st and then flew on to Mersa Matruh. Temlett was with 'C' Flight, which was attached to 73 Squadron in the Western Desert. On June 15 he destroyed a Bf 109 and on the 26th damaged a Ju 87.

The squadron went to Nicosia in July and returned to the Western Desert in December 1941. On July 3 1942 five Hurricanes of 213 were scrambled over Alamein. They were jumped by four Bf 109s of l/JG 27. Temlett and two other British pilots were killed and a fourth wounded.

Temlett is buried in El Alamein War Cemetery, Egypt.

PO 23.12.39   FO 23.12.40   FL 23.12.41

PATRICK HUGH RICHARD RUNCIMAN TERRY

1190615   Sgt   Pilot   British   72 and 603 Squadrons

Joined the RAF on a short service commission in January 1936 (Officer's No 37725). After completing his flying training Terry joined 19 Squadron at Duxford on October 25 1936. He was posted to the SHQ staff at Halton on September 16 1937 and on February 2 1939 went to 111 Squadron at Northolt.

Terry resigned his commission on September 12 1939. He joined 72 Squadron as a Sergeant-Pilot on October 3 1940 and moved to 603 Squadron at Hornchurch later in the month. He was shot down by Bf 109s in combat over Canterbury on November 5. Terry was admitted to Charlton Hospital, Canterbury, wounded.

No further service details traced.

APO 30.3.36   PO 3.2.37   FO 3.11.38

PHILLIP HARRY TEW

49065   F/Sgt   Pilot   British   54 Squadron

Born on February 19 1913, Tew was a pre-war airman pilot with 65 Squadron. He was posted to 54 Squadron in early 1940 and over Dunkirk on May 26 he probably destroyed a Bf 110.

On August 8 Tew claimed a Bf 109 destroyed and shared in the destruction of a Bf 110.

Commissioned in May 1942, Tew was awarded the AFC (10.6.48) and retired from the RAF on February 19 1963, as a Squadron Leader. He died in 1984.

*PO 17.5.42   FO 17.11.42   FL 17.5.44   FL 17.11.46
SL 1.1.55*

DAVID JOHN THACKER

85273   PO   Pilot   British   32 Squadron

Joined 32 Squadron at Acklington in October 1940. Thacker embarked on HMS 'Furious' for an unknown destination on December 17. With other pilots, he flew a Hurricane off to Takoradi on January 9 1941. They flew up to Cairo in stages, covering more than 4000 miles in six days. They flew via Lagos, Kano, El Geneina, Khartoum, Wadi Halfa and Abu Sueir. Thacker flew across to Malta on January 29 and joined 261 Squadron.

On February 12 he was shot down by Bf 109s of 7/JG 26 and baled out, wounded, into St Paul's Bay. Thacker was out of action for a month. When 261 was disbanded in May he returned to the Middle East and later went to ADU, Takoradi on ferrying duties.

Thacker was awarded the AFC (8.6.44) and he was with 151 Squadron in 1944/45, as a Flight Commander. He was released in late 1946, as a Squadron Leader.

PO 22.9.40   FO 22.9.41   FL 22.9.42

ALEC JOHN THEASBY

1161473   Sgt   Radar Operator   British   25 Squadron

Theasby, of Malton, joined 25 Squadron at North Weald in October 1940. He was killed on November 16 1940, when the Blenheim he was in crashed and burned out near Ingatestone during a night patrol, cause unknown. The other two crew members were also killed.

Theasby was 23. He is buried in Norton Cemetery, Yorkshire.

JOHN GRAHAM THEILMANN

37701   FL   Pilot   British   234 Squadron

Joined the RAF on a short service commission in January 1936. Theilmann was posted to 9 FTS, Thornaby on April 4 and joined 41 Squadron at Catterick on October 11.

When 234 Squadron was reformed at Leconfield on October 30 1939 Theilmann was appointed 'A' Flight Commander. He relinquished this on August 7 1940, then being non-effective sick, suffering from asthma.

Theilmann was released from the RAF in 1946, as a Squadron Leader.

*APO 23.3.36   PO 27.1.37   FO 27.7.38   FL 27.7.40
SL 1.12.41*

ALEXANDER HENRY THOM

114075　Sgt　Pilot　British　79 Squadron

Thom joined the RAFVR on June 24 1939 and did his weekend flying at 11 E&RFTS, Perth. Called to full-time service at the outbreak of war he was posted to 3 ITW, Hastings on October 2, moved to 15 EFTS, Redhill on April 29 1940 and then to 15 FTS on June 15, firstly at Brize Norton and later at Chipping Norton.

On September 29 Thom went to 6 OTU, Sutton Bridge and after converting to Hurricanes he joined 79 Squadron at Pembrey on October 6, moving to 87 Squadron at Exeter on the 31st.

Commissioned in early December 1941, Thom was appointed 'B' Flight Commander on July 10 1942 and awarded the DFC (14.8.42). He was then credited with two enemy aircraft destroyed and a He 111 probably destroyed.

In November 1942 87 Squadron went to North Africa. Thom was posted away on May 7 1943, to be a flying control officer at Bone. He returned to 87 Squadron, then at Tingley, and took command on June 27 1943. He was again posted away on September 27, this time to return to the UK.

On November 17 Thom became an instructor at 55 OTU, Annan. He moved to 53 OTU, Kirton-in-Lindsey on March 12 1944. He was appointed Flight Commander, Fighter Affiliation Flight at 84 (Bomber) OTU at Husbands Bosworth on May 19 1944 and remained there until October 10, when he went to RAF Peterhead, as adjutant.

Thom's final posting was to HQ 13 Group, Inverness on May 8 1945, as a staff officer. He was released from the RAF on December 4 1945, as a Flight Lieutenant.

PO 3.12.41　　FO 1.10.42　　FL 27.9.43

———— THOMAS

No unknown　Sgt　Aircrew　British　236 Squadron

Joined 236 Squadron in early August 1940.
No further service details traced.

CHARLES RAYMOND DELAUNEY THOMAS

40031　FO　Pilot　British　236 Squadron

Joined the RAF on a short service commission in June 1937. Thomas was posted to 10 FTS, Tern Hill on August 21 and after completing his training he joined the FAA Pool at RAF Gosport on October 10 1938.

In June 1940 Thomas was with 236 Squadron. On July 18 he was captain of Blenheim L 6779, which failed to return from a photo-reconnaissance sortie over Le Havre. The weather was bad and intense flak was encountered over Cap de la Hague. It is believed that the Blenheim was shot down by Major Schellmann of JG 2.

Thomas was 22. He is buried in Quiberville churchyard, France.

APO 9.8.37　　PO 31.5.38　　FO 31.1.40

ERIC HUGH THOMAS

39138　FL　Pilot　British　222, 19 and 266 Sqdns

Born in Tunbridge Wells in 1917, Thomas joined the RAF on a short service commission in July 1936. He was posted to 6 FTS, Netheravon on September 19 and joined 19 Squadron at Duxford on May 22 1937.

In early 1940 Thomas was a flying instructor at Cranwell and in early July was with 222 Squadron at Kirton-in-Lindsey. He moved to 19 Squadron at Fowlmere on August 19 and then to 266 Squadron at Wittering on the 24th. Thomas rejoined 222, then at Hornchurch, on September 15 and on this day shared in the destruction of a Do 17. On October 9, 25 and 29 Thomas claimed Bf 109s destroyed.

On April 4 1941 he destroyed a Ju 88. Thomas took command of 611 Squadron at Rochford in June 1941. He left the squadron in early November to command 133 Squadron at Eglinton. Thomas was awarded the DFC (25.11.41).

He probably destroyed a FW 190 on June 5 1942. In early August Thomas was appointed Wing Leader at Biggin Hill and led the Wing over Dieppe on August 19. On the 31st he was posted to lead the Hornchurch Wing.

Thomas was awarded a Bar to the DFC (18.9.42). He was posted away from Hornchurch on November 27 and awarded the DSO (2.2.43). He left the RAF in late 1944, as a Wing Commander, and died in 1972.

APO 31.8.36　　PO 10.7.37　　FO 10.4.39　　FL 3.9.40
SL 1.12.41

FREDERICK MYTTON THOMAS

37133　FL　Pilot　British　152 Squadron

Born on October 10 1915, Thomas joined the RAF on a short service commission in March 1935. He was posted to 3 FTS, Grantham on the 30th and joined 29 Squadron at North Weald on February 1 1936. Thomas went to the Station Flight at Mildenhall on May 10 1937 and was posted to 73 Squadron at Digby on September 13 1937. He was the Officers RAF Featherweight Boxing Champion in 1936, 1938 and 1939 and Imperial Service Champion in 1939.

When 152 Squadron was reformed at Acklington on October 1 1939 Thomas joined it, as a Flight Commander. In November he was detached with four Gladiators to Sumburgh as OC Fighter Flight, Shetland. He was recalled to 152 in December.

Thomas served as 'B' Flight Commander at Warmwell throughout the Battle of Britain. He was promoted to Squadron Leader and posted to Middle Wallop in November 1940, as Sector Controller. In 1942 Thomas was loaned to the RCAF to advise on setting up an Air Defence system on the east and west coasts.

In 1943 he did a twin-engine conversion course at Grantham. After a spell at Air Ministry Thomas was posted to Palam, India, in late 1944, as Wing Commander Flying. In 1947 he was at HQ 12 Group, as Wing Commander Night Ops.

Thomas retired from the RAF on December 29 1958, as a Wing Commander.

APO 15.3.35　　PO 15.3.36　　FO 15.9.37　　FL 15.9.39
SL 1.12.40　　WC 1.3.42　　WC 1.7.47

GORDON SINCLAIR THOMAS

175847　Sgt　Air Gunner　British　604 Squadron

Joined 604 Squadron, AuxAF in 1936, after being in the Territorial Army. Thomas flew with Flying Officer AS Hunter in Demons before the war.

Called to full-time service on August 24 1939, Thomas continued to fly with Hunter and on June 18 1940 they shot down a He 115 floatplane off the French coast, 604's first victory.

In May 1941 Thomas was posted away to 109 Squadron, a hush-hush unit formed from the Wireless Intelligence Unit at Boscombe Down, concerned with the development of radio counter-measures and new radar aids.

Commissioned from Warrant Officer in March 1944, Thomas was released from the RAF in 1946, as a Flying Officer.

PO 24.3.44   FO 24.9.44

RICHARD CEREDIG THOMAS

82731   PO   Observer   British   235 Squadron

Thomas, of Cardiff, joined 235 Squadron on August 16 1940. He was a member of the crew of Blenheim N 3530, which failed to return after a combat with enemy aircraft over the Channel on October 9 1940. All three men on board were lost.

Thomas' body was recovered and he is buried in Cathays Cemetery, Cardiff.

PO 28.7.40

ROBERT TUDOR THOMAS

754426   Sgt   Pilot   British   247 Squadron

Thomas, of Battersea, London, joined the newly-formed 247 Squadron at Roborough on August 14 1940. He wrote off Gladiator N 5701 on the 27th, after flying through trees at Werrington, Devon on a landing approach after a night patrol over Plymouth, unhurt.

During a night patrol on November 21 Thomas lost his bearings, flew into Will Hay's Height, Okehampton and was killed, aged 22. He is buried in St Stephen's churchyard, Bodfari, Flintshire.

SAMUEL RICHARD THOMAS

42029   PO   Pilot   British   264 Squadron

Joined the RAF on a short service commission in March 1939. Thomas was posted to 264 at Sutton Bridge on November 6, soon after its reformation. He took part in operations over Dunkirk and during the Battle of Britain.

When he was awarded the DFC (29.5.42) the citation credited him with three enemy aircraft destroyed in daylight and another damaged. Thomas was awarded the AFC (2.6.43).

He stayed on in the RAF after the war. Thomas' name disappears from the Air Force List after July 1962.

APO 29.4.39   PO 6.11.39   FO 6.11.40   FL 6.11.41
SL 1.7.45   SL 1.8.47   WC 1.7.55

ANTONY ROBERT FLETCHER THOMPSON

84965   PO   Pilot   British   85 and 249 Squadrons

Thompson was born on October 14 1920. He joined 85 Squadron at Church Fenton on September 29 1940 and moved to 249 Squadron at North Weald on October 17. Thompson shared in the destruction of a Ju 88 on October 28 and destroyed a Bf 109 on the 30th.

In May 1941 249 went to Malta. The squadron flew off 'Ark Royal' on the 21st, in two groups. On August 5 Thompson joined the Malta Night Fighter Unit, then being formed at Ta Kali. He damaged a BR 20 at night on November 11. The Unit became 1435 (Night Fighter) Flight on December 2.

Thompson was posted to 71 OTU, Gordon's Tree, Sudan on March 3 1942. He returned to operations on October 1, joining 73 Squadron in the Western Desert. In mid-November he was promoted and appointed 'A' Flight Commander. At the end of December Thompson was posted to Cairo and in February he went to 206 Group,

as a test pilot. He was awarded the DFC (23.3.43).

On March 10 1944 Thompson was seconded to BOAC and he took his release in Cairo on January 26 1946, as a Flight Lieutenant. The next day he signed a contract with BOAC, as a Captain. He retired from British Airways on October 14 1975.

PO 7.9.40   FO 7.9.41   FL 7.9.42

FRANK NOBLE THOMPSON

78258   PO   Observer   British   248 Squadron

Thompson was born in 1917. He was with 248 Squadron in early July 1940.

He was released from the RAF in 1946, as a Flight Lieutenant.

PO 24.3.40   FO 24.3.41   FL 24.3.42

JAMES ROBERT THOMPSON

755146   Sgt   Air Gunner   British   236 Squadron

Thompson, of Kings Heath, Birmingham, joined 236 Squadron in mid-August 1940.

He was killed on March 10 1941, as a Sergeant with 272 Squadron, probably flying with Pilot Officer AAL van Wayenberghe. Thompson was 24. He is remembered on the Runnymede Memorial, Panel 53.

JOHN MARLOW THOMPSON

34183   SL   Pilot   British   111 Squadron

Thompson was born on August 16 1914 at Keynsham, Somerset and educated at Bristol Grammar School. He joined the RAF on a short service commission in March 1934, was posted to 5 FTS, Sealand on April 3 and with training completed he joined 29 Squadron at North Weald on March 4 1935. Thompson went to 151 Squadron at its reformation at North Weald on August 4 1936. He was appointed a Flight Commander in September 1937.

Thompson was promoted and given command of 111 Squadron at Drem in January 1940. In patrols over France in May he claimed a He 111 destroyed on the 13th, a Bf 110 and probably a second on the 18th and a He 111 probably destroyed on the 19th. In this engagement Thompson was shot down by escorting Bf 110s, unhurt. He made his way back to England. Over Dunkirk on May 31 he damaged a Bf 109. On June 10 he damaged a Do 17 and on the 11th destroyed a Bf 109, probably another and also probably destroyed a Ju 88.

On August 13 Thompson claimed a Do 17 destroyed, on the 15th a Bf 110 and another Do 17, on the 16th a Do 17 and on September 7 a He 111. He was awarded the DFC (6.9.40).

In October 1940 Thompson was posted away from 111 Squadron. He returned to operations on June 30 1941, taking command of 131 Squadron at its reformation at Ouston. The squadron had a high number of Belgian pilots. After the squadron became operational in October Thompson was posted away in November in company with twelve Belgian pilots to form 350 Squadron at Valley on the 13th. He commanded the squadron until March 1942.

In the summer of 1942 Thompson was posted to Malta to lead a Spitfire Wing. He probably destroyed a Ju 88 on August 27 1942, a Bf 109 on October 11 and a Ju 88 on the 16th. He was awarded a Bar to the DFC (4.12.42), the Belgian Military Cross (1st Class)(1.1.43) and the DSO (14.5.43).

Thompson held a series of appointments and commands in the postwar RAF. He was invested with the Danish Order of Dannebrog in 1951 and awarded the AFC (1.1.52). He retired on September 14 1966, as an Air Commodore.

APO 16.3.34   PO 16.3.35   FO 16.9.36   FL 19.9.37
SL 1.6.40   WC 1.3.42   WC 1.7.47   GC 1.7.53
AC 1.7.59

JOSEPH BECKETT THOMPSON

566058   Sgt   Pilot   British   25 Squadron

Thompson, of Magheragall, was with 25 Squadron at Martlesham Heath in early July 1940.

On July 31 Thompson was captain of Blenheim L 1408, which collided with Blenheim L 6722 of 29 Squadron over the Bristol Channel during a test of the AI radar system. He and two MU personnel were lost.

Thompson was 24. He is buried in the Church of Ireland churchyard, Magheragall, Co Antrim, Northern Ireland.

PETER DOUGLAS THOMPSON

84697   PO   Pilot   British   32 and 605 Squadrons

Born on September 7 1920. Thompson joined the RAFVR in January 1939 and began elementary flying training at 20 E&RFTS, Gravesend. Called to full-time service at the outbreak of war, Thompson was posted to 5 EFTS, Hanworth. In January 1940 he went to 3 FTS, South Cerney and after completing the course in June he was sent to 6 OTU, Sutton Bridge to convert to Hurricanes.

Thompson joined 32 Squadron at Acklington in August 1940 and moved to 605 Squadron at Croydon on September 20. He was posted away on October 31. During the Battle of Britain he is believed to have destroyed three enemy aircraft.

On April 27 1941 Thompson was one of twenty-four pilots who flew Hurricanes off HMS 'Ark Royal' to Hal Far, Malta. He joined 261 Squadron and was wounded on May 6 but landed safely. When 261 was disbanded in May he went to the newly-reformed 185 Squadron on the 12th. Thompson shared in destroying a Cant Z 1007 on July 25, shared a SM 79 on the 27th and destroyed a Bf 109 on December 29.

He returned to the UK in January 1942 and was awarded the DFC (30.1.42). In early 1943 Thompson joined 601 Squadron in the Western Desert, as a Flight Commander, moving with it later to Sicily and Italy. He returned to the UK in early 1944 and in July took command of 129 Squadron, operating from Ford with Mustangs.

Thompson led the squadron until April 1945. He stayed on in the RAF, retiring on September 7 1975, as a Wing Commander, retaining the rank of Group Captain.

PO 24.8.40   FO 24.8.41   FL 24.8.42   FL 1.9.45
SL 1.1.49   WC 1.7.56

WILLIAM WATSON THOMPSON

48812   Sgt   Pilot   British   234 Squadron

In the thirties Watson applied to join the RAF as a trainee wireless operator. There were no vacancies so he became an armourer and was eventually promoted to LAC. Watson volunteered for pilot training, was selected and qualified as a Sergeant Pilot.

He was then posted to the Armament School at Catfoss as a staff pilot. In December 1939 Watson joined 603 Squadron at Prestwick and in April 1940 moved to 234 Squadron at Leconfield. On July 31 he crashed on landing at St Eval after a routine night patrol, in Spitfire P 9365. Watson crashed into a stone wall and was badly injured. He was admitted to the Royal Cornish Infirmary.

Watson did not fly again. He was commissioned in the Technical Branch (Armament) in May 1942 and finished his service in the RAF as an Armament Officer. He was released in 1946, as a Flight Lieutenant. He died in 1986.

PO 27.5.42   FO 24.12.42   FL 1.7.45

JAMES ANDERSON THOMSON

37599   FL   Pilot   British   245 and 302 Squadrons

Born on January 18 1916, Thomson joined the RAF on a short service commission in November 1935. He was posted to 11 FTS, Wittering on February 22 1936 and joined 56 Squadron at North Weald on August 24.

Thomson joined 245 Squadron when it was reformed at Leconfield on October 30 1939. Over Dunkirk on May 30 1940 he damaged a Do 17 and on June 1 damaged a Bf 109. He was posted to 302 Squadron at its formation at Leconfield on July 13, as a Flight Commander. On October 29 Thomson collided with Flight Lieutenant JT Czerny during a routine patrol over Brooklands. He baled out, slightly injured. His Hurricane, P 3085, crashed at Penny-Pot Hill, Chobham. Thomson was posted away from 302 on December 28 1940.

In September 1941 he was posted to command 258 Squadron at Martlesham Heath. The squadron flew to Debden on October 3 to prepare for overseas. Leaving their Hurricanes behind the twenty-two pilots went to Abbotsinch on the 30th and two days later sailed in HMS 'Athene' for Gibraltar, with wing-detached Hurricanes on board. After arriving on the 21st the aircraft were to be unloaded, to be taken by 'Ark Royal' to Malta later. However the carrier was sunk returning to Gibraltar so other plans were made for the 258 pilots.

They left on Christmas Eve 1941, on the 'Athene'. They berthed at Takoradi on January 1 1942 and disembarked. The 'Athene' left, taking their Hurricanes with her. On the 3rd they flew on the Middle East ferry route in a DC 3 and arrived at Port Sudan, from where they sailed south in HMS 'Indomitable' on the 9th, with Hurricanes aboard. They flew off on the 28th and later in the morning arrived at Airfield P2 at Palembang, Sumatra. In the afternoon they went on to Seletar airfield, Singapore and flew their first operation on January 31.

On February 10 1942 the three surviving Hurricanes of 258 were withdrawn to Palembang. Of the fifteen surviving pilots six were required to remain behind there to fly with a reformed 605 Squadron. One was nominated, two volunteered and the other three were selected by cutting cards. Thomson was one of the nine pilots evacuated from Java to Ceylon in the SS 'Kota Gede'. His command of 258 Squadron ceased on February 28 1942.

Thomson stayed on in the RAF. He was released on December 18 1957, as a Squadron Leader, retaining the rank of Wing Commander.

APO 3.2.36   PO 25.10.36   FO 25.6.38   FL 25.6.40
SL 1.9.41   SL 1.9.45

RONALD ALEXANDER THOMSON

39398   FL   Pilot   New Zealander   72 Squadron

Thomson was born in Gore on August 11 1910, the son of a chemist. After leaving the High School there he entered his father's business. In early 1936 he won a flying scholarship, sponsored by a newspaper, the prize for which was training to solo standard followed by some further flying. With four hours dual and thirteen hours total Thomson decided to go to England to apply for an RAF short service commission, although he was above the qualifying age. At that time the New Zealand scheme for processing candidates had not been started.

In July 1936 Thomson sailed from Bluff to Sydney and then travelled steerage from there to the UK. On arrival he went to Air Ministry, applied and was provisionally accepted. He began his ab initio course at 11 E&RFTS, Perth on November 16 1936 and was posted to 11 FTS, Wittering on February 8 1937. He completed his training in early September and joined 72 Squadron at Church Fenton on the 4th.

Thomson was still with the squadron in June 1940. On the 26th he destroyed a Ju 88 caught in searchlights, one of the few night victories gained in a Spitfire. On September 1 Thomson was flying one of twelve Spitfires despatched from Croydon to intercept enemy aircraft. The squadron was surprised by Bf 109s and Thomson's aircraft was severely damaged by cannon fire and he was wounded in the chest, lungs, stomach, hands and one leg by shell splinters. With a dead engine he glided down for a belly-landing near Leeds Castle, selected an ideal-looking field but on his final approach saw anti-invasion steel hawsers stretched across it. With no choice he flew under the hawsers at 120 mph and lost speed by lowering the Spitfire's nose into the ground to come to a halt before hitting tall trees at the far end of the field. His aircraft skidded to a stop, its fin and rudder sliced off, Thomson climbed out and was taken to Leeds Castle military hospital. He rejoined 72 at Biggin Hill on October 11.

In early 1941 Thomson was posted to 2 CFS, Cranwell for an instructor's course. He qualified as an A 2 Elementary Instructor and went to 7 EFTS, Desford in June 1941 to instruct on Tiger Moths. Thomson was sent to ECFS, Hullavington in November 1941 for a Senior Instructor's Course and in March 1943 he was appointed CFI at 11 (P) AFU, Condover, a pre-conversion unit doing day and night flying in Oxfords.

On November 20 1943 Thomson went to Canada as a CFI and when the Empire Air Training Scheme began to run down he returned to England on June 4 1944. He was posted to the Aircrew Officers Training School at Hereford to instruct on ground subjects.

Thomson transferred to the RNZAF in 1945 and sailed for New Zealand with his family in June 1946. After a long spell on the sick list he was released in June 1947, as a Squadron Leader.

APO 25.1.37   PO 16.11.37   FO 16.5.39   FL 3.9.40
SL 1.12.41

THOMAS RUSSELL THOMSON

85246   PO   Pilot   British   607 and 213 Squadrons

Joined the RAFVR in April 1939. Thomson was called to full-time service at the outbreak of war and with training completed he joined 607 Squadron at Tangmere on October 9 1940, moving to 213 Squadron, also at Tangmere, on the 21st.

On October 29 Thomson became a casualty and was in hospital during 1941. He resumed active service in 1942 and went into Flying Control. He was released from the RAF on August 16 1946, as a Wing Commander. Thomson received a Mention in Despatches in 1944 and was made an OBE (1.1.72) for services to aviation.

PO 7.9.40   FO 7.9.41   FL 1.1.43

EDWARD ROLAND THORN

46957   Sgt   Pilot   British   264 Squadron

A pre-war airman pilot, Thorn was born in Portsmouth in 1913. He joined 264 Squadron at Sutton Bridge at its reformation on October 30 1939. He teamed up with LAC FJ Barker and they later became the most successful Defiant partnership of the war.

Over Dunkirk on May 28 1940 they destroyed three Bf 109s, the following day two Ju 87s and a Bf 110 and on May 31 a He 111 and another shared. Thorn was awarded the DFM (14.6.40).

When 264 Squadron moved south to Hornchurch on

August 21 1940 Thorn and Barker were again in action. On the 26th they destroyed two Do 17s and as they went for a third they were attacked by a Bf 109. With their aircraft damaged Thorn spun down and prepared to make a crash-landing. At 500 feet the Bf 109 attacked again, this time setting the Defiant on fire. Before crashing Barker shot the enemy fighter down and it crashed a short distance away. Thorn and Barker escaped with slight injuries. For this action they were each awarded a Bar to the DFM (11.2.41).

They destroyed a He 111 at night on April 9 1941. The partnership broke up when Thorn was commissioned from Warrant Officer in October 1941 and posted to 32 Squadron at Angle. He took command of the squadron in April 1942 and led it until September. At the completion of his tour he was awarded the DFC (22.9.42).

Thorn later served with 169 Squadron, as a Flight Commander, and was awarded a Bar to the DFC (8.12.44). He was killed in a flying accident on February 12 1946 and is buried in St Peter's churchyard, Bishops Waltham, Hampshire.

PO 11.10.41   FO 26.2.42   FL 6.7.42

LAURENCE ARTHUR THOROGOOD

107939   Sgt   Pilot   British   87 Squadron

Born on May 13 1919, Thorogood was an engineering apprentice when he joined the RAFVR at Luton in December 1938. After a few hours dual on Magisters at 29 E&RFTS he was sent on a two months course at 9 E&RFTS, Ansty, after which he returned to Luton to train on Harts.

Called to full-time service at the outbreak of war, Thorogood went to No 1 ITW Cambridge, based at Pembroke College. He was posted to 2 FTS, Brize Norton on March 1 1940, was awarded his flying badge on April 25 and joined 87 Squadron at Church Fenton on June 14. Thorogood destroyed a Ju 88 on August 25.

He shared a Do 18 with Ian Gleed on May 24 1941, was commissioned in August and posted away from the squadron in April 1942. During his rest period Thorogood served firstly as a judge's marshal and then went on a Specialist Armament Officer's Course. He was posted to India in July 1943, to be OC of a gunnery flight at Poona. Thorogood was sent in March 1944 for a course at the Air Fighting Training Unit at Amarda Road.

In July he joined 9 (IAF) Squadron at Comilla, as a Flight Commander. He had carried out 56 operational sorties when his tour ended in January 1945. After a spell with 607 Squadron to gain Spitfire experience Thorogood took command of 273 Squadron on Ramree Island in April 1945, moving on May 9 to Mingaladon. He went to Tangmere in July for a Fighter Leaders' Course and rejoined 273 in Saigon. With the disbandment of the squadron imminent Thorogood was posted to 155 Squadron at Tengah in September 1945.

He led the squadron to Indonesia in February 1946, to support the Indian Army in operations against the Indonesians and to cover the withdrawal of the Dutch. Thorogood was awarded the DFC (4.6.46), disbanded his squadron in September and returned to the UK. He retired from the RAF on June 1 1964, as a Flight Lieutenant, retaining the rank of Squadron Leader.

PO 14.8.41   FO 14.8.42   FL 14.8.43   FL 14.2.45

PETER THORPE

754556   Sgt   Pilot   British   145 Squadron

Joined 145 Squadron at Drem on August 22 1940.

Thorpe was shot down by Bf 109s on October 12 over Hastings and baled out, injured. He landed at Coghurst and was taken to Buchanan Hospital, Hastings. His Hurricane, P 3896, crashed in Blackbrooke Wood, Guestling.

No further service details traced.

ALFRED ROBERTS TIDMAN

86345   PO   Pilot   British   64 Squadron

Tidman, of Lincolnshire, joined 64 Squadron at Biggin Hill on October 11 1940.

He was posted away to 123 Squadron on May 10 1941, at its reformation at Turnhouse. Later Tidman was posted to 602 Squadron at Kenley to gain operational experience. He was shot down and killed on September 17 1941, on his fourth flight with the squadron.

Tidman was 23. He is buried in Bergen-op-Zoom War Cemetery, Netherlands.

PO 14.9.40

JOHN TILL

552090   Sgt   Aircrew   British   248 Squadron

Till, of Bradford, Yorkshire, joined 248 Squadron in mid-July 1940.

He was killed on June 12 1941, as a Sergeant with 248, aged 19. He is remembered on the Runnymede Memorial, Panel 53.

RUPERT CLAUDE TILLARD

Lieutenant (FAA)   Pilot   British   808 Squadron

Tillard, of Wimborne, Dorset, was a Sub-Lieutenant in the Navy when he was seconded to the RAF in January 1932, becoming a Flying Officer. On the 17th he was posted to the RAF Training Base at Leuchars for flying instruction. On September 4 1932 Tillard went to RAF Gosport for further training, after which he joined 812 Squadron on April 19 1933, based at Hal Far, Malta and on HMS 'Glorious'.

On April 8 1935 Tillard was posted to 811 (Fleet Torpedo-Bomber) Squadron, based at Gosport and on HMS 'Furious'. He moved to 714 (Catapult) Flight on July 15 1936, with the 4th Cruiser Squadron in the East Indies. Tillard was appointed a Flying Examining Officer at 26 (Training) Group, Hendon on July 16 1938. He was recalled to the Navy at the outbreak of war.

In early July 1940 Tillard was commanding 808 Squadron at Wick, flying Fulmars on dockyard defence. He embarked with the squadron on HMS 'Ark Royal' on October 22 1940. South of Sardinia on November 8 Tillard destroyed a SM 79, on the 9th he shot down a Cant Z 506B and a SM 79, on the 27th shared a SM 79, on January 9 1941 he destroyed two more SM 79s. For this action he was later awarded the DSC.

On April 3 1941 Tillard shared in probably destroying a Cant Z 506B. On May 8 he was leading an attack on sixteen SM 79s when his Fulmars were jumped by the CR 42 escort. Tillard was shot down into the sea and he and his observer, Lieutenant MF Somerville, were lost.

Tillard was 31. He is buried in Enfidaville War Cemetery, Tunisia.

Midshipman 1.9.27   Sub-Lt 16.9.30   Lt 1.12.32
FO 17.1.32   FL 1.1.37   Lt-Cdr 1.12.40

JAMES TILLETT

33454   PO   Pilot   British   238 Squadron

Tillett entered RAF College, Cranwell in September 1937 as a flight cadet. He graduated in July 1939.

He joined 238 Squadron at St Eval on September 7 1940. Tillett was shot down and killed on November 6 1940, possibly by Major Helmut Wick. His Hurricane, V 6814, crashed and burned out at Park Gate, Fareham.

Tillett is buried in Ann's Hill Cemetery, Gosport.

PO 29.7.39

EDWARD GEORGE TITLEY

86334   PO   Pilot   British   609 Squadron

Titley, of Northam, Devon, joined 609 Squadron at Middle Wallop on October 20 1940.

He was killed on July 17 1943, as a Squadron Leader, aged 31. The unit he was serving with is not known. Titley is buried in St Margaret's churchyard, Northam.

PO 7.9.40   FO 7.9.41   FL 7.9.42

EUGENE QUIMBY TOBIN

81622   PO   Pilot   American   609 Squadron

Tobin, of Los Angeles, learned to fly in the late thirties, paying for his lessons by working as a guide and messenger at the MGM Studios in Hollywood. In late 1939 Tobin volunteered to fly in the war in Finland. When that war ended he was told he would fly with l'Armée de l'Air. With fellow-Americans, A Mamedoff and VC Keough, he went to Paris, via Canada.

The May 1940 blitzkrieg had already started when they arrived and the three men were virtually ignored. They joined two Czech pilots in a scheme to steal two Potez bombers to fly to England but the attempt failed and the Czechs were killed by French guards.

The Americans made their way to St Jean de Luz, where they managed to get a ship. They eventually reached London and after some initial problems were accepted by the RAF. They went to 7 OTU, Hawarden on July 7 1940 and joined 609 at Middle Wallop on August 8. Tobin shared in the destruction of a Bf 110 on the 25th and shared a Do 17 on September 15.

When the first Eagle Squadron, 71, was reformed at Church Fenton on September 19 1940 the three Americans from 609 were the first pilots to arrive. Tobin was killed on September 7 1941, on 71 Squadron's first sweep over France, after an attack by Bf 109s. He was 24 years old and is buried in Boulogne Eastern Cemetery, France.

PAUL ANTHONY TOMLINSON

44198   PO   Pilot   British   29 Squadron

Tomlinson was born on November 3 1921. He entered RAF College, Cranwell in September 1939 as a flight cadet. He did a shortened course and graduated on July 21 1940, with a Permanent Commission.

He joined 29 Squadron at Digby on August 20. Two days later, during an RDF trial flight, his Blenheim was struck by lightning. Tomlinson and his gunner were unhurt and returned safely to base.

Tomlinson retired from the RAF on March 31 1945, as a Flight Lieutenant, retaining the rank of Squadron Leader.

PO 21.7.40   FO 21.7.41   FL 21.7.42

REGINALD ELLIS TONGUE

78551   PO   Pilot   British   3 and 504 Squadrons

Tongue made his first flight in 1931, in a Tiger Moth from Barton Airport, Manchester. He went up to Oxford, where he joined the University Air Squadron. He soloed in July 1932 at the annual camp at Eastchurch.

In July 1935 Tongue left the squadron, did a little more flying in 1936 and then bought his own Leopard Moth in 1937. He was a well-known motor-racing driver before the war, winning places in important events in Britain and on the Continent from 1934 to 1939.

Tongue joined the RAF in early 1940, went to 9 FTS, Hullavington on April 10 and was posted directly to 3 Squadron at Wick on July 27. A week later he was sent to 5 OTU, Aston Down and after converting to Hurricanes he returned to Wick on September 2. Tongue was posted to 504 Squadron at Filton on the 28th. He made a forced-landing near Whitchurch on October 16, running into a pond in Hurricane R 4178.

On November 10 1940 Tongue went to 249 Squadron at North Weald, moving to 46 Squadron there on the 16th. Apart from a five week attachment to 71 Squadron in March/April 1941 Tongue remained with 46 until May 1. He then went overseas, spent two months at Takoradi and was back in the UK at the end of August.

On October 8 1941 Tongue was posted to 55 OTU, Usworth, as an instructor. He went to Rolls Royce Ltd on March 7 1942, as Fighter Command liaison officer. He was put on the Special Duties List on November 11 1942 and became a test pilot at Rolls Royce. Tongue continued this until October 19 1945. He was released from the RAF on December 14, 1945, as a Flight Lieutenant.

APO 10.4.40   PO 27.7.40   FO 27.7.41   FL 27.7.42

LEONARD VIVIAN TOOGOOD

758096   Sgt   Pilot   British   43 Squadron

Joined 43 Squadron at Usworth on September 28 1940.

Toogood was killed on October 27 when he dived vertically from 20000 feet during high altitude aerobatics. The Hurricane, L 1963, crashed at Congburn Dean, Edmondsley. The cause is unknown but could have been oxygen failure.

He was 20 and is buried in Kingston Cemetery, Portsmouth.

JOHN RICHARD TOOMBS

179612   Sgt   Wop/AG   British   264 and 236 Squadrons

With 264 Squadron at Duxford in early July 1940. Toombs was posted to 236 Squadron in August, as a Wop/AG.

He was commissioned in July 1944 and released from the RAF in 1946, as a Flight Lieutenant.

PO 12.7.44   FO 12.1.45

JOHN GROVES TOPHAM

41882   FO   Pilot   British   219 Squadron

Born in Bradford on March 18 1917, Topham joined the RAF on a short service commission in February 1939. He was with 219 Squadron at Catterick in early July 1940. On August 15 he probably destroyed a Ju 88.

In September 219 began to convert to Beaufighters and Topham teamed up with Sergeant HWW Berridge, a partnership that was to last for over three years. On March 13 1941 they destroyed a He 111 at night and on June 14 an unidentified enemy aircraft. Topham was awarded the DFC (3.3.42). On May 8 1942 they destroyed a He 111, on June 9 a Ju 88 and on July 6 a Do 217. Topham received a Bar to the DFC (14.7.42).

On July 26 the team destroyed two unidentified enemy aircraft and a Do 217 on September 19. Topham was posted away for a rest in early 1943. He returned to operations in October, taking command of 125 Squadron at Exeter, with Berridge as his navigator.

On April 27 1944 they destroyed a Ju 188, on the 28th a Ju 88 and on June 18 two more. Topham was awarded the DSO (1.9.44).

He retired from the RAF on August 20 1968, as an Air Commodore. Topham died in 1987.

APO 1.4.39   PO 23.10.39   FO 23.10.40   FL 23.10.41
SL 7.5.43   SL 1.9.45   WC 1.1.52   GC 1.7.58
AC 1.1.65

JULIUSZ TOPOLNICKI

76722   FO   Pilot   Polish   601 Squadron

Joined 601 Squadron at Tangmere on August 18 1940. Topolnicki shared in the destruction of a Bf 109 on September 6 but was then shot down himself in combat over Mayfield. He baled out, slightly wounded, and was admitted to Leeds Castle Hospital. His Hurricane, P 3382, crashed at Boyton Court, Sutton Valence.

Topolnicki was killed on September 21 when he crashed taking off from Exeter. His Hurricane, L 1894, burned out. Topolnicki was 30. He is buried in Exeter Higher Cemetery, Heavitree, Devon. He was awarded the KW (1.2.41).

FO 27.1.40

DONALD FRANK TOUCH

116513   Sgt   Pilot   British   235 Squadron

Joined 235 Squadron in early October 1940.

In July 1941 Touch was in Malta with a detachment of 272 Squadron. On July 27 he took part in a strafing attack on Borizzo airfield in Sicily, claiming two enemy aircraft destroyed on the ground and another damaged. On August 2, in another attack on Borizzo, he damaged Italian aircraft on the ground.

Commissioned in November 1941, Touch was awarded the AFC (3.4.45). On October 2 1945 he was posted to command 27 Squadron at Akyab but this proved to be an error and he went to a Liberator squadron.

Touch was released from the RAF in 1946, as a Squadron Leader. He died on April 10 1948.

PO 5.11.41   FO 1.10.42   FL 5.11 43

WILLIAM TOWERS-PERKINS

75869   PO   Pilot   British   238 Squadron

Joined 238 Squadron at Middle Wallop on July 13 1940.

Towers-Perkins was shot down in an action with Ju 88s south of Tunbridge Wells on September 11 1940. He baled out, wounded and burned, and was admitted to Tunbridge Wells Hospital. His Hurricane, P 3096, is believed to be that which crashed near Withyham Post Office.

Later transferred to Queen Victoria Hospital, East Grinstead, Towers-Perkins was a founder-member and the first secretary of the Guinea Pig Club. He was released from the RAF in 1946.

PO 18.11.39   FO 18.11.40   FL 18.11.41

PETER WOOLDRIDGE TOWNSEND

33178   SL   Pilot   British   85 Squadron

Born in Rangoon on November 22 1914, Townsend was educated at Wychwood Preparatory School, Bournemouth and Haileybury College. He entered RAF College, Cranwell in September 1933 as a flight cadet. He was a Prize Cadet in that year.

On graduation in July 1935 Townsend joined No 1 Squadron at Tangmere. He was posted to 36 (Torpedo Bomber) Squadron in Singapore in January 1936 but was posted back to the UK for health reasons. He joined 43 Squadron at Tangmere on June 27 1937.

Later in the year Townsend was sent for a course to the School of Navigation, Manston and afterwards posted to 217 (Coastal Command) Squadron at Tangmere. He became ill, threatened to resign and after a long sick leave he rejoined 43 Squadron in September 1938.

Townsend was appointed a Flight Commander in September 1939. He shared in the destruction of a He 111 on February 3 1940. It crashed near Whitby, the first enemy aircraft to fall on English soil during the war. He claimed He 111s destroyed on February 22 and April 8. Townsend was awarded the DFC (30.4.40).

On May 23 1940 he was posted to Debden to command 85 Squadron, which had just returned from France. On July 11 Townsend was shot down into the sea three miles off Southwold during an attack on a Do 17, in Hurricane P 2716. He was rescued by the 'Cap Finisterre' and landed at Harwich.

On August 11 Townsend claimed a Do 17 destroyed, on the 18th two Bf 109s and a Bf 110, on the 26th he shared two Do 17s, on the 28th and 30th destroyed Bf 109s and on the 31st destroyed a Bf 109 and probably a second. In this engagement Townsend was shot down by a Bf 110 over Tunbridge Wells. He baled out, wounded in the foot, landed at Cranbrook Road, Hawkhurst and was admitted to Hawkhurst Cottage Hospital and later transferred to Croydon. His Hurricane, P 3166, crashed at Bedgebury Park, near Badgers Oak, Goudhurst.

PW Townsend (continued)

Townsend was awarded a Bar to the DFC (6.9.40) and rejoined 85 at Church Fenton in mid-September. After the Battle of Britain the squadron went over to night-fighting. On February 25 1941 he destroyed a Do 17, 85's first night victory and on April 10 and 11 he probably destroyed Ju 88s. He was awarded the DSO (13.5.41) and posted to HQ 12 Group, as Wing Commander Night Operations.

In April 1942 Townsend was made Station Commander at Drem and in June he took command of the reformed 605 Squadron at Ford. He went to RAF Staff College in October and in January 1943 took command of RAF West Malling. Later in the year he commanded 23 ITW and then went to 2 FIS, Montrose for an instructor's course.

In mid-February 1944 Townsend was appointed Equerry to the King. He was created a CVO in 1947 and served until the King's death in February 1952, continuing then as Comptroller to the Queen Mother until July 1953, when he was appointed Air Attaché in Brussels. Townsend retired from the RAF on November 18 1956, as a Group Captain. He was a Commander in the Order of Orange Nassau, an Officer of the Légion d'Honneur and a Chevalier in the Danish Order of Dannebrog.

PO 27.7.35   FO 27.1.37   FL 27.1.39   SL 1.9.40
WC 1.12.41   WC 1.7.47   GC 1.1.53

THOMAS WILLIAM TOWNSHEND

801555   Sgt   Air Gunner   British   600 Squadron

Joined 600 Squadron at Northolt in early July 1940.
No further service details traced.

OWEN VINCENT TRACEY

42774   PO   Pilot   New Zealander   79 Squadron

Born in Dunedin on March 15 1915, Tracey learned to fly privately at the Otago Aero Club and obtained his 'A' license in early 1937. He made several applications for a short service commission in the RAF and was finally accepted in April 1939. He sailed for the UK in the 'Rimutaka' on June 27.

Tracey began his elementary flying training at 19 E&RFTS, Fair Oaks on August 8. He went to 3 ITW, Hastings on October 9 and moved on to 3 FTS, South Cerney on the 21st. At the end of the course he was posted to HQ Reserve Command for an instructor's course. On May 29 1940 Tracey went to 6 OTU, Sutton Bridge and after converting to Hurricanes he joined 79 Squadron at Biggin Hill on July 6.

He claimed a He 111 destroyed on August 15, a Do 17 destroyed, a He 111 probably destroyed and a Bf 109 damaged on the 28th, a He 111 destroyed on the 30th, a Do 17 destroyed on the 31st and Do 17s probably destroyed on September 5 and 21.

Tracey was sent to No 1 PDC, Bournemouth on January 29 1941 for overseas. He embarked for the Middle East on March 4 and joined 274 Squadron in the Western Desert on April 5. He destroyed a Ju 52 over Crete on May 26 and was then chased by a Bf 109. Tracey dived steeply and pulled out but the pursuing enemy fighter did not and crashed into the sea. On the 29th he shared in destroying a Ju 88.

On August 26 Tracey was appointed a Flight Commander. When the squadron was engaged in the Sidi Rezegh area on December 1 he saw one of 274's Hurricanes go down and make a forced-landing in no-man's land. Tracey landed, picked up the pilot, Lieutenant Hoffe of the SAAF and successfully carried him back to base.

274 Squadron was detailed to give top cover to Blenheims bombing five miles south-west of El Adem on December 8 1941. Over the target enemy fighters were seen and 274 turned towards them. Other enemy fighters joined in and 274 was heavily outnumbered. Tracey was shot down by a Mc 200. His Hurricane turned over at low level and dived into the ground five miles south of El Adem, bursting

into flames. Sometime later some South African soldiers reported finding a grave beside the wrecked Hurricane. On the cross was a flying helmet and Tracey's identity discs.

Tracey was awarded the DFC (6.10.42) with effect from December 7 1941. After the war his remains were re-interred in Halfaya Sollum War Cemetery.

APO 9.10.39   PO 28.4.40   FO 28.4.41

CHARLES WARREN TREVENA

C 787   FO   Pilot   Canadian   1 (RCAF) Squadron

Trevena joined 120 Squadron, RCAF Auxiliary in December 1936, as an AC 2 on general duties. He obtained his Private Pilot's License in April 1937 and was commissioned in the Auxiliary in July. Trevena began flying Gypsy Moths, then Tiger Moths and at the summer camp he flew Westland Wapitis.

On June 5 1939 he began full-time service with 120 Squadron and in September and October carried out advanced flying training at Camp Borden. Trevena joined 2 (Army Co-operation) Squadron at Ottawa on November 2. He sailed from Halifax with the squadron on February 15 1940 and after arrival at Old Sarum on the 25th the squadron was renumbered 110.

On August 18 Trevena was posted to 5 OTU, Aston Down and after converting to Hurricanes he joined No 1 (RCAF) Squadron at Northolt on September 1. He left the squadron in early March 1941 to be Deputy CO of 403 Squadron, then forming at Baginton. Trevena was posted to Digby on June 30 1941, to form and command 412 Squadron. The squadron became operational in September but after only three sweeps over France he was posted away in November and sailed for Canada on December 23 1941.

In January 1942 Trevena went to Eastern Air Command RCAF to supervise fighter operations. He took command of 25 (RCAF) Squadron at Sydney, Nova Scotia on May 13 1942 but having only four Hurricanes he said he no longer wished to command. Trevena was then sent to BGS, Paulson, Manitoba as a staff pilot. He retired on medical grounds on October 9 1943, as an Acting Squadron Leader.

RICHARD MACKLOW TROUSDALE

42163   PO   Pilot   New Zealander   266 Squadron

Trousdale was born on January 23 1921 at the Old Mission House at Waimate North. In February 1938 he applied for a short service commission and after being provisionally accepted in November he sailed for the UK on February 1 1939 in the RMS 'Tainui'.

On March 16 Trousdale began his ab initio course at 11 E&RFTS, Perth, went to Uxbridge for a short induction course on May 13 and then to 9 FTS, Hullavington on the 27th. He applied for training as a heavy bomber pilot and at the end of the course Trousdale was sent to 10 AOS, Warmwell for a month's practical bombing and air firing.

Trousdale was posted to 266 Squadron at Sutton Bridge on November 6 1939. In late May the squadron began flying patrols over Dunkirk. On June 2 Trousdale probably destroyed a Bf 110. He destroyed a Bf 109 on August 16, probably another on the 18th, shared a Do 17 on September 7 and destroyed another Bf 109 on October 29.

He was posted away on November 23 1940 to 255 Squadron, then reforming with Defiants at Kirton-in-Lindsey, as a Flight Commander. He destroyed a He 111 off Spurn Head at night on February 10 1941, was awarded the DFC (4.3.41) and destroyed two more He 111s on May 9 during a raid on Hull.

On July 20 1941 Trousdale was posted to HQ 12 Group for staff duties connected with night operations. He returned to operations on October 1, joining 409 Squadron at Coleby Grange as a Flight Commander. Trousdale destroyed a He 111 on March 8 1942 and a Do 217 on April 4. He was awarded a Bar to the DFC (8.5.42).

Promoted to Acting Wing Commander, Trousdale went to Church Fenton on July 9 to form and command 488 Squadron. On February 18 1943 he destroyed a railway engine on an intruder operation and damaged two barges. Trousdale was posted to HQ 13 Group on the 20th, as Wing Commander Training. He left on March 13 1944 to go to the A&AEE at Boscombe Down, where he flew a great variety of aircraft, from Tiger Moths to Lancasters. He also attended technical courses and took a test pilot's course.

Trousdale transferred to the RNZAF on January 19 1945. He was posted to TFU, Defford on March 5, where he flew many twin and four-engined types of aircraft. He returned to New Zealand in January 1946 with his family. Trousdale was granted a Permanent Commission in the RNZAF on April 29 1947.

In May he went to the UK with another pilot to collect two Mosquitos and ferry them back to New Zealand. On May 16 he was acting as second pilot carrying out a dual instrument and flight check in a Mosquito from RAF Pershore, with an RAF officer as instructor. Whilst going through an exercise involving single-engined flight at a low altitude the aircraft stalled and crashed. Both men were killed.

APO 13.5.39   PO 6.11.39   FO 6.11.40   FL 20.10.41
SL 9.10.42   SL (RNZAF) 29.4.47

ALEC ALBERT GRAY TRUEMAN

40766   PO   Pilot   Canadian   253 Squadron

Born at Sackville, New Brunswick in 1914, Trueman joined the RAF on a short service commission in March 1938. After completing his training at 6 FTS, Netheravon he served in Bomber Command at Waddington and Hemswell.

In June 1940 Trueman converted to Hurricanes at 6 OTU, Sutton Bridge and joined 253 Squadron at Turnhouse on July 20. He damaged a Bf 109 on September 2.

Trueman was shot down and killed in combat over Kenley on September 4. His Hurricane, V 6638, crashed in Tudor Close, Banstead. He was 26 and is buried in St Luke's churchyard, Whyteleafe, Surrey.

APO 7.5.38   PO 7.3.39

JAN TRUHLAR

82643   Sgt   Pilot   Czechoslovakian   312 Squadron

Truhlar joined 312 Squadron at Duxford on September 5 1940.

Commissioned in March 1941, he was shot down over St Omer on June 9 and captured. Truhlar returned to Czechoslovakia and died there on October 25 1973.

FO 1.3.41

ANTHONY JOHN TRUMBLE

37137   FL   Pilot   British   264 Squadron

Born on December 15 1915, Trumble joined the RAF on a short service commission in March 1935. He was posted to 5 FTS, Sealand on the 30th and after completing his training he joined 56 Squadron at North Weald on February 28 1936.

Trumble was attached to RAF Gosport on June 22 for floatplane conversion and then No 1 FTS, Leuchars for an FAA conversion course. He joined 801 (Fleet Fighter) Squadron on September 25 1936, based at Southampton and on HMS 'Furious', moved to 800 (Fleet Fighter) Squadron on May 6 1937 and to 803 (Fleet Fighter) Squadron on December 1 1938, as 'A' Flight Commander.

On March 31 1939 the Navy took over the FAA and Trumble was posted to staff duties at HQ 23 Group. On August 26 1939 he went on staff duties at the RAF Component of the Field Force, destined for France. After Dunkirk Trumble joined 264 Squadron at Duxford, as 'B' Flight Commander.

He left the squadron on July 18 and joined a group of pilots on board HMS 'Argus' at Greenock. They then became 418 Flight and their destination was Malta. The 'Argus' sailed on the 23rd and on August 2 1940 they flew their Hurricanes off to Luqa, Malta. The Flight was renumbered as 261 Squadron on August 16 and Trumble was promoted to Acting Squadron Leader on December 10 and took command.

On February 25 1941 Trumble was posted to HQ Middle East for staff duties on Fighter Plans. He was attached to RAF Crete on April 1 for fighter operations but these were cancelled following the German invasion of Greece. Trumble subsequently became Station Commander at Heraklion. The station was taken by German airborne troops and he was captured. He was in many different camps from Greece to Poland but most of his time as a PoW was spent in Stalag Luft III.

Trumble returned to the UK on May 10 1945. After an Air Ministry attachment for debriefing he went to 7 FIS, Upavon for a refresher flying course and after another course at the School of Air Transport he took command of the Metropolitan Communications Squadron at Hendon on August 10 1945. He was made an OBE (28.12.45) for services as a PoW. Trumble retired on May 3 1966, as a Group Captain. He was made an officer of the Order of Leopold II of Belgium for services to the Belgian Air Force.

APO 15.3.35   PO 15.3.36   FO 15.9.37   FL 15.9.39
SL 1.12.40   WC 1.3.42   WC 1.7.47   GC 1.1.56

ANTHONY JOHN JAMIESON TRURAN

91019   PO   Pilot   British   615 Squadron

Born on April 28 1920, Truran was at Rugby School from 1933 to 1937. He worked for Sir William Crawford, Advertising Agents in Holborn, London. Truran joined 615 Squadron, AuxAF in 1939 and was called to full-time service on August 24.

After completing his training Truran rejoined 615 Squadron, then at Kenley, in late July 1940. On August 15 his Hurricane, L 1829, was badly damaged in combat with Bf 109s over Folkestone but he returned to base, with slight injuries.

Truran was killed on November 25 1940, when he crashed in a Magister at Sunningdale after a wing fell off at 200 feet. Pilot Officer JAP McClintock was also killed. They were both cremated at St John's Crematorium, Woking.

APO 24.8.39   PO 13.7.40

ROBERT ROLAND STANFORD TUCK

37306   FL   Pilot   British   92 and 257 Squadrons

Born in Catford, London on July 1 1916, Tuck was educated at St Dunstan's Preparatory School and College, Reading. After leaving in 1932 he went to sea as a cadet with Lamport and Holt.

In September 1935 Tuck joined the RAF on a short service commission. He was posted to 3 FTS, Grantham on the 28th and joined 65 Squadron at Hornchurch on August 5 1936. In April 1938 Tuck collided with Flying Officer LC Bicknell whilst they were doing aerobatics. Bicknell baled out safely.

In late 1938 Tuck was chosen to represent 65 Squadron at the service initiation of the Spitfire. On May 1 1940 he was posted to 92 Squadron at Croydon, as a Flight Commander. Over Dunkirk on May 23 Tuck claimed two Bf 110s and a Bf 109, on the 24th two Do 17s, on the 25th he shared a Do 17 and on June 2 he claimed a He 111 and a Bf 109. He was awarded the DFC (11.6.40), which he received from the King at a special ceremony at Hornchurch on June 28.

In late June Tuck shot down a Ju 88 at night. On August 13 he shared in the destruction of another Ju 88, on the 14th he destroyed two more and on the 18th another. Tuck was shot down by return fire from a Ju 88 on this day. He baled out over Horsmonden and was

407

RRS Tuck (continued)

slightly injured in a heavy landing. His Spitfire, N 3040, crashed by Tucks Cottages, Park Farm. On August 25 Tuck claimed a Ju 88 destroyed. His Spitfire, N 3268, was severely damaged on this day in an attack on a Do 215 off St Gowan's Head. He glided fifteen miles to land on a dead engine and made a forced-landing, writing off the aircraft.

On September 11 Tuck was posted to command 257 Squadron at Debden. On the 15th he claimed a Bf 110 destroyed, on the 23rd a Bf 109, on October 4 a Ju 88 and on the 12th and 25th Bf 109s. Tuck was awarded a Bar to the DFC (25.10.40). On October 28 he claimed a Bf 109, on December 9 a Do 17, on the 12th a Bf 109 and on the 29th another Do 17. He was awarded the DSO (7.1.41).

On March 2 1941 Tuck claimed a Do 17. He received a second Bar to the DFC (11.4.41). On April 9 he claimed a Ju 88 at night and on May 11 another Ju 88. After shooting down two Bf 109s on June 21 Tuck was himself shot down into the Channel. He was picked up after two hours in his dinghy by a coal barge from Gravesend.

In early July 1941 he was appointed Wing Leader at Duxford. Tuck was sent to the USA on a liaison trip in October, with five other pilots, including Malan and Broadhurst. Back in the UK he became Wing Leader at Biggin Hill. On January 28 1942 he was shot down by flak whilst on a low-level strafe just outside Boulogne.

Tuck was in various PoW camps. After several attempts he finally escaped on February 1 1945, with Flight Lieutenant Z Kustrzynski. They were found by the Russians in mid-February and spent two weeks fighting alongside them. The two men made their way into Poland and later into Russia, eventually reaching the British Embassy in Moscow. They were put on a ship at Odessa for Southampton.

Tuck was awarded the DFC (US)(14.6.46). He retired from the RAF on May 13 1949, as a Wing Commander. He died on May 5 1987.

APO 16.9.35   PO 16.9.36   FO 15.9.38   FL 3.9.40
SL 1.12.41   WC 1.7.44   WC 1.7.47

AIDAN BOYS TUCKER

70683   FO   Pilot   British   151 Squadron

Born on January 11 1912, Tucker was commissioned in the RAFO in July 1931. He was commissioned in the RAF in July 1939 and was with 151 Squadron at Martlesham Heath in early July 1940.

On August 12 Tucker was shot down by Bf 109s off Ramsgate and crashed into the sea, in Hurricane P 3302. He was rescued by a launch and admitted to Ramsgate Hospital, with back wounds.

He retired from the RAF on February 10 1958, as a Flight Lieutenant. Tucker died in 1987.

PO (RAFO) 2.7.31   FO (RAFO) 28.3.33   PO 1.7.39
FO 3.9.40   FL 3.9.41   FL 1.9.45

BERNARD ERIC TUCKER

86349   PO   Pilot   British   266 and 66 Squadrons

Joined 266 Squadron at Wittering on October 7 1940 and moved to 66 Squadron at West Malling on the 25th.

Tucker was released from the RAF in 1946, as a Flight Lieutenant. He later joined the RAFVR.

PO 22.9.40   FO 21.9.41   FL 21.9.42
FO (RAFVR) 21.2.48

FRANK DAY TUCKER

61014   Sgt   Observer   British   236 Squadron

Joined 236 Squadron on July 21 1940.

Commissioned in February 1941, Tucker was released from the RAF in 1946, as a Flight Lieutenant. He died in May 1982.

PO 12.2.41   FO 12.2.42   FL 12.2.43

RONALD YEAMAN TUCKER

55271   Sgt   Air Gunner   British   235 Squadron

Tucker, of Leadgate, Cumberland, joined 235 Squadron on July 12 1940.

He was a member of the crew of Blenheim N 3541, which failed to return from an operational sortie on July 18 1940. All three men on board were lost.

Tucker was 18 years old. He is remembered on the Runnymede Memorial, Panel 20.

DOUGLAS RICHARD TURLEY-GEORGE

41336   FO   Pilot   British   54 Squadron

Born in Middlesex on August 8 1918, Turley-George joined the RAFVR in 1937 and did his weekend flying at 19 E&RFTS, Gatwick. He joined the RAF on a short service commission in August 1938. With training completed he was posted to the Test Flight at RAF Henlow.

Turley-George joined 54 Squadron at Rochford on July 15 1940. He crash-landed near Dover on the 25th after a combat with Bf 109s and wrote off Spitfire P 9387. On August 12 he crash-landed at Denton after being damaged in combat with Bf 109s. Turley-George was admitted to the Kent and Canterbury Hospital, with shrapnel wounds to the head and eye.

After leaving hospital he was grounded and sent on a 2nd Class Navigator's Course, after which he was posted to 54 OTU as a navigation instructor. He later regained his full operational category and was posted to the MSFU in September 1941.

In June 1942 Turley-George was senior pilot on the Camship 'Empire Tide', in Russian convoy PQ 17. The convoy was ordered to scatter when it was thought an attack by German warships was imminent. After the scatter order came the ships were subjected to six days of bombing and torpedo attacks, after which only eleven remained of the original forty-two. The 'Empire Tide' was one of the survivors. It lay over in a bay for two weeks, joined a small Russian convoy and finally reached Archangel on July 24 1942.

Late in the year Turley-George went to the newly-reformed 198 Squadron at Digby, as a supernumerary Flight Lieutenant. In early 1943 he was attached to 231 Squadron as an instructor. It was originally an army co-operation unit which had converted to a fighter-reconnaissance role. In March 1943 he went on to the squadron strength as 'A' Flight Commander. Turley-George was wounded in November during a ground-attack sortie over Normandy. He was awarded the DFC (3.10.44).

In December 1944 he was posted to 88 Group Communications Squadron at Turnhouse, as a Flight Commander. The unit later moved to Fornebu, Norway. In December 1945 Turley-George took command of the Reserve Command Communications Squadron.

He was released to the RAFO in November 1949, as a Squadron Leader, and became a test pilot with an aircraft company. Turley-George was awarded the Norwegian Medal of Liberation.

APO 29.10.38   PO 29.8.39   FO 3.9.40   FL 3.9.41
SL 1.7.44

ROBERT NESBIT TURNBULL

171858   Sgt   Air Gunner   British   25 Squadron

Joined 25 Squadron at North Weald in late September 1940.

With the increasing use of AI equipment and the advent of the Beaufighter Turnbull retrained as a Radio Observer and later as a Navigator Radar.

In late 1942 he was with 89 Squadron in the Middle East. On December 4 he assisted in the destruction of a He 111, on the 6th two He 111s over Algiers, on March 9 1943 a Ju 88 and on April 13 two more Ju 88s. Turnbull was awarded the DFC (25.5.43), as a Warrant Officer.

Commissioned in January 1944, he was released in 1945, as a Flying Officer. Turnbull died on September 18 1980.

PO 20.1.44   FO 20.7.44

DONALD ERIC TURNER

32254   FL   Pilot   British   238 Squadron

Born in Port Stanley in the Falkland Islands on July 31 1910, Turner went to England at the age of 10. He was educated at the King Edward VI Grammar School at Bury St Edmunds. He worked for Barclays Bank and was a member of the Artists Rifles Territorials.

In September 1932 Turner joined the RAF on a short service commission. He was posted to 3 FTS, Grantham on October 8 and with training completed he joined 19 Squadron at Duxford on September 16 1934, to 74 Squadron, also at Hornchurch, on September 3 1935 and to 87 Squadron at Debden on March 22 1937.

Turner went on to the Reserve in August 1938. He was recalled to the RAF on September 1 1939. He joined 238 Squadron at Middle Wallop on July 13 1940. Turner destroyed a Bf 109 on the 20th and shared in the destruction of a Bf 110 on the 21st. He was shot down in combat over the convoy 'Peewit' south of the Isle of Wight on August 8 1940, in Hurricane P 3823, and was reported 'Missing'.

Turner is remembered on the Runnymede Memorial, Panel 5.

APO 23.9.32   PO 23.9.33   FO 23.3.35   FL 23.3.37
FL (RAFO) 18.8.38   FL 1.9.39

GUY TURNER

50155   F/Sgt   Pilot   British   32 Squadron

Born on January 18 1912, Turner was a pre-war airman pilot. He was with 32 Squadron at Biggin Hill in early July 1940.

Turner was shot down in combat over Dover on July 19 and baled out, badly burned. He was admitted to Dover Hospital. His Hurricane, P 3144, crashed at Hougham. Turner later went to Queen Victoria Hospital, East Grinstead for plastic surgery and became a Guinea Pig.

Commissioned in November 1942, he was released from the RAF in 1946 and later rejoined. Turner served in the Technical Branch (Engineering) and retired on January 18 1961, as a Flight Lieutenant, retaining the rank of Squadron Leader. He died on December 5 1982.

PO 19.11.42   FO 7.10.43   FL 8.12.46

PERCIVAL STANLEY TURNER

41631   PO   Pilot   Canadian   242 Squadron

Born in Ivybridge, Devon on September 3 1913, Turner went to Canada as a child. He lived in Toronto and did an engineering course at the university there. He joined 110 Squadron, RCAF Auxiliary, as an airman.

In 1938 Turner went to England and joined the RAF on a short service commission in November. He completed his flying training in September 1939 and was sent to No 1 Fighter Training School at St Athan. Turner was posted to 219 Squadron at Catterick at its reformation on October 4 1939

and moved to 242 at Church Fenton on November 20.

He was sent to France on May 14 1940 and attached to 607 Squadron, moved to 615 Squadron on the 16th and returned to England on the 19th, when 615 was withdrawn. Over Dunkirk between May 28 and June 1 Turner destroyed four Bf 109s and damaged a fifth.

On June 8 242 Squadron went to France to help cover the retreat of the Army to the Atlantic ports. Turner destroyed two Bf 109s on the 9th. The squadron was withdrawn on the 16th.

Turner was promoted on September 15 and appointed 'B' Flight Commander and on this day he claimed two Do 17s destroyed and a Bf 109 probably destroyed. He was awarded the DFC (8.10.40). On February 8 1941 Turner destroyed a Do 17. He was posted to command 145 Squadron at Tangmere on April 13. He destroyed a Bf 109 on July 23 and was awarded a Bar to the DFC (5.8.41).

On October 22 1941 Turner was posted to HQ 42 Group, Northern Ireland on staff duties. He was given command of 411 Squadron at Hornchurch on December 17. In February 1942 Turner was posted to Malta to command 249 Squadron. He destroyed a Bf 109 on the 22nd and on the 23rd was shot down, crashing near Luqa and going to hospital. He rejoined the squadron on March 10. Turner destroyed another Bf 109 on the 18th and was posted away in April to take charge of the Fighter Control Room at Valetta.

In late August 1942 Turner went to RAF Heliopolis and on September 10 was sent as an observer on HMS 'Coventry' on a combined operation against Tobruk. The ship was sunk and Turner was rescued from the sea by a destroyer. In January 1943 he took command of 134 Squadron at Shandur and in June took over 417 Squadron at Ben Gardane. The squadron moved to Malta in July, to prepare for the invasion of Sicily.

On November 19 1943 Turner became Wing Leader of 244 Wing. He was awarded the DSO (23.5.44) and posted to HQ Desert Air Force on May 26 1944, as a staff officer. In June he went to Corsica for the invasion of southern France. In October 1944 Turner returned to the UK, was promoted to Group Captain and given command of 127 (RCAF) Wing.

Turner sailed in the 'Mauretania' for Canada on March 22 1946. He remained in the RCAF until 1965 and died in Ottawa on July 23 1985.

APO 14.1.39   PO 3.9.39   FO 3.9.40   FL 16.7.41
SL 14.6.42   WC 15.7.45

ROBERT CHARLES TURNER

751362   Sgt   Air Gunner   British   264 Squadron

Turner was educated at Christ's Hospital, Horsham. He was with 264 Squadron at Duxford in early July 1940.

He went with the squadron to Hornchurch on August 21 for what proved to be 264's final spell of day-fighting. In action on the 24th Turner's Defiant, L 7021, was severely damaged in the tail by return fire from a Ju 88. He and his pilot, Pilot Officer D Whitley, were both unhurt and returned safely to base.

On the 28th they were shot down and killed by a Bf 109 over Thanet. The Defiant, N 1574, crashed in Kingswood, Challock Forest. Turner was 25. He is buried in Henley Road Cemetery, Eye and Dunsden, Berkshire.

LESLIE JOHN TWEED

138195   Sgt   Pilot   British   111 Squadron

Tweed was born on October 17 1920. He joined 111 Squadron at Croydon on July 27 1940.

Following a combat with Ju 88s over Kenley on September 6 Tweed crash-landed in Hurricane L 1892, injured.

Commissioned in June 1942, he was released from the RAF in 1946 but rejoined later. Tweed retired from the RAF on October 21 1972, as a Flight Lieutenant. He died on February 4 1985.

PO 19.6.42   FO 19.3.43   FL 19.9.44   FL 2.4.48

FRANCIS JOHN TWITCHETT

115346　Sgt　Pilot　British　43 and 229 Squadrons

Joined the RAFVR in London in July 1939. Called to full-time service at the outbreak of war, Twitchett went to No 1 ITW, Cambridge in September. He was posted to 10 EFTS, Yatesbury in December and in May 1940 went to 3 FTS, South Cerney.

In August Twitchett moved to 6 OTU, Sutton Bridge and after converting to Hurricanes he joined 43 Squadron at Usworth in mid-September, moving to 229 Squadron at Northolt in October.

Twitchett was posted to 145 Squadron at Tangmere in December 1940. He was commissioned from Flight Sergeant in January 1942 and went with the squadron to the Middle East in February. At the end of his operational tour in September 1942 Twitchett was posted to 103 MU, Aboukir, on test and ferry duties. On December 24 1942 he joined 74 Squadron at Teheran but it did not become operational until August 1943, flying from Edku on defence duties.

In September Twitchett was posted to 134 Squadron at Bersis. It moved to India in November and was operational by December 5. Twitchett completed his second tour in September 1944 and then returned to the UK. He joined 287 Squadron at Gatwick on anti-aircraft co-operation duties. In mid-1946 he went as an instructor to 7 FIS, Kirton-in-Lindsey. Twitchett instructed at 226 OCU, Bentwaters from May 1948 and then at 203 AFT, Driffield from August 1949 until August 1950, when he was released to the RAFO.

Twitchett flew Chipmunks for the ATC from June 1966 until November 1972.

PO 7.1.42　FO 1.10.42　FL 7.1.44　FL 1.9.45
FO (RAFVR) 17.10.66

EDWARD TYRER

47504　Sgt　Pilot　British　46 Squadron

Joined 46 Squadron at Digby in early July 1940. Tyrer shared in the destruction of a Do 17 on September 15 and shared a Bf 109 on the 27th.

Commissioned in November 1941, Tyrer was released from the RAF in 1945, as a Flight Lieutenant. He died on April 1 1946.

PO 29.11.41　FO 1.10.42
FL 29.11.43

FRANK HASTINGS TYSON

26248　SL　Pilot　British　3 and 312 Squadrons

Born on February 14 1912, Tyson entered RAF College, Cranwell in January 1930 as a flight cadet. On graduation in December 1931 he joined 29 Squadron at North Weald. On March 2 1933 Tyson was posted to 802 (Fleet Fighter) Squadron, based at Hal Far, Malta and on HMS 'Glorious'. He was supernumerary at RAF Gosport on August 22 1935 and on December 16 joined the instructing staff at 7 FTS, Peterborough.

Tyson was posted to 603 Squadron, AuxAF on January 1 1937, as Flying Instructor and Adjutant. He formed and then briefly commanded 245 Squadron at Leconfield from late October 1939. On August 6 1940 Tyson joined 3 Squadron at Wick, as supernumerary Squadron Leader. He took command of 312 Squadron at its formation at Digby on August 29 and remained with the squadron until April 1941, when it became an all-Czech unit. He was awarded the Czech Military Cross (14.4.42).

In September 1942 Tyson was Deputy Station Commander at Luqa, Malta. He retired from the RAF on February 14 1962, as a Group Captain. He died on December 30 1979.

PO 19.12.31　FO 19.6.33　FL 19.6.36　SL 1.2.39
WC 1.3.41　GC 1.7.44　WC 1.10.46　GC 1.1.54

JOHN WINDSOR UNETT

638891　Sgt　Wop/AG　British　235 Squadron

Unett, of Exeter, joined 235 Squadron on August 4 1940.

He was killed on December 27 1940, as a Sergeant with 22 Squadron, aged 28. He is buried in Sage War Cemetery, Oldenburg, Germany.

GEORGE CECIL UNWIN

46298　F/Sgt　Pilot　British　19 Squadron

Unwin, of Bolton-on-Dearne, Yorkshire, was born on January 18 1913. He joined the RAF in April 1929 as an apprentice clerk at RAF Records, Ruislip. On April 24 1931 he was posted to HQ Fighting Area, Uxbridge as an LAC Clerk GD.

He volunteered for pilot training, was selected and on November 25 1935 began his ab initio course at 8 E&RFTS, Woodley. He moved on to 11 FTS, Wittering on February 17 1936 and after completing his training joined 19 Squadron at Duxford.

Over Dunkirk on May 27 1940 Unwin destroyed a Hs 126, on the 28th a Bf 109 and on June 1 a Bf 110 and probably another. On a later patrol that day he shared a probable He 111.

On August 16 Unwin claimed a Bf 110 and a Bf 109 destroyed, on September 3 a Bf 110, on the 7th two Bf 109s, on the 11th a probable He 111, on the 15th three Bf 109s, on the 18th a Bf 110 and on the 27th another Bf 109. He was awarded the DFM (1.10.40). On November 5 Unwin claimed a Bf 109 destroyed, on the 15th he shared a Bf 110 and on the 28th shared a Bf 109. He was awarded a Bar to the DFM (6.12.40) and on December 29 went to 2 CFS, Cranwell for an instructor's course.

Posted to 16 EFTS, Derby on February 23 1941, Unwin was commissioned from Warrant Officer in July 1941 and moved to 2 FIS, Montrose on March 3 1942. He instructed there until October 19 1943, when he was posted to 12 (P) AFU, Grantham to convert to Mosquitos. After a spell at 60 OTU, High Ercall Unwin joined 613 Squadron at Lasham on April 5 1944.

With his tour completed he went to CGS, Catfoss on October 30 1944 and moved to CGS, Leconfield on November 18 1945. Unwin was posted to 608 Squadron, RAuxAF at Thornaby on June 12 1946, as Chief Instructor. He had a staff job at HQ 23 Group from September 27 1947 until January 11 1949 and another at HQ 12 Group until August 18 1949. Unwin was then posted overseas and on September 9 took command of 84 Squadron at Habbaniya.

The squadron moved to Tengah on April 8 1950 and began operations in support of the Army against terrorists in Malaya. Unwin led the squadron until August 24 1951, when he broke a leg and returned to the UK. For distinguished service in Malaya he was awarded the DSO (21.3.52).

Unwin retired from the RAF on January 18 1961, as a Wing Commander.

PO 31.7.41　FO 1.12.41　FL 1.12.42　FL 1.9.45
SL 1.8.47　WC 1.1.54

HAMILTON CHARLES UPTON

42544   PO   Pilot   British   43 and 607 Squadrons

Upton was born in Manchester and brought up in Vancouver. He joined the RAF on a short service commission in June 1939 and after completing his training he joined 43 Squadron at Wick in February 1940.

On July 12 Upton shared in destroying a He 111 and on August 8 he claimed two Ju 87s. Immediately after destroying the second Ju 87 Upton's engine seized and he glided back to the Isle of Wight and made a forced-landing at Ford Farm, Whitwell. On August 13 Upton claimed a Do 17 destroyed, on the 15th a Ju 88 and on the 16th three Ju 87s. In this combat his oil system was damaged by return fire and he crash-landed on Selsey Beach, in Hurricane P 3216. Upton claimed a Ju 87 and a Bf 109 destroyed on August 18 and a Bf 110 on September 4.

He was posted to 607 Squadron at Tangmere on September 24 1940, as a Flight Commander. In late 1940 Upton went to instruct at an OTU. He was awarded the DFC (29.4.41).

In 1945 Upton transferred to the RCAF, serving with it until 1953. He is believed to have died in 1965.

APO 19.8.39   PO 1.2.40   FO 1.2.41   FL 1.2.42

WITOLD URBANOWICZ

76735   FO   Pilot   Polish   145 and 303 Squadrons

Born in Olszanka, Bialystok on March 30 1908, Urbanowicz joined the PAF in 1930 and graduated from the Air Force College in 1932 as a 2nd Lieutenant.

In 1936 Urbanowicz shot down a Russian reconnaissance aircraft over eastern Poland, whilst serving with the Kosciuszko Squadron. Later in the year he was posted to the Fighter School at Deblin as an instructor. After the fall of Poland he escaped to Roumania with fifty cadets. They made their way through the Balkans and boarded a ship for France.

Urbanowicz arrived in Britain on January 27 1940. After converting to Hurricanes he joined 145 Squadron at Westhampnett on August 4 1940. He claimed a Bf 110 destroyed on the 8th and a Ju 88 on the 12th. On the 21st Urbanowicz was posted to 303 Squadron at Northolt, as a Flight Commander. When the CO was shot down on September 6 Urbanowicz took command. He claimed a Bf 110 destroyed on September 6, a Do 17 and a probable Bf 109 on the 7th, two Do 17s on the 15th, a He 111 on the 26th, a Do 17, a Bf 109 and two Ju 88s on the 27th and three Bf 109s and a Do 17 on the 30th.

On October 20 1940 Urbanowicz was posted to HQ 11 Group on staff duties. He was awarded the VM (5th Class)(23.12.40) and the KW and three Bars (1.2.41). In mid-April 1941 he began to organise the first all-Polish Wing at Northolt, made up of 303, 306 and 308 Squadrons. Urbanowicz was posted away in June and sent to the USA to recruit Americans of Polish descent for the PAF in England. Whilst there he lectured on tactics at USAAC bases.

On July 27 1942 Urbanowicz was posted to 2 FIS, Montrose for an instructor's course. He went to 16 FTS, Newton on September 23 but on November 3 he was appointed Assistant Air Attaché at the Polish Embassy in Washington. In Spring 1943 Urbanowicz met General C Chennault, who invited him to China. He flew there from October 23 to December 15, firstly in P40s from Kunming and later with the 75th Fighter Squadron, USAAF in eastern China. He

destroyed two Japanese aircraft on December 11 1943.

After further service in Washington Urbanowicz returned to Kunming in early 1944 and then returned to the UK. In August he returned to Washington as Polish Air Attaché. He returned again to Britain in early July 1945 and was released from the PAF on October 18. Urbanowicz went to the USA, as a political emigré and settled there. He died in 1987. He was awarded the DFC (30.10.41), the Air Medal (US)(25.9.44) and the Chinese Flying Cross. Urbanowicz's portrait was drawn by Cuthbert Orde in September 1940.

FL 1.3.41

JOHN DUNLOP URIE

90164   SL   Pilot   British   602 Squadron

Joined 602 Squadron, AuxAF in June 1935. Urie was called to full-time service on August 25 1939. He shared in the destruction of a He 111 fifteen miles east of May Isle on December 22. The enemy aircraft was on a mine-laying operation.

In April 1940 Urie was appointed a Flight Commander. He damaged a Ju 88 on July 9, ten miles east of Fifeness. On August 1 Urie tore a wing off Spitfire P 9461, landing at Drem in heavy ground mist, unhurt. On the 18th he landed back at Westhampnett minus flaps and with one burst tyre after his Spitfire, X 4110, was severely damaged in combat with Bf 109s over Ford. Urie was wounded in both legs.

On November 13 he shared in the destruction of a Ju 88. In December 1940 he was posted to 52 OTU, Aston Down. Urie later commanded 151 Wing in Russia.

He was released from the RAF in 1945, as a Wing Commander. He rejoined the RAuxAF in 1946.

PO (AuxAF) 21.6.35   FO (AuxAF) 21.12.36   FL 25.8.39
SL 1.9.40   WC 1.3.42   FL (RAuxAFRO) 4.9.46

JOHN RONALD URWIN-MANN

42281   PO   Pilot   Canadian   238 Squadron

Born in Victoria, British Columbia on July 29 1920, Urwin-Mann entered the RAF on a short service commission in March 1939. In December he was posted to 253 Squadron at Manston, later joining 238 Squadron at its reformation at Tangmere on May 12 1940.

On July 11 and 13 Urwin-Mann shared in probably destroying Bf 110s, on the 20th he destroyed a He 59 three miles off Cherbourg, on August 11 and 13 Bf 109s, on the 21st a Ju 88, on September 15 a He 111, on the 25th two more, on the 26th a Bf 110 and on October 7 a Ju 88. Urwin-Mann was awarded the DFC (26.11.40).

In May 1941 he went with the squadron to the Middle East, as a Flight Commander. He was promoted and given command of 80 Squadron at El Adem on January 14 1942. For services with 238 Urwin-Mann was awarded a Bar to the DFC (7.4.42).

On April 4 he was posted away from 80 Squadron and did not return to operations until mid-October 1942, when he took command of 126 Squadron at Luqa, Malta. Urwin-Mann probably destroyed a Me 210 on January 28 1943. At the completion of his tour in May he was awarded the DSO (14.5.43).

In early 1944 Urwin-Mann was at HQ Fighter Command, in the Tactics and Training Branch. He retired from the RAF on March 15

JR Urwin-Mann (continued)

1959, as a Flight Lieutenant, retaining the rank of Squadron Leader. His portrait was done by Cuthbert Orde in 1940.

APO 1.5.39   PO 27.12.39   FO 27.12.40   FL 27.12.41
FL 1.9.45

FRANK USMAR

115914   Sgt   Pilot   British   41 Squadron

Born on September 16 1915, Usmar was studying accountancy when he joined the RAFVR on June 30 1938. He began his weekend flying at 23 E&RFTS, Rochester. Called to full-time service at the outbreak of war, Usmar was posted to 4 ITW, Bexhill on October 30, moved to 6 FTS, Little Rissington on December 9 and was awarded his flying badge on April 29 1940.

After completing the course Usmar went on leave prior to going to 6 OTU, Sutton Bridge. When he arrived home a telegram was waiting, telling him to report to 41 Squadron at Catterick, which he did on June 18. Conversion to Spitfires was carried out on the squadron.

On August 15 Usmar destroyed a He 111 and damaged a Bf 110 and a Do 17, on September 6 he damaged a Bf 110, on the 9th he claimed a Bf 109 probably destroyed and on the 18th he had two Bf 109s confirmed.

Usmar was shot down on September 27, when 41 Squadron was jumped by Bf 109s. With his cockpit in flames and wounded in the right leg, he managed to bale out, intending to make a delayed drop. However, he pulled his ripcord almost immediately and as he floated down he beat out his burning tunic and used his wireless lead as a tourniquet to stop his right leg bleeding. Usmar landed in an apple-orchard and was approached by hop-pickers, who mistook him for a German. Once convinced he was not they took him to the doctor at Yalding. He was taken to Preston Hall Hospital, Maidstone. Usmar's home was at West Malling and his parents had watched him come down, not realising who it was.

In June 1941 he volunteered for night fighters and was posted to 141 Squadron at Ayr, moving later to 410 (RCAF) Squadron at Drem. Commissioned in December 1941, Usmar came off operational flying in April 1942 and became a Blind Approach instructor. In August 1944 he transferred to Admin duties and was appointed Station Adjutant at 61 OTU.

Usmar went into the Accountancy Branch in 1946 and was granted a Permanent Commission in 1948. He retired from the RAF on September 16 1964, as a Squadron Leader.

PO 15.12.41   FO 24.9.42   FL 24.9.43   SL 1.8.47

ALBERT EMMANUEL ALIX DIEUDONNE JEAN GHISLAIN van den HOVE d'ERTSENRIJCK

83699   PO   Pilot   Belgian   43 and 501 Squadrons

After leaving Belgium in May 1940 van den Hove d'Ertsenrijck went to France. On June 21 the French signed an Armistice with the Germans and the Belgians were told to stay put. With other pilots van den Hove d'Ertsenrijck reached Port Vendres, where with the help of a British destroyer and the support of the Belgian Embassy in London they caught a passing convoy and embarked on the SS 'Apapa' on the 24th. They arrived in Liverpool on July 7 and he was commissioned on the 19th.

Van den Hove d'Ertsenrijck was posted to 43 Squadron at Tangmere on August 5. He claimed a Ju 87 destroyed on the 16th, a Bf 109 on the 26th and a Bf 110 on September 4. In this latter combat his glycol tank was damaged and he forced-landed at Ford, following a mid-air fire.

On September 11 van den Hove d'Ertsenrijck was posted to 501 Squadron at Kenley. On the 15th, on his first patrol with the squadron, he was killed when his aircraft exploded over Ashford after being damaged by Bf 109s during an attack on Do 17s. The wreckage of

the Hurricane, P 2760, fell into the River Stour.

Van den Hove d'Ertsenrijck was 32. He was buried in St Stephen's churchyard, Lympne, Kent. On October 20 1949 his remains were exhumed and re-interred in the Pelouse d'Honneur Cemetery of Brussels at Evere.

PO 19.7.40

WILLI van LIERDE

83700   PO   Pilot   Belgian   87 Squadron

Van Lierde was in the pre-war Belgian Air Force and flew Fairey Foxes in Groupe de Chasse 3/IIe. He joined 87 Squadron at Church Fenton on August 12 1940 and was posted to 609 Squadron at Biggin Hill on April 7 1941.

No further service details traced.

BRIAN van MENTZ

70826   FO   Pilot   South African   222 Squadron

Born in Johannesburg, van Mentz joined the RAF on a short service commission in October 1937. He was posted to 8 FTS, Montrose on December 11 and joined 213 Squadron at Wittering on July 9 1938.

In May 1940 van Mentz was posted to 504 Squadron and went to France with it on the 12th. During the ten days of the squadron's stay he destroyed at least two enemy aircraft.

On September 3 van Mentz claimed a Bf 110 destroyed, on the 7th a probable Bf 109, on the 11th a Ju 88 and on the 23rd another Bf 110. He was awarded the DFC (25.10.40) and on November 29 destroyed a Do 17.

Van Mentz was decorated by the King in a ceremony at Bircham Newton on January 28 1941. Three days later he probably destroyed a He 111 and on March 18 shared a Do 17. He was killed on April 26 1941, when the Ferry Inn, near Coltishall was hit by a bomb. He was 24 and is buried in Brookwood Cemetery, Woking.

APO 24.12.37   PO 19.10.38   FO 19.5.40

ARTHUR ALBERT LEOPOLD van WAYENBERGHE

81629   PO   Pilot   Belgian   236 Squadron

Joined 236 Squadron on August 5 1940.

Van Wayenberghe was killed on March 10 1941, as a Pilot Officer with 272 Squadron. He is remembered on the Runnymede Memorial, Panel 35.

GEORGE WALLACE VARLEY

85670   PO   Pilot   British   79 and 247 Squadrons

Joined 79 Squadron at Pembrey in early October 1940 and moved to 247 Squadron at Roborough on the 26th.

In mid-1941 Varley was with the MSFU at Speke. On November 1 he was launched from the 'Empire Foam' on an Atlantic crossing. A FW Condor was sighted and as Varley became airborne it turned towards the convoy. Sighting the Hurricane the German pilot broke away, went down to sea level and then escaped into a cloud. Varley returned to circle the convoy and after patrolling for an hour another four-engined aircraft was sighted ahead of the convoy. It was a Liberator. With his fuel nearly exhausted Varley baled out, not without some difficulty. Within a few minutes of going into the sea he was rescued.

Varley was awarded the DFC (29.6.45), as a Flight Lieutenant with 222 Squadron. He was released from the RAF in 1946, as a Flight Lieutenant. He died on February 11 1982.

PO 22.9.40   FO 21.9.41   FL 21.9.42

ALOIS VASATKO

83233   PO   Pilot   Czechoslovakian   312 Squadron

Vasatko was in France at the outbreak of war. He served as a Captain in Groupe de Chasse I/5, l'Armée de l'Air and was credited with twelve enemy aircraft destroyed in France. He was awarded the C de G with five palms.

On June 20 1940 the unit flew to Algeria and Vasatko made his way to England. He joined 312 Squadron at Duxford on September 5 and shared in the destruction of a Ju 88 on October 8.

Vasatko probably destroyed a Bf 109 on July 9 1941. He took command of the squadron later in the month and led it until April 1942, when he was promoted to lead the Exeter Wing. Vasatko probably destroyed a FW 190 on June 3.

He was killed on June 23 and is remembered on the Runnymede Memorial, Panel 64. Vasatko was awarded the DFC.

FL 1.3.41

ANTONIN VELEBNOVSKY

82581   PO   Pilot   Czechoslovakian   1 Squadron

Joined No 1 Squadron at Wittering on October 22 1940.

Velebnovsky damaged a Bf 109 on May 21 1941. He was killed in a night flying accident on July 16. Around midnight he was on a searchlight co-operation flight. After receiving directions from base Velebnovsky was not heard from again. His body was found the next day in his wrecked Hurricane in a wood near Graffham, eight miles from Tangmere. He had apparently flown into the top of a hill.

Velebnovsky was 26. He is buried in Chichester Cemetery. His portrait was done by Cuthbert Orde.

FO 27.12.40

FRANCOIS AUGUST VENESOEN

107235   Sgt   Pilot   Belgian   235 Squadron

Joined 235 Squadron on August 27 1940.

Commissioned in July 1941, Venesoen joined 350 Squadron at its formation at Valley on November 13. Over Dieppe on August 19 1942 he claimed two FW 190s destroyed, on November 16 he shared in destroying a Ju 52 over France, on March 29 1943 destroyed a FW 190 and on September 24 shared a Bf 110.

Venesoen was killed on D Day, June 6 1944, as a Flight Lieutenant with 350 Squadron. He is remembered on the Runnymede Memorial, Panel 203. He was awarded the DFC.

PO 17.7.41   FO 17.7.42   FL 17.7.43

JACK ALBERT CHARLES VENN

84023   PO   Observer   British   236 Squadron

Enlisted in the RAF in September 1939 as a trainee observer. Venn was posted to No 1 ITW, Cambridge on January 11 1940, moved to 6 ANS, Staverton on February 1 and then to 3 BGS, Aldergrove on April 1.

With training completed Venn went to No 1 (Coastal) OTU at Silloth on June 1 and joined 236 Squadron at Thorney Island on July 1. He was posted to 272 Squadron at Aldergrove on September 1, remaining with it until May 1 1941, when he joined 235 Squadron at Bircham Newton.

Venn went to 2 (Coastal) AFU at Millom on July 1 1941 as an instructor. After a short Senior Navigation Instructor's course at Cranage he was posted to 10 AFU, Dumfries on September 1 1942. Venn volunteered for pilot training and on July 1 1943 went to 13 ITW, Torquay. He did his grading course at Shellingford and was posted to Canada on November 1 1943. He went to 34 EFTS, Assiniboia on the 27th and moved to 33 FTS, Carberry on February 28 1944, completing the course on October 20.

After returning to the UK Venn was posted to 107 OTU, Leicester East on March 18 1945, went for a glider-pulling course at Ibsley on May 6 and joined 512 Squadron, a Dakota transport unit on the 20th. Venn was released from the RAF in September 1945, as a Flight Lieutenant. He joined the RAFVR in July 1948 and instructed at 22 RFS, Filton until June 30 1952. Venn continued to fly at the Bristol and Wessex Flying Club until August 1974.

PO 30.6.40   FO 30.6.41   FL 30.9.42   FO (RAFVR) 17.6.48

VICTOR BOSANQUET STRACHAN VERITY

42164   PO   Pilot   New Zealander   229 Squadron

Born in Timaru on November 5 1919, Verity was educated at the Boys' High School there, after which he worked on his father's farm. He applied for a short service commission in the RAF in early 1938, was provisionally accepted in September and sailed for the UK in the RMS 'Tainui' on February 1 1939.

Verity began his ab initio course at 11 E&RFTS, Perth on March 16 and after a short induction course at Uxbridge he was posted to 9 FTS, Hullavington on May 30. Verity joined 229 Squadron at Digby on November 25 1939. The squadron was then equipped with Blenheims but began to receive Hurricanes in March 1940.

On May 14 Verity and two other pilots were attached to 615 Squadron in France. He destroyed two He 111s on the 20th but was then immediately shot down himself by escorting Bf 110s and crash-landed at his base at Norrent Fontes. Verity was ordered to return to England. He travelled to Cherbourg by road and then went by steamer to Southampton, reaching Digby on the 23rd. The next day 229 moved south to Biggin Hill.

Over Dunkirk on May 31 Verity destroyed a Bf 110 but was again shot down, this time rescued from the sea by a paddle steamer, the captain of which confirmed Verity's victory. He rejoined the squadron, which returned to Digby on June 5.

On September 11 he claimed a He 111 destroyed and damaged a Bf 110 and on October 4 claimed a Ju 88 destroyed. Verity volunteered for night fighters and was posted to 422 Flight at Shoreham. This unit was controlled by FIU at Ford and often operated by night from Tangmere. On November 6 Verity damaged a Ju 88 and on the 13th shared in destroying a Ju 88 and damaging a second.

On December 7 the Flight moved to Cranage and became the nucleus of 96 Squadron, charged with the night defence of Liverpool, Manchester and Birmingham. In March 1941 the squadron began to replace its Hurricanes with Defiants. Verity teamed up with Sergeant FW Wake. On May 3 they destroyed a Ju 88, on the 6th a He 111 and probably a Ju 88, on the 7th another Ju 88 and probably a second and on July 8 another He 111. Verity was awarded the DFC (8.8.41).

In April 1942 he was posted to the Middle East and in June joined 73 Squadron in the Western Desert. To gain experience on Beaufighters Verity went to ADU, Cairo on September 6 and in January 1943 he was posted to 89 Squadron at Abu Sueir. He was crewed up with Warrant Officer Farquharson and after being detached to Benina they were sent to 89's detached flight at Luqa, Malta. On April 10 1943 the flight was absorbed into 108 Squadron at Luqa, for the night defence of Malta and intruder patrols.

On April 17 Verity and Farquharson destroyed a He 111 off Trapani. In late June Verity returned to the UK and was posted to HQ Fighter Command, to become one of three controllers of the night-fighter intruder force operating against German night-fighter bases. In November Verity went to 1622 Flight at Gosport but was soon afterwards given command of 650 Squadron at Grange-over-Sands, engaged in target-towing for anti-aircraft training for the Army, in preparation for D Day. Its work completed, the squadron was disbanded at the end of June 1944.

Verity was posted to 62 OTU, Ouston in early August 1944, as Squadron Leader Flying. In June 1945 he went to HQ 12 Group and later in the month moved to a staff job at RAF Hereford. In November 1945 Verity returned to New Zealand and went on to the Reserve in January 1946. He returned to farming until 1959, when he took his family to England and started a roofing business in Northampton. Verity returned to New Zealand in 1969 and died in Wellington on February 2 1979.

APO 13.5.39   PO 6.11.39   FO 6.11.40   FL 6.11.41

VLASTIMIL VESELY

83234   PO   Pilot   Czechoslovakian   312 Squadron

Born on September 20 1913. Vesely joined 312 Squadron at Duxford on September 5 1940.

Awarded the DFC during the war, Vesely stayed on in the RAF. He was awarded the AFC (10.6.54) and retired on October 3 1968, as a Squadron Leader.

He later settled in Australia.

PO 17.8.40   FO 27.12.40
FL 17.8.42   SL 1.1.58

JAMES ANDERSON VICK

90274   SL   Pilot   British   607 Squadron

Vick was born in 1908. He joined 607 Squadron, AuxAF in March 1932 and obtained his 'A' License in the summer of 1933.

Called to full-time service on August 24 1939, Vick flew to Merville from Croydon on November 16 1939 in an Ensign, in charge of the ground party. The squadron was withdrawn from France on May 20 1940 and the remnants re-assembled at Croydon on the 22nd. Vick took command of the squadron in June and led it until October 12 1940, when he was posted to HQ 14 Group as Wing Commander Training.

In early 1942 Vick was released from the RAF to join BOAC on the organisation and administrative side. He remained with the airline until his retirement.

PO (AuxAF) 4.9.33   FO (AuxAF) 4.3.35   FL (AuxAF) 4.3.37
FL 24.8.39   SL 1.3.40

TIMOTHY ASHMEAD VIGORS

33554   PO   Pilot   British   222 Squadron

Born in Hatfield, Hertfordshire on March 22 1921, Vigors was educated at Eton. He entered RAF College, Cranwell in January 1939. The course was shortened because of the war and Vigors graduated in December 1939.

In early 1940 Vigors was with 226 Squadron, based at Rheims with Battles. In May 1940 he was posted to 222 Squadron at Digby. Over Dunkirk on May 31 he probably destroyed a He 111 and on June 1 claimed a Bf 110.

On August 30 Vigors probably destroyed a Bf 109, on the 31st and September 1 Bf 109s, on the 3rd a Bf 110, on the 9th another Bf 109 and on October 8 a Ju 88. He was awarded the DFC (1.10.40) and on October 30 he claimed two Bf 109s probably destroyed.

Vigors was posted to the Far East in early 1941 and joined 243 Squadron at Kallang at its reformation on March 11, as a Flight Commander. In December he went to 453 Squadron at Sembawang. The squadron was assigned to the defence of the fleet and on December 10 1941 Vigors led eleven Buffalos to fend off attacks on HMS 'Repulse' and 'Prince of Wales'. Both ships were already sunk before they arrived. On the 13th Vigors was in action, intercepting a raid. His petrol tank was hit and he baled out, with burns.

After the fall of Singapore Vigors went to India and spent the next three years on staff and training duties. He returned to the UK in 1945 and took part that year in the Battle of Britain flypast. He retired from the RAF on November 8 1946, as a Squadron Leader, retaining the rank of Wing Commander.

PO 23.12.39   FO 23.12.40   FL 23.12.41   SL 24.1.44

LESLIE WILLIAM VILES

126694   Sgt   Aircrew   British   236 Squadron

Joined 236 Squadron in late August 1940.

Commissioned in May 1942, Viles was released from the RAF in 1945, as a Flight Lieutenant.

PO 22.5.42   FO 22.11.42   FL 22.5.44

JOHN WOLFERSTAN VILLA

39768   FL   Pilot   British   72 and 92 Squadrons

Villa was born in South Kensington, London. He joined the RAF on a short service commission in March 1937. He was posted to 11 FTS, Wittering on June 5 and joined 2 AACU at Lee-on-Solent on March 26 1938.

In early July 1940 Villa was with 72 Squadron at Acklington, as a Flight Commander. On September 2 he claimed a Bf 110 destroyed and probably a second, on the 4th a Bf 110, on the 7th a probable He 111, on the 10th shared Do 215, on the 14th a shared He 111, on the 15th a Do 17 and a shared He 111, on the 27th a He 111 and on the 28th a Bf 109. Villa was awarded the DFC (8.10.40). On the 11th he claimed a Do 17 and two days later was posted to 92 Squadron at Biggin Hill.

On October 20 Villa shared in destroying a Bf 110. His Spitfire, N 3113, was damaged by return fire in this engagement and he made a forced-landing at Waterfield, near Tonbridge, unhurt. On October 25 Villa claimed a Bf 109, on the 29th a Bf 110 and on November 18 and December 1 Bf 109s. He was awarded a Bar to the DFC (26.11.40).

In June 1941 Villa was instructing at 58 OTU, Grangemouth. He took command of 65 Squadron at Kirton-in-Lindsey in September and led it until December. He commanded 504 Squadron at Ballyhalbert from June to September 1942 and 198 Squadron from its reformation at Digby on December 8 1942 until May 1943.

Villa came off operations because of increasing sinus trouble. He was released from the RAF in 1946, as a Squadron Leader. He died in 1983.

APO 18.5.37   PO 26.3.38   FO 26.10.39   FL 26.10.40
SL 1.12.41

STANLEY FLAMANK VINCENT

09109   GC   Pilot   British   257 and 229 Squadrons

Vincent was born on April 7 1897. He was educated at King's College Choir School, Cambridge and Lancing College. He learned to fly at Brooklands in 1915 and was commissioned in the RFC in December 1915. Vincent carried out further training at Beaulieu and CFS, Upavon before joining 60 Squadron at its formation at Gosport on April 30 1916.

The squadron went to France on May 5. Vincent claimed the squadron's first victory, shooting down an LVG two-seater in July. When he returned to England on March 17 1917 Vincent had destroyed three enemy aircraft, probably three more and had received two Mentions in Despatches. He was appointed a Flight Commander at the Instructors' School at Gosport. In late April 1917 Vincent was in a crash which put him into hospital for seven months.

In early 1918 he was given command of 110 Squadron. Later in the year Vincent formed the Special Instructors' Flight at Shoreham. In November the Flight was disbanded and he was awarded the AFC (1.1.19) for his work. Vincent was posted to 24 Squadron at Croydon to give ex-PoWs refresher courses. Whilst there he taught the Prince of Wales to fly.

In October 1920 Vincent went to the Flying Wing at RAF College, Cranwell as an instructor. He was posted to 30 Squadron in Iraq in September 1923 and in late 1925 went to Heliopolis to command the

Communications Flight but after three weeks he joined 2 Armoured Car Company, Palestine.

Vincent returned to the UK in January 1928 and was posted to No 1 Squadron at Tangmere on the 30th. He took command of 41 Squadron at Northolt on July 7 1931, going overseas again on April 29 1933, to command 84 Squadron at Shaibah, Iraq. Vincent again returned to the UK in February 1935 and on March 5 he went to the Air Armament School at Northolt for a course.

In January 1936 Vincent became CO of AFDU, Northolt and at the end of the year he was promoted to Wing Commander and appointed Station Commander there. On January 3 1938 he went to Air Ministry, in the Directorate of Training as Training (Armament) Staff Officer. Vincent was sent to the Royal Naval Staff College at Greenwich for a course in April 1938, after which he was posted to HQ Plymouth as Controller.

In March 1940 Vincent returned to Northolt as Station Commander. During July he flew occasional operational sorties with 257 Squadron. Flying with 229 Squadron on September 30 he claimed a Bf 109 destroyed. Vincent also flew on sorties alone. He was awarded the DFC (25.10.40). In March 1941 he moved to command RAF North Weald and in July went to HQ 11 Group as Group Captain Ops.

In late 1941 Vincent was posted to HQ Fighter Command. In January 1942 he flew out to Singapore and when that fell he moved to Sumatra. When operations against the Japanese ceased he flew to Australia, later going to New Zealand, then the USA, arriving back in the UK in early 1943. Vincent was posted to the Operations Room at Fighter Command, moving after five months to HQ 13 Group.

Vincent flew to Delhi on February 2 1944 to take command of 221 Group. He led the Group until May 1945, throughout the strenuous campaign against the Japanese, including the operations in the Imphal Valley. He elected not to retire but stay in the valley and fight back from there. Vincent was made a CB (5.6.45).

In June 1945 he was posted to HQ Fighter Command as SASO. He was appointed AOC 11 Group in 1948 and remained there until retiring on February 6 1950, as an Air Vice-Marshal. Vincent was made a Commander of the Legion of Merit (US)(1945). He died on March 13 1976.

2nd Lt (RFC) 7.12.15   FL 30.6.22   SL 30.6.31   WC 1.1.37
GC 1.3.40   AC 1.6.42   AVM 1.1.46   AVM 1.7.47

FRANTISEK VINDIS

158968   Sgt   Pilot   Czechoslovakian   310 Squadron

Joined 310 Squadron at Duxford in October 1940. Vindis crashed at Sudbury on November 1 in Hurricane P 8809, cause unknown.

Commissioned in June 1943, he was at some time awarded the DFC.

Vindis served in the RAF after the war and last appears in the Air Force List for July 1961.

PO 20.6.43   FO 20.6.44   FL 20.6.45   FO 26.2.48
FL (RAFRO) 3.11.59 (No 787550).

FREDERICK FENTON VINYARD

748089   Sgt   Pilot   British   64 Squadron

Vinyard, of Erdington, Birmingham, joined 64 Squadron at Leconfield in mid-September 1940.

During a routine section patrol on October 6 Vinyard was lost when he crashed into the sea in Spitfire R 6683, cause unknown. He was 24 and is remembered on the Runnymede Memorial, Panel 20.

ARTHUR FRANK VOKES

79559   PO   Pilot   British   19 Squadron

Vokes, of Birmingham, joined 19 Squadron at Duxford in June 1940.

He was killed on September 5 1941, as a Flight Lieutenant with 19 Squadron, aged 23. Vokes is buried in St James' churchyard, Great Ellingham, Norfolk.

PO 2.6.40   FO 2.6.41

JOSEF VOPALECKY

102581   WO   Pilot   Czechoslovakian   310 Squadron

Joined 310 Squadron at its formation at Duxford on July 12 1940.

Vopalecky was commissioned in 1941. No further service details traced.

ADOLF VRANA

83235   PO   Pilot   Czechoslovakian   312 Squadron

Joined 312 Squadron at Duxford on September 5 1940.
No further service details traced.

FO 27.12.40

TOMAS VYBIRAL

83236   PO   Pilot   Czechoslovakian   312 Squadron

Vybiral served as a Lieutenant in Groupe de Chasse I/5, l'Armée de l'Air and was credited with eight victories in France. He made his way to England after the French collapse and joined 312 Squadron at Duxford on September 5 1940.

On a flight from Speke on October 15 Vybiral lost his bearings and having run low on fuel he baled out over Dalton-in-Furness. His Hurricane, V 6811, crashed at Gleaston.

In early 1942 Vybiral was posted to 41 Squadron, as a Flight Commander. He shared in the destruction of a FW 190 on May 4. From January to November 1943 he commanded 312 Squadron. During 1944 Vybiral led the Czech Wing from North Weald. He was awarded the DFC in July 1944 and the DSO in December 1944.

Vybiral was released from the RAF as a Wing Commander. He died in February 1981.

FO 27.12.40

KAREL JAN VYKOUKAL

81902   PO   Pilot   Czechoslovakian   111 and 73 Sqdns

Joined 111 Squadron at Drem on September 12 1940 and moved to 73 Squadron at Castle Camps on the 25th.

Vykoukal was killed on May 21 1942, as a Flight Lieutenant with 41 Squadron. He is remembered on the Runnymede Memorial, Panel 66.

FO 27.12.40

JOHN WADDINGHAM

40867   FO   Pilot   British   141 Squadron

Joined the RAF on a short service commission in April 1938. Waddingham was posted to 9 FTS, Hullavington on June 18 and after completing the course he went to No 1 AOS, North Coates as a staff pilot.

In early July 1940 Waddingham was with 141 Squadron. On September 16, flying with Sergeant AB Cumbers as his gunner, he destroyed a He 111 and probably shot down another into the sea. He was awarded the DFC (18.3.41).

In 1942 Waddingham was with 89 Squadron in the Middle East. He was killed on September 27 1942, as a Flight Lieutenant with the 89 Squadron detachment at Ta Kali, Malta.

Waddingham is buried in the Naval Cemetery, Capuccini, Malta.

APO 4.6.38   PO 4.4.39   FO 3.9.40   FL 3.9.41

TREVOR SIDNEY WADE

78984   PO   Pilot   British   92 Squadron

Wade was born in 1920 and educated at Tonbridge School. He joined the RAFVR in 1938 and learned to fly at 19 E&RFTS, Gatwick. Called to full-time service at the outbreak of war, he completed his training and was commissioned in late April.

In May 1940 Wade joined 92 Squadron at Croydon. On July 28, with deteriorating weather conditions and R/T failure during a night patrol over Swansea Bay, he baled out over Exeter. His Spitfire, N 3287, crashed two miles south-west of Chudleigh. On August 19 Wade shared in destroying a Ju 88 but his Spitfire, R 6703, was hit by return fire and he made a forced-landing at Norton, Selsey, escaping before the aircraft exploded.

On August 20 Wade shared a Ju 88, on September 10 shared a Do 17, on the 11th claimed a He 111 destroyed and on the 27th a Do 17. In this engagement over Brighton Wade's Spitfire, P 9544, was hit by return fire and he forced-landed on Macehill, Lewes Race Course. The aircraft overturned and Wade was trapped upside down in the cockpit but fortunately the aircraft did not catch fire. On October 12 he claimed a Bf 109 destroyed and probably a second, on the 26th a probable Bf 109, on the 29th a probable Bf 110 and on November 21 a Do 17.

Wade destroyed a Bf 109 on May 9 1941, shared another on the 16th, destroyed one on June 16 and shared another on the 21st. He was posted away in late June 1941 to join 123 Squadron at Turnhouse. He was awarded the DFC (15.7.41) and joined 602 Squadron at Kenley in September 1941. Wade was shot down on the 17th but was unhurt.

After leaving 602 Wade was posted to instruct at an OTU. He did an instructor's course at CFS and then went to CGS, Sutton Bridge as a gunnery instructor. He was later posted to HQ 9 Group as Gunnery Officer, responsible for gunnery instruction at fighter OTUs. In late 1943 Wade was appointed OC Flying at AFDU, testing the performance of captured enemy fighters and comparing them to their Allied counterparts. For this work he was awarded the AFC (1.9.44). In early 1945 Wade went to the USA to test captured Japanese fighters and to gain experience on new American types.

Wade was released from the RAF in 1946, as a Squadron Leader. He joined the editorial staff of 'The Aeroplane', concerned with testing new types of light civil aeroplanes. In late 1947 Wade was offered the job of assistant test pilot at Hawker Aircraft. A few months later he took over as test pilot, flying the new Hawker jets. After a spell in the USA on an exchange scheme he returned to Hawkers and resumed testing.

On April 3 1951 Wade was killed when he crashed at Ringmer, Sussex, whilst testing the P 1081.

PO 30.4.40   FO 30.10.41   FL 30.10.42

JOHN VICTOR WADHAM

742598   Sgt   Pilot   British   601 and 145 Squadrons

Wadham, of the Isle of Wight, was educated at Ryde School and Newport Grammar School. He worked as an apprentice with a furnishing firm in Southampton and joined the RAFVR there.

Called to full-time service at the outbreak of war, Wadham completed his training and joined 601 Squadron at Tangmere on August 3 1940. He moved to 145 Squadron at Drem on the 20th. Wadham was shot down and killed by Bf 109s over Hastings on October 12. His Hurricane, V 7426, crashed

at Courseham Farm, Chittenden, near Cranbrook.

Wadham was 21. He is buried in Carisbrooke Cemetery, Newport, Isle of Wight.

PETER HARRY WAGHORN

745800   Sgt   Pilot   British   249 and 111 Squadrons

Initially with 249 Squadron, Waghorn was posted to 111 Squadron at Debden on August 21 1940.

Waghorn flew off HMS 'Ark Royal' to Malta on April 3 1941 and joined 261 Squadron. After sharing a Ju 88 on the 11th Waghorn and Pilot Officer P Kennett were jumped by Bf 109s and shot down. Both lost their lives in the sea.

Waghorn is buried in the Naval Cemetery, Capuccini, Malta.

ALAN DEREK WAGNER

65993   Sgt   Pilot   British   151 Squadron

Wagner, of Croydon, was educated at Whitgift School. He joined 151 Squadron at Digby in October 1940.

Flying a Defiant on the night of April 8 1941 Wagner sighted a He 111 and attacked but his gun turret jammed in the beam position. By skilful manoeuvring he enabled his gunner to shoot the enemy aircraft down and damage another later in the patrol.

Commissioned in May 1941, Wagner joined 30 Squadron in the Western Desert later in the year and sailed with it to Ceylon in February 1942, in HMS 'Indomitable'. When the Japanese made their carrier-based attack on Colombo on April 5 Wagner destroyed two of their bombers. Later in the year he returned to the UK and rejoined 151 Squadron, then at Wittering. Wagner was awarded the DFC (5.3.43).

In October 1943 he was posted to 605 Squadron at Bradwell Bay. He destroyed an unidentified enemy aircraft on December 23, damaged another on February 4 1944 and on March 5 he destroyed a FW 190 and two Me 410s, one of which he attacked at such close range that his Mosquito was enveloped in burning oil and petrol, damaging the outer skin. Wagner was awarded a Bar to the DFC (28.4.44).

He was killed on July 17 1944, as a Flight Lieutenant with 108 Squadron, aged 29. Wagner is buried in Folkestone New Cemetery, Hawkinge.

PO 1.5.41   FO 1.5.42   FL 1.5.43

ALEX GEORGE WAINWRIGHT

84675   PO   Pilot   British   151 Squadron

Joined 151 Squadron at Martlesham Heath in August 1940. On the 29th, during a routine patrol, Wainwright baled out and was admitted to Epping Hospital with broken ribs. His Hurricane, P 3882, crashed near Basildon.

In January 1941 Wainwright was with 73 Squadron in the Western Desert. On the 21st the squadron escorted Blenheims to bomb Tobruk. The Hurricanes got into a dogfight with Fiat G 50s and Wainwright was shot down and killed.

He is remembered on the Alamein Memorial, Column 241.

PO 4.8.40

MICHAEL TERRY WAINWRIGHT

40346   FO   Pilot   British   64 Squadron

Born on March 15 1919, Wainwright joined the RAF on a short service commission in September 1937. He was posted to 64 Squadron at Church Fenton on September 27 1938.

Wainwright served with 64 throughout the Battle of Britain. He was awarded the AFC (1.1.51) and retired from the RAF on March 31 1958, as a Squadron Leader.

APO 30.11.37   PO 27.9.38   FO 27.6.40   FL 27.6.41
SL 1.7.43   FL 1.12.42   SL 1.7.53

FREDERICK WILLIAM WAKE

No unknown   Sgt   Air Gunner   British   264 Sqdn

Joined 264 Squadron at Kirton-in-Lindsey in September 1940.

In early 1941 Wake was with the newly-formed 96 Squadron at Cranage, equipped with Defiants. He teamed up with Flying Officer VBS Verity. On May 3 they destroyed a Ju 88 at night, on the 6th a He 111 and probably a Ju 88, on the 7th a Ju 88 and probably a second and on July 8 a He 111. For his part in these victories Wake was awarded the DFM (8.8.41).

No further service details traced.

HERBERT KENNETH WAKEFIELD

78267   PO   Observer   British   235 Squadron

A well-known rugby player before the war, Wakefield joined the RAFVR in February 1938, as a trainee observer.

Called to full-time service at the outbreak of war, Wakefield was posted to 7 ANS, Perth in October 1939 and moved on to the ABGS at West Freugh in February 1940. He joined 235 Squadron at North Coates in late March.

Wakefield generally flew with Flying Officer RJ Peacock. On June 26 they shot down a Bf 109, on August 11 another and on the 18th a Ju 87. Wakefield was awarded the DFC (22.10.40). He was on a sortie on October 25, when four He 115s were attacked.

He was released from the RAF in 1946, as a Flight Lieutenant.

PO 24.3.40   FO 24.3.41   FL 24.3.42

ERNEST CECIL JOHN WAKEHAM

41883   PO   Pilot   British   145 Squadron

Wakeham joined the RAF on a short service commission in February 1939. After completing his training at 11 FTS, Shawbury he joined 145 Squadron at Croydon on October 23. Then equipped with Blenheims, 145 began to receive Hurricanes in March 1940.

In May the squadron began ferrying Hurricanes to France and supporting squadrons there. On the 18th Wakeham destroyed a He 111 over Dunkirk and on the 19th destroyed another. On the 27th he was stunned by a glancing bullet whilst attacking enemy aircraft and lost consciousness. Wakeham came to after falling 5000 feet and returned to the attack. Later in the day he was shot down, making a forced-landing between Ostend and Dunkirk. Wakeham was awarded the DFC (21.6.40).

On July 7 he shared in destroying a Ju 88, on the 11th claimed a He 111, on the 19th shared a Do 17, on the 29th shared a Ju 88 and on August 1 claimed a Hs 126. Wakeham failed to return from an action with Ju 87s and Bf 110s over a convoy south of the Isle of Wight on August 8, in Hurricane P 2957.

Wakeham was 19. He is remembered on the Runnymede Memorial, Panel 10.

APO 1.4.39   PO 23.10.39

SIDNEY RICHARD ERNEST WAKELING

741505   Sgt   Pilot   British   87 Squadron

Wakeling was born in 1919 and educated at Latimer Grammar School, Kensington. He was with 87 Squadron at Church Fenton in early July 1940.

In combat over Portland on August 25 Wakeling was shot down and killed. His Hurricane, V 7250, is believed to have crashed at New Barn, near Dorchester. Wakeling is buried in Holy Trinity churchyard, Warmwell.

STUART CROSBY WALCH

40063   FO   Pilot   Australian   238 Squadron

Born in Hobart, Tasmania on February 16 1917, Walch joined the RAAF in 1936 and did his flying training in Australia.

He transferred into the RAF in August 1937 and went for a short course to 11 FTS, Wittering on September 18. Walch was posted to 151 Squadron at North Weald on January 8 1938. He moved to 238 Squadron, when it was reformed at Tangmere on May 12 1940.

Walch claimed a Bf 110 destroyed on July 11, shared a Bf 109 on the 20th, a Bf 110 destroyed on the 21st and a Bf 109 on the 26th. He was shot down into the Channel during a combat two miles east of Weymouth on August 11, in Hurricane R 4097. Walch is remembered on the Runnymede Memorial, Panel 5.

PO 26.8.37   FO 24.3.39

GEORGE ARTHUR WALKER

113499   Sgt   Pilot   British   232 Squadron

Walker was born on June 4 1917. He joined 232 Squadron at Castletown on September 14 1940.

He was one of twelve pilots who flew Hurricanes off HMS 'Ark Royal' on April 3 1941, bound for Malta. Walker joined 261 Squadron. During a patrol on May 7 Walker collided with Sergeant HH Jennings. He was slightly injured and Jennings was killed.

When 261 was disbanded later in May Walker went to the Middle East. He was commissioned in July, released from the RAF in 1946, later rejoining. Walker retired on June 4 1972, as a Squadron Leader.

PO 20.9.41   FO 20.9.42   FL 20.9.43   FO 6.1.49
FL 23.4 51   SL 1.7.65

JAMES ARTHUR WALKER

40768   FO   Pilot   Canadian   111 Squadron

Walker, of Gleichen, Alberta, joined the RAF on a short service commission in March 1938. He was posted to 2 FTS, Brize Norton on May 21 and joined 111 Squadron at Northolt on December 17.

Patrolling over France on May 8 1940 Walker destroyed two He 111s, on the 31st a Bf 109 over Dunkirk, on June 7 a Bf 109 and on the 11th a Do 17.

Walker claimed a Do 17 destroyed on August 13 and a Bf 109 on the 16th. He was awarded the DFC (6.9.40). On January 1 1941 he probably destroyed a Ju 88.

In May 1941 Walker was posted to 603 Squadron at Hornchurch and moved to 610 Squadron at Westhampnett in August, as a Flight Commander. In April 1942 he was with 94 Squadron in the Western Desert and in 1943 with 31 (Transport) Squadron in India.

Walker was killed in a flying accident on February 8 1944, as a Flight Lieutenant with 31 Squadron. He is remembered on the Singapore Memorial, Column 432.

APO 7.5.38   PO 7.3.39   FO 3.9.40   FL 3.9.41

JAMES IAN BRADLEY WALKER

NZ 40211   **Sgt**   **Air Gunner**   **New Zealander**   **600 Sqdn**

Walker was born in New Plymouth on February 20 1920. He volunteered for aircrew duties at the outbreak of war and after initial rejection was accepted as a trainee air gunner.

He reported to the Ground Training School at Weraroa on January 15 1940, moved to the Air Observers' School, Ohakea for a gunnery course in February and sailed for the UK on March 23 in the SS 'Akaroa'.

On June 3 Walker was posted to 264 Squadron at Duxford for further training. He did no flying with 264 and was posted to 5 OTU, Aston Down at the end of the month. After nine hours on Blenheims he was awarded his air gunner's badge, promoted to Sergeant and joined 600 Squadron at Manston on July 10 1940.

In early September the squadron began to convert to Beaufighters and by the end of the year the air gunners were doing little flying. In early 1941 Walker and others asked for a transfer to Bomber Command and on February 6 he was posted to 11 OTU, Bassingbourn. After crewing-up and converting to Wellingtons Walker was posted to 115 Squadron at Marham in mid-April. He flew his first operation on the 25th, as rear gunner on a seven hour flight to raid Wilhelmshaven. On May 3 he escaped unhurt when his Wellington crashed at Oakington after returning from operations.

On the night of August 5/6 1941 Walker's crew was detailed to attack Cologne. On the way back the Wellington was caught in searchlights and one engine put out of action by flak. This caused Walker's turret to be inoperable, with guns unable to fire. The aircraft lost height and when the second engine failed it crashed into a wood near Louvain, Belgium.

Walker's leg was broken below the knee. The crew were taken to a village by Belgians, where they were taken into custody by the Germans. Walker spent three months in hospital in Louvain, Brussels and Antwerp. After a month in Frankfurt, for interrogation he was sent to a PoW camp, the first of several he was to be in during his captivity. In 1942, at a time when his leg looked extremely unsightly, Walker was seen by Swiss medical observers from the International Red Cross and recommended for repatriation.

Having heard nothing by mid-1943 Walker escaped with another prisoner and they were at liberty for eight days before being caught and returned to the camp. After being threatened with shooting they got off with a sentence of fourteen days solitary confinement.

In August 1943 his repatriation came through. The repatriates went on a train to Marseilles, then in an Italian ship to Barcelona, where the man-for-man exchange of prisoners took place on the wharf. Walker went to Alexandria and a month later boarded a Dutch hospital ship at Port Tewfik. The voyage to New Zealand was made via Australia and Walker landed at Wellington on December 13 1943.

He took the option of release from the RNZAF and was discharged on March 15 1944, as a Warrant Officer.

JAMES RICHARD WALKER

41500   **FO**   **Pilot**   **Canadian**   **611 and 41 Squadrons**

Walker, of Oak Bay, British Columbia, joined the RAF on a short service commission in October 1938.

He joined 611 Squadron at Tern Hill on July 27 1940 and moved to 41 Squadron at Hornchurch on September 29. Walker claimed Bf 109s destroyed on October 7 and 9.

In October he volunteered for service in the Middle East. In mid-November 1940 the carrier HMS 'Argus' sailed from Gibraltar with Hurricanes for Malta. Walker was one of six pilots, who flew off on November 16, led by a FAA Skua. A series of mishaps saw the Hurricanes run out of fuel and fall one by one into the sea, with the loss of all six pilots.

Walker is remembered on the Runnymede Memorial, Panel 6.

APO 14.12.38   *PO 3.9.39*   *FO 3.9.40*

JOHN HAROLD GILBERT WALKER

40036   **FO**   **Pilot**   **British**   **25 Squadron**

Walker, of Nottingham, entered the RAF on a short service commission in June 1937. He was posted to 3 FTS, South Cerney on August 21 and joined the staff at the School of Naval Co-operation at Ford on March 26 1938.

In early July 1940 Walker was with 25 Squadron at Martlesham Heath and served with the squadron throughout the Battle of Britain.

He was killed on May 9 1942, as a Squadron Leader with 118 Squadron, aged 23. He is buried in St Leonard's churchyard, Wollaton, Nottinghamshire.

APO 9.8.37   *PO 24.5.38*   *FO 24.11.39*   *FL 24.11.40*
SL 1.12.41

NORMAN MacDONALD WALKER

745818   **Sgt**   **Pilot**   **British**   **615 Squadron**

Walker, of Motherwell, Lanarkshire, joined 615 Squadron at Prestwick on September 30 1940.

In May 1941 Walker was with 46 Squadron. On the 21st the squadron's pilots and aircraft went on board HMS 'Argus', bound for Gibraltar. There they were transferred to HMS 'Ark Royal' and 'Furious'. On June 6 they flew off to Hal Far, Malta, for service there.

Walker damaged a SM 79 on the 11th. He was shot down into the sea by a CR 42 on June 12 and a search found no trace of him. He is remembered on the Malta Memorial, Panel 2, Column 1.

ROBERT JAMES WALKER

39915   **FO**   **Pilot**   **British**   **72 Squadron**

Born on December 6 1911, Walker joined the RAF on a short service commission in May 1937. He was posted to 5 FTS, Sealand on July 17 and joined 72 Squadron at Church Fenton on April 23 1938.

Walker served with 72 throughout the Battle of Britain. He was awarded the DSO (12.6.45), as an Acting Wing Commander with 45 Squadron, operating in Mosquitos from Joari, India. He retired from the RAF on November 28 1964, as a Group Captain.

APO 5.7.37   *PO 10.5.38*   *FO 10.11.39*   *FL 10.11.40*
SL 1.12.41   *SL 1.9.45*   *WC 1.7.52*   *GC 1.1.59*

STANLEY WALKER

751643   **Sgt**   **Aircrew**   **British**   **236 Squadron**

Joined 236 Squadron in early August 1940.

Walker was killed on February 12 1942, as a Flight Sergeant with 407 (RCAF) Squadron. He is remembered on the Runnymede Memorial, Panel 76.

WILLIAM LOUIS BUCHANAN WALKER

82662   **PO**   **Pilot**   **British**   **616 Squadron**

Born on August 24 1913, Walker joined the RAFVR on September 2 1938 at Kidlington, Oxford and flew his first solo there on the 28th. He moved to Romford and continued his weekend flying at 21 E&RFTS, Stapleford.

Walker was called to full-time service at the outbreak of war and posted to No 1 ITW, Cambridge on November 15 1939. He went to 2 FTS, Brize Norton on February 17 1940 and at the end of the course was posted directly to 616 Squadron at Leconfield on June 18.

In combat off Dover on August 26 Walker was shot down in Spitfire R 6701 and baled out, wounded in the foot. He was rescued by the Royal Navy and admitted to Ramsgate Hospital, going the next day to RAF Hospital, Halton. Walker rejoined 616 at Tangmere on May 1 1941. He was attached to No 1 ADF at Hendon from the 20th.

Walker returned to hospital at Halton on September 23 1941 and after convalescence at Torquay he rejoined No 1 ADF on November 17. He was posted to 116 Squadron at Heston on July 8 1942, on anti-aircraft co-operation duties. Walker remained with the squadron until July 6 1944. He then went to the Sector Gunnery Flight at Gatwick until October 4, when he rejoined No 1 ADF. Walker served with the unit at various locations until released from the RAF at Uxbridge on September 1 1945, as a Flight Lieutenant.

PO 18.6.40   FO 18.6.41   FL 18.6.42

FRANCIS RICHARD WALKER-SMITH

64872   Sgt   Pilot   British   85 Squadron

Walker-Smith, of Stanley Common, Derbyshire, was born on January 29 1917. He joined the RAFVR on June 13 1937 as an AC 2 Fitter but remustered to Sergeant u/t pilot on January 8 1938.

Called to full-time service on September 1 1939, Walker-Smith was posted to 9 FTS, Hullavington on December 6. He passed out on April 11 1940 and after converting to Hurricanes at 5 OTU joined 85 Squadron in France on May 15.

Walker-Smith claimed two Bf 110s destroyed on August 18, a Do 17 on the 26th and a Bf 109 on the 28th. He was shot down in combat with Bf 109s off the Sussex Coast on the 29th. He baled out, wounded in the foot, landing at Hawkhurst. The Hurricane, V 7350, crashed on Underwood Farm, near the River Dudwell, Etchingham.

In March 1941 Walker-Smith was commissioned. On the 13th he took off in a Havoc from Debden, flying as second pilot to Geoffrey Allard and with Pilot Officer WH Hodgson as passenger. Shortly afterwards the aircraft crashed at Mill Field Ley, just south of Wimbish. The three pilots were killed. It is believed that an insecurely-fastened nose panel flew off and jammed in the rudder, causing the aircraft to became uncontrollable.

Walker-Smith is buried in Saffron Walden Borough Cemetery.

PO 6.3.41

CLARENCE ALFRED BLAKE WALLACE

C 1371   PO   Pilot   Canadian   3 Squadron

Born in North Vancouver, British Columbia, Wallace joined the RCAF on November 6 1939. He was posted to 3 Squadron at Turnhouse in October 1940.

Wallace was reported 'Missing' on air operations on October 27 1941, as a Flying Officer with 401 (RCAF) Squadron. He is remembered on the Runnymede Memorial, Panel 59.

PO 13.7.40   FO 13.7.41

THOMAS YOUNG WALLACE

149635   Sgt   Pilot   South African   610 and 111 Sqdns

Wallace was born in Johannesburg. He was posted to 610 Squadron at Gravesend in June 1940 and moved to 111 Squadron at Croydon on July 17.

He claimed a Bf 110 destroyed and another shared on August 15, a Bf 109 on the 16th, a Do 17 on the 18th, shared a Do 17 on the 26th, destroyed a Bf 110 on the 31st and a Bf 109 on September 4. Wallace's aircraft was severely damaged by a Bf 109 over the Channel on September 7. He glided back to the English coast and baled out south of Ashford, slightly wounded. The Hurricane, P 3025, crashed on Gammons Farm, Newchurch. Wallace was awarded the DFM (25.10.40).

Commissioned from Warrant Officer in March 1943, he commanded 609 Squadron from September 17 1944 to November 11, when he was shot down by flak over Dunkirk and killed. Wallace was 28 years old. He is buried in Pihen-les-Guines War Cemetery, France.

PO 10.3.43   FO 10.9.43

DENNIS STANLEY WALLEN

77347   FO   Air Gunner   British   604 Squadron

Wallen was commissioned in February 1940 and was with 604 Squadron at Gravesend in early July.

He was made an OBE (1.1.46) and released from the RAF in 1946, as a Wing Commander.

PO 4.2.40   FO 10.5.40   FL 10.5.41   SL 3.9.45

RONALD WALTER WALLENS

70708   FO   Pilot   British   41 Squadron

Joined the RAF on a short service commission in June 1937. Wallens was posted to 8 FTS, Montrose on August 21 and joined 41 Squadron at Catterick on March 26 1938.

Still with 41 in August 1940, Wallens claimed three Bf 109s destroyed on the 8th, shared a Ju 88 on the 11th and claimed another Bf 109 on September 5. On this day his aircraft was severely damaged during an attack on Do 17s. Wallens baled out, badly wounded in the leg by a cannon shell, and landed at Carpenter's Arms, Rawreth. His Spitfire, X 4021, is believed to have crashed south-east of Nevendon Hall.

In 1944 Wallens was commanding 277 (ASR) Squadron. He was awarded the DFC (15.8.44), being then credited with at least four enemy aircraft destroyed and having been responsible for rescuing a number of men from the sea.

Wallens was released in 1946, as a Squadron Leader.

APO 9.8.37   PO 7.10.38   FO 7.7.40   FL 7.7 41
SL 1.7.43

GEORGE ALFRED WALLER

149145   Sgt   Air Gunner   British   29 Squadron

Joined 29 Squadron at Digby in early July 1940.

Waller was in Blenheim L 1371 on September 28 when it was hit in the starboard wing by British anti-aircraft fire during an evening patrol. He and Pilot Officer J Buchanan were unhurt and returned safely to Digby.

After the advent of the Beaufighter and greatly-improved AI equipment Waller retrained as a Radio Observer. Commissioned from Warrant Officer in June 1943, he was awarded the DFC (20.10.44), as a Flying Officer with 604 Squadron. Waller had then assisted in the destruction of three enemy aircraft.

He was released from the RAF in 1950, as a Flight Lieutenant, and died in 1983.

PO 24.6.43   FO 24.12.43   FL 24.6.45   FL 24.12.46

PETER KENNETH WALLEY

819018   Sgt   Pilot   British   615 Squadron

Born in Barnes on November 20 1919, Walley was an apprentice toolmaker. He joined the AuxAF in March 1938, as an aircrafthand and air gunner. In August he transferred to 615 Squadron and by the time he was called up at the outbreak of war he had been selected for pilot training.

Walley did his intermediate and advanced training at 3 FTS, South Cerney and 5 FTS, Sealand, was awarded his wings on July 11 and after converting to Hurricanes he rejoined 615 Squadron, then at Kenley, on August 6 1940.

He shared in probably destroying a Bf 109 on August 16. Two days later Walley was shot down and killed by Bf 109s of JG 3. He was 20 and is buried in St Luke's churchyard, Whyteleafe, Surrey.

There is a memorial plaque to Walley at Merton Technical College.

DONALD SYLVESTER WALLIS

754744   Sgt   Pilot   British   235 Squadron

Joined 235 Squadron on September 19 1940.

Wallis, of Hendon, was killed on February 22 1941, as a Sergeant with 235, aged 20. He is remembered on the Runnymede Memorial, Panel 54.

HAROLD WILLIAM WALMSLEY

755997   Sgt   Observer   British   248 Squadron

Walmsley, of Blackpool, was with 248 Squadron in early July 1940.

On December 13 Walmsley was one of the crew of a Blenheim detailed to fly from Sumburgh to Wick for operations. Whilst formating his aircraft collided with another Blenheim, crashed into the sea and sank. The crew of three and two ground staff men were all lost.

Walmsley was 24. He is remembered on the Runnymede Memorial, Panel 20.

EDMUND WALSH

131632   Sgt   Air Gunner   British   141 Squadron

Born in Manchester on August 22 1918, Walsh joined the RAFVR in 1938. He was called to full-time service on September 22 1939.

In early 1940 Walsh was posted to 4 ITW, Bexhill, moved on to CGS, Warmwell for a gunnery course and then converted to Defiants at 5 OTU, Aston Down. He joined 141 Squadron at Turnhouse in early September 1940.

In August 1941 the squadron began to convert to Beaufighters and Walsh was sent to the Airborne Radar School at Newton-on-Ayr. After qualifying as a Radio Observer he returned to 141 and resumed operational flying with Warrant Officer RC Hamer (qv).

In the early hours of September 9 1942 they were directed to a He 111 fifteen miles south-east of St Alban's Head. The enemy aircraft was destroyed but Hamer was wounded and the Beaufighter's starboard engine set alight. He flew the aircraft back over the Isle of Wight and then ordered Walsh to bale out. Hamer flew on to his death. They had flown 219 times together.

Walsh, who had been commissioned from Warrant Officer in August 1942, left 141 in early 1943. He had flown 131 hours on Defiants and 514 on Beaufighters. He was transferred to the Administrative Branch on Special Duties. Walsh was posted to 225 Group in India and appointed OC 853 AMES. When the unit was disbanded in Burma Walsh continued as OC No II Opening Party in the Central Provinces of India.

He was released from the RAF on February 23 1946, as a Flight Lieutenant.

PO 26.8.42   FO 26.2.43

JOHN JOSEPH WALSH

42547   PO   Pilot   Canadian   615 Squadron

Walsh, of Bassano, Alberta, joined the RAF on a short service commission in June 1939. He was posted to 615 Squadron at Prestwick on September 23 1940.

In January 1941 Walsh was in Egypt, having come up from Takoradi. He and three other pilots flew to Malta in a Sunderland on the 20th, to reinforce 261 Squadron.

On February 25 Walsh damaged a Do 215. Later in the day he was shot down by Bf 109s of 7/JG 26 over St Paul's Bay and baled out. He was picked up by a destroyer, with a leg broken in four places and a broken arm. He died in hospital on March 2 1941 from pneumonia, possibly brought on by shock. Walsh was 23. He is buried in the Naval Cemetery, Capuccini, Malta.

APO 19.8.39   PO 1.2.40   FO 1.2.41

ROBERT WILLIAM MEADE WALSH

Sub-Lieutenant (FAA)   Pilot   British   111 Squadron

Walsh is believed to have served with 142 Squadron at Eastchurch. He moved to 111 Squadron at Drem on September 22.

After rejoining the FAA Walsh was posted to Dekheila, Egypt and served with 805 Squadron in the Western Desert. He destroyed a G 50 on September 28 1941 and probably a SM 79 on November 23.

In 1944 Walsh was back in the UK. For the invasion he was with 885 Squadron, in 3 Wing at Lee-on-Solent. In 1945 he became CO of 1831 Squadron, formed in the US with Corsairs. The squadron later embarked in HMS 'Glory' for service in the Pacific.

After the war Walsh served at Lossiemouth and Lee-on-Solent as Lieutenant Commander Flying, as Flight Deck Officer on HMS 'Vengeance' and as FDO and Lieutenant Commander Flying on HMS 'Theseus'. When he retired on February 10 1958 Walsh was Officer i/c the Safety Equipment School at Seafield Park.

Actg Sub-Lt 13.9.39   Sub-Lt 14.3.40   Lt 11.3.42
Lt-Cdr 11.3.50

HERBERT WALTON

51843   Sgt   Pilot   British   87 Squadron

Walton was born in 1916. He was with 87 Squadron at Church Fenton in early July 1940. He was slightly wounded on September 30 and returned to Exeter with aircraft damage.

Promoted to Warrant Officer on October 1 1941, Walton was commissioned in January 1943. He was released from the RAF in 1946, as a Flight Lieutenant.

PO 25.1.43   FO 25.7.43   FL 25.1.45

WILLIAM HUDSON WANT

745927   Sgt   Observer   British   248 Squadron

With 248 Squadron in early July 1940.

On August 3 he was a member of the crew of a Blenheim which made a forced-landing in a field at Tranent, cause unknown. On the 19th he was in a Blenheim which failed to return from a reconnaissance of the south Norwegian coast. All three men on board were lost.

Want was 28. He is remembered on the Runnymede Memorial, Panel 20.

STEFAN WAPNIAREK

P 1291   PO   Pilot   Polish   302 Squadron

Wapniarek was born on February 23 1916. As a cadet officer he destroyed at least two German aircraft during the fighting in Poland in September 1939.

He joined 302 Squadron at Leconfield on July 30 1940. Wapniarek claimed a Ju 88 destroyed on September 18. After a patrol in bad weather conditions on October 18 he was killed attempting a forced-landing at Nutwood Farm, Thames Ditton, in Hurricane P 3872.

Wapniarek was 24. He is buried in Northwood Cemetery, Middlesex and is remembered on the Polish Air Force Memorial at Northolt. He was awarded the KW (1.2.41) and the VM (5th Class)(31.10.47).

DEREK HARLAND WARD

40786   FO   Pilot   New Zealander   87 Squadron

Born at Whangarei on July 31 1917, Ward learned to fly at Waikato Airport, Hamilton in early 1937. He applied for a short service commission in the RNZAF in March and reported to Wigram on May 23. Ward began flying training a month later.

He was awarded his flying badge on December 10. After completing the course on April 1 1938 he sailed for the UK on the 23rd in the SS 'Tamaroa'. Ward transferred to the RAF on June 1 1938, with a five year short service commission. He joined 151 Squadron at North Weald on the 15th.

Ward was still with 151 in May 1940. On the 16th, in company with five other ferry pilots, he delivered a new Hurricane to 87 Squadron at Lille-Seclin. The squadron had suffered heavy losses and with no definite orders the six pilots decided to remain in France with 87. On the 18th Ward destroyed a Hs 126 and on the 19th damaged a Do 17.

The squadron was withdrawn on the 20th and he made his way to England in a badly-damaged Hurricane, reaching Debden after a few narrow escapes. Ward was taken on to the strength of 87 Squadron. On August 11 he was appointed 'B' Flight Commander and claimed a Bf 110 destroyed on the 15th.

From the beginning of September 1940 'A' and 'B' flights alternated at Bibury, on night duties. On the 3rd Ward damaged an enemy aircraft at night. During the flat period after the Battle of Britain Ward organised a squadron aerobatic team, comprising of himself, Pilot Officer RP Beamont and Flight Sergeant IJ Badger, who had flown in a 151 Squadron aerobatic team before the war. The team became very proficient and its displays contributed greatly to squadron morale. Ward was awarded the DFC (17.10.41).

He was posted overseas on September 20 1941 and joined 73 Squadron at El Gamil at the end of the month as a supernumerary. Ward took command in early October. From mid-November a flight of 73 operated from landing grounds in the Western Desert, as part of Wing Commander EW Whitley's 'Whitforce'. Ward himself led this flight on bomber escorts, offensive sweeps, scrambles and ground-strafing operations. On December 8 he destroyed a Ju 88 and two days later damaged another. The flight was withdrawn for a rest on December 11.

Operating with the squadron from El Adem on February 9 1942 Ward destroyed a He 111, on the 13th he probably destroyed a Bf 109 over Tobruk and on May 1 he shot down a four-engined enemy aircraft, probably a FW Condor, during a strafing attack on Barce airfield. Ward was awarded a Bar to the DFC (22.5.42).

After a three-week leave he rejoined the squadron at Gambut on June 1 and the next night damaged a Ju 88 over Gasr-el-Arid. Soon after mid-day on June 17 Ward led the squadron off, as part of a fighter escort covering Bostons. After returning and very low on fuel the Hurricanes were jumped by four Bf 109s as they were about to land. The Germans were led by Oberleutnant H-J Marseille. He shot down two Hurricanes on his first pass. Not realising what had happened most of the Hurricanes landed but Ward went back to cover the pilots coming down by parachute. Marseille returned and shot Ward down, almost certainly killing him instantly. His Hurricane crashed two miles south of Gambut and he was buried nearby, in a grave marked by a small wooden cross.

Ward was later re-interred in the Halfaya Sollum War Cemetery. His DFC and Bar were presented to his parents by the Governor-General of New Zealand at a ceremony in Auckland on May 31 1944.

PO (RNZAF) 23.5.37   PO 1.6.38   FO 1.1.40   FL 1.1.41

The Hon EDWARD FREDERICK WARD

32144   SL   Pilot   British   601 Squadron

Ward was born on November 20 1907, the third son of the 2nd Earl of Dudley. He was sponsored by King Edward VII, educated at Eton and entered the Army as a 2nd Lieutenant 10th Hussars.

He joined 601 Squadron, AuxAF in 1931. Ward was commissioned in the RAF in February 1932 and posted to 57 Squadron at Upper Heyford. He went to 811 Squadron on August 11 1933, based at Gosport and on HMS 'Furious'.

Ward joined the staff at RAF Gosport on October 17 1934 and remained there until February 11 1937, when he went on to the Reserve. He was recalled to full-time service on August 26 1939.

After being attached to 601 Squadron at Tangmere on July 28 1940, Ward took command on August 10 but he was posted away to the Tangmere Sector Operations Room on the 19th.

Ward was released from the RAF in 1945, as a Group Captain. He died in April 1987.

PO 11.2.32   FO 11.8.33   FL 11.8.36   FL (RAFO) 11.2.37
FL 26.8.39   SL 1.3.40   WC 1.3.42

JOHN LEWIS WARD

84018   PO   Pilot   British   32 Squadron

Ward, of Merthyr Tydfil, Glamorgan, joined 32 Squadron at Acklington in late September 1940.

He was killed on March 20 1942, as a Flying Officer with 127 Squadron, operating from St Jean in Palestine with Hurricanes. Ward was 26. He is buried in Khayat Beach War Cemetery, Israel.

PO 24.8.40   FO 24.8.41

RUFUS ARTHUR WARD

740193   Sgt   Pilot   British   616 and 66 Squadrons

Born in Croydon on February 2 1917, Ward was educated at Stanley Technical School and was an aircraft engineer. He joined the AuxAF on March 3 1936 and transferred to the RAFVR in September 1937 as a Sergeant u/t pilot.

Called to full-time service at the outbreak of war, Ward was awarded his flying badge on May 20 1940. He completed his training, converted to Spitfires, joined 616 Squadron at Kenley on September 5 and moved to 66 Squadron at Gravesend on the 29th.

Over North Kent on October 8 1940 Ward was shot down and killed by Bf 109s. His Spitfire, N 3043, crashed near Valley View Road, Borstal, near Rochester. Ward is buried in Mitcham Road Cemetery, Croydon.

WILLIAM BARLOW WARD

516760   Sgt   Aircrew   British   604 Squadron

No service details traced.

NOEL PROCTOR WARDEN

100592   Sgt   Pilot   British   610 Squadron

Joined 610 Squadron at Acklington on October 6 1940.

Commissioned in June 1941, Warden was killed on October 1, as a Pilot Officer with 91 Squadron. He is remembered on the Runnymede Memorial, Panel 35.

PO 12.6.41

PETER WARD-SMITH

100039   Sgt   Pilot   British   610 Squadron

Joined 610 Squadron at Acklington on September 16 1940.

Commissioned in June 1941, Ward-Smith was released from the RAF in 1946, as a Flight Lieutenant.

PO 19.6.41   FO 19.6.42   FL 19.6.43

RALPH TAVERHAM WARE

52938   Sgt   Pilot   British   3 Squadron

Ware, of Teignmouth, Devon, was with 3 Squadron at Wick in early July 1940.

He was promoted to Warrant Officer on October 1 1941 and commissioned in June 1943. Ware was killed on January 21 1945, as a Flying Officer with No 1 OADU Transit Flight. He was 30 and is remembered on the Runnymede Memorial, Panel 268. Ware received a Mention in Despatches.

PO 18.6.43   FO 18.12.43

MICHAEL PERCY WAREHAM

85269   PO   Pilot   British   1 and 242 Squadrons

Initially with No 1 Squadron, Wareham joined 242 Squadron at Duxford on October 17 1940.

He was posted to 73 Squadron at Castle Camps on November 6, embarked soon afterwards on HMS 'Furious' for West Africa and flew off to Takoradi on the 29th. The squadron then flew to Heliopolis, via Lagos, Accra, Kano, Maidugari, Khartoum, Wadi Halfa and Abu Sueir. During December the pilots were attached to 274 Squadron in the Western Desert. The squadron began to operate on its own account in early January 1941.

On February 1 Wareham destroyed a Caproni Ghibli on the ground at Apollonia airfield, on April 22 he destroyed a Ju 87, on July 4 he was the only one of six Hurricanes to return from strafing airfields and on the 15th he destroyed a Ju 87 and a Bf 110. Wareham was awarded the DFC (12.12.41).

He remained in the RAF after the war and died on November 16 1948, as a Squadron Leader.

PO 22.9.40   FO 22.9.41   FL 22.9.42   SL 1.8.47

PHILLIP THOMAS WAREING

155258   Sgt   Pilot   British   616 Squadron

Born in 1915, Wareing was educated at Bishops Vesey's Grammar School, Sutton Coldfield. He joined the RAFVR in 1939 and was called to full-time service at the outbreak of war.

Wareing was with 616 Squadron at Leconfield in early July 1940. On August 22 he claimed a Bf 109 destroyed. Three days later he failed to return from a combat with Bf 109s over the Canterbury area, in Spitfire K 9819, and was later reported to be a prisoner.

On December 16 1942 Wareing escaped from Schukin camp, 150 miles west of Warsaw. After many adventures he stowed away on a Swedish ship and eventually reached the British Legation in Stockholm, who arranged his repatriation to England.

Commissioned from Warrant Officer in July 1943, Wareing was awarded the DCM (14.12.43). He was released from the RAF after the war as a Flight Lieutenant. He died in May 1987.

PO 13.7.43   FO 13.1.44   FL 13.7.45

WILLIAM WARING

615629   Sgt   Aircrew   British   23 Squadron

Joined 23 Squadron at Wittering in August 1940.
No other service details traced.

WILLIAM HENRY CROMWELL WARNER

90344   FO   Pilot   British   610 Squadron

Joined 610 Squadron, AuxAF in 1937. Warner was called to full-time service on August 24 1939.

He failed to return from combat with Bf 109s off Dungeness on August 16 1940, in Spitfire R 6802, as an Acting Flight Lieutenant.

Warner was 21. He is remembered on the Runnymede Memorial, Panel 5.

PO (AuxAF) 7.5.37   FO (AuxAF) 7.11.38   FO 24.8.39

CHARLES WARREN

33482   FO   Pilot   British   152 Squadron

Born on November 15 1918, Warren entered RAF College, Cranwell in January 1938 as a flight cadet. On graduation he joined 152 Squadron at Acklington on October 1 1939.

Warren shared in the destruction of a Do 17 on August 22 1940.

He was awarded the DFC (10.9.43), as an Acting Squadron Leader with 466 Squadron and was later made an MBE (12.6.47). Warren retired from the RAF on December 14 1957, as a Squadron Leader, retaining the rank of Wing Commander.

PO 1.10.39   FO 1.10.40   FL 1.10.41   SL 1.7.45
SL 1.7.45

DOUGLAS ALBERT PALMER WARREN

78259   PO   Observer   British   248 Squadron

Warren, of Cheam, Surrey, joined 248 Squadron on August 26 1940.

He was killed on February 9 1941, still with 248, aged 24. He is buried in Mandal churchyard, Norway.

PO 24.3.40

JOHN BENJAMIN WILLIAM WARREN

628894   AC 1   Radar Operator   British   600 Squadron

Warren, of Chelmsford, joined 600 Squadron at Manston in July 1940.

He was a member of the crew of Blenheim L 8665, which was shot down by Oberleutnant Sprick of III/JG 26 on August 8 and crashed in flames into the sea off Ramsgate. All three men aboard were killed.

Warren was 19. He is buried in Calais Southern Cemetery, France.

STANLEY WARREN

754897   Sgt   Pilot   British   1 Squadron

Warren, of Hull, joined No 1 Squadron at Wittering in mid-September 1940.

He failed to return from a section cloud formation over the Wash on October 9, in Hurricane V 7376. Warren was 22 and is remembered on the Runnymede Memorial, Panel 20.

THORNTON ARROWSMITH WARREN

61015   Sgt   Observer   British   236 Squadron

Joined 236 Squadron in late September 1940.

Warren was commissioned in February 1941 and released from the RAF in 1945, as a Squadron Leader.

PO 12.2.41   FO 12.2.42   FL 12.2.43

ROBIN McGREGOR WATERSTON

90197   FO   Pilot   British   603 Squadron

Waterston, of Edinburgh, joined 603 Squadron, AuxAF in 1937. He was then studying in Scotland for an engineering degree.

Called to full-time service on August 24 1939, Waterston was with 603 in early July 1940. On the 20th he shared a Do 17, shot down into the North Sea thirty miles east of Aberdeen. He claimed a Bf 109 destroyed on August 30 over Canterbury and returned to Hornchurch with a punctured oil tank after being attacked by Bf 109s.

The next day Waterston was killed in a combat over London and is believed to have been shot down by Bf 109s of I/JG 3. His Spitfire, X 4273, broke up over Woolwich and crashed near Repository Road.

Waterston was 23. He was cremated at Warriston Crematorium, Edinburgh.

PO (AuxAF) 3.2.37   FO (AuxAF) 3.8.38   FO 24.8.39

DOUGLAS HERBERT WATKINS

90363 FL Pilot British 611 Squadron

Watkins, of Heswall, Cheshire, joined 611 Squadron, AuxAF in 1938. He was called to full-time service on September 21 1939.

Over Dunkirk on June 2 1940 Watkins damaged a Bf 109. He destroyed a Do 17 on August 21, shot down into the sea off Scolt Head, Brancaster Roads, and returned to Digby with his aircraft damaged by return fire. He claimed another Do 17 destroyed on October 11 and a Bf 109 on February 25 1941.

Watkins was awarded the DFC (29.4.41). He took command of 611 Squadron in November 1941, destroyed a FW 190 over Dieppe on August 19 1942 and left the squadron in September.

He was released from the RAF in 1945, as a Wing Commander, and died in 1969.

PO (AuxAF) 21.3.38   FO 21.9.39   FL 21.9.40   SL 1.12.41

ARTHUR BASIL WATKINSON

42921 PO Pilot South African 66 Squadron

Joined the RAF on a short service commission in August 1939. With training completed Watkinson joined 66 Squadron at Coltishall on July 26 1940.

He claimed a Do 17 destroyed on September 11. He was shot down in combat over Mayfield on the 28th and baled out, wounded in the shoulder and leg. His Spitfire, X 4322, crashed at Batts Wood, Bivelham Forge Farm, Mayfield.

Watkinson was released from the RAF in 1945, as a Flight Lieutenant. He died in South Africa on October 18 1985.

APO 23.10.39   PO 6.7.40   FO 6.7.41   FL 6.10.42

WILLIAM CHARLES WATLING

44186 PO Pilot British 92 Squadron

Watling, of St Jacques, Guernsey, entered RAF College, Cranwell in September 1939 as a flight cadet. After a shortened course he graduated with a Permanent Commission in July 1940 and joined 92 Squadron at Pembrey.

He claimed a share in the destruction of a Ju 88 on August 13. He was shot down in combat with enemy aircraft over Biggin Hill on September 9, in Spitfire P 9372, and baled out, badly burned on face and hands.

Watling probably destroyed a Bf 109 on November 2 and damaged another on December 1. He was killed on February 7 1941, still with 92, aged 20. Watling is buried in St Mary Cray Cemetery, Orpington, Kent.

PO 14.7.40

———— WATSON

No unknown PO Pilot British 64 Squadron

Joined 64 Squadron at Biggin Hill on October 15 1940. No further service details traced.

ARTHUR ROY WATSON

44187 PO Pilot British 152 Squadron

Watson, of Nottingham, entered RAF College, Cranwell in September 1939 as a flight cadet. After a shortened course he graduated with a Permanent Commission in July 1940 and joined 152 Squadron at Warmwell.

On September 15 he claimed a He 111 destroyed and on the 27th a Ju 88 and a Bf 110. Watson was shot down in combat with Bf 109s on November 28 1940. He baled out but fell dead after his parachute fouled his aircraft and tore. The Spitfire, R 6597,

crashed near Wareham.

Watson was 19 years old. He is buried in Nottingham Southern Cemetery.

PO 14.7.40

EDWARD JAMES WATSON

81374 PO Pilot British 605 Squadron

Watson, of Dundee, joined 605 Squadron at Drem on August 5 1940.

Over north Kent on September 16 Watson was attacked by Major Mölders of JG 51 and his aircraft severely damaged. He made a forced-landing at Detling, wounded.

Watson was killed on February 26 1942, as a Flight Lieutenant with 135 Squadron, operating with Hurricanes from Mingaladon, Burma. He is remembered on the Singapore Memorial, Column 412.

PO 6.7.40   FO 6.7.41

FREDERICK STANLEY WATSON

C 1372 PO Pilot Canadian 3 and 1 (RCAF) Sqdns

Born in Winnipeg on February 10 1915, Watson joined the RCAF on November 6 1939.

Initially with 3 Squadron at Castletown, Watson was posted to No 1 (RCAF) Squadron, also at Castletown, on October 21 1940.

In 1941 Watson was with 409 (RCAF) Squadron. He was killed in a flying accident on October 11 and is buried in Scopwick Burial Ground, Lincolnshire.

JOHN GORDON WATSON

1002548 AC2 Radar Operator British 604 Squadron

Joined 604 Squadron at Middle Wallop in July 1940. Watson flew operationally with the squadron throughout the Battle of Britain without flying badge or rank.

He was posted away in December 1940 to a radar course at Yatesbury and did not fly again.

LIONEL GEORGE WATSON

78702 PO Air Gunner British 29 Squadron

Born in 1909, Watson joined the RAF with a direct-entry commission as a trainee air gunner. He was with 29 Squadron at Digby in early July 1940.

Watson later transferred to the Administrative Branch and was released from the RAF in 1945, as a Squadron Leader.

APO 6.4.40   PO 14.5.40   FO 14.5.41   FL 14.5.42

RAFAEL WATSON

40581 FO Pilot British 87 Squadron

Joined the RAF on a short service commission in December 1937. Watson was posted to 5 FTS, Sealand on March 5 1938 and joined 87 Squadron at Debden on September 17.

Watson served with the squadron in France and throughout the Battle of Britain. He was released from the RAF in 1947, as a Squadron Leader, and died in 1986.

APO 19.2.38   PO 6.12.38
FO 3.9.40   FL 3.9.41
SL 1.1.44

JOSEPH WATTERS

44123　PO　Pilot　New Zealander　236 Squadron

Born in Waikino on February 2 1916, Watters was educated at Waihi and Whangarei High Schools and after leaving school he was employed on the civil engineering staff of the Public Works Department. In March 1939 Watters applied for a short service commission in the RNZAF and was accepted in July.

On September 20 he reported to the Ground Training School at Rongotai, went to No 1 EFTS, Taieri in October and then to No 1 FTS, Wigram on January 16 1940. With flying training completed in early May Watters sailed for the UK on the 24th in the SS 'Mataroa'. On arrival he transferred into the RAF and after converting to Blenheims at the coastal OTU at Prestwick he joined 236 Squadron at St Eval on August 27.

On a sortie to Ushant on February 24 1941 Watters sighted two German destroyers. Unable to shadow them because of an engine giving trouble he radioed their position and as he approached St Eval aircraft were taking off to attack them. As he came in the faulty engine failed and he spun in. The Blenheim hit the ground and cartwheeled. Watters had a fractured spine but the two members of his crew escaped with bad bruises.

After return to duty he lost his operational category but regained it later, also his crew, who asked to fly with him again. On August 30 1941 Watters was posted to Dyce, to convert to Beaufighters and on September 24 he was ordered to join 272 Squadron at Edku, Egypt. He flew his own Beaufighter out, via Gibraltar and Malta. Watters took part in operations in the Western Desert and from Malta. One day in mid-November 1941 he was flying one of six Beaufighters, which arrived over Tmimi airfield just after five Ju 52s had taken off. All five were shot down and four other aircraft were left in flames on the ground. Two German reconnaissance planes were destroyed and a column of troops shot up before the Beaufighters set course for base.

Watters was posted away on March 15 1942 and in late May sailed for Capetown and thence to the UK. He went to 9 OTU, then forming at Aldergrove, as an instructor. After an instructor's course at CFS, Hullavington he returned to 9 OTU, then at Crosby-on-Eden, where he flew Oxfords on the Receiving Squadron.

On August 27 Watters was posted to 603 Squadron in the Middle East. He flew a Beaufighter out and joined the squadron in Egypt on September 29 1942, as Senior Flight Commander. Before leaving the squadron on March 23 1944 Watters had shot down one enemy aircraft and forced an Arado floatplane down on the sea and sunk it. He went to the RAF Staff College at Haifa in June, after which he was posted to HQ Middle East as Ops 1.

Watters transferred to the RNZAF on July 11 1945. He returned to the UK for repatriation to New Zealand, arrived home on February 28 1946 and went on to the Reserve on July 2. He rejoined the PWD, worked for Quantas-Empire Airways from 1948 to 1950, and then rejoined PWD.

After retiring in March 1979 Watters died on April 18 1981.

APO 18.1.40　　PO 10.7.40　　FO 10.7.41　　FL 10.7.42
SL 2.7.46

EDWIN LESLIE WATTS

755917　Sgt　Air Gunner　British　248 Squadron

Watts, of Paignton, Devon, was with 248 Squadron in early July 1940.

He was killed on April 13 1943, as a Warrant Officer with 20 Squadron. He is remembered on the Runnymede Memorial, Panel 134.

REGINALD DOUGLAS HAIG WATTS

746868　Sgt　Wop/AG　British　235 Squadron

Watts, of Far Colton, Northamptonshire, was with 235 Squadron in early July 1940.

On September 11 he was one of the crew of a Blenheim shot down into the sea by a Bf 109 during an escort operation for FAA Albacores attacking Calais. All three men on board were lost. Watts was 35. He is remembered on the Runnymede Memorial, Panel 20.

ROY FREDERICK WATTS

36142　FL　Pilot　British　253 Squadron

Born on September 13 1914, Watts joined the RAF in 1938 on one of the few direct-entry Permanent Commissions offered each year to university graduates. He was posted to 7 FTS, Peterborough on June 4 and with training completed he joined the staff of the School of Naval Co-operation at Ford.

Watts was posted to 253 Squadron at Kirton-in-Lindsey on July 1 1940. He was shot down by a Bf 109 on December 1 and crash-landed near Ashford, in Hurricane V 6881. Watts commanded 253 Squadron from November 1941 to May 1942 and 488 Squadron from October 1944 to April 1945.

He retired from the RAF on October 4 1964, as a Group Captain.

PO 4.6.38　　FO 4.9.38　　FL 3.9.40　　SL 1.12.41
WC 1.7.45　　WC 1.7.47　　GC 1.7.57

BASIL HUGH WAY

33402　FO　Pilot　British　54 Squadron

Way, of Hinton St George, Somerset, entered RAF College, Cranwell in January 1937 as a flight cadet. Whilst there he won the Groves Memorial Prize as the best all-round pilot. On graduation in December 1938 Way was posted to 54 Squadron at Hornchurch.

On February 13 1940 he shared in destroying a He 111 off the north Kent coast. In May he was appointed 'B' Flight Commander and over Dunkirk on the 25th he probably destroyed a Bf 110 and on the 26th damaged a Ju 88.

On July 3 Way shared a Do 215, on the 8th he claimed a Bf 109 destroyed and shared another, on the 11th a Bf 109, on the 24th two probable Bf 109s and on the 25th another Bf 109 destroyed. Immediately after this victory Way was shot down and killed, crashing into the Channel in Spitfire R 6707.

Way was 22 years old. He is buried in Oostdunkerke Communal Cemetery, Belgium.

PO 17.12.38　　FO 17.6.40

LEWIS BENJAMIN ROGER WAY

77132　PO　Pilot　British　229 Squadron

Joined 229 Squadron at Northolt on September 23 1940. During a squadron patrol on the 30th Way baled out of Hurricane P 3037, possibly shot down, unhurt.

Way was released from the RAF in 1946, as a Squadron Leader.

APO 15.1.40　　PO 17.8.40　　FO 17.8.41　　FL 17.8.42

ANTONI WCZELIK

P 1419   PO   Pilot   Polish   302 Squadron

Wczelik was born on October 4 1906. He arrived in England on July 12 1940 and joined 302 Squadron at Leconfield on August 20.

He made a forced-landing at Detling on November 8 after his radiator was damaged by a Bf 109, unhurt. Wczelik was awarded the KW (23.12.40).

He was posted to 317 Squadron at Squires Gate on March 6 1941, as a Flight Commander. Wczelik took command of 306 Squadron at Northolt on September 1. He was killed on April 14 1942 during a bomber escort to Caen, in Spitfire AB 182.

Wczelik is remembered on the Polish Air Force Memorial at Northolt. He was awarded a Bar to the KW (5.5.42) and a second Bar (31.10.47).

PO 5.8.40   FO 1.3.41   FL 1.3.42

PERCY STEVENSON WEAVER

70719   FO   Pilot   British   56 Squadron

Weaver, of Chippenham, Wiltshire, joined the RAF on a short service commission in October 1936. He was posted to 8 FTS, Montrose on January 16 1937 and joined 56 Squadron at North Weald on September 13. He went to the SHQ staff at North Weald on August 26 1938 but later rejoined 56 Squadron.

On July 20 1940 Weaver shared in the destruction of a Ju 88, on the 29th he claimed a Bf 109 destroyed, on August 12 a Do 17, on the 13th a Bf 110, on the 16th a shared Do 215, on the 18th a Bf 110 and a He 111, on the 24th another He 111 and on the 28th a Bf 109. On this day Weaver's aircraft was damaged by return fire from a Do 17 engaged over the Thames Estuary and he made a forced-landing at Scocles Farm, Eastchurch.

Weaver was shot down by enemy fighters over Colchester on August 31. He crashed into the River Blackwater at West Point, Osea Island in Hurricane V 7378 and was reported 'Missing'. He was 25 years old and is remembered on the Runnymede Memorial, Panel 5. Weaver was awarded the DFC (1.10.40).

APO 21.12.36   PO 10.9.37   FO 10.3.39

PAUL CLIFFORD WEBB

90171   FL   Pilot   British   602 Squadron

Born on March 10 1918, Webb was educated at Kelvinside Academy, Glasgow. He joined 602 Squadron, AuxAF in late 1937 and was called to full-time service on August 24 1939. At that time he was working for the National Bank of Scotland.

On July 1 1940 Webb attacked and damaged a Ju 88, which jettisoned its bombs in the sea off Dunbar. It later crashed at Melun-Villaroche in France. On August 16 he claimed a Bf 110 destroyed, on the 25th two more, on the 26th a He 59, on September 7 a Bf 110 and on the 9th an unidentified enemy aircraft. On this day Webb's Spitfire, K 9910, was damaged in combat with Bf 109s over Mayfield and he crash-landed in a wood at Crocker Hill, Boxgrove, with slight injuries and a broken wrist.

In early 1941 Webb was posted to 58 OTU, Grangemouth as an instructor. He later went to 123 Squadron at Drem, as a Flight Commander. On November 22 1941 Webb took command of 416 (RCAF) Squadron, then forming at Peterhead. He led the squadron until March 1942, when he was posted to the Middle East.

Webb commanded 253 Squadron in Italy from May to September 1944, when he was promoted and posted away to command a Wing. He was awarded the DFC (17.10.44) and later served in Yugoslavia.

After the war Webb commanded 612 Squadron, spent four years as Air Attaché in Turkey, was made a CBE (1.1.63) and retired from the RAF on March 18 1973, as a Group Captain, retaining the rank of Air Commodore.

PO (AuxAF) 23.1.38   FO 24.8.39   FL 3.9.40
SL 1.12.41   SL 1.9.45   WC 1.1.52   GC 1.7.63

WYNDHAM FREDERICK PEIRSON WEBBER

79222   PO   Air Gunner   British   141 Squadron

Joined the RAF on a direct-entry commission as a trainee air gunner. Webber was with 141 Squadron at Turnhouse in early July 1940.

He stayed on in the RAF, in the Secretarial Branch, and went on to the RAFO in 1954, as a Squadron Leader.

APO 20.4.40   PO 15.6.40   FO 15.6.41   FL 15.6.42
FL 1.9.45   SL 1.7.48

FRANTISEK WEBER

82584   PO   Pilot   Czechoslovakian   145 Squadron

Joined 145 Squadron at Drem on September 11 1940. Weber was shot down by Bf 109s on October 27, baled out and was rescued from the sea by an MTB. His Hurricane, V 7592, crashed into the Solent.

Weber commanded 310 Squadron from June 1941 to April 1942. He was released from the RAF after the war as a Squadron Leader.

PO 2.8.40   FL 1.3.41

JACK WEBER

115547   Sgt   Pilot   British   1 and 145 Squadrons

Joined the RAFVR on July 3 1939 and began his weekend training at 13 E&RFTS, White Waltham.

Weber was called up at the outbreak of war and after completing his training he joined No 1 Squadron at Wittering on September 23 1940. He moved to 145 Squadron at Tangmere on October 13. Weber was shot down by a Bf 109 on November 6 over the Isle of Wight and baled out of Hurricane R 4177, unhurt.

Commissioned in January 1942, Weber went with the squadron to the Middle East in February. In July it was in the Western Desert. On the 15th 145 was acting as top cover for Kittyhawk fighter-bombers. It was attacked by Bf 109s and Weber was shot down. He baled out and broke his arm on landing.

Weber was released from the RAF in November 1945, as a Flight Lieutenant. He died in 1988.

PO 7.1.42   FO 7.1.43   FL 7.1.44

ERNEST REGINALD WEBSTER

158315   Sgt   Pilot   British   85 Squadron

Born in 1917, Webster was in the RAFVR before the war. He was with 85 Squadron at Martlesham Heath in early July 1940.

Commissioned from Warrant Officer in October 1943, Webster was released from the RAF in 1947, as a Flying Officer.

PO 4.10.43   FO 5.4.44

FRANK KINNERSLEY WEBSTER

82682   PO   Pilot   British   610 Squadron

A pre-war member of the RAFVR, Webster joined 610 Squadron at Acklington on July 28 1940.

His Spitfire, R 6595, was severely damaged by a Bf 109 in combat over Folkestone on August 26. Webster was killed, when he crashed in flames attempting to land at Hawkinge.

He was 26 and is buried in Sandown Cemetery, Isle of Wight.

PO 27.7.40

HERBERT GARTH WEBSTER

519739   Sgt   Pilot   British   73 Squadron

A pre-war airman pilot, Webster was with 73 Squadron at Church Fenton in early July 1940.

On September 9 Webster was shot down in combat with Bf 110s over Sheppey and baled out, unhurt. His Hurricane, P 2796, crashed at Coldblow Lane, Detling.

In November the squadron embarked on HMS 'Furious' for West Africa and flew off to Takoradi on the 29th. The pilots then flew their Hurricanes in stages to Heliopolis, via Lagos, Accra, Kano, Maidugari, Khartoum, Wadi Halfa and Abu Sueir. During December the pilots were attached to 274 Squadron in the Western Desert. The squadron began to operate on its own account in early January 1941.

On April 10 Webster's aircraft was damaged by flak and he crash-landed at El Gubbi. On the 14th he was shot down and killed by a Bf 110 after he and Flying Officer GE Goodman had destroyed a Hs 126.

Webster was a Flight Sergeant at the time of his death. He is buried in Tobruk War Cemetery, Libya.

JOHN TERRANCE WEBSTER

37436   FO   Pilot   British   41 Squadron

Webster was born in Liverpool. He joined the RAF on a short service commission in August 1935. He was posted to 11 FTS, Wittering on November 2 and joined 17 Squadron at Kenley on May 11 1936. Webster went to 80 Squadron at its reformation at Kenley on March 8 1937 and moved to 41 Squadron at Catterick on April 11 1938.

Over Dunkirk on May 31 Webster destroyed a Bf 109 and shared a He 111 and on June 1 destroyed a Do 215 and probably another.

On July 27 Webster claimed a Bf 109 destroyed. The next day he is believed to have severely damaged two Bf 109s of JG 51. The first landed back at Wissant, with pilot unhurt. The second made a belly-landing beyond the French coast and was written off. The pilot, Major W Mölders, was wounded. On the 29th Webster claimed a Bf 109 destroyed and crashed on landing back at Manston.

He claimed four Bf 109s destroyed on August 8 and two on September 5. On this day Webster collided with Squadron Leader HRL Hood during a combat with Do 17s and Bf 109s over the Thames Estuary. Webster baled out but fell dead. His Spitfire, R 6635, crashed in flames opposite Markham Chase School, Laindon.

He was 24 and was cremated at Darlington Crematorium, Co Durham. Webster was awarded the DFC (30.8.40).

APO 21.10.35   PO 26.8.36   FO 25.8.38

JEFFERSON HEYWOOD WEDGWOOD

37645   FL   Pilot   British   253 Squadron

Wedgwood was born in London on May 28 1917. He was educated at Holyrood School, Bognor and Lancing College. He joined the RAF on a short service commission in March 1936. Wedgwood was posted to 5 FTS, Sealand on March 21, joined the staff of 2 Air Armament School, North Coates on April 15 1937 and moved to the staff of RAF Lee-on-Solent on September 3 1938. He was later with 65 Squadron, after which he instructed at Aston Down.

In June 1940 Wedgwood joined 253 Squadron at Kirton-in-Lindsey. On September 4 he claimed a Bf 110 destroyed. He was posted away on September 26 to the Vickers Supermarine works at Eastleigh as a test pilot.

In 1941 Wedgwood joined the Flying Flight at the Czech Depot at Cosford. He took command of 92 Squadron at Digby in January 1942. The squadron departed for the Middle East in February and arrived at Fayid, Egypt in April. It had no aircraft for several months and from July 2 the pilots were attached to 80 Squadron in the Western

Desert to gain operational experience. On the 27th Wedgwood destroyed a Ju 87 and damaged a Bf 109.

In early August 1942 the squadron's Spitfires arrived. Between August 14 and November 2 Wedgwood destroyed seven Bf 109s and probably another. He was awarded the DFC (2.10.42).

On December 2 he handed over the squadron, tour-expired. Wedgwood was on his way back to the UK on December 17 1942 as a passenger in a Halifax of 138 Squadron when the aircraft was shot down by anti-aircraft fire over Malta and all on board were killed.

Wedgwood is buried in the Naval Cemetery, Capuccini, Malta. He was awarded a Bar to the DFC (5.2.43), being then credited with thirteen enemy aircraft destroyed.

APO 9.3.36   PO 6.1.37   FO 6.7.38   FL 6.7.40
SL 1.9.41

GORDON VICTOR WEDLOCK

115579   Sgt   Observer   British   235 Squadron

With 235 Squadron in early July 1940.

Wedlock was awarded the DFM (17.1.41). Commissioned in January 1942, he was released from the RAF in 1946, as a Squadron Leader.

PO 22.1.42   FO 1.10.42   FL 5.9.43

MARIAN WEDZIK

P 1917   Sgt   Pilot   Polish   302 Squadron

Born in Guc, Lodz on November 3 1913, Wedzik joined the PAF in 1931. He went to the NCOs Training School at Bydgoszcz and qualified in 1934 as an aircraft mechanic with elementary flying training. He went on to complete his training at the Air Force Officers' Training Centre at Sadkow, after which he served with 162 Fighter Squadron and later 121 Fighter Squadron.

Before the war Wedzik was instructing at No 1 Training Centre at Deblin. In the September 1939 fighting he flew with the Deblin Fighting Team until evacuated to Roumania. Wedzik made his way to France and joined l'Armée de l'Air. After the French collapse he escaped to England.

On July 23 1940 Wedzik joined 302 Squadron at Leconfield. He claimed a Do 17 destroyed on September 15 and was himself shot down in flames over Chatham on October 15. He baled out and was admitted to Chatham Hospital. His Hurricane, P 2572, crashed at Walnut Tree Farm, Stoke. Wedzik was awarded the KW (1.2.41), shared a Ju 88 on February 16 1941, received a Bar to the KW (19.2.42), was commissioned in May 1942 and probably destroyed a FW 190 on July 26.

Wedzik was awarded a second Bar to the KW (20.8.42) and left 302 on November 2 1942, going to 58 OTU, Grangemouth as an instructor. He returned to operations on May 12 1943, joining 317 Squadron at Martlesham Heath. Wedzik destroyed a FW 190 on July 14. He was posted away on October 22 1943 to be air traffic controller at HQ 131 Airfield. Wedzik was awarded the VM (5th Class)(20.12.43). He went to 306 Squadron at Coolham on April 28 1944 and moved to 316 Squadron at Andrews Field on December 30, serving with it as a Flight Commander until April 5 1945.

After a spell at the PAF Depot at Blackpool Wedzik went to 25 EFTS on May 25 for an instructor's course. He was awarded the DFC (1.6.45) and then a third Bar to the KW (15.6.45). He remained at 25 EFTS until January 5 1946, when he was posted to Blackpool to await repatriation to Poland.

Wedzik returned home on June 1 1946. He flew with the Polish airline, Lot, until his retirement in 1972. He died in Warsaw on October 10 1977.

PO 31.5.42   FO 31.5.43   FL 31.5.44

ARCHIBALD NIGEL CHARLES WEIR

73593   PO   Pilot   British   145 Squadron

Weir was born in Hythe, Kent, on June 2 1919, the son of a serving RAF officer, who later went to Oxford as the first adjutant of the University Air Squadron. Weir was educated at Abberley Hall, Worcester and Winchester College. In 1937 he went up to Christ Church College, Oxford, where he learned to fly with the University Air Squadron.

Commissioned in the RAFVR in June 1939, Weir was called to full-time service at the outbreak of war. He completed his training at 2 FTS, Brize Norton and at end of February 1940 went to the Harvard Flight there for operational training. On April 8 Weir was posted to Penrhos for bombing and gunnery exercises, after which he was briefly with 504 Squadron before joining 145 Squadron at Tangmere on May 12.

Near Dunkirk on June 1 1940 Weir destroyed a Bf 110 and probably a Bf 109. On July 18 he shared a He 111, on the 22nd shared a Do 17 and on August 8 claimed two Bf 109s and a Ju 87 destroyed.

On August 11 Weir's aircraft was damaged in combat with enemy fighters south of Swanage and he made a forced-landing near Christchurch, unhurt. He was awarded the DFC (30.8.40). Weir was lost on November 7 1940 when he was shot down into the sea off Ventnor by a Bf 109 of JG 2. The Hurricane, P 2720, sank immediately. He is remembered on the Runnymede Memorial, Panel 6. His portrait was done by Cuthbert Orde.

Weir's father was killed on April 30 1941, when the troopship on which he was OC troops was torpedoed. Weir's younger brother was killed in action with the Scots Guards at Anzio on February 28 1944.

PO (RAFVR) 21.6.39   PO 9.9.39

ERIC WELCH

1050617   AC2   Radar Operator   604 Squadron

Welch, of Marple, Cheshire, joined 604 Squadron in July 1940.

After the advent of the Beaufighter and the increasing use of airborne radar Welch retrained as a Radio Observer. He was killed on December 17 1941, as a Sergeant, aged 21. He is buried in All Saints' churchyard, Marple.

GEORGE HENRY ETTRICK WELFORD

90756   PO   Pilot   British   607 Squadron

Joined 607 Squadron, AuxAF in 1939. Called to full-time service, Welford completed his training and rejoined 607, then at Usworth, in June 1940.

He was shot down on September 17 by Hauptmann Neumann of I/JG 27 and made a forced-landing at Tuesnoad Farm, Bethersden, slightly wounded.

Welford was released from the RAF in 1945, as a Squadron Leader.

APO (AuxAF) 7.5.39   APO 24.8.39   PO 1.6.40
FO 1.12.40   FL 1.12.41

EDWARD PRESTON WELLS

| 58786 | PO | Pilot | New Zealander | 266 and 41 Sqdns |

Wells was born in Cambridge, New Zealand on July 26 1916. He was educated at the High School there and after leaving he went farming. In October 1938 Wells applied for a short service commission in the RNZAF, was accepted in mid-April 1939 but was not called until October 26, when he reported to the Ground Training School at Weraroa.

On November 20 Wells went to 2 EFTS, New Plymouth, moved to 2 FTS, Woodbourne on January 15 1940 and with his flying training completed he sailed for the UK on June 7 in the RMS 'Rangitata'. Wells went to 7 OTU, Hawarden on August 4 and after converting to Spitfires he joined 266 Squadron at Wittering on the 26th. He was posted to 41 Squadron at Hornchurch on October 2.

Wells claimed a Bf 109 destroyed on October 17, a probable Bf 109 on the 29th and one confirmed on November 2. He became the first British-based fighter pilot to engage the Italians when he chanced on some CR 42s over the Channel on the 11th. Wells destroyed a Bf 109 near Dymchurch on the 27th.

When 485 Squadron began to form at Driffield in March 1941 Wells joined it on the 15th. He scored the squadron's first victory on July 5, a Bf 109 shot down during a close-cover escort for Stirlings to Lille. On the 24th Wells destroyed another Bf 109. He was awarded the DFC (7.8.41). On August 19 he probably destroyed a Bf 109, on September 18 another, on the 21st two Bf 109s and on October 2 a probable Bf 109. Wells was awarded a Bar to the DFC (6.11.41) and took command of 485 Squadron on November 22.

He led the squadron in the operations against the 'Scharnhorst' and 'Gneisenau' on February 12 1942. Wells destroyed FW 190s on April 16 and 24 and damaged another on the 25th. He was promoted to Acting Wing Commander on May 5 and appointed Wing Leader at Kenley. Wells was awarded the DSO (28.7.42) and posted back to New Zealand on loan to the Government.

He returned to the UK on April 4 1943 and in late May was sent to a course at RAF Staff College, after which he again took over the Kenley Wing, leading it until mid-November, when he went to HQ 11 Group as Wing Commander Training.

Wells was posted to lead the Tangmere Wing on March 20 1944 and he destroyed a Me 410 on the ground on the 28th. During the next few months he led both the Detling and West Malling Wings. On November 1 1944 Wells went to CFE, Wittering to command the Day Fighter Leaders' School.

He was released from the RNZAF in the UK on February 13 1947, to take up a Permanent Commission in the RAF. Wells retired on June 15 1960, as a Group Captain.

APO 26.10.39   PO 28.5.40   FO 28.5.41   FL 22.2.42
SL 1.7.44   SL 1.9.45   WC 1.1.52   GC 1.1.59

MALCOLM LESLIE WELLS

| 78260 | PO | Observer | British | 248 Squadron |

With 248 Squadron in early July 1940.

On August 7 Wells was a member of the crew of Blenheim L 9456, which ditched off St Abb's Head when it ran out of fuel. The aircraft was towed in by a trawler, which picked the crew up from their dinghy and landed them at South Shields. The aircraft was salvaged.

Wells was awarded the DFC (26.9.41), as a Flying Officer with 69 Squadron in Malta. He was released from the RAF in 1945, as a Squadron Leader. He died in 1983.

PO 24.3.40   FO 24.3.41   FL 24.3.42

PATRICK HARDY VESEY WELLS

| 72098 | FO | Pilot | British | 249 Squadron |

Wells was commissioned in the RAFVR in February 1938 and called to full-time service at the outbreak of war. On January 1 1940 he was posted to Cranwell to complete his flying training, went to No 1 School of Army Co-operation at Old Sarum on June 2 but eight days later moved to 5 OTU, Aston Down. Wells converted to Hurricanes and joined 249 Squadron at Leconfield on June 23.

During an attack on a He 111 on September 7 Wells' Hurricane, P 3594, caught fire and he baled out over Goodnestone Court, Faversham, landing at Dunkirk, Kent. He was admitted to Chartham Hospital, wounded, and was listed as 'Missing' for five days at the squadron.

On November 11 Wells shared in the destruction of a He 59 floatplane and on the 28th he was shot down by Bf 109s and baled out, burned and injured. He underwent plastic surgery at Queen Victoria Hospital, East Grinstead and became a Guinea Pig.

In May 1941 249 Squadron embarked on HMS 'Furious' for the Middle East. At Gibraltar pilots and aircraft were transferred on to HMS 'Ark Royal' and on the 21st they flew off to Malta, arriving at Luqa in the middle of a raid.

Wells was wounded in the leg when Bf 109s shot up Ta Kali airfield on May 25. He returned to operational flying on July 30. With his tour completed Wells left Malta in a Sunderland for Egypt on September 26 1941.

In 1944 Wells was a Flight Commander in 255 Squadron in Italy. He was awarded the DSO (23.5.44). He was released from the RAF in 1946, as a Squadron Leader, and later went to live in South Africa.

PO (RAFVR) 15.2.38   FO 11.4.40   FL 2.6.41   SL 1.7.43

GEOFFREY HARRIS AUGUSTUS WELLUM

| 42925 | PO | Pilot | British | 92 Squadron |

Born in Walthamstow, Essex on August 14 1921, Wellum joined the RAF on a short service commission in August 1939. With training completed he was posted to 92 Squadron at Northolt in May 1940.

On September 11 Wellum claimed a He 111 destroyed and on the 27th he shared in the destruction of a Ju 88. In early August 1941 he was posted away to 52 OTU, Aston Down as an instructor. He was awarded the DFC (5.8.41), being then credited with at least three enemy aircraft destroyed and several others damaged.

In March 1942 Wellum was posted to 65 Squadron at Debden as a Flight Commander. He was posted to Malta in August and led eight Spitfires off HMS 'Furious' to Luqa.

After returning to the UK Wellum became a test pilot at Gloster Aircraft, testing Typhoons. He later became a gunnery instructor, continuing this duty until the end of the war.

Wellum retired from the RAF on June 30 1961, as a Flight Lieutenant, retaining the rank of Squadron Leader.

APO 23.10.39   PO 20.5.40   FO 20.5.41   FL 20.5.42
FL 1.9.45

TERENCE DEANE WELSH

42033   PO   Pilot   British   264 Squadron

Joined the RAF on a short service commission in February 1939. Welsh joined 264 Squadron at Sutton Bridge in November 1939.

Over Dunkirk on May 27 1940 he shared a He 111 and on the 29th he claimed a Bf 109, a Bf 110 and two Ju 87s destroyed. During 264 Squadron's last spell of day-fighting at Biggin Hill Welsh claimed the destruction of a Ju 88 on August 24.

He was awarded the DFC (11.2.41) and on March 12 1941 he destroyed a He 111 at night. Welsh was posted away in June to join 125 Squadron, then forming at Colerne. He left the squadron in November 1941 to be an instructor at 60 OTU.

Welsh was released from the RAF in 1945, as a Flight Lieutenant. He died in 1980.

APO 29.4.39   PO 6.2.40   FO 6.2.41   FL 6.2.42

KENNETH VICTOR WENDEL

40651   FO   Pilot   New Zealander   504 Squadron

Born in Auckland on May 8 1916, Wendel was educated at King's College there. After school he worked for an accountant but in 1934 he joined the RNZAF as a stores accounting clerk. Whilst stationed at Hobsonville Wendel joined the Auckland Aero Club and obtained his 'A' License.

He applied for a short service commission in the RAF in May 1937, was accepted and sailed for the UK on December 1 in the RMS 'Ruahine'. Wendel began his ab initio course at 13 E&RFTS, White Waltham on January 17 1938. After a short induction course at Uxbridge he went to 8 FTS, Montrose on April 9.

After completing his flying training on October 29 1938 Wendel was posted to No 1 Electrical and Wireless School, Cranwell as a staff pilot. He left on December 10 1939, going then to 12 Group Pool for advanced flying training.

Wendel joined 504 Squadron at Debden on January 23 1940. He went with it to France on May 12 and returned to England when it was withdrawn to Filton on the 22nd, after suffering severe losses. The squadron went north to Wick to reform and was assigned to the defence of Scapa Flow. On September 5 504 went south to Hendon.

On the 7th it began operations. Wendel was leading the rear section on a patrol south of the Thames Estuary when it was jumped by five Bf 109s out of the sun. After firing short bursts they made off before the remainder of the squadron turned to meet them. No one saw Wendel go down but witnesses on the ground reported that his Hurricane, L 1615, went down completely out of control, crashing at Sandbanks Farm, Graveney, near Faversham.

Wendel was badly burned and died of his injuries the same day. He is buried in Faversham Cemetery.

APO 26.3.38   PO 17.1.39   FO 3.9.40

DONAL ROCK WEST

42087   PO   Pilot   British   141 Squadron

Born on January 1 1921, West joined the RAF on a short service commission in March 1939.

He joined 141 Squadron at Grangemouth on July 24 1940.

West was awarded the DFC (8.9.44), as an Acting Squadron Leader with 256 Squadron. He retired from the RAF on December 1 1961, as a Flight Lieutenant, retaining the rank of Squadron Leader.

APO 27.5.39   PO 18.11.39   FO 18.11.40   FL 18.11.41
FL 1.9.45

HAMISH WEST

34058   SL   Pilot   British   41 and 151 Squadrons

Joined the RAF on a short service commission in March 1933. West was posted to 3 FTS, Grantham on April 8 and joined 32 Squadron at Biggin Hill on March 11 1934. He moved to 801 (Fleet Fighter) Squadron on September 4 1935, based at Gosport and on HMS 'Furious'.

West joined 803 (Fleet Fighter) Squadron on October 3 1936, based on HMS 'Furious' in the Far East. He was at RAF Gosport from May 4 1937 and was posted to CFS, Upavon on January 22 1939 for an instructor's course.

In early July 1940 West was supernumerary Squadron Leader with 41 Squadron at Hornchurch. He took command of 151 Squadron at Digby on September 8 and led it until December 1940.

West formed and then commanded 122 Squadron at Turnhouse from May 22 until August 1941. He commanded 80 Squadron briefly in the Western Desert in April 1942.

He was released from the RAF in 1947, as a Wing Commander.

APO 24.3.33   PO 24.3.34   FO 24.9.35   FL 24.9.37
SL 1.6.40

WILLIAM HENRY JAMES WESTCOTT

155543   Sgt   Observer   British   235 Squadron

With 235 Squadron in early July 1940.

Westcott was with 23 Squadron in Malta in February 1943. He was commissioned from Warrant Officer in July 1943 and released from the RAF in 1946, as a Flight Lieutenant.

PO 26.7.43   FO 26.1.44   FL 26.7.45

GEORGE HERBERT WESTLAKE

84019   PO   Pilot   British   43 and 213 Squadrons

Born on April 21 1918, Westlake joined 43 Squadron at Usworth on September 21 1940 and moved to 213 Squadron at Tangmere on the 29th. He claimed a Bf 109 destroyed on November 15.

In May 1941 the squadron embarked on HMS 'Furious' for the Middle East. It flew off to Malta on the 21st and went on to Mersa Matruh later the same day.

During the campaign in Syria Westlake was attached to 80 Squadron. He destroyed a Vichy Dewoitine D 520 on June 9 1941 and a Ju 88 on July 18.

Back with 213, he was appointed a Flight Commander. On August 26 1941 Westlake destroyed a Cant Z 1007, on June 16 1942 a Bf 109 and on July 5 a Bf 110. He was posted away to 244 Wing on August 24 but before he could leave the CO, Squadron Leader MH Young, was taken ill and on the 31st Westlake took temporary command. He was awarded the DFC (18.9.42).

In 1944/45 Westlake led a Wing in the Mediterranean area. He was awarded the DSO (22.6.45), being then credited with eleven enemy aircraft destroyed.

Westlake retired from the RAF on July 25 1969, as a Group Captain.

PO 24.8.40   FO 24.8.41   FL 24.8.42   SL 1.9.45
WC 1.7.52   GC 1.7.61

RICHARD DOUGLAS WESTLAKE

43347   PO   Pilot   British   235 Squadron

Westlake was born in 1916. He joined 235 Squadron on August 1 1940.

He was released from the RAF in 1945, as a Squadron Leader.

PO 1.4.40   FO 1.4.41   FL 1.4.42

INNES BENTALL WESTMACOTT

40488 FO Pilot British 56 Squadron

Born in Heybridge, Essex on September 20 1913, Westmacott was the son of a naval officer. His father became the first regular naval officer killed in action in the war, on HMS 'Arethusa' on August 28 1914.

Westmacott was educated at Repton and Jesus College, Cambridge. In 1936 he began a course in aeronautical engineering at the De Havilland Aeronautical Technical School and whilst there he learned to fly at the London Aeroplane Club.

In November 1937 Westmacott joined the RAF on a short service commission. After completing his ab initio course at 4 E&RFTS, Brough he was posted to 4 FTS, Abu Sueir on February 19 1938. In September Westmacott joined 80 Squadron at Ismailia. He returned to the UK in December and on January 23 1939 went to CFS, Upavon for an instructor's course. In March he was posted to 610 Squadron, AuxAF, as Assistant Adjutant and Flying Instructor.

At the outbreak of war Westmacott was posted to 2 FTS, Brize Norton, where he instructed on Oxfords. He made several applications to return to fighters and finally in late June 1940 was posted to 6 OTU, Sutton Bridge. After converting to Hurricanes Westmacott joined 56 Squadron at North Weald on August 3. He shared a Bf 110 and damaged another on the 18th, destroyed a Bf 110 on the 26th, shared a Do 17 on the 27th and destroyed a Bf 110 on the 30th.

Westmacott was shot down by Bf 110s whilst attacking Do 17s over the Blackwater Estuary on the 31st. He baled out, badly burned by his reserve tank blowing up. After landing in a clearing in a wood at Little Baddow Westmacott was taken to Chelmsford Hospital. He returned to 56 Squadron later in the year.

In early April 1941 Westmacott was on HMS 'Ark Royal' heading for Malta. He led the second flight of six Hurricanes off on the 3rd and joined 261 Squadron. He claimed a Bf 109 destroyed on April 28 and a He 111 probably destroyed on May 6. 'C' Flight of 261 provided the nucleus for 185 Squadron, reformed at Hal Far on May 12 1941 and Westmacott was appointed 'B' Flight Commander.

On May 13 Westmacott was shot down and baled out, wounded in the elbow. He returned to duty on July 30 but was made Fighter Controller and then Senior Intelligence Officer at Luqa. He protested in November 1941 and asked to go back on flying. When the Malta Night Fighter Unit was re-named 1435 (Night Fighter) Flight on December 2 Westmacott was given command.

In April 1942 he was posted to Egypt for a rest. He became Controller of the Defence Wing, Alexandria and went to sea to acquaint the Navy with fighter direction. Later he went on to the Air Staff at Air HQ, Cairo. On November 28 1942 Westmacott returned to Ta Kali to be Wing Commander Flying and Deputy Station Commander.

On March 20 1943 he was given the job of building the airfield at Safi and commanded it until its closure on November 8. Westmacott then went to Air HQ, Malta as Group Training Instructor. He returned to the UK on March 15 1944 and joined Leigh-Mallory's staff, Allied Expeditionary Air Forces, Stanmore. Westmacott was sent to RAF Staff College on September 25 1944 and at the end of the one year course he was posted to Air Ministry on Personnel Staff.

Westmacott retired from the RAF on May 1 1958, as a Wing Commander.

APO 2.2.38   PO 25.11.38   FO 25.5.40   FL 25.5.41
SL 1.6.42   WC 1.7.47

THOMAS EMRYS WESTMORELAND

741143 Sgt Pilot British 616 Squadron

Westmoreland was born at Huddersfield on June 5 1913. He obtained his 'A' License on January 5 1937.

In early July 1940 Westmoreland was with 616 Squadron at Leconfield. On August 15 he claimed a Ju 88 destroyed. He failed to return from a combat with Bf 109s over Canterbury on the 25th, in Spitfire R 6966.

Westmoreland was 27. He is remembered on the Runnymede Memorial, Panel 20.

BASIL EWART PATRICK WHALL

740484 Sgt Pilot British 602 Squadron

Joined the RAFVR in 1936. Called to full-time service at the outbreak of war, Whall joined 605 Squadron at Tangmere in late 1939.

He was posted to 263 Squadron at Filton in April 1940. On the 21st the squadron embarked on HMS 'Furious', landing on a frozen lake in Norway three days later. By nightfall on the 26th all the Gladiators were either unserviceable or destroyed so 263 re-embarked and returned to the UK.

In May a second expedition to Norway was made and on the 21st the squadron began patrolling. Whall destroyed a Do 17 on the 23rd and before the squadron was withdrawn on June 6 he had destroyed another two enemy aircraft.

Whall was posted to 602 Squadron at Drem on July 5 1940. He shared a Do 17 on August 15 and destroyed two Ju 87s on the 18th. In this engagement his Spitfire, L 1019, was hit by return fire and he ditched at Elmer Sands, Middleton, writing the aircraft off. On August 26 Whall claimed two He 111s destroyed, on September 7 a Bf 109, on the 9th a Do 17, on the 30th shared a Ju 88 and on October 7 shared a probable Do 17. On this day his Spitfire, X 4160, was damaged by a Ju 88 off Beachy Head. Whall spun in near Court Farm, Lullington whilst attempting a forced-landing.

He was taken to Princess Alice Hospital, Eastbourne, severely injured, and died on admission. Whall was 22. He is buried in St Mary's churchyard, Amersham, Buckinghamshire.

NIGEL RONALD WHEATCROFT

74695 PO Pilot British 604 Squadron

Wheatcroft, of Idridgehay, Derbyshire, was born on July 21 1919. He was educated at Winchester College and Trinity College, Cambridge, where he read Modern Languages. Wheatcroft learned to fly with the University Air Squadron and was called to full-time service in October 1939.

He joined 604 Squadron at Northolt on July 8 1940. Wheatcroft was captain of Blenheim L 6728, which crashed at Danebury Hill during an evening flight on November 26 1940. He and Sergeant RHW Taylor were killed. Wheatcroft is buried in St James' churchyard, Idridgehay.

PO 3.10.39

NORMAN JOHN WHEELER

82668   PO   Pilot   British   600 and 615 Squadrons

Joined 600 Squadron at Manston in July 1940 and moved to 615 Squadron at Prestwick on August 28.

Wheeler was awarded the AFC (11.6.42) and released from the RAF in 1945, as a Flight Lieutenant.

PO 11.7.40   FO 11.7.41   FL 11.7.42

JOHN WHELAN

52561   Sgt   Pilot   British   64 and 19 Squadrons

Born on July 10 1915. Whelan was with 64 Squadron at Kenley in early July 1940. He crash-landed there on August 11 in Spitfire P 9450, after being damaged in combat with Bf 109s off Dover. Whelan moved to 19 Squadron at Fowlmere in October.

Commissioned from Warrant Officer in June 1943, he was awarded the AFC (14.6.45) and made an MBE (1.1.59). Whelan retired from the RAF on September 15 1966, as a Wing Commander.

PO 5.6.43   FO 5.12.43   FL 5.6.45   FL 5.12.46
SL 1.7.56   WC 1.7.63

MAURICE TOLLER WHINNEY

82686   PO   Pilot   British   3 Squadron

After completing his training at 9 FTS, Hullavington and converting to Hurricanes Whinney joined 3 Squadron at Wick on August 21 1940. He was posted away on November 21 to be an instructor.

In March 1941 Whinney was put on Special Duties and in September was attached to 161 Squadron, Bomber Command. He was made an OBE (15.6.45), as a Squadron Leader. He was then employed in a department of the Foreign Office. Whinney was released in 1945, as a Squadron Leader.

PO 27.7.40   FO 27.7.41   FL 27.7.42

GEORGE ALBERT WHIPPS

741028   Sgt   Pilot   British   602 Squadron

Joined 602 Squadron at Drem on June 21 1940.

Whipps was shot down in combat with Bf 109s over Hailsham on September 6 and baled out, unhurt. His Spitfire, N 3227, crashed and burned out at Pelsham Farm, Peasmarsh. On October 29 he claimed a Bf 109 destroyed.

In August 1941 Whipps was a Flight Sergeant instructor at 61 OTU, Heston. On the 26th he was with a pupil in Master W 8583. They were both killed when a Belgian pilot took off in a Spitfire, did not check that the runway was clear and took the hood off the Master. The Belgian was killed himself on November 6, when a Spitfire landed on top of his taxying aircraft.

Whipps is buried in St Mary's churchyard, Theydon Bois, Essex.

HERBERT LAURANCE WHITBREAD

42034   PO   Pilot   British   222 Squadron

Whitbread was born in Ludlow in 1914 and educated at the Grammar School there. He joined the RAF on a short service commission in March 1939.

He carried out his flying training at Cranwell and was then posted to 222 Squadron at Duxford on November 6 1939. Whitbread claimed a Bf 109 destroyed on September 9 1940. He was shot down and killed in a surprise attack by Bf 109s on the 20th. The Spitfire, N 3203, crashed at Pond Cottage, Hermitage Farm, Higham, Rochester.

Whitbread was 26. He is buried in Ludlow New Cemetery, Shropshire.

APO 29.4.39   PO 6.11.39

ALFRED WHITBY

45721   Sgt   Pilot   British   79 Squadron

Born in Liverpool on May 19 1912, Whitby was a pre-war airman pilot. He was with 79 Squadron at Manston in early 1940. The squadron went to France on May 10, to support the squadrons there.

On the 12th Whitby shared a Do 17, on the 14th destroyed a Do 17, on the 17th probably destroyed a Bf 109 and on the 20th two Do 17s. The squadron was withdrawn to Biggin Hill on the 22nd. Whitby destroyed a Hs 126 on June 7. He was awarded the DFM (28.6.40) and was decorated by the King in a special ceremony at Biggin Hill on June 27.

Whitby shared in destroying a He 111 on August 30. He was commissioned in May 1941, served with 219 Squadron in 1944 and 157 Squadron later the same year. Whitby retired from the RAF on June 29 1962, as a Squadron Leader.

PO 1.5.41   FO 1.11.41   FL 1.5.43   FL 1.9.45
SL 1.1.53

BLAIR EUSTACE GALLOWAY WHITE

41510   FO   Pilot   British   504 Squadron

White, of Exmouth, Devon, joined the RAF on a short service commission in October 1938.

He served with 504 Squadron in the Battle of Britain. On September 15 he claimed a Do 17 destroyed and on the 27th a Bf 110.

White was killed on July 5 1943, as a Squadron Leader with 229 Squadron in Malta. He was 28 and is remembered on the Malta Memorial, Panel 6, Column 1.

APO 14.12.38   PO 3.9.39   FO 3.9.40   FL 3.9.41

FRANCIS LAWRENCE WHITE

05192   SL   Pilot   British   74 Squadron

Born on February 18 1905, White joined the RAF in May 1931. On the 29th he was posted to 15 Squadron at Martlesham Heath. He joined the staff at the RAF Training Base at Leuchars on June 10 1933 and on December 8 went to the staff at SHQ Hal Far, Malta, later joining the Station Flight there and becoming adjutant.

White was posted to the staff of RAF College, Cranwell on February 28 1938, moving to the Air Staff at HQ 21 Group, Sleaford on December 1. He joined 74 Squadron at Rochford on February 25 1940 as supernumerary Squadron Leader and took command on March 1.

Whilst sharing in the destruction of a Hs 126 over the French coast on May 23 White's aircraft was hit by return fire from the gunner and he made a forced-landing at Calais-Marck airfield. He was rescued by Flight Lieutenant JA Leathart of 54 Squadron (qv).

On August 8 1940 White was posted to HQ Fighter Command and did not fly operationally again. He retired from the RAF on September 9 1952, as a Group Captain.

PO 29.5.31   FO 29.11.32   FL 1.4.36   SL 1.12.38
WC 1.3.41   GC 1.7.44   GC 1.7.47

JACK WHITE

184793   Sgt   Air Gunner   British   248 Squadron

With 248 Squadron in early July 1940.

Commissioned in August 1944, White died on March 16 1945.

PO 31.8.44

JOHN WHITE

741363   Sgt   Pilot   British   72 Squadron

White, of Lanarkshire, joined 72 Squadron at Gravesend on June 19 1940.

He claimed a Do 17 destroyed on September 2 and probably destroyed a He 111 on the 7th. In this engagement his Spitfire, R 7022, was damaged and he made a forced-landing at Eynsford, slightly injured in the forehead and one leg. On the 11th White claimed a Do 17 destroyed, on the 14th he shared a He 111, on the 15th destroyed a He 111 and shared a second, on the 23rd probably destroyed a Bf 109 and on the 27th probably a Do 17. On this day White made a forced-landing after his header tank was damaged in combat with Bf 109s over Sevenoaks. He was awarded the DFM (24.12.40).

In June 1941 White was a Flight Sergeant with 73 Squadron in the Western Desert. On the 14th he was one of six pilots who went to strafe Gazala. Heavy flak was encountered and White's Hurricane, V 7383, was damaged. Whilst attempting to land he spun in and crashed at Sidi Barrani. He died of his injuries, aged 25.

White is buried in Halfaya Sollum War Cemetery, Egypt.

JOHN SIDNEY WHITE

128434   Sgt   Pilot   British   32 Squadron

With 32 Squadron in early July 1940.

Commissioned in July 1942, White was released from the RAF, as a Flying Officer. He died in 1985.

PO 15.7.42   FO 15.1.43

JOHN WILLIAM WHITE

43833   PO   Pilot   British   3 Squadron and FIU

Born on January 29 1914, White joined the RAF at Halton in September 1929, as an aircraft apprentice. After passing out in August 1932 he was posted to 35 Squadron, equipped with Fairey Gordons, at Bircham Newton. The squadron later went to the Sudan and White became an air gunner.

He volunteered for pilot training, was selected and began his course at 6 FTS, Netheravon. He qualified as a Sergeant-Pilot in December 1936 and was posted to 32 Squadron at Biggin Hill in January 1937. Commissioned in April 1940, White took part in operations over the Low Countries, France and Dunkirk and destroyed one Do 215 and a Bf 109.

In early July 1940 White was posted to 3 Squadron at Wick, as a Flight Commander. He went to the Fighter Interception Unit at Tangmere on September 5 and whilst serving with it was shot down by a German raider at night.

In January 1941 White went to hospital and was subsequently declared unfit for further flying because of lung damage. From April to August 1941 he was a student at the Officers' Engineering College and transferred to the Engineer Branch.

White was Engineer Officer with 264 Squadron from September to December 1941, Flight Commander of the Repair Section at 58 MU until April 1943 and OC of 235 (Mobile) MU at Netheravon until February 1944. In March he was promoted to Wing Commander and took command of No 1 Heavy Glider Servicing Unit at Netheravon. He later was appointed to command RAF Netheravon, doing so until October 1945.

Made an MBE (1.1.45), White held a series of appointments at home and overseas before retiring from the RAF on November 12 1966, as a Group Captain. He joined Rolls Royce in 1968 in an executive capacity and remained there until 1980.

PO 25.4.40   FO 25.4.41   FL 25.4.42   SL 10.7.44
WC 1.7.47   GC 1.1.58

ROBERT WHITE

552576   Sgt   Wop/AG   British   235 Squadron

Born on January 31 1922, White enlisted as a Boy Entrant on May 22 1938. He chose to be trained as a wireless operator and was posted to No 1 Electrical and Wireless School at Cranwell.

He completed his training on May 24 1940 and volunteered for aircrew duties. White was posted on flight maintenance to 5 OTU, Aston Down but on June 29 he went to 9 BGS, Penrhos for a gunnery course. He was reclassified Wop/AG on July 20, promoted to Sergeant and posted to No 1 (Coastal) OTU, Silloth.

White joined 235 Squadron at Bircham Newton on September 16. His flight, 'B', became part of 272 Squadron when it was reformed at Aldergrove on November 5. The squadron converted to Beaufighters in May 1941 and White and all other Wop/AGs were posted to other squadrons. He joined 407 (RCAF) Squadron at Thorney Island on the 21st and operated in Hudsons until March 6 1942, when he was posted to 279 (ASR) Squadron at Bircham Newton.

On June 29 1942 White was grounded and returned to being a wireless operator. He served at HQ Signals, Aldermaston until May 5 1943 and then at HQ RAF Chigwell until July 7 1944, when he was posted to 5763 Mobile Signals Unit at Kumbhirgram in Burma. The unit was disbanded in Rangoon in March 1946 and after a spell in Saigon White was repatriated to the UK on August 1. He was released from the RAF when his engagement was up on January 31 1949, nine years from his eighteenth birthday.

CLIFFORD WHITEHEAD

45299   F/Sgt   Pilot   British   56 Squadron

A pre-war airman pilot from Sheffield, Whitehead was with 56 Squadron at North Weald at the outbreak of war.

On May 16 1940 Whitehead went with 'B' Flight to Vitry-en-Artois to support the squadrons in France. On the 17th he destroyed a He 111 east of Cambrai and damaged another and on the 18th he destroyed two Bf 110s south of Vitry. On the evening of the 18th the flight evacuated Vitry and went to Norrent Fontes. Whitehead and Sergeant FW Higginson were sent back to destroy the remaining aircraft and stores. When they finally left Vitry the Germans were only three to four miles away.

Over Dunkirk on May 29 Whitehead probably destroyed a Bf 109. On July 10 he claimed a Bf 110 destroyed, on the 28th a probable Do 17, on August 16 a shared Do 215 and on the 18th a Bf 110. During a combat with enemy fighters over Colchester on the 31st Whitehead baled out of Hurricane V 6628, unhurt. He was awarded the DFM (30.8.40).

Commissioned in January 1941, Whitehead was killed on July 4 1942, as a Flying Officer instructor. He was 27 and is buried in Arnold Cemetery, Nottinghamshire. His portrait was done by Cuthbert Orde in December 1940.

PO 22.1.41   FO 22.1.42

ROBERT OLIVER WHITEHEAD

118049   Sgt   Pilot   British   151 and 253 Squadrons

Joined 151 Squadron at Stapleford on August 26 1940 and moved to 253 Squadron at Kenley in September.

Whitehead was commissioned in November 1941 and posted away from 253. He was released from the RAF in 1946, as a Flight Lieutenant. Whitehead served in the RAFVR from June 1949.

PO 25.11.41   FO 1.10.42   FL 25.11.43
FO (RAFVR) 30.6.49

————— WHITEHOUSE

No unknown   PO   Pilot   British   32 Squadron

Joined 32 Squadron at Acklington on August 22 1940.

No further service details traced.

SIDNEY ANTHONY HOLLINGSWORTH WHITEHOUSE

88438   Sgt   Pilot   British   501 Squadron

Whitehouse, of Harrow-on-the-Hill, was born on December 18 1919. He was educated at Harrow and Keble College, Oxford.

He joined 501 Squadron at Kenley on August 26 1940.

Whitehouse is believed to have been shot down in combat with Bf 109s over Cranbrook on October 25, in Hurricane P 5193. He destroyed a Bf 109 on November 8.

Commissioned in November 1940, Whitehouse served later in India and Burma. He was released from the RAF in 1946, as a Wing Commander.

PO 27.11.40   FO 27.11.41   FL 27.11.42   SL 28.2.45

JOSEPH JAMES WHITFIELD

526295   Sgt   Pilot   British   56 Squadron

Whitfield, of Goldthorpe, Yorkshire, was with 56 Squadron at North Weald in early July 1940.

He was shot down by Oberleutnant Fözö of 4/JG 51 in combat over the Channel off Calais on July 13 and was reported 'Missing', aged 25. Whitfield is remembered on the Runnymede Memorial, Panel 21.

DAVID WHITLEY

42036   PO   Pilot   British   264 Squadron

Joined the RAF on a short service commission in February 1939. After completing his training Whitley joined the newly-reformed 264 Squadron at Sutton Bridge on November 6 1939.

Over Dunkirk on May 24 1940 Whitley and his gunner shared in the destruction of a Bf 110, on the 27th shared a He 111 and on the 29th destroyed a Ju 87. Whitley collided with Pilot Officer MH Young over Dunkirk on the 31st and crash-landed on the beach.

On August 21 264 went to Hornchurch for what was to be its final spell of day fighting. Whitley's Defiant, L 7021, was severely damaged by return fire from a Ju 88 attacked over Manston on the 24th. He returned safely to base.

Whitley was shot down by a Bf 109 over Thanet on August 28 and he and his gunner, Sergeant RC Turner, were killed. The Defiant, N 1574, crashed in Kingswood, Challock Forest. Whitley was 21. He is buried in Bedford Cemetery.

APO 29.4.39   PO 6.11.39

ERIC WILLIAM WHITLEY

29195   SL   Pilot   New Zealander   245 Squadron

Whitley was born in Auckland on August 17 1908. He was educated at King's College there. In May 1930 he left for the UK to join the RAF. He successfully applied for a short service commission and entered the service in December.

On the 19th Whitley was posted to 4 FTS, Abu Sueir, making his first flight there on January 7 1931. He joined 84 Squadron at Shaibah, Iraq on November 10. He returned to the UK in late 1933 and in late January 1934 was posted to 17 Squadron at Upavon. Whitley was appointed 'C' Flight

Commander in April 1935. In mid-September he went to CFS, Upavon for an instructor's course.

On January 1 1936 he was posted to 10 FTS, Tern Hill and became a Flight Commander in January 1937. Whitley took command of RAF Marham on December 5 1938, remaining there until November 6 1939, when he went to Leconfield to form and command 245 Squadron. It became operational with Hurricanes on April 25 1940 and moved north to Drem in May.

After being detached to Hawkinge to take part in operations over Dunkirk 245 returned to Scotland but was detached to Hawkinge again in June to carry out patrols and bomber escorts to France. On the 20th Whitley led a successful low-level attack on the airfield at Rouen-Boos, in which many aircraft were destroyed on the ground. For this action he was awarded the DFC (30.7.40).

Whitley was posted away to HQ 13 Group, Newcastle on December 6 1940 and in early June 1941 he went to Uxbridge for overseas, arriving in the Middle East at the end of the month. He took

command of 259 Wing in Palestine in mid-July and planned the air defence of Cyprus and the Syrian coast.

On October 19 1941 Whitley went on attachment to Air HQ Libya. He was given command of a diversionary force, made up of one Hurricane and one Blenheim squadron, together with an armoured car unit to guard the airfields from which the aircraft would operate. 'Whitforce' operated from bases in the heart of the Cyrenaican desert, with the task of attacking Rommel's supply lines south of Benghazi. Although completely isolated and with its landing grounds under frequent attack by enemy bombers 'Whitforce' destroyed several hundred enemy vehicles and more than thirty enemy aircraft on the ground and in the air. The force was disbanded in early January 1942 and Whitley became Wing Leader 234 Wing in the Western Desert. He took command of the Wing on May 23, as an Acting Group Captain, received a Mention in Despatches (11.6.42) and the DSO (18.9.42).

Whitley went to 212 Group on December 26 and moved to 209 Group in early February, planning fighter operations from Palestinian and Syrian bases. He moved to 210 Group on October 9 1943 and remained there until mid-April 1944, when he returned to the UK. After a short spell at HQ 9 Group Whitley took command of the Fighter Leaders' School at Milfield on July 24, moved to CFE in mid-October, remaining there until March 12 1945, when he was posted to command 58 OTU.

Whitley retired from the RAF on September 9 1952, as a Group Captain. He died on October 25 1973.

PO 5.12.30   FO 5.7.32   FL 1.4.36   SL 1.12.38
WC 1.3.41   GC 1.7.44   GC 1.7.47

DOUGLAS MITCHELL WHITNEY

A 391885   PO   Pilot   New Zealander   245 Squadron

Whitney was born in Sydney, Australia on June 20 1914. His family moved to Wellington, New Zealand in 1915.

In June 1939 he applied to join the Civil Reserve of Pilots, was accepted in August and made his first solo flight on September 3. Whitney volunteered for aircrew duties and reported to the Ground Training School at Weraroa on December 18. He went to No 1 EFTS, Taieri on January 15 1940, moved to No 1 FTS, Wigram on March 10 and with training completed sailed for the UK on July 12 in the RMS 'Rangitane'.

On September 14 Whitney was posted to 6 OTU, Sutton Bridge and after converting to Hurricanes he joined 245 Squadron at Aldergrove on the 28th. He went to 17 Squadron at Martlesham Heath on November 12 but volunteered for overseas soon afterwards. Whitney embarked on HMS 'Furious' on December 17, sailing south for an unknown destination. He flew a Hurricane off to Takoradi on January 8 1941. The Hurricanes then flew in stages to Abu Sueir, via Lagos, Accra, Kano, Maidugari, Khartoum and Wadi Halfa.

Whitney went into the Fighter Pilots Pool until March 6, when he flew a Hurricane to Ta Kali, Malta and joined 261 Squadron. On March 22 he destroyed a Bf 109 and on April 11 he claimed a Bf 109 shot down and crash-landed himself. Whitney flew back to Egypt as a passenger on May 20 1941. He went to Takoradi on June 14 and began ferrying duties. In mid-July he was posted to 128 Squadron, then about to reform at Hastings, Sierra Leone.

On March 1 1942 Whitney was attached to Air HQ West Africa, to help set up a Fighter Operations Control Room at Tower Hill. He returned to 128 and on June 28 was appointed a Flight Commander. Whitney was posted way on November 28 and after a protracted and eventful journey he finally reached New Zealand on June 9 1943. He served as an instructor at 2 (Fighter) OTU, Ohakea until October, when he became Flight Commander of the Communications Flight at Rongotai. He later served at 2 FTS, Woodbourne and finally No 1 FTS, Wigram.

Whitney was released from the RNZAF in July 1945 and went on to the Reserve on November 15, as a Flight Lieutenant. He died in Wellington in 1981.

PO 28.6.40   FO 28.6.41   FL 28.6.42

ALFRED DANIEL WHITSON

746745   Sgt   Aircrew   British   236 Squadron

Joined 236 Squadron on July 19 1940.

Whitson was killed on May 6 1941, as a Sergeant with 59 Squadron. He is remembered on the Runnymede Memorial, Panel 54.

HARRY GEORGE WHITTICK

116055   Sgt   Air Gunner   British   604 Squadron

Joined 604 Squadron at Middle Wallop in August 1940.

Commissioned in February 1942, Whittick was released from the RAF in 1946, as a Flight Lieutenant.

PO 2.2.42   FO 1.10.42   FL 2.2.44

CHARLES DEREK WHITTINGHAM

70734   FO   Pilot   British   151 Squadron

Whittingham was commissioned in the RAFO in June 1931 and transferred to the RAFVR in January 1938.

Called to full-time service at the outbreak of war, Whittingham was with 151 Squadron at Martlesham Heath in early July 1940. On January 29 1941 he led six Hurricanes from the Middle East to Hal Far, Malta and they joined 261 Squadron at Ta Kali.

On February 1 Whittingham claimed a CR 42 destroyed. He was appointed 'B' Flight Commander on the 23rd and destroyed a Do 215 on the 25th. He took command of 261 Squadron in early May 1941 and was credited with a He 111 destroyed, a Ju 88 probably destroyed and another damaged on the 6th. 261 Squadron was disbanded on May 21 and Whittingham returned to the Middle East.

One source states that he was over 40 when he commanded 261 Squadron in Malta. It is believed that Whittingham did not return to operational flying. He was released from the RAF in 1945, as a Squadron Leader. He died on April 8 1958.

PO (RAFO) 2.6.31   FO (RAFO) 2.12.32   FO (RAFVR) 1.1.38
FO 6.3.40   FL 22.6.41

WILLIAM HUBERT RIGBY WHITTY

90288   FL   Pilot   British   607 Squadron

Whitty joined 607 Squadron, AuxAF in 1938. He was called to full-time service with the squadron in September 1939.

On October 16 Whitty was one of a section of three Gladiators which sighted a Do 18 flying boat twenty-five miles out to sea. They attacked and it crashed into the sea fifty miles out, the crew being picked up by a trawler.

The squadron flew from Acklington to Croydon on November 13 1939 and two days later flew on to Merville in France. Whitty was there with 607 until it was withdrawn to Croydon on May 20 1940. He served with the squadron throughout the Battle of Britain.

Whitty was awarded the DFC (26.10.45), as a Squadron Leader with 640 Squadron, operating in Halifaxes from Leconfield. He was also awarded the DFC (US) (14.6.46). He was released from the RAF in 1946, as a Squadron Leader, and later went to live in Canada.

PO (AuxAF) 7.3.38   FO 7.9.39   FL 7.9.40   SL 1.12.41

PETER COULSON WHITWELL

NZ 40613   Sgt   Air Gunner   British   600 Squadron

 Whitwell was born in Hartlepool, Co Durham on August 16 1920. He was educated at King's School, Bruton, Somerset and after leaving he served in the Scots Greys before going to New Zealand in late 1938. He joined the New Zealand Artillery and was serving with the 1st Battery at Fort Dorset, Seatoun when he volunteered for aircrew duties in the RNZAF on November 28 1939.

On February 13 1940 Whitwell reported to the Ground Training School at Weraroa, moved to the Air Observers' School, Ohakea on March 11 for a gunnery course and after completing it he sailed for the UK on April 26 in the RMS 'Rangitiki'.

After disembarking on June 8 Whitwell went to the RAF Depot at Uxbridge, where he was promoted to Sergeant. He was posted to 5 OTU, Aston Down on July 17 and after further training was awarded his air gunner's badge. Whitwell joined 600 Squadron at Hornchurch on September 18.

When the squadron began to receive Beaufighters the air gunners did little flying and Whitwell and others requested transfer to Bomber Command. He went to 11 OTU, Bassingbourn on February 6 1941 and after crewing-up and converting to Wellingtons he joined 7 Squadron at Oakington on May 11. Soon afterwards the squadron re-equipped with Stirlings, the first in the RAF to do so.

On the night of July 2 Whitwell was rear gunner in an aircraft, which was on its way to raid Bremen when it was attacked by a Bf 110, which he shot down in flames. On another occasion Whitwell was in one of two Stirlings making a daylight attack on ships off Borkum. They were intercepted over the convoy by eight Bf 109s. Whitwell warded off eight attacks and probably destroyed two Bf 109s. For these two actions he was awarded the DFM (16.12.41), as a Flight Sergeant.

Commissioned in January 1942, Whitwell was posted to 11 OTU, as an instructor. He returned to 7 Squadron on September 10 to begin his second tour of operations. His crew failed to return from a mine-laying operation off the Friesian Islands on the night of November 6/7 1942 and were reported 'Missing'.

Whitwell is remembered on the Runnymede Memorial, Panel 114.

PO 27.1.42   FO 1.9.42

PETER CLAUDE WICKINGS-SMITH

42929   PO   Pilot   British   235 Squadron

Wickings-Smith, of Bedford, joined the RAF on a short service commission in August 1939. After completing his training he joined 235 Squadron on August 5 1940.

On September 11 Wickings-Smith was captain of a Blenheim shot down into the sea by a Bf 109 during an escort operation for FAA Albacores attacking Calais. All three men on board were lost.

Wickings-Smith was 22. He is remembered on the Runnymede Memorial, Panel 10.

APO 23.10.39   PO 13.7.40

ARTHUR STANLEY WICKINS

47997   Sgt   Pilot   British   141 Squadron

Wickins was born on April 12 1912 and joined the RAF at Halton on July 23 1927, as an aircraft apprentice. After qualifying as a Fitter Aero Engine he was posted to 7 Squadron at Worthy Down on June 28 1930, as an AC1.

On November 23 1934 Wickins returned to Halton for a course to convert him to Fitter I. He joined 21 Squadron at Bircham Newton on November 25 1935. During his time with the squadron Wickins became a navigator, was promoted to Corporal and later to Sergeant. He went to 90 Squadron at Bicester on August 24 1937 and whilst there volunteered for pilot training.

On July 25 1938 Wickins began his ab initio course at 7 E&RFTS, Desford. He moved on to 7 FTS, Peterborough on September 30 and with training completed was posted to BGS, Aldergrove, as a staff pilot.

Wickins went to Turnhouse on October 7 1939 to join 141 Squadron at its reformation. He served with the squadron until May 16 1941, when he was posted to 54 OTU at Church Fenton, as an instructor, moving later to East Fortune, where he was commissioned from Warrant Officer in February 1942.

In late October 1943 Wickins was posted to 2 OADU, Filton. He flew a Beaufighter out to the Middle East and joined 227 Squadron there on July 15 1944. The squadron moved to Biferno, Italy on August 18. Wickins was shot down on September 10 and became a PoW. He was awarded the DFC (9.1.45), to date with effect from September 9 1944.

After returning to the UK on May 22 1945 Wickins was in various hospitals. He returned to duty on April 4 1946, when he was sent for an armament course at Henlow. Wickins held various appointments in the Technical Branch before retiring from the RAF on April 12 1961, as a Squadron Leader.

PO 28.2.42   FO 1.10.42   FL 28.2.44   FL 1.9.45
SL 1.1.53

BRYAN JOHN WICKS

40774   **FO**   **Pilot**   **British**   **56 Squadron**

Wicks, of Totnes, Devon, joined the RAF on a short service commission in March 1938. He was posted to 6 FTS, Netheravon on May 21 and joined 56 Squadron at North Weald on December 17.

During the fighting in France in May 1940 'B' Flight of 56 Squadron was sent to Vitry-en-Artois on the 16th, to support the squadrons in France. Wicks destroyed an enemy aircraft but was himself shot down on the 22nd, making a forced-landing near the Belgian frontier. He managed to evade capture for ten days and got into Dunkirk, where he was arrested by the French on suspicion of being a spy. Wicks was eventually passed to the British authorities and taken to England in an MTB. He was questioned at the Admiralty and Air Ministry, where his identity was established and he was allowed to rejoin his squadron.

On August 24 Wicks destroyed a Bf 109. He was shot down two days later by a Bf 109 over Canterbury and baled out, unhurt. His Hurricane, V 7340, crashed in the River Stour, near Grove Ferry, Upstreet.

Wicks was posted away from 56 in May 1941 and awarded the DFC (6.6.41). He took command of 610 Squadron at Leconfield in November 1941 and moved to lead 64 Squadron at Hornchurch in December, doing so until March 1942.

In August Wicks went to Malta to command 126 Squadron at Luqa. He was killed on October 12 1942, aged 22. He is remembered on the Malta Memorial, Panel 2, Column 1.

APO 7.5.38   PO 7.3.39   FO 1.9.40   FL 3.9.41

STANLEY CHARLES WIDDOWS

26218   **SL**   **Pilot**   **British**   **29 Squadron**

Born at Bradfield, Berkshire on October 4 1909, Widdows was educated at St Bartolomew's School, Newbury. He joined the RAF at Halton in 1926 as an aircraft apprentice. He entered RAF College, Cranwell in September 1929 as a flight cadet. On graduation in July 1931 Widdows was posted to 43 Squadron at Tangmere. In 1932 he served with 29 Squadron at North Weald.

On February 28 1933 he went to 45 Squadron at Helwan, Egypt, moving in November to 47 Squadron, Khartoum. Widdows was posted to RAF Ramleh, Palestine on August 14 1936. He returned to the UK in 1937 and on September 1 went as a test pilot to A&AEE, Martlesham Heath, where he carried out extensive performance tests on the first production Hurricane, L 1547, and the first production Spitfire, K 9787.

On July 16 1940 Widdows took command of 29 Squadron at Digby. He destroyed a Ju 88 at night on March 13 1941, which crashed at Smiths Farm, Dovedale, near Louth, Lincolnshire. He was awarded the DFC (4.4.41) and posted away in June 1941 to command RAF West Malling. In 1942 Widdows became Group Captain Night Ops at HQ 11 Group and 12 Group. He was SASO 85 Group in 1943/44 and Group Captain Organisation at Supreme HQ Allied Expeditionary Air Forces later in 1944.

Widdows held a series of appointments and commands in the post-war years. He was made a CB (1.1.59) and retired from the RAF on December 29 1958, as an Air Commodore.

PO 25.7.31   FO 25.1.33   FL 1.4.36   SL 1.12.38
WC 1.3.41   GC 1.7.44   GC 1.1.49   AC 1.1.55

RONALD GEORGE WIGG

41229   **FO**   **Pilot**   **New Zealander**   **65 Squadron**

Born in Auckland on October 20 1914, Wigg worked for an insurance company after leaving school. He travelled to England in April 1938, applied for a short service commission in the RAF and was provisionally accepted.

Wigg began his ab initio course at 8 E&RFTS, Woodley on July 25 and was posted to 7 FTS, Peterborough on October 1, moving on November 21 to 8 FTS, Montrose. He finished his training at 2 FTS, Brize Norton and 6 ATS, Warmwell.

On August 5 1939 Wigg joined 65 Squadron at Hornchurch. In late May 1940 he took part in operations over Dunkirk. On August 12 at Manston the squadron was lined up for take off, in vics of three, with engines running. Unable to hear, the pilots did not realise the airfield was being bombed. As they raced across the grass, tails up, bombs exploded amongst them. Blast from one which burst near Wigg overcame the Spitfire's slipstream and stopped the propellor, leaving him in the middle of a smoke-swept field. He exited rapidly and went to shelter.

Wigg was posted away to 55 OTU, Aston Down on February 25 1941, as an instructor. On November 12 Wigg sailed from Liverpool on his way to 73 OTU at Aden, finally arriving there on January 4 1942.

In mid-September Wigg was posted to the Middle East and joined No 1 (SAAF) Squadron in the Western Desert on the 25th. He flew with the squadron throughout the operations before and during the Battle of Alamein. In late January 1943 Wigg went to HQ 206 Group, Aboukir to be a test pilot on Hurricanes and Spitfires. He remained there until late July 1945, when he was posted for return to the UK.

On August 1 Wigg transferred to the RNZAF. He sailed for New Zealand on November 30 1945 and was released from the RNZAF on April 14 1946, as a Squadron Leader. He died at Kawakawa on August 4 1976.

APO 17.9.38   PO 5.8.39   FO 3.9.40   FL 3.9.41
SL 1.7.45

JOHN SPENCER WIGGLESWORTH

42930   **PO**   **Pilot**   **British**   **238 Squadron**

Wigglesworth, of Buckinghamshire, joined the RAF on a short service commission in August 1939.

He was with 238 Squadron at Middle Wallop in early July 1940. On the 21st Wigglesworth shared in the destruction of a Do 17, on September 25 he claimed a He 111 destroyed and on the 26th a Bf 110.

He was killed on February 6 1942, as a Flying Officer with 67 Squadron, operating in Buffalos from Toungoo. Wigglesworth was 21 years old. He is buried in Rangoon War Cemetery, Burma.

APO 23.10.39   PO 11.5.40   FO 11.5.41

RONALD DEREK GORDON WIGHT

34187   **FL**   **Pilot**   **British**   **213 Squadron**

Born in Skelmorlie, Ayrshire, Wight joined the RAF on a short service commission in March 1934. He was posted to 5 FTS, Sealand on April 3.

Wight joined 64 Squadron at Martlesham Heath on March 16 1936, remaining with it until June 10 1938, when he went to the SHQ staff at RAF Wittering. He was posted to 213 Squadron there on February 7 1939, as a Flight Commander.

The squadron was sent to Merville on May 17 1940 to support the hard-pressed squadrons in France. On the 19th Wight shared in the destruction of two Hs 126s and on the 20th he destroyed a Hs 126 and shared a Do 17. The squadron withdrew on the 21st, Wight's flight going to Manston. Over Dunkirk on the 27th he destroyed two Bf 109s,

RDG Wight (continued)

on the 28th another Bf 109 and two probables, on the 30th he shared in probably destroying a Do 17 and on the 31st destroyed another two Bf 109s. Wight was awarded the DFC (21.6.40).

He failed to return from a combat over Portland on August 11 1940, in Hurricane N 2650. Wight was 22. He is buried in Cayeux-sur-Mer Communal Cemetery, France.

APO 16.3.34   PO 28.8.35   FO 28.2.37   FL 28.2.39

OWEN MAURICE WIGHTMAN

Midshipman (FAA)   Pilot   British   151 Squadron

Wightman, of Colchester, was loaned to the RAF in mid-June 1940 and after converting to Hurricanes he joined 151 Squadron at North Weald on July 1.

He claimed a Bf 109 destroyed on July 9 and was then shot down himself by a Bf 109 over the Thames Estuary. He baled out and was picked up safely by a trawler.

On February 4 1941 Wightman joined 807 Squadron. The unit embarked on HMS 'Ark Royal' in early May and Wightman was killed on June 30, on a convoy operation from the carrier, as an Acting Sub-Lieutenant. Wightman was 20. He is buried in North Front Cemetery, Gibraltar.

Midshipman 1.7.39

CHARLES WILCOCK

46167   Sgt   Air Gunner   British   248 Squadron

Wilcock, of Lancashire, joined 248 Squadron in mid-July 1940. He flew with Flying Officer EH McHardy from September 1940 until posted away from 248 in July 1941, when the squadron converted to Beaufighters.

Commissioned in July 1941, Wilcock died on May 21 1942, as a Pilot Officer with 62 (GR) Squadron. He was 20 and is remembered on the Singapore Memorial, Column 413.

PO 3.7.41

EDGAR JOHN WILCOX

70830   FO   Pilot   British   72 Squadron

Born in Croydon in 1917, Wilcox was educated at Winton House School and Croydon High School. He joined the RAF on a short service commission in September 1937.

Wilcox was posted to 8 FTS, Montrose on December 11 and joined 72 Squadron at Church Fenton on July 9 1938. Over Dunkirk on June 2 1940 he destroyed a Ju 87 and on July 1 claimed a share in the destruction of a He 59.

On August 31 Wilcox was shot down and killed in combat over Dungeness. His Spitfire, P 9457, crashed in Hungerford Field, Checkenden Farm, Staplehurst. Wilcox was 23. He is buried in All Saints' churchyard, Staplehurst.

APO 24.11.37   PO 24.10.38   FO 24.5.40

TIMOTHY SEDDON WILDBLOOD

33478   PO   Pilot   British   152 Squadron

Born in Egypt on March 3 1920, Wildblood was educated at Colmes Rectory, Allton 1926 to 28, The Towers, Crowthorne 1928 to 33 and Wellington College from 1933 to 37. He won a King's Cadetship to RAF College, Cranwell and entered 'B' Squadron there on January 1 1938.

On graduation Wildblood joined 152 Squadron, then forming at Acklington, on October 1 1939.

He claimed a Bf 109 destroyed on August 11 1940, a Bf 110 on the 12th and a Ju 87 and another shared on the 18th.

Wildblood failed to return from combat over the Channel on August 25, in Spitfire R 6994. He is remembered on the Runnymede Memorial, Panel 10. He received a Mention in Despatches (17.3.41).

PO 1.10.39

DENIS CLIFTON WILDE

83291   PO   Observer   British   236 Squadron

Joined 601 Squadron, AuxAF in 1932 and served as an AC1 air gunner until 1936. Wilde joined the RAFVR at Bristol in 1938, as a trainee observer.

He was called to full-time service at the outbreak of war and after qualifying Wilde joined 236 Squadron at Thorney Island. After completing his operational tour in 1941 he was posted to Port Albert, Ontario, for a Specialist Navigator's Course. On return to the UK Wilde went to North Coates, as Senior Navigation Officer, a post he held for two years.

He was eventually posted to 575 Squadron at Bradwell Bay, a unit of Transport Support Command, where he qualified as a co-pilot on Dakotas. Wilde was released from the RAF in August 1946, as a Squadron Leader. He then served as a King's, later Queen's, Foreign Service Messenger for thirteen years. He died in 1989.

PO 30.6.40   FO 30.6.41   FL 30.6.42

GEOFFREY NORMAN WILKES

741315   Sgt   Pilot   British   213 Squadron

Wilkes, of Horley, Surrey, was with 213 Squadron at Exeter in early July 1940.

On August 12 he failed to return from combat with enemy aircraft off Bognor, in Hurricane P 2854. Wilkes was 21. He is remembered on the Runnymede Memorial, Panel 21.

KENNETH ASTILL WILKINSON

172142   Sgt   Pilot   British   616 and 19 Squadrons

Wilkinson joined the RAFVR in March 1939 and carried out his weekend flying at 31 E&RFTS, Staverton.

Called to full-time service at the outbreak of war, Wilkinson went to ITW and did not reach 5 EFTS, Hanworth until March 26 1940. He was at 10 (Advanced) EFTS, Yatesbury from May 25 until June 7, moving then to complete his flying training at 8 FTS, Montrose.

On September 1 Wilkinson went to 7 OTU, Hawarden and after converting to Spitfires he joined 616 Squadron at Kirton-in-Lindsey on October 1, moving to 19 Squadron at Fowlmere on the 17th. Tour-expired, Wilkinson was posted to 56 OTU, Sutton Bridge, on January 27 1941 as an instructor.

On October 23 1941 Wilkinson joined 1488 Flight at Shoreham. He was sent on a course to CGS, Sutton Bridge on May 10 1942 to become a pilot gunnery instructor, after which he was posted to 11 Group Practice Camp at Martlesham Heath. Wilkinson went to 61 OTU, Rednal on February 23 1943 for a refresher course on Spitfires before joining 234 Squadron on April 23 at Skeabrae. He moved to 165 Squadron at Ibsley on July 8.

Wilkinson was posted away to 53 OTU, Hibaldstow on December 27 1943, was commissioned in February 1944 and remained there until June 7. He went to 24 OTU, Honeybourne on August 28 and moved on to 10 OTU, Abingdon on May 27 1945. Wilkinson was released from the RAF in November 1945, as a Flying Officer. He served in the RAFVR from 1947.

PO 4.2.44   FO 4.8.44   FO (RAFVR) 21.11.47

RODNEY LEVETT WILKINSON

26192   SL   Pilot   British   266 Squadron

Wilkinson, of Rotherfield, Sussex, entered RAF College, Cranwell in January 1929 as a flight cadet. On graduation in December 1930 he joined 3 Squadron at Upavon.

On October 1 1932 Wilkinson was posted to the staff of HQ Transjordan and Palestine, Jerusalem. He returned to the UK in 1934 and joined the Station Flight at Duxford on October 22, moving on April 19 1937 to the staff of CFS, Upavon.

On July 6 1940 Wilkinson was given command of 266 Squadron at Wittering. He claimed a Do 17 destroyed on August 12 and a Ju 88 on the 15th. He was shot down and killed in combat with Bf 109s on the 16th. His Spitfire, R 6768, crashed and burned out at Eastry Court.

Wilkinson was 30. He is buried in Margate Cemetery, Kent.

PO 20.12.30   FO 20.6.32   FL 1.4.36   SL 1.12.38

ROYCE CLIFFORD WILKINSON

44125   FO   Pilot   British   3 Squadron

Born in Mexborough, Yorkshire on November 26 1913, Wilkinson joined the RAF at Halton in January 1930 as an aircraft apprentice. After qualifying as a Fitter Aero Engine he was posted to Aboukir in 1933.

Wilkinson volunteered for pilot training and after returning to the UK in 1936 he began the course in July. After passing out he joined 3 Squadron at Kenley in May 1937.

On May 10 1940 the squadron went to France, attached to 63 Wing. Wilkinson shared in destroying two Hs 126s on the 12th, destroyed a He 111 on the 13th, two Bf 109s on the 14th and a Hs 126 on the 20th. The squadron was withdrawn to Kenley the same day. Wilkinson received the double award of DFM and Bar (31.5.40). His commission was gazetted whilst he was in France.

In October 1940 he was posted to the newly-formed 71 (Eagle) Squadron at Church Fenton, as a Flight Commander. Wilkinson went to Kirton-in-Lindsey on May 14 1941 to join 121 (Eagle) Squadron about to be formed there, as a Flight Commander. He was posted away on March 3 1942 to form and command 174 Squadron at Manston, which he did until May.

Wilkinson commanded No 1 Squadron at Acklington and Biggin Hill from August 1 1942 to May 30 1943, when he was appointed to lead the Gravesend Wing. In March 1944 he was given command of HQ 149 Airfield, in 11 Group.

In August 1944 Wilkinson was sent to Australia on special duties. After return to the UK he went to a staff appointment at Air Ministry

in December 1945. Wilkinson was released in April 1946, as a Wing Commander OBE.

PO 15.5.40   FO 15.8.40   FL 15.8.41   SL 21.8.43

WILFRED ARTHUR WILKINSON

49914   Sgt   Pilot   British   501 Squadron

Born on August 10 1915, Wilkinson joined the RAF on November 5 1934. After four months at No 1 RAF Depot, Uxbridge he was posted to RAF Gosport. On November 6 1935 Wilkinson went for a course to the S of TT, Manston, after which he was posted to RAF Cranwell.

Wilkinson volunteered for pilot training, was selected and on June 12 1939 he began his ab initio course at 22 E&RFTS, Cambridge, moving on August 19 to 6 FTS, Little Rissington. He qualified as a Sergeant-Pilot on March 23 1940 and went to 6 OTU, Sutton Bridge on April 27.

After converting to Hurricanes Wilkinson was posted to 501 Squadron in France on May 22. The squadron was withdrawn on June 19 and re-assembled at Croydon on the 21st. Landing at Gravesend in poor visibility on August 7 Wilkinson collided with Sergeant EF Howarth.

Wilkinson was posted away on August 12 to No 1 (Coastal) OTU at Silloth, where he converted to Ansons. He joined 48 Squadron at Hooton Park on September 6 and remained with it until May 6 1941, being then posted to 2 CFS, Cranwell for an instructor's course on Oxfords. As a QFI Wilkinson went to 6 FTS, Little Rissington on June 16. After a short BAT course at 7 FIS, Upavon he moved to 6 (P) AFU, also at Little Rissington, on May 6 1942.

Commissioned from Warrant Officer in August, Wilkinson returned to 7 FIS on October 5, this time to be an instructor. He moved to 3 FIS, Lulsgate Bottom on February 23 1945, remaining there until being posted to the instructing staff at CFS, Little Rissington on April 28 1946.

Wilkinson transferred to the Secretarial Branch in February 1948. He retired from the RAF on August 10 1970, as a Squadron Leader.

PO 14.8.42   FO 14.2.43   FL 14.8.44   FL 14.2.47
SL 1.4.57

DEREK ALAN WILLANS

41089   FO   Pilot   British   23 Squadron

Joined the RAF on a short service commission in June 1938. Willans was posted to 23 Squadron at Collyweston on July 24 1940.

He was awarded the DFC (18.2.41), the citation stating that one night in January 1941 he displayed great courage in attacking an enemy aircraft over the aerodrome at Poix, continuing his attack down to 500 feet, although aware of the heavy anti-aircraft defences.

Willans was killed on May 28 1941, as a Flying Officer with 23. He is buried in St Mary's churchyard, Clymping, Sussex.

APO 20.8.38   PO 27.6.39   FO 3.9.40

PETER HAMILTON WILLCOCKS

742044   Sgt   Pilot   British   610 and 66 Squadrons

Willcocks, of South Croydon, was educated at Selhurst Grammar School. He worked for the County of London Electricity Supply Co and began with the Iraq Petrol Co one week before the war started.

After completing his flying training Willcocks joined 610 Squadron at Biggin Hill on July 27 1940. He moved to 66 Squadron at Kenley on September 10. Willcocks made a forced-landing one mile south-east of Gravesend on the 14th due to engine failure, writing the aircraft off. On the 29th he made a forced-landing after a combat with enemy fighters, slightly wounded.

On October 11 Willcocks crashed near Newhook, as he approached Eastchurch in bad visibility, unhurt. He was killed on November 28 1940, when he collided with Pilot Officer HR Allen over Edenbridge and crashed in Spitfire P 7491. Willcocks was 20. He was cremated at South London Crematorium, Mitcham.

CEDRIC WATCYN WILLIAMS

26219   SL   Pilot   British   17 Squadron

Williams entered RAF College, Cranwell in September 1929 as a flight cadet. On graduation in July 1931 he joined 32 Squadron at Kenley. He was posted to 84 Squadron at Shaibah, Iraq on February 28 1933. Williams returned to the UK in early 1935 and on February 20 he joined the staff at 3 Armament Training Camp at Sutton Bridge.

On March 30 1936 Williams went to the staff at RAF College, Cranwell and moved to the Deputy Directorate of Intelligence at Air Ministry on July 14 1938. Williams was given command of 17 Squadron at Debden on July 18 1940.

He claimed a Do 17 destroyed on August 18 and a Ju 88 on the 21st. Williams was killed on the 25th, when his port mainplane was shot off in a head-on attack on a Bf 110. His Hurricane, R 4199, crashed into the sea. He was 30 years old and is remembered on the Runnymede Memorial, Panel 4.

PO 25.7.31   FO 25.1.33   FL 1.4.36   SL 1.12.38

DENNIS CONON WILLIAMS

41230   FO   Pilot   British   141 Squadron

Williams, of Bromsgrove, joined the RAF on a short service commission in July 1938. He was with 141 Squadron at Turnhouse in early July 1940.

He generally flew with Pilot Officer GF Pledger as his gunner. They were killed together on April 4 1941. Williams was cremated at Birmingham Crematorium, Perry Bar.

APO 17.9.38   PO 25.7.39   FO 3.9.40

DESMOND GORDON WILLIAMS

41890   PO   Pilot   British   92 Squadron

Joined the RAF on a short service commission in February 1939. Williams was posted to the newly-reformed 92 Squadron at Tangmere on October 23 1939. The squadron initially had Blenheims but began to receive Spitfires in March 1940.

In William's first action, on May 23 over the French coast, he claimed a Bf 110 destroyed and two others probably destroyed. Over Dunkirk on June 2 he destroyed a He 111.

On July 10 Williams claimed a He 111 destroyed, on the 26th a shared Ju 88, on August 14 and September 11 He 111s, on the 15th another He 111 and a shared Do 17 and on the 30th a probable Do 17.

Williams was killed on October 10 1940. He collided with Flying Officer JF Drummond during an attack on a Do 17 near Tangmere. His Spitfire, X 4038, crashed east of Brighton, pieces falling at Fallowfield Crescent, Hove. Williams was 20 years old. He is buried in London Road Cemetery, Salisbury.

APO 1.4.39   PO 23.10.39

ERIC EDWARD WILLIAMS

562960   F/Sgt   Pilot   British   46 Squadron

A pre-war airman pilot, Williams was with 46 Squadron at Digby in early July 1940.

He landed at Debden on September 3 with damage sustained in combat off the Essex coast, wounded. Williams was shot down by Bf 109s over the Thames Estuary on October 15. His Hurricane, V 6550, crashed at Barton's Timber Wharf, Gravesend.

Williams was reported 'Missing'. He was 28 years old and is remembered on the Runnymede Memorial, Panel 11.

GWILYM TREVOR WILLIAMS

48736   Sgt   Air Gunner   British   219 Squadron

Williams was born on October 11 1916. He joined 219 Squadron at Catterick in May 1940.

After the arrival of the Beaufighter and the increasing use of airborne radar Williams retrained as a Radio Observer. He was awarded the DFM (30.5.41), as a Flight Sergeant with 219. He had then assisted in the destruction of three enemy aircraft at night.

Promoted to Warrant Officer on March 1 1942, Williams was commissioned in May. He was made an OBE (13.6.46), as an Acting Squadron Leader.

Williams retired from the RAF on October 11 1972, as a Squadron Leader.

PO 1.5.42   FO 1.10.42   FL 1.10.43   FL 1.10.45
FL 1.11.46   SL 1.7.53

MARK ALAN WILLIAMS

79953   PO   Pilot   British   604 Squadron

With 604 Squadron at Northolt in early July 1940.

William's name last appears in the January 1941 Air Force List and he has not been traced as a casualty so presumably he left the RAF.

PO 2.6.40

THOMAS DRAPER WILLIAMS

90658   PO   Pilot   British   611 Squadron

Joined 611 Squadron, AuxAF in early 1939. Williams was called to full-time service at the outbreak of war and after completing his training he rejoined 611 Squadron in April 1940.

On October 11 Williams claimed a share in the destruction of a Do 17. He was awarded the DFC (15.7.41), being then credited with destroying at least three enemy aircraft and damaging others. One day in June 1941 he shot down a Bf 109 when it was attempting to attack a British bomber, which had been damaged by flak. Williams then escorted the bomber to the English coast, flying at low level.

On July 23 1941 Williams was posted to 602 Squadron at Kenley, as a Flight Commander. He was released from the RAF in 1946, as a Squadron Leader.

APO (AuxAF) 12.3.39   PO 6.4.40   FO 3.12.40   FL 3.12.41

WILLIAM DUDLEY WILLIAMS

78985   PO   Pilot   British   152 Squadron

Williams was born in East Grinstead, Sussex. He joined the RAFVR in 1938 and was called to full-time service at the outbreak of war. He joined 152 Squadron at Acklington in May 1940.

On September 25 Williams claimed a Ju 88 and a Bf 110 destroyed, on the 27th another Bf 110 and on the 30th yet another, with a second shared. He was awarded the DFC (7.1.41), being then credited with at least five enemy aircraft destroyed.

In October 1941 Williams was posted away to OTU as an instructor. He commanded 121 (Eagle) Squadron from August 1 to September 29 1942, when it was transferred to the USAAC as 355 (Pursuit) Squadron.

Williams commanded 615 Squadron at Feni, India from January to March 1943. He was released from the RAF in 1945, as a Squadron Leader. He died in Sussex in April 1976. Williams' portrait was done by Cuthbert Orde in December 1940.

PO 30.4.40   FO 30.4.41   FL 30.4.42

WYCLIFF STUART WILLIAMS

42173   **PO**   **Pilot**   **New Zealander**   **266 Squadron**

Born in Dunedin on September 28 1920, Williams was a bank clerk when he applied for a short service commission in the RAF in June 1938. He was provisionally accepted in November and sailed for the UK on February 1 1939 in the RMS 'Tainui'.

Williams began his ab initio course at 11 E&RFTS, Perth on March 13, moved to 9 FTS, Hullavington on May 26, was awarded his flying badge on August 29 and joined the newly-reformed 266 Squadron at Sutton Bridge on November 6 1939. The squadron was to have Battles but in January 1940 it began to receive Spitfires.

On August 12 1940 Williams attacked a Ju 88, setting it on fire. His Spitfire, N 3175, was then badly damaged and he made a belly-landing at Bembridge, Isle of Wight. The aircraft was in flames and Williams just managed to scramble clear before it exploded. He destroyed a Bf 109 over Dover on the 18th and on September 7 shared in destroying a Do 17, shot down in flames over the Scheldt Estuary after a chase across the Channel.

On October 21 Williams took off in Spitfire X 4265 from Wittering, to intercept a raid on Cambridge. After the action he landed at Stradishall to refuel. He took off again and according to a witness he flew low across the airfield and then seemed to stall. His engine cut and unable to pull out he crashed and was killed.

Williams is buried in St Margaret's churchyard, Stradishall. He received a Mention in Despatches (17.3.41).

APO 13.7.39   PO 6.11.39

RONALD FRANK WILLIS

1003600   **Sgt**   **Radar Operator**   **British**   **219 Squadron**

Willis, of Cardiff, joined 219 Squadron at Catterick in early October 1940.

He was killed on February 8 1941, still with 219, aged 25.

Willis is buried in Cathays Cemetery, Cardiff.

WILLIAM OWEN WILLIS

NZ 40930   **Sgt**   **Air Gunner**   **New Zealander**   **600 Sqdn**

Willis was born in Ahipara on October 6 1910. After leaving school he trained as a linotype operator and worked for various newspapers around the country. Although he served in the Territorial Army for four years Willis volunteered for aircrew duties at the outbreak of war.

He was in his thirtieth year when he reported to the Ground Training School on April 9 1940, an advanced age for a trainee air gunner. In early May Willis went to the Air Observers' School, Ohakea for a gunnery course. He sailed for the UK on June 7 in the RMS 'Rangitata'. On July 30 Willis went to 5 OTU, Aston Down and after converting to Blenheims he was awarded his air gunner's badge and posted to 600 Squadron at Redhill on September 21.

When the squadron began to receive Beaufighters the air gunners did little flying and Willis and others requested transfer to Bomber Command. He went to 11 OTU, Bassingbourn on February 6 1941 and after crewing-up and converting to Wellingtons he joined 9 Squadron at Honington on April 18.

With his tour completed Willis was posted to 27 OTU, Lichfield on September 4 1941, as an instructor. Commissioned in September 1942, he was repatriated to New Zealand in May 1943, disembarking on August 3. He joined 2 Squadron at Ohakea but was transferred to No 1 OTU, as Gunnery Leader.

Willis was medically discharged on December 7 1943. He returned to newspapers but after the war went on a sheep-farming course at Massey University. His health was not up to it and he once again returned to newspapers. He died on April 23 1969.

PO 3.9.42   FO 4.3.43

WILLIAM CLAUDE WILLS

740355   **Sgt**   **Pilot**   **British**   **3 and 73 Squadrons**

Joined 3 Squadron at Wick in early July 1940 and moved to 73 Squadron at Castle Camps on September 25.

In November Wills embarked with the squadron on HMS 'Furious' for West Africa and flew off to Takoradi on the 29th. The pilots then flew their Hurricanes in stages to Heliopolis, via Lagos, Accra, Kano, Maidugari, Khartoum, Wadi Halfa and Abu Sueir. During December the pilots were attached to 274 Squadron in the Western Desert. The squadron began to operate on its own account in early January 1941.

On February 1 Wills shot down a CR 42 south-west of Cirene. He flew with Sergeant Gideon on an early morning offensive reconnaissance of El Adem on April 12 1941. Both Hurricanes were shot down. Gideon was captured but Wills was killed by a flak burst. He is buried in Knightsbridge War Cemetery, Acroma, Libya.

ALBERT ALFRED WILSDON

501613   **Sgt**   **Air Gunner**   **British**   **29 Squadron**

Wilsdon, of Bradford, Yorkshire, joined 29 Squadron at Digby on August 9 1940.

On the 24th Wilsdon was flying as gunner to Pilot Officer JRD Braham when they intercepted a Do 17 over the Humber area. Braham drew alongside and Wilsdon fired long bursts until the Dornier caught fire and peeled away with its port engine alight. The enemy aircraft was claimed by the Humber anti-aircraft guns but Braham and Wilsdon were eventually credited with it.

On December 19 1940 Wilsdon was in Blenheim L 6612, which is believed to have hit a tree during low flying. It crashed two miles south-west of Digby airfield and all four men on board were killed. Wilsdon is buried in Rose Hill Cemetery, Doncaster.

DONALD FRASER WILSON

41891   **FO**   **Pilot**   **New Zealander**   **141 Squadron**

Wilson was born in Wairoa on August 27 1916 and worked as a costing clerk in Wellington. In June 1938 he applied for an RAF short service commission, was provisionally accepted and sailed for the UK on December 16 in the RMS 'Rangitata'.

On January 23 1939 Wilson began his ab initio course at 13 E&RFTS, White Waltham. He was posted to 13 FTS, Drem on April 15 and after completing the course he joined the newly-formed 141 Squadron at Turnhouse on October 21.

Wilson served with the squadron throughout the Battle of Britain. He received a Mention in Despatches (17.3.41). On May 5 1941 he damaged a He 111 at night over Glasgow. Wilson was posted to command 1451 Flight at Hunsdon on January 1 1942. This was a Turbinlite Havoc unit, which achieved no successes.

In early June 1942 Wilson was posted to Air Ministry as a Deputy Technical Officer. He was there until June 30 1943, going then to 62 OTU, as an instructor. Wilson transferred to the RNZAF on January 1 1944 and moved to 51 OTU, Bedford on March 28 for a refresher course on night Beaufighters. He joined 219 Squadron at Bradwell Bay on June 7 but went to 277 (ASR) Squadron on July 20. Wilson was appointed Deputy Director of the School of Air-Sea Rescue at 19 Group on February 1 1945.

Wilson was posted away for repatriation to New Zealand on January 13 1947. Later in the year he relinquished his RNZAF commission and rejoined the RAF. He retired on April 1 1958, as a Squadron Leader OBE.

APO 1.4.39   PO 21.10.39   FO 21.10.40   FL 21.10.41
SL 1.7.45   SL 1.1.50

DOUGLAS STRACHAN WILSON

90342   FL   Pilot   British   610 Squadron

Joined 610 Squadron, AuxAF in 1936. Wilson was called to full-time service with the squadron on August 26 1939.

He claimed Bf 109s destroyed on July 25 1940 and August 26.

Wilson was released from the RAF in 1945, as a Wing Commander. He died in 1985.

PO (AuxAF) 24.10.36
FO (AuxAF) 24.8.38
FO 26.8.39   FL 3.9.40
SL 6.2.43

LEONARD DONALD WILSON

44307   PO   Air Gunner   British   29 Squadron

Wilson was born on May 31 1907. He was with 29 Squadron at Digby in early July 1940 and in September was Gunnery Leader.

Flying with Squadron Leader SC Widdows in a Beaufighter one night in early April 1941 Wilson had a remarkable escape from death. They had been scrambled but the engines were not right and Widdows could not maintain height so he ordered Wilson to bale out. Wilson unplugged his radio lead and prepared to go but could not open the rear hatch. Thinking him gone, Widdows made his own preparations to jump but looking back he saw Wilson struggling with the hatch. The aircraft was now down to 1000 feet. Widdows climbed back into his seat and prepared for a crash-landing. Wilson thought himself to be alone and knew the aircraft was low. Widdows made a good landing but a second or two before touchdown Wilson got the hatch open and put one foot out. He suffered severe injuries to the foot and after time in hospital he rejoined the squadron but suffered a permanent limp.

Wilson transferred to the Technical Branch (Engineering) in 1942. He retired from the RAF on March 30 1948, as a Flight Lieutenant. He died in 1987.

PO 9.5.40   FO 9.5.41   FL 9.5.42   FL 1.9.45

ROBERT ROY WILSON

41513   PO   Pilot   Canadian   111 Squadron

Wilson, of Moncton, New Brunswick, joined the RAF on a short service commission in October 1938.

He was posted to 111 Squadron at Digby in May 1940. Over Dunkirk on June 2 Wilson destroyed a Bf 109 and damaged another. His own aircraft was damaged and he made for home. Fumes forced him to bale out just short of the English coast and although the Hurricane went into the sea he landed about one mile from Manston.

On July 25 Wilson claimed a Bf 109 destroyed. He failed to return from a combat with Bf 109s over Margate on August 11 and is presumed to have crashed into the sea.

Wilson was 20. He is remembered on the Runnymede Memorial, Panel 10.

WILLIAM WILSON

553328   Sgt   Aircrew   British   235 Squadron

Joined 235 Squadron on July 13 1940. He may have been awarded the DFM at some time.

No further service details traced.

WILLIAM CHARLES WILSON

910832   Sgt   Aircrew   British   29 Squadron

Joined 29 Squadron at Digby in mid-July 1940.

No further service details traced.

VICTOR JOHN WINGFIELD

801551   Sgt   Air Gunner   British   29 Squadron

Wingfield, of Middlesex, joined 29 Squadron at Digby in late July 1940.

He was killed on May 11 1941, as a Sergeant, aged 25. Wingfield is buried in Maidstone Cemetery, Kent.

CHARLES VIVIAN WINN

40586   FO   Pilot   British   29 Squadron

Winn was born on April 20 1918 and educated at St Peter's School, Weston-super-Mare and Wycliffe College. He joined the RAF on a short service commission in November 1937. Winn was posted to 7 FTS, Peterborough on March 5 1938 and joined 29 Squadron at Debden on September 17.

He served with the squadron throughout the Battle of Britain. In early 1942 Winn was with 1459 Flight at Hibaldstow, flying Turbinlite Havocs and operating with 253 Squadron Hurricanes. On the night of May 1 Winn was vectored on to a He 111, which Flight Lieutenant Yapp of 253 attacked and damaged.

Later in the month Winn took command of 1459 Flight. On July 28 he probably got a Do 17 near Mablethorpe, with the assistance of Flight Lieutenant JLW Ellacombe of 253. On August 11 he participated in the probable destruction of an enemy aircraft, with Flight Sergeant McCarthy of 253. Winn was awarded the DFC (29.9.42). The Flight was re-numbered 538 Squadron on September 8 and Winn commanded it until its disbandment on January 25 1943.

Winn rejoined 29 Squadron at West Malling in March 1943, as a Flight Commander. He commanded 141 Squadron from June 1944 until its disbandment at Little Snoring on September 7 1945. He was awarded the DSO (3.7.45). Winn was made an OBE (1.1.51), received the Queen's Commendation for Bravery in 1953, was made a CBE (1.1.63) and retired from the RAF on July 1 1974, as an Air Vice-Marshal.

APO 19.2.38   PO 29.11.38   FO 29.8.40   FL 29.8.41
SL 1.7.43   SL 1.9.45   WC 1.7.51   GC 1.1.59
AC 1.7.65   AVM 1.1.72

ARCHIBALD LITTLE WINSKILL

84702   PO   Pilot   British   72 and 603 Squadrons

Winskill was born in Penrith, Cumberland on January 24 1917. He joined the RAFVR in April 1937 and was called to full-time service at the outbreak of war.

From September 1939 to June 1940 Winskill was a staff pilot at BGS, Catfoss. He was commissioned in August and after converting to Spitfires at 7 OTU, Hawarden he was posted to 72 Squadron on October 4, moving to 603 Squadron at Hornchurch on the 17th. Winskill claimed a Bf 109 probably destroyed on the 28th, shared a He 111 on November 21 and two CR 42s destroyed on the 23rd.

In January 1941 Winskill was posted to 41 Squadron at Hornchurch and later became a Flight Commander. He destroyed a Bf 109 on August 14 and later in the month was shot down near Calais. With the help of the French Resistance he evaded capture and returned to England in December 1941, via Spain and Gibraltar. Winskill was awarded the DFC (6.1.42), being then credited with at least three enemy aircraft destroyed.

He formed 165 Squadron at Ayr on April 6 1942 and commanded it until August. He then took command of 222 Squadron at Drem until September, when he became CO of 232 Squadron at Turnhouse. Winskill took the squadron to North Africa in November.

On a sweep over the Mateur area on January 18 1943 he was shot down, probably by FW 190s, and after ditching in the sea he swam ashore. Winskill destroyed a Ju 87 and shared another on April 7 and destroyed a Ju 88 on the ground at La Sebala airfield on May 7. With his tour completed Winskill was awarded a Bar to the DFC (27.7.43) and returned to the UK.

He commanded CGS, Catfoss from September 1943 to December 1944. He then went to Army Staff College, Camberley for a course, after which he was posted to a staff job at Air Ministry in June 1945. Winskill was made a CBE (11.6.60) and retired from the RAF on December 18 1968, as an Air Commodore. He was Captain of the Queen's Flight from 1968 to 1972 and was created a KCVO in 1980 (CVO 1973).

PO 15.8.40   FO 15.8.41   FL 14.7.42   SL 21.6.44
SL 1.9.45   WC 1.1.53   GC 1.7.59   AC 1.7.63

JOHN WINSTANLEY

52550   Sgt   Pilot   British   151 Squadron

Winstanley was born on July 26 1916. He joined 151 Squadron at Stapleford on September 4 1940. Pursuing a He 111 through low cloud on the 17th Winstanley flew into the ground, writing off Hurricane R 4185 and putting himself into hospital with injuries.

In 1941 Winstanley was in Russia with 151 Wing. He was commissioned in April 1943 and retired from the RAF on July 26 1966, as a Flight Lieutenant.

PO 29.4.43   FO 29.10.43   FL 29.4.45   FL 29.10.47

DOUGLAS CYRIL WINTER

43372   PO   Pilot   British   72 Squadron

Winter, of South Shields, joined the RAF in 1930 as an aircraft apprentice. After qualifying in his trade he served in Egypt and Palestine.

He volunteered for pilot training and after passing out as a Sergeant-Pilot he joined 72 Squadron at Church Fenton. Winter was commissioned in April 1940. Over Dunkirk on June 2 he probably destroyed a Ju 87.

On August 15 he claimed two Bf 110s destroyed and on September 1 a Bf109. Winter was shot down by a BF 109 on September 5 and was killed when he attempted to bale out too low. His Spitfire, X 4013, crashed into Covert Wood, Elham.

Winter was 26. He is buried in Harton Cemetery, South Shields.

PO 1.4.40

RICHARD ARTHUR WINTER

73015   FO   Pilot   British   247 Squadron

Winter was commissioned in the RAFVR in March 1939. He was called to full-time service at the outbreak of war and was with 247 Squadron at Roborough in early July 1940.

On October 28 Winter intercepted a He 111 over Plymouth at night but without result. He damaged another on November 6.

Winter was released from the RAF in 1945, as a Squadron Leader. He died in 1970.

PO (RAFVR) 29.3.39   PO 3.9.39   FO 3.9.40   FL 3.9.41
SL 1.7.45

JOHN FRANCIS WISE

746875   Sgt   Air Gunner   British   141 Squadron

With 141 Squadron at Turnhouse in early July 1940.

The squadron flew south to West Mlling on the 12th. Shortly after 09.00 hrs on the 19th twelve Defiants moved to the forward airfield at Hawkinge. At 12.23 hrs they were ordered off to carry out an offensive patrol twenty miles south of Folkestone. Three were left behind with engine trouble. During the patrol the nine Defiants were surprised by a force of Bf 109s of III/JG 51. Wise's aircraft, L 6983, was hit in the engine. The pilot, Flying Officer IN MacDougall, ordered Wise to bale out. He then managed to get the aircraft back to West Malling.

Wise was never heard of again. He was 20 years old and is remembered on the Runnymede Memorial, Panel 21.

WILLIAM DOUGLAS WISEMAN

82719   PO   Air Gunner   British   600 Squadron

With 600 Squadron at Northolt in early July 1940.

Wiseman was released from the RAF in 1946, as a Squadron Leader.

PO 9.5.40   FO 9.5.41   FL 9.5.42

DENIS HEATHCOTE WISSLER

42665   PO   Pilot   British   17 Squadron

Joined the RAF on a short service commission in July 1939. With training completed Wissler was posted to 85 Squadron in France in March 1940. He returned to Debden on May 22, when the squadron was withdrawn.

Wissler was posted to 17 Squadron at Martlesham Heath on June 8 and flew out to join it at Le Mans in France the next day. He returned to Debden with the squadron on June 19.

He shared in the destruction of a He 111 on July 29. Wissler was wounded in the left arm in combat with a Bf 109 over the Thames Estuary on September 24 and crashed on landing at Debden, in Hurricane P 3168. He was admitted to Saffron Walden Hospital.

On November 11 1940 Wissler was shot down during an attack on Ju 87s off Burnham. He crashed into the sea in Hurricane V 7570 and was reported 'Missing'. Wissler is remembered on the Runnymede Memorial, Panel 10.

APO 2.9.39   PO 28.2.40

LATHAM CARR WITHALL

39361   FL   Pilot   Australian   152 Squadron

Joined the RAF on a short service commission in October 1936. Withall was posted to 8 FTS, Montrose on January 16 1937 and joined 19 Squadron at Duxford on August 7.

In early July 1940 Withall was with 152 Squadron at Acklington. He failed to return from combat with enemy aircraft south of the Isle of Wight on August 12, in Spitfire P 9456. Withall was 29. He is remembered on the Runnymede Memorial, Panel 5.

APO 21.12.36   PO 12.10.37   FO 12.4.39   FL 31.5.40

STEFAN WITORZENC

76730   PO   Pilot   Polish   501 Squadron

Born on January 2 1908, Witorzenc joined the PAF in 1930. He was posted to 501 Squadron at Gravesend on August 6 1940.

Witorzenc claimed two Ju 87s destroyed on the 15th, a Bf 109 on the 18th, a Do 17 on September 2 and a Do 215 shared on the 11th. He was posted away to 306 Squadron at Tern Hill on November 22, as a Flight Commander. Witorzenc was awarded the VM (5th Class)(1.2.41).

He went to 302 Squadron at Kenley on May 14 1941, initially as a Flight Commander but he became CO on the 27th. Witorzenc destroyed a Bf 109 on September 4 and was awarded the KW (30.10.41). On February 28 1942 he was appointed Wing Leader of No 1 Polish Wing and was awarded the DFC (1.6.42). Witorzenc led the Wing until September 25, being then posted to HQ 11 Group.

He moved to HQ Fighter Command on February 18 1943 as Polish Liaison Officer. On April 24 1944 Witorzenc went to 61 OTU as Wing Commander Flying. He took command of 25 EFTS, Hucknall on January 7 1945 and on promotion to Acting Group Captain Witorzenc was made CO 131 Wing.

In January 1947 he was released from the PAF and repatriated to Poland.

PO 27.1.40   FO 1.3.41   WC 1.9.44

BOLESLAW ANDRZEJ WLASNOWOLSKI
76736   PO   Pilot   Polish   32, 607 and 213 Squadrons

Wlasnowolski was born on November 29 1916. He was in the PAF before the war and is believed to have shared in destroying a German aircraft in the September 1939 fighting in Poland.

On August 8 1940 Wlasnowolski joined 32 Squadron at Biggin Hill. He claimed a Bf 109 destroyed on the 15th and a Bf 109 and a Do 215 on the 18th. Wlasnowolski went to 607 Squadron at Tangmere on September 13 and claimed a Do 17 destroyed on the 15th. He moved on to 213 Squadron, also at Tangmere, on the 17th.

Wlasnowolski claimed a Bf 109 destroyed on October 15. He was killed on November 1 1940, crashing at Liphook Game Farm, Stoughton following combat with Bf 109s off Portsmouth, in Hurricane V 7221. He is buried in Chichester Cemetery, Sussex. Wlasnowolski was awarded the VM (5th Class) (1.2.41) and the KW (31.10.47).

PO 6.8.40

ANTONI WOJCICKI
780525   Sgt   Pilot   Polish   213 Squadron

Born on August 1 1914. Wojcicki joined 213 Squadron at Exeter on August 19 1940.

He was shot down into the Channel one mile off Selsey Bill on September 11 during a combat with Bf 110s, in Hurricane V 6667. Wojcicki is remembered on the Polish Air Force Memorial at Northolt.

MIROSLAW WOJCIECHOWSKI
781062   Sgt   Pilot   Polish   303 Squadron

Born on March 6 1917. Wojciechowski joined 303 Squadron at Northolt on August 15 1940.

He claimed two Bf 109s destroyed and a Do 17 shared on September 15 and another Bf 109 destroyed on the 17th. Wojciechowski was awarded the KW and Bar (1.2.41) and a second Bar (10.9.41).

On November 11 1942 he was posted away to 2 FIS, Montrose for an instructor's course. He was awarded the VM (5th Class)(15.11.42). Wojciechowski returned to 303 Squadron on February 17 1943 but went to 25 EFTS, Hucknall on April 4 as an instructor. He remained there until November 14 1945 and was released from the PAF soon afterwards, as a Warrant Officer.

STEFAN WOJTOWICZ
P 5024   Sgt   Pilot   Polish   303 Squadron

Born in Wynich on June 19 1916, Wojtowicz entered the PAF NCOs School at Bydgoszcz in 1936. He qualified as a fighter pilot at Krosno in 1939 and was posted to the 1st Air Force Regiment, Warsaw, joining 111 Fighter Squadron. Wojtowicz was evacuated to Roumania on September 18 1939 and eventually made his way to France, where he joined l'Armée de l'Air. In May 1940 he was in a Polish formation defending the base at Nantes. When France collapsed Wojtowicz escaped to Britain. He joined 303 Squadron at

Northolt at its formation on August 2 1940. His engine was damaged in combat with Bf 109s over the Channel on September 3 and Wojtowicz landed at Woodchurch, near Tenterden, in Hurricane R 2688, slightly injured. On the 7th he claimed two Do 17s destroyed and on the 11th a Bf 109 and another probable.

Wojtowicz was shot down and killed on the 11th, in combat south of London. His Hurricane, V 7242, crashed and burned out on Hogtrough Hill, Westerham. He is buried in Northwood Cemetery, Middlesex and remembered on the Polish Air Force Memorial at Northolt.

EDWARD CHATHAM WOLFE
37705   FL   Pilot   British   219 and 141 Squadrons

Joined the RAF on a short service commission in January 1936. Wolfe was posted to 9 FTS, Thornaby on April 4 and joined 64 Squadron at Martlesham Heath on October 11.

Wolfe was with 219 Squadron at Catterick in early July 1940. He was posted to command 141 Squadron at Turnhouse in September. In May 1941 he shot down an enemy bomber at night. Wolfe was awarded the DFC (30.5.41) and posted away from the squadron in July.

He took command of 456 Squadron at Valley in March 1942. On July 30 he shot down a He 111, which crashed on the beach at Pwllheli. Wolfe was released from the RAF in 1946, as a Wing Commander. The Norwegians awarded him the King Haakon Vll Freedom Cross (9.9.46).

APO 23.3.36   PO 27.1.37   FO 27.10.38   FL 3.9.40
SL 1.12.41   WC 1.7.44

RALPH WOLTON
45487   Sgt   Pilot   British   152 Squadron

Born on July 26 1914, Wolton joined the RAF in July 1932 for ground duties. After recruit training he went to the Torpedo Development Flight at Gosport. After nine months Wolton was sent to No 1 Electrical and Wireless School at Cranwell for a wireless operator's course, which lasted fourteen months.

After passing out Wolton was posted to 58 Squadron at Worthy Down and became a Wop/part-time air gunner. In September 1935 he went to 142 Squadron, which was sent out to Mersa Matruh at the time of the Abyssinian crisis. The squadron returned to the UK but Wolton was posted to 45 Squadron at Helwan.

He volunteered for pilot training and returned to the UK in September 1938 and began his ab initio course at 9 E&RFTS, Ansty. He moved on to 10 FTS, Tern Hill, completing his training in October 1939 and joining 152 Squadron, then forming at Acklington. The squadron moved south to Warmwell on July 7 1940. On July 25 Wolton shot down a Do 17, which crashed and burned out at East Fleet Farm, Fleet, Dorset.

On August 15 Wolton was shot down into the sea off Chesil Beach. He got out of the Spitfire, uninjured, and swam to a buoy, from where he was picked up. He claimed a Ju 88 destroyed on September 26. Wolton was thrown out of his aircraft when a wing fell off at 15000 feet on October 11. His parachute was damaged and he was unable to open it until he was down to 1000 feet.

On December 16 1940 Wolton went to CFS, Upavon for an instructor's course. He was afterwards posted to 16 FTS, Newton, instructing Polish pupils. Commissioned in March 1941, Wolton moved to 51 OTU, Cranfield on April 8 1942 to instruct on night fighters. He joined 153 Squadron at Ballyhalbert on January 20 1943 and when it was disbanded on March 13 he went to 96 Squadron at Honiley.

From May 18 to August 6 1943 Wolton was attached to 417 Squadron, USAAF to convert its crews to Beaufighters. He then went to 63 OTU at Honiley until October 27, when he rejoined 96 Squadron, then at Drem. The squadron was disbanded on December 17 1944 at Odiham and Wolton went to 239 Squadron at West Raynham, flying Mosquitos on radio countermeasures.

Wolton was released from the RAF on July 24 1946 but he rejoined on March 3 1947 for a further eighteen months, finally retiring on September 4 1948, as a Flight Lieutenant. His portrait was done by Cuthbert Orde.

PO 12.3.41   FO 30.9.41   FL 1.1.43

KENNETH RUSSELL WOOD

759352   Sgt   Air Gunner   British   23 Squadron

Wood, of Leeds, Yorkshire, joined 23 Squadron at Ford on October 1 1940.

He was killed on July 10 1941, as a Sergeant with 7 Squadron, operating in Stirlings from Oakington. Wood was 22 years old. He is remembered on the Runnymede Memorial, Panel 55.

STANLEY VICTOR WOOD

649800   Sgt   Wop/AG   British   248 Squadron

Joined 248 Squadron in September 1940.

Wood was a member of the crew of Blenheim P 6952, detailed to carry out a reconnaissance off the south-west coast of Norway on October 20 1940. After engaging and shooting down a Do 215 the Blenheim was attacked by three Bf 109s. One engine was put out of action and the cockpit filled with smoke. The captain, Pilot Officer GM Baird (qv), got down to low level, flying blind and skimming the sea, feeling for the surface at a speed of 150 mph.

The aircraft struck and the silence was complete as the fuselage filled with water. Baird freed himself and saved Sergeant DL Burton but was unable to rescue his observer, Sergeant R Copcutt. Wood, although having a bullet through his foot, got out of the sinking aircraft and launched the dinghy. After capture he was taken away to hospital and did not see the other members of the crew again.

Wood was released from the RAF after the war as a Warrant Officer.

JOSEPH ERIC WOODGATE

155878   Sgt   Air Gunner   British   141 Squadron

Woodgate, of Burton-on-Trent, was with 141 Squadron at Turnhouse in early July 1940.

Commissioned in July 1943, Woodgate was killed on August 24 1943, as a Pilot Officer with 101 Squadron, operating in Lancasters from Ludford Magna. He was 28 years old and is remembered on the Runnymede Memorial, Panel 134.

PO 6.7.43

DAVID NOEL WOODGER

42666   PO   Pilot   British   235 Squadron

Woodger, of Old Coulsdon, Surrey, joined the RAF on a short service commission in July 1939. He was posted to 235 Squadron in March 1940.

He was captain of Blenheim T 1804, which was attacked and shot down by Hurricanes of No 1 (RCAF) Squadron over Thorney Island on August 24 1940. The aircraft crashed into Bracklesham Bay. Sergeant DL Wright was killed and Woodger was reported 'Missing'.

He was 20 years old and is remembered on the Runnymede Memorial, Panel 10.

APO 2.9.39   PO 2.3.40

NORMAN NAYLOR WOODLAND

902981   Sgt   Observer   British   236 Squadron

Joined the RAF on September 12 1939, aged 27. Woodland was sent home until November 24, being then called to Uxbridge and posted to No 1 ITW, Cambridge.

In January 1940 he went to 6 ANS, Staverton, as an LAC. He moved to 3 BGS, Aldergrove in May and at the end of the course in July he was promoted to Sergeant and posted to No 1 (Coastal) OTU, Silloth.

Woodland joined 236 Squadron at St Eval on August 8. He generally flew with Pilot Officer AFY Lees. On January 29 1941 he was in a Blenheim captained by Flying Officer DVC Cotes-Preedy, which crashed shortly after taking off.

In July 1941 Woodland was posted to 413 (RCAF) Squadron, at its formation with Catalinas. He went to 210 Squadron at Sollum Voe, Shetlands in March 1942 and to 190 Squadron, also at Sollum Voe, in March 1943. On May 27 Woodland made his longest flight, an ice reconnaissance north of Spitzbergen, with a flying time of 23 hrs, 30 mins.

In May 1944 Woodland arrived at 45 Air School, Oudtshoorn, South Africa, as a navigation instructor. He returned to the UK and was released from the RAF in 1945, as a Warrant Officer.

CHARLES ANTHONY WOODS-SCAWEN

40778   PO   Pilot   British   43 Squadron

Woods-Scawen, of South Farnborough, Hampshire, was born in Karachi, India in 1918. He was educated at the Salesian College, Farnborough and joined the RAF on a short service commission in March 1938. He was posted to 6 FTS, Netheravon on May 21 and joined 43 Squadron at Tangmere on December 17.

Over Dunkirk on May 31 1940 Woods-Scawen's Hurricane, L1592, was damaged in combat with Bf 109s. He returned to Tangmere with a rapidly-overheating engine and made a belly-landing. On June 1 he damaged a Bf 109. Woods-Scawen baled out over France on the 7th, after a combat near Dieppe. He landed in German-held territory and had walked twenty miles before falling in with a retreating British column. Evacuated from Cherbourg, Woods-Scawen arrived back at Tangmere eight days after he took off.

On August 8 he claimed a Bf 110 destroyed ten miles south of the Isle of Wight but his own aircraft was damaged and he landed back at Tangmere with slight shell splinter wounds in the legs. On the 13th Woods-Scawen claimed two He 111s destroyed over Petworth but was himself shot down by return fire and baled out, unhurt. His Hurricane, R 4102, crashed and burned out on Northend Farm, Milland, near Midhurst. Woods-Scawen claimed another He 111 destroyed on the 15th and two Ju 87s on the 16th. On this day Woods-Scawen was shot down by a Bf 109 off the Sussex coast and baled out, slightly injured. His Hurricane, N 2621, crashed near Parkhurst, Isle of Wight.

Woods-Scawen claimed a Bf 109 destroyed on August 30. He was shot down in combat with Bf 109s on September 2 and baled out too low and was killed. His Hurricane, V 7420, crashed at Fryland, near Ivychurch.

He is buried in Folkestone New Cemetery, Kent. Woods-Scawen was awarded the DFC (6.9.40). He was the younger brother of PP Woods-Scawen.

APO 7.5.38   PO 7.4.39

PATRICK PHILIP WOODS-SCAWEN

40452   FO   Pilot   British   85 Squadron

Woods-Scawen, of South Farnborough, Hampshire was born in Karachi, India in 1916. He was educated at the Salesian College,

PP WOODS-SCAWEN (continued)

Farnborough and joined the RAF on a short service commission in October 1937. Woods-Scawen was posted to 11 FTS, Wittering on January 9 1938 and joined 85 Squadron at Debden on August 20.

He went to France with the squadron at the outbreak of war. On May 10 1940 Woods-Scawen shared in destroying a Ju 86 and on the 19th claimed three Bf 109s destroyed as well as another unidentified enemy aircraft. The squadron withdrew to Debden on May 22. Woods-Scawen was awarded the DFC (25.6.40). The citation credited him with six enemy aircraft destroyed in France and stated that he had baled out, slightly wounded, after destroying two enemy aircraft in a large formation.

On July 29 Woods-Scawen damaged a Do 17 forty miles east of Felixstowe and had his own aircraft damaged by return fire. He claimed a Bf 109 probably destroyed and two Do 17s shared on August 26, a Bf 109 destroyed on the 28th, a Bf 110 on the 30th and three Bf 109s on the 31st. Woods-Scawen was shot down in combat with Bf 109s in the Kenley area on September 1. He baled out but was killed when his parachute failed, his body not being found until the 6th, in the grounds of The Ivies, Kenley Lane.

Woods-Scawen was buried in Caterham and Warlingham Burial Ground, Surrey. Elder brother of CA Woods-Scawen.

APO 9.1.38   PO 25.10.38   FO 25.5.40

HERBERT JOHN WOODWARD

70833   FO   Pilot   British   64 and 23 Squadrons

Woodward, of Heckmondwike, was born in Harefield, Middlesex in 1916, the son of a soldier killed at Passchendaele on October 30 1917. He joined the RAF on a short service commission in September 1937.

He was posted to 8 FTS, Montrose on December 11 and joined 64 Squadron at Church Fenton on July 9 1938. Over Dunkirk on May 31 1940 Woodward destroyed a Do 17.

In a combat over Dover on July 19 he collided with a Bf 109 and returned to Kenley with a damaged wingtip. On August 5, 8 and 12 Woodward claimed Bf 109s destroyed and on the 13th a Do 215. He was awarded the DFC (1.10.40) and posted away to 23 Squadron at Ford later in the month.

On October 30 Woodward was captain of Blenheim L 6721, which crashed at Orchard Way Road, South Berstead, after having R/T failure in deteriorating weather conditions after a routine night patrol. All three men on board were killed.

Woodward is buried in Heckmondwike Cemetery, Yorkshire.

APO 24.11.37   PO 23.9.38   FO 23.3.40

ROBERT SINCKLER WOODWARD

74698   FO   Pilot   British   600 Squadron

Woodward, of Goring-on-Thames, Oxfordshire, learned to fly with the Oxford University Air Squadron when he was at Corpus Christi College. He was called to full-time service in October 1939 and joined 600 Squadron at Catterick on September 25 1940.

In late April 1941 Woodward, with Sergeant AJ Lipscombe as his operator, destroyed a Ju 88 near Shepton Mallett. On the night of May 9/10 their Beaufighter was attacked by another night fighter, probably from 604 Squadron, when far out at sea. Woodward flew the burning aircraft back to Britain before he and Lipscombe baled out. On July 9 Woodward shot down a He 111 near Abergavenny, again assisted by Lipscombe. He was awarded the DFC (29.8.41).

In March 1942 Woodward was given command of 263 Squadron, operating in Whirlwinds from Fairwood Common. He led the squadron until reported 'Missing' on December 7 1942. Woodward was 23. He is remembered on the Runnymede Memorial, Panel 65.

PO 3.10.39   FO 3.10.40   FL 3.10.41

ARTHUR WILLIAM WOOLLEY

67602   Sgt   Pilot   British   601 Squadron

From the outbreak of war Woolley was a Sergeant Pilot with 604 Squadron. He was posted to 601 Squadron at Tangmere on July 5 1940.

On the 11th his aircraft was set alight by a bullet in the gravity tank during an attack on He 111s over the Channel off Selsey. He baled out, wounded and burned. His Hurricane, P 3681, crashed at Cranmore, Isle of Wight. On August 26 Woolley is believed to have crashed near Captain's Wood, Great Totham during a routine patrol. The Hurricane, V 7238, burned out.

After a combat with Bf 109s off Gravesend on August 31 Woolley baled out, burned, and was admitted to hospital. The Hurricane, N 2602, crashed and burned out.

Commissioned in May 1941, Woolley later transferred to the Administrative Branch. He was released from the RAF in 1948, as a Flight Lieutenant. He joined the RAFVR in 1951.

PO 27.5.41   FO 27.5.42   FL 27.5.43   FO (RAFVR) 8.2.51

ERNEST WAITE WOOTTEN

42667   PO   Pilot   British   234 Squadron

Born in Aberbeeg on November 5 1918, Wootten joined the RAF in 1938 and began a short service commission in July 1939. He did his ab initio course at 12 E&RFTS, Prestwick, his intermediate at 9 FTS, Hullavington and advanced at 15 FTS, Lossiemouth.

In late February 1940 Wootten was posted to 9 AOS, Penrhos as a staff pilot. He joined 4 Continental Ferry Pilots Pool at Cardiff and Kemble in May, ferrying aircraft from MUs to squadrons in France and at home

Wootten was posted to 234 Squadron at Warmwell in late August. On October 9 he shared in destroying a Ju 88, had another confirmed on November 25, a Do 17 on December 19, a shared Bf 110 on March 11 1941, two Bf 109s on March 19 and another on July 14. He was appointed a Flight Commander in August and awarded the DFC (29.8.41).

On November 10 1941 Wootten was posted to command 2 Delivery Flight at Colerne, moving on January 14 1942 to HQ 10 Group as Squadron Leader Tactics. He returned to operations on June 8, taking command of 118 Squadron at Ibsley, part of the Middle Wallop Wing. Wootten damaged a FW 190 on January 23 1943. At the end of April Wootten was appointed Wing Commander Flying at Coltishall, destroyed a FW 190 and damaged another on May 3 and on June 1 moved to Fairwood Common to lead the Wing there. He was awarded a Bar to the DFC (4.6.43).

In January 1944 Wootten moved to HQ Mediterranean Allied Air Forces in Algiers, as Wing Commander Tactics, later moving to MAAF Advanced HQ at La Marsa, Tunisia. In March the HQ moved to Caserta, near Naples. Wootten went to 244 Wing Desert Air Force in June 1944 as supernumerary to the Wing Leader and was given his own Wing, 322, in July at Calenzana, Corsica for the invasion of southern France. On August 23 the Wing moved to Frejus in France and went northward until it met the cross-Channel invasion forces in October 1944. The Wing was then disbanded and Wootten was given 324 Wing Desert Air Force at Florence. He returned to the UK in December 1944 and on January 4 1945 was posted to the Pentagon in Washington as RAF Liaison Officer to the USAF.

In August 1945 Wootten was appointed Wing Commander Flying RAF Dorval, Montreal. He returned to the UK in January 1946. He was awarded the AFC (2.1.50), made a CBE (1.1.71) and retired from the RAF on November 5 1973, as an Air Commodore. He was also awarded the Venezuelan Air Force Cross in 1963.

Wootten joined Hawker Siddely Dynamics Ltd in their Space Division, which was later nationalised as British Aerospace. After retiring in 1984 he set up as an Aerospace Consultant.

APO 2.9.39   PO 2.3.40   FO 2.3.41   FL 2.3.42
SL 1.8.47   WC 1.1.57   GC 1.1.64   AC 1.7.68

DOUGLAS KENNETH ALFRED WORDSWORTH

41517   FO   Pilot   British   235 Squadron

Joined the RAF on a short service commission in October 1938. Wordsworth joined 235 Squadron on August 1 1940.

He was killed on October 30 1941, as a Flight Lieutenant with 272 Squadron. He is remembered on the Alamein Memorial, Column 240. Wordsworth was awarded the DFC (28.7.42), with effect from October 22 1941.

APO 14.12.38   PO 3.9.39   FO 3.9.40   FL 3.9.41

JOHN WORRALL

26151   **SL**   **Pilot**   **British**   **32 Squadron**

Born on April 9 1911, Worrall was educated at Cranleigh and entered RAF College, Cranwell in January 1930 as a flight cadet. On graduation in December 1931 he joined No 1 Squadron at Tangmere. Worrall was posted to 208 (Army Co-operation) Squadron at Heliopolis on February 28 1933, remaining with it until October 7 1936, when he went to the School of Oriental Studies in Peking for language studies.

Worrall returned to the UK in 1939 and in May 1940 he was given command of 32 Squadron at Biggin Hill. On July 20 the engine and gravity tank of his Hurricane, N 2532, were badly damaged in a combat off Dover. He made a forced-landing near Hawkinge and the aircraft burned out. He was awarded the DFC (6.8.40). On August 15 Worrall shared in the destruction of a Do 17. Later in the month he was posted to the Control Room at Biggin Hill as Senior Controller.

For the remainder of the war Worrall was on staff duties at Fighter and Transport Commands. He received a Mention in Despatches in 1944. He went to RAF Staff College in 1945. Worrall was made a CB in 1963 and retired from the RAF on August 5 1963, as an Air Vice-Marshal. He later went to live in Spain and died on January 14 1988.

PO 19.12.31   FO 19.6.33   FL 19.6.36   SL 1.2.39
WC 1.3.41   GC 1.7.44   GC 1.1.49   AC 1.1.55
AVM 1.1.58

PYERS ARTHUR WORRALL

42291   **PO**   **Pilot**   **British**   **85 and 249 Squadrons**

Joined the RAF on a short service commission in April 1939. Worrall was posted to 85 Squadron at Martlesham Heath on July 21 1940.

He shared in the destruction of a Do 17 on August 26 and claimed a Bf 110 destroyed on the 31st. In this combat over Tunbridge Wells he was himself shot down, baled out, slightly wounded in the thigh, and was admitted to Croydon Hospital. His Hurricane, V 6581, crashed on Court Lane Farm, Newenden.

On September 13 Worrall was posted to 249 Squadron at North Weald. He claimed a Bf 109 destroyed on October 25 and another probably destroyed on November 8.

Worrall arrived in Malta in a Sunderland from the Middle East on January 20 1941 and joined 261 Squadron at Hal Far. He returned to the Middle East in May and in 1942 was in Burma with 136 Squadron, as a Flight Commander. Worrall was killed in a flying accident on June 8 1942, aged 21. He is buried in Bhowanipore Cemetery, Calcutta.

APO 24.6.39   PO 10.12.39   FO 10.12.40   FL 10.12.41

THOMAS VICTOR WORRALL

Sub-Lieutenant (FAA)   **Pilot**   **British**   **111 Squadron**

Worrall, of Runcorn, Cheshire, joined 111 Squadron at Debden on September 22 1940.

He returned to the FAA in early 1941 and was posted to 809 Squadron on February 4. Worrall was killed on February 21 1941, serving with HMS 'Daedalus'. He was 19 and is buried in Runcorn Cemetery.

Midshipman 1.7.39   Actg Sub-Lt 14.3.40

KENNETH WILSON WORSDELL

33497   **PO**   **Pilot**   **British**   **219 Squadron**

Worsdell, of Bracknell, Berkshire, was educated at Wellington College and entered RAF College, Cranwell in April 1938 as a flight cadet. He was a Prize Cadet in 1938 and graduated in September 1939.

In early July 1940 Worsdell was with 219 Squadron at Catterick. He was captain of Beaufighter R 2065, which hit trees trying to locate Redhill in bad visibility on October 30 1940. The aircraft crashed and exploded 150 yards south of Balcome Place, killing Worsdell and Sergeant EC Gardiner.

Worsdell was 20. He is buried in Nutfield Cemetery, Surrey.

PO 21.10.39

ALEC SILLAVAN WORTHINGTON

72080   **FO**   **Pilot**   **British**   **219 Squadron**

Commissioned in the RAFVR in December 1937. Worthington was called to full-time service in September 1939 and was with 219 Squadron at Catterick in early July 1940.

He was released from the RAF in 1946, as a Squadron Leader.

PO (RAFVR) 28.12.37   PO 25.9.39   FO 25.1.40
FL 20.4.41   SL 1.9.42

HAROLD JOHN WOTTON

745641   **Sgt**   **Pilot**   **British**   **234 Squadron**

Wotton, of Reading, Berkshire, was born in April 1920 and educated at Whitgift Middle School, Croydon.

He joined 234 Squadron at Middle Wallop on August 19 1940. Wotton was killed in an air raid on January 25 1941. He is buried in St Eval churchyard, Cornwall.

ALEXANDER JAMES WRIGHT

Lieutenant (RM)   **Pilot**   **British**   **804 Squadron**

Wright was commissioned in the Royal Marines in January 1936. In early July 1940 he was with 804 Squadron at Hatston, flying Sea Gladiators on dockyard defence.

On November 24 Wright went to 803 Squadron for HMS 'Formidable', operating in the Mediterranean covering Malta convoys and searching for the Italian fleet. In late May 1941 Wright was posted to 805 Squadron at Dekheila, Egypt to fly Martlets in the Naval Fighter Wing.

After instructing at the Fighter School at Yeovilton Wright took command of 809 Squadron on August 7 1943, which embarked on HMS 'Unicorn' for operations at Salerno on September 9 to 12.

Wright later served as Lieutenant Commander Flying on HMS 'Patroller' and then on HMS 'Arbiter', which was used as a back-up carrier in operations against Japan in July and August 1945. He returned to duty with the Royal Marines on August 15 1949 and retired on July 26 1958, as a Major. He received a Mention in Despatches (2.12.41) for service in 805 Squadron and another (19.5.44) for Salerno.

2nd Lieutenant 1.1.36   Lt 1.2.38   Capt 12.8.43
Major 30.6.51

ALLAN RICHARD WRIGHT

33499   **FO**   **Pilot**   **British**   **92 Squadron**

Born in Teignmouth, Devon on February 12 1920, Wright entered RAF College, Cranwell in April 1938 as a flight cadet. After completing air gunnery and bombing training at West Freugh he was commissioned on October 23 1939 and posted to 92 Squadron at Tangmere.

Over the French coast on May 23 1940 Wright destroyed a Bf 110 and over Dunkirk on June 2 a Bf 109. On August 14 he claimed a Bf 109 destroyed and another probably destroyed, on the 29th he shot down a He 111 at night over Bristol, on September 11 he claimed a He 111, on the 26th a Ju 88 and on the 27th another Ju 88 and a shared He 111.

On September 27 Wright was appointed 'B' Flight Commander. Three days later his Spitfire, X 4069, was damaged by a Bf 109 off Brighton. He made a forced-landing at Shoreham, slightly wounded by cannon shell splinters in the thigh and was admitted to Southlands Hospital. Wright was awarded the DFC (22.10.40).

AR WRIGHT (continued)

On May 16 1941 he shared a Bf 109, on June 17 and 25 probably destroyed Bf 109s and on the 26th had another confirmed. Wright was awarded a Bar to the DFC (15.7.41) and posted away to 59 OTU, Crosby-on-Eden, to be OC 'B' Flight. In September he went to HQ 9 Group, on air tactics, moving in October to HQ Fighter Command.

In February 1942 Wright was appointed Chief Instructor at the Pilot Gunnery Instructor School, then forming at CGS, Sutton Bridge. He was sent on a training tour of USAAF squadrons across the USA in October 1942. Wright went on a night fighter refresher course at 54 OTU, Charter Hall in December. He was posted to 29 Squadron at West Malling in March 1943, as 'A' Flight Commander, and destroyed a Ju 88 on April 3.

After a short spell as Fighter Tactics Officer at HQ 92 Group Wright was appointed OC Demonstration Squadron at AFDU, Wittering in November 1943 and took command of the unit in December. Wright went to Army Staff College, Camberley in August 1944, was awarded the AFC (1.9.44) and in December appointed Wing Commander Single Engine Training at HQ 12 Group, Watnall. In February 1945 he was posted to Egypt, as OC ABGS at El Ballah.

Wright retired from the RAF on February 12 1967, as a Wing Commander, retaining the rank of Group Captain.

PO 23.10.39   FO 23.10.40   FL 23.10.41   SL 10.3.44
SL 1.8.47   WC 1.7.52

B WRIGHT

No unknown   Sgt   Pilot   British   616 and 66 Squadrons

Joined 616 Squadron at Kenley on September 2 1940 and moved to 66 Squadron, also at Kenley, on the 17th.

No further service details traced.

DANIEL LESLIE WRIGHT

552618   Sgt   Wop/AG   British   235 Squadron

Wright, of Lichfield, Staffordshire, joined the RAF as a boy entrant at 16. He trained as a wireless operator, later volunteered for aircrew duties and qualified after taking a gunnery course. He was with 235 Squadron in early July 1940.

On August 24 Wright was in Blenheim T 1804, which was shot down in error by Hurricanes of No 1 (RCAF) Squadron. The aircraft crashed into Bracklesham Bay. Wright was killed and Pilot Officer DN Woodger reported 'Missing'.

Wright was 18 years old. He is buried in St Ann's churchyard, Chasetown, Burtonwood, Staffordshire.

ERIC WILLIAM WRIGHT

64870   Sgt   Pilot   British   605 Squadron

Born in Cherry Hinton, Cambridgeshire on September 21 1919, Wright joined 605 Squadron at Drem on July 8 1940. He shared in destroying a Bf 110 on September 9, shared a Do 17 on the 12th, claimed a Do 17 on the 15th, a probable Bf 110 on the 27th, probably destroyed one on November 1 and claimed another on the 15th. Wright was awarded the DFM (26.11.40).

Commissioned in December 1940, Wright went to the Far East with the squadron in December 1941. In January 1942 he was posted to 232 Squadron at Seletar, Singapore, as a Flight Commander. Wright took command of the squadron when the CO was killed on February 7 1942. Soon afterwards Wright was given the job of reforming 605 Squadron from the remnants of 258 and 488 Squadrons. He was captured by the Japanese in early March.

After release from captivity Wright returned to the UK. He was awarded the DFC (1.10.46) 'in recognition of gallant and distinguished services rendered during operations against the Japanese in Malaya and the Netherlands East Indies, terminating in March 1942'.

Wright walked in Churchill's funeral procession, was made a CBE (1.1.64) and retired from the RAF on July 21 1973, as an Air Commodore.

PO 18.12.40   FO 23.10.41   FL 6.5.42   FL 1.9.45
SL 1.1.49   WC 1.7.55   GC 1.7.60   AC 1.7.66

JOHN WRIGHT

522272   Sgt   Pilot   British   79 Squadron

Joined 79 Squadron at Biggin Hill on July 9 1940.

Wright's Hurricane, P 3676, was severely damaged in an action over Biggin Hill on September 4 and he was wounded. After crashing at Surbiton he was admitted to hospital, where he died the next day. Wright was 24 years old and is buried in New Kilpatrick Cemetery.

ROBERT RONALD WRIGHT

60514   Sgt   Pilot   British   248 Squadron

Joined 248 Squadron on September 5 1940.

Commissioned in January 1941, Wright was awarded the DFC (14.4.44), as a Flight Lieutenant with 235 Squadron. He was released from the RAF in 1946, as a Flight Lieutenant.

PO 8.1.41   FO 8.1.42   FL 8.1.43

WILLIAM WRIGHT

77373   PO   Air Gunner   British   604 Squadron

Wright, of Middlesex, was with 604 Squadron at Northolt in early July 1940.

He was killed on August 26 1941, as a Flying Officer with 40 Squadron, operating in Wellingtons from Alconbury. Wright was 31. He is buried in Hanazame Communal Cemetery, Belgium.

PO 16.3.40

ZBIGNIEW WROBLEWSKI

P 1285   PO   Pilot   Polish   302 Squadron

Born on December 25 1914. Wroblewski arrived in England on June 21 1940 and joined 302 Squadron at Leconfield on August 23.

He destroyed Bf 109s on May 8 and 21 1941 and June 25. He was awarded the KW (10.9.41) and a Bar (15.11.42). On February 25 1943 Wroblewski was posted to 317 Squadron at Kirton-in-Lindsey, as a Flight Commander. He destroyed a FW 190 on July 26.

On September 5 he went to the PAF Staff College. Wroblewski was awarded a second Bar to the KW (20.10.43) and the VM (5th Class) (20.12.43). After a spell at HQ PAF he was posted to 16 FTS, Newton on September 5 1944 for a refresher course and then became a staff pilot there.

On December 20 Wroblewski joined 602 Squadron at Matlask and was posted away on June 9 1945 to Coltishall as Station Adjutant. He was released from the PAF in December 1945, as a Flight Lieutenant.

Wroblewski was awarded a third Bar to the KW (31.10.47). He became a captain for a British airline.

PO 1.3.41   FO 1.3.42   FL 1.3.43

KAZIMIERZ WUNSCHE

P 2096   F/Sgt   Pilot   Polish   303 Squadron

Born on June 5 1919, Wunsche was in the PAF before the war. He joined 303 Squadron at Northolt at its formation on August 12 1940.

Wunsche claimed Bf 109s destroyed on August 31, September 5 and 6. He was shot down on September 9 by Bf 109s in combat over Beachy Head, baled out with slight burns and after landing near Devil's Dyke was admitted to Hove Hospital. His Hurricane, P 3700, crashed and burned out at Saddlescombe Farm, Poynings, Newtimber. Wunsche was awarded the VM (5th Class) (23.12.40), destroyed a Bf 109 on June 23 1941 and received the KW (10.9.41). He shared in the destruction of a Ju 88 on July 3 1942, was awarded a Bar to the KW (20.8.42) and was posted away to 58 OTU, Grangemouth on September 6 as an instructor. Wunsche was commissioned in December 1942.

He rejoined 303 Squadron, then at Debden, on March 17 1943. He left the squadron on October 1 for duties at the PAF Depot, Blackpool and was awarded a second Bar to the KW (20.12.43). On April 18 1944 Wunsche joined 315 Squadron at Coolham. He became a Flight Commander on December 6, was awarded a third Bar to the KW (30.12.44) and remained with the squadron until August 24 1945, being then posted to RAF Coltishall on staff duties.

He was released from the PAF in December 1946 and was repatriated to Poland. He died there in 1980.

PO 31.12.42   FO 1.7.43   FL 15.4.45

JOHN PILE WYATT

915837   LAC   Observer   British   25 Squadron

Joined 25 Squadron at Martlesham Heath in late July 1940.

Wyatt was killed on September 15, possibly in a collision between a Blenheim and a Beaufighter near Biggin Hill. He was 32 and is buried in Christ Church churchyard, Melplash, Netherbury, Dorset.

PETER WYATT-SMITH

41768   FO   Pilot   British   263 Squadron

Wyatt-Smith, of Lanarkshire, joined the RAF on a short service commission in January 1939. He flew with 263 Squadron in Norway in May 1940.

He arrived in Malta from the Middle East in a Sunderland on January 20 1941 and joined 261 Squadron. Wyatt-Smith returned to the Middle East in May 1941 and served later with 73 Squadron.

He was killed on January 5 1945, as a Flight Lieutenant with 165 Squadron, aged 26. Wyatt-Smith is buried in Haycombe Cemetery, Englishcombe, Somerset.

APO 4.3.39   PO 23.9.39   FO 23.9.40   FL 23.9.41

BRONISLAW WYDROWSKI

P 0316   PO   Pilot   Polish   615 and 607 Squadrons

Wydrowski was born on September 1 1916. In September 1939 he was with the 3rd Air Regiment, PAF.

He arrived in England on June 22 1940. Wydrowski joined 615 Squadron at Prestwick in September and moved to 607 Squadron at Turnhouse on October 9. After a week with 229 Squadron in late November Wydrowski returned to 615, then at Northolt.

On May 16 1941 he joined 302 Squadron at Jurby. Wydrowski damaged a Bf 109 on April 17 1942 and was posted away to 2 ADF on July 27. He left the PAF on October 19 1942 and went into the Polish Army.

Wydrowski was repatriated to Poland in 1946.

PO 1.3.41

RICHARD EDWARD NEY WYNN

81375   PO   Pilot   British   249 Squadron

Wynn was the son of Group Captain AHWE Wynn OBE. He was at Wellington College from 1930 to 1934.

He joined 249 Squadron at Church Fenton on August 4 1940. Wynn made a forced-landing near Whitchurch on the 31st, in Hurricane L 2067, after engine failure during a routine patrol, unhurt.

After a combat with enemy fighters over Rochester on September 2 Wynn crash-landed near Chartham, in Hurricane V 7352, wounded.

He was killed on April 7 1941, crashing at Langford Bridge Farm, Ongar, Essex. Wynn is buried in St Andrew's churchyard, North Weald Bassett.

PO 6.7.40

DEREK SYDNEY YAPP

41975   PO   Pilot   British   245 and 253 Squadrons

Joined the RAF on a short service commission in February 1939. Yapp started his ab initio course at 9 E&RFTS, Ansty on the 6th, moved to 6 FTS, Little Rissington on April 30 and with flying training completed joined the newly-reformed 245 Squadron at Leconfield on November 6.

Yapp went to Belgium on May 16 1940, when 'A' Flight was attached to 615 Squadron, returning to Drem on the 21st. He was posted away to 253 Squadron at Kenley on October 1 1940. Yapp remained with the squadron until May 10 1941, being then posted to 124 Squadron, then reforming at Castletown.

Tour-expired, he went to 54 OTU at Church Fenton on October 27 1941 but his stay was short and he rejoined 253 Squadron, then at Hibaldstow, on December 23, as a Flight Commander. Yapp damaged a He 111 at night on May 1 1942 whilst co-operating with a 1459 Flight Turbinlite Havoc. He took command of 253 later in the month and led it with distinction during the Dieppe operation on August 19, for which he was awarded the DFC (29.9.42).

Yapp moved to 59 OTU, Milfield on September 15 1942 as a supernumerary. He was appointed CFI at 57 OTU, Eshott on November 7. In preparation for a return to operations he went on a night-fighter course at 54 OTU, Charter Hall on April 20 1943 and

DS YAPP (continued)

then joined 68 Squadron at Coltishall on July 15, remaining with it until March 1 1944 when he was posted to HQ 12 Group, Watnall.

From April 24 until July 4 1944 Yapp served with 4 ADF, York. He then went to SHQ Church Fenton until November 6 1944 when he was released from the RAF, as a Squadron Leader, to go into civil aviation.

APO 15.4.39   PO 6.11.39   FO 6.11.40   FL 6.11.41

GORDON YATES

631756   Sgt   Air Gunner   British   248 Squadron

Joined 248 Squadron in late July 1940.

On August 3 Yates was a member of the crew of a Blenheim, which made a forced-landing in a field at Tranent, cause unknown.

No further service details traced but it is known that Yates was released from the RAF after the war as a Warrant Officer.

WILLIAM YATES

1002549   AC2   Radar Operator   British   604 Squadron

Yates, of Newburn, volunteered for the RAF in December 1939 and was called up in 1940.

He volunteered for aircrew duties and was sent to Yatesbury for a short radar course, after which he joined 604 Squadron on August 2 1940.

After being on operations throughout the Battle of Britain and after Yates was promoted to Sergeant in early 1941. He later went home on leave and when he woke there the first morning he was paralysed, with his arms locked behind his head. He was examined by four doctors and then sent back to Middle Wallop, from where, after further stringent tests, he was invalided out of the RAF with psycho-neurosis.

Yates was told that he should never have been in, taking into account the broken back, seven broken ribs, broken thigh and broken ankle that he had sustained in a serious accident in 1934.

RONALD LEWIS YORK

758009   Sgt   Pilot   British   610 Squadron

York, of Weston Favell, joined 610 Squadron at Acklington on September 23 1940.

In late 1940 York was with 74 Squadron at Biggin Hill. He was killed on March 28 1942, as a Flight Sergeant, aged 22. The unit he was serving with is not known.

York is buried in the churchyard of St Peter and St Paul, Abington, Northampton.

CECIL REGINALD YOUNG

42372   PO   Pilot   British   615, 607 and 46 Squadrons

Joined the RAF on a short service commission in May 1939. Young was with 615 Squadron at Kenley in early July 1940. He claimed a He 111 destroyed on August 16 and a Do 17 on the 18th.

Young moved to 607 Squadron at Tangmere on September 13 and then to 46 Squadron at Stapleford on October 16. He was killed on December 5 1940, crashing at Daughton House, near Wrotham, Kent, in Hurricane V 7617. He is buried in Thanet Cemetery, Minster.

PO 22.7.39   PO 1.2.40

JAMES HAROLD YOUNG

42175   PO   Pilot   British   234 Squadron

Joined the RAF on a short service commission in March 1939.

Young served with 234 Squadron in the Battle of Britain. No service details have been traced and his name last appears in the January 1945 Air Force List but no trace of him as a casualty has been found.

APO 13.5.39   PO 10.4.40   FO 10.4.41   FL 10.1.43

JAMES HUGH ROUMIEU YOUNG

42670   PO   Pilot   British   74 Squadron

Joined the RAF on a short service commission in July 1939. Young was posted to 74 Squadron at Hornchurch on April 13 1940.

He was killed on July 28, shot down into the Channel, possibly by Oberleutnant Müncheberg of III/JG 26. The Spitfire, P 9547, crashed near the Goodwin Sands. Young was 22. He is buried in Pihen-les-Guines Cemetery, France.

APO 2.9.39   PO 6.4.40

JOHN REGINALD CASS YOUNG

70766   FO   Pilot   British   249 Squadron

Young was born on July 19 1915. His early attempt at a naval career was frustrated by his having had peritonitis in 1929. He joined the RAFO, Class AA, in 1937. Young did his ab initio course at 11 E&RFTS, Perth and then went to 8 FTS, Montrose on August 21 1937, finishing up at 10 Squadron, Dishforth for 2nd pilot navigation training.

In 1938 Young got his Mechanical Science Tripos at St Catherine's College, Cambridge, having partly financed his studies by being an assistant instructor at the Blackburn Flying School at Brough. Young graduated from CFS on July 13 1939 and was posted as instructor to 41 Squadron and its satellite AuxAF squadrons, 603 and 609.

In October Young was posted to 603 Squadron at Turnhouse. He went to 249 Squadron at Church Fenton at its formation on May 16 1940. He made a forced-landing at Wellburn Hall, Yorkshire on July 20, following engine failure due to misunderstanding of petrol system in Hurricane P 3154, unhurt.

After the Battle of Britain Young had a roving commission, assisting newly-formed squadrons. In November 1940 he went to 308 Squadron at Baginton, in March 1941 to 317 at Acklington and in April to 406, forming at Acklington. Young was later OC 289 Squadron and Station Commander at RAF Kirknewton. He was awarded the AFC (1.1.42) and received a Mention in Despatches (15.7.44).

In April 1945 Young returned to his Reserve status, as a Wing Commander and joined BOAC.

APO (RAFO) 9.8.37   PO (RAFO) 31.5.38   FO 30.11.39
FL 30.5.41   SL 1.6.42

JOHN STEWART YOUNG

39362   FL   Pilot   Canadian   234 Squadron

Joined the RAF on a short service commission on October 12 1936 and began his ab initio course at 6 E&RFTS, Sywell. Young was posted to 10 FTS, Tern Hill on January 16 1937 and joined 10 Squadron at Dishforth on August 7.

Young went to the Ferry Pilots Pool at Filton on September 8 1939 and then to 7 BGS, Stormy Down on October 27, as a Flight Commander. In August 1940 he was posted to 7 OTU, Hawarden and after converting to Spitfires he joined 234 Squadron at Middle Wallop.

On December 29 1940 Young went to 15 FTS, Kidlington as an instructor. He moved to West Kirby for overseas on June 2 1941, going first to Reykjavik, Iceland and then to 34 SFTS, Medicine Hat and later to 36 SFTS, Penfold, Alberta. Young returned to the UK in mid-1943, took a refresher course at Brize Norton and then went to 105 (Transport) OTU at Bramcote on August 17. In November he was posted to HQ 45 (Atlantic Transport) Group at Dorval, Montreal.

Young was sent to Nassau on January 30 1944 to operate on the South Atlantic ferry route. He returned to Dorval on September 23, transferred to the RCAF on July 23 1945 and returned again to the UK on October 1, joining the 'Missing' Research Enquiry Unit in Brussels.

On June 25 1947 Young returned to Canada. He retired from the RCAF in October 1962, as a Squadron Leader.

APO 21.12.36   PO 12.10.37   FO 12.7.39   FL 3.9.40

MICHAEL HUGH YOUNG

42040   PO   Pilot   British   264 Squadron

Joined the RAF on a short service commission in February 1939. After completing his training Young joined the newly-formed 264 Squadron at Sutton Bridge on November 6.

Young claimed a Ju 88 destroyed on May 12 1940 during a patrol off the Dutch coast. Over Dunkirk on May 27 he shared in the destruction of a Bf 109 and a He 111, on the 28th he claimed a Bf 109 destroyed, on the 29th another Bf 109, a Bf 110, two Ju 87s and a shared Bf 110 and on the 31st another Bf 109 destroyed. On this day Young collided with Pilot Officer D Whitley over Dunkirk and he and his gunner baled out when their Defiant broke up.

During 264's last spell of day-fighting Young claimed a He 111 destroyed on August 24. He was awarded the DFC (11.2.41) and destroyed a Bf 110 on a night intruder sortie over France on May 8 1941.

In 1942 Young was with 73 Squadron in the Western Desert, as a Flight Commander. On May 18 he took command of 213 Squadron there. On November 15 he destroyed a Ju 88 and two CR 42s on the ground at Gialo landing ground. Young was posted to 244 Wing on November 24, as Squadron Leader Flying. He left the Wing on February 5 1943.

Young was released from the RAF in 1946, as a Squadron Leader.

APO 29.4.39   PO 6.11.39   FO 6.11.40   FL 6.11.41
SL 1.7.45

RANDOLPH CHARLES YOUNG

49995   Sgt   Pilot   British   23 Squadron

Young was born on September 4 1911. He was with 23 Squadron at Collyweston in early July 1940.

He was promoted to Warrant Officer on September 1 1941 and commissioned in September 1942. Young transferred to the Equipment Branch after the war. He was released in 1950 but rejoined, retiring on September 4 1960, as a Squadron Leader.

PO 17.9.42   FO 17.3.43   FL 17.9.44   FL 17.3.47
SL 1.7.51

ROBERT BETT MIRK YOUNG

NZ 40197   Sgt   Air Gunner   New Zealander   264 Sqdn

Born in Palmerston North on August 1 1918, Young worked as a bank clerk. He volunteered for aircrew duties after the outbreak of war and reported to the Ground Training School at Weraroa on January 15 1940. Young moved on to the Air Observers' School, Ohakea in February for a gunnery course. He sailed for the UK on March 23, in the SS 'Akaroa'.

Young was posted to 264 Squadron at Duxford on June 4 for further training. He completed his training with the squadron, was promoted to

Sergeant on August 7 and received his air gunner's badge on the 15th.

The squadron went south to Hornchurch on the 21st. Young shared in destroying a Ju 88 on the 24th and probably destroyed a Do 17 on the 26th. The remnants of 264 were withdrawn to Kirton-in-Lindsey on the 29th.

In the late evening of October 8 Young and his pilot, Pilot Officer HI Goodall, were patrolling from Halton to Maidenhead at 10000 feet. At 21.20 hrs Goodall reported that he was going to investigate a suspected enemy aircraft. Nothing more was heard and at 21.40 hrs it was reported that a Defiant, N 1627, had crashed at Marlow and the crew were killed. The aircraft had suspected bullet holes, so enemy aircraft may have been engaged. The colour cartridge of the hour had been fired.

Young is buried in Northwood Cemetery, Middlesex.

ARTHUR McLEOD YUILE

C 1328   FO   Pilot   Canadian   1 (RCAF) Squadron

Born in Montreal on June 6 1917, Yuile joined 115 (Auxiliary) Fighter Squadron there on September 15 1939 for training. He soloed on the 23rd. From February to May 1940 Yuile carried out his intermediate and advanced training at Camp Borden and later Trenton.

In early June he joined No 1 (RCAF) Squadron at Dartmouth, Nova Scotia for embarkation. It arrived in the UK on the 20th and underwent operational training, firstly at Middle Wallop and then Croydon, before being declared operational at Northolt on August 17.

Yuile was shot down in an action with Do 17s on September 1 and baled out, unhurt. His Hurricane, R 4171, crashed near West Malling. He claimed a He 111 destroyed on the 11th and on the 15th returned to Northolt with his Hurricane, L 1973, severely damaged after a combat with Bf 109s and He 111s south of London. Yuile was wounded in the shoulder. He damaged a Do 215 on the 27th.

He served with the squadron until mid-February 1941, when he was repatriated to Canada. Yuile joined 118 (RCAF) Squadron at Rockcliffe, Ottawa. On April 27 1942 he took command of 126 (RCAF) Squadron at Dartmouth on east coast defence. Yuile returned to 118 Squadron on June 15 1942, to command. He took it 4000 miles across Canada to Annette Island, Alaska, where it formed part of the force protecting the Canadian railhead port of Prince Rupert.

On February 27 1943 Yuile was posted to HQ Western Air Command, Vancouver, as liaison between the growing number of fighter squadrons and the Operations Rooms, which were predominantly bomber/reconnaissance. In May he moved to HQ 2 Group, Victoria, British Columbia as Fighter Operations Staff Officer. Yuile returned to HQ Western Air Command in November 1943 as Senior Fighter Staff Officer.

In February 1944 he was posted to command No 1 Flight Engineers' School at Arnprior, Ontario. Yuile resigned his commission on September 13 1944 to complete his studies at McGill University. He graduated in May 1945 and emigrated to the USA in April 1963.

PO 15.9.39   FO 12.7.40   FL 12.7.41   SL 15.6.42

ROBERT DUNCAN YULE

33502   PO   Pilot   New Zealander   145 Squadron

The son of a dental surgeon, Yule was born in Invercargill on January 2 1920. In early 1938 he won a national scholarship to RAF College, Cranwell. He sailed in the RMS 'Rangitiki' on March 10 and began as a flight cadet on April 28.

The course was shortened because of the outbreak of war. Yule went into the RAF on September 7 1939, was granted a Permanent Commission on October 23 and joined 145 Squadron at Croydon on November 1. Then equipped with Blenheims, it began to receive Hurricanes in March 1940 and became operational in May, ferrying Hurricanes to France and assisting squadrons there.

Yule destroyed a He 111 over Brussels on May 18, a Ju 88 on the 22nd and a Bf 110 over Dunkirk on June 1. He shared in destroying Do 17s on July 1 and 10, claimed a Ju 88 on the 12th, shared another Do 17 on the 19th and damaged Ju 88s on August 1, 13 and 17.

On October 25 Yule was shot down in a combat with Bf 109s over Tenterden. He made a forced-landing at Barn Farm, Brightling, wounded in the leg, and was admitted to Pembury Hospital. His Hurricane, P 3926, was a write-off. Yule returned to the squadron on February 17 1941. He was posted away to 53 OTU, Heston on March 10, moving to 61 OTU at the end of June.

Yule returned to operations in early November 1941, joining 501 Squadron at Ibsley, as a Flight Commander. He was awarded the DFC (17.4.42). On June 22 1942 he took command of 66 Squadron, also at Ibsley. Leading the squadron on a sweep over Cherbourg on July 15 Yule destroyed a FW 190 and probably another.

On November 17 Yule went to HQ 10 Group on staff duties and was awarded a Bar to the DFC (20.11.42). He was promoted to Wing Commander on August 8 1943 to lead 15 Wing. Yule's final victory was a FW 190, destroyed on January 6 1944. He was posted to 83 Group Control Centre on March 9, responsible for planning and controlling many of the operations of 2nd TAF fighter wings.

Yule was awarded the DSO (16.3.44) and posted to RAF Staff College on January 8 1945, after which he was posted to Air Ministry on staff duties.

On September 11 1953 Yule was rehearsing for the Battle of Britain flypast over London. His aircraft collided with another jet. In his line of emergency descent lay a densely-populated area. Yule steered his aeroplane to Woolwich Arsenal and crash-landed between rows of buildings there. Some workers were injured and buildings damaged. Yule was killed but by his selfless action he undoubtedly saved many lives.

PO 23.10.39   FO 23.10.40   FL 23.10.41   SL 9.11.43
SL 1.8.47   WC 1.7.51

WALERIAN ZAK

P 1390   FO   Pilot   Polish   303 Squadron

Born in Bobrka on April 14 1911, Zak was in the PAF before the war. He arrived in England on June 27 1940 and joined 303 Squadron at Northolt on August 21.

He claimed a Do 17 destroyed on September 15 and a He 111 on the 26th. He was shot down in combat over the Horsham area on the 27th, baled out and was admitted to Leatherhead Hospital, with burns. Zak was awarded the KW and Bar (1.2.41) and posted for a rest to the 303 Operations Room on May 22

1941. He was appointed a Flight Commander in the squadron on July 9 and posted away to 58 OTU, Grangemouth on December 4, as an instructor

Zak rejoined 303, then at Northolt, on April 7 1942, as a Flight Commander, was made CO on May 6 and was posted away on the 15th. He took command of 308 Squadron at Hutton Cranswick on May 27. Zak was awarded the VM (5th Class) (15.11.42), probably destroyed a FW 190 on February 3 1943 and was posted away to HQ 12 Group on the 13th. as Polish liaison officer. On June 29 Zak was appointed Wing Leader of the Polish Wing at Kirton-in-Lindsey, moving on to lead 18 Wing on October 4 1943.

He was posted away to HQ 11 Group on February 15 1944 and awarded two more Bars to the KW (15.2.44). Zak went to HQ ADGB on April 24 and was awarded the DFC (15.5.44). He moved to 61 OTU on January 8 1945 and then to RAF Coltishall on July 18. Zak's final posting was to 5 RU on January 15 1947 as Senior Admin Officer. He was repatriated to Poland later.

FO 1.3.41   FL 1.3.42   SL 1.3.43

JERZY ZALUSKI

781415   Sgt   Pilot   Polish   302 Squadron

Zaluski was born on August 16 1916. After converting to Hurricanes at 6 OTU, Sutton Bridge he joined 302 Squadron at Leconfield on September 23 1940.

He was killed on October 17, when he overturned attempting a forced-landing at Colliers End in Hurricane V 7417. Zaluski is buried in Northwood Cemetery. He was awarded the Bronze Cross of Merit with Swords (31.10.47).

VALDIMIR ZAORAL

81903   PO   Pilot   Czechoslovakian   310 Squadron

Joined 310 Squadron at Duxford in October 1940 and claimed a Bf 109 destroyed on the 25th.

Zaoral was killed in a flying accident on November 19 1941, as a Flying Officer with 310, aged 27. He is buried in Dyce Old Churchyard, Aberdeen.

FO 27.12.40

ANTONIN ZAVORAL

787660   Sgt   Pilot   Czechoslovakian   151 and 1 Sqdns

Joined 151 Squadron at Digby in late September 1940 and moved to No 1 Squadron at Wittering on October 6.

Zavoral was killed on October 31 1941, as a Sergeant with 607 Squadron. He is remembered on the Runnymede Memorial, Panel 55.

PAWEL ZENKER

76714   PO   Pilot   Polish   501 Squadron

Zenker was born on December 25 1914. He joined 501 Squadron at Gravesend on August 7 1940.

He claimed a Ju 87 destroyed on the 12th and a Bf 109 on the 18th. Zenker was reported 'Missing' after an action with Do 17s and Bf 109s four miles north-west of Dover on August 24. When the German formation broke Zenker is believed to have chased an enemy aircraft out to sea, in Hurricane P 3141. He is remembered on the Polish Air Force Memorial at Northolt.

Zenker was awarded the KW and Bar (1.2.41) and a second Bar (31.10.47).

RUDOLF ZIMA

No unknown   **Sgt**   **Pilot**   **Czechoslovakian**   **310 Sqdn**

Joined 310 Squadron at Duxford on August 6 1940.

No further service details traced. Zima was repatriated to Czechoslovakia on July 18 1945 and is believed to have died there in the early seventies.

STANISLAV ZIMPRICH

81904   **PO**   **Pilot**   **Czechoslovakian**   **310 Squadron**

Joined 310 Squadron at its formation at Duxford on July 10 1940. Zimprich claimed a Do 17 destroyed on September 9.

He was killed on April 12 1942, as a Flight Lieutenant, aged 26. The unit he was serving with is not known.

Zimprich is buried in St Augustine's churchyard, Heanton Punchardon, Devon.

FO 27.12.40

ALEKSIEJ ZUKOWSKI

P 1292   **PO**   **Pilot**   **Polish**   **302 Squadron**

Zukowski was born on March 28 1911. He arrived in England on July 12 1940 and joined 302 Squadron at Leconfield on August 20.

He was killed on October 18, when he crashed at Harp Farm, Boxley, near Detling after losing his bearings in deteriorating weather and running out of fuel, in Hurricane V 6571. Zukowski is buried in Northwood Cemetery, Middlesex. After his death he was awarded the KW (23.12.40).

JAN EUGIENIUS LUDWIK ZUMBACH

P 1382   **PO**   **Pilot**   **Polish**   **303 Squadron**

Zumbach was born in Ursynow, Warsaw on April 14 1915. He joined the Polish Army in 1934, transferred to the Air Force in 1936 and was posted to the Officers' Training School at Deblin. He graduated on November 2 1938 and was posted to 111 Fighter Squadron.

When Poland was invaded Zumbach was recovering from a flying accident and so was not with his squadron. In mid-September he escaped by air to Roumania, then made his way to the Bulgarian port of Baltchik. With 299 other men he got on a ship bound for Beirut and arrived there on October 21 1939. After three days Zumbach sailed for Marseilles.

With other Poles he joined l'Armée de l'Air but they were not used by the French. On June 18 1940 Zumbach sailed in a Polish collier for Plymouth and reported to the PAF Depot at Blackpool. He joined 303 Squadron at Northolt at its formation on August 2. Zumbach claimed two Do 17s destroyed on September 7, Bf 109s on the 9th, 11th and 15th, a He 111 and another Bf 109 on the 26th and a Bf 109 on the 27th. He was awarded the VM (5th Class)(23.12.40) and the KW (1.2.41).

On July 2 1941 Zumbach destroyed a Bf 109 and probably a second and two more on October 13 and 24. He was awarded a Bar to the KW (10.9.41) and the DFC (30.10.41). On December 4 Zumbach was posted to 58 OTU, Grangemouth as an instructor. On March 23 1942 he was promoted and rejoined 303 at Northolt, as a Flight Commander. He probably destroyed a FW 190 on April 27.

Zumbach took command of 303 on May 18 and over Dieppe on August 19 he destroyed a FW 190, probably shared another and shared a He 111. He was awarded a second Bar to the KW (20.8.42), a third (15.11.42) and a Bar to the DFC (15.11.42). He was posted to HQ 9 Group, Preston on December 1 1942 as Polish Liaison Officer. On April 15 1943 Zumbach was appointed Wing Leader of the Polish Wing at Kirton-in-Lindsey. Later in the year he went on a course to the Polish Staff College, after which he went to Coltishall to resume leading his Wing. He probably destroyed a FW 190 on September 25 1944.

Zumbach was posted to HQ 84 Group on January 30 1945 as an operations officer. He was eventually released from the PAF in October 1946. Although born in Poland Zumbach had a paternal grandfather who had come from Switzerland and after he was released he obtained a Swiss passport.

The immediate post-war years were occupied with smuggling watches and other scarce commodities. Zumbach later flew in the wars in the Congo and Biafra. He finally gave up in 1967 and retired to France. He died there in 1986.

FO 1.3.41   *FL 1.9.42*   *SL 1.9.44*

JANUSZ ZURAKOWSKI

76715   **PO**   **Pilot**   **Polish**   **234 and 609 Squadrons**

Zurakowski was born on September 12 1914 and joined the PAF in 1935. He arrived in England in June 1940 and on July 21 was posted to 5 OTU, Aston Down. After converting to Spitfires he joined 234 Squadron at Middle Wallop in early August.

On the 15th Zurakowski claimed a Bf 110 destroyed. He was shot down in combat on the 24th and crashed on the Isle of Wight in Spitfire N 3239, unhurt. On September 5 he claimed a Bf 109 and on the 6th another. In this action Zurakowski's Spitfire, N 3279, was damaged by a Bf 109 over Beachy Head and he crashed on landing back at Middle Wallop. He shared in the probable destruction of a Bf 110 on September 29.

Zurakowski was posted to 609 Squadron, also at Middle Wallop, on October 4. He was awarded the KW and Bar (1.2.41) and left 609 on March 7 1941 to go to 57 OTU, Hawarden as an instructor. During the course of the next eight months Zurakowski served at various OTUs, finishing up at 58, at Grangemouth.

He returned to operations on December 8 1941, when he joined 315 Squadron at Northolt. Zurakowski moved to 306 Squadron at Church Stanton on April 11 1942, as a Flight Commander. He was given command of 316 Squadron at Heston on June 6 and led it until December 28 1942, when he was posted to SHQ Northolt. Zurakowski was awarded a second Bar to the KW (20.2.43). He was appointed Squadron Leader Flying at Northolt on July 4, holding the appointment until October 30 1943, going then to HQ Fighter Command.

Zurakowski was awarded the VM (5th Class)(20.12.43). On May 17 1944 he went to the Empire Test Pilots' School for a course, after which he was posted to the A&AEE, Boscombe Down on December 18 1946 for flying duties in 'A' Squadron, with the RAF rank of Acting Squadron Leader.

In 1950 Zurakowski was a test pilot with Gloster Aircraft and in 1952 he went to Canada to test the CF 100 for Avro (Canada). He became Chief Test Pilot there and settled in Canada.

FO 1.3.41   *FL 1.6.42*   *SL 1.9.44*

THE MEMORIALS

Many references have been made in the book to men being remembered on memorials around the world because they have no known graves.

The memorials each cover operations in specific areas and record the names of those men lost whilst operating from bases in those areas, as follows:

THE RUNNYMEDE MEMORIAL   The United Kingdom, Faroe Islands, Northern Ireland, France, Holland, Belgium, Germany, Denmark, Norway, Finland, Luxembourg, Czechoslovakia and Russia.

THE ALAMEIN MEMORIAL   Egypt, Libya, Syria, Lebanon, Iraq, Persia, Greece, Crete and the Aegean, Ethiopia, Eritrea and the Somalilands, the Sudan, East Africa, Aden and Madagascar.

THE MALTA MEMORIAL   Austria, Italy, Sicily, Islands of the Adriatic and the Mediterranean, Malta, Tunisia, Algeria, Morocco, West Africa, Yugoslavia and Gibraltar.

THE SINGAPORE MEMORIAL   The whole of southern and eastern Asia and the surrounding seas and oceans, or who died in captivity, or were being transported as prisoners-of-war from Malaya to imprisonment elsewhere.

THE OTTAWA MEMORIAL   Canada, British West Indies and the United States.

THE FLEET AIR ARM MEMORIAL   Situated at Lee-on-Solent and remembering all Fleet Air Arm personnel lost in all theatres of war and having no known grave.

SQUADRON ROLLS

Where a man served with more than one squadron or unit during the Battle of Britain period his name appears in each. He may not have flown operationally with every unit.

1 SQUADRON

Sgt J Arbuthnot
F/Sgt FG Berry
FO CN Birch
PO PV Boot
SL H Broadhurst
FL MH Brown
PO DOM Browne
Sgt N Cameron
PO CAC Chetham
PO JA Chevrier
PO E Cizek
PO AV Clowes
PO JAJ Davey
Sgt MP Davies
2nd Lt J Demozay
PO RH Dibnah
FO JA Dixon
Sgt J Dygryn
PO JFD Elkington
FO F Fajtl
FL JFF Finnis
PO GE Goodman
PO BA Hanbury
PO NPW Hancock
FO HBL Hillcoat
Sgt CG Hodson
FO JB Holderness
PO MG Homer
PO V Jicha
PO A Kershaw
Sgt B Kratkoruky
PO F Kordula
Sgt KM Kuttelwascher
FO RG Lewis
PO HJ Mann
FO PGH Matthews
Sgt HJ Merchant
PO JGP Millard
Sgt WT Page
Sgt O Pavlu
SL DA Pemberton
Sgt HW Pettit
Sgt J Prihoda
FO JCE Robinson
FO HNE Salmon
Sgt MM Shanahan
PO RH Shaw
PO CM Stavert
Sgt J Stefan
PO A Velebnovsky
PO MP Wareham
Sgt S Warren
Sgt J Weber
Sgt A Zavoral

1 SQUADRON (RCAF)

PO EWB Beardmore
FO CE Briese
FO de P Brown
PO JAJ Chevrier
PO BE Christmas
FL VB Corbett
FO J-PJ Desloges
FO RL Edwards
PO BA Hanbury
PO FW Hillock
FO GG Hyde
PO BV Kerwin
FO TB Little
FO PW Lochnan
FL GR McGregor
SL EA McNab
FO WBM Millar

FO H deM Molson
FO AD Nesbitt
FO RW Norris
FO JD Pattison
PO OJ Peterson
FO PB Pitcher
FL EM Reyno
FO BD Russel
FO R Smither
FO WP Sprenger
FO CW Trevana
PO FS Watson
FO AM Yuile

3 SQUADRON

PO JJFH Bandinel
FO NJM Barry
PO DL Bisgood
Sgt AF Butterick
Sgt ET Cosby
Sgt Fletcher
PO EG Ford
Sgt Fotheringham
FO CN Foxley-Norris
Sgt Francis
PO AHB Friendship
Sgt RH Furneaux
Sgt PP Gallus
Sgt WA Gardiner
SL SF Godden
Sgt HC Grove
Sgt J Hammerton
PO PA Harris
FO BAH Hitchings
PO JB Hobbs
PO CGStD Jeffries
FO DAE Jones
PO P Kennett
PO LN Landels
PO J Lonsdale
PO R McDougall
Sgt RJ McNair
FL R Miller
Sgt HR Mitchell
Sgt AR Moore
PO AG Osmand
Sgt GCR Pannell
PO AMW Scott
PO JA Sims
PO HA Sprague
FO MM Stephens
Sgt GS Taylor
PO CB Temlett
PO RE Tongue
SL FH Tyson
PO CAB Wallace
Sgt RT Ware
PO FS Watson
PO MT Whinney
PO JW White
FO RC Wilkinson
Sgt WC Wills

17 SQUADRON

Sgt LH Bartlett
FL AWA Bayne
FO GR Bennette
FO HAC Bird-Wilson
FL HP Blatchford
FO CPN Brett
PO HWA Britton
Sgt N Cameron

PO M Chelmecki
Sgt CA Chew
SL WE Coope
FO Count MB Czernin
PO PL Dawbarn
Sgt WJ Etherington
FO F Fajtl
Sgt D Fopp
Sgt G Griffiths
WC RK Hamblen
FO DHW Hanson
FO WJ Harper
Sgt RD Hogg
PO F Kordula
PO TL Kumiega
PO DC Leary
FO AP Innes
SL RIG MacDougall
PO K Manger
SL AG Miller
PO P Niemiec
Sgt DJ North-Bomford
Sgt GCC Palliser
FO GE Pittman
PO JK Ross
Sgt DA Sewell
PO ND Solomon
PO LW Stevens
Sgt GA Steward
SL CW Williams
PO DH Wissler

19 SQUADRON

PO RAC Aeberhardt
Sub-Lt AG Blake
Sgt RA Boswell
FO FN Brinsden
PO E Burgoyne
Sgt HW Charnock
FL WG Clouston
FL JB Coward
Sgt DGSR Cox
PO W Cunningham
PO F Dolezal
Sgt D Fulford
Sgt PS Hawke
FO LA Haines
PO PI Howard-Williams
PO F Hradil
Sgt BJ Jennings
PO RL Jones
FL BJE Lane
PO WJ Lawson
Sgt DE Lloyd
Sgt AN MacGregor
Sgt F Marek
FO DT Parrott
FL PC Pinkham
Sgt S Plzak
Sgt JA Potter
Sgt HAC Roden
Sgt GW Scott
F/Sgt H Steere
PO IW Sutherland
F/Sgt C Sydney
FL EH Thomas
F/Sgt GC Unwin
PO AF Vokes
Sgt J Whelan
Sgt KA Wilkinson

23 SQUADRON

Sgt WN Addison
Sgt CR Aindow
Sgt ED Ainge
Sgt S Ainsworth
Sgt J Angus
Sgt HT Archer
PO AA Atkinson
Sgt CC Bailey
PO CCM Baker
Sgt D Bell
SL LC Bicknell
Sgt JJ Booth
Sgt JS Brennan
F/Sgt CG Burton
Sgt K Butterworth
Sgt DB Campbell
Sgt B Capel
PO CF Cardnell
Sgt JC Cheetham
Sgt HR Crooke
Sgt RW Cullen
Sgt JE Dann
Sgt AMS Dargie
PO SS Duff
FL RMBD Duke-Woolley
Sgt CR Durrant
FO PSB Ensor
Sgt WT Fletcher
Sgt CLM Forsyth
Sgt J Francis
Sgt WE Gaunt
FO AA Gawith
Sgt JV Gill
PO JL Gillespie
PO HE Grellis
PO GJ Grogan
FL NM Harding
SL GFW Heycock
F/Sgt WRK Hughes
FO J Hunter-Tod
Sgt AE Johnson
Sgt GB Johnson
Sgt LR Karasek
FL RAL Knight
Sgt L Langley
Sgt WC McAdam
Sgt PJ McAllister
Sgt JA McDermott
Sgt HI MacRory
Sgt JW Mathers
PO K Mathews
Sgt SF Miles
Sgt AJ Miller
Sgt JB Mills
Sgt G Mitchell
Sgt PH Murray
Sgt TGF Nicholls
Sgt W Nixon
Sgt RRJ Nute
Sgt GD Oliver
PO E Orgias
Sgt E Parry
Sgt EE Parsons
PO AJS Pattinson
AC2 RI Payne
F/Sgt VWF Penford
Sgt HT Perry
Sgt A Pilkington
PO GR Pushman
Sgt CC Reilly
Sgt EC Roberts
Sgt JS Rose
Sgt WS Ruddock
Sgt A Sampson
Sgt JN Senior
Sgt J Smallman

23 SQUADRON (cont)

Sgt G Southall
Sgt C Stephens
Sgt WR Stevens
Sgt M Stuart
Sgt F Sumner
Sgt W Waring
FO DA Williams
Sgt KR Wood
FO HJ Woodward
Sgt RC Young

25 SQUADRON

PO R Ambrose
Sgt DH Baddeley
Sgt WE Barrett
Sgt A Bennison
Sgt B Bent
Sgt RC Berwick
Sgt JE Bignall
Sgt F Blenkharn
Sgt PW Broom
PO AW Brown
FO CH Bull
PO RJ Candy
FO E Cassidy
Sgt G Charnock
Sgt JW Compton
PO NH Corry
Sgt G Cottam
Sgt W Cowen
Sgt RG Crossman
Sgt JD Culmer
Sgt FW Curtis
Sgt JW Ditzel
Sgt Draby
FL WAC Emmett
Sgt F Fildes
Sgt JR Friend
Sgt Gothorpe
PO MJ Herrick
Sgt AM Hill
Sgt WH Hodds
PO DW Hogg
Sgt EJ Hollis
Sgt SV Holloway
Sgt KB Hollowell
FO BG Hooper
PO B Howe
FL JM Hughes
Sgt CA Johnson
Sgt JFR Jones
Sgt G Kensall
FL RG Ker-Ramsay
Sgt A Lamb
FO HMS Lambert
Sgt WG Lewis
PO JG Lingard
SL WW Loxton
FO HS Lusk
Sgt KR Lusty
FL AM Lyall
Sgt J Lynch
Sgt JB McCormack
Sgt HR Main
Sgt JCO Medworth
FO MJ Miley
Sgt TH Miller
SL HM Mitchell
PO EWJ Monk
Sgt J Phillip
Sgt RRC Pound
Sgt E Powell
Sgt JS Pugh

Sgt JW Pye
Sgt PG Rich
Sgt DF Roberts
FO BJ Rofe
Sgt AL Romanis
PO PR Smith
WO WG Snape
PO AT Sword-Daniels
Sgt AJ Theasby
Sgt JB Thompson
Sgt RN Turnbull
FO JHG Walker
LAC JP Wyatt

29 SQUADRON

FL JS Adams
PO DJ Anderson
Sgt J Ashworth
Sgt AT Austin
Sgt EH Bee
FO CA Bell
SL ER Bitmead
FO JRD Braham
FO CPN Brett
PO J Buchanan
Sgt RF Bumstead
PO P Byng-Hall
FL AM Campbell
PO KM Carver
Sgt J Cunningham
Sgt T Cupitt
Sgt AG Dannatt
FO RB Davies
Sgt WS Dossett
Sgt Duncan
Sgt F Edwards
Sgt GC Everitt
Sgt DR Fawcett
Sgt JF Fizel
Sgt L Fox
Sgt RP Freeman
Sgt PF Freer
Sgt TL French
Sgt HR Gilyeat
Sgt RJ Gouldstone
Sgt WJ Gregory
Sgt Hall
Sgt ND Harding
FO JD Humphreys
Sgt DJ Hunter
Sgt DW Isherwood
AC2 A Jackson
AC2 N Jacobson
Sgt RH James
Sgt E Jones
FO LGH Kells
Sgt R Lilley
FO AJA Llewellyn
Sgt Lloyd
PO OA Logie
Sgt PJ McAllister
Sgt RS Mallett
Sgt JW Mathers
Sgt TN Menage
Sgt RC Moss
F/Sgt WS Munn
Sgt N Neer
Sgt EF Newton
Sgt DJ Parr
Sgt R Pearce
PO PE Penfold
PO HA Pippard
Sgt J Price
PO RA Rhodes
Sgt AJA Roberts

PO DL Ryalls
Sgt A Service
Sgt VH Skillen
Sgt OK Sly
Sgt RE Stevens
Sgt S Stokoe
Sgt EF Taylor
Sgt K Taylor
PO PA Tomlinson
Sgt GA Waller
PO LG Watson
SL SC Widdows
Sgt AA Wilsdon
Sgt LD Wilson
Sgt WC Wilson
Sgt V Wingfield
FO CV Winn

32 SQUADRON

PO KR Aldridge
PO SE Andrews
Sgt DK Ashton
Sgt DJ Aslin
Sgt WH Banks
PO ARH Barton
Sgt EA Bayley
Sgt HE Black
FL PM Brothers
Sub-Lt GGR Bulmer
FL RFH Clerke
PO WC Connell
FL MN Crossley
PO S Czternastek
PO B Davey
FO VG Daw
PO Comte RGC
  de Hemricourt de Grunne
FO AF Eckford
FO JP Falkowski
PO J Flinders
FO RC Fumerton
FO PM Gardner
Sgt AW Gear
Sgt RJK Gent
PO KR Gillman
FO CL Gould
FO DH Grice
Sgt Griffiths
Sgt B Henson
PO NB Heywood
Sgt DT Hick
Sgt WB Higgins
Sgt OV Houghton
Sgt HN Hoyle
FL JBW Humpherson
PO PC Humphreys
PO RR Hutley
PO Z Janicki
Sgt K Korber
FL BK Kosinski
PO LN Landels
Sgt SE Lucas
PO WW McConnell
Sgt AH Milnes
PO JF Pain
Sgt RJ Parrott
Sgt LHB Pearce
PO JP Pfeiffer
Sgt TG Pickering
PO K Pniak
PO JE Proctor
FO J Rose
PO JH Rothwell
FL H a'B Russell
Sgt W Sasak

PO EGA Seghers
Sgt A Seredyn
Sgt HFW Shead
FO RF Smythe
Sgt GA Stroud
PO DJ Thacker
PO PD Thompson
F/Sgt G Turner
PO JL Ward
Sgt JS White
PO Whitehouse
PO BA Wlasnowolski
SL J Worrall

41 SQUADRON

PO DA Adams
PO ES Aldous
PO FJ Aldridge
Sgt JW Allison
Sgt RA Angus
Sgt AC Baker
FO HC Baker
Sgt CS Bamberger
Sgt RA Beardsley
PO GH Bennions
PO RJ Boret
FO JG Boyle
FO MP Brown
Sgt RA Carr-Lewty
Sgt LR Carter
PO HH Chalder
PO GW Cory
Sgt EV Darling
PO GGF Draper
SL DO Finlay
Sgt RC Ford
FO DR Gamblen
Sgt LA Garvey
Sgt TWR Healy
SL HRL Hood
Sgt IE Howitt
PO GA Langley
PO JG Lecky
SL RCF Lister
Sgt PD Lloyd
PO ES Lock
FO ADJ Lovell
Sgt J McAdam
FO JN Mackenzie
PO DE Mileham
FO OB Morrogh-Ryan
FO DH O'Neill
FL EN Ryder
F/Sgt JE Sayers
FL WJM Scott
PO EA Shipman
Sgt F Usmar
FO JR Walker
FO RW Wallens
FO JT Webster
PO EP Wells
SL H West

43 SQUADRON

F/Sgt KM Allen
FL MR Atkinson
Sgt CAH Ayling
SL JVC Badger
Sgt HJR Barrow
Sgt HE Bennett
Sgt V Brejcha
PO GC Brunner

43 SQUADRON (cont)

Sgt JA Buck
PO FR Carey
FO MK Carswell
PO RI Chaffe
Sgt JL Crisp
PO J Cruttenden
Sgt V Cukr
Sgt ALM Deller
PO RA de Mancha
PO DG Gorrie
PO CK Gray
FO B Groszewski
PO EM Gunter
PO HJL Hallowes
FO JFJ Haworth
FL CB Hull
Sgt CAL Hurry
Sgt G Jefferson
Sgt GW Jefferys
PO EW Jereczek
Sgt ER Jessop
Sgt RA Johnson
FO JI Kilmartin
PO R Lane
PO EC Langdon
PO DARG le Roy du Vivier
PO KW Mackenzie
Sgt B Malinowski
Sgt JP Mills
Sgt HF Montgomery
FL TFD Morgan
Sgt JP Morrison
PO K Mrazek
Sgt D Noble
FO HL North
PO JRS Oelofse
Sgt GCC Palliser
Sgt J Pipa
Sgt R Ptacek
PO J Redman
FL RC Reynell
Sgt AG Russell
FO LH Schwind
Sgt J Sika
FL JWC Simpson
FO J Stenhouse
Sgt DR Stoodley
Sgt LV Toogood
Sgt FJ Twitchett
PO HC Upton
PO AEA van den Hove
 d'Ertsenrijck
PO GH Westlake
PO CA Woods-Scawen

46 SQUADRON

PO CF Ambrose
Sgt S Andrew
FO F Austin
PO JCLD Bailey
PO RH Barber
Sgt HE Black
Sgt E Bloor
FO NW Burnett
Sub-Lt JC Carpenter
SL AR Collins
PO AM Cooper-Key
PO JD Crossman
Sgt RE de Cannaert d'Hamale
FO JF Drummond
Sgt RL Earp
Sgt GH Edworthy
FL WR Farley

Sgt AT Gooderham
PO PS Gunning
Sgt CAL Hurry
Sgt GW Jefferys
PO AE Johnson
FO PW Lefevre
PO PG Leggett
Sgt RH Lonsdale
FO RA McGowan
FO PR McGregor
FO H Morgan-Gray
Sgt JP Morrison
PO K Mrazek
SL AD Murray
Sgt JK Norwell
PO WB Pattulo
Sgt WA Peacock
Sgt LHB Pearce
FO RP Plummer
FL AC Rabagliati
PO R Reid
PO EGA Seghers
Sgt RF Sellers
Sgt E Tyrer
F/Sgt EE Williams
PO JR Young

54 SQUADRON

Sgt HA Aitken
FO JL Allen
PO W Armstrong
PO HND Bailey
PO S Baker
PO GH Batchelor
Sgt A Black
Sgt JS Bucknole
Sgt AA Burtenshaw
PO GD Calderhead
PO ARM Campbell
FO EFJ Charles
PO C Colebrook
PO EJ Coleman
Sgt GR Collett
PO GW Couzens
Sgt J Davis
FO AC Deere
PO PG Dexter
FL FPR Dunworth
PO EF Edsall
SL DO Finlay
PO A Finnie
Sgt A Gavan
Sgt DG Gibbins
Sgt JN Glendinning
FO CW Goldsmith
FL WE Gore
FO CF Gray
FO DG Gribble
PO DJ Hammond
FO JS Hart
Sgt LW Harvey
PO WP Hopkin
PO J Howard
PO P Howes
FO JL Kemp
Sgt W Klozinski
PO W Krepski
Sgt NA Lawrence
FL JA Leathart
Sgt JC Lockwood
PO L Martel
FO HKF Matthews
FL ST Meares
PO PR Mildren
Sgt N Morrison

Sgt WJ Noble
Sgt JK Norwell
PO RH Robbins
Sgt BL Robertson
FO D Secretan
PO MM Shand
Sgt DJ Steadman
PO C Stewart
Sgt GW Swanwick
Sgt L Switon
F/Sgt PH Tew
FO DR Turley-George
FO BH Way

56 SQUADRON

PO GG Bailey
Sgt RD Baker
FO REP Brooker
PO M Chelmecki
FO JH Coghlan
FO MH Constable Maxwell
F/Sgt CJ Cooney
Sgt JR Cowsill
FO PFM Davies
FO PDM Down
FL RSJ Edwards
Sgt PH Fox
FL EJ Gracie
PO LW Graham
PO TF Guest
Sgt VW Heslop
PO FW Higginson
Sgt P Hillwood
PO J Himr
Sgt J Hlavac
Sgt RD Hogg
PO MR Ingle-Finch
PO CCO Joubert
FO HK Laycock
FO EC Lenton
PO DC Mackenzie
SL GAL Manton
PO KJ Marston
Sgt CV Meeson
PO MH Mounsdon
Sgt DH Nichols
PO Z Nosowicz
FO AG Page
SL MH Pinfold
PO G Radwanski
Sgt RW Ray
Sgt Robertson
Sgt PEM Robinson
Sgt G Smythe
FO FB Sutton
Sgt Szafraniec
FO PS Weaver
FO IB Westmacott
Sgt C Whitehead
Sgt JJ Whitfield
FO BJ Wicks

64 SQUADRON

FO CJD Andrae
PO PH Beake
Sgt AE Binham
Sgt H Bowen-Morris
PO HR Case
Sgt DF Chadwick
Sgt HW Charnock
Sgt MPC Choron
Sgt HA Cordell

Sgt X de Cherade
 de Montbron
PO AG Donahue
Sgt JK Down
Sgt LA Dyke
PO GE Ellis
Sgt D Fulford
PO EG Gilbert
Sgt RD Goodwin
PO T Gray
Sgt PS Hawke
FL LF Henstock
FL DB Hobson
Sgt CL Hopgood
Sgt LR Isaac
FO AJO Jeffrey
PO RL Jones
PO PF Kennard-Davis
PO LFD King
FO AFA Laing
PO AF Laws
PO J Lawson-Brown
Sgt AC Leigh
Sgt ER Limpenny
Sgt DE Lloyd
PO JP Lloyd
SL ARD MacDonnell
Sgt J Mann
Sgt IW Matthews
SL NC Odbert
Sgt TG Oldfield
FO JJ O'Meara
Sgt KB Parker
FO HPF Patten
Sub-Lt FD Paul
Sgt J Pickering
PO JG Pippet
PO HRG Poulton
Sub-Lt GB Pudney
PO HW Reilley
FO R Roberts
PO JH Rowden
PO WNC Salmond
Sgt TW Savage
Sgt GW Scott
FO PJ Simpson
Sgt JW Slade
Sgt JWC Squier
PO DA Stanley
Sub-Lt JHC Sykes
FO DM Taylor
PO AR Tidman
Sgt FF Vinyard
FO MT Wainwright
PO Watson
Sgt J Whelan
FO HJ Woodward

65 SQUADRON

FO CG Chappell
Sgt RN Cooper
PO B Drobinski
PO BEF Finucane
PO WH Franklin
PO ED Glaser
FO SB Grant
PO FS Gregory
FO F Gruszka
PO NE Hancock
PO KG Hart
Sgt CR Hewlett
Sgt G Hill
Sgt MH Hine
SL AL Holland
Sgt M Keymer

65 SQUADRON (cont)

Sgt JR Kilner
Sgt DI Kirton
PO EB Lyons
F/Sgt RR MacPherson
FL WH Maitland-Walker
Sgt P Mitchell
FO JBH Nicholas
PO RKC Norwood
FL CGC Olive
Sgt HC Orchard
F/Sgt NT Phillips
FO LL Pyman
FO JK Quill
FL GAW Saunders
SL HC Sawyer
FO T Smart
Sgt RL Stillwell
PO W Szulkowski
Sgt GW Tabor
FO RG Wigg

66 SQUADRON

PO HR Allen
SL HGL Allsop
PO ANRL Appleford
Sgt CAH Ayling
PO S Baker
PO CAW Bodie
FL HF Burton
F/Sgt M Cameron
Sgt DCO Campbell
FL EW Campbell-Colquhoun
Sgt LR Carter
FO GP Christie
Sgt HR Clarke
PO LW Collingridge
Sgt H Cook
PO CA Cooke
Sgt P Copeland
PO GH Corbett
Sgt WJ Corbin
Sgt DF Corfe
PO IJA Cruickshanks
FL FPR Dunworth
FL AS Forbes
Sgt DH Forrest
FL KM Gillies
Sgt SA Goodwin
PO HMT Heron
Sgt J Hopewell
Sgt BW Hopton
Sgt DAC Hunt
Sgt RJ Hyde
PO JB Kendal
FO HC Kennard
PO PJC King
SL RHA Leigh
PO CA McGaw
PO JR Mather
PO PR Mildren
FO RW Oxspring
Sgt DK Parker
Sgt CA Parsons
PO JH Pickering
PO HW Reilley
Sgt RH Robbins
Sgt FN Robertson
Sgt AD Smith
PO JAP Studd
PO BE Tucker
Sgt RA Ward
PO AB Watkinson
Sgt PH Willcocks
Sgt B Wright

72 SQUADRON

Sgt HJ Bell-Walker
PO BW Brown
PO HR Case
SL AR Collins
FO PJ Davies-Cooke
FO TDH Davy
PO Douthwaite
PO RD Elliott
FL TAF Elsdon
Sgt JS Gilders
Sgt N Glew
FL E Graham
Sgt M Gray
PO DF Holland
Sgt MAW Lee
SL RB Lees
Sgt AC Leigh
PO AI Lindsay
PO JP Lloyd
PO EE Males
Sgt N Morrison
PO NR Norfolk
FO JJ O'Meara
FO O StJ Pigg
Sgt RE Plant
Sgt MH Pocock
PO PD Pool
PO IR Ritchie
FO NCH Robson
Sgt WTE Rolls
FO D Secretan
FL DFB Sheen
FL FM Smith
Sgt RCJ Staples
F/Sgt J Steere
PO N Sutton
Sgt PHRR Terry
FL RA Thomson
FL JW Villa
FO RJ Walker
Sgt J White
FO EJ Wilcox
PO AL Winskill
PO DC Winter

73 SQUADRON

FL MLff Beytagh
Sgt JJ Brimble
PO PEG Carter
Sgt P Copeland
Sgt DF Corfe
PO HW Eliot
Sgt RV Ellis
Sgt RH Furneaux
Sgt GW Garton
Sgt JJ Griffin
Sgt J Hopewell
Sgt BW Hopton
PO DS Kinder
PO NC Langham-Hobart
Sgt ME Leng
FL RE Lovett
PO A McFadden
PO CA McGaw
FL JAF MacLachlan
Sgt AL McNay
PO RA Marchand
Sgt AE Marshall
PO KM Millist
SL JWC More
SL AD Murray
Sgt P O'Byrne
Sgt FS Perkin

Sgt R Plenderleith
SL MWS Robinson
PO RD Rutter
Sgt AE Scott
FO DS Scott
FO JD Smith
FO JE Storrar
PO KJ Vykoukal
Sgt HG Webster
Sgt WC Wills

74 SQUADRON

PO W Armstrong
Sgt DH Ayers
FO RJE Boulding
FL S Brzezina
F/Sgt FP Burnard
PO P Chesters
PO EWG Churches
PO DG Cobden
FO DHT Dowding
PO BV Draper
Sgt W Eley
Sgt CW Francis
FO WDK Franklin
FO JC Freeborn
Sgt LE Freese
Sgt IN Glendinning
PO HR Gunn
PO D Hastings
Sgt CG Hilken
PO J Howard
Sub-Lt DA Hutchison
SL DPDG Kelly
Sgt TB Kirk
FL AG Malan
WO E Mayne
FL WEG Measures
Sgt N Morrison
Sgt EA Mould
FO JC Mungo-Park
Sgt J Murray
FO WH Nelson
Sgt WB Parkes
FO AL Ricalton
FO PCB St John
Sgt JA Scott
Sgt WM Skinner
PO AJ Smith
PO DNE Smith
Sgt HJ Soars
PO RL Spurdle
PO HM Stephen
PO PCF Stevenson
PO H Szczesny
SL FL White
PO JHR Young

79 SQUADRON

PO GG Bailey
Midshipman MA Birrell
Sgt HA Bolton
F/Sgt FS Brown
FO LT Bryant-Fenn
FO RW Clarke
FL RFH Clerke
FO DG Clift
Sgt DC Deutzer
PO TF Guest
FL GDL Haysom
SL JH Heyworth
PO J Himr

Sgt J Hlavac
FO HK Laycock
FO PF Mayhew
PO WH Millington
PO PJ Morgan
FO EJ Morris
Sgt W Mudry
FO GH Nelson-Edwards
PO BR Noble
FO TC Parker
Sgt LA Parr
FO GCB Peters
PO S Piatkowski
PO GL Roscoe
PO DWA Stones
Sgt AH Thom
PO OV Tracey
PO GW Varley
Sgt A Whitby
Sgt J Wright

85 SQUADRON

PO G Allard
Sgt HH Allgood
PO PW Arbon
FO JRA Bailey
Sgt TCE Berkley
PO JL Bickerdike
Sgt GB Booth
Sgt TM Calderwood
FO WF Carnaby
PO GCT Carthew
Sgt AH Deacon
WO FHEJA de Labouchere
FO IB Difford
Sgt JHM Ellis
PO CE English
Sgt WR Evans
FO FE Fayolle
Sgt G Goodman
FO AV Gowers
Sgt KW Gray
FL HR Hamilton
Sgt CE Hampshire
FO JA Hemingway
PO WH Hodgson
Sgt HN Howes
Sgt RS Hutton
FL J Jefferies
Sgt WJ Johnson
Sgt HDB Jones
Sgt KH Jones
Sgt L Jowitt
PO NLD Kemp
FO MC Kinder
Sgt S Kita
FO RHA Lee
PO AG Lewis
FO J Lockhart
FO JE Marshall
Sgt KA Muchowski
Sgt DBF Nicholls
PO G North
PO FA Robshaw
FO BA Rogers
Sgt CA Rust
FO SP Stephenson
PO ARF Thompson
SL PW Townsend
Sgt FR Walker-Smith
Sgt ER Webster
FO PP Woods-Scawen
PO PA Worrall

87 SQUADRON

F/Sgt IJ Badger
FO RP Beamont
FO JC Carver
FO JR Cock
PO PW Comely
Sgt J Cowley
Sgt JH Culverwell
PO CWW Darwin
FO WD David
PO FXE de Spirlet
WC JS Dewar
FL IR Gleed
FO RL Glyde
Sgt FV Howell
PO DT Jay
FO RV Jeff
FO Laycock
SL TG Lovell Gregg
PO ACR McLure
PO R Malengreau
Sgt RA Milburn
FL RS Mills
PO HT Mitchell
FO RMS Rayner
PO GL Roscoe
FO KW Tait
Sgt LA Thorogood
PO W van Lierde
Sgt SRE Wakeling
Sgt H Walton
FO DH Ward
FO R Watson

92 SQUADRON

Sgt JW Allison
Sgt LC Allton
Sgt SM Barraclough
PO AC Bartley
Sgt H Bowen-Morris
PO J Bryson
PO HD Edwards
Sgt WT Ellis
Sgt PR Eyles
Sgt RH Fokes
Sgt ETG Frith
PO FN Hargreaves
Sgt RE Havercroft
PO HP Hill
PO RH Holland
FL JA Kent
FO MC Kinder
Sgt DE Kingaby
FO CBF Kingcome
SL RCF Lister
PO JW Lund
PO HW McGowan
SL AM MacLachlan
Sgt J Mann
PO J Mansel-Lewis
PO R Mottram
SL JS O'Brien
Sgt TG Oldfield
Sgt KB Parker
FO JA Paterson
PO AJS Pattinson
FO JG Pattison
PO HS Sadler
SL PJ Sanders
PO CH Saunders
PO TBA Sherrington
F/Sgt C Sydney
FL RRS Tuck
FL JW Villa

PO TS Wade
PO WC Watling
PO GHA Wellum
PO DG Williams
FO AR Wright

111 SQUADRON

PO GSP Bain
Sgt J Bayly
SL AJ Biggar
WO PM Blaize
FO BH Bowring
PO RJW Brown
FL DC Bruce
Sgt RF Bumstead
Sgt R Carnall
FO SDP Connors
PO JHH Copeman
Sgt JB Courtis
Sgt JT Craig
Sgt EE Croker
Sgt K Dawick
Sgt AH Deacon
Sgt WL Dymond
Sgt VH Ekins
FO HM Ferriss
FO AGA Fisher
FO BM Fisher
FL HS Giddings
Midshipman PRJ Gilbert
PO KAG Graham
Sgt AH Gregory
Sgt CE Hampshire
PO HG Hardman
FO TPK Higgs
PO O Hruby
PO JK Kay
PO M Kellett
Sgt O Kestler
Sgt VA Kopecky
Sgt O Kucera
FO Z Kustrzynski
Sgt CW MacDougal
Sgt M Maciejowski
PO J Macinski
PO AG McIntyre
PO JW McKenzie
SL EA McNab
Sgt B Malinowski
Sgt MJ Mansfeld
Sgt HS Newton
Sgt DJ North-Bomford
Sgt B Olewinski
Sgt AD Page
PO J Poplawski
Sgt OW Porter
FL RPR Powell
Sub-Lt DH Richards
PO JR Ritchie
Sgt J Robinson
Sgt RF Sellers
PO LM Sharp
Sgt FH Silk
Sgt RB Sim
FO PJ Simpson
Sgt RH Smyth
SL JM Thompson
Sgt LJ Tweed
PO KJ Vykoukal
Sgt PH Waghorn
FO JA Walker
Sgt TY Wallace
Sub-Lt RWM Walsh
PO RR Wilson
Sub-Lt TV Worrall

141 SQUADRON

Sgt LH Allen
PO CIR Arthur
Sgt AE Ashcroft
Sgt FPJ Atkins
Sgt AF Beechey
PO JG Benson
Sgt LD Bowman
Sgt WT Chard
FO AN Constantine
Sgt JH Coxon
Sgt DG Cresswell
Sgt R Crombie
PO WA Cuddie
Sgt AB Cumbers
Sgt AG Curley
Sgt JJ Daly
FO RLF Day
FO IDG Donald
PO E Farnes
Sgt EH Ferguson
FO TB Fitzgerald
PO JR Gard'ner
Sgt HE Green
PO AB Halliwell
Sgt RC Hamer
PO AC Hamilton
Sgt CR Hill
Sgt AJB Hithersay
Sgt JSA Hodge
Sgt JH Hogg
Sgt AGV Holton
PO CG Houghton
PO RA Howley
PO DL Hughes
PO JR Kemp
PO R Kidson
Sgt LA Komaroff
Sgt WL Lackie
PO A Lammer
PO FCA Lanning
Sgt G Laurence
Sgt FWR Litson
FL MJ Loudon
PO RMMD Lucas
FO IN MacDougall
Sgt R McGugan
Sgt AD Meredith
Sgt WH Mott
PO SJ Pearman
PO GFC Pledger
Sgt EF Porter
Sgt SWM Powell
Sgt RW Richardson
SL WA Richardson
PO JM Ritchie
PO Russell
Sgt E Salway
PO LW Simpson
PO DM Slatter
FO AW Smith
PO EJ Stevens
Sgt Swanwick
FO HN Tamblyn
FO J Waddingham
Sgt E Walsh
PO WFP Webber
PO DR West
Sgt AS Wickins
PO DC Williams
PO Wilsch
FO DF Wilson
Sgt JF Wise
FL EC Wolfe
Sgt JE Woodgate

145 SQUADRON

PO JH Bachmann
Sgt ED Baker
FL AH Boyd
FO GR Branch
Sgt J Budzinski
FL RW Bungey
PO GCT Carthew
WC RA Chignell
PO BMG de Hemptinne
PO PW Dunning-White
FL RG Dutton
FO DN Forde
PO J Gil
PO WJ Glowacki
Sgt JK Haire
PO JH Harrison
FO DSG Honor
Sgt WJ Johnson
PO ARIG Jottard
F/Sgt J Kwiecinski
Sub-Lt IH Kestin
Sgt J McConnell
PO J Machacek
FL JAF MacLachlan
FO MA Newling
PO JHM Offenberg
FO A Ostowicz
FL CL Page
FL W Pankratz
SL JRA Peel
FO RW Rabone
FL W Riley
FL RMB Rowley
PO LA Sears
FO Lord Shuttleworth
Sub-Lt FA Smith
FO JE Storrar
Sgt DB Sykes
PO JM Talman
Sgt P Thorpe
FO W Urbanowicz
Sgt JV Wadham
PO ECJ Wakeham
PO F Weber
Sgt J Weber
PO ANC Weir
FO RD Yule

151 SQUADRON

Sgt HH Adair
PO JWE Alexander
FO JHL Allen
PO R Ambrose
Sgt G Atkinson
PO Austin
WC FV Beamish
Sub-Lt HW Beggs
PO RWG Beley
FL KH Blair
PO DH Blomeley
Sgt GT Clarke
FO RNH Courtney
PO F Czajkowski
Sgt L Davies
PO KBL Debenham
WC EM Donaldson
PO GAF Edmiston
PO JLW Ellacombe
FL WR Farley
FO TRH Finch
FO AD Forster
Sgt F Gmur
Sgt AT Gooderham

151 SQUADRON (cont)

SL JAG Gordon
Sgt IAC Grant
PO JR Hamar
PO FC Harrold
PO JK Haviland
Sgt D Haywood
Sgt R Holder
Sgt WB Holroyd
PO JM Horrox
PO MR Ingle-Finch
PO JT Johnson
PO TW Kawalecki
SL EB King
Sgt A Laing
PO OE Lamb
Sgt GGS Laws
Sgt PRC McIntosh
Sgt J McPhee
FO RM Milne
Sgt DBF Nicholls
PO WB Pattullo
PO RF Philo
PO JB Ramsay
PO M Rozwadowski
Sgt JE Savill
PO IS Smith
FL RL Smith
FO VR Snell
PO JJ Solak
Sgt DO Stanley
Sgt L Staples
Sgt G Stevens
PO RP Stevens
PO F Surma
Sgt W Szafraniec
FO AB Tucker
Sgt AD Wagner
PO AG Wainwright
SL H West
Sgt RO Whitehead
FO CD Whittingham
Midshipman OM Wightman
Sgt J Winstanley
Sgt A Zavoral

152 SQUADRON

PO HJ Akroyd
PO CG Bailey
Sgt JK Barker
FO IN Bayles
FO GT Baynham
PO W Beaumont
FL DPA Boitel-Gill
Sgt JM Christie
FO GJ Cox
FL EC Deanesly
SL PK Devitt
PO DH Fox-Male
PO RMD Hall
PO NE Hancock
FL ES Hogg
PO RM Hogg
Sgt KC Holland
PO FH Holmes
PO PH Humphreys
FO RF Inness
PO JSB Jones
Sgt AW Kearsey
Sgt Z Klein
PO ES Marrs
Sgt EH Marsh
FL PGStG O'Brian
PO FH Posener

PO G Radwanski
Sgt LAE Reddington
Sgt DN Robinson
PO DC Shepley
Sgt EE Shepperd
Sgt WG Silver
Sgt J Szlagowski
Sgt GW Tabor
FL FM Thomas
FO C Warren
PO AR Watson
PO TS Wildblood
PO WD Williams
FL LC Withall
Sgt R Wolton

213 SQUADRON

Sgt HH Adair
PO HD Atkinson
PO R Atkinson
Sgt HJR Barrow
Sgt IKJ Bidgood
SL GDM Blackwood
Sub-Lt HGK Bramah
PO MSHC Buchin
Sgt GD Bushell
Sgt SL Butterfield
FO HD Clark
PO HW Cottam
Sgt ME Croskell
FO WD David
Sgt MP Davies
WC JS Dewar
PO RD Dunscombe
FO M Duryasz
F/Sgt C Grayson
PO RR Hutley
Sub-Lt DM Jeram
PO PJ Kearsey
PO JEP Laricheliere
Sgt RT Llewellyn
FO J Lockhart
FL DS MacDonald
SL HD McGregor
Sub-Lt WJM Moss
Sgt PP Norris
PO AG Osmand
PO JAL Philippart
FO LH Schwind
FL JEJ Sing
FO WM Sizer
Sgt EG Snowden
Sgt G Stevens
FL JM Strickland
Sgt SG Stuckey
PO JM Talman
PO TR Thomson
PO GH Westlake
FL RDG Wight
Sgt GN Wilkes
PO B Wlasnowolski
Sgt A Wojcicki

219 SQUADRON

Sgt A Aitken
Sgt S Austin
Sgt TH Banister
PO RV Baron
Sgt R Bell
Sgt GW Benn
Sgt HWW Berridge
Sgt C Beveridge

PO T Burkett
Sgt C Browne
Sgt DC Bunch
FO JC Carriere
Sgt CEP Castle
Sgt JA Clandillon
Sgt WTM Clark
SL AE Clouston
Sgt RV Cook
Sgt E Coombes
Sgt HK Crook
PO HR Crowley
Sgt CW Dodge
PO JH Duart
Sgt OA Dupee
Sgt BE Dye
Sgt EC Gardiner
Sgt VD Gee
FO HG Goddard
Sgt C Goodwin
Sgt AE Gregory
Sgt KG Gresty
Sgt EG Grubb
Sgt HF Grubb
PO RC Hall
Sgt CB Hamilton
Sgt J Hardcastle
FO TP Harnett
Sgt ARJ Harrison
PO GM Head
Sgt DO Hendry
PO DO Hobbis
Sgt AJ Hodgkinson
PO H Jacobs
Sgt J Keatings
Sgt ER Lacey
PO DM Lake
PO WGM Lambie
Sgt T le Dong
Sgt GM Leslie
PO JG Lingard
FL JH Little
Sgt W Lowther
AC2 JP McCaul
Sgt TR Marshall
PO FG Nightingale
Sgt H Owen
Sgt DJ Pearcy
Sgt CC Pyne
Sgt REB Sargent
Sgt GE Shepperd
PO J Sinclair
Sgt L Smith
Sgt RB Summmers
FO JG Topham
Sgt GT Williams
Sgt RF Willis
FL EC Wolfe
PO KW Worsdell
FO AS Worthington

222 SQUADRON

PO WR Assheton
PO FB Bassett
Sgt S Baxter
Sgt OR Bowerman
Sgt RA Breeze
PO JW Broadhurst
Sgt JHB Burgess
PO JMV Carpenter
Sgt DJ Chipping
PO IH Cosby
FO JW Cutts
PO AE Davies
PO GGA Davies

Sgt PO Davis
Sgt JT Dunmore
PO HPM Edridge
PO EF Edsall
Sgt DG Gibbins
Sgt RH Gretton
FO ILM Hallam
SL JH Hill
Sgt I Hutchinson
Sgt JI Johnson
Sgt RB Johnson
FO DAP McMullen
Sgt RG Marland
FL GC Matheson
SL HW Mermagen
Sgt LF Patrick
Sgt RB Price
Sgt NHD Ramsay
Sgt JW Ramshaw
FL AI Robinson
Sgt E Scott
Sgt AWP Spears
PO C Stewart
FL EH Thomas
FO B van Mentz
PO TA Vigors
PO HL Whitbread

229 SQUADRON

PO POD Allcock
Sgt J Arbuthnot
SL AJ Banham
PO RE Bary
Sdt EG Bidgood
SL ER Bitmead
FO VM Bright
FO RC Brown
Sub-Lt JC Carpenter
PO KM Carver
PO JMF Dewar
PO GLJ Doutrepont
PO RAL Duviver
Sgt JR Farrow
FL JFF Finnis
FO JW Hamill
FO JB Holderness
Sgt JW Hyde
PO EW Jereczek
Sgt GB Johns
FO AS Linney
FO DBH McHardy
SL HJ Maguire
Sgt SW Merryweather
Sgt RR Mitchell
Sgt DJ North-Bomford
Sgt RJ Ommaney
PO V Ortmans
PO J Poplawski
PO M Ravenhill
FO RF Rimmer
PO FA Robshaw
FL FE Rosier
FO HNE Salmon
Sgt GF Silvester
FO GM Simpson
PO E Smith
FO RR Smith
FO WA Smith
PO NK Stansfeld
PO S Stegman
Sgt FJ Twitchett
PO VBS Verity
GC SF Vincent
PO LBR Way

232 SQUADRON

Adj Y Briere
Sgt AF Butterick
Sgt RA Draper
PO EG Ford
Adj CP Guerin
Sgt Hardie
PO JB Hobbs
Sgt GV Hoyle
PO CGStD Jeffries
PO R McDougall
PO JV Marshall
Sgt PB Nicholson
FL AW Pennington-Legh
Sgt JK Pollard
Sgt EA Redfern
PO JA Sims
FO MM Stephens
Sgt GA Walker

234 SQUADRON

Sgt GJ Bailey
SL RE Barnett
FO GT Baynham
Sgt CH Bell
SL MV Blake
PO MCB Boddington
PO MF Briggs
Sgt PGF Brown
FO FHP Connor
PO KS Dewhurst
PO RFT Doe
PO IH Edwards
PO WHG Gordon
PO GK Gout
PO CE Hamilton
PO R Hardy
Sgt AS Harker
PO CH Hight
PO DN Hookway
Sgt WH Hornby
PO PW Horton
FO PC Hughes
FO CP Igglesden
FO TM Kane
Sgt Z Klein
PO KA Lawrence
PO R MacKay
PO EB Mortimer-Rose
SL JS O'Brien
FO Z Olenski
FL CL Page
PO V Parker
FO GL Ritcher
Sgt GW Rogers
Sgt H Sharpley
Sgt JB Shepherd
Sgt LE Smith
Sgt J Szlagowski
FL JG Thielmann
Sgt WW Thompson
PO EW Wootten
Sgt HJ Wotton
PO JH Young
FL JS Young
PO J Zurakowski

235 SQUADRON

Sgt ATR Aslett
Sgt CSF Beer
Sgt KLO Blow
Sgt RW Brookman
Sgt OV Burns
Sgt AR Cain
FL WJ Carr
PO JTR Chamberlain
Sgt C Chrystall
SL RN Clarke
PO J Coggins
Sgt DC Cooper
Sgt ND Copeland
PO HH Crawford
Sgt AS Davis
PO JT Davison
Sgt T Dawson
Sgt OJ Dee
Sgt RJG Demoulin
Sgt WH Dulwich
Sgt IL Dunn
Sgt CR Evans
Sgt AD Everett
Sgt J Farthing
Sgt JL Feather
PO JO Fenton
SL AW Fletcher
FL FW Flood
FL WB Goddard
PO HAC Gonay
Sgt S Gordon
Sgt GL Gould
Sgt EA Graves
PO AWV Green
Sgt RV Gridley
Sgt Hall
PO GS Hebron
Sgt L Heimes
Sgt RW Hillman
Sgt SJ Hobbs
Sgt Howard
PO DC Howe
Sgt BFR Hubbard
PO LLG Javaux
Sgt RKH Johnson
PO JA Keard
Sgt GE Keel
PO RD Kent
PO JC Kirkpatrick
FO JH Laughlin
Sgt JT Lawrence
Sgt OG Lejeune
PO AG Little
Sgt JP McCarthy
Sgt TF McCarthy
Sgt GSM McLeod
Sgt JR McMahon
Sgt ARD Maconochie
Sgt TB Marshall
PO AW Martin
Sgt TA Maslen
Sgt W Mason
Sgt JC Merrett
Sgt ACA Michiels
Sgt W Middlemiss
Sgt KE Naish
Sgt HT Naughton
F/Sgt D Nelson
Sgt EA Newham
Sgt DV Newport
Sgt TW Oaks
Sgt WG Owen
PO FG Paisey
Sgt JG Parsons
PO RL Patterson
Sgt HJ Pavitt

FO RJ Peacock
Sgt W Peebles
PO ER Phillips
Sgt SG Preater
PO L Prevot
PO JS Priestley
Sgt PR Prosser
Sgt BH Quelch
Sgt JS Ramsay
Sgt CA Ream
Sgt LHM Reece
Sgt WC Richards
Sgt HW Ricketts
Sgt LPVJ Ricks
PO NA Sadler
Sgt BR Sharp
PO NB Shorrocks
Sgt NHJ Smith
Sgt DA Sobey
Sgt GA Southorn
Sgt JH Spires
Sgt NM Stanger
Sgt RM Steele
FL PAM Stickney
Sgt RR Stretch
Sgt HR Sutton
Sgt RF Tatnell
PO R Taylor
PO RC Thomas
Sgt DF Touch
Sgt RY Tucker
Sgt JW Unett
Sgt FA Venesoen
PO HK Wakefield
Sgt DS Wallis
Sgt RDH Watts
Sgt GV Wedlock
Sgt WHJ Westcott
PO RD Westlake
Sgt R White
PO PC Wickings-Smith
Sgt W Wilson
PO DN Woodger
FO DKA Wordsworth
Sgt DL Wright

236 SQUADRON

Sgt EH Adams
Sgt EA Alexander
Sgt S Archer
Sgt LV Baker
Sgt NPG Barron
Sgt C Boyle
Sgt DR Briggs
Sgt CWD Brown
Sgt WR Burns
PO LG Burton
PO GL Campbell
PO H Capstick
PO AK Chappell
Sgt DWE Chapple
Sgt CFJ Cole
Sgt H Corcoran
PO DVC Cotes-Preedy
Sgt GP Cox
PO RF Crockett
Sgt PE Davis
Sgt HG Deadman
PO LJ Dejace
FL RW Denison
Sgt DA Denton
PO JM Derbyshire
PO G Dieu
SL PE Drew
Sgt HDB Elsdon

Sgt G Emmett
PO HAC Evans
Sgt E Gant
Sgt G Garside
Sgt CM Gibbons
Sgt JE Goldsmith
Sgt J Graham
Sgt GG Green
PO GH Hannan
Sgt RA Haylock
Sgt FAP Head
PO BH Herrick
PO AH Hiles
PO GA Holder
PO ARdeL Inniss
PO HJ Jeffcoat
Sgt HR Jeffery-Cridge
Sgt RRG Keeler
Sgt WH Kellitt
Sgt JD Keynes
PO WL King
PO HG Lascot
Sgt L Ledger
PO AFY Lees
Sgt FT Lerway
Sgt EE Lockton
Sgt Long
Sgt J Lowe
PO DTM Lumsden
FL MR MacArthur
Sgt RI McChesney
PO BM McDonough
Sgt DD MacKinnon
Sgt BM Mansfield
Sgt DE Mansfield
Sgt WC Marsh
Sgt HG Matthews
PO GH Melville-Jackson
Sgt RHR Meyer
Sgt EE Miles
Sgt DA Monk
FL GW Montagu
FO WS Moore
PO B Nokes-Cooper
PO SG Nunn
PO CBG Peachment
Sgt WJ Pearce
Sgt LL Pearse
Sgt DE Pearson
Sgt WD Penfold
Sgt B Pennycuick
Sgt AH Piper
FL RM Power
PO AO Price
Sgt NAJ Price
Sgt WGV Puxley
Sgt J Quinn
Sgt JD Riddell-Hannam
PO RH Rigby
PO F Riley
PO RAL Robb
PO CL Roman
Sgt GW Rouse
PO GH Russell
Sgt RJ Sharp
Sgt H Sheard
Sgt WJP Sheppard
Sgt S Sheridan
Sgt Shewel
AC 2 J Smallman
Sgt PR Smith
Sgt RC Smith
PO WG Snow
Sgt A Spiers
Sgt JE Symonds
Sgt GN Taylor
Sgt Thomas
FO CRD Thomas

236 SQUADRON (cont)

Sgt JR Thompson
Sgt JR Toombs
Sgt FD Tucker
PO AAL van Wayenberghe
PO JAC Venn
Sgt LW Viles
Sgt S Walker
Sgt TA Warren
PO J Watters
Sgt AD Whitson
PO DC Wilde
Sgt NN Woodland

238 SQUADRON

SL CEJ Baines
Sgt ES Bann
Sgt LG Batt
Sgt FA Bernard
SL MV Blake
PO FN Cawse
FO RW Clarke
PO BG Collyns
PO BB Considine
PO AR Covington
PO CT Davis
PO RFT Doe
Sgt M Domagala
Sgt S Duszynski
SL HA Fenton
Sgt G Gledhill
Sgt ENL Guymer
PO DS Harrison
Sgt V Horsky
FL DP Hughes
Sgt J Jeka
FO JC Kennedy
PO RA Kings
Sgt J Kucera
Sgt R Little
FL JHG McArthur
FO DC MacCaw
PO A McInnes
Sgt JW McLaughlin
Sgt HJ Marsh
FL WEG Measures
PO PJ Morgan
FL JA O'Neill
Sgt C Parkinson
Sgt P Pearson
Sgt L Pidd
WC DN Roberts
FL ML Robinson
PO RB Rohacek
PO W Rozycki
Sgt EW Seabourne
Sgt FA Sibley
PO VC Simmonds
FO MJ Steborowski
PO J Tillett
PO W Towers-Perkins
FL DE Turner
PO JR Urwin-Mann
FO SC Walch
PO JS Wigglesworth

242 SQUADRON

Sgt JF Armitage
PO R Atkinson
SL DRS Bader
FL GE Ball

WC PR Barwell
PO J Benzie
Sgt GW Brimble
PO MK Brown
PO CR Bush
PO NN Campbell
FL JG Cave
FO GP Christie
Sub-Lt RJ Cork
PO D Crowley-Milling
FO LE Cryderman
PO RH Dibnah
FO AF Eckford
Lt RE Gardner
FO RD Grassick
PO N Hart
SL HL Hayes
PO MG Homer
PO NLD Kemp
PO JB Latta
Sgt RH Lonsdale
PO WL McKnight
Sgt AD Meredith
PO JGP Millard
Sgt DBF Nicholls
Midshipman PJ Patterson
Sgt JA Porter
FL GSff Powell-Shedden
Sgt E Richardson
PO BA Rogers
Sgt JE Savill
PO KM Sclanders
PO NK Stansfeld
FO HN Tamblyn
PO PS Turner
PO MP Wareham

245 SQUADRON

Sgt WH Banks
Adj HJ Bouquillard
Sgt CB Brown
FO GA Brown
PO RI Chaffe
PO VB de la Perrelle
Capt CJMP de Scitivaux
de Greische
PO ER Edmunds
PO WT Eiby
Sgt SA Fenemore
Sgt V Foglar
PO DJ Hammond
Sgt M Hare
Sgt LW Harvey
PO AL Hedges
PO GE Hill
PO GL Howitt
Sgt AJ Hughes
Sgt RWE Jarrett
Sgt P Killick
PO TR Kitson
Sgt J Kucera
Adj H Lafont
PO PG Leggett
PO WW McConnell
PO KW McGlashan
PO G Marsland
Sgt AR Moore
Adj RGOJ Mouchotte
FO NJ Mowat
PO DA Pennington
Sgt RB Price
PO J Redman
Sgt GF Silvester
PO JS Southwell
PO DJ Spence

SL HM Starr
Sgt DJ Steadman
FL CAC Stone
FL JA Thomson
SL EW Whitley
PO DM Whitney
PO DS Yapp

247 SQUADRON

SL GF Chater
Sgt DC Deuntzer
FO NAR Doughty
Sgt Edwards
Sgt RJ Fowler
FO NIC Fowler
FO TW Gillen
Sgt DN Lawford
Sgt Makins
FL PGStG O'Brian
Sgt JV Renvoise
Sgt RT Thomas
PO GW Varley
FO RA Winter

248 SQUADRON

PO CJ Arthur
PO GB Atkinson
FL GM Baird
Sgt H Bashford
Sgt EJ Bayliss
PO CC Bennett
Sgt GB Brash
Sgt DL Burton
Sgt GS Clarke
Sgt R Copcutt
Sgt RCR Cox
Sgt FS Day
Sgt MP Digby-Worsley
PO JD Dodd
Sgt DA Easton
Sgt HH Edwards
PO FRC Elger
Sgt CF Fenn
Sgt HL Flower
PO AL Fowler
Sgt JH Fripp
PO SR Gane
Sgt WJ Garfield
PO AHH Garrad
Sgt E Gillam
PO MD Green
PO WC Hall
PO AL Hamilton
Sgt JS Hamilton
PO RH Haviland
PO AE Hill
Sgt EL Holmes
Sgt A Hook
Sgt R Ivey
Sgt RSS James
PO AHE Kahn
Sgt A Kay
PO EGC Leathem
Sgt JC Lumsden
PO EH McHardy
Sgt EJ McKie
Sgt K Massey
Sgt BW Mesner
FL REG Morewood
PO J Morris
Sgt RI Mowat
Sgt HFJ Moynham

Sgt NN Palmer
FL AW Pennington-Legh
PO AH Pettet
PO RJ Powell
Sgt DH Proudman
Sgt DN Rains
PO VA Ricketts
Sgt EA Ringwood
Sgt JH Round
Sgt J Rourke
PO EC Schollar
PO HR Sharman
Sgt WG Sharratt
Sgt IR Sims
Sgt NJ Stocks
SL VCF Streatfield
PO FN Thompson
Sgt J Till
Sgt HW Walmsley
Sgt WH Want
PO DAP Warren
Sgt EL Watts
PO ML Wells
Sgt J White
Sgt C Wilcock
WO SV Wood
Sgt RR Wright
Sgt G Yates

249 SQUADRON

FO RGA Barclay
FL RA Barton
Sgt EA Bayley
WC FV Beamish
Sgt JMB Beard
FO HJS Beazley
Adj HJ Bouquillard
PO PR-F Burton
FO E Cassidy
PO JT Crossey
Sgt HJ Davidson
Sgt WL Davis
Sgt WR Evans
PO RDS Fleming
SL J Grandy
Sgt CE Hampshire
SL RG Kellett
Sgt FWG Killingback
SL EB King
PO MA King
PO AG Lewis
FO KT Lofts
PO PA Loweth
PO WW McConnell
Sgt M Maciejowski
Sgt RJ McNair
Sgt J McPhee
Sgt ADW Main
PO JRB Meaker
PO WH Millington
Sgt JP Mills
PO TF Neil
FL JB Nicolson
Sgt GCC Palliser
FO DG Parnall
PO WB Pattullo
Sgt LHB Pearce
Adj GC Perrin
Sgt PA Rowell
Sgt CA Rust
Sgt R Smithson
Sgt RH Smyth
PO JJ Solak
Sgt GA Stroud
PO ARF Thompson

249 SQUADRON (cont)

Sgt PH Waghorn
FO PHV Wells
PO RENE Wynn
FO JRC Young

253 SQUADRON

Sgt KM Allen
Sgt HH Allgood
Sgt JA Anderson
PO ARH Barton
FO DB Barton
PO EG Bidgood
SL ER Bitmead
FO GA Brown
FO WP Cambridge
PO GCT Carthew
Sgt ICC Clenshaw
PO JKG Clifton
Sgt SF Cooper
PO AH Corkett
Sgt V Cukr
Sgt JH Dickinson
Sgt AS Dredge
FL RMBD Duke-Woolley
FO AF Eckford
FL GR Edge
Sgt A Edgley
PO CD Francis
SL TP Gleave
PO RC Graves
PO JPB Greenwood
PO DJ Hammond
Sgt WB Higgins
Sgt RA Innes
PO DNO Jenkins
Sgt ER Jessop
Sgt EHC Kee
SL EB King
Sgt S Kita
Sgt VA Kopecky
PO G Marland
Sgt J Metham
Sgt PJ Moore
PO LC Murch
PO T Nowak
FO SR Peacock-Edwards
PO DA Pennington
PO WMC Samolinski
SL HM Starr
FO JT Strang
FO AAG Trueman
FL RF Watts
FL JH Wedgewood
Sgt RO Whitehead
PO DS Yapp

257 SQUADRON

F/Sgt KM Allen
PO SE Andrews
Sgt DJ Aslin
Sgt LD Barnes
SL DW Bayne
FL HRA Beresford
Sgt HE Black
FO HP Blatchford
PO CR Bonseigneur
FL WS Bowyer
FL PM Brothers
PO CFA Capon
PO JAG Chomley

PO AC Cochrane
FO The Hon DA Coke
FO BWJ D'Arcy-Irvine
PO B Davey
WC AD Farquhar
Sgt RV Forward
Sgt DN Francis
Sgt RHB Fraser
PO CG Frizell
Sgt AG Girdwood
PO KC Gundry
SL H Harkness
PO AL Hedges
FO JAM Henderson
Sgt B Henson
PO NB Heywood
Sgt HN Hoyle
Sgt DJ Hulbert
PO DW Hunt
Sgt ER Jessop
PO JK Kay
Sgt SE Lucas
PO WW McConnell
PO GH Maffett
FO JC Martin
FO LRG Mitchell
PO PA Mortimer
PO G North
Sgt RC Nutter
Sgt AD Page
Sgt AJ Page
PO JP Pfeiffer
PO K Pniak
PO J Redman
Sgt PT Robinson
FO LH Schwind
Sgt HFW Shead
Sgt KB Smith
PO F Surma
FL RRS Tuck
GC SF Vincent

263 SQUADRON

FO AWN Britton
PO RF Ferdinand
SL CB Hull
FL RS Mills
FO TP Pugh
FL W Riley
Sgt CP Rudland
FL WOL Smith
PO D Stein
FL CAC Stone
FO P Wyatt-Smith

264 SQUADRON

Sgt RT Adams
Sgt MR Andrews
FL RCV Ash
FO JRA Bailey
Sgt B Baker
SL AJ Banham
Sgt FJ Barker
PO EG Barwell
SL LG Belchem
Sgt A Berry
PO PD Bowen
Sgt A Campbell
FL EW Campbell-Colquhoun
PO S Carlin
FO WF Carnaby
Sgt VR Chapman

PO MC Corner
Sgt WE Cox
Sgt VWJ Crook
FO NR Dobree
PO CC Ellery
Sgt CS Emeny
SL GD Garvin
Sgt F Gash
PO RS Gaskell
PO HI Goodall
PO GH Hackwood
Sgt OA Hardy
Sgt LH Hayden
FO FD Hughes
SL PA Hunter
PO CE Johnson
PO JT Jones
PO DHS Kay
PO PL Kenner
PO FH King
FO WRA Knocker
Sgt AJ Lauder
Sgt P Lille
Sgt WH Machin
PO MH Maggs
Sgt A Martin
Sgt W Maxwell
FO JC Melvill
PO WR Moore
Sgt WJ Murland
PO A O'Connell
FO DKC O'Malley
FO HH Percy
PO WA Ponting
Sgt LAW Rasmussen
PO G Robinson
Sgt LP Russell
Sgt WJ Scott
FO IG Shaw
Sgt FW Shepherd
PO LW Simpson
FL AM Smith
Sgt GE Smith
PO DMA Smythe
FO IR Stephenson
PO RW Stokes
PO AJ Storrie
PO FC Sutton
PO KR Sutton
PO SR Thomas
Sgt ER Thorn
Sgt JR Toombs
FL AJ Trumble
Sgt RC Turner
Sgt FW Wake
PO TD Welsh
PO D Whitley
PO MH Young
Sgt RBM Young

266 SQUADRON

Sgt JW Allen
Sgt LC Allton
PO DL Armitage
PO DG Ashton
Sgt RGV Barraclough
FL SH Bazley
Sgt MA Beatty
SL ER Bitmead
Sgt RA Boswell
PO NG Bowen
Sgt RA Breeze
PO NW Burnett
PO FW Cale
PO HH Chalder

Sgt H Cook
Sgt TA Cooper
FO TDH Davey
Sgt JT Dunmore
Sgt AW Eade
Sgt WT Ellis
Sgt SA Goodwin
PO RC Gosling
Sub-Lt H laF Greenshields
Sgt RH Gretton
Sgt FB Hawley
PO HMT Heron
FO MR Hill
PO AH Humphrey
FL PG Jameson
PO WR Jones
Sgt DE Kingaby
PO C Logan
Sgt AN MacGregor
SL HW Mermagen
PO WA Middleton
PO PHG Mitchell
FO JG Pattison
PO PD Pool
PO HAR Prowse
PO RJB Roach
PO JF Soden
SL DGH Spencer
F/Sgt C Sydney
FL EH Thomas
PO RM Trousdale
PO BE Tucker
PO EP Wells
SL RL Wilkinson
PO WS Williams

302 SQUADRON

Sgt A Beda
PO B Bernas
FO J Borowski
PO PEG Carter
PO SJ Chalupa
FL TP Chlopik
PO M Czerniak
FL JT Czerny
PO T Czerwinski
FL JNW Farmer
PO W Gnys
FL F Jastrzebski
PO WE Karwowski
PO S Kleczkowski
Sgt W Kosarz
Sgt J Kowalski
FO W Krol
FL P Laguna
PO S Lapka
FO K Lukaszewicz
Sgt A Lysek
PO J Malinski
Sgt A Markiewicz
WC M Mumler
Sgt EJA Nowakiewicz
Sgt J Palak
Sgt E Paterek
PO ER Pilch
FL W Riley
SL WAJ Satchell
Sgt A Siudak
PO S Skalski
FL JA Thomson
PO S Wapniarek
PO A Wczelik
Sgt M Wedzik
PO Z Wroblewski
Sgt J Zaluski
PO A Zukowski

303 SQUADRON

Sgt T Andruszkow
Sgt M Belc
FO FN Brinsden
Sgt M Brzezowski
FO A Cebrzynski
PO JKM Daszewski
PO M Feric
FL AS Forbes
Sgt J Frantisek
Sgt PP Gallus
FO B Grzeszczak
FO Z Henneberg
FO MR Hill
PO J Jankiewicz
FO W Janusewicz
F/Sgt J Kania
Sgt S Karubin
SL RG Kellett
FL JA Kent
Sgt J Kowalski
SL Z Krasnodebski
PO W Lapkowski
PO W Lokuciewski
PO B Mierzwa
PO W Miksa
Sgt J Palak
PO JH Palusinski
FO LW Paszkiewicz
Sgt E Paterek
FO M Pisarek
PO J Radomski
Sgt J Rogowski
FO T Sawicz
Sgt A Siudak
Sgt H Skowron
Sgt L Switon
Sgt E Szaposznikow
FO W Urbanowicz
Sgt M Wojciechowski
Sgt S Wojtowicz
F/Sgt K Wunsche
FO W Zak
PO JEL Zumbach

310 SQUADRON

PO V Bergman
SL ER Bitmead
SL GDM Blackwood
FO JE Boulton
PO F Burda
Sgt A Dvorak
PO E Fechtner
PO S Fejfar
PO EA Foit
Sgt B Furst
PO V Goth
PO JJ Hanus
SL A Hess
PO F Hradil
Sgt J Hubacek
PO JE Hybler
PO S Janouch
FL J Jefferies
F/Sgt M Jiroudek
Sgt J Kaucky
F/Sgt J Kominek
Sgt J Kopriva
Sgt J Koukal
PO M Kredba
PO J Machacek
PO JM Maly
Sgt F Marek
Sgt S Plzak

Sgt EM Prchal
Sgt R Puda
Sgt J Rechka
PO F Rypl
Sgt K Seda
FL GL Sinclair
PO J Sterbacek
F/Sgt J Strihavka
Sgt F Vindis
WO J Vopalecky
PO V Zaoral
Sgt R Zima
PO S Zimprich

312 SQUADRON

PO JK Ambrus
PO J Bartos
Sgt F Chabera
FL HAG Comerford
PO J Duda
PO RD Dunscombe
FL DE Gillam
Sgt O Hanzlicek
PO A Hlobil
FL NL Ievers
PO JA Jaske
Sgt J Keprt
Sgt V Slouf
Sgt J Stehlik
Sgt J Truhlar
SL FH Tyson
PO A Vasatko
PO V Vesely
PO A Vrana
PO T Vybiral

501 SQUADRON

PO HC Adams
PO KR Aldridge
FO NJM Barry
PO JW Bland
FO PAN Cox
Sgt DB Crabtree
PO RC Dafforn
Sgt FJP Dixon
PO RS Don
PO BL Duckenfield
Sgt EJ Egan
Sgt VH Ekins
Sgt PCP Farnes
Sgt SA Fenemore
Sgt RJK Gent
FL JAA Gibson
Sgt A Glowacki
PO V Goth
Sgt WJ Green
Sgt HC Grove
PO EM Gunter
PO PR Hairs
PO FC Harrold
Sgt WB Henn
PO DA Hewitt
SL HAV Hogan
FL E Holden
SL AL Holland
Sgt WB Holroyd
Sgt OV Houghton
Sgt EF Howarth
Sgt DJ Hulbert
Sgt RWE Jarrett
FO DAE Jones
PO F Kozlowski

Sgt JH Lacey
Sgt GGS Laws
FO KNT Lee
Midshipman PL Lennard
Sgt RH Lonsdale
Sgt JE Loverseed
FO K Lukaszewicz
Sgt DAS MacKay
PO KW MacKenzie
Sgt M Marcinkowski
F/Sgt PF Morfill
Sgt KA Muchowski
SL AD Murray
Sgt P O'Byrne
PO EG Parkin
Sgt LJ Patterson
F/Sgt AD Payne
Sgt GW Pearson
Sgt TG Pickering
FL AR Putt
PO EB Rogers
FO AT Rose-Price
Sgt JE Savill
Sgt CJ Saward
PO S Skalski
FO VR Snell
FL GEB Stoney
PO EJH Sylvester
PO AEADJG van den Hove
d'Ertsenrijck
Sgt SAH Whitehouse
Sgt WA Wilkinson
PO S Witorzenc
PO P Zenker

504 SQUADRON

Sgt WH Banks
PO W Barnes
Sgt BM Bush
PO AW Clarke
FO EM Frisby
PO JV Gurteen
FO JR Hardacre
Sgt C Haw
Sgt D Haywood
Sgt DA Helcke
Sgt RT Holmes
PO HN Hunt
FO M Jebb
Sgt HDB Jones
PO AJ McGregor
PO PT Parsons
FL AH Rook
FO M Rook
FO MEA Royce
FL WB Royce
SL J Sample
Sgt GH Spencer
PO CM Stavert
Sgt GA Stroud
PO RE Tongue
FO KV Wendel
FO BEG White

600 SQUADRON

Sgt AV Albertini
PO R Atkinson
Sgt DH Ayers
PO P Baker
PO GL Barker
Sgt EC Barnard
FO JGC Barnes

PO CE Blair
Sgt JJ Booth
FO BH Bowring
FO ADM Boyd
Sgt JW Brown
PO JC Bull
Sgt AG Burdekin
Sgt PS Burley
Sgt AW Canham
FL JG Cave
FL DL Clackson
SL DdeB Clark
Sgt RJ Coombs
AC2 CF Cooper
Sgt LEM Coote
PO HR Crowley
PO GA Denby
PO Dermott
Sgt L Dixon
Sgt HPD Dyer
PO KC Edwards
Sgt EJ Egan
PO JL Frost
PO AJ Glegg
PO KAG Graham
Sgt EJF Grant
Sgt FWW Green
FO DN Grice
PO RC Haine
Sgt WRH Hardwick
FL TN Hayes
Sgt FG Hindrup
PO CA Hobson
Sgt RM Holland
PO GH Holmes
Sgt BW Hopton
PO HBL Hough
Sgt PE Huckin
Sgt DE Hughes
PO PRS Hurst
Sgt HS Imray
PO H Jacobs
PO SFF Johnson
PO JR Juleff
Sgt FJ Keast
PO M Kramer
PO RL Lamb
PO BD Larbalestier
FL SP le Rougetel
Sgt CS Lewis
Sgt AJ Lipscombe
SL P Little
SL HL Maxwell
Sgt EW Moulton
Sgt AE Owen
Sgt PG Pearce
Sgt FS Perkin
FL CA Pritchard
FO AJ Rawlence
Sgt H Reed
Sgt AH Riseley
PO JR Ritchie
Sgt RG St James-Smith
PO FH Schumer
FO GET Scrase
Sgt B Senior
Sgt A Smith
Sgt EC Smith
FL ES Smith
Sgt EF Taylor
Sgt FJ Tearle
Sgt TW Townsend
Sgt JIB Walker
AC1 JBW Warren
PO NJ Wheeler
Sgt PC Whitwell
Sgt WO Willis
PO WD Wiseman
PO RS Woodward

601 SQUADRON

FL The Hon JWM Aitken
PO AJM Aldwincle
Sgt R Beamish
Sgt FA Bernard
PO JW Bland
Sgt Bomford
PO P Challoner-Lindsey
FO GNS Cleaver
FL WP Clyde
Sgt HW Coussens
FO CR Davis
FO RS Demetriadi
PO WG Dickie
Sgt CAW Dixon
FO MD Doulton
PO GGF Draper
Sgt A Edgley
PO SG Fenwick
PO WML Fiske
FO HT Gilbert
FO J Gillan
FL DL Gould
FO T Grier
Sgt LN Guy
Sgt RP Hawkings
Sgt EL Hetherington
PO JH Hoare-Smith
SL WFC Hobson
FL Sir AP Hope
FL TE Hubbard
Sgt FHR Hulbert
PO J Jankiewicz
PO RC Lawson
WC RJ Legg
Sgt TA McCann
Sgt AS MacDonald
PO JKUB McGrath
PO A McInnes
PO HC Mayers
Sgt RA Milburn
PO HG Niven
PO DB Ogilvie
FL JA O'Neill
F/Sgt AHD Pond
Sgt JA Rees
FO WH Rhodes-Moorhouse
FL CJH Riddle
FO HJ Riddle
PO AJ Rippon
FL ML Robinson
FO PB Robinson
PO RB Rohacek
PO JH Rothwell
FO JW Seddon
PO JL Smithers
Sgt Starll
FO WW Straight
Sgt N Taylor
FO J Topolnicki
Sgt JV Wadham
SL EF Ward
Sgt AW Woolley

602 SQUADRON

PO EW Aries
Sgt CF Babbage
FO PPC Barthropp
FL RF Boyd
Sgt Bracton
FO WH Coverley
Sgt AW Eade
FO AL Edy
Sgt DW Elcome
FL PJ Ferguson

FO G Fisher
PO DH Gage
F/Sgt J Gillies
PO OV Hanbury
FO JS Hart
PO WP Hopkin
FL DM Jack
SL AVR Johnstone
PO WR Jones
PO A Lyall
Sgt A McDowall
FL CH MacLean
PO HW Moody
FL CJ Mount
PO HG Niven
Sgt VD Page
PO RA Payne
Sgt RFP Phillips
Sgt J Proctor
PO TGF Ritchie
PO SN Rose
Sgt MH Sprague
SL JD Urie
FL PC Webb
Sgt BEP Whall
Sgt GA Whipps

603 SQUADRON

Sgt IK Arber
Sgt GJ Bailey
PO NJV Benson
PO R Berry
FL JC Boulter
FO JE Boulton
Sgt AD Burt
PO JR Caister
FO BJG Carbury
PO PM Cardell
FL JLG Cunningham
Sgt AS Darling
SL GL Denholm
PO RB Dewey
PO PG Dexter
FO GK Gilroy
FO CW Goldsmith
FL JGE Haig
FO PM Hartas
FO RH Hillary
PO P Howes
PO KA Lawrence
PO DK MacDonald
FL HK MacDonald
FO BR MacNamara
PO JFJ MacPhail
PO LA Martel
FO HKF Matthews
PO DA Maxwell
FO JS Morton
PO P Olver
FO AP Pease
FO CD Peel
FO DJC Pinckney
PO HAR Prowse
PO WPH Rafter
PO WAA Read
FL IS Ritchie
FL FW Rushmer
Sgt AR Sarre
FO FDS Scott-Malden
PO JF Soden
FO BG Stapleton
PO D Stewart-Clark
Sgt J Stokoe
Sgt PHRR Terry
FO RM Waterston
PO AL Winskill

604 SQUADRON

AC2 JD Anderson
SL MF Anderson
LAC AL Austin
PO D Bayliss
AC2 WH Blane
AC2 RS Brown
FL GO Budd
Sgt JD Cameron
AC2 B Cannon
FO RE Chisholm
Sgt GP Clark
Sgt AW Cook
FO ED Crew
FL J Cunningham
Sgt RW Dalton
SL JA Davies
Sgt GW Dutton
Sgt Edwards
Sgt GJ Evans
Sgt WG Fenton
Sgt JGB Fletcher
Sgt JH Folliard
FO KI Geddes
PO T Genney
Sgt MV Goodman
Sgt NH Guthrie
Sgt C Haigh
Sgt Hatton
Sgt SN Hawke
FL PWD Heal
Sgt L Hird
FL AS Hunter
Sgt PF Jackson
PO IKS Joll
Sgt RW Kennedy
Sgt ES Lawler
FL PCF Lawton
PO AC MacLaren
Sgt AC Metcalfe
Sgt AC Miller
Sgt DG Moody
LAC AA O'Leary
Sgt ME Parry
LAC AG Patston
Sgt A Phillips
LAC JR Phillipson
Sgt JT Pickford
Sgt ERL Poole
FL JHM Rabone
Sgt CF Rawnsley
Sgt WG Ripley
FL P Ruston
Sgt AK Sandifer
FL RH Scott
FO JB Selway
Sgt SHJ Shirley
FL CDE Skinner
FL SH Skinner
PO EL Smith
Sgt F Smith
FL H Speke
Sgt CND Stewart
AC2 E Stock
Sgt CHS Sumpter
Sgt Tate
Sgt RHW Taylor
Sgt GS Thomas
FO DS Wallen
Sgt WB Ward
AC2 JG Watson
Sgt E Welch
PO NR Wheatcroft
Sgt White
Sgt HG Whittick
PO MA Williams
PO W Wright
Sgt W Yates

605 SQUADRON

Sgt J Budzinski
SL WM Churchill
FO TPM Cooper-Slipper
FO PG Crofts
PO CF Currant
FL GR Edge
PO CE English
FO J Fleming
FO DN Forde
PO GM Forrester
PO RW Foster
Sgt B Furst
PO WJ Glowacki
FO JCF Hayter
FO R Hope
Sgt HN Howes
PO JS Humphreys
PO A Ingle
Sgt KH Jones
PO RE Jones
PO P Kennett
Sgt PRC McIntosh
FL AA McKellar
PO SJ Madle
PO JA Milne
PO IJ Muirhead
FO PL Parrott
FO CW Passy
Sgt DC Peacock
Sgt WH Pettit
Sgt R Puda
Sgt LF Ralls
Sgt RD Ritchie
PO JH Rothwell
PO K Schadtler-Law
PO AMW Scott
SL DR Scott
Sgt LC Sones
PO PD Thompson
PO EJ Watson
Sgt EW Wright

607 SQUADRON

FL W Baranski
Sgt LD Barnes
Sgt HJR Barrow
FL JM Bazin
FL WF Blackadder
FL CE Bowen
Sgt N Brumby
Sgt PA Burnell-Phillips
PO VA Carter
FL GD Craig
Sgt WG Cunnington
FO IB Difford
PO GJ Drake
PO GJ Elliot
PO D Evans
FO AD Forster
FL J Frey
FO AK Gabszewicz
FL WE Gore
PO M Gorzula
FO DL Gould
Sgt GA Hewett
PO NB Heywood
PO MR Ingle-Finch
FO MM Irving
PO PJ Kearsey
FO MC Kinder
FO Z Kustrzynski
Sgt J Landesdell
FO W Lazoryk

607 SQUADRON (cont)

PO JD Lenahan
PO SV McCall
PO WW McConnell
PO AR Narucki
PO WP Olensen
PO J Orzechowski
PO SB Parnall
Sgt EA Redfern
PO AMW Scott
Sgt RA Spyer
PO PJT Stephenson
PO JM Storie
PO JE Sulman
PO F Surma
Sgt W Szafraniec
PO TR Thomson
PO HC Upton
SL JA Vick
PO GHE Welford
FL WHR Whitty
PO BA Wlasnowolski
PO B Wydrowski
PO CR Young

609 SQUADRON

PO N leC Agazarian
PO MJ Appleby
PO PA Baillon
PO FHR Baraldi
FL PH Barran
FL SG Beaumont
PO JD Bisdee
FO AJ Blayney
PO JR Buchanan
FO CG Chappell
PO DM Crook
PO J Curchin
SL HS Darley
FO JC Dundas
FL AR Edge
Sgt AN Feary
FL THT Forshaw
PO GN Gaunt
FO HM Goodwin
FO EL Hancock
PO SJ Hill
FL FJ Howell
Sgt JA Hughes-Rees
PO VC Keough
FL BW Little
FL JHG McArthur
PO A Mamedoff
Sgt RTD Mercer
PO RFG Miller
PO GTM Mitchell
FO JC Newbery
FO T Nowierski
PO AK Ogilvie
FO Z Olenski
FO P Ostaszewski-Ostoja
FO CN Overton
WC DN Roberts
FL ML Robinson
PO ME Staples
PO EG Titley
PO EQ Torbin
PO J Zurakowski

610 SQUADRON

PO ES Aldous
PO FJ Aldridge
Sgt SJ Arnfield
FO CH Bacon
Sgt AC Baker
Sgt CS Bamberger
Sgt RA Beardsley
PO BW Brown
Sgt RL Carter
Sgt HH Chandler
Sgt HR Clarke
Sgt JE Cooper
Sgt RN Cooper
Sgt WJ Corbin
Sgt DF Corfe
PO IH Cosby
PO KH Cox
Sgt EW Cranwell
PO AE Davies
FO PJ Davies-Cooke
Sgt HD Denchfield
PO WA Douglas
PO NG Drever
FL J Ellis
Sgt P Else
PO CR Fenwick
FO FT Gardiner
Sgt BGD Gardner
PO DM Gray
FL ILM Hallam
Sgt RF Hamlyn
Sgt FG Homer
FO G Keighley
FL MT Kirkwood
FL PG Lamb
PO JG Lecky
PO P Litchfield
Sgt E Manton
PO C Merrick
PO DE Mileham
Sgt J Murray
Sgt WJ Neville
FO SC Norris
Sgt VD Page
Sgt CA Parsons
Sgt AD Payne
FO COJ Pegge
Sgt W Raine
Sgt NHD Ramsay
FO BV Rees
Sgt RW Richardson
PO AR Ross
FL AT Smith
FL EBB Smith
Sgt WA Sutcliffe
F/Sgt JH Tanner
Sgt TY Wallace
Sgt NP Warden
Sgt P Ward-Smith
FO WHC Warner
PO FK Webster
Sgt PH Willcocks
FL DS Wilson
Sgt RL York

611 SQUADRON

PO DA Adams
Sgt JW Allison
Sgt RA Angus
SL ER Bitmead
FO MP Brown
Sgt AD Burt
PO CAW Carter

Sgt AS Darling
PO RB Dewey
Sgt LE Freese
Sgt ETG Frith
Sgt JE Gadd
FO IBDE Hay
Sgt TWR Healy
FL B Heath
PO CAT Jones
Sgt EN Kelsey
FL WJ Leather
Sgt SA Levenson
PO JW Lund
SL JE McComb
PO CH MacFie
PO DA Maxwell
FO DH O'Neill
WC IR Parker
Sgt KC Pattison
Sgt RE Plant
FO PSC Pollard
PO HS Sadler
Sgt JA Scott
FO FDS Scott-Malden
Sgt FER Shepherd
FL KM Stoddart
PO JRG Sutton
PO N Sutton
FO JR Walker
FL DH Watkins
PO TD Williams

615 SQUADRON

Sgt LD Barnes
Adj H Bouquillard
FO J Brewster
Sgt N Brumby
PO LH Casson
FO P Collard
Sgt ET Cosby
FO PG Crofts
FO ND Edmond
PO ER Edmunds
Sgt EJ Egan
PO D Evans
FO A Eyre
FL LM Gaunce
FL JRH Gayner
FL HS Giddings
FL AP Gray
Sgt DW Halton
Sgt J Hammerton
FO JCF Hayter
PO DH Hone
Sgt BW Hopton
PO GL Howitt
FO PH Hugo
SL JR Kayll
PO DS Kinder
Adj HG Lafont
PO LN Landels
PO PG Leggett
FO KT Lofts
FO DJ Looker
PO JAP McClintock
PO J McGibbon
PO SJ Madle
PO KM Millist
PO CR Montgomery
Sgt AR Moore
Adj RGOJ Mouchotte
PO MR Mudie
FL J Orzechowski
FO SR Peacock-Edwards
Sgt FS Perkin

Adj GC Perrin
FL RD Pexton
Sgt JA Porter
FO R Roberts
PO EB Rogers
FL JG Sanders
Sgt CJ Saward
FO DGA Stewart
PO JM Storie
PO CD Strickland
PO AJJ Truran
Sgt NM Walker
Sgt PK Walley
PO JJ Walsh
PO NJ Wheeler
PO B Wydrowski
PO CR Young

616 SQUADRON

FO JS Bell
FO J Brewster
F/Sgt FP Burnard
FL HF Burton
PO LH Casson
Sgt P Copeland
Sgt HA Cordell
Sgt JK Down
FO HSL Dundas
FL DE Gillam
FO PM Hartas
FL RO Hellyer
PO JM Hewson
Sgt RV Hogg
FO K Holden
Sgt J Hopewell
Sgt TC Iveson
Sgt R Ivey
PO JE Johnson
PO CAT Jones
Sgt J le Cheminant
PO PH Leckrone
FO CH MacFie
FO R Marples
FO GE Moberley
PO TB Murray
Sgt DK Parker
PO HRG Poulton
Sgt M Ridley
SL M Robinson
PO JH Rowden
FL EF St Aubyn
PO DS Smith
PO WLB Walker
Sgt RA Ward
Sgt PT Wareing
Sgt TE Westmoreland
Sgt KA Wilkinson
Sgt B Wright

421 FLIGHT

Sgt CAH Ayling
FO HC Baker
FL B Drake
Sgt DH Forrest
F/Sgt J Gillies
FL CP Green
FO PM Hartas
PO KA Lawrence
Sgt MAW Lee
Sgt DAS McKay
FO JJ O'Meara
FO DT Parrott
Sgt FS Perkin
Sgt AWP Spears
FO JE Storrar

422 FLIGHT

Sgt CE Hampshire
FO PW Rabone
Sgt AE Scott

FIGHTER INTERCEPTION UNIT

PO DG Ashfield
Sgt EL Byrne
WC GP Chamberlain
PO CAG Clark
Sgt G Dixon
Sgt JF Fizel
FL RG Ker-Ramsay
Sgt EF le Conte
Sgt RH Leyland
Sgt IN MacRae
SL AG Miller
PO GE Morris
PO DL Ryalls
PO JW White

FLEET AIR ARM

804 SQUADRON

Lt RA Bird
Midshipman MA Birrell
Sub-Lt SH Bunch
LT RHP Carver
Sub-Lt PCS Chilton
Lt-Cdr JC Cockburn
Sub-Lt D Grant
Sub-Lt DA Hutchison
Sub-Lt RR Lamb
Lt AM MacKinnon
Lt TJ Mahoney
Lt AE Marsh
Sub-Lt WR Nowell
Sub-Lt TRV Parke
Lt B Paterson
Sub-Lt NH Patterson
Sub-Lt J Reardon-Parker
Lt GF Russell
Petty Officer FJ Shaw
Lt JW Sleigh
Petty Officer WEJ Stockwell
Lt AJ Wright

808 SQUADRON

Lt JP Coates
Lt RC Cockburn
Petty Officer RE Dubber
Lt GC Guthrie
Midshipman P Guy
Lt RC Hay
Lt ATJ Kindersley
Sub-Lt RMS Martin
Midshipman GW Roberts
Petty Officer DE Taylor
Lt EWT Taylour
Lt RC Tillard

BIBLIOGRAPHY

All books published in London unless otherwise stated.

AIR MINISTRY   *The Battle of Britain*   HMSO 1941
ALLEN, WC HR   *Battle for Britain*   Barker 1973
————   *Who won the Battle of Britain?*   Barker 1974
————   *Fighter Squadron   A Memoir 1940-1942*   Kimber 1979
ANON   *The Air Battle of Malta*   HMSO 1944
ANTHONY, GORDON   *Air Aces*   Home and Van Thal 1944
AUSTIN, AB   *Fighter Command*   Gollancz 1941
BADER, GC DRS   *Fight for the Sky*   Sidgwick and Jackson 1973
BAILEY, JIM   *The Sky Suspended*   Hodder (1965)
BAKER, ECR   *The Fighter Aces of the RAF 1939-1945*   Kimber 1962
BARCLAY, GEORGE   *Fighter Pilot   A Self-portrait*   Kimber 1976
BARKER, RALPH   *The Hurricats*   Pelham 1978
BARNHAM, DENIS   *One Man's Window   Malta April 13th to June 21st 1942*   Kimber 1956
BARRYMAINE, NORMAN   *The Story of Peter Townsend*   Davies 1958
BARTHROPP, WC PATRICK   *Paddy*   Baker 1987
BARTLEY, SL ANTHONY   *Smoke Trails in the Sky*   Kimber 1984
BEAMONT, ROLAND   *Testing Years*   Allan 1980
BEEDLE, J   *43 Squadron*   Beaumont 1985
BEKKER, CAJUS   *The Luftwaffe War Diaries*   Macdonald 1966
BICKERS, RICHARD TOWNSEND   *Ginger Lacey   Fighter Pilot*   Hale 1962
BISHOP, EDWARD   *The Battle of Britain*   Allen and Unwin 1960
————   *The Guinea Pig Club*   Macmillan 1963
————   *Their Finest Hour   Battle of Britain 1940*   Pan/Ballantine 1972
BOLITHO, HECTOR   *Combat Report*   Batsford 1943
BOWYER, CHAZ   *The Flying Elephants   History of 27 Squadron*   Macdonald 1972
————   *Hurricane at War*   Allan 1976
————   *For Valour   The Air VCs*   Kimber 1978
————   *Fighter Command 1936-1968*   Book Club Associates 1980
————   *Supermarine Spitfire*   Bison 1980
————   *Fighter Pilots of the RAF 1939-1945*   Kimber 1984
————   and CHRISTOPHER SHORES   *Desert Air Force at War*   Allan 1981
BOWYER, MJF AND JDR RAWLINGS   *Squadron Codes 1937-56*   Cambridge, Stephens 1979
BRAHAM, WC JRD   *'Scramble!'*   Muller 1961
BRANDON, SL LEWIS   *Night Flyer*   Kimber 1969
BRENNAN, PO PAUL and PO RAY HESSELYN   *Spitfires over Malta*   Jarrolds 1942
BRICKHILL, PAUL   *The Great Escape*   Faber 1951
————   *Reach for the Sky*   Collins 1954
————   and CONRAD NORTON   *Escape to Danger*   Faber 1953
BROOKES, AJ   *Fighter Squadron at War*   Allan 1980
BROWN GEORGE and MICHEL LAVIGNE   *Canadian Wing Commanders*   Canada, Battleline 1984
BRYANT, ARTHUR and EDWARD SHANKS   *The Battle of Britain*   Daily Sketch 1948
CAMERON, NEIL   *In the midst of Things*   Hodder and Stoughton 1984
CHILDERS, JAMES SAXON   *War Eagles*   Heinemann 1943
CHISHOLM, RODERICK   *Cover of Darkness*   Chatto 1953
CLOUSTON, AC AE   *These Dangerous Skies*   Cassell 1954
CLUETT D, J BOGLE and B LEARMONTH   *Croydon Airport and the Battle of Britain*   Sutton Library 1984
COLLIER, BASIL   *Leader of the Few   Lord Dowding*   Jarrolds 1957
————   *Eagle Day*   Fontana 1974
CROOK, DM   *Spitfire Pilot*   Faber 1942
CYNK, JERZY B   *History of the Polish Air Force   1918-1968*   Osprey 1972
DARLINGTON, ROGER   *Night Hawk   Karel Kuttlewascher*   Kimber 1985
DAVIS, BRIAN L   *Luftwaffe Air Crews   Battle of Britain 1940*   Arms and Armour Press 1974
DEERE, ALAN C   *Nine Lives*   Hodder 1959
DEIGHTON, LEN   *Fighter*   Cape 1977
————   *Battle of Britain*   Cape 1980
DICKSON, LOVAT   *Richard Hillary*   Macmillan 1950
DONAHUE, ARTHUR GERALD   *Tally-Ho! Yankee in a Spitfire*   Macmillan 1942
————   *Last Flight from Singapore*   Macmillan 1944
DORMAN, GEOFFREY   *British Test Pilots*   Forbes and Robertson 1950
DUKE, NEVILLE   *Test Pilot*   Wingate 1953
ELLAN, BJ (SL BJE Lane)   *Spitfire*   Murray 1942
EVERSON, DON   *The Reluctant Messerschmitt*   Portcullis 1978
FAIRCLOTH, NW   *New Zealanders in the Battle of Britain*   Wellington 1950
FIEDLER, ARKADY   *Squadron 303*   Davies 1942
FIELD, PETER J   *Canada's Wings*   Lane 1942
FORBES, WC ATHOL and SL HUBERT ALLEN   *Ten Fighter Boys*   Collins   1942
FORRESTER, LARRY   *Fly for your life   Story of Stanford Tuck*   Muller 1956
FOXLEY-NORRIS, CHRISTOPHER   *A Lighter Shade of Blue*   Allan 1978

FRANKS, NORMAN   *Double Mission   Story of Manfred Czernin*   Kimber 1976
————   *Fighter Leader   Story of Ian Gleed*   Kimber 1978
————   *Wings of Freedom*   Kimber 1980
————   *Sky Tiger   Story of Sailor Malan*   Kimber 1980
————   *Battle of Britain*   Bison 1981
————   *The Air Battle of Dunkirk*   Kimber 1983
FRASER, FL W   *The History of RAF Manston*   Manston 1971
GALLAND, ADOLF   *The First and the Last*   Methuen 1955
GALLICO, PAUL   *The Hurricane Story*   Joseph 1959
GARDNER, CHARLES   *AASF*   Hutchinson 1940
GELB, NORMAN   *Scramble   A Narrative History*   Joseph 1986
(GLEAVE, TP)   *I had a Row with a German*   Macmillan 1941
GLEED, WC IAN   *Arise to Conquer*   Gollancz 1942
GNYS, WLADEK   *First Kill*   Kimber 1981
GREEN, WILLIAM   *Aircraft of the Battle of Britain*   Pan 1969
GREER, LOUISE and HAROLD ANTHONY   *Flying Clothing*   Airlife 1979
GRIBBLE, LEONARD R   *Heroes of the Fighting RAF*   Harrap 1941
————   *Epics of the Fighting RAF*   Harrap 1943
GRIFFITH, HUBERT   *RAF in Russia*   Hammond 1942
HALL, ROGER   *Clouds of Fear*   Folkestone, Bailey Bros 1975
HALLIDAY, HUGH   *242 Squadron   The Canadian Years*   Ontario 1981
HALPENNY, BRUCE   *Fight for the Sky*   Wellingborough 1986
HALSTEAD, IVOR   *Wings of Victory*   Right Book Club 1941
HAMILTON, ALEXANDER   *Wings of Night*   Kimber 1977
HANCOCK, KENNETH   *New Zealand at War*   Wellington 1946
HAUGHLAND, VERN   *Eagle Squadrons   1940-1942*   David and Charles 1979
HELD, WERNER   *Fighter!*   Arms and Armour Press 1979
HESS, WN   *The Allied Aces of World War 11*   New York, Arco 1966
HILLARY, RICHARD   *The Last Enemy*   Macmillan 1942
HOUART, VICTOR   *Lonely Warrior*   Souvenir Press 1956
————   *Desert Squadron*   Souvenir Press 1959
HOUGHTON, GW   *They flew through Sand*   Cairo 1942
HOWARD-WILLIAMS, JEREMY   *Night Intruder*   Purnell 1976
HUNT, LESLIE   *Defence until Dawn*   Southend 1949
————   *Twenty-One Squadrons   RAuxAF 1925-1957*   Garnstone Press 1972
JACKSON, ROBERT   *Air War over France   1939-40*   Allan 1974
————   *Douglas Bader*   Barker 1982
JOHNSON, FRANK (Editor)   *RAF over Europe*   Eyre and Spottiswoode 1946
JOHNSON, GC JE   *Wing Leader*   Chatto 1956
JOHNSTONE, AVM SANDY   *Where no Angels dwell*   Jarrolds 1969
————   *Enemy in the Sky   My 1940 Diary*   Kimber 1976
————   *Adventure in the Sky*   Kimber 1978
JONES, WC IRA   *Tiger Squadron*   Allen 1954
JUBELIN, ANDRE   *The Flying Sailor*   Hurst and Blackett 1954
JULLIAN, MARCEL   *The Battle of Britain*   Cape 1967
KELLY, TERENCE *Hurricane over the Jungle*   Kimber 1977
KENNINGTON, ERIC   *Drawing the RAF*   OUP 1942
KENT, GC JA   *One of the Few*   Kimber 1971
KNIGHT, DENNIS   *Harvest of Messerschmitts*   Warne 1981
KROL, WACLAW   *Polski Skrzydla W Inwazju na Francje*   Warsaw 1983
LANCHBERY, EDWARD   *Against the Sun   The Story of Roland Beamont*   Cassell 1955
LEE, ASHER   *The German Air Force*   Duckworth 1946
LEWIS, PETER   *Squadron Histories   RFC, RNAS & RAF since 1912*   Putnam 1968
LLOYD, FHM   *Hurricane   The story of a Great Fighter*   Harborough 1945
LUCAS, PB   *Flying Colours   Story of Douglas Bader*   Hutchinson 1981
MacCLURE, VICTOR   *Gladiators over Norway*   Allen 1942
McKEE, ALEXANDER   *Strike from the Sky*   Souvenir Press 1960
MACKENZIE, WC KW   *Hurricane Combat*   Kimber 1987
MACKERSAY, IAN   *Into the Silk*   Hale 1956
MACMILLAN, Capt NORMAN   *The Royal Air Force in the World War 4 Vols*   Harrap 1942-50
McROBERTS, ALEXANDER   *Lions Rampant   Story of 602 Squadron*   Kimber 1985
MASON, FRANCIS K   *Battle over Britain*   McWhirter   1969
————   *The Hawker Hurricane*   Aston 1987
MASTERS, DAVID   *'So Few'*   Eyre and Spottiswoode 1942
MICHIE, ALLAN A (Editor)   *Their Finest Hour*   Allen and Unwin 1941
MIDDLETON, DREW   *The Sky Suspended*   Secker and Warburg 1960
MITCHELL, ALAN W   *New Zealanders in the Air War*   Harrap 1945
MONKS, NOEL   *Squadrons Up*   Gollancz 1940
MOSLEY, LEONARD   *Faces from the Fire*   Weidenfeld 1962
MOUCHOTTE, RENE   *The Mouchotte Diaries*   Staples 1956
MOULSON, TOM   *The Flying Sword*   Macdonald 1964
MOYES, PHILIP   *Bomber Squadrons of the RAF*   Macdonald 1964
MUSCIANO, WA   *Messerschmitt Aces*   New York, Arco 1982

NANCARROW, FG   *Glasgow's Fighter Squadron*   Collins 1942
NARRACOTT AH   *War News had Wings*   Muller 1941
OBERMAIER, ERNST   *Die Ritterkreuztrager der Luftwaffe Jagdflieger 1939-1945*   Mainz 1966
——————   *Die Ritterkreuztrager der Luftwaffe Stuka und Schlactflieger*   Mainz 1976
——————   and WERNER HELD   *Jagdflieger, Oberst Werner Molders*   Stuttgart 1982
ORANGE, VINCENT   *Sir Keith Park*   Methuen 1984
ORDE, Capt CUTHBERT   *Pilots of Fighter Command*   Harrap 1942
OXSPRING, GC RW   *Spitfire Command*   Kimber 1984
PAGE, GEOFFREY   *Tale of a Guinea Pig*   Pelham 1981
PAYNE, AC LGS   *Air Dates*   Heinemann 1957
PHILPOTT, BRYAN   *German Fighters over the Mediterranean*   Stephens 1979
POOLMAN, KENNETH   *Faith, Hope and Charity*   Kimber 1954
——————   *The Catafighters*   Kimber 1970
PRICE, ALFRED   *The Hardest Day*   Macdonald   1979
PRUSZYNSKI, KSAWERY   *Poland fights back*   Hodder 1941
RAMSEY, WINSTON (Editor)   *The Battle of Britain*   *Then and Now MK 11*   After the Battle 1982
RAWLINGS, JOHN   *Fighter Squadrons of the RAF*   Macdonald 1978
RAWNSLEY, CF and ROBERT WRIGHT   *Night Fighter*   Collins 1957
(RCAF)   *The RCAF Overseas*   *The First Four Years*   Toronto 1944
REID, JPM   *Some of the Few*   Macdonald 1960
——————   *The Battle of Britain*   Liverpool 1960
REVELL ALEX   *The Vivid Air*   Kimber 1978
RICHARDS, DENIS and H StG SAUNDERS   *Royal Air Force 1939-45 3 Vols*   HMSO 1974-75
RICHEY, PAUL   *Fighter Pilot*   Batsford 1941
ROBERTSON, BRUCE   *Spitfire*   *Story of a famous Fighter*   Harleyford 1961
ROLLS, WTE   *Spitfire Combat*   Kimber 1987
ROTHENSTEIN, Sir WILLIAM   *Men of the RAF*   OUP 1942
SADLOWSKA, SLAWA   *Album of Polish Airmen*   Letchworth 1947
SHARP, CM and MJF BOWYER   *Mosquito*   Faber 1971
SHAW, MICHAEL   *Twice Vertical*   *Story of No 1 Squadron*   Macdonald 1971
SHORES CHRISTOPHER and CLIVE WILLIAMS   *Aces High*   Spearman 1966
——————   and HANS RING   *Fighters over the Desert*   Spearman 1969
——————   *Fighters over Tunisia*   Spearman 1975
——————   and BRIAN CULL with NICOLA MALIZIA   *Malta: The Hurricane Years 1940-41*   Grub Street 1987
SIMS, EDWARD H   *The Fighter Pilots*   Cassell 1967
SMITH, GC DUNCAN   *Spitfire into Battle*   Murray 1981
SMITH, PETER C   *Stuka at War*   Allan 1980
SPAIGHT, JM   *The Battle of Britain 1940*   Bles 1941
STOKES, DOUGLAS   *Wings Aflame*   Kimber 1985
SUTTON, BARRY   *The Way of a Pilot*   Macmillan 1943
——————   *Jungle Pilot*   Macmillan 1946
SUTTON, SL HT   *Raiders Approach*   Gale and Polden 1956
(TANGMERE)   *Military Aviation Museum*   Derby 1984
TAYLOR, JWR and KENNETH MUNSON   *The Battle of Britain*   NEL 1976
——————   and MAURICE ALLWARD   *Spitfire*   Harborough 1946
THOMAS, GIL   *Shoulder the Sky*   Barker 1959
THOMPSON, WC HL   *New Zealanders in the Royal Air Force 3 Vols*   Wellington 1953-59
TIDY, DOUGLAS   *I fear no Man*   *A history of 74 Squadron*   Macdonald 1972
TOLIVER, Colonel RF and TJ CONSTABLE   *Fighter Aces of the Luftwaffe*   California, Aero Publishers 1977
TOWNSEND, PETER   *Duel of Eagles*   Weidenfeld and Nicolson 1970
——————   *Time and Chance*   Collins 1978
VADER, JOHN   *Spitfire*   Pan/Ballantine 1972
VAN ISHOVEN, ARMAND   *The Luftwaffe in the Battle of Britain*   Allan 1980
VINCENT, AVM SF   *Flying Fever*   Jarrolds 1972
WAKEFIELD, KENNETH   *Luftwaffe Encore*   Kimber 1979
WALKER, OLIVER   *Sailor Malan*   Cassell 1953
WALLACE, GRAHAM   *RAF Biggin Hill*   Putnam 1957
WHELAN, JA   *Malta Airmen*   Wellington 1951
WILLIAMS, PETER and TED HARRISON   *McIndoe's Army*   Pelham 1979
WILLIS, JOHN   *Churchill's Few*   Joseph 1985
WINCHESTER, BARRY   *Eighty-Four Days*   Horsted Keynes, Selma Press 1974
WOOD, DEREK   *Target England*   Jones 1980
——————   and DEREK DEMPSTER   *The Narrow Margin*   Hutchinson 1961
WOOD, TONY and BILL GUNSTON   *Hitler's Luftwaffe*   Salamander 1977
WRIGHT, NICHOLAS   *The Bump*   *Biggin Hill*   RAF 1980
WRIGHT, ROBERT   *Dowding and the Battle of Britain*   Macdonald 1969
WYKEHAM, PETER   *Fighter Command*   Putnam 1960
WYNN, KENNETH G   *A Clasp for the Few*   Auckland 1981
YOUNG, SL AJ and FL DW WARNE   *Sixty Squadron 1916-1966*   Singapore 1967
ZIEGLER, FRANK H   *The Story of 609 Squadron*   Macdonald 1971
ZUMBACH, JEAN   *On Wings of War*   Deutsch 1975

GLOSSARY

AACU	Anti-Aircraft Co-operation Unit
A&AEE	Aeroplane and Armament Experimental Establishment
AASF	Air Advanced Striking Force
ABGS	Advanced Bombing and Gunnery School
AC	Air Commodore
ACH	Aircrafthand
ACM	Air Chief Marshal
AC 2	Aircraftsman 2nd Class
ADF	Aircraft Delivery Flight
ADGB	Air Defence Great Britain
ADU	Aircraft Delivery Unit
AEA	Air Efficiency Award
AEAF	Allied Expeditionary Air Force
AFC	Air Force Cross
AFDU	Air Fighting Development Unit
AFM	Air Force Medal
AFTS	Advanced Flying Training School
AFTU	Air Fighting Training Unit
AFU	Advanced Flying Unit
AGS	Air Gunners' School
AI	Airborne Interception
AM	Air Marshal
AMES	Air Ministry Experimental Station
AOC	Air Officer Commanding
AONS	Air Observers' Navigation School
AOS	Air Observers' School
APC	Armament Practice Camp
APO	Acting Pilot Officer
ASR	Air Sea Rescue
ATS	Advanced Training Squadron
AuxAF	Auxiliary Air Force
AVM	Air Vice-Marshal
BEA	British European Airways
BEM	British Empire Medal
BGS	Bombing and Gunnery School
BOAC	British Overseas Airways Corporation
CAM	Catapult-Armed Merchant Ship
CB	Companion of the Bath
CBE	Commander of the Order of the British Empire
C de G (Belg)	Croix de Guerre (Belgian)
C de G (Fr)	Croix de Guerre (French)
CFE	Central Fighter Establishment
CFI	Chief Flying Instructor
CFS	Central Flying School
CGS	Central Gunnery School
CVO	Commander of the Royal Victorian Order
DFC	Distinguished Flying Cross
DFM	Distinguished Flying Medal
DSO	Companion of the Distinguished Service Order
ECFS	Empire Central Flying School
EFTS	Elementary Flying Training School
E&RFTS	Elementary and Reserve Flying Training School
FAA	Fleet Air Arm
FCU	Flying Control Unit
FIS	Flying Instructors' School
FIU	Fighter Interception Unit
FL	Flight Lieutenant
FO	Flying Officer
F/Sgt	Flight Sergeant
FTS	Flying Training School
GC	George Cross
GCA	Ground Controlled Approach
GCB	Knight Grand Cross of the Bath
GCI	Ground Controlled Interception
GM	George Medal
GRS	General Reconnaissance School
GRU	General Reconnaissance Unit
GSU	Group Suport Unit
HMT	His Majesty's Transport
IAF	Indian Air Force
ITW	Initial Training Wing
KCB	Knight Commander of the Bath
KCVO	Knight Commander Royal Victorian Order
KT	Knight of the Thistle
KW	Krzyz Walecznych
LAC	Leading Aircraftsman
Lt	Lieutenant
Lt-Cdr	Lieutenant Commander
MAAF	Mediterranean Allied Air Forces
MBE	Member of the Order of the British Empire
MRAF	Marshal of the Royal Air Force
MSFU	Merchant Ship Fighter Unit
MU	Maintenance Unit
OADU	Overseas Aircraft Delivery Unit
OBE	Officer of the Order of the British Empire
OCU	Operational Conversion Unit
OTU	Operational Training Unit
OUAS	Oxford University Air Squadron
PA	Personal Assistant
PAF	Polish Air Force
PHU	Personnel Holding Unit
PO	Pilot Officer
PoW	Prisoner of War
PRU	Photographic Reconnaissance Unit
QFI	Qualified Flying Instructor
RAAF	Royal Australian Air Force
RAE	Royal Aircraft Establishment
RAFO	Reserve of Air Force Officers
RAFRO	Royal Air Force Reserve of Officers
RAFVR	Royal Air Force Volunteer Reserve
RAN	Royal Australian Navy
RANAS	Royal Australian Naval Air Station
RAuxAF	Royal Auxiliary Air Force
RAuxAFRO	Royal Auxiliary Air Force Reserve of Officers
RCAF	Royal Canadian Air Force
RFC	Royal Flying Corps
RFS	Reserve Flying School
RHAF	Royal Hellenic Air Force
RM	Royal Marines
RNZAF	Royal New Zealand Air Force
RU	Repair Unit
SAAF	South African Air Force
SASO	Senior Air Staff Officer
SFTS	Service Flying Training School
Sgt	Sergeant
SHAEF	Supreme Headquarters Allied Expeditionary Force
SHQ	Station Headquarters
SL	Squadron Leader
S of TT	School of Technical Training
SPSO	Senior Personnel Staff Officer
SRAF	Southern Rhodesian Air Force
Sub-Lt	Sub-Lieutenant
TAF	Tactical Air Force
TAF	Turkish Air Force
TEU	Tactical Exercise Unit
USAAC	United States Army Air Corps
USAAF	United States Army Air Force
USAF	United States Air Force
VM	Virtuti Militari
WC	Wing Commander
Wop/AG	Wireless Operator/Air Gunner